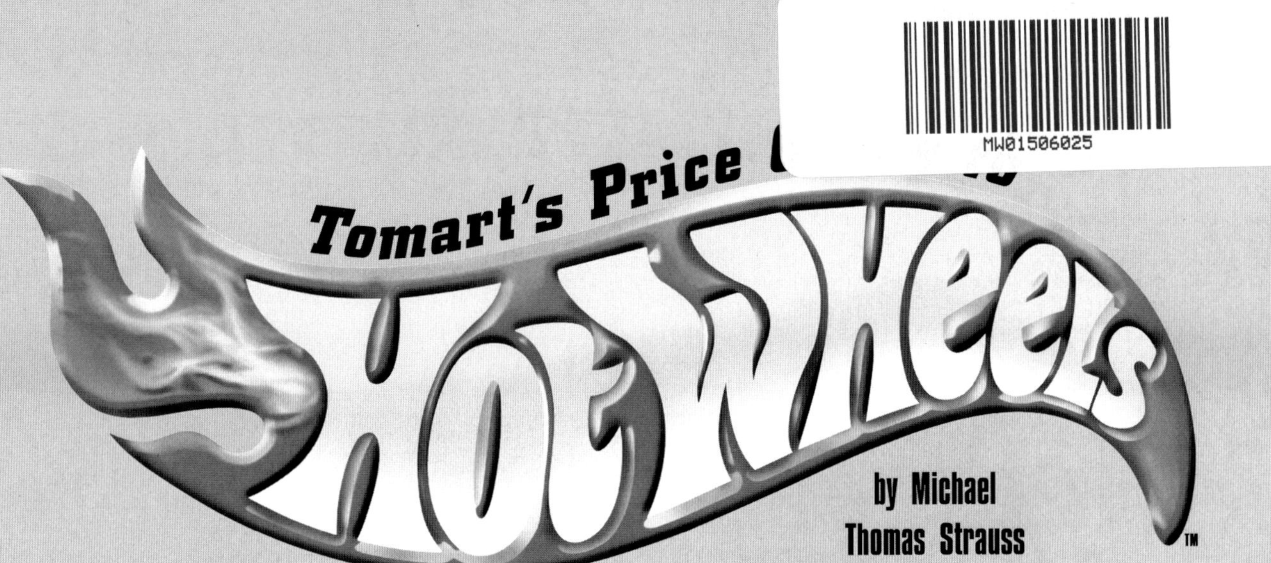

by Michael
Thomas Strauss

Updated 5th Edition

Photography by Tom Schwartz and Chris Hall

TOMART PUBLICATIONS
division of Tomart Corporation
Dayton, Ohio

This book is dedicated to my wife Diane and my sons Michael and Steven.
They are and always will be my true Passion.

Acknowledgements

Special thanks to the following dedicated and knowledgeble collectors who gave their time and experience to this edition: Bryan Hladek, "DW" Steve Stephenson, Dan Koechel, Dave Lopez, Steve Tscherter, Mike Stephenson, Chuck Gaughn, Mark Winkelman, Tom Engen and Luis, Franklin and Erasmo Ouchida for their help throughout the book Also a big thank you goes to all who helped in the first four editions and to all of the collectors who wrote in with additions/corrections to the previous books.

My appreciation goes to Larry Wood, Ira Gilford, and Harry Bradley for their recollections of the early Hot Wheels days—without them there would be no Hot Wheels. Special thanks are due to all the collectors and dealers who have shared their enthusiasm, knowledge, and finds over the years. There is no hobby without you.

Special thanks go to Michael Dewart, Robert Walsh, and Mattel, Inc., for the rights to produce this book, and for providing many color photographs of Hot Wheels cars through the years. In addition, Heather Schneider provided invaluable assistance for this edition. To Tom Tumbusch, Tom Schwartz and Chris Hall for color and black and white photography. This book would not have been possible without the multi-talented Tomart Staff: image editors Nathan Hanneman and Adam Parks for color-correction; Robert Welbaum for sorting out the scattered pieces of manuscript; Elizabeth Jones for cheerfully talking to all those people on the phone; and Josh Becker for fulfillment and shipping. Final layout and production was managed by T.N.Tumbusch of Digital Dynamite, Inc.

Prices listed in this guide are averaged from sales across the U.S. They are derived from dealers and collectors reports of prices paid in the months prior to publication, and are presented as a guide for information purposes only. No one is obligated in any way to buy, sell, or trade according to these prices. Condition, rarity, demand and the reader's desire to own determine the actual price paid. No offer to buy or sell at the prices listed is intended or made. Buying and selling is conducted at the reader's risk. Neither the author, publisher, nor Mattel, Inc. assume any liability for any losses suffered for use of, or any typographic errors contained in, this book.

All value estimates are presented in U.S. dollars. The dollar sign is omitted to avoid needless repetition.

First printing, 2002

Cruise by the Hot Wheels℠ Web site @ www.hotwheels.com

Published by Tomart Publications, Dayton, Ohio.

Library of Congress Control Number: 92-82853

ISBN: 0-914293-52-4

Manufactured in the United States of America

1 2 3 4 5 6 7 8 9 0 8 7 6 5 4 3 2 1 9 0

INTRODUCTION TO THE UPDATED 5th EDITION

This book is an identification and value guide to Hot Wheels products...a new toy idea when it was introduced in 1968, and the leading die-cast vehicle collectible nearly thirty-five years later. This fifth edition updates values and adds car information not found in the previous editions. It is the only such book authorized by Mattel, which means it has the most up-to-date information available anywhere. Every casting and variation known to the author is listed by the name of the original design in the year it was first sold. All subsequent paint, decoration, or model-number changes are listed under the original name. Similar castings produced under another name are cross-referenced.

The simple key to becoming a Hot Wheels expert is knowing the name of the car and the year it was first produced. Every vehicle from 1968 through cars produced for 2002 is pictured in this book. Most cars from the beginning through 1982 have the name on the bottom of the car, as do several post-1982 cars. That still leaves several hundred cars without any name identification. The year imprinted on the bottom of a car is often misleading. It is the copyright date rather than the year of production. This is at least one year off...and can be up to 20 years different. There are, however, many other clues to narrow down the picture comparison if the name and first year of production are not known. For example, the type of paint, country of origin, and, most importantly, wheel design, all help pinpoint the location of each car listed in this book.

Be sure to read the introductory pages. It only takes a few minutes, and you'll have a much better understanding of the value of Hot Wheels collecting...and how to use this guide.

COLLECTING MINIATURE DIE-CAST VEHICLES

Collecting model die-cast vehicles is one of the most popular but under-publicized hobbies in America. More than 200 million are purchased each year. These tiny cars have an average length of three inches and mirror interests in our civilization.

Die-cast cars are as American as apple pie, being an outgrowth of the Linotype machines introduced at the Columbian Exposition in Chicago in 1893. The first die-cast cars were produced by Samuel Dowst, the founder of Tootsietoys, who used such a machine to make small promotional miniature vehicles. By the turn of the century he had a thriving toy-car business.

Die-cast car collecting began in earnest in England where long winters and an inborn sense of history tend to make one passionate about collecting. The English, not considering themselves merely accumulators, are with very few exceptions completists (collecting every variation). Within the last decade this die-cast car-collecting phenomenon has become a world-wide passion, reaching Japan, Germany and Australia.

COLLECTING HOT WHEELS VEHICLES

By the late '80s, Hot Wheels became the most desirable of all die-cast vehicles to collect. They have also proven to be the most difficult to find in mint condition, to complete as sets, and even to fully document (as production records are not generally released by Mattel).

On the whole, it would be hard to imagine any collectible that has appreciated in value as much as these fanciful miniature cars. Lionel trains command high prices and some engines now sell for thirty times their original value. Imagine, however, the Hot Wheels Classic Cord which sold for as little as 79 cents in 1971 and is now going for as much as $800...over a thousand times its original value!

It's been estimated there are more than 50,000 Hot Wheels accumulators and well over 15,000 serious collectors in the U.S. The average collector has over two thousand cars in his collection and spends a great amount of his time searching for missing pieces. He (or she) is an astute collector, investor and trader who has proven to be quite perplexing to those dealers not familiar with Hot Wheels vehicles. Hot Wheels collectors can be found at almost every toy show. Many dealers now specialize in Hot Wheels cars. There are also several publications devoted exclusively to Hot Wheels collecting. At the annual Hot Wheels Newsletter Convention held each fall, hundreds of collectors from across the U.S. take over several floors of a hotel to buy, sell and trade.

Hot Wheels collectors are careful to protect their vehicles and treat them with reverence. However, they only preserve a very small number of the cars produced. Many get stepped on, are lost in sand boxes or are broken in play. One mother said "When my son was little, he sure liked those little Hot Wheels cars. They were everywhere and every time you moved you would be stepping on them. But now that he is grown, I can't get him to part with any he has left." Future archaeologists may determine a great deal about us by studying these fanciful jewel-like vehicles.

Why are Hot Wheels vehicles such a good collectible? They meet several tests for what constitutes a "collectible."

1. It is easy to get a collection started. They are available in almost any toy store and older models can be found at most toy shows. Bargains are still available at flea markets and garage sales.

2. They offer a challenge to the serious collector. There are over four thousand variations; it may take years and miles of searching to put together a complete collection.

3. They are relatively easy to describe and catalog. Collections can even be custom-tailored to an individual by only purchasing a specific type: Corvette models, fire equipment or red-stripe-wheeled vehicles, for example.

4. Since the oldest Hot Wheels vehicles are nearly thirty-five years old, the average child enthusiast is now in his or her thirties. This is the age group with both a growing disposable income and an inclination to start collecting something. Thus many other adults can be expected to enter the hobby.

5. The typical vehicle offers ready associations or memories of the past. Remember Hot Wheels cars were traded in the school yard with as much vigor as baseball cards.

6. Hot Wheels vehicles display well (there are several case manufacturers) and they take up very little room to store in contrast to other items such as large toy trucks, movie-related items or promotional glasses.

7. There are collectors' groups throughout the U.S., England and Australia and several publications to keep collectors informed. Many magazines have articles about the hobby's growth and there has been a very successful museum exhibit.

8. Vehicles are easily bought & sold, and there is a ready market for any you may wish to sell.

9. They have been an uncommonly good investment, appreciating at least 20% per year from 1987 to 1997.

10. The hobby is still under-publicized. Many fine collections have been built at reasonable costs by advertising for vehicles in local papers or seeking them at garage sales and flea markets.

11. Even today, the vehicle on your local toy store's shelf may be a limited-run item. Many cars are changed during a production run either by the Mattel marketing department or at the plant, giving collectors many highly-prized variations each year.

12. Many promotional models are made each year for companies ranging from pest exterminators to cereal companies and by Mattel for sales and promotional reasons. Some of these cars are produced in very limited numbers. Historically, these have been very good purchases and have appreciated greatly. This book included all promotional models up to press time. Information about new promotional cars and their availability can be obtained by reading collector publications.

STORY OF THE HOT WHEELS BRAND

The Hot Wheels story is one of pride, extreme attention to detail and teamwork by a host of professionals: designers, model makers, engineers, tool makers, production people, artists, copywriters and marketing wizards.

Hot Wheels cars start life on an artist's drawing board. The designer may sketch hundreds of drawings as he conceives different ideas for new vehicles. Some designs are based on actual cars or trucks. In this case, photos are used. If it's a classic or older model, manufacturers and owners are often consulted. Completed drawings for many cars have been test-marketed with focus groups of children and adults.

Photographs or renderings of the selected models are sent to the Engineering Department so detailed mechanical drawings can be made. Model-makers use the engineering drawings to create an Alias 3D computer model, which is sent to a Stereo Lithography machine to create a 3:1 model of the car. In this way, the designers make certain all parts are in scale and possess the fine, authentic detailing that has made Hot Wheels products famous. Finally, door handles, emblems, logos, headlights or multi-color pad-printing are added to give each vehicle a special look and personality. The cars are then packaged and shipped in assortments to toy stores everywhere.

A HISTORY TIMELINE

1966

Matchbox cars from the Lesney Corporation in England dominated the die-cast toy car market. Elliot and Ruth Handler, Mattel's founders, had watched their grandchildren playing with these small foreign cars. Shortly afterward, Elliot, Mattel's Chairman of the Board, purchased a die-cast manufacturing vendor who had produced small parts for Mattel. Elliot summoned Jack Ryan, head of Research and Development, and asked him to develop something different for die-cast cars.

Back in 1966, Mattel was the leading toy manufacturer in the U.S. It seemed logical a company so successful with the famous Barbie doll would move more strongly into the growing boys' toy market.

Jack Ryan, who was something of a mechanical genius and had experience with Navy missiles, called in Harvey LaBranch, head of engineering, and Howard Newman, Mattel's top designer, to form a toy-car development team.

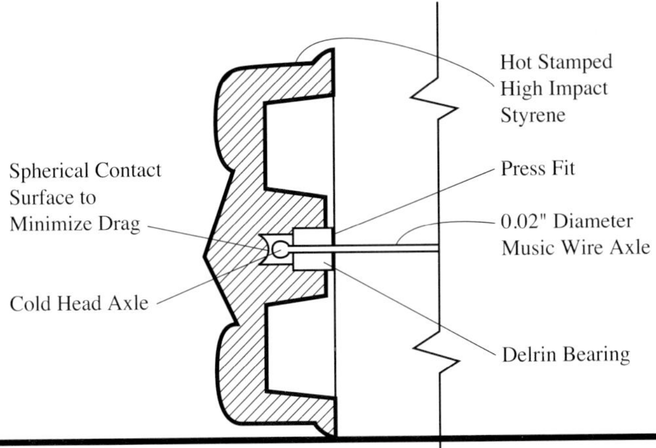

Howard Newman's Original Hot Wheels wheel design

One of their first actions was to place an ad in a Detroit paper to recruit a top auto designer. Harry Bradley, who had designed the Deora show car and was working in the Chevrolet design department, answered the ad. Mattel, as Harry tells it, offered him five percent above his current salary. He had just quit his job at GM to work at a substantially higher salary at Chrysler, which was coincidentally trying to steal away GM auto stylists. He then left Chrysler after one day for Mattel, parlaying this job shuffling into a much nicer salary.

That fall, the design team spent about two weeks hitting the toy stores, buying all the different die-cast vehicles they could find. They gathered over a thousand different vehicles and mounted them on large wallboards to study, hoping to think of something to make their cars different. First, they noticed the cars all looked basically the same. Second, they were not very exciting. They did not roll well and few American models were represented.

Marketing research had told them children loved to roll these cars and often raced them. So one of their goals was to make these cars faster than any others sold at the time. Races were held by the designers and engineers to see who could develop the fastest car.

One of Howard Newman's designs used a 0.020" music-wire axle. He devised a torsion-bar spring-action layout which was later incorporated into production designs. This feature improved durability. When dropped, the wheels moved upward until they contacted the underside of the fenders, so impact loads went from the wheel onto the car body without damaging the axle.

The wheels were designed by many people, including Harvey LaBranch. His design incorporated a tiny paper-thin lip on the inside edge which was all that touched the surface, minimizing friction and giving the fastest possible speeds.

After much debate, Elliot narrowed the design ingredients down to five major points.

1. A California look, which meant having a rake (larger tires in the rear and smaller tires in the front).
2. Hood scoops, to suggest powerful engines.
3. Exposed and chromed exhaust headers.
4. Mag wheels with a red stripe around the tires which were in vogue at the time.
5. Exciting candy-color paint jobs.

Harry Bradley drove a yellow customized El Camino to work every day and Elliot saw it in the parking lot. It had a distinctive California look and Elliot immediately decided this was how he wanted the cars to look. He suggested Harry make his own El Camino one of the first Hot Wheels designs.

Elliot was under constant pressure from Mattel's Board of Directors to prove the project's viability. The marketing department's research indicated there would not be many sales for a toy targeted to retail at 98 cents when competitors' cars were selling for 49 cents. They also predicted the market would not be very large and set an unusually low production quota of 16 million units. The consumer safety department expressed concerns as well. But Elliott persisted. Eventually all manufacturing and safety problems were solved. But no one except Elliot was sure how these little cars would sell.

After calling their creations die-cast cars or even Matchbox cars for months, Jack Ryan finally came up with the name "Hot Wheels." He said "I have been thinking about it and I want to pick up the Hot Rod theme and express our wheels and suspension. We'll call them Hot Wheels."

1967

The engineering staff, on a rather tight budget because of the Board of Directors' resistance, built the prototypes by assembling store-bought plastic models and customizing them. These models were then sent to the manufacturing plant to be pantographed. A pantograph machine moves over the model with a steel figure (probe) and cuts the trace into a steel die. It can also reduce the size of a model by as much as 75%.

According to Harry Bradley, the design team wanted to produce the new Chevrolet Corvette, but no drawings had been released to the public and a written request had been turned down by the GM Styling Center. Harry remembered the Styling Center always had a door unlocked for easy access to the cafeteria. Harry made arrangements with an old friend at the center and within a few days made a trip to Detroit and returned with purloined plans. The Custom Corvette was released by Mattel before the real car hit the street. Harry was severely rebuked and threatened by GM. However, Mattel and the new Corvette both greatly benefited by the premature exposure.

After Harry Bradley had designed eleven of the first sixteen cars, one of his bosses, convinced the Hot Wheels line would fail, reassigned him to designing staples of the Mattel line (Jack-in-the-Box, See 'N Say, etc.). Harry, whose heart was really in automobiles, resisted this reassignment and was eventually fired. He is now an instructor at the Art Center College of Design in Pasadena, California. Ironically, he designed the Oscar Meyer Wienermobile found in the 25th Anniversary year Hot Wheels line.

Harvey LaBranch recalls a meeting in Elliott Handler's office with a toy buyer from J.C. Penney. "A long section of track was laid out with an initial drop of three feet. Several cars from other manufacturers were rolled down the track. Then the Hot Wheels cars were rolled. They far out-performed the competition. The buyer was impressed. Ruth Handler, president of Mattel at the time, asked the buyer how many units he thought J.C. Penney might sell. He checked some numbers in his briefcase and then said, 'I think we might sell 12 to 15 million.' Ruth turned to Elliott and said 'Did you hear that?' The next day Ruth called a meeting of the manufacturing staff and shortly thereafter a team of people left for Hong Kong to set up a parallel production facility to the existing one in the U.S."

The Custom Firebird on the original Hot Wheels card design

Hot Wheels cars were introduced packaged individually and included in five playsets, but "Accessory Paks" soon became basic to Hot Wheels product marketing. These are particularly interesting to collectors if found in the original package.

Ira Gilford, who had worked for the Chevrolet design team the previous four years, was hired to replace Harry. Ira designed the remainder of the 1968 line, including the Custom Volkswagen, plus the entire 1969 line and part of the 1970 designs. He developed the Heavyweights and many of the Spoilers. He was also responsible for the long, low and sleek look necessary to hold cars close to the Hot Wheels track and handle the short curves. Mattel began putting great effort into sets as they were becoming very popular and enhancing car sales. Ira worked for Mattel through early 1969 when he left for private consulting.

1968

The Hot Wheels concept, aided by extensive television advertising, had taken the market by storm. Touted as the fastest metal cars in the world, they became an overnight phenomenon. The sixteen original models were manufactured in both Hong Kong and the United States. There are discernible differences between the two castings.

These first models had Spectraflame paint jobs, mag-style wheels with red-line tires and positive-action torsion-bar suspensions. Originally planned to be released in only two colors, each was issued in a least eight and as many as fourteen. Several were based on concept cars from two of the most famous hot rod builders of the decade: Bill Cushenberry and Ed "Big Daddy" Roth.

The original package was designed by Rick Irons around the idea of using bright colors to look "hot." Rick also designed the metal buttons included with each package and the boxes for many of the earlier sets.

By the end of 1968, the Hong Kong plant was swinging into production. However, Hot Wheels sales were seven times original projections and the sales and marketing departments were more than a year behind in filling their booked orders. Matchbox sales plummeted until a new, faster wheel was produced a year later.

Harry Bradley recalls driving through the Hawthorne, California, area and seeing people selling black-market cars from the backs of their trunks for prices up to four dollars. People would stop and wave as they recognized his now-famous truck. According to Harry, Hot Wheels vehicles became the biggest-selling toy in the history of the world.

1969

Howard Rees, another automotive designer, replaced Ira Gilford. Howard headed the department for eight months and designed many of the 1970 Hot Wheels models. But his interests were elsewhere and he accepted a chance to head Mattel's new space toy department. Howard later devoted himself to a very successful western-art painting career.

Howard brought a few Hot Wheels cars to a party in Van Nuys as presents for a friend's children. Also attending the party was Larry Wood. Howard and Larry had been fellow students at the Art Center in Los Angeles. In Detroit, Howard had become reacquainted with Larry while working on the Ford Mustang. Larry, who had since moved back to Los Angeles, saw the cars and his eyes got glassy. Howard said, "I told Larry of the Hot Wheels design spot and the rest is history. Of all of the designers who have ever worked for Mattel, only Larry deserves a T-shirt that says 'Mr. Hot Wheels.' Gasoline truly flows through his veins."

Larry Wood continued as the principal designer of the Hot Wheels product line. For many years he was the only designer. Larry is as passionate at the time of this writing as he was when he was a teenager dreaming of designing cars. On any given weekend Larry can be found at car shows and automotive swap meets, garnering ideas for the next new car, swapping stories or just talking cars with Hot Wheels collectors. Harry Bradley, who is a good friend, believes Larry has designed more cars than any other living person.

1970

Mattel sponsored two very popular drag racers: Don "The Snake" Prudhomme and Tom "The Mongoose" McEwen. Hot Wheels cars had become ubiquitous with a Saturday morning television show, comic books, sheets and bedspreads, lunch boxes and watches. They

One of the Heavyweights, introduced in 1970

Mongoose and Snake Dragster Pack

The Hot Wheels Collectors Club Kit, issued in 1970

garnered critical placements and yards of aisle space in almost every toy store. A child could furnish his room with a Hot Wheels garbage can, listen to an LP of the soundtrack of the Hot Wheels television show, or wake up to a Hot Wheels alarm clock. Thousands of kids joined the Hot Wheels collectors' club and received the Hot Wheels

The 1970 Jack-In-The-Box promo car

Club Kit which contained a collector's book, Hot Wheels patch, membership certificate and a special chrome-plated car. The line also expanded to include Spoilers and Heavyweights.

This year was the first time a promotional (or giveaway) model (with special decal sheet) was issued. The honor went to Jack-in-the-Box, a West Coast fast-food chain.

Two of the better-known Hot Wheels designs by Tom Daniel. Right: S'Cool Bus. Below: Red Baron.

1971

Mattel was riding the crest of the Hot Wheels phenomenon. They purchased Monogram, the model-kit company which had a well-known designer named Tom Daniel. Several of Tom's more popular designs were incorporated into the Hot Wheels line, including S'Cool Bus and the Red Baron.

1972

Mattel discontinued collector buttons in packages and began moving away from the bright spectraflame colors. Only seven new models were issued, although some earlier models were reissued in new packages. Hot Wheels cars were now exclusively manufactured in Hong Kong.

Left: Jet Threat, a Shell Promotional car.
Right: New packaging design introduced in 1973.

1973

Worldwide inflation and the gas crisis forced Americans to think of their cars as more than status icons. For the first time Mattel suffered the effects of inflation and a slump in the toy industry. The situation was complicated by internal problems. Cost-cutting moves were made across the entire line and only three new castings were made. Although twenty-one of the old castings were reissued, car quality suffered. The cars were now painted in rather unexciting enamel colors. Many collectors quit buying the now somewhat drab Hot Wheels vehicles and sales dropped. Mattel, in turn, cut production. The 1973 models were only issued for one year, making them among the most expensive and difficult to find.

Also this year, Mattel produced a series of ten promo cars for Shell Oil Company.

Flying Colors (1974)

Flying Colors (1976)

1974

Mattel revamped the entire Hot Wheels line with a completely new look that added "wild" designs. They were called Flying Colors and came on a very distinctive blistercard with a white background. The enamel paint-jobs were now enlivened with special designs imprinted on the cars. This was done by a pad-press machine known as a "tampo," named for the German company which developed the equipment. Mattel issued the entire line in only one basic color per car. Some models, however, had short runs of alternate colors, which can make them very expensive in the collector's market.

1975

The Hot Wheels line was expanded by 25 new, exciting models, including the only two motorcycles ever included in the basic line. Mattel also produced the first promotional vehicle for one of its largest customers, Toys "R" Us. Promotional models are never part of the normal line and in many cases can be quite rare. Larry Wood designed the Ramblin' Wrecker and the vehicle was inadvertently produced with his real phone number on the side. He received many calls from small children.

1976

Mattel celebrated the bicentennial by creating four very special editions in red, white and blue. A new blistercard pictured Fire-Eater, black Super Van and the P-917. It was the work of Arvin Carlson, who had been designing packages for the company since 1969.

1977

This was the tenth year of Hot Wheels production. It was also the year Mattel phased out one of its best known trademarks: the redline tire. By the end of the production year, all-new models came with black sidewall tires only. Some 1977 models with red-stripe tires are extremely difficult to find and are among the most expensive Hot Wheels vehicles.

Left: Super Streeters package with patch offer. Right: Marvel Heroes package.

1978

Seven versions of a new blistercard were issued. These cards showed seven different cloth patches naming the seven new groups of Hot Wheels vehicles for the year: Super Streeters, Drag Strippers, Oldies But Goodies, Rescue Team, Classy Customs, Speedway Specials and Heavies. One could send away to Mattel for the patches.

1979

This year's line included Marvel comic characters' vehicles called Heroes, which became very popular among collectors. The Scene Machine vehicles each had a special magnifier rear window, through which a picture corresponding to the vehicle's theme could be viewed. Each Scene Machine came with its own distinctive blistercard.

1980

Hi-Rakers and Workhorses were introduced. Hi-Rakers had a rear axle that could be raised or lowered to increase the rake of the car.

The 1981 Collectors' Book 3-pack

1981

Gold hubs (gw) were included with all-new Hot Ones series. These new wheels and thinner axles helped regain some of the speed that had made the first Hot Wheels cars so famous. The package sticker read, "The Hot Ones - Fastest non-powered metal cars." Mattel also issued its first collector's handbook which was available only in a special three-pack.

The 1983 15th Anniversary 3-pack

1982

Hot Wheels cars were also produced in a new Malaysian plant; it would eventually become Mattel's largest production facility. Hot Wheels cars made their first appearance at McDonald's with 24 standard models.

1983

Mattel celebrated the 15th anniversary of Hot Wheels cars with a remake of the 1968 Custom Camaro and a belt buckle. The new Real Riders series with real rubber tires and a new package quickly became popular with collectors.

Also this year Mattel began producing Hot Wheels vehicles in Mexico for its domestic market and in France for the European Community. These cars were never sold in the U.S.

1984

Mattel held a penny sale with a mail-in offer for four cars, two of which were special. The Ultra Hots were introduced. They were said to be the fastest breed of Hot Wheels cars and had a new paint style similar to the 1968 spectraflame colors. Several regular-line cars were marketed only in Canada and very few made their way back across the border, making them very special to collectors.

1985

Kellogg's sponsored a mail-in promotion for the first Hot Wheels cereal cars.

1986

A new line called Speed Demons was advertised as creepy, crawly fantasy vehicles. Mattel stopped production in France for the European market. The Real Riders line was discontinued.

1987

Mattel discontinued production in both Mexico and Hong Kong. Malaysia would now be the principal Hot Wheels production location. The first Hot Wheels price guide was published and prices for collector cars began to escalate at a rapid rate. The first Hot Wheels collectors' convention was held in Toledo, Ohio, in October. Over one hundred people attended.

1988

This year marked the 20th anniversary of Hot Wheels vehicles. The event was celebrated with a chrome and gold-chrome series of vehicles with the 20th year cast into the cars. The Dinosaur Mud Pit set was unexpectedly withdrawn from the market, making it highly desired by collectors.

The Dinosaur Mud Pit, discontinued in 1988.

20th Anniversary 3-pack

1989

The Malaysian plant changed the colors of all cars painted purple or containing purple in their tampos for safety reasons. The Park 'n Plates series was introduced. Mattel published a new, expanded collector's handbook. Production also began on an ongoing series of cars for Getty Oil Co. This series would be changed every year.

1990

Malaysia produced the first casting solely for the International division which distributes cars worldwide. Over the years, Hot Wheels packages have been produced in Japanese, Italian, French, Spanish and German. Hot Wheels cereal was on grocery-store shelves. The first aircraft, a helicopter, appeared in the regular Hot Wheels lineup. The California Customs were also introduced this year. They had the latest paint styles, wild tampos, custom wheels and buttons.

1991

Mattel and McDonald's restaurants hit a grand slam with a Happy Meal Promotion featuring both Hot Wheels and Barbie. Hot Wheels sales flourished and production needed six months to catch up with

Display for the 1991 Hot Wheels/Barbie Happy Meal promotion.

the backlog. A Hot Wheels cartoon series once again gained popularity. A video tape with a special car could be purchased at local toy stores. Kool-Aid and Kay Bee toy stores combined on a promotion to redeem Kool-Aid proofs of purchase for a special car at Kay Bee. Gold ultra hot wheels appeared. Apparently the factory ran out of silver foil and substituted gold foil instead. They were produced in very small numbers, found mainly in Canada and quickly commanded a premium price among collectors. Mattel's premium's department gave away a pair of Corvette Stingrays at the National Premium Show in Chicago. This was the first such giveaway in sixteen years. These cars had the shortest run of any production car since the 1970s and are quite scarce.

Left: Roberto Guerrero car from Pro Circuit series. Right: 1992-93 packaging style.

1992

The Goodyear Blimp appeared on the shelves and proved very popular among collectors. Second in what hopefully will be a series of aircraft, it already has seven variations. This year also marked the first time special cars were produced for the collector and they proved extremely popular. The long-awaited Pro Circuit line with special foiled cards was also introduced. These cars were replicas of real race cars and were produced by a subcontractor in China. The Tattoo Machines line with wild designs and a set of matching body tattoos was introduced at the end of the year. The Hot Wheels brand name began appearing on many other wheeled vehicles made by Mattel. The Museum of American Heritage in Palo Alto, California, honored Mattel with the first exhibit of Hot Wheels vehicles and a special car was produced for the occasion.

Above: To commemorate the 25th Anniversary of Hot Wheels cars, 8 of the original cars were reissued in replica packaging as a Toys "Я" Us exclusive. Right: Some Revealers included tokens for exclusive cars and other prizes.

1993

Mattel celebrated the 25th Anniversary of the Hot Wheels brand with a commemorative line exclusively for Toys "Я" Us. Eight of the original cars were re-tooled and re-issued in packaging reminiscent of the 1968 Hot Wheels cars. The cars were produced with tampoed "redline" tires, plastic buttons, and Spectraflame-like paint jobs. This was the first line designed for collectors, with colors changing each month just like the original Hot Wheels models. The series achieved instant popularity.

Revealers, cars covered by dissolvable car covers, were numbered one through twelve. Each bag contained one of three color variations. There were 36 different cars in all. One in 72 packages contained a blue token which could be redeemed for a special set of ten cars. Approximately 1,000 contained a gold token good for a free Hot Wheels bike and gold chrome Lamborghini Countach.

1994

Only one new series was introduced: the Vintage Collection. This was really a continuation of the 1993 25th Anniversary collector's series with the same packaging, buttons, etc. The series included eight new vehicles (all Toys "Я" Us exclusives). Each model, including 1993 25th Anniversary cars, had the Hot Wheels logo and "Vintage" embossed on the base. Mattel decided all cars would have the Hot Wheels logo somewhere. The logo would not always be the same color and it would be in different places on the car. Also introduced was a new top-fuel dragster and some re-designed earlier Hot Wheels vehicles.

1995

This year Mattel introduced the Treasure Hunt cars and the 1995 Model Series. The Treasure Hunt cars were issued monthly and were limited to 10,000 of each model. They caused quite a commotion with speculators buying all they could find, then selling them for $25 to $100 each. The 1995 Model Series used a new casting and was also issued monthly. The Segment Series were also introduced, with twelve different series of four cars each in the same theme. Three different series were issued every three months. Six new wheels were introduced: three-spoke (sp3), five-spoke (sp5), six-spoke (sp6), seven-spoke (sp7), hot hubs (hh), and the progressive oval wheels (pow). The six-spoke and progressive ovals were each used for only one vehicle.

The 1995 Treasure Hunt Series

One of 4 Holiday Hot Wheels cars released in 1996 30th Anniversary Deora

1996

Mattel began re-issuing basic cars from China. Most were from the late 1980s and early 1990s with new colors and tampos. Vehicles made from the old Corgi tools also appeared. Other introductions were the VW bus, 1970 Dodge Daytona Charger, and Radio Flyer Wagon, all favorites among collectors. Many cars were again issued in a series (Treasure Hunt, Dark Rider II, 1996 Model Series). More new wheels appeared, including the lace wheel (lw), directional wheel (dw), and five-hole wheel (ho5). Many cars would get all three plus a few from prior years.

1997

Kyle Petty and PE[2] signed licensing agreements with Mattel. As a result, Hot Wheels returned to the racing scene with the introduction of the Pro Racing series, featuring cars from the NASCAR® circuit. The line was divided into two segments: basic cars for kids, and more elaborate models targeted at collectors. The basic cars had plastic bases and wheels, came packaged on a card shaped like the number "1," and sold for about $1.99. The collector's line was more detailed, with metal bases and synthetic rubber tires. Each included a collector's card and retailed for approximately $2.99. Apart from the Treasure Hunt cars, the hot releases this year were the Scorchin' Scooter, the 1970 Plymouth Barracuda, the Excavator, and the '59 Chevy Impala.

Larger scale cars were added to the Pro Racing line in 1998

Pro Racing cars, basic and collector series (1997-98)

1998

For the 30th Anniversary of Hot Wheels cars, Mattel issued 40 new castings instead of the usual 12. The NASCAR® line was hotter than the previous year. The Pro Racing line was also expanded late in the year to include 1/43rd- and 1/24th-scale cars. Almost all of the popular vehicles for this year were from the 1998 model series.

This was the first year that Mattel produced the souvenir cars for the national collector's convention. There were four different cars, each blisterpacked, a McDonald's charity car (proceeds went to Ronald McDonald House Charities) and one giveaway. Convention exclusives also included a series of 25 unpainted Zamak cars, each limited to 500 and separately blisterpacked, plus a four-car Zamak set.

In 1999 the Hot Wheels line saw a major expansion of vehicles in larger scales. There were also a larger-than-average number of limited edition and premium cars.

1999

This year brought some huge additions to the Hot Wheels line, including cars in 1/43rd scale, 1/24th scale and 1/18th scale. The racing line added additional segments as well as limited editions. Mattel and Ferrari signed an exclusive licensing agreement so that 1/43rd-scale and 1/24th-scale Ferraris were added to the line as well as the basic 1/64th-scale line. The collectible line continued going strong with more than thirty new castings added in various two-, three- and four-car sets. There were more than sixty different limited editions/premiums available, including six different involving Major League Baseball teams. The 1999 convention featured three collectible line 1/64-scale cars, a 1/18th-scale car, the official convention car and a McDonald's car (the last two were 1/64-scale basic-line cars).

2000

Numbered blisterpacks continued, although Mattel went to a new card with a yearly format: numbers started at #001 for each new year and were placed on the card's front. Mattel obtained the license for Harley-Davidson, issuing cars in the basic & collectible lines, plus a 1/10th-scale series. Convention cars were continued and there were also some set cars. A new series was taken from NASCAR, using basic-line cars with teams' sponsorship tampos. The Action Packs and 1/43-scale cars (other than the Ferrari line) were discontinued. In the racing series, Mattel for the first time produced a Treasure Hunt series. Also, the Radical Rides came out in the NASCAR line. The 1/18th-scale cars and the collectible line continued.

2001

The Final Run line was introduced and 12 basic-line cars were discontinued. Also discontinued were the Mystery Cars. The Collectibles-line box was revamped and was more popular than ever. April saw the first Nationals, a convention for the eastern half of the U.S. The Hot Wheels Convention celebrated its 15th Anniversary. It was also the 15th Anniversary of the Newsletter, which had a limited-edition Passion exclusive for subscribers. Hotwheelscollectors.com, an addition to hotwheels.com, came on board, issuing a Rodger Dodger as its first car.

2002

Mattel had basically the same selection as 2001. A Passion, the first-ever limited edition produced for the foreign market, was made for the Japanese Collector's Club. Also, hotwheelscollectors.com introduced the Redline Club, an exclusive club that gives members first choice of the limited editions sold online. This is the year Mattel started numbering the Collectible singles and only issued two-car sets.

VALUES AND PRICES

Cars that are mint (meaning new and unused condition) or are in the original package demand the highest prices. Worn or badly abused cars are generally not worth much and are usually put in a collection in lieu of a better-condition model (these are called "space fillers"). However, there are several years, 1973 and 1974 in particular, where even extremely worn cars have value because of their rarity. Like other collectibles, vehicle price is based on supply and demand.

Supply

Supply depends upon production, attrition, and the willingness to sell. Several years ago Mattel produced its billionth car and recently Mattel's production runs were estimated to be about 250,000 of each car. On average, Mattel replaces or changes about 25% to 50% of its line each year. However some of the more popular cars may have lives of seven to eight years. The collector is always on the lookout for those models that are only in the line for short periods of time or have had a short-lived change. The life span of a car is quixotic at best. Many cars have been taken out of production or their colors quickly changed because of a marketing decision or, as in the case of the A-OK, mold breakage. Other reasons for variations are the overseas manufacturing facility not following the plans with exactness on first runs or simply substituting parts for those out of stock. Whatever the reasons, the variety produced over the years have made Hot Wheels cars extremely challenging and collectible.

Demand

Demand is somewhat fickle and can be trendy. Popularity challenges every marketing department. What was desirable ten years ago isn't necessarily desirable today. Sometimes a car appeals to several collectors' groups. The Snake and Mongoose set has Coca-Cola logos and is sought by Coca-Cola collectors. The McDonald's display containing eight Barbie figures and eight Hot Wheels cars is pursued by three distinct collecting groups. Even though this promotional display is from 1991, prices escalated rapidly. Some die-cast enthusiasts collect fire trucks, others police cars and still others only Corvette or Volkswagen models. But in general, the older the model, the more likely there are fewer copies available and demand often escalates accordingly.

TIPS FOR FINDING HOT WHEELS CARS

There are several publications and events focused on Hot Wheels cars. They can also be found at many toy shows, swap meets, and antique flea markets.

Hot Wheels Newsletter
26 Madera Ave.
San Carlos, CA 94070
Contact: Mike Strauss
(650) 591-6482 (after 6 p.m. PST)
$30 for 6 quarterly issues. Information on past and present Hot Wheels, premiums, promotions, limited editions, free subscriber ads and world-wide Collector's Club.

The Annual Hot Wheels Collector's Convention, sponsored by the Hot Wheels Newsletter, is held each fall in the western part of the U.S. The Annual Hot Wheels Collector's Nationals, sponsored by the Hot Wheels Newsletter, is held each spring in the eastern U.S. For more information, please contact Mike Strauss (650) 591-6482 (after 6 pm PST).

WHEELS

Fast wheels were responsible for the success and the name of the original Hot Wheels product. The concept design and a description of the wheel variations used during the first 30 years of Hot Wheels history appear below.

Wheel Variations

Type A red-stripe tires (rsw), removable, 1968-1970
These come in three types: A, B and E. The first type is removable. (To tell if a wheel is removable, turn the car over and look where the axle enters the wheel. There will be a white or pink bushing pressed into the wheel.) On the wheel's outside is an embossed red circle. The center is silver. On the inside is a small lip about 1/32". With the car sitting on a flat surface, only the lip will make contact (not the entire wheel). These were issued in three sizes: 1/8" by 5/16", 3/16" by 3/8" and 3/16" by 7/16". The smallest were only used on the front.

Type B red-stripe tires (rsw), split wheel, 1970-1974
These look like Type A but do not have the bushing pressed into the wheel. The wheel joins together at a lip with the outside half being removable and the inside half remaining attached to the axle. These also come in three sizes: 3/16" by 3/8", 3/16" by 7/16" and 9/32" by 3/8". The larger wheels vary because the lips are on the outside (rather than the inside). These wheels were only used on the 1970 and 1971 Heavyweights.

Type C large basic wheels with black sidewall tires (bwl), 1971
These are the same as large Type B and were only used as the back wheels on the Snake and Mongoose rail dragsters.

Type D small spoke wheels (sw), 1970-1978
These were only used in the front on dragsters. They are not removable and came in two variations, solid black and clear. Both variations measure 1/16" by 3/8".

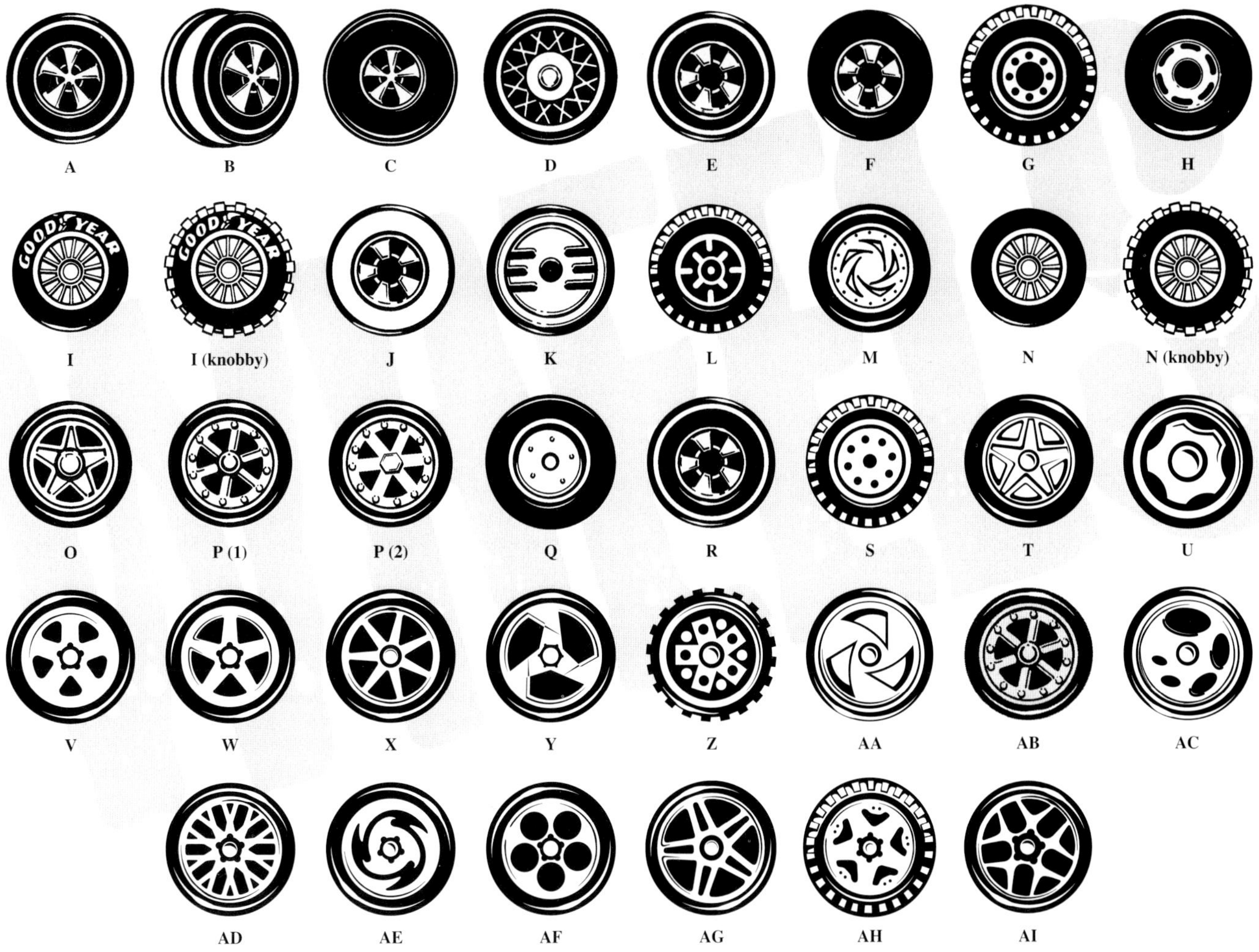

A B C D E F G H

I I (knobby) J K L M N N (knobby)

O P (1) P (2) Q R S T U

V W X Y Z AA AB AC

AD AE AF AG AH AI

Wheel variations from 1968-2002, not shown to scale.

Type E red-stripe tires (rsw), 1973-1977
The last of the rsw, these are unremovable. Like the earlier rsw, there is a red circle embossed around the tire. There's also a hole in the center of the spokes. This was the last wheel with an inside lip. The axle goes through and is beveled. There are three sizes: 3/16" by 3/8", 3/16" by 7/16", & 3/16" by 9/16".

Type F basic blackwall tires (bw), 1977 to present
These are basically the same as Type E except there is no red stripe. They are used on some military vehicles with black (bwbk) or tan spokes (bwt) and have also been used in white (bww) and yellow (bwy). They come in the same sizes as Type E.

Type G construction tires (ct), 1980 to present
These unremovable truck wheels come with a knobby tread. They were originally issued with yellow hubs (cty). Later models came in silver, orange (cto), gold (ctgd), white (ctw), yellow (cty), large (ctl) and large yellow (ctly).

Type H gold Hot Ones wheels (gw), 1980 to present
These are the same as Type F except the hubs look slightly different. They were first issued in 1981 for the Hot Ones series and use a thinner axle. They were originally only issued with gold hubs (gw) but in 1992 were made with chrome hubs (hoc). There are two sizes: 3/16" by 3/8" and 3/16" by 7/16".

Type I Goodyear Tires (gyt), 1983 to present
Mattel called cars with these wheels Real Riders™. The tires are removable, but the wheels are not. The wheel is a truck type, recessed with fifteen spokes. They were first issued in 1983 with gray hubs (gyg), then in 1984 with white hubs (gyw). "GOODYEAR" is printed in white on the sides. The hubs are issued in two sizes: 1/4" by 5/16" and 3/16" by 1/4". The tires come three ways: 1/4" by 9/16" knobby tires, 1/4" by 1/2" treaded tires, and 3/16" by 7/16" treaded tires.

Type J white wall tires (ww), 1983 to present
These were the same as the basic wheels except the tires were painted white. They were mainly used on classic-type vehicles and were issued in two sizes: 3/16" by 3/8" and 3/16" by 7/16" treaded tires.

Type K Ultra Hot wheels (uh), 1984-1995
These were originally made only for the Ultra Hot series, although they are now used for other cars. A hole in the center exposes the axle. A 1/16" chrome-plated circle runs around the side. Inside the circle, the wheel center is chrome-plated with six black slots cut into the tire. The cuts run parallel and 1/16" apart, three on each side of the center hole. These come in either chrome (uh) or gold (uhgd), and in the same sizes as ww.

Type L construction tires, 8-spoke (cts), 1985 to present
These are unremovable wheels with knobby treads. A hole in the center exposes the axle. The wheel measures 9/32" by 5/8" and has a chrome-plated circle in the center with four spokes sticking up and four sticking down. They were also issued in yellow (ctsy) or black (ctsb) instead of chrome.

Type M turbo wheels (tw), 1989 to present
These mag-style wheels were introduced with the California Customs series. They have a center design, silver rim, and black plastic tire. Turbo wheels have been found in chrome (tw), blue (twb), red (twr), and yellow (twy). There are two sizes: 3/16" by 15/32" and 5/32" by 7/16".

Type N Real Riders wheels (rr), 1989 to present
These are similar to Type I wheels because they come with the same hubs and synthetic rubber tires. Unlike earlier tires, they do not have "GOODYEAR" on the sides and are a glossy black. The hubs have been issued in gray (rrgy), red (rrr), two different shades of yellow (rry), and orange (rro). They were only used for California Customs. There are two sizes: 1/4" by 15/32" and 3/16" by 7/16".

Type O Pro Circuit wheels (pc), 1992 to present
These are produced for the Pro Circuits cars. They are plastic with plastic tires and come with five large spokes in chrome (pc), gray (pcg), red (pcr), or white (pcw). There are two sizes: 1/4" by 15/32" and 3/16" by 7/16".

Type P Pro Circuit Indy Wheels (iw), 1992 to present
These were produced for the Pro Circuit Indy cars. They are plastic with plastic tires and were issued with six thin spokes in either chrome (iw) or gray (iwg). There are two sizes: 1/4" by 15/32" and 3/16" by 7/16"

Type Q race car tires (rt), 1992 to present
These wheels come with synthetic rubber tires and were made with refurbished tooling exclusively for the collector's edition cars. A center hole exposes the axle. The wheel is a recessed race type with five bolts in a circle on the hub. They were issued with "GOODYEAR" in white on the sides (rtg) or without (rt). All hubs were gray or chrome (rtch) and all tires were black. They come in two sizes: 1/4" by 15/32" and 5/32" by 7/16".

Type R new red-line tires (nrl), 1993
These are basically the same as Type E except there is a red line tampoed (rather than embossed) around the wheel. They were produced exclusively for the 25th Anniversary cars.

Type S construction tire (ctel), 1992 to present
These are very similar to type G tires, except they are about twice as large. They were first found on the 1992 Tractor.

Type T lime wheels (liw), 1993
These plastic experimental wheels were only used for two cars, the BMW 850i and the Mazda MX-5 Miata. They had yellow hubs and black tires.

Type U micro wheels or dragster wheels (mw), 1993 to present
The same style as on Mattel's Planet Micro cars, these have only been found as the front tires on dragsters and Rail Rodder. They have black plastic tires with chrome center designs and rims.

Type V five-spoke hubs (sp5), 1995 to present
One of the replacements for uh wheels for more realism, these have five spokes in the hubs and smooth plastic tires. They've been found in 7/16" & 1/2" sizes, and white (sp5w) & gold (sp5gd) colors.

Type W large five-spoke hubs (sp5-large), 1995 to present
These are found in the backs of dragsters and some cars having sp5 wheels in front. They have five-spoke hubs and smooth tires. This wheel has been found in the 9/16" size and white (sp5w) & gold (sp5gd) colors.

Type X seven-spoke hubs (sp7), 1995 to present
One of the replacements for uh wheels for more realism, these have seven spokes in the hubs and smooth plastic tires. They have been found in 7/16" & 1/2" sizes, and gold (sp7gd) & orange (sp7o) colors.

Type Y three-spoke hubs (sp3), 1995 to present
One of the replacements for uh wheels for more realism, these have three spokes in the hubs and smooth plastic tires. They have been found in 7/16" & 1/2" sizes, and chrome (sp3), gold (sp7gd), and white (sp3w).

Type Z screamin' wheels (scw), 1993 to present
These have only been found on set cars. They have grooves in the tires so they make a whistling (screaming) sound when rolled down the track.

Type AA hot hub wheels (hh), 1995 to present
These plastic wheels were first introduced in the Hot Hubs Series. They have been found in blue (hhb), green (hhgn), and yellow (hhy) hubs, and have different color tires.

Type AB six-spoke wheels (sp6), 1995 to present
At this time, these have only been found in green (sp6gn) on Vampyra in the Hot Hubs Series. They are plastic and have black tires.

Type AC progressive oval wheels (pow), 1995 to present
These have only been found on the Suzuki QuadRacer and only in yellow. The hubs are flat and have five holes, each hole getting progressively smaller. They are plastic with black plastic tires.

Type AD lace wheels (lwch), 1996
Called lace wheels by Mattel, these were modeled after the BBS wheels used by Mercedes and other foreign luxury cars.

Type AE directional wheels (dw3), 1996
These have three spokes all going in the same direction. They have been found in chrome (dw3), orange (dw3o), and yellow (dw3y) colors, in two sizes, and are also found with construction tires (dw3ct).

Type AF five-hole wheels (ho5), 1996
These deep-dish wheels come with five holes in the hub cap. They have been found in two sizes, and have been released in chrome (ho5) & white (ho5w).

Type AG Phil Riehlman wheels (Pr5s), 2001
This wheel was named for its designer: Phil Riehlman. It has five double spokes. Originally issued in chrome, it comes in medium, large, large wide, extra large, extra large wide and assorted colors.

Type AH off-road wheels/tires (ort), 2002
This wheel was also designed by Phil Riehlman. It comes in only two sizes, large and extra large.

Type AI five y's tires (y5t), 2002
At this time, this wheel has only been found on the Ballistik. It should be out in medium and large.

Wheel and Tire Abbreviations

Wheel and tire abbreviations are letter-number combinations describing both type (with variations) and color. For example, "dw3cty" means directional wheels, three-spoke, with yellow construction tires.

bw basic wheels (Type F)
bwl basic wheels, large (Type C)
ct construction tires (Type G)
ctel construction tires, extra large (Type S)
ctl construction tires, large (Type G)
cts construction tires, 8-spoke (Type L)
dw3 directional wheels, three-spoke (Type AE)

gy Goodyear tires
gyt Goodyear tires (Type I)
hh Hot Hubs (Type AA)
ho5 five-hole wheels (Type AF)
ho Hot Ones wheels (Type H)
iw Pro Circuit Indy wheels (Type P)
liw lime wheels (Type T)
lw lace wheels (Type AD)
mw micro wheels (Type U)
nrl new redline tires (tampoed stripe, Type R)
pc Pro Circuit wheels (Type O)
pow progressive oval wheels (Type AC)
rr Real Rider wheels (Type N)
rt race car tires (Type Q)
rtg race car tires with Goodyear on sides (Type Q)
scw screamin' wheels (Type Z)
sp3 three-spoke wheels (Type Y)
sp5 five-spoke wheels (Type V)
sp5-large five-spoke wheels, large (Type W)
sp6 six-spoke wheels
sp7 seven-spoke wheels (Type X)
sw small spoke wheels (Type D)
tw turbo wheels (Type M)
uh Ultra Hot wheels (Type K)
ww white wall tires (Type J)

Tire Variations

gw gold hubs (Hot Ones) wheels (Type H)
rsw red stripe around tire
ws white stripe around tire

Wheel Color Abbreviations

bk black
bl blue
bn brown
gy gray
gd gold
gn green
lg light green
mg magenta
o orange
pk pink
pp purple
rd red
t tan
wt white
yw yellow

Other Abbreviations Used in Listings

Anniv. Anniversary
bp blisterpack
camo camouflage
dk. dark
ed edition
excl. exclusive
fluor. fluorescent
int. interior
Intl. International
lt. light
ltd limited
mtlc metallic
mtlfk metalflake
NA not applicable
pkg package
POC price of car(s)
promo promotion
sig. signature
sm small
w/ with
w/o without

ABOUT THIS BOOK

From 1968 through 1972, most models were issued in the same assorted colors every year and used just one stock number per car. The stock-numbering system, vehicle names and spectraflame paints were consistent over the first five years. These cars are listed by name with all changes. Mattel's marketing philosophy in these early years was to produce the same model in as many as fourteen different colors. Also, enamel paints were used sparingly. They usually appeared when they made the car more prototypical, as British racing green on British racing models. Since not every color has been found for every model, space has been left in the listings for missing colors. If ever located, they will be included in future editions.

The year 1973 saw some major changes. Castings were reissued in new enamel colors, some models had new names and all had new stock numbers. In the following years models were reissued with designs (tampos) and many of the stock numbers were changed. Some models were reissued with more than thirty variations. When a name changed, all vehicles using the same casting are listed under "Similar castings."

Since most collectors only collect one of each of the early models, there is not a great price disparity among different colors. The exception being colors which are very scarce (Custom Camaro in white enamel) or much more desirable (pink). There never seems to be enough of these to go around to satisfy the color collectors. Later models (1974 to the present) were generally issued in only one color per year and therefore most collectors try to accumulate all colors.

The Mattel Toy Club is a retail outlet. Although most cars in stock are sold at regular retail prices, there are periodic clearance sales of cars which normally come from sets.

The term "tampo" refers to the pad-press decoration found on some vehicles.

The country of manufacture is normally found on the vehicle's base and is identified in the listings. If a vehicle was only sold outside the U.S., the country is indicated after the year.

Words within quotation marks are found on the vehicle.

Three numbers appear in the listings. The Mattel part number is given at the beginning. The number at the end preceded by a "#" is the collector number. The year of issue appears in parentheses.

Determining Value

The prices listed in this guide are averaged from sales across the U.S. They are derived from collectors' and dealers' reports of prices paid in the months prior to publication. Auction results are not used in averaging.

The first price listed is the price for a mint-condition vehicle, the second for a mint-condition vehicle in its original package. Prices drop dramatically for cars that are not in mint condition. Restored cars have no value. There are reproduction parts available, but their use should be to increase a collector's personal pleasure, not to increase resale value. Some people knowingly or unknowingly sell or trade cars with reproduction parts. Beware! Serious collectors consider this counterfeiting. Also beware of vehicles with many decals; decals can be used to hide scratches or dark spots.

If a car was accompanied by another item, such as a video tape or trophy, this item normally must be included in comparable condition to command the full listed value. This will be noted in the listings. For example: "w/trophy."

To help provide a more objective determination of grade, the following point system is suggested:

1 small, barely noticeable scratch
1 slight wear on decal
1 slightly tarnished base
1 minor wear on wheel (one point for each wheel)
2 up to three barely noticeable scratches

2 noticeable wear on decals
2 slightly crooked tampo
3 clearly crooked tampo
3 substantial wear on decals
3 tarnished base
3 wheels show considerable wear (3 points for each wheel)
5 small noticeable scratches
5 up to two small dark spots
10 very noticeable dark spots
14 very obvious scratches
20 reproduction parts
40 most of paint is missing
50 parts missing

Add all the points together and locate the vehicle's condition on the following table. For collectors who prefer a 1-10 numeric scale, the corresponding numbers are in parentheses.

0 points - mint (m) (10)
1 - near mint to mint (nm-m) (9)
2 - near mint (nm) (8)
6 - excellent to near mint (exc-nm) (7)
9 - excellent (exc) (6)
20 - fine (fn) (5)
25 - very good to fine (vg-fn) (4)
30 - very good (vg) (3)
35 - good to very good (g-vg) (2)
40 - good (g) (1)

Prices for a $100 mint car (10) would correspond to other conditions as follows:
near mint to mint (nm-m) (9) - $85
near mint (nm) (8) - $80
excellent to near mint (exc-nm) (7) - $65
excellent (exc) (6) - $50
fine (fn) (5) - $30
very good to fine (vg-fn) (4) - $20
very good (vg) (3) - $15
good to very good (g-vg) (2) - $10
good (g) (1) - $5

LOCATING A CAR IN THIS BOOK

Remember, all Hot Wheels cars known to have been produced from 1968 through 2002 and Toy Fair announcements are listed in this book. The key to finding any individual vehicle is knowing its name and year of introduction. Of course, you could compare the car in question to each photo in the book until you have a match, but the valuable introductory material preceding this paragraph will help you use wheel design and other factors to narrow down a positive identification much faster. The value range shown after each car or variation is a representation in U.S. dollars. The dollar signs have been removed to avoid needless repetition.

J.C. Penney Treasure Hunt Sets

The rare Mongoose and Snake funny car Drag Race Set from 1970.

1968 - 1972 Spectraflame Colors

Metallic Aqua

Metallic Blue

Metallic Brown

Metallic Gold

Metallic Green

Metallic Light Blue

Metallic Light Green

Metallic Magenta

Metallic Olive

Metallic Orange

Metallic Pink

Metallic Purple

Metallic Red

Metallic Yellow

Metallic Lime

Metallic Lavender

Metallic Salmon

1968

The 1968 Hot Wheels line of sixteen models included custom cars, race cars, and show cars. All were released in eight spectraflame colors, some in as many as fourteen not counting shades. These are the models that have been positively verified as of this writing. Color shades can vary for several reasons: changing intensities in the spray booth, age and storage are all factors.

Note: Custom Camaro (white enamel), Custom Volkswagen (green enamel) and Ford J-Car (white enamel) were the only cars issued in anything but the normal spectraflame colors.

All 1968 models were made in both the U.S. and Hong Kong. All differ between production facilities, some more than others. Hong Kong versions have blue-tinted windows and more chassis detail, whereas U.S. cars have clear windows and are less detailed.

6217-a

Beatnik Bandit 6217 - 59 mm - 1968-1971

This model is based on the show car designed and built by Ed "Big Daddy" Roth. It has a metal chassis, exposed metal engine, plastic interior (assorted colors), plastic dome roof and rsw. The Hong Kong version has two headlights sticking through holes under the fender, an engine with supercharger sitting on the chassis, a grille sticking through the body, a round steering wheel instead of a steering rod as in the real model and longer taillights than the U.S. version. The U.S. version has flat headlights inside holes under the fenders, an engine with two carburetors sitting on the body casting and a steering rod instead of a steering wheel. The grille does not stick through the body.

Similar casting: 5714 Beatnik Bandit (1993)

a. metallic aqua $60 - 100
b. metallic blue 40 - 80
c. metallic brown 75 - 120
d. metallic gold 40 - 80
e. metallic green 40 - 80
f. metallic light blue 125 - 200
h. metallic magenta 125 - 200
i. metallic olive 60 - 100
j. metallic orange 50 - 110
k. metallic pink 750 - 1500
l. metallic purple 50 - 110
m. metallic red 40 - 80
n. metallic yellow 60 - 100
o. metallic lavender 300 - 400
p. metallic lime 60 - 100

6211-c

Custom Barracuda 6211 - 77mm - 1968-1969

This 1967 Plymouth Barracuda fastback has a metal chassis, plastic interior (assorted colors), rsw and a lift-up hood. The Hong Kong version has longer hood scoops, a large black steering wheel sticking through the interior and a flat dashboard. The U.S. version has shorter hood scoops, a small steering wheel as part of the interior and a raised dashboard. This car is difficult to find in blisterpack.

a. metallic aqua $120 - 350
b. metallic blue 200 - 450
c. metallic brown 100 - 300
d. metallic gold 120 - 300
e. metallic green 140 - 350
f. metallic light blue 300 - 600
i. metallic olive 350 - 650
j. metallic orange 300 - 800
l. metallic purple 200 - 500
m. metallic red 300 - 650
o. metallic lavender 600 - 1000
p. metallic lime 200 - 600

6208-b

Custom Camaro 6208 - 70mm - 1968-1969

This 1967 Chevrolet Camaro has a metal chassis, plastic interior (assorted colors), rsw and a lift-up hood. Some of the models were issued with a black roof. The Hong Kong version has a flat dashboard, large black steering wheel sticking through the interior and smaller taillights. The U.S. version has a raised dashboard and a small steering wheel as part of the interior. The Camaro is rumored to be the first Hot Wheels car produced, but this cannot be true because Mattel originally came out with an assortment of 1968 cars.

Note: There is a white enamel version of the Camaro which is quite rare and sells for at least ten times more. Only about 15 are presently known to exist; none are blisterpacked.

Similar casting: 3913 '67 Camaro (1983)

a. metallic aqua $150 - 450
b. metallic blue 120 - 300
c. metallic brown 200 - 600
d. metallic gold 350 - 800
e. metallic green 175 - 400
f. metallic light blue 500 - 1000
i. metallic olive 350 - 650
j. metallic orange 300 - 800
l. metallic purple 200 - 500
m. metallic red 300 - 650
n. metallic yellow 200 - 550
o. metallic lavender 750 - 1200
p. metallic lime 200 - 450
q. white enamel 2200 - NA

6215-m

Custom Corvette 6215 - 70mm - 1968-1971

This 1968 Chevrolet Corvette has a metal chassis, plastic interior (assorted colors), rsw and a lift-up hood. The Hong Kong version has the rear panel in the body casting, a flat dashboard and a large black steering wheel sticking through the interior. The U.S. version has the rear panel as part of the chassis, a raised dashboard and a small steering wheel as part of the interior. Although not rare, this model's popularity with Chevy and Corvette collectors makes it one of the more desirable models in the Hot Wheels line.

Note: The Hot Wheels version of the Custom Corvette was in stores before the full-size Corvettes were in the showrooms.

a. metallic aqua $140 - 375
b. metallic blue 125 - 300
c. metallic brown 350 - 600
d. metallic gold 150 - 350
e. metallic green 150 - 350
f. metallic light blue 450 - 900
h. metallic magenta 400 - 1000
i. metallic olive 300 - 500
j. metallic orange 200 - 425
l. metallic purple 250 - 550
m. metallic red 110 - 300
n. metallic yellow 150 - 350
p. metallic lime 200 - 450

6205-i

Custom Cougar 6205 - 73mm - 1968-1969

This 1967 Mercury Cougar has a metal chassis, plastic interior (assorted colors), rsw and a lift-up hood. Some models were issued with a black roof. The Hong Kong version has no dashboard, a large black steering wheel sticking through the interior and larger taillights. The U.S. version has a dashboard and small steering wheel as part of the interior. This is one of the most difficult models to find in blisterpack.

a. metallic aqua $225 - 550
b. metallic blue 125 - 350
c. metallic brown 400 - 800
d. metallic gold 225 - 500
e. metallic green 175 - 450
f. metallic light blue 400 - 900
i. metallic olive 200 - 400
j. metallic orange 200 - 400
l. metallic purple 350 - 850
m. metallic red 600 - 1200
n. metallic yellow 175 - 400
p. metallic lime 225 - 450

6218-a

Custom Eldorado 6218 - 78mm - 1968-1971

This 1967 Cadillac Eldorado Coupe de Ville has a metal chassis, plastic interior (assorted colors), rsw, a lift-up hood and a black roof. The Hong Kong version has a flat dashboard and a large black steering wheel sticking through the interior. The U.S. version has a raised dashboard and a small steering wheel as part of the interior.

a. metallic aqua $80 - 200
b. metallic blue 70 - 200
c. metallic brown 90 - 250
d. metallic gold 80 - 225
e. metallic green 75 - 200
f. metallic light blue 325 - 525
g. metallic light green 350 - 550
h. metallic magenta 110 - 300
i. metallic olive 90 - 250
j. metallic orange 85 - 250
k. metallic pink 350 - 750
l. metallic purple 125 - 350
m. metallic red 100 - 250
n. metallic yellow 85 - 250
o. metallic lavender 200 - 600
p. metallic lime 125 - 275

6212-e

Custom Firebird 6212 - 72mm - 1968-1969

This 1968 Pontiac Firebird convertible has a metal chassis, a plastic interior (assorted colors), rsw and a lift-up hood. The Hong Kong version has a larger, thinner hood scoop, small windshield cowl vent, flat dashboard and a large black steering wheel sticking through the interior. The seats are at an angle, there is no door outline and the body casting is higher. The U.S. version has a large windshield cowl vent, a shorter, thicker hood scoop, raised dashboard and a small steering wheel as part of the interior. The seats are straight up and the door is outlined.

Note: This is the first convertible produced by Mattel. The red version with red interior and the blue version with blue interior, although not too difficult to find, are quite popular and a little more expensive than other models.

a. metallic aqua $100 - 225
b. metallic blue 85 - 210
c. metallic brown 135 - 340
d. metallic gold 100 - 250
e. metallic green 85 - 240
f. metallic light blue 300 - 500
i. metallic olive 100 - 275
j. metallic orange 125 - 300
l. metallic purple 140 - 350
m. metallic red 85 - 240
o. metallic lavender 400 - 600
p. metallic lime 150 - 400
q. metallic blue - blue interior 175 - 450

6212-r

r. metallic red - red interior 175 - 450

6213-d

Custom Fleetside 6213 - 78mm - 1968-1969

This customized Chevrolet El Camino pickup truck has a metal chassis, plastic interior (assorted colors), black roof and a black plastic cover on the truck bed. The Hong Kong version has a smooth black cover over the truck bed, flat dashboard, a large black steering wheel sticking through the interior and vertical taillights. The U.S. version has a mold mark on the black cover, a raised dashboard, a small steering wheel as part of the interior and horizontal taillights.

Note: This was modeled after Harry Bradley's own car, which he drove to work every day. Harry was the first Hot Wheels designer; this was the first car he designed for Mattel.

Similar casting: 6436 Sky Show Fleetside (1970, with ramp)

a. metallic aqua $80 - 200
b. metallic blue 225 - 375
c. metallic brown 250 - 500
d. metallic gold 100 - 250
e. metallic green 100 - 250
f. metallic light blue 350 - 700
j. metallic orange 75 - 225
l. metallic purple 75 - 250
m. metallic red 150 - 375
n. metallic yellow 125 - 275
p. metallic lime 150 - 300

6206-d

Custom Mustang 6206 - 71mm - 1968-1969

This 1967 Ford Mustang fastback has a metal chassis, plastic interior (assorted colors), rsw, lift-up hood, black roof and was available with either open or closed hood scoops. It was also issued in smooth or louvered rear-window versions. The Hong Kong casting has a flat dashboard, large black steering wheel sticking through the interior, black rear panel with red taillights and no fuel cap. There are no vertical bars or black on the front grill. The U.S. version has a raised dashboard, small steering wheel as part of the interior and is only black in the center by the taillights. The fuel tank cap is outlined and the black front grill has vertical bars. The open hood scoop model is from Hong Kong and has the taillight section as part of the body.

Values are shown in U.S. dollars, first price is for mint, second is for mint packaged vehicles only. See pages 15-16 for grading guide to determine value for cars in lesser conditions.

Although not rare, the Custom Mustang's popularity with Ford and Mustang collectors makes it one of the most desirable models in the Hot Wheels line.

Similar casting: 10496 Custom Mustang (1994)

Note: The Mustang with open hood scoops is very rare and has only been found in red or gold. The Mustang with the louvered back window is just as difficult to find and has only been seen in red, blue, orange, & yellow.

a. metallic aqua $175 - 450
b. metallic blue 150 - 400

6206-b2

b2. mtlc blue, louvered rear window 550 - 1100
c. metallic brown 175 - 450
d. metallic gold 150 - 400
d2. metallic gold, open hood scoops 1100 - 1400
e. metallic green 225 - 500
f. metallic light blue 450 - 800
i. metallic olive 200 - 475
j. metallic orange 200 - 475
j2. mtlc orange, louvered rear window 500 - 1100
l. metallic purple 300 - 650
m. metallic red 150 - 400

6206-m2

m2. metallic red, open hood scoops 550 - 1350
m3. mtlc red, louvered rear window 600 - 1100
n. metallic yellow 165 - 475
n2. mtlc yellow, louvered rear window 500 - 1100
o. metallic lavender 600 - 1050
p. metallic lime 175 - 475

6207-m

Custom T-Bird 6207 - 78mm - 1968-1969

This 1967 Ford Thunderbird has a metal chassis, plastic interior (assorted colors), rsw and a lift-up hood. Some models came with a black roof. The Hong Kong version has no dashboard, a large black steering wheel sticking through the interior, wider taillights and no black on a larger front grill. The U.S. version has a dashboard, a small steering wheel as part of the interior and black on a smaller front grill.

a. metallic aqua $75 - 225
b. metallic blue 90 - 250
c. metallic brown 100 - 250
d. metallic gold 110 - 275
e. metallic green 95 - 275
f. metallic light blue 325 - 900
i. metallic olive 165 - 450
j. metallic orange 125 - 275
l. metallic purple 200 - 400
m. metallic red 110 - 250
o. metallic lavender 200 - 400
p. metallic lime 200 - 425

Custom Volkswagen 6220 - 56mm - 1968-1971

This 1967 Volkswagen has a metal chassis, exposed engine, plastic interior (assorted colors), rsw and a plastic sliding sun roof.

6220-j

The Hong Kong version has no dashboard, an engine with smaller valve covers sitting on the frame and a large, short black steering wheel sticking through the interior. The headlights are part of the chassis and stick through holes in the fenders. The U.S. version has a dashboard, an engine with larger valve covers sitting on the body casting, a long, small steering wheel as part of the interior and headlights painted in silver on the fenders.

Note: The dark green enamel and magenta enamel versions are more difficult to find and worth more than any other color. This model has been found in Europe without a sunroof.

a. metallic aqua $60 - 125
b. metallic blue 60 - 135

6220-b2

b2. metallic blue, no sunroof 900 - 2000
c. metallic brown 60 - 135
d. metallic gold 75 - 190
e. metallic green 65 - 135
e2. metallic green, no sunroof 900 - 2000
f. metallic light blue 275 - 600
h. metallic magenta 200 - 450
i. metallic olive 100 - 200
j. metallic orange 90 - 200
k. metallic pink 650 - 1250
l. metallic purple 150 - 275
m. metallic red 85 - 180
n. metallic yellow 110 - 250
o. metallic lavender 275 - 650
p. metallic lime 115 - 275
q. dark green enamel 175 - 375
q2. green enamel, no sunroof 750 - 2200
r. magenta enamel 245 - 500

6210-e

Deora® 6210 - 70mm - 1968-1969

This model is based on the custom surfing truck designed by Harry Bradley for Dodge and built by the Alexander brothers. It has a metal chassis, plastic interior (assorted colors), rsw and orange & yellow plastic surfboards on a black flat bed. These removable surfboards stick through the rear window. The Hong Kong version has no dashboard, a large black steering wheel attached to the side of the interior, large front bumper, deep inset grill area, flat headlights and a frame which is part of the front bumper assembly. The U.S. version has a dashboard with a small steering wheel as part of the interior, small front bumper, shallow inset grill area and ribbed headlights. The front is part of the frame and is painted in the car's color.

Similar casting: 10495 Deora (1994)

a. metallic aqua $75 - 325
b. metallic blue 700 - 1500
d. metallic gold 85 - 300
e. metallic green 175 - 500
j. metallic orange 90 - 350
l. metallic purple 100 - 375
m. metallic red 200 - 450
n. metallic yellow 100 - 350
p. metallic lime 125 - 350

6214-a

Ford J-Car 6214 - 62mm - 1968-1971

Based on the Ford factory racing machine designed and raced by Carroll Shelby, this model has a metal chassis, plastic interior (assorted colors), rsw and lift-up hood. The Hong Kong version has only been seen with no louvers on the rear fenders. It also has a large, short black steering wheel that sticks through the interior, a base painted in white enamel, and a body casting going halfway down the sides. The U.S. version has louvers on the rear fenders, a body casting going all the way down the sides, a long, small steering wheel on the right side and an unpainted base.

a. metallic aqua $40 - 85
b. metallic blue 45 - 85
c. metallic brown 45 - 95
d. metallic gold 45 - 85
e. metallic green 45 - 85
f. metallic light blue 110 - 235
i. metallic olive 55 - 95
j. metallic orange 45 - 85
k. metallic pink 300 - 600
l. metallic purple 65 - 150
m. metallic red 45 - 85
n. metallic yellow 45 - 85
o. metallic lavender 175 - 250
p. metallic lime 65 - 125
q. white enamel 70 - 140
r. light blue enamel 600 - 1000

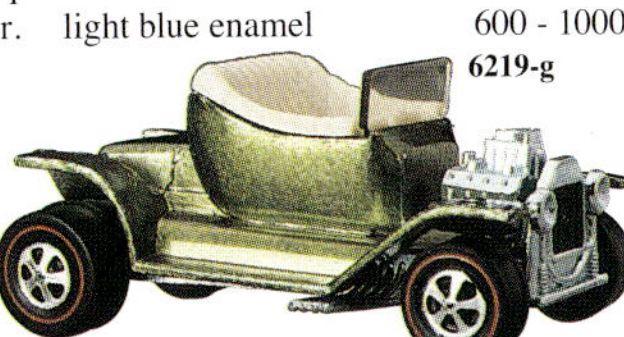
6219-g

Hot Heap™ 6219 - 55mm - 1968-1971

This model is based on the Model T Roadster convertible known as "Tognotti's T." It has a metal chassis, exposed metal engine, a plastic interior (assorted colors) and rsw. The Hong Kong version has an engine sitting back on the chassis, a large black steering wheel sticking through the floor, a longer trunk and a short rear spring brace. The U.S. version has an engine sitting forward on the body casting, a small steering wheel in the interior and a long rear spring brace.

a. metallic aqua $50 - 90
b. metallic blue 45 - 80
c. metallic brown 125 - 250
d. metallic gold 45 - 80
e. metallic green 45 - 80
f. metallic light blue 200 - 325
g. metallic light green 200 - 400
h. metallic magenta 150 - 300
i. metallic olive 50 - 85
j. metallic orange 50 - 100
k. metallic pink 450 - 700
l. metallic purple 100 - 175
m. metallic red 50 - 90
n. metallic yellow 60 - 100
o. metallic lavender 225 - 300
p. metallic lime 65 - 125

6216-n

Python 6216 - 64mm - 1968-1971

Based on Car Craft Magazine's "Dream Car" designed by Bill Cushenberry, this model has a metal chassis, exposed metal engine, plastic interior (assorted colors), rsw and a black roof. The Hong Kong version has a smaller rear window, no dashboard, large black front grill, sloping interior seats and a large black steering wheel sticking through the interior. The supercharged engine sits on the chassis. The body hangs over the chassis in front and back. The U.S. version has a dashboard, small black front grill, straight interior seats and a small steering wheel in the interior. The two-carburetor engine sits on the body casting. The body hangs halfway over the chassis in front but has no overhang in back.

Underside of the Cheetah

Note: Mattel originally called this the Cheetah but only three models with this name are known to exist. Whether this is a prototype or public issue is uncertain. It cannot be valued without a sales history.

a. metallic aqua $45 - 90
b. metallic blue 45 - 90
c. metallic brown 125 - 225
d. metallic gold 50 - 100
e. metallic green 45 - 100
f. metallic light blue 175 - 325
h. metallic magenta 185 - 375
i. metallic olive 75 - 145
j. metallic orange 50 - 100
k. metallic pink 450 - 800
l. metallic purple 75 - 200
m. metallic red 45 - 95
n. metallic yellow 60 - 120
o. metallic lavender 250 - 350
p. metallic lime 65 - 125

6209-l

Silhouette™ 6209 - 69mm - 1968-1971

Based on Bill Cushenberry's custom car, this model has a metal chassis, exposed chrome plastic engine, plastic interior (assorted colors), rsw, plastic dome roof and a painted base (same color as the car). The Hong Kong version has a large black steering wheel which sticks through the interior and longer, thinner side pipes sticking outside the body. The U.S. version has the steering wheel as part of the interior and shorter, fatter side pipes showing through holes on the sides.

Note: Very popular in 1968, this is probably the most remembered car of the era (especially the purple Silhouette).

Similar casting: 5715 Silhouette (1993)

a. metallic aqua $40 - 80
b. metallic blue 35 - 80
c. metallic brown 125 - 265
d. metallic gold 35 - 80
e. metallic green 35 - 80
f. metallic light blue 140 - 250
g. metallic light green 165 - 275
h. metallic magenta 110 - 240
i. metallic olive 75 - 150
j. metallic orange 50 - 80
k. metallic pink 350 - 500
l. metallic purple 40 - 80
m. metallic red 40 - 80
n. metallic yellow 40 - 90
o. metallic lavender 150 - 275
p. metallic lime 50 - 100

1969

Sales of Hot Wheels cars were ten times the first year projection, so Mattel expanded the line to include 24 additional cars. This brought the 1969 model total to

Values are shown in U.S. dollars, first price is for mint, second is for mint packaged vehicles only. See pages 15-16 for grading guide to determine value for cars in lesser conditions.

40. The Grand Prix series was introduced along with Indy, Can-Am and endurance cars. Another popular line was Street Rods which included the Classic '31 Ford Woody, the Classic '32 Ford Vicky and the Classic '36 Ford Coupe. These joined the popular Hot Heap from 1968. Two muscle cars were introduced, the Custom AMX and the Custom Charger. Several luxury cars were also included as well as the Classic '57 T-Bird and the highly sought Volkswagen Beach Bomb in two versions. This is also the first year cars came with paper decals. Models were again produced in both Hong Kong and the U.S., although not all models were made in both locations. Designers for 1969 included Ira Gilford and Howard Rees.

6264-c

Brabham-Repco F1 6264 - 73mm - 1969-1971 (Grand Prix)
This Hong Kong-made model is based on the Formula 1 racer designed by John Cooper, built by Geoff Brabham, and driven by Jack Brabham. It has a metal chassis, plastic interior (assorted colors), exposed plastic engine, plastic tailpipe, blue-tinted windshield, and rsw. It has been found with plastic detachable fuel tanks. The white-interior version is very difficult to find and is worth about four times the mint price and two times the blisterpack price of the dark-interior version.
Note: The real car was painted in British racing green.
Similar casting: 7616 Rash 1 (1974)
a. metallic aqua $35 - 80
b. metallic blue 35 - 80
c. metallic brown 55 - 125
e. metallic green 35 - 80
i. metallic olive 60 - 125
j. metallic orange 45 - 95
l. metallic purple 50 - 100
m. metallic red 40 - 85
o. dark green enamel (racing green) 80 - 150

6256-o

Chapparal 2G 6256 - 60mm - 1969-1971 (Grand Prix)
Based on the Can-Am racer built and raced by Jim Hall, this model has a metal chassis, dark brown or black plastic interior (assorted colors), blue-tinted windshield, removable white plastic spoiler in the back, rsw, a lift-up back to reveal a metal engine and was made in both Hong Kong and the U.S. Other than the window and base, the only difference between the two is the exhaust headers on the Hong Kong versions are longer. Also the headers on some U.S. versions don't meet at the rear.
Note: The plastic spoiler has been reproduced.
Similar casting: 7618 Winnipeg (1974)
a. metallic aqua $40 - 85
b. metallic blue 40 - 80
c. metallic brown 55 - 110
d. metallic gold 40 - 80
e. metallic green 80 - 75
f. metallic light blue 100 - 225
g. metallic light green 125 - 225
h. metallic magenta 100 - 225
i. metallic olive 60 - 160
j. metallic orange 40 - 85

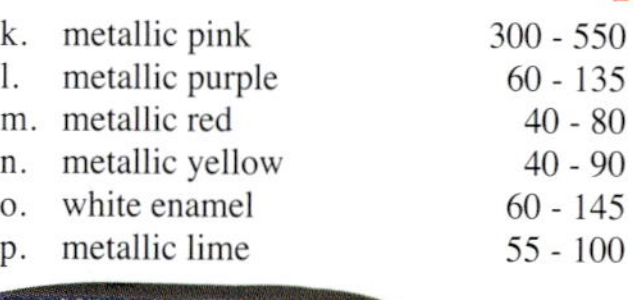

k. metallic pink 300 - 550
l. metallic purple 60 - 135
m. metallic red 40 - 80
n. metallic yellow 40 - 90
o. white enamel 60 - 145
p. metallic lime 55 - 100

6251-b

Classic '31 Ford Woody 6251 - 62mm - 1969-71
This customized 1931 Ford Woody station wagon has a metal chassis, plastic interior (assorted colors), exposed metal engine, clear or blue-tinted windshield, smooth or textured black roof, rsw and was made in the U.S.
Note: This model was so popular Mattel came out with the '40s Woodie in 1980.
a. metallic aqua $55 - 110
b. metallic blue 45 - 100
c. metallic brown 2000 - NA
d. metallic gold 50 - 90
e. metallic green 50 - 90
f. metallic light blue 125 - 275
h. metallic magenta 75 - 175
i. metallic olive 60 - 100
j. metallic orange 45 - 90
k. metallic pink 400 - 450
l. metallic purple 80 - 130
m. metallic red 50 - 90
n. metallic yellow 50 - 100
o. metallic lavender 125 - 300
p. metallic lime 60 - 110

6250-a

Classic '32 Ford Vicky 6250 - 62mm - 1969-71
This U.S.-made customized 1932 Ford Victoria has a metal chassis, plastic interior (assorted colors), exposed metal engine, clear windows, smooth black roof and rsw.
Similar casting: 10494 '32 Ford Vicky (1994)
a. metallic aqua $50 - 110
b. metallic blue 50 - 100
c. metallic brown 65 - 120
d. metallic gold 50 - 100
e. metallic green 50 - 100
f. metallic light blue 125 - 240
g. metallic light green 200 - 375
h. metallic magenta 125 - 210
i. metallic olive 55 - 110
j. metallic orange 55 - 125
k. metallic pink 575 - 900
l. metallic purple 75 - 140
m. metallic red 50 - 110
n. metallic yellow 50 - 100
p. metallic lime 65 - 110

6253-m

Classic '36 Ford Coupe 6253 - 65mm - 1969-71
This customized 1936 Ford Coupe has a metal chassis, plastic interior (assorted dark colors), exposed metal engine, opening rumble seat, clear windows, smooth black roof, rsw and was made in the U.S.
Note: Blue is very common in blisterpack.
a. metallic aqua $50 - 100
b. metallic blue 45 - 75
c. metallic brown 100 - 250
d. metallic gold 50 - 120
e. metallic green 50 - 120
g. metallic light green 250 - 425
h. metallic magenta 125 - 250
i. metallic olive 90 - 150
j. metallic orange 60 - 140
k. metallic pink 400 - 850
l. metallic purple 80 - 170
m. metallic red 65 - 135
n. metallic yellow 60 - 150
p. metallic lime 85 - 150

6252-l

Classic '57 T-Bird 6252 - 1969-1971
This 1957 Ford Thunderbird convertible has a metal chassis, plastic interior (assorted colors), lift-up hood to reveal a metal engine, clear windows, rsw and was made in the U.S.
a. metallic aqua $65 - 150
b. metallic blue 60 - 140
c. metallic brown 100 - 200
d. metallic gold 65 - 150
e. metallic green 65 - 140
f. metallic light blue 135 - 220
g. metallic light green 175 - 300
h. metallic magenta 135 - 250
i. metallic olive 75 - 150
j. metallic orange 65 - 150
k. metallic pink 425 - 700
l. metallic purple 80 - 175
m. metallic red 65 - 150
n. metallic yellow 65 - 135
p. metallic lime 85 - 170

6267-a

Custom AMX 6267 - 70mm - 1969-1971
Based on the American Motors AMX, this model has a metal chassis, white plastic interior, lift-up hood to reveal a metal engine, clear windows, rsw. Made in U.S. Very few mint pieces exist.

In 1970 in England this model was driven in races and a special model of the race car driven by Ed Shaver was issued. The model was only issued in blue and had Ed Shaver decals in the pack.
a. metallic aqua $90 - 200
b. metallic blue 110 - 225
b2. blue w/Ed Shaver decals 3000 - 4500
d. metallic gold 75 - 235
e. metallic green 75 - 220
g. metallic light green 200 - 350
h. metallic magenta 160 - 260
j. metallic orange 130 - 265
k. metallic pink 200 - 360
l. metallic purple 175 - 325
m. metallic red 100 - 225
n. metallic yellow 90 - 200
o. metallic salmon 175 - 350
p. metallic lime 160 - 260

6268-l

Custom Charger 6268 - 80mm - 1969-1971
This U.S.-made Dodge Charger has a metal chassis, white plastic interior, lift-up hood to reveal a metal engine, clear windows and rsw.
a. metallic aqua $175 - 350
b. metallic blue 150 - 275
c. metallic brown 2000 - NA
d. metallic gold 150 - 250
e. metallic green 165 - 300
g. metallic light green 175 - 375
h. metallic magenta 190 - 350
j. metallic orange 200 - 350
k. metallic pink 300 - 450
l. metallic purple 325 - 500
m. metallic red 165 - 300
n. metallic yellow 165 - 325
p. metallic lime 225 - 375

6266-h

Custom Continental Mark III 6266 - 80mm - 1969-1971
This U.S.-made Lincoln features a metal chassis, plastic interior (assorted colors), lift-up hood to reveal a metal engine, clear windows, & rsw.
Note: Most cars have white interiors; black-interior models are approximately three times more valuable.
a. metallic aqua $70 - 135
b. metallic blue 70 - 150
d. metallic gold 70 - 150
e. metallic green 75 - 150
f. metallic light blue 150 - 200
g. metallic light green 120 - 175
h. metallic magenta 120 - 165
i. metallic olive 135 - 240
j. metallic orange 80 - 165
k. metallic pink 250 - 400
l. metallic purple 90 - 190
m. metallic red 70 - 150
n. metallic yellow 70 - 150

6269-a

Custom Police Cruiser 6269 - 77mm - 1969-72
This U.S.-made Plymouth Fury police car has a metal chassis, black hood & trunk, black tampo with star & "Police" on the sides, white plastic interior, clear windows, and rsw.
Note: This was the first model with a tampo. A prototype has been found with black fenders.
Similar casting: 6469 Fire Chief Cruiser (1970)
a. white, clear red plastic dome light $75 - 150
a2. white, opaque dome light 90 - 150

6257-j

Ford Mark IV 6257 - 70mm - 1969-71 (Grand Prix)
Based on a Grand Prix race car, this model has a metal chassis, black & white stickers with "1" & stripes, plastic interior (dark brown or black), lift-up back to reveal a metal engine, clear or blue-tinted windows and rsw. The Hong Kong version has blue-tinted windows, raised outlines of the lights, gas tanks, etc, and slightly larger tailpipes. The U.S. version has clear windows and the outlines are inverted.
a. metallic aqua $35 - 80
b. metallic blue 35 - 80
c. metallic brown 40 - 90
d. metallic gold 35 - 80
e. metallic green 25 - 45
f. metallic light blue 60 - 110
h. metallic magenta 60 - 120
i. metallic olive 35 - 80
j. metallic orange 35 - 80
l. metallic purple 40 - 90
m. metallic red 30 - 80
n. metallic yellow 30 - 80
o. red enamel 30 - 70

Values are shown in U.S. dollars, first price is for mint, second is for mint packaged vehicles only. See pages 15-16 for grading guide to determine value for cars in lesser conditions.

6263-l

Indy Eagle 6263 - 75mm - 1969-71
(Grand Prix)

Based on Dan Gurney's Eagle racer, this model has a metal chassis, plastic interior (assorted colors), exposed chrome plastic engine, rear spoiler, blue-tinted windshield, rsw & was made in Hong Kong. It has been found with plastic detachable fuel tanks. The white interior version is very difficult to find and is worth about four times the mint price and two times the blisterpack price of the dark interior version.

Note: Mattel issued a gold-chrome version. Although not rare, it's very collectible.

a. metallic aqua $35 - 75
b. metallic blue 30 - 75
c. metallic brown 45 - 85
e. metallic green 35 - 75
i. metallic olive 75 - 110
j. metallic orange 50 - 80
l. metallic purple 50 - 90
m. metallic red 35 - 85

6263-o

o. gold chrome 140 - 285

6254-c

Lola GT70 6254 - 70mm - 1969-71
(Grand Prix)

Based on a Grand Prix racer, this model has a metal chassis, plastic interior (dark brown or black), lift-up back to reveal a metal engine, clear or blue-tinted windshield and rsw. The Hong Kong version has a different engine compartment, larger taillights and shallower outlines of lights, doors, etc. (some lines are barely noticeable or completely gone). The car looks like it was painted after the lines were made. The U.S. version has clearly defined lines. The lines look like they were made after painting.

Note: The real car was British racing green.

a. metallic aqua $30 - 70
b. metallic blue 30 - 70
c. metallic brown 40 - 90
d. metallic gold 30 - 70
e. metallic green 30 - 70
f. metallic light blue 100 - 150
h. metallic magenta 50 - 80
i. metallic olive 35 - 90
j. metallic orange 35 - 85
k. metallic pink 650 - 1800
l. metallic purple 50 - 110
m. metallic red 30 - 70
n. metallic yellow 35 - 70
o. dark green enamel (British racing green) 35 - 70
p. metallic lavender 200 - 650
q. metallic lime 60 - 100

6262-l

Lotus Turbine 6262 - 68mm - 1969-1971
(Grand Prix)

This Hong Kong-made Indy-style race car has a metal chassis, plastic interior (assorted colors), blue-tinted windshield and rsw. It has been found with plastic detachable fuel tanks. The white interior version is very difficult to find and is worth about five times the mint price and three times the blister-

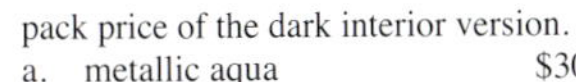

pack price of the dark interior version.

a. metallic aqua $30 - 70
b. metallic blue 30 - 80
c. metallic brown 45 - 80
e. metallic green 25 - 70
i. metallic olive 45 - 90
j. metallic orange 30 - 80
l. metallic purple 40 - 85
m. metallic red 30 - 75

6277-b

Maserati Mistral 6277 - 70mm - 1969-1971

This Hong Kong-made model has a metal chassis & engine, lift-up hood, plastic interior (assorted colors), blue-tinted windshield and rsw. Some models come with a black roof.

a. metallic aqua $90 - 190
b. metallic blue 90 - 200
c. metallic brown 90 - 200
e. metallic green 90 - 200
i. metallic olive 135 - 230
j. metallic orange 90 - 200
l. metallic purple 135 - 275
m. metallic red 130 - 275
p. metallic lime 150 - 275

6255-j

McLaren M6A 6255 - 68mm - 1969-1971
(Grand Prix)

Based on a Can-Am racer, this model has a metal chassis, lift-up back to reveal a metal engine, plastic interior (dark brown or black), clear or blue-tinted windshield and rsw. The Hong Kong version has small taillights, poorly-defined door-lines and no fender vents. The U.S. version has flat taillights, more noticeable door-lines and rectangular fender vents.

Note: The real car was painted in orange enamel; this color has never been found in blisterpack.

a. metallic aqua $30 - 70
b. metallic blue 30 - 70
c. metallic brown 35 - 75
d. metallic gold 30 - 70
e. metallic green 30 - 70
f. metallic light blue 60 - 100
g. metallic light green 60 - 100
h. metallic magenta 45 - 80
i. metallic olive 30 - 70
j. metallic orange 30 - 70
l. metallic purple 40 - 75
m. metallic red 30 - 70
n. metallic yellow 30 - 70

6255-o

o. orange enamel 45 - 90
q. metallic lime 45 - 90

6275-l

Mercedes-Benz 280SL 6275 - 67mm - 1969-71

This model has a metal chassis & engine, lift-up hood, plastic interior (assorted colors), blue-tinted windows, rsw and was made in Hong Kong. Some models come with a black roof.

Similar casting: 6962 Mercedes 280SL (1973, enamel colors)

a. metallic aqua $45 - 95
b. metallic blue 45 - 95
c. metallic brown 50 - 115
e. metallic green 45 - 95
f. metallic light blue 150 - 200
i. metallic olive 50 - 90
j. metallic orange 45 - 95
l. metallic purple 60 - 115
m. metallic red 45 - 90

6276-m

Rolls-Royce Silver Shadow 6276 - 82mm - 1969-1971

This model has a metal chassis & engine, lift-up hood, plastic interior (assorted colors), blue-tinted windows, rsw and was made in Hong Kong. Some come with a black roof.

Note: The gray enamel version is very common. The ratio of gray cars to all other colors combined is about two to one.

a. metallic aqua $85 - 180
b. metallic blue 80 - 175
d. metallic gold 100 - 190
e. metallic green 80 - 180
g. metallic light green 80 - 190
j. metallic orange 100 - 190
k. metallic pink 1000 - 2000
l. metallic purple 400 - 600
m. metallic red 90 - 180
n. metallic yellow 100 - 210
o. gray enamel 40 - 100

6265-b

Shelby Turbine 6265 - 66mm - 1969-1971 (Grand Prix)

Based on the turbine-powered racer driven by Mario Andretti, this Hong Kong-made model has a metal chassis, plastic interior (assorted colors), blue-tinted windshield and rsw. It has been found with plastic detachable fuel tanks. The white interior version is very difficult to find and is worth about five times the mint price and three times the blisterpack price of the dark interior version.

a. metallic aqua $30 - 75
b. metallic blue 30 - 70
c. metallic brown 45 - 90
e. metallic green 30 - 75
g. metallic light green 150 - 300
i. metallic olive 75 - 135
j. metallic orange 40 - 75
l. metallic purple 40 - 90
m. metallic red 30 - 70

6261-c

Splittin' Image® 6261 - 75mm - 1969-1971

This U.S.-made concept car was designed by Ira Gilford. It has a metal chassis, plastic interior (assorted colors), clear plastic windows, and rsw.

Similar castings: Splittin' Image (1973 Shell Promo), 5708 Splittin' Image (1993)

a. metallic aqua $30 - 80
b. metallic blue 30 - 80
c. metallic brown 35 - 90
d. metallic gold 30 - 80
e. metallic green 30 - 80
f. metallic light blue 60 - 145
h. metallic magenta 65 - 120
i. metallic olive 35 - 80
j. metallic orange 35 - 80
l. metallic purple 45 - 90
m. metallic red 30 - 80
n. metallic yellow 30 - 80
o. metallic lavender 110 - 175
p. metallic lime 45 - 95

6260-c

Torero 6260 - 70mm - 1969-1971

This concept car was designed by Ira Gilford. It has a metal chassis and engine, lift-up hood, plastic interior (assorted colors), clear plastic windows, rsw and was made in the U.S.

a. metallic aqua $30 - 80
b. metallic blue 35 - 80
c. metallic brown 50 - 100
d. metallic gold 30 - 80
e. metallic green 30 - 80
f. metallic light blue 90 - 160
g. metallic light green 90 - 160
h. metallic magenta 60 - 135
i. metallic olive 40 - 90
j. metallic orange 30 - 80
k. metallic pink 350 - 650
l. metallic purple 70 - 150
m. metallic red 30 - 80
n. metallic yellow 30 - 80
o. metallic lavender 160 - 275
p. metallic lime 45 - 85

6259-n

Turbofire® 6259 - 72mm - 1969-1971

Designed by Ira Gilford, this U.S.-made concept car has a metal chassis, lift-up rear hood to reveal a metal engine, plastic interior (assorted colors), clear plastic windows, & rsw.

a. metallic aqua $30 - 85
b. metallic blue 30 - 80
c. metallic brown 40 - 95
d. metallic gold 30 - 80
e. metallic green 30 - 85
f. metallic light blue 75 - 145
g. metallic light green 185 - 300
h. metallic magenta 60 - 125
i. metallic olive 45 - 100
j. metallic orange 30 - 80
k. metallic pink 350 - 600
l. metallic purple 60 - 140
m. metallic red 30 - 80
n. metallic yellow 30 - 80
p. metallic lime 40 - 100

6258-d

TwinMill® 6258 - 72mm - 1969-1971

This concept car was designed by Ira Gilford. It has a metal chassis, two chrome plastic engines, plastic interior (assorted colors), clear plastic windows, rsw and was made in the U.S.

Similar castings: TwinMill (1973 Shell Promo), 8240 TwinMill 2 (1976), 5709 TwinMill (1993)

a. metallic aqua $35 - 90
b. metallic blue 30 - 90
c. metallic brown 130 - 225
d. metallic gold 30 - 90
e. metallic green 30 - 90
f. metallic light blue 150 - 300
g. metallic light green 175 - 350
h. metallic magenta 150 - 300
i. metallic olive 100 - 200
j. metallic orange 35 - 90
k. metallic pink 325 - 600
l. metallic purple 70 - 165
m. metallic red 30 - 90
n. metallic yellow 30 - 90

Values are shown in U.S. dollars, first price is for mint, second is for mint packaged vehicles only. See pages 15-16 for grading guide to determine value for cars in lesser conditions.

o. metallic lavender 150 - 300
p. metallic lime 60 - 110

6274-f

Volkswagen Beach Bomb 6274 - 65mm - 1969-1971
This Hong Kong-made customized van has a metal chassis, plastic interior (assorted colors), blue-tinted plastic windows, an orange & a yellow plastic surfboard sticking through the rear window, and rsw. This might be a pre-production model and may not have been sold in stores. It has never been found in blisterpack.
Note: This model is the most desired vehicle and is easily the most expensive. A pink prototype has also been seen.

a.	metallic blue	$15,000 - NA
b.	metallic gold	15,000 - NA
c.	metallic green	15,000 - NA
e.	metallic purple	17,000 - NA

6274-f

f.	metallic red	15,000 - NA
g.	metallic yellow	15,000 - NA
o.	metallic light blue	16,000 - NA

6274-a

Volkswagen Beach Bomb 6274 - 65mm - 1969-1971
This Hong Kong-made customized van has a metal chassis, plastic interior (assorted colors), blue-tinted plastic windows, an orange & a yellow plastic surfboard in side slots, and rsw.
Note: The surfboards have been reproduced in resin.

a.	metallic aqua	$130 - 325
b.	metallic blue	130 - 325
c.	metallic brown	180 - 425
e.	metallic green	130 - 325
g.	metallic light green	275 - 550
i.	metallic olive	200 - 400
j.	metallic orange	300 - 550
l.	metallic purple	235 - 500
m.	metallic red	275 - 450
n.	metallic yellow	300 - 500

1970

Thirty-three new vehicles were introduced. These included Sky Show Fleetside, which was only available in a race set. This was the first year Mattel produced a model exclusively for a race set. Mattel also introduced Spoilers, Heavyweights and Club Kit cars. Spoilers were souped-up cars with large exposed engines plus front and rear spoilers. They came in their own special blistercard. Heavyweights were futuristic trucks. They were all designed by Ira Gilford and came with wraparound windshields. Some were issued in a two-part cab and trailer combination, a first for Hot Wheels. The series was issued on three different blistercards: one pictured the Fire Engine, another the Cement Mixer and the third showed the Tow Truck.

Club Kit models included three different Spoiler cars: Boss Hoss, King 'Kuda and Heavy Chevy. They were all issued in chrome and only sold as part of the Hot Wheels Club Kit, never in blisterpack. These kits were originally sold exclusively through the mail, but later they could be found in stores. The Club Kit box measures 11" by 5-1/2" by 2-1/4."

This year Mattel sponsored two race cars, "The Snake," driven by Don Prudhomme and "The Mongoose," driven by Tom McEwen. They were also part of the 1970 line and had their own blistercards picturing both the cars and their drivers. Some 1970 vehicles were again made in both the U.S. and Hong Kong, although most were made in only one country.

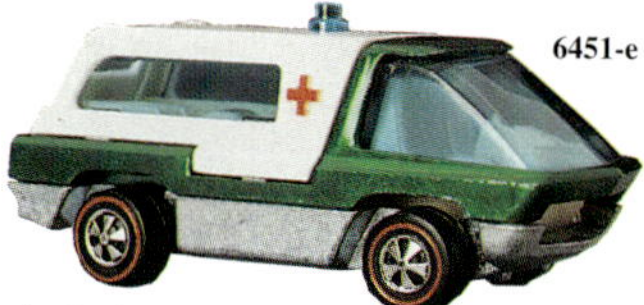
6451-e

Ambulance 6451 - 75mm - 1970-1972 (Heavyweights)
This Hong Kong-made concept model has a cab designed by Ira Gilford, metal chassis, white plastic body with a raised red cross, clear blue emergency light on top, opening rear door, blue-tinted plastic windows, plastic interior (assorted colors) and rsw.

a.	metallic aqua	$55 - 125
b.	metallic blue	55 - 125
c.	metallic brown	70 - 140
e.	metallic green	55 - 125
g.	metallic light green	85 - 140
h.	metallic magenta	100 - 225
i.	metallic olive	55 - 150
j.	metallic orange	75 - 160
k.	metallic pink	250 - 500
l.	metallic purple	75 - 150
m.	metallic red	90 - 175
n.	metallic yellow	55 - 125
o.	white enamel	250 - 400

6499-a

Boss Hoss 6499 - 72mm - 1970-1971
This customized Ford Mustang Boss 302 has a metal chassis, blue-tinted plastic windows, louvered rear window, brown plastic interior, two black stripes on top, rsw and was made in Hong Kong. This was one of three models given away with the Hot Wheels Club Kit.
Note: The complete Club Kit is very tough to find and is getting quite expensive. The Kit has to be opened to see which car it contains. Unlike other Club Kit cars, Boss Hoss was issued a year earlier than the regular line car.
Similar castings: 6499 Boss Hoss (1971), 7644 Mustang Stocker (1975)

a.	chrome, in Club Kit	$80 - 375

6420-k

Carabo 6420 - 72mm - 1970-1971
This "gull wing" sports car is based on the Carabo show car. It has a black metal chassis, "gull wing" opening doors, plastic interior (assorted colors) and rsw. The Hong Kong version has blue-tinted plastic windows and the rear panel is shinier, has deeper embossing and is larger than the U.S. version which has clear plastic windows.
Similar casting: 7617 Carabo (1974, enamel colors)

b.	metallic blue	$65 - 140
e.	metallic green	50 - 130
g.	metallic light green	65 - 130
h.	metallic magenta	70 - 135
k.	metallic pink	225 - 400
m.	metallic red	75 - 140
n.	metallic yellow	60 - 135
o.	metallic lavender	75 - 140

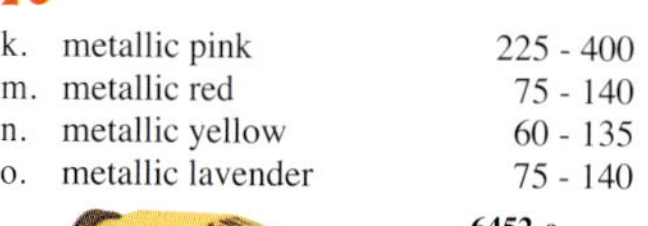

6452-c

Cement Mixer 6452 - 85mm - 1970-1972 (Heavyweights)
This concept model was designed by Ira Gilford. It has a metal chassis, brown or orange plastic truck bed, rotating orange plastic barrel with red Hot Wheels logo decal & "Cement Co." in black on the barrel, blue-tinted plastic windows, plastic interior (assorted colors), rsw and was made in Hong Kong.

a.	metallic aqua	$50 - 90
b.	metallic blue	50 - 90
c.	metallic brown	50 - 90
e.	metallic green	50 - 90
g.	metallic light green	50 - 130
i.	metallic olive	60 - 150
j.	metallic orange	50 - 135
l.	metallic purple	70 - 160
m.	metallic red	50 - 135
n.	metallic yellow	45 - 120
o.	white enamel	200 - 250

6404-m

Classic Nomad 6404 - 70mm - 1970-1971
This 1955 Chevrolet Nomad station wagon has a metal chassis, lift-up hood with a metal engine, clear plastic windows & sun roof, white plastic interior, rsw. Made in the U.S.
Similar castings: 6968 Alive '55 (1973), 5743 Classic Nomad (1993), 2098 '55 Nomad (1991)

a.	metallic aqua	$100 - 190
b.	metallic blue	85 - 175
c.	metallic brown	250 - 450
e.	metallic green	80 - 170
g.	metallic light green	110 - 225
h.	metallic magenta	150 - 250
i.	metallic olive	200 - 300
j.	metallic orange	100 - 200
k.	metallic pink	150 - 325
l.	metallic purple	150 - 250
m.	metallic red	85 - 190
n.	metallic yellow	70 - 160

6401-e

Demon, The 6401 - 75mm - 1970-1971
Based on the "Lil' Coffin" show car, this model has a metal chassis, black roof, blue-tinted plastic windows, plastic interior (black or white), rsw and was made in Hong Kong.
Note: The Demon with a white interior is difficult to find and worth about twice as much as the dark-interior version.
Similar castings: 6965 Prowler (1973), 5730 The Demon (1993)

a.	metallic aqua	$35 - 90
b.	metallic blue	35 - 90
c.	metallic brown	50 - 120
e.	metallic green	35 - 90
g.	metallic light green	60 - 120
i.	metallic olive	50 - 120
j.	metallic orange	40 - 110
l.	metallic purple	55 - 110
m.	metallic red	35 - 90
n.	metallic yellow	40 - 100

6453-e

Dump Truck 6453 - 98mm - 1970-1972 (Heavyweights)
This concept model was designed by Ira Gilford. It has a metal chassis, brown or orange plastic truck bed with an orange or yellow lift-up plastic dumper, blue-tinted plastic windows, plastic interior (assorted colors), rsw and was made in Hong Kong.

a.	metallic aqua	$45 - 100
b.	metallic blue	45 - 100
c.	metallic brown	50 - 120
d.	metallic gold	75 - 120
e.	metallic green	45 - 100
g.	metallic light green	60 - 110
j.	metallic orange	55 - 100
l.	metallic purple	60 - 135
m.	metallic red	90 - 175
n.	metallic yellow	45 - 100
o.	white enamel	250 - 400

6417-n

Ferrari 312P 6417 - 70mm - 1970-1971 (Grand Prix)
This race-car model has a metal chassis, exposed metal engine, lift-up back, black rear panel, red taillights, plastic windshield, plastic interior (assorted colors), and rsw. The Hong Kong version has a blue-tinted windshield, protruding outlines of doors, lights, etc. and a shiny black rear panel. The U.S. version has a clear windshield, recessed outlines of doors, lights, etc., and a dull black rear panel.
Note: Models with white interiors are very rare and to date have only been found in metallic red.
Similar casting: 6973 Ferrari 312P (1973)

a.	metallic aqua	$50 - 100
b.	metallic blue	40 - 85
c.	metallic brown	125 - 250
e.	metallic green	40 - 80
g.	metallic light green	60 - 125
h.	metallic magenta	80 - 150
i.	metallic olive	75 - 140
j.	metallic orange	45 - 85
k.	metallic pink	100 - 225
l.	metallic purple	90 - 150
m.	metallic red	40 - 85
m2.	metallic red, white interior	550 - 1000
n.	metallic yellow	40 - 85
o.	metallic salmon	80 - 140
p.	red enamel	45 - 85

6469-a

Fire Chief Cruiser 6469 - 77mm - 1970-71
This U.S.-made Plymouth Fury fire chief car has a metal chassis, "Chief" & a shield on the sides, blue transparent light on top, clear plastic windows, white plastic interior, and rsw.
Similar casting: 6269 Custom Police Cruiser (1969)

a.	red	$45 - 90
a2.	dark red	45 - 90

6454-a2

Fire Engine 6454 - 100mm - 1970-1972 (Heavyweights)
Designed by Ira Gilford, this Hong Kong-made concept model comes with a cab,

Values are shown in U.S. dollars, first price is for mint, second is for mint packaged vehicles only. See pages 15-16 for grading guide to determine value for cars in lesser conditions.

detachable trailer and rsw. The cab has a metal chassis, blue-tinted plastic windshield and plastic interior (white or black). The trailer is red plastic with white hoses and has "Fire Dept." & a shield in white on the side and a removable black ladder.

a. red; black interior $60 - 135
a2. red; white interior 75 - 160
a3. red enamel; black interior 140 - 325
a4. red enamel; white interior 175 - 350

6408-j

Heavy Chevy 6408 - 70mm - 1970-71 (Spoilers)

Based on the Chevrolet Camaro, this Hong Kong-made model has a metal chassis, exposed metal engine, stickers with numbers on the sides, two white stripes on top, blue-tinted plastic windows, plastic interior (assorted colors), & rsw.

Similar castings: 6189 Heavy Chevy (1970, chrome), 7619 Heavy Chevy (1974)

a. metallic aqua $90 - 180
b. metallic blue 90 - 180
c. metallic brown 100 - 220
e. metallic green 85 - 175
i. metallic olive 150 - 275
j. metallic orange 110 - 240
l. metallic purple 150 - 300
m. metallic red 100 - 220

6189-a

Heavy Chevy 6189 - 70mm - 1970-1971

This model is 6408 with a chrome finish, two black stripes on top & a brown plastic interior.

Similar castings: 6408 Heavy Chevy (1970), 7619 Heavy Chevy (1974)

Note: This is one of three models given away with the Hot Wheels Club Kit.

a. chrome, in Club Kit $90 - 375

6421-a

Jack "Rabbit" Special 6421 - 65mm - 1970-71

This convertible concept car has a metal chassis, opening trunk, light blue stripe down the middle, clear plastic windshield, plastic interior (black or white), and rsw.

Note: This model was "Bunny Car" in the cartoon series. Also, the Jack-in-the-Box decal sheet has been reproduced.

Similar casting: 6974 Sand Witch (1973)

a. white; black interior $35 - 80
a2. white; white interior 35 - 80
a3. white; black or white int., lt. blue decal sheet stapled to plastic baggy. 2 sets of 3 red stripes on sheet, red & black Jack-in-the-Box logo, black "1" in red circle, red Hot Wheels logo, red & black "Jack "Rabbit" Special" & black " Jack-in-the-Box;" picture of car w/decals; unopened $300 - 350

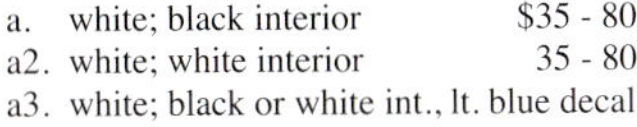
6421-a3

a4. white; same as a, blue-tinted windows, Hong Kong 200 - 300

6411-c

King 'Kuda 6411 - 75mm - 1970-71 (Spoilers)

Based on a Plymouth Barracuda as customized and reproportioned by Ira Gilford, this model has a metal chassis, exposed metal engine, stickers with numbers on the sides, a sticker with two white stripes on the back, blue-tinted plastic windows, plastic interior (assorted colors), rsw and was made in Hong Kong. Gold and yellow versions of this car have been found as prototypes only.

Similar casting: 6190 King 'Kuda (1970, chrome)

a. metallic aqua $90 - 190
b. metallic blue 90 - 190
c. metallic brown 150 - 250
e. metallic green 80 - 190
i. metallic olive 125 - 300
j. metallic orange 150 - 275
l. metallic purple 150 - 310
m. metallic red 125 - 210

6190-a

King 'Kuda 6190 - 75mm - 1970-1971

This model is 6411 with a chrome finish, two black stripes on top and a brown or white plastic interior.

Note: This is one of three models given away with the Hot Wheels Club Kit.

Similar casting: 6411 King 'Kuda (1970)

a. chrome; in Club Kit $90 - 400

6412-b

Light My Firebird 6412 - 75mm - 1970-1971 (Spoilers)

This Hong Kong-made model is based on a Pontiac Firebird convertible as customized and reproportioned by Ira Gilford. It has a metal chassis, exposed metal engine, stickers with numbers on the sides, blue-tinted plastic windshield, plastic interior (assorted colors), and rsw.

a. metallic aqua $75 - 125
b. metallic blue 75 - 110
c. metallic brown 90 - 170
e. metallic green 65 - 125
g. metallic light green 500 - 1000
i. metallic olive 80 - 160
j. metallic orange 85 - 175
l. metallic purple 110 - 235
m. metallic red 75 - 170

6423-k

Mantis 6423 - 75mm - 1970-1971

This concept car was designed by Ira Gilford and Howard Rees. It has a metal chassis, exposed metal engine, two plastic opening canopies, plastic interior (assorted colors) and rsw. The Hong Kong version has a smaller nose wrapping down the sides of the base and a shorter steering rod. The U.S. version's body doesn't extend over the sides but stops at the base casting.

Similar castings: 6975 Double Vision (1973), 7299 Speed Seeker (1984), 15258 Speed Machine (1996)

a. metallic aqua $60 - 100
b. metallic blue 40 - 80
c. metallic brown 65 - 110
e. metallic green 40 - 80
g. metallic light green 50 - 90
h. metallic magenta 75 - 135
i. metallic olive 50 - 90
j. metallic orange 65 - 110
k. metallic pink 100 - 180
l. metallic purple 150 - 250
m. metallic red 40 - 85
n. metallic yellow 40 - 85

6414-a

Mighty Maverick 6414 - 70mm - 1970-71

This model is based on the Ford Maverick as customized and reproportioned by Howard Rees. It has a metal chassis, lift-up hood to reveal a metal engine, black plastic rear spoiler, a white or black stripe on the roof, plastic windows, plastic interior (assorted colors) and rsw. The Hong Kong version has a thin stripe on the roof, unpainted headlights, and the top rear sides of the chassis by the taillights extend upward. The U.S. version has a thick stripe on the roof, black headlights, and the top of the rear chassis is straight.

Note: The black-striped version is much tougher to find and worth about twice as much as the white-striped version.

Similar castings: 6971 Street Snorter (1973), 7653 Mighty Maverick (1975)

a. metallic aqua $110 - 200
b. metallic blue 95 - 170
c. metallic brown 150 - 240
d. metallic gold 145 - 210
e. metallic green 95 - 175
g. metallic light green 100 - 175
h. metallic magenta 130 - 220
i. metallic olive 130 - 200
j. metallic orange 145 - 265
k. metallic pink 195 - 350
l. metallic purple 150 - 250
m. metallic red 100 - 170
n. metallic yellow 100 - 170
o. metallic salmon 175 - 300

6456-e

Mod Quad 6456 - 80mm - 1970-1971

Designed by Howard Rees, this concept model has a metal chassis, four exposed unpainted metal engines (two in front & two in back), a hinged opening plastic canopy, plastic interior (assorted colors) and rsw. The Hong Kong version has a blue-tinted canopy. The U.S. version has a clear canopy with a molded circle.

a. metallic aqua $125 - 160
b. metallic blue 40 - 120
d. metallic gold 40 - 100
e. metallic green 40 - 100
g. metallic light green 60 - 120
h. metallic magenta 120 - 175
k. metallic pink 200 - 325
l. metallic purple 125 - 175
m. metallic red 45 - 100
n. metallic yellow 40 - 85
o. metallic salmon 160 - 250
p. metallic lime 175 - 250

6410-a

Mongoose 6410 - 80mm - 1970

Based on Tom (The Mongoose) McEwen's Plymouth Duster funny car, this model has a metal chassis, black plastic interior, blue-tinted plastic window, rsw and white stickers with red, blue, yellow, & orange colors. The side stickers have the Hot Wheels logo, a mongoose and "Tom (The Mongoose) McEwen." The top has a blue stripe with yellow stars, "Plymouth" twice and "Enjoy Coca Cola" twice. There is no major difference between the Hong Kong and U.S. versions.

Note: The Mongoose had its own blister-card.

Similar castings: 5954 Mongoose 2 (1971), 10497 Snake (1973), 10783 Mongoose (1994)

a. red, made in Hong Kong $85 - 200
a2. red, made in U.S. 85 - 200

6455-a

Moving Van 6455 - 95mm - 1970-1972 (Heavyweights)

A concept model with a detachable cab, designed by Ira Gilford. It has a metal chassis, gray or white plastic trailer with the Hot Wheels logo & "Van Lines" in turquoise on a gold rectangle on the sides, opening gold plastic rear trailer doors, no tampo on the cab, plastic interior (assorted colors), rsw and was made in Hong Kong.

a. metallic aqua $70 - 150
b. metallic blue 70 - 150
e. metallic green 70 - 150
g. metallic light green 125 - 190
i. metallic olive 70 - 150
l. metallic purple 125 - 225
m. metallic red 70 - 150
n. metallic yellow 85 - 160

6405-e

Nitty Gritty Kitty™ 6405 - 73mm - 1970-1971 (Spoilers)

Based on a Mercury Cougar as customized and reproportioned by Ira Gilford, this Hong Kong-made model has a metal chassis, exposed metal engine, blue-tinted plastic windows, two white stripes on top, plastic interior (assorted colors) and rsw.

a. metallic aqua $100 - 190
b. metallic blue 100 - 190
c. metallic brown 150 - 265
e. metallic green 90 - 190
i. metallic olive 135 - 250
j. metallic orange 125 - 200
l. metallic purple 175 - 350
m. metallic red 130 - 200

6402-a

Paddy Wagon 6402 - 64mm - 1970-1979

This model is based on the show car designed by Tom Daniel for Monogram. It has a metal chassis, exposed metal engine, clear plastic windows, dark blue plastic top with "3" & "Police" imprinted on the sides of the top, brown metal interior, rsw & was made in the U.S.

Similar castings: 6966 Paddy Wagon (1973), 5707 Paddy Wagon (1993)

a. dark blue, "3" & "Police" in silver $40 - 80
a2. dark blue, "3" & "Police" in gold 40 - 80
a3. dark blue, same as a2, Hong Kong 60 - 80

Values are shown in U.S. dollars, first price is for mint, second is for mint packaged vehicles only. See pages 15-16 for grading guide to determine value for cars in lesser conditions.

Paddy Wagon-a4

a4. same as a, shorter blue top, no writing on sides. Only found in Great Getaway Set (1971) 500 - NA

6419-k

Peepin' Bomb 6419 - 75mm - 1970-1971
This convertible concept car was designed by Howard Rees. It has a metal chassis, exposed metal engine, clear plastic windshield, plastic interior (assorted colors) with a lever that raises and lowers the headlight covers, rsw and was made in the U.S. It has been found with a Hong Kong base which is worth about twice the value of U.S. models.
Similar casting: Peeping Bomb (1973 Shell Promo)

a.	metallic aqua	$40 - 75
b.	metallic blue	40 - 75
e.	metallic green	40 - 85
g.	metallic light green	45 - 90
h.	metallic magenta	45 - 90
i.	metallic olive	80 - 125
j.	metallic orange	40 - 100
k.	metallic pink	85 - 175
l.	metallic purple	80 - 125
m.	metallic red	35 - 75
n.	metallic yellow	35 - 75
o.	metallic salmon	45 - 90

6416-g

Porsche 917 6416 - 68mm - 1970-1971 (Grand Prix)
This race-car model has a metal chassis, opening rear-engine cowling with window showing a metal engine, plastic windows, plastic interior (assorted colors) and rsw. The Hong Kong version has blue-tinted plastic windows, a thinner rectangle on the front fenders, larger headlights, shorter side pipes & a shorter rear engine cover. The U.S. version has clear plastic windows.
Similar casting: 6972 Porsche 917 (1973)

a.	metallic aqua	$125 - 200
b.	metallic blue	50 - 100
e.	metallic green	50 - 100
g.	metallic light green	55 - 110
h.	metallic magenta	75 - 135
k.	metallic pink	125 - 200
l.	metallic purple	200 - 300
m.	metallic red	50 - 100
n.	metallic yellow	50 - 100
o.	metallic salmon	75 - 110
p.	gray enamel	90 - 150

6459-b

Power Pad 6459 - 73mm - 1970-1971
This U.S.-made model is based on a customized pickup truck with a white plastic camper shell. Designed by Ira Gilford, it also has a metal chassis, exposed metal engine, clear plastic windows, black plastic interior, and rsw.
Note: Originally called Dream Camper, the name was changed before production began.

b.	metallic blue	$135 - 175
e.	metallic green	65 - 130
g.	metallic light green	75 - 130
h.	metallic magenta	75 - 135
k.	metallic pink	110 - 225
m.	metallic red	65 - 130
n.	metallic yellow	65 - 130

6400-a

Red Baron 6400 - 55mm - 1970-1979
This concept model was originally designed by Tom Daniel for Monogram. It has a metal chassis, exposed metal engine, unpainted metal helmet with a black iron cross on the side & sharp point on top, plastic interior, rsw, and was made in Hong Kong.
Similar castings: 6964 Red Baron (1973), 5700 Red Baron (1993)
Note: The white-interior version is very rare and has not been seen in blisterpack. Tom Daniels worked for Monogram plastic models which was owned by Mattel at the time. Later a full-size, working show-car version was built.

a.	red; black interior	$40 - 80
a2.	red; white interior, mint	1800 - NA

6403-k

Sand Crab 6403 - 60mm - 1970-1971
This concept model was originally designed by Tom Daniel for Monogram. It has a metal chassis, clear windshield & sun roof, black plastic interior, rsw and was made in the U.S. It has been found with a Hong Kong base which is worth about three times the value of U.S. models.
Similar casting: 6967 Dune Daddy

a.	metallic aqua	$50 - 95
b.	metallic blue	35 - 80
e.	metallic green	35 - 80
g.	metallic light green	35 - 80
h.	metallic magenta	40 - 90
j.	metallic orange	800 - 1200
k.	metallic pink	90 - 200
m.	metallic red	35 - 80
n.	metallic yellow	35 - 80
o.	metallic salmon	90 - 165

6413-l

Seasider 6413 - 81mm - 1970-1971
This U.S.-made model is based on a customized Chevrolet Fleetside pickup. Designed by Howard Rees, it has a metal chassis, exposed metal engine, clear windshield, black plastic interior, detachable plastic boat (either red over white or white over red) in the bed and rsw.
Note: The plastic boat has been reproduced.

b.	metallic blue	$130 - 225
e.	metallic green	100 - 225
g.	metallic light green	110 - 225
h.	metallic magenta	110 - 225
j.	metallic orange	1000 - 2500
k.	metallic pink	135 - 275

6413-l, detail

l.	metallic purple	1350 - 2800
m.	metallic red	110 - 225
n.	metallic yellow	100 - 200

6436-a

Sky Show Deora 6436 - 70mm - 1970
This is the 1968 Deora with a red plastic ramp. It was only available in the Sky Show set.

a.	aqua	$1600 - 2000
b.	metallic purple	2000 - 2400

6436-m

Sky Show Fleetside 6436 - 78mm - 1970-71
This U.S.-made model is based on a customized Chevy pickup. Designed by Harry Bradley and Howard Rees, it has a metal chassis, a black & white sticker on the sides with "Sky Show" in blue, clear plastic windows, plastic interior, a red plane ramp in the bed and rsw. This model was only available in the Sky Show or Flying Circus sets. The second price is for a mint set. There are three planes in the set in blue, yellow & light green, worth $35.00 each in mint condition.
Note: Ramp & stickers have been reproduced.

a.	metallic aqua	$350 - 800
b.	metallic blue	360 - 750
d.	metallic gold	400 - 800
e.	metallic green	375 - 800
g.	metallic light green	375 - 800
h.	metallic magenta	400 - 950
i.	metallic olive	550 - 1100
j.	metallic orange	425 - 900
k.	metallic pink	550 - 1200
l.	metallic purple	550 - 1100
m.	metallic red	360 - 850
n.	metallic yellow	360 - 850

6409-a2

Snake 6409 - 75mm - 1970
Based on Don "The Snake" Prudhomme's Plymouth Barracuda funny car, this model has a metal chassis, black plastic interior, blue-tinted plastic windows, rsw, white stickers with red, blue, yellow & orange colors and side stickers with the Hot Wheels logo, a snake and "Don (The Snake) Prudhomme." The top has a blue stripe with yellow stars, "Plymouth" twice and "Enjoy Coca Cola" twice. The Hong Kong version has blue-tinted plastic windows. The U.S. version has clear plastic windows.
Note: The Snake had its own blistercard.
Similar castings: 5953 Snake 2 (1971), 6969 Snake (1974), 6970 The Mongoose (1974), 7630 Top Eliminator (1974), 10497 Snake (1993), '70 Plymouth Barracuda Funny Car (1997)

a.	yellow, made in Hong Kong	$90 - 325
a2.	yellow, made in the U.S.	90 - 325

6422-g

Swingin' Wing 6422 - 83mm 1970-1971
Designed by Ira Gilford, this concept car features a metal chassis, plastic windows, plastic interior (assorted colors), rsw and large white plastic flexible wing in back. The Hong Kong version has blue-tinted windows, a black interior and slightly larger headlights. The U.S. version has clear windows and a light interior.
Similar casting: Swingin' Wing (1973 Shell Promo, no wing)
Note: The Hong Kong black-interior version is much harder to find and worth about twice the price of the U.S. version.

a.	metallic aqua	$65 - 135
b.	metallic blue	55 - 90
e.	metallic green	50 - 125
g.	metallic light green	50 - 100
h.	metallic magenta	60 - 100
k.	metallic pink	125 - 180
l.	metallic purple	100 - 155
m.	metallic red	50 - 90
n.	metallic yellow	50 - 90
o.	metallic salmon	90 - 125

6407-e

TNT-Bird 6407 - 80mm - 1970-71 (Spoilers)
This model is based on a 1968 Ford Thunderbird as customized and reproportioned by Ira Gilford. It has a metal chassis, exposed metal engine, stickers with numbers on the sides, a black roof with a white stripe, blue-tinted plastic windows, plastic interior (assorted colors), rsw and was made in Hong Kong.

a.	metallic aqua	$85 - 150
b.	metallic blue	80 - 150
c.	metallic brown	100 - 185
e.	metallic green	80 - 150
i.	metallic olive	140 - 250
j.	metallic orange	90 - 165
l.	metallic purple	160 - 270
m.	metallic red	90 - 185

6450-b

Tow Truck 6450 - 74mm - 1970-1972 (Heavyweights)
Designed by Ira Gilford, this Hong Kong-made concept model has a metal chassis with yellow plastic bed & cowling around the bed, white plastic tow bar & metal towing hook, decal with a black Hot Wheels logo & "Tow Service" on the cowling sides, blue-tinted plastic windows, plastic interior (assorted colors) and rsw.

a.	metallic aqua	$60 - 100
b.	metallic blue	60 - 100
c.	metallic brown	75 - 125
e.	metallic green	60 - 120
g.	metallic light green	60 - 110
h.	metallic magenta	120 - 175
i.	metallic olive	70 - 125
j.	metallic orange	65 - 120
k.	metallic pink	225 - 325
l.	metallic purple	80 - 150
m.	metallic red	60 - 120
n.	metallic yellow	60 - 120
o.	metallic salmon	150 - 170

6424-h

Tri Baby 6424 - 72mm - 1970-1971
This concept car was designed by Larry Wood, his first for Mattel. It has a metal chassis, swing-up rear engine cover, plastic windows, plastic interior (assorted colors) and rsw. The Hong Kong version has the rear engine cover sitting directly on the chassis, blue-tinted windows and a dark interior. The U.S. version has the rear engine cover sitting on part of the body, clear windows and a light interior.
Similar casting: 6976 Buzz Off (1973)

a.	metallic aqua	$100 - 120
b.	metallic blue	55 - 90
d.	metallic gold	55 - 100
e.	metallic green	50 - 100
g.	metallic light green	55 - 100
h.	metallic magenta	75 - 135
k.	metallic pink	125 - 200
m.	metallic red	50 - 95
n.	metallic yellow	50 - 95
o.	metallic salmon	150 - 175

6457-n

Whip Creamer® 6457 - 79mm - 1970-1971
This concept car was designed by Paul Tam. It has a metal chassis, sliding plastic canopy, orange plastic turbine that spins when blown upon, plastic interior (assorted colors) and rsw. The Hong Kong version has a blue-tinted plastic canopy. The U.S. version has a clear plastic canopy.
Similar casting: 11523 Whip Creamer (1994)
Note: The white-interior version is extremely hard to find and worth about twice the price of the black-interior version.

a.	metallic aqua	$60 - 110
b.	metallic blue	50 - 100
e.	metallic green	50 - 90
g.	metallic light green	60 - 95
h.	metallic magenta	75 - 120
k.	metallic pink	100 - 210
l.	metallic purple	120 - 200
m.	metallic red	80 - 130
n.	metallic yellow	80 - 130
o.	metallic salmon	80 - 130

1971

Mattel introduced thirty-five new models. There were two new Spoilers, seven new Heavyweights and new Snake and Mongoose funny cars. Also available were two new front-engine dragsters which were issued together, either in their own blister-pack or the Wild Wheelie set. As in previous years, some models were made in both the U.S. and Hong Kong. But this was the last year Hot Wheels cars were made in the U.S.

6460-2/l

AMX/2 6460 - 67mm - 1971
Based on an American Motors experimental show car, this U.S.-made model has a metal chassis, two black plastic pop-up engine covers, tinted windows, black plastic interior and rsw.
Similar castings: 6977 Xploder (1973), 7654 Warpath (1975), 9534 Redliner (1985), 1510 Road Torch (1987)

b.	metallic blue	$225 - 340
e.	metallic green	85 - 160
g.	metallic light green	75 - 150
h.	metallic magenta	80 - 160

k.	metallic pink	150 - 300
l.	metallic purple	170 - 325
m.	metallic red	70 - 125
n.	metallic yellow	70 - 125
o.	metallic salmon	120 - 200

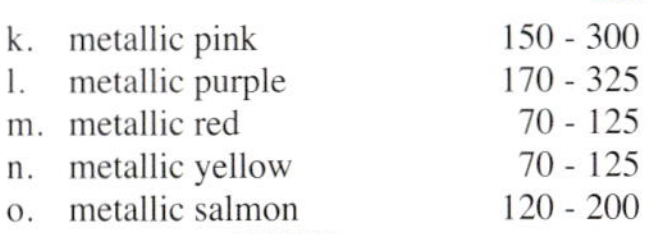

6407-k

Boss Hoss 6407 - 72mm - 1971 (Spoilers)
Based on a '68-'69 Ford Mustang Boss 302, this model has a metal chassis, exposed metal engine, blue-tinted windows, ribbed rear window, plastic interior (assorted colors), rsw, and was made in Hong Kong. It comes with either two black stripes on top or a black roof.
Similar castings: 6499 Boss Hoss (1970), 7644 Mustang Stocker (1975)

a.	metallic aqua	$150 - 325
b.	metallic blue	175 - 375
c.	metallic brown	200 - 450
e.	metallic green	150 - 320
i.	metallic olive	275 - 450
j.	metallic orange	250 - 475
k.	metallic pink	750 - 1200
l.	metallic purple	400 - 700
m.	metallic red	175 - 400

5178-h

Bugeye 5178 - 74mm - 1971-1972
Designed by Larry Wood, this concept car has a metal chassis, lift-up rear hood (two variations) to expose a metal engine, plastic interior (assorted colors) and rsw. The Hong Kong version has tinted windows and a dark interior. The U.S. version has clear windows and a light interior.
Similar casting: Bugeye (1973 Shell Promo)

a.	metallic aqua	$75 - 160
b.	metallic blue	55 - 130
d.	metallic gold	140 - 230
e.	metallic green	80 - 170
g.	metallic light green	60 - 150
h.	metallic magenta	60 - 150
k.	metallic pink	225 - 360
l.	metallic purple	200 - 300
m.	metallic red	60 - 150
n.	metallic yellow	60 - 150

6187-h

Bye-Focal 6187 - 75mm - 1971-1972
This concept car is based on a Dodge Challenger. Designed by Larry Wood, it has a metal chassis, clear or blue-tinted plastic lift-up engine cover to reveal two metal engines, blue-tinted windows, light or dark brown plastic interior, rsw and was made in Hong Kong. It also has red, black & white stickers with "Bye Focal" and eyes in glasses between the words.
Similar casting: 6982 Show Off (1973)
Note: This model is not difficult to find in lesser condition but mint or packaged models are extremely rare.

a.	metallic aqua	$150 - 325
b.	metallic blue	200 - 450
e.	metallic green	200 - 400
f.	metallic light blue	350 - 700
g.	metallic light green	250 - 525
h.	metallic magenta	175 - 375
i.	metallic olive	325 - 700
l.	metallic purple	1250 - 2000
m.	metallic red	1250 - 2100
n.	metallic yellow	650 - 650

6472-m

Classic Cord 6472 - 76mm - 1971-1972
Based on the 1937 Cord 812, this Hong Kong-made model was designed by Larry Wood. It has a metal chassis, metal engine sticking through a lift-up hood, removable black plastic roof, clear windows, black plastic interior and rsw.
Note: This is a favorite among collectors. The plastic roof has been reproduced.

b.	metallic blue	$300 - 600
d.	metallic gold	700 - 1300
e.	metallic green	300 - 600
g.	metallic light green	275 - 500
h.	metallic magenta	275 - 500
k.	metallic pink	1400 - 2300
l.	metallic purple	800 - 1400
m.	metallic red	350 - 700
n.	metallic yellow	325 - 600
o.	metallic salmon	1000 - 1850

6466-g

Cockney Cab 6466 - 63mm - 1971-1972
This model is based on an English Austin Taxi Cab. Designed by Howard Rees, it has a metal chassis, metal engine sticking through the hood, no door on the left side, a sticker with the British flag & "Cockney Cab" on the back, a plastic interior and rsw. The Hong Kong version has tinted windows, a slightly smaller rear window and a slightly lower interior. The U.S. version has clear windows.

a.	metallic aqua	$150 - 235
b.	metallic blue	135 - 220
c.	metallic brown	375 - 450
e.	metallic green	90 - 175
g.	metallic light green	95 - 180
h.	metallic magenta	95 - 200
k.	metallic pink	225 - 350
m.	metallic red	95 - 175
n.	metallic yellow	95 - 175

6471-b

Evil Weevil® 6471 - 70mm - 1971-72 (Spoilers)
This Volkswagen-based concept car designed by Paul Tam has a metal chassis, two exposed metal engines (front & back), blue-tinted windows, sun roof, plastic interior (assorted colors), rsw, and was made in Hong Kong.

a.	metallic aqua	$150 - 275
b.	metallic blue	100 - 185
e.	metallic green	125 - 175
g.	metallic light green	150 - 240
h.	metallic magenta	350 - 750
i.	metallic olive	145 - 200
l.	metallic purple	400 - 1400
m.	metallic red	125 - 175
n.	metallic yellow	135 - 250

Fuel Tanker 6018 - 85mm - 1971 (Heavyweights)
This Hong Kong-made concept model was designed by Ira Gilford. It has a metal chassis, plastic fuel tank with two retractable black plastic hoses, blue-tinted windshield, a sticker with the Hot Wheels logo and "Racing Fuel" on the sides, plas-

6018-a

tic interior (assorted colors) and rsw.

a.	white enamel	$115 - 225

6461-k

Grass Hopper 6461 - 65mm - 1971
This U.S.-made Jeep-style concept car designed by Larry Wood has a metal chassis, front & rear mounted metal engines, removable white plastic roof covering the interior & rear engine, gray-tinted windshield, black plastic interior and rsw.
Similar casting: 7622 Grass Hopper (1974)

a.	metallic aqua	$70 - 130
b.	metallic blue	80 - 140
e.	metallic green	65 - 130
g.	metallic light green	65 - 130
h.	metallic magenta	65 - 130
k.	metallic pink	125 - 225
l.	metallic purple	120 - 200
m.	metallic red	70 - 130
n.	metallic yellow	65 - 130
o.	metallic salmon	110 - 200

6458-b

Hairy Hauler 6458 - 75mm - 1971
This U.S.-made concept car designed by Paul Tam has a metal chassis, exposed metal engine in back, opening canopy with a clear windshield, white plastic interior and rsw.

a.	metallic aqua	$60 - 110
b.	metallic blue	50 - 90
e.	metallic green	50 - 90
f.	metallic light blue	175 - 250
g.	metallic light green	45 - 100
h.	metallic magenta	60 - 100
k.	metallic pink	135 - 250
l.	metallic purple	180 - 300
m.	metallic red	60 - 125
n.	metallic yellow	60 - 125
o.	metallic salmon	100 - 145

6175-k

Hood, The 6175 - 70mm - 1971-1972
This concept car was designed by Larry Wood. It has a metal chassis, exposed metal engine, black plastic retractable roof, dark plastic interior (assorted colors) and rsw. The Hong Kong version has a blue-tinted windshield and smaller side windows. The U.S. version has a clear windshield.
Similar casting: 6979 Hiway Robber (1973)

a.	metallic aqua	$100 - 200
b.	metallic blue	65 - 135
d.	metallic gold	100 - 180
e.	metallic green	110 - 225
g.	metallic light green	75 - 160
h.	metallic magenta	70 - 135
i.	metallic olive	120 - 200
k.	metallic pink	350 - 650
l.	metallic purple	125 - 260
m.	metallic red	70 - 150
n.	metallic yellow	65 - 130

Values are shown in U.S. dollars, first price is for mint, second is for mint packaged vehicles only. See pages 15-16 for grading guide to determine value for cars in lesser conditions.

6184-a

Ice "T" 6184 - 70mm - 1971-1972
This Hong Kong-made model is based on Tom Daniel's show-car design for Monogram. It has a metal chassis, yellow plastic roof with an embossed "Ice T" in black & two ice blocks in the back, exposed metal engine, black plastic interior and rsw.
Similar casting: 6980 Ice 'T' (1973)

a. yellow $50 - 200

6179-a

Jet Threat® 6179 - 81mm - 1971-1972
Designed by Larry Wood, this Hong Kong-made concept car has a metal chassis, lift-up cover on a metal engine to reveal an orange plastic turbine blade, blue-tinted windshield, unpainted metal interior, stickers in orange, black & white with "15" in a circle and rsw.
Similar castings: Jet Threat (1973 Shell Promo), 8235 Jet Threat 2 (1976)
Note: Stickers on the sides demand a 10% premium.

a. metallic aqua $75 - 175
b. metallic blue 75 - 185
d. metallic gold 75 - 180
e. metallic green 100 - 200
g. metallic light green 75 - 175
h. metallic magenta 150 - 285
l. metallic purple 200 - 350
m. metallic red 150 - 325
n. metallic yellow 90 - 200

6410-a2

Mongoose 2 5954 - 79mm - 1971-1972
This model is based on Tom McEwen's Plymouth Duster funny car sponsored by Mattel. It has a metal chassis, lift-up body to reveal a metal engine, black plastic interior, black body-support struts, and rsw. It comes with white stickers on the sides with the Hot Wheels logo, "Tom McEwen" & "the Mongoose II," red flame stickers on top, "Plymouth" on the hood, and "Coca Cola" on the trunk.
Similar casting: 6410 Mongoose (1970), 10783 Mongoose (1994)
Note: The Snake 2 and Mongoose 2 have their own blistercards. A lot of Mongoose 2 cars have mottled spots under the paint and deteriorating glue tends to ruin the stickers. This even happens to blister-packed cars.

a. mtlc blue, blue-tinted window, Hong Kong $115 - 325
b. mtlc blue, clear window, U.S. 115 - 325

5952-a2

Mongoose Rail Dragster 5952 - 106mm - 1971-1972
This model is based on Tom McEwen's front-engine dragster. It has a metal chassis, plastic nose, exposed metal engine, separate wheelie wheels, a white sticker on the nose with the Hot Wheels logo, "Tom McEwen" & "Mongoose I," a white sticker on the front of the cockpit with "Tom McEwen" & "Mongoose I," a white driver in the cockpit, bw in the back, small bicycle-type wheels in front and was made in the U.S.
Similar casting: 5951 Snake Rail Dragster 1971
Note: The Mongoose and Snake Rail Dragsters were only available together in their own blisterpack. (See multi-packs)

a. mtlc blue; clear fr wheels $90 - 1300
a2. mtlc blue; black fr wheels 90 - 1300

6185-a

Mutt Mobile 6185 - 72mm - 1971-1972
Designed by Larry Wood, this Hong Kong-made concept car has a metal chassis, exposed metal engine, white plastic top with "Mutt Mobile" embossed on the sides, two white plastic dogs in a black plastic cage in back, black plastic interior & rsw.
Similar castings: 6981 Odd Job (1973), 11524 Mutt Mobile (1994)

a. metallic aqua $65 - 200
b. metallic blue 90 - 250
d. metallic gold 125 - 300
f. metallic light blue 225 - 335
h. metallic magenta 225 - 340
m. metallic red 225 - 325

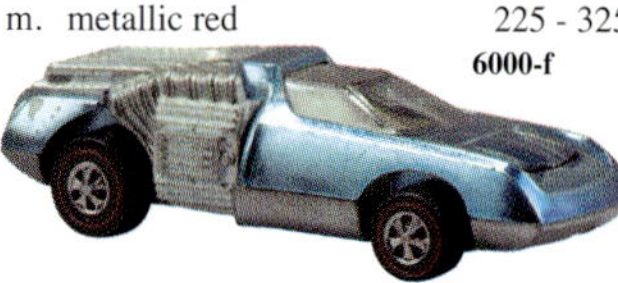
6000-f

Noodle Head 6000 - 80mm - 1971-1972
This concept car was designed by Howard Rees. It has a metal chassis, enormous exposed metal engine, hidden lift-up headlights, plastic interior (assorted colors) and rsw. The Hong Kong version has a blue-tinted windshield, smaller pipes and the back does not extend to the pipes. The U.S. version has a clear windshield and the back extends to the pipes.

a. metallic aqua $100 - 250
b. metallic blue 90 - 220
e. metallic green 100 - 220
f. metallic light blue 175 - 320
g. metallic light green 125 - 235
h. metallic magenta 90 - 220
k. metallic pink 250 - 400
m. metallic red 90 - 210
n. metallic yellow 90 - 210
o. metallic salmon 200 - 300

6467-b

Olds 442 6467 - 75mm - 1971
This U.S.-made model is based on the 1968 Oldsmobile 442 Coupe as customized and reproportioned by Larry Wood. It has a metal chassis, lift-up hood with a metal engine, soft removable plastic spoiler in back, clear windows, white stickers with blue stars, a plastic interior (assorted colors) and rsw.
Similar castings: 6963 Police Cruiser (1973), 7665 Chief's Special (1975), 9184 Maxi Taxi (1976), 9521 Army Staff Car (1976)

b. metallic blue $600 - 1000
e. metallic green 700 - 1100
f. metallic light blue 1200 - 2000
g. metallic light green 650 - 1200
h. metallic magenta 500 - 1000
k. metallic pink 2000 - 4000
l. metallic purple 3500 - 6000
m. metallic red 650 - 1100
n. metallic yellow 500 - 1000
o. metallic salmon 1400 - 2500

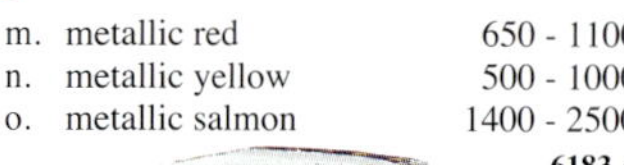

6183-a

Pit Crew Car 6183 - 75mm - 1971-1972
This Hong Kong-made concept car designed by Larry Wood and Howard Rees has a metal chassis, opening trunk with embossed assorted tools, stickers with the Hot Wheels logo & "Pit Crew" on the sides, blue stripes & yellow stars on top, blue-tinted windows, plastic interior (assorted colors) and rsw.

a. white enamel $125 - 350

6194-a

Racer Rig 6194 - 110mm - 1971 (Heavyweights)
This vehicle is a concept race-car hauler. The detachable cab was designed by Ira Gilford and the trailer was designed by Larry Wood. The cab has an unpainted metal chassis, blue-tinted windshield, black plastic interior, rsw, and was made in Hong Kong. The trailer has an opening tool box in front and a sticker with the Hot Wheels logo on the sides.

a. metallic red $125 - 325
b. white enamel 175 - 425

6186-n

Rocket-Bye-Baby 6186 - 80mm - 1971-72
This Hong Kong-made concept car was designed by Bob Lovejoy. It has a metal chassis, metal rocket on the roof, plastic interior (assorted colors), black plastic pull-out tailpipes, pop-up engine covers, blue-tinted windshield & rsw.
Note: Almost all the metal rockets are tarnished. This does not detract from the value because they are easily cleaned.

a. metallic aqua $75 - 185
b. metallic blue 75 - 200
d. metallic gold 175 - 350
e. metallic green 90 - 225
g. metallic light green 200 - 350
h. metallic magenta 175 - 350
m. metallic red 200 - 375
n. metallic yellow 150 - 300

6468-a

S'Cool Bus® 6468 - 77mm - 1971 (Heavyweights)
This is Tom Daniel's design of a funny-car dragster based on a school bus. It has a metal chassis, lift-up body to reveal a metal engine with orange plastic air scoop, black plastic interior, black struts to support the body, "S'Cool Bus" tampo on the sides, stickers (black stripes), sun roof, rsw, and was made in Hong Kong.
Similar casting: 11522 S'Cool Bus (1994)
Note: Tom Daniels worked for Monogram (owned by Mattel) and several of his designs were used for the Hot Wheels line, but he never worked in the Hot Wheels design department.

a. yellow enamel $225 - 825

6193-e

Scooper 6193 - 79mm - 1971 (Heavyweights)
This Hong Kong-made concept front-loading dump truck was designed by Ira Gilford. It has a metal chassis, yellow plastic bed, moveable yellow plastic scoop on white arms, plastic interior (assorted colors), blue-tinted windshield and rsw.

a. metallic aqua $110 - 220
b. metallic blue 100 - 210
c. metallic brown 125 - 200
d. metallic gold 90 - 185
e. metallic green 90 - 185
g. metallic light green 100 - 200
h. metallic magenta 150 - 250
i. metallic olive 100 - 200
l. metallic purple 150 - 245
m. metallic red 120 - 220
n. metallic yellow 100 - 210

6176-a

Short Order 6176 - 70mm - 1971-1972
Howard Rees designed this Hong Kong-made '50s Ford pickup concept model. It has a metal chassis, exposed metal engine, shortened pickup bed with an orange plastic tailgate, blue-tinted windows, black plastic interior and rsw.
Similar casting: Short Order (1973 Shell Promo)

a. metallic aqua $80 - 160
b. metallic blue 150 - 250
d. metallic gold 80 - 160
e. metallic green 85 - 165
g. metallic light green 80 - 165
h. metallic magenta 175 - 275
l. metallic purple 225 - 340
m. metallic red 125 - 200
n. metallic yellow 75 - 155

6003-d

Six Shooter 6003 - 76mm - 1971-1972
This Hong Kong-made concept car designed by Paul Tam has a metal chassis, two exposed metal engines in back, six wheels, plastic interior (assorted colors), blue-tinted windshield and rsw.

a. metallic aqua $100 - 225
b. metallic blue 120 - 250
d. metallic gold 140 - 325
f. metallic light blue 200 - 350
h. metallic magenta 225 - 385
n. metallic yellow 150 - 260

5953-a

Snake 2 5953 - 73mm - 1971-1972
This model is based on Don Prudhomme's funny car sponsored by Mattel. It has a metal chassis, lift-up body to reveal a metal engine, black plastic interior, body-support struts, blue stickers on the sides with "Don Prudhomme," the Hot Wheels logo & "the Snake II," red flame stickers on top, "Plymouth" on the hood, "Coca Cola" on the trunk and rsw.
Similar castings: 6409 Snake (1970), 10497 Snake (1973), 7630 Top Eliminator

Values are shown in U.S. dollars, first price is for mint, second is for mint packaged vehicles only. See pages 15-16 for grading guide to determine value for cars in lesser conditions.

(1974), 6969 Snake (1974), 6970 Mongoose (1974), '70 Plymouth Barracuda Funny Car (1997).

Note: Snake 2 and Mongoose 2 had their own blistercards.

a. white enamel; blue-tinted window, Hong Kong $85 - 285
a2. white enamel; clear window, U.S. 85 - 285

5951-a

Snake Rail Dragster 5951 - 106mm - 1971-72

This model is based on Don Prudhomme's front-engine dragster. It has a plastic nose, exposed metal engine, separate wheelie wheels, a blue sticker on the nose with "Don Prudhomme," the Hot Wheels logo and "Snake I," a white sticker in front of the cockpit with "Don Prudhomme" and "Snake I," a white driver in the cockpit, bw in back, bicycle-type wheels in front, and was made in the U.S.

Note: The Mongoose and Snake Rail Dragsters were only available together in their own blisterpack. (See Multipacks)

Similar casting: 5952 Mongoose Rail Dragster

a. white enamel with clear front wheels $90 - 1300
a2. white enamel with black front wheels 90 - 1300

6020-n

Snorkel 6020 - 74mm - 1971 (Heavyweights)

This concept cherry picker or telephone repair truck was designed by Ira Gilford and Larry Wood. It has a metal chassis, white plastic bed with red plastic hydraulic arms and a red plastic basket, plastic interior (assorted colors), blue-tinted windshield, and rsw. Made in Hong Kong.

Note: The metal will deteriorate and corrode; it just falls apart, even in blisterpacks. This is especially true of the white enamel version.

a. metallic aqua $100 - 210
b. metallic blue 100 - 210
c. metallic brown 115 - 235
d. metallic gold 105 - 225
e. metallic green 100 - 210
g. metallic light green 100 - 220
h. metallic magenta 105 - 235
i. metallic olive 125 - 265
k. metallic pink 300 - 450
m. metallic red 110 - 235
n. metallic yellow 100 - 210
o. white enamel 250 - 450

6006-a

Special Delivery 6006 - 65mm - 1971-1972

This concept mail car was designed by Larry Wood. It has a metal chassis, two exposed metal engines, black grill, no tampo, red, white, & blue stickers with "U.S. Mail" on the sides, white plastic interior, rsw, and was made in Hong Kong.

Note: Without complete stickers this model is worth 25% less.

a. metallic light blue $70 - 260
b. metallic blue 85 - 285

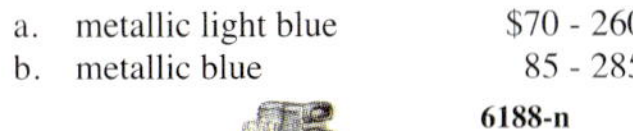

6188-n

Strip Teaser 6188 - 79mm - 1971-1972

Larry Wood designed this Hong Kong-made concept model. It has a metal chassis, exposed metal engine with exhaust headers, a driver's compartment with lift-up lid, black stickers with "7" on the sides & hood, a black plastic interior and rsw.

Similar casting: Strip Teaser (1973 Shell Promos)

a. metallic aqua $65 - 200
b. metallic blue 90 - 250
d. metallic gold 100 - 260
f. metallic light blue 225 - 475
g. metallic light green 225 - 450
h. metallic magenta 300 - 600
n. metallic yellow 125 - 300

6418-k

Sugar Caddy 6418 - 76mm - 1971 (Spoilers)

This Hong Kong-made model is based on the 1967 Cadillac Eldorado. Designed by Ira Gilford, it has a metal chassis, exposed metal engine sticking through the lift-up hood, stickers with numbers on the sides, plastic interior (assorted colors), blue-tinted windows & rsw.

a. metallic aqua $80 - 190
b. metallic blue 80 - 190
c. metallic brown 135 - 250
e. metallic green 85 - 190
g. metallic light green 90 - 200
i. metallic olive 140 - 250
j. metallic orange 135 - 250
k. metallic pink 400 - 550
l. metallic purple 130 - 240
m. metallic red 95 - 190
n. metallic yellow 85 - 190

6177-e

T-4-2 6177 - 62mm - 1971-1972

This Hong Kong-made concept car of two Model T Ford front ends stuck together was designed by Larry Wood. It has a metal chassis, two exposed metal engines (front & back) with black grills, "?" cast on the sides, dark plastic interior, blue windows and rsw.

a. metallic aqua $90 - 185
b. metallic blue 90 - 175
d. metallic gold 130 - 235
e. metallic green 85 - 180
g. metallic light green 85 - 180
h. metallic magenta 160 - 265
m. metallic red 125 - 240
n. metallic yellow 80 - 165

6019-a

Team Trailer 6019 - 108mm - 1971 (Heavyweights)

This concept racing-team camper has rsw and was made in Hong Kong. The detachable cab was designed by Ira Gilford and has a metal chassis, blue-tinted windshield and a black plastic interior. The white plastic trailer was designed by Larry Wood and has a light blue interior, blue-tinted windows, a metal chassis, sticker with the Hot Wheels logo & "Racing Team" on the sides and a light blue opening door.

a. metallic red $110 - 260
b. white enamel 125 - 325

6192-a

Waste Wagon 6192 - 85mm - 1971 (Heavyweights)

A Hong Kong-made concept trash truck, the cab was designed by Ira Gilford and the orange plastic container with moveable black plastic scoop was designed by Larry Wood. It has a metal chassis, sticker with "Dept. of Sanitation" in black on the sides, plastic interior (assorted colors), blue-tinted windshield, and rsw.

a. metallic aqua $100 - 235
b. metallic blue 100 - 225
c. metallic brown 125 - 250
e. metallic green 100 - 210
g. metallic light green 100 - 200
h. metallic magenta 110 - 250
j. metallic orange 110 - 250
k. metallic pink 200 - 400
m. metallic red 140 - 240
n. metallic yellow 110 - 225

6001-h

What-4 6001 - 79mm - 1971-1972

Designed by Bob Lovejoy, this Hong Kong-made concept car has a metal chassis, four exposed metal engines (two on each side), blue-tinted cockpit window, plastic interior (assorted colors), moveable white plastic fin in back, and rsw.

a. metallic aqua $100 - 250
b. metallic blue 110 - 260
d. metallic gold 140 - 300
e. metallic green 100 - 250
g. metallic light green 375 - 700
h. metallic magenta 275 - 360
l. metallic purple 350 - 500
m. metallic red 200 - 400

1972

Mattel began this year with an overstock of earlier models. Since Hot Wheels cars had not been selling as fast as before, there was no desire to spend much money on new castings. Therefore, Mattel issued only seven new models in 1972. Three of the new models were issued in only one color.

The Hot Wheels buttons were discontinued, as were two popular series, Heavyweights and Spoilers. Instead of buttons, each model came with drive-wheel mounts that could be used with a Drivin' Gear, one of the separately-purchased accessories. All of the new models from 1972 were only issued for one year and are very difficult to find.

6012-m

Ferrari 512S 6021 - 70mm - 1972

This model was designed by Paul Tam. It has a metal chassis, lift-up hood over the rear engine, opening cockpit cover, blue-tinted windshield, black on the rear hood, black plastic interior, and rsw. Hong Kong.

Similar casting: Ferrari 512S (1973 Shell Promo)

a. metallic aqua $150 - 320
b. metallic blue 175 - 330
d. metallic gold 140 - 330
g. metallic light green 125 - 265
h. metallic magenta 125 - 265
m. metallic red 150 - 300
n. metallic yellow 120 - 300

6005-a

Funny Money 6005 - 65m - 1972

Based on an armored truck, this Hong Kong-made funny-car model designed by Larry Wood blue, yellow & white sticker with "Funny Money Truck," an orange plastic bumper, black plastic interior and rsw.

Similar casting: 7621 Funny Money (1974)

a. gray $85 - 300

6169-g

Mercedes-Benz C-111 6169 - 75mm - 1972

Another Larry Wood design, this Hong Kong-made model has a black painted metal chassis, opening gull wing doors, blue-tinted windshield, plastic interior (assorted colors) & rsw.

Similar casting: 6978 Mercedes-Benz C-111 (1973)

a. metallic aqua $180 - 375
b. metallic blue 165 - 350
d. metallic gold 165 - 340
g. metallic light green 130 - 290
h. metallic magenta 135 - 300
l. metallic purple 275 - 450
m. metallic red 360 - 600
n. metallic yellow 150 - 325

5881-n

Open Fire 5881 - 70mm - 1972

Designed by Paul Tam, this Hong Kong-made model comes with a Gremlin-style body and has a metal chassis, exposed engine, blue-tinted windows, black plastic interior and six rsw.

b. metallic blue $375 - 600
d. metallic gold 180 - 385
h. metallic magenta 250 - 375
m. metallic red 250 - 475
n. metallic yellow 240 - 400

5699-a

Rear Engine Mongoose 5699 - 107mm - 1972

Based on Tom McEwen's rear-engine dragster, this model was designed by Larry Wood. It has a metal chassis, opening rear-engine cover, a red, white & blue sticker with "Tom McEwen" and "The Mongoose," black plastic interior, two rsw wheels in back, two thin wheels in front, and was made in Hong Kong.

Similar casting: 5856 Rear Engine Snake (1972)

a. blue; clear wheels in front $200 - 550
a2. blue; black wheels in front 200 - 550

Values are shown in U.S. dollars, first price is for mint, second is for mint packaged vehicles only. See pages 15-16 for grading guide to determine value for cars in lesser conditions.

5856-b

Rear Engine Snake 5856 - 107mm - 1972
Based on Don Prudhomme's rear-engine dragster, this model was designed by Larry Wood. It has a metal chassis, opening rear engine cover, a red, yellow & blue sticker with "Don Prudhomme" and "The Snake," black plastic interior, two rsw in back, two thin wheels in front, & was made in Hong Kong.
Similar casting: 5699 Rear Engine Mongoose (1972)

a.	yellow w/clear wheels in front	$200 - 550
a2.	yellow w/black wheels in front	200 - 550

6022-m

Side Kick® 6022 - 80mm - 1972
Designed by Larry Wood, this concept car has a metal chassis, exposed engine, slide-out cockpit, rear pipes, blue-tinted windshield, metal interior, rsw, and was made in Hong Kong.

a.	metallic aqua	$150 - 350
b.	metallic blue	150 - 325
d.	metallic gold	140 - 325
g.	metallic light green	130 - 300
h.	metallic magenta	150 - 320
m.	metallic red	175 - 350
n.	metallic yellow	150 - 325

1973

This year's line provides collectors with some of the hardest Hot Wheels cars to find. The average price for a 1973 issue is higher than for any other year. Included are two of the rarest models: the Snake and Mongoose funny-car dragsters. There were only three new castings: Double Header, Superfine Turbine and Sweet 16. All 1973 issues were sold either on a dark blue blistercard depicting the P-917, Superfine Turbine and Sweet 16 on two pieces of track or on a plastic bag which holds two cars and has a dark blue header card on top which says "2-Pak." Both packs say "Race 'em! Collect 'em!"

In an effort to reduce vehicle cost, Mattel switched from the more expensive spectraflame-paint schemes to enamels and took out extras found in earlier models. All 1973 models were only issued in enamel colors. None had tampos (they would first appear in 1974). Three of the cars did have stick-on labels (Snake, Mongoose, and Police Cruiser).

Body colors offered were dark blue, fluorescent lime green, fluorescent pink, dark green, lemon yellow, light blue, light green, orange, plum, red and yellow. Not all models have been found in all colors. If a particular color has not been located, that color has been omitted from the listing but may be added later. Interior colors varied. One oddity is the Mongoose funny car. Even though the full-size dragster (as well as the 1970 and 1971 Hot Wheels models) was based on the Plymouth Duster, the 1973 Mongoose was based on the Plymouth Barracuda. This was the same casting used for the Snake models. Mattel even gave the 1973 Mongoose a different stock number (6970). However, since both models were based on the Snake casting, the stock number on the underside of the roof is the same as the Snake model (6969). The reason Mattel used the Snake casting for the 1973 Mongoose is unknown.

Alive '55 6968 - 70mm - 1973
Based on a 1955 Chevy Nomad station wagon, this Hong Kong-made model has a metal chassis, lift-up hood, blue-tinted

6968-h

plastic windows, plastic interior (assorted colors) and rsw.
Similar castings: 6404 Classic Nomad (1970), 2098 '55 Nomad (1991), 5743 Classic Nomad (1993), 2098

a.	dark blue	$165 - 525
b.	fluorescent lime green	175 - 540
c.	fluorescent pink	275 - 670
d.	dark green	200 - 565
e.	lemon yellow	200 - 565
f.	light blue	185 - 550
g.	light green	200 - 550
h.	orange	350 - 775
i.	plum	365 - 800
j.	red	175 - 525
k.	yellow	175 - 540

6968-l

l.	dk. green; yellow, lt. green & dk. blue tampo: "Chevrolet" (1974)	125 - 200
l2.	same as l, bw (1983) France	200 - 250
l3.	same as l2, yellow & dk. blue tampo (1983), France	200 - 250
l4.	same as l2, dk. blue & lt. green tampo (1983), France	200 - 250

Alive '55-m

m.	light blue, same as l. (1974)	200 - 750

9210-n

n.	9210, chrome, same as a, black plastic int., yellow, blue, green tampo Super Chromes (1976)	75 - 100
n2.	same as n, hood cast shut (1977)	30 - 35
n3.	same as n2, bw (1977)	20 - 25

6976-c

Buzz Off™ 6976 - 72mm - 1973
This concept car has a metal chassis, swing-up rear engine cover, blue-tinted plastic windows, plastic interior (assorted colors), rsw. Made in Hong Kong.
Similar casting: 6424 Tri Baby (1970)

a.	dark blue	$175 - 500
b.	fluorescent lime green	200 - 500
c.	fluorescent pink	250 - 625
e.	lemon yellow	200 - 575
f.	light blue	200 - 525
j.	red	200 - 525

6976-l

l.	dk. blue; yellow pinstripe tampo (1974)	70 - 100
l2.	med. blue, same as l (1974)	70 - 100
l3.	dk. blue; same as l, black plastic base (1976)	90 - 120
l4.	dk. blue, same as l3, bw (1977)	100 - 145
m.	dk. blue, same as n; yellow & lt. green tampo-like beetle, may be prototype, never in bp (1977)	1000 - NA

1973 Enamel Colors (Show-Off)

Dark Blue
Fluorescent Lime Green
Fluorescent Pink
Dark Green
Lemon Yellow
Light Blue
Light Green
Orange
Plum
Red
Yellow

Values are shown in U.S. dollars, first price is for mint, second is for mint packaged vehicles only. See pages 15-16 for grading guide to determine value for cars in lesser conditions.

Buzz Off-m

6976-n

n. gold chrome; red, dk. red & black tampo: "The Gold One" on hood, black plastic base (1977) 40 - 50
n2. same as n, bw (1977) 25 - 30

5880-d

Double Header 5880 - 79mm - 1973
This concept car has a metal chassis, two engines (one on each side), blue-tinted plastic windows, plastic interior (assorted colors), rsw. Made in Hong Kong.
Note: This model, one of only three new castings for 1973, was designed by Paul Tam and Larry Wood. This was the only year it was used.

a.	dark blue	$180 - 500
b.	fluorescent lime green	225 - 575
d.	dark green	185 - 525
e.	lemon yellow	225 - 575
f.	light blue	225 - 550
g.	light green	250 - 550
h.	orange	200 - 550
i.	plum	250 - 650
j.	red	185 - 500
k.	yellow	185 - 500

6975-b2

Double Vision™ 6975 - 75mm - 1973
This concept car, originally called the Mantis, was designed by Ira Gilford and Howard Rees. The Mantis was issued with an exposed engine in back, but except for a fluorescent green version, no Double Visions were issued that way. This model has a metal chassis, two blue-tinted movable plastic canopies, plastic interior (assorted colors), rsw. Made in Hong Kong.
Similar castings: 6423 Mantis (1970), 7299 Speed Seeker (1984), 15258 Speed Machine (1996)

a.	dark blue	$150 - 475
b.	fluor. lime green	175 - 500
b2.	fluor. lime green (engine in back)	200 - 500
c.	fluor. pink	300 - 650
d.	dark green	225 - 550
e.	lemon yellow	225 - 525
f.	light blue	200 - 500
g.	light green	200 - 525

6975-h

h.	orange	200 - 525
i.	plum	250 - 575
j.	red	200 - 475
k.	yellow	200 - 525
l.	blue, black interior, bw (1983), France	120 - 150

6975-m

m. dk. blue, black int., bw, (1983), France 120 - 150

6967-k

Dune Daddy 6967 - 60mm - 1973
Designed by Tom Daniel, this concept dune buggy was originally called the Sand Crab. It has a metal chassis & roll bar, blue-tinted plastic windshield, plastic interior (white, tan, dark brown, black), rsw. Made in Hong Kong.
Similar casting: 6403 Sand Crab (1970)

a.	dark blue	$100 - 325
b.	fluorescent lime green	100 - 325
c.	fluorescent pink	150 - 375
d.	dark green	125 - 350
e.	lemon yellow	100 - 325
f.	light blue	100 - 325
g.	light green	100 - 325
i.	plum	200 - 475
j.	red	100 - 325
k.	yellow	150 - 365

6967-l

l. lt. green; orange, yellow & blue flower tampo (1975) 60 - 85

6967-m

m. orange, same as l, red instead of orange in tampo (1975) 350 - 550

Dune Daddy-n

n. no #, dk. blue, same as l, black plastic base, lt. green instead of blue, Wisconsin Toy Co, plastic bag w/header card only (1980) 10 - 12

6967-o

o. blue, no tampo, black plastic base, no windshield, bw (1983), France 70 - 90
p. lt. green, same as o, France 60 - 80
p2. same as p, chrome plastic base, Mexico (1983) 60 - 80

6973-f

Ferrari 312P 6973 - 70mm - 1973
This race-car model has a metal chassis, lift-up rear engine cover, blue-tinted plastic windshield, plastic interior (assorted colors), rsw. Made in Hong Kong.
Similar casting: 6417 Ferrari 312P (1970)

a.	dark blue	$300 - 700
b.	fluorescent lime green	350 - 725
c.	fluorescent pink	450 - 850
e.	lemon yellow	350 - 775
f.	light blue	300 - 675
j.	red	275 - 650

6973-l

l. red w/blue & white tampo (1974) 50 - 90
l2. same as l, black plastic base (1976) 40 - 55
l3. same as l2, bw (1977) 20 - 25

6979-j

Hiway Robber 6979 - 70mm - 1973
This Hong Kong-made concept car designed by Larry Wood has a metal chassis, blue-tinted plastic windshield, plastic interior (assorted colors) and rsw.
Similar casting: 6175 The Hood (1971)

a.	dark blue	$150 - 400
b.	fluorescent lime green	175 - 450
c.	fluorescent pink	240 - 550
d.	dark green	175 - 450
e.	lemon yellow	150 - 425
f.	light blue	150 - 400
g.	light green	150 - 425
h.	orange	225 - 550
i.	plum	300 - 600
j.	red	150 - 425
k.	yellow	160 - 450

6980-a

Ice "T" 6980 - 70mm - 1973
Based on Tom Daniel's show car, this Hong Kong-made model has a metal chassis, white plastic roof with "Ice T" imprinted, exposed metal engine, black plastic interior and rsw.
Similar casting: 6184 Ice "T" (1971)

a.	dark blue	$200 - 525
b.	fluorescent lime green	200 - 525
e.	lemon yellow	200 - 535
f.	light blue	200 - 525
j.	red	240 - 600
k.	yellow	200 - 550

6980-l

l. lt. green, orange & olive tampo (1974) 50 - 90
l2. same as l, bw (1977) 40 - 65

6980-m

m. yellow w/orange & olive tampo (1974) 350 - 650
n. blue, same as a, bw, (1983), France 75 - 100

6980-o

o. lt. red-brown, no tampo, bw (1983), France 75 - 100
p. yellow, same as o, bw, (1983), France 60 - 80

p2. same as p, yellow roof (1983) France 65 - 90
p3. same as p, no roof (1983), France,on pkg 80 - NA

6980-q

q. dk. green, same as a, bright yellow plastic roof, bw (1983), Mexico 55 - 75

6962-b

Mercedes-Benz 280SL 6962 - 68mm - 1973
This Hong Kong-made model has a metal chassis, lift-up hood, blue-tinted plastic windshield, plastic interior (assorted colors) and rsw.
Similar casting: 6275 Mercedes-Benz 280SL (1969)

a.	dark blue	$150 - 450
b.	fluorescent lime green	175 - 475
c.	fluorescent pink	325 - 600
d.	dark green	175 - 475
e.	lemon yellow	175 - 475
f.	light blue	150 - 450
g.	light green	200 - 500
h.	orange	250 - 550
i.	plum	325 - 600
j.	red	175 - 500
k.	yellow	175 - 450

6978-b

Mercedes-Benz C-111 6978 - 75mm - 1973
This Hong Kong-made model has a metal chassis, gull-wing opening doors, blue-tinted plastic windshield, plastic interior (assorted colors), and rsw.
Similar casting: 6169 Mercedes-Benz C-111 (1972)
Note: The 1976 model with chrome base may be a prototype. Only six have been reported.

a.	dark blue	$350 - 800
b.	fluorescent lime green	450 - 850
c.	fluorescent pink	800 - 1200
e.	lemon yellow	400 - 875
f.	light blue	400 - 850
j.	red	400 - 825

6978-l

l. red; yellow, white & blue tampo, black int (1974) 60 - 100
l2. same as l, black plastic base (1976) 30 - 45
l3. same as l, chrome plastic base, never in bp (1976) 600 - NA
l4. same as l2, bw (1977) 25 - 30

6970-a

Mongoose 6970 - 75mm - 1973
Based on Tom McEwen's Plymouth Barracuda funny car, this model features a metal chassis, lift-up body, stickers, black plastic interior, rsw. Made in Hong Kong.
Similar castings: 6409 Snake (1970), 5953 Snake 2 (1971), 7630 Top Eliminator

Values are shown in U.S. dollars, first price is for mint, second is for mint packaged vehicles only. See pages 15-16 for grading guide to determine value for cars in lesser conditions.

(1974), 6969 Snake (1974), 10497 Snake (1974), '70 Plymouth Barracuda Funny Car (1997)

Note: Of all vehicles sold in blisterpack, the 1973 Mongoose is one of the two most difficult to find (along with the 1973 Snake). Their values are comparable to the 1974 Road King Truck. This is the only time the Mongoose was issued without plastic windows. The best way to identify a 1973 Mongoose is to lift up the body and look for the number 6969 on the roof's underside.

a. blue $700 - 1350
b. red 950 - 1650

6981-a

Odd Job™ 6981 - 72mm - 1973

This Hong Kong-made concept car was modeled after the Mutt Mobile. It has a metal chassis, exposed engine, black plastic interior and rsw.

Similar casting: 6185 Mutt Mobile (1971), 1524 Mutt Mobile (1994)

a. dark blue $165 - 525
b. fluorescent lime green 165 - 525
c. fluorescent pink 300 - 700
d. dark green 200 - 550
e. lemon yellow 225 - 575
f. light blue 185 - 535
g. light green 200 - 525
h. orange 225 - 535
i. plum 300 - 725
j. red 185 - 535
k. yellow 200 - 550

7966-a

Paddy Wagon 6966 - 64mm - 1973

This show-car model has a metal chassis, exposed engine, "Police" & "3" imprinted in gold on a dark blue roof, metal interior, rsw. Made in Hong Kong.

Note: Paddy Wagon (along with Red Baron) is the least expensive 1973 model. Since it was issued in the U.S. for ten years, many collectors don't care which version they have.

Similar castings: 6402 Paddy Wagon (1970), 5707 Paddy Wagon (1993)

a. dark blue $65 - 240

7966-a2

a2. same as a, black plastic base (1976) 40 - 50
a3. same as a2, bw (1977) 15 - 20
a4. same as a2, bw, (1983), France 20 - 35
a5. same as a4, metal base, (1983), France 70 - 85

6965-c

a6. same as a3, light blue roof, "Police" & "3" imprinted in white, bw, (1983), Mexico 80 - 100
b. brown, same as d, tan roof w/ "Police" & "3" (1983), France 95 - 120
c. tan, same as b. (1983), France 95 - 120

6963-a

Police Cruiser 6963 - 77mm - 1973

This Olds 442 muscle-car version of a police car has a metal chassis, opening engine cover, blue-tinted windows, stickers on the sides with a badge & "Police" red plastic light on top, police sirens cast on roof, black plastic interior, rsw. Made in Hong Kong.

Note: This is one of only three 1973 cars to come with stickers, the other two being Snake and Mongoose.

Similar castings: 6467 Olds 442 (1971), 7665 Chief's Special (1975), 9184 Maxi Taxi (1976), 9521 Army Staff Car (1976)

a. white $250 - 600

6963-b

b. white, same as a, yellow & black police tampo (1974) 85 - 110

6963-b2

b2. same as b, blue light on top, hood cast shut (1976) 75 - 85
b3. same as b2, bw (1977) 50 - 60

6972-b

Porsche 917 6972 - 68mm - 1973

This Hong Kong-made race-car model has a metal chassis, opening engine cover, blue-tinted windows, black plastic interior & rsw.

Similar casting: 6416 Porsche 917 (1970)

a. dark blue $275 - 550
b. fluorescent lime 300 - 575
c. fluorescent pink 450 - 725
e. lemon yellow 300 - 550
f. light blue 300 - 575
j. red 300 - 675

6972-l

l. orange w/yellow, purple & red tampo: "Porsche" twice on top, "9" on hood (1974) 60 - 90

6972-l2

l2. same as l, "P-917" replaces "Porsche;" black plastic chassis (1976) 50 - 70
l3. same as l2, bw (1977) 25 - 30
m. red, same as l (1974) 500 - 850
m2. same as l2 (1976) 800 - 1200

9204-n

n. 9204, chrome, same as l, black plastic chassis, Super Chromes (1976) 65 - 100
n2. same as l2, (1976) 65 - 100

6965-e

Prowler 6965 - 65mm - 1973

Based on the Lil Coffin show car, this Hong Kong-made model has a metal chassis, exposed chrome plastic engine, blue-tinted windshield, plastic interior (assorted colors) and rsw.

Similar castings: 6401 The Demon (1970), 5730 The Demon (1993)

a. dark blue $325 - 700
b. fluorescent limegreen 350 - 725
d. dark green 350 - 725
e. lemon yellow 325 - 725
f. light blue 375 - 735
g. light green 375 - 750
h. orange 400 - 800
i. plum 550 - 900
j. red 400 - 775

6965-l

l. orange, devil, red & yellow flame tampo (1974) 70 - 100
l2. same as l, bw (1983), France 70 - 80

6965-m

m. green, same as l. (1974) 650 - 950

9207-n

n. 9207, chrome, same as l, Super Chromes (1976) 55 - 80
n2. same as n, bw, (1977) 45 - 60

9207-o

o. 9207, chrome, red, white & black tampo: "Prowler" & burglar on roof, bw, Super Chromes (1978) 40 - 50
p. orange, same as o, red & black tampo (1983) France 350 - 550
q. white, same as o, France 300 - 500

6964-a

Red Baron 6964 - 55mm - 1973

This Hong Kong-made show car has a metal chassis, exposed engine, sharp point atop a metal helmet, black plastic interior and rsw.

Note: Unlike the original, the 1973 version does not have the iron cross on the helmet's side. The 1974 version is missing both the cross and the helmet's sharp point. The Red Baron (along with Paddy Wagon) is the least expensive of the 1973 models. This vehicle was issued in the U.S. for ten years.

Similar castings: 6400 Red Baron (1970), 5700 Red Baron (1993)

6964-a2

a. red $65 - 190
a2. same as a, dull point on top of helmet (1974) 15 - 35
a3. same as a2, bw (1977) 15 - 25

6974-d

Sand Witch 6974 - 65mm - 1973

This concept convertible sports car has a metal chassis, lift-up hood on a rear engine, blue-tinted windshield, black plastic interior, rsw. Made in Hong Kong.

Similar casting: 6421 Jack "Rabbit" Special (1970)

a. dark blue $165 - 450
b. fluorescent lime green 150 - 450
c. fluorescent pink 190 - 550
d. dark green 185 - 475
e. lemon yellow 165 - 475
f. light blue 150 - 475
g. light green 190 - 500
h. orange 190 - 525
i. plum 225 - 575
j. red 165 - 475
k. yellow 165 - 475
l. burgundy, bw (1983), France 120 - 250
m. red, bw (1983) Mexico 85 - 150

6982-a

Show-Off® 6982 - 75mm - 1973

This customized Dodge Challenger has a metal chassis, exposed engine, blue-tinted windows, plastic interior (assorted colors), rsw. Made in Hong Kong.

Similar casting: 6187 Bye-Focal (1971)

a. dark blue $250 - 550
b. fluorescent limegreen 250 - 550
c. fluorescent pink 350 - 700
d. dark green 275 - 550
e. lemon yellow 250 - 550
f. light blue 250 - 550
g. light green 225 - 550
h. orange 275 - 600
i. plum 450 - 800
j. red 225 - 525
k. yellow 275 - 575

6969-a

Snake 6969 - 75mm - 1973

Based on Don Prudhomme's Plymouth Barracuda funny car, this Hong Kong-made model has a metal chassis, lift-up body, stickers, black plastic interior and rsw.

Similar castings: 6409 Snake (1970), 5953 Snake 2 (1971), 7630 Top Eliminator (1974), 6969 Snake (1974), 10497 Snake (1974), '70 Plymouth Barracuda Funny Car (1997)

Note: Of all vehicles sold in blisterpack, the 1973 Snake is one of the two most difficult to find (along with 1973 Mongoose). Their values are comparable to the 1974 Road King Truck. This is the only time the Snake was issued without plastic windows. The best way to identify a 1973 Snake is to lift up the body and look for the number 6969 on the roof's underside.

a. white $700 - 1350
b. yellow 950 - 1650

Values are shown in U.S. dollars, first price is for mint, second is for mint packaged vehicles only. See pages 15-16 for grading guide to determine value for cars in lesser conditions.

6971-a

Street Snorter 6971 - 66mm - 1973
This customized Ford Maverick has an unpainted metal chassis, lift-up hood, blue-tinted windows, plastic interior (assorted colors), rsw. Made in Hong Kong.
Note: Unlike the 1970 Mighty Maverick, the 1973 Street Snorter and all later castings do not come with the black plastic rear spoiler.
Similar castings: 6414 Mighty Maverick (1970), 7653 Mighty Maverick (1975)

a. dark blue $200 - 500
b. fluorescent limegreen 225 - 525
c. fluorescent pink 325 - 700
d. dark green 235 - 550
e. lemon yellow 250 - 550
f. light blue 250 - 550
g. light green 235 - 525
h. orange 250 - 550
i. plum 300 - 650
j. red 210 - 535
k. yellow 250 - 550

6004-a

Superfine Turbine 6004 - 58mm - 1973
Designed by Larry Wood, this Hong Kong-made concept car has a metal chassis, exposed metal engine, black plastic interior and rsw.
Note: This casting was used only in 1973.

a. dark blue $425 - 800
b. fluorescent lime 475 - 875
c. fluorescent pink 1050 - 1500
e. lemon yellow 450 - 875
f. light blue 450 - 850
j. red 450 - 900

6007-c

Sweet 16™ 6007 - 76mm - 1973
This Hong Kong-made concept car was designed by Paul Tam. It has a metal chassis, exposed engine, opening trunk, black plastic interior, & rsw.

a. dark blue $200 - 600
b. fluorescent lime 225 - 650
c. fluorescent pink 300 - 700
d. dark green 325 - 750
e. lemon yellow 250 - 650
f. light blue 250 - 650
g. light green 300 - 700
h. orange 350 - 800
i. plum 475 - 925
j. red 250 - 625
j2. same as j; limited ed. for 30th Anniv. w/blistercard in windowbox (1998) 5 - 7
k. yellow 225 - 600
l. mtlfk blue; white int., bw. In box w/2 pins from K•B Toys (1999) 15 - 18
m. mtlfk gold; black int., bw. In box w/2 pins from K•B Toys (1999) 15 - 18
n. black w/red int., silver & red tampo with "Sweet 16" on sides, flames on fenders, Malaysia, #220 (2000) 2 - 4
o. mtlfk green, tan int., gold & white design on front & back fenders, "Sweet 16" on sides, bw. From Avon Vintage Hot Rods 3-pack (2000) 6 - NA
p. white w/gold int., black & gold tampo on sides & top, "Sweet 16" on sides, lwch, Malaysia, #129 (2002) 2 - 4

6977-b

Xploder 6977 - 67mm - 1973
Based on the American Motors experimental car AMX/2, this model has a metal chassis, two black plastic pop-up engine covers, blue-tinted windows, black plastic interior, rsw. Made in Hong Kong.
Similar castings: 6460 AMX/2 (1971), 7654 Warpath (1975), 9534 Redliner (1985), 1510 Road Torch (1987)

a. dark blue $185 - 500
b. fluorescent limegreen 240 - 550
c. fluorescent pink 300 - 650
d. dark green 275 - 600
e. lemon yellow 275 - 650
f. light blue 185 - 525
g. light green 190 - 575
h. orange 300 - 675
i. plum 350 - 725
j. red 190 - 550
k. yellow 250 - 600

Shell Promos
In 1973, Mattel made some special models for a nationwide Shell gasoline-dealer promotion. Ten models were issued in seven colors. They were packed in small plastic bags with dark blue cardboard tops showing both the Shell emblem and the Hot Wheels logo. All ten were listed on the back. Mattel used several cost-cutting measures to create these cars. All were made from previous castings.
Note: The second price is for a mint car in an unopened bag. Some have been found on a 1973 blistercard and are worth about twice the price of a mint model.

Bugeye-g

Bugeye - 74mm - 1973
Designed by Larry Wood, this concept car has a metal chassis, lift-up rear hood to expose the engine, blue-tinted plastic windows, black plastic interior, rsw. Made in Hong Kong.
Similar casting: 6178 Bugeye (1971)

a. dark blue $90 - 125
b. fluorescent green 90 - 125
c. fluorescent lime 150 - 200
d. fluorescent pink 150 - 200
e. light blue 90 - 125
f. red 110 - 125
g. yellow 150 - 200

Ferrari 512S-d

Ferrari 512P - 70mm - 1973
This race car has a metal chassis, lift-up hood over the rear engine, opening cockpit cover, blue-tinted plastic windshield, black plastic interior, rsw. Made in Hong Kong.
Similar casting: 6021 Ferrari 512S (1972)

a. dark blue $120 - 135
b. fluorescent green 120 - 135
c. fluorescent lime 150 - 200
d. fluorescent pink 175 - 225
e. light blue 120 - 135
f. red 130 - 180
g. yellow 150 - 200

Jet Threat-b

Jet Threat® - 81mm - 1973
This Hong Kong-made concept car was designed by Larry Wood. It has a metal chassis, blue-tinted plastic windshield, painted metal interior (same color as car), and rsw.
Note: Unlike the 1971 Jet Threat, the cover doesn't open.
Similar castings: 6179 Jet Threat (1971), 8235 Jet Threat 2 (1976)

a. dark blue $110 - 125
b. fluorescent green 110 - 125
c. fluorescent lime 200 - 275
d. fluorescent pink 200 - 275
e. light blue 110 - 125
f. red 110 - 125
g. yellow 150 - 200

Peeping Bomb-d

Peepin' Bomb - 75mm - 1973
Designed by Howard Rees, this convertible concept car has a metal chassis, exposed metal engine, blue-tinted plastic windshield, black or brown plastic interior, rsw. Made in Hong Kong.
Note: Unlike the 1970 Peepin' Bomb, this version doesn't have retractable headlight covers.
Similar casting: 6419 Peepin' Bomb (1970)

a. dark blue $90 - 125
b. fluorescent green 90 - 125
c. fluorescent lime 155 - 200
d. fluorescent pink 155 - 200
e. light blue 110 - 125
f. red 100 - 125
g. yellow 90 - 125

Rocket-Bye-Baby-d

Rocket-Bye-Baby - 80mm - 1973
Designed by Bob Lovejoy, this concept car has a metal chassis, metal rocket on the roof, black plastic interior, no tailpipes or engine covers, blue-tinted windshield, rsw. Made in Hong Kong.
Similar casting: 6186 Rocket-Bye-Baby (1971)

a. dark blue $90 - 125
b. fluorescent green 90 - 125
d. fluorescent pink 150 - 175
e. light blue 150 - 175
f. red 110 - 125
g. yellow 110 - 125

Short Order-a

Short Order - 70mm - 1973
This Hong Kong-made model is based on a 1950's Ford pickup. Designed by Howard Rees, it has a metal chassis, exposed metal engine, shortened pickup bed, orange plastic tail gate, blue-tinted windows, black plastic interior, and rsw.
Similar casting: 6176 Short Order (1971)

a. dark blue $125 - 150
b. fluorescent green 125 - 150
d. fluorescent pink 200 - 250
e. light blue 125 - 150
f. red 125 - 105
g. yellow 150 - 175

Splittin' Image-d

Splittin' Image - 75mm - 1973
This Hong Kong-made concept car was designed by Ira Gilford. It has a metal chassis, chrome plastic engine, plastic interior, dark blue-tinted plastic windows, and rsw.
Similar casting: 6261 Splittin' Image (1969), 5708 Splittin' Image (1993)

a. dark blue $90 - 125
b. fluorescent green 90 - 125
d. fluorescent pink 175 - 200
e. light blue 100 - 125
f. red 100 - 125
g. yellow 110 - 125

Strip Teaser-c

Strip Teaser - 79mm - 1973
Designed by Larry Wood, this concept car has a metal chassis, exposed metal engine, lift-up top to the driver's compartment, black plastic interior, rsw. Made in Hong Kong.
Similar casting: 6188 Strip Teaser (1971)

a. dark blue $125 - 150
b. fluorescent green 135 - 160
c. fluorescent lime 250 - 350
d. fluorescent pink 200 - 250
e. light blue 125 - 150
f. red 125 - 150
g. yellow 170 - 200

Swingin' Wing- g

Swingin' Wing - 83mm - 1973
Designed by Ira Gilford, this concept car has a metal chassis, dark blue plastic windows, plastic interior and rsw. Hong Kong.
Note: Unlike the 1970 version, this model had no plastic wing.
Similar casting: 6422 Swingin' Wing (1970)

a. dark blue $110 - 125
d. fluorescent pink 175 - 200
e. light blue 110 - 125
f. red 110 - 125
g. yellow 125 - 150

Swingin' Wing-h

h. yellow; black plastic base, orange & magenta tampo on top, dk. blue tinted windows; Wisconsin Toy Co. promo, plastic bag with header card only (1980) 6- 8

Twinmill-b

TwinMill® - 72mm - 1973
This Hong Kong-made concept car was designed by Ira Gilford. It has a metal chassis, two chrome plastic engines, black plastic interior, dark blue-tinted plastic windows & rsw.
Similar castings: 6258 TwinMill (1969), 8240 TwinMill II (1976), 5709 TwinMill (1993)

a. dark blue $110 - 125
b. fluorescent green 90 - 125
d. fluorescent pink 175 - 200
e. light blue 110 - 125
f. red 150 - 175
g. yellow 110 - 125

Values are shown in U.S. dollars, first price is for mint, second is for mint packaged vehicles only. See pages 15-16 for grading guide to determine value for cars in lesser conditions.

1974

Mattel stepped up the line's marketing. Seven new and eight embellished castings were issued. This was the first year all vehicles were issued in enamel colors with designs called tampos. As in 1973, many of the models were based on previous castings.

All 1974 models were issued on new blistercards. These cards were white with "Flying Colors" in red and pictured three models: Baja Bruiser, Heavy Chevy, and Porsche 917.

This marked the first year models were not issued in many colors, although some were re-issued in other colors in later years. Some 1974 cars were issued in alternate colors. These have been documented because they are very rare collectibles.

Alternate Colors: Due to random paint changes, some cars have been found in unexpected colors. For example, a plant may have temporarily run out of a color, or a production run may have changed because of a marketing decision. These changes are still happening today. Depending upon how many were produced, some alternate colors can be worth more than ten times normal value.

8258-a

Baja Bruiser 8258 - 69mm - 1974
This Hong Kong-made customized 1956 Ford pickup has a metal base, exposed metal engine, black plastic interior and rsw.
a. orange; red, white & blue tampo: "5," "Baja" & racing decals on sides, "Mattel" cast on back $65 - 100
a2. same as a, chrome plastic base (1976) 65 - 100

8258-b

b. yellow, same as a 600 - 1200
b2. same tampo design as b; red, white & magenta tampo 600 - 1200

8258-c

c. green, same as a2 (1976) 850 - 1000

8258-d

d. dk. blue, chrome plastic base; yellow, white & red tampo: "Baja Bruiser," "American," "711" & racing decals on sides (1977) 50 - 75
d2. same as d, bw (1977) 45 - 55

8258-e

e. white; chrome plastic base, dk. red, yellow, blue tampo: "6" & racing decals on sides, bw (1982) 12 - 18
e2. same as e, lt. red in tampo, Malaysia (1982) 10 - 16

8262-a

Breakaway Bucket 8263 - 75mm - 1974
This Hong Kong-made 1973 Pontiac Grand Am Pickup has a metal chassis, blue-tinted windshield, black plastic interior, and rsw.
a. blue; orange & yellow tampo $100 - 150

7617-a

Carabo 7617 - 70mm - 1974
This Hong Kong-made show car has a metal chassis, working gull-wing doors, blue-tinted windshield, black plastic interior and rsw.
Similar casting: 6420 Carabo (1970)
a. lt. green; orange & blue tampo $65 - 100
a2. same as a, bw (1977) 90 - 140

7617-b

b. yellow, same as a 800 - 1200

8273-a2

El Rey Special 8273 - 75mm - 1974
Based on a Grand Prix-style racer, this model has a metal chassis & interior, rsw. Made in Hong Kong.
Similar castings: 9037 Formula P.A.C.K. (1976), 9037 Malibu Grand Prix (1982)
a. green; yellow & orange tampo: "Dunlop," "1" & "76" on top $60 - 125
a2. light green, same as a 100 -175

8273-b

b. dark blue, same as a 350 - 750

8273-c

c. light blue, same as a 800 - 1200

7621-a

Funny Money 7621 - 73mm - 1974
Based on an armored truck, this funny-car model has a metal chassis, black interior, rsw. Made in Hong Kong.
Similar casting: 6005 Funny Money (1972)
a. plum; yellow, green & orange flower tampo $85 - 110
b. gray; yellow, white & blue Brink's armored car tampo (1977) 50 - 75

7621-b2

b2. same as b, bw (1977) 30 - 35

Grass Hopper 7622 - 65mm - 1974
This Hong Kong-made customized Jeep has a metal chassis, exposed metal engine, black interior, blue-tinted windshield and rsw.

7622-a

Similar casting: 6461 Grass Hopper (1971)
Note: Two dark green versions exist but are thought to be prototypes.
a. lt. green; orange & blue tampo: "Grass Hopper" on sides $50 - 95

7622-b

b. same as a, no engine showing (1975) 100 - 300

7619-a

Heavy Chevy 7619 - 70mm - 1974
Based on a Chevrolet Camaro, this model has a metal chassis, exposed chrome metal engine, black interior, blue-tinted plastic windows, rsw. Made in Hong Kong.
Similar casting: 6408 Heavy Chevy (1970)
a. yellow; dk. red, lt. orange & dk. orange tampo: "7" on sides $125 - 175

7619-b

b. lt. green, same tampo as a 800 - 1200

9212-c

c. 9212, chrome, same tampo as a (1976), Super Chromes 100 - 135
c2. same as c, olive; green & yellow tampo (1977) 90 - 125
c3. same as c2, bw (1977) 70 - 110

7616-a

Rash 1 7616 - 72mm - 1974
Based on the Brabham racer, this model has a metal chassis, chrome plastic engine in the rear, black interior, blue-tinted windshield, rsw. Made in Hong Kong.
Similar casting: 6264 Brabham-Repco F1 (1969)
a. green; yellow, white & red tampo: "Lucas" & "31" on hood $75 - 140
a2. same as a, white interior 600 - NA
a3. light green, same as a 150 - 225

7616-b

b. dark blue, same as a 600 - 1000

7615-a

Road King Truck 7615 - 94mm - 1974
This side-dumping gravel truck has a metal chassis, blacked-out windows, rsw. Made in Hong Kong. The detachable trailer, dumper & handle are yellow plastic.
Note: Issued only in the Mountain Mining set, this is the most valuable Hot Wheels model that's not a variation.
a. yellow, no tampo $800 - NA

8259-a

Rodger Dodger 8259 - 75mm - 1974
This Hong Kong-made concept car has a metal chassis, exposed metal engine, black interior, blue-tinted windows and rsw.
a. plum; orange & yellow flame tampo $70 - 130
a2. same as a, chrome plastic base (1976) 65 - 100
a3. same as a; limited ed. for 30th Anniv. w/blistercard in windowbox (1998) 8 - 10
b. blue, same as a 2000 - 2500

8259-c

c. gold chrome; magenta, white & red striped tampo on top (1977) 50 - 60
c2. same as c, bw (1977) 30 - 35
d. white; tinted window; black int.; black, orange & silver tampo: stripes & "426" on sides & hood; 1998 Convention logo on trunk; rrch w/white stripe around tire. Limited to 5000. Sold at 1998 Hot Wheels Convention (1998) 30 - 35

8259-e

e. white w/black int., blue-tinted windows, blue & gray tampo w/"Detroit Police" & emblem on trunk, rrch. From Cop Rods Series 2 (2000) 7 - 9

8259-f

f. black w/chrome chassis; red int.; clear windows; gold & white emblem on rear fender; red, orange & yellow flames on top; rrchww; Malaysia; #4 in 2001 Treasure Hunt series, #004 (2001) 18 - 25
g. yellow w/chrome chassis, black int., dk.-tinted windows, black roof, black & orange flames on sides, sp5, #186 (2001) 2 - 3

8259-h

h. yellow w/chrome chassis; black int.; dk.-tinted windows; black, red, orange & white tampo w/Hot Wheels logo, "collectors*com" on sides & stripes over top; limited run from Mattel's Web site (2001) 25 - 30

8259-i

i. green w/tan int.; clear windows; black, white, orange & gold tampo on sides, hood & roof w/"Lila's Bowl-A-Rama" on sides & roof; sp5; Malaysia; #3 in Spares 'n Strikes series; #061 (2002) 2 - 3

Values are shown in U.S. dollars, first price is for mint, second is for mint packaged vehicles only. See pages 15-16 for grading guide to determine value for cars in lesser conditions.

j. green, same as g, limited run from Mattel's Web site (2001) 75 - 250

8259-k

k. red; black int, clear windows; blue, white & gray tampo w/flames & JC Whitney logo on sides, flag tampo on roof, JC Whitney logo on trunk, gych. Boxed limited ed. (2002) 15 - 18

8261-a

Sir Rodney Roadster 8261 - 60mm - 1974
This concept model is based on the Lotus Super Seven. It has a metal base & interior, exposed metal engine, removable brown plastic roof, rsw, & was made in Hong Kong.
a. yellow w/red flame tampo $50 - 100
a2. lt. yellow, same as a, bw (1977) 75 - 100
a3. yellow, dk. brown roof, different & darker tampo, bw (1983), Mexico 75 - 110

8261-b

b. green, same as a 400 - 600

8261-c

c. orange-brown, same as a 500 - 800
d. metal, duller brown roof, different flame tampo, bw (1983), France 75 - 100

8261-d2

d2. same as d, beige roof (1983), France 75 - 100

8260-a

Steam Roller 8260 - 72mm - 1974
A Can-Am racer with metal chassis & interior, exposed metal engine in back, rsw. Hong Kong. Prototypes of a & b exist with a chrome plastic base.
a. white; red & blue tampo: "3" & 3 stars in front, "3" & racing decals in back $50 - 75

8260-a 8260-a2

a2. same as a, 7 stars in tampo 350 - 500

9208-b

b. 9208, chrome, as a, black plastic chassis, red & plum tampo black plastic int. (1976), Super Chromes 35 - 40
b2. as b, yellow & blue tampo (1976) 35 - 40
b3. as b2, bw (1977) 35 - 40
b4. as b3, 7 stars in tampo (1976) 250 - 400

8260-c

c. yellow, same as a, black plastic chassis, red & plum tampo, bw (1978) 25 - 35

7630-a

Top Eliminator 7630 - 75mm - 1974
Based on a Plymouth Barracuda funny car, this Hong Kong-made model has a metal chassis, black plastic interior and rsw.
Similar castings: 6409 Snake (1970), 5953 Snake 2 (1971), 6970 Mongoose (1974), 6969 Snake (1974), 10497 Snake (1993), '70 Plymouth Barracuda Funny Car (1997)
a. dk. blue; orange, green & yellow tampo w/"Hot Wheels," "Flying Colors" & racing decals on sides $80 - 150

7630-b

b. gold chrome; red, blue & magenta tampo on sides: "Hemi Hauler" & racing decals, blue Ancel decal on rear fender (1977) 50 - 60
b2. same as b, bw (1977) 60 - 75

7630-b3

b3. same as b, red AC decal on rear fender, bw (1978) 30 - 35

7630-c

c. red; tan int., black, yellow & white tampo w/"Radical Racer," "301" & racing decals on side, bw, Malaysia (1982) 18 - 20
c2. same as c but lighter, France (French) 30 - 40
d. no number, plum, no tampo, Speed Machines (1983) 15 - 18
e. dk. green, no tampo, Malaysia (Italy) (1983) 200 - 225

7630-f

f. white, same as e, red flame tampo, France (1985) 145 - 200

7620-a

Volkswagen 7620 - 56mm - 1974
This model has a metal chassis, blue-tinted windows, exposed engine, black plastic interior, rsw. Made in Hong Kong.
Note: This model was originally issued with stripes on the hood, roof and trunk, but the tampo was changed because of difficulty in lining up the stripes.
a. orange; black, white & yellow stripe top tampo $600 - 1000
b. orange; black, yellow & green bug on roof 75 - 125

7620-b

7620-b2

b2. same as b, same tampo: yellow "Herfy's" tampo on sides, in plastic bag with header card 300 - 350
b3. same as b, black plastic base, Wisconsin Toy Co, plastic bag with header card only (1980) 25 - 35

7618-a

Winnipeg 7618 - 60mm - 1974
Based on the Chapparal 2G, this model has a metal chassis, blue-tinted windshield, black plastic interior, removable plastic orange spoiler on the back which lifts to reveal a metal engine, rsw. Made in Hong Kong.
Similar casting: 6256 Chapparal 2G (1969)
a. yellow; blue & orange tampo on top: blue "33" on nose & orange "33" on both sides behind driver's seat $125 - 200

1975

This year, 23 new models were introduced into the Hot Wheels "Flying Colors" line. New editions included military and emergency vehicles, van models, and the only two motorcycles ever in the regular line. Other highlights were: Mattel continued the practice of issuing some models in harder-to-find alternate colors. The Ramblin' Wrecker actually had Larry Wood's phone number on the sides (which was removed in later issues). The first promotional model for the Toys "R" Us toy store chain was introduced. Promotional models for the Herfy's restaurant chain were also issued. Finally, this was the last year white blistercards were used.

7662-a

American Victory 7662 - 75mm - 1975
Based on a McLaren racer, this Hong Kong-made model has a chrome plastic chassis & interior, exposed metal engine and rsw.
a. lt. blue; red & white tampo: stars & "9" on sides $35 - 50
a2. same as a, bw 20 - 25

7662-b

b. magenta; yellow, orange & red tampo: "10" & racing decals on sides, bw (1978) 12 - 18
b2. lt. magenta, same as b (1978) 15 - 20
b3. magenta, same as b, "Made in France" on base (1983) 25 - 30
c. dk. red, same as b, yellow & red tampo (1983), France 20 - 25

7662-d

d. lt. blue, same as b, dk. blue tampo (1983), France 35 - 60

7662-e

e. dk. green, yellow plastic chassis & int., no tampo, Speed Machines 18 - 20
f. mtlfk dk. green, Malaysia (Italy) (1983) 80 - 100
g. dark blue, same as a (1984), Mexico 25 - 50

7670-a

Backwoods Bomb 7670 - 80mm - 1975
This Hong Kong-made pickup truck has a chrome plastic chassis, white plastic camper shell, black plastic interior and rsw.
a. lt. blue; yellow & lt. green tampo: "Keep on Camping" on sides, blue-tinted windshield $65 - 125
a2. same as a, dk. gray-tinted windshield 65 - 125

7670-b

b. dk. green; yellow & red dragon on sides, dk. gray-tinted windshield (1977) 40 - 45
b2. same as b, bw (1977) 35 - 40

7671-a

Chevy Monza 2+2 7671 - 72mm - 1975
This Hong Kong-made Chevrolet hatchback has a black plastic chassis, blue-tinted windows and interior, and rsw.
a. orange; black & white tampo: "Monza" on hood $50 - 110
a2. same as a, no white in tampo, gray-tinted window, clear plastic interior, bw (1983), France 60 - 75

7671-a3

a3. same as a2, white shield: "BP" on top (1983), France 125 - 150
a4. same as a, gray-tinted windows, clear plastic int., France on base, bw (1984), Mexico 55 - 75
a5. same as a, orange-tinted windows, bw, Mexico 55 - 75
a6. same as a, no tampo, orange-tinted windows, bw (1987), Mexico 110 - 145

7671-b

Values are shown in U.S. dollars, first price is for mint, second is for mint packaged vehicles only. See pages 15-16 for grading guide to determine value for cars in lesser conditions.

a7. same as a, no tampo, orange-tinted windows, ww (1987), Mexico 120 - 150
b. light green, same as a 400 - 700

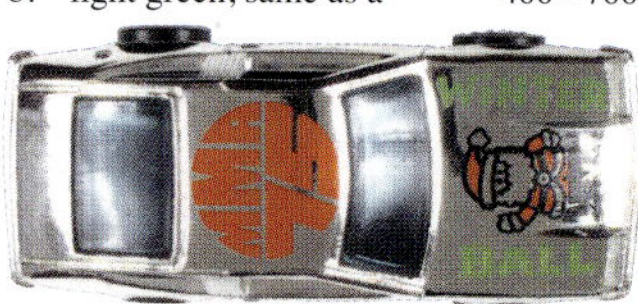

Chevy Monza 2+2-c

c. chrome, no #, red "MMA," green "Winter Ball" & Santa in black & red on roof, given to Mattel Managers about 1975 at Mattel Managers Christmas Ball, 200 made 2500 - NA
d. 9202, chrome, same as a, yellow & black tampo, Super Chromes (1976) 40 - 50

9202-d2

d2. same as d, bw, Super Chromes (1977) 35 - 45
e. beige, same as a4, (1985), Mexico 65 - 85
e2. same as e, yellow not white in tampo (1985), Mexico 65 - 85
e3. same as e, no tampo (1986), Mexico 65 - 85
e4. same as e3, ww (1987), Mexico 90 - 125

7665-a

Chief's Special 7665 - 77mm - 1975
An Olds 442 muscle-car version of a fire chief's car, this Hong Kong-made model has a chrome plastic chassis, blue-tinted windows, black plastic interior, blue-tinted light on top and rsw.
Similar castings: 6467 Olds 442 (1971), 6963 Police Cruiser (1973), 9184 Maxi Taxi (1976), 9521 Staff Car (1976)
a. red; yellow & white fire chief tampo on sides $50 - 90

7665-a2

a2. same as a, yellow "Herfy's" side tampo, plastic bag w/Herfy's Restaurant header card only 275 - 325
a3. same as a, red bar instead of blue light (1976) 50 - 60

7665-a4

a4. red, same as a3, bw 20 - 25

7650-a

Emergency Squad 7650 - 77mm - 1975
This concept paramedic vehicle has a chrome plastic chassis, blue-tinted windshield, clear blue plastic interior, rsw. Made in Hong Kong.
Similar castings: 7666 Ranger Rig (1975), 2537 Rescue Ranger (1986)
a. red; yellow & white emergency squad tampo on sides, dk. blue hoses, lights, etc. $20 - 50

a2. same as a, gray-tinted windows, black int. (1976) 20 - 50
a3. same as a2, bw (1977) 10 - 12
a4. same as a3, Malaysia (1982) 10 - 12
a5. same as a4, "Made in France" on base 20 - 40
a6. same as a5, "Masters of the Universe" on hood, logo in white 135 - NA

9529-b

b. 9529; yellow; red, white & blue tampo w/Hot Wheels logo & "Race Rescue" on sides, gray-tinted windshield; black interior; red hoses, lights etc; Malaysia; bw (1985) 20 - 25

Emergency Squad-c

c. red; blue-tinted windows; chrome plastic int.; blue lights & hoses; white, gold & black tampo w/"Fire Dept.," "Emergency," "51" & emblem on sides; sp7; Fire Fighting 5-packs (1998) 2 - NA
c2. same as c, ho5 2 - NA
c3. same as c, sp5 2 - NA

7652-a

Gremlin Grinder 7652 - 59mm - 1975
Based on the American Motors Gremlin, this model has a metal chassis, exposed metal engine, blue-tinted windows, black plastic interior, rsw. Made in Hong Kong.
a. green; orange, yellow & black tampo: gremlin on roof $45 - 95

7652-a2

a2. same as a, yellow "Herfy's" side tampo, plastic bag w/Herfy's Restaurant header card only 275 - 325
b. 9201; chrome; same as a; red, green & black tampo; Super Chromes (1976) 35 - 50
b2. same as b, bw (1977) 30 - 35

7664-a

Gun Slinger 7664 - 63mm - 1975
This Hong Kong-made army vehicle has a black plastic chassis & window frame, black plastic interior with gun in back and rsw.
a. olive; white army tampo on hood $50 - 60

7664-a2

a2. same as a, gun clip on window frame (1976) 35 - 45
a3. same as a, bw (1977) 30 - 35

8272-a

Large Charge® 8272 - 75mm - 1975-1984
This Hong Kong-made concept model has a metal chassis, blue-tinted windows, metal interior, and rsw.
Similar castings: 9535 Silver Bullet (1985), 1781 Aeroflash (1992 Gleam Team)
a. green; black, yellow & orange tampo: circuit board, lightning bolts & "High Voltage" 40 - 85

9211-b

b. 9211, chrome, same as a, (1976) Super Chromes 45 - 55
b2. same as b, bw (1977) 25 - 35

8272-c

c. orange, purple, white tampo: "4," bw (1979) 15 - 20
d. orange; same as a; black, yellow, purple tampo: yellow inside purple, bw (1984); Mexico 40 - 60
d2. same as d, purple inside yellow in tampo, bw (1985), Mexico 40 - 60

7653-a

Mighty Maverick 7653 - 66mm - 1975
This Hong Kong-made customized Ford Maverick has a metal chassis, blue-tinted windows, black plastic interior and rsw.
Similar castings: 6414 Mighty Maverick (1970), 6971 Street Snorter (1973)
a. dk. blue with orange & white tampo $75 - 110

7653-b

b. lt. green, same as a, blue & white tampo 175 - 300
c. 9209, chrome, same as a, yellow & blue tampo, Super Chromes (1976) 60 - 80

9209-c2

c2. same as c, bw (1977) 50 - 65

7660-a

Monte Carlo Stocker 7660 - 76mm - 1975
This Hong Kong-made Chevrolet stock car has a chrome plastic chassis, blue-tinted windows, black plastic interior and rsw.
Similar casting: 9185 Lowdown (1976)
a. yellow; blue, red & white tampo: "38," "Chevrolet" & racing decals on sides $75 - 125
a2. lemon yellow, same as a 100 - 175
a3. same as a2, bw (1977) 50 - 60

7660-b

a4. yellow, same as a, bw. (1977) 70 - 85
b. dk. blue; green, yellow & white tampo on sides & top; "38" & racing decals on sides; "355" twice on hood; bw (1979) 60 - 75
c. blue; green, white & yellow stripes on top; "355" twice on hood; "Lowdown" on base; bw (1983); Mexico 35 - 45

7660-c2

c2. same as c, gw (1983), Mexico 35 - 45
c3. same as c2, black plastic base (1986), Mexico 75 - 100

7668-a

Motocross 1 7668 - 68mm - 1975
This is one of the first Hot Wheels motorcycles ever produced. It has a red plastic gas tank & rear fender, black plastic seat, front fender & handlebars. Made in Hong Kong.
a. red & black; yellow circle: "1" under seat $130 - 200

7644-a

Mustang Stocker 7644 - 72mm - 1975
Based on a Ford Mustang fastback, this model has a metal chassis, blue-tinted plastic windows, louvered back window, black plastic interior, rsw. Made in Hong Kong.
a. yellow; orange & magenta tampo w/"Ford" twice on roof & "450 HP" twice on hood $150 - 250

7644-a2

a2. same as a, blue & red tampo 400 - 700
a3. same as a, yellow int., bw (1983), France 300 - 350
a4. same as a3, no tampo (1984), France 100 - 125

7644-b

b. white, same as a, blue & red tampo 700 - 1200

7644-b2

b2. same as b, red & yellow tampo, white int., bw (1984) Mexico 225 - 275
c. 9203, chrome, same as a, Super Chromes (1976) 100 - 150
d. chrome, same as c; red, white & blue stars & stripes tampo, Super Chromes (1977) 60 - 85
d2. same as d, bw (1977) 55 - 70

Values are shown in U.S. dollars, first price is for mint, second is for mint packaged vehicles only. *See pages 15-16 for grading guide to determine value for cars in lesser conditions.*

9203-d2

7644-e

e. white; two blue stripes on top, tan int., bw, Malaysia (1982) 70 - 90
e2. same as e, yellow int., bw (1983), France 120 - 180

7644-f

f. black, same as e, gray plastic chassis, 2 yellow stripes on top, white int., Speed Machines (1983) 45 - 50

7648-a

P-911 7648 - 70mm - 1975
This Hong Kong-made Porsche 911 has a metal chassis, gray-tinted windows, black plastic interior, "Porsche" cast above the rear bumper, "Porsche Carrera" on the base & rsw.
a. yellow; red & blue striping tampo on top: "911" on hood $75 - 100
a2. yellow, same as a, "P-911" not "Porsche Carrera" on base (1976) 40 - 70

7648-a3

a3. same as a2, red "Herfy's" tampo on sides, plastic bag w/Herfy's Restaurant header card only 325 - 375

P-911-b

b. white, same as a 2000 - NA
c. gold chrome w/o tampo, given to Mattel's top salesmen w/plaque 1300 - NA
d. 9206, chrome, same as a, red & lt. green tampo, Super Chromes (1976) 40 - 50

9206-e

e. chrome same as d, red, orange swirl tampo, Super Chromes (1976) 35 - 40
e2. same as e, bw (1976) 30 - 35

7648-f

f. black, same as e, bw (1977), only in set 450 - NA
g. white; red, black & aqua stripes on top & sides; "Turbo" & "6" on hood; racing decals & "6" on sides; gw (1980) 10 - 12

7648-i

h. black, same as g, bw 15 - 18
i. black; red, yellow & white stripes on top & sides; "95" on hood & sides; gw (1982) 6 - 8
i2. same as i, gold bw (1982) 10 - 12
i3. same as i, made in Malaysia (1982) 5 - 7
i4. same as i3, bw 6 - 8
i5. same as i. (1984), France 6 - 8
j. 9345, red, same as i, Stamper 3-pack only (1985) 10 - NA
k. 3968, black, issued as P-911 Turbo, no tampo (1988) 12 - 15

3969-l

l. 3969; white; issued as P-911 Turbo; black, red & yellow stripes on top & sides; "95" & racing decals on sides; gold bw (1988) 6 - 8

P-911-l2

l2. same as l; "95" added to hood tampo; bw; Ziploc promo; never in bp; in bag (1989) 15 - 18

2108-m

m. 2108; P-911 Turbo; chrome magenta; pink, blue & yellow tampo on sides & hood; yellow "Cal Custom" on roof; black-tinted windows; black int.; twy; California Custom (1990) 15 - 20
m2. same as m, red replaces pink, twl (1990) 12 - 15
n. 2108; P-911 Turbo; bright red; black, green & blue tampo on hood & sides; "Cal Custom" in blue on roof; twl; California Custom (1991) 15 - 20

2108-n2

n2. same as n, twch (1991) 15 - 20
o. 15789, red; clear window, black int., sp5 #590 (1996) 2 - 4
o2. same as o, ho5. #590 (1997) 2 - 4
o3. same as o, dw3. #590 (1997) 2 - 4
o4. same as o, sp7. #590 (1997) 2 - 4
o5. same as o, sp3. #590 (1997) 2 - 4
o6. same as o, dw3. China, Target excl. set (1999) 4 - 6

P-911-p

p. purple; red-tinted windows & int., sp5; Toys "R" Us 5-pack 6 - NA

P-911-q

q. blue; tinted windows; black int.; white, orange & silver tampo on sides w/"Baurspeed Rennsport ag. Racebait Turbolager Technologies"; sp3. #3 of 4 in European pack (1998) 4 - 6
r. yellow; black int., tinted window, sp5; #995 (1999) 2 - 4
s. gray, black int., clear windows, small purple Hot Wheels logo on hood, dw3, China. Power Launcher pack (2000) 4 - 6
t. dk. mtlfk blue, dk. blue chassis, black int., clear windows, white stripe with "Final Run" on sides, pcch. #6 in 2001 Final Run series (2001) 4 - 6

7661-a

Paramedic 7661 - 70mm - 1975
Based on a standard delivery van, this Hong Kong-made model has a chrome plastic chassis, gray-tinted windshield, black plastic interior and rsw.
Similar castings: 7649 Super Van (1975), 9183 Khaki Kooler (1976)
a. white; red & yellow striping tampo: red cross, "Paramedic" & "Ambulance" on sides $55 - 95
a2. same as a, blue-tinted windows 55 - 95
b. yellow, same as b, white not yellow in tampo (1977) 35 - 55
b2. same as b, metal chassis (1977) 35 - 55

7649-b3

b3. same as b2, bw (1977) 25 - 35

7659-a

Ramblin' Wrecker® 7659 - 70mm - 1975
This tow truck has a chrome plastic chassis, blue plastic wrecker with a tow-bar/hook in the bed, gray-tinted windshield, clear blue plastic interior, rsw. Made in Hong Kong.
Note: Larry Wood used his own phone number on the sides of the original version.
a. white; blue & yellow tampo: "Larry's 24 hr Towing," "375-1670" & shield on sides $50 - 75
a2. as a, blue-tinted windshield 40 - 65
a3. as a, no phone #, bw (1977) 15 - 20

7659-b

b. yellow; blue, orange & white tampo: "24 Hour Towing" on sides & round AAA emblem on door; black int.; bw; Malaysia (1983) 15 - 20

7666-a

Ranger Rig 7666 - 77mm - 1975
This forest ranger truck has a chrome plastic chassis, gray-tinted windshield, brown plastic interior, red hoses, lights, etc., rsw. Made in Hong Kong.

Similar castings: 7650 Emergency Squad (1975), 2537 Rescue Ranger (1986)
a. green; yellow Forest Ranger tampo on sides 55 - 80
a2. same as a, blue-tinted windows 55 - 80

7651-a

Sand Drifter 7651 - 62mm - 1975
This customized pickup truck has a metal chassis, black plastic int., opening black plastic truck-bed cover with tools cast into the bed, rsw. Made in Hong Kong.
a. yellow; orange & magenta flame tampo on hood & front fenders 65 - 90
a2. same as a, bw (1983), France 75 - 125
a3. same as a2, no tampo (1983), France 70 - 100
b. green, same as a 350 - 700
c. orange, bw, no tampo (1983), France 70 - 100

7651-c2

c2. same as c, ww (1983), France 110 - 130
c3. same as c, white shield & "BP" on hood 150 - 200

7669-a

Street Eater 7669 - 66mm - 1975
This was one of the first Hot Wheels motorcycles produced. It has a yellow plastic gas tank & rear fender, black plastic seat, metal handlebars. Made in Hong Kong.
a. yellow; red & orange flame tampo on gas tank 110 - 200

7649-a

Super Van 7649 - 70mm - 1975
This delivery van has a chrome plastic chassis, gray-tinted windshield, black plastic interior, rsw. Made in Hong Kong.
Similar castings: 7661 Paramedic (1975), 9183 Khaki Kooler (1976), 2880 Thor (1979)
a. black; red & yellow flame tampo on sides 60 - 100
a2. as a, blue-tinted windshield 60 - 100

7649-a3

a3. same as a2; orange "62 KGW Radio" on sides, plastic bag w/Herfy's Restaurant header card only 300 - 350
a4. same as a2; "King Radio" in orange on sides, plastic bag w/Herfy's restaurant header card only 350 - 450

Values are shown in U.S. dollars, first price is for mint, second is for mint packaged vehicles only. See pages 15-16 for grading guide to determine value for cars in lesser conditions.

Super Van-a4

a5. same as a, unpainted metal chassis 75 - 110
a6. black, same as a, bw (1977) 25 - 35

Super Van-b

b. white; red, yellow & black tampo: flames, Mattel emblem, "Hot Wheels Flying Colors" & "Toy Fair '75" on sides; given to key accounts at 1975 Toy Fair, about 200 produced 2200 - NA

Super Van-c

c. chrome, same as b, 1975 Toy Fair 4500 - NA

7649-d

d. blue, same as a, blue-tinted windshield 1350 - NA

7649-e

e. plum; yellow, orange & blue stripe tampo: flames behind driver on one side; motorcycle rider on sides 125 - 225
e2. same as e, blue-tinted windshield 125 - 225

7649-f

f. white; orange, black & purple tampo: "Toys "R" Us Giraffe & "Geoffrey" on sides; only at Toys "R" Us (1976) 200 - 300
f2. same as f, bw (1977) 300 - 400
g. 9205, chrome, same as a, Super Chromes (1976) 45 - 60
g2. same as g, black plastic chassis (1976) 45 - 60
g3. same as g, bw (1977) 40 - 45

9205-h

h. 9205; chrome; red, black & yellow tampo, hot rod & "California Cruisin" on sides; bw; Super Chromes (1979) 25 - 30

7649-i

i. white; red & orange flame tampo, bw (1980) 15 - 20
i2. same as i, made in Malaysia (1980) 15 - 20

9205-j

j. 9205; mtlfk gray; unpainted metal chassis; red, black & yellow tampo: hot rod & "California Cruisin" on sides; bw; Malaysia (1979) 15 - 20

7649-k

k. red; yellow & white flame tampo on sides, gray plastic chassis, gray-tinted plastic windows, black plastic int., bw, Speed Machines (1983) 20 - 25

7649-l

l. mtlfk blue; yellow & white flame tampo: red "Super Van" on sides; blue-tinted windows; bw; Malaysia; Kellogg's promo (1985) 30 - NA

7649-m

m. black; orange stripe on sides, blue-tinted window & int., plastic base, bw, issued w/Dynamite Crossing Set or found loose at Mattel Toy Club 8 - NA

7647-a

Torino Stocker 7647 - 75mm - 1975
This Hong Kong-made Ford racer features a chrome plastic chassis, blue-tinted windshield, black plastic interior & hood scoop, and rsw.
Similar castings: 9793 Thrill Driver Torino (1979), 9533 Torino Tornado (1985)
a. red; yellow, blue & white tampo, "23" & racing decals on sides $60 - 100
a2. red, same as a, bw (1977) 60 - 100
b. black; yellow, orange & white stripe tampo, "3" & racing decals on sides; arrow on hood; bw (1979) 25 - 40

7647-b2

b2. same as b, gw (1982) 25 - 35

b3. same as b2, Malaysia (1982) 20 - 25
b4. same as b2, duller colors than U.S. version, gw (1983), Mexico 20 - 30
b5. black, same as b4, bw (1985), Mexico 20 - 30

7655-a2

Tough Customer 7655 - 78mm - 1975
This Hong Kong-made army tank has an olive plastic chassis, plastic movable turret with long gun barrel, small black wheels and was issued with & without "Tough Customer" on the base.
Similar castings: 5272 Battle Tank (1982 Megaforce), 4920, 9372 Big Bertha (1985)
a. shiny olive, white army tampo on top $25 - 75
a2. dull olive, same as a 25 - 75

7658-a

Vega Bomb 7658 - 80mm - 1975
This Hong Kong-made Chevrolet Vega funny-car dragster has a metal chassis, black plastic interior, lift-up body to reveal a metal engine and rsw.
a. orange; red, yellow & blue tampo: "Vega Bomb," racing decals on sides $60 - 125
a2. orange, same as a, bw (1977) 85 - 125

7658-b

b. light green, same as a 900 - 1500

7658-c

c. red, same as a2, yellow & blue tampo, lt. brown int., bw (1983), France 160 - 200
d. lt. orange-brown, same as c, (1983) France 175 - 225
e. maroon, no tampo, lt. brown int., bw (1983), France 40 - 80
e2. same as e, orange int., bw (1983), France 40 - 80
f. dk. green; no tampo, bw, Speed Machines (1983) 18 - 20
g. white, black int., bw, Malaysia (1983), Italy 200 - 300

7654-a

Warpath® 7654 - 65mm - 1975
Based on the American Motors experimental car AMX/2, this Hong Kong-made model has a metal chassis, blue-tinted plastic windows, black plastic interior, two black plastic engine covers and rsw.
Similar castings: 6460 AMX/2 (1971), 6977 Xploder (1973), 9534 Redliner (1985), 1510 Road Torch (1987)
a. white; red & blue stars & stripes tampo on top $65 - 100

7654-a2

a2. same as a, red "Herfy's" side tampo, plastic bag w/Herfy's Restaurant header card only 350 - 400

a3. same as a, black plastic base 65 - 100
a4. same as a3, (1983), France 65 - 110
a5. same as a3, chrome plastic base, darker tampo colors, bw (1983), Mexico 85 - 125

7654-b

b. red, same as a3, blue & white tampo, Wisconsin Toy Co., plastic bag with header card (1980) 6 - 8
c. lt. blue, same as c, no tampo, bw (1983) France 150 - 200
d. blue, same as a4, (1983), France 150 - 200

1976

The "Flying Colors" line continued with several new additions. Two were semi-truck models, one a dump truck and the other a box-style cargo truck. These were painted red, white and blue with white stars: a flag-style tampo in honor of our country's 200th birthday. Also done in red, white and blue was a race car, Formula 5000 with "76" in the tampo, and a street rod, Neet Streeter.

This year Super Chromes were introduced. This was a line of eighteen chrome models, twelve in individual blisterpacks and six which were only issued in a 6-pack. There were also four more military vehicles. All were issued in both a blister-pack and a 6-pack, except the Army Staff Car which only came in the 6-pack.

9118-a

American Hauler 9118 - 68mm - 1976
This moving van has a metal chassis, white plastic box, dark gray-tinted windows, rsw and was made in Hong Kong.
a. blue; red & blue tampo: "American Hauler," "Coast to Coast" & 3 stars on sides of box $35 - 55
a2. same as a, bw (1977) 25 - 30

9089-a

American Tipper 9089 - 65mm - 1976
This dump truck has a metal chassis, white plastic dumper, dark gray-tinted windows, rsw, and was made in Hong Kong.
a. red; red & blue tampo: "American Tipper" & 3 stars on sides $55 - 65
a2. same as a, bw (1977) 35 - 45

9243-a

Aw Shoot 9243 - 62mm - 1976
This Hong Kong-made large-caliber tank has an olive plastic chassis & gun, and small black wheels.
Similar casting: 2518 Shell Shocker (1986)
a. olive; white star & army tampo on front $30 - 40

Values are shown in U.S. dollars, first price is for mint, second is for mint packaged vehicles only. See pages 15-16 for grading guide to determine value for cars in lesser conditions.

9120-a

Cool One 9120 - 81mm - 1976
This Hong Kong-made concept rear-engine dragster has a metal chassis, chrome plastic interior & exposed engine, rsw in back & small black bicycle wheels in front.
Similar casting: 9186 Inferno (1976)

a. plum; yellow & white tampo: lightning bolt & "Zap" on nose; "Cool One" in large letters & "Moon" in small letters on front spoiler $55 - 75
a2. same as a, bw (1977) 50 - 65

9120-b

b. green; yellow, orange & black tampo: striping & "Cool One" on nose; bw (1978) 40 - 60

9241-a2

Corvette Stingray 9241 - 76mm - 1976
This model has a metal chassis, blue-tinted windows, blue clear plastic interior, rsw and was made in Hong Kong.

a. red; blue, yellow, white stripe tampo on top $60 - 100
a2. red, same as a, bw (1977) 30 - 35
a3. same as a; darker tampo colors, Hot Wheels 30th Anniv. logo in gold on rear fender; limited ed. for 30th Anniv. w/blistercard in window box (1998) 4 - 6

9206-b

b. 9206, chrome, same as a, only in Super Chromes 6-pack (1976) 100 - NA
b2. same as b, bw (1977) 80 - NA

9241-c

c. gray; black, orange & white tampo; bw (1978) 500 - 800
d. yellow, same as c (1979) 15 - 20
e. no #, gold chrome, same as d, Golden Machines 6-packs only (1979) 40 - NA

9241-f

f. orange; black, yellow & magenta tampo, bw (1980) 18 - 22
f2. orange, same as f, gw (1980) 15 - 20

9241-g

g. black; red, orange & yellow stripe tampo: "Corvette" on sides; gw (1982); Hot Ones 3-pack only 12 - NA

9241-h

h. red; same as g; white, orange & yellow tampo (1982) 10 - 12
h2. mtlfk red, same as h (1983) 8 - 10
h3. mtlfk red, same as h, Malaysia (1983) 8 - 10

Corvette Stingray-i

i. no #; red; yellow, blue & white stripe tampo on top & sides; bw; Kellogg's mail-in only (1985) 30 - NA

9525-j

j. 9525; white; red, blue & black tampo: "35," "Corvette" & 2 winner's flags on hood; "35," "Corvette" & racing decals on sides; bw; Malaysia (1985) 15 - 20
j2. 3973, white, same as j, gw (1988) 10 - 12

1448-k

k. 1448; mtlfk gray; yellow, orange & magenta stripes & "Corvette" twice on top; "Stingray," stripes & racing decals on sides; bw; Malaysia (1988) 10 - 12
k2. same as k, black replaces magenta (1990), International series only 15 - 18

3974-l

l. 3974; yellow; dk. blue, orange & magenta stripes on top & sides; "Stingray" on sides; bw; Malaysia (1988) 10 - 12

9252-m

m. 9252, gold chrome; blacked-out windows, black int., bw, w/trophy for 20th Hot Wheels Anniv. only (1990) 6 - 8

Corvette Stingray-n

n. no #, orange; blue & black stripes on top & "Corvette" twice on hood, Hot Wheels cereal only (1990) 10 - NA

Corvette Stingray-o

o. no #, red; black plastic base, white "NPS" on roof, given at 1991 Chicago National Premiums Show, less than 2,000 made (1991) 40 - NA

Corvette Stingray-p

p. no #, white; black plastic base, black "NPS" on roof, given at 1991 Chicago National Premiums Show, less than 2000 made (1991) 40 - NA

1793-q

q. 1793, lt. green chrome, no tampo, bw, Gleam Team, #192 (1992) 10 - 22
r. 1793, chrome, same as q, Gleam Team, #192 (1992) 6 - 12
r2. 1793, chrome, same as r, uh. #192 (1995) 4 - 10
r3. chrome, same as r, sp5. Lucky Supermarkets 2-packs only (1995) 5 - NA
s. no #, lt. blue; white Hot Wheels logo on rear fender, lt. blue windows & int., uh. Chevrolet 5-Pack only (1995) 6 - NA
s2. no #, lt. blue, same as s, sp5. Chevrolet 5-Pack only (1995) 7 - NA
t. 12925, white; blue Hot Wheels logo on rear fender, lt. blue windows & int., sp5, #450 3 - 6
t2. same as t, uh. Chevrolet 5-packs only (1995) 2 - NA

12925-t3

t3. 12925, white, same as t, sp3, #450 (1996) 2 - 4
t4. 12925, white, same as t, sp7, #450 (1996) 6 - 15

13308-u

u. 13308, mtlfk aqua, clear windows, gray int., gold Hot Wheels logo on rear bumper, gyg, #4 in Real Riders Series, #321 (1995) 65 - 75
v. mtlfk green; green tinted windows & int., gygd. History of Hot Wheels II 8-pack from FAO Schwarz (1996) 10 - NA

Corvette Stingray-w

w. no #, bronze; clear plastic int., clear windows & gych. FAO Schwarz Olympic 3-pack only (1996) 75 - NA

Corvette Stingray-x

x. 16933, white; blue-tinted windows, black int.; red, yellow & black tampo of bird head (roof)& claws (hood); dw3y, #4 in Street Beast series. #560 (1997) 2 - 4

Corvette Stingray-y

y. red; blacked-out windows; white, lt. purple, lt. blue & yellow rainbow design on sides & hood, Lucky Charms logo on hood & "Lucky Charms" on trunk; sp5. General Mills mail-in (1997) 8 - NA
y2. same as y, "Lucky Charms" on hood has black outline (1998) 8 - NA

Corvette Stingray-z

z. orange; yellow & black design on sides, sp3. #4 in Tattoo Machines series. #688 (1998) 2 - 5
z2. same as z, dw3 #688 (1998) 2 - 4

Corvette Stingray-aa

aa. white; blue-tinted windows & int., gold, black, white & blue tampo: "Moran's Surf Shop Xpress" on sides; sp3; Thailand; Ocean Blasters 5-pack (1999) 2 - NA

9241-ab

ab. mustard yellow; clear windows, black int., black, white & orange tampo on sides & hood; lwgd. China #1056 (1999) 2 - 3

9241-ac

ac. yellow; clear windows, black int., black & red tampo: pinstripes on sides & top, "Corvette Central" on trunk, gych, limited edition for Corvette Central, Thailand (1999) 15 - 20
ad. blue w/black windows; white, yellow & orange tampo on sides; ho5; China; #154 (2000) 2 - 3
ad2.same as ad, sp3, China, #154 (2000)
ae. black w/black int.; tinted windows; orange, yellow & turquoise flame tampo on sides & hood; sp5; Malaysia; #135 (2001) 2 - 3

9119-a2

Formula 5000 9119 - 76mm - 1976
This Formula One race car has a metal chassis & interior, exposed metal engine, rsw and was made in Hong Kong.

a. white; blue, red & white tampo: "76" & racing decals on spoiler; striping & "76" 3 times on top $30 - 50
a2. white, same as a, bw (1977) 10 - 15
a3. same as a2, "France" on base (1983) 15 - 35
a4. 8199, white, same as a2, Mexican pack. (1984) 10 - 30
b. 9511, chrome, same as a, only in Super Chromes 6-pack (1976) 50 - NA
b2. 9511, chrome, same as b, bw (1977) 40 - NA

9037-a2

Formula P.A.C.K. 9037 - 75mm - 1976
This Formula One race car has a metal chassis & interior, exposed metal engine, rsw, and was made in Hong Kong.
Similar castings: 8273 El Rey Special (1974), 9037 Malibu Grand Prix (1982)

a. black; orange & yellow tampo: "P.A.C.K." on spoiler & twice on top; "5" & lightning bolt on nose $45 - 50

Values are shown in U.S. dollars, first price is for mint, second is for mint packaged vehicles only. See pages 15-16 for grading guide to determine value for cars in lesser conditions.

9037-b

a2. same as a, bw 100 - 120
b. black; yellow tampo: "8" 3 times & pinstripe trim on top; bw (1978) 20 - 25

9090-a2

Gun Bucket 9090 - 78mm - 1976
This army half-track has a black plastic chassis, black plastic twin guns mounted on rear, olive plastic interior, rsw in front, small black wheels in rear. Hong Kong.
Similar casting: 9374 Tank Gunner (1985)
a. olive; white tampo: "Army," a star & numbers on hood $30 - 50
a2. same as a , Malaysia
a3. same as a, bw (1977) 25 - 40

9186-a2

Inferno 9186 - 81mm - 1976
This Hong Kong-made concept rear-engine dragster has a metal chassis, chrome plastic interior & exposed engine, rsw in back & small black bicycle wheels in front.
Similar casting: 9120 Cool One (1976)
a. yellow; orange, purple & red flame tampo on nose, "Inferno" on front spoiler $60 - 85
a2. same as a, bw (1977) 45 - 65

8235-a2

Jet Threat II 8235 - 81mm - 1976
This concept car has a metal chassis & exposed engine, blue-tinted windshield, plum interior, and rsw. Made in Hong Kong.
Similar castings: 6179 Jet Threat (1971), Jet Threat (1973 Shell Promo)
a. plum with yellow flame tampo $40 - 50
a2. same as a, bw (1977) 20 - 25

8235-b

b. blue; orange & yellow tampo: "Jet Threat" on sides; blue int.; bw (1978) 20 - 25

9183-a

Khaki Kooler 9183 - 70mm - 1976
Based on a standard delivery van, this Hong Kong-made model has a chrome plastic chassis, gray-tinted windshield, black plastic interior, and rsw.
Similar castings: 7661 Paramedic (1975), 7649 Super Van (1975)
a. olive; white "Military Police" & military tampo on side $40 - 60
a2. same as a, metal base 35 - 55
b. same as a2, bw (1977) 25 - 30

Lowdown 9185 - 76mm - 1976
This Hong Kong-made Chevrolet Monte

9185-a

Carlo stock car has a chrome plastic chassis, blue-tinted windows, black plastic interior, and rsw.
Similar castings: 7660 Monte Carlo Stocker (1975)
a. lt. blue; plum, yellow & white tampo on top; "Flyin Low" twice on hood $65 - 75

9185-b

b. gold chrome; red, white & blue ribbon on top (1977) 35 - 45
b2. same as b, bw (1977) 30 - 40

9185-c

c. white; same as b2, black plastic chassis; blue, red & yellow ribbon tampo on top (1983) France 130 - 175
d. blue; same as c, black plastic chassis; white, dk. red & yellow striping tampo on top (1983); France 130 - 175

9185-e

e. red; same as c, gray plastic chassis; white, orange & yellow tampo; white plastic int.; Speed Machines (1983) 22 - 28

9184-a

Maxi Taxi 9184 - 75mm - 1976
This Hong Kong-made Olds 442 muscle-car version of a taxi has a chrome plastic chassis, black plastic interior, blue-tinted windows, and rsw.
Similar castings: 6467 Olds 442 (1971), 6963 Police Cruiser (1973), 7665 Chief's Cruiser (1975), 9521 Army Staff Car (1976)
a. yellow; red, white & black taxi tampo: "Maxi Taxi" on sides $50 - 75
a2. same as a, bw (1977) 35 - 50
a3. lemon yellow, same as a2 (1977) 45 - 60

9244-a2

Neet Streeter® 9244 - 65mm - 1976
This customized 1936 Ford Coupe has a metal chassis, black plastic interior & hood scoop, rsw, and was made in Hong Kong.
a. lt. blue; red, white & blue striping tampo on top; "Ford" & "Oldie but a Goodie" on trunk $60 - 70
a2. lt. blue, same as a, bw (1977) 30 - 35
a3. lt. blue, same as a, magenta replaces blue in tampo, bw (1983), Mexico 65 - 85
b. 9510, chrome, same as a, Super Chromes 6-pack only 75 - NA
b2. 9510, chrome, same as b, bw (1976) 70 - NA
c. plum, same as a, bw (1980) 20 - 25
d. mtlfk dk. red, same as a, bw (1983) 15 - 20
d2. mtlfk dk. red, same as d, Malaysia 15 - 20
e. mtlfk magenta, same as a, darker tampo, bw (1985), Mexico 55 - 70
e2. mtlfk magenta, same as e, bw, made in Malaysia on base (1985), Mexico 55 - 70

9244-f

f. turquoise; red & yellow flame tampo on sides; white rectangle: red Hot Wheels logo in back; orange int. & spoiler; bw; "India" on metal base. FAO Schwarz History of Hot Wheels 8-pack (1995) 12 - NA

Neet Streeter-g

g. yellow; black int. and hood scoops magenta in blue tampo on sides, bw. India #526 (1997) 7 - 9

9240-a

Poison Pinto 9240 - 72mm - 1976
This Ford Pinto wagon has a black plastic chassis, chrome plastic interior & exposed engine, blue-tinted windows, and rsw (rear wheel size may vary). Made in Hong Kong.
Similar casting: 2882 The Thing (1979)
a. lt. green; yellow, black & white tampo: "Poison Pinto," skull & crossbones on sides $35 - 50
a2. lt. green, same as a, bw (1977) 15 - 20
a3. same as a2, blue-green-tinted window, France (1984) 70 - 90
a4. lt. green, same as a3, lime green not yellow in tampo (1984), France 70 - 90
b. 9508, chrome, same as a, Super Chromes 6-pack only 55 - NA

9508-b2

b2. same as b, bw (1977) 50 - NA

9240-c

c. red, same as a2, black plastic chassis, gray int., bw, Speed Machines (1983) 30 - 35
d. blue-green, no tampo, "France" on base (1985) 40 - 55

9507-b

Rock Buster™ 9088 - 67mm - 1976
This Hong Kong-made Baja-style dune buggy has a metal chassis, metal engine in back, black plastic interior, roll bar and rsw.
a. yellow; red, white & blue tampo: lightning bolts on sides of the top; "10" & racing decals on hood $40 - 60
a2. yellow, same as a, bw (1977) 20 - 25
a3. yellow, same as a2, black replaces blue, chrome plastic base & rear engine, "Made in Mexico" on base (1983) 80 - 100
b. 9507, chrome, same as a, Super Chromes 6-pack & Super Chromes Race set only 50 - NA
b2. same as b, bw (1977) 40 - NA

9088-c

c. green, same as a. (1980) 15 - 20
c2. same as c, made in Malaysia 15 - 20

9088-d

d. white, same as c, black plastic chassis, no tampo, Speed Machines (1983) 80 - 100

9088-d2

d2. same as d, red int. & roll bar (1983) 15 - 18

9521-a

Staff Car 9521 - 75mm - 1976
This Olds 442 muscle-car version of an army staff car has a chrome plastic chassis, black plastic interior, blue-tinted windows, rsw, and was made in Hong Kong.
Note: This model was only sold in the Military 6-pack.
a. olive; white star, flag & "Staff Car" tampo on sides $700 - NA
a2. same as a, bw (1977) 850 - NA

9242-a

Street Rodder 9242 - 60mm - 1976
This Hong Kong-made customized 1932 Ford roadster has a metal chassis, exposed chrome plastic engine, gray plastic interior and rsw.
a. black; red & yellow flame tampo on sides $75 - 100
a2. same as a, bw (1977) 35 - 40

Values are shown in U.S. dollars, first price is for mint, second is for mint packaged vehicles only. See pages 15-16 for grading guide to determine value for cars in lesser conditions.

b. white, same as a, red & orange tampo, bw (1981) 15 - 20
b2. same as b, bw, Malaysia (1981) 15 - 20
b3. same as b2, gyg (1982) 40 - 50
b4. same as b2, darker tampo (1984), Mexico 30 - 40

Twin Mill 8240 - 72mm - 1976
This concept car has a metal chassis, two exposed chrome plastic engines on the sides, black plastic interior, blue-tinted windows, and rsw. Made in Hong Kong.
Similar castings: 6258 TwinMill (1969), TwinMill (1973 Shell Promo), 5709 TwinMill (1993)
a. orange; red, white & blue tampo $35 - 50
a2. orange, same as a, bw (1977) 20 - 25
b. 9509, chrome, same as a, only in Super Chromes 6-pack 50 - NA
b2. same as b, bw (1977) 45 - NA

1977

There were 69 vehicles with 12 new castings and changes on 10 previously issued models. This year Mattel started phasing out "redlines" or red-stripe tires (rsw). All 1977 standard-line models were available with both rsw and basic wheels (bw). Several are extremely hard to find in rsw and very valuable. The Thrill Driver Torinos, released later in the year in a "set," were the sole vehicles to have only bw. This year also marked the introduction of the popular gold-chrome vehicles. These are listed in earlier years because they were re-issues of older castings.

'31 Doozie 9649 - 76mm - 1977
This Hong Kong-made 1931 Duesenberg Dual Cowl Phaeton has a metal chassis, dark brown plastic interior & fenders, removable cream-colored plastic top, blue-tinted plastic windows and rsw.
a. orange, no tampo $35 - 50
a2. same as a, bw 18 - 20
a3. same as a, brown plastic int. & fenders, bw (1978) 18 - 20

a4. same as a, green plastic int. & fenders, bw (1981) 250 - 400

b. green, green plastic int. & fenders, yellow tampo on sides, bw (1981) 6 - 8
b2. same as b, lt. green tampo, bw (1981) 10 -12
b3. same as b2, Malaysia (1981) 10 - 12
c. red, red-brown plastic int. & fenders, ww, Malaysia, Extras series (1983) 8 - 10

c2. same as c, red plastic int. & fenders (1983) 60 - 75
d. maroon, same as a, #11 (1986) 10 - 12

e. 13361, yellow; black plastic roof & fenders, black int., red Hot Wheels logo on side, sp6y, #12 in Treasure Hunt series, #364 (1995) 35 - 65

f. chrome, chrome int., black plastic top, red Hot Wheels logo on side, rsw. Service Merchandise 16-piece Classic American Car Collection only, limited to 5,000 (1995) 12 - NA

g. dk. pearl purple, lt. purple design on hood & sides, clear windshield, purple int., rtch. American Classics 3-pack only (1996) 12 - NA
h. white, white int., blue tinted windshield, black roof & fenders, purple tampo design on sides, lwch. Issued as Duesenberg 1931, #3 of 4 in International line. (1997) 4 - 6
i. mtlfk green, lt. green sides, lt. brown top & int., white headlights, rrchww. FAO Schwarz Classic Collection. (1999) 10 - NA
j. mtlfk red w/clear windshield, black int. & roof, lwch, #1097 (2000) 2 - 3

k. dk. mtlfk red w/extra window behind front seat, tinted windows, black int., sp5, #176 (2001) 2 - 4

'56 Hi-Tail Hauler 9647 - 70mm - 1977
This 1956 Ford pickup comes with a chrome plastic chassis, black plastic interior, two black plastic motorcycles in the bed, blue-tinted plastic windows, rsw, and was made in Hong Kong.
Similar casting: 9641 Good Ol' Pick-Um-Up (1985)
a. orange; yellow & blue flame tampo on hood & roof $50 - 75
a2. same as a, bw 30 - 40
a3. same as a, no roof tampo, bw (1978) 10 - 15

b. lt. blue; yellow & dk. red flame tampo on hood, bw (1979) 80 - 100

b2. same as b, yellow motorcycles & int., yellow-tinted windshield, bw (1979) 12 - 15

c. 4341, mtlfk lt. blue, same as b, white plastic camper top, Extras series (1983) 10 - 12

'57 Chevy 9638 - 73mm - 1977
This 1957 Chevrolet Bel Air hardtop has a chrome plastic chassis, clear blue plastic interior, blue-tinted plastic windows, rsw, and was made in Hong Kong.
a. red; yellow & white striping tampo w/"57 Chevy" on sides $85 - 110
a2. same as a, bw 20 - 30
a3. same as a; ltd ed for 30th Anniv. w/blistercard in window box (1998) 5 - 7
b. black, same as a, bw (1978) 20 - 25
b2. same as b, gw (1982) 15 - 18
c. mtlfk red, same as a, gw (1983) 10 - 12
c2. same as c, gw, Malaysia (1983) 10 - 12

d. yellow, exposed metal engine, black stripe, red & white flame tampo on sides, gw, Malaysia (1984) 15 - 20
d2. same as d, bw (1984) 15 - 20
d3. same as d, uh, #157 (1991) 10 - 20
d4. same as d, hoc, #157 (1992) 12 - 30

e. 1538; mtlfk blue; exposed metal engine; white, yellow & black striping tampo with "57 Chevy" on sides; gw; Malaysia (1987) 25 - 30
e2. same as e, no "57 Chevy" (1987) 10 - 12
e3. same as e2, uh, 20-pack only (1988) 25 - NA
f. turquoise; exposed metal engine; red, yellow & black striping tampo with "57 Chevy" on sides; gw; Malaysia (1989) 8 - 10
f2. same as f, no "57 Chevy" (1989) 6 - 8
f3. same as f2, uh, #47 (1990) 10 - 12

f4. same as f2, hoc, Canada in box only (1993) 10 - 12

g. 2178, mtlfk dk. red, same as e, yellow tinted int., Park 'n Plates (1989) 10 - 12

g2. same as g, no "57 Chevy" (1989) 8 - 10
h. 1297; bright orange; magenta, pink & blue tampo; black "Cal Custom" on roof; rrgy; California Custom (1990) 10 - 15
h2. same as h, blue "Cal Custom" 10 - 15
h3. same as h, yellow "Cal Custom," twgn (1991) 10 - 15
h4. same as h3, blue "Cal Custom" 10 - 15

i. 1256; white; black, red & blue tampo: "22," "Frank Stricklin Motors" & racing decals on sides; "260 H.P." twice, "Smith Motor Co.," 2 stripes & "Fireball Roberts" twice on roof; no engine showing; rrgy; in special blistercard; limited to 12,000 (1992) 20 - 25

j. aqua; yellow, orange & brown side tampo; uh; #213 (1993) 10 - 18
j2. same as j, lower part of side tampo missing, #213 (1994) 10 - 20
j3. 13586, same as j2, uhgd, #213 (1994) 10 - 18
j4. 4311, same as j2, sp5 #213 (1995) 4 - 8
j5. same as j2, gray-tinted windows (1998) 4 - 6

k. lt. purple; dk. red, pink & white tampo on sides; gray-tinted windows; black int.; uh; 25th Anniv. Chevy 5-pack only (1993) 10 - NA

l. no #; red; "World Cup USA" & Hot Wheels logo in white on sides; brown, black, blue & white World Cup mascot on roof; clear windows & int.; uh; World Cup 5-Pack only (1994) 8 - NA

m. black, white stripe w/yellow on rear fender, black Hot Wheels logo on rear window, yellow-tinted windows, clear windows, exposed metal engine, uh, Chevrolet Pack only (1995) 3 - NA
m2. same as m, sp5 (1995) 3 - NA
m3. same as m, sp7 (1995) 10 - NA
m4. same as m, bw (1995) 3 - NA
n. 13277; mtlfk blue: "57" in silver; silver, blue & pink tampo on sides; blue-tinted windows & int.; uh; #4 of Steel Stamp series; #290 (1995) 6 - 12
n2. same as n, sp5, #290 5 - 10

Values are shown in U.S. dollars, first price is for mint, second is for mint packaged vehicles only. See pages 15-16 for grading guide to determine value for cars in lesser conditions.

n3. same as n2, gray-tinted windows & black int., #290 (1995) 20 - 50
n4. same as n, sp7, #290 (1995) 3 - 5

9638-o

o. chrome w/blue-tinted int. & windows, red Hot Wheels logo on back window, rsw. Service Merchandise 16-piece Classic American Car Collection only, limited to 5000 (1995) 12 - NA

13636-p

p. 13636, aqua, yellow design & white "Malt-O-Meal" on sides, blue-tinted windows, plastic base, sp5, limited edition from Malt-O-Meal (1995) 15 - 18
p2. same as p, sp7 (1997) 15 - 18
q. yellow plastic body, black & silver tampo on sides, black-tinted windows, black int., sp5, 50's Favorites 5-pack (1996) 3 - NA
q2. same as q, body is die cast (1996) 3 - NA
q3. same as q2, dw3 (1996) 3 - NA
q4. same as q2, sp3 (1997) 3 - NA
q5. same as q4, gray base (1997) 3 - NA
q6. same as q2, gray base, sp5 (1997) 3 - NA
q7. same as q2, gray base, dw3 (1997) 3 - NA

15235-r

r. #15235, mtlfk blue, Hot Wheels Race Team tampo: "Vijay" on sides, sp5, #3 in Race Team Series II, #394 (1996) 5 - 10

9647-s

s. orange, chrome plastic base, black roof, black & gray tampo on sides, clear windows, clear plastic int., rrch; white stripe around tire. Fabulous 57s 2-pack by Bloomingdales (1996) 125 - NA

15080-t

t. 15080, mtlfk purple, black & silver tampo on rear fender, purple-tinted windows & int., gych. Car #7 in Treasure Hunt Series, #434 (1996) 35 - 65
u. 15270, chrome plastic body, orange-tinted windows, sp5. Car #3 in Silver Series II, #422 (1996) 5 - 10
v. no #, aqua; black int., blue tinted windows; silver, gold & black striping tampo; sp5gd. Cruisin' America 6-pack only (1997) 3 - NA

'57 Chevy-w

w. no #; black; clear window; black int.; gold hood & roof; gold, white, black & red tampo: "Smokey's 'Best Darn Garage in Town'," "3" & racing decals on sides; "3" on roof & trunk; rrgd. 40th Anniv. of the '57 Chevy 4-pack only (1997) 12 - NA

'57 Chevy-x

x. no #, red, clear windows, black int., yellow & orange flame tampo on hood and sides, pcch. 40th Anniversary of '57 Chevy only (1997) 12 - NA

'57 Chevy-y

y. no #; lt. yellow; blue-tinted window; black int.; silver, red & black tampo: stripes, "Fuel Injection," "1957" & 2 racing flags on sides; rrch. 40th Anniv. of '57 Chevy 4-pack (1997) 12 - NA

'57 Chevy-z

z. no #, mc blue, white roof, blue int., gray Chevy stripe on sides, rrch. 40th Anniversary of '57 Chevy 4-pack only (1997) 12 - NA

'57 Chevy-aa

aa. no #; black; red roof & trunk; clear windows; red int.; yellow, black, white & red tampo: "07," "Sunoco Special" & racing decals on sides, Sunoco logo on hood; "07" & "Jack Flash" on roof; red chrome bw. FAO Schwarz History of Hot Wheels III 8-packs only (1997) 12 - NA

'57 Chevy-ab

ab. black; yellow, orange & red flames; "Airwalk" on sides; sp5. Limited to 10,000, given at Nordstrom stores with purchase of Airwalk shoes (1998) 30 - 35

'57 Chevy-ac

ac. red; white, yellow, orange & blue tampo w/flames on sides, "Norwalk Raceway Park" on roof & "Norwalk Express" on trunk; gych; Thailand. Norwalk Raceway exclusive on special card, limited to 12,000 20 - 25

'57 Chevy-ad

ad. blue, metal base, lt. blue int., blue-tinted windows, gray & black striping tampo: "Bel-Air" on sides, flame tampo on hood & sides, sp5. China. FAO Schwarz Cruisin' The '50s 8-packs only (1998) 8 - NA
ae. mtlfk purple; black int.; tinted window; black, red & white tampo: "'57 Chevy" on sides; dw3; #787 (1998) Thailand 3 - 8

'57 Chevy-ae

'57 Chevy-af

af. gray plastic body; metal base; black int.; tinted window; orange, black, white & red tampo: face on sides, white dots on roof & trunk; dw3. #2 in Artistic License Series #730 (1998) 2 - 4

'57 Chevy-ag

ag. mtlfk green; gold chrome base; yellow-tinted int. & window; gold, black & gray tampo on sides; sp3; #10 in 1998 Treasure Hunt Series #758 (1998) 20 - 35
ah. unpainted, black int., tinted window, dw3, 1998 Hot Wheels Convention #787 (1998) 100 - 150

'57 Chevy-ai

ai. blue, exposed engine, blue-tinted int. & window, gold & white flame tampo on sides & roof, "Custom Rod" on sides, sp3gd, Thailand, '50s Cruisers 5-pack only (1999) 2 - NA
ai2. same as ai, Malaysia 2 - NA
ai3. same as ai; gold, red & white tampo w/"Big Kids Toys" & "SEMA '99" on roof; sp3; only in baggie; SEMA Show (1999) 40 - NA
aj. mtlc red, chrome base, blue-tinted window, sp5, China, Train Set (1998) 8 - NA
ak. mtlc dk. green; chrome base, tinted window; sp5. K•B Toys exclusive Deluxe Highway set (1998) 6 - NA
al. purple enamel, chrome base, tinted window, sp5, China. Shell Gas station play set (1999) 8 - NA
am. yellow enamel, black base, blue-tinted window, sp5, China, Arco Hauler set (1999) 6 - NA
an. red enamel, chrome base, blue-tinted window, sp5, China, Target exclusive w/Arco Hauler set (1999) 8 - NA

'57 Chevy-ao

ao. white; chrome base; black int.; tinted window; black roof & trunk; black, red, blue & gold tampo w/stripes, Columbus, OH Police Dept logo, "162," "Emergency" on sides; "Columbus, Ohio Police" on logo on roof; "162" on trunk, rrch. Limited to 25,000 in Cop Rods series for K•B Toys (1999) 6 - 8
ap. red, same as ai, lwgd, #1077 (2000) 2 - 3

9638-aq

aq. turquoise with mtlfk silver base, gold & white tampo design on sides & roof, ho5, Malaysia, #105 (2000) 2 - 3
aq2.same as aq, unpainted base 2 - 3

9638-ar

ar. turquoise w/black windows; black, orange, white & red tampo: face w/balloon caption on sides, dots on roof & trunk; #105 (2000) 6 - 8

9638-as

as. mtlfk red-orange w/black, purple & white tampo design on sides & hood; sp5; Malaysia; #228 (2000) 4 - 6
at. purple w/white int., blue-tinted windows, dk. blue & lt. violet tampo on sides & hood, rrch, Thailand, Target Exclusive Editor's Choice series (2000) 6 - 8
au. pink, exposed engine, blue-tinted windows. sp5, K mart Long Haulers 2-pack only (2000) 4 - 6
av. yellow, exposed engine; black int.; tinted windows; black & orange flame tampo on sides, roof & trunk; dw3; Target Exclusive Drive-In Hot Nights 4-car set (2000) 6 - NA
aw. black w/engine sticking thru hood, tinted windows, black int., white & gold tampo w/"Kostyas Taxi Service Fleet" on sides & roof, " No. 3" on sides, sp3, Malaysia, #1 in Turbo Taxi Series, #053 (2001) 2 - 3

9638-ax

PHOENIX FIRE DEPT.

ax. red; exposed engine; clear windows; white int.; white on sides, hood, roof & trunk; dk. red, gold & black tampo w/flames, "No. 8," "Arizona F.D." & Phoenix Fire Dept. emblem on sides, "Phoenix Fire Dept." on roof & trunk, "No. 8" on trunk, "Arizona F.D." in back; rrch; Fire Rods series (2001) 6 - 8

9638-ay

ay. black w/black int., red-tinted windows, black & white tampo w/"Bel Air" on sides, yellow & orange spray mask in front, red & white JC Whitney logo on trunk, gych. JC Whitney boxed limited edition (2001) 15 - 20
az. red, black int., tinted windows, black & white tampo w/"Bel Air" on sides, blue & white JC Whitney logo on trunk, gych. JC Whitney boxed limited edition (2001) 15 - 20
ba. yellow, exposed engine; chrome int.; clear windows; black, purple & red tampo on sides; sp5; China; Kool Toyz Power Launcher pack (2001) 4 - 6
bb. yellow, exposed engine, chrome int., clear windows, black & red flame tampo w/"57" on sides, sp5, China, Power Launcher pack (2001) 4 - 6
bc. yellow, exposed engine, black int., tinted windows, black & red flame tampo, sp5, China, Pavement Pounder pack (2001) 4 - 6

Values are shown in U.S. dollars, first price is for mint, second is for mint packaged vehicles only. See pages 15-16 for grading guide to determine value for cars in lesser conditions.

bd. mtlfk blue, black int., blue-tinted windows, white & gold tampo w/flames & "Custom Rod" on sides, sp5gd, China, Stop 'n Go Hot Rod Magazine set. (2001) 4 - 6

be. mtlfk red-brown, tinted windows, black int., yellow & black tampo on sides, sp5, China, Pavement Pounder pack (2001) 4 - 6

bf. mtlfk yellow, exposed engine, black & gray tampo on sides, sp5, China, K•B Downtown Roadway Set (2001) 6 - NA

bg. black, red roof, black int, tinted windows, red, yellow and white tampo, "25", "UAW-Delphi" and race decals on sides, "UAW-Delphi" on hood, "25" on roof. "UAW-Delphi" and race decals on trunk, "UAW-Delphi" in back and rrgych. Thailand. #2 in NASCAR '57 Chevy series (2002) 5 - 7

bh. yellow, gray int, blue tinted windows, blue, red and white tampo, "55", "Square D" and race decals on sides, "D" in square on hood, "55" on roof. "Square D" on trunk and in back and rrgych. Thailand. #3 in NASCAR '57 Chevy.series (2002) 5 - 7

'57 Chevy-bi

bi. green, white roof and int, clear windows, white, yellow and light green flame tampo on sides and hood and rrch. Wal-Mart excl. Cruisin' America series. (2002) 5 - 7

9640-a2

Fire-Eater™ 9640 - 75mm - 1977
Based on an American La France fire pumper truck, this model has a chrome plastic chassis, clear blue plastic interior, blue plastic hoses, tools, light on top, etc., blue-tinted plastic windows, rsw, and was made in Hong Kong.

a. red; yellow & white fire engine tampo on sides $18 - 45
a2. same as a, bw 6 - 10
a3. same as a, bw, Malaysia, #82 (1982) 5 - 8
a4. same as a2, France (1984) 10 - 12
a5. 4000, same as a3, Malaysia (1988) 5 - 8
a6. same as a3, sp7, #82 (1997) 5 - NA
a7. same as a3, sp5, #82 (1997) 2 - 4
a8. same as a6, sp7, gray plastic base 2 - 4

4001-b

b. 4001; yellow; red hoses, tools, light on top, etc.; red & black fire engine tampo on sides; bw; Malaysia (1988) 10 - 12

13309-c

c. 13309, chrome, same as f, tampo colors are black & yellow, #1 in Silver Series, #322 (1995) 3 - 6
c2. same as c, sp7, #322 (1995) 5 - 10

9640-d

d. fluor. lime; red & black fire engine tampo; red plastic lights, hoses, etc; black Hot Wheels logo in back; sp5. In Then & Now 8-Pack (1995) 6 - NA
e. 15276; red; yellow & black tampo: "Fire Dept." on hood; City of Hot Wheels logo on sides; blue-tinted int. & windows; sp5; #4 in Fire Squad series; #427 (1996) 2 - 4
e2. same as e, sp7, #427 (1996) 2 - 6
f. lime yellow, tinted windshield, red int. & hoses, black & red tampo design, emblem on sides, sp5, #82 (1997) 2 - 4
f2. same as f, dw3, #82 (1998) 2 - 4
g. dk. mtlc red, clear window, black int., red light, yellow & black tampo on sides, sp5. Fire 'n Rescue Action Pack only (1999) 8 - NA

9640-h

h. red, clear window, yellow int. & light, black & white tampo: "Metro 122" on sides, sp5. City Center 5-pack (1999) 2 - NA
i. white, black int., red-tinted windows, red lights & hoses, red & black fire engine tampo w/"Metro 122" on sides, sp3, Virtual Collection, Malaysia, #145 (2000) 2 - 3
j. fluor. lime yellow, black int., clear windows, red lights & hoses, red & black fire engine tampo w/"Metro 122" on sides, ho5, Malaysia, #237 (2001) 2 - 3
j2. as j, sp5, Thailand, #237 (2002) 4 - 6
k. mtlfk silver; clear int.; yellow-tinted windows; yellow hoses & lights; black, red & white tampo w/"Fire Eater No. 5" & fire engine deco on sides; sp5; Thailand. Heat Fleet 5-pack (2002) 2 - NA

9645-a

GMC Motor Home 9645 - 77mm - 1977
This model has a metal chassis, white plastic int., blue-tinted plastic windows, rsw, and was made in Hong Kong.
Note: The rsw model has never been found in blisterpack.
Similar castings: 2851 Captain America Van (1979), Airport Transportation (1983, France)

a. orange; blue & white striping tampo on sides: "Palm Beach," blue palm tree & yellow sun; rsw $500 - NA
a2. same as a, bw 20 - 25
a3. same as a, chrome plastic chassis, bw (1979) 18 - 20

GMC Motor Home-b

b. no #, gold chrome, same as a2, never in bp, Mattel promo (1978) 1200 - NA
c. green, same as a3, black replaces blue in tampo, chrome plastic chassis, bw (1980) 25 - 30
c2. dk. green, same as c, Mexico (1983) 40 - 50

9645-c

GMC Motorhome-d

d. mtlfk blue; gray plastic chassis; clear window; white int.; yellow, red & white tampo: Hot Wheels logo & "Team Racing" on sides, India, #524 (1998) 12 - 15
e. red, same as a, black plastic chassis, clear windows, ho5 (1999) 12 - 15
f. red & black; red chassis; white int.; tinted windows; yellow, white, black & red tampo with "97," "Drive Thru," McDonald's logo & race decals on sides, "97" on roof; bw w/white Goodyear tampo; Thailand; #1 in NASCAR RV series (2001) 6 - 8
g. blue; same as f; blue chassis; multicolored tampo w/"Jasper Engines," "77" & race decals on sides & roof; Thailand; #2 in NASCAR RV series (2001) 6 - 8
h. blue, blue chassis, white int., tinted windows, multicolored tampo w/"44" & race decals on sides & roof, bw with white Goodyear tampo, Thailand. #3 in NASCAR RV Series (2001) 8 - 10

9645-i

i. dk. green; same as f; lt. green chassis; lt. green, black & white tampo with "Conseco," "14" & race decals on sides & roof; Thailand; #4 in NASCAR RV series (2001) 6 - 8

9643-a2

Letter Getter 9643 - 70mm - 1977
This Hong Kong-made mail truck has a metal chassis, black plastic interior, opening back doors, blue-tinted plastic windows and rsw.
Similar castings: 2854 S.W.A.T. Van (1979), 2850 The Incredible Hulk (1979), 3303 Racing Team (1981), 9643 Delivery Van (1984), 2519 Combat Medic (1986), 2808 Delivery Truck (1989), 9114 The Simpson's Homer's Nuclear Waste Van (1990)

a. white ; blue & red striping tampo: "U.S. Mail" & postal emblem on sides; never in bp $500 - NA
a2. same as a, bw 12 - 15
a3. same as a, black plastic base, bw (1979) 7 - 10
a4. same as a3, Malaysia (1979) 5 - 8

9642-a

Odd Rod™ 9642 - 80mm - 1977
This Hong Kong-made rear-engine dragster has a plastic body, metal chassis, unpainted metal interior, exposed metal engine in back, clear plastic windshield & nose, and rsw.

a. yellow; flame tampo on nose $75 - 100
a2. same as a, bw 25 - 30
a3. same as a, dk. red tampo, bw (1984), Mexico 30 - 35
a4. same as a3, "Made in France" on base (1984) 45 - 55
b. plum, same as a 450 - 750

9642-b2

b2. same as b, bw 450 - 750

9644-a

Second Wind® 9644 - 70mm - 1977
Based on a sports roadster, this concept model has a black plastic chassis, black plastic interior, blue-tinted plastic windshield, rsw, and was made in Hong Kong.

a. white; red, yellow & purple stripe tampo on top, "5" on hood $75 - 100
a2. same as a, bw 30 - 40
a3. same as a, bw, France (1983) 30 - 50
a4. white, same as a2, black replaces blue in tampo, bw (1984) Mexico 50 - 75

9644-b

b. orange; same as a2; white, dk. red & dk. blue tampo, "5" on top; bw; Speed Machines (1983) 15 - 20
c. white, bw (1986) Mexico 65 - 90

9644-d

d. blue; red & white tampo on sides; white oval w/red Hot Wheels logo in back; blue-tinted windshield; black int.; bw; "India" on black plastic base. FAO Schwarz History of Hot Wheels 8-pack (1995) 10 - NA

Second Wind-e

e. 16810, white, blue plastic base, black int., blue-tinted windshield, bw, #527 (1997) 3 - 5

9646-a

Show Hoss II 9646 - 71mm - 1977
Based on a Mustang II funny-car dragster, this model has a metal chassis, black plastic interior, lift-up body to show an unpainted metal engine, and rsw. Hong Kong.

a. yellow; dk. red, white & black tampo on top; "Show Hoss II," horse & racing decals on hood $400 - 550
a2. same as a, bw 55 - 75
a3. same as a2, tan int. (1983) France 110 - 135
b. green; blue, white & black tampo with "Mustang II," horse's head & racing decals on sides; bw (1979) 40 - 50

9646-b

c. yellow, tan int., bw (1983), France 100 - 125
d. dk. blue, bw (1984), Mexico 60 - 75

9646-e

e. lt. blue, same as b, blue & white tampo, Speed Machines (1983) 80 - 90
f. dk. blue, black int., bw, Malaysia (Italy) (1983) 200 - 225

9641-a2

Spoiler Sport 9641 - 76mm - 1977
This Hong Kong-made customized van with a large rear spoiler has a metal chassis, clear blue plastic interior, blue-tinted plastic windows, two small windows in back, and rsw.
Similar castings: 2878 The Incredible Hulk (1979), 9536 Street Scorcher (1985)
a. green; black, yellow & dk. red tampo with "Spoiler Sport" & sunset design on sides $25 - 40
a2. same as a, bw 12 - 18
a3. same as a2, one large back window, bw (1980) 8 - 12
a4. same as a3 (1983), France 12 - 20
b. no #, gold chrome, same as a, orange replaces yellow in tampo, bw, Golden Machines 6-pack only (1979) 25 - NA
b2. same as b, one large back window, Golden Machines 6-pack only (1979) 25 - NA

9641-c

c. white; one large back window; blue, yellow & magenta flame design on sides; bw (1982) 8 - 10
c2. same as c, Malaysia (1982) 8 - 10

9641-d

d. pink, same as c, bright red in tampo, (1983) Mexico 300 - 400
e. lt. blue; black plastic chassis; yellow, lt. green & dk. blue flame tampo on sides; clear plastic window; black plastic int.; Speed Machines (1983) 18 - 25
e2. same as e, blue base, Speed Machines (1983) 25 - 35

9648-a

T-Totaller 9648 - 58mm - 1977
Based on a customized Model T panel truck, this Hong Kong-made model has a metal body, golden chrome plastic chassis, unpainted metal pipes, black plastic interior, and rsw.
Note: Never found in blisterpack with rsw.
a. black; orange tampo with "No. 3," "Your Basic Trucking Company" & "Est. 1901" in white & "Express" in blue on sides $550 - NA
a2. same as a, bw 15 - 20

9648-b

b. brown, same as a, bw (1979) 12 - 15
b2. dk. brown, same as b, yellow & red tampo, gw (1984), Mexico 60 - 75
b3. same as b2, bw (1985) Mexico 60 - 75
c. red, same as a, yellow replaces orange in tampo, bw (1980) 8 - 10
d. magenta; same as b; yellow plastic chassis; yellow, white & blue tampo; pinkish tan int. & rear doors; gray plastic pipes; bw; Speed Machines (1983) 12 - 15

9793-b

Thrill Drivers Torino 9793 - 75mm - 1977
This Ford Torino stunt car has a chrome plastic chassis, black plastic interior & hood scoop, blue-tinted plastic windows, bw, was made in Hong Kong and was issued only in the Thrill Drivers Corkscrew set.
Similar castings: 7647 Torino Stocker (1975), 9533 Torino Tornado (1985)
a. white; blue & red stripes w/"Thrill Drivers" in yellow on sides $120 - NA
a2. 7191; white; orange not red in tampo; found in bp (1983) Mexico 125 - 225
b. red, same as a, white not red in tampo 150 - NA
b2. 7192; red; orange not red in tampo; found in bp (1983); Mexico 140 - 250

9639-b

Z Whiz 9639 - 70mm - 1977
This Datsun Z car features a metal chassis, clear blue plastic interior, blue-tinted plastic windows, louvered window in back, rsw, and was made in Hong Kong.
a. gray; orange, yellow & blue stripe tampo on top, "Datsun Z" on hood $40 - 60
a2. same as a, bw 12 - 15
b. white, same as a 1900 - NA
c. gold chrome, same as a, white not yellow in tampo, bw, Golden Machines 6-pack only (1979) 25 - NA
d. green; same as a; dk. green, lt. green & white tampo; bw (1980) 8 - 10
d2. same as d, Malaysia 12 - 15

9639-e

e. blue; dk. red, orange & yellow tampo w/"15" & racing decals on sides; bw (1982) 35 - 60

9639-f

f. black, white tampo similar to original design, bw (1983) France 85 - 120
g. lt. green; same as a; gray plastic chassis; yellow, orange & blue tampo; black-tinted plastic windshield; black plastic int.; Speed Machines (1983) 10 - 12
g2. same as g, red not orange in tampo, (1983) 25 - 35
h. mtlfk dk. red, black chassis, blue-tinted windows & int., bw, Malaysia (Italy) (1983) 175 - 225
i. mtlfk green, Malaysia (Italy) (1983) 175 - 225
j. dk. green; same as c; dk. red, yellow & black tampo; bw (1984), Mexico 60 - 85
k. dk. green, same as c, large bw rear wheels (1984), Mexico 60 - 85

1978

Twelve new models were introduced and ten sported new colors or tampos. This was the first year all models were issued with basic black-wall tires (bw). A new blistercard featured seven different cloth patches with seven groups of vehicles: Super Streeters, Drag Strippers, Oldies But Goodies, Rescue Team, Classy Customs, Speedway Specials, and Heavies. The patches were only available by mail and are worth about ten dollars each.

2013-a

'57 T-Bird 2013 - 70mm - 1978
This 1957 Ford Thunderbird has a metal chassis, blue-tinted plastic windows, porthole behind the side window, clear blue plastic interior, bw, and was made in Hong Kong.
a. white; red & blue stripe tampo on top; black emblem w/ "Thunderbird" on hood $30 - 40
a2. white, same as a, blue stripe on roof much darker, limited for 30th Anniv. w/card in window box (1998) 4 - 6
b. yellow, same as a 15 - 18

2013-b2

b2. same as a, no porthole, Malaysia 10 - 15
c. metallic red, no tampo (1982) 90 - 120
c2. same as c, no porthole (1982) 4 - 6
c3. same as c2, Malaysia (1982) 4 - 6
c4. 4357, same as c2, gyg (1982) 25 - 30
c5. same as c4, gyw (1982) 40 - 50

9522-d

d. 9522, red, no porthole, blue & yellow stripe tampo on top, "T-Bird" in yellow & magenta on hood, black int., Malaysia (1985) 10 - 12
e. 2536; black; same as d; red, magenta & blue tampo; Hong Kong (1986) 10 - 12
e2. same as e, gyg, made in Malaysia (1986) 30 - 35

3992-f

e3. same as e, gyw (1986) 85 - 175
f. 3992, turquoise, no porthole, red & magenta stripe top tampo, clear plastic int., Hong Kong (1988) 10 - 12

3993-g

g. 3993, white, no porthole, red & blue stripe top tampo, Hong Kong (1988) 10 - 12

2072-h

h. 2072; turquoise; as d; purple, yellow & dk. blue tampo; ww; Park 'n Plates (1990) 10 - 12
h2. same as h, bw (1990) 40 - 50
h3. same as h, orange replaces purple in tampo, (1991) 20 - 25

1677;1610-i

i. 1677; 1610; red; no porthole; gray plastic chassis; green, blue & pink stripe tampo on sides; red-tinted window; red int.; McDonald's give-away in U.S. & sold in bp in Intl. line (1991) 6 - 8
j. turquoise; same as i; yellow, magenta & white stripes; blue-tinted plastic windows & int.; McDonald's give-away in U.S. & sold in bp in Intl. line (1991) 6 - 8
k. gold chrome, no tampo, bw, issued in different shades of gold, Gleam Team, #190 (1992) 4 - 10

'57 T-Bird-l

l. no #, vacuum metal silver; black 25th Anniv. logo on roof, red-tinted window, chrome plastic base, bw. Service Merchandise 16-pack only (1994) 15 - NA

'57 T-Bird-m

m. no #, turquoise; orange, white & dk. blue Gulf logo on hood; lightly-tinted window; black int.; bw. Gulf Service Stations only. Baggies only, never on blistercard (1994) 4 - 6

2013-n

n. black; white Hot Wheels logo in back, yellow-tinted window & int., pcgd. In 16-piece FAO Schwarz Gold Series Collection, limited to 3000 (1994) 15 - NA
o. no #, yellow, clear window & int., yellow Hot Wheels logo on rear window, bw. Ford 5-pack only (1995) 3 - NA

Values are shown in U.S. dollars, first price is for mint, second is for mint packaged vehicles only. See pages 15-16 for grading guide to determine value for cars in lesser conditions.

o2. same as o, sp7. (1995) 3 - NA

o3. same as o, sp3 (1996) 2 - NA

13352-p

p. 13352; mtlfk black; white Hot Wheels logo on rear window; black int.; clear window; rr w/white stripe & gray hubs; #4 of Treasure Hunt series #356 (1995) 45 - 75

q. chrome; blue-tinted int. & window; red Hot Wheels logo on back window; rsw. Service Merchandise 16-piece Classic American Car Collection only, limited to 5000 (1995) 12 - NA

r. mtlfk silver, slightly tinted window, black int., red Hot Wheels logo in back, sp7. Then & Now 8-pack (1995) 8 - NA

15223-s

s. 15223; pearl white; orange & lt. green flames on sides & top; clear plastic int. & window; sp7; #1 of Flamethrower series; #384 (1996) 4 - 8

s2. same as s, pink replaces orange in flames, #384 4 - 8

s3. same as s, shorter flames, #384 Hot Wheels logo on sides (1996) 4 - 10

s4. same as s, sp3 (1997) 2 - NA

s5. same as s4, China, Long Hauler or train set (1998) 2 - NA

t. mtlfk green, plastic base, green-tinted window & int., sp7, '50s Favorites 5-pack only (1996) 3 - NA

t2. same as t, sp5 (1996) 3 - NA

t3. same as t, dw3 (1997) 2 - NA

t4. same as t, sp3 (1997) 2 - NA

t5. same as t4, gray base (1997) 2 - NA

2013-u

u. red, chrome plastic base, mtlfk silver top, clear window, clear plastic int., rrch white stripe around tire, Bloomingdales' Fabulous 57s 2-pack (1996) 125 - NA

'57 T-Bird-v

v. no #, mtlfk dk. red, white top, gray int., clear window, rrch white stripe, 40th Anniv. of 2-Seat Thunderbird 2-pack only (1997) 10 - NA

'57 T-Bird-w

w. mtlc blue, blue-tinted windows, blue int., white & black design on sides & hood, sp3, #1 in Tattoo Machines series, #685 (1998) 2 - 3

x. turquoise; white roof; white int.; clear window; gray tampo on sides & hood; ww; China. FAO Schwarz Cruisin' the '50s pack only (1998) 6 - NA

2013-y

y. black; clear int.; orange-tinted window; yellow, orange & white tampo design on sides & hood; lwgd; Thailand; '50s Cruisers 5-pack only (1999) 2 - NA

y2. same as y, lwch, Malaysia (1999) 2 - NA

z. mtlfk purple; clear int.; blue-tinted windows; white, yellow & orange tampo on sides & hood; lwch; #217 (2000) 2 - 3

15223-aa

aa. mtlfk green, clear int., yellow-tinted windows, black & gray tampo w/2000 Treasure Hunt logo on sides & hood, rrch, #8 in 2000 Treasure Hunt series, #056 (2000) 15 - 20

15223-ab

ab. yellow; small round back window; clear int.; orange-tinted windows; orange, black, gray & white tampo w/"Tad's Taxi" on sides & hood; sp3; #3 in Turbo Taxi series; Malaysia; #055 (2001) 2 - 3

ab2. same as ab, no porthole, #3 in Turbo Taxi Series, Malaysia, #055 (2001) 25 - 30

ac. blue, gray int., clear windows, yellow flame tampo on sides, sp3, China, Kool Toyz Super Race Rigs pack, (2001) 5 - 7

ad. mtlfk purple, same as ac, sp3, China, Kool Toyz Power Launcher pack (2001) 5 - 7

ae. red, clear windows & int., green & white tampo w/"9" on sides, sp3, China, Pavement Pounder pack (2001) 5 - 7

ae2. same as ae, olive not green in tampo, Pavement Pounder pack (2001) 5 - 7

af. red, clear windows & int., gold tampo on sides & hood, sp3, China, Power Launcher pack (2001) 5 - 7

ag. orange; tinted windows; black int.; black, gray & gold tampo w/"TH" on sides; sp3; China; Pavement Pounder pack (2001) 15 - 18

ah. white, plastic chassis, clear int. & windows, orange & red tampo design on sides, sp3, China, Pavement Pounder pack (2001) 5 - 7

ai. maroon, plastic chassis, clear int. & windows, silver & black tampo on sides, sp3, Rock & Roll Cafe set (2001) 6 - NA

15223-aj

aj. yellow, black int., blue-tinted windows, multicolored tampo w/"10" & "Nestle Nesquik" on sides & top, rrch w/white stripe, #4 in NASCAR '57 T-Bird Series (2002) 6 - 8

ak. reddish pink, black int., clear windows, olive & gold tampo on sides & hood, sp3, K mart Deluxe Downtown six-car set (2001) 6 - NA

ak2. same as am, clear int. (2001) 6 - NA

al. blue; white roof; white int.; clear windows; white, gold & dk. blue tampo w/"Automobile Milestones 2002" on trunk; rrch w/white stripe. Auto Milestones series (2002) 6 - 8

am. mtlfk dk. blue; blue-tinted windows & int.; red, white, black & gray tampo w/Hot Wheels logo, "Racing" & race decals on sides; "Hot Wheels Racing," "7" & race decals on black roof; sp5; Malaysia; #165 (2002) 2 - 4

an. black, white hood, white int, blue tinted windows, white, red and blue tampo, "12", "Alltel" and race decals on sides, "Alltel" and "Mobil II" on hood, "12" on roof. "Print by Sony" on trunk, "Alltel" in back and rrchws. Thailand. #4 in NASCAR '57 T-Bird Series. (2002) 2 - 4

2016-a

A-OK 2016 - 66mm - 1978

This Ford Model A 2-door sedan has a metal chassis, clear plastic windshield, chrome plastic engine, olive green interior & fenders, bw, and was made in Hong Kong.

a. green; olive, black & yellow tampo "Early Times Delivery" on sides $15 - 20

b. dk. mtlc red, same as a, dk. red int. & fenders, red replaces olive in tampo (1981) 10 - 12

b2. same as b, dk. maroon int. & fenders, Malaysia (1981) 10 - 12

4358-b3

b3. 4358, same as b2, gyg (1981) 200 - 500

2023-a

Army Funny Car 2023 - 75mm - 1978

Based on Don "The Snake" Prudhomme's funny car sponsored by the U. S. Army, this Hong Kong-made model comes with a metal chassis, lift-up body, metal interior, and bw.

Similar castings: 2881 Human Torch, 2023 Pepsi Challenger (1982), 9521 Screamin' (1985)

a. white; red, black & blue tampo "Don 'The Snake' Prudhomme," "Army," snake & racing decals on sides; "Army" & snake on hood $25 - 30

2022-a

Baja Breaker 2022 - 72mm - 1978

This 4-wheel drive Ford van has a metal chassis, blue-tinted plastic windows, two black plastic rear windows, black plastic interior & lift-up hood, metal engine, top luggage rack, and bw. Made in Hong Kong.

Similar castings: 2853 Motocross Team (1979), 3303 Circus Cats (1981), 9113 The Simpson's Family Camper (1990), 3490 Open Wide (1993 Tattoo Machines)

a. gray; red, blue & yellow tampo "Baja Breaker" on sides $12 - 18

2022-b2

b. green; same as a; yellow, blue & white tampo (1980) 8 - 10

b2. same as b, olive replaces blue in tampo (1980) 250 - 350

c. mtlfk orange; same as a; yellow, blue & white tampo (1983) 5 - 7

c2. same as c, Malaysia (1983) 5 - 7

c3. 4360, same as c2, gyg (1983) 25 - 30

d. 4360, black, orange stripe on sides, shut black plastic hood, Malaysia (1984) 4 - 6

d2. same as d, gyg (1984) 25 - 30

2022-d3

d3. same as d, gyw (1984) 55 - 70

d4. same as d, shut metal hood, ct (1989) 12 - 15

d5. black, same as d3, bw 8 - 10

1517-e

e. 1517; white, red & yellow striping w/"Racing Team," "A.T.V.," "Suzuki" & racing decals on sides; shut metal hood; Malaysia; bw (1989) 8 - 10

e2. same as e, ct, #10 (1989) 4 - 15

e3. same as e2, orange replaces yellow in tampo, ct (1989) 4 - 5

f. purple, clear window, red int., yellow polka dots on sides, bw, China (1997) 4 - 10

2019-a

Highway Patrol 2019 - 75mm - 1978

This Hong Kong-made police car has a metal chassis, blue-tinted plastic windows & dome light, black plastic interior and bw.

Similar castings: 2639 Fire Chaser (1979), 2019 Sheriff Patrol (1982), no number, Airport Security (1983)

a. white; black & yellow Highway Patrol tampo w/"12" in front of door $30 - 40

2019-a2

a2. same as a, black "12" added to roof (1979) 11 - 15

2014-a

Hot Bird® 2014 - 74mm - 1978

Based on the Pontiac Firebird, this Hong Kong-made model has a metal chassis, blue-tinted plastic windows, tan plastic interior and bw.

Similar casting: 2879 Captain America (1979)

a. black; orange & yellow stripe tampo on top; yellow Firebird emblem on hood $8 - 10

a2. same as a, gw (1982) 4 - 5

a3. same as a2, hoc #37 (1990) 15 - 18

a4. same as a2, Malaysia (1982) 4 - 5

a5. same as a, red int., gw, #37 (1990) 18 - 25

Values are shown in U.S. dollars, first price is for mint, second is for mint packaged vehicles only. See pages 15-16 for grading guide to determine value for cars in lesser conditions.

b. no #, gold chrome, same as a, blue replaces yellow in tampo, Golden Machines 6-pack only (1979) 30 - NA

2014-c

c. brown, same as a (1980) 125 - 150
d. blue, same as a (1980) 75 - 100

Hot Bird-e

e. no #; mtlfk blue; orange & gray tampo on top & sides; hot bird on hood; gray int.; gw; Double Barrel Stunt set only (1989) 10 - NA
e2. same as e, tan interior (1989) 10 - NA

2014-f

f. mtlfk blue; yellow, orange & white flame tampo on sides & top; "Firebird" on sides; firebird on hood; tan plastic int.; gw; #37 (1989) 6 - 10
f2. same as f, gray plastic interior, gw (1989) 25 - 55
f3. same as f, uh, #37 (1990) 4 - 5

2014-g

g. white; red int.; red & blue stars-&-stripes tampo on hood & sides; "All American Fire Bird" on sides; gw; #37; (1990) 6 - 10
g2. same as g, uh, #37 (1990) 10 - 15
g3. same as g, tan int., uh (1990) 20 - 35
g4. same as g, turquoise replaces blue in tampo, uh, #37 (1991) 8 - 12
g5. white, same as g4, uhgd, Intl. line, #37 (1991) 10 - 12

Hot Bird-h

h. no #; mtlfk gray; red & blue flames & yellow firebird outlined in red on hood; clear window; tan int.; Hot Wheels cereal (1990) 10 - NA

0462-i

i. 0462, black, multicolored glitter, no tampo, pink-tinted window, pink int., uh, #178 (1992) 6 - 12

15978-j

j. 15978; mtlfk gold; gray-tinted window; beige int.; red Hot Wheels logo on rear license plate; sp5; China; #469 (1996) 2 - 6
j2. same as j, black int., black Hot Bird on hood, #469 (1996) 2 - 4
j3. same as j2, lwch, #469 (1997) 2 - 4
k. yellow; black Hot Bird logo on hood; clear window; black int.; iw; 100th Anniv. of the Auto gift pack (1996) 15 - NA

Hot Bird-l

l. black; gold Hot Bird on hood; blue-tinted window; cream int.; sp5gd; China; K mart exclusive 70th Anniv. of the Pontiac set only; limited to 7000 (1996) 15 - NA

2012-a

Jaguar XJS 2012 - 78mm - 1978
This Hong Kong model has a metal chassis, blue-tinted plastic windows, black plastic interior and front & rear fenders, & bw.

a. gray; red, yellow & black tampo with "XJS" & jaguar on sides; black triangle behind rear side window $15 - 18
b. no #, same as a, gold chrome, no yellow in tampo, Golden Machines 6-pack only (1979) 30 - NA
c. blue, same as a (1980) 6 - 8
c2. same as c, Malaysia (1982) 5 - 7

2012-d

d. mtlfk brown, same as a, Malaysia (1983) 50 - 60
d2. same as d, France on base, Mexico
d3. same as a, no black triangle behind rear window, Mexico (1984) 60 - 75
d4. same as a, Mexico (1984) 70 - 85
d5. same as d, uh, Mexico (1987) 130 - 180
e. gray, no tampo, France (1983) 40 - 50
f. white, black int., blue-tinted windows, bw, Malaysia (Italy) (1983) 75 - 125

2012-g

g. mtlfk brown; yellow, green & black tampo with "10," "Bell," "Hooker," "Moon" & "Goodyear" on hood; gw; Mexico (1986) 90 - 120

2012-h

g2. same as g, bw, Mexico (1986) 90 - 120
g3. same as g, uh, Mexico (1986) 130 - 180
h. white; same tampo as f but yellow, blue & black; gw; Mexico (1986) 90 - 120
h2. same as h, bw, Mexico (1986) 90 - 120
h3. same as h2; yellow, red & black tampo; bw; Mexico (1986) 130 - 180

2017-a

Lickety Six 2017 - 68mm - 1978
Based on the Tyrrell six-wheel Grand Prix Racer, this model has a metal chassis, chrome plastic interior, engine & fuel tanks, bw, and was made in Hong Kong.

a. dk. blue; red & white tampo with "6" & racing decals in front $18 - 25
a2. dk. blue; same as a (different shade); black plastic int., engine & fuel tanks; France (1983) 70 - 85
b. gray-blue, same as a (different shade), Mexico (1983) 35 - 40

2017-c

c. white, same as a, red & blue tampo, 4-pack only, Mexico (1986) 100 - NA

2015-a

Packin' Pacer 2015 - 66mm - 1978
This American Motors Pacer has a metal chassis, yellow-tinted plastic windows, chrome plastic interior, chrome plastic engine in back, bw, and was made in Hong Kong.

a. yellow; red, magenta & blue stripe tampo on top, "Packin' Pacer" on roof $8 - 10
b. orange, same as a, darker red & lighter magenta tampo (1980) 5 - 7

2015-c

c. white; magenta, red & yellow stripe tampo & "427" twice on hood (1982) 10 - 12
d. lt. blue; gray plastic chassis; yellow-tinted plastic window; yellow plastic int.; bw; Speed Machines (1983) 8 - 10
e. lt. yellow; same as c; dk. magenta, red & orange tampo; milky yellow plastic window; Mexico (1984) 40 - 45

2021-a

Race Bait 308 2021 - 70mm - 1978
This Ferrari 308 GTB has a black metal chassis & interior, blue-tinted plastic windows, bw, and was made in Hong Kong. Similar castings: 7295 Quik Trik (1984), 9538 Street Beast (1985), 3494 Hot Wheels (1993 Tattoo Machines), 17962 Ferrari 308 GTB (1997)

a. red; black, yellow & white tampo with Ferrari emblem,"308" & "G.T.B." on hood $12 - 15
a2. same as a, black plastic base 12 - 15

Race Bait 308-b

b. no #, gold chrome, same as a, no yellow in tampo, Golden Machines 6-pack only (1979) 30 - NA
c. gray; red, yellow & black tampo w/Ferrari emblem, "308" & turbo on sides; gw (1982) 30 - 35

2021-d

d. mtlfk gray, same as c (1982) 8 - 10
d2. same as d, bw (1982) 8 - 10
d3. 4359, same as d, gyg (1982) 25 - 30

2018-a2

Science Friction 2018 - 67mm - 1978
This futuristic police car has a metal chassis, exposed chrome plastic engine, chrome plastic windows, orange plastic radar, light & guns, bw, and was made in Hong Kong. Similar castings: 7293 Flame Runner (1984), 2544 Back Burner (1986), 3510 Lightning Storm (1993, Tattoo Machines)

a. white; black, yellow & red tampo on sides, "Space Cop" on doors $10 - 12
a2. same as a, gw (1982) 6 - 8
b. magenta; red, blue and light blue striping tampo on sides; gw; Malaysia (1982) 8 - 10

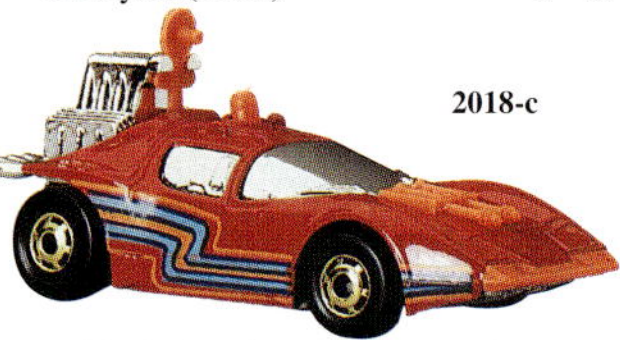
2018-c

c. mtlfk dark red, same as b (1983) 5 - 7

2020-a

Stagefright 2020 - 73mm - 1978
This Hong Kong-made concept stagecoach dragster has a metal chassis, metal engine inside the coach, black plastic roof, interior & steering wheel, black top, and bw.

a. brown; yellow and orange tampo on sides $10 - 15
a2. same as a, Malaysia (1982) 10 - 15

2020-a3

a3. dk. brown, same as a, darker color & tampo, Mexico (1983) 70 - 90

1979

There were eighteen new listings and twelve models in new colors and/or tampos. Mattel continued the seven themes introduced in 1978 and added three new series: Golden Machines, Heroes, and Scene Machines. Golden Machines was a 6-pack of gold-chrome cars from old castings; the cars were never sold in single blisterpacks. The Heroes series was based on Marvel Comics characters; each vehicle had the character's name and picture on the sides or top. Scene Machines had a photo inside which was viewed through a lens in the rear of the vehicle.

2505-a

Auburn 852 2505 - 78mm - 1979
This Hong Kong-made 1934 convertible has a metal chassis, clear plastic windshield, dark brown interior & fenders and bw.

a. red $8 - 10
a2. same as a, Hot Wheels 30th Anniv. logo in gold on front fender. Limited for 30th Anniv. w/card in window box (1998) 4 - 6
b. yellow (1981) 5 - 7
b2. same as b, brown interior & fenders (1981) 5 - 7

Values are shown in U.S. dollars, first price is for mint, second is for mint packaged vehicles only. See pages 15-16 for grading guide to determine value for cars in lesser conditions.

b3. same as b, red-brown int. & fenders (1981) 12 - 15
b4. same as b, Malaysia (1981) 5 - 7
c. mtlfk gold, black int. & fenders, Malaysia (1983) 5 - 7
c2. same as c, ww (1983) 5 - 7
d. white, white int. & fenders, ww, Malaysia (1984) 8 - 10
e. 2527, green, darker green int. & fenders, ww, Malaysia (1986) 6 - 8
f. red; red fenders & interior; ww; #94 (1991) 10 - 15
f2. same as f, bw, #94 (1992) 150 - 175
g. 4341, red; black fenders, ww, #215 (1993) 10 - 15
g2. same as g, sp5. #215 (1997) 6 - 8

2505-h

h. chrome, chrome int., red Hot Wheels logo in back, rsw. Service Merchandise 16-piece Classic American Car Collection only, limited to 5000 (1995) 12 - NA

Auburn 852-i

i. 15083; gold; black speckles in paint; gold plastic fenders & int.; clear windshield; Hot Wheels logo in white rectangle behind seat; rrgd with white stripe around wheel; #2 in Treasure Hunt Series #437 (1996) 35 - 45

Auburn 852-j

j. mtlfk red; silver on top of hood & trunk; clear windshield; red int.; rtch. American Classics 3-pack only (1996) 12 - NA

2505-k

k. mtlfk silver, black tampo on top, clear windshield, black int., lwch, #1 in International line (1997) 2 - 4
l. unpainted, black int. & fenders, clear windshield, sp5, 1998 Hot Wheels Convention, #215 (1998) 50 - 95

2505-m

m. black; gold fenders & int.; tinted windshield; gold tampo on top; lwgd; #793 (1999) 2 - 4

2505-n

n. black, gray on top, white int. & fenders, pink & black tampo on top, lwch, #4 in Pinstripe Power series, #956 (1999) 2 - 3
o. white, white fenders, tan int., mtlfk gold on top, rrchww, FAO Schwarz Classic Collection (1999) 8 - NA
p. white, dark red on sides & top, black fenders & int., clear windshield, silver & black pinstripes on top, lwch, Malaysia, #116 (2001) 2 - 3
q. mtlfk red; red fenders; tan int.; clear windshield; white, gold & black tampo w/"Automobile Milestones 2002" on trunk; rrwwch. '33 1935 Auburn Boat Tail Speedster in Auto Milestones series (2002) 6 - 8

2511-a

Bubble Gunner 2511 - 78mm - 1979
This Hong Kong-made concept car has a metal chassis, exposed chrome plastic engine, yellow-tinted plastic dome, chrome plastic interior, and bw.
a. magenta; orange, yellow & white striping tampo; stars on top $10 - 12
b. lt. green, same as a, blue replaces orange in tampo (1980) 10 - 12
b2. same as b, Malaysia (1980) 10 - 12

2511-c

c. yellow; black plastic chassis; white, dk. red & orange tampo on top; clear plastic bubble red plastic int.; bw; Speed Machines (1983) 10 - 20
c2. same as c, maroon plastic chassis (1983) 50 - 60

2509-a

Bywayman 2509 - 71mm - 1979
This Hong Kong-made Chevrolet pickup has a metal chassis, gray-tinted plastic windshield & skylight, black plastic interior & truck bed, and bw. Some earlier models were issued with or without tool boxes cast in the truck bed. The values of these variations do not differ.
Similar castings: 1129 Super Scraper (1980), 5113 Power Plower (1986)
a. lt. blue; yellow, black & white tampo: "Eagle," eagle & stars on sides $20 - 25

1337-b

b. 1337; white; purple, orange & black tampo w/Toys "R" Us giraffe & "Geoffrey" on sides 85 - 100
c. lt. green, same as a (1980) 12 - 18
c2. same as c, Malaysia (1982) 8 - 12
d. metalflake blue, same as a, Malaysia (1983) 5 - 7
d2. 4361, same as d, gyg (1983) 25 - 30
d3. same as d, gyw (1984) 30 - 40
d4. same as d, ct (1989) 15 - 20
d5. same as d, red int. & truck bed, #77 (1992) 100 - 125
e. 9349, yellow, same as a, black & red tampo, gyw, Malaysia, Stamper 3-pack only (1985) 40 - NA
f. maroon, same as a, ct, Malaysia, #77 (1989) 30 - 45
f2. same as f, ctw, #77 (1989) 100 - 175
g. black, same as c, blue replaces black in tampo, red int. & truck bed, ct, #77 (1990) 14 - 18
g2. same as g, turquoise replaces blue in tampo, #77 (1991) 4 - 6

9230-h

h. 9230; white; orange, green & blue stripes on sides; red plastic int. & truck bed; blue-tinted windows; Park 'n Plates (1991) 25 - 30
h2. same as h, blue interior & truck bed, (1991) 35 - 40
h3. same as h2, ctw, (1991) 85 - 100

Bywayman-i

i. no #; yellow; magenta, red & white tampo: "Getty" on sides; black int. & truck bed; ct; never in bp (1992) 6 - NA

2509-j

j. white; orange & pink tampo on sides & hood, blue int., clear windows, ct, #220 (1993) 3 - 6
j2. same as j, black int. & truck bed, #220 (1995) 3 - 6
j3. same as j, dw3ct (1997) 2 - 6

Bywayman-k

k. no #; black; same as a; yellow int., truck bed & Shell logo; red & white on hood. Shell dealers in Ohio & Massachusetts only, baggie only (1994) 4 - 6

2509-l

l. white; black int. & truck bed; red tampo w/blue "Dinty Moore" on sides. Hormel, baggie only, (1995) 4 - 6

Bywayman-m

m. no #, black, same as h, red "Truck Guard" on sides. Shell Service Stations only (1995) 4 - 6
n. 13323; gray chrome; red & white tampo: "1," "Chevrolet," Hot Wheels logo & racing decals on side; "Chevrolet," "Goodyear" twice & Chevy logo on hood; yellow "Hot Wheels" on windshield; tinted windows; red int. & bed; black metal base; ct; #1 in Racing Metals series; #336 (1995) 5 - 10

13323-n

n2. same as n, about half race decals deleted, mtlc black base 5 - 10

2509-o

o. mtlfk blue; white on sides, int. & truck bed; red & yellow Hot Wheels logo, "1," racing decals & "Arun" on sides; Hot Wheels logo, "Goodyear" & Chevy logo on hood; clear windows; ct; #4 in Race Team Series II; #395 (1996) 3 - 8
o2. same as o, dw3ct #395 (1997) 6 - 12

Bywayman-p

p. no #, white, gold int. & bed, gold chrome grill, blue-tinted windshield, red & dk. blue stars & stripes, pcgd. American Spirit 4-pack only (1997) 8 - NA

2509-q

q. red; white int. & truck bed; tinted windows; gray, black, gold & white tampo: "Hi Bank racing," "Pit Crew" & "Crew Chief" on sides; dw3ct; Thailand; #876 (1999) 2 - 3

2509-r

r. lt. brown; black int. & truck bed; clear windows; black, white, silver & orange tampo w/"99," "Alba"& race decals on sides; dw3ct; Thailand; Baja Blazers 5-pack (1999) 2 - NA

2509-s

s. black, mtlfk gray chassis, tinted windows, gray int. & truck bed, orange & white tampo w/"Tony & Noah Construction Contractors" & "We Knock it Down & Rebuild it" on sides, dw3ct, Malaysia, #187 (2001) 2 - 3

Values are shown in U.S. dollars, first price is for mint, second is for mint packaged vehicles only. See pages 15-16 for grading guide to determine value for cars in lesser conditions.

2879-a

Captain America 2879 - 74mm - 1979 (Heroes)
Based on the Pontiac Firebird and Marvel Comics superhero, this model has a metal chassis, blue-tinted plastic windows, red plastic interior, and bw. Made in Hong Kong.
Similar casting: 2014 Hot Bird (1978)
a. white; red & blue tampo w/"Captain America" on doors, stars-&-stripes design on top $20 - 25
a2. same as a, orange plastic int. 18 - 20
a3. same as a, gw 18 - 20

2851-a

Captain America Van 2851 - 77mm - 1979 (Scene Machines)
This Hong Kong-made motor home has a red plastic base, clear windows, light blue interior, and bw.
Similar castings: 9645 GMC Motor Home (1977), Airport Transportation (1983 France)
a. white; red, blue & black tampo with "Captain America" & Captain America on sides $85 - 100

2507-a

Dumpin' A 2507 - 70mm - 1979
This Hong Kong-made Model A Ford dump truck has a metal chassis, exposed chrome plastic engine, brown plastic interior & fenders, movable red dumper and bw.
a. yellow; olive, light green & dark red tampo with "A Truck'n" & "Dump" on sides $8 - 10
b. orange; same as a; yellow dumper; dark red, dark orange & yellow tampo (1980) 8 - 10
b2. same as b, plum int. & fenders, Malaysia, (1980) 25 - 35
b3. same as b; lt. brown interior & fenders; yellow, purple & red tampo (1984), Mexico 35 - 45

2507-c

c. gray; same as a; blue dumper, fenders & int.; no tampo; gray plastic exposed engine; Speed Machines (1983) 15 - 18
c2. same as c, chrome engine (1983) 50 - 60
c3. same as c, "Hot Wheels" on base (1983) 30 - 35

2639-a

Fire Chaser 2639 - 75mm - 1979
This Hong Kong-made fire chief's car has a metal chassis, blue-tinted plastic windows & light on top, black plastic interior and bw.
Similar castings: 2019 Highway Patrol (1978), 2019 Sheriff Patrol (1982), no number, Airport Security (1983)
a. red; yellow, black & white tampo w/"Fire Chief" & "5" on sides $8 - 10
a2. same as a, Malaysia (1982) 5 - 7
b. no #; red; yellow & black tampo w/"Fire Chief" & "1" on sides; black int.; only in 5-pack (1989) 6 - NA

Fire Chaser-b2

b2. same as b, tan int., only in 5-pack (1989) 30 - NA

2506-a

Flat Out 442 2506 - 77mm - 1979
This Hong Kong-made Oldsmobile 442 race car has a metal chassis, black plastic hood scoop, gray-tinted plastic windows, louvered black window in back, metal interior, and bw.
a. orange; blue, maroon & white tampo w/"442," racing decals & blue pentagon on sides $10 - 12
a2. same as a, no pentagon 8 - 10
b. yellow, same as a, orange replaces white in tampo (1980) 10 - 12
b2. same as b, no pentagon (1982) 6 - 8
b3. same as b2, gw (1982) 5 - 7
c. mtlfk gold, same as b3 (1983) 4 - 6
c2. same as c, Malaysia (1983) 4 - 6

2506-d

d. lt. green; same as c2; dk. green, yellow & white tampo (1984); bp found only in Canada 110 - 165

2502-a

Greased Gremlin 2502 - 73mm - 1979
This Hong Kong-made American Motors Gremlin has a yellow metal chassis & interior, large rear spoiler, black plastic roll cage, & bw.
a. red; blue, yellow & white tampo w/"5" & racing decals on sides $25 - 30
a2. same as a, Malaysia (1982) 20 - 25
a3. same as a, yellow & white in tampo reversed, gyw (1987), Mexico 800 - 1000

2504-a

Hare Splitter 2504 - 70mm - 1979
This Monte Carlo rally car has a metal chassis, red plastic tire rack with wheel on roof, dark gray plastic windows, black plastic interior & lift-up hood, white metal engine, bw, and was made in Hong Kong.
a. white; red, black & plum tampo w/"3," "Monte Carlo Rally" & racing decals on sides $10 - 12
a2. same as a, orange tire rack, Malaysia (1982) 8 - 10
a3. same as a, darker tampo, "France" on base (1984), Mexico 25 - 30
a4. same as a2, no roof rack (1984) 30 - 35
b. yellow, same as a2 (1982) 8 - 10

2504-c

c. lt. blue, gray plastic chassis, no tampo or tire rack, Speed Machines (1983) 12 - 15
d. white, black chassis, red hood & int., blue-tinted windows, bw, Malaysia (Italy) (1983) 100 - 125

2881-a

Human Torch 2881 - 75mm - 1979 (Heroes)
Based on the Firebird Funny Car and Marvel Comics superhero, this model has a metal chassis, lift-up body to show a metal engine & interior, and bw. Hong Kong.
Similar castings: 2023 Army Funny Car (1978), 2023 Pepsi Challenger (1982), 9521 Screamin' (1985)
a. black; red & yellow tampo, "The Human Torch" on sides, Human Torch & flames on top $25 - 30

2878-a

Incredible Hulk, The 2878 - 76mm - 1979 (Heroes)
Based on a customized van and the Marvel Comics superhero, this model has a metal chassis, large rear spoiler, blue-tinted plastic windows, clear blue plastic interior, two small rear windows, and bw. Hong Kong.
Similar casting: 9641 Spoiler Sport (1978)
a. yellow; green, black & white tampo w/"The Incredible Hulk" & Incredible Hulk on sides $25 - 35
a2. same as a, one large rear window (1980) 18 - 20

2850-a

Incredible Hulk, The 2850 - 70mm - 1979 (Scene Machines)
This Hong Kong-made model uses the same casting as Letter Getter. It has a black plastic chassis, clear windows, black interior, & bw.
Similar castings: 9643 Letter Getter (1977), 2854 S.W.A.T. (1979), 3303 Racing Team (1981), 9643 Delivery Van (1984), 2519 Combat Medic (1986), 2808 Delivery Truck (1989), 9114 The Simpson's Homer's Nuclear Waste Van (1990)
a. white; green, black & red tampo w/"The Incredible Hulk" on sides $90 - 110

2510-a

Inside Story 2510 - 73mm - 1979
This Hong Kong-made concept van has a black plastic chassis, blue-tinted plastic windows, chrome plastic interior, vent on top, and bw.
Similar casting: 2852 Spider-Man (1979 Scene Machines), 16811 Beach Blaster (1997)
a. gray; red, yellow & blue striping tampo on sides $12 - 15

2510-b

b. yellow, same as a, green replaces yellow in tampo (1980) 8 - 10
b2. same as b, dk. blue-tinted windows (1980) 6 - 8
b3. same as b2, Malaysia (1980) 5 - 7
c. red, no tampo, yellow-tinted windows, white int., bw, Malaysia, Speed Machines (1983) 12 - 15
c2. same as c, chrome plastic int., blue tinted window (1983) 25 - 30

2510-d

d. gray-tan; blue, red & yellow tampo on sides; yellow-tinted window; white int.; Mexico (1984) 100 - 120
e. black, same as d, orange-tinted windows, white int., Mexico (1987) 125 - 150

2853-a

Motocross Team 2853 - 72mm - 1979 (Scene Machines)
This four-wheel drive Ford truck has a metal chassis, gray-tinted windows, black plastic interior, vent & a porthole on the side in back, bw, and was made in Hong Kong.
Similar castings: 2022 Baja Breaker (1978), 3303 Circus Cats (1981), 9113 The Simpson's Family Camper (1990), 3490 Open Wide (1993 Tattoo Machines)
a. red; yellow, black & white tampo with Hot Wheels logo, "Motocross Team" & bike rider on sides $100 - 125

2501-a

Royal Flash 2501 - 72mm - 1979
This Lotus Esprit has a metal chassis, blue-tinted plastic windows, black plastic interior, bw, and was made in Hong Kong.
a. white; red & blue striping tampo on roof, "Lotus" & flag design on hood $7 - 9
a2. same as a, gray-tinted plastic windows 7 - 9
a3. same as a, Malaysia (1982) 6 - 8
a4. same as a, lt. blue replaces blue in tampo, brown-tinted plastic windows, white plastic int. (1983), France 20 - 25

2501-b

b. orange; purple, yellow & black tampo on top, "33" on hood & twice on roof, Malaysia (1982) 5 - 7
c. mtlfk orange, same as b (1983) 4 - 6

Values are shown in U.S. dollars, first price is for mint, second is for mint packaged vehicles only. See pages 15-16 for grading guide to determine value for cars in lesser conditions.

d. orange, same as a, black-tinted plastic window, dk. blue replaces blue in tampo (1985), Mexico 30 - 35
d2. same as d, blue-tinted plastic windows (1987), Mexico 35 - 40

2855-a

Space Van 2855 - 75mm - 1979 (Scene Machines)
This Hong Kong-made concept model has a chrome plastic chassis and interior, clear windows, white plastic top, and bw.
Similar castings: 3304 Rescue Squad (1981), 5273 Tac-Com (1982), 2855 Space Van (1984)
a. gray $120 - 130

2503-a

Spacer Racer 2503 - 75mm - 1979
This Hong Kong-made concept futuristic space vehicle has a chrome plastic chassis, yellow plastic interior, gray gun on top, chrome plastic hood, and bw.
a. red; black, yellow & white tampo: circuit board on hood; "M-8" & "Rescue" on sides $18 - 20
a2. same as a, large wheels, Mexico (1984) 40 - 45
a3. same as a, Mexico (1987) 18 - 25
b. mtlc red, same as a 7 - 9
b2. same as b, Malaysia (1982) 5 - 7

2503-c

c. yellow; black plastic chassis; black, lt. green & white tampo on top; red plastic int.; Speed Machines (1983) 15 - 18

2877-a

Spider-Man 2877 - 74mm - 1979 (Heroes)
Based on the Marvel Comics superhero, this Hong Kong-made concept model has a metal chassis & interior, red-tinted plastic dome, and bw.
a. black; red & white tampo: web & "Spider-Man" $15 - 20
a2. same as a, orange-tinted plastic dome 15 - 20
a3. same as a, yellow-orange-tinted plastic dome, redder tampo. Malaysia on base, Mexico (1984) 15 - 20

2852-a

Spider-Man 2852 - 73mm - 1979 (Scene Machines)
This concept van has a blue plastic chassis, red interior & headlights, clear windows, vent on top, & bw. Made in Hong Kong.
Similar casting: 2510 Inside Story (1979)
a. white; red, blue & black tampo w/"The Amazing Spider-Man" & Spider-Man on sides $80 - 90

2854-a

S.W.A.T. Van 2854 - 70mm - 1979 (Scene Machines)
This Hong Kong-made model has a black plastic chassis, clear windows, brown interior, and bw.
Similar castings: 9643 Letter Getter (1977), 2850 The Incredible Hulk (1979), 3303 Racing Team (1981), 9643 Delivery Van (1984), 2519 Combat Medic (1986), 2808 Delivery Truck (1989), 9114 The Simpson's Homer's Nuclear Waste Van (1990)
a. dk. blue; orange & white tampo: "S.W.A.T.," "Guard Dogs Inside" & insignia on side $80 - 90

2882-a

Thing, The 2882 - 72mm - 1979 (Heroes)
Based on the Ford Pinto wagon and Marvel Comics superhero, this Hong Kong-made model has a black plastic chassis, blue-tinted plastic windshield, chrome plastic interior, and bw.
Similar casting: 9240 Poison Pinto (1977)
a. dk. blue; orange, black & white tampo: "The Thing" & Thing on sides $20 - 25

2880-a

Thor 2880 - 70mm - 1979 (Heroes)
Based on a standard delivery van and the Marvel Comics superhero, this Hong Kong-made model has a metal chassis, dark gray-tinted plastic windshield, black plastic interior & bw.
Similar castings: 7649 Super Van (1975), 7661 Paramedic (1975), 9183 Khaki Cooler (1976)
a. yellow; red, tan & blue tampo: "The Mighty Thor" & Thor on sides $12 - 18

2500-a

Upfront 924 2500 - 70mm - 1979
This Porsche 924 has a metal chassis, dark gray-tinted plastic windows, black plastic interior, black plastic strip on the bottom of each side, bw, and was made in Hong Kong.
a. yellow; red, orange & black stripe tampo on top; "924" & Porsche emblem on hood $8 - 10
b. orange, same as a, yellow replaces orange in tampo (1980) 5 - 7
b2. same as b, Malaysia (1982) 5 - 7
b3. same as a (1983), France 10 - 15

2500-c

c. black; red & yellow stripe tampo w/"Turbo 924" on sides, Malaysia (1982) 10 - 12

4339-d

d. 4339; mtlfk gold; red, black & yellow tampo; orange plastic ski rack on rear window; Malaysia; Extras series (1983) 5 - 7
d2. same as d, gray plastic ski rack on rear window, white plastic int., white plastic strip on bottom of sides, bw, Mexico (1984) 30 - 35
d3. same as d2, gray plastic int., gray plastic strip on bottom of sides, bw, Mexico (1987) 30 - 35
d4. same as d3, ww, Mexico (1987) 75 - 100
d5. same as d3, no tampo, Mexico (1987) 65 - 75
d6. same as d4, no tampo, Mexico (1987) 65 - 75
e. white, same as a, no orange in tampo, brown-tinted windows, France (1984) 15 - 20
e2. same as e, 4 holes in rear window for ski rack, France (1984) 15 - 20
e3. same as e, black BP logo on roof (1984) 75 - 90
e4. same as e, blue ski rack (1984) 15 - 20

2508-a

Vetty Funny 2508 - 80mm - 1979
This Corvette Stingray funny car was driven by Tom "Mongoose" McEwen and has a metal chassis, slightly-tinted plastic windshield, lift-up body to show a metal engine & interior, bw, and was made in Hong Kong.
Similar castings: 2528 Poppa Vette (1986), 2102 Corvette Funny Car (1990)
a. gray; red, yellow & black striping tampo w/"Tom 'Mongoose' McEwen" & racing decals on sides; "Mongoose" & mongoose on hood $30 - 35

2508-a2

a2. same as a, white replaces red in tampo 450 - 600
a3. same as a, Malaysia (1982) 20 - 25

2508-b

b. white; red, yellow & purple striping tampo on top & sides; "Corvette Fever" & Hot Wheels logo on sides (1983) 20 - 25

2508-c

c. lime green; red, magenta & blue ribbon tampo w/"Corvette Fever" & red Hot Wheels logo on sides; metal int., engine & side pipes; yellow-tinted window; bw. FAO Schwarz History of Hot Wheels 8-pack (1995) 10 - NA

1980

Theme groupings of Hot Wheels cars continued but the only two carry-overs were Heroes and Scene Machines. Two new categories were added: Workhorses and Hi-Rakers. Workhorses included construction vehicles and a forklift. Hi-Rakers had attachments in their bases to raise and lower the cars' backs.

1123-a

3-Window '34" 1132 - 70mm - 1980 (Hi-Rakers)
This Hong Kong-made 1934 Ford 3-Window Coupe has a metal chassis, lightly-tinted plastic windows, plastic engine sticking out on the sides, brown plastic interior & fenders, & bw.
a. red; yellow flame tampo on trunk, yellow lines, "Hot Rod" & black rectangle on roof $15 - 18
a2. same as a, Malaysia (1982) 15 - 18
a3. 4352, same as a, gyg (1982) 30 - 40
b. mtlfk red, same as a (1983) 10 - 12
b2. same as b, Malaysia (1983) 10 - 12
b3. same as b, gyg (1983) 25 - 30
b4. same as b2, gyg (1983) 25 - 30
b5. same as b2, gyw (1985) 45 - 60
c. 4352; black; white, yellow & black flames on sides; black plastic int., fenders & running board; Malaysia; bw (1984) 12 - 15

1132-c2

c2. same as c, gyg (1984) 40 - 50
c3. same as c, gyw (1984) 100 - 150
c4. same as c3, brown fenders 100 - 150

1473-d

d. 1473; red; gray-tinted windows; yellow, black & white lines (like a Z) on sides; black plastic int. & running board; red plastic fenders; Malaysia; bw; no longer a Hi-Raker (1987) 25 - 30
d2. same as d; red, yellow & white flame tampo on sides; large rear wheels (1988) 20 - 25

1473-d3

d3. same as d2, small rear wheels (1988) 12 - 15

1132-e

e. purple; red, blue & lt. green stripe tampo w/"34" on sides; #57 (1989) 18 - 20
f. 2225; mtlc blue; red, yellow & white flame tampo on sides; black plastic int.; large back bw; small front bw; Park 'n Plates (1989) 12 - 15
f2. same as f, small back bw (1989) 12 - 15

Values are shown in U.S. dollars, first price is for mint, second is for mint packaged vehicles only. See pages 15-16 for grading guide to determine value for cars in lesser conditions.

1299-g

g. 1299; mtlc blue; white, lt. green & pink tampo w/"Pro Street '34" on sides & "Cal Custom" in white on roof; blue int. & fenders; rrgy; California Custom (1990) 15 - 18
h. 1299; fluor. lime; same as g; orange, blue & dk. blue tampo; California Custom (1990) 15 - 18

1132-h2

h2. same as h, tw 12 - 15
h3. same as h2, black replaces blue in tampo 12 - 15

2334-i

i. white; pink plastic fenders; pink, black & orange lines & star on sides; #196 (1993) 70 - 80
i2. same as i, purple fenders, purple not pink in tampo, #196 (1993) 15 - 18

3-Window '34-j

j. lime yellow; plastic purple fenders; black running boards; orange, magenta & light green tampo on sides, #196 (1993) 110 - 225
j2. same as j, dk. purple fenders, 25th Anniv. 5-pack only (1993) 4 - NA

12033-k

k. 12033, black, yellow plastic fenders, red flame tampo w/"Malt O Meal" in yellow & black on sides, tinted window, chrome int., bw. Malt-O-Meal limited edition (1994) 15 - 18
k2. same as k, sp7 (1995) 15 - 18

12350-l

l. 12350; mtlfk silver; yellow, orange & red flames on trunk & sides; gray plastic fenders; black-tinted window; red Hot Wheels logo in rear window; chrome int.; bw; #257 (1995) 12 - 15
l2. same as l, sp7, #257 (1995) 7 - 10
l3. same as l, sp3, #257 (1997) 2 - 4
l4. same as l, all small wheels 4 - 6
l5. same as l3; no tampo, China w/Arco Hauler set only (1999) 6 - NA
m. 13635; yellow; yellow fenders; "Early Times '95 Hemet" in orange, black & pink on roof; tinted window; chrome

13635-m

int.; pc. Early Times Car Club (1995), limited to 7000 35 - 40
n. pink; pinkish chrome engine, pink-tinted window, pink fenders & int., black Hot Wheels logo underneath trunk, bw. Ford 5-pack only (1995) 3 - NA
n2. same as n, all small wheels 6 - 8

3-Window '34-n3

n3. same as n, sp7, #451 (1995) 8 - 10
n4. same as n, sp3, #451 (1996) 10 - 12
n5. same as n, dw3. Ford 5-pack only (1996) 2 - NA

13299-o

o. 13299; turquoise chrome; turquoise plastic fenders & int.; blue-tinted windows; sp7; #1 in Speed Gleamer series; #312 (1995) 10 - 12

1132-p

p. chrome, black int., black plastic running boards, red Hot Wheels logo on back window, rsw. Service Merchandise 16-piece Classic American Car Collection only, limited to 5000 (1995) 20 - NA

3-Window '34-q

q. no #, purple chrome, pinkish chrome engine, pink-tinted window, pink interior & fenders, sp7. Ford 5-pack only (1996) 40 - NA
r. 16908; blue; white, red & yellow flames; racing tampo on sides & hood; black int.; tinted window; sp5; #3 in Race Team Series III; #535 (1997) 6 - 8

3-Window '34-s

s. orange, clear window, yellow & red flames on sides, ho5, #4 in Treasure Hunt Series (1998) 30 - 35

3-Window '34-u

u. black; black int.; clear window; white & red tampo design on sides, hood & roof; "Lexmark" on sides; "Print Lexmark" on trunk; gyw. Limited to 10,000 for Lexmark, in box (1998) 18 - 25
v. unpainted, clear window, gray interior, sp7, 1998 Hot Wheels Convention, #257 (1998) 160 - 190

3-Window '34-w

w. mtlfk gold; black fenders & int.; red & purple flames on sides, hood & roof; ho5. Target Exclusive Street Rods set (1999) 8 - NA

3-Window '34-x

x. purple, purple fenders & int., lt. blue & gold tampo on sides, sp5. #1 in Pinstripe Power series, #953 (1999) 4 - 5

3-Window '34-y

y. white; black int.; clear window; black, yellow, purple & red tampo w/"Lexmark" on sides & trunk, gych. Limited to 25,000 for Lexmark, in box (1999) 18 - 25

3-Window '34-z

z. black; gold, black & white tampo w/Jefferson City, MO Police Dept. police shield on sides, "Jefferson City Police" on trunk, "30" on roof; pc. Limited to 25,000 in Cop Rods Series for K•B Toys (1999) 5 - 7

3-Window '34-ac

aa. mtlc gray; gray fenders & int.; tinted window; sp3. Sold w/Long Hauler (1999) 5 - NA
ab. mtlfk green, white int., yellow-tinted windows, gold & orange tampo on sides & hood, sp3, Malaysia, #132 (2000) 2 - 3
ac. red; white fenders & roof; chrome & red int.; clear windows; white, gray, black & gold logo with "Official Unit Fire Chief," "3120" & North Pole Fire Department emblem on sides; design on hood; red square on roof; "Fire Chief" & North Pole Fire Department logo on trunk; rrch w/white stripe; Fire Rods series (2001) 6 - 8

3-Window '34-ad

ad. black; clear windows; black int.; red, white, yellow & blue tampo w/"Astros" & star on sides; logo in back; sp5; for Houston Astros baseball (2001) 15 - 18

3-Window '34-ag

ae. green; black chassis, fenders, running board & int.; clear windows; gold, orange & black tampo on sides; sp5; Thailand; #196 (2001) 2 - 3
af. black, gray int. & fenders, clear windows, orange & yellow flame tampo, sp3, in baggie in cake-decorating kit or City Center set (2001) 6 - NA
ag. green; black chassis, fenders & int.; clear windows; black & white tampo on sides; "Editor's Choice" in black, white & yellow on trunk; pc; Thailand; Target Exclusive Editor's Choice (2001) 6 - 8
ah. green, white fenders & interior, clear windows, black & white tampo on sides, sp3, China, in Pavement Pounder pack (2001) 6 - NA
ai. mtlfk gray, gray fenders & int., tinted windows, sp3, China, in Pavement Pounder pack (2001) 6 - NA
aj. blue, white int., blue-tinted windows, red & white stars-&-stripes tampo on sides & hood, dw3. #2 in Star-Spangled series, #080 (2002) 2 - 3

1131-a

'40s Woodie™ 1131 - 77mm - 1980 (Hi-Rakers)

This Hong Kong-made 1940 Ford Woodie wagon has a metal chassis, chrome plastic engine sticking thru the hood, blue-tinted plastic windows, tan plastic interior, dark brown plastic wood panels, black plastic top, & bw.

a. orange, smooth wood panels $15 - 18

1131-a2

a2. same as a, wood-grain panels (1981) 30 - 35
a3. orange, same as a, Hot Wheels 30th Anniv. logo in gold on rear side window, limited edition for 30th Anniv. w/card in window box (1998) 4 - 6
b. blue, same as a2 (1982) 15 - 18
b2. same as b, Malaysia (1982) 12 - 15
c. mtlfk blue, same as b (1983) 6 - 8
c2. same as b2 (1983) 6 - 8
c3. 4351, same as c, gyg (1983) 30 - 35
c4. same as c3, made in Malaysia 30 - 35
c5. same as c2, gyw 40 - 50
d. yellow, same as b2, black interior (1986) 85 - 100
d2. same as d, lt. brown wood panels (1986) 10 - 12
d3. same as d2, no longer Hi-Raker, #51 (1987) 10 - 12

Values are shown in U.S. dollars, first price is for mint, second is for mint packaged vehicles only. See pages 15-16 for grading guide to determine value for cars in lesser conditions.

1131-d2

d4. same as d3, small rear wheels, #51 (1987) 10 - 12

1229-e

e. 1229, bright red, yellow interior, yellow "Cal Customs" on roof, clear windows, rrr, California Custom (1990) 18 - 20
e2. same as e, bwy (1990) 12 - 15
e3. same as e2, blue-tinted windows (1990) 12 - 15

1131-f

f. no #, bright yellow-green, same as e3, yellow "Cal Custom," black int., bwy, California Custom (1990). Wild Wave set only w/roof rack & surfboards, later sold separately at Mattel Toy Club (1990), w/o surfboards 12 - NA
with surfboards 30 - NA
f2. same as f, pink int. (1990), w/o surfboards 5 - NA
with surfboards 18 - NA
g. 1229, turquoise, same as n, pink wood panels, California Custom (1990) 12 - 15
h. 9226, mtlc ruby red, same as n, black int., ww, Park 'n Plates (1990) 60 - 75

4316-i

i. 4316, black, turquoise box, yellow int., exposed plastic chrome engine, yellow & maroon tampo on rear fenders & hood, clear windshield, metal base, bw, #217 (1993) 5 - 8
i2. same as i, sp7, #217 (1995) 5 - 8
i3. same as i, sp5, #217 (1997) 3 - 6
i4. same as i, ho5, #217 (1997) 2 - 4

13896-j

j. 11896, Day-Glo red, black int., tinted window, lt. brown sides, rr, red "Early Times 94" & gray "Hot Rods To Hemet" on roof, #217 (1994) 30 - 35

15074-k

k. 15074, Day-Glo yellow, lt. brown sides, black int., black-tinted window, brown Hot Wheels logo on side window, rry, yellow circle on tire & yellow rims, #1 in Treasure Hunt Series, #428 (1996) 35 - 45
k2. same as k, silver wheel rims, #428 (1996) 55 - 75
k3. same as k, gold wheel rims, #428 (1996) 80 - 100

16017-l

l. 16017; black; dk. beige box "Back to the Fifties 1996 Weekend" & "MSRA" in orange, yellow & blue on roof; rrch. Limited to 10,000 as Back to the Fifties '40s Woodie (1996) 18 - 20
m. 15269, chrome, chrome base, clear window, black int., sp5, #2 in Silver Series II, #421 (1996) 8 - 10
m2. same as m, sp7 (1997) 16 - 20

'40s Woodie-n

n. no #, dk. mtlc red, black roof, clear window, black int., lt & dk. brown panels, 2 surfboards on roof, bw. Target Motorin' Music 4-pack only (1997) 18 - NA
o. unpainted, lt. brown side panels, black int., clear window, ho5, 1998 Hot Wheels Convention, #217 (1998) 100 - 150

'40s Woodie-p

p. white; lt. brown box; clear window; black int.; black, orange & gold tampo design on sides of hood & roof; sp5; #803 (1999) 3 - 6

'40s Woodie-q

q. white; black int.; dk. brown sides; "JC Whitney" in blue on side of hood & in white on roof; 2 white surfboards on roof: "Visit Us" in blue on one, Internet address in red on other, rrch; boxed; limited edition for JC Whitney (1999) 15 - 18

'40s Woodie-r

r. red, same as q, box in limited edition for JC Whitney (1999) 18 - 25

'40s Woodie-s

s. mtlfk purple; blue-tinted window; black int.; yellow, orange, black & white tampo on roof & front fenders; sp5; Malaysia; #1 in Surf 'n Fun series; #961 (1999) 3 - 6
t. mtlc blue, gray int., lt. brown box, 2 white surfboards on roof, lwch, China, Surfs Up Action Pack only (1999) 20 - NA
t2. same as t; one red & one blue surfboard (1999) 8 - NA

'40s Woodie-u

u. white; black int.; blue tinted window; white box; white, red, & gray tampo w/"24" on sides, "Police" on sides & hood, "24" & "El Segundo Police" on roof; rrch. Limited to 25,000; K•B Toys' Cop Rods series (1999) 6 - 8

'40s Woodie-v

v. black, red int., clear windows, orange surfboards on top, "Padres" in white on sides, "San Diego Padres" in blue on surfboards, rrch, Padres' premium 15 - 18
w. mtlfk orange-brown, mtlfk gray chassis, clear windows, black int., black & white tampo on front fenders & roof w/"Linked" in red on roof, lwch, China, #193 (2001) 2 - 3
x. orange, lt. brown box, white roof, tinted windows, gray int., "33" & star on sides & roof, lwch, Thailand, Skateboarders 5-pack (2001) 3 - NA

1172-a

Bulldozer 1172 - 72mm - 1980
This Hong Kong-made model has a yellow plastic chassis, interior & lift, movable blade and black plastic tread.
a. yellow $5 - 7
a2. same as a, Malaysia, #34 5 - 7

Bulldozer-a3

a3. same as a2; black, white & red tampo w/"CAT" on sides. Large bp w/vial of dirt only (1998) 4 - 6

1168-a

CAT Forklift 1168 - 68mm - 1980
This model has a metal chassis, "Caterpillar" cast on the back, black plastic interior & roof guard, yellow plastic movable forklift, bw, and was made in Hong Kong.
a. yellow, "Cv80" on black & white tampo $15 - 20
a2. same as a, "Cv80" cast in sides 10 - 12
a3. same as a2, Malaysia (1982) 10 - 12
a4. same as a3, Mexico (1986) 10 - 15
a5. 16042, same as a, red Hot Wheels logo on sides, bw in front, sp5 in back, China #475 (1996) 2 - 4
a6. no #, yellow, same as f, red Little Debbie logo & "Snacks" in blue on sides. Little Debbie Bakery Series II 3-pack only (1997) 4 - NA

1168-b

b. green, same as a3, Intl. line, 5-pack only (1991) 55 - NA
c. white, blue seat & roll cage, black lift, large bw in front, sp5 in back, #642 (1999) 2 - 3
d. orange; black seat, roll cage & lift; black, white & blue-gray tampo w/"Marcus Construction" on sides; sp5; Virtual Collection vehicle; #110 (2000) 2 - 3
e. red; black seat, roll cage & lift; yellow, blue, black & white tampo w/"TAK" on sides; sp3; China; #122 (2001) 2 - 3

1133-a

Dodge D-50 1133 - 75mm - 1980 (Hi-Rakers)
This Hong Kong-made Dodge D-50 pickup truck has a metal chassis, chrome plastic interior & engine sticking thru the hood, blue-tinted plastic windows, white plastic camper shell and bw.
a. red; black, orange & yellow stripe tampo w/"Dodge" on sides $10 - 12
a2. same as a, Malaysia (1982) 10 - 12
b. mtlfk blue, same as a2 (1983) 5 - 7
b2. 4353, same as a, gyg (1983) 20 - 25
b3. same as b2, gyw (1985) 30 - 35

9540-c

c. 9540; white; red & yellow flame tampo on hood & sides; "Hot" on sides; red plastic int. & engine; Malaysia; gyw (1985) 40 - 45
c2. same as c, bw, Mexico (1986) 30 - 35

1171-a

Dump Truck 1171 - 76mm - 1980
This Hong Kong-made model has a metal chassis, yellow metal dumper tipping backward, black plastic interior, and cty.
a. yellow, "C 777" on black & white tampo on left side $5 - 7
a2. same as a, "C 777" cast in left side 5 - 7
a3. same as a2, Malaysia, #38 (1982) 5 - 7

Values are shown in U.S. dollars, first price is for mint, second is for mint packaged vehicles only. See pages 15-16 for grading guide to determine value for cars in lesser conditions.

a4. same as a3, ctgd (1987) 45 - 55
a5. same as a3, plastic dumper, #38 (1992) 3 - 5
a6. same as a5, dw3cty 2 - 4
b. 15268, chrome, chrome base, black interior, dw3, #1 in Silver Series II, #420 (1996) 25 - 30
b2. same as b, black dumper, #420 (1997) 6 - 8

Dump Truck-c

c. yellow; same as a; black, white & red tampo w/"Caterpillar" on front edge of dump & "CAT" on sides. Lever in front lifts dumper; large bp w/vial of dirt only (1998) 4 - 6

1127-a

Greyhound MC-8 1127 - 80mm - 1980
This Hong Kong-made Greyhound bus has a metal chassis & interior, sunroof, brown-tinted plastic windows and bw.
a. white; top half painted & bottom half unpainted metal; blue & red striping tampo on top & sides w/"Greyhound," "Americruiser" & greyhound; top tampo extends over sides of roof $35 - 40
a2. same as a, Malaysia 25 - 30

1127-a3

a3. same as a, darker tampo which doesn't go over sides, Mexico (1983) 90 - 120

Hammer Down-a

Hammer Down - no # - 80mm - 1980
This Hong Kong-made Peterbilt tractor has a metal chassis, gray-tinted plastic windows, unpainted metal interior, bw, and was only in The Great American Truck Race set. See also 1169 Peterbilt Cement Mixer (1980)
a. red, no blue sticker w/ "Hammer Down" in white on chassis $100 - NA

1174-a

Hiway Hauler® 1174 - 83mm - 1980
(Workhorses)
This short bobtail inter-city delivery truck has a metal chassis, white plastic box on the chassis with opening doors, browned-out plastic windows, & bw. Hong Kong. Similar casting: Movin' On (1980)
a. white; red & blue design w/"North American Van Lines" on box sides $25 - 50
a2. same as a, small "Van Lines" on cab 45 - 50

1174-b

a3. same as a, France (1985) 20 - 25
b. yellow; white box; red, yellow & black Pennzoil design on sides; gray-tinted windshield; black int. (1982) 30 - 35

1174-c

c. green, same as b, white box, green & red Mountain Dew design on sides (1983) 25 - 30

1174-d

d. yellow; same as b; yellow box; red, olive green & black Mayflower design (1984) 20 - 25

9549 -e

e. 9549; white; same as c; white box; red, yellow & blue stripe design; Hot Wheels logo & "Racing Team" on sides (1985) 30 - 35

2548-f

f. 2548; white; same as c; white box; red, turquoise & black design; "Masters of the Universe Toy Delivery" on sides (1986) 20 - 25

1565-g

g. 1565; dk. blue; same as c; white box; red, black & blue design; "Goodyear Racing Tires" & race car on sides (1987) 12 - 15

5144-h

h. 5144, white, same as c, white box, red & blue design, "NASA" & "Space Shuttle Ground Support" on sides, black int. (1988) 12 - 15

2806-i

i. 2806, red, same as c, white box, red & blue 36mm-long Pepsi design on sides (1989) 15 - 20

2806-i2

i2. same as i, Pepsi design is 53mm long, #24 (1989) 8 - 30

1174-j

j. turquoise; same as c; white box; red, turquoise & yellow design; "Ocean Pacific Delivery" on sides; blue-tinted windshield; tan int.; #24 (1990) 18 - 20

4969-k

k. 4969, blue, same as m, white box, blue & red tampo, "Goodyear" on sides, Intl. boxed line only (1991) 20 - 25

1174-l

l. no #, white, blue tampo w/"Wal-Mart" & "Low Prices Every Day" on sides, Wal-Mart & Wal-Mart Playset only (1991) - 2nd price for playset 15 - 20

1174-m

m. white; white box w/"Jewel" in yellow, black circle w/"Freshness Guaranteed" in white & multi-colored produce; dk.-tinted windows, sp5, China, Jewel 2-pack only (1996) 5 - 7

Movin' On-a

Movin' On - no # - 60mm - 1980
This Kenworth tractor has a metal chassis, browned-out plastic windows, bw and was made in Hong Kong. It was only issued in The Great American Truck Race set.
Similar casting: 1174 Hiway Hauler (1980)
a. white; red sticker w/"Movin' On" in white on chassis $110 - NA

1169-a

Peterbilt Cement Mixer 1169 - 80mm - 1980
This model has a metal chassis, dark gray-tinted plastic windows, gray plastic lift-up truck bed, white plastic rotating cement drum, six bw, and was made in Hong Kong. Similar casting: Hammer Down (1980)
a. red, no tampo $8 - 10
a2. same as a, different exhaust stacks, Malaysia, #78 (1985) 6 - 8
a3. same as a, Malaysia (1985) 6 - 8

1136-a

Split Window '63 1136 - 70mm - 1980
(Hi-Rakers)
This Hong Kong-made 1963 Corvette Coupe has a metal chassis, lightly-tinted plastic windows, tan plastic interior, and bw. Similar casting: 3092 Corvette Split Window (1993)
a. gray; red, white & blue tampo with "Corvette" twice on hood & "Chevrolet Corvette" inside emblem on roof $12 - 15

1136-b

b. yellow; same as a; red, blue & magenta tampo on top (1982) 15 - 18
b2. same as b, Malaysia (1982) 11 - 15
c. metalflake gold, same as b (1983) 6 - 8
c2. same as c, Malaysia (1983) 6 - 8
c3. 4354, same as c, gyg (1983) 20 - 30
c4. 4354, same as c2, gyw (1983) 45 - 55

4354-d

d. 4354; black, yellow, red & blue tampo; white int.; Malaysia; bw (1984) 12 - 15
d2. same as d, gyg (1984) 30 - 35
d3. same as d2, Malaysia 25 - 35
d4. same as d, gyw (1985) 45 - 50

1486-e

e. 1486; magenta; lt. green, white & yellow flame tampo on hood & sides; bw; tan int.; Hong Kong (1987) 18 - 20
e2. same as e, Malaysia (1987) 10 - 15

3983-f

f. 3983; black; red, yellow & blue flame tampo on sides; bw; tan int.; Hong Kong (1988) 12 - 15

Values are shown in U.S. dollars, first price is for mint, second is for mint packaged vehicles only. See pages 15-16 for grading guide to determine value for cars in lesser conditions.

3985-g

g. 3985; gray; maroon & magenta stripe tampo on top; bw; tan int.; Hong Kong (1988) 12 - 15
g2. same as g, Malaysia (1988) 12 - 15

Split Window '63-h

h. no #; white; blue & yellow stripe tampo w/red flames; blue "Corvette" twice on hood; 5-pack only (1989) 25 - NA

9252-i

i. 9254, gold chrome, chromed windows, bw, issued for billionth car promotion & only sold w/trophy (1990) 6 - 8

1305-j

j. 1305; chrome rose; blue & orange stripes on top & sides; "Cal Custom" in orange on sides; clear windows; blue int.; rry; California Custom (1990) 15 - 18
j2. same as j, bw 10 - 12

Split Window '63-k

k. no #, hot pink, same as j2, bw, California Custom Freeway Frenzy set only, later sold at Mattel Toy Club, never in blisterpack (1990) 6 - NA

1416-l

l. 1416; black; purple & yellow tampo on sides; gray plastic base; McDonald's promotion; later in bp (1991) 8 - 10
l. in McDonald's baggy 8 - NA

1486-m

m. 1486 or 1671; lt. green; blue, yellow & red tampo on top; McDonald's promotion; later in bp (1991) 8 - 10
m. in McDonald's baggy 8 - NA
n. same as m; magenta replaces blue in tampo (1991) 8 - 10
n. in McDonald's baggy 8 - NA

Split Window '63-o

o. no #; pearl white; orange, pink & blue stripe tampo on top & sides; "Kool-Aid" on sides; clear windows; pink int.; gray plastic base; bw; Malaysia; Kaybee's Toy Store give-away for Kool-Aid points; never in bp (1992) 10 - NA

Split Window '63-p

p. no #; black; red, yellow & white tampo w/"Getty" on sides; red int.; bw; never in blisterpack (1991) 6 - NA

1126-a

Stutz Blackhawk 1126 - 77mm - 1980
This model has a metal chassis, gray-tinted plastic windows, black plastic interior, bw, and was made in Hong Kong.
a. gray; yellow, white & blue stripe tampo on top, "Stutz" twice on hood $8 - 10

1126-b

b. black; lt. blue, blue & red stripe tampo on top (1982) 10 - 12
b2. same as b, Malaysia (1982) 10 - 12
b3. same as b2, black replaces lt. blue in tampo 10 - 12
c. mtlfk brown; same as b2; yellow, orange & red tampo (1983) 5 - 7
c2. same as c; white, blue & red tampo (1983) 18 - 24

1126-c3

c3. same as c; yellow, orange & white tampo (1984), Malaysia on base, Mexico ("Stutz Open" on package) 18 - 24
d. mtlfk gold, white int., blue-tinted windows, bw, Malaysia (Italy) (1983) 150 - 175
e. mtlfk blue, Malaysia (Italy) (1983) 150 - 175
f. gray; (1985), produced in France, "Made in Malaysia" on base 25 - 30

2106-g

g. 2106; neon red; orange, yellow & pink stripe design on sides & hood; "Stutz" on sides; yellow "Cal Custom" on windshield; clear window; yellow int.; twy; California Custom (1991) 8 - 10
h. white, clear window, tan int., uh, FAO Schwarz The History of Hot Wheels 8-pack (1995) 8 - NA

13355-i

i. 13355, black, clear window, red int., chrome rt w/red stripes, #7 in Treasure Hunt series, #359 (1995) 60 - 70
j. aqua, magenta-tinted windows, gray int., lwch. Designer Collection 5-pack (General Mills mail-in, 1997) 4 - NA

Stutz Blackhawk-k

k. red w/black metal-flakes, tinted windows, white int., white tampo on sides, sp3, #3 in Tattoo Machines, #687 (1998) 2 - 4

Stutz Blackhawk-l

l. pearl white; gold chassis; white int.; tinted window; silver & gold tampo design on sides, hood & trunk w/"Stutz Blackhawk" on sides; rrgd w/white stripe around tire. #6 in Final Run Series, limited to 35,000 (1999) 8 - 10

1129-a

Super Scraper 1129 - 71mm - 1980
This Hong Kong-made Chevrolet pickup has a metal chassis, gray-tinted plastic windows, sun roof, red plastic interior & truck bed, & bw.
Similar castings: 2509 Bywayman (1979), 9242 Pavement Pounder (1985), 5113 Power Plower (1986)
a. yellow; orange, black & blue stripe tampo w/"Speedy Removal," "Snow Dirt Sand" & truck on sides $8 - 10
a2. same as a, Malaysia (1982) 8 - 10

1129-b

b. black; yellow, orange & red stripe tampo & "Henry's Hauling" on sides (1983) 5 - 7
b2. 4350, same as b, gyg (1983) 25 - 30
b3. 4350, same as b, gyw (1985) 35 - 40

1130-a

Tricar X8 1130 - 79mm - 1980
Based on a jet-powered race car, this model has a white metal chassis, yellow-tinted plastic windshield, bw in back with one small thin wheel in front. Hong Kong.
a. white; red & blue stars & stripes tampo on top; blue soft plastic nose, tail fin & tailpipe $5 - 7
a2. same as a, Malaysia (1982) 5 - 7

1130-b

b. red; red metal base; black, yellow & white flame tampo on top; white soft plastic nose, tail fin & tailpipe; clear plastic windshield, white int. (1983) 4 - 6

Tricar X8-c

c. no #; red; red, white & blue stars-&-stripes tampo on top; white rubber nose & fin; clear window; white int.; bw. Kellogg's cereal mail-in; never in blisterpack; Malaysia (1985) 8 - NA

2525-d

d. 2525; mtlfk gray; maroon metal base; orange, maroon & yellow tampo w/"X8" on top; maroon soft plastic nose, tail fin & tailpipe; clear plastic windshield; maroon int.; Hong Kong (1986) 8 - 10
d2. same as d, Malaysia (1986) 8 - 10

5112-e

e. 5112; yellow; red metal base; red, maroon & white striping tampo on top; red soft plastic nose, tail fin & tailpipe; gray-tinted plastic windshield; red int.; Malaysia (1988) 4 - 6
e2. same as e, yellow metal base (1988) 40 - 50

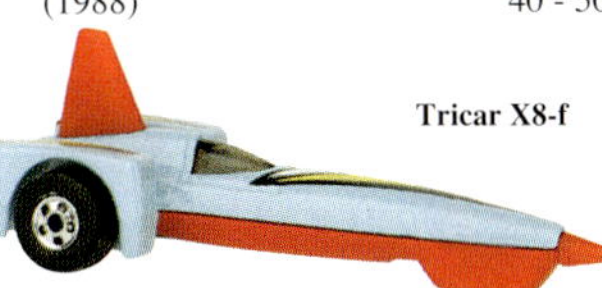
Tricar X8-f

f. no #; turquoise; yellow, black & white tampo on top; red plastic nose & fin; gray-tinted window; red int.; never in bp; planned for Hot Wheels cereal but never used for safety reasons, some later sold directly to collectors (1989) 8 - NA

1125-a

Turbo Mustang 1125 - 73mm - 1980
This Ford Mustang has a yellow metal chassis, gray-tinted plastic windshield, red interior, bw, and was made in Hong Kong.
Similar casting: 9531 Mustang S.V.O. (1985)
a. yellow; orange, red & black tampo on top, "Mustang" twice on hood $8 - 10
a2. same as a, gw (1982) 6 - 8

1125-b

b. orange; same as a; orange chassis; red, black & yellow stripe tampo w/"Cobra" on sides; black & yellow cobra design & "Cobra" on hood; 1981 black Collector's Book 3-pack only (1981) 12 - NA
c. 3361, red, same as b, red chassis, dk. red not red in tampo, gw (1982) 6 - 8
c2. same as c; black, yellow, orange & blue tampo; sold w/Cobra set or in Canadian bp (1982) 25 - 45
c3. same as c2, Malaysia 25 - 45
c4. same as c3, lighter red int., darker yellow in tampo, no country on base, never in bp, Mexico (1983) 100 - NA
d. mtlfk red, same as c, mtlfk red chassis (1983) 5 - 7
e. same as c4, no tampo, never in bp, Mexico (1983) 75 - NA

3361-f

Values are shown in U.S. dollars, first price is for mint, second is for mint packaged vehicles only. See pages 15-16 for grading guide to determine value for cars in lesser conditions.

f. mtlfk blue; same as c; mtlfk blue chassis; yellow, black & lt. blue tampo; yellow int. (1984) 80 - 100

3361-g

g. 3361; white; yellow chassis; yellow, lt. blue & black tampo w/"31" & racing decals on sides; "Mustang GT" & "31" on hood; red int. (1984) 8 - 10
g2. same as g, Malaysia (1984) 8 - 10

1134-a

Turbo Wedge 1134 - 77mm - 1980 (Hi-Rakers)
This concept racer has a metal chassis & interior, exposed metal engine, yellow plastic rear spoiler, clear plastic windows, bw, and was made in Hong Kong.
a. light green $5 - 7
b. orange, same as a (1982) 4 - 6
b2. same as b, Malaysia (1982) 4 - 6
c. yellow, same as b2, gray plastic chassis & exposed engine, black-tinted windows, Speed Machines (1983) 7 - 9

1135-a

'Vette Van 1135 - 67mm - 1980 (Hi-Rakers)
A Hong Kong-made customized Chevrolet Corvette van with a metal chassis, gray-tinted plastic windows, tan plastic interior, & bw.
Similar casting: 3301 Iron Man (1981)
a. black; yellow, red & white tampo, "Vette-Van" on sides $20 - 525
a2. same as a, Malaysia (1982) 12 - 15

1135-b

b. red; yellow, white & blue ribbon on sides (1982) 15 - 18
b2. same as b, Malaysia (1982) 15 - 18

Vette Van-c

c. no #; plum; gray plastic chassis; yellow, white & red ribbon tampo on sides; dk. blue plastic int.; Speed Machines (1983) 20 - 25

1173-a

Wheel Loader 1173 - 80mm - 1980
This Hong Kong-made front-wheel loader has a yellow metal chassis, black plastic interior, yellow plastic movable scoop and cty.
a. yellow, "C988" on black & white tampo $5 - 7
a2. same as a, Malaysia (1982) 5 - 7
a3. same as a2, no tampo, Malaysia (1982) 5 - 7
a4. same as a2, cts (1986) 4 - 6
a5. same as a2, ctsy (1986) 10 - 12
a6. same as a2, ctgd (1989) 35 - 50
a7. same as a3, yellow plastic base, cty, #3 (1990) 4 - 6

Wheel Loader-a8

a8. same as a2; black, white & red tampo "CAT" on sides. Loader lifts when large stack is pressed. Large bp w/vial of dirt only (1998) 4 - 6

Wheel Loader-b

b. orange, black top, gray scoop, cts, China, #641 (1998) 2 - 4
c. red, white scoop & top, black int., dw3ct. Virtual Collection, #111 (2000) 2 - 3
d. gray; mtlfk blue top, black scoop & int.; dw3ct; China; #123 (2001) 2 - 3

1981

Twelve new models were introduced. These included Hot Ones which featured new gold-colored wheels (gw) on old-style axles from the late 1960s. With the introduction of Hot Ones, Mattel once again claimed "The Fastest Non-Powered Die-Cast Metal Cars." Hot Ones were first released with stickers on existing blister-cards, but were issued on their own cards later in the year. Mattel continued Heroes and Scene Machines through 1981, but this would be the last year for these lines.

1696-a

'37 Bugatti 1696 - 80mm - 1981
This 1937 Bugatti Royale has a metal chassis, two spare tires in back, blue-tinted plastic windows, chrome plastic interior, bw, and was made in Hong Kong.
a. black; red tampo on sides $6 - 8
a2. same as a, red tampo added to hood (1982) 6 - 8
a3. same as a2, ww, Malaysia (1982) 5 - 7
b. 2526, yellow, same as a3; bw (1986) 8 - 10
b2. same as b, ww (1986) 5 - 7
b3. same as b, yellow plastic fenders, #28 (1989) 4 - 6
b4. same as b3, ww, #28 (1989) 4 - 6

1696-c

c. blue, gray tampo on sides, yellow plastic fenders, ww, #28 (1991) 8 - 10
c2. same as c, blue plastic fenders, #28 (1991) 3 - 5
c3. same as c2, sp7, #28 (1995) 3 - 5
c4. same as c2, bw, #28 (1996) 15 - 40
d. yellow; black Hot Wheels logo in back; clear window; gold-plated int., headlights & radiator; iwgd. 16-piece FAO Schwarz Gold Series Collection, limited to 3000 (1994) 8 - NA

15085-e

e. 15085, mtlfk blue, blue plastic fenders, clear window, red int., iw. #12 in Treasure Hunt Series, #439 (1996) 25 - 40

'37 Bugatti-f

f. black, black int., clear window, yellow side tampo, lwch, #1098 (1999) 2 - 3
g. white, clear windows, gold chrome int., black tampo w/"Classic" on sides, "Classic 1937" on hood, ho5, #163 (2001) 2 - 3
h. red & yellow; black trunk & fenders; chrome int.; clear windows; white, gold & black tampo w/"Automobile Milestones 2002" on roof, rrch. '33 Bugatti in Auto Milestones series (2002) 6 - 8

1699-a

Airport Rescue 1699 - 85mm - 1981
This model has a metal chassis, two black plastic hose nozzles on the roof (one in front & one in back), blue-tinted plastic windows, eight bw, and was made in Hong Kong.
a. yellow; red-orange & black tampo w/"Rescue" & "Airport Fire Dept." on sides $15 - 18
a2. same as a, Malaysia (1982) 15 - 18
a3. same as a2; lt. orange & black tampo, Mexico (1985) 30 - 35

1699-b

b. red, same as a, yellow & black tampo, France (1983) 125 - 150

1690-a

Bronco 4-Wheeler 1690 - 75mm - 1981
This Hong Kong-made Ford Bronco has a metal chassis, blue-tinted plastic windows, chrome plastic interior, chrome plastic motorcycle in back, black plastic camper shell, & bw.
Similar casting: 5270 Personnel Carrier (1982 Megaforce)
a. black; red, yellow & orange stripe tampo on sides & top; "Ford Bronco" & horse on hood $8 - 10
a2. same as a, clear windows 8 - 10
a3. same as a, Malaysia (1982) 8 - 10

1690-b

b. white; yellow, orange & black tampo of Toys "R" Us giraffe & "Geoffrey" on sides; "4x4 Bronco" on hood; bp 85 - 95
c. red; yellow, black & white stripe tampo w/"21" & racing decals on sides, "21" on hood (1982) 45 - 55

4355-c2

c2. 4355, same as c, gyg (1982) 90 - 100

1690-c3

c3. same as c2, white camper shell (1982) 4 - 6
c4. same as c3, gyg (1982) 25 - 30
c5. same as c3, gyw (1985) 40 - 45

1520-d

d. 1520; white; red, yellow & blue stripe tampo w/"Ford," "Built Tough" & "Bronco" on sides; red & yellow flame tampo on hood; black-tinted windows; red plastic int.; red plastic motorcycle in rear; bw; Malaysia (1987) 6 - 8
d2. same as d, some stripes removed (1990) 4 - 6
d3. same as d2, ct, #56 (1990) 4 - 6

Bronco 4-Wheeler-e

e. no #; white; different camper shell; black stripe on sides, "Guaranteed Pest Elimination," "Ecolab" & phone # in blue & red on camper sides & rear; given by Ecolab Pest Control Co., later sold by mail (1991) 20 - NA
e2. same as e, ct (1991) 15 - NA
e3. same as e, sp5 (1997) 15 - NA
e4. same as e, dw3 (1997) 15 - NA

4355-f

f. turquoise; red & white stripe tampo w/"Bronco" on doors; red int.; motorcycle in back; ct; #56 5 - 10
g. no #; mtlfk blue; clear window; white int., camper shell & motorcycle; white "Ford" & Hot Wheels logo on side

Values are shown in U.S. dollars, first price is for mint, second is for mint packaged vehicles only. See pages 15-16 for grading guide to determine value for cars in lesser conditions.

Bronco 4-Wheeler-g

window of shell; ct; Ford 5-pack only (1995) 3 - NA

g2. same as g, dw3ct, Just Trucks 5-pack only (1997) 2 - NA

g3. same as g, silver base, dw3ct, Ford 5-pack only (1998) 2 - NA

Bronco 4-Wheeler-h

h. white; green canopy; clear window; tan int. & motorcycle; pink, black & gold tampo w/"Farm Fresh Local Delivery," "CountryFarm Products," "Best of the West," pig on sides; dw3ct; Farm Country 5-pack (1997) 2 - NA

h2. same as h, silver base (1997) 2 - NA

Bronco 4-Wheeler-i

i. red; white camper top; black-tinted windows; black & white tampo design w/"Alaska Trek" on sides; dw3ct; #859 (1998) 2 - 3

i2. same as i, Thailand (1998) 2 - NA

Bronco 4-Wheeler-j

j. black; red camper shell, tan int. & bike; clear window; "Wash ME" on rear window; gold, red & white tampo w/"Mudster" on sides; dw3ct; Thailand; Baja Blazers 5-pack (1999) 2 - 3

k. white; green canopy; black int; clear windows; gray, purple, gold & magenta tampo w/"Santa Fe" on sides; dw3ct; Thailand; #198 (2000) 2 - 3

Bronco 4-Wheeler-l

l. black; tinted windows; gray int. & motorcycle; gray, orange & white tampo on sides & hood w/"Harley-Davidson" on sides, Harley-Davidson logo on hood; dw3ct; Thailand; Harley-Davidson 5-pack (2001) 2 - NA

1691-a

Cannonade 1691 - 72mm - 1981
This concept model has a black plastic chassis, chrome plastic interior & exposed engine, clear plastic windshield, opening canopy, bw, and was made in Hong Kong.
Similar casting: 9587 Snake Busters Car (1985)

a. yellow; red, purple & orange striping tampo "3" on sides $6 - 8

a2. same as a, gw (1982) 4 - 6

a3. same as a2, darker tampo, Mexico (1983) 15 - 18

1691-b

b. red; same as a2; white, yellow & orange tampo; Malaysia (1983) 4 - 6

1691-c

c. maroon, same as b; Mexico (1986) 50 - 60

1693-a

Chevy Citation 1693 - 70mm - 1981
This Hong Kong-made model has a metal chassis, clear plastic windows, red plastic interior, and bw.

a. white; dk. red & black stripe, "X11" on sides $6 - 8

a2. same as a, gw (1982) 4 - 6

a3. same as a, red replaces dk. red in tampo, France (1983) 15 - 25

a4. same as a3, black BP logo on roof, France 75 - NA

a5. same as a3, black interior, France (1985) 40 - 45
available in Mexico 8 - 10

a6. same as a5, black BP logo on roof, France 75 - NA

1693-b

b. red; white, black & yellow striping tampo & "Citation X11" on sides; tan int.; 1981 collector's book 3-pack only (1981) 15 - NA

c. yellow; same as b; orange, black & white tampo; red int.; gw (1982) 4 - 6

c2. same as c, red replaces orange in tampo, Malaysia (1982) 4 - 6

d. 3362, mtlfk red-brown, same as c2, dk. red replaces red in tampo (1983) 4 - 6

d2. same as d, bw, made in France, Mexico (1984) 8 - 10

d3. same as d, black & yellow tampo, bw, made in France, Mexico only (1985) 15 - 20

3303-a

Circus Cats 3303 - 72mm - 1981 (Scene Machines)
This four-wheel drive Ford truck has a metal chassis, gray-tinted windows, black plastic interior, vent & a porthole on the side in back, bw, and was made in Hong Kong.
Similar castings: 2022 Baja Breaker (1978), 2853 Motocross Team (1979), 9113 The Simpson's Family Camper (1990), 3490 Open Wide (1993 Tattoo Machines)

a. white; yellow, black & orange tampo w/"Ringling Brothers Barnum and Bailey Circus" & tiger on sides 125 - 150

3364-a

Dixie Challenger 3364 - 75mm - 1981
This Hong Kong-made Dodge Challenger has a chrome plastic chassis, blue-tinted plastic windows, black plastic interior and bw.

a. orange; blue, red & white rebel flag roof tampo w/"426 Hemi" twice & "Dixie Challenger" on hood $8 - 10

a2. same as a, Malaysia (1982) 8 - 10

3364-a

3364-a3

a3. same as a2, blue & red roof tampo (1982) 12 - 15

a4. same as a3, darker tampo, Mexico (1986) 20 - 25

3301-a

Iron Man 3301 - 67mm - 1981 (Heroes)
This Hong Kong-made customized Corvette van with Marvel Comics® Iron Man character has a metal chassis with Hi-Raker attachment, clear plastic windows, tan plastic interior and bw.
Similar casting: 1135 'Vette Van (1980)

a. white; yellow, red & black tampo w/Iron Man & "The Invincible Iron Man" on sides $18 - 20

a2. same as a, red int., Malaysia (1982) 40 - 45

1697-a

Minitrek 1697 - 76mm - 1981
This Hong Kong-made concept camper has a brown metal chassis, clear plastic windows, sun roof, red plastic interior and bw.

a. tan; yellow & orange stripe tampo on sides $6 - 8

1697-b

b. white; blue & red stripe tampo w/"Good Time Camper" on sides; Malaysia (1983) 80 - 100

b2. same as b, black metal chassis (1983) 6 - 8

c. gray, unpainted metal chassis, dk. red stripe tampo on sides, tan int., France (1984) 60 - 80

1697-c2

c2. same as c, "Le Club des Maitres" (Masters of the Universe) in blue on roof, not in bp, France (1986) 110 - NA

1697-d

d. black, same as c, yellow & orange tampo, orange int., Mexico (1987) 110 - 140

1700-a

Mirada Stocker 1700 - 81mm - 1981
This Dodge Mirada race car has a metal chassis, clear plastic windows, tan plastic interior, bw, and was made in Hong Kong.

a. red; black, yellow & white tampo w/"10" & racing decals on sides; "10," "Dodge" twice & "355 cu. in." on hood $10 - 12

a2. same as a, gw (1982) 10 - 12

a3. same as a, lighter yellow in tampo, France (1987), Mexico only 20 - 25

b. yellow, same as a2, red replaces yellow in tampo (1982) 8 - 12

c. metalflake gold, same as b (1983) 7 - 9

1700-d

d. red, white int., blue-tinted windows, gw, Malaysia (Italy) (1983) 110 - 150

e. blue, white int., blue-tinted windows, gw, Malaysia (Italy) (1983) 125 - 175

f. red, black int., France (1985) 25 - 40

1695-a

Old Number 5® 1695 - 82mm - 1981
This Hong Kong-made Ahrens Fox Pumper fire engine has a red painted metal chassis, two black plastic ladders, tan plastic interior & bw.

a. red; black & yellow tampo w/"No. 5" & "Fire Dept" twice on hood $20 - 25

a2. same as a, louvers on hood 6 - 8

a3. same as a2, Malaysia, #1 (1982) 6 - 8

a4. same as a2, foreign package, France (1983) 8 - 10

a5. same as a2, limited Hot Wheels 30th Anniv. w/blistercard in window box (1998) 4 - 6

12536-b

b. 12536, yellow, same as a, yellow chassis, black & red tampo, iwy, limited to 7000 (1994) 35 - 40

1695-c

c. chrome; chrome base; red int.; black ladders; gold-plated radiator, headlights, etc.; red Hot Wheels logo on hood; rsw. Service Merchandise 16-piece Classic American Car Collection only, limited to 5000 (1995) 12 - NA

Values are shown in U.S. dollars, first price is for mint, second is for mint packaged vehicles only. See pages 15-16 for grading guide to determine value for cars in lesser conditions.

1695-d

d. dk. yellow; black int.; red ladders; gold-plated headlights, radiator, etc.; red Hot Wheels logo in back; sp7y. Then & Now 8-pack (1995) 8 - NA

1695-e

e. white, white base, red int., gold ladders, chrome front, iwgd, 100th Anniv. of Auto gift pack (1996) 12 - NA

Old Number 5-f

f. mtlc gold; gold-plated front; red int., ladders & tampo w/"97" on hood; red iw; tree & elves on top. '97 Holiday Hot Wheels gift pack (1997) 15 - 20

Old Number 5-g

g. mtlc red, gold-plated front, black int., tan ladders, gold tampo w/"97" on hood, gold iw, tree & elves on top. '97 Holiday Hot Wheels gift pack (1997) 15 - 20

1692-a

Omni 024 1692 - 67mm - 1981
This Dodge has a black metal chassis, blue-tinted plastic windows, red plastic interior, bw, and was made in Hong Kong.
a. gray; orange & black stripe and "024 Omni" on sides $5 - 7
a2. same as a, Malaysia (1982) 5 - 7
b. mtlfk blue, same as a (1983) 8 - 10

1692-c

c. mtlfk gold; purple, yellow & red stripe on sides & hood (1983) 15 - 18

1692-c2

c2. as c, red & purple colors reversed, darker tampo colors, made in France (1984), Mexico 40 - 45
c3. as c2, unpainted metal base, Mexico (1987) 40 - 45
c4. as c3, no tampo, Mexico (1987) 55 - 65
d. orange, unpainted base, bw, France 50 - 60
e. dk. blue, red int., blue-tinted windows, bw, Hong Kong (Italy) (1983) 75 - 90
f. mtlfk gold, Hong Kong (Italy) (1983) 85 - 120

1689-a

Peterbilt Tank Truck 1689 - 87mm - 1981
This model has a metal chassis, gray-tinted plastic windows, red plastic interior, six bw, and was made in Hong Kong.
Similar castings: 1169 Peterbilt Cement Mixer (1980), 4017 Peterbilt Dump Truck (1983), 2076 Tank Truck (1992)
a. orange; metal tank; orange, white & black tampo w/"California Construction Company," "est 1932" & "3rd & Main" on sides $5 - 7
a2. same as a, Malaysia 5 - 7

2547-b

b. 2547; red; red, blue & yellow tampo on tank; Hot Wheels logo & "Railroad" on sides (1986) 6 - 8
b2. same as b, unpainted tank (1986) 6 - 8

2800-c

c. 2800; orange; red & yellow tampo w/"Shell" & Shell logo on tank sides (1989) 8 - 10
d. yellow, same as c, #15 (1989) 4 - 6
e. 2800, yellow, same as b (1989) 80 - 100
f. no #, blue, same as b, Mattel Toy Club only, never in bp (1991) 10 - NA

2800-g

g. green, gray plastic tank, lt. green & white "Helium Gas Careful!" on sides, black "Airbase Support Team" & blue blimp on doors, gray plastic windshield. Blimp & Support Team 5-pack only (1994) 8 - NA

3305-a

Racing Team 3305 - 70mm - 1981 (Scene Machines)
This delivery truck has a black plastic chassis, clear windows, brown interior, bw, and was made in Hong Kong.
Similar castings: 9643 Letter Getter (1977), 2854 S.W.A.T. (1979), 2850 The Incredible Hulk (1979), 9643 Delivery Van (1984), 2519 Combat Medic (1986), 2808 Delivery Truck (1989), 9114 The Simpson's Homer's Nuclear Waste Van (1990)
a. yellow; red, white & black tampo with Hot Wheels logo, "1," "Racing Team" & racing decals on sides $110 - 120

Rescue Squad 3304 - 75mm - 1981 (Scene Machines)
This Hong Kong-made concept model has

3304-a

a chrome plastic chassis & interior, clear windows, red plastic top and bw.
Similar castings: 2855 Space Van (1979, 1984), 5273 Tac-Com (1982)
a. red $130 - 150

3300-b

Silver Surfer 3300 - 72mm - 1981 (Heroes)
Based on a concept van and the Marvel Comics superhero, this Hong Kong-made model has a blue plastic chassis, blue-tinted plastic windows, top vent, red plastic interior and bw.
Similar castings: 2510 Inside Story (1979), 2852 Spider-Man (1979 Scene Machines)
a. chrome; black & red tampo w/"Silver Surfer" & character on sides 18 - 20
a2. same as a, dk. blue-tinted window, Malaysia (1982) 18 - 20

1694-a

Turismo 1694 - 72mm - 1981
Based on the DeLorean sports car, this concept model has a metal chassis, blue-tinted plastic windows, tan plastic interior, bw, and was made in Hong Kong.
a. red; white, yellow & black tampo on top & sides; "10" & racing decals on sides $6 - 8
a2. same as a, black int., Malaysia 5 - 7

1694-b

b. yellow; purple, orange & black stripe tampo on sides; black int. (1983) 6 - 8
b2. as b, black-tinted windows (1983) 6 - 8
b3. as b2, plum int. (1983) 4 - 6
b4. as b2, red not purple & orange in tampo, blue-tinted window, "France" on base, Mexico (1984) 40 - 45
c. gray-blue, black int., blue-tinted windows, bw, Malaysia (Italy) (1983) 75 - 90
d. mtlfk gold, Malaysia (Italy) (1983) 90 - 120

1694-e

e. dk. maroon; white stripe on roof & hood; black int.; "France" on base; France (1985) 65 - 75

1982

Of the 51 models issued, 23 were new releases. This was the first year Hot Wheels cars were manufactured in both Hong Kong and Malaysia. All blistercards remained the same as 1981. A Hot Ones 3-pack was issued with a cloth patch; two vehicles (yellow Datsun 200 SX and black Corvette Stingray) were only available in the 3-pack.

3252 -a

'35 Classic Caddy 3252 - 82mm - 1982
This Hong Kong-made 1935 Cadillac Cabriolet Towne Car has a metal chassis, clear plastic windows, brown plastic interior & bw.
a. tan, tan plastic fenders $8 - 10
a2. same as a, Malaysia 8 - 10
b. burgundy, burgundy plastic fenders, brown plastic interior (1983) 5 - 7
b2. same as b; lighter fenders, ww (1983) 5 - 7
c. mtlfk dark blue, dk. blue plastic fenders, tan int., ww, #44 (1986) 5 - 7
c2. same as c, sp5 #44 (1996) 3 - 5
c3. same as c, dw3 #44 (1997) 2 - 4
d. 1543, mtlfk silver, pink plastic fenders, beige plastic int., ww (1989) 25 - 30

3371-e

e. 3371, gold chrome, dk. blue fenders, "Studio Limo" in blue & white on sides, blue "Cal Custom" on roof, red int., California Custom (1990) 15 - 18
e2. same as e, gold fenders 15 - 20

4901-f

f. 4901; white; blue fenders & stars; red "Museum of American Heritage" on sides; Hot Wheels logo with blue "25th Anniversary" on roof; limited to 5000 (1992) 20 - 25
f2. same as f, red fenders, limited to 5000 (1992) 20 - 25

13357-g

g. 13357, mtlfk green, black fenders, clear window, tan int., red Hot Wheels logo on front fender, gold iw, #9 in Treasure Hunt Series, #361 (1995) 50 - 60
h. chrome, red int., red Hot Wheels logo on side, rsw. Service Merchandise 16-piece Classic American Car Collection only, limited to 5000 (1995) 12 - NA

'35 Classic Caddy-i

i. dk. mtlfk aqua, clear windshield, gray int., rtch. American Classics 3-pack only (1996) 12 - NA

'35 Classic Caddy-j

j. red; tan int.; tinted window; black fenders; red, white, yellow & lt. green tampo w/"Friendly Tour Guide" & "Jammin Tours" on sides; lwch;

Values are shown in U.S. dollars, first price is for mint, second is for mint packaged vehicles only. See pages 15-16 for grading guide to determine value for cars in lesser conditions.

#3 in Tropicool Series; #695 (1998) 3 - 5
j2. same as j, sp3, #695 (1998) 2 - 4
k. mtlfk dk. red, red fenders, tan int., black top, rrchww, Thailand, FAO Schwarz Classic Collection (1999) 8 - NA

'35 Classic Caddy-l

l. purple, black fenders & int., tinted windshield, white & silver tampo w/"Aldo's Tuxedo Centre" on sides, stripes on hood, lwch, Thailand, Show Biz 5-pack (1999) 2 - NA
m. mtlfk gold, black fenders, white int., clear windshield, white & dk. red tampo on sides & roof, "35 Cadillac" on roof, lwch, Malaysia, #115 (2001) 2 - 3

5179-a

'55 Chevy 5179 - 72mm - 1982
This Hong Kong-made Chevrolet Bel Air Coupe has a metal chassis, black hood scoop, black-tinted plastic windows and gw.
a. red; orange & yellow flame tampo on hood; orange cross w/"55 Chevy Fever" in yellow & black on sides $12 - 15
a2. same as a, Malaysia 12 - 15

2523-b

b. 2523, red & white, blacked-out windows (1986) 40 - 50

'55 Chevy-c

c. no #; mtlc dk. red; white, blue & orange tampo w/"55" & "Chevy" on sides; Hot Wheels cereal only; not in bp (1990) 30 - NA

'55 Chevy-c2

c2. same as c; yellow, black & white tampo (1990) 125 - NA

5179-d

d. white; gray plastic chassis; red, yellow & magenta stripe design on sides; blacked-out window; McDonald's promo, later sold in bp #95 (1991) 10 - 30

5179-e

e. yellow; gray plastic chassis; orange, blue & magenta stripes & lines on sides; McDonald's promo; later sold in blisterpack #95 (1991) 10 - 20

4991-f

f. 4991; blue; "92," "Smokey's Best Dam Garage in Town" & racing decals on sides; "92" & "Herb Thomas" twice on roof; "240 H.P." twice on hood; white, black & red tampo; blacked-out window; rrgy; limited to 12,000 (1992) 20 - 25

2294-g

g. 2294, black, "3" & "Smokey's Best Dam Garage in Town" on sides, "3" & "Paul Goldsmith" twice on roof, "240 H.P." twice on hood, white tampo, grayed-out window, rrgy, limited to 12,000 (1992) 20 - 25

4965-h

h. 4965; black; "Tim Flock" twice on roof; orange "3," white "Smokey's Best Dam Garage in Town," "Purelube" inside white design on bottom of sides; gray window; bwbk; Malaysia (1992) 10 - 12

11266-i

i. 11266, red, white roof, chromed window, rrgy w/red stripe, limited to 5000 (1993) 45 - 50
j. mtlfk plum, white Hot Wheels logo on license plate, blacked-out window, pcgd. 16-piece FAO Schwarz Gold Series Collection, limited to 3000 (1994) 15 - NA

15255-k

k. 15255, orange, red base, red paint splatter on car, red-tinted window, sp5, #3 in Splatter Paint series, #410 (1996) 3 - 5
k2. same as k, dw3, #410 (1996) 3 - 5

15955-l

l. 15955; yellow & white; black & silver trim on sides; red & blue "JC Whitney Warshawsky" on trunk; tinted window; gych; in box; only 10,000 (1996) 18 - 25
m. 16812, aqua & white, same as n, limited to 10,000 (1996) 18 - 25
n. 16948, blue, blacked-out window, silver Hot Wheels logo on trunk, sp3, #3 in Blue Streak series, #575 (1997) 2 -4
n2. same as n, China, Target exclusive set (1999) 6 - NA
o. red, white roof, black & white tampo w/"Toy Cars and Vehicles" on sides & trunk, gych. In box for Toy Cars and Vehicles magazine (1999) 15 - 18

'55 Chevy-p

p. dk. mtlfk red; blue, white & black tampo; decals on sides; "Ride Yourself Wild" on roof; sp3; #3 in Surf 'n Fun series; #963 (1999) 5 - 6

'55 Chevy-q

q. lt. blue; white roof & trunk; chrome window; silver & black stripes on sides; "Old Cars" in black & lt. blue on trunk; gych. Limited, in box for Old Cars Weekly News & Marketplace (1999) 15 - 18

'55 Chevy-r

r. white; black window; blue, gray, yellow & red tampo w/"Boston Police Department," logo & "Police" on sides, "Boston Police Department" on roof; rrgy. Limited to 25,000 in Cop Rods series for K•B Toys (1999) 5 - 7
s. yellow, black windows, red tampo w/black stripes on sides, sp5, China. Power Launcher pack (2000) 5 - 7
t. red, black windows, black flame tampo on sides, sp3, China. Power Launcher pack (2000) 5 - 7
u. dark blue, black windows, yellow & silver flame tampo on sides, sp3, Hot Rod Boulevard set (2001) 10 - NA
u2. same as u, no tampo, Malaysia, sold only in Mexico (2001) 8 - 10
v. black, tinted windows, yellow & purple striping tampo on sides, sp3, China, Kool Toyz Power Launcher pack (2001) 5 - 7
w. dark blue, black windows, yellow tampo on hood & roof, sp3, China, Power Launcher pack (2001) 5 - 7
x. black, clear windows, red & gold flame tampo on sides, sp3, China, Power Launcher pack (2001) 5 - 7
y. blue, black windows, yellow & light blue racing tampo on sides, sp3, China, Pavement Pounder pack (2001) 5 - 7

'55 Chevy-z

z. white, white chassis, black windows, orange spray mask on hood & sides, gych, #2 in 2001 Final Run (2001) 8 - 10

3258-a

Aries Wagon 3258 - 72mm - 1982
This Dodge station wagon has a metal chassis, gray-tinted plastic windows, brown interior, bw, and was made in Hong Kong.
a. yellow, wood-grain tampo on sides $6 - 8
a2. same as a, lighter tampo, red-brown int., Mexico (1984) 6 - 8

1698-a

Cadillac Seville 1698 - 80mm - 1982
This 1977 model has a metal chassis, gray-tinted plastic windows, sun roof, red interior, bw, and was made in Hong Kong.
a. gray, purple tampo on sides $6 - 8
a2. same as a, Malaysia 6 - 8
b. mtlfk gold, blue-tinted plastic window (1983) 4 - 6
b2. 4356, same as b, gyg (1983) 20 - 25
b3. same as b, purple tampo on sides, blue-tinted window, Canadian 3-pack only (1983) 70 - NA
b4. same as b, red int., Mexico (1986) 60 - 70
b5. same as b, ww, Mexico (1987) 125 - 150
b6. same as b; gyg, Mexico (1987) 80 - 100
c. gray, gyg, France (1983) 70 - 80

1698-c2

c2. gray, same as c, blue tampo "Le Club Des Maitres" (Masters of the Universe) on hood, never in bp, France (1986) 110 - NA
c3. same as c2, "Le Club Des Maitres" in yellow 150 - NA
d. tan, same as f, blue-tinted window, gray int., no country of origin on base, Mexico (1984) 6 - 12

5182-a

Camaro Z-28 5182 - 77mm - 1982
This Hong Kong-made Chevrolet has a metal chassis, black-tinted plastic windows, and gw.
a. white; purple, red & yellow tampo on top & sides; "Z-28" on sides 5 - 7
a2. same as a, "Camaro" on base 5 - 7

5182-b

b. gray; 2 small orange stripes on hood; orange & red stripe with "Z-28" on sides (1983) 30 - 35
c. mtlfk gray, same as b (1983) 6 - 8
c2. same as c, Malaysia (1983) 6 - 8
d. 5892, gold chrome, 2 small orange stripes on hood, orange & red stripe w/"Z-28" on sides, Mattel mail-in: 1¢ & 2 proofs of purchase, never found in bp (1984) 20 - NA
e. mtlfk dark red; same as e; white, yellow & blue tampo (1984) 6 - 8

9344-f

f. 9344; white; red, yellow & black stripe tampo w/"Camaro" & "Z-28" on sides; Stamper 3-pack only (1985) 15 - NA
g. red; blue, black & yellow tampo with "Camaro Z-28" on sides; #33 (1986) 20 - 40

Values are shown in U.S. dollars, first price is for mint, second is for mint packaged vehicles only. See pages 15-16 for grading guide to determine value for cars in lesser conditions.

Camaro Z-28-g

g2. same as g, uh, #33 (1991) 6 - 8
g3. same as g, black plastic base, bw, #33 (1992) 8 - 12
g4. same as g3, uh, #33 (1992) 8 - 30
g5. same as g4, black metal base, #33 (1992) 15 - 18
h. 2179; orange; purple, yellow & blue tampo w/"Camaro Z-28" on sides; blacked-out plastic window; Park 'n Plates (1989) 6 - 8
h2. same as h, black replaces purple in tampo (1990) 20 - 25
h3. same as h, uh, 20-car gift pack only (1990) 20 - 25
h4. same as h3, black base, #33 (1992) 20 - 75

Camaro Z-28-i

i. no #; white; red & blue stripes, yellow "1" & "Getty" outlined in red on sides; Getty station give-away only, never in bp (1989) 8 - NA

Camaro Z-28-j

j. no #; white; blue, orange & black stripe tampo on top & sides; blacked-out windows; gw. Double Barrel Stunt set only (1989) 10 - NA

5182-k

k. purple; yellow, white & green tampo w/"Camaro Z-28" on sides; Hot Wheels cereal only; never in bp (1990) 10 - NA

5182-l

l. purple; black plastic chassis; orange, lt. green & yellow tampo on sides; blacked-out windows; bw. McDonald's promo, later in bp, #33 (1991) 10 - 12

5182-m

m. orange; yellow, magenta & blue tampo on sides. McDonald's promo, later in bp, #33 (1991) 10 - 20

Camaro Z-28-n

n. no #; blue; red, pink & yellow tampo on sides & hood; blacked-out windows; uh. Track set only, never in bp 8 - NA

5182-o

o. orange, "Camaro" in orange on windshield, red Hot Wheels logo on rear window, blue-tinted windows, black metal base, bw. Chevrolet 5-Pack only (1995) 3 - NA
o2. same as o, uh (1995) 2 - NA
o3. same as o, sp7 (1995) 2 - NA
o4. 12922, same as o, sp5, #449 (1996) 8 - 10
o5. same as o4, sp3, #449 (1996) 4 - 6

Camaro Z-28-p

p. blue plastic body, metal base, yellow & orange flames, blacked-out windows, orange Hot Wheels logo on windshield, scw. Criss-Cross Crash set only (1995) 8 - NA
q. 15775, white, black metal base, blue-tinted windows, sp5, #504 (1996) 4 - 6
q2. same as q, sp3, #504 (1997) 2 - 4
q3. same as q, sp7, #504 (1997) 2 - 4
r. lime green plastic body; black metal base; blacked-out windows; red, black, dk. blue & white tampo design; "4" & "Crossover Setup" on sides, sp5. Figure 8 Racers 5-pack only (1998) 2 - NA
r2. same as r, ho5, #853 (1998) 3 - 5
r3. same as r2, unpainted base 2 - 3

Camaro Z-28-s

s. mtlfk blue; red, white & gold stars-&-stripes tampo on sides & hood; "30" on roof; sp3; #1078 (1999) 2 - 3

Camaro Z-28-t

t. white; black, orange & purple tampo w/"Alienz" on hood; sp5. Alien Attack 5-pack, Thailand (1999) 2 - 3
t2. same as t, Malaysia 2 - 3

Camaro Z-28-u

u. black; black metal chassis; black plastic windows; red, white & gold stars-&-stripes tampo on sides & hood; "30" on roof; lwgd; #124 (2000) 2 - 3

Camaro Z-28-v

v. mtlfk gray; black metal chassis; black plastic windows; red, yellow, white & black tampo with face & "Fire-Eater" on sides & hood; dw3; #2 in Mad Maniax Series; #018 (2000) 25 - 30
v2. same as v, lwch, #2 in Mad Maniax Series, #018 (2000) 2 - 3
w. white; black metal chassis; black plastic windows; dark blue, gray & yellow tampo w/"5" on sides; "Big Air Stunt Ramp" on hood; scw; Malaysia; Big Air Stunt Set (2001) 10 - NA

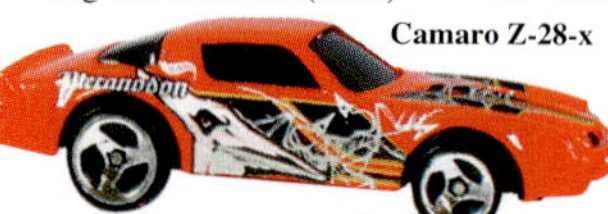
Camaro Z-28-x

x. red; chassis & windows; gray, black & pink tampo on sides & hood w/"pterandoon" on sides; #4 in Fossil Fuel Series; Malaysia; #044 (2001) 2 - 3
y. purple, metal chassis, black & white design on sides & hood, sp5, #146 (2001) 3 - 5
y2. same as y, mtlfk gray chassis, #146 (2001) 2 - 3
z. red, black windows, gray & black tampo on sides & hood, sp5, China. Pavement Pounder pack, sold in Disneyland (2001) 8 - 10

3254-a

Construction Crane 3254 - 85mm - 1982
This Hong Kong-made 8-wheel heavy-duty crane has a black plastic chassis & interior, black movable boom and eight bw.
a. yellow $15 - 18
a2. same as a, made in Malaysia 10 - 12
a3. same as a, made in France (1983) 25 - 30

3255-a

Datsun 200SX 3255 - 76mm - 1982
This model has a metal chassis, lift-up hood to show a metal engine, black plastic interior & bumpers, blue-tinted plastic windows, gw, and was made in Hong Kong.
a. white; orange, red-orange & yellow tampo w/"200-SX" & "Datsun" on sides 5 - 7
a2. same as a, dk. red replaces red-orange in tampo, made in Malaysia 20 - 25
b. yellow; same as a; black, purple & blue tampo; Hot Ones 3-pack only 15 - NA
c. mtlfk gold, same as a2 (1983) 4 - 6

5083-d

d. 5083; maroon; white, yellow & black tampo w/"Datsun 200 SX" & racing decals on sides (1984); Canada only; bp w/2 winner's flags pictured 100 - 135
e. red-brown, same as d, Mexico (1985) 90 - 115

3250-a2

Firebird Funny Car 3250 - 79mm - 1982
This Hong Kong-made concept funny-car dragster has a metal chassis & interior, lift-up body to show an unpainted metal engine, engine top sticking through the hood & windshield, blue-tinted plastic windows and bw. Similar castings – 12795 Side-Splitter (1995), 11390 Spawnmobile (1995)
a. magenta; yellow, orange & black bird on sides; orange & black bird on hood; yellow & black headlights $10 - 12
a2. same as a; bird on hood is yellow & black; white & black headlights 8 - 10
a3. same as a2, Malaysia 8 - 10

3250-b

b. white; red, yellow & black flame tampo w/"Fireball" & racing decals on sides; red & yellow flame tampo on hood; black headlights 10 - 12
b2. same as b, Malaysia 10 - 12
c. mtlfk magenta, same as a2, small flames added to side of fenders (1983) 4 - 6
c2. same as c, limited for 30th Anniv. w/card in window box (1998) 4 - 6

Firebird Funny Car-d

d. no #; black; same as c; orange, purple & red side tampos; orange & purple hood tampo w/purple & white headlights; first only thru Kellogg's mail-in offer, later 50¢ at Mattel Toy Club (1986) 8 - NA

1483-e

e. 1483; mtlfk blue; yellow, red & black tampo on hood & sides; "The Speed Monster" & racing decals on sides; black & white headlights (1987) 12 - 15

5121-f

f. 5121; yellow; orange, magenta & blue striping tampo on sides & top; "2" & racing decals on sides (1988) 6 - 8
f2. 5121, yellow, same as f, black replaces magenta in tampo (1989) 6 - 8
f3. same as f2, orange & blue in roof tampo are reversed (1990) 45 - 60
g. no #, chrome, "20th Hot Wheels Anniversary" engraved on top, only in 3-packs (1988) 10 - 12
h. no #, gold chrome, "20th Hot Wheels Anniversary" engraved on top, only in 3-packs (1988) 10 - 12

Firebird Funny Car-i

i. no #, lemon yellow, same as c, "Pennzoil" on sides & hood, pink metal base, 3-pack only (1991) 8 - NA
i2. same as i, yellow metal base (1991) 8 - NA

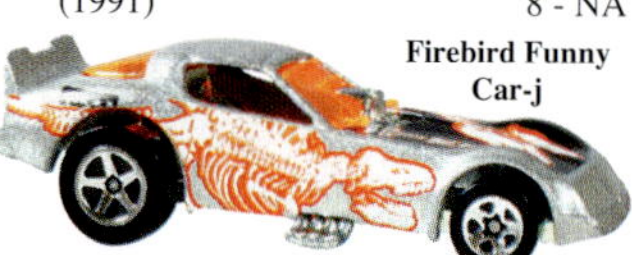
Firebird Funny Car-j

j. mtlfk gray; orange-tinted windows; orange, white & black tampo with "TRex" & dinosaur on sides & hood; sp5; #3 in the Fossil Fuel Series; Malaysia; #043 (2001) 2 - 4

3253-a

Ford Dump Truck 3253 - 76mm - 1982
This Hong Kong-made model has a metal chassis, gray plastic lift-up dumper, chrome plastic interior, clear plastic windows, & bw.
a. green; yellow, white & black tampo "Sunset Trucking" on sides $7 - 9

a2. same as a, Malaysia 7 - 9

3257-a

Front Runnin' Fairmont 3257 - 76mm - 1982
This Ford Fairmont stock car has a metal chassis, gray plastic windows, black plastic interior, gw, and was made in Hong Kong.
Similar casting: 2620 Race Ace (1986)
a. red; yellow, white & black tampo w/Hot Wheels logo, "27" & race decals on sides; white, yellow, & orange flame tampo w/"27" on hood; "Fireball Jr." twice on roof $10 - 12
a2. same as a, Malaysia 10 - 12

3259-a

Jeep CJ-7 3259 - 68mm - 1982
This Hong Kong-made model has a metal chassis, clear plastic windshield, black plastic interior, black roll bar, black spare tire in back, and bw.
Similar casting: 9375 Roll Patrol Jeep CJ (1985)
a. white; orange, red & black bird tampo on hood; white windshield frame $5 - 7
a2. same as a, Malaysia 5 - 7
a3. 3953, same as a, no white windshield frame (1988) 4 - 6
b. mtlfk red-brown, same as a2, no white windshield frame (1983) 10 - 12
b2. same as b, white frame around window (1983) 10 - 12
b3. same as b, tan int. & spare tire (1983) 4 - 6
b4. 4362, same as b, gyg (1983) 25 - 30
b5. 4362, same as b, gyw (1985) 35 - 45

9543-c

c. 9543; yellow; black, green & red snake tampo on hood; gyw (1985) 25 - 30

2539-d

d. 2539; white; maroon, orange & red ribbon w/"Jeep" twice on hood; red int. & spare tire; bw (1986) 5 - 7
d2. same as d, gyw (1986) 30 - 35
d3. same as d, ct (1989) 12 - 15
e. no #, yellow, same tampo as c, orange & white tampo. Kellogg's promo (1985) 8 - NA
g. 3954, yellow, same as d; purple replaces maroon in tampo (1988) 5 - 7

3260-a

Land Lord 3260 - 70mm - 1982
This Hong Kong-made racer concept model has a metal chassis, exposed plastic engine, unpainted metal spoiler in front, yellow-tinted plastic dome roof, chrome plastic interior, and bw.
a. orange; lt. orange, red & black tampo on top; "Street is Neat" on spoiler $5 - 7
a2. same as a, Malaysia 5 - 7

9037-a

Malibu Grand Prix 9037 - 75mm - 1982
This Hong Kong-made Grand Prix concept racer has a metal chassis & interior, exposed metal engine and bw.
Similar castings: 8273 El Rey Special (1974), 9037 Formula P.A.C.K. (1976), 4372 Lightning Gold (1984)
a. black; yellow, red & blue tampo on top; "1" & "Malibu Grand Prix" in front; "Goodyear" on spoiler $5 - 7
a2. same as a, Malaysia 5 - 7
a3. 4372, same as a2, gyg 20 - 25

Malibu Grand Prix-b

b. no #, mtlc blue, Hot Wheels logo on rear spoiler, red stripes & white "2" w/black outline on front & sides, Malaysia. Kellogg's promo only or sold at Mattel Toy Club (1985) 8 - NA

3261-b

Mercedes 380 SEL 3261 - 77mm - 1982
This Hong Kong-made model has a black metal chassis, clear windows, tan plastic interior and gw.
a. gray $25 - 30
a2. same as a, white int., no country on base, Mexico (1984) 20 - 25
b. mtlfk silver, same as a 5 - 7
b2. same as b, bw 5 - 7
b3. 4363, same as b, gyg 20 - 25
c. black, same as b, unpainted metal base, white interior, France, Europe only (1984) 20 - 25
c2. same as c, gyg 90 - 110
c3. same as c2, white BP logo on roof 125 - NA
c4. 3856 or 9986, same as c2, black metal base, uh, #92 (1990) 15 - 18
c5. same as c3, gw, #92 (1990) 40 - 45
c6. 9220, same as c4, Park 'n Plates (1990) 10 - 12
c7. 9986, same as c3, uhgd (1991) 18 - 25
c8. same as c6, hoc, #92 (1991) 18 - 20
d. 4206, white, same as a, white metal base, Malaysia, uh (1989) 5 - 7

Mercedes 380 SEL-e

e. 3368; chrome; black, yellow & pink design w/black "Mercedes" on sides; yellow "Cal Custom" on windshield; pink metal base & int.; tw; California Custom (1990) 15 - 18
f. no #, mtlfk blue, gray int., silver metal chassis, uh, City Bank Sto & Go set only 5 - 7
g. blue, blue glitter, yellow-tinted windows, yellow int., metal base, uh, #184 (1992) 3 - 5
g2. same as g, hoc, #184 8 - 10

3261-h

h. mtlfk silver; blue, pink & purple tampo; gray-tinted windows; tan int.; uho; Malaysia; Revealers 3 - 5
i. white, same as h, black int., uhr, Revealers 3 - 5
j. Day-Glo yellow, same as h, gray int., uho, Revealers 3 - 5
k. pink; red metalflakes, black-tinted windows, black int., uh, #229 (1993) 5 - 8
l. 12346, dark metalflake red, uh, #253 (1994) 4 - 6
l2. same as l, sp5, #253 (1995) 4 - 6
l3. same as l, dw3, #253 (1996) 2 - 4
l4. same as l, sp7, #253 (1996) 2 - 4
l5. same as l, sp7gd, Canada only (1997) 2 - 4
l6. same as l4, silver base, #253 (1997) 2 - 4

Mercedes 380 SEL-m

m. white, gold painted base, tan int., tinted windows, dw3, #767 (1998) 2 - 4

Mercedes 380 SEL-n

n. black, mtlfk gold chassis, lt. brown int., tinted windows, gold stripe & "Custom 380 SL" on sides, lchgd. Showroom Specials 5-pack only (1998) 2 - NA
n2. same as n, Thailand, #889 (1999) 2 - 4

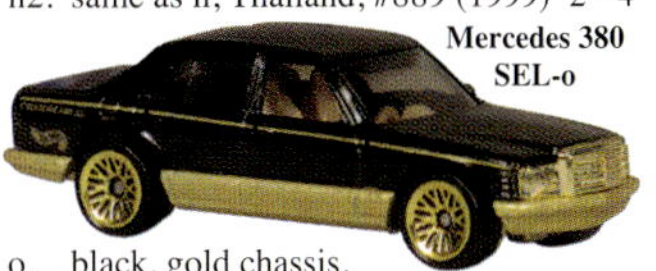
Mercedes 380 SEL-o

o. black, gold chassis, clear windows, tan int., gold stripe w/"Custom 380 SL" on sides, lwgd, Thailand, #889 (1999) 2 - 3

Mercedes 380 SEL-p

p. purple, black chassis & int., tinted windows, gray tampo on sides & rear window, black & white license plate, "AVTAZYN" in back, sp6pp. #2 in Final Run Series, limited to 35,000 (1999) 5 - 7

3911-a

Mercedes 540K 3911 - 80mm - 1982
Based on the classic 1937 Mercedes, this model has a metal chassis, clear windshield, black plastic interior, tan plastic removable roof, bw, and was made in Hong Kong.
a. red $6 - 8
a2. same as a, ww, Malaysia 5 - 7
a3. dk. red, same as a, France, Europe only (1983) 8 - 10

Mercedes 540K-b

b. black, same as a, Malaysia, #18 (1988) 6 - 8
b2. black, same as a, ww (1988) 4 - 6
c. no #, chrome, "20th Hot Wheels Anniversary" engraved on hood, 3-packs only (1988) 12 - NA
d. no #, gold chrome; "20th Hot Wheels Anniversary" engraved on hood, 3-packs only (1988) 12 - NA
e. white, same as a2, red interior, #134 (1990) 3 - 5
f. blue, red glitter, lt. blue plastic roof, red int., bw #164 4 - 6
f2. same as f, sp5, #164 (1995) 2 - 4
f3. same as f, sp7, #164 (1995) 2 - 4
f4. same as f, sp3, #164 (1996) 2 - 4
f5. same as f, dw3, #164 (1996) 2 - 4
f6. same as f, ho5, #164 (1996) 2 - 4

Mercedes 540K-g

g. mtlfk red, white Hot Wheels logo in back, tan top & int., clear windshield, gold-plated headlights & radiator, iwgd. 16-piece FAO Schwarz Gold Series Collection, limited to 3000 (1994) 12 - NA
h. gold-plated, gold-plated base, clear windshield, red int., black plastic roof, iwgd. FAO Schwarz 24K Gold Classics 3-pack only (1995) 12 - NA
i. no #, mtlfk gold, green roof & int., clear windshield, sp7. 2-pack only sold by Avon (1997) 4 - NA

Mercedes 540K-j

j. no #, mtlfk green, tan roof & int., clear windshield, rrch. 60th Anniversary '37 European Classics 2-car set (1997) 8 - NA

Mercedes 540K-k

k. no #, white, tan roof & int., clear windshield, gold pipes, lwgd. Target Cruisin' America 6-pack only (1997) 8 - NA

Mercedes 540K-l

l. mtlfk purple, black int., clear windshield, turquoise roof, turquoise stripe on sides, large lwch, #788 (1998) 2 - 4
l2. same as l, small lwch, #788 (1998) 2 - 4
l3. same as l, sp3, #788 (1998) 2 - 4
m. red; black roof & int.; clear windshield; black & gold tampo on sides, hood & trunk; "TH" on trunk; sp5. #1 in 1999 Treasure Hunt Series, #929 (1999) 12 - 15

Mercedes 540K-m

Mercedes 540K-n

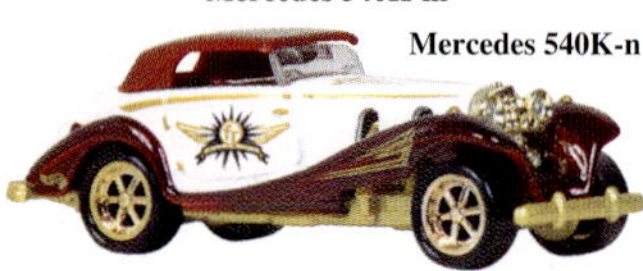

n. white, gold chassis, mtlfk dk. red fenders, dk. red plastic roof, tan int., clear windshield, gold & black tampo on sides, hood & trunk w/"Final Run" on sides, black & white license plate, "540FINL-RN" in back, iwgd. #9 in Final Run Series, limited to 35,000 (1999) 5 - 7

5180-a

P-928 (Porsche 928) 5180 - 75mm - 1982
This Hong Kong-made Porsche 928 has a metal chassis, metal headlights sticking thru the body, black plastic windows, and bw.
Similar castings: 7292 Predator (1984), 9537 Nightstreaker (1985)

a. red; yellow & orange tampo on top & sides; "Turbo" on hood; "928 Turbo" on sides $12 - 15
a2. same as a, gw 10 - 12
a3. 4371, same as a, gyg 30 - 35

5180-b

b. white; yellow, red & black tampo w/"928" on hood & sides; 3-pack only (1983) 15 - NA
c. no #, green, sp5. Porsche 5-pack only (1997) 2 - NA
c2. same as c, lwch (1997) 2 - NA
c3. same as c, dw3 (1997) 2 - NA
d. white, black windows & lwch, #817 (1998) 2 - 4

P-928-e

e. gray; black, white, red & yellow tampo w/Porsche logo & "World Racers 9" on sides & hood, race decals on sides; Thailand. Flag Flyers 5-pack only (1998) 2 - NA
f. mtlfk gold, ho5, #1085 (1999) 2 - 3
g. mtlfk green; mtlfk gray base; black windows; black, gold & dark red design on sides; ho5; China; #103 (2001) 2 - 3

2023-a

Pepsi Challenger 2023 - 75mm - 1982
This Hong Kong-made funny-car dragster has a metal chassis, lift-up body to show a metal engine & interior, and bw.
Similar castings: 2023 Army Funny Car (1978), 2881 Human Torch (1979), 9521 Screamin' (1985)

a. yellow; red, white & blue tampo w/"Don 'Snake' Prudhomme," " Pepsi Challenger," Pepsi logo, race sponsor decals & Hot Wheels logo on sides; headlights, snake, Pepsi logo & "Pepsi Challenger" on front $15 - 20
a2. same as a, Malaysia 15 - 20

2023-a3

a3. same as a2, no "Don 'Snake' Prudhomme" on sides or snake on hood 25 - 30

3281-a

Peugeot 505 3281 - 75mm - 1982
This model has a metal chassis, black plastic interior & bumpers, clear plastic windows, bw, and was made in Hong Kong.

a. dark blue $5 - 7
b. mtlfk gold, same as a (1983) 4 - 6

3281-c

c. blue, same as a, Mexico (1983) 50 - 60
c2. blue, same as c, blue-tinted windows, Hong Kong (Italy) (1983) 75 - 100
d. mtlfk red, black int., blue-tinted windows, Hong Kong (Italy) (1983) 75 - 100
e. black, same as a, Mexico (1983) 60 - 70
e2. black, same as e, brown plastic fenders & bottom border (1985) 75 - NA
f. lt. brown, same as a, never in bp, France (1985), Europe & Canada only 35 - NA

3256-a

Rapid Transit 3256 - 82mm - 1982
This Hong Kong-made city bus concept model has a plastic body, metal chassis & interior, unpainted metal headlights sticking thru the body, blue-tinted plastic windshield & left front side window, black-tinted plastic windows on sides, and bw.
Similar casting: 3502 Bus Boys (1993 Tattoo Machines)

a. white; red, orange & yellow stripe on sides & back; red "RTD" on sides; black tampo in back w/"Get the news first in the City Gazette" in red & yellow $30 - 35

3256-a2

a2. same as a, black tampo is blue 8 - 10
a3. same as a2, Malaysia 8 - 10

3256-b

b. yellow; chrome int.; black tampo w/"School Bus No. 3," "Stop When Lights Flash," "City of Hot Wheels" & "Max. Cap. 52" on sides; no back tampo; clear windows (some packages may call this Team Bus) (1984) 8 - 10
b2. same as b; black-tinted windows, Pop 'n Play set only (1988) 4 - 5
b3. same as b2, black interior (1985) 4 - 5

3875-c

c. 3875; white; same as b; red & blue tampo w/"American Football Team" & stars on sides; chrome int.; blue-tinted windows; International series as Team Bus only (1990) 30 - 35
c2. same as c, black int. (1990) 25 - 30

2019-a

Sheriff Patrol 2019 - 75mm - 1982
This Hong Kong-made model has a metal chassis, blue-tinted plastic windows, black interior, and bw.
Similar castings: 2019 Highway Patrol (1978), 2639 Fire Chaser (1979), no number - Airport Security (1983)

a. black; 4 white doors; "Sheriff," "701" & yellow sheriff's star on sides; yellow "Sheriff" & white "701" rectangle on top $4 - 6
a2. same as a, Malaysia 4 - 6
a3. 4004, same as a, only front doors are white (1988) 4 - 6

9526-b

b. 9526, mtlfk blue, same as a, only front doors are white (1985) 4 - 6
b2. same as b, #59 (1985) 4 - 6
b3. same as b, four white doors (1985) 4 - 6
b4. same as b2, tan int. (1985) 35 - 40
b5. no #, mtlfk blue, same as b2, no roof tampo, Hot Wheels cereal only, not in bp (1990) 8 -NA
c. black; yellow, blue & white tampo w/"Police," "Radar Equipped," "To Serve and Protect," "123" & star on sides; "Police 123" on roof; star on hood; tan int.; #59 (1990) 8 - 10

2019-c2

c2. same as c, turquoise not blue in tampo, #59 (1991) 10 - 12
c3. same as c2, sp7, #59 (1996) 12 - 15
c4. same as c2, black int. (1996) 2 - 4
d. 9228, same as a2, tan int., "104" not "701" & "Police" not "Sheriff" in tampo, Park 'n Plates (1990) 8 - 10
e. no #, blue mtlfk, same as c, gray int., black not blue in tampo, City Police Station Sto & Go set only (1996) 5 - 7

1691-f

f. 1691, chrome, no tampo, pattern etched on plastic body, black int., gray-tinted windows, bw, #59 (1992) 4 - 6
f2. 1691, gray-chrome, same as f, tan int., gray-tinted windows (1992) 3 - 5

Sheriff Patrol-g

g. no #; black; black int.; tinted windows; white side doors; "Police" in blue, "To Protect & Serve" in black on doors; "96" in black on white roof; sp5. Action Pack Police Force set only (1997) 5 - NA

3251-a

Sunagon 3251 - 73mm - 1982
This Hong Kong-made Volkswagen Vanagon Camper has a metal chassis, tan plastic removable top, clear plastic windows, brown plastic interior & motorcycle in back and bw.

a. orange & tan $10 - 12
a2. same as a, Malaysia 8 - 10
b. 4340, mtlfk blue & lt. blue, same as a, lt. blue removable roof, tan int. & motorcycle (1983), Extras series 8 - 10
c. blue, same as b, light blue removable roof, white int. & motorcycle, Mexico (1985) 30 - 35
d. dk. blue, same as c, Mexico (1986) 30 - 35
e. metalflake blue, same as c, Mexico (1987) 25 - 30

5181-a3

Taxi 5181 - 72mm - 1982
This model has a metal chassis, black plastic taxi sign on top, black-tinted plastic windows, gw, and was made in Hong Kong.

a. yellow; red, black & white tampo w/"U.S.A. Taxi Service," "555-2745" & "Radio Dispatched" on sides $8 - 10
a2. same as a, made in Malaysia 8 - 10
a3. same as a, no white or black in tampo, no "Radio Dispatched" on sides, clear windows, no int., France (1986), Europe & Canada only 12 - 15

3912-a

Trash Truck 3912 - 82mm - 1982
This Hong Kong-made model has a black plastic chassis & exhaust stack, white-tinted plastic windows, and bw.

a. orange; green, black & lt. blue tampo; "Dept. of Sanitation" on sides $10 - 12
a2. same as a, made in Malaysia 10 - 12
a3. same as a2; black, blue & green tampo (1985) 18 - 20
a4. same as a2, black & yellow tampo, Mexico (1987) 35 - 45

MEGAFORCE SERIES (1982)

This series was issued on its own blistercard which pictured Tac-Com, Megadestroyer 1 and a never-issued Motorcycle. The package read "Megaforce - From the Motion Picture" but did not mention Hot Wheels anywhere. Since the movie bombed, Mattel stopped production and some of these vehicles are difficult to find.

5272-a

Battle Tank 5272 - 78mm - 1982
This Malaysia-made model has an olive plastic base, movable olive plastic turret with

Values are shown in U.S. dollars, first price is for mint, second is for mint packaged vehicles only. See pages 15-16 for grading guide to determine value for cars in lesser conditions.

long gun barrel, and small black wheels.
Similar castings: 7655 Tough Customer (1975), 9372 Big Bertha (1985)

a. olive; green & tan camouflage tampo on top $20 - 25

5268-a

Megadestroyer 1 5268 - 73mm - 1982
This Malaysia-made military sprint buggy has a light brown metal chassis, blacked-out plastic windshield, black plastic guns on the sides, movable rockets on top, a movable black machine gun in back, and black bw.
Similar castings: 5269 Megadestroyer 2 (1982 Megaforce), 9373 Super Cannon (1985), 15968 Enforcer (1996)

a. lt. brown; brown, dk. brown & black tampo $20 - 25

5269-a

Megadestroyer 2 5269 - 73mm - 1982
This Malaysia-made military sprint buggy has a black metal chassis, blacked-out plastic windshield, black plastic guns on the sides, movable rockets on top, a movable black machine gun in the back, and black bw.
Similar castings: 5268 Megadestroyer 1 (1982 Megaforce), 9373 Super Cannon (1985), 15968 Enforcer (1996)

a. black $35 - 40

5270-a

Personnel Carrier 5270 - 75mm - 1982
Based on a Ford Bronco, this Hong Kong-made model has a metal chassis, blue-tinted plastic windows, chrome plastic interior & motorcycle in back, dark red plastic camper shell and bw.
Similar casting: 1690 Bronco 4-Wheeler (1981)

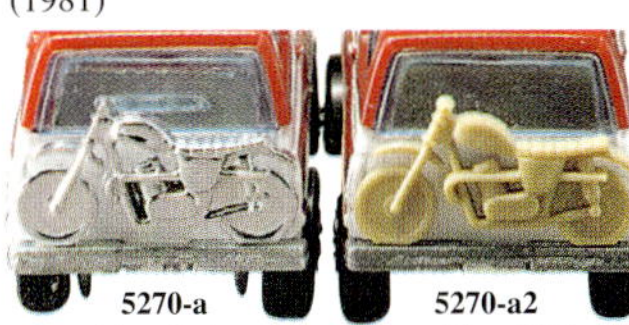
5270-a 5270-a2

a. white; dark red tampo on sides $60 - 80
a2. same as a; tan int. & motorcycle 20 - 25

5273-a

Tac-Com 5273 - 75mm - 1982
This concept model has a black plastic chassis & interior, black-tinted windows, bwbk, and was made in Hong Kong.
Similar castings: 2855 Space Van (1979, 1984), 3304 Rescue Squad (1981)

a. lt. brown; brown & dk. brown tampo on sides $25 - 30

1983

There were ninety-six total models. Twenty new models and almost fifty new colors and/or tampos were introduced. A new line with synthetic rubber tires with "Goodyear" on the sides first sold as Real Riders. Another new series was Extras: models which could be modified with various extra parts in the package. All groups were issued in their own special blister-packs. Mattel also reissued Hot Ones and Workhorses.

3919-a

'40s Ford 2-Door 3919 - 77mm - 1983
This 1940 Ford sedan has a metal chassis, tan plastic interior, clear plastic windows, bw, and was made in Hong Kong.
Similar casting: 9523 Fat Fendered '40 (1985)

a. black; red, yellow & orange flame tampo on sides & hood $15 - 18
a2. same as a 15 - 18
a3. same as a2, gyg 40 - 50
a4. same as a3, gyw 70 - 85

3913-a

'67 Camaro 3913 - 70mm - 1983
This Hong Kong-made model has a metal chassis, lift-up hood, black plastic interior, clear plastic windows, and bw.
Similar casting: 6208 Custom Camaro (1968)

a. red; yellow, white & black flame tampo w/"67 Camaro" on sides $60 - 85
a2. same as a, Malaysia 55 - 75

3913-b

b. mtlfk lime yellow, no tampo, black roof, 15th Anniv. Belt Buckle 3-pack only (1983) 45 - NA

2103-c

c. 2103; mtlfk blue; white, pink & lt. green splash tampo on sides & top; pink int.; yellow "Cal Custom" on windshield; clear window, silver tw, California Custom (1991) 50 - 70

'67 Camaro-d

d. no #, mtlfk blue, 2 white stripes on hood & trunk, clear plastic window, white int., red-stripe rr. Mattel give-away, limited to 5000, baggie only (1995) 60 - 70

13351-e

e. 13351, white, orange stripes on hood & trunk, white Hot Wheels logo on rear window, orange int., clear window, gyg, #3 in Treasure Hunt series, #355 (1995) 200 - 350

3913-f

f. gold-plated, white int., red FAO Schwarz logo, black "FAO Schwarz" on trunk, pcgd. 16-piece FAO Schwarz Gold Series Collection II, limited to 4000 (1995) 20 - NA
g. chrome, tinted window, red int. & Hot Wheels logo on back window, rsw. Service Merchandise 16-piece Classic American Car Collection only, limited to 5000 (1995) 15 - NA
h. mtlfk dk. red, white int., tinted window, bw. Chevy 5-pack only (1995) 20 - NA
i. white, clear plastic window, blue int., red Hot Wheels logo on rear window, sp5. Then & Now 8-pack (1995) 8 - NA

'67 Camaro-j

j. 13845; black; 2 large white stripes on hood & trunk; "Greater Seattle Toy Show 1995" in red, white & blue on roof; clear window; black int.; iwgd; limited to 8000 (1995) 25 - 30

14874-k

k. 14874, white, black stripes across front of hood, clear window, black int., pc. Pat's Collectibles, limited to 7000 (1995) 35 - 40

'67 Camaro-l

l. yellow, metal base, black int., tinted window, 2 black stripes on hood & trunk, yellow Hot Wheels logo on rear window, sp5, #448 (1995) 6 - 8
l2. same as l, sp7, 60s Muscle Cars 5-pack only (1997) 2 - NA
l3. same as l, ho5, #448 6 - 8
m. 15242; green; red wavy lines, red & yellow Hot Wheels logos on sides & top; clear window; red int.; sp5; #4 in Mod Bod Series, #399 (1996) 6 - 10
m2. same as m, sp7 (1996) 60 - 75

'67 Camaro-m3

m3. same as m, tinted windows, #399 (1996) 20 - 30

3913-n

n. red; white stripes all over; "USA" & five Olympic circles in red, green, yellow, black & blue on sides; tan int.; clear window; pcgd. American Victory Olympic 3-pack only (1996) 45 - NA

'67 Camaro-o

o. orange, white stripes on sides, clear window, black int. & grill, gych. '60s Muscle Cars 4-pack only (1996) 12 - NA

'67 Camaro-p

p. 15929, blue, white top & int., white trim on sides, clear window, gych. Issued in black box by Hill's Dept. Stores as limited edition (1996) 40 - 45
q. mtlfk gray, clear window, black int., sp7; Camaro 5-pack only (1996) 3 - NA
q2. same as q, sp5 (1997) 2 - NA
q3. same as q, sp3 (1997) 2 - NA

'67 Camaro-r

r. no #; green; clear windows; black & white int.; white stripes on hood & front fenders; "Camaro" in white & red, black & white racing flags on sides; silver door handles; gych. 30th Anniv. of '67 Muscle Cars 3-pack (1997) 8 - NA

'67 Camaro-s

s. no #; dk. blue; clear windows; white int.; black, white & yellow tampo w/"15" on sides, hood, & trunk; "Sunoco Camaro" & "Penske" on sides; rrch. 30th Anniv. of Camaro gift set only (1997) 8 - NA
t. pearl white, tinted windows, black interior, sp7 w/red stripe. Designer Collection 5-pack, General Mills mail-in (1997) 6 - NA

'67 Camaro-u

u. red, same as r, sp5 w/"Goodyear" & "Eagle." Limited to 15,000 for M & D Toys for Camaro Enthusiasts Magazine, 1967 RS/SS Camaro (1998) 20 - 25

'67 Camaro-v

v. black; mtlfk gold top; black metal base; black int.; clear window; red & white tampo w/"13" on sides, hood & trunk; gych. Limited to 10,000 for Edelbrock, '68 Trans-Am Camaro (1998) 20 - 25

'67 Camaro-w

w. mtlfk blue; white int.; clear window; red, yellow & white tampo; Hot Wheels logo, "1" & race decals on sides; "Hot Wheels" & "1" on roof;

Values are shown in U.S. dollars, first price is for mint, second is for mint packaged vehicles only. See pages 15-16 for grading guide to determine value for cars in lesser conditions.

'67 Camaro-y

sp5. #1 in Race Team Series IV, #725 (1998) 4 - 6

w2. same as w, China, playset only (1999) 6 - NA

w3. same as w, sp3, #725 (1999) 2 - 3

x. unpainted, yellow int., clear window, sp5. #1 in Race Team Series IV, 1998 Hot Wheels Convention, #725 (1998) 175 - 300

y. blue; white int.; tinted window; orange, yellow & white tampo design on sides, hood & roof; flames on sides; sp5. #3 in X-Ray Cruiser series, #947 (1999) 3 - 6

y2. same as y; sp3 (1999) 2 - 4

'67 Camaro-z

z. white; black top; yellow, orange, black, blue & white tampo w/El Paso, TX Police Dept. shield, stripes & "12" on sides; "El Paso, Texas Police" on trunk; "12" on roof; "Dedicated To Serve" on hood; pc. Limited to 25,000 in Cop Rods Series for K•B Toys (1999) 5 - 7

'67 Camaro-aa

aa. white; blue int.; blue-tinted window; dk. blue & red tampo w/Cubs logo on sides & roof; "3" on hood; different Cubs logo on trunk; sp5. Limited edition 2-pack give-away at Chicago Cubs baseball game (1999) 15 - NA

ab. gray; blue-tinted windows; black int.; red, yellow & black tampo w/"Stunt 99" & race decals on sides & hood; sp5; #1014 (2000) 2 - 3

'67 Camaro-ac

ac. red; clear windows; white int. & roof; white, yellow & red tampo w/"Kookie" on sides, stripes on hood & trunk, Kookie figure on roof, "Otter Pops" on trunk; rrrd; Otter Pops premium (2000) 20 - 25

'67 Camaro-ad

ad. orange; black int.; clear windows; red, black & white tampo w/"Camaro" on sides; stripes on top; Editor's Choice logo on trunk; pc; Thailand; Target Exclusive Editor's Choice series (2000) 6 - 8

'67 Camaro-ae

ae. red; white int.; clear windows; yellow, black & white tampo w/"Ronald McDonald House Charities" & logo on sides & top; rrch; limited to 5000; in baggie for 14th Annual Convention (2000) 30 - 35

'67 Camaro-af

af. white; black roof & int.; clear windows; black, yellow, red & gray tampo w/"Official Convention" & race decals on sides; "Irvine Street Burner 2000" on hood & trunk; 14th Annual Hot Wheels Convention logo on roof; pc. Limited to 2,000 cars, in baggie, 14th Annual Convention (2000) 125 - NA

ag. white, white int., clear windows, red & black tampo w/"Stunt 99" on sides & hood, sp5, China, Power Launcher pack (2001) 5 - 7

ah. turquoise, white int., clear windows, orange & yellow bird tampo on sides, sp5, China, Pavement Pounder pack (2001) 5 - 7

ai. magenta; black int.; clear windows; yellow, black & purple bird tampo on sides; sp3; China; Target Pavement Pounder pack (2001) 5 - 7

aj. magenta; black int.; clear windows; gray, black & blue tampo; sp5; China; Kool Toyz Power Launcher pack (2001) 5 - 7

ak. mtlfk red, white int., clear windows, yellow & black tampo w/"31" on sides, sp5, China, Pavement Pounder pack (2001) 5 - 7

al. mtlfk gray, black int., tinted windows, sp3, China, Pavement Pounder pack (2001) 5 - 7

'67 Camaro-am

am. red, white int., tinted windows, black & white tampo on sides & hood, "Punk Rock" on sides, dw3, Thailand. Issued in Motorin' Music 5-pack (2001) 4 - NA

an. dk. gray-blue; black chassis; black hood; gray int.; clear windows; red & white tampo w/"1," Hot Wheels logo & "Racing" on sides & hood; sp3; China; #139 (2002) 2 - 3

ao. chrome; black int.; chrome windows; red, white & black tampo with Hot Wheels Collectors.com logo on sides, Red Line Club logo on roof, two red stripes on hood & trunk; rrchrl; China. Ltd ed of 5000 by Hot Wheels Collectors.com (2002) 100 - 175

ao2. same as a, stripes are blue. Ltd ed of 10,000 by Hot Wheels Collectors.com (2002) 50 - 100

3928-a

'80s Corvette 3928 - 71mm - 1983

This 1980 Chevrolet Corvette has a gray metal chassis, lift-up hood, tan & red plastic interior, black-tinted plastic roof, clear plastic windows, an gw. Made in Hong Kong. Similar casting: 16306 Corvette Coupe (1996)

a. gray $30 - 35

b. mtlfk gray, same as a, mtlfk gray chassis 8 - 10

c. red, same as a, red chassis, yellow & brown int. (1984) 8 - 10

c2. same as c, black top (1984) 8 - 10

3928-d

d. white, white chassis, orange & black tampo w/"Fuel Injected" & "Corvette" twice on hood, tan & orange int., Turbo Trax set, later at Mattel Toy Club for 50¢ (1986) 20 - NA

1457-e

e. 1457, black, black chassis, red & pink "Corvette" on sides, red & gray int., gray bag in back, Malaysia (1987) 6 - 8

e2. same as e, red bag in back (1989) 15 - 18

e3. same as e, red & tan int., tan bag in back (1989) 15 - 18

3928-f

f. blue; blue chassis; red, white & yellow tampo w/"88" & "Corvette" on sides; red & white tampo on hood; tan & red int.; tan bag in back; #30 (1989) 6 - 8

f2. same as f, red bag in back (1989) 6 - 8

f3. same as f, no hood tampo, tan bag in back (1989) 6 - 8

f4. same as f3, red bag in back (1989) 6 - 8

2170-g

g. 2170, red, red metal chassis, yellow & red stripe w/"Corvette" on sides, black plastic roof, black & red plastic int., red bag in back, gw, Park 'n Plates (1989) 10 - 12

g2. same as g, black bag in back (1989) 15 - 20

h. 9250, gold chrome,, chromed windows, black int., hood cast shut, gw (1988). Billionth Car Anniversary, only sold w/trophy 5 - 7

i. 15781, mtlfk red, black roof, clear windows, gray int., sp5, #503 (1996) 2 - 4

i2. same as i, sp3, #503 (1996) 2 - 4

i3. same as i, lwch, #503 (1997) 2 - 4

i4. same as i, dw3, #503 (1997) 2 - 4

'80s Corvette-j

j. 16909; blue; metal base; white, red & yellow tampo w/"1" & racing decals on sides; Hot Wheels logo on hood; blue-tinted roof; white int.; clear windows; sp5; #4 in Race Team Series III; #536 (1997) 3 - 6

j2. same as j, ho5, #536 (1997) 2 - 4

'80s Corvette-k

k. mtlfk green; black int.; tinted windows; black, white & yellow tampo w/signs & signals on sides; lwch; #2 in Mixed Signals Series; #734 (1998) 2 - 3

l. white, white chassis, white & black int., clear windows, "Corvette Central" in black on hood & trunk, rrch, limited edition for Corvette Central, Malaysia (1999) 15 - 18

m. mtlfk gold, metal base, black interior, tinted windows, lwch, Malaysia, #1103 (1999) 2 - 3

n. mtlfk orange, black roof, gray int., tinted windows, dk. red & gray flame tampo on sides, pr5s, Malaysia, #219 (2001) 2 - 3

n2. same as n, sp5 (2001) 2 - 3

'80s Corvette-o

o. yellow, white int., clear windows, dk. red & green tampo w/"Egypt" on sides, sp3, Thailand, World Tour 5-pack (2001) 3 - NA

3918-a

'80s Firebird 3918 - 75mm - 1983

This Pontiac Firebird has a black plastic chassis, tan plastic interior, clear plastic windows, gw, and was made in Hong Kong.

a. red, yellow firebird tampo on hood $5 - 7

a2. same as a, Malaysia 5 - 7

a3. same as a, darker red card, white tampo, France (1983), Europe only 8 - 15

3918-b

b. chrome, same as a, red tampo, Mattel mail-in, sold for 1¢ & 2 proofs of purchase (1984) 15 - NA

c. black, same as a, red int. (1984) 6 - 8

c2. same as c, bw 6 - 8

c3. same as c, Malaysia (1984) 4 - 6

d. 9341, mtlfk blue, white firebird on hood, Hot Ones Stamper 3-pack only (1985) 15 - NA

9341-d2

d2. same as d, red int. (1985) 50 - NA

5128-e

e. 5128, black, yellow "Formula" on sides, red int., bw (1988) 3 - 5

e2. same as e, bwgd 6 - 8

f. 3971, mtlfk blue, silver firebird on hood, black int., bw (1988) 4 - 6

9341-f2

f2. same as e, bwgd 6 - 8

g. 3972, black, same as d, yellow Firebird on hood, Hong Kong, bw, #23 (1988) 16 - 20

3848-h

h. 3848; mtlfk dk. red; yellow & blue firebird on hood (different design); tan int.; bw; Intl. line only (1990) 8 - 10

h2. same as h, gray int., Intl. line only (1990) 30 - 35

3918-i

i. 3854, yellow, same as h, blue & gray tampo, blue-tinted windows, gray int., Intl. line only (1990) 8 - 10

j. 9227, mtlfk dk. red, same as i, yellow tampo, beige int., bw, Park 'n Plates (1990) 12 - 15
k. yellow; green, black & red tampo w/"30" & bird on hood; red int.; bw; #23 (1990) 15 - 18
k2. same as k, black plastic taillights, #23 (1991) 30 - 35

3918-l

l. orange; pink & magenta lightning tampo on sides; #167 (1992) 25 - 30

3918-l2

l2. orange, same as l; extra lightning bolt on sides; #167 (1992) 30 - 35

'80s Firebird-m

m. no #; pink; yellow, blue & black flame tampo on sides; gray int.; shopping mall give-away in 2-pack; later bought by dealers (1992) 10 - 12

'80s Firebird-n

n. no #; white; red, yellow & black logo w/"Chuck E. Cheese Pizza" on sides; red int.; bw. Chuck E. Cheese exclusive, never in bp 10 - NA

3918-o

o. same as a; white; blue & red "V" on sides & hood, Heroes on Hot Wheels video tapes only (1993) 12 - NA

12349-p

p. 12349; fluor. rose red; lt. green, blue & yellow ribbon tampo on sides & hood; lt. green Firebird logo on hood; white Hot Wheels logo on trunk; blacked-out windows; yellow int.; black plastic base; bw; #256 (1995) 16 - 20

3918-q

q. mtlfk blue, blue plastic base, clear windows, white int., sp5, China, #462 (1996) 6 - 8
q2. same as q, lwch (1997) 2 - 4

'80s Firebird-r

r. black, gold plastic base, tan int., lightly tinted windows, gold stripes on sides, gold design on hood, lwgd, Park 'n Plates box by Avon, China (1998) 6 - 8

'82 Supra 3925 - 75mm - 1983
This Hong Kong-made Toyota hatchback coupe has a black metal chassis, tan plastic interior, clear plastic windows and gw.

3925-a

a. black; yellow, red & blue tampo w/"Supra" & "Toy" above rear bumper $5 - 7
a2. black, same as a, Malaysia 5 - 7

3925-b

b. black, white int., no country on base (1983), Mexico (pkg reads "Celica Supra") 55 - 70

3925-c

c. red; yellow int.; yellow, black & blue striping tampo w/"Toyota" on sides; gw; Malaysia (1984) 4 - 6

'82 Supra-d

d. dk. red, clear windows, black int., bw, Sto 'n Go set only (1993) 8 - 10

3925-e

e. green, same as d, Sto 'n Go set only (1993) 8 - 10

Airport Food Service-a

Airport Food Service - no # - 70mm - 1983
This delivery truck has a metal chassis, clear plastic windshield, black plastic interior, white & light blue plastic box, six bw, was made in France and was only in the European line.
a. blue, "Food Service" & turquoise-&-yellow airplane on sides of box $110 - 125

Airport Security-a

Airport Security - no # - 77mm - 1983
Based on an airport police car and using the same casting as Highway Patrol (1978), this model has a metal chassis, blue-tinted plastic windows & light on top, black plastic interior, and bw. Made in France, it was issued only in Europe.
Similar castings: 2019 Highway Patrol (1978), 2639 Fire Chaser (1979), 2019 Sheriff Patrol (1982)
a. dk. blue; yellow & black tampo w/airplane, "Airport Security" & "301" on sides $80 - 95

Airport Security-a2

a2. same as a; "Le Club de Maitres de L'Univers" (Masters of the Universe) in gray on hood 110 - 125

4708-a

Airport Transportation 4708 - 77mm - 1983
This GMC Motor Home has a metal chassis, blue plastic interior, clear plastic windows, and six bw. Made in France, it was issued only in Europe.
Similar castings: 9645 GMC Motor Home (1977), 2851 Spider-Man (1979 Scene Machines)
a. white; blue & yellow tampo w/"Airport Transportation" & plane on sides $110 - 125

4368-a

Beach Patrol 4368 - 73mm - 1983
This Hong Kong-made Chevrolet pickup has a metal chassis, blue plastic interior & truck bed with two surfboards on the sides & assorted beach gear in the bed, clear windows and bw.
Similar castings: 5348 Surf Patrol (1991), 2534 Path Beater (1986)
a. white; yellow, red & blue striping tampo w/"Sandee Beach Patrol" in circle design on sides $8 - 10
a2. same as a, Malaysia 8 - 10
a3. same as a2, gyg 20 - 25
a4. same as a2, gyw (1985) 30 - 35

4368-a5

a5. same as a, no yellow in tampo, tampo colors are different shade, bw, France (1985), Europe only 20 - 25

2101-b

b. 2101; fluor. green; magenta wave tampo w/white-&-pink lines on sides; magenta wave tampo & pink-&-white "Surfs Up" on hood; magenta "Cal Custom" on roof; red int. & bed; large twy; California Custom (1990) 12 - 15
b2. same as b, small twy (1990) 18 - 20

3289-a

BMW M1 3289 - 78mm - 1983
This Malaysia-made car has a red metal chassis, black plastic interior, black plastic opening hatch in back, clear plastic windows and gyg.
Similar castings: 7296 Wind Splitter (1984), 3501 Street Dog (Tattoo Machines)
a. red; yellow, black & white stripe tampo on top; "BMW" on hood $30 - 35
a2. same as a, darker yellow in tampo, bw, France (1984), Europe & Canada only 18 - 20
a3. red, same as a2, orange replaces yellow in tampo, France (1984), Europe & Canada only 18 - 20

BMW M1-b

b. 15963, green, green metal base, gray-tinted windows, gray int. & rear window, sp5, China, #473 (1996) 2 - 4

BMW M1-c

c. 15963, mtlfk silver, gray chassis, black int., sp5, China, #473 (1996) 2 - 4

4703-a

Cargo Lift 4703 - 80mm - 1983
This airport freight container truck has a metal chassis, black-tinted plastic windows, black plastic interior, two white plastic removable containers (It has also been found with only one plastic container), and six bw. Made in France, it was issued only in Europe.
a. yellow with two containers $80 - 90
b. yellow with one container 60 - 150

3923-a

Classic Cobra (Shelby Cobra 427 S/C) 3923 - 67mm - 1983
Based on Carroll Shelby's Ford-powered Shelby Cobra 427 S/C, this model has a metal chassis, lift-up hood, black plastic interior, clear plastic windshield, bw, and was made in Hong Kong.
a. blue, 2 white stripes on top $25 - 30
a2. 4369, same as a, gyg 35 - 40
a3. same as a2, gyw (1985) 75 - 100
a4. same as a2, smaller wheels, Mexico (1985) 135 - 160
a5. same as a4, yellow stripes, Mexico (1985) 150 - 190
a6. same as a4, yellow stripes, bw, Mexico (1985) 135 - 160

2535-b

b. 2535; red; yellow, black & white striping tampo w/"427" twice & "Cobra" twice on hood; gyg (1986) 25 - 30
b2. same as b, bw (1986) 6 - 8
b3. same as b2, no "427" on hood, #31 (1988) 5 - 10
b4. same as b3, metal base, sp7, #31 (1995) 15 - 25
b5. same as b3, black plastic base, sp7, #31 5 - 10
b6. same as b3, black metal base, sp7, #31 4 - 6

2055-c

Values are shown in U.S. dollars, first price is for mint, second is for mint packaged vehicles only. See pages 15-16 for grading guide to determine value for cars in lesser conditions.

c. 2055; black; orange, yellow & red tampo w/"Cobra" twice on hood; red plastic int.; Park 'n Plates (1989) 18 - 20

1296-d

d. 1296; white; red & black stripes & gray "7" in black circle on sides; black "7," "Cobra" twice on hood; black "Cal Custom" on windshield; blue plastic int.; rrgy; California Custom (1990) 12 - 15

d2. same as d, yellow "Cal Custom" on windshield (1990) 12 - 15

d3. white, same as d2, bw (1990) 8 - 10

e. 1296; lime yellow; same as d; dk. red, blue & gray tampo; red int.; bw; California Custom (1990) 10 - 12

3923-f

f. pearl white, blue stripes on top, orange cobra w/ magenta spots on hood & sides; white "Revealers" on windshield, Malaysia, bw, Revealers 10-pack only 10 - NA

f2. white, same as f, Revealers 10-pack only 10 - NA

Classic Cobra-g

g. no #; lt. gray-blue; same tampo as b2; tampo colors are orange, dk. orange & white; white int.; 25th Anniv. Ford 5-pack only (1993) 6 - NA

3923-h

h. red, white Hot Wheels logo in back, clear windshield, black int., pcgd. 16-piece FAO Schwarz Gold Series Collection, limited to 3000 (1994) 10 - NA

13292-i

i. 13292, lime yellow, black plastic base & pipes, silver lines crisscrossing all over, tinted windshield, gray int., sp7, #3 in Roarin' Rods, #305 (1995) 10 - 15

i2. same as i, metal base & pipes, #305 (1995) 5 - 10

i3. same as i, black metal base & pipes, #305 (1995) 5 - 10

i4. same as i3, sp5 30 - 65

13360-j

j. 13360, dk. mtlc green, 2 gold stripes on hood & trunk, tan int., clear windshield, gold pc, #11 in Treasure Hunt series, #363 (1995) 100 - 125

k. black, white Hot Wheels logo in back, black-tinted windshield, black plastic base & int., sp5, Target Stores excl., Black Convertible Collection only (1995) 8 - NA

l. mtlfk red, black plastic base, clear windshield, white int., 2 gold stripes over top, sp7, 60s Muscle Cars 5-pack only (1995) 4 - NA

l2. same as l, sp5 (1997) 45 - NA

14014-m

m. 14014; mtlfk gray; white & black tampo w/"98" & "AP" on sides, "98" in front of hood; issued as 1965 Shelby Cobra 427 S/C; limited to 10,000 (1995) 40 - 45

n. gold-plated, black metal base, clear windshield, black int., pcgd, in JC Penney gold-plated 2-pack (1995) 65 - NA

3923-o

o. yellow, black plastic base, two black stripes on top, clear windshield, black int., rrgd. FAO Schwarz History Of Hot Wheels II 8-pack (1996) 10 - NA

15250-p

p. 15250; pearl white; black, blue & red tampo w/net & flying soccer ball on sides; soccer player & soccer ball on hood; black metal base; black int.; clear windshield; sp7. Shelby Cobra 427 SC, #3 in Sports Car series, #406 (1996) 6 - 10

p2. same as p, sp5, #406 (1996) 85 - 90

Classic Cobra-q

q. no #, red, gray int., clear windshield & gray rim, 2 white stripes over top, sp5. Open engine shown. Target Motorin' Music 4-packs only (1997) 15 - NA

Classic Cobra-r

r. white; tan int.; clear windshield; lt. brown tampo design on sides; purple, lt. blue, lt. green & red "Cinnamon Crunch" on sides & trunk; "French Toast Crunch" on hood; sp5. General Mills mail-in (1997) 3 - 5

s. dk. blue, same as a3, gyw. Limited edition for 30th Anniv., w/blister card in window box (1998) 6 - 8

Classic Cobra-t

t. mtlfk blue; white int.; tinted windshield; red, yellow & white tampo w/Hot Wheels logo, "1" & race decals on sides, "Hot Wheels" & "1" on hood; sp5. #3 in Race Team Series IV, #727 (1998) 2 - 4

u. unpainted, gray int., tinted windshield, sp5, Shelby Cobra 427 S/C, #3 in Race Team Series IV, 1998 Hot Wheels Convention, #727 (1998) 120 - 150

Classic Cobra-v

v. white; tinted windshield; black int.; orange & black tampo on sides, hood & trunk w/"47" & "Celebrity Tour de Milan" on hood; sp5; Thailand; #1024 (1999) 5 - 7

w. white, blue-tinted windshield, blue int., black & blue tampo w/"Speed" on sides, sp5, Thailand, #4 in Speed Blaster Series, #40 (2000) 2 - 3

x. mtlfk dark red, tan int., clear windshield, orange & black flame tampo on sides, lwch, Malaysia, #224 (2001) 2 - 3

y. blue, black int., clear windshield, two white stripes on top, gych. Auto Milestones series (2002) 10 - 12

3923-z

z. mf blue, black int, clear windshield, white, red and black tampo, decal on sides, two white stripes over the top and rrgygy. Issued as a limited edition for the Japanese Collector's Club. (2002) 20 - 25

3920-a

Classic Packard 3920 - 78mm - 1983
This Hong Kong-made 1934 sedan has a metal chassis, black plastic interior & fenders, clear plastic windshield, ww, and comes with either "Classic Packard" or "'34 Packard" on the base.

a. black $10 - 12

a2. same as a, Malaysia 10 - 12

a3. same as a, (1983), Mexico only 10 - 60

Classic Packard-a4

a4. same as a, sp5, China, #625 (1997) 8 - 10

3291-a

Double Deck Bus 3291 - 80mm - 1983
This European double-decker bus has a metal chassis, clear plastic windows, tan plastic interior, bw, and was made in France. It was never issued in the U.S.

a. white, blue stripe, red & blue Pepsi logo, yellow & red Shell logo, Europe only $100 - 125

3291-b

b. red, Mexico only (package reads "Autobus") 90 - 110

3287-a

Fiat Ritmo (Strada) 3287 - 70mm - 1983
This model has a black metal chassis, clear plastic windows, brown plastic interior, bw and was made in France. Never issued in the U.S.

a. gray, thin black stripe, "Abarth 2000" on sides, France $30 - 35

a2. same as a, no tampo, Europe only 50 - 60

b. silver gray, same as a, Europe only 35 - 40

b2. same as b, no tampo (1987), Mexico only 40 - 45

Fireball Torino-a

Fireball Torino - no # - 76mm - 1983
This Mexican-made Torino stock car has a chrome plastic chassis, blue-tinted windows, black plastic interior and bw. Similar castings: 7647 Torino Stocker (1975), 9533 Torino Tornado (1985)

a. white; red & yellow flames on hood & sides; Mexico only $100 - 125

3288-a

Ford Escort 3288 - 72mm - 1983
This model features a metal chassis, black plastic interior, clear plastic windows, bw, and was made in Malaysia.

a. black, orange stripe & "XR3" on sides $4 - 6

a2. same as a, brown tampo, France (1983) 12 - 20

a3. same as a, gold tampo, France (1983) 12 - 20

a4. same as a, no tampo (1983), Europe only 12 - 20

3288-b

b. yellow; red, blue & white tampo w/"Escort G.T." & Ford logo on sides (1984) 40 - 65

b2. lemon yellow, same as b, darker tampo, "Escort G.T." is larger, Mexico (1985) 70 - 90

3288-c

c. red, same as b2, no red in tampo (1985), Mexico only 90 - 100

c2. same as c, yellow & blue tampo (1985), Mexico only 90 - 100

d. white, same as b2, red & lt. blue tampo (1985), Mexico only 90 - 100

Ford Stake Bed Truck 4018 - 67mm - 1983
This Malaysia-made model has a metal chassis, tan plastic stake bed, chrome plastic interior, clear plastic windshield and six bw.

a. blue; yellow, black & white tampo w/"Sunset Trucking" on sides of cab; Extras series $5 - 7

Values are shown in U.S. dollars, first price is for mint, second is for mint packaged vehicles only. See pages 15-16 for grading guide to determine value for cars in lesser conditions.

4018-a

9551-b

b. 9551; mtlfk red; yellow plastic stake bed; yellow, blue & white tampo with "Rapid Delivery" on sides (1986) 15 - 18

4018-c

c. mtlfk blue, same as b, chrome plastic chassis, different truck bed, #99 (1991) 10 - 12
d. red, same as c, yellow & white tampo, #237 (1993) 6 - 8
d2. same as d, sp7, #237 (1996) 4 - 6
d3. same as d, sp5, #237 (1997) 4 - 6
d4. same as d, tinted window, sp3, #237 (1997) 6 - 8
d5. same as d, sp3, #237 (1997) 2 - 4
d6. same as d, dw3, #237 (1997) 2 - 4
d7. same as d, clear window, gray plastic base, sp7, #237 (1997) 2 - 4
d8. same as d7, tinted window, #237 (1997) 2 - 4

Ford Stake Bed Truck-e

e. blue; clear windshield; chrome int.; tan stake bed; green, yellow & brown tampo w/"Citrus Groves," tree on sides of cab; sp7. Farm Country 5-packs (1997) 2 - NA
e2. same as e, sp3, #237 (1998) 2 - 4
e3. same as e, dw3 (1998) 2 - NA
e4. same as e, sp5 (1998) 2 - NA

Ford Stake Bed Truck-f

f. red; white stake bed; yellow-tinted windshield; chrome int.; black, white & yellow tampo w/"Crash Barrier Constructors" on sides; sp3. Rad Rigs 5-packs only (1998) 2 - NA
g. aqua, chrome int., clear window, gray stake bed, ho5, Malaysia, #1010 (1999) 2 - 3
h. yellow, same as g, sp5, in Pop 'n Play set 5 - NA
i. mtlfk dark red; clear window; chrome int.; black steak bed; orange, white, yellow & black tampo w/cat & "Fatcat Moving Company" on sides of cab; sp3; China; #191 (2001) 2 - 3

Ford Stake Bed Truck-h

j. mtlfk dk.blue; clear window; chrome int.; gray stake bed; white, yellow, black & red tampo w/"Crash Barrier Constructors" on sides; ho5; Malaysia; #228 (2001) 2 - 3

3915-a

Formula Fever 3915 - 75mm - 1983
This Indy-style racer has a metal chassis & engine, metal spoiler in back, red plastic interior, bw, and was made in Hong Kong. Similar castings: 9545 Thunderstreak (1985), 2698 #26 Quaker State Indy Car (1992 Pro Circuit)

a. yellow; red plastic sides; black & red tampo w/"12" in front; yellow, black & white tampo w/"12" & racing decals on sides $6 - 8
a2. 4366, same as a, gyg 20 - 25
a3. same as a2, Malaysia 20 - 25
a4. same as a3, gyw 40 - 50

4370-b

Jeep Scrambler 4370 - 78mm - 1983
This Hong Kong-made Jeep utility truck has a metal chassis, black roof, tan plastic interior & truck bed, clear plastic windows and gyg. Similar casting: 16808 Trailbuster (1997)

a. gray; yellow & orange stripe on sides $35 - 40
b. metalflake gray, same as a 15 - 18
b2. same as b, Malaysia 15 - 18
b3. same as b2, gyw (1984) 80 - 100

4370-c

c. black, same as b, red & yellow tampo, gyw (1984) 30 - 40

9547-d

d. 9547; plum; red int. & truck bed; white, yellow & blue tampo w/"13" & "Jeep" on sides; "13" & "Jeep" twice on hood; gyw (1985) 25 - 35
e. 2541; mtlfk blue; same as d; gray int. & bed; yellow, black & white tampo; gyw (1986) 25 - 35
e2. same as e, bw (1987) 7 - 9

5146-f

f. 5146; mtlfk dk. red; black int. & bed; orange, yellow & blue stripe w/"Jeep" on sides (1988) 5 - 7
f2. same as f, ct 5 - 7

3768-a

Long Shot 3768 - 84mm - 1983
Based on a semi-tractor made for racing, this model has a chrome plastic chassis, maroon plastic interior & truck bed, clear plastic windshield, and six bw. Hong Kong.

a. white; yellow, red & black tampo on sides & top, "1" and race decals on sides $5 - 7
a2. same as a, Malaysia 5 - 7
b. yellow, same as a, purple replaces yellow in tampo, 15th Anniv. Belt Buckle 3-pack only (1983) 15 - NA
c. white, same as a2, darker red & lighter yellow in tampo, Mexico (1985) 15 - 18

3927-a

NASCAR Stocker 3927 - 78mm - 1983
This racing model has a metal chassis, black plastic interior, black-tinted plastic windows, and was made in Hong Kong. Similar casting: 2522 Stock Rocket (1986)

a. white; lt. green, yellow, black & red tampo on sides & top w/"11," "Mountain Dew" & race decals on sides; "Give me a Dew" & "Mountain Dew" on hood; "11" on roof; "Nascar Stocker" on base & package $110 - 135
a2. same as a, "Mountain Dew Stocker" on base & package 120 - 145
a3. same as a, darker green in tampo, "Racing Stocker" on base 30 - 35
a4. same as a3, Malaysia 30 - 35

4017-a

Peterbilt Dump Truck 4017 - 88mm - 1983
This model has a metal chassis, gray movable dump bed with an opening rear door, black plastic interior, gray-tinted plastic windows, six bw, and was made in Malaysia.

a. yellow, Extras series $5 - 7
b. 9550, mtlfk blue, same as a, white dump bed, clear windows (1985) 5 - 7
c. red, same as a, bw, #100 (1989) 4 - 7
c2. same as c, bww, #100 (1995) 75 - 100
c3. same as c, sp7, #100 (1996) 3 - 6
c4. same as c, sp3, #100 (1998) 2 - 4
c5. same as c, dw3, #100 (1998) 2 - 4

Peterbilt Dump Truck-d

d. 13304, lime yellow, yellow plastic dump bed, blacked-out window, black int., rr w/lime hubs, #1 of Real Riders Series, #317 (1996) 20 - 25
e. orange; gray dump bed; tinted window; black, yellow & white tampo w/"Road Dept." & logo on sides; sp5; Europe; #1 of 4 (1998) 5 - 7
f. orange; tinted window; black, red, & white tampo with "38" and logo on

Peterbilt Dump Truck-e

sides; sp3. Road Repair 5-packs only (1997) 2 - NA
g. lt. blue; orange dump bed; orange-tinted windshield & int.; orange, black, & white tampo w/"AE" & "Asphalt Engineering" on sides; sp3. Rad Trucks 5-packs only (1998) 2 - NA

Peterbilt Dump Truck-h

h. yellow; clear plastic int. & window; red, black & white "CAT Diesel Power" on doors; sp7; baggie only (1998) 3 - NA
i. yellow, clear window, black dump bed, sp7. In Pop 'n Play set 5 - NA
j. blue, blue-tinted window, white dump bed, sp5, #1009 (1999) 2 - 3

Peterbuilt Dump Truck-k

k. aqua; blue dump bed; mtlfk gray chassis; black int.; tinted windshield; white, black & yellow tampo w/"HWCT" & "Hot Wheels Transporter" on sides; sp3; China; #190 (2000) 2 - 3
l. orange; blue dump, black int.; tinted windows; black & white tampo w/"HW Trans" on sides, "HW Trans" & "Maintenance Service" on hood; sp3; Thailand. Asphalt Assault 5-pack (2002) 2 - NA

3917-a

Pontiac J-2000 3917 - 76mm - 1983
Based on Pontiac's "J-Car," this model has a metal chassis, red plastic interior, gray-tinted plastic windows, ribbed rear window, sun roof, bw, and was made in Hong Kong.

a. yellow; black & red-orange stripe tampo w/"J-2000" & "Pontiac" on sides; red-orange, orange & purple stripe on top; 8mm-wide sun roof $8 - 10
a2. same as a, 5mm-wide sun roof, Malaysia 6 - 8

3917-a3

a3. same as a2; no side tampos, top tampo colors darker than U.S. model, clear windows, Mexico (1983) 55 - 65
a4. same as a3, gw, Mexico (1983) 55 - 65

3917-b

b. green; black, red & yellow dragon

Values are shown in U.S. dollars, first price is for mint, second is for mint packaged vehicles only. See pages 15-16 for grading guide to determine value for cars in lesser conditions.

tampo on sides; red & yellow hood design, Canada (1984) 135 - 160

b2. same as b, dk. red in tampo, gw, Mexico (1985) 100 - 110

b3. same as b2, "Made in Mexico" on base, Mexico (1985) 100 - 110

b4. same as b2, bw, Mexico (1985) 100 - 110

b5. same as b3, bw, Mexico (1985) 100 - 110

c. white, same as b5, red-tinted windows, Mexico (1985) 125 - 150

3917-c2

c2. same as c, blue replaces red in tampo, Mexico (1985) 160 - 200

d. red, same as c, bw, Mexico (1986) 135 - 160

3292-a

Renault LeCar 3292 - 60mm - 1983

This model has a black plastic chassis, clear windows & sunroof, tan interior, bw and was made in France. It was never issued in the U.S.

a. red; black stripe tampo & "Renault" on sides, France, Europe only $20 - 25

a2. same as a, no tampo, white int., Mexico (1987) 40 - 50

b. black, no tampo, France, Europe only 45 - 50

3292-c

c. lt. blue, no tampo, never in bp, Europe & Canada only 40 - NA

d. lt. olive green, no tampo, never in bp, Europe & Canada only 40 - NA

3916-a

Rig Wrecker® 3916 - 72mm - 1983

This wrecker for towing semi-tractors has a metal chassis, red plastic boom arm & hook in back, chrome plastic interior, clear plastic windows, and six bw. Hong Kong. Similar casting: 16913 Ramblin' Wrecker (1997)

a. white; red & blue tampo w/"Steve's 24 Hour Towing" on sides; red & blue tampo in front $6 - 8

a2. same as a, Malaysia 4 - 6

a3. same as a2, chrome plastic base, #46 (1989) 4 - 6

Rig Wrecker-b

b. white; same as a3; red lines & "Airship Tug" on sides; black "Airship Support Team" & blue blimp on doors; gray plastic boom arm & hook. Blimp & Support Team 5-pack only (1994) 3 - NA

Rig Wrecker-c2

c. white, same as b, thick blue stripe, Hot Wheels logo on doors, red & yellow "Auto-City Tow" on sides, sp5. Auto City 5-packs (1996) 2 - NA

c2. same as c, sp3 (1997) 2 - NA

c3. same as c, sp7 (1997) 2 - NA

c4. same as c, gray plastic base (1997) 2 - NA

c5. same as c4, sp7 (1997) 2 - NA

d. no #; mtlfk dk. blue; orange chassis, boom, int. & lights; tinted windshield; white stripe w/orange "24 Hr Towing" on sides; orange "86," "Emergency," "Radio Dispatch" & black, orange, & white logo on sides; sp5; 5-pack only (1997) 2 - NA

Rig Wrecker-d2

d2. same as d, sp7 (1997) 2 - NA

d3. same as d, dw3 (1997) 2 - NA

Rig Wrecker-e

e. mtlfk blue; white chassis, boom, int. & lights; tinted windshield; red, yellow, & white Hot Wheels Race Team on sides; sp5; 5-packs only (1997) 2 - NA

e2. same as e, sp3 2 - NA

e3. metalflake dark blue, same as e, sp3 (1997) 2 - NA

Rig Wrecker-f2

f. white; black plastic chassis; red boom; chrome int.; tinted window; black, red & blue tampo w/"Hi Bank Racing," "Pit Crew Tow Rig" & "#1" on sides; ho5; Thailand; #872 (1999) 2 - 3

f2. same as f, dw3, #872 (1999) 2 - 3

Rig Wrecker-g

g. yellow, chrome chassis, blue boom, black int., clear window, gray & black tampo w/"Finish Line Towing" & logo on sides, Malaysia, #1087 (1999) 2 - 3

h. black, clear windows, gold int., white boom, white & gold tampo w/"M&C" on sides, sp3gd, #206 (2000) 2 - 3

Rig Wrecker-i

i. white, black boom, blue & dk. blue on sides, multicolored tampo w/"Daytona" & race decals on sides, Treasure Hunt logo on roof, gych, Thailand, #1 in NASCAR 2001 Treasure Hunt Series (2001) 18 - 22

j. white; black boom; dk. blue, red & magenta tampo w/"Darlington a NASCAR Tradition" & "Rapid Response" on sides, Treasure Hunt logo on roof, gych, Thailand, #2 in NASCAR 2001 Treasure Hunt Series (2001) 18 - 22

k. black, white boom, red cab, black & white tampo w/"California Speedway" & "Rapid Response" on sides, Treasure Hunt logo on roof, gych, Thailand, #3 in NASCAR 2001 Treasure Hunt Series (2001) 18 - 22

l. black; white boom; blue, red & white tampo w/"Talladega 500" & "Rapid Response" on sides; Treasure Hunt logo on roof; gych; Thailand; #4 in NASCAR 2001 Treasure Hunt Series (2001) 18 - 22

m. dark blue, white boom, chrome chassis & int., clear windshield, multicolored tampo w/"Daytona International Speedway" & race decals on sides, "Daytona" in front, "Treasure Hunt" on the roof, gych, Thailand, #5 in NASCAR 2001 Treasure Hunt Series (2001) 18 - 22

n. red, gold chrome chassis & int., clear windshield, multicolored tampo w/"Watkins Glen Thunder Road" & race decals on sides, "Watkins Glen" in front, "Treasure Hunt" on roof, gygd, Thailand, #6 in NASCAR 2001 Treasure Hunt Series (2001) 18 - 22

o. black; gold chrome chassis & int.; clear windshield; olive & white tampo w/"Kansas," "Kansas Speedway" & race decals on sides, "Kansas" in front, "Treasure Hunt" on roof; gygd; Thailand; #7 in NASCAR 2001 Treasure Hunt Series (2001) 18 - 22

p. blue; black boom; black, red & white tampo w/"Talladega Superspeedway" & "Rapid Response" on sides; Treasure Hunt logo on roof; gych; Thailand; #8 in NASCAR 2001 Treasure Hunt Series (2001) 18 - 22

q. black; chrome chassis & int.; clear windshield; blue, white & orange tampo w/"Phoenix International Speedway" & race decals on sides, "Phoenix" in front, "Treasure Hunt" on roof; gych; Thailand; #9 in NASCAR 2001 Treasure Hunt Series (2001) 18 - 22

Rig Wrecker-r

r. lt. purple; chrome chassis & int.; clear windshield; multicolored tampo w/"Miami Rapid Response," "Homestead Miami Speedway" & race decals on sides, "Miami" in front, "Treasure Hunt" on roof; gych; Thailand; #10 in NASCAR 2001 Treasure Hunt Series (2001) 18 - 22

s. black; chrome int.; red-tinted windows; yellow boom & lights on top; white, orange & yellow tampo w/"Rescue Rig," "Unit 7" & "Rescue Network" on sides; sp5; Thailand; Rescue Rods 5-pack (2001) 18 - 22

3924-a

Thunder Roller™ 3924 - 82mm - 1983

Based on a cabover-style semi-tractor, this model comes with a chrome plastic chassis, red plastic interior, gray-tinted plastic windows, six bw, and was made in China.

a. yellow; brown, red & black tampo w/"2" & eagle on sides $5 - 7

a2. same as a, Malaysia 5 - 7

a3. same as a2, ribbed roof 5 - 7

b. 16054, dk. mtlfk red, same as a3, tinted windows, tan int., sp5 in front, bw in back, China, #483 (1996) 6 - 8

Thunder Roller-c

c. no #, white, clear windows, white int., red & blue stripes, blue McKee logo on sides, sp5 in front & bw in back, China, Little Debbie Bakery Series II 3-packs only (1997) 4 - NA

3914-a

Turbo Streak® 3914 - 75mm - 1983

This Indy-type racer has a metal chassis & interior, bw, and was made in Hong Kong. Similar casting: 9544 Black Lightning (1985)

a. yellow; orange, red & black tampo w/"Elf" & "Michelin" on sides; "7" on top $4 - 6

a2. same as a, Malaysia 4 - 6

a3. 4365, same as a2, gyg 20 - 25

3914-a4

a4. same as a2, no "Elf" & "Michelin" in tampo 4 - 6

a5. same as a4, gyg 20 - 25

a6. same as a4, gyw 25 - 30

Turbo Streak-b

b. no #; yellow; red, white & blue stripe tampo & "20" on sides & front; Kellogg's mail-in only (1985) 20 - NA

b2. same as b, gyg, Kellogg's mail-in (1985) 60 - NA

Values are shown in U.S. dollars, first price is for mint, second is for mint packaged vehicles only. *See pages 15-16 for grading guide to determine value for cars in lesser conditions.*

Turbo Streak-c

c. no #; white; red & blue tampo w/Hot Wheels logo & "20th Anniversary" on sides; logo backwards on one side, bw; 20th Anniversary 3-pack or 20-pack only (1988) 30 - NA

3914-c2

c2. same as c; Hot Wheels logo backwards & blue "20th Anniversary" on one side; yellow & black wheel w/wings & "Indy 500" in red & black on sides; 1988 Hot Wheels Mall Tour giveaway only (1988) 150 - NA

3914-d

d. bright red; white & blue tampo w/"Tuneup Masters," blue Tuneup Masters logo & "1" on sides; "Tuneup Masters" & pink logo on back spoiler; "1" on nose; #104 (1991) 85 - 110

d2. same as d, blue spoiler logo, #104 (1991) 65 - 75

d3. same as d, spoilers are unpainted & no tampo on rear spoiler, #104 (1991) 4 - 6

d4. same as d3, white emblem on sides (1991) 18 - 20

Turbo Streak-e

e. no #; white; black & red tampo w/"V" & "1" on sides, "1" on hood; Heroes on Hot Wheels video tapes only (1993); w/video 10 - NA

4639-f

f. 4639, Day-Glo yellow, Hot Wheels logo on sides #235 (1994) 4 - 6

Turbo Streak-g

g. no #, yellow, 2 racing stripes, red "1" & Shell emblem on sides. Sold by Shell dealers in OH & MA only, baggie only (1994) 4 - NA

3914-g2

g2. same as g; no "1" & racing stripes; "Formula Shell" in yellow & white on black background. Sold by Shell dealers in OH & MA only, baggie only (1995) 3 - 5

Turbo Streak-h

h. no #; orange; same as g; orange, white & dk. blue Gulf logo on sides. Gulf exclusive, baggie only (1994) 3 - 5

3914-i

i. turquoise, "3" & lightning in white & red on sides & top, racing decals on sides. In box w/Aquafresh Toothpaste only (1994) 10 - 20

j. yellow, no tampo, made for unproduced game, baggies only (1995) 6 - NA

k. red, no tampo, made for unproduced game, baggies only (1995) 6 - NA

15979-l

l. 15979; white; dk. blue sides; red & yellow Hot Wheels logo on spoiler; sp5; China; #470 (1996) 2 - 4

15979-l2

l2. same as l, "1" & lines in magenta on sides, white metal base & white plastic spoiler, China, #470 (1996) 2 - 4

Turbo Streak-m

m. no #; dk. blue; metal base; chrome int.; sp5; Union 76 logo in orange, white & blue on sides & hood, "Performance" in white on black on sides. Baggie from Union 76 dealers only (1996) 5 - NA

Turbo Streak-n

n. no #, orange, blue sides, "Unocal 76" on sides, "Unocal" on spoiler & racing decals on painted wing, FAO Schwarz 8-packs only (1997) 8 - NA

1984

Eighteen new models were introduced with the total number of vehicles remaining at ninety-six. Two were never sold in the U.S.: Pontiac J-2000 in green and Datsun 200SX in maroon. Also, the Frito Lay van and Flat Out 442 in green were only found in the U.S. in a 6-pack. These four models, although scheduled for the domestic market, were only released in blisterpacks in Canada. This was also the year Ultra Hot Wheels cars, referred to as the fastest breed of Hot Wheels cars, were introduced.

5908-a

'65 Mustang Convertible 5908 - 87mm - 1984

This model has a metal chassis, lift-up hood, clear plastic windshield, tan interior, ww, and was made in Hong Kong.

a. red $6 - 8

a2. same as a, Malaysia 5 - 7

a3. same as a2, sp3gd. Avon Father & Son Collector 2-pack only (1997) 4 - NA

a4. same as a2, gold Hot Wheels 30th Anniv. logo on rear fender. Limited for 30th Anniv. w/blistercard in window box (1998) 4 - 6

5908-b

b. black; white tampo w/"Mustang," logo & 2 white stripes on sides (1987) 50 - 60

b2. same as b, white interior, sp5, #455 (1998) 3 - 5

c. lt. blue, same as b, black tampo, #26 (1987) 25 - 35

c2. same as c, black int. (1987) 18 - 20

c3. same as c2, Hong Kong (1987) 18 - 20

2194-d

d. 2194; white; red striping w/"Mustang" & logo on sides; clear plastic windshield; red plastic int.; ww; Park 'n Plates (1989) 15 - 25

d2. same as d, tan plastic int., found in single blister, #26 (1990) 15 - 235

1241-e

e. 1241; green; blue, dk. blue & white wave tampo on sides & hood; black "Cal Custom" on clear windshield; blue int.; rry; California Custom (1990) 12 - 15

e2. same as e, yellow "Cal Custom" on windshield 10 - 12

e3. same as e2, hood tampo colors reversed, twy (1990) 10 - 12

e4. same as e3, black "Cal Custom" on windshield 10 - 12

e5. same as e4, black replaces dk. blue in tampo 10 - 12

'65 Mustang Convertible-f

f. no #; orange; lt. blue, dk. blue & white tampo on sides & hood; orange "Cal Custom" on blue-tinted windshield; pink int.; twb; Freeway Frenzy Cal Custom set, later at Mattel Toy Club, never in blisterpack (1990) 6 - NA

f2. same as f, black replaces dk. blue in tampo 12 - 15

g. mtlc blue, same tampo as b, #26 25 - 30

h. red, same as b, yellow tampo, #162 10 - 15

h2. same as h, sp7, #162 (1995) 6 - 8

h3. same as h, sp5, #162 (1995) 4 - 6

5908-i

i. Day-Glo yellow; pink, turquoise & red stripe tampo on sides; black int., white "Revealers" on clear windshield, ww; Malaysia, Revealers 10-pack only 10 - NA

j. no #, dk. green, same tampo as b, tan int., 25th Anniv. Ford 5-pack only (1993) 4 - NA

k. no #, mtlfk purple, same as b, yellow tampo, Day-Glo yellow int., sc. Only in set (1995) 4 - NA

'65 Mustang Convertible-k

14903-l

l. 14903, white, red stripes on sides, black "Happy 65th Birthday," red "Fisher Price" in red circle on hood, red int., clear windshield, ww, limited to 8000 (1994) 15 - 18

m. chrome, red int., red Hot Wheels logo on windshield, rsw. Service Merchandise 16-piece Classic American Car Collection only, limited to 5000 (1995) 8 - NA

n. mtlfk black, gold Hot Wheels logo on black-tinted windshield, metal base, black plastic int., sp7. Target-exclusive Black Convertible Collection only (1995) 6 - NA

5908-o

o. 14042; black; red stripes & "Mustang" on sides; red, white & blue "Greater Seattle Toy Show 1995" on hood; clear windshield; white int.; iwgd; limited to 8000 (1995) 18 - 20

p. fluor. red, yellow tampo, same design as b, white int., clear windshield, scw. Double Barrel set only (1995) 6 - NA

p2. same as p, tan int., sp7, Ford 5-pack only (1996) 40 - NA

q. 13871, mtlfk gold, same tampo as b, white int., tinted windshield, sp5, #455 (1995) 8 - 12

q2. same as q, sp7, #455 (1996) 9 - 15

q3. same as q, sp3, #455 (1996) 7 - 10

'65 Mustang Convertible-r

r. no #, lt. yellow, clear windshield, black int., black & yellow license plate "1965" front & back, rrch w/red stripe. Four Decades of Pony Power set only (1997) 10 - NA

s. white, red int., clear windshield, two stripes, "Mustang" & logo on sides, lwgd. Father & Son Collector 2-packs by Avon only, China (1997) 4 - NA

'65 Mustang Convertible-t

t. mtlc dk. blue, white int., clear windshield, white tampo w/"Mustang" & stripes on sides, sp5, #455 (1998) 2 - 4

'65 Mustang Convertible-u

u. red, tinted windshield, white int., white & black tampo w/"Toy Cars and Vehicles" on sides & trunk; rrch w/red stripe around tire. In box as limited edition for Toy Cars and Vehicles magazine (1999) 15 - 18

Values are shown in U.S. dollars, first price is for mint, second is for mint packaged vehicles only. See pages 15-16 for grading guide to determine value for cars in lesser conditions.

'65 Mustang Convertible-v

v. black, tan int., tinted windshield, orange & yellow flame tampo on sides & hood w/"Mustang" & mustang in white on hood, China, #1051 (1999) 2 - 3

'65 Mustang Convertible-w

w. white; blue int.; blue-tinted windshield; red, blue & gold tampo w/"Coca Cola" on sides, stripes on top; round logo on hood w/"35 Great Years 65, 99" & Astros logo on hood; Coca Cola logo on trunk; rrch w/white stripe. Houston Astros baseball limited give-away (1999) 15 - 20

x. green; yellow-tinted windows; yellow int.; yellow, black, white & red tampo on sides, hood & trunk w/"Classic Rock" on trunk; dw3; Thailand; #201 (2001) 2 - 3

y. mtlfk silver, white int., tinted windshield, black & white tampo w/"4" on sides, sp5, Thailand, #147 (2002) 2 - 3

z. lt. blue, white int., clear windshield, two white stripes over top, black & orange tampo w/"Automobile Milestones 2002" on trunk, rrch w/white stripe, Thailand. Auto Milestones series (2002) 10 - 12

Army Convoy - see Troop Convoy (1984)

5907-a

Baja Bug 5907 - 57mm - 1984
This Hong Kong-made off-road racing Volkswagen has a metal chassis & engine in back, black plastic interior and gyg. Similar casting: 2990 VW Baja (1990 California Custom)

a. yellow; red, purple & white tampo w/"Baja Bug" & race decals on sides $20 - 25
a2. same as a, Malaysia 8 - 10
a3. same as a2, gyw 35 - 40
a4. same as a2, bw 5 - 7
b. 9548; red; same as a3; orange, white & yellow tampo; red int. (1985) 25 - 30

9548-c

c. 9548, red, red int., orange & white flame tampo, "Blazin' Bug" on sides, gyw (1985) 25 - 30
c2. 3888, same as c, yellow & white flames, blue "Blazin' Bug," bw (1990) 6 - 8
c3. same as c2, black interior 6 - 8
c4. same as c2, purple "Blazin' Bug," only in Intl. line (1990) 8 - 10

d. 9343, black, same as c, orange & yellow flames, white "Blazin' Bug," tan int., gyw, Stamper 3-pack only (1985) 35 - NA
e. white, same as c, red and orange flames, purple "Blazin' Bug," bw, #36 (1987) 6 - 8

Baja Bug-e2

e2. white, same as e, gyw (1987) 30 - 35
f. 3876, purple, same as c2, red "Blazin' Bug," red int., Intl. line only (1990) 8 - 10

Baja Bug-g

g. no #; mtlc dk. red; orange & yellow flame tampo, blue "Blazin' Bug" on sides; red int.; Hot Wheels cereal, later K•B Toys give-away w/Kool-Aid points & Heroes on Hot Wheels video tapes (1990); w/tape 15 - NA

1238-h

h. 1238; fluor. pink; pink back half of car; yellow, blue & black tampo on sides & hood; black "Cal Custom" on hood; yellow int.; rry; California Custom (1990) 18 - 20
h2. same as h, bw (1990) 10 - 12
i. 4325; red; red & dk. red metalflakes #223; (1993) 18 - 35
j. no #; white; red metal base; black, blue, gray, yellow & red tampo in front & on sides; red int.; gw. Track System Gift Pack only (1995) 3 - NA

Baja Bug-j2

j2. same as j, sp5gd (1995) 2 - NA

15234-k

k. 15234; blue; red, white & yellow racing team tampo; sp5; #2 in Race Team Series II; #393 (1996) 6 - 8

Baja Bug-l

l. no #, mtlfk dark red, white interior, black & white card tampo on hood & sides, sp5, #3 Dealer's Choice Series, #567 (1997) 6 - 8
l2. same as l, silver painted base, #3 Dealer's Choice Series, #567 (1998) 6 - 8

Baja Bug-m

m. 18670; yellow; dk. blue int.; blue, black, white & red tampo w/"JC Whitney" on sides; rrw in front, rrw w/knobby tires in back; JC Whitney only, limited to 10,000 (1997) 20 - 25

Baja Bug-n

n. white; red int.; red, black, yellow & green design w/"Bug 'n Taxi" on sides & hood; sp5; #2 in Tropicool Series; #694 (1998) 2 - 4

Baja Bug-o

o. mtlfk blue; white int.; red, yellow & white Hot Wheels logo & "Nithia" on sides; bw; India; #835 (1998) 3 - 6

Baja Bug-p

p. red; tan int.; black & yellow tampo design w/"Dakar" & "Rally 1" on sides; bw; #835 (1998) 5 - 10

Baja Bug-q

q. red; purple int.; white, yellow & lt. purple tampo w/"The Original UNO" on sides & hood; sp5. Hot Wheels Cars-Timeless Toys 4-pack (1998) 6 - NA

Baja Bug-r

r. mtlfk blue; orange int.; black, yellow & orange tampo on sides & hood w/butterfly on sides; sp5; #4 Buggin' Out Series; #944 (1999) 4 - 6
s. mtlfk gray; black int.; yellow, black & red lightning tampo w/race decals on the sides & hood; #174 (2001) 3 - 5
s2. same as s, mtlfk gray painted chassis, #174 (2001) 2 - 3

4920-a

Battle Tank 4920 - 78mm - 1984
This Hong Kong-made army tank has a tan plastic chassis, tan plastic movable turret with gun on top and small black wheels. Similar casting: 9371 Command Tank (1985)

a. tan; dark green, white & brown camo tampo $5 - 7
b. same as a, Malaysia 5 - 7

5910-a

Blazer 4x4 5910 - 70mm - 1984
This Chevrolet S-10 Blazer has a metal chassis, opening doors, yellow-tinted plastic windows & lights on top, yellow plastic interior, and ct. It was made in Hong Kong.

a. black; yellow, red & white tampo w/"4x4 Blazer" on sides & hood $5 - 7
a2. same as a, Malaysia, #6 5 - 7
a3. same as a2, cts, #6 (1987) 5 - 7

Blazer 4X4-b

b. no #, olive, yellow tampo on hood, yellow "Digger Douglas Dinosaur Digger" on sides; yellow-tinted windows, yellow interior, Dinosaur Mud Pit set only (1988) 20 - NA

9231-c

c. 9231; lt. green; yellow, orange & blue tampo w/"4x4 Blazer" on sides; "4x4" on hood; yellow int.; yellow-tinted windows; Park 'n Plates (1990) 30 - 35
d. blue; orange, lt. green & dk. blue tampo w/"Blazer" twice on hood; "Blazer 4x4" on sides; gray int.; #6 (1991) 6 - 12

Values are shown in U.S. dollars, first price is for mint, second is for mint packaged vehicles only. See pages 15-16 for grading guide to determine value for cars in lesser conditions.

5910-d

d2. same as d, cts, #6 (1991) 8 - 15
e. blue, black mtlfks, yellow int., green-tinted windows, ct, #222 (1993) 6 - 8

Blazer 4x4-f

f. no #; pearl white; red, orange & blue tampo on sides & hood; blue-tinted windows, blue int., ct. 25th Anniv. Chevy 5-pack only (1993) 3 - NA

Blazer 4x4-g

g. no #; white; black World Cup mascot on sides; brown, black & blue "World Cup USA" & Hot Wheels logo on hood; blue-tinted windows; blue int.; ct. World Cup 5-pack only (1994) 6 - NA

12351-h

h. 12351; gray-blue; dk. red, yellow & blue stripes on sides; blue-tinted windows; gray int.; red Hot Wheels logo on side window; ct; #258 (1995) 3 - 6
h2. same as h, ctb, #258 (1996) 15 - 20
h3. same as h, cto, #258 (1996) 2 - 4

Blazer 4x4-i

i. 15972, mtlfk blue, yellow int., blue-tinted windows, ct, China, #464 (1997) 2 - 6
i2. same as i, cts (1998) 2 - 6

5901-a

Blown Camaro Z-28 5901 - 75mm - 1984
This Hong-Kong made customized 80s Camaro has a metal chassis, chrome plastic engine, clear plastic windows & sunroof, red plastic interior and gw.
Similar castings: 2115 #25 Hot Wheels (1992 Pro Circuit), 2738 #33 Duracell (1992 Pro Circuit)
a. black; yellow, red & orange striping on sides $8 - 10
a2. same as a, Malaysia 8 - 10

5901-b

b. no #, blue, white glow-in-dark tampo on hood & sides, plastic engine shows thru hood, clear window, red int., Malaysia. Turbotrax Turboglo set only (1987) 15 - NA

5901-c

c. turquoise; magenta, white & yellow tampo w/"Z-28" & "Camaro" on sides; "Z-28" on hood; gray int.; blue-tinted windows (1988) 6 - 8
c2. same as c, blue replaces magenta in tampo, #58 (1990) 3 - 5
c3. same as c2, uh, #58 (1990) 3 - 5
c4. same as c2, gw, #58 (1990) 3 - 5
c5. same as c2, bw, #58 3 - 5

5138-c6

c6. same as c2, no hood tampo, uh, Intl. line only (1992) 10 - 12
c7. same as c5, black replaces blue in tampo, Intl. line only (1992) 10 - 12
c8. same as c5, hoc (1992) 12 - 15
c9. same as c5, uhgd 250 - 350

Blown Camaro Z-28-d

d. no #, dk. mtlfk red; yellow, lt. blue & purple tampo w/"I.R.O.C. Camaro" & racing decals on sides; "Camaro" twice on hood; tan int.; uh; set or 20-pack only (1989) 15 - NA
d2. same as d, red int. 12 - NA
d3. same as d2, gray int., Canada only 10 - 12
d4. same as d2, bw, set or 20-pack only, loose at Mattel Toy Club (1989) 4 - NA
d5. same as d2, orange replaces purple in tampo (1989) 10 - NA
d6. same as d5, bw, set or 20-pack (1989) 10 - NA

Blown Camaro Z-28-e

e. no #; black; yellow, red & white stripes & white "Getty" in red & white square on sides; clear window; red int.; bw (1990) 5 - NA
e2. same as e, uh (1990) 20 - NA

1289-f

f. 1289; dk. red; orange, pink, lt. & dk. blue striping w/red "Cal Custom" on sides; yellow "Cal Custom" on windshield; black int.; black-tinted window; rrgy; California Custom (1990) 50 - 60

1289-g

g. white, same as f, California Custom (1990) 12 - 15
g2. as g, orange int. (1990) 10 - 12
g3. as g2, silver turbo wheels (1990) 5 - 7
g4. as g3, clear windows (1990) 65 - 75

9643-a

Delivery Van 9643 - 70mm - 1984
This Malaysia-made model has a black plastic chassis & interior, blue-tinted plastic windows, black plastic opening doors in back, and bw.
Similar castings: 9643 Letter Getter (1977), 2854 S.W.A.T. Van (1979), 2850 The Incredible Hulk (1979), 3303 Racing Team (1981), 2519 Combat Medic (1986), 2808 Delivery Truck (1989), 9114 The Simpson's Homer's Nuclear Waste Van (1990)
a. white; beige, red & brown stripe tampo w/"Frito Lay" on sides $100 - 125

5903-a

Dodge Rampage 5903 - 73mm - 1984
This Hong Kong-made concept El Camino-style Dodge truck has a metal chassis, clear plastic windows, yellow plastic interior, yellow 3-wheel ATV in the bed & gyg.
a. red; yellow, black & white stripe tampo with "Rampage" on sides, "2.2" on hood $15 - 18
a2. same as a, gyw, Malaysia 25 - 35
a3. same as a2, darker color & tampo, Mexico (1986) 45 - 60

5909-a

Dream Van XGW 5909 - 73mm - 1984
This concept customized futuristic van has a metal chassis, lift-up opening side door, clear plastic windows, tan plastic interior, gyg, and was made in Hong Kong.
a. mtlfk blue; yellow, lt. green & white stripe tampo on sides $25 - 30
a2. same as a, Malaysia 25 - 30
a3. same as a2, gyw 30 - 35
b. 9546; lt. green; same as a2; blue, red & yellow tampo; yellow-tinted plastic window; yellow int. (1985) 20 - 25
b2. same as b, darker tampo, orange-tinted windows, Mexico (1986) 70 - 80

9360-c

c. 9360; maroon; same as b; orange, red & yellow tampo; Stamper 3-pack only (1985) 30 - NA

Flame Runner 7293 - 67mm - 1984 (Ultra Hots)
This Hong Kong-made concept car has a metal chassis, exposed black plastic engine in back, red plastic front bumper & hood ornament, blacked-out plastic windows and uh.
Similar castings: 2018 Science Friction (1978), 3510 Lightning Storm (1993)

7293-a

a. mtlc gold; white, orange & dk. red flame tampo on top $6 - 8
a2. same as a, Malaysia 5 - 7

9346-b

b. 9346; unpainted; same as a2; yellow replaces orange in tampo; Ultra Hots Stamper 3-pack only (1985) 15 - NA

5904-a

Good Humor Truck 5904 - 68mm - 1984
This Hong Kong-made ice cream truck has a black plastic chassis, blue plastic interior & figure by the window, and bw.
Similar casting: 27110 Ice Cream Truck
a. white; blue, red & black tampo with "Good Humor" & ice cream types (including "Popsicle"), prices & flavors on sides $10 - 12
a2. same as a, Malaysia 8 - 10
a3. same as a2, "Popsicle" blacked-out (1986) 65 - 90
a4. same as a3, "Strawberry" replaces "Popsicle," Malaysia (1986) 5 - 7

5904-a5

a5. same as a3, blue & red reversed in tampo, #5 (1988) 6 - 12

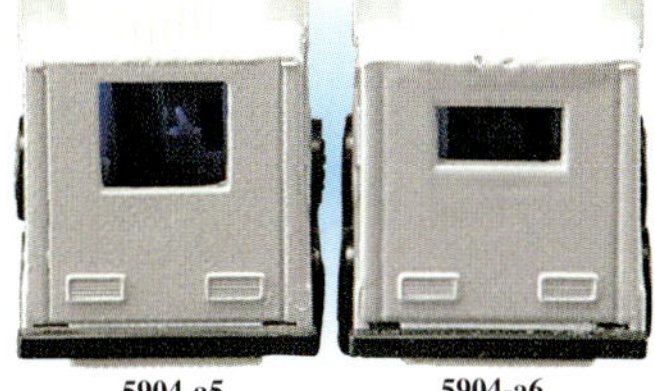
5904-a5 5904-a6

a6. same as a5, small rear window, #5 (1992) 4 - 6
a7. same as a6, sp5, #5 (1995) 4 - 6
a8. same as a5, dw3, #5 (1996) 3 - 5
a9. same as a6, sp7 (1996) 14 - 16

5904-b

b. red; yellow, blue & white tampo w/Pepsi logo, "Candy," "Cola," "Ice Cream," "Hot Dogs," "Pizza," "Hamburgers" & different foods shown on sides; tan plastic int.; Intl. line only (1990) 10 - 12

Values are shown in U.S. dollars, first price is for mint, second is for mint packaged vehicles only. See pages 15-16 for grading guide to determine value for cars in lesser conditions.

5904-b2

b2. same as b, no Pepsi logo (1992) 4 - 6

3206-c

c. 3206; lime green; same as b; orange, black & green tampo with "Skateboard," "Rental," "Cool" & 2 skateboarders on sides; green int.; bwgn. Issued as Ice Cream Truck, Canada, box only (1993) 15 - 18

Good Humor Truck-d

d. white; black plastic base; clear windows; lt. green int.; yellow, red, green & black tampo w/"Rasta Fruits and Veggies" on sides; #1 in Tropicool Series; #693 (1998) 3 - 5

d2. same as d, "Rasta" only on sides, #1 in Tropicool series, #693 (1998) 3 - 5

Good Humor Truck-e

e. white; orange chassis; lt. green int.; clear windows; lt. green, orange & black tampo w/"Espresso Stop" & coffee cup on sides; sp5; City Center 5-pack (1999) 2 - NA

Good Humor Truck-e2

e2. same as e; no coffee cup on sides (1999) 2 - NA

4372-a2

Lightning Gold 4372 - 75mm - 1984

This concept Grand Prix-type racer has a metal chassis & interior, rear spoiler, gyg, and was made in Malaysia.

Similar castings: 8273 El Rey Special (1974), 9037 Formula P.A.C.K., 9037 Malibu Grand Prix (1982)

a. yellow; red, white & black tampo w/"2" in front, "2" & race decals on sides, Hot Wheels logo on spoiler $20 - 25

a2. same as a, gyw 25 - 30

a3. same as a2, bw (1985) 8 - 10

5905-a2

Oshkosh Snowplow 5905 - 88mm - 1984

This Hong Kong-made dump truck with orange plastic detachable snow plow has a metal chassis, orange metal interior and ct.

a. orange $15 - 18

a2. as a, cto, #42, Malaysia 5 - 7

a3. as a2, plastic cab, #42 & #201 (1991) 6 - 8

a4. 2902, as a3, ctb, #201 (1995) 6 - 15

a5. as a4, dw3o, #201 (1995) 2 - 6

b. green, as a2, ct, color may vary, #42 (1990) 10 - 25

b2. as b, cts, color may vary, #42 (1990) 10 - 25

b3. as b, plastic cab, #42 (1990) 8 - 15

b4. as b2, plastic cab, #42 (1990) 8 - 15

c. 15226; black; yellow & turquoise flames on sides & hood; black int.; ct; #4 in Flamethrower series; #387 (1996) 3 - 6

5905-c2

c2. same as c, ctb 6 - 10

Oshkosh Snowplow-d

d. 2902, mtlfk red, gray plastic cab & dumper, "Fresno Feed Co." on sides, dw3ct, #201 (1997) 3 - 6

Oshkosh Snowplow-e

e. white; orange cab & bed; white int.; "K34," "Road Dept" & logo on sides; dw3ct; Road Repair 5-pack only (1998) 2 - NA

Oshkosh Snowplow-g

f. mtlfk blue, white cab & bed, gray plow in bed, blue int., dwct, Oshkosh P-Series, #765 (1999) 2 - 3

g. white; gray cab & bed; white int.; black, light blue, white & red tampo with "Avalanche Resort" & "Maintenance" on sides; dw3ct; Thailand; Snow Patrol 5-pack (2000) 2 - NA

h. dark yellow; black cab & dump; dark yellow int.; red, white & yellow tampo w/"Hank's Hauler" on sides; dw3ct; #233 (2000) 2 - 3

5609-a

Phone Truck 5906 - 82mm - 1984

This Hong Kong-made model has a metal chassis, clear plastic windows, interior & lights on top, yellow plastic boom and bw.

a. white; orange, yellow & black stripe tampo with "Mark's Phone Co." on sides $7 - 9

a2. same as a, Malaysia 7 - 9

5906-a3

a3. same as a2, no "Mark's" on sides 12 - 15

a4. same as a3, Mexico (1986) 12 - 20

7292-a

Predator 7292 - 75mm - 1984 (Ultra Hots)

Based on the Porsche 928, this model has a metal chassis, black-tinted plastic windows, uh, and was made in Hong Kong.

Similar castings: 5180 P-928 (1982), 9537 Nightstreaker (1985)

a. mtlc green; lt. green, yellow & white lightning bolt tampo on sides $8 - 10

a2. same as a, Malaysia 8 - 10

7295-a

Quik Trik 7295 - 70mm - 1984

Based on the Ferrari 308 GTB, this Hong Kong-made model has a black metal chassis, black-tinted plastic windows and uh.

Similar castings: 17962, Ferrari 308 GTB (1997), 2021 Race Bait 308 (1978), 9538 Street Beast (1985), 3494 Hot Wheels (1993 Tattoo Machines)

a. mtlc magenta; orange, lt. orange & white tampo on top; "Ultra Hots" on hood $5 - 7

a2. same as a, Malaysia 5 - 7

3290-a2

Rolls-Royce Phantom II 3290 - 78mm - 1984

This Malaysia-made 1935 roadster has a metal chassis, tan plastic removable top, black interior, clear plastic windshield & bw.

a. metalflake light blue $6 - 8

a2. same as a, ww, #50 10 - 12

3290-b

b. mtlfk silver, taller & shorter top, taller windshield, bw, "France" on base, (1985), Europe only 120 - 140

b2. gray, same as b, "France" on base, (1985), Europe only 60 - 70

b3. same as b2, ww, (1985), Europe only 60 - 70

3290-b2

13356-c

c. 13356, dk. mtlfk red, tan plastic roof, metal running boards, red int. & wheel covers, Hot Wheels logo in white oval in back, sp6r, #8 in Treasure Hunt series, #360 (1995) 50 - 75

d. gold-plated, gold-plated base, clear windshield, black int., tan plastic roof, iwgd. FAO Schwarz 24K Gold Classics 3-pack only (1995) 60 - NA

5902-a

Sol-Aire® CX4 5902 - 75mm - 1984 (Ultra Hots)

This Hong Kong-made concept racer has a metal chassis, rear wing, opening rear hood, black-tinted plastic windshield & uh.

a. unpainted; yellow, red & orange stripe tampo w/"Ultra Hots" in front $5 - 7

a2. same as a, Malaysia 5 - 7

b. metallic silver, same as a2 5 - 7

9342-c

c. 9342; mtlc dk. red; yellow, white & black lightning-style tampo w/"Ultra Hots" on sides; Ultra Hots Stamper 3-pack only (1985) 15 - NA

Sol-Aire CX4-d

d. no #; red; white, yellow & blue stripe tampo on top & sides w/arrow point in front; Turbotrax set only (1986) 15 - NA

e. red, same as b; purple not red in tampo (1988) 6 - 8

e2. same as e; blue replaces red in tampo (1989) 4 - 6

1494-f

f. 1494; black; magenta, orange & yellow stripe tampo on top & sides; "33" on sides & top in front & back; blacked-out window (1989) 10 - 12

f2. same as f, yellow-tinted window, unpainted metal int. (1989) 4 - 6

f3. same as f2, blue replaces purple in tampo, #2 (1989) 3 - 5

f4. same as f3, hoc, #2 (1991) 8 - 10

f5. same as f3, turquoise replaces blue in tampo 3 - 5

f6. same as f5, uhgd, #2 6 - 8

f7. same as f5, hoc 6 - 8

2200-g

g. 2200; yellow; red, orange & dk. blue tampo w/"13 GTS" on sides; blacked-out windows; Park 'n Plates (1989) 8 - 10

g2. same as g, blue-tinted plastic

windows, chrome plastic int. (1989) 8 - 10
g3. 9232, same as j, in Park 'n Plates under name "Fast GT" (1989) 8 - 10

5902-h

h. 5902; red; magenta, yellow & orange stripe tampo on top w/"Ultra Hots" in front; blacked-out windows (1989) 10 - 12
i. 5902, red, same as a, blue not magenta in tampo, Intl. line only (1990) 8 - 10

2105-j

j. 2105; bright pink-red; yellow, pink & blue tampo on sides & top: "2" on sides & hood; yellow-tinted windows, gray int., tw; California Custom (1991) 10 - 12
j2. same as j, lt. blue metal base, California Custom (1991) 50 - 60

5902-k

k. red; same as g; yellow, orange & black tampo, Heroes of Hot Wheels tapes only, never in bp; w/video 12 - 15

5902-l

l. blue; orange, purple & dk. red tampo on sides & top w/"2" on sides & hood; clear windows; chrome int.; uh; #169 (1992) 20 - 25
l2. same as l, black plastic chassis & int., hoc, #169 (1992) 15 - 20
l3. same as l2, uh, #169 (1992) 8 - 12
l4. same as l3, plastic base, #169 (1992) 2 - 4

5902-m

m. white; red, black & blue playing-card-suits tampo; black-tinted windows; black int.; gray plastic base; uhgn; Malaysia; Revealers 4 - 6
n. Day-Glo yellow; same as m; uhp; Revealers 4 - 6
o. candy blue, same as m, uhy, Revealers 4 - 6
p. no #; Day-Glo orange; same as m; dk. red, blue & green tampo; black plastic base. 25th Anniv. Dream Car 5-pack only (1993) 3 - NA
q. 13578; mtlfk blue; white base & sides w/"1" & red & yellow Hot Wheels logo; "1," Hot Wheels logo & Chevrolet emblem in front; yellow "Hot Wheels" on spoiler; clear windows; white int.; uhgd; #254 (1994) 4 - 6

13578-q2

q2. same as q, tinted windows, uh, 5-pack only (1995) 3 - NA

Sol-Aire CX4-s

q3. same as q2, clear windows, #254 (1995) 3 - 5
q4. same as q3, sp7, #254 (1995) 4 - 6
q5. blue, same as q, lwgd, #254 (1996), Collector, #823 (1998) 4 - 6
q6. same as q5, lwch, Race Team Hauler 3-pack only (1998) 4 - NA
r. dk. blue, same as q, sp7, Hot Wheels Race Team 5-pack only (1995) 3 - NA
s. 16928, mtlfk dk. red, white sides, black spy design & blue "Infiltration" on sides, blacked-out windows, dw3. Car 3 in Spy Print Series, #555 (1997) 2 - 4
s2. same as s, sp3, #3 in Spy Print Series, #555 (1997) 2 - 4

Sol-Aire CX4-u

u. white, blue chassis & int., clear windows, red & blue flag tampo on sides & top, lww. #8 in 1998 Treasure Hunt Series, #757 (1998) 18 - 25
v. yellow; black chassis & int.; clear windows; black, red & gray tampo design on sides, hood & wing; sp5. #3 in Flyin' Aces Series, #739 (1998) 2 - 3

Sol-Aire CX4-v2

v2. same as v, ho5, #739 (1999) 6 - 8
v3. same as v, sp3, #739 (1999) 2 - 3

Sol-Aire CX4-w

w. white; black plastic chassis; blue-tinted windows; red & dk. blue tampo; logo on sides & hood; "Skip Bo" on sides & rear spoiler; sp3; Malaysia. #3 in Classic Games Series, #983 (1999) 2 - 3

Sol-Aire CX4-x

x. white; black int.; yellow-tinted windows; black, orange & yellow tampo on sides & top with "Birdhouse" on sides; sp3. #2 in Tony Hawk Skate Series, Malaysia, #042 (2000) 2 - 3
y. mtlfk purple; black int.; purple engine; yellow, black & red tampo on sides; lwch; China; Kool Toyz Power Launcher pack (2001) 5 - 8
z. mtlfk dark blue, white chassis & interior, clear windows, red & white tampo w/"41" on sides, lwch, China, Pavement Pounder pack (2001) 4 - 7
aa. dk. blue; gray chassis & int.; clear windows; white, blue, red & black tampo on sides; sp3; #153 (2002) 2 - 3

Space Vehicle 2855 - 75mm - 1984
This Hong Kong-made concept model has a chrome plastic chassis & interior, clear windows, and bw. Mexico only.
Similar castings: 2855 Space Van (1979), 3304 Rescue Squad (1981), 5273 Tac-Com (1982 Megaforce)

2855-a

a. gray; red & white lightning on sides (1984) $50 - 60

2855-a2

a2. gray, no tampo (1984) 70 - 80

7299-a

Speed Seeker 7299 - 75mm - 1984 (Ultra Hots)
This concept car has a metal chassis, two black-tinted movable plastic canopies, uh, and was made in Hong Kong.
Similar castings: 6423 Mantis (1970), 6975 Double Vision (1973), 15258 Speed Machine (1996)
a. mtlc dk. red; black, yellow & white lightning bolt tampo in front $10 - 12
a2. same as a, Malaysia 10 - 12

9348-b

b. 9348, mtlc gold, same as a2, red replaces black in tampo, yellow-tinted canopies, yellow plastic int., Ultra Hots Stamper 3-pack only (1985) 15 - NA

1512-c

c. 1512; white; red & green snake tampo on hood (1987) 6 - 8

Team Bus 3256 - see Rapid Transit (1982)

5900-a

Thunderbird Stocker 5900 - 78mm - 1984
This Ford stock car has a metal chassis, clear plastic windows, black plastic interior, gw, and was made in Hong Kong.
Similar castings: 1456 Thunderburner (1987), 2565 #6 Valvoline (1992 Pro Circuit), 2568 #21 Citgo (1992 Pro Circuit), 16039 Velocitor (1996)
a. white; dk. blue tampo covering back; red, blue & dk. blue tampo w/"21," "Valvoline" & race decals on sides, "21" on roof, "V" & "Valvoline" on hood $30 - 35
a2. same as a, Malaysia 30 - 35

4921-a

Troop Convoy (Army Convoy) 4921 - 78mm - 1984
This Hong Kong-made army convoy truck has a tan metal chassis & interior, tan plastic truck bed with matching removable cover and beige bw.
a. tan; white tampo w/star & "U.S. Army" on hood $4 - 6
a2. same as a, Malaysia, bwbk 4 - 6

4921-b

b. olive; same as a2; green, brown & tan camo tampo on top of cover; white hood tampo; black bw #7 (1985) 6 - 8
b2. same as b, no tampo on top (1987) 4 - 6

4921-c

c. lt. brown; same as b; brown, white & black camo tampo; #195 (1993) 6 - 8
c2. same as c, olive roof & cover, star & "U.S. Army" twice on hood, bww. Action Command 5-pack only (1994) 3 - NA
d. 16296, mtlfk gray, black metal base, orange roof & trailer, black canopy, gray int., sp5, China, #487 (1996) 4 - 6

Troop Convoy-e

e. 16296, mtlfk aqua, same as d, "Luis' Ranch Markets" in lt. blue & lt. brown on sides, aqua base, tan canopy, sp5, #487 (1997) 2 - 4

5911-a

Turbo Heater 5911 - 70mm - 1984
This Hong Kong-made Dodge Daytona has a metal chassis, blue-tinted plastic windows, beige plastic interior and bw.
Similar casting: 2524 Highway Heat (1986)
a. magenta; white & yellow stripe tampo; "Turbo" outlined in red on hood $8 - 10
a2. same as a, lighter blue-tinted windows, Malaysia 8 - 10

9524-b

b. 9524, mtlfk blue, same as a2, lt. blue not red in tampo, yellow int. (1985) 8 - 10

7296-a

Wind Splitter 7296 - 78mm - 1984 (Ultra Hots)
This Hong Kong-made BMW M1 has a metal chassis, black plastic-ribbed rear window, blacked-out plastic windows, black plastic interior and uh.
Similar castings: 3289 BMW M1 (1983), 3501 Street Dog (1993 Tattoo Machines)
a. mtlc blue; white & dk. blue lightning bolt tampo on top $6 - 8
a2. same as a, Malaysia 6 - 8

Values are shown in U.S. dollars, first price is for mint, second is for mint packaged vehicles only. See pages 15-16 for grading guide to determine value for cars in lesser conditions.

7296-b

b. 9539, mtlc green, same as a2, yellow & black tampo (1985) 5 - 7

Wind Splitter-c

c. no #; yellow; blue, orange & magenta tampo on top, "Turbo" twice on hood; only in set or sold at Mattel Toy Club (1987) 6 - NA

d. mtlc aqua, same as c, yellow & black tampo (1985) 6 - 8

1985

A special model, Snake Busters Car (a metalflake version of Cannonade with a special tampo) was issued in the Masters of the Universe set. Army vehicles reappeared with the Action Command series. The six vehicles included tanks, trucks and a jeep. Indy-style vehicles were also reintroduced after a six- or seven-year absence. Stamper 3-packs were issued with three combinations: Real Riders, Ultra Hots and Hot Ones. These packs included models never sold in a single blisterpack.

9372-a

Big Bertha 9372 - 78mm - 1985
This army tank has an olive plastic base & movable turret with long gun barrel, small black wheels, and was made in Malaysia. Similar castings: 7655 Tough Customer (1975), 5272 Battle Tank (1982 Megaforce)

a. olive; green, brown & tan camo tampo, #79 $5 - 7

9372-b

b. tan, same as a, tan not olive in base & turret, white not tan in tampo (1988) 5 - 7

9372-c

c. lt. gray-brown; same as b; brown, black & white tampo; #159 (1992) 6 - 8

d. 19309; dk. mtlfk gray; orange turret & gun; China; #489 (1996) 2 - 4

16309-e

e. 16309; black; fluor. magenta camo tampo; China; #489 (1997) 2 - 4

9544-a

Black Lightning 9544 - 75mm - 1985
This Indy-style racer has a metal base, unpainted metal front & back spoilers, metal engine in back, unpainted metal figure in cockpit, gyg, and was made in Malaysia. Similar casting: 3914 Turbo Streak (1983)

a. black; white, yellow & red lightning tampo on top & sides; "3" in front, "3" & racing decals on sides $25 - 30

a2. same as a, bw (1987) 8 - 10

9371-a

Command Tank® 9371 - 78mm - 1985
This army tank has an olive plastic base & movable turret with short gun barrel & small black wheels, and was made in Malaysia. Similar casting: 4920 Battle Tank (1984)

a. olive; green, brown & tan camo tampo, #27 $4 - 6

Command Tank-b

b. no #, black, same as a, black metal chassis, lt & dk. gray tampo w/black spider on yellow circle, Battleground 4-pack (1985) 30 - NA

c. white; same as a; gray, black & tan tampo; #160 (1992) 6 - 8

d. no #, dk. green, olive plastic base, lt. olive turret & gun, sm black wheels, 5-pack only (1995) 3 - NA

e. no #; lt. green; same as d; olive, lt. brown & brown camo tampo; dk. green turret & gun; 5-pack only (1995) 8 - NA

9371-e2

e2. same as e; green & black camouflage tampo w/dk. red, yellow & black bullet holes w/flames on sides (1995) 75 - NA

9371-f

f. black; fluor. magenta camo tampo & "Night Force" in gray on sides; China; #486 (1997) 2 - 4

f2. same as f, no "Night Force," 486 (1997) 2 - 4

9523-a

Fat Fendered '40™ 9523 - 77mm - 1985
This 1940 Ford sedan has a metal base, clear plastic windows, black plastic interior, bw, and was made in Malaysia. Similar casting: 3919 '40s Ford 2-Door (1983)

a. mtlc red; white, yellow & turquoise stripe tampo on sides $30 - 35

b. mtlc plum, no tampo, dk. gray int., Mexico (1986) 40 - 50

4315-c

c. 4315, purple, yellow flames outlined in dk. red on sides, clear windows, black int., metal base, bw, #216 (1993) 20 - 25

Fat Fendered '40-d

d. no #, vacuum metallized silver, 25th Anniv. logo on roof, black int., 25th Anniv. Ford 5-pack only (1993) 18 - NA

12275-e

e. 12275; white; yellow, red & orange flames on sides & hood; blue "Steadly Quikwheels" on roof; tinted windows; tan int.; red-line rr. Limited to 7000, card reads "Limited Edition Steadly Tudor" (1994) 25 - 35

11267-f

f. 11267; yellow; red & black flame tampo on sides, hood & fenders; black Hot Wheels logo on trunk; tan int.; tinted windows; rt. Limited to 7000, packaged in black 25th Anniv. box, Mattel mail-in and Toy Club only (1994) 40 - 45

g. chrome, red int., red Hot Wheels logo on back, rsw. Service Merchandise 16-piece Classic American Car Collection only, limited to 5000 (1995) 10 - NA

15022-h

h. 15022; mtlfk blue; yellow, orange & black flame design w/"Warshawsky JC Whitney" in flames; blue-tinted window; red int.; sp5; limited to 7000; in box (1995) 30 - 35

15568-i

i. 15568; dk. mtlfk blue; yellow, orange & red flame logo from front toward back; "Early Times Mid-Winter 96 Rod Run" in red, yellow & gold on roof; clear windows; gray int.; pc; limited to 8000 (1996) 40 - 50

9523-j

j. dk. mtlfk red, clear windows, tan int., iwgd, in 100th Anniv. of Auto gift pack (1996) 12 - NA

Fat Fendered '40-k

k. 17930; turquoise; clear windows; black int.; magenta, red & yellow stripes; sp5; China; #607 (1997) 8 - 12

Fat Fendered '40-l

l. ruby red; tinted windows; black int.; yellow, orange & blue flames; "Firebird Raceway" in white; "Ignitor Sedan" in yellow; iw. Ignitor Sedan limited edition of 10,000 (1998) 18 - 24

Fat Fendered '40-m

m. red, clear windows, white int., black & white tampo on sides & hood w/"Lexmark" on sides & "Optra" on rear side window, gyw. Lexmark premium, limited edition of 10,000, China, box only (1998) 20 -25

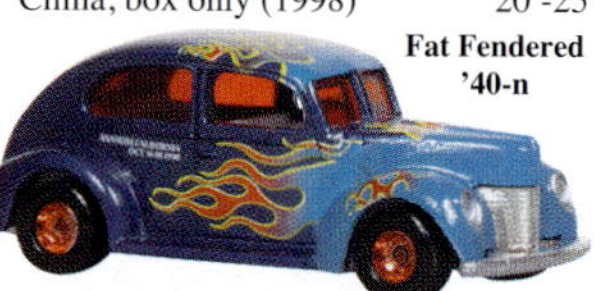
Fat Fendered '40-n

n. lt. blue & dk. blue; red-tinted windows; white int.; yellow & red flames; "Anaheim California Oct. 16-18, 1998" in white on sides; 1998 Convention logo on roof; rr in red chrome; 1998 Hot Wheels Convention (1998) 20 - 25

Fat Fendered '40-o

o. lt. blue; dk. blue top; blue int.; clear windows; yellow, dk. blue & lt. blue tampo on sides & hood w/"Blue Angels" written on roof twice & Blue Angel logo on trunk; rrch w/white stripe around tire. M & D Toys' limited edition for Blue Angels (1998) 20 - 25

Fat Fendered '40-p

p. white; black fenders; dk. blue, black & blue tampo; Providence, RI Police Dept. shield; "Providence Police" & "Patrol Bureau" on sides; "Providence Police" & "Pride in Providence" on roof; rrch. Limited to 25,000 in Cop Rods Series for K•B Toys (1999) 5 - 7

Fat Fendered '40-q

q. black; white int.; yellow, red & blue spray mask flame tampo on hood & sides w/"Showtime Forty" on sides;

Values are shown in U.S. dollars, first price is for mint, second is for mint packaged vehicles only. See pages 15-16 for grading guide to determine value for cars in lesser conditions.

Boise Roadster Show logo on trunk; rrch w/white wall tires; limited to 15,000 for Boise Roadster Show (2000) 15 - 20

Fat Fendered '40-r

r. blue; clear windows; tan int.; black, silver & orange tampo w/"The Weise Brothers" on sides; lwch; #3 in Circus on Wheels series; Malaysia; #27 (2000) 3 - 5
r2. same as r, dw3, #27 (2000) 2 - 3

Fat Fendered '40-s

s. gray; white int.; red-tinted windows; black, white, orange & red tampo with "Chuck E. Cheese's" on sides; sp5; for Chuck E. Cheese's Pizza (2001) 10 - 12

Fat Fendered '40-t

t. black; white int; tinted windows; white sides; gold, black & white tampo with "Police 10746" & emblem on sides; license plate w/"Hope" in back; for Los Angeles Police Dept. (2001) 12 - 15
u. black; white int.; clear windows; red, white, orange & gray tampo on sides; sp3; Thailand; Hot Rods 5-pack 3 - NA

Fat Fendered '40-v

v. dark mtlfk red; white top & int.; clear windows; orange, yellow & turquoise flames on sides; ww; Target Exclusive Elvis Drive-In 4-pack (2001) 6 - NA
w. mtlfk blue; blue-tinted windows; white int.; yellow & black design on sides, hood & roof; Editor's Choice logo on trunk; rrch; Target Exclusive Editor's Choice series (2001) 20 - 25
x. mtlfk black; white int., yellow-tinted windows; white, gray, red & yellow tampo w/"Lightning Fast Delivery" on sides & roof; sp5; Malaysia; Truck Stoppers 5-pack (2001) 4 - NA
y. turquoise, black fenders and int, clear windows, purple, blue and gray flames on sides and roof , black and white Motor City Classics logo on trunk and rrch. Wal-Mart excl. Motor City Classics series. (2002) 4 - NA

7527-a

Fiero 2M4 7527 - 68mm - 1985
This Hong Kong-made Pontiac two-seater sports car has a black metal chassis, clear plastic sun roof & windows, black plastic interior, and gw.
a. white; red, yellow & black tampo with "Fiero" on sides, "Fiero" & shield on hood $8 - 10
a2. same as a, Malaysia 8 - 10
b. 1458; red; white & blue stars & stripes on sides & hood, "Fiero" on sides (1987) 3 - 5

1458-b3

b2. same as b, uh, #114 6 - 12
b3. same as b2, no hood tampo, in Hot Wheels cereal (1990) 4 - 5

1458-b4

b4. same as b, bw, #114 (1991) 25 - 75
b5. same as b4, uh, #114 (1991) 4 - 6

9552-c

c. black; red, yellow & blue confetti tampo on sides, "Fiero" on hood, metal chassis; red int.; uh; #114 (1991) 6 - 15
c2. same as c, bw, #114 (1991) 10 - 25
c3. same as c, hoc, #114 (1992) 10 - 22
c4. same as c2, black metal base, #114 (1991) 8 - 12
d. lt. green, gold glitter, metal base, clear windows, yellow interior, uh, #181 (1992) 6 - 8
d2. same as d, hoc #181 15 - 20

Fiero 2M4-e

e. no #; black; yellow, orange & red tampo on sides & hood; red int.; uh (1993) 6 - NA
f. mtlfk lime, metal base, clear windows, black int., sp5, China, #463 (1996) 3 - 6

195962-f2

f2. same as f, black stripe on sides, black logo & "Fiero" on hood, China, #463 (1997) 3 - 6
f3. same as f2, lwch, #463 (1997) 2 - 3
g. no #, dk. mtlc red, same as f, tinted windows, sp5gd, China. Kmart exclusive 70th Anniv. of Pontiac only, limited to 7,000 (1996) 10 - NA

9541-a

Good Ol' Pick-Um-Up 9541 - 70mm - 1985
This Malaysia-made 1956 Ford pickup truck has a chrome plastic chassis, clear plastic windshield, red plastic interior, two red plastic motorcycles in the truck bed, and gyw. Similar casting: 9647 '56 Hi-Tail Hauler (1977)
a. plum; white, blue & black tampo with star & "Good 'Ol Pick-Um-Up" on hood $50 - 60
b. mtlc plum, same as a, lighter blue in tampo, bw, Mexico (1987) 130 - 160

Gulch Stepper® 7532 - 65mm - 1985
This Hong Kong-made concept vehicle of a high-rise 4x4 pickup has a metal chassis, black plastic windows, spare tire on the hood and ct.

7532-a

a. yellow; orange, red & purple stripe; tan roof $4 - 6
a2. same as a, cts 4 - 6
a3. same as a, orange roof 4 - 6
a4. same as a2, orange roof 4 - 6

1516-b

b. red; white, lt. blue & yellow stripe with "15" & racing decals on sides; Malaysia; #49 (1987) 15 - 18
b2. same as b, no Pennzoil in tampo, #49 (1987) 20 - 22
b3. same as b, cts, #49 (1987) 20 - 22

Gulch Stepper-c

c. no #; white; lt. green, dk. green & pink design on sides; shopping-mall give-away in 2-pack, later bought by dealers (1992) 8 - NA
d. fluor. green-yellow; same as b; red, black & orange tampo; #219 (1993) 8 - 10

7532-e

e. bright green, "Hormel Foods" & stripes in red & white on sides, blacked-out windows, ct. Hormel exclusive in baggies only, never in bp (1995) 4 - NA

12343-f

f. 12343; red; yellow & black tampo on sides & roof, yellow Hot Wheels logo on front fender; blacked-out windows; ct; #251 (1995) 4 - 6

12343-g 12343-g2

g. 12343, black, same as f, red & yellow tampo, roof has yellow inside red, #251 (1995) 10 - 12
g2. same as g, roof tampo reversed, #251 (1995) 45 - 50

Gulch Stepper-h

g3. same as g, dw3ct, #251 (1997) 4 - 6
h. mtlc yellow; black windows; magenta, black & white tampo w/"Gulch Stepper" on sides; dw3ct; #884 (1998) 2 - 3

Gulch Stepper-i

i. red; black, yellow, blue & white tampo w/"27," Mojave Racing & race decals on sides; dw3ct; Thailand; Baja Blazers 5-pack (1999) 2 - NA

Gulch Stepper-j

j. yellow, yellow chassis, black windows, black & white tampo on sides & top with "85 Gulch Stepper" on sides, "Final Run" on windshield, dw3ct with "Final Run" in white around tires, #3 in Final Run series (2001) 5 - 7

7528-a

Jet Sweep X5 7528 - 76mm - 1985
This Hong Kong-made concept race car has a metal chassis, lift-up body to show a metal jet engine, black plastic window & rear spoiler, and uh.
a. mtlc yellow; white, orange & dk. orange lightning tampo on top $5 - 7
a2. same as a, Malaysia 5 - 7
b. unpainted, same as a2, purple replaces dk. orange in tampo, red-tinted plastic spoiler & window (1986) 5 - 7

9531-a

Mustang S.V.O. 9531 - 73mm - 1985
This model has a black metal chassis, gray-tinted plastic windows, red interior, gw, and was made in Malaysia.
Similar casting: 1125 Turbo Mustang (1980)
a. black; white, yellow & red stripe on top & sides; "S.V.O." & "Mustang" on sides $12 - 15

Nightstreaker 9537 - 75mm - 1985
Based on the Porsche 928, this model has a metal chassis, black-tinted plastic windows, uh, and was made in Malaysia. Similar castings: 5180 P-928 (1982), 7292 Predator (1984)

Values are shown in U.S. dollars, first price is for mint, second is for mint packaged vehicles only. See pages 15-16 for grading guide to determine value for cars in lesser conditions.

9537-a

a. mtlc magenta; white, yellow & turquoise lightning tampo on top $8 - 10
a2. same as a, gray windows 12 - 15

9537-b

b. 1497; mtlfk gray; yellow, orange & purple stripe; "928" & "Porsche" on sides (1987) 8 - 10

7529-a

Nissan 300ZX 7529 - 74mm - 1985
This Hong Kong-made model has a red metal chassis, opening side doors, clear plastic windows, black plastic interior, and gw.
a. red; white, yellow & black tampo on sides & top; "Nissan 300ZX" on sides; "300ZX" & "Turbo" twice on hood $8 - 10
a2. same as a, Malaysia 8 - 10

Nissan 300ZX-b

b. no #, mtlfk dk. blue, blue metal chassis, yellow & purple stripes on top, white "Turbo" outlined in purple on hood. In Turbotrax Speed Trigger or sold loose at Mattel Toy Club (1986) 4 - NA

1454-c

c. 1454; yellow; yellow metal chassis; red, white & blue stripes on top; "300ZX" twice on hood (1987) 5 - 7
c2. same as c, uh, 20-car gift pack only (1989) 10 - NA

7529-d

d. white; white metal chassis; blue, yellow & red tampo w/"Nissan" & "300" on sides, stripes on top,"300 ZX" on hood; gw; #54 (1989) 100 - 200
d2. same as d, uh, #54 (1989) 15 - 28

2140-e

e. 2140; white; red, yellow & blue tampo on top; "300 ZX" twice on hood; unpainted metal base; black int.; Park 'n Plates (1989) 20 - 25
e2. same as e, white metal base (1989) 10 - 12
e3. same as e, red int., (1989) 18 - 20

Nissan 300ZX-f

f. no #; white; metal base; red, yellow & blue stripes on roof & hood; white "Getty" in red square on hood; red int.; Getty promo (1990) 5 - NA
f2. same as f, white metal base (1990) 5 - NA

Nissan 300ZX-g

g. 16363, mtlc purple, clear windows, purple int., gold & black on hood & rear fender, sp5, China, #506 (1997) 2 - 6

9542-a

Pavement Pounder 9542 - 77mm - 1985
This Malaysia-made Chevrolet pickup truck has a metal chassis, clear plastic windows & sun roof, black plastic interior & truck bed, and gyw.
Similar castings: 2509 Bywayman (1979), 1129 Super Scraper (1980), 2538 Power Plower (1986)
a. lt. green; yellow, dk. green & black tampo w/"Henry's Hauling" on sides $20 - 25

9534-a

Redliner 9534 - 65mm - 1985
Based on the American Motors experimental car AMX/2, this model has a black plastic chassis & interior, black plastic windows, uh, and was made in Hong Kong.
Similar castings: 6460 AMX/2 (1971), 6977 Xploder (1973), 7654 Warpath (1975), 1510
a. mtlc gold; white, orange & dk. orange lightning tampo on top $6 - 8

9375-a

Roll Patrol® Jeep CJ-7 9375 - 68mm - 1985
This model has an olive plastic chassis & interior, black roll bar, clear plastic windshield, bwbk, and was made in Malaysia.
Similar castings: 3259 Jeep CJ-7 (1982), 5636 Trailbuster (1991). New casting: 9560 Roll Patrol (1991)
a. olive; tan, green & brown camouflage tampo on hood; #12 $6 - 8

9375-b

b. tan, same as a, tan base & seats, white replaces tan in tampo (1988) 12 - 15
b2. same as b, beige seats (1988) 12 - 15
b3. same as b, black int., bw 6 - 8
c. olive, same as b, new casting, #115 (1991) 16 - 25

9375-c

d. lt. gray-brown; same as c; black, lt. brown & white tampo; black int.; clear windshield; ct; #161 (1992) 6 - 18
d2. same as d, ctb, #161 (1992) 4 - 12
d3. same as d, bwbk, #161 (1992) 4 - 10
d4. same as d, new tampo, star on hood, ctb, #161 (1992) 4 - 18

13291-e

e. 13291, white, black-tinted metal base, black zebra stripes, black Hot Wheels logo on sides, tinted windshield, black int., cty, #2 in Roarin' Rods, #304 (1995) 3 - 8
e2. 3291, same as e, ct, #304 (1995) 20 - 35
f. black, gold Hot Wheels logo in back, black metal base, clear windshield, black plastic int., ct. Target-exclusive Black Convertible Collection only 6 - NA

15261-g

g. 15261; lt. brown; orange metal base; red, white & black tampo w/gorilla face on hood & hair on sides; clear windshield; orange int. & spare tire; cty. #4 in Street Eaters, #415 (1996) 2 - 10
g2. same as g, dw3y, #415 (1996) 2 - 6
g3. same as g, ct, #415 (1996) 16 - 20

Roll Patrol Jeep CJ-7-h

h. white, black int., clear windshield, brown mud tampo w/blue & red "JC Whitney" on hood & sides, rrch. Limited to 10,000, in box (1997) 15 -20

Roll Patrol Jeep CJ-7-i

i. lt. blue; tinted windshield; black int.; red, white, dk. blue tampo w/"Roll Patrol" in circle & "6" on sides; dw3ct. Off-Road 4x4's 5-pack only (1998) 2 - NA
j. mtlfk purple; blue int.; clear windshield; white, lt. blue & black tampo w/"Avalanche Resort" & "Guest

Roll Patrol-j

Services" on sides & hood; dw3ct; Thailand; Snow Patrol 5-pack (2000) 3 - NA

Roll Patrol-k

k. yellow; tan int.; tinted windshield; gray, blue & black tampo on sides & hood w/"30," "Mudcat" & race decals on sides; dw3ct; #1037 (1999) 6 - 12
l. red; tinted windshield; tan int.; black, white, orange & gray tampo with "Hawaii" on sides; w3ct; Thailand; #199 (2001) 2 - 3
m. blue; red int.; blue-tinted windshield; yellow, orange & black tampo with "Coast Rescue," "Unit 5" & "Rescue Network" on sides; dw3ct; Thailand; #194 (2001) 2 - 3

9521-a

Screamin' 9521 - 75mm - 1985
This Dodge funny-car dragster has a metal chassis, lift-up body, metal engine & interior, bw, and was made in Malaysia.
Similar castings: 2023 Army Funny Car (1978), 2881 Human Torch (1979), 2023 Pepsi Challenger (1982)
a. red; lt. blue, orange & yellow tampo on top & sides; "Screamin'" on sides 15 - 20

2532-b

b. 2532; green; same as a; dk. green, yellow & white tampo (1986) 30 - 35

9535-a

Silver Bullet 9535 - 75mm - 1985
This concept model has a metal chassis, blacked-out plastic windows, uh, and was made in Hong Kong.
Similar castings: 8272 Large Charge (1975), 1781 Aeroflash (1992 Gleam Team)
a. unpainted; yellow, orange & purple lightning on top, "Ultra Hots" in back $10 - 12
a2. same as a, Malaysia 5 - 7
b. mtlfk silver, same as a, Malaysia 5 - 7
c. black plastic body, mtlfk dark red chassis, red-tinted windows, red & white tampo on top, dw3, Thailand, #229 (2001) 2 - 3

Snake Busters Car 1691 - 72mm - 1985
This Hong Kong-made concept model has a blue plastic chassis, purple plastic interior & engine sticking out the back, opening canopy, clear plastic windows and uh. It was only sold in the Snake Mountain

Values are shown in U.S. dollars, first price is for mint, second is for mint packaged vehicles only. See pages 15-16 for grading guide to determine value for cars in lesser conditions.

1691-b2

Challenge set, although b. & c. were sold loose at the Mattel Toy Club. It was never issued in blisterpack.
Similar casting: 1691 Cannonade (1981)

a. unpainted; yellow, red & black tampo w/Masters of the Universe logo on sides $20 - NA
b. mtlfk silver, same as a 6 - NA
b2. same as b, gw 6 - NA

9538-a

Street Beast™ 9538 - 70mm - 1985
This Hong Kong-made Ferrari 308 GTB has a black metal chassis, black-tinted plastic windows, black plastic interior and uh.
Similar castings: 2021 Race Bait 308 (1978), 7295 Quik Trik (1984),17962 Ferrari 308 GTB (1997), 3494 Hot Wheels (1993 Tattoo Machines)

a. mtlc blue; white, red & yellow tampo on top w/"Ultra Hots" on hood $6 -8
a2. same as a, bwgd 8 - 10
a3. same as a, Malaysia 6 - 8

3975-b

b. 3975; red; black, yellow & blue stripe tampo w/"308" on sides; gw (1988) 5 - 7
b2. same as b, small lip under front fender (1988) 5 - 7
c. 3976, mtlfk silver, same as b, red replaces blue in tampo (1988) 5 - 7
c2. same as c, small lip under front fender (1988) 5 - 7

Street Beast-d

d. red; yellow & black Ferrari logo on hood; plastic body; black metal chassis; clear windows; black int.; white Hot Wheels logo on rear bumper; bw; Ferrari 5-Pack only (1995) 5 - NA
d2. same as d, metal body, Ferrari 5-Pack (1995) 3 - NA
e. green, clear windows, black int., gift set only (1995) 8 - NA

9536-a

Street Scorcher 9536 - 76mm - 1985
This Hong Kong-made custom van with a large rear spoiler has a metal chassis, blacked-out plastic windows, black plastic interior, & uh.
Similar castings: 9641 Spoiler Sport (1977), 2878 The Incredible Hulk (1979)

a. mtlc red; white, orange & yellow lightning tampo with l"Ultrahots" on sides $18 - 20
b. brown, same as a, Mexico (1986) 15 - 18

Super Cannon 9373 - 73mm - 1985
Based on a military sprint buggy, this

9373-a

Malaysia-made concept model has an olive metal chassis, blacked-out plastic windows, black plastic guns on the sides, movable rockets on top, a movable black machine gun in the back, and black bw.
Similar castings: 5269 Megadestroyer 1 (1982 Megaforce), 15968 Enforcer (1996)

a. olive; lt. green, brown & tan camo tampo $6 - 4
a2. same as a; car is a little darker, tampo colors are yellow, green and brown; bww. Action Command 5-pack only (1994) 3 - NA
a3. 11378, same as a, yellow replaces lt. green in tampo, different camo design, bww, #274 (1994) 4 - 6

11378-a4

a4. same as a3, sp5 in front & sp5-large in back, #274 (1995) 4 - 6

9373-b

b. no #, black, same as a, black metal chassis, lt. & dk. gray tampo w/black spider on yellow circle, gray guns & rockets, gray plastic window, Battleground 4-pack only (1985) 25 - NA
c. no #, tan, same as a, white replaces tan in tampo, 5-pack only 8 - NA

7530-a

Tall Ryder 7530 - 66mm - 1985
Based on a high-rise 4-wheel drive minivan, this Hong Kong-made concept car has a metal chassis, black plastic fenders & border around the bottom, blacked-out plastic windows and ct.

a. gray; yellow, purple & red stripe w/"Tall Ryder" on sides $8 - 10
a2. same as a, cts 6 - 8
b. mtlfk silver, same as a, Malaysia, #43 (1987) 6 - 8
b2. same as b, cts, #43 (1987) 6 - 8
b3. same as b, blue replaces purple in tampo, ct (1997) 2 - 4
b4. same as b2, blue replaces purple in tampo, cts (1997) 2 - 4
c. no #, chrome, "20th Hot Wheels Anniversary" engraved on top, two 3-packs only (1988) 8 - NA

16050-e

d. 16050, mtlfk green, chrome windows, cts, China, #481 (1996) 4 - 6
e. 16050; dk. yellow; same as d; magenta & lt. green tampo w/"Rocky Mountain Rescue," Hot Wheels logo on side; cts; China; #481 (1997) 4 - 6

9374-a

Tank Gunner 9374 - 78mm - 1985
This army half-track vehicle has an olive plastic chassis & interior, movable olive plastic twin guns in back, black bw in front & small black wheels in back. Hong Kong.
Similar casting: 9090 Gun Bucket (1976), 16299 Swingfire (1996)

a. olive; green, brown & tan camo tampo, tan star on hood, #83 $8 - 10
a2. same as a, bww 3 - 5
b. tan, same as a, white not tan (1987) 6 - 8

9545-a

Thunderstreak® 9545 - 75mm - 1985
This formula-type Indy racer has a metal chassis, unpainted metal rear spoiler, white plastic sides, white figure with a red helmet in the cockpit, gyg, & was made in Malaysia.
Similar castings: 3915 Formula Fever (1983), 2698 #26 Quaker State Indy Car (1992 Pro Circuit)

a. red; yellow, orange & red tampo w/"8" & race decals on sides; orange, yellow & black tampo w/"8" in front $20 - 25
a2. same as a, orange "8" in front 35 - 40
a3. same as a, gyw 30 - 40

Thunderstreak-b

b. 2540; maroon; same as a; purple sides; white, red & yellow tampo; purple figure; maroon hat in cockpit (1987) 15 - 18
b2. 1491 or 3998, same as b, bw (1988) 7 - 9
c. 3999; blue; yellow sides; blue, red & white tampo w/"Kraco," "18" & race decals on sides; yellow, white & red tampo w/"18," "Kraco," "Stereo" & STP decal on front; yellow figure w/blue helmet in cockpit (1988) 5 - 7

3999-c2

c2. 2199, same as c, Park 'n Plates (1989) 5 - 8
c3. same as c, no "STP" in tampo (1990) 4 - 6

Thunderstreak-d

d. no #; dk. blue; green plastic sides; red stripe in front, "1" & "Dow" inside stripe; "Ziploc" on each side of front spoiler; yellow, white & blue "Ziploc Brand Sandwich Bags"; green figure w/blue helmet in seat; Ziploc mail-in only (1989) 20 - NA
d2. same as d, olive replaces green, Ziploc mail-in offer only (1989) 60 - NA

9545-d2

Thunderstreak-e

e. no #; white; red & blue tampo w/"Cefotaxime Sodium" & "Claforan 500" on sides; given to pharmacists by wholesale distributor; Park 'n Plates package (1991) 35 - 45

9545-f

f. yellow; red & black tampo w/"Pennzoil" on sides & wings; "4" on front; race decals; #153 (1992) 10 - 12

Thunderstreak-g

g. no #; white; green & white sides; red & black tampo w/"Fuji" & "Fuji Film" on sides & spoiler; "2" on sides & nose; "Fuji" on nose; green int.; iwc; "Hot Wheels" & "Mattel Inc." on base; China; Corgi U.K. Fuji Film promo (1993) 85 - 110

9545-h

h. dk. blue, olive sides, blue tampo, red & white Hot Wheels logo on sides, white-on-red "1" in front, #153 (1994) 8 - 10
h2. same as h, no tampo in front, #153 (1994) 8 - 10

Thunderstreak-i

i. turquoise; red, white & blue tampo w/"Aquafresh" & "Waterpik" on sides & front spoiler; "61" on nose; "Waterpik" on rear spoiler. Sold in box w/Aquafresh Kids Toothpaste only (1994) 4 - 6
i2. same as i, "Aquafresh" on rear spoiler. Sold in box w/Aquafresh Kids Toothpaste only (1994) 4 - 6

Thunderstreak-j

j. red, white sides, green & red "Hormel Foods" on sides, green "1" on sides of rear spoiler. Hormel exclusive in baggies only, never in bp (1995) 3 - NA

15245-k

k. 15245, mtlfk black, black chrome sides, silver Hot Wheels logo on nose, sp7. #3 in Dark Rider Series II, #402 (1996) 4 - 6
l. yellow; black sides; red, white, magenta tampo w/"Zap," "Racing," & "8" on sides; sp5. Racing World 5-pack only (1997) 2 - NA

Values are shown in U.S. dollars, first price is for mint, second is for mint packaged vehicles only. See pages 15-16 for grading guide to determine value for cars in lesser conditions.

l2. same as l, dw3 (1997) 2 - NA
l3. same as l, sp7 (1997) 2 - NA

Thunderstreak-l4

l4. same as l, ho5, Thailand (1997) 2 - NA

Thunderstreak-m

m. black, same as l, sp5 (1997) 2 - NA

Thunderstreak-n

n. dk. mtlfk red; blue sides & int.; yellow, black & blue tampo w/"Thunderstreak" & race decals on sides, "Thunderstreak" on rear spoiler; sp5bk w/"Goodyear" & "Eagle" in yellow on tires; China; #1057 (1999) 2 - 3
o. maroon; maroon int.; blue, white & orange tampo w/"Sun" & "6" on sides; lwch; Virtual Collection; China; #135 (2000) 2 - 3
p. dk. blue, black int., red & white tampo w/"Hot Wheels Racing" & "3" on sides & spoiler, lwch, China, #131 (2002) 2 - 3
p2. mf blue, same as p. #131 (2002) 2 - 3

9533-a

Torino Tornado 9533 - 75mm - 1985
This Malaysia-made Ford race car has a chrome plastic chassis, black-tinted plastic windows, black plastic interior and gw.
Similar castings: 7647 Torino Stocker (1975), 9793 Thrill Driver Torino (1979)

a. yellow; blue, white & red tampo on sides & top; "17," Hot Wheels logo & race decals on sides; "17" on hood $15 - 18
a2. same as a; yellow, blue & red much darker, Mexico only (1986) 40 - 50
a3. same as a2, no tampo on sides, "Made in Mexico" on base, Mexico only (1986) 60 - 75

7531-a

XT-3® 7531 - 80mm - 1985
This Hong Kong-made concept three-wheel race car has a black metal chassis & interior, metal engine on top, metal spoiler in back, yellow-tinted plastic canopy, & bw.

a. black; yellow, white & red tampo on sides & top; "XT3" on spoiler; Hong Kong $4 - 6
a2. same as a, Malaysia 4 - 6
a3. same as a2, gold 30th Anniv. logo on side. Limited edition for 30th Anniv., w/blistercard (1998) 4 - 6

1484-b

b. purple; purple base; red, white & yellow flame tampo on sides, top & spoiler; blacked-out canopy; #4 (1989) 3 - 5
c. 1484, black, same tampo as b (1989) 45 - 50

1484-c2

c2. same as c, yellow-tinted canopy (1989) 45 - 50

XT-3-d

d. no #; purple; orange, white & black flame tampo on top; blacked-out window; purple metal chassis. Made for Hot Wheels cereal, never put in boxes for safety reasons. Sold directly to collectors (1990) 12 - NA
e. white; yellow & red flame tampo; white chassis; red-tinted window; #230 (1993) 6 - 8

XT-3-e2

e2. same as e, blue-tinted canopy, #230 (1995) 50 - 55
f. mtlfk blue, same as e2, #230 (1995) 4 - 6
f2. same as f, more metalflakes & greenish tint, #230 (1995) 4 - 6
f3. mtlfk blue, same as f2, sp5-large in back, #230 4 - 6

XT-3-g

g. mtlfk aqua; yellow & purple flames on sides & top; yellow nose & int.; yellow-tinted window; sp5. Designer Collection 8-pack, Target only (1996) 6 - NA

XT-3-h

h. 16924, blue, white base, orange nose & int., tinted window, white spray on sides & fenders, sp5. #3 in Speed Spray Series, #551 (1997) 2 - 4

XT-3-i

i. gray; orange chassis; black window & nose; black, red, white & green tampo design on sides & top; "XT-3" on sides; sp5. #4 in Flyin' Aces Series, #740 (1998) 2 - 3

XT-3-j

j. orange; black chassis, window & nose; black & grey tampo on sides & top; "Rocky" on sides; sp5gd. #2 in Car-Toon Friends Series #986 (1999) 2 - 4
k. mtlfk dark red; yellow chassis; black, silver & yellow design on sides & top; sp5; #215 (2000) 2 - 3

XT-3-l

l. black, black chassis & window, orange & white tampo on sides & top w/"Final Run" on sides & "FR" on wing, pr5, Thailand, #11 in 2001 Final Run Series (2001) 6 - 8

1986

A new line of fantasy models called Speed Demons was introduced. There were six vehicles with plastic bodies and Ultra Hot Wheels. Some of these were released late in the year. They are always difficult to find and have been steadily increasing in price.

2544-a

Back Burner 2544 - 76mm - 1986
This is a Malaysia-made concept car with a metal chassis, "Flame Runner" on the base, chrome plastic windows & exposed engine, black plastic guns on the hood, and uh.
Similar castings: 2018 Science Friction (1978), 7293 Flame Runner (1985), 3510 Lightning Storm (1993 Tattoo Machines)

a. mtlc dk. red; white, yellow & blue lightning-bolt tampo on top $5 - 7

2058-a

Cargoyle 2058 - 68mm - 1986 (Speed Demons)
Shaped like a gargoyle, this Hong Kong-made concept car has a plastic body, metal chassis, chrome plastic interior, exposed engine and uh.
Similar casting: 16055 Grizzler (1996)

a. orange; black eyes & spots on back $5 - 7

2058-b

b. yellow, same as a, orange in eyes, Speed Demons set only (1986) 15 - NA
c. orange, same as a, magenta eyes & spots on back, Speed Demons 5-pack only, Malaysia (1994) 3 - NA

2519-a

Combat Medic 2519 - 70mm - 1986
This army ambulance has a black plastic chassis & interior, clear plastic windows, black bw, and was made in Malaysia.
Similar castings: 9643 Letter Getter (1977), 2854 S.W.A.T. Van (1979), 2850 The Incredible Hulk (1979), 3303 Racing Team (1981), 9643 Delivery Van (1984), 2808 Delivery Truck (1989), 9114 The Simpson's Homer's Nuclear Waste Van (1990)

a. olive; tan, green & brown camo tampo w/"Medical Unit" & tan cross $4 - 6
b. tan, same as a, white replaces tan in tampo (1988) 4 - 6

Combat Medic-c

c. no #, gold chrome, "20th Hot Wheels Anniversary" engraved on sides, horizontal lines on sides, 3-pack only (1988) 35 - NA

Combat Medic-c2

c2. same as c, no side horizontal lines 45 - NA

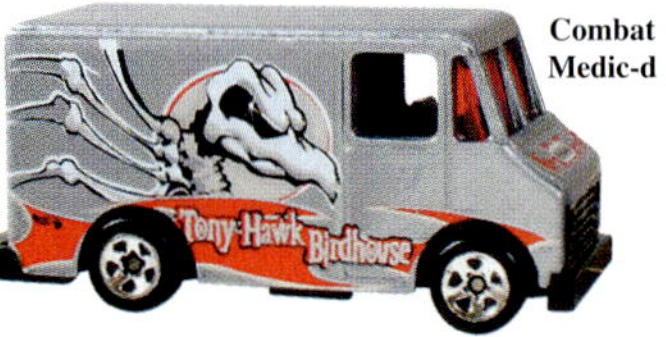

Combat Medic-d

d. gray; red-tinted windows; black int.; dk. red, black & white tampo w/bird & "Tony Hawk Birdhouse" on sides, "Birdhouse" in front; sp5; Thailand; #4 in Tony Hawk Skate series; #044 (2000) 2 - 3

2057-a

Double Demon® 2057 - 75mm - 1986 (Speed Demons)
Based on a two-headed dragon (one in front & one in back), this Hong Kong-made model has a plastic body, metal chassis, chrome plastic windows & exposed engine, and uh.

a. red; yellow spots on back $5 - 7
a2. same as a, Malaysia 5 - 7

2057-b

b. lt. green, same as a, Speed Demons set only (1986) 15 - NA
b2. same as b, white spots 15 - NA
c. 2850, fluor. lime, same as a, spots on back are lt. green, #199 (1993) 4 - 6
c2. same as c, black plastic windows, #199 (1993) 4 - 6
d. 2850, yellow, same as b2, black spots on back, #199 (1995) 4 - 6
d2. same as d, lighter yellow, chrome plastic window, black spots 2 - 4
e. 16046, lt. green, black chassis, red chrome int. & engine, sp5; China, #477 (1996) 2 - 4

Eevil Weevil 2062 - 68mm - 1986 (Speed Demons)
Based on a scorpion, this concept model has a plastic body, metal chassis, unpainted metal

2062-a

legs & pincers, black seat with steering wheel on top, uh, & was made in Hong Kong.

a. blue, pink plastic eyes, yellow & lt. green tampo on top of head $5 - 7
a2. same as a, Malaysia 5 - 7
a3. blue, same as a2, bw (1988) 15 - 18
b. yellow, same as a2, red eyes, orange & purple tampo, uh (1988) 5 - 7
b2. same as b, bw (1989) 5 - 7
c. purple, same as b, yellow plastic eyes, Speed Demons 5-pack only (1994) 2 - NA
d. 16056, orange, red metal base & pincers, lt. green eyes, sp5, China, #485 (1996) 2 - 4

2059-a

Fangster 2059 - 80mm - 1986 (Speed Demons)
Based on a lizard, this Hong Kong-made concept car has a plastic body, metal chassis & exposed engine, red plastic eyes and uh.
Similar casting: 16047 Dragon Wagon (1996)

a. light green $6 - 8
a2. same as a, Malaysia 5 - 7
a3. same as a, bw, Malaysia (1988) 10 - 12

2524-a

Highway Heat 2524 - 70mm - 1986
This Dodge Daytona has a metal chassis, yellow-tinted plastic windows, beige interior, gw, and was made in Malaysia.
Similar casting: 5911 Turbo Heater (1984)

a. orange; yellow, red & black tampo $30 - 35

2534-a

Path Beater 2534 - 73mm - 1986
This Chevrolet S-10 pickup has a metal chassis, clear plastic windows, red interior & bed, gyw, and was made in Malaysia.
Similar castings: 4368 Beach Patrol (1983), 5348 Surf Patrol (1991)

a. black; yellow, red & white tampo with "Chevy s10" & race decals on sides; "s10" & "350 H.P." twice on hood $25 - 30
a2. same as a, bw (1989) 7 - 9
a3. same as a, gold 30th Anniv. logo on sides, limited edition for 30th Anniv. w/blistercard in window box (1998) 4 - 6

Path Beater-b

b. black; lt. green int. & truck bed; clear windows; red, yellow & white tampo with "1" & "Path Beater" on sides; dw3ct; Off-Road 4x4's 5-pack only (1998) 2 - NA

Path Beater-c

c. black; black int. & truck bed; clear windshield; red & white tampo with "Police Beach Patrol," "1030" & logo on sides; "Police" on roof; dw3ct; Thailand; City Police 5-pack (1999) 2 - NA

2528-a

Poppa 'Vette 2528 - 80mm - 1986
Based on a Corvette Stingray funny car, this model has a metal chassis with lift-up body, gray-tinted plastic windows, metal interior & engine, bw, and was made in Malaysia.
Similar castings: 2508 Vetty Funny (1979), 2102 Corvette Funny Car (1990)

a. white; yellow, red & black tampo on top & sides, "Corvette" on sides $35 - 40

2538-a

Power Plower® 2538 - 77mm - 1986
This Chevrolet pickup truck has a metal chassis, blue-tinted plastic windows & sunroof, blue plastic interior & truck bed, orange plastic plow in front, gyw. Made in Malaysia.
Similar castings: 2509 Bywayman (1979), 1129 Super Scraper (1980), 9542 Pavement Pounder (1985)

a. red; yellow, purple & blue tampo with "Brian's Snow and Dirt Removal" design on sides $30 - 35
a2. same as a, large bw 6 - 8

5113-b

b. 5113, black; orange, red & purple stripe & "Midnight Removal" on sides; gray-tinted windows & sunroof; red int. & bed; red plow; bw (1989) 4 - 6
b2. same as b, ct, #40 (1990) 6 - 8

9580-c

c. mtlfk purple; orange, yellow & blue tampo on sides & hood; yellow plastic int., plow & bed; ct; #127 (1990) 10 - 25
c2. same as c, turquoise replaces blue in tampo, #127 (1990) 8 - 15
d. purple, same as c2, #127 (1990) 8 - 12

2781-e

e. 2781; Day-Glo lt. green; red, blue & white tampo & "Ecology Recycle Center" on sides; gray int., truck bed & plow; ct; #198 (1993) 5 - 10
e2. same as e, ctb, #198 8 - 18
e3. same as e, dw3ct, Pathbeater, #198 (1997) 2 - 4

Power Plower-f

f. purple; no plow; orange int. & truck bed; clear windows; orange, white & black tampo with "Piranha" on sides & hood; dw3ct; #2 in Attack Pack series; #022 (2000) 2 - 3

Power Plower-g

g. mtlfk green; no plow; lt. green int. & truck bed; clear windows; orange & white tampo w/"Oak Bros. Earth Pros," "Landscaping," "Tree Trimming," "Mulching" & "Bio Recycling" on sides; dw3ct; #1081 (2000) 2 - 3
h. mtlfk dark red; gray bed & int.; clear windows; white, black & gold tampo on sides & hood; dw3ctgd; Malaysia; #058. #4 in Wild Frontier series (2002) 2 - 3
h2. same as h, ortgd, #4 in Wild Frontier series, #058 (2002) 2 - 3

2520-a

Race Ace 2520 - 76mm - 1986
This Ford Fairmont stock car has a metal chassis with "Frontrunnin' Fairmont" on base, clear plastic windows, black plastic interior, gw, and was made in Malaysia.
Similar casting: 3257 Front Runnin' Fairmont (1982)

a. white; yellow, purple & orange stripe tampo w/"13" & race decals on sides, "13" on hood $30 - 35

2537-a

Rescue Ranger 2537 - 77mm - 1986
This Malaysia-made concept forest ranger's truck has a chrome plastic chassis, yellow plastic lights on top, yellow plastic hoses & other fire-fighting equipment in the back, outlines of compartments on the sides, gray-tinted plastic windshield, black plastic interior, and gyw.
Similar castings: 7650 Emergency Squad (1975), 7666 Ranger Rig (1975)

a. green; yellow & lt. green tampo; "Forest Service," "Help Prevent Forest Fires" & compartment names on sides $25 - 30
a2. same as a, bw 6 - 8

5145-b

b. red; black, yellow & white tampo w/"Hot Wheels Rescue Unit" on doors; "Emergency," "First Aid" & "Oxygen" on sides; #45 (1988) 6 - 8
b2. red, same as b, sp7, Emergency Squad 5-pack only (1995) 3 - NA

2537-c

c. yellow; same as b; black "Airship Support Team" & blue blimp on doors; "Oxygen, First Aid," red cross & "Emergency" inside black stripe on sides; red plastic not yellow; Blimp & Support Team 5-pack only (1994) 5 - NA
c2. same as c; "Oxygen, First Aid" & cross are white (1994) 10 - NA
c3. same as c; "Oxygen, First Aid" & cross are black; 5-pack only (1994) 3 - NA

2537-d

d. red; black int.; tinted windshield; yellow hoses, emergency lights, etc.; white "Emergency, Oxygen and Fisrt Aid," black "Baywatch," yellow & black Baywatch logo on sides; sp7; Baywatch 5-pack only (1995) 5 - NA
d2. red, same as d, "First" spelled correctly 3 - NA
e. 15253; orange; blue & yellow paint splattered over vehicle; tinted windshield; blue int., lights & hose; sp5; #1 in Splatter Paint Series; #408 (1996) 2 - 7
e2. same as e, dw3, #408 (1996) 2 - 4

15253-e3

e3. same as e, black interior, sp5, #408 (1997) 2 - 4
e4. same as e, dw3, #408 (1997) 2 - 4

15274-f

f. 15274; yellow; chrome plastic base; black & red tampo w/"Official Car" & "Fire Dept" on sides, "Fire Dept." on hood; red hoses; gray-tinted window & int.; sp5; #2 in Fire Rescue Series; #425 (1996) 2 - 4
g. no #; yellow; black int., & windshield; red hoses, emergency lights, etc.; red, black & white tampo w/"Rescue," "Paramedic," "Radio Dispatch Unit 3" & logo on sides; sp7; Rescue Squad 5-pack only (1997) 2 - NA
g2. same as g, sp5, #425 (1998) 2 - 4

Rescue Ranger-g3

g3. same as g, dw3ct (1998) 2 - NA
g4. same as g, ho5 (1998) 2 - NA
h. black; yellow-tinted int. & windshield; lime & yellow hoses & lights; yellow, red & white tampo w/"Biohazard

Values are shown in U.S. dollars, first price is for mint, second is for mint packaged vehicles only. See pages 15-16 for grading guide to determine value for cars in lesser conditions.

Rescue Ranger-h

Removal," "Unit 3," "Emergency Supplies," "Code 03-51951" & logo on sides; sp5; #4 in Biohazard Series; #720 (1998) 2 - 3
h2. same as h, ho5, #720 2 - 3

Rescue Ranger-i

i. white; blue-tinted window & int., red lights & hoses, red & black tampo w/"Bomb Squad Emergency Detonation Team" & logo on sides; sp5; Thailand; City Police 5-pack (1999) 2 - NA
i2. same as i, ho5, #1048 (1999) 2 - 3
i3. same as i, China, #1048 (1999) 2 - 3
j. white; red-tinted windows; red plastic chassis, int., lights & hoses; red, gold & black tampo w/"Fire Department," "Emergency," "51" & emblem on sides; ho5; China; #1061 (1999) 2 - 3
k. mtlfk silver, black int., clear windshield, red lights & hoses, black & red tampo with "Bomb Squad" & "Emergency Detonation Team" on sides, sp3, China, #218 (2000) 2 - 3

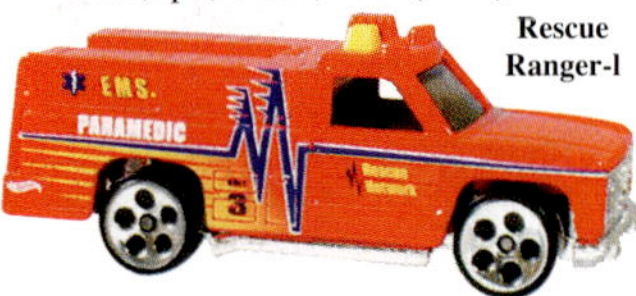
Rescue Ranger-l

l. red; black int.; tinted windows; yellow lights & hoses; blue, white & yellow tampo with "EMS," "Paramedic" & "Rescue Network" on sides; ho5; China; #193 (2001) 2 - 3
l2. same as l, Thailand, Rescue Rods 5-pack (2001) 2 - NA
m. white; chrome chassis; yellow int., hoses & lights; yellow-tinted windows; black, orange & yellow tampo w/"Unit 7," Hot Wheels logo, emblem & "Code H110201" on sides; sp5; Thailand. Heat Fleet 5-pack (2002) 2 - NA

2518-a

Shell Shocker 2518 - 67mm - 1986
This army armored gun has an olive plastic chassis, olive movable plastic cannon, small bw, and was made in Malaysia.
Similar casting: 9243 Aw Shoot 1975
a. olive, tan star & "53571" on front $5 - 7

2518-b

b. tan, same as a, white star & "623385" on front (1987) 5 - 7

2522-a

Stock Rocket 2522 - 78mm - 1986
This Malaysia-made stock car has a metal chassis with "Racing Stocker" on the base, gray-tinted plastic windows, black plastic interior, and gw.
Similar casting: 3927 NASCAR Stocker (1983)
a. red; yellow, black & white tampo w/"17," "Buick" & race decals on sides; "17" & Hot Wheels logo on hood; black & white "17" on roof $25 - 30

2061-a

Turboa® 2061 - 80mm - 1986 (Speed Demons)
Based on a snake, this concept model has a plastic body, metal chassis, exposed metal engine in the middle, chrome plastic interior, uh, and was made in Hong Kong.
a. yellow, green spots on top, #155 $8 - 10
a2. same as a, Malaysia
a3. same as a2, hoc, #155 (1992) 12 - 15
a4. same as a, sp5, China, Snake Pit playset only (1998) 5 - NA

13268-b

b. 13268; purple; fluor. orange lines; orange pipes, engine & int.; uh; #2 in Krackle Car Series; #281 (1995) 4 - 6
b2. purple, same as b, sp7, #281 (1995) 6 - 8
b3. same as b, silver paint base, #281 (1998) 6 - 8

Turboa-c

c. mustard yellow; black, red & silver tampo on top; sp5; China; #598 (1998) 2 - 4

2060-a

Vampyra® 2060 - 65mm - 1986 (Speed Demons)
Based on a vampire-type bird, this model has a plastic body, metal chassis, exposed metal engine in the middle, chrome plastic interior, uh, and was made in Hong Kong.
a. purple; white, red & orange tampo on wings; orange & white eyes $5 - 7
a2. same as a, Malaysia, #8 5 - 7
a3. same as a2, bw, #8 (1991) 3 - 5

0444-b

b. black; purple & lt. green eyes; purple, lt. green & yellow tampo on wings (purple on top); bw; #166 (1992) 3 - 5
b2. black, same as b, yellow in tampo is on top, #166 (1992) 3 - 5
b3. same as b2, hoc, #166 (1992) 25 - 30
b4. same as b2, uh, #166 (1992) 4 - 6
b5. 0444, same as b, no tampo on wings, lt. green & yellow eyes, #166 (1995) 3 - 5
c. white; yellow, lt. green & purple tampo on wings; lt. green eyes; uh; Speed Demons 5-pack only (1994) 8 - NA

2060-d

d. purple, black metal base, red & yellow eyes, gold Hot Wheels logo on side, gold engine, hhgn w/black tires, #2 in Hot Hubs series, #308 (1995) 8 - 10
d2. same as d, sp6gn, #308 (1995) 12 - 15
d3. same as d, lwch, China, #308 (1997) 2 - 4
d4. same as d, sp5, China, #308 (1997) 2 - 4

1987

Twelve new models were issued, bringing the total to 38. One popular car was the Ferrari Testarossa, even though it already had 21 variations in the last five years. Mattel also released the Turbo Trax Turbo Glo set which featured two cars with glow-in-the-dark tampo for the first and only time.

3338-a

Assault Crawler 3338 - 56mm - 1987
Based on the army vehicle Tracked Artillery Prime Mover, this model has an olive plastic chassis & interior, plastic gun on top, small bw, and was made in Malaysia.
a. olive; green, tan & brown camouflage tampo $8 - 10
a2. same as a, China, #624 (1997) 2 - 4

3338-b

b. tan, same as a, tan base & int., white replaces tan in tampo (1988) 20 - 25

3715-a

CAT Earth Mover 3715 - 82mm - 1987
This Malaysia-made Caterpillar construction vehicle has a yellow plastic body, yellow metal chassis, black plastic interior and cty.
Note: The Earth Mover with gold construction tires was only available for a short time and is more expensive.
a. yellow, #16 $10 - 12
a2. same as a, ctgd (1989) 30 - 35
a3. 16053, same as a, cts, China, #482 (1996) 2 - 4

3853-a

CAT Road Roller® 3853 - 76mm - 1987
This heavy-duty steam roller has a black plastic chassis & interior, five bars in the operator safety railing, two black plastic movable rollers in place of wheels, and was made in Malaysia.
Note: The original Road Roller with five bars was only out for a short time and is sells for a premium price.
a. yellow; black stripe tampo w/Caterpillar logo & "CB-614" in black & white on sides $30 - 35
a2. same as a, 3 bars in safety railing 6 - 8

3853-a3

a3. yellow, same as a2, no tampo, #55 6 - 8

CAT Road Roller-b

b. yellow; black plastic base & int.; black, red & white tampo w/"CAT" on sides; 3 interchangeable rollers, one with embossed Hot Wheels & CAT logos; large bp w/vial of dirt only (1998) 4 - 6

1897-a

Ferrari Testarossa 1897 - 71mm - 1987
This Malaysia-made model has a black metal chassis, red & black plastic interior & bumpers, clear plastic windows and uh.
Similar casting: Ferrari Testarossa (1988 20th Anniv.)
Note: The black version had only been available for a short time when it was replaced by the white version. The 1989 red version with the all-tan interior & bumper is very scarce. Even more difficult is the red-&-black interior/bumper variation. At present, only about fifteen have been reported.
a. black $18 - 20
b. white; white chassis; red & white int. & bumpers 5 - 7

Ferrari Testarossa-c

c. no #; red; red chassis, interior & bumpers; white glow-in-dark arrow tampo on top; Turbo Trax Turbo Glo set only (1987) 15 - NA
d. no #; yellow; yellow chassis; yellow & black int. & bumpers; blue tampo

Values are shown in U.S. dollars, first price is for mint, second is for mint packaged vehicles only. See pages 15-16 for grading guide to determine value for cars in lesser conditions.

Ferrari Testarossa-d

w/racing decals on sides & hood; "75" on hood & roof; "Ferrari" & Ferrari emblem on roof; Speedshift 500 set or Mattel Toy Club only (1988) 6 - NA

e. no #, chrome, "20th Hot Wheels Anniversary" engraved on top, 3-pack only (1988) 8 - NA

5111-f

f. red; red metal chassis; black & red int. & bumpers; yellow & black tampo with "Ferrari" & Ferrari logo on hood; uh; #35 (1989) 3 - 5

f2. same as f, tan & red int. & bumpers, #35 (1989) 3 - 5

f3. 5111, same as f2, bw 3 - 5

f4. same as f, all-tan int. & bumpers (1989) 40 - 50

f5. same as f, tan & black int. & bumpers (1989) 55 - 70

f6. 2048, red, same as f, Park 'n Plates (1990) 12 - 15

f7. same as f, red Hot Wheels logo on rear window, sp5, Then & Now 8-pack (1995) 5 - NA

g. 2048, mtlfk silver, mtlfk silver chassis, red & gray int. & bumpers, Park 'n Plates (1989) 8 - 10

g2. same as g, gray & tan int. & rear bumpers (1989) 8 - 10

g3. same as g, white & tan int. & rear bumpers, Park 'n Plates (1989) 65 - 75

Ferrari Testarossa-h

h. no #; mtlc dk. red; yellow & red stripes on hood & roof; white square outlined in red; "Getty" in red; clear windows; black & red int.; uh (1989) 5 - NA

3835-i

i. 3835, white, same as d, white chassis, white & black int. & bumpers, red tampo, no tampo on sides, Intl. line only (1990) 4 - NA

i2. 1897, white, same as i, tan int., no tampo, Intl. line only (1991) 6 - 8

1302-j

j. 1302, chrome magenta, pink stripe on hood & roof, yellow "3" & "Ferrari" on hood, black "Cal Custom" on windshield, red & blue int. & rear bumper, rry, California Custom (1990) 10 - 12

1302-k

k. 1302, neon red, same as j, blue tampo stripe, yellow & red int. & bumper, California Custom (1991) 12 - 15

k2. same as k, blue replaces yellow in int. & bumper (1991) 30 - 35

k3. same as k, tw (1991) 10 - 12

1897-l

l. Day-Glo pink; blue, black & white tampo on top & sides; clear windows; black & pink int., uho; Malaysia; Revealers 3 - 5

m. Day-Glo orange, same as v, orange & black int., uhp, Revealers 3 - 5

n. Day-Glo green, same as v, green & black int., uhy, Revealers 3 - 5

1897-o

o. candy purple; orange & black tampo on top; white horse's head on hood; yellow int.; white "Revealers" on clear window; uh; Malaysia; Revealers 10-pack only 10 - NA

p. no #; yellow; magenta, lt. green & orange tampo on hood & roof; clear windows; yellow & black int.; uh; Jumpbusters set only (1993) 6 - NA

1897-q

q. pearl white; black & yellow tampo w/Ferrari logo & "Ferrari" on hood; black-tinted window; gray & white int.; 25th Anniv. Exotic Car 5-pack only (1993) 4 - NA

r. no #, Day-Glo green, same tampo as f, metal chassis, lime & black int. & bumpers, Criss-Cross Crash set only (1993) 6 - NA

s. red; yellow & black Ferrari emblem on hood; red metal base; black & red int.; uh; Ferrari 5-Pack only (1995) 3 - NA

s2. same as s, sp5 (1995) 2 - NA

13576-t

t. 13576, black, "Ferrari" & yellow logo on hood, uhgd, #35 (1995) 4 - 6

t2. 5111, same as t, uh, Canada only (1995) 5 - 7

t3. same as t, sp3g, #35 (1996) 6 - 8

t4. same as t, lwgd, #35 (1996) 2 - 4

t5. same as t4, black int., #35 (1996) 45 - 55

t6. same as t, bw, India, #834 (1996) 2 - 5

Ferrari Testarossa-u

u. mtlfk silver, mtlfk silver base, yellow & black Ferrari emblem on hood, yellow & gray int., clear windows, sp5, Ferrari 5-pack only (1996) 3 - NA

v. mtlfk dk. red, dk. red chassis, clear plastic int. & windows, pcgd. FAO Schwarz History of Hot Wheels 8-pack only (1996) 6 - NA

w. mtlfk silver; black base & int.; clear windows; Ferrari logo in yellow-&-black rectangle on hood; sp5; #784 (1998) 2 - 4

w2. same as b, ho5, #784 (1998) 2 - 4

3716-a

Monster 'Vette 3716 - 75mm - 1987

This Malaysia-made Corvette Stingray has a metal chassis, black-tinted plastic windows, black plastic interior, and large ct. Similar casting: 3491 Street Beast (1993 Tattoo Machines)

a. yellow; red & purple flame tampo on sides & hood; #39 $6 - 8

a2. same as a, cts, #39 6 - 8

a3. same as a, blue-tinted windows 8 - 10

Monster 'Vette-b

b. no #, chrome, "20th Hot Wheels Anniversary" engraved on top, 3-pack only (1988) 15 - NA

b2. same as b, cts, 20th Anniv. 20-pack only (1988) 18 - NA

c. no #, gold chrome, "20th Hot Wheels Anniversary" on top, 3-pack only (1988) 12 - NA

2177-d

d. purple, same as a, red & blue tampo, #39 (1990) 10 - 12

d2. purple, same as d, cts, #39 (1990) 12 - 15

3851-a

Phantomachine 3851 - 74mm - 1987 (Speed Demons)

This concept car looks like a reclining robot. It has a chrome plastic body, metal chassis, exposed bluish-chrome plastic engine, uh, and was made in Malaysia. Similar casting: 16048 Computer Warrior (1996)

a. chrome; red, blue & orange tampo on chest & face 5 - 7

1500-a

Road Torch 1500 - 67mm - 1987

Based on the American Motors experimental car AMX/2, this model has a black plastic chassis, yellow interior, clear plastic windshield, uh, and was made in Malaysia. Similar castings: 6460 AMX-2 (1971), 6977 Xploder (1973), 7654 Warpath (1975), 9534 Redliner (1985)

a. red; black, white & yellow tampo w/"8" & race decals on sides $8 - 10

3286-a

Sharkruiser® 3286 - 75mm - 1987 (Speed Demons)

Shaped like a shark, this Malaysia-made concept car has a gray metal chassis, chrome plastic exposed engine, teeth, a seat and uh.

a. gray, #32 $8 - 10

a2. same as a, hoc, #32 15 - 20

a3. same as a, sp5, Shark Lair playset only, China (1998) 4 - NA

a4. same as a, gold 30th Anniv. logo on fin. Limited edition for 30th Anniv., w/blistercard in window box (1998) 3 - 5

13267-b

b. 13267; aqua; thin yellow lines all over body; fluor. yellow plastic pipes, int. & teeth; silver metal base; uh; #1 in Krackle Car Series; #280 (1995) 2 - 4

b2. same as b, sp7, #280 (1995) 6 - 8

b3. same as b2, silver base, #280 (1995) 2 - 4

Sharkruiser-c

c. no #; red; chrome int., teeth & engine. From movie Honey, I Shrunk Ourselves, China (1997) 10 - NA

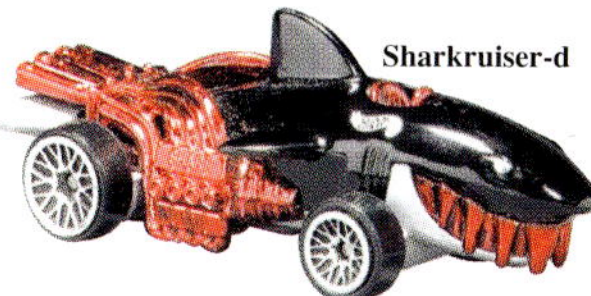
Sharkruiser-d

d. 18554; black; red chrome int., teeth & engine; lwch; China; #602 (1997) 2 - 4

e. orange; black & white tampo on top; dw3gd; Thailand; #147 (2001) 2 - 3

3209-a

Suzuki QuadRacer 3209 - 55mm - 1987

This all-terrain vehicle (ATV) has a yellow plastic body, metal chassis, exposed metal engine under a blue plastic seat, black handlebars, and was made in Malaysia.

a. yellow, #17 $4 - 6

a2. same as a, ctsy, #17 4 - 6

b. white, same as a, #129 (1991) 12 - 15

b2. same as b, ct, #129 (1991) 8 - 10

c. pink, same as a, ct, #165 (1992) 10 - 12

Suzuki QuadRacer-d

d. no #, turquoise, same as a, purple seat, Kool-Aid Wacky Warehouse 2-pack only 7 - NA

e. 13298, yellow, black-tinted metal base & engine, purple seat, red Hot Wheels logo on rear fender, hhy w/black tires, #4 in Hot Hubs Series, #311 (1995) 8 - 10

e2. lime green, same as e, #311 (1995) 35 - 40

e3. same as e2, pow (1995) 65 - 75

e4. yellow, same as e, black handlebars & seat, red "Baywatch" behind seat, 2

13298-e3

3209-e4

red Hot Wheels logos on each side of seat, cty. Baywatch 5-pack only (1995) 3 - NA
e5. same as e, blue seat (1996) 50 - 60

Suzuki QuadRacer-e6

e6. same as e, cts, China, #311 (1997) 2 - 4

Suzuki QuadRacer-f

f. lt. green; purple seat & handlebars; black, orange & white tampo on rear fenders; cts. Off-Road Racing 4-pack (1998) 6 - NA

Tail Gunner-a2

Tail Gunner 5T 4059 - 70mm - 1987 (Action Command)
This customized Ford stepside pickup truck has an olive metal chassis, olive dual plastic guns in back, gray-tinted plastic windows, black plastic interior, & ctb. Made in Malaysia.

a. olive; green, tan & brown camouflage, #29 $8 - 10
a2. same as a, ctsb, #29 8 - 10
b. tan, same as a, tan base, white replaces tan in tampo (1987) 8 - 10
b2. same as b, ctsb (1987) 8 - 10

4059-c

c. white; metal base; gray guns & bumper; gray, blue & black camouflage tampo; ctw. Action Command 5-pack only (1994) 3 - NA
c2. same as c, ctb (1995) 3 - NA
d. 11376; white; gray, black & blue camo tampo; gray plastic guns; blacked-out windows; ctw; #273 (1995) 8 - 10
e. red w/black rear; white int.; blue-tinted windows; gray, black, white & red tampo w/"45" & race decals on sides; "Sprint" on hood; "SprintPCS, "45" & "1-888-45-petty" on truck bed; "Sprint" & "45" in back; dw3ct w/white tampo; Thailand. #1 in NASCAR Tail Gunner series (2001) 5 - 7

Tail Gunner-f

f. white; no guns; white int.; blue-tinted windows, multicolored tampo w/"33" & race decals on sides, "Oakwood Homes" on hood, "33" on truck bed; dw3ct w/white tampo; Thailand; #2 in NASCAR Tail Gunner Series (2001) 5 - 7
g. white; no guns; dk. blue rear; white int.; blue-tinted windows; multicolored tampo w/"10" & race decals on sides, "Valvoline" & logo on hood, "10," "Valvoline" & "Eagle 1" on truck bed; dw3ct w/white tampo; Thailand; #3 in NASCAR Tail Gunner Series (2001) 5 - 7
h. red; clear windows; red int.; yellow, black & white tampo w/"96" & race decals on sides, McDonald's M & "Coca Cola" on hood, "96" & "Drive Thru" on truck bed, "www.ppi.racing.com" in back; gold dw3ct w/white tampo; Thailand. #4 in NASCAR Tail Gunner series (2001) 5 - 7

1456-a

Thunderburner 1456 - 78mm - 1987
This new model uses the Thunderbird Stocker casting and has a metal chassis, clear plastic windows, black plastic interior, gw, and was made in Malaysia. Similar castings: 5900 Thunderbird Stocker (1984), 16039 Velocitor (1996)

a. black, "The Black Knight" in yellow, yellow knight w/red feather $8 - 10
a2. black, same as a, uh (1989) 20 - 25

5139-b

b. 5139; white; red & blue tampo w/"1," Hot Wheels logo & race decals on sides; "1," "T Bird" & race decals on hood; blue stripes on roof 15 - 20
b2. same as b, bw (1989) 15 - 20
b3. same as b, uh (1990) 15 - 20

Thunderburner-c

c. no #, yellow, purple flames on hood & roof, white "Getty" in red & white square on hood, bw (1990) 5 - NA
d. no #; blue; same as a; yellow, white & red tampo; Hot Wheels cereal only 6 - NA

Thunderburner-d

Thunderburner-e

e. no #; black; yellow, lt. green & purple tampo w/"4" on hood & sides; pink int.; uh; set only (1993) 8 - NA

Thunderburner-f

f. no #; black; silver plastic grill; gray int.; clear windows; white doors & roof; blue, yellow, & black star tampo w/"Police" on sides & hood; sp5; China; Police Station or Police Chase sets only (1997) 4 - NA

3852-a

Zombot® 3852 - 75mm - 1987 (Speed Demons)
This Malaysia-made concept car is a reclining robot with a gold-chrome plastic body, metal chassis, red-chrome plastic gun, & uh.

a. gold chrome, red, blue & black tampo on chest & face; #53 $4 - 6
a2. same as a, hoc, #53 4 - 6

Zombot 3852-b Phantomachine 3851-a

b. blue chrome, same as a, #224 (1993) 10 - 14
b2. black chrome, same as b, #224 (1995) 8 - 10
b3. same as b2, fluor. orange gun, #224 (1995) 3 - 5
b4. same as b3, sp7, #224 (1995) 3 - 5

3852-c

c. dk. gray, orange chassis & gun, mtlfk silver head, sp5, China, #460 (1996) 2 - 4

1988

Thirteen new models were introduced. Also available were three models with different colors/tampo that could only be found in race sets. The Speed Shift 500 set contained the blue Porsche 959 and the yellow Testarossa. The Dinosaur Mud Pit set had the olive green Blazer 4x4. Also introduced were color-changer models. These would change color when heated or cooled. Two models, Alien & Talbot Lago, were introduced in temporary short-run colors before being issued in other hues.

Since 1988 was the 20th Anniversary of Hot Wheels cars, Mattel issued special collectors'-edition vacuum-metallized models. These were available in gold, silver or both. Each special edition was packaged with two regular models on a special blistercard.

5026-a

Alien 5026 - 71mm - 1988
This Malaysia-made concept car has a metal base, two engines in back, plastic top holding a blacked-out window, silver metalflake interior and uh.

a. mtlfk gray, dark blue top $10 - 12
b. same as a, red top, #62 5 - 10
b2. same as b, sp5, #62 (1995) 3 - 5
b3. same as b, sp7, #62 (1997) 3 - 5
c. mtlfk blue; red top w/lt. purple, lt. green & yellow "Alien" on hood; white "Revealers" on black-tinted window; uh; Malaysia; Revealers 10-pack only 10 - NA
d. no #, same as a, black, bright green top, 25th Anniv. Dream Car 5-pack only (1993) 4 - NA

15230-e

e. 15230; pearl white; blue top; black plastic canopy; red, orange & white tampo w/"Rescue" on sides; "HWSA Hot Wheels Space Administration" in front; Hot Wheels logo in back; sp5; #3 in Space Series; #390 (1996) 2 - 4

Alien-f

f. 16927; blue; white top; black & white int.; tinted dome; red & black spy tampo w/"HUD," "Spy Scan," & "Heads Up Display" in front; sp3. #2 in Spy Print Series, #554 (1997) 2 - 4
f2. same as f, dw3, #554 (1997) 2 - 4

Alien-g

g. white; white int.; tinted dome; red, yellow & black tampo w/"Alien" on sides & top; sp3. #1 in Artistic License Series, #729 (1998) 2 - 3
g2. pearl white, same as g, #729 (1999) 2 - 3

Alien-h

h. mtlfk orange; black on top; gold, black & white tampo, Final Run logo on hood, "Powered by Millennium Capacitors" on trunk, "9921350" in back; rrgd. #12 in 1999 Final Run Series (1999) 5 - 7

Values are shown in U.S. dollars, first price is for mint, second is for mint packaged vehicles only. See pages 15-16 for grading guide to determine value for cars in lesser conditions.

5027-a

Flame Stopper 5027 - 82mm - 1988
This Malaysia-made concept fire vehicle has a yellow water cannon, black winch, blacked-out windows, red plastic base, and ct.
a. red; "Unit 31" & "Fire Dept." in yellow & white on sides $6 - 8
a2. same as a, cts 6 - 8
a3. same as a, cty. Blimp & Support Team 5-pack only (1994) 3 - NA
b. 15275; yellow; black plastic chassis; red & black tampo w/"Fire Dept. City of Hot Wheels" & "3" on sides; yellow-tinted windows; yellow int.; large sp3; #3 in Fire Rescue Series; #426 (1996) 2 - 4
b2. same as b, dw3cty, #426 4 - 6

15275-b2

b3. same as b, cty, #426 8 - 10
b4. same as b, cts, #426 (1997) 10 - 15

Flame Stopper-c

c. red; black plastic base; gray water cannon; gold, black & white tampo w/"Fire Dept," "31" & logo on sides; dw3ct; #761 (1998) 3 - 5

Flame Stopper-d

d. pinkish red; black plastic chassis, windows & water cannon; "Unit 2," "Flammable Materials Control" & logo on sides; dw3cty; Malaysia; #2 in Biohazard Series; #718 (1998) 2 - 4
d2. same as d, Thailand 2 - 4
d3. same as d, China, #718 2 - 3

Flame Stopper-e

e. white; black base, water cannon & winch; dk. yellow, red & black tampo w/"Airport Fire and Rescue Team" & "Emergency" on sides; dw3ct; Malaysia; #1012 (1999) 2 - 3
e2. China, #1012 (1999) 2 - 3
f. orange; black chassis & windows; gray water cannon & winch; gold, black & red tampo w/"Airport" on sides; dw3ct; Virtual Collection; China; #113 (2000) 2 - 3

Flame Stopper-g

g. red-brown; black chassis & windows; white water cannon & winch; yellow, black & white tampo w/"Stand Clear," "Emergency Corrosive Crew," "Toxic" & "Unit 31" on sides; dw3cty; China; #188 (2001) 2 - 3
g2. same as g, dw3ct y
h. orange; black chassis, windows, water cannon & winch; white, black & red tampo w/Hot Wheels logo, "Flame Stopper," "Unit 02" & "851811241" on sides; dw3ct; Thailand. Heat Fleet 5-pack (2002) 2 - 3

4384-a

Lamborghini Countach 4384 - 70mm - 1988
This model has a white metal base, attached rear spoiler, black-tinted windows, red interior, uh, and was made in Malaysia.
a. white $4 - 6

4384-b

b. white; red, blue & yellow tampo w/"Lamborghini" twice & emblem on hood; "LP500S" & "Countach" on sides (1989) 10 - 12
b2. same as b, no hood tampo, #60 (1989) 6 - 8
b3. same as b, black windows, #60 6 - 8
b4. same as b2, black windows, #60 6 - 8
b5. same as b2, rear spoiler is part of body, #60 3 - 5
b6. same as b3, blue gray replaces blue in tampo. #60 3 - 5
b7. same as b5, uhgd, #60 6 - 8
c. 9222; red, clear windows, white int., Park 'n Plates (1990) 20 - 25

4384-d

d. white; black & red tampo w/yellow coins all over; black-tinted window; red int.; uhgn; Malaysia; Revealers 3 - 5
e. silver, same as d, uhy, Revealers 3 - 5
f. Day-Glo red, same as d, black int., uhp, Revealers 3 - 5

4384-g

g. vacuum-metallized gold, given w/bike, Revealers' 1st prize 125 - NA
h. no #, mtlfk dk. gray, clear windows, red int., 25th Anniv. Exotic Car 5-pack only (1993) 4 - NA
h2. same as h; rear spoiler is part of body 4 - NA
i. 4553, red, white & black tampo, same tampo design as b2, tan int., red base, #232 (1993) 6 - 8
i2. same as i, black interior, #232 3 - 5
i3. same as i2, rear spoiler is part of body, #232 3 - 5
i4. same as i, uhgd, #232 (1994) 6 - 10
i5. same as i, no tampo, mail-in offer from Tony's Pizza 5 - NA

15075-j

j. 15075, candy red, black tampo in back on top, clear windows, tan interior, iw, #10 in Treasure Hunt Series, #429 (1996) 30 - 35
k. 4384, white, red int., black-tinted windows, ho5, #232 (1997) 4 - 6
k2. same as k, clear windows, #232 18 - 20

4392-a

Nissan Hardbody (Truck) 4392 - 77mm - 1988
This four-wheel drive pickup truck has a metal base, large chrome plastic engine in the truck bed, black roll bar, grill & interior, clear windows, ct, & was made in Malaysia.
a. white, red in back, red truck bed, red & blue tampo w/"Nissan 4x4" in back & on hood $12 - 15
a2. same as a, cts 12 - 15

4392-b

b. same as a, white truck bed, blue stripe in back, red "Nissan" on side (1989) 5 - 7
b2. same as b, cts, #21 5 - 7
b3. same as b, black plastic base, #21 5 - 7
b4. same as b2, black plastic base, #21 (1991) 5 - 7
b5. same as b4, pink interior, ct, #131 (1992) 20 - 60
c. black; black plastic base; lt. green, lt. blue & pink striping tampo w/"10" on sides, hood & roof; black truck bed; pink int., grill & roll bar; ct; #131 (1991) 10 - 15

9588-c2

c2. same as c, cts, #131 10 - 15
c3. same as c, metal base, #131 10 - 15
c4. same as c3; yellow, lt. green & blue tampo; yellow int.; #131 (1992) 6 - 12
c5. same as c3, dw3ct, #131 (1997) 6 - 10
c6. same as c4, black chrome hubs, #131 6 - 8
d. no #; white; gray-blue, pink & green tampo w/"Kool-Aid" on sides; splash tampo on hood; Kool-Aid Wacky Warehouse only (1993) 10 - NA

Nissan Hardbody-d

11595-e

e. 11595; white; yellow, blue & red tampo w/"Cheesasaurus Rex" & orange, blue & red Cheesasaurus on hood; orange int. & bed; chrome plastic engine on bed; clear window; ct. Kraft send-away offer, card reads "C. Rex Mobile" 10 - 12

15221-f

f. 15221; mtlfk blue; issued as Nissan Truck on blistercard; red & white tampo w/"Nissan Racing" on sides & hood; "8," Hot Wheels logo & racing decals on sides; "8" on roof; "Nissan" on windshield; gray int.; clear windows; ct; #4 in Race Truck Series; #383 (1996) 3 - 7
f2. same as f, ctb, #383 (1996) 10 - 20
f3. same as f, yellow int. & front grill, #383 65 - 135
g. 9588; red; "#1" & checkerboard flag tampo on sides & hood; racing decals on sides; black int.; dw3ct; #131 (1997) 3 - 6

Nissan Hardbody-g2

g2. same as g, dw3ctb, Racing World 5-pack only (1997) 2 - 4
g3. same as g, darker red, Thailand, Racing World 5-pack only (1998) 2 - NA
h. 16947, blue, black plastic base & int., blue-tinted windows, silver Hot Wheels logo on hood, dw3ct. #2 in Blue Streak Series, #574 (1997) 18 - 35

Nissan Hardbody-i

i. mtlfk red; black plastic base, int. & truck bed; clear windshield; black, yellow & white tampo w/street signs on sides; dw3ct. #3 in Mixed Signals Series, #735 (1998) 2 - 3
j. dk. mtlfk blue; black chassis; white int.; tinted windows; gold, black & white tampo with "17," "Sandswarm," "JT Motor Sport" & race decals on

Values are shown in U.S. dollars, first price is for mint, second is for mint packaged vehicles only. See pages 15-16 for grading guide to determine value for cars in lesser conditions.

Nissan Hardbody-j

sides; dw3ct; Thailand; Baja Blazers 5-pack (1999) 2 - NA

k. brown; black chassis; gray int.; orange, black & white tampo w/tigers on sides & "Tiger" on hood; #1 in Attack Pack Series; #021 (2000) 2 - 3

4631-a

Porsche 959 4631 - 70mm - 1988

Based on one of the most high-tech vehicles ever produced, this Malaysia-made model has a metal base, clear windows, tan interior, & uh.

Similar casting: 3493 Eye-Gor (1993 Tattoo Machines)

a. mtlfk red; orange & yellow tampo w/"Porsche" twice & "959" on hood; "Porsche 959" on sides; #80 $10 - 22

a2. same as a, ltd ed for 30th Anniv., w/blistercard in window box (1998) 7 - 9

4631-b

b. mtlc blue; white headlights; black "7" in white circle w/white "Porsche" underneath on hood & sides; red & white "Porsche" on rear spoiler; Speedshift 500 set or at Mattel Toy Club only 6 - NA

4631-c

c. 3808, blue, same as b, no "Porsche" on spoiler, Intl. series only (1989) 5 - 7

d. 2038, white, same as a, blue & red tampo, black int., uh, Park 'n Plates (1989) 8 - 10

d2. same as d, blue-tinted windows 8 - 10

2038-d3

d3. same as d, bw 25 - 30

d4. same as d2, bw 25 - 30

d5. same as d, tan int., uh 45 - 50

d6. same as d2, blue int., uh 8 - 10

d7. same as d6, bw 8 - 10

e. 1403, red, same as c, gray interior (1990) 6 - 8

e2. 9519, same as e, turquoise replaces blue in tampo, #80 (1991) 6 - 22

e3. same as e2, uhgd, #80 10 - 12

e4. same as e2, hoc, #80 20 - 30

1403-f

f. 1403, red, gray headlights, "Porsche 959" on hood, yellow "59" w/blue border on hood & sides, #80 (1990) 10 - 18

Porsche 959-g

g. no #; yellow; red, white & blue stripes & white "Getty" in red rectangle on sides; clear windows; red int.; bw (1991) 3 - NA

0463-h

h. 0463; purple; yellow, gray & pink tampo on sides, hood & top; "5" & "Porsche" on sides; "Porsche" twice on hood; chromed-out windows; uh; #179 (1992) 4 - 8

h2. same as h, hoc, #179 10 - 20

i. 1794, pink chrome, design etched into body, blacked-out windows, uh, Gleam Team, #193 (1995) 4 - 10

i2. same as i, sp5, Lucky Supermarkets 2-pack only (1995) 6 - 10

1794-i3

i3. same as i, uhgd, Track System Gift Pack only (1996) 6 - NA

4631-j

j. chrome, design etched into body, uh, Gleem Team, #193 (1995) 8 - 10

j2. same as j, silver chassis, Power Loop set, in baggie 5 - NA

k. no #; white; unpainted metal base; blue-tinted windows; white int.; black, gray, red & blue tampo on sides, hood & roof; red Hot Wheels logo on rear fender; uhgd; Track System Gift Pack only (1995) 5 - NA

Porsche 959-k2

k2. same as k, sp5g 3 - NA

k3. same as k, sp3g 3 - NA

4631-l

l. yellow, clear windows, gray int., orange flame tampo on sides, bw, parking garage set only 12 - NA

m. 15790, lt. powder blue, dk.-tinted windows, black int., sp5, #591 (1996) 2 - 4

m2. same as m, dw3, #591 (1997) 2 - 4

m3. same as m, ho5, #591 (1997) 2 - 4

m4. same as m, sp5, China, #591 (1997) 2 - 4

Porsche 959-n

n. white; black int.; tinted windows; red & black tampo w/"2," "High Bank Racing" on sides; dw3; #854 (1998) 2 - 3

n2. same as n, sp3, #854 (1998) 2 - 3

n3. same as n, lwch, China, #854 (1998) 2 - 3

o. black, clear windows, tan int., lwch, China, #1054 (1999) 2 - 3

Porsche 959-p

p. gray; black int.; blue-tinted windows; red, black & white tampo w/"959" & "Twin Turbo" on sides, Porsche logo & "Twin Turbo" on hood; ho5; #1030 (2000) 2 - 3

q. black; same as p; gray, white & dk. red tampo colors; China; #232 (2000) 2 - 3

r. red; white int.; tinted windows; yellow, black & orange tampo w/Hot Wheels logo on sides, flames on hood & roof, "Twin Turbo' on spoiler; sp5; Thailand; #148 (2002) 2 - 3

5022-a

Radar Ranger® 5022 - 70mm - 1988

Based on a six-wheel all-terrain vehicle, this Malaysia-made model has a metal chassis, metal base, chrome plastic radar dish on top, black interior, clear windshield and ct.

a. mtlc silver; red & blue tampo w/"Radar" in black on top, #63 $6 - 12

a2. same as a, cts, #63 18 - 40

a3. same as a, ctb, #63 18 - 40

a4. same as a, dw3ct, #63 (1997) 3 - 8

a5. same as a, antenna dish is gray plastic, dw3ct, #63 (1997) 2 - 4

a6. same as a, silver base, dw3ct, #63 (1997) 2 - 4

15228-b

b. 15228; white; black metal chassis; blue, orange & red tampo w/"Advanced Communication" on sides,"HWSA Hot Wheels Space Administration" on hood, orange int.; clear plastic window; ct; #1 in Space Series; #388 (1996) 3 - 6

Radar Ranger-c

c. no #; orange; black chassis; tinted window; orange & black int.; black, red & blue tampo; "Radar" on top; black antenna dish; dw3ct; Toys "R" Us 10-car set (1997) 6 - NA

d. lt. green; black base & antenna dish; purple engine; tinted window; black, white & purple tampo on sides; dw3ct; #4 in Techno Bits series; #692 (1998) 2 - 3

e. mtlfk gold, black int., clear window, black & white tampo w/"Radar Ranger" & "11" on sides, "Radar Ranger" & "6" on top, dw3ct, #782 (1998) 2 - 3

Radar Ranger-d

Radar Ranger-e

Radar Ranger-f

f. mtlfk purple; blue int.; blue-tinted windshield; black radar dish; yellow, black & white tampo on sides & top; "Webspinner" on sides; dw3ct. #3 in Buggin' Out Series, #943 (1999) 2 - 3

g. mtlfk blue; black int.; red-tinted window; black, red & white tampo w/"oo" & "Alien Detector" on top; dw3ct; Thailand; Star Explorers 5-pack (1999) 2 - 3

h. aqua, same as e, clear window, white int. & radar dish, dw3ct, #1101 (2000) 2 - 3

Radar Ranger-i

i. chrome; white chassis; yellow-tinted window; black, gold, white & red tampo w/"System 3rdStone" & "FR" on sides, "Radar Ranger" & "Final Run" on top; dw3ct; Thailand; #9 in 2001 Final Run Series; (2001) 4 - 6

5028-a

Ratmobile 5028 - 74mm - 1988 (Speed Demons)

This Malaysia-made concept model has a plastic body, metal base, gray teeth, black nose, red & black eyes, chrome plastic engine in the middle of its back, white plastic seat and uh.

a. white, #81 $3 - 4

a2. same as a, hoc, #81 (1992) 3 - 12

13302-b

b. 13302, black, same as a, gray nose, red & white eyes, #3 in Speed Gleamer series, #315 (1995) 3 - 5

b2. same as b, sp7, #315 (1995) 3 - 6

Values are shown in U.S. dollars, first price is for mint, second is for mint packaged vehicles only. See pages 15-16 for grading guide to determine value for cars in lesser conditions.

Rocketank 9380 - 64mm - 1988

This army rocket-launching tank has an olive base, olive removable plastic rocket, no wheels, and was made in Malaysia.
Similar casting: 16298 Rocket Shot (1996)

a. olive, #20 $5 - 7
b. tan, same as a; tan base 5 - 7

Rodzilla® 4389 - 76mm - 1988

This Malaysia-made dragon has a plastic body with a chrome engine on its back, movable head, white teeth, yellow eyes and uh.

a. purple, purple metal base, #156 $3 - 6
a2. same as a, red base, #156 4 - 15
a3. same as a2, red eyes 45 - 55
a4. same as a2, hoc, #156 (1992) 10 - 20
b. green, same as a, gold-plated engine, uh, Speed Demons 5-pack only (1994) 3 - NA

c. 13310, chrome, gold-plated engine, uh, #2 in Silver Series, #323 (1995) 3 - 5
c2. same as c, sp7, #323 3 - 8
c3. same as c, silver base, #323 3 - 12
c4. same as c, sp5, China, #323 (1997) 2 - 4
c5. white eyes & teeth, lwgd, China, #991 (1999) 2 - 3
d. green, gold engine, sp3gd, Virtual Collection, #126 (2000) 2 - 3
d2. same as d, light gold engine, Virtual Collection, #126 (2000) 2 - 3

Shadow Jet® 4699 - 75mm - 1988

This Malaysia-made race car has a metal base, black-tinted plastic windshield, yellow interior, rear spoiler, and bw.

a. yellow; red & magenta tampo w/"Inter Cooled" on spoiler; "F-3" twice in back; #19 $6 - 8
a2. same as a, blue replaces magenta in tampo, #19 18 - 20
b. blue, yellow "Super Turbo" in back, white square outlined in red, "Getty" on each side of wing (1989) 6 - NA

c. mtlc purple, same tampo as a, "Inter Cooled" in green, "F-3" in yellow, #133 (1990) 5 - 8
c2. same as c, small front wheels, #133 20 - 25
c3. same as c, tampo colors reversed, #133 (1991) 25 - 30

d. no #; pink; black tampo w/3 lines & "Inter" on one side of spoiler, 3 lines & "cooled" on other side; Heroes on Hot Wheels tape only; never in bp (1991); w/video 10 - 12
e. green, same as a, blue & green tampo, #182 (1992) 4 - 6
e2. same as e, yellow & blue tampo, #182 4 - 6
e3. same as e, sp5, #182 (1996) 4 - 6

f. 13297, lt. green, gold metalflakes, yellow-tinted dome, dk. red "Inter Cooled" & stripes on spoiler, "F-3" twice & red Hot Wheels logo on front of spoiler, chrome engine, yellow hhy, purple tires, #3 in Hot Hubs series, #310 (1995) 4 - 6
f2. same as f, bluish-chrome engine 65 - 75
g. 16935, white, yellow-tinted dome, chrome engine, sp5, #2 in White Ice Series, #562 (1997) 2 - 4
g2. same as g, silver base, #562 2 - 4

h. purple, tinted dome, gold & white tampo on top & sides, "Racer" on sides, sp5, #4 in Techno Bits series, #691 (1998) 2 - 4

i. yellow; tinted dome; blue, red & black tampo w/"Raceway 2000" on sides; writing on wings; #2 in Game Over Series; Malaysia; #958 (1999) 2 - 3

j. yellow; yellow int.; red-tinted dome; orange, black & white tampo w/"Ezroj" on sides, "ME25" on top; sp5; Thailand; Star Explorers 5-pack; (1999) 2 - NA
k. mtlfk gray; tinted dome; red, white & black tampo on sides & top w/"85720" on sides, "Caution" on top; sp5; Malaysia (2001) 2 - 3

Sting Rod® 5025 - 76mm - 1988

This Malaysia-made army off-road attack vehicle has an olive metal base, two black plastic rockets in back, black plastic machine guns through the hood & on the sides, black plastic interior, and ctb.

Note: Few olive models surfaced in the first two-three years and their value was $35-45. In 1991 (two years after discontinuation), Toys "R" Us marketed hundreds of cases, each with six models, across the country, causing the value to drop to its present level.
Similar casting: 3527 Ammo (1993 Tattoo Machines)

a. olive; dk. green, brown & tan camouflage tampo $10 - 12
a2. same as a, ctsb 15 - 18

b. tan; same as a; olive, brown & white camouflage tampo 15 - 18
b2. same as b, ctsb 20 - 25

c. 16297, mtlfk gray, red chassis, orange int. & guns, cts, China, #488 (1996) 2 - 4

Talbot Lago 4741 - 83mm - 1988

This 1930's model has a metal base, brown-tinted windows, light brown interior, ww, and was made in Malaysia.

Note: This was the first model with the wheels pulled in & hidden in the body (like fender skirts).
Similar Casting: 3479 Spiderider (1993 Tattoo Machines)

a. burgundy $8 - 10
b. white, same as a, #22 6 - 8

c. black, red glitter, red-tinted windows, #163 (1992) 18 - 20

d. white, black Hot Wheels logo in back, gray-tinted windows & int., gold-plated headlights & radiator; iwgd. One of 16 in FAO Schwarz Gold Series, limited to 3000 (1994) 10 - NA
e. 12342, mtlfk black, clear windows & int., red Hot Wheels logo in white oval in back, ww, #250 (1995) 5 - 8
e2. same as e, sp7, #250 3 - 5
f. 13282, pearl blue, red Hot Wheels logo in white oval in back, ww, blue-tinted windows, #1 in Pearl Driver series #295, (1995) 4 - 6
f2. same as f, sp7, #295 6 - 8
g. gold-plated, gold-plated base, clear windows, chrome int., iwgd, FAO Schwarz 24K Gold Classics 3-pack only (1995) 50 - NA

h. no #, purple, lt. gray int., clear windows, rrch, 60th Anniv. '37 European Classics 2-car set only (1997) 8 - NA
i. red, tan int., rrch ww, FAO Schwarz Classic Collection (1999) 10 - NA

j. blue, black chassis, blue-tinted windows, black tampo on sides of fenders, lwch, China, #714 (1999) 300 - 375
k. red, chrome int., clear windows, gray tampo on sides, lwch, Malaysia, #173 (2001) 2 - 3

1989

Mattel introduced Park 'N Plates: small plastic see-through boxes with colored see-through lids displaying the vehicle's name. These were issued with their own line and were never in a single blisterpack. This year also saw the introduction of three models destined to become popular with non-Hot Wheels collectors: '32 Ford Delivery (street rod collectors), Custom Corvette (Corvette collectors), and Ferrari F40 (Ferrari/race-car collectors). Mattel also repeated the strategy used in 1988 with the Talbot Lago and Alien (issue a short-run body color, then switch to a more readily available color). GT Racer was initially issued in hard-to-find light blue metalflake and School Bus first came with a two-line tampo on its sides. T-Bucket also had a short-run color and Custom Corvette was first issued with a blue-tinted windshield, but these two variations aren't hard to find. Finally, there are different shades of blue in many cars' tampo.

'32 Ford Delivery 7672 - 62mm - 1989

This sedan delivery truck was patterned after Larry Wood's own truck. It has a metal chassis, yellow plastic fenders, clear windows, yellow interior, bw, & was made in Malaysia.

a. yellow; orange, red & magenta stripe on bottom of sides; Hot Wheels logo & "Delivery" on top behind side window $10 - 12
a2. same as a, blue replaces magenta in tampo, #67 8 - 10

Values are shown in U.S. dollars, first price is for mint, second is for mint packaged vehicles only. See pages 15-16 for grading guide to determine value for cars in lesser conditions.

a3. same as a2, blue tampo darker, gold 30th Anniv. logo in back. Ltd ed for 30th Anniv., w/blistercard in window box (1998) 4 - 6

9599-b

b. 9599; white; turquoise fenders; turquoise, pink & blue tampo on sides, pink varies from dull to bright; #135 (1991) 6 - 15

'32 Ford Delivery-b2

b2. no #, same as b, blue "Warshawsky & Company" on sides. Limited to 7000, never in bp, Warshawsky & Co. give-away only w/purchase worth $75 (1995) 35 - 40
b3. same as b, sp7, #135 (1995) 4 - 10
b4. same as b, sp5, City Action 5-pack (1997) 4 - NA
b5. same as b, ho5, #135 (1998) 2 - 4

9599-c

c. same as b, purple & orange tampo w/"Early Times Car Club" on sides, rt, #135 (1993) 35 - 50

9599-c2

c2. same as c; black, pink & red tampo w/"Temecula-"I Drove"-Rod Run '93" on roof; #135 125 - 200

'32 Ford Delivery-d

d. no #, pink, dk. blue plastic window, tan & blue tampo on sides, dk. blue int., 25th Anniv. Ford 5-pack only (1993) 10 - NA

12034-e

e. 12034, yellow, red plastic fenders, red stripes w/"Malt O Meal" in white on sides, clear window, red int., bw. Ltd ed from Malt O Meal (1994) 18 - 20
e2. same as e, sp7 (1996) 18 - 20

'32 Ford Delivery-f2

f. no #, white, red plastic fenders, blue "McKee Bakery" on front doors, Little Debbie logo on back. Little Debbie Bakery exclusive (1995) 6 - NA
f2. same as f, sp7 4 - NA

7672-g

g. dk. blue, clear window, dk. blue int. & fenders, white "Ford" on sides, white Hot Wheels logo in back, bw. Ford 5-pack only (1995) 3 - NA
g2. same as g, sp7, #446 (1996) 4 - 15
g3. same as g, sp3, #446 (1996) 2 - 4
g4. same as g, sp5, Ford 5 pack only (1997) 2 - NA
g5. same as g, dw3, #446 (1997) 2 - 4

14012-h

h. 14012; black; black fenders, window & int.; pc; "Hot Delivery" & yellow, red & blue flame tampo on sides. #9502 in M&D Toys Ltd Ed series, 9000 made (1995) 25 - 30

'32 Ford Delivery-i

i. chrome, black int., black plastic running boards & fenders, red Hot Wheels logo on back, rsw. Service Merchandise Classic American Car Collection only, limited to 5000 (1995) 10 - NA

'32 Ford Delivery-j

j. 16813; mtlfk dk. red; yellow, orange & blue flames on hood & sides; "Firebird Raceway" in white rectangle on sides; "Nightfire Delivery" in white; yellow Hot Wheels logo in back; clear window; tan int.; pc. Limited to 10,000 (1997) 20 - 25

16813-k

k. mtlc dk. red; black top; yellow, red & blue flames w/Hot Wheels logo on sides. JC Penney 1/24th scale bank (1996) 30 - 35

'32 Ford Delivery-l

l. no #; white; blue plastic fenders & int.; clear windshield; red & black design; red, black, & lt. green "Toys "R" Us" on sides; "Geoffrey" in white & orange logo on black tampo roof; sp7 w/white stripe. Toys "R" Us 10-car set (1997) 8 - NA

'32 Ford Delivery-m

m. lt. green; same as l; purple plastic fenders & int.; red, orange & purple tampo; Toys "R" Us 10-car set only (1997) 8 - NA

'32 Ford Delivery-n

n. mtlfk dk. red, red int., clear window, gold & blue flame tampo on sides & roof, lwgd. Target Exclusive Street Rods set only (1999) 6 - NA

'32 Ford Delivery-o

o. lt. blue; black int.; lt. blue-tinted window; gray & dk. blue tampo on sides & rear w/"Hot Wheels Delivery"; lwch; #996 (1999) 3 - 6

'32 Ford Delivery-p

p. white; black fenders; black, blue & red tampo w/"Newark Police," "103," "Emergency Police & Medical" on sides; "Newark Police" & "103" on hood, "Command Operation Center" on roof; rrch. Limited to 25,000 in Cop Rods Series for K•B Toys (1999) 5 - 7

'32 Ford Delivery-q

q. mtlfk gold; clear window; purple int. & fenders; red, white & black tampo w/"T. Hunter" on doors, "Hunter Delivery" on side panels, design on hood & roof; sp5gd; Malaysia; #9 in 1999 Treasure Hunt Series #937 20 - 30

'32 Ford Delivery-r

r. red & black; black chassis; gray fenders & int.; red, black & white tampo with 14th Annual Hot Wheels Convention logo on sides & roof; pc. Limited to 4000 for 14th Hot Wheels Convention (2000) 30 - 35

'32 Ford Delivery-s

s. black; mtlfk gray chassis; green int. & fenders; clear windshield; green, yellow, black & white tampo w/"Circus" & "Alectra" on sides; lwch. #2 in Circus on Wheels Series, Malaysia, #026 (2000) 2 - 3

t. same as a, unpainted chassis, #2 in Circus on Wheels series, Malaysia, #026 (2000) 2 - 3

'32 Ford Delivery-u

u. white & mtlfk red, white int., clear window, black flame tampo on sides, white flame tampo on hood, Editor's Choice logo in back, iw, Malaysia, Target Exclusive Editor's Choice series, (2000) 6 - 8
v. yellow; w/gray fenders & int.; clear window; red, black & gray tampo w/flames on sides & roof; "Get Real Hot Wheels" & two skulls on sides; dw3; Thailand; Skateboarders 5-pack (2001) 2 - NA

'32 Ford Delivery-w

w. black; beige fenders & int.; clear windshield; red, white & brown tampo on sides & roof w/"The Good, the Bad & the Speedy" on sides; sp3; Thailand; #2 in Wild Frontier series; #056 (2002) 2 - 3

1792-a

Ambulance 1792 - 70mm - 1989
This Chevrolet box-style ambulance has a black plastic base, white plastic opening doors in back, blue-tinted plastic windows, white interior, bw, and was made in Malaysia.

a. white; red, blue & black tampo with "Oxygen Supplies," "American Ambulance Service" & "First Aid" on sides; #71 $8 - 10
a2. same as a, different casting, bw, China, Hospital Sto 'n Go set only (1993) 4 - NA
a3. same as a, sp7, #71 (1996) 18 - 22
a4. same as a, dw3, #71 (1996) 3 - 6
a5. same as a, sp3, #71 (1997) 2 - 4
a6. same as a, sp5. China. Target exclusive set (1999) 5 - NA
b. no number; yellow; same as a; red, blue & white tampo; City Hospital Sto & Go set only (1990) 5 - NA
b2. same as b, white center stripe (1990) 40 - NA

15273-c

c. 15273, green, chrome plastic base, yellow & black tampo with "Fire Dept." & City of Hot Wheels logo on sides, white int., blue-tinted windows, sp5, #1 in Fire Rescue Series, #424 (1996) 8 - 10
c2. same as c, sp7 (1997) 2 - 4
d. red, same tampo as c, sp7, #424 (1997) 2 - 6
d2. same as d, sp3, #424 2 - 4
d3. same as d, sp5, #424 2 - 4

Values are shown in U.S. dollars, first price is for mint, second is for mint packaged vehicles only. See pages 15-16 for grading guide to determine value for cars in lesser conditions.

Ambulance-d

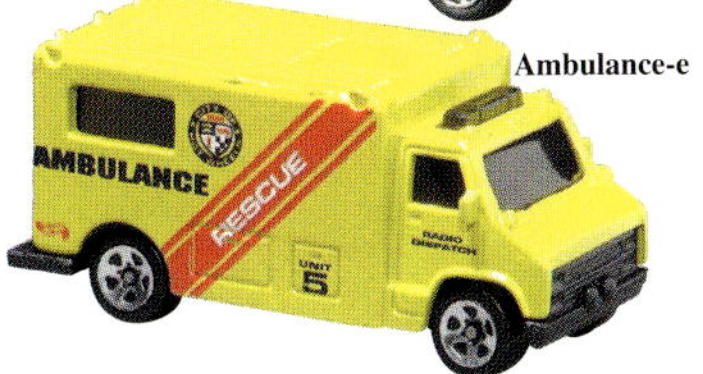
Ambulance-e

e. yellow; black plastic chassis; blacked-out windows; red, black & white tampo with "Rescue," "Ambulance," "Unit 5" & logo on sides; sp5; #71 (1997) 6 - 8
e2. same as e, sp7, #71 2 - 4
e3. same as e, ho5, #71 2 - 4
e4. same as e, dw3, Rescue Squad 5-pack (1997) 2 - NA

Ambulance-f

f. no #; dk. gray; black plastic base; blue-tinted windows; white int.; white "Armored Truck;" City of Hot Wheels logo in gold, white, black & red; bw; Target Holiday gift set; China (1997) 8 - NA

Ambulance-g

g. white; red base; blue-tinted windows; white int.; red, gold & black tampo w/"Ambulance," "Fire Dept," "18" & logo on sides; sp7; Fire Fighting 5-pack (1998) 4 - NA
g2. same as g, ho5 4 - NA
g3. same as g, dw3 4 - NA

Ambulance-h

h. white, blue-tinted windshield, white int., red & black tampo w/"Fire Dept" & City of Hot Wheels logo, bw. Sold w/Long Hauler only, China (1998) 4 - NA

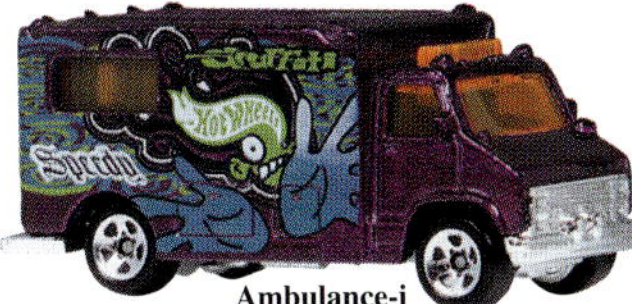
Ambulance-i

i. mtlfk purple; orange-tinted windows & lights; blue, lt. green, white & black tampo with " Graffiti," "Speedy" & Hot Wheels logo on sides; sp5; #3 in Street Art Series; #951 (1999) 2 - 3
i2. same as i, sp3, #951 (1999) 2 - 3
j. white; chrome chassis; white int.; yellow-tinted windows; red stripe; gold & black tampo with "Ambulance," "Fire Dept.," City of Hot Wheels logo, "Burn Kit" &"CPR" on sides; sp5; Fire 'n Rescue Action Pack only (1999) 6 - NA
k. red; white int.; blue-tinted windows & lights; blue, yellow & black tampo with Hot Wheels logo & "Post Office" on sides; sp5; China; Americas Highway Set (1999) 6 - NA

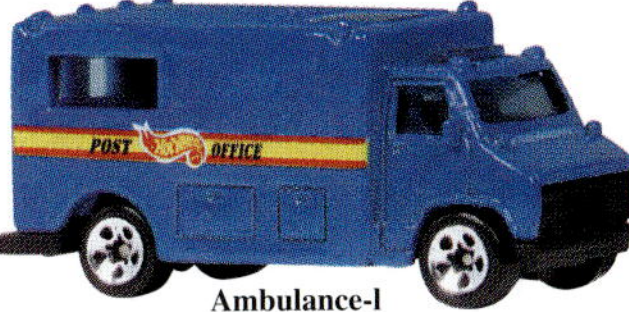
Ambulance-l

l. blue, same as k, red not blue in tampo, Deluxe Downtown set (1999) 6 - NA

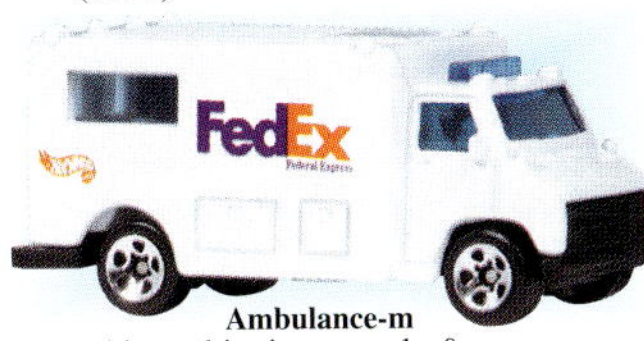
Ambulance-m

m. white; white int.; purple & orange tampo with "FedEx" on sides; sp5 (1999) 2 - NA
n. gray; same as k; white, yellow, red & black tampo with "Armored Truck" & City of Hot Wheels logo on sides; bw; Super Police Set 10 - NA

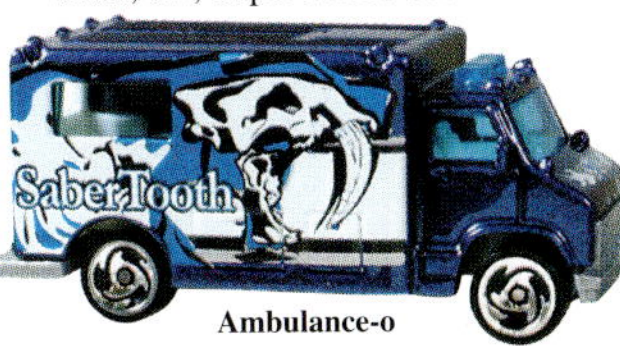
Ambulance-o

o. dk. purple; gray plastic chassis; white int.; blue-tinted windows; blue, black & white tampo with "Saber Tooth" on sides; dw3; Malaysia; #2 in Fossil Fuel series; #042 (2000) 2 - 3

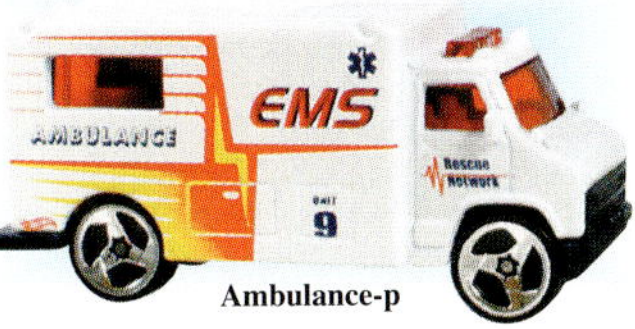
Ambulance-p

p. white; black chassis; red int.; red-tinted windows; orange, yellow, dk. blue & black tampo w/"Ambulance," "EMS," "Unit 9" & "Rescue Network" on sides; sp3; Thailand; Rescue Rods 5 pack (2001) 2 - 3

1790-a

Big Rig 1790 - 81mm - 1989
This is a Malaysia-made Kenworth T 600A tractor rig with a sleeper cab, black plastic chassis, gray plastic windows, and bw. Similar castings: 15219 Ford LTL (1996), 15219 Kenworth T-600 (1996)
a. black; blue, red & orange stripe tampo on sides; red is over orange $3 - 5
a2. same as a, orange is over red 3 - 5

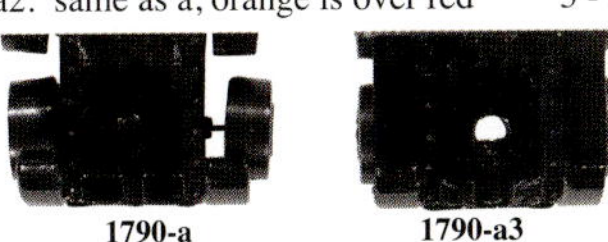
1790-a 1790-a3

a3. same as a, new casting (back of sleeper missing 2 struts, hitch changed shape), #76 (1990) 5 - 7

Big Rig-b

a4. same as a3, orange is over red (1990) 3 - 5
a5. same as a, casting change (rear mud flaps part of fenders & hitch has hole) (1991) 3 - 5
a6. same as a5, sp7, #76 (1995) 5 - 7
a7. same as a5, dw3, #76 (1997) 4 - 6
b. no #; yellow; yellow plastic chassis; black windows; black, red, blue & white stars-&-stripes tampo on sides; bw; Big Rigger Stunt Show set only (1990) 20 - NA

Big Rig-c

c. white; blue plastic base; blacked-out windows; red, yellow, blue tampo with "Action News KHWW," "Field Transport Rig" & "1" on side; sp5; Action News Team 5-pack (1998) 2 - NA
c2. same as c, ho5 2 - NA

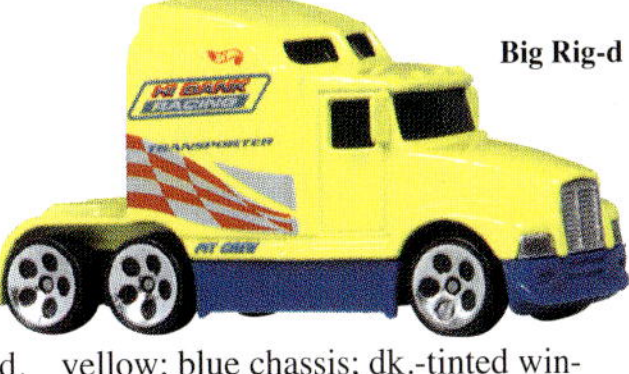
Big Rig-d

d. yellow; blue chassis; dk.-tinted windows; gray, red & blue tampo with "Hi Bank Racing," "Transporter" & "Pit Crew on sides; ho5; Thailand; Race Team Crew 5-pack only (1999) 2 - NA

1791-a2

Chevy Stocker 1791 - 76mm - 1989
This Chevrolet NASCAR stock car has a metal base, clear windows, gray interior, bw, and was made in Malaysia.
Similar casting: 15266 Crunch Chief (1996)
a. black; yellow, red & white stripe tampo with "3" & race decals on sides, "Chevrolet 350" twice & Chevy logo on hood, gray & red "3" on roof; larger bw in back; #70 $30 - 35
a2. same as a, 4 small bw, #70 30 - 35
a3. same as a2, Union & V in tampo missing, #70 15 - 20

Chevy Stocker-b

b. no #; turquoise; same as a; side tampo is red, yellow & white; no tampo on roof or hood; Hot Wheels cereal only (1990) 12 - NA
c. 0452; orange; gold metalflakes; yellow plastic interior; #170 12 - 15
c2. same as c, uhgd, #270 10 - 12
c3. 13575, same as c2, red int., tinted windows, uhgd, #270 60 - 65

1791-d

d. fluor. lime; orange, red & dk. red tampo: flames, Hot Wheels logo, "Track System" & racing decals on sides; flames & "New York Toy Fair" on hood; "95" & flames on roof; "Hot Wheels" on trunk; "Track System" in back; clear windows, black int., iw. 1995 Toy Fair give-away only; Park 'n Plates plastic box w/piece of track only (1995) 300 - NA
e. black; red & white tampo with "Chevrolet," "1" & Hot Wheels logo on sides; "Chevrolet," Chevy logo & "Goodyear" on hood; "1" on roof; clear windows; red int. & roll cage; bw; Chevrolet 5-Pack only (1995) 3 - NA

1791-e2

e2. same as e, sp7, #441 (1996) 6 - 8
f. 13575, mtlfk gold, tinted windows, red int., red Hot Wheels logo on rear bumper, uhgd, #270 (1995) 45 - 50
f2. same as f, sp7, Racing Team 5-pack 4 - NA
g. white; same tampo color & design as d, st, Criss Cross Crash set only (1995) 8 - NA
h. 16918; red; blacked-out windows; black, yellow & white design on sides & hood; "Hurricane" on sides; sp3; #1 in Quicksilver Series; #545 (1997) 2 - 4
h2. same as h, silver base, #545 (1998) 2 - 4
i. blue plastic body; black metal base; black int.; tinted windows; orange, black & white tampo with "7" & "Track Jumper" on sides; sp5; Figure 8 Racers 5-pack only (1998) 2 - NA
i2. same as i, ho5 2 - NA

Chevy Stocker-j

j. white; clear windows; black int.; silver, red & dk. blue tampo with "1," "Huffman Racing" & race decals on sides; "Huffman Racing" on hood; sp5; #618 (1998) 20 - 22

Chevy Stocker-k

k. purple plastic body; black metal base; blacked-out windows; orange, black, gray & white tampo with skulls on sides; dw3gd; Malaysia; Volcano Blowout 5-pack only (1999) 2 - NA
k2. same as k, Thailand, #870 (1999) 2 - 3

Values are shown in U.S. dollars, first price is for mint, second is for mint packaged vehicles only. See pages 15-16 for grading guide to determine value for cars in lesser conditions.

Chevy Stocker-l

l. purple plastic body; metal base; black windshield; orange, white & black tampo with "Smash Champs" & "4777" on sides; dw; Criss Cross Crash 5-pack (1999) 2 - NA
m. red, black windows, sp3, Malaysia, Mexico only (2001) 10 - 12
n. white plastic body; black windows; yellow, black & gold tampo w/"Yellow Jacket" on sides & hood; dw3gd; Thailand; #153 (2001) 2 - 3
o. red; black windows; yellow, purple & white tampo on sides, hood & roof w/"Demolition Derby" on sides; dw3; Thailand; Demolition Derby playset (2001) 2 - 3

7670-a

Custom Corvette 7670 - 74mm - 1989
This Malaysia-made Corvette convertible has a black plastic chassis, tan plastic interior, blue-tinted plastic windshield, and uh.
a. mtlc dk. red; yellow, white & lt. blue stripes; "Corvette" once on sides & twice on hood; ZR-1 in stripe $10 - 12
a2. as a, clear windshield 15 - 18
a3. as a, no ZR-1 in stripe, #66 10 - 12

Custom Corvette-b

b. no number; black; yellow stripes; red flames & "Getty" on white square on hood; Getty service stations exclusive (1989) 8 - NA
c. 9246, gold chrome, no tampo, gray plastic chassis, chrome plastic int., clear windshield, 20th Hot Wheels Anniv., only sold w/trophy (1990), w/trophy 6 - 8

1301-d

d. 1301; chrome blue; pink, yellow & white stripes on sides; "Corvette" in pink & white on hood; black "Cal Custom" on windshield; pink int.; rry; California Custom (1990) 15 - 18
d2. same as d, tw 30 - 35

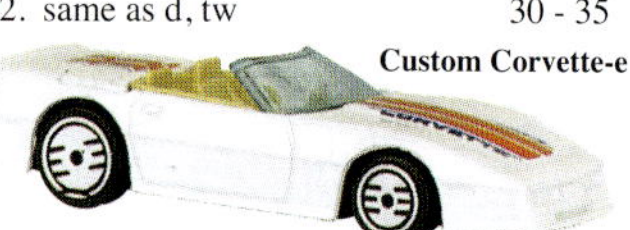
Custom Corvette-e

e. no #, white; red & blue stripes on hood & trunk; blue "Corvette" twice on hood; Hot Wheels cereal only (1990) 8 - NA

1301-f

f. 1301, orange, same as d, tw, California Custom (1991) 15 - 18

2898-g

g. 2898; pearl white; clear windshield; red int.; red stripes on sides; "Corvette" in yellow; "Corvette" & Chevy logo in red, black & yellow on hood; black plastic base; uh; #200 (1993) 6 - 8

Custom Corvette-h

h. no #; lt. brown; brown, aqua & lt. green tampo on sides; "Corvette" on hood; blue-tinted windshield; blue int.; black plastic base; uh; 25th Anniv. Chevy 5-pack only (1993) 6 - NA

7670-i

i. white; orange & yellow fireball design on top & sides; orange int.; rose uh; tinted windshield; Revealers series 4 - 6
j. gray; orange, white & yellow fireball design on top & sides; yellow int.; tinted windshield; lime green uh; Revealers series 4 - 6
k. blue; orange, white & yellow ribbon design on top & sides; red interior; tinted windshield; orange uh; Revealers series 4 - 6

Custom Corvette-l

l. no #; white; red, black & blue tampo with "World Cup USA 94" & Hot Wheels logo on sides, "World Cup USA 94" and soccer ball on hood; clear windshield; red int.; uh; World Cup 5-pack only (1994) 6 - NA
m. 15249, dk. mtlfk purple, red Hot Wheels logo on clear windshield, gray int., black plastic base, uh, #200 (1995) 6 - 8
m2. same as m, tan int., #200 (1995) 6 - 8

2898-m3

m3. 2898, same as m2, sp5, #200 (1995) 6 - 8
m4. same as m2, lwch, #200 (1997) 4 - 6
m5. same as m2, sp7, #200 8 - 12
m6. same as m2, sp7gd, Canada only (1997) 3 - 5
n. no #, yellow, gray int., tinted windshield, uh, Chevrolet 5-Pack only (1995) 2 - NA
n2. same as n, clear windshield, uh 4 - NA
n3. same as n, sp5 2 - NA
n4. same as n, sp7 (1996) 3 - NA
o. black, gold Hot Wheels logo in back, black-tinted windshield, black plastic base & int., sp5. Black Convertible Collection only, Target exclusive 6 - NA
p. mtlfk silver; red int., black-tinted windshield, sp5, Corvette 5-pack only (1996) 3 - NA
p2. same as p, sp7 2 - NA
p3. same as p, sp3 2 - NA

15249-q

q. 15249; mtlfk purple; green, brown, yellow & white tampo w/football field & helmet on sides, football field in back & football on hood; gray int.; black-tinted windshield; sp7; #2 in Sports Car Series; #405 (1996) 6 - 8

Custom Corvette-r

q2. same as q, red int., #405 50 - 60
r. 16929; black; gray int.; tinted windshield; yellow, red, white tampo with buildings, circle & arrows on hood; sp3; #4 in Spy Print Series; #556 (1997) 2 - 4

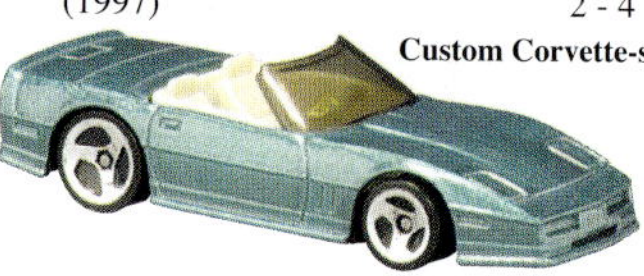
Custom Corvette-s

s. no #, mtlfk aqua, beige int., tinted windshield, sp3, Father & Son Collector 2-pack by Avon only (1997) 4 - NA

Custom Corvette-t

t. green, blue int., tinted windshield, black & white tampo w/"Tour'd Inland" on sides, sp3. Issued as Corvette Convertible, #4 in Tropicool Series, #696 (1998) 2 - 4

Custom Corvette-u

u. mtlc purple; white int.; tinted windshield; orange, silver, black & white tampo w/"98 Bonus car" & "Q3" on sides & hood; baggie only; Malaysia; 1998 Mystery Car #3 (1998) 6 - NA

Custom Corvette-v

v. mtlfk dk. blue; black chassis; tinted windshield; white int.; gold & white tampo with stripes & Final Run logo on hood, "Final Run" on trunk, "Corvette" in back; iwgd; #10 in 1999 Final Run Series (1999) 6 - 8
w. bright green, black chassis, blue int., tinted windshield, sp3, Malaysia, sold in Mexico only (2000) 10 - 12

2808-a

Delivery Truck 2808 - 70mm - 1989
Based on a generic stepside bread delivery van, this Malaysia-made model has a black plastic base, black plastic opening doors in back, clear windshield, black interior, & bw. Similar castings: 9643 Letter Getter (1977), 2854 S.W.A.T. Van (1979), 2850 The Incredible Hulk (1979), 3303 Racing Team (1981), 9643 Delivery Van (1984), 2519 Combat Medic (1986), 9114 The Simpson's Homer's Nuclear Waste Van (1990), 19580 Pit Crew Truck (1999)

1578-b

a. white; red, blue & yellow tampo with "Wonder" & "Twinkies" in red, blue "Hostess" on sides $12 - 15
b. white; red, yellow & blue tampo with Hot Wheels logo, "Larry's Mobile Tune-Up" & ad on sides; #52 (1990) 8 - 10

4970-c

c. 4970, white, same as a, red & blue tampo with "Air France Cargo" on sides, red doors & int., Intl. box line only 12 - 15
d. no #; white; white plastic doors; clear windshield; white int.; red & blue stripes w/Little Debbie logo on sides. Sold or give-away as Little Debbie Bakery 3-pack (1995) 6 - NA

Delivery Truck-d2

d2. same as d, sp7 4 - NA

14975-e

e. 14975; red; yellow tampo w/"Bob's Toy Show," "A Collectible Meet for the Miniature Car Collector," "Holiday Inn Foster City CA," "13" & Hot Wheels logo on sides; "Bob's Toy Show" & phone # on front; black-tinted windshield; black int.; gych. Limited to 10,000, #13 (1996) 20 - 25

Delivery Truck-f

f. no #; dk. blue; gray chassis; blue-tinted windshield; black int.; red, white & gold tampo w/"SWAT," "Police," "86" & logo on sides; sp7; Police Force 5-pack only (1997) 2 - NA
f2. same as f, dw3 (1998) 2 - NA
f3. same as f2, Thailand 2 - NA

Delivery Truck-g

g. white; black plastic base & int.; clear windshield; red, yellow, blue tampo w/"Action News KHWW," "Broadcast Van" & "1" on sides; sp5; Action News Team 5-pack (1998) 2 - NA
g2. same as g, sp3 2 - NA
g3. same as g, ho5 2 - NA
h. blue; black plastic chassis & int.; blue-tinted windshield; white, black & orange tampo w/"Stinky's Diaper Cleaners," flames & fly on sides; dw3; House Calls 5-pack only (1999) 2 - NA

Values are shown in U.S. dollars, first price is for mint, second is for mint packaged vehicles only. See pages 15-16 for grading guide to determine value for cars in lesser conditions.

Delivery Truck-h

i. pearl gray; black int.; orange-tinted windshield; blue, orange & black tampo w/"Blue X Emergency" on sides; sp5; Malaysia; Truck Stoppers 5-pack (2001) 2 - NA

1468-a

Ferrari F40 1468 - 72mm - 1989
This Malaysia-made model has a metal base, rear spoiler, clear windows, tan interior, & uh.

a. red; yellow tampo with "Ferrari" twice and "F40" on hood; "F40" on sides; #69 $6 - 8
a2. same as a, uhgd, #69 (1994) 8 - 10
a3. same as a, sp5, #69 (1995) 3 - 5
a4. same as a, sp5g, #69 (1995) 3 - 5
a5. same as a, sp3g, #69 (1995) 3 - 5
a6. same as a, lwgd, #69 (1997) 3 - 5

1468-b

b. candy red; blue & white flag tampo on sides & top; yellow "F40" on hood; clear windows; tan int.; uhy; Malaysia, Revealers 3 - 5
c. metallic red, same as a, Revealers 3 - 5
d. yellow, same as a, "F40" in white, black int., uhp, Revealers 3 - 5
e. no #, yellow, same as a, blue tampo & int., 25th Anniv. Exotic Car 5-pack only (1993) 6 - NA
f. red; yellow & black Ferrari logo on hood; tan int.; white Hot Wheels logo on rear bumper; uh; Ferrari 5-pack only (1995) 2 - NA

Ferrari F40-g

g. 12935; pearl white; yellow & black Ferrari logo on hood; tinted windows; tan int.; sp7; #442 (1996) 4 - 6
g2. same as g, sp5, #442 2 - 4
g3. same as g, ho5w, #442 10 - 12
g4. same as g, ho5, #442 (1997) 2 - 4
g5. same as g, dw3, #442 (1997) 2 - 4
h. 17963, red, Ferrari logo in yellow & black on hood, "Ferrari" in yellow on spoiler, sp5, small European blister-card only, #3 in Ferrari Series (1997) 4 - 6
h2. same as h, grayish tan int. 4 - 6

Ferrari F40-i

i. mtlfk gold; tan int.; tinted windows; black & white tampo w/"Banca d Italia," "Centomila" & shield on sides, "Centomila" & shield on hood; lwgd; #2 in Dash 4 Cash Series; #722 (1998) 2 - 3
j. unpainted, tan int., tinted windows, lwch, #2 in Dash 4 Cash Series, sold at 1998 Hot Wheels Convention, #722 (1998) 75 - 85

Ferrari F40-k

k. black, tinted windows, red interior, yellow Ferrari logo on hood, sp5, #1003 (1999) 2 - 3
l. yellow, clear windows, black int., sp5, #122 (2000) 2 - 3
m. pearl blue, clear windows, black int., yellow & black Ferrari logo on hood, pr5s. Malaysia. #209 (2001) 2 - 3
n. red, black int, clear windows, yellow, black and white tampo, Ferrari logo on hood, Auto Milestones logo on roof and pc. Thailand. Auto Milestones series. (2002) 2 - 3

1789-a

GT Racer 1789 - 79mm - 1989
This endurance-style concept car has a metal base, chrome plastic rear spoiler, blacked-out plastic windows and uh. Malaysia.

a. purple; orange, blue & white stripe tampo w/"5" on sides & top; #74 $15 - 18

1789-a2

a2. as a, one decal missing, #74 10 - 12
a3. as a2, bw, #74 12 - 15

1789-b

b. blue metalflake, same as a 50 - 60
c. 9224; red; same as a; blue, white & yellow tampo; gray int.; blue-tinted windows; Park 'n Plates (1990) 20 - 25

GT Racer-d

d. no #; pearl white; orange, pink & magenta tampo on top & sides; black-tinted windows; black int.; bw; only in set (1991) 8 - NA
d2. same as d, dk. blue replaces magenta in tampo 8 - NA
e. 0450; black; same as a; yellow, pink & red tampo; grayed-out windows; bw; #168 (1992) 8 - 10

GT Racer-f

f. no #; mtlfk silver; yellow, white & magenta stripes on top; "5" on hood; clear windows; black int.; Heroes on Hot Wheels video tapes only (1993); w/video 8 - NA

1789-g

g. Day-Glo blue; orange, yellow & magenta striping; "3" on sides & top; gold windows; white "Revealers" on windshield; bw; Malaysia; Revealers 10-pack only 10 - NA
h. 15964; day-glow orange; black windows & spoiler; red, yellow & white

15964-h

Hot Wheels logo; sp5; China; #468 (1996) 2 - 4

15964-h2

h2. same as h; dk. green stripe, "Goodyear," "Danger Flame Arrester" & "Nitrogen Purged Injection" on sides; China; #468 (1997) 2 - 4
h3. same as h, lwch, #468 (1997) 2 - 4

GT Racer-i

i. gold; tinted windows; black & gold int.; black engine & spoiler; red stripe & black tampo w/"Danger Flame Arrester," "Nitrogen Purged Induction" & race decals on sides; sp5; China; #468 (1999) 2 - 4
j. lime yellow; black interior & spoiler; tinted windows; black, blue, white & gray tampo on sides; dw3; Malaysia; Max Steel 5-pack 2 - NA
k. blue, chrome int., yellow-tinted windows, red & yellow flame tampo on sides & roof, ho5, Malaysia, #220 (2001) 2 - 3

1469-a

Peugeot 205 Rallye 1469 - 74mm - 1989
Based on the factory-built high-performance car that dominated European Rallyes for years, this Malaysia-made model has a metal base, clear windows, gray interior, and bw.
Note: Originally for the International line, it appeared in the U.S. about the same time as in Canada.

a. white; red, blue, yellow & black tampo w/"2" & racing decals on hood & sides; #105 $12 - 15

1469-b

b. same as a; red, lt. blue & black tampo w/"3" on sides, hood & top; race decals on sides; Intl. line only (1992) 8 - 10

Peugeot 205 Rallye-c

c. black in back, lt. blue in middle, magenta in front; orange metal chassis, gray int., clear windows, silver tampo w/"205" & race decals on sides, sp5, China, #507 (1998) 8 - 18
c2. as c, unpainted metal chassis 8 - 18

1796-a

Pontiac Banshee 1796 - 70mm - 1989
Based on Pontiac's prototype futuristic show car, this Malaysia-made model has a metal base, black-tinted windows with a red plastic roof insert, black plastic interior & hood, & uh.
Note: The first Banshees had "Pontiac" imprinted on the backs, but because of tooling problems the imprint became unreadable and was removed.

1796-a 1796-a2

a. red, "Pontiac" imprinted on back $8 - 10
a2. same as a, "Pontiac" imprint removed, #75 (1990) 3 - 5
a3. same as a2, uhgd, #75 10 - 225
a4. same as a, clear windows, pc, Demolition Man series w/Cryo-Cube only 4 - 6
a5. same as a2, sp5, #75 (1995) 2 - 6
a6. same as a2, sp7, #75 (1996) 2 - 6
a7. same as a2, bw, Canada only (1996) 2 - 4

1303-b

b. 1303, gold chrome, orange plastic roof insert, orange "Pontiac" twice in front, yellow "Cal Custom" on windshield, rry, California Custom (1990) 10 - 12
b2. same as b; red plastic int., roof inset & hood (1991) 10 - 12
b3. same as b2; pink plastic insert, white "Cal Custom" on window (1991) 10 - 12
b4. 1303, same as b2, tw (1991) 10 - 12

Pontiac Banshee-c

c. no #; blue; yellow & blue tampo on sides; blacked-out windows; uh; Heroes on Hot Wheels tapes only (1993) w/tape 10 - NA

1796-d

d. candy red; yellow, pink & purple tampo w/"Banshee" on sides; white hood; black-tinted windows; "Revealers" in white on windshield; uh; Malaysia; Revealers 10-pack only 10 - NA
e. black, lt. green int., clear windshield, sp5, China, #457 (1996) 2 - 6
e2. same as e, lwch, #457 (1997) 2 - 4
e3. same as e, red int., Launcher pack only (1998) 3 - NA

Pontiac Banshee-e4

e4. no #, same as e, sp5, red int. & hood, Target excl. holiday set only 5 - NA

Values are shown in U.S. dollars, first price is for mint, second is for mint packaged vehicles only. See pages 15-16 for grading guide to determine value for cars in lesser conditions.

Pontiac Banshee-f

f. yellow, "Banshee" in red under doors, black int., clear windows, black plastic roof inserts, sp5, China, Kmart excl., 70th Anniv. of the Pontiac set only, limited to 7000 (1996) 12 - NA
g. mtlfk purple, black int., clear dome, black plastic roof insert, sp5, China, #457 (1999) 2 - 4

Pontiac banshee-h

h. orange; clear windows; black int.; black & silver tampo w/flames on sides & top, "Custom Car Designer CD ROM" & "Design" on trunk; ho5; Malaysia; #4 in CD Customs series; #32 (2000) 2 - 3
i. blue, gray int., blue-tinted dome, gray & black tampo on top & sides w/Hot Wheels logo on sides, sp5, #2 in Loco-Motive Series, #074 (2001) 2 - 3

1795-a

School Bus 1795 - 80mm - 1989
This Ford school bus has a black plastic chassis, clear windows, black interior, bw, and was made in Malaysia.
a. yellow, black tampo, thick black line & "School Bus" on sides, #72 $3 - 6

1795-a2

a2. same as a, lighter yellow & thinner line on sides in back only 6 - 8

School Bus-a3

a3. no #, same as a, tan int., "City School" & 2 stripes in black on sides, City School Sto & Go Set only 5 - NA
a4. same a3, black int. (1992) 5 - NA
b. 13315, chrome, same as a, tinted windows, gray int., #4 in Silver Series, #328 (1995) 15 - 35
b2. same as b, clear windows, #328 (1995) 2 - 18
b3. same as b2, sp7, #328 (1995) 2 - 8

13315-b4

b4. same as b2, sp3, #328 (1995) 5 - 15
b5. same as b2, sp5, #328 (1996) 2 - 8

15239-c

c. 15239; mtlfk purple; yellow, orange & lt. green tampo w/"Love" & Hot Wheels logo on sides, "Love" & "Peace" on roof; clear windows; orange int.; yellow base; sp7; #2 in Mod Bod Series; #397 (1996) 2 - 6
d. 16911; mtlfk aqua; white & yellow flames; sides & roof outlined in red; white int.; sp5; #2 in Heat Fleet Series; #538 (1997) 2 - 5

School Bus-d2

d2. same as d, sp3, #538 2 - 5
d3. same as d, sp7, #538 (1997) 20 - 25
d4. same as d, ho5, #538 2 - 4
d5. same as d, sp5, bars on windows, #538 25 - 30
d6. same as d, sp5, China (1998) 2 - 4
e. 1795; black; white, gold & red tampo w/"Police," "Prisoner Transport," "013" & logo on sides; sp7; silver stripes on side & rear windows; bus on package; #72 (1997) 2 - 8

School Bus-e2

e2. same as e, ho5, #72 (1998) 2 - 8
e3. same as e, ho5, Thailand, #72 2 - 8

School Bus-f

f. yellow; black int.; tinted windows; black, white, red & green tampo w/street signs on sides; ho5; #4 in Mixed Signal Series; #736 (1998) 2 - 3
f2. same as f, Thailand, #736 (1998) 2 - 3

School Bus-g

g. yellow; red-tinted windows; orange, black & olive tampo w/"Graffiti Transport" on sides; ho5; #4 in Street Art Series; #952 (1999) 2 - 3

School Bus-h

h. gray, same as g, #4 in Street Art Series, #952 (1999) 2 - 3

School Bus-i

i. yellow; blue chassis; red int.; clear windows; red, white & blue tampo w/Fisher Price logo on sides; dw3; Toys "R" Us Timeless Toys II 4-pack (1999) 5 - NA
j. black; black chassis; red-tinted windows; white, gold & purple tampo w/"Graphics" on sides, flames & wheel w/"Hot Wheels" twice on roof; ho5; China; #1055 (2000) 2 - 3
k. dk. blue; gray chassis & int.; clear windows; multicolored tampo w/"44," Hot Wheels logo & race decals on sides, "44" & Hot Wheels logo on hood; gyrd; Thailand; #1 in NASCAR School Bus series (2000) 6 - 10
l. yellow; same as k; multicolored tampo w/"22," "Caterpillar" & race decals on sides, "CAT" on hood; gybk; Thailand; #2 in NASCAR School Bus series (2000) 6 - 10

School Bus-m

m. red; same as k; multicolored tampo w/"94," "McDonald's" & race decals on sides, McDonald's M on hood; gybk; Thailand; #3 in NASCAR School Bus series (2000) 6 - 10
n. dk. blue; same as k; lt. blue roof; multicolored tampo w/"43," "Cheerios," STP logo & race decals on sides, STP logo on hood; gybl; Thailand; #4 in NASCAR School Bus series (2000) 8 - 12
o. red; white int.; blue-tinted windows; black, gray & white tampo w/"Graphics" on sides, flames & "Hot Wheels" on roof wheel; Thailand; #216 (2000) 2 - 3
p. green; yellow int.; clear windows; gray, black & white tampo w/dinosaur on sides & top, "Triceratops" on sides; ho5; #1 in Fossil Fuel series; #041 (2001) 2 - 3

1470-a

Street Roader® 1470 - 68mm - 1989
Based on a Suzuki Samurai four-wheel drive road vehicle, this model has a metal base, clear windshield, black plastic interior & truck bed, ct, and was made in Malaysia.
a. white; magenta, orange & blue stripe on hood & sides; "4x4" on sides; "4x4" twice on hood $6 - 8
a2. same as a, cts 6 - 8
a3. same as a, cty 8 - 10
a4. same as a2, pink replaces magenta in tampo, #73 8 - 12
a5. same as a, black replaces magenta in tampo, #73 2 - 3
a6. same as a5, cts 15 - 18

1287-b

b. 1287; white; lt. blue back; yellow, blue & orange tampo on sides & hood; black "Cal Custom" on windshield; orange int. & truck bed; cto; California Custom (1990) 8 - 10
b2. same as b, ct, yellow "Cal Custom" (1990) 8 - 10
b3. same as b2, cts (1990) 8 - 10
b4. same as b2, red int. & truck bed, ct 8 - 10
b5. same as b4, pink interior and truck bed, ct 8 - 10
b6. same as b4, cto 8 - 10
b7. same as b4, black "Cal Custom" on windshield, cts 8 - 10
c. orange; same as b; dk. blue, white & red tampo; no lt. blue in back; ct; California Custom (1991) 30 - 35

1287-c

1470-c2

c2. same as c, red in back 8 - 10
c3. same as c2, cts 12 - 15

Street Roader-d

d. no #; fluor. lime-yellow; magenta, pink & white tampo on sides; pink int.; clear windshield; ct; Heroes on Hot Wheels tapes only (1993), w/video 12 - NA

4318-e

e. 4318; mtlc green; same tampo as a; magenta, orange & aqua colors; gray int. & truck bed; ct; #218 (1993) 4 - 6

12344-f

f. 12344; white; pink & blue tampo on sides & hood; blue "Beach Patrol" on hood; blue bed & int.; blue-tinted windshield; ct; #252 (1995) 2 - 4
f2. same as f, cto, #252 (1996) 2 - 4
f3. same as f, dw3ct, #252 (1996) 2 - 4

13290-g2

g. 13290, orange, black zebra stripes, black int. & Hot Wheels logo on sides, tinted windshield, cto, #1 in Roarin' Rods series, #303 (1995) 6 - 8
g2. same as g, ct, #303 40 - 50

Values are shown in U.S. dollars, first price is for mint, second is for mint packaged vehicles only. See pages 15-16 for grading guide to determine value for cars in lesser conditions.

Street Roader-h

h. 16923, white, red int. & bed, clear windshield, gold spray tampo w/"Dirty Dog" red on sides & hood, dwct, #2 in Speed Spray series, #550 (1997) 2 - 4

Street Roader-i

i. white; blue plastic int., bed & grille; tinted windshield; red, yellow, lt. green & blue design on sides; gray, orange & red "Chuck E Cheese" & logo on hood; dw3ct; Chuck E. Cheese promo 6 - 8

Street Roader-j

j. white; yellow int. & truck bed; tinted windshield; yellow, red & black tampo w/street signs; dw3ct; #1 in Mixed Signals series; #733 (1998) 2 - 3

Street Roader-k

k. dk. mtlc red; black chassis; white border, bed & int.; clear windshield; white flames on sides; black, white & gold tampo w/"Michael's Lil Firecracker" on sides & hood; black & gold tampo in back; dwctw; "Final Run" on tires; #5 in Final Run series, limited to 35,000 (1999) 3 - 5

7673-a2

T-Bucket 7673 - 65mm - 1989
This Ford Model T Roadster hot rod has a metal chassis, chrome plastic supercharged engine & side pipes, red plastic interior, clear windshield, and bw. Made in Malaysia.

a. orange; red & blue flame tampo on sides $8 - 10
b. yellow, same as a, #68 10 - 12
c. same as b, sp5, #68 (1995) 8 - 10

9223-c2

c2. 9223, purple, same as a, lt. blue & orange tampo, orange int., Park 'n Plates (1991) 30 - 35
c3. same as c2, clear windows, red interior 65 - 75
d. no #, fluor. lime-yellow, same as c; red & dk. red tampo, pink int., Heroes on Hot Wheels tapes only (1991), w/video 8 - 10

T-Bucket-e

e. 12276; black; orange & yellow flames on sides; clear windshield; tan int.; gyg; limited to 7000 (1994) 35 - 40

T-Bucket-f

f. 13300, dk. purple, rose chrome engine, black-tinted metal base & pipes, purple-tinted windshield, white int., sp5, #2 in Speed Gleamer series, #313 (1995) 4 - 6
f2. same as f, clear windows 40 - 45
f3. same as f, sp7, #313 (1996) 12 - 15
f4. same as f, blue chrome engine, sp7 10 - 12

T-Bucket-g

g. mtlc red, gold sparkle flames on sides, green-tinted windshield, green int., iw w/green hubs, Santa in driver's seat, toy sack in back. Issued w/ornament in red display box w/plastic top for Christmas (1995) 15 - 20

T-Bucket-h

h. mtlc green, same as l, white int., iw w/red hubs. Issued w/ornament in red display box w/plastic top for Christmas (1995) 15 - 20
i. black, clear windshield, purple int., gold-plated radiator, chrome engine, iw, 100th Anniversary of Auto gift pack (1996) 12 - NA

T-Bucket-j

j. no #, white, gold int., blue-tinted windshield, chrome engine, red & dk. blue stars & stripes all over, pcgd, American Spirit 4-pack gift set only (1997) 10 - NA
k. purple; clear windshield; black int.; yellow, orange & lt. blue flame tampo; sp5; FAO Schwarz History of Hot Wheels III 8-pack only (1997) 8 - NA

l. red w/orange in middle & lt. blue rear; chrome engine; tinted windshield; gray int.; multicolored tampo w/"66," "Big K" & race decals on sides, "Route 66" & "Big K" on trunk & in back; sp5; Thailand; #1 in NASCAR Hot Rod series (2000) 6 - 8
m. orange; same as l; black, white & blue tampo w/"21," Citgo logo & race decals on sides, "21" & "Citgo" on trunk & back; sp5; Thailand; #2 in NASCAR Hot Rod series (2000) 6 - 8
n. red; same as l; black, white & yellow tampo w/"94," "Drive Thru," McDonald's M & race decals on sides, McDonald's M on trunk & back; sp5; Thailand; #3 in NASCAR Hot Rod series (2000) 6 - 8

T-Bucket-o

o. orange; same as l; yellow, white & dk. blue tampo w/"32," "Tide" & race decals on sides, "Tide" & "32" on trunk & back; sp5; Thailand; #4 in NASCAR Hot Rod series (2000) 6 - 8

7671-a

VW Bug 7671 - 60mm - 1989
This Malaysia-made 1966 Volkswagen has a metal base, metal headlights sticking thru the body, gray-tinted windows, tan interior, & bw.

a. turquoise; magenta, orange & yellow striping tampo on sides & roof; #65 $12 - 15
a2. same as a, blue replaces magenta in tampo (1990) 12 - 15

2149-b

b. red; yellow, white & blue flame tampo on sides, hood & roof (different shades of blue in tampo); white int.; #65 12 - 15
b2. same as b, turquoise replaces blue in tampo, #65 (1991) 20 - 25

7671-c

c. no #; lt. green; yellow stripes & "Getty" in red & white square on roof, clear windows, yellow int., bw, Getty (1990) 5 - NA
d. 9225; yellow; same as a; orange, blue & green tampo; blue-tinted windows; dk. blue int.; Park 'n Plates (1991) 50 - 60

0453-e

e. purple; orange, green & yellow tampo on sides, hood & roof; red int.; bw; #171 (1992) 15 - 18
e2. same as e, sp7, U.S. playset or European single pack (1997) 4 - 6
e3. same as e, sp3, #171 (1997) 2 - 4
e4. same as e2, China (1998) 4 - 6

11810-f

f. 11810, pink, black top, "Randy's Stuff" in black & white on sides, clear windows, cream int., rt. Only 3000 made, issued on white card (1994) 50 - 60

11810-g

g. 11810, purple, same as f, only 7000 made (1994) 35 - 45

VW Bug-h

h. no #, mtlfk black, tinted windows, tan int., rrgy. 1993 SEMA Show give-away only, never in bp (1993) 80 - NA
i. 13280, pearl pink, Hot Wheels logo in white oval in back, clear windows, gray int., bw. #3 in Pearl Driver series, #293 (1995) 8 - 10

VW Bug-i2

i2. same as i, sp7, #293 8 - 10
i3. same as i, sp5, #293 20 - 25

13353-j

j. 13353, lt. green, red Hot Wheels logo in yellow oval in back, purple tw, #5 in Treasure Hunt series, #357 (1995) 130 - 160

15240-k

k. 15240; mtlfk blue; yellow, lt. green & dk. red galactic tampo on sides, hood & roof; clear windows; green int.; sp7; #3 in Mod Bod Series; #398 (1996) 8 - 10

VW Bug-l

l. 16917; green; clear windows; black int.; yellow, orange, black & white tampo w/"Kasplat" on sides, "Swat" on hood,

Values are shown in U.S. dollars, first price is for mint, second is for mint packaged vehicles only. See pages 15-16 for grading guide to determine value for cars in lesser conditions.

"Thwaack!" on roof; sp5; #4 in Biff! Bam! Boom! series; #543 (1997) 6 - 8
12. same as l, sp7 (1997) 40 - 50

VW Bug-m

m. 18669, red, clear windows, black int., gray stripes on sides & hood, rrch, JC Whitney ltd ed of 10,000 (1997) 15 - 20

VW Bug-n

n. pearl white; black int.; blue-tinted windows; black, lt. green & red tampo on sides & roof; ho5; #3 in Artistic License series; #731 (1998) 4 - 6
o. unpainted, lt. green int., clear windows, ho5, #3 in Artistic License Series, 1998 Hot Wheels Convention, #731 (1998) 250 - 300

VW Bug-p

p. blue; tinted windows; white int.; lt. green, dk. blue & white tampo on sides & hood, "Olas Del Sol" on sides; sp5; #2 in Surf 'n Fun series; #962 (1999) 4 - 6

VW Bug-q

q. turquoise, gray int., clear windows, sp7, China, Car Crusher Playset (1999) 6 - NA

VW Bug-r

r. mtlc brown, same as q, China, Car Crusher Playset (1999) 6 - NA
s. flat dark red; mtlfk gray chassis; clear windows; red int.; black, orange & yellow flame tampo on sides & roof; ho5; China; #175 (2001) 3 - 5
t. mtlfk purple; black int.; blue-tinted windows; yellow, red, black, silver, pink & white tampo w/flames on sides, hood, roof & trunk; 2nd Annual Nationals logo on roof; rrch w/white stripe. Ltd ed of 4000 for 2nd Annual Nationals (2002) 25 - 40

7671-u

u. black, same as t, white int., red-tinted windows. Ltd ed of 2000 for 2nd Annual Nationals (2002) 100 - 125

1990

The big news was the Purple Passion. For the first nine months of production, this model could not be located on toy store shelves. Collectors and dealers grabbed every one they could find. Some collectors panicked, paying up to twenty dollars at toy shows, only to see prices plummet as Mattel filled the distribution pipeline. This was also the year the California Custom series was introduced. These models had hot paint jobs, wild tampos, custom wheels and a collectors' button. Hot Wheels cereal was also in grocery stores, the first time Mattel actually put cars in cereal boxes. Finally, the first aircraft, a helicopter, appeared in the regular line.

9726-a

BMW 323 9726 - 75mm - 1990
This BMW 323 Cabriolet convertible has a black plastic chassis, "BMW" imprinted in the license plate, tan interior, clear plastic windshield, uh, and was made in Malaysia. Similar casting: 3492 Skull Rider (1993 Tattoo Machines)
a. black, "M3" in white, small blue & red stripe on sides, #150 $8 - 15
a2. same as a, no BMW in license plate, #150 6 - 12
a3. same as a2, bw, #150 (1991) 6 - 12
a4. same as a2, hoc, #150 (1992) 10 - 22

9726-b

b. 2100; white; lt. blue in back; yellow, blue & magenta tampo on sides w/"Cal Custom" in blue on windshield; blue plastic chassis & int.; blue tw; California Custom 12 - 15

9726-c

c. blue, black plastic base, beige int., clear windshield, red stripe on sides, bw, Parking Garage set only (1995) 15 - NA

2102-a

Corvette Funny Car 2102 - 78mm - 1990
This Corvette drag racer has a metal chassis, engine & interior, blue-tinted plastic windows, bw, and was made in Malaysia. Similar castings: 2508 Vetty Funny (1979), 2508 Poppa 'Vette (1986)
a. white; lt. blue, pink & lt. green tampo w/"Cal Custom" on sides & roof, "12" on sides; California Custom $15 - 18
a2. same as a, dk. blue replaces lt. blue in tampo, California Custom 15 - 18

4005-a

Fire Chief 4005 - 75mm - 1990
This Malaysia-made 1978 Dodge Monaco has a metal chassis, blue-tinted windows & light on top, black interior, and bw.
a. red; yellow, black & white tampo with "5" & "Fire Chief" on sides $4 - 6

Fire Chief-b

b. no #; red; same as a; different tampo, yellow, black & white tampo w/"Fire Chief" & "1" on sides; 5-pack only 6 - NA
b2. same as b, tan int., 5-pack only 20 - NA

2104-a

Firebird 2104 - 75mm - 1990
This Trans Am series-style racer has a metal chassis, painted spoiler, chromed windows, tw, and was made in Malaysia. Similar casting: 18551 Camaro Wind (1997)
a. fluor. lime green; red in back; blue, white & red tampo w/"3" & race decals on sides, "3" on hood, "Goodyear" on spoiler, blue "Cal Custom" on windshield 8 - 10

2104-b

b. chrome; yellow & purple stripes on hood & roof; red & yellow Hot Wheels logo on hood; black metal base; blacked-out windows; bw; Racing Team 5-pack only (1995) 12 - NA
b2. same as b, mtlc silver metal base, Racing Team 5-pack only (1995) 12 - NA
b3. chrome, same as b, unpainted metal base, Racing Team 5-pack only (1995) 12 - NA

2099-a

Mini Truck 2099 - 70mm - 1990
This generic mini truck has a turquoise plastic chassis, blue plastic interior, chrome plastic exposed engine, speakers, spoiler in back, clear windshield, uh, & was made in Malaysia.
a. turquoise; magenta, blue & yellow striping tampo on sides (magenta comes in different shades); #89 $8 - 10
a2. same as a, hoc, #89 25 - 100
b. no #; yellow; blue, lt. green & pink striping on sides; yellow chassis; blue plastic int.; City Burger Stand Sto & Go set only 6 - NA
b2. same as b, uhgd 12 - NA

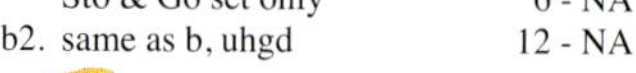

9546-c

c. 4546; orange; gray-blue, black & white tampo all over; #231 (1993) 6 - 8
c2. same as c, dw3, #231 (1996) 2 - 4
c3. same as c, ho5, #231 (1996) 4 - 6
c4. same as c, ho5w, #231 (1996) 14 - 18
c5. same as c, sp5, #231 (1997) 4 - 6

13289-d

d. 13289, lt. brown, lt. brown plastic base & int., dk. brown paw prints, tinted windshield, sp5, #3 in Roarin' Rods series, #302 (1995) 4 - 6
d2. same as d, uh, #302 (1995) 6 - 8
d3. same as d, orange plastic base (1995) 50 - 60
d4. same as d, sp7, #302 (1996) 6 - 8
e. 16914; red; black plastic base & int.; tinted windshield; white, yellow & black tampo w/"Boom" on sides & hood; sp3; #1 in Biff! Bam! Boom! series; #541 (1997) 3 - 5

Mini Truck-e

e2. same as e, sp5 (1997) 2 - 4

Mini Truck-e3

e3. same as e, dw3 (1997) 2 - 4
f. no #, green, black plastic base, purple int., tinted windshield, orange & maroon tampo on sides, sp3. Just Trucks 5-pack only (1997) 2 - NA

Mini Truck-f2

f2. same as f, sp5 (1997) 2 - NA

Mini Truck-g

g. lime yellow; black plastic base & int.; tinted windshield; black, green & orange tampo on sides & hood; sp3gd. #1 in Low 'n Cool series, #697 (1998) 4 - 6

Mini Truck-h

h. black, black chassis & int., clear windshield, orange & black tampo w/"Mini Truck" on sides & hood, dw3. #1 in Street Art series, #949 (1999) 2 - 3
i. black, red int., gold-plated engine & speakers, lwgd, #1102 (2000) 2 - 3
j. mtlfk green; black int.; clear windshield; yellow, brown & red brown tampo on sides; dw3; #4 in Kung Fu Series; Malaysia; #36 (2000) 2 - 3
k. lime yellow, black chassis & int., tinted windshield, sp3gd, Malaysia. Sold only in Mexico (2001) 12 - 15
l. mtlfk burnt orange; black chassis, bed & interior; clear windshield; black & gold tampo on sides; sp5; China; #227 (2001) 2 - 3

7609-a

Nissan 300ZX or Nissan Custom "Z" 7609 - 70mm - 1990
A new casting, this model has a metal chassis, opening side doors, tan plastic interior, clear plastic windows, uh, & was made in Malaysia.
a. mtlc dk. red; yellow stripes & "300ZX" on hood; #54 $15 - 18
a2. same as a, #98 (1991) 9 - 15
a3. same as a2, uhgd, #98 (1992) 200 - 260
a4. same as a2, hoc, #98 (1992) 18 - 25

7609-b

b. mtlfk black; green & white $1000 bills, orange & white flames on hood; orange & white

Values are shown in U.S. dollars, first price is for mint, second is for mint packaged vehicles only. See pages 15-16 for grading guide to determine value for cars in lesser conditions.

flames on roof; bills & flames on sides; red int.; black-tinted windows; uhpk; Malaysia; Revealers 3 - 5

c. purple, same as b, tan int., uhy, Revealers 3 - 5

d. Day-Glo yellow, same as b, uho, Revealers 3 - 5

e. 4628, mtlfk purple, yellow "300ZX" twice on hood, uh. #234 4 - 8

f. 13584, mtlfk purple, same as b, uhgd, #234 (1994) 4 - 8

f2. same as f, sp5g, #234 (1995) 2 - 4

f3. same as f, sp3g, #234 (1995) 2 - 4

f4. same as f, lwgd, #234 (1996) 2 - 4

g. 18552; blue; clear windows; black int.; red, black & silver on sides; lwch; China; #600 (1997) 3 - 6

18552-g2

g2. lt. blue, same as g, sp5, #600 (1997) 20 - 30

g3. same as g, sp5, #600 (1997) 2 - 4

7608-a

Probe Funny Car 7608 - 80mm - 1990

This Malaysia-made model has a metal chassis with lift-up body showing a metal engine & interior, plastic body prop, dark-tinted windows, and bw (small front, large back). Similar castings: 2743 Castrol GTX Funny Car (1992 Pro Circuit), 2841 King Kenny Funny Car (1992 Pro Circuit); Funny Car (1997)

a. red; white & blue tampo, race decals & "Motorcraft Quality Parts" on sides & hood; 3-pack only $8- NA

a2. same as a, no body prop, #84 22 - 55

a3. same as a, mtlc lime metal chassis & int., 3-pack only 8 - NA

Probe Funny Car-b

b. no #; white; same as a; red, green & black tampo w/"Castrol GTX," "Jolly Rancher" & race decals on sides & hood; blue metal base; 3-pack only 10 - NA

b2. same as b, rose metal chassis 8 - NA

b3. white, same as b2, no "Jolly Rancher" or "JR" in tampo 8 - NA

15254-c

c. 15254; white; red & orange paint splattered on car; clear windows; sp5. Funny Car name on package, #2 in Splatter Paint Series, #409 (1996) 2 - 4

16202-d

d. 16202; red; white front; yellow, black & white tampo w/"McDonald's," McDonald's M & racing decals on sides; McDonald's M on hood; "Pontiac" on roof; black-tinted windows; black engine; sp5. Kellogg's Raisin Bran mail-in only (1996) 6 - 8

e. 16925; plum; clear windows; yellow, black & white spray tampo w/"Bullet Bonneville," & racing decals on sides; sp5; #4 in Speed Spray series; #552 (1997) 3 - 5

Probe Funny Car-f

f. yellow; tinted windows; black int.; red, black & white flame tampo w/"Hot Stuff" & racing decals on sides; sp5. Exclusive Funny Car Racing Team 4-pack (1997) 4 - NA

Probe Funny Car-g

g. red; tinted windows; black int.; red, lt. purple, aqua, yellow, blue & white tampo fruit design on sides; Trix rabbit on hood; "Trix" on roof; General Mills premium (1997) 10 - NA

Probe Funny Car-h

h. blue; white nose; white & lt. blue tampo w/"Coronet" on sides & nose; sp5. Coronet Paper & Atlanta charity only (1997) 10 - NA

Probe Funny Car-i

i. white; black windows; brown & gray tampo w/"Milk Chocolate" & "Hershey's" on sides & hood; sp5; #2 in Sugar Rush Series; Funny Car; #742 (1998) 2 - 3

Probe Funny Car-j

j. lime green; yellow-tinted windows; gray, black & orange tampo w/"3" & "Team Bousquette" on sides; sp5; #1 in Mega Graphics series; Funny Car; #973 (1999) 2 - 3

Probe Funny Car-k

k. white, clear windows, w/CD-ROM, Avon (1999) 10 - NA

Probe Funny Car-l

l. white; red-tinted windows; lt. green, black, orange & red tampo w/"Chuck E. Cheese's" on sides, "CEC Entertainment Inc." on hood, "Chuck E." on roof; sp5. Chuck E. Cheese's Pizza only 10 - 12

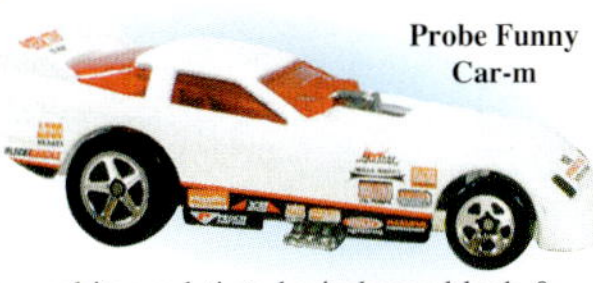

Probe Funny Car-m

m. white; red-tinted windows; black & red tampo w/race decals on sides, "Interactive Tattoo CD ROM" on top & in front; sp5. Only issued with Tattoo Designer CD-ROM (2001) 10 - 15

n. black; metal int.; clear windows; silver, orange & red tampo on sides; sp5; Thailand; Forces of Nature 5-pack (2001) 2 - 3

9112-a

Propper Chopper® 9112 - 74mm - 1990

Based on a helicopter, this Malaysia-made model has a blue plastic base & interior, white plastic tail, gray plastic rotors, and blue-tinted windows.

Similar casting: Propper Chopper (Helicopter) Racing Series (2000)

a. white; red, blue & yellow tampo w/"2," small yellow triangle & "Newschopper" on sides; #86 $10 - 40

a2. same as a, w/o yellow triangle, #86 10 - 15

0492-b

b. white; black plastic; black, yellow & red tampo w/"Police" & "Unit 45" on sides; #185 (1992) 3 - 8

b2. same as b, clear-coated, #185 3 - 5

c. 13312, chrome, same as c, #3 in Silver Series, #325 (1995) 2 - 8

Propper Chopper-d

d. white; orange int., base, blades, tail, etc.; black-tinted windows; red, black & yellow tampo w/Baywatch & Hot Wheels logo, "Baywatch" & "Search" on sides; Baywatch 5-pack (1995) 2 - NA

15260-e

e. 15260; blue; orange, red & white tampo w/mouth & teeth on sides & eyes in front; orange base & int.; blue-tinted windows; lt. blue blades & tail; orange skis; #3 in Street Eater Series; #414 (1996) 4 - 6

e2. same as e, clear windows, #414 (1997) 2 - 4

e3. same as e, China, #414 (1997) 2 - 4

f. 0492; yellow; black plastic chassis, tail, blades & windows; red, black & white tampo with "Rescue," "Search & Rescue" & "Unit 4" logo on sides; #185 (1997) 6 - 12

f2. same as f; red chassis, skis & tail; #185 (1997) 3 - 8

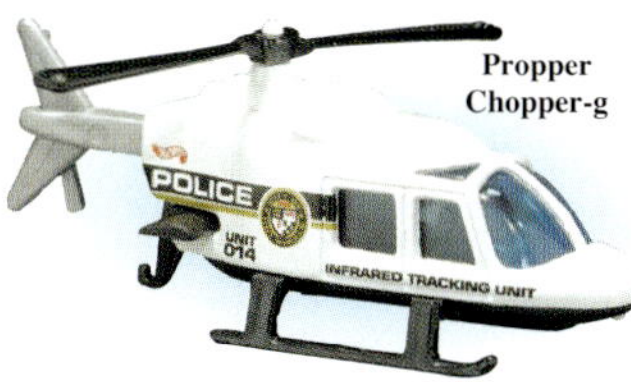

Propper Chopper-g

g. no number; white; black plastic chassis, skis & int.; blue-tinted windows; black, gold & red tampo w/"Police," "Unit 14," "Infrared Tracking Unit" & logo on sides; Police Force 5-pack only (1997) 2 - NA

Propper Chopper-h

h. blue; black int., base & tail; gray blades; blue-tinted windows; yellow, red & white tampo w/"Action News KHWW," "1," "Helicam" on sides; #798 (1998) 2 - 3

Propper Chopper-i

i. black; black base & int.; yellow-tinted windows; green, gold & white tampo design w/"Graffiti" on sides & nose; #2 in Street Art Series; #950 (1999) 2 - 3

Propper Chopper-j

j. blue; black base, propeller & tracks; gold stripe; black & white tampo w/"Hot Wheels Air 13," "Police," "Emergency Call 911," "To Serve and Protect," "Pilot" & pilot's name on sides. Sky Search Action Pack only (1999) 6 - NA

Propper Chopper-k

k. red; black chassis; yellow blades; black int.; yellow-tinted windows; gray, yellow & black tampo w/"Unit 3" & "Trackside Assistance" on sides; #1 in Seein' 3-D Series; Malaysia; #009 (2000) 2 - 3

l. black; maroon skis, tail, int. & blades; red, gray & yellow tampo w/"Sky Spy" on sides; #241 (2000) 2 - 3

Propper Chopper-m

m. dk. blue; black blades; white chassis, skis & int.; tinted windows; white, lt. blue & red tampo w/"33," "Oakwood Homes" & race decals on sides, Oakwood Homes logo on nose;

Values are shown in U.S. dollars, first price is for mint, second is for mint packaged vehicles only. See pages 15-16 for grading guide to determine value for cars in lesser conditions.

Thailand; #1 in NASCAR Helicopter series (2000) 5 - 7

n. black; black blades, chassis, skis & int.; tinted windows; white, lt. blue & magenta tampo w/"99," "Exide" & race decals on sides, "Exide" on nose; Thailand; #2 in NASCAR Helicopter series (2000) 5 - 7

o. black; yellow blades, tail, chassis, skis & int.; tinted windows; red, white & blue tampo w/"22," "Caterpillar" & race decals on sides, "CAT" on nose; Thailand; #3 in NASCAR Helicopter series (2000) 5 - 7

p. orange; white blades, tail, chassis, skis & int.; tinted windows; white, lt. blue, yellow & black tampo w/"32" & "Tide" on sides, "Tide" on nose; Thailand; #4 in NASCAR Helicopter series (2000) 5 - 7

q. blue; black chassis & int.; yellow tail & blades; yellow, gray, black & red tampo w/"222" & "The Sky is Falling" on sides; #4 in Rod Squadron series; #068 (2001) 2 - 3

Propper Chopper-r

r. white; black blades; blue tail; white skis & int.; blue-tinted windows; black, blue & dark blue tampo w/"Los Angeles Police" & "N211LA" on sides. Limited edition sold by Los Angeles Police Historical Society (2001) 10 - 15

2173-a

Purple Passion® 2173 - 75mm - 1990
Based on a 1951 chopped and channeled Mercury, this model has a chrome plastic chassis, red interior, clear plastic windows, ww, and was made in Malaysia.

a. purple; lt. green & dk. green striping tampo on hood & sides; #87 $12 - 20

a2. same as a, bw, white stripe, gold Hot Wheels 30th Anniv. logo on rear window, ltd ed for 30th Anniv., w/blistercard in window box (1998) 10 - 12

Purple Passion-b

b. no #, black, same as a, orange & red tampo, City Mini Market Sto & Go only 30 - NA

c. no #, white, same as b, City Mini Market Sto & Go only 35 - NA

Purple Passion-d

d. no #; gold chrome; red & black flames on sides & hood; "New York Toy Fair 1992" on roof; 1992 Toy Fair give-away, in plastic bags only 65 - 75

2469-e

e. 2469, ruby red, tan int., yellow & turquoise flames on sides & hood, limited to 10,000 (1992) 45 - 50

f. purple, same as e, clear windows, #87 (1993) 10 - 15

2173-g

g. candy blue; pink, magenta & orange tampo on sides & hood; white int.; clear windows; "Revealers" in white; ww; Malaysia; Revealers 10-pack only 20 - NA

Purple Passion-h

h. no #, yellow, same as a, red tampo of Shell logo on sides, Shell logo & "Shell" on hood. Shell dealers in OH & MA only; baggie only (1994) 15 - NA

11816-i

i. 11816; red; same as h; white & red tampo on hood; orange & white tampo on sides; tinted windows; white int.; Passion in Rod & Custom series; limited to 7000 (1994) 30 - 35

j. 12537; pink; same as i; red, white & purple tampo on sides & hood; tinted windows; white int.; 9404 Pink Passion in ltd ed 8000, Custom Rods series (1994) 30 - 35

k. gold-plated, black Hot Wheels logo on side, FAO Schwarz logo in red & "FAO Schwarz" in black in back, clear windows, red int., wwgd. One of 16 FAO Schwarz Gold Series Collection, limited to 3000 (1994) 15 - NA

12356-l

l. 12356; green; gold & blue flames on sides & hood; tinted windows; white interior; #263 Mean Green Passion (1995) 25 - 30

13350-m

m. 13350; gold; black mtlfk; black, gold & violet tampo on sides & hood; clear windows; white int.; gold-chrome plastic base; rr with white stripe & gold hubs; #2 in Treasure Hunt series; #354 (1995) 120 - 135

n. 13272; mtlfk black; same as j; red, silver & gold tampo on sides & hood; clear windows; red int.; Steel Passion; #1 in Steel Stamp series; #285 (1995) 10 - 12

n2. same as n, sp7, #285 (1995) 8 - 10

o. 13279, pearl purple, tinted windows, yellow int., ww. #2 in Pearl Driver series, #292 (1995) 4 - 8

o2. 13279, pearl purple, same as o, sp7, #292 (1995) 5 - 10

p. chrome, red int., clear windows, red Hot Wheels logo on side, rsw. Service Merchandise 16-piece Classic American Car Collection only, limited to 5000 (1995) 8 - NA

13908-q

q. 13908; black; yellow & blue tampo w/flames on both sides & hood, "Sweet 16," & "The Rebel Run Car Show 1995" on roof; clear windows; tan int.; ww. Limited to 7000; sold at Rebel Run Car Show (1996) 25 - 30

14971-r

r. 14971; pearl white; magenta & gold flames on sides, hood & trunk; tinted windows; tan int.; sp5 w/white stripe on tires; limited to 8000; #48 (1996) 25 - 40

s. no #; purple; blue int.; clear windows; yellow, orange, red flames; blue outline on sides; ww; China; Cruisin America 6-pack only (1997) 8 - NA

t. purple, tinted windows, tan roof, black & silver side tampo, gold striping tampo on hood & sides, "Kustom Kings" on rear window, ww, China, Cruisin' The '50s 8-pack from FAO Schwarz (1998) 6 -NA

2173-u

u. mtlfk purple; lt. brown roof; white & black tampo on sides & front; "Purple Passion" on sides & rear window; 13th Annual Hot Wheels Convention logo on trunk; rrch w/white stripe. Limited to 2,000 in baggie for 13th Annual Hot Wheels Convention (1999) 100 - 125

Purple Passion-v

v. white; clear windows; black int.; dk. blue roof; dk. blue, gray, gold & white tampo w/"Springfield Police" & logo on sides; "27" & "Springfield Police" on roof; rrch w/white stripe. Limited to 25,000 in Cop Rods series for K•B Toys (1999) 5 - 7

Purple Passion-w

w. white; black int.; clear windows; purple, orange & yellow tampo on sides, hood & roof; "Optra" & "Lexmark" on sides, "Optra" on roof; rrch w/white stripe. Ltd ed in box by Lexmark (1999) 18 - 25

Purple Passion-x

x. lt. blue; clear windows; white int. & roof; white, black, yellow & red tampo w/stripes & "Louie Bloo" on sides, figure on roof, "Otter Pops" on trunk; rrch; Otter Pops premium (2000) 10 - 15

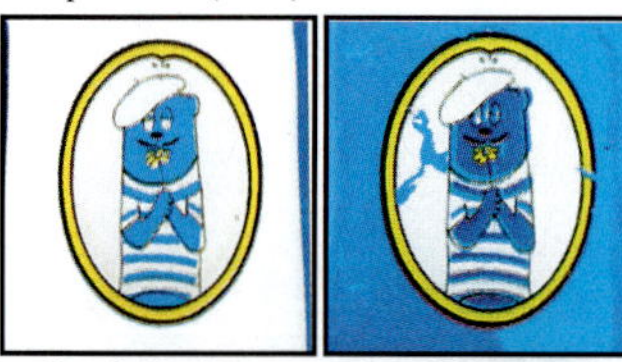
Purple Passion-x Purple Passion-x2

x2. same as x, blue roof (2000) 10 - 15

Purple Passion-y

y. white, white int., blue-tinted windows, blue & gold tampo on sides & hood with "Purple Passion" on sides, dw3, Vintage Hot Rods 3-pack from Avon (2000) 6 - NA

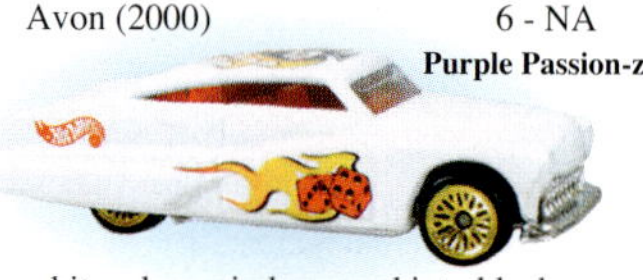
Purple Passion-z

z. white; clear windows; red int.; black, red & yellow tampo w/dice on sides, "13" on roof; Thailand; #200 (2000) 3 - 5

aa. black; white roof; tinted windows; red int.; red, white & gold tampo on sides & hood; ww; Target Exclusive Drive-In Hot Nights 4-car set (2000) 6 - NA

Purple Passion-ab

ab. red; clear windows; white int.; white, lt. green, black & lt. brown tampo w/eyeballs & flame tampo on sides, monster on roof; sp5gd; Thailand; #4 in Monster Series; #080 (2001) 2 - 4

Purple Passion-ac

ac. black; clear windows; white int.; purple & white flames on sides & hood; red, yellow, gray & white tampo w/Hot Wheels Newsletter logo & "15 Years by Collectors, For Collectors" on roof, 15th Annual Collector's Convention logo on trunk; rrch w/white stripe; limited to 2000 for 15th Annual Collector's Convention Dinner in Irvine, CA (2001) 45 - 55

Purple Passion-ad

ad. yellow, same as ab, purple-tinted windows, no Convention logo on trunk, limited to 8000, for 15th Anniversary of Hot Wheels Newsletter (2001) 30 - 40

ae. mtlfk white; red int.; clear windows; yellow, red & black tampo w/dice on sides, "#13" & flames on roof; lwgd; Thailand; Motorin' Music 5-pack (2001) 2 - NA

Purple Passion-af

af. yellow; white roof & int.; yellow-tinted windows; black, white, orange & gray tampo w/"13," "Always Ready, Proud to Serve," "Miami-Dade Florida Fire Rescue" & emblem on sides, emblem on roof, "Miami-Dade Florida Fire Rescue" on trunk; rrch w/white stripe; Fire Rods Series 2 (2001) 10 - 12

ag. white; black int.; clear windows; black, orange & yellow flame tampo on sides, hood & roof; sp5; Target Exclusive Elvis Drive-In 4-pack (2001) 6 - NA

Purple Passion-ah

ah. primer black; clear windows; red int.; red & white spray mask tampo with Mooneyes logo on sides; rrww; ltd ed of 20,000 for Collector's Club in Japan (2001) 20 - 30

Values are shown in U.S. dollars, first price is for mint, second is for mint packaged vehicles only. See pages 15-16 for grading guide to determine value for cars in lesser conditions.

Purple Passion-ai

ai. blue, white int., clear windows, yellow & orange flame spray mask in front, "JC Whitney" in white on trunk, gych, in box for JC Whitney. (2002) 15 - 20
aj. red, same as ai, in box for JC Whitney (2002) 15 - 20
ak. mtlfk purple with a white roof and interior, clear windows, an orange, white and black tampo on the sides, hood and trunk with "California Custom" on the sides and "Automobile Milestones 2002" on the trunk; rrch with a white stripe. Auto Milestones series (2002) 15 - 18

2173-al

al. red; gold chassis; white roof & int.; yellow-tinted windows; white, yellow, dk. red & black tampo w/flames & "Ronald McDonald House Charities" on sides, flames on hood, logo on roof, 2nd Annual Nationals on trunk; rrch w/white stripe. Sold at 2nd Annual Nationals in baggie (2002) 30 - 35

2173-am

am. red; white int.; clear windows; yellow, orange & blue flame spray mask; "Fire Passion" in white & yellow on sides; Firebird Raceway logo in white & blue on sides; rrwwch. Ltd ed of 6000 for Firebird Raceway (2002) 18 - 20
an. white; same as am; side tampo is yellow, orange & black; trunk tampo is red & blue. Ltd ed of 6000 for Firebird Raceway (2002) 18 - 20
ao. flat black; white int.; orange-tinted windows; silver, yellow & orange flame tampo w/"Toy Fair 2003" & Hot Wheels Highway 35 logo on roof; rrchww. Limited run in plastic Cool Collectibles box for Mattel's June 2002 Toy Fair (2002) 150 - 200
ap. metallic pink, white int, clear windows, white stripe on sides and sp5rl. Target excl. Originals Series. (2001) 9 - 15

9738-a

Range Rover 9738 - 70mm - 1990
This British Leyland Range Rover 4x4 has a black plastic base, tan interior, clear windows, ct, and was made in Malaysia.
a. white, black window frames, thin red stripe & blue stripe with "Range Rover" on sides, #103 $3 - 6

Range Rover-b

b. no #, yellow, "Cadbury's Flake" in purple on hood 1000 - NA
c. no #, purple, "Cadbury" in white on sides 1000 - NA
d. no #; white; blue, yellow & red striping tampo with "Getty" inside red rectangle; red int. (1991) 4 - NA

Range Rover-c

Range Rover-d

4322-e

e. 4322, black, black plastic base, orange stripe, white "Range Rover" on sides, #221 (1993) 3 - 6
e2. same as e, gray plastic base, dw3ct, #221 (1996) 2 - 5
e3. same as e, dw3ct, #221 (1997) 2 - 5

15225-f

f. 15225; red; gold & purple flames on sides, hood & roof; chrome plastic base; clear windows; tan int.; ct; #3 in Flamethrower series; #386 (1996) 2 - 6
f2. 15225, red, same as f, part of flame replaced by Hot Wheels logo, #386 (1996) 4 - 8

Range Rover-g

g. 16916; plum; chrome plastic base; gray int.; clear windows; orange, black, white & blue tampo w/"Screeeech!" on sides, "Vroom" on hood & roof; dw3ct; #3 in Biff! Bam! Boom! series; #544 (1997) 2 - 4

Range Rover-k

k. dk. green; chrome plastic base; tan int.; tinted windows; red, white, gold & dk. blue UK flag tampo w/"Land Rover" & "World Racers 15" on sides & hood, "Zafferoil" on sides, "Norris Precision" on roof, race decal on car; dw3ct; Thailand; #868 (1998) 2 - 3
l. unpainted, tan int., tinted windows, dw3ct, 1998 Hot Wheels Convention, #868 (1998) 65 - 85

Range Rover-m

m. green; gold chrome chassis; black, gold & white tampo, stripes & Final Run logo on hood; "Final Run" & small logo in back; gygd; #1 in 1999 Final Run series (1999) 5 - 7

9113-a

Simpson's Family Camper, The 9113 - 72mm - 1990 (Scene Machines)
Based on a four-wheel drive Ford truck, this model has a metal chassis, clear plastic windows, white plastic interior & top luggage rack, ct, and was made in Malaysia.
Similar castings: 2022 Baja Breaker (1978), 2853 Motocross Team (1979), 3303 Circus Cats (1981), 3490 Open Wide (1993 Tattoo Machines)
a. blue; yellow stripes & signs on sides $10 - 12

9113-a2

a2. same as a, thicker stripes 12 - 15
a3. same as a, cty 10 - 12
a4. same as a2, cty 12 - 15
a5. same as a, ctw 10 - 12
a6. same as a2, ctw 12 - 15

9114-a

Simpson's Homer's Nuclear Waste Van, The 9114 - 70mm - 1990 (Scene Machines)
Based on a delivery truck, this Malaysia-made model has a black plastic chassis, white plastic interior, clear plastic windows and bw.
Similar castings: 9643 Letter Getter (1977), 2854 S.W.A.T. (1979), 2850 The Incredible Hulk (1979), 3305 Racing Team (1981), 9643 Delivery Van (1984), 2519 Combat Medic (1986), 2808 Delivery Truck (1989)
a. yellow; red, black & magenta design w/"Danger Nuclear Waste," "Driver Homer Simpson" & "Free Delivery" on sides $10 - 12
a2. same as a, bwy 10 - 12
a3. same as a, bww 10 - 12

5900-a

T-Bird Stocker ('90 T-Bird) 5900 - 78mm - 1990
This new casting of a Ford stock car has a black plastic chassis, clear windows, black interior, bw, and was made in Malaysia.
a. red; "Motorcraft Quality Parts" & blue Ford logo on hood & sides; white "Goodyear" on sides; #88 (1990) $15 - 18
a2. same as a, small back wheels, #88 18 - 20

5900-b

b. white; black in back; blue, red, yellow & black tampo w/"Havoline," "28" & race decals on sides; "Havoline," Ford & Texaco logos on hood; "28" on roof; uh; #88 (1991) 18 - 22
b2. same as b, bw, #88 (1991) 200 - 300
b3. same as b, turquoise replaces blue in tampo, #88 (1992) 18 - 22

2456-c

c. 2456; white; green, red & black tampo w/"64," "Sunny King Foods" & race stickers on sides, "Elmo" on hood, "64" on roof; ltd ed of 25,000 (1992) 15 - 18

5298-d

d. 5298; black; same as c; yellow, red & white tampo w/"Havoline," "28," & racing decals on sides; "Havoline" & Texaco logo on hood; "28" on roof; clear windows; gray int.; roll bars; uh; Germany only (1993) 150 - 175

5900-e

e. orange, same as c, dk. blue "76" w/white border on sides & hood, clear windows, blue int. & roll cage, Unocal stations only, baggie only (1994) 5 - NA

T-Bird Stocker-f

f. no #; fluor. lime yellow; orange, red & purple tampo w/Hot Wheels logo, "Track System," track & racing decals on sides, "Hot Wheels" on trunk, "Track System" in back; blacked-out windows; uhgd; Track System Gift Pack only (1995) 5 - NA
f2. same as f, sp5g (1995) 4 - NA
f3. same as f, sp3 (1995) 4 - NA
f4. same as f, sp7gd (1995) 2 - NA
g. 16921; blue; blacked-out windows; yellow, orange & black lightning bolt tampo on sides & hood; "Lightning" on sides; sp5; #4 in Quicksilver series; #548 (1997) 2 - 4

T-Bird Stocker-g2

g2. same as g; silver base 2 - 4
h. orange; black base & windows; white, black & magenta tampo w/"Xtreme Ramp Jump" on sides; sp5; #857 (1998) 2 - 3
h2. same as h, ho5, #857 (1998) 2 - 3

T-Bird Stocker-h3

h3. same as h, ho5, Thailand, #857 (1999) 2 - NA
i. yellow plastic body; black metal base; blacked-out windows; black, orange & white tampo design on sides; sp3gd;

Values are shown in U.S. dollars, first price is for mint, second is for mint packaged vehicles only. See pages 15-16 for grading guide to determine value for cars in lesser conditions.

T-Bird Stocker-i

Thailand; Volcano Blowout 5-pack only (1999) 2 - NA

T-Bird Stocker-j

j. blue; gray chassis; yellow int.; clear windows; black, red, white & yellow tampo with "12," "T. Hunter" & race decals on sides, "T. Hunter" & race decals on hood, "12" on roof; sp5; #2 in 1999 Treasure Hunt Series; #930 (1999) 12 - 15
k. chrome; black-tinted windows; orange, magenta, black & white tampo w/"Xtreme" on sides; lwgd; #102 (2000) 2 - 3
l. mtlfk brown; black chassis; yellow int. & roll cage; clear windows; white, yellow & orange flame tampo on sides; pr5s; Thailand; Forces of Nature 5-pack (2000) 2 - NA

1991

This was the last year for Park 'n Plates. There were two new California Custom castings. This series was replaced by Super Cal Customs. Five California Custom and eleven Park 'n Plates models were originally sold outside the U.S. They were highly sought by collectors until the following year, when they were found in the U.S. at various Mid-West discount houses for a dollar each. Ramp Truck was taken from Crack-Ups and re-cast as a regular model. Buick Stocker was produced exclusively for Roses Department Stores. This model was raced by Tommy Houston in the Busch Grand National Races.

2098-a

'55 Nomad 2098 - 70mm - 1991

This Malaysia-made Chevrolet station wagon has a metal chassis, yellow plastic interior, clear plastic windows & sunroof, and rtw.

a. rose red; blue, white, yellow & green tampo on hood & sides; "Nomad" on sides; "Cal Custom" on sunroof; California Custom $20 - 25

10153-b

b. 10153; purple; same as a; yellow, turquoise & red tampo w/"Nomad" in red on sides; yellow & red lightning on hood; red int.; blue-tinted windows; ww; limited to 6000 (1993) 30 - 35
b2. 10092, same as b, gyg, ltd ed of 6000 (1993) 40 - 45

2097-a

'59 Caddy (Eldorado) 2097 - 85mm - 1991

This Malaysia-made 1959 Cadillac Eldorado convertible has a chrome plastic chassis and grille, white interior, clear windshield and ww.

a. pink; blue, magenta, white & yellow tampo on sides, hood & trunk; black "Cal Custom" on windshield; California Custom $45 - 50
b. pearl white, no tampo, red int., #154 (1991) 6 - 8
b2. same as a, ltd ed for 30th Anniv. w/blistercard in window box (1998) 5 - 7
c. 7218, gold chrome, no tampo, red int., ltd ed of 5000 (1992) 20 - 25
c2. 7220, same as c, no tampo, white int., ltd ed of 5000 (1992) 20 - 25
d. 12359, lt. purple, white int., clear windshield, red Hot Wheels logo, ww, #266 7 - 10
d2. same as d, sp7, #266 (1995) 6 - 8

'59 Caddy-e

e. chrome, red int., clear windshield, red "Service" & white "Merchandise" on black stripe on sides, red Hot Wheels logo on windshield, rsw. Service Merchandise 16-piece Classic American Car Collection only, limited to 5000 (1995) 8 - NA
f. 13307, mtlfk pink, clear windshield, red Hot Wheels logo, white int., rr w/chrome hubs & white stripe, #3 in Real Riders series, #320 (1995) 30 - 35

'59 Caddy-g

g. mtlfk black, silver stripe, red int., clear windshield, sp7 w/white stripe, 50s Favorites 5-pack only (1996) 2 - NA
g2. same as g, light gray base & grill (1997) 2 - NA

15079-h

h. 15079, red, silver stripe on sides, clear windshield, tan int., rt w/white stripe, #5 in 1996 Treasure Hunt series, #432 (1996) 50 - 60

15251-i

i. 15251; mtlfk black; red, orange, yellow, white & brown tampo w/basketball, flames, basket & "Slam Dunk" on sides; white int.; clear windshield; sp7; #4 in Sports Car series; #407 (1996) 6 - 8

'59 Caddy-j

j. blue; black int.; tinted windshield; gold, black & pink design w/"Low Rider" on sides; lwgd; #266 (1997) 3 - 6
j2. same as j, Thailand (1998) 3 - NA

'59 Caddy-k

k. red, white interior, tinted windshield, blue & yellow tampo on sides & hood, lwgd, #3 in Low 'n Cool series, #699 (1998) 2 - 4
l. pink, white int., clear windshield, silver-stripe tampo on sides & hood, "Eldorado" on sides, ww, China, FAO Schwarz Cruisin' The '50s 8-pack only (1998) 6 - NA

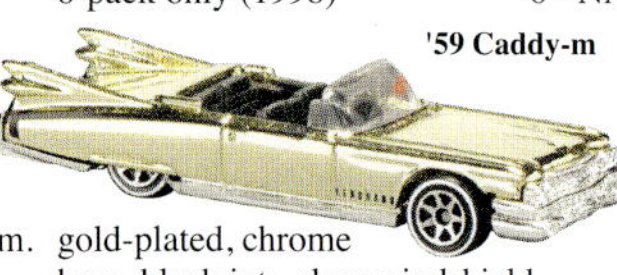
'59 Caddy-m

m. gold-plated, chrome base, black int., clear windshield, black-stripe tampo w/"Eldorado" on sides, sp7 w/white stripe, Mattel mail-in, baggie only (1997) 8 - NA
n. unpainted, black plastic base, white int., tinted windshield, lwgd, #3 in Low 'n Cool Series, 1998 Hot Wheels Convention, #699 (1998) 70 - 85

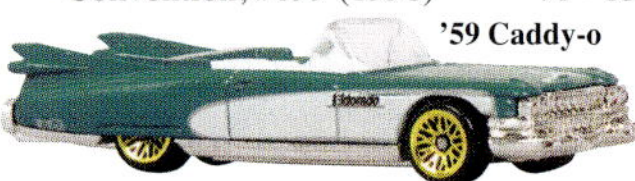
'59 Caddy-o

o. aqua, white int., clear windshield, white & gray tampo on sides & hood w/"Eldorado" in black on sides, lwgd, Thailand, '50s Cruisers 5-pack only (1999) 2 - NA
p. blue, black int., tinted windshield, lwgd, China, set only (1999) 5 - NA
q. mtlfk blue, white int., blue-tinted windshield, white & black tampo w/"Eldorado" on sides, lwch. Blistercard reads '59 Eldorado, #1076 (2000) 2 - 3

'59 Caddy-r

r. mtlfk blue; white int.; clear windshield; white tampo on sides, hood & trunk; sp7ww; Target Exclusive Drive-In Hot Nights 4-car set 6 - NA

'59 Caddy-s

s. mtlfk green; gray int.; yellow-tinted windshield; yellow, black & white tampo w"Creature Screamer" on sides, head on hood, eye & crossbones on trunk; sp5gd; Thailand; #3 in Monster series; #079 (2001) 2 - 3
s2. same as s, Malaysia, #3 in Monster series, #079 (2001) 2 - 3
t. mtlfk blue, chrome chassis, black int., tinted windshield, lwch, China, Super Highway Playset (2001) 3 - NA
u. mtlfk blue; gold chassis; gray int.; tinted windshield; gold, red, black & white tampo on hood & trunk; "Hip Hop" on trunk; lwgd; Thailand; Motorin' Music 5-pack (2001) 3 - NA
v. mtlfk blue, chrome chassis, black int., tinted windshield, lwgd, China, Super Highway set (2001) 5 - NA
w. lt. green, chrome chassis, black int., tinted windshield, lwch, Kool Toys Racing Pack (2001) 5 - NA
x. dark red; white int.; clear windows; white & silver tampo on sides & hood; black, white & orange tampo w/"Automobile Milestones 2002" on trunk; rrch w/white stripe. Auto Milestones series (2002) 7 - 9
y mf gold, white int, clear windows, dark red and white tampo design on sides, hood and trunk and rrgdww. Wal-Mart excl. Cruisin' America series. (2002) 7 - 9

BMW 850i 5667 - 73mm - 1991

This Malaysia-made model has a blue plastic chassis, clear windows, tan interior & uh. Similar casting: 16305 BMW 850i (1996)

5667-a

a. blue, white stripes, pink & yellow design on sides, #149 $4 - 8
a2. same as a, hoc, #149 10 - 15
a3. same as a, liw, #149 (1993) 6 - 10
a4. same as a, bw, #149 (1993) 4 - 6

BMW 850i-b

b. no #; red; yellow & white stripes on hood & roof, white "Getty" outlined in white on hood; clear windows; black int.; bw; never in blisterpack 5 - NA
c. 13581, dk. mtlfk blue, red int., tinted windows, red Hot Wheels logo on rear window, uh, #255 (1994) 2 - 4
c2. same as c, clear windows 2 - 4
c3. same as c, uhgd, #255 (1994) 2 - 6
c4. same as c2, uhgd, #255 (1996) 2 - 6
c5. same as c2, sp3g, #255 (1996) 2 - 6
c6. same as c2, lwgd, #255 (1996) 3 - 6
c7. same as c2, sp5, Sto 'n Go Parking Garage 3 - NA
d. yellow; black int.; tinted windows; lt. green, silver & black tampo w/"Klausner Tuning" on sides; lwgd; California Dreamin' 5-pack only (1997) 2 - NA
d2. as d, sp3gd, Thailand (1998) 2 - NA
e. mtlfk gold, gold chassis, black int., tinted windows, lwch, Malaysia, #1093 (1999) 2 - 3
f. lt.blue, dk. blue chassis, clear windows, black int., sp3, Malaysia, #159 (2000) 2 - 3

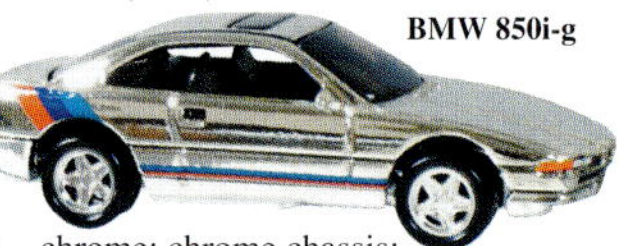
BMW 850i-g

g. chrome; chrome chassis; black int.; tinted windows; blue, dk. blue & red tampo on sides; "FR" on rear window; pc; Thailand; #10 in 2001 Final Run Series (2001) 7 - 9

9258-a

Buick Stocker 9258 - 70mm - 1991

Based on a Grand National stock car driven by Tommy Houston, this Malaysia-made model has a black plastic chassis, clear windows, white plastic interior and bw. It was issued on a special blistercard and sold only at Roses Department stores.

a. blue; white & red tampo w/"Buick" & "Roses Discount Stores" on hood; Buick's racing insignia on roof, "Roses" on trunk, "Roses" & Buick's racing insignia on sides $10 - 12

9258-a2

a2. same as a, "6" replaces Buick's racing insignia in tampo (1992) 6 - 8

Buick Stocker-b

b. no #; yellow; red tampo w/"3" on hood, roof & sides; only w/Heroes on Hot Wheels video tapes (1993), w/video 10 - NA

Values are shown in U.S. dollars, first price is for mint, second is for mint packaged vehicles only. See pages 15-16 for grading guide to determine value for cars in lesser conditions.

c. 16040; yellow; black base, interior & grill; clear windows; sp5; China; #472 (1996) 2 - 4

16042-c2

c2. same as c; "97," "Morey" & racing decals in red on sides & turquoise on hood; China; #472 (1997) 2 - 4
c3. same as c, lwch, #472 (1997) 2 - 3

9258-d

d. mtlfk lime; "96," "Hot Wheels" & race decals on sides; red "96" on roof; black metal base; clear windows; black int.; sp5; China; grocery store Hiway Hauler 2-packs only (1996) 5 - 7
d2. same as d, lwch (1996)

Buick Stocker-e

e. white; fade to purple; blue, green & black tampo w/"Coronet" & logo on hood & sides; Coronet paper give-away (1996) 8 - NA

Buick Stocker-f

f. black, green int., orange-tinted windows, yellow racing tampo w/"97" on sides, blue racing tampo w/"97" on hood, sp5, Action-pack racing set (1997) 6 - NA
g. no #; black; silver base; gray int.; clear windows; white doors & roof; blue, yellow & black star tampo w/"Police" on sides & hood; sp5. Target excl. Police Station & Police Chase sets only (1997) 6 - NA
h. mtlc blue; red metal base; blue-tinted windows; red int. & nose; red, white & yellow tampo w/"51" on sides, roof & hood, "Kool-Aid," "the Big Man" & figure on sides, "the Big Man," on roof; sp5bk w/"Goodyear" in white on sides; China; Wacky Warehouse premium 5 - 7

5665-a

Ferrari 250 (Classic Ferrari) 5665 - 70mm - 1991

This convertible is based on the Grand Prix car driven by Phil Hill. It has a chrome plastic base, black plastic interior, clear windshield, bw, and was made in Malaysia.

a. yellow, "7" in black circle on hood & sides, "Ferrari" in red on sides & twice on hood, #117 $15 - 20
a2. same as a, yellow plastic base, #117 10 - 12
a3. same as a2, black plastic sidepipes, #117 (1995) 6 - 8
a4. same as a3, sp7, #117 (1995) 4 - 6
b. red; yellow & black Ferrari logo on hood; red plastic base; blue int.; blackish chrome side pipes; white Hot Wheels logo on rear bumper; bw; Ferrari 5-pack only (1995) 3 - NA

5665-b

b2. same as b, black int. (1996) 3 - NA
b3. same as b, black interior & tail pipes (1995) 3 - NA
b4. same as b3, sp7 (1997) 2 - NA
c. dk. mtlc red, dk. red base, blackish chrome plastic pipes, clear windshield, tan interior, Hot Wheels logo in white rectangle in back, sp7, Then & Now 8-pack (1995) 4 - NA

5665-d

d. mtlfk aqua, aqua plastic base, yellow & black Ferrari logo on hood, tan int., clear windshield, sp7, #452 (1996) 4 - 6
d2. same as d, sp5, #452 (1997) 4 - 6
d3. same as d, ho5, #452 (1997) 2 - 4
d4. same as d, ho5w, #452 (1997) 2 - 4

15076-e

e. 15076, gray, red stripe on top, red interior, clear windshield, gray base, rrch, #3 in Treasure Hunt Series, #430 (1996) 40 - 45
f. mtlfk black, black plastic chassis, tan int., clear windshield, rrgd, FAO Schwarz History of Hot Wheels 8-pack only (1996) 8 - NA
g. 17961, mtlfk silver, gray base, clear windshield, red int., yellow & black Ferrari logo on hood, sp5. Small European blistercard only, #1 in Ferrari series (1997) 5 - 7

Ferrari 250-h

h. gold, black metalflakes, clear windshield, black int., sp5, Toys "R" Us 10-pack (1997) 4 - NA
i. mtlfk gold; black plastic base & int.; tinted windshield; black, white & yellow tampo w/"16" & "Classic Racer" on sides, Ferrari logo on hood; lwch; Malaysia; #866 (1998) 2 - 3
i2. same as i, Thailand, #866 (1998)

Ferrari 250-j

j. red, red base, black int., clear windshield, yellow & black Ferrari logo on hood & rear fenders, sp5, Thailand, Show Biz 5-pack (1999) 2 - NA
k. gray, black chassis & int., clear windshield, lwch, #218 (2001) 2 - 3

5666-a

Ferrari 348 5666 - 72mm - 1991

This model has a black plastic chassis, black and yellow interior, clear plastic windows, uh, and was made in Malaysia.

a. yellow; white & blue striping tampo on hood & roof; red "Ferrari 348" on hood; different blues in tampo; #118 $8 - 10
a2. same as a, uhgd 6 - 8
a3. same as a, hoc, #118 18 - 20

0459-b

b. 0459; pearl white; pink, red & dk. red striping tampo on roof & hood; black-tinted windows; red & white int.; "Ferrari 348" on hood; hoc; #175 (1992) 15 - 18
b2. same as b, uh, #175 (1992) 4 - 6

5666-c

c. white, red dollar sign on hood, green & black dollar bills all over, tinted windows, red & white int., uhpk, Malaysia, Revealers 3 - 5
d. Day-Glo orange, same as c, uho, Revealers 3 - 5
e. bronze, same as c, gray & red int., uhgn, Revealers 3 - 5
f. 4348; Day-Glo red; same as b; black, white & yellow tampo; uh, #226 (1993) 4 - 6

5666-g

g. fluor. lime; purple, black & white lightning & spiral tampo on top; clear windows; lime & black int.; uh. Only in Power Loop set (1995) 8 - NA
g2. same as g, pink replaces purple in tampo (1995) 8 - NA

5666-h

h. fluor. lime; same as a; white, dk. blue & lt. green tampo; lime & black int.; uh. In box w/Aquafresh Kids Toothpaste only (1994) 6 - 8

5666-i

i. red; yellow & black Ferrari logo on hood; black plastic base; tan & red int.; uh; Ferrari 5-Pack only (1995) 3 - NA
i2. same as i, sp5 (1995) 2 - NA
i3. same as i, sp5, #226 (1995) 4 - 6
j. 4348, black, same as i, yellow & white tampo, sp5, #226 (1995) 4 - 6
j2. same as j, sp7, #226 (1996) 8 - 10
k. 12933; mtlfk black; yellow & black Ferrari logo on hood; red & black int.; clear windows; sp5; #443 (1996) 4 - 6
k2. same as k, sp7, #443 (1996) 6 - 8
k3. same as k, ho5, #443 (1996) 2 - 4

Ferrari 348-l

l. yellow, black chassis, black & yellow int., tinted windows, black Ferrari logo on hood, sp5, #993 (1999) 2 - 3

m. red, black chassis, tan int., clear windows, yellow & black Ferrari logo on hood, ho5, China, Ferrari Dealership Sto 'n Go set (1999) 5 - NA
n. black, light brown int., tinted windows, yellow & black Ferrari logo on hood, sp3, #106 (2000) 2 - 3
o. black, black chassis, red int., clear windows, yellow Ferrari logo on hood, ho5, China, Pavement Pounder pack (2001) 4 - 6
p. yellow, black chassis & int., tinted windows, black Ferrari logo on hood, sp3, Thailand, #137 (2002) 2 - 3

4695-a

Ford Aerostar 4695 - 70mm - 1991

This minivan has a metal chassis, chromed windows, bw, and was made in Malaysia.

a. mtlfk purple, yellow splash tampo on sides, #151 $6 - 10

9767-b

b. 9767; white; red & black tampo: "Qantas" in black & Qantas logo & stripes in red on sides; Intl. boxed line 8 - 10

0546-c

c. white; red, yellow & blue tampo with "Speedie Pizza"& phone # on sides, #186 12 - 15
c2. same as c, no phone #, #186 8 - 10

4640-d

d. 4640; black; purple, yellow, red & aqua tampo w/"Rollerblade" & skate on sides; chromed windows; #236 (1993) 10 - 12

Ford Aerostar-e

e. white; red stripe & "Kinko's The Copy Center" in blue & red on sides; "Kinko's" on hood. In baggie only, Kinko's excl., limited to 30,000 (1994) 12 - NA

13318-f

f. 13318; white; chrome windows; orange-brown, black & yellow photo tampo of capitol building; #1 of Photo Finish Series; #331 (1995) 10 - 12

Values are shown in U.S. dollars, first price is for mint, second is for mint packaged vehicles only. See pages 15-16 for grading guide to determine value for cars in lesser conditions.

9713-a

Holden Commodore 9713 - 73mm - 1991
This British sedan has a white plastic chassis, black-tinted windows, red interior, bw, and was made in Malaysia; International line only.
Similar casting: 15785 Police Cruiser (1996)
a. white; yellow, pink & black striping tampo & "SV" on sides; several pinks in tampo $6 - 8

5672-a

Lamborghini Diablo 5672 - 68mm - 1991
This model has a red metal chassis, rear spoiler, tan & red interior, black-tinted windows, uh, and was made in Malaysia.
a. red, yellow "Diablo" on sides, #123 $10 - 12

0460-b

b. blue, multicolored glitter, metal chassis, red-tinted windows, red int., dk. blue plastic rear spoiler, uh, #176 (1992) 12 - 15
b2. same as b, light blue spoiler, #176 6 - 8

5672-c

c. candy red; red spoiler; orange, pink & white striping on sides; tan int.; tinted windows; uhy; Malaysia; Revealers 3 - 5
d. mtlfk blue, same as c, black spoiler, uhgn, Revealers 3 - 5
e. black, same as c, orange spoilers, uhp, Revealers 3 - 5

5672-f

f. Day-Glo red, blue spoiler, gold & purple tampo on sides, yellow interior, black-tinted windows, "Revealers" in white, uh, Malaysia, Revealers 10-pack only 10 - NA
g. no #, black, same as a; red "Diablo" on sides, clear windows, red interior, 25th Anniversary Exotic Car 5-pack only (1993) 6 - NA
h. 4406, yellow, red-tinted windows, black "Diablo" on sides, uh, #227 (1994) 4 - 6
h2. same as h, sp5, #227 (1995) 6 - 8
i. 4406, mtlc purple, blue int., sp5 4 - 6
i2. same as i, clear windows, dw3, #227 (1997) 2 - 4
i3. same as i2, ho5, #227 (1997) 2 - 4
j. mtlfk red, black metal base, tan int., tinted windows, ho5, #781 (1998) 2 - 4
j2. same as j, sp5 2 - 4

Lamborghini Diablo-k

k. mtlfk dk. green, black base, black int., tinted windows, black & white tampo on sides & hood, sp5, #2 in X-Ray Cruiser series #946 (1999) 2 - 3

l. mtlfk blue, mtlfk blue chassis, white int., clear windows, ho5, Virtual Collection, #114 (2000) 2 - 3
m. mtlfk purple; metal chassis; black int.; clear windows; gold, gray & black tampo w/"Lamborghini Diablo" on sides; sp3; Malaysia; #124 (2001) 2 - 3
m2. same as m, mtlfk gray chassis, #124 (2001) 2 - 3

5638-a

Limozeen 5638 - 80mm - 1991
This model has a chrome plastic chassis, white-tinted interior, gray-tinted windows, sunroof, ww and was made in Malaysia.
a. white; pink, orange & dk. blue stripe tampo w/"vj" & "Classic Limo Service" on sides, pink varies dull to bright; #112 $10 - 12

5638-b

b. turquoise w/glitter, gold metal chassis, clear windows, yellow interior, #174 (1992) 6 - 8

5638-c

c. black, multicolored metalflakes, red int., clear windows, ww, #225 (1994) 6 - 8
d. 13303, gold, tinted windows, white int., ww, #4 in Speed Gleamer series, #316 (1995) 12 - 15
d2. same as d, sp7, #316 (1995) 12 - 15

16915-e

e. 16915; blue; chrome plastic base; white int.; tinted windows; red, magenta & silver tampo w/"Brrrrrratata" on sides, "Blam!" on hood, "Bang" on roof; sp5; #2 in Biff! Bam! Boom! series; #542 (1997) 2 - 4

Limozeen-f

f. mtlfk black, white int., tinted windows, turquoise & gold tampo w/"Limozeen" on sides, lwgd, #4 in Low 'n Cool series, #716 (1998) 2 - 4
g. unpainted, gold chrome base, gray int., tinted windows, lwgd, #4 in Low 'n Cool Series, 1998 Hot Wheels Convention, #716 (1998) 60 - 70

Limozeen-h

h. gray; blue int.; tinted windows; yellow, white & dk. blue tampo w/"Hollywierd" on sides; lwch; Thailand; Show Biz 5-pack (1999) 2 - NA
h2. same as h, Malaysia, Toys "R" Us 10-pack (1999) 2 - NA

Limozeen-i

i. black, chrome chassis, white int., lwch. Malaysia. Mexico only (2000) 12 - 15

j. mtlfk green; gold chassis; tinted windows; white int.; black, white & gold tampo w/"Dele's Exclusive Service" & "Taxi" on sides & hood; dw3gd; #2 in Turbo Taxi series; Thailand; #054 (2001) 2 - 3
j2. same as j, Malaysia, #054 (2001) 2 - 3
j3. same as j, sp5gd, Thailand, #054 (2001) 2 - 3
k. red; chrome chassis; white int.; tinted windows; green, black, white & orange tampo w/"Happy Birthday" on sides; lwch; Birthday Cake 5-pack (2001) 3 - NA

2920-a

Mazda MX-5 Miata 2920 - 65mm - 1991
This Malaysia-made convertible has a red metal chassis, tan interior, clear windshield and bw.

2920-a

a. red; yellow, pink & turquoise tampo on hood & driver's side; "Miata" in large letters & "Mazda MX-5" in small letters on hood; #116 $10 - 15
a2. same as a, no tampo, #116 8 - 10

2920-a3

a3. same as a, no tampo on side, #116 8 - 10

2920-b

b. yellow; pink int.; pink, black & blue tampo w/"Miata Mazda MX-5" on sides; #172 (1992) 6 - 8
b2. same as b, liw, #172 (1993) 12 -18
b3. same as b, sp7, #172 (1996) 55 - 60

Mazda MX-5 Miata-c

c. no #; bright red; yellow, lt. blue & white striping tampo on top; "Getty" on trunk; yellow int.; never in bp (1992) 5 - NA

Mazda MX-5 Miata-d

d. no #, Day-Glo orange, same as a, silver plastic base, blue & magenta stripe on sides, pink int., scw. Only in G-Force set (1994) 35 - NA
e. black, gold Hot Wheels logo on black-tinted windshield, black metal base, black plastic int., sp7. Black Convertible Collection only, Target Stores excl. 6 - NA
f. 0454, dk. mtlfk red car & base, clear windshield, tan interior, sp7, #172 (1995) 3 - 5
f2. same as f, tinted windshield, yellow & orange stripe on sides, sp5, #172 (1997) 3 - 5
f3. same as f2, sp3, #172 (1997) 2 - 4
g. mtlfk black, same as e, sp7gd, Canada only (1996) 3 - 5

h. no #; green; gold glitter; orange base & int.; tinted windshield; yellow & magenta stripes on sides; scw. G Force & Double Barrel set only (1996) 6 - NA

Mazda MX-5 Miata-i

i. no #, mtlfk aqua, gold metal base, clear windshield, gold int., sp7gd, Toys "R" Us 10-car set only (1997) 6 - NA

Mazda MX-5 Miata-j

j. bluish green, white interior, tinted windshield, blue & silver tampo with "Surf Runner" & Miata logo on sides, dw3, California Dreamin' 5-pack only (1997) 4 - NA
j2. same as j, Thailand (1997) 2 - NA

Mazda MX-5 Miata-k

k. orange; orange chassis; black int.; tinted windshield; yellow & dk. brown tampo w/"Reese's" & " 2 Peanut Butter Cups" on sides & trunk, "Reese's Milk Chocolate" on hood; sp5. #1 in Sugar Rush Series, #741 (1998) 2 - 3
l. unpainted, blue int., clear windshield, sp5, #1 in Sugar Rush series, 1998 Hot Wheels Convention, #741 (1998) 70 - 75

Mazda MX-5 Miata-m

m. blue, lt. green int., clear windshield, black & yellow tampo on sides & hood, lwch, #4 in X-Treme Speed series, #968 (1999) 2 - 3
n. turquoise, turquoise chassis, white int., tinted windshield, dw3, China, Car Crashers set (1999) 5 - NA

Mazda Miata MX-5-o

o. white; black chassis & int.; tinted windshield; lavender, black & gray tampo w/"Pang Racing" on sides, "Pang Racing Official Pace Car" on hood, "Car 23" on trunk; Malaysia; #1084 (2000) 2 - 3

9770-a

Mercedes-Benz SL 9770 - 80mm - 1991
This Malaysia-made convertible has a black plastic chassis extending halfway up the side, blue interior, clear windshield, and uh.
Similar casting: 13601 Mercedes 500SL
a. chrome, Intl. line only $8 - 10
a2. same as a, hoc 12 - 15
b. 13610, red, red chassis, clear windshield, tan int., uh, #2 in 1995 Model Series, #342 (1995) 6 - 8

Values are shown in U.S. dollars, first price is for mint, second is for mint packaged vehicles only. See pages 15-16 for grading guide to determine value for cars in lesser conditions.

b2. same as b, sp5, #342 (1995) 6 - 8

c. black, red Hot Wheels logo on white rectangle, black-tinted windshield, black int., black plastic base, sp5, Black Convertible Collection only, Target Stores excl. 4 - NA

d. 13610, mtlfk black, gray plastic chassis, red int., clear windshield, sp5, #2 in 1995 Model series, #342 (1996) 5 - 7

d2. same as d, tan int., #342 (1996) 40 - 50

d3. same as d, sp7gd, Canada only (1996) 3 - 5

d4. same as d, sp7, #342 (1996) 4 - 8

d5. same as d, lwch, 342 (1997) 2 - 4

Mercedes-Benz SL-e

e. 16677, black, clear windshield, white int., "SL 500" on sides, white lines on trunk, sp5, Mercedes 500 SL, #3 in 1997 Treasure Hunt series, #580 (1997) 20 - 25

f. no #, mtlfk dk. red, red chassis & int., clear windshield, sp5, Avon Father & Son Collector 2-pack only (1997) 6 - NA

Mercedes-Benz SL-g

g. white, red plastic chassis, black int., tinted windshield, yellow & black design on sides, sp3, California Dreamin' 5-pack only (1997) 2 - NA

g2. same as g, Thailand (1997) 2 - NA

h. mtlfk blue, gray chassis, black int., clear windshield, ho5, #134 (2000) 2 - 3

h2. same as h, blue chassis, #134 (2000) 2 - 3

5673-a

Mercedes-Benz Unimog 5673 - 55mm - 1991

This Malaysia-made utility truck has a metal chassis with red plastic fenders & gas tanks, a white plastic cover, red interior, clear windshield, and ct.

a. white; lt. green & red tampo w/red "Castrol Research Team" on sides of cover; #158 $8 - 12

4643-b

b. 4643; tan; brown, black & orange camouflage tampo; tan int.; metal base; ctw; #239 (1993) 6 - 8

b2. same as b, ctb, #239 (1994) 8 - 10

b3. same as b, ct, #239 (1994) 10 - 12

b4. same as b, dw3ctw, #239 (1996) 4 - 6

b5. same as b, dw3ct, #239 (1997) 2 - 4

c. 13305; gray; orange canopy, fenders, int. & bumpers; tinted windshield; knobby rro; #2 in Real Riders series; #318 (1995) 20 - 25

d. 16930, black, red plastic on sides, tan plastic canopy, black & red bear on sides, red int., clear windshield, dw3ct, #1 in Street Beast series, #557 (1997) 4 - 6

e. red, black canopy & interior, clear windshield, dw3ct, Malaysia, #1005 (1999) 2 - 3

f. mtlfk dark red, tan canopy, tinted windshield, black int., dw3ct, Virtual Collection car, #133 (2000) 2 - 3

Mercedes-Benz Unimog-g

g. mtlfk dark green; black chassis; orange fenders; black cover; orange int.; clear windshield; white, black, orange & yellow tampo w/"U" on cover, "U" & "Unimog" on sides & hood; Final Run Logo in back; dw3ct w/"Final Run" in white around tires; #1 in Final Run series (2001) 5 - 7

5670-a

Peugeot 405 5670 - 70mm - 1991

This French standard street coupe/sedan has a black plastic chassis, red grill & border around the sides, clear windows, red interior, bw, and was made in Malaysia.

a. black $5 - 7

a2. same as a, sp5 5 - 7

3204-b

b. 3204; blue; same as a; yellow grill, border & int.; red, white & black tampo w/"Rally 21," "Goodyear" & racing decals on sides, striping on hood & roof; Canada only 5 - 7

c. 15977, mtlfk dk. green, green plastic base, clear windows, white int., white border along bottom, sp5, China, #467 (1996) 2 - 6

d. 15977, mtlfk gray, same as c, black plastic base, orange & magenta tampo on sides, China, #467 (1997) 2 - 6

d2. same as d, lwch, #467 (1997) 2 - 6

7607-a

Porsche 930 7607 - 70mm - 1991

This Malaysia-made model has a metal chassis, tinted windows, black interior, and bw.

a. dk. mtlc red; yellow & black stripes; black "Turbo" inside stripes; "Porsche 930" in white on sides $20 - 30

b. no #, lt. green, same as a, black "Porsche 930," Turbo Tube set only (1991) 10 - NA

c. purple, same as b, yellow "Porsche 930," #148 (1991) 60 - 90

7607-d

d. red, same as a, #148 (1991) 8 - 12

d2. red, same as d, sp5, #148 (1996) 4 - 6

7607-e

e. mtlfk dk. blue; orange, yellow & white tampo all over; grayed-out windows; gray int.; uhy; Malaysia; Revealers 3 - 5

f. mtlfk green, same as e, Revealers 3 - 5

g. mtlfk red, same as e, uhp, Revealers 3 - 5

h. Day-Glo orange, no tampo, black int., black-tinted windows, "Revealers" in white; bw, Malaysia, Revealers 10-pack only 10 - NA

7607-i

i. no #; mtlfk lt. green; blue, yellow & red tampo on sides, hood & roof; rose int.; rose-tinted windows; scw; Double Barrel set only (1994) 30 - NA

7607-i2

i2. 7607, same as i, slightly different tampo, bw, #148 (1995) 70 - 110

15248-j

j. 15248; mtlfk silver; white, red, black, purple & yellow tampo w/baseball flying thru hole on sides & hood, "Home Run" on roof; black-tinted windows; black int.; sp7; #1 in Sports Car Series; #404 (1996) 4 - 8

Porsche 930-k

k. no #; mtlfk purple; yellow, orange & lt. green scribbly design on sides, hood & roof; green-tinted windows; black interior; scw; Double Barrel Loop set (1996) 8 - NA

l. 15792, blue, black int., tinted windows, sp5, #592 (1997) 2 - 4

l2. same as l, ho5, Porsche 5-pack only (1997) 2 - NA

l3. same as l2, sp7 (1997) 2 - NA

l4. same as l, dw3, #592 (1997) 2 - 4

Porsche 930-l5

l5. same as l, pink window & int., sp5, Porsche 5-pack only (1997) 2 - NA

m. dk. mtlc green; clear windows & int.; gold, silver & magenta tampo w/"97 Bonus Car" on sides & roof, "Q4" on sides & hood; sp3; Mattel's 4th quarter bonus car only (1997) 8 - NA

Porsche 930-n

n. 16945; dk. mtlfk green; black int.; tinted windows; yellow, orange & white guitar on sides, hood & roof; "Rock n Roll" on hood; sp5; #4 in Rockin' Rods series; #572 (1997) 2 - 4

n2. same as n, ho5, #572 (1998) 2 - 4

Porsche 930-o

o. pearl white; black-tinted windows & int.; "G-Force" in red, yellow & blue on sides; Double Barrel & G-Force sets only (1997) 6 - NA

Porsche 930-p

p. dk. mtlc red; tinted windows; black int.; orange, black & white tampo w/"Zero G" on sides; sp3; Thailand; #856 (1998) 2 - 3

Porsche 930-q

q. mtlfk blue; black interior; tinted windows; red, white & yellow tampo w/Hot Wheels logo, "Marilou" & race decals on sides; lwch; Thailand; Race Team III 5-pack (1999) 2 - NA

Porsche 930-r

r. mtlfk gold; dk. brown int.; tinted windows; orange, black & white tampo w/"2" on sides & roof; sp3; Alien Attack 5-pack; Thailand (1999) 2 - NA

s. white; black int.; tinted windows; black, red & yellow tampo with Porsche logo on hood; sp3; #125 (2000) 2 - 3

t. black, mtlfk gray chassis, black int., clear windows, white & yellow tampo w/"Police" & "Unit 7" on sides & hood, sp3 gray, China, Cyborg City 5-pack (2001) 3 - NA

5343-a

Ramp Truck 5343 - 79mm - 1991

Based on a Kenworth Cabover truck with car-carrying bed, this Malaysia-made model has a metal base, white plastic ramp, clear plastic windows, no interior, and bw. Note: This model was first issued in The Crack-Ups line.

a. white; yellow & red tampo on ramp sides w/blue stripe & "International Dream Cars Racing Team"; #108 $15 - 25

Values are shown in U.S. dollars, first price is for mint, second is for mint packaged vehicles only. See pages 15-16 for grading guide to determine value for cars in lesser conditions.

a2. same as a, blue-gray not blue in tampo, blacked-out windows, #108 8 - 18

0700-b

b. yellow; Hot Wheels logo & "24hr Emergency Towing" in yellow, red & blue-gray on ramp sides; #187 (1992) 5 - 12
b2. 0700, same as b, sp7, #187 (1996) 3 - 6
b3. same as b, dw3, #187 (1996) 4 - 6
c. 13324; purple chrome; yellow & red Hot Wheels logo on cab roof & ramp sides; #2 in Racing Metals series; #337 (1995) 4 - 10

13324-c2

c2. pink chrome, same as c, #337 (1995) 6 - 15

15233-d

d. 15233; mtlfk blue; white ramp; blue "#1 in Racing" & "Not For Hire"; red & yellow Hot Wheels logo on sides; clear windows; sp5; #1 in Race Team Series II; #392 (1996) 4 - 8
d2. same as d, sp7, #392 (1996) 12 - 25
d3. same as d, black windows, China, #392 (1998) 2 - 4

Ramp Truck-e

e. lt. blue; blacked-out windows; white ramp; gold & black tampo w/"Fischer Motors Limited" & logo on ramp sides; dw3; Showroom Specials 5-pack only (1998) 2 - NA
e2. dk. blue, same as e 2 - NA

Ramp Truck-f

f. mtlfk dk. aqua; gray ramp; blue, yellow & red tampo w/Hot Wheels logo & "24 Hr. Emergency Towing" on sides, large Hot Wheels logo on roof; sp5; #774 (1998) 2 - 3
g. black, same as f, yellow ramp, ho5, #1060 (2000) 2 - 3

Ramp Truck-h

h. mtlfk gold; black chassis, ramp & windows; gold, black & red tampo w/"FR" & "24/7 Towing" on sides, "FR" on roof; flames on ramp; rrch; #4 in 2001 Final Run (2001) 7 - 9

9749-a

Renault 5 Turbo 9749 - 64mm - 1991
This Malaysia-made model has a blue plastic chassis, clear windows, tan interior, and bw.
a. blue; yellow, orange & white tampo w/"GT" & "Renault 5 Turbo" on sides, "Turbo" on hood $5 -7

3205-b

b. 3205; white; same as a; purple chassis; gray int.; black, yellow & green stripe tampo on sides, hood & roof; "Goodyear" & "Rally 17" on sides; Canada only 6 - 8

5640-a

Speed Shark™ 5640 - 68mm - 1991
Based on a shark, this Malaysia-made concept car has a chrome plastic chassis, windshield & engine, pink interior & gills & bw.
a. maroon; yellow, white & pink tampo on sides & top; #113 $60 - 65

5640-b

b. purple, same as a, #113 6 - 8
c. no #, white, no tampo, blue chassis, red int. & gills, only w/Heroes on Hot Wheels tapes (1991), w/tape 8 - 10

Speed Shark-d

d. no #; mtlfk gray; black, orange & blue tampo; black int. & gills; 25th Anniv. Dream Car 5-pack only (1993) 8 - NA
e. 5640; black; yellow, orange & red tampo on sides & hood; red int. & engine; orange windshield & headlights; bw; #113 (1995) 2 - 4
e2. same as e, sp5 (1996) 3 - 5

Speed Shark-f

f. 15969; mtlc lavender; purple int. & windshield; sp5; China; #458 (1997) 2 - 4
g. red; chrome chassis & windshield; gray int.; gray, black & white tampo on sides & top; sp3; Thailand; #148 (2001) 2 - 3
h. mtlfk gray; chrome chassis; magenta int.; orange windshield; black, red, yellow & blue tampo on top; sp5; Cosmic Blast playset (2001) 2 - 3

Speed Shark-i

i. mtlfk orange; chrome chassis & windshield; gray int.; black, gray & white tampo on sides & top, "Venom Strike" on sides; sp5; Malaysia; #2 in Cold Blooded Series #076 (2002) 2 - 3

5637-a

Street Beast 5637 - 80mm - 1991
Based on a combination Studebaker-Plymouth convertible, this Malaysia-made model has a metal base with turquoise plastic above the base, turquoise plastic interior, clear windshield, metal tire in back, and ww.
a. white; blue & pink tampo on hood, pink varies dull to bright; #111 $6 - 8

Street Beast-b

b. mtlfk blue, white plastic sides & int., white Hot Wheels logo on back of seats, blue-tinted windshield, pcgd, "'50s Dream Car" in 16-piece FAO Schwarz Gold Series Collection, limited to 3000 (1994) 10 - NA
c. 15244, mtlfk black, black metal base, black int., clear windshield, sp7b, #2 in Dark Rider Series II, #401 (1996) 4 - 6
d. mtlfk purple, gray-tinted windshield, gray sides & int., lwgd, Designer Collection 8-pack, sold by Target 5 - NA
e. 16939; white; gold plastic sides & int.; clear windshield; red, black & gold tampo w/diamonds w/"K" & king of diamonds playing card on sides, king of diamonds playing card on hood; ho5; #2 in Dealer's Choice Series; #566 (1997) 2 - 4
e2. same as e, sp7, #2 in Dealer's Choice Series, #566 (1997) 2 - 4
f. plum, gray sides, gray & pink int., clear windshield, gray tampo on hood, ww, China, Cruisin' the '50s 8-pack from FAO Schwarz only (1998) 6 - NA
g. unpainted, pink int. & sides, clear windshield, dw3, 1998 Hot Wheels Convention, #214 (1998) 90 - 95

Street Beast-h

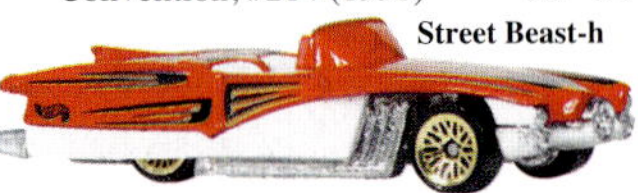

h. red; white sides & int.; red-tinted windshield; gold & black tampo on sides, hood & roof; lwgd; #7 in 1998 Treasure Hunt series; #755 (1998) 22 - 25

Street Beast-i

i. white; gold sides & int.; clear windshield; brown fenders; gold & black tampo w/"Final Run" on hood, "Street Beast" in back of seats; rrch w/white stripe; #4 in Final Run series, limited to 35,000 (1999) 5 - 7

5348-a

Surf Patrol™ 5348 - 73mm - 1991
This Malaysia-made Chevy pickup has a red interior & truck bed, and clear windshield.
Similar casting: 4368 Beach Patrol (1983)
a. yellow; red, white & black striping tampo w/"Rescue," "Radio Dispatched" & "Emergency Support Vehicle" on sides; #102 $6 - 8

Surf Patrol-a2

a2. same as a; red circle w/"Baywatch," "Lifeguard" and black & white scene in circle on hood; Baywatch Lifeguard Station Pop 'n Play set only (1995) 4 - 8
b. mtlfk blue; same as a; pink truck bed & int.; yellow, red & white tampo; in box w/Aquafresh Kids Toothpaste only (1994) 6 - NA

Surf Patrol-c

c. yellow; tinted windshield; red int. & truck bed; red & black tampo w/"Rescue," "Baywatch" & Baywatch logo on sides; Hot Wheels logo in back; Baywatch 5-pack only (1995) 3 - NA

Surf Patrol-d

d. yellow; red int. & truck bed; tinted windshield; black, red & white tampo w/"Rescue," "Lifeguard," "Radio Dispatch," "Unit 2" & logo on sides; dw3ct; #102 (1997) 2 - 4
e. gray; purple int. & truck bed; purple-tinted windshield; purple, lt. blue & black tampo w/"Storm Chaser" on sides; dw3ct; Thailand; #203 (2001) 2 - 3
f. yellow; red bed & int.; blue-tinted windshield; red & black tampo with "Disaster Network," "Unit 1" & "Rescue Network" on; sides dw3ct; Thailand; Rescue Rods 5 pack (2001) 2 - NA

5669-a

Toyota MR-2 Rally 5669 - 72mm - 1991
This model has a black plastic chassis, rear spoiler, red plastic interior, clear windows, uh, and was made in Malaysia.
a. white; red, yellow & orange tampo w/"Toyota" & "Toyota MR-2" on sides, "MR-2" on hood, "Toyota" on roof; black plastic headlights; #122 $35 - 40
a2. same as a, chrome headlights, #122 10 - 12
a3. white, same as a2, hoc, #122 18 - 20

Toyota MR-2 Rally-b

b. no #; blue; red, yellow & white stripe tampo on top, "Getty" on hood; red int.; never in bp (1992) 4 - NA

Values are shown in U.S. dollars, first price is for mint, second is for mint packaged vehicles only. See pages 15-16 for grading guide to determine value for cars in lesser conditions.

c. 4609; white; red, purple & pink tampo w/"Europa/Asia" & "34" on sides, "34" on hood; red int.; clear windows; black plastic base; uh; #233 (1993) 6 - 8

4609-c2

c2. same as c, sp3, #233 (1996) 6 - 8
c3. same as c, dw3, #233 (1996) 2 - 4
c4. same as c, ho5, #233 (1996) 2 - 4

5669-d

d. no #; Day-Glo pink; white, lt. brown & red tampo on sides & hood; Criss-Cross Crash set only (1994) 8 - NA

5669-e

e. red; same as a2; black, white & yellow tampo; in box w/Aquafresh Kids Toothpaste only (1994) 5 - NA

Toyota MR-2 Rally-f

f. fluor. pink; same as g; white, yellow & orange tampo, in box w/Aquafresh Kids Toothpaste only (1994) 5 - NA

4609-g

g. black, same as c, sp5, #233 (1995) 35 - 130
g2. same as g, uh, #233 (1995) 65 - 77
g3. same as g, sp3, #233 (1996) 65 - 85

Toyota MR-2 Rally-h

h. 4609; white; purple, blue & lt. green tampo w/"Midnite Racers 2" on sides; blue int.; blue-tinted windows; lwch; #233 (1997) 2 - 4
h2. same as h, mtlc blue in tampo, #233 (1997) 2 - 4
h3. same as h2, sp3, Thailand, Racing World 5-pack only (1998) 2 - 4
h4. same as h3, lwch (1998) 2 - 4

Toyota MR-2 Rally-i

i. white; tinted windows; black, red & gray tampo w/"Toyota," "World Racers 31" & race decals on sides, hood & roof; lwch; #894 (1998) 2 - 3
i2. white, same as i, blue-tinted windows, blue interior, China, Road Race Set (1999) 10 - NA
j. purple; black chassis; gray int.; clear windows; gray, white & orange tampo w/"4" & "MR2" on sides, "4" on roof; sp3; Malaysia; #1086 (1999) 2 - 3

Toyota MR-2 Rally-j

Toyota MR-2 Rally-k

k. black, purple int., blue-tinted windows, lwch, China, Target excl. w/Arco Hauler (1999) 5 - NA
l. orange, orange base, white int., tinted windows, lwch, China, Deluxe Downtown Set (1999) 5 - NA
l2. orange, same as l, black base, blue int., issued w/Power Launcher (1999) 5 - NA
m. red, black base, blue int., blue-tinted windows, lwch, China, issued w/Long Hauler (1999) 5 - NA
n. mtlfk silver, same as m, issued w/Power Launcher (1999) 5 - NA

Toyota MR-2-o

o. black; black chassis; red int.; clear windows; white, orange & brown tampo on sides & hood; sp3; Malaysia; #1 in Kung Fu Force series; #033 (2000) 2 - 3
p. red; white int.; tinted windows; yellow, black & white lightning tampo with "Toyota," Hot Wheels logo & race decals on sides, "Toyota" & Toyota logo on hood; sp3; #145 (2001) 2 - 3
q. white; black chassis, int. & windows; red & black tampo w/"27" on sides; lwch; China; Pavement Pounder pack (2001) 5 - 7
r. red, chrome chassis, black int., clear windows, silver & black flame tampo, lwch, China, Power Launcher pack (2001) 5 - 7
s. orange, black chassis, blue int., clear windows, red "Nitro Fuel" on sides, lwch, Kool Toys Racing Pack (2001) 5 - 7
t. lt. green; black chassis; gray int.; tinted windows; orange-brown, dk. blue & black tampo w/"Radio Dispatched 24 Hrs.," "HW Trans," "5" & "Maintenance Service" on sides, "HW Trans" on hood; ho5; Thailand. Asphalt Assault 5-pack (2002) 2 - NA

5636-a

Trailbuster® 5636 - 65mm - 1991
Based on a Jeep, this model has a clear windshield, pink interior & spare tire, metal body, metal base, ct, and was made in Malaysia. Similar casting: 9375 Roll Patrol Jeep CJ-7 (1985)

a. turquoise; blue, yellow & pink splash tampo; #110 $10 - 15
a2. same as a, lt. blue replaces blue in tampo, #110 10 - 15
a3. same as a, black replaces blue in tampo, #110 30 - 35
b. no #; purple; blue, orange & yellow tampo w/"Kool Aid" on sides; yellow int.; 2-pack; Kool-Aid Wacky Warehouse only (1993) 10 - NA
b2. same as b, plastic body, 2-pack, Kool-Aid Wacky Warehouse only 12 - NA

Trailbuster-b

Trailbuster-c

c. no #; white; yellow, orange & purple tampo w/"Chuck E Cheese's" on sides & Chuck E Cheese on hood; orange int.; Chuck E Cheese's pizza only (1993) 8 - 10
d. blackish chrome; lt. green int. & spare tire; ct; Off Road Explorers 5-pack only (1994) 8 - NA

Trailbuster-e

e. Day-Glo pink, black metal base & int., tinted windshield, black "Baywatch" & "Rescue" on sides, black & yellow Baywatch logo on hood, ct, Baywatch 5-pack only (1995) 3 - NA
f. yellow; red int.; tinted windshield; red, white & black tampo w/"Rescue," "Unit 1," "Patrol" & logo on car; dw3ct; Rescue Squad 5-pack only (1997) 2 - NA

Trailbuster-g

g. white; blue int.; tinted windshield; red, yellow & blue tampo w/"Action News KHWW" & "1" on sides & hood, "Off-Road Reporter" on sides; dw3ct; Action News Team 5-pack (1998) 2 - NA

Trailbuster-h

h. mtlfk blue; white int. & spare tire; white, red & yellow tampo w/"1" & Hot Wheels logo on sides & roof; race decals on sides; dw3ct; Off-Road Racing 4-pack (1998) 5 - NA

Trailbuster-i

i. yellow; tan int.; tinted windshield; black, gray & lt. blue tampo on sides & hood; "30," "Mud Cat" & race decals on sides; dw3ct; Thailand; Baja Blazers 5-pack (1999) 5 - NA

9557-a

VW Golf 9557 - 65mm - 1991
This Malaysia-made model has a pink plastic chassis & interior, clear windows, and bw.

a. white; pink, lt. green & blue tampo; #106 $55 - 65

9714-b

b. red; black chassis; tan int.; red, white & black striping tampo w/Volkswagen logo & "GTi" on sides; #106 12 - 15

9557-c

c. mtlc silver, yellow & red flames, white "Getty" inside red rectangle, black plastic chassis, yellow int., never in bp 3 - NA
d. black, green glitter, no tampo, chrome plastic chassis, yellow-tinted windows, yellow int., bw, #183 (1992) 30 - 35
e. pink, same as d, silver glitter, #183 (1992) 18 - 20
e2. same as e, black plastic chassis (1992) 7 - 10
f. 16041, mtlfk black, clear windows, red int., white Hot Wheels logo on rear window, sp5, China, #474 (1996) 4 - 8

16042-f2

f2. same as f, "Fahrvergnugen" in gray & outline of driver in red on sides, #474 (1997) 2 - 4
f3. same as f2, lwch, #474 (1997) 2 - 4

5674-a

Zender Fact 4 5674 - 67mm - 1991
This Malaysia-made German high-dollar sports car has a black plastic base & interior, light-gray-tinted windows & lights, and uh.

a. mtlc silver, yellow "Fact 4" on front & sides, #125 $10 - 12
a2. same as a, no tampo on sides, #125 6 - 8
a3. same as a2, uhgd, #125 20 - 25
a4. same as a2, hoc, #125 15 - 18

0461-b

b. magenta; multicolored glitter; no tampo; clear windows; orange chassis, int. & headlights; #177 (1992) 4 - 6
b2. same as b, hoc, #177 (1992) 15 - 18
c. no #; purple; lt. green & yellow tampo w/"36" on hood & sides; clear windows; gray int.; only w/Heroes

Values are shown in U.S. dollars, first price is for mint, second is for mint packaged vehicles only. See pages 15-16 for grading guide to determine value for cars in lesser conditions.

Zender Fact 4-c

on Hot Wheels video tapes (1993), w/video 8 - NA

5674-d

d. black; yellow, pink & white tampo on top & sides; black-tinted windows; black int.; uhy; Malaysia; Revealers 3 - 5
e. mtlc green, same as d, Revealers 3 - 5
f. candy purple, same as d, uhgn, Revealers 3 - 5

4007-g

g. 4407, mtlfk dk. blue, white "Zender" & yellow "Fact 4" on hood, black-tinted windows, uh, #228 (1993) 8 - 10
g2. same as g, clear windows, gray int., #228 (1993) 15 - 20

Zender Fact 4-h

h. no #, vacuum metallized silver, black 25th Anniv. logo on roof, gray interior, 25th Anniv. Dream Car 5-pack only (1993) 8 - NA

Zender Fact 4-i

i. no #, red, black-tinted windshield, yellow & white Shell logo on sides, yellow "Shell" on windshield. Sold by Shell dealers in OH & MA only, baggie only 4 - NA

5674-j

j. Day-Glo green; orange, black & white tampo on roof & hood; blacked-out windows; #228 (1994) 10 - 12
j2. same as j, clear windows, black int., #228 (1994) 25 - 30
j3. same as j2, yellow replaces orange in tampo, #228 (1994) 8 - 10
k. red, yellow "Hormel Chili" & orange flames on sides, white "Zender" in front, yellow "Fact" above left headlight. Hormel only, in baggies, never in blisterpack (1995) 4 - NA

Zender Fact 4-k2

k2. same as k, white "Fact," yellow "Zender." Hormel only, in baggies (1995) 5 - NA
l. 13274; mtlfk black; gold stripes; blue & red flakes on sides & hood; gold Hot Wheels logo on rear spoiler; tinted windows; white int.; uh; #2 in Steel Stamp series; #287 (1995) 6 - 8

13274-l2

l2. same as l, sp5, #287 (1995) 2 - 4
l3. same as l, clear windows, white int., #287 (1995) 18 - 20
l4. same as l, sp3, #287 (1996) 2 - 4
m. 13867, pearl white, gray plastic base & int., blue-tinted windows, blue "Zender" above front bumper, gold "Fact 4" over left headlight, blue Hot Wheels logo on rear spoiler, sp5, #454 (1996) 2 - 4
m2. same as m, sp7, #454 (1996) 2 - 4
m3. same as m, dw3, #454 (1996) 2 - 4

13867-n

n. no #, white, black plastic base, blacked-out windows, sp5, orange Union 76 logo, white & blue on sides & hood, white "Performance" on windshield. In baggie only at Union 76 stations (1996) 3 - NA

4407-o

o. 4407, mtlc burgundy, clear windows, tan int., gold & black tampo on sides & hood, sp5, China, #228 (1997) 4 - 6
p. dk. blue, clear windows, silver interior, sp5, Toys "R" Us playset only, China (1998) 5 - NA

Zender Fact 4-q

q. mtlfk dk. green, clear windows, black int., black & gold tampo on sides & hood, lwch, #820 (1998) 2 - 3
r. red; gray chassis & int.; orange-tinted windows; black, yellow & gray tampo w/"Flamer Destruction" on sides, flames on hood & roof; Thailand; Tornado Twister 5-pack (1999) 2 - NA
s. red; gray plastic base & int.; orange-tinted windows; yellow, orange, black & gray flame tampo on hood & roof; "Flames of Destruction" on sides; dw3; Thailand; #208 (2001) 2 - 3
t. white; black chassis & int.; clear windows; green, orange & yellow tampo w/"Flame Proof" on sides & front; sp3; China; Cyborg City 5-pack (2001) 2 - NA

1992

Mattel introduced three new series. The first had metallic-flake paint jobs with rather large speckles and used castings from the regular line. The second series, called Gleam Team, had regular-line cars retooled with plastic upper bodies. They had embossed metallic designs over the entire length of the car. The Pro Circuit line re-created the more popular race cars from the world of motor sports. Each came with its own individual trading card. Mattel sponsored the Hot Wheels SCCA Trans-Am car in which Jack Baldwin won the 1992 Championship. The company also issued a blimp with six distinct variations within six months and caused a stir among collectors. The Hiway Hauler casting was changed after a run of twelve years and twelve major variations. This was also the first year several cars were produced for collectors. These included several historical race cars and the popular Ruby Red Passion.

2029-a

'56 Flashsider 2029 - 75mm - 1992
Based on the 1956 Chevrolet Stepside truck, this model has a chrome plastic chassis, blacked-out windows, flat truck bed, uh, and was made in Malaysia.

a. turquoise; blue, pink & yellow tampo on sides; #136 $8 - 10

2029-a2

a2. same as a, hoc, #136 25 - 30
a3. same as a, ho5, #136 (1996) 5 - 8
a4. same as a, sp5, #136 (1996) 3 - 6
a5. same as a, lt. gray plastic base, ho5w, #136 (1997) 3 - 6
a6. same as a, chrome windows, ho5, #136 (1997) 18 - 20
b. 10250, black, same as a, no tampo, grayed-out windows, ww, limited to 5000, Seattle Toy Show giveaway 20 - 25

10250-b2

b2. same as b; "Greater Seattle Toy Show" in red, white & blue on bed; limited to 5000, Toy Show giveaway 20 - 25
c. 13276; mtlfk maroon; turquoise, gold & magenta tampo on sides; gold Hot Wheels logo on rear fender; chromed windows; uh; #3 in Steel Stamp series; #289 (1995) 8 - 10

13276-c2

c2. same as c, sp5, #289 (1995) 6 - 8
c3. same as c, sp7, #289 8 - 10

13637-d

d. 13637; purple; lt. green & white stripe tampo on sides, Malt O Meal & lt. green stripe on bed; blacked-out windows; plastic base; sp5. Ltd ed from Malt O Meal (1995) 15 - 18

'56 Flashsider-e

e. red; gold, red & magenta flame tampo w/Hot Wheels logo & gold "The Toy Club" on bed; gyt w/gold hubs; in box for Mattel Toy Club, limited to 7000 35 - 40
f. chrome, blue-tinted windows, chrome int., red Hot Wheels logo on rear window, rsw. Service Merchandise 16-piece Classic American Car Collection only, limited to 5000 (1995) 8 - NA

15220-g

g. 15220; black; gray, red & white tampo w/"1" & racing decals on sides, "Chevrolet" & Chevy logo on hood & truck bed, "1" on roof; chrome plastic base & windows; black sp7 w/yellow "Goodyear #1" & "Eagle" on sides. #3 in Race Truck series, #382 (1996) 6 - 10
g2. same as g, sp7 w/o tampo on wheels, #382 (1996) 10 - 15
h. mtlfk purple, purple windows & int., sp5, 50's Favorites 5-pack only (1996) 3 - NA
h2. same as h, dw3 (1996) 2 - NA
h3. same as h, sp3 (1997) 2 - NA
h4. same as h, gray plastic base, sp5 (1997) 4 - NA
h5. same as h, gray plastic base, dw3 (1997) 4 - NA

15025-i

i. 15025, white, blue chrome windows, red & blue "JC Whitney Everything Automotive" on sides & truck bed, sp5. Ltd ed of 20,000 (1996) 20 - 25

16675-j

j. 16675, dk. green, chrome windows, pink & orange tampo on hood, sp5. #1 in 1997 Treasure Hunt Series, #578 (1997) 30 - 35
k. yellow, same as a, ho5, #771 (1998) 2 - 3

'56 Flashsider-l

l. yellow, black windows, orange & black flame tampo on sides, logo & black "White's Guide Exclusive" on bed, sp5. Ltd ed of 10,000 15 - 18
m. green; chrome plastic base; white top & truck bed cover; blacked-out windows; yellow & silver design on sides, top & rear; sp7; white-side-wall tires; China; Cruisin' the 50s 8-pack from FAO Schwarz (1998) 6 - NA

'56 Flashsider-n

n. gray; chrome base; black windows; red, yellow, dk. blue & white tampo w/flames, large Hot Wheels logo, "My other Hot Wheel is a car" & "Hot Wheels fan" on sides; sp5; Thailand; #899 (1998) 3 - 5

Values are shown in U.S. dollars, first price is for mint, second is for mint packaged vehicles only. See pages 15-16 for grading guide to determine value for cars in lesser conditions.

o. unpainted, black plastic base, orange-tinted windows, sp5. 1998 Hot Wheels Convention, #899 (1998) 150 - 170

'56 Flashsider-p

p. mtlfk gold; same as l; black, red & white tampo. Ltd ed of 10,000 for White's Guide magazine (1998) 12 - 15

'56 Flashsider-q

q. yellow; chrome base; black windows; black, orange & white tampo on sides & hood w/"Hot Rod Handyman" & race decals on sides; sp3; Thailand; #1028 (1999) 3 - 5

'56 Flashsider-r

r. mtlfk black; gold windows; gold & white tampo w/"Mystery Car" on sides, design on hood, "Q1" on truck bed; 1999 First Quarter Mystery car; in baggie; Thailand (1999) 8 - NA

'56 Flashsider-s

s. white; black top; chrome windows; red, white & black tampo w/"Police," "Emergency" & "Santa Fe" on sides, "Santa Fe Police" on hood, "Emergency" & Santa Fe Police emblem on truck bed cover; rrch; Cop Rods Series 2 (2000) 6 - 8

'56 Flashsider-t

t. dark mtlfk red; gold chrome chassis; black windows; black, yellow, orange & red tampo w/"Circus on Wheels" on hood, "Imperio the Fireeater" on truck bed; ho5gd; Malaysia; #1 in Circus on Wheels series; #025 (2000) 2 - 3

u. gray; black windows; black & orange tampo on sides, hood & cover; Editor's Choice logo in black; pc; Thailand; Target Exclusive Editor's Choice series (2000) 6 - 8

'56 Flashsider-v

v. lt. blue; black windows; white & orange tampo on sides & truck bed cover w/"Tony & Noah's Auto Parts" on sides & cover, "Free Delivery" on sides; sp5; Malaysia; Truck Stoppers 5-pack (2001) 4 - NA

w. dark blue, black windows, white roof and truck bed, white flames on sides and hood, blue, red and yellow Brach's logo on truck bed and pr5s. Brach's mail-in premium, baggie (2002) 12 - NA

x. black, gray hood, chrome windows, white, red and gray tampo design on sides, roof and truck bed and rrchrl. Wal-Mart excl. Cruisin' America series. (2002) 9 - 12

1781-a

Aeroflash® 1781 - 75mm - 1992 (Gleam Team®)

This concept car has a plastic body, metal chassis, blacked-out windows, metal interior, uh, and was made in Malaysia.

Similar castings: 8727 Large Charge 1975, 9535 Silver Bullet (1985)

a. pink, etched design, #191 $8 - 12

a2. 13580, as a, uhgd, #191 (1994) 6 - 10

a3. as a2, silver base, #191 (1995) 16 - 20

b. no #; white; pink metal base & int.; red-tinted windows; yellow, green & blue tampo all over; red Hot Wheels logo on rear fender; uhgd. Track System Gift Pack only (1995) 3 - NA

b2. white, same as b, sp5g (1995) 3 - NA

1781-b3

b3. white, as b, sp3g (1995) 3 - NA

b4. 13232, as b, sp7gd, #444 (1996) 2 - 5

b5. 13232, as b, sp5, #444 (1996) 2 - 4

c. 16919, purple, white chassis, plastic windows, snow w/skis, white & black "Blizzard" on top, sp3, #2 in Quicksilver series, #546 (1997) 2 - 4

d. green plastic body; metal int.; blue tinted windows; black, orange & yellow tampo w/circuit board, lightning bolts & "High Voltage" on top (same as original Large Charge); nrsw. Ltd ed for 30th Anniv., w/blistercard in window box (1998) 5 - 7

Aeroflash-e

e. milky white; glow-in-dark plastic body; metal base; yellow, orange & red flame tampo on sides & top; sp3. Volcano Blowout set only (1998) 6 - NA

Aeroflash-f

f. green; black chassis & int.; clear windows; black, orange & white tampo w/"3" in back; sp3; #1031 (1999) 2 - 3

Aeroflash-g

g. blue; white chassis & int.; yellow-tinted windows; white, yellow & black tampo on sides & top; lwch; Thailand; Tornado Twister 5-pack (1999) 3 - NA

1384-a

Blimp 1384 - 80mm - 1992

This model has a metal gondola with a gray fuselage, "Goodyear" on the right side, and was made in Malaysia.

Note: The tail turns 180 degrees and there are two different messages on the left side. Only the gondola color is listed.

Similar casting: 1384 Blimp (1994)

a. white, black tampo, gray blimp, "Goodyear" in black on right side, "Rev It Up! Rip It Up" & Hot Wheels logo in red & yellow on left side, #137 $4 - 6

1384-a2

a2. same as a, "Goodyear #1 in Tires" on left side, #137 or #194 3 - 5

a3. same as a2; "Goodyear #1 in Tires" on both sides; yellow, aqua & blue; #194 3 - 5

a4. same as a3, "Rev It Up! Rip It Up" & Hot Wheels logo in red & yellow on left side, #194 3 - 5

5518-a5

a5. 5518, same as a3, left side has "The Best Tires In The World..." "Have Goodyear Written All Over Them" in black, Goodyear Service Centers only 6 - 8

a6. same as a, Hot Wheels 30th Anniv. logo in gold on bottom of blimp. Ltd ed for 30th Anniv., w/blistercard in window box (1998) 4 - 6

Blimp-b

b. no #, white, chrome blimp, red Mattel logo on right side & "Mattel Toys/the toys kids love/the products parents trust/the Brands that mean Business" in black on 4 lines & tail, message doesn't turn, SEMA show give-away in Las Vegas only 75 - NA

Blimp-c

c. white, blue fuselage, red flames, yellow & white "Leading the Way" on one side, red Hot Wheels logo on other. Inside turning apparatus: white & yellow Hot Wheels logo on one side, gold & white "Treasure Hunt '97" on other. #10 in 1997 Treasure Hunt series, #587 (1997) 20 - 25

d. metalflake silver, same as a4, #194 (1998) 2 - 4

Blimp-e

e. black; gold, black & white tampo: "Police Air Surveillance" on sides. Blue blimp w/gold stripe around middle, black & white tampo: "Caution Pressurized Helium" on sides, "Hot Wheels Air 13" in winged logo inside blimp. Sky Search Action Pack only (1999) 5 - NA

f. red, white fuselage w/red & yellow Hot Wheels logo, Virtual Collection, Malaysia, #142 (2000) 2 - 3

Blimp-g

g. red; dk. blue fuselage w/white int. with multicolored "Mobil 1," "12," "Jeremy Mayfield" & race decals; Thailand; #1 in NASCAR Blimp series (2001) 5 - 7

h. black, yellow fuselage w/black int., multicolored tampo w/"Dewalt 17" & race decals, Thailand, #2 in NASCAR Blimp series (2001) 5 - 7

i. orange; orange, yellow & white fuselage; orange tail & int.; multicolored tampo w/race decals on fuselage & #32 car inside fuselage; Thailand; #3 in NASCAR Blimp series (2001) 5 - 7

j. orange; dk. blue int. w/multicolored tampo w/Citgo logo, "99," Jeff Burton's signature & race decals; Thailand; #4 in NASCAR Blimp series (2001) 5 - 7

k. orange, tan fuselage, orange tail, black int. w/orange & white Hot Wheels logo, #210 (2001) 2 - 3

Blimp-l

l. red, red fuselage, white & black tampo with "Saturn" on sides & fuselage. Ltd ed on Saturn Starship blistercard & given at car shows (2002) 8 - 10

m. gray; dk. red fuselage; blue, white, red & black tampo w/"HWSL Hot Wheels Sports League" on sides,"Touchdown" inside blimp; Thailand. Sports 5-pack (2002) 3 - NA

3765-a

Bulldozer 3765 - 69mm - 1992

This Malaysia-made model has a yellow plastic chassis & blade, metal body, black plastic tracks, black interior and small black wheels.

a. yellow, #146 $3 - 5

5675-a

Chevy Lumina 5675 - 75mm - 1992

This Malaysia-made all-purpose van has a black plastic base, clear windows with black plastic frame, tan interior and bw.

Similar casting: 12352 Lumina Minivan

a. red; yellow, blue & pink striping tampo on sides; #126 $25 - 30

a2. same as a, smaller bw, #126 6 - 8

a3. same as a2, black int., #126 (1994) 20 -25

Flashfire® 3156 - 73mm - 1992

This futuristic sports car has a black plastic chassis, red plastic interior, spoiler & side

Values are shown in U.S. dollars, first price is for mint, second is for mint packaged vehicles only. See pages 15-16 for grading guide to determine value for cars in lesser conditions.

1992

3156-a

grilles, yellow-tinted dome, exposed chrome plastic engine, & hoc. Malaysia.

a. black; pink, yellow & green striping tampo on sides; #140 $16 - 20
a2. same as a, uh, #140 6 - 8
a3. same as a, dw3, #140 (1996) 2 - 4
a4. same as a, sp5, #140 (1997) 12 - 15
a5. same as a, ho5, #140 (1997) 10 - 12
a6. same as a, ho5, Thailand, #802 (1998) 2 - 4

Flashfire-b

b. no #; pink; magenta, turquoise & yellow stripes on sides; pink base; blue plastic int., spoiler & side grills; only w/Heroes on Hot Wheels video tapes (1993), w/video 8 - NA
c. no #; pink; blue, black & green tampo on sides; gray int., side grills & spoiler; clear dome; pink base; uh; 25th Anniv. Dream Car 5-pack only (1993) 6 - NA

13271-d

d. 13271; purple; thin yellow lines all over body; yellow side pipes, wing & int.; yellow plastic dome w/dk. red Hot Wheels logo on top; black plastic base; uh; #4 of Krackle Car Series; #284 (1995) 4 - 6
d2. same as d, sp5, #284 (1996) 2 - 4
d3. same as d, orange dome & wing, #284 (1996) 22 - 25

Flashfire-e

e. no #, green, red int., red-tinted dome, chrome engine, black tampo, green Hot Wheels logo on top of dome, uhgd, Track System Gift Pack only (1995) 3 - NA
e2. same as e, sp5g (1995) 2 - NA
e3. same as e, sp3g (1995) 2 - NA
e4. same as e, yellow dome, yellow plastic on sides, Intl. line only (1995) 15 - NA
e5. same as e, sp5gd (1997) 2 - NA

Flashfire-f

f. mtlfk gold; tan plastic base; tinted dome; black spoiler & plastic design on sides; pink, yellow & lt. green tampo w/"Turbo" on sides; ho5; Thailand; #802 (1998) 2 - 4

Flashfire-g

g. mtlfk orange; black chassis; gold int., spoiler & sides; tinted dome; black, gold, white & dk. red tampo on sides & top; sp3gd; Thailand; Alien Attack 5-pack (1999) 2 - NA

Flashfire-h

h. mtlfk blue; white int.; clear dome; red, white & yellow tampo w/Hot Wheels logo, "KS" & race decals on sides, "Hot Wheels 1" on nose; sp5; Thailand; Race Team III 5-pack (1999) 2 - NA

Flashfire-i

i. white; black chassis; gray sides, interior & wing; clear dome; black, yellow & light green tampo w/"934" & "Inter Galatic Rider" on sides; sp3; Thailand; #177 (2000) 2 - 3
i2. same as i, sp5, #177 (2000)
j. black; orange int., sides & spoiler; tinted dome; orange & gray tampo on sides & top w/"Anders" in front; lwch; #165 (2001) 2 - 3
j2. same as j, ho5, #165 (2001) 2 - 4
k. orange; black chassis; red int., sides & spoiler; purple-tinted dome; blue, red & white tampo on sides; sp5. Super Soakin' playset (2002) 5 - NA

3782-a

Hiway Hauler 3782 - 80mm - 1992

A different casting than the original Hiway Hauler, this model has a chrome plastic chassis, blacked-out windows, white plastic box, six bw, and was made in Malaysia.

a. red; white box w/blue, yellow & red tampo w/"Kool-Aid Wacky Warehouse" on sides; #142 $12 - 15

3782-a2

a2. same as a, slightly different design, #142 (1993) 12 - 15

4642-b

b. 4642; purple; same as a; red & yellow Hot Wheels logo; purple, blue, green & black "Delivery" on sides of box; #238 (1994) 10 - 12
b2. 4642, purple, same as b, red Hot Wheels logo on front license plate, #238 (1995) 25 - 30

Hiway Hauler-c

c. no #; red; white box w/"Dinty Moore" & can of Dinty Moore Beef Stew on sides; chrome plastic base; blacked-out windows; bw. Hormel give-away, never in bp (1994) 4 - NA

13487-d

d. 13487; yellow; white box w/red Hot Wheels logo; red, yellow & black McDonald's Happy Meal tampo on box. Blistercard reads, "Commemorating 5 Years of Mattel & McDonald's Happy Meal Promotions 1991-1995." Limited to 7000 (1995) 20 - 25

Hiway Hauler-e

e. no #, white, white box w/red & blue stripes, McKee logo on sides, Little Debbie Snacks logo on sides & back. Only given away or sold in 3-pack by Little Debbie Bakery (1995) 6 - NA

13771-f

f. 13771; red; white box w/red & yellow Hot Wheels logo, "Newsletter," "Delivery" & a car in red, yellow & blue on sides; gyg. Limited to 7000, #9 (1995) 30 - 35

Hiway Hauler-g

g. blue; white box w/Spam & Spam Lite can on sides. Hormel only, in baggies (1995) 4 - NA

14408-h

h. 14408; black; white box w/"Kool-Aid Soft Drinks Brand" & "Wacky Warehouse 5 Year Celebration Limited Edition" in black, blue & red on sides; chromed windows; iwc; limited to 8000 (1995) 15 - 20

Hiway Hauler-i

i. red, white box w/red & black H.E.B. logo on sides, 2-pack by H.E.B. stores only, for 90-year anniv. (1995) 8 - 10

13322-j

j. 13322, mtlc green, white box w/multi-colored photo of Statue of Liberty & New York City skyline, sp7, #4 of Photo Finish Series, #335 (1995) 8 - 10

14989-k

k. red; white box w/red "Lucky," black "The Low Price Leader Every Day," green, red, orange & black fruits & vegetables on sides; sp7. Lucky Supermarkets 2-pack only (1995) 8 - 10

14988-l

l. 14988; black; white box w/red & black tampo w/90th anniversary logo & "Davis Printing Quality Printing Since 1906" on sides; chrome windows; sp5 (1996) 12 - 15

14904-m

m. 14904; gold-plated; black box w/1968 Hot Wheels & Mattel logos on one side & 1995 Hot Wheels & Mattel logos on other; black-tinted windows; pcgd; limited to 8000 (1996) 15 - 20

14989-n

n. 14989; black; white box w/black & red "Feed The Children," blue Feed the Children logo & white "Feed The Children" on sides of cab; pc. Limited run of 10,000 (1996) 12 - 15

3782-o

o. white; white box w/red & blue patriotic design & "H.E.B. Serving More Texans Better Every Day" on box; "H.E.B." on cab; dk.-tinted windows; sp5; China; H.E.B. 2-pack only (1996) 6 - 8
p. white; white box w/brown, black, green & orange steak & seafood

Hiway Hauler-p

design; red "Lucky" on box; dk.-tinted windows; sp5; China; Lucky stores 2-pack only (1996) 5 - 7

3728-q

q. red, white box w/red "Woolworth," dk.-tinted windows, sp5, China, Woolworth 2-pack (1996) 5 - 7

Hiway Hauler-r

r. white, white box w/red "Vons" & black "Produce," dk.-tinted windows, sp5, China, Vons 2-pack only (1996) 5 - 7

3782-s

s. white, white box w/"Hughes Family Market" & blue stripes, dk.-tinted windows, sp5, China, Hughes 2-pack only (1996) 5 - 7

3782-t

t. red; yellow box w/black & orange ShopRite logo & black "ShopRite always save" on sides; white "ShopRite" on cab; dk.-tinted windows; sp5; China; ShopRite 2-pack only (1996) 12 - 15

3782-u

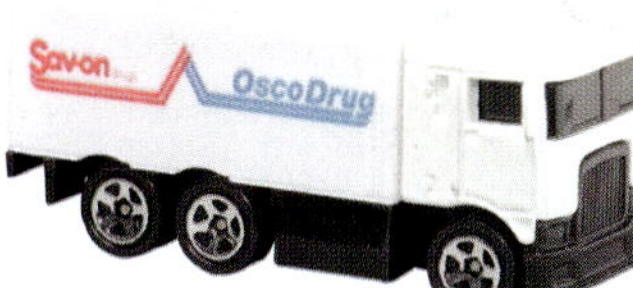

u. white; white box w/pink "Sav-on Drugs" & lt. blue "Osco Drug"; dk.-tinted windows; sp5; China; Osco Drug & Sav-on Drugs 2-pack only (1996) 5 - 7

v. 16898; mtlfk blue; white box w/"Van de Kamp's," "Fish-O-Saurs" & fish sticker; dk.-tinted windows; sp5; China. Van de Kamp's offer on fish sticks pkg only (1997) 5 - 7

16898-v

Hiway Hauler-w

w. white; white box w/"Albertson's" & logo on sides; white cab; blue-tinted windows; sp5. Albertson's Supermarkets 2-pack only 4 - 6

Hiway Hauler-x

x. lt. blue; white box w/multi-colored tampo on sides: Count Chocula & Reese's Peanut Butter Puffs logos on one side, Cookie Crisp & Cocoa Puffs on other; blacked-out windows; sp5; China; General Mills mail-in (1997) 6 - NA

Hiway Hauler-y

y. white; white box w/red, lt. blue & dk. blue tampo w/Kroger logo & "Quality Guaranteed" on sides; dk.-blue-tinted windows; sp5; China; Kroger Supermarket 2-pack only (1997) 4 - 6

Hiway Hauler-z

z. red; white box w/black & red tampo w/Ralphs logo & "Lower Prices Higher Standards" on sides; blacked-out windows; sp5; China; Ralphs Supermarket 2-pack only (1997) 4 - 6

aa. blue; white box w/blue & red tampo w/Rite Aid logo & "For your life, Rite Aids got it" on sides; blacked-out windows; sp5; China; Rite Aid 2-pack only (1998) 4 - 6

ab. white; white box with red tampo with"the Spirit of H.E.B." on box, H.E.B. logo on cab; blacked-out windows; China; H.E.B. Supermarket 2-pack only (1998) 4 - 6

Hiway Hauler-ac

ac. blue; blue box w/lt. blue & white tampo w/"Yamahauler Racing Team" on sides; gych; China. Helpful Hauler, limited to 10,000 (1998) 12 - 15

Hiway Hauler-ad

ad. red; white box w/yellow, blue, black, red & dk. red tampo w/"H.E.B. 1905-2000," "95th Anniversary Celebration" & "Go Home a Hero" on sides; sp5; H.E.B. Supermarkets 2-pack only (2000) 4 - 6

Hiway Hauler-ae

ae. dk. green; yellow box w/green & white tampo w/"Athletics," "Baseball A's Style" & Mr. Peanut on sides, "A's" & Mr. Peanut in back, "Champions" on sides of cab; sp5. Issued in box by Oakland A's baseball team (2001) 10 - 15

af. red, white box w/"Cub Foods" in red on sides, pr5s, Cub Stores 2-pack (2001) 4 - 6

0773-a

Hummer 0773 - 63mm - 1992

This "Hummvee" military vehicle has a black plastic chassis, metal body with a top-mounted tan plastic gun turret, blacked-out windows, no interior, ct; made in Malaysia.

a. tan; brown, white & black camo tampo on sides & hood; #188 $8 - 10

0773-a2

a2. lt. brown; dk. brown, orange & black camouflage tampo on sides & hood; #188 (1993) 6 - 8

a3. tan, same as a2, black metal base & plastic body, no tampo on hood, #188 (1995) 4 - 6

a4. same as a3, black plastic chassis & body, no tampo on hood, Russell Stover 2-pack only (1995) 8 - 10

a5. same as a3, dw3ct, no gun on roof, #188 (1996) 3 - 5

15238-b

b. 15238; hot pink; yellow, lt. green & dark red flower design w/"Love" & Hot Wheels logo on sides, "Love" & "Peace" on roof; dark green windows; purple base; ct; #1 in Mod Bod Series; #396 (1996) 6 - 8

b2. same as b, dw3ct 20 - 25

Hummer-c

c. 16906; blue; metal base; white, red & yellow racing tampo w/racing decals & "1" on sides, 2 Hot Wheels logos & "1" on roof; grayed out windows; dw3ct; #1 in Race Team Series III; #533 (1997) 4 - 6

c2. same as c, silver base, #533 (1997) 4 - 6

Hummer-d

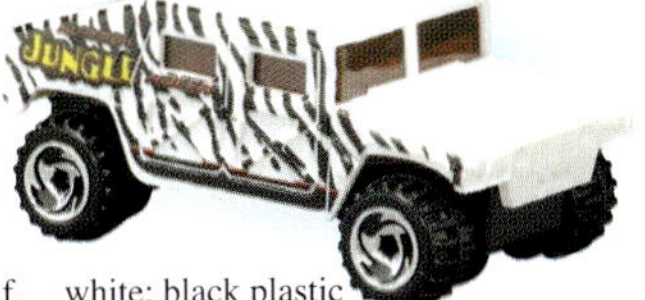

d. 16814; dk. blue; red, white & blue tampo w/U.S. flag on sides & roof, "405" on sides, "U.S. Charities Racing Team" on hood; rrch w/knobby tires. Ltd ed 10,000 for U.S. Charities Racing Team (1997) 25 - 30

e. 0773; white; blue, gold & red tampo w/"Police," "17," "Anti Drug Unit" & logo on sides; dw3ct; #188 (1997) 3 - 5

e2. same as e, silver base, #188 (1997) 3 - 5

Hummer-f

f. white; black plastic base; red-tinted windows; black, red & yellow zebra stripe tampo w/"Hummer Racer" & "Jungle" on sides; dw3ct; Malaysia; #858 (1998) 2 - 3

Hummer-g

g. aqua; gray plastic windows; gray, black & yellow tampo w/"Hummer" on sides, "Humvee," "Man" & "B" on top; dw3ct; #1080 (1999) 2 - 3

h. white, black chassis, red-tinted int. & windows, dw3ct, Malaysia. Only in Mexico (2000) 12 - 15

i. yellow; black chassis; gray windows; black & red tampo w/"Camron" on sides & roof, "Rescue" on sides, "012" on roof; dw3ct; Malaysia; #162 (2001) 2 - 3

j. lt. brown; black chassis; gray windows; dk. green & brown camouflage; white, blue & orange tampo w/"USMC" on sides, "Padres SD" & Union 76 service station logo on top; ort, Malaysia. Ltd ed for San Diego Padres baseball team only (2002) 8 - 10

2074-a

Oshkosh Cement Mixer Truck 2074 - 80mm - 1992

This Malaysia-made model has a blue plastic base, white plastic body, red plastic drum, and bw.

Values are shown in U.S. dollars, first price is for mint, second is for mint packaged vehicles only. See pages 15-16 for grading guide to determine value for cars in lesser conditions.

a. white, #144 $4 - 8
b. 12362, yellow, black drum, red Hot Wheels logo on white rectangle in front, yellow plastic base, bw, #269 (1995) 4 - 8

13262-b2

b2. same as b, sp5, #269 (1995) 2 - 6
b3. same as b, sp7, #269 (1996) 4 - 8
b4. same as b, sp3, #269 (1996) 2 - 4
b5. same as b, dw3, #269 (1997) 2 - 4
b6. same as b, revised casting w/smaller diamond plate around cab & smooth front bumper, sp7 (1997) 2 - 4
b7. same as b6, black plastic base, Toys "R" Us 10-pack (1997) 4 - NA

Oshkosh Cement Mixer-c

c. orange; gray chassis & int.; black drum; white, yellow & red tampo w/"Cement," "53," & logo on drum; sp5; Road Repair 5-pack only (1998) 2 - NA
d. lime yellow, black plastic base & drum, yellow & lt. green tampo on sides of drum, Oshkosh Concrete Mixer, #863 (1998) 2 - 3
e. orange, same as c, black plastic base, orange fenders & int., red & white tampo w/"49" & City of Hot Wheels logo on drum, sp5, European only (1998) 2 - 4

Oshkosh Cement Mixer-f

f. mtlfk dk. red; black base, cab & drum; mtlfk dk. red interior; dw3; #1011 (1999) 2 - 3
g. black; green chassis, int. & drum w/black & yellow tampo & "Cement Mixer" on drum; ho5; Virtual Collection; #123 (2000) 2 - 3
h. yellow w/black chassis & drum; gray fenders & int.; yellow tampo w/"Constructo Concrete 24 Hour Service," "14" & "Satellite Dispatched" on drum; sp3; Malaysia; #134 (2001) 2 - 3

2073-a

Recycling (Garbage) Truck 2073 - 80mm - 1992
This garbage truck has a black plastic chassis, metal cab with orange plastic dumper & container, blacked-out windows, no interior, bw, and was made in Malaysia.
a. orange, "Recycler," in turquoise & pink on sides, #143 $4 - 8
a2. orange, same as a, sp7, #143 4 - 6
a3. same as a, dw3, Construction Crew 5-pack only 2 - NA

Recycling Truck-b

b. lt. green; white plastic chassis; lt. green dumper & container w/white stripe, "Recycling" in red, "Dept. of Sanitation," "45" & logo in red, white & black on sides; sp7; #143 (1997) 4 - 6
b2. same as b, no black outline, sp7, #143 (1997) 2 - 4
b3. same as b2, dw3, #143 (1997) 2 - 4

Recycling Truck-c

c. lime yellow; black plastic chassis & windows; red, black, yellow & white tampo w/"Caution Biohazard Waste," logo & "Max Load 8,000 Lbs." on sides; dw3; #3 in Biohazard series; #719 (1998) 2 - 3

Recycling Truck-d

d. green; white container; lt. green, black & blue tampo w/"Metro Recycle" on sides of container; ho5; City Center 5-pack only (1999) 2 - NA
e. mtlfk black; gray plastic chassis; orange, gray, black & white tampo w/brick wall & garbage cans on sides; dw3; Virtual Collection; #143 (2000) 2 - 3

Recycling Truck-f

f. white; gold chrome chassis & windows; black scoop; orange, red & black tampo w/"Hot Wheel Recycler" & "Stand Clear" on sides, Final Run logo on roof, "Final Run" in back; rrch; #8 in Final Run series (2001) 7 - 11

3164-a

Shock Factor 3164 - 68mm - 1992
This Malaysia-made off-road-racing sprint buggy has a metal chassis, pink plastic interior, driver & sides, rear spoiler, and ct.
a. black; yellow, red & blue tampo w/"7" on sides, "7" & racing decals on spoiler; pink may vary; #141 $10 - 12

Shock Factor-b

a2. black, same as a, red replaces pink on sides, #141 (1995) 55 - 60
b. red; white "FX" & blue & white eye on sides; Nintendo logo on wing; clear windshield; red int.; ct. Cereal give-away only (1994) 12 - NA

Shock Factor-c

c. no #; lt. green; blue metal base; black-tinted windshield & black int.; dk. blue, lt. blue & white wave tampo on sides & rear wing; ct. Toy Story pack only, w/disc (1996) 15 - NA

Shock Factor-c2

c2. same as c, sp5, Toy Story Action Pack (1999) 8 - NA
d. yellow; blue sides & int.; black, red & white tampo w/"5" on sides, "Shock Factor Racing" on wing; bw; China; #700 (1998) 2 - 4

Shock Factor-e

e. yellow; black int. & driver; orange, black & gray tampo w/"2" & race decals on sides, "2" & "Goodyear" on wing; bw. Off-Road Racing 4-pack (1998) 4 - NA

Shock Factor-f

f. black; black int.; gold & silver tampo w/"Mystery Car" on sides, "Q2" on spoiler; bw; #2 in 1999 Mystery Cars; China (1999) 6 - NA

Shock Factor-g

g. yellow, purple int., large Hot Wheels logo on wing. In Toy Story game or K•B Toys (1999) 6 - NA
h. red; black int. & engine; white, gray & black tampo w/"Tyco RC" on wing; dw3ct; Toys "R" Us Timeless Toys II 4-pack (2000) 6 - NA
i. fluor. lime yellow; black int. & engine; black, gray & gold tampo on sides, roof & wing; dw3ct; #121; Malaysia (2002) 2 - 3

2076-a

Tank Truck 2076 - 80mm - 1992
This gas truck has a red plastic chassis, red metal cab, chrome plastic tank, chromed windows, bw, and was made in Malaysia.
a. red; "Unocal" in blue, "76" logo on tank sides; #147 $10 - 12
a2. same as a, sp7, #147 (1995) 6 - 8

Tank Truck-b

b. no #; orange; gray plastic tank; orange, white & dk. blue Gulf logo on sides; chromed windows; black plastic base; bw. Gulf Service Stations in baggies only (1994) 4 - NA

Tank Truck-c

c. no #, orange, same as a, dk. blue "Unocal" & dk. blue "76" in orange circle on tank. Union stations in baggie only (1994) 4 - NA

Tank Truck-d

d. red; white tank; red plastic base; yellow, green & black tampo w/blue "Toxic Waste" on tank sides. Construction Crew 5-pack only (1995) 6 - NA

13320-e

e. 13320, lt. blue, white tank w/multicolored photo of Mt. Rushmore, sp7. #3 in Photo Finish Series, #333 (1995) 4 - 6

Tank Truck-f

f. no #, orange, same as b, orange rectangle & blue & gray "76" in orange ball on sides. Union 76 Stations only, baggie only (1995) 3 - NA
g. orange, same as a, sp7, #147 (1996) 3 - 5
g2. same as h, dw3, #147 (1996) 3 - 5
h. 16912, mtlfk dk. red, chrome base & windows, dk. purple tank, yellow to orange flames w/orange outline on tank, sp7, #3 in Heat Fleet series, #539 (1997) 4 - 8
h2. same as h, sp5 3 - 5
h3. same as h, dw3 2 - 4
h4. same as h, black chassis, ho5, Malaysia, #864 (1998) 2 - 3

Tank Truck-i

i. white; black tank; orange plastic chassis, blacked-out windows, yellow, white, black & red tampo w/"Water Dust Control" on tank, "Road Dept.," logo on doors; sp5; #147 (1997) 2 - 4

Values are shown in U.S. dollars, first price is for mint, second is for mint packaged vehicles only. See pages 15-16 for grading guide to determine value for cars in lesser conditions.

i2. same as i, sp3, #147 (1998) 2 - 4
j. black; blue base; chrome tank & windows; white, orange & dk. blue tampo on sides of cab; orange & dk. blue stripe w/"Trans H2O Water Systems" on sides of tank; ho5; #864 (1998) 2 - NA

Tank Truck-k

k. mtlfk gold; gray plastic chassis; gold chrome tank; orange, black & white tampo w/Final Run logo on hood, "Final Run Fluid Technologies Transport" on sides, pinstripes on door; rrgd; #11 in 1999 Final Run series (1999) 5 - 7

2075-a

Tractor 2075 - 79mm - 1992
This Malaysia-made construction tractor has a yellow plastic base, roof & fenders, metal body & blade, yellow interior, ct in front, and ctly in back.
a. yellow, #145 $12 - 15

2075-b

b. red, ct in front, ctl in back, #145 4 - 6
b2. same as b, dw3ct in front, ctly in back, #145 (1996) 2 - 4

Tractor-c

c. yellow; same as a; green base, int., engine & scoop; ctly in back, dw3cty in front 12 - 15
c2. same as c, shorter stack on hood, #145 (1997) 2 - 4

Tractor-d

d. yellow, same as c; blue base & int.; ctl in back, dw3ct in front. Toys "R" Us 10-pack only 8 - NA

Tractor-e

e. black, same as c, red base & int., black plastic roof & arms, ctl in back, dw3ct in front 12 - 15

f. unpainted, unpainted int., blue roof & arms, ctly in back, dw3cty in front, 1998 Hot Wheels Convention, #145 (1998) 70 - 85

Tractor-g

g. gray, gray int., black roof & arms, ctl in back, dw3ct in front, #795 (1999) 2 - 3
h. black; blue tracks; purple nose; white, lt. blue & red tampo w/"Avalanche Resort" & "Search & Rescue" on sides; Thailand; Snow Patrol 5-pack (2000) 2 - NA
i. fluor. lime green, black plastic roof & arms, dw3ct, Virtual Collection, #103 (2000) 2 - 3

1993

Mattel introduced three new series. The most popular among collectors is the 25th Anniversary collectors' series which replicates eight cars from the first three years. Each comes with a plastic button in a replica of the 1968 blisterpack. The cars have red-stripe tires and Spectraflame paint. The blistercards carry the 25th Anniversary logo in the upper left hand corner. The logo is also embossed into the underside of the base. These cars were released throughout the year in one color per car per month. Other than Red Baron and Paddy Wagon, there are eleven distinct colors per car on a blistercard and one totally different series of colors in an eight-pack. These are the first cars to be produced in so many different colors in the same year since 1973. The second series is Tattoo Machines. These have unusual tampos and the package contains a packet of corresponding tattoos for kids. There are twelve models in the series and all were made in China.

Third is Revealers, with thirty-six different vehicles. Each comes on a separate blistercard and is wrapped in a rice-paper bag which dissolves in water. These bags are numbered one through twelve. Each bag contains one of three different-colored vehicles. Plus one out of seventy-two has a blue token which can be redeemed for a set of ten completely different vehicles. Approximately one thousand bags contain a gold token which wins the lucky buyer a free Hot Wheels bike and vacuum-metallized Lamborghini Countach.

3021-a

'93 Camaro 3021 - 75mm - 1993
a. chrome; red, white & yellow Hot Wheels logo on sides; "New York Toy Fair 1993" in yellow, orange & black on hood; 25th Anniv. logo on rear window $150 - NA

3021-b

b. purple, "Camaro" in yellow & orange on sides, #202 6 - 8
b2. same as b, white int., #202 (1994) 4 - 6
b3. purple, same as b2, clear windows, #202 8 - 12
c. Day-Glo green; yellow, pink & blue tampo on sides; tan int.; gray-tinted

3021-c

windows w/white "Revealers" on windshield; uh. Malaysia; Revealers 10-pack only 8 - NA
d. no #, vacuum-metallized silver, chrome-plated plastic base, red int., blacked-out windows, white 25th Anniv. logo on rear window, 25th Anniversary Chevy 5-pack only (1993) 6 - NA
e. 11243; mtlfk blue; white on sides; red & yellow Hot Wheels logo, red & black "1," black 25th Anniv. logo on sides; 2 red & yellow logos on top of wing; red Chevy logos on roof & hood; white "Jack Baldwin" twice on roof; red & white Hot Wheels logo on hood; clear windows w/white "Camaro" on windshield; white int.; bw; #242 (1994) 6 - 8
e2. same as e, uh, #242 (1994) 150 - 175

11253-e3

e3. dk. blue, same as e, #242 (1994) 20 - 35
e4. dk. blue, same as e2, #242 (1994) 110 - 150

13583-e5

e5. 13583, same as e, uhgd, #262 (1994) 4 - 6

3021-e6

e6. mtlfk blue, same as e, red "1", no 25th Anniv. logo on sides, uh, FAO Schwarz History of Hot Wheels 8-pack (1995) 8 - NA
e7. mtlfk blue, same as e6, bw, FAO Schwarz History of Hot Wheels 8-pack (1995) 8 - NA

'93 Camaro-e8

e8. dk. blue, same as e, no Jack Baldwin on roof, pc, Avon kit only (1996) 5 - NA
e9. same as e8, tw, Avon kit only (1996) 5 - NA

11837-f

f. 11837, gold-plated, same as d, red rtgd in front, rtgd in back, black int., 25th Anniv. logo on blistercard, commemorative ed, limited to 7000 (1994) 40 - 45
g. 12355, red, no tampo, white int., clear windows, uh, #262 (1993) 8 - 10
g2. same as g, bw, #262 12 - 15
g3. same as g, tan int., #262 (1995) 8 - 12
g4. same as g3, sp5, #262 (1995) 4 - 6
g5. same as g3, gray plastic base, #262 (1995) 25 - 30
g6. same as g3, sp7, #262 (1995) 40 - 55

'93 Camaro-h

h. no #; mtlfk blue; yellow "Spam" & red & white "37" on sides & hood; "Spam" twice on wing; clear windows; red int.; bw. Promo model from Spam, baggie only (1994) 35 - NA

'93 Camaro-i

i. no #; dk. mtlc red; "World Cup USA 94" & white Hot Wheels logo on sides; brown, black, blue & white World Cup mascot kicking black & white soccer ball on hood; clear windows; white int.; uh. World Cup 5-pack only (1994) 5 - NA

13250-j

j. 13250; pink; red & yellow Hot Wheels logo, white stripe & "1" on sides; "Barbie" & "35th Anniversary" on hood; "Hot Wheels" & 2 Hot Wheels logos on rear spoiler; clear windows; white int.; gych. Commemorated 35th Anniv. of Barbie dolls, limited to 7000 (1995) 85 - 100

13250-j2

j2. mtlfk pink, same as j, limited to 8000 cars (1995) 45 - 50

14011-k

k. 14011; blue; orange, white & dk. green tampo w/"C. Rex Racer" on sides, "Kraft Cheese & Macaroni Treasures" on hood, "C. Rex Racer" & stripes on roof; gray plastic base; white int.; clear windows; pc5. Kraft give-away, "C. Rex Racer" figure & free pog as part of card (1995) 25 - 30
k2. same as k, red replaces green in tampo. Kraft give-away w/pog as part of card (1995) 8 - 10
l. white, clear plastic windows, dk. blue int., blue Hot Wheels logo on rear bumper, sp5. Then & Now 8-pack (1995) 3 - NA

'93 Camaro-m

m. dk. blue; white stars all over; "USA" & five Olympic circles in red, green, yellow, black & blue on sides; red int.; clear windows; pcgd. American Victory Olympic 3-pack only (1996) 6 - NA
n. 15776, mtlfk black, black base, tan int., clear windows, sp5, #505 (1996) 6 - 8
n2. same as n, lwch, #505 (1997) 2 - 4
n3. same as n, dw3, #505 (1997) 3 - 6

Values are shown in U.S. dollars, first price is for mint, second is for mint packaged vehicles only. See pages 15-16 for grading guide to determine value for cars in lesser conditions.

'93 Camaro-n4

n4. same as n, sp7bk w/Goodyear tires, Camaro 5-pack only (1997) 2 - NA

'93 Camaro-o

o. no #, dk. blue, white tampo of bubbles & red "Chuck E. Cheese" on sides, tinted windows, red int. & roll cage, sp5. Ltd for Chuck E. Cheese Pizza (1996) 5 - 7

'93 Camaro-p

p. no #; orange; black on sides; red & black tampo w/"1," "Duracell" & Hot Wheels logo on sides; "Duracell," battery & "Goodyear" on hood; Chevy logo on roof; "Duracell" on rear wing. Baggie only, mail-in (1996) 40 - NA

'93 Camaro-q

q. no #; dk. blue; yellow top & trim; red, white, yellow & black tampo w/"3," Sunoco logo, racing decals on sides & hood, "Camaro" on windshield, Chevy logo & "Ron Fellows" on roof, "AER Mfg." on spoiler; gray int.; lwy. 30th Anniv. of Camaro Collectible line gift pack only (1997) 12 - NA

'93 Camaro-r

r. yellow, black int., tinted windows, red flames on sides, lt. brown Cheerio & "1" in purple on sides & hood, "Cheerios" in black & 2 Hot Wheels logos on trunk, sp5. General Mills mail-in (1997) 5 - NA

'93 Camaro-s

s. lt. green, tinted windows, white int., black & lighter green tampo on sides, sp3, #2 in Tattoo Machines, #686 (1998) 2 - 5

'93 Camaro-t

t. gray; black chassis; gold, orange, black & white tampo w/Final Run logo on hood & sides, "Final Run" & logo in back; rrgy w/"Final Run" on sides; #8 in 1999 Final Run Series (1999) 5 - 7

Ammo 3527 - 76mm - 1993 (Tattoo Machines)
This army off-road attack vehicle has a black metal base, two black plastic rockets mounted in back, black plastic machine

3527-a

guns on the sides & sticking through the hood, a black plastic interior, metallic blue windshield, ctsb, and was made in China.
Similar casting: 5025 Sting Rod (1988)
a. gray; red, yellow, green & black tampo w/guns & bullets all over $5 - 7

10159-a

Auto Palace/AC Delco 10159 - 76mm - 1993
This Pontiac Stocker has a black plastic base, clear windows, gray interior and roll bars, pcb, and was made in China.
Similar castings: 2628 #42 Mello Yello (1992), 2623 #43 STP (1992), 2630 #2 Pontiac Excitement (1993), 12873 Pontiac Stocker (1995)
a. blue; white hood & back; "9," "Auto Palace" & racing decals on sides; "Auto Palace The Automotive Super Store" & winner's flag on hood; "9" on roof $8 - 10

5250-a

Avus Quattro 5260 - 75mm - 1993
Based on the German car of the same name, this Malaysia-made model has a black plastic base, clear windows, red interior, and uh.
a. metalflake gray, #208 $3 - 6
a2. same as a, sp5, #208 (1995) 2 - 4
a3. same as a, bw, Canada only (1996) 3 - 5

13868-b

b. 13868, red, same as a, tan int., red & black tampo on windows, sp5, #453 (1996) 2 - 4
b2. same as b, sp7, #453 (1996) 2 - 4
b3. same as b, dw3, #453 (1997) 2 - 4

Avus Quattro-c

c. 16686, mtlfk gold, tan int., tinted dome, "Avus" in black on sides, dw3, #11 in Treasure Hunt series, #588 (1997) 15 - 20
d. metalflake gray, same as a, "Avus" in red on sides, sp7, Toys "R" Us set only (1997) 5 - NA

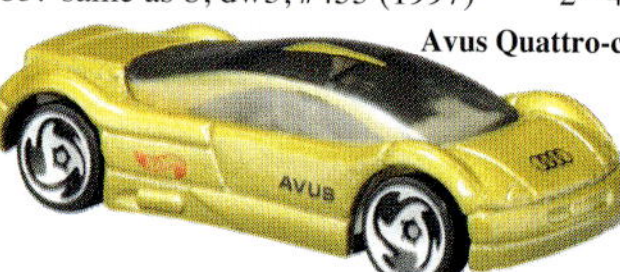
Avus Quattro-e

e. black; tinted dome outlined in gold; tan int.; white, purple & yellow tampo with "Banknote," "50" & "Funfzig Deutsche Mark" on sides; lwgd; Thailand. #3 in Dash 4 Cash series, #723 (1998) 2 - 3
f. unpainted, black interior, green-tinted & red dome, sp5. #3 in Dash 4 Cash Series, 1998 Hot Wheels Convention, #723 (1998) 60 - 70

Avus Quattro-g

g. black, dk. red base, white int., clear dome, mtlfk red spotting tampo, lwgd. #4 in Tech Tones series, Malaysia, #748 (1999) 2 - 3

Avus Quattro-h

h. chrome, black base, mtlfk gray tampo, sp5, Malaysia, #1096 (1999) 2 - 3
i. mtlfk dk. purple; tan int.; tinted dome; red, black & white tampo w/"Avus" on sides; pr5s; Malaysia; #104 (2001) 2 - 3

5414-a

Beatnik Bandit 5414 - 59mm - 1993
This Chinese-made model is based on the show car designed and built by Ed "Big Daddy" Roth. It has a metal chassis, exposed metal engine, white plastic interior, blue-tinted plastic dome roof and nrl. The Hot Wheels logo and "25th Anniversary" are etched on the base.
Similar casting: 6217 Beatnik Bandit (1968)
a. metallic light blue $3 - 5
b. metallic magenta 3 - 5
c. metallic orange 3 - 5
d. metallic green 3 - 5
e. metallic olive 3 - 5
f. metallic red 3 - 5
g. metallic brown 3 - 5
h. metallic gold 3 - 5
i. metallic lavender 3 - 5
j. metallic lime 3 - 5
k. metallic purple 3 - 5
l. metallic aqua, Toys "R" Us 8-pack only 2 - NA

Beatnik Bandit-m

m. metalflake purple, gold-plated engine, white int., clear plastic dome, black steering wheel, white Hot Wheels logo in back, rsw, gold hubs. 1 of 16 FAO Schwarz Gold Series Collection, limited to 3000 (1994) 6 - NA
n. metalflake magenta 3 - 5
o. white 3 - 5
p. metalflake black 3 - 5
q. metalflake yellow 3 - 5
r. metalflake blue 3 - 5
s. burnt orange 3 - 5
t. metalflake turquoise 3 - 5
u. metalflake silver 3 - 5
v. metalflake light green 3 - 5
w. metalflake burgundy 3 - 5
x. metalflake aqua 3 - 5

11089-a

Buick Wildcat 11089 - 75mm - 1993
This futuristic model has a gray plastic base, black hood dome and engine with a black vent on each side and bw; Malaysia.
a. red, Demolition Man series only, w/Cryo-Cube $4 - 6
a2. 8366, same as a, black base, no black vent, sp7, #597 (1997) 2 - 6
a3. same as a2, sp3, #597 (1998) 2 - 4

16683-b

b. 16683, mtlfk silver, gray plastic base, blacked-out dome, thick red stripes on hood & rear, sp3. #9 in 1997 Treasure Hunt series, #586 (1997) 20 - 22

Buick Wildcat-c

c. mtlc green, gray base, chrome plastic engine, sp3, #597 (1997) 2 - 4
c2. same as c, gray plastic engine 2 - 4

Buick Wildcat-d

d. same as c, "Wildcat" in brown on sides, 2-pack (1998) 2 - 3

Buick Wildcat-e

e. black, lt. green chassis, gray dome, chrome engine, mtlfk green tampo design, sp3. #1 in Tech Tones series, #745 (1998) 2 - 3

Buick Wildcat-f

f. black, black plastic base & window, gold & silver tampo w/"Q3" on sides & nose, "Mystery Car" behind rear engine. In baggie, #3 Mystery Car (1999) 5 - NA
g. lt. green; black chassis & dome; chrome engine; black, yellow & white tampo design on sides; sp3; Thailand; #183 (2000) 2 - 3
h. mtlfk purple, black chassis & dome, chrome engine, black & silver tampo on sides, sp3, China, #138 (2002) 2 - 3

3502-a

Bus Boys 3502 - 82mm - 1993 (Tattoo Machines)
This Chinese-made concept city bus has a plastic body, metal chassis, unpainted metal headlights sticking through the body, clear plastic windows, chrome plastic interior & bw.
Similar casting: 3256 Rapid Transit (1982)
a. yellow; "Cool" in purple, orange & turquoise all over $10 - 12
b. white, same as a 5 - 7

11098-a

Chevrolet ACC Camaro 11090 - 78mm - 1993
This futuristic Camaro has a black plastic chassis, blacked-out windows, black plastic interior and pc; Malaysia.
a. red, black roof & headlights, Demolition Man series only, w/Cryo-Cube $6 - 8

Values are shown in U.S. dollars, first price is for mint, second is for mint packaged vehicles only. See pages 15-16 for grading guide to determine value for cars in lesser conditions.

5743-a

Classic Nomad 5743 - 70mm - 1993
This model, a remake of the 1974 issue, is based on the 1955 Chevrolet Nomad station wagon. It has a metal chassis, lift-up hood with metal engine, clear plastic windows & sun roof, white plastic interior, nrl and was made in China. The Hot Wheels logo and "25th Anniversary" are etched on the base. Similar castings: 6404 Classic Nomad (1970), 6968 Alive '55 (1973)

a. metallic lime $3 - 5
b. metallic purple 4 - 6
c. metallic aqua 4 - 6
d. metallic light blue 4 - 6
e. metallic magenta 4 - 6
f. metallic orange 4 - 6
g. metallic green 4 - 6
h. metallic olive 4 - 6
i. metallic red 4 - 6
j. metallic brown 4 - 6
k. metallic gold 4 - 6
k2. dark blue 5 - 7
l. metallic lavender, Toys "R" Us 8-pack only 2 - NA

Classic Nomad-m

m. metalflake turquoise, white int., clear plastic windows, white Hot Wheels logo on top, rsw, gold hubs. 1 of 16 FAO Schwarz Gold Series Collection, limited to 3000 (1994) 4 - NA
n. metalflake blue 4 - 6
o. metalflake yellow 4 - 6
p. metalflake turquoise 4 - 6
q. metalflake aqua 4 - 6
r. metalflake pink 4 - 6
s. metalflake black 4 - 6

13523-t

t. 13523, black, white top, clear windows, red int., bwgd w/white striped tires, Seattle Toy Show, limited to 7000 (1995) 25 - 30

13359-u

u. 13359, mtlfk aqua, white int., slightly tinted windows, Hot Wheels logo on windshield, tw, #10 in Treasure Hunt series, #362 (1995) 60 - 80
v. gold-plated, white int., clear windows, red Hot Wheels logo in back of roof, rsw w/gold hubs. 1 of 16 FAO Schwarz Gold Series Collection II, limited to 4000 (1995) 4 - NA
x. 15770, mtlfk dk. red, tan int., clear windows, sp7g, #502 (1996) 6 - 8

Classic Nomad-y

y. mtlfk blue; yellow, white, red & black tampo w/"1," "Hot Wheels" & racing decals on sides; clear windows; white int.; black grill; bw w/white "Goodyear" & "Eagle" on sides; Vintage Series 4-pack (1996) 12 - NA

Classic Nomad-z

z. turquoise, clear windows, white roof & int., bw. Mattel bonus car in baggie, mail-in only (1996) 8 - NA

Classic Nomad-aa

aa. mtlc gold; red sparkle flames on sides & hood; red "1996" on sun roof; green, white & brown Christmas tree on roof; clear windows; red int.; presents in back; rsw w/green hubs. Red display box w/ornament, plastic top for 1996 Christmas season (1996) 15 - 20

Classic Nomad-ab

ab. mtlc blue, same as aa, gold sparkle flames, yellow int., rsw w/red hubs. Red display box w/ornament, plastic top for 1996 Christmas season (1996) 15 - 20
ac. no #, orange; gold flames outlined in purple w/dk. magenta outline on sides, roof & front, tinted windshield, magenta int.; sp5. Real Rods limited set only. K•B exclusive (1996) 15 - NA
ad. mtlc green, same as g, ltd ed for 30th Anniv. w/blistercard in window box (1998) 5 - 7

Classic Nomad-ae

ae. yellow; white roof; tinted windows; tan int.; silver tampo on sides, hood & rear; ww; China; FAO Schwarz Cruisin' the '50s 8-pack only (1998) 6 - NA

Classic Nomad-af

af. mtlc aqua; same as c; red, silver, black, yellow & white tampo w/Hot Wheels logo; redline wheels & smoke on door. JC Penney; only w/Hot Wheels watch (1997) 55 - NA

Classic Nomad-ag

ag. mtlfk dk. red; white roof; white int.; clear windows; white, silver & black tampo w/"Red Pyro," 1998 Convention logo & race decals on sides, "Red Pyro" & "G. Swisher 427" on hood, "G. Swisher" on both sides of roof; rrch w/red stripe. 1998 Hot Wheels Convention (1998) 20 - 25

Classic Nomad-ah

ah. white; black roof & hood; gold, black, blue, red & white tampo w/police shield from Pueblo, CO Police Department, "City of Pueblo Colorado," "742" & "Police" on sides, "City of Pueblo Colorado" & "Police" on roof, "Police" in back, "743" & stripes on hood; rrch. Limited to 25,000 in Cop Rods Series for K•B Toys (1999) 5 - 7

Classic Nomad-ai

ai. white; white int.; tinted windows; black, gold & red flame tampo w/"Spike Surfboards" & "Westride" on sides, "Westride" on hood; sp5gd. #4 in Surf 'n Fun Series, #964 (1999) 4 - 6
aj. mtlfk dk. red, tan int., tinted windows, lwch, China. Surfs Up Action Pack w/gray or blue surfboard 5 - NA

Classic Nomad-aj2

aj2. same as aj, clear windows, sp5, Malaysia. Toy Story 2 Super Stunt Set (1999) 5 - NA

Classic Nomad-ak

ak. yellow, white int., aqua-tinted windows, white roof, JC Whitney logo in black & white on sides, gych. Ltd ed in box by JC Whitney (1999) 15 - 20

Classic Nomad-al

al. turquoise, same as ak (1999) 15 - 20

Classic Nomad-am

am. red, white int., clear windows, white & yellow flame tampo on sides, ww. Target V-8 3-pack (1999) 8 - NA

Classic Nomad-an

an. black & white; gold chrome int.; clear windows; gold, black & white tampo w/"Sacramento Police" on sides, "Police" & shield on hood, "Police" on roof & in back; rrch; Cop Rods Series 2 only (2000) 7 - 9
ao. orange; clear windows; white int.; white, red & yellow tampo w/Hot Wheels logo on sides, Hot Wheels logo & ".com" on hood; sp3gd; China; issued as Chevy Nomad; #196 (2000) 2 - 3
ao2. same as ao, sp3, .com 5-pack only 3 - NA
ap. black, white roof & int., tinted windows, white & orange flame tampo on sides & hood, sp3, Ames Stores exclusive Cruise Night 4-pack. (2000) 6 - NA

Classic Nomad-aq

aq. mtlfk green; white int.; yellow-tinted windows; black, white, orange & red tampo w/"Noyes Wheels" on sides & hood; Thailand; Skateboarders 5-pack (2001) 3 - NA

3092-a2

Corvette Split Window (Corvette Stingray ('63 'Vette)) 3092 - 70mm - 1993
This Malaysia-made 1963 Corvette Coupe has a plastic chassis, lightly tinted plastic windows, red plastic interior, and bw. Similar casting: 1136 Split Window '63 (1980)

a. lt. blue; yellow, lt. brown & magenta tampo on top; #197 $18 - 22
a2. same as a, ww, #197 6 - 10
a3. same as a, sp5, #197 (1995) 4 - 6

Corvette Split Window-b

b. no #; red; yellow, blue & pink tampo on sides; gray-tinted windows; yellow int.; chrome plastic base; ww; 25th Anniv. Chevy 5-pack only (1993) 6 - NA

Corvette Split Window-c

c. no #; mtlfk blue; "World Cup USA 94" & Hot Wheels logo on sides, World Cup mascot in brown, black, blue, red & white on hood; clear windows; white int.; bw. World Cup 5-pack only (1994) 6 - NA

13269-d

d. 13269, aqua, orange crackly lines all over body, orange-tinted windows, bw, "'63 Split Window," #3 of Krackle Car Series, #282 (1995) 3 - 6
d2. same as d, sp5, #282 (1995) 3 - 6
d3. same as d, gray plastic base (1997) 4 - 6
d4. same as d, sp7, #282 10 - 15

13354-e

e. 13354, mtlfk blue, white int., clear windows, Hot Wheels logo on windshield, rrgy, #6 in Treasure Hunt series, #358 (1995) 80 - 95
f. chrome, red int., clear windows, red Hot Wheels logo on windshield, rsw. Service Merchandise only in 16-piece Classic American Car Collection, limited to 5000 (1995) 10 - NA

Values are shown in U.S. dollars, first price is for mint, second is for mint packaged vehicles only. See pages 15-16 for grading guide to determine value for cars in lesser conditions.

Corvette Split Window-i

g. 13874, green, plastic base, beige int., clear windows, red Hot Wheels logo on w, sp5, '63 Split Window, #447 (1996) 2 - 4
g2. same as g, sp7, #447 (1996) 6 - 8
g3. same as g, sp3, #447 (1996) 3 - 5
g4. same as g, lt. blue-gray plastic base, sp7, #447 (1997) 2 - 4
g5. same as g4, sp3 2 - 4
h. mtlfk purple, chrome plastic base, white int., clear windows, rrgd w/white stripe. FAO Schwarz History of Hot Wheels 8-pack only (1996) 8 - NA
i. no #, chrome, chrome base, clear windows, red interior, gych w/red stripe. FAO Schwarz Olympic 3-pack only (1996) 50 - NA

16815-j

j. 16815; powder blue; white "614" in dk. blue circle w/white border on sides, hood & trunk; Edelbrock logo & "Washburn Chevrolet" in blue & white on sides; clear windows; red int.; gych. 1963 Corvette Sting Ray, limited to 10,000 (1997) 20 - 25
k. mtlc blue, chrome base, tan int., sp5. Corvette 5-pack only (1996) 25 - NA
k2. same as k, sp7 25 - NA
l. mtlfk aqua; chrome plastic base; clear windows; gray int.; gold, silver & dk. red tampo w/"97 Bonus Car Q1" on sides & top; sp3. Mystery Car #1 (1997) 8 - NA

Corvette Split Window-m

m. no #, black, tan int., clear windows, sp5. Avon Father & Son 2-pack only (1997) 5 - NA
n. 16941; black; red plastic base & int., clear windows; red, white & gold card tampo on sides & top; ho5. #4 in Dealer's Choice series, #568 (1997) 2 - 4
o. blue; chrome plastic base; tan int.; tinted windows; red, white & yellow tampo w/Hot Wheels logo on sides & hood, "1" on sides, hood & roof, "Hot Wheels" on roof; sp5. '63 Corvette & #4 in Race Team Series IV, #728 (1998) 2 - 3
p. gray, chrome base, red int., clear windows, gray on sides, red Corvette Central logo on roof. Ltd ed of 10,000 for Corvette Central (1998) 15 -18

Corvette Split Window-q

q. mtlfk black, gold chassis, clear windows, tan int., gold tampo on sides & hood, sp5gd, Malaysia. #1 in X-Ray Cruiser Series, #1114 (1999) 2 - 3

Corvette Split Window-r

r. gray; black chassis & int.; clear windows; black, yellow, white & lt. green tampo on sides, hood & roof; "Extreme Rider" on sides & hood; ho5; #1079 (1999) 2 - 3
r2. same as r, lwch, #114 (2000) 2 - 3
s. black, same as r, white int., dw3, #174 (2000) 2 - 3
t. white; black chassis, int. & roof; clear windows; dark blue, gold & black tampo w/"Police Hartford," "10" & emblem on sides, "Police" on roof, emblem on roof; gych; Cop Rods Series 2 (2000) 6 - 8

Corvette Split Window-u

u. green; white int.; yellow-tinted windows; lt. green, yellow & black tampo w/"Funky Speed" on sides & hood; sp5; Malaysia; #2 in Hippie Series; #090 (2001) 2 - 3

Corvette Split Window-v

v. black; red int.; clear windows; red & white tampo w/"02," "Pep Boys" & race decals on sides; "02" & "Manny, Moe and Jack Team Racing" on hood; "Pep Boys," "Manny, Moe and Jack" & 3 faces on roof; sp5 w/white stripe; reads "Corvette Stingray" on base; Malaysia; Pep Boys 2-pack (2001) 3 - NA

Corvette Split Window-w

w. red; tan int.; tinted windows; black & white tampo w/flames & "Corvette" on sides, flames & "Sixty-Three" on hood; sp3; Malaysia. #4 in Corvette series #070 (2002) 2 - 3
x. mtlfk red; chrome chassis; black int.; clear windows; black & white "63" on sides; silver & black tampo w/"Automobile Milestones 2002" on roof; rrch w/white stripe; Thailand. Auto Milestones series (2002) 9 - 12

11085-a

Corvette Stingray III 11085 - 70mm - 1993
This futuristic Corvette convertible has a red plastic base, tan plastic interior, clear windshield, and pc; Malaysia.
a. dk. red, Demolition Man series only, w/Cryo-Cube $6 - 8
b. 18364, purple, gray int., clear windshield, sp5, #595 (1997) 2 - 4
b2. same as b, sp7, #595 (1997) 2 - 4
b3. same as b, sp3, #595 (1997) 2 - 4

Corvette Stingray III-c

c. dk. blue, black plastic base, tinted windshield, white int., sp3, #595 (1997) 2 - 4

Corvette Stingray III-d

d. gray; red int.; tinted windshield; black & white tampo on sides; two red, white & black racing flags on hood; sp3. #11 in 1998 Treasure Hunt Series, #759 (1998) 20 - 25

Corvette Stingray III-e

e. red; white int.; tinted windshield; black, white & gold tampo w/"Enviro Hydro," "E," "6" & "Ostendorf Testing Equip." on sides, "E" on hood; sp3gd; Thailand. Ocean Blasters 5-pack (1999) 2 - NA

Corvette Stingray III-f

f. black; black chassis; orange int.; tinted windshield; orange, white & blue tampo w/"76" on sides, "Padres" on hood, 76 Union oil logo on trunk. San Diego baseball team promotion (2000) 10 - 15
g. mtlfk gray; black chassis; white int.; tinted windshield; yellow, green & black tampo on sides & hood; lwch; Malaysia; #180 (2001) 2 - 3
g2. same as g, yellow int., lwch, Power Launcher 2-pack (2001) 3 - NA

Corvette Stingray III-h

h. mtlfk gold; gold chassis; white int.; tinted windshield; orange, yellow, black & white tampo w/"Davis Tigers" on sides; sp3; Thailand; Sports Stars 5-pack (2001) 3 - NA

5730-a

Demon, The 5730 - 75mm - 1993
Based on the "Lil Coffin" show car, this model has a metal chassis, black roof, blue-tinted plastic windshield, black plastic interior, nrl, and was made in China. Hot Wheels logo & "25th Anniversary" are etched on base.
Similar castings: 6401 The Demon (1970), 6965 Prowler (1973)
a. metallic purple 3 - 5
b. metallic aqua 3 - 5
c. metallic light blue 3 - 5
d. metallic magenta 3 - 5
e. metallic orange 3 - 5
f. metallic green 3 - 5
g. metallic olive 3 - 5
h. metallic red 3 - 5
i. metallic brown 3 - 5
j. metallic gold 3 - 5
k. metallic lavender 3 - 5
k2. dark blue 5 - 7
l. metallic lime, Toys "R" Us 8-pack only 2 - NA

Demon-m

m. metalflake dark blue; red, white & yellow tampo w/Hot Wheels logo & "Toy Fair "94" on roof. 1994 New York Toy Fair promo, limited to 2500, baggie only (1994) 125 - NA

Demon-n

n. mtlfk magenta, gold-plated engine, white int., clear windshield, black roof, white Hot Wheels logo on top, rsw w/gold hubs. 1 of 16 FAO Schwarz Gold Series Collection, limited to 3000 cars (1994) 6 - NA
o. metalflake light green 3 - 5
p. metalflake silver 3 - 5
q. white 3 - 5
r. metalflake aqua 3 - 5
s. metalflake black 3 - 5
t. metalflake yellow 3 - 5
u. metalflake magenta 3 - 5
v. burnt orange 3 - 5
w. metalflake turquoise 3 - 5
x. metalflake pink 3 - 5
y. metalflake burgundy 3 - 5

Demon-z

z. gold-plated, chrome engine, black int., red Hot Wheels logo on roof, rsw w/gold hubs. 1 of 16 FAO Schwarz Gold Series Collection II, limited to 4000 (1995) 6 - NA
aa. no #; lt. green; gold flames; purple w/dk. magenta outline on sides, roof & front; tinted windshield; magenta int.; sp5. Real Rods ltd ed set only, K•B excl. (1996) 10 - NA

Demon-ab

ab. mtlc purple, same as a, 30th Anniv. logo in silver on roof. 30th Anniv. G-Force set only 8 - NA
ac. mtlfk magenta; white int.; clear windshield; white roof w/red, black & gray 14th Annual Hot Wheels Convention logo; rrch w/white walls. Issued as Lil Coffin for 14th Hot Wheels convention (2000). Limited to 4000. 25 - 40
ad. blue; gray roof & front; tinted windshield; black int.; multicolored tampo with "6," Pfizer & race decals on sides & top; Thailand. #1 in NASCAR Demon Series (2001) 7 - 9
ae. yellow; tinted windshield, black int.; black, red, white & blue tampo w/"22," "Caterpillar" & race decals on sides, "Cat" in front of engine, "22" on roof, "Polaris ATV's" in back; sp3; Thailand. #2 in NASCAR Demon series (2001) 7 - 9
af. neon red, mtlfk silver sides & front, tinted windshield, black int., multicolored tampo with "40" & race decals on sides & top, Thailand. #3 in NASCAR Demon series (2001) 7 - 9
ag. red; tinted windshield; black int.; black & white tampo w/"21," "Motorcraft" & race decals on sides & top; Thailand. #4 in NASCAR Demon series (2001) 7 - 9
ah. black, clear windshield, red int., red & silver flames on sides & roof, sp3, Thailand, #105 (2001) 2 -3
ah2.same as ah, Malaysia, #105 (2001) 2 -3

Values are shown in U.S. dollars, first price is for mint, second is for mint packaged vehicles only. See pages 15-16 for grading guide to determine value for cars in lesser conditions.

5265-a

Dodge Viper RT/10 5265 - 71mm - 1993
This Malaysia-made convertible is based on the limited production sports car of the same name. It has a black plastic base, clear windshield, and uh.

a. red, #210 $6 - 8
a2. 13585, same as a, uhgd, #210 (1995) 15 - 20
a3. same as a2, sp5, #210 (1995) 90 - 100
a4. same as a, lwch, China. Mispackaged in Treasure Hunt blistercard (1997) 15 - 20

Dodge Viper-a5

a5. same as a4, #210 (1998) 4 - 6
a6. same as a, uh. Ltd ed for 30th Anniv., w/blistercard in window box, #210 (1998) 4 - 6
b. yellow, same as a, uhgd, #210 (1995) 8 - 10
b2. same as b, sp5 2 - NA
b3. same as b, sp7. Super Show Cars 5-pack only (1995) 4 - NA
c. 13585, dk. mtlc aqua, same as b, #210 (1995) 6 - 8
c2. same as c, sp5g, #210 (1995) 8 - 10
c3. same as c, sp3g, #210 (1995) 4 - 6
c4. same as c, lwgd, #210 (1996) 3 - 5
c5. same as c, sp5, #210 (1997) 2 - 4
d. black, silver headlights, gold Hot Wheels logo on black-tinted windshield, black plastic base & int., sp5. Target excl. Black Convertible Collection only 6 - NA
e. red, black plastic base, black int., clear windshield, iwgd. FAO Schwarz History of Hot Wheels 8-pack only (1996) 8 - NA

15079-f

f. 15079, white, black plastic base, blue stripes on top, clear windshield, black int., iww. #5 in Treasure Hunt Series #433 (1996) 70 - 75
g. mtlfk black, 2 silver stripes on hood & back, clear windshield, black int., pc. Dodge 3-pack only (1996) 12 - NA
h. mtlc dk. purple, gray int., tinted windshield, sp3. California Dreamin' 5-pack only (1997) 2 - NA
h2. same as h, Thailand (1997) 2 - NA

Dodge Viper-i

i. red, black plastic base, black int., clear windshield, two yellow stripes over hood & trunk, yellow logo on driver's side, sp5y, China. Park 'n Plates box only (1998) 6 - 8
j. white; black plastic base; red int.; tinted windshield; mtlc blue tampo w/"20" & "United States" on sides, red & black design, "20" on hood; dw3; Thailand. #4 in Dash 4 Cash series, #724 (1998) 2 - 3
j2. same as j, China (1998) 2 - 3

Dodge Viper-k

k. black, clear windshield, 2 yellow stripes over top, rry. Ltd ed of 25,000 for All Tune & Lube (1998) 12 - 15
l. unpainted, tan int., tinted windshield, dw3. #4 in Dash 4 Cash series. 1998 Hot Wheels Convention, #724 (1998) 150 - 200

Dodge Viper-m

m. mtlfk blue, black int., tinted windshield, white tampo w/"Viper RT/10" on sides & 2 stripes over top, #1006 (1999) 2 - 3
m2. same as m, China, #1006 (1999) 2 - 3
m3. same as m2, w/sticker, NY Mets baseball team only (1999) 2 - 8

Dodge Viper-n

n. gray, black int., clear windshield, two black stripes over top, sp3. Ames Stores excl. 4-pack only (1999) 4 - NA

Dodge Viper-o

o. white; black chassis; blue int.; blue-tinted windshield; blue & red tampo w/"LA" on sides, "Dodgers" & stripes on hood; iw. Limited to 30,000 for LA Dodgers baseball team (1999) 10 - 12

Dodge Viper-p

p. lt. green, gray chassis & int., tinted windshield, sp3, China, w/Power Launcher 5 - NA
q. yellow, same as p, sp3, w/Long Hauler (1999) 5 - NA

Dodge Viper-r

r. mtlc purple, same as p, sp3 w/Power Launcher (1999) 5 - NA

Dodge Viper-s

s. mtlfk gray; black chassis & int.; clear windshield; black, blue, white & red tampo w/"Team Benjamin," "27" & race decals on sides & hood; sp3; China; #1038 (1999) 2 - 3
t. gray; black int.; blue-tinted windshield; black, white, blue & yellow tampo w/"Jaws Water Polo" on sides; sp3; China; #178 (2000) 2 - 3
u lime yellow; black chassis & int.; tinted windshield; black, red & white tampo w/"Anti De Construct" on sides & hood; pr5s; China; #177 (2001) 2 - 3
v. gray; black base & int.; blue-tinted windshield; black, yellow & lt. blue tampo w/"Jibason Jaws Water Polo" on sides; sp3; Thailand; Sports Stars 5-pack (2001) 2 - NA
w. gold, black chassis & int., tinted windshield, black & blue tampo on sides, sp3, China, Pavement Pounder pack (2001) 3 - 5
x. black, black chassis, gray int., yellow-tinted windshield, silver & red tampo on sides, sp3, China, Kool Toyz Super Race Rigs pack (2001) 3 - 5
y. black, same as i, green-tinted windshield, green replaces red in tampo on sides, sp3, China, Kool Toyz Power Launcher pack (2001) 3 - 5
z. orange, black chassis & int., tinted windows, silver & black tampo on sides, sp3, China, Power Launcher pack (2001) 3 - 5
aa. blue, gray chassis & int., tinted windshield, yellow & white checkerboard tampo on sides, sp3, China, Pavement Pounder pack (2001) 3 - 5
ab. black, tan int., tinted windshield, yellow & white tampo w/"27" on sides, sp3, China, Pavement Pounder pack (2001) 3 - 5
ac. dk. gold, black chassis & int., tinted windshield, purple & lt. blue tampo on sides, sp3, China, Pavement Pounder pack (2001) 3 - 5
ad. blue, black chassis, gray int., clear windshield, white stripes on top, sp3, China, Gas Station pack (2001) 3 - 5
ae. lt. blue, black chassis & int., clear windshield, white tampo w/"Viper RT/10" on sides, stripes over top, sp3, China, Power Launcher pack (2001) 3 - 5
af. pink, black chassis, gray int., clear windshield, white stripes outlined in silver over top, sp3, Kmart City Service 6-car set (2001) 6 - NA
ag. mtlfk dk. blue; black int.; clear windshield; white, gold & lt. blue tampo w/"Automobile Milestones 2002" on trunk, 2 white stripes over top; rrch w/white stripe. Auto Milestones series (2002) 8 - 10

3438-a

Dragon Wagon® 3438 - 72mm - 1993 (Tattoo Machines)
This concept model has a green plastic base, chrome plastic windows & engine in back, bw, and was made in China.
Similar casting: 13609 Speed Blaster (1995)

a. green; yellow in back; yellow, green & red dragons all over $5 - 7

3493-a

Eye-Gor 3493 - 70mm - 1993 (Tattoo Machines)
Based on the high tech Porsche 959, this model has a metal base, clear windows, gray interior, bw, and was made in China.
Similar casting: 4631 Porsche 959 (1988)

a. yellow; green in back; white, blue, red & black eyes all over $5 - 7

1691-a

Gleamer Patrol 1691 - 75mm - 1993
This sheriff's car has a metal chassis, blue-tinted plastic windows, black interior, bw, and was made in Malaysia.
Similar castings: 2019 Highway Patrol (1978); 2639 Fire Chaser (1979); 2019 Sheriff Patrol (1982); no number, Airport Security (1983)

a. chrome, pattern etched on plastic body, black int., gray-tinted windows, bw, #189 (1992) $4 - 10
b. gray-chrome, same as a, tan int., clear windows, #189 (1992) 12 - 18
b2. same as b, tinted windows 4 - 8

11084-a

GM Lean Machine 11084 - 70mm - 1993
This futuristic General Motors car from the movie Demolition Man has a black metal chassis, black-tinted plastic canopy, plastic sides, two uh in back and a small plastic wheel in front. It was made in Malaysia.

a. gray, gray sides, Demolition Man series only, w/Cryo-Cube $5 - 7
b. 12361; lime yellow & black; black plastic chassis; black-tinted canopy; lime yellow int.; white Hot Wheels logo in back; uh; #268 4 - 6
b2. same as b, sp7 in back, #268 3 - 5
b3. same as b, sp5, #268 (1996) 3 - 5
b4. same as b, dw3, #268 (1997) 2 - 4
b5. same as b, ho5, #268 (1997) 2 - 4
b6. same as b, sp3 (1997) 2 - 4

15229-c

c. 15229; blue; white top; black canopy; metal base; white, orange & blue tampo w/"Search" on sides & "HWSA Hot Wheels Space Administration" on front; sp5. #2 in Space series, #389 (1996) 4 - 6

GM Lean Machine-d

d. 16679, chrome, mtlfk red top, chrome canopy, "HTW 3/7" & black design on sides, sp5. #5 in Treasure Hunt series, #582 (1997) 15 - 20
e. mtlfk aqua; metal base; black bottom half; blacked-out canopy; gold, silver & dk. red tampo w/"97 Bonus Car Q3" on top; sp3. Mystery Car #3 (1997) 8 - NA
f. mtlfk gold, turquoise top, gold int., tinted canopy, dw3, #812 (1998) 2 - 3

GM Lean Machine-g

g. purple; black canopy; lt. green, yellow & white tampo w/"Star Commander" on sides; sp5; Malaysia. #1 in Game Over series, #957 (1999) 2 - 3

11083-a

GM Ultralite 11083 - 70mm - 1993
This General Motors model has a black plastic chassis, blacked-out metal windows, uh, and was made in Malaysia.

Values are shown in U.S. dollars, first price is for mint, second is for mint packaged vehicles only. See pages 15-16 for grading guide to determine value for cars in lesser conditions.

a. white; black doors, wheel covers & windows; "SAPD" in white on doors; white futuristic police logo on back wheel covers, different black logo on front. Demolition Man series only, w/Cryo-Cube $5 - 7
a2. same as a, back of car is black, sp7, #594 (1997) 6 - 8
a3. same as a2, no tampo, #594 (1997) 4 - 6
a4. same as a3, ho5 #594 (1997) 2 - 4

GM Ultralite-a5

a5. same as a3, sp3 #594 (1997) 4 - 6
a6. same as a; white plastic chassis; yellow, orange & white tampo w/star logo on back wheel covers, "To Protect and Serve" and "Unit 3" on sides; sp3; Thailand. Police Squad 5-pack only (1999) 2 - NA

GM Ultralite-b

b. white, red front & back, gray & black tampo w/"Police" on sides, rrch. #5 in 2001 Final Run (2001) 9 - 12

3494-a

Hot Wheels 3494 - 70mm - 1993 (Tattoo Machines)
This Ferrari 308 GTB has a black metal chassis, clear plastic windows, black plastic interior, bw, and was made in China. Similar castings: 2021 Race Bait 308 (1978), 7295 Quik Trik (1984), 9538 Street Beast (1985), 17962 Ferrari 308 GTB (1997)
a. blue; red, yellow & white with Hot Wheels logos $8 - 10

3026-a

Jaguar XJ220 3026 - 74mm - 1993
This Malaysia-made model has a black plastic chassis & interior, clear windows & uh.
a. mtlfk silver, open rear spoiler, #203 $8 - 10
a2. same as a, closed rear spoiler, #203 6 - 8
a3. same as a2, uhgd, #203 (1994) 30 - 35
b. candy red, clear windows, black int., uhy, Revealers 3 - 5
c. candy blue, same as a, uhgn, Revealers 3 - 5
d. candy purple, same as a, Revealers 3 - 5
e. no #, vacuum metallized silver, blacked-out windows w/white 25th Anniv. logo on rear window. 25th Anniv. Exotic Car 5-pack only (1993) 4 - NA
f. 3026, mtlfk dk. blue, same as a2, #203 (1995) 6 - 8
f2. same as f, uhgd, #203 (1995) 18 - 20
f3. same as f, clear windows, gray int., lwgd, #203 (1997) 8 - 10
f4. as f3, black int., #203 (1997) 8 - 10
g. 13283, pearl white, white Hot Wheels logo on rear window, black-tinted windows, black plastic base, uh. #4 in Pearl Driver series, #296 (1995) 6 - 8
g2. same as g, sp5, #296 (1995) 5 - 7
g3. same as g, sp7, #296 (1996) 10 - 12
g4. same as g, sp3, #296 (1996) 4 - 6

h. mtlfk purple, same as g, red Hot Wheels logo on rear window, sp5. Super Show Cars 5-pack only (1995) 10 - NA
i. mtlc green, same as h, #445 (1995) 6 - 8
i2. same as i, dw3, #445 (1996) 8 - 10
i3. same as i, sp7, #445 (1996) 12 - 15

15077-j

j. 15077, dk. mtlfk green, blacked-out windows, gold Hot Wheels logo on rear window; iwgd. #4 in Treasure Hunt series, #431 (1996) 35 - 40

Jaguar XJ220-k

k. 16931; orange; clear windows; black int.; black & yellow tampo w/claw & claw marks on sides, wildcat on hood; dw3y. Street Beast #2, #558 (1997) 2 - 4
l. gray; clear windows; purple int.; black & red tampo w/"Fast Cash" & "L10" on sides, "L10" on hood; sp3. #1 in Dash 'n Cash series, #721 (1998) 2 - 3
l2. same as l, lwch, #721 (1998) 2 - 3

Jaguar XJ220-l3

l3. same as l, dw3 2 - 3
m. unpainted, tan int., clear windows, sp3. #1 in Dash 4 Cash series. 1998 Hot Wheels Convention, #721 (1998) 65 - 75

Jaguar XJ220-n

n. yellow, blue int., clear windows, black tampo outlining insides of car, sp3. #4 in X-Ray Cruiser series, #948 (1999) 2 - 3

Jaguar XJ220-o

o. mtlc gold; tinted windows; gold int.; blue, black & white tampo w/"Jaguar XJ220" on rear fender; sp3gd; Malaysia; #1082 (1999) 2 - 3
p. red, black base & int., blue-tinted windows, lt. blue & white tampo w/"XJ220" & "Jaguar" on sides, lwgd, #160 (2000) 2 - 3

Jaguar XJ220-q

q. black, tan int., yellow-tinted windows, gold tampo on sides, gold & silver tampo on hood w/"Jaguar" on sides, sp3gd, Malaysia. #1 in Company Cars series, #085 (2001) 2 - 3

5263-a2

Lexus SC400 5263 - 70mm - 1993
This Malaysia-made model has a black plastic base, white interior, clear windows, & uh.
a. black, #209 $4 - 6
a2. same as a, bw, Canada only 3 - 5

b. 12357, dk. mtlfk red, same as a, tan int., white Hot Wheels logo in back, #264 (1995) 4 - 6
b2. same as b, sp5, #264 (1995) 4 - 6
b3. same as b, bw, #264 (1995) 2 - 4
b4. same as b, sp3, #264 (1996) 4 - 6
b5. same as b, dw3, #264 (1996) 2 - 4
b6. same as b, ho5, #264 (1996) 3 - 5
b7. same as b, uh, #264 (1996) 2 - 4
b8. same as b, ho5w, #264 (1996) 12 - 15
b9. same as b, sp7, #264 (1997) 2 - 4
b10.same as b; sp7gd, #264 (1997) 2 - 4

Lexus SC400-c

c. mtlfk aqua, clear windows, tan int., sp5. Toys "R" Us 10-pack only (1997) 5 - NA

Lexus SC400-d

d. mtlfk purple, tan int., tinted windows, lwch, #770 (1998) 2 - 4

Lexus SC400-e

e. mtlfk dk. green, white int., tinted windows, silver striping tampo w/"Lexus Special Edition" on sides, sp3. Showroom Specials 5-pack only (1998) 2 - NA

Lexus SC400-f

f. black; white int.; yellow-tinted windows; red, white, yellow & lt. green tampo w/"4" on hood; sp3gd. Alien Attack 5-pack, Thailand (1999) 2 - 3

Lexus SC400-g

g. yellow; black chassis; white int.; tinted windows; orange, gray & black tampo on sides; sp3. #3 in Seein' 3-D series #011 (2000) 2 - 3
h. mtlfk blue, tan int., tinted windows, dw3, #210 (2000) 3 - 5
h2. same as h, lwch, #210 (2000) 2 - 3

3510-a

Lightning Storm 3510 - 67mm - 1993 (Tattoo Machines)
This Chinese-made futuristic car has a metal chassis, chrome plastic windows & exposed engine, red plastic light & guns, & bw. Similar castings: 2018 Science Friction (1978), 7293 Flame Runner (1984), 2544 Back Burner (1986)
a. mtlc dk. blue; lt. blue, pink, lt. green & black lightning bolts all over $6 - 8

11082-a

Olds 442 W-30 11082 - 72mm - 1993
A replica of the car from the Warner Brothers movie Demolition Man, this model has a chrome plastic base, black interior, clear windows, and bw; Malaysia.
a. red, 2 thick black stripes on hood, thin black stripe on sides, Demolition Man series only, w/Cryo-Cube $12 - 15

11897-b

b. 11897; black; 2 white stripes on hood; red, white & blue tampo w/"Greater Seattle Toy Show 1994" on roof; clear windows; white int.; gyg; limited to 7000 (1994) 25 - 30

12360-c

c. 12360, yellow, 2 black stripes on hood, thin black stripe on sides, red Hot Wheels logo on rear window, clear windows, black int., bw, #267 (1995) 6 - 8
c2. same as c, sp7, #267 (1995) 4 - 6
c3. same as c, sp5, #267 (1997) 3 - 5
c4. same as c, gray plastic base, sp7 (1997) 3 - 5
c5. same as c, gray plastic base, sp5 (1997) 3 - 5

13349-d

d. 13349, blue, same as c, white stripes & int., red-striped rr. #1 in Treasure Hunt series, #353 (1995) 75 - 130
e. chrome, gray int., clear windows, red Hot Wheels logo on back window, rsw. Service Merchandise in 16-piece Classic American Car Collection only, limited to 5000 (1995) 8 - NA
f. mtlc silver, same as a, red tampo, plastic base, clear windows, red int., sp7. '60s Muscle Cars 5-pack only (1995) 3 - NA
f2. same as f, sp3 (1995) 3 - NA
f3. same as f, sp5 (1996) 2 - NA
g. gold-plated, gold-plated base, tinted windows, black int., pcgd. JC Penney gold-plated 2-pack (1995) 60 - NA
h. black, white roof, 2 white stripes on hood, thin stripe on sides, clear windows, white int., gygd. '60s Muscle Cars 4-pack only (1996) 10 - NA

Olds 442-i

i. no #, black, tan int., clear windows, gold stripes, "422" in white on sides, sp5. Cruisin' America 6-pack only (1997) 6 - NA
j. #16946, blue, black int., blue-tinted windows, silver Hot Wheels logo on trunk, sp3. #1 in Blue Streak series, #573 (1997) 4 - 6
k. mtlfk blue; white int.; tinted windows; red, yellow & white tampo w/Hot Wheels logo, "1," "Richard" & race decals on sides; sp5; Thailand; #871 (1998) 3 - 10

Olds 442-l

l. green; white int.; clear windows; yellow, black & blue tampo w/"Olds 442" on sides; sp3. #4 in Seein' 3-D series, #012 (2000) 2 - 3

m. white, clear windows, tan int., gold & black tampo on sides & hood, pr5s, Malaysia, #242 (2000) 2 - 3

m2. same as m, sp5, #242 (2000) 2 - 3

Olds 442-n

n. mtlfk blue; white int.; clear windows; white tampo on sides & hood w/"445" on hood; orange, black & white Treasure Hunt logo on sides; rrch. #9 in 2001 Treasure Hunt series, #009 (2001) 15 - 20

o. mtlfk blue; white int.; tinted windows; orange & white tampo w/large Hot Wheels logo, "1" & race decals on sides; and sp5; Malaysia. Sto 'n Go Shell Gas Station set (2001) 5 - NA

p. mtlfk dk. red, black int., tinted windows, black & white tampo w/"442" & "DJ" on sides, sp3, Malaysia, #154 (2002) 2 - 3

10566-a

Oldsmobile Aurora 10566 - 72mm - 1993
This Malaysia-made futuristic model has a black plastic base, tan interior, clear windows, and bw.

a. gray, Demolition Man series only, w/Cryo-Cube $12 - 15

b. 12358; pearl green; white Hot Wheels logo in back; gray plastic base, int. & tinted window; #265 (1994) 15 - 28

b2. as b, clear windows, #265 12 - 18

Oldsmobile Aurora-c

c. 16681, mtlc purple, gray int., clear windows, silver stripe w/"Aurora" on sides, Aurora logo on hood, sp5. #7 in Treasure Hunt series, #584 (1997) 20 - 25

Oldsmobile Aurora-d

d. 12358; black; blue-tinted windows; white int.; white, gold & red tampo w/"Police K-9 Unit," "54" & logo on sides, "54" on white roof & "Police" on trunk; sp7b; #265 (1997) 4 - 6

d2. same as d, sp7, Metro-Tech Police Force set & Highway Police Chase set (1999) 6 - NA

e. blue; black plastic base & int.; tinted windows; yellow, white & red tampo w/"Action News KHWW" & "1" on sides & hood, "On Site Reporter" on sides; sp5. Action News 5-pack (1998) 2 - NA

Oldsmobile Aurora-e2

e2. blue, same as e, sp3 2 - NA

f. white; blue chassis; blue int.; blue-tinted windows; black, red & gold tampo w/logo, "Sheriff" & "Safety and Service" on sides, stripes & logo on

Oldsmobile Aurora-f

hood; sp5; Thailand. Police Squad 5-pack only (1999) 2 - NA

g. black; tan int., clear windows, white & gold tampo w/"39" on sides & roof, logo, "Police" & "Unit L9" on sides; ho5; Thailand; #1047 (1999) 2 - 3

Oldsmobile Aurora-g2

g2. same as g, sp5 2 - NA

Oldsmobile Aurora-h

h. blue, same as h, sp7, Police playset 5 - NA

Oldsmobile Aurora-i

i. yellow; black chassis; red int.; clear windows; black, red & white tampo w/"1" & "Hot Wheels" on sides; lwch; China; #230 (2001) 2 - 3

i2. yellow, same as i, Thailand, #230 (2002) 2 - 3

j. maroon; black int.; blue-tinted windows; gold & dk. green tampo w/"Paris" on sides; ho5; Thailand. World Tour 5-pack (2001) 2 - NA

k. purple, black chassis, white int., clear windows, yellow & gold lightning tampo on hood & roof, sp7. McDonald's Drive Thru pack (2001)

l. lt. green, same as k, Kmart City Service 6-car set (2001) 3 - NA

m. lt. blue; black chassis; gray int.; lt.-blue-tinted windows; white, red & gold Police tampo with "Police," "54" & emblem on sides, "54" on roof, "Police" on trunk. Kmart City Service 6-car set (2001) 3 - NA

n. mtlfk dk. red; white chassis & int.; orange-tinted windows; black, dk. red & white tampo w/Hot Wheels logo, "Arson Investigator" & "Unit 12" on sides, flames on white roof; ho5; Thailand. Heat Fleet 5-pack (2002) 2 - NA

3490-a

Open Wide® 3490 - 72mm - 1993 (Tattoo Machines)
Based on a four-wheel-drive Ford truck, this model has a metal chassis, clear plastic windows, bw, and was made in China.
Similar castings: 2022 Baja Breaker (1978), 2853 Motocross Team (1979), 3303 Circus Cats (1981), 9113 The Simpson's Family Camper (1990)

a. dk. maroon, yellow in front & back, red & white mouths w/teeth all over $5 - 7

Oscar Mayer Wienermobile 3029 - 78mm - 1993
The Wienermobile was designed by Harry Bradley. Its most prominent features are a tan base and an orange-brown wiener with a yellow band. "Oscar Mayer" appears in red and white on the band. It also has black-tinted windows, bwbk, and was made in Malaysia.

3029-a

a. tan, bwbk, #204 $4 - 6

a2. same as a, bw, #204 (1993) 2 - 6

a3. same as a, sp7, #204 (1993) 2 - 6

a4. same as a, ho5, #204 (1997) 2 - 6

a5. same as a, sp5, #204 (1997) 2 - 4

b. 15271, chrome, yellow belt w/red & white Oscar Mayer logo, gray-tinted windows, sp5bk. #4 in Silver Series II, #423 (1996) 2 - 4

5707-b

Paddy Wagon 5707 - 64mm - 1993
Based on a show car, this model has a metal chassis & interior, exposed engine, "Police" & "3" imprinted in gold on a dark blue roof, nrl and was made in China. The Hot Wheels logo & "25th Anniversary" are etched on the base.
Similar castings: 6402, 6966 Paddy Wagon (1970, 1973)

a. black $3 - 5

a2. black, blue top 3 - 5

b. magenta 3 - 5

c. blue 3 - 5

d. brown 3 - 5

e. gold 3 - 5

f. mtlfk aqua, gold-plated engine, white int., clear windshield, black plastic roof w/white Hot Wheels logo on top, gold "Police" on sides, rsw w/gold hubs. 1 of 16 FAO Schwarz Gold Series Collection, limited to 3000 (1994) 6 - NA

g. metalflake burgundy 3 - 5

h. metalflake aqua 3 - 5

i. metalflake light green 3 - 5

j. metalflake silver 3 - 5

k. metalflake magenta 3 - 5

l. white 3 - 5

m. metalflake pink 3 - 5

n. metalflake black 3 - 5

o. metalflake yellow 3 - 5

p. metalflake blue 3 - 5

q. burnt orange 3 - 5

r. gold-plated, chrome engine, metal int., blue-tinted windshield, black plastic roof, "Police 3" on sides, red Hot Wheels logo on top, rsw, gold hubs. 1 of 16 FAO Schwarz Gold Series Collection II, limited to 4000 (1995) 6 - NA

Paddy Wagon-s

s. black; white plastic top w/black sides; gold, red, white & blue logo, "Police 3" & "Los Angeles Police Dept." in white on sides; "Police Patrol" in white over windshield; iwgd; China. Ltd ed of 10,000 for L.A. police (1998) 25 - 30

Paddy Wagon-s2

s2. same as s, rrgd (1999) 55 - 60

3036-a

Pipe Jammer™ 3036 - 73mm - 1993
This concept race car has a black plastic chassis, chrome plastic interior, driver & rear engine, uh, and was made in Malaysia.
Similar casting: 12354 Cyber Cruiser (1994)

a. yellow, #206 $5 - 10

11087-a

Pontiac Salsa 11087 - 68mm - 1993
Made in Malaysia, this Pontiac convertible has a black plastic chassis, tan interior, gray painted windshield & headlights, and bwo.

a. orange, Demolition Man series only, w/Cryo-Cube $6 - 8

a2. #18365, same as a, sp7, #596 (1997) 2 - 4

a3. same as a, sp3, #596 (1997) 2 - 4

a4. same as a, chrome plastic base, sp3 (1997) 10 - 18

Pontiac Salsa-a5

a5. orange, same as a, dw3, #596 (1997) 2 - 4

Pontiac Salsa-b

b. dk. mtlc green; black int.; gold, silver & magenta tampo w/"97 Bonus Car" on sides, "02" on hood; sp3. Mattel 2nd quarter bonus car giveaway only (1997) 8 - NA

Pontiac Salsa-c

c. mtlfk dk. red; black int.; yellow & blue tampo w/"Ram" on sides; ho5; #862 (1998) 2 - 3

Pontiac Salsa-d

d. yellow, black chassis & int., black-tinted windows, black & white tampo, license plate w/"LAST-SALZA99," sp6y. #7 in Final Run Series, limited to 35,000 (1999) 5 - 7

Red Baron 5700 - 55mm - 1993
This model, a remake of the 1974 issue, has a metal chassis, exposed engine, dull point on top of a metal helmet, black plastic interior, nrl, and was made in China. The Hot Wheels logo & "25th Anniversary" are etched on the base.

Values are shown in U.S. dollars, first price is for mint, second is for mint packaged vehicles only. See pages 15-16 for grading guide to determine value for cars in lesser conditions.

5700-a

Similar castings: 6400, 6964 Red Baron (1970, 1973)

a. metallic red $3 - 5
b. mtlfk dk. blue-green, gold-plated engine, white int., white Hot Wheels logo in front, metal helmet, rsw w/gold hubs. 1 of 16 FAO Schwarz Gold Series Collection, limited to 3000 (1994) 8 - NA
c. mtlfk aqua 3 - 5
d. mtlfk turquoise 3 - 5
e. mtlfk silver 3 - 5
f. mtlfk magenta 3 - 5
g. white 3 - 5
h. mtlfk pink 3 - 5
i. mtlfk black 3 - 5
j. mtlfk burgundy 3 - 5
k. mtlfk blue 3 - 5
l. burnt orange 3 - 5
m. mtlfk yellow 3 - 5
n. gold-plated, chrome engine & helmet, black int., red Hot Wheels logo in front, rsw w/gold hubs. 1 of 16 FAO Schwarz Gold Series Collection II, limited to 4000 (1995) 6 - NA
o. dk. red, white int., rsw. Target Stores excl. 4-pack only (1996) 6 - NA

3489-a

Road Pirate 3489 - 72mm - 1993 (Tattoo Machines)

This model has a black plastic base, chrome plastic windows, chrome plastic engine in back, and bw; China.

a. magenta & yellow; black & white bones, skulls, swords, etc. all over $4 - 6
b. dk. red, same as a, no tampo, set only (1993) 4 - NA

Silhouette-m

Silhouette 5715 - 69mm - 1993

Based on Bill Cushenberry's custom car, this model has a metal chassis & exposed engine, brown plastic interior, nrl, plastic dome roof and the base is the same color as the car. The Hot Wheels logo and "25th Anniversary" are etched on the base.

Similar casting: 6209 Silhouette (1968)

a. metallic aqua $3 - 5
b. metallic light blue 3 - 5
c. metallic magenta 3 - 5
d. metallic orange 3 - 5
e. metallic green 3 - 5
f. metallic olive 3 - 5
g. metallic red 3 - 5
h. metallic brown 3 - 5
i. metallic gold 3 - 5
j. metallic lavender 3 - 5
k. metallic lime 3 - 5
k1. dk. blue 5 - 7
l. metallic purple, Toys "R" Us 8-pack only 4 - NA
m. mtlfk red-brown, gold-plated engine, white int., clear plastic dome, white Hot Wheels logo in back, rsw, gold hubs. 1 of 16 FAO Schwarz Gold Series Collection, limited to 3000 (1994) 8 - NA
n. metalflake silver 3 - 5
o. metalflake magenta 3 - 5
p. metalflake pink 3 - 5
q. white 3 - 5
r. metalflake burgundy 3 - 5
s. metalflake blue 3 - 5
t. burnt orange 3 - 5
u. metalflake yellow 3 - 5
v. metalflake black 3 - 5
w. metalflake light green 3 - 5
x. metalflake turquoise 3 - 5
y. gold-plated, chrome engine, black int., tinted dome, red Hot Wheels logo in back, rsw, gold hubs. 1 of 16 FAO Schwarz Gold Series Collection II, limited to 4000 (1995) 8 - NA

Silhouette II-d

Silhouette II 5267 - 73mm - 1993

This new design of the 1968 Silhouette has a chrome plastic engine, clear plastic dome, white interior, uh, and was made in Malaysia.

a. mtlfk purple, #212 $4 - 6
a2. same as a, gray plastic base, #212 6 - 8
a3. same as a2, ho5 (1997) 4 - 6
b. 13286, mtlfk black, black plastic base, red Hot Wheels logo in back, chrome black engine, iwb. #3 Dark Rider series, #299 (1995) 12 - 15
b2. same as b, chrome plastic base, #299 18 - 20
b3. same as b, black plastic base, sp7, #299 8 - 10
c. 15259; mtlfk purple; red plastic base; green, red & white tampo w/mouth & teeth on sides; mouth, teeth & eyes on nose; green on sides; sp5. #2 in Street Eaters series, #413 (1996) 2 - 4
d. mtlfk dk. blue, chrome engine, blue-tinted dome, white int., dw3gd. Designer Collection 8-pack only, sold by Target Stores (1996) 6 - NA

Silhouette II-e

e. 16685, white, blue plastic dome, blue chrome plastic engine, sp3w. #2 in Treasure Hunt series (1997) 20 - 25
f. 16938, blue, black plastic base, gold plastic engine & int., clear plastic dome, white & red playing-card tampo on sides & hood, ho5. #1 in Dealer's Choice series, #565 (1997) 2 - 4

Silhouette II-g

g. black, purple chassis, white int., clear dome, mtlfk red tampo, ho5. #2 in Tech Tones series, #746 (1998) 2 - 3
h. unpainted, ho5. Hot Wheels 1998 conventioneers' questionnaire mail-in, baggie (1999) 60 - NA

Silhouette II-i

i. lt. blue gray, white int., blue-tinted dome, chrome engine, white & red tampo w/"Toss Across" on sides, red pinstripes, ho5. #2 in Classic Games series, #982 (1999) 2 - 3
j. red; white int.; yellow-tinted dome; chrome engine; yellow, black, blue & white tampo w/"Super Launcher" on sides; lwch; Thailand; Super Launcher 5-pack (2001) 3 - NA
k. lime; white int.; clear dome; chrome engine; orange, black & white tampo on sides; sp3; Thailand; #152 (2002) 2 - 3
l. purple; white int.; blue-tinted dome; white & lt. blue tampo; sp3. Super Soakin' playset (2002) 8 - NA

3492-a

Skull Rider 3492 - 75mm - 1993 (Tattoo Machines)

Based on the BMW 323 Cabriolet, this Chinese-made convertible model has a black plastic chassis, tan interior, clear plastic windshield, and bw.

Similar casting: 9726 BMW 323 (1990)

a. magenta; green, black & white tampo w/snakes & skulls all over $5 - 7

3479-a

Spiderider 3479 - 83mm - 1993 (Tattoo Machines)

Based on the 1930's Talbot Lago, this Chinese-made model has a metal base, red-tinted windows, chrome interior, and ww.

Similar casting: Talbot Lago (1988)

a. white; black & red spiders all over $5 - 7

5708-b

Splittin' Image 5708 - 75mm - 1993

Designed by Ira Gilford, this concept car has a metal chassis, brown plastic interior, clear plastic domes, nrl, and was made in China. The Hot Wheels logo and "25th Anniversary" are etched on the base.

Similar castings: 6261 Splittin' Image (1969), Splittin' Image (1973 Shell Promo)

a. metallic orange $3 - 5
b. metallic green 3 - 5
c. metallic olive 3 - 5
d. metallic red 3 - 5
e. metallic brown 3 - 5
f. metallic gold 3 - 5
g. metallic lavender 3 - 5
h. metallic lime 3 - 5
i. metallic purple 3 - 5
j. metallic aqua 3 - 5
k. metallic light blue 3 - 5
l. metallic magenta, Toys "R" Us 8-pack only 4 - NA
m. mtlfk green, gold-plated engine, white int., clear plastic domes, white Hot Wheels logo in back, rsw w/gold hubs. 1 of 16 FAO Schwarz Gold Series Collection, limited to 3000 (1994) 8 - NA
n. metalflake pink 3 - 5
o. metalflake burgundy 3 - 5
p. metalflake turquoise 3 - 5
q. metalflake light green 3 - 5
r. metalflake silver 3 - 5
s. metalflake magenta 3 - 5
t. white 3 - 5
u. burnt orange 3 - 5
v. metalflake aqua 3 - 5
w. metalflake yellow 3 - 5
x. metalflake blue 3 - 5
y. gold-plated, chrome engine, white int., blue-tinted domes, red Hot Wheels logo in back, rsw, gold hubs. 1 of 16 FAO Schwarz Gold Series Collection II, limited to 4000 (1995) 6 - NA
z. mtlc dk. red, gold engine & pipes, blue-tinted domes, lt. gold int., sp5gd, China. In box w/wrist watch by JC Penney (1998) 30 - NA
aa. lime, white int., blue-tinted domes, chrome engine, sp5, Malaysia, #170 (2002) 2 - 3

3491-a

Street Beast (3rd version) 3491 - 75 mm - 1993 (Tattoo Machines)

Based on the Corvette Stingray, this Chinese-made model has a metal chassis, clear plastic windows, black plastic interior, and large cts.

Similar casting: 3716 Monster 'Vette (1987)

a. yellow; orange, black, white & pink tampo w/tigers on hood & trunk $4 - 6

3501-a

Street Dog 3501 - 78mm - 1993 (Tattoo Machines)

Based on a German prototype, this model has a black metal chassis, black plastic interior & grill in back, clear plastic windows, bw, and was made in China.

Similar castings: 3289 BMW-M1 (1983), 7296 Wind Splitter (1984)

a. blue-gray; red, white, gray & blue dog heads $4 - 6

4312-a

Swingfire® 4312 - 80mm - 1993

A Malaysia-made Studebaker/Plymouth convertible with metal base and metal tire in back.

Similar casting: 5637 Street Beast (1991)

a. mtlfk blue, white plastic on bottom, metal base, yellow & white tampo on hood, white int., ww, #214 (1994) $6 - 8
a2. same as a, sp7, #214 (1995) 4 - 6
b. mtlfk blue, white sides, clear domes, white interior, yellow & white tampo on hood, dw3, Street Beast, #214 (1998) 2 - 4

3035-a

Treadator® 3035 - 82mm - 1993

This Malaysia-made futuristic tank has a black plastic base, chrome plastic engine & canopy, black tank tracks and small black wheels.

a. red, #205 $3 - 6
b. 3035; fluor. green; purple plastic engine & canopy; #205 (1995) 3 - 6
c. 15231; bluish gray; blue chrome engine & canopy; orange nose. #4 in Space Series, #391 (1996) 3 - 6

15231-d

d. 15231, white, same as c, #391 (1996) 40 - 45

Values are shown in U.S. dollars, first price is for mint, second is for mint packaged vehicles only. See pages 15-16 for grading guide to determine value for cars in lesser conditions.

Treadator-f

e. green; purple plastic engine & canopy; black tracks; #205 (1997) 2 - 4
f. metalflake purple; light green tracks; silver & black tampo on sides; #851 (1998) 2 - NA

Treadator-g

g. red; yellow & black tampo on sides & wing; "Anteater" on wing; Thailand. #1 in Buggin' Out series, #941 (1999) 2 - 3

Treadator-h

h. mtlfk blue, black tracks, white nose, chrome engine, #791 2 - 3

Treadator-i

i. black, blue tracks, chrome engine, white & light blue tampo w/"Search & Rescue" & "Avalanche" on sides, Thailand, #1049 (1999) 2 - 3
j. mtlfk gold; chrome engine & windows; red, lt. green & black tampo on sides & top; Thailand; #231 (2001) 2 - 3
j2. as j, Malaysia, #231 (2001) 2 - 3

5709-a

TwinMill 5709 - 72mm - 1993
Designed by Ira Gilford, this concept car has a metal chassis, two chrome plastic engines, white plastic interior, clear plastic windshield, nrl, and was made in China. The Hot Wheels logo and "25th Anniversary" are etched on the base. Similar castings: 6258 TwinMill (1969), TwinMill (1973 Shell Promo), 8240 TwinMill II (1976)

a. metallic magenta $3 - 5
b. metallic orange 3 - 5
c. metallic green 3 - 5
d. metallic olive 3 - 5
e. metallic brown 3 - 5
f. metallic gold 3 - 5
g. metallic lavender 3 - 5
h. metallic lime 3 - 5
i. metallic purple 3 - 5
j. metallic aqua 3 - 5
k. metallic lt. blue, Toys "R" Us 8-pack only 4 - NA
l. mtlfk gray, 2 gold-plated engines, white int., clear plastic windshield, white Hot Wheels logo on top, rsw w/gold hubs. 1 of 16 FAO Schwarz Gold Series Collection, limited to 3000 (1994) 8 - NA
m. metalflake black 3 - 5
n. metalflake pink 3 - 5
o. white 3 - 5
p. metalflake blue 3 - 5
q. burnt orange 3 - 5
r. metalflake silver 3 - 5
s. metalflake light green 3 - 5
t. metalflake turquoise 3 - 5
u. metalflake burgundy 3 - 5
v. metalflake aqua 3 - 5
w. metalflake magenta 3 - 5
x. gold-plated, chrome engines, black int., blue-tinted windshield, red Hot Wheels logo on roof, rsw w/gold hubs. 1 of 16 FAO Schwarz Gold Series Collection II, limited to 4000 (1995) 8 - NA
y. yellow, clear windshield, black int., bw. Mattel bonus car, in baggie, mail only (1996) 6 - NA

5709-z

z. blue; white, red & yellow tampo w/"1" & Hot Wheels logo on top & sides; blue metal chassis; clear windshield; white int.; bw w/white "Goodyear" & "Eagle" on sides. Vintage Series 4-pack (1996) 10 - NA

TwinMill-aa

aa. mtlfk dk. red, black metal base, gold-plated engines & pipes, white int., clear windshield, black & gold flame tampo w/"New York Toy Fair 1998" & Toy Fair logo on nose, "Twinmill" & Toy Fair logo on rear, bwgd. Park 'n Plates box, ltd ed 5000 for 1998 Toy Fair (1998) 100 - 110
ab. mtlc purple, purple metal base, chrome engines & pipes, white int., clear windshield, rsw. 30th Anniv. pin on blistercard in window box 7 - 9
ac. metallic red, same as ab 7 - 9
ad. lime yellow, same as ab 7 - 9

TwinMill-ae

ae. mtlfk dk. red, black int., tinted windshield, gold tampo, Ira Gilford's signature & "Original Twin Mill Designer 1968," rrch w/red stripe. 1998 Hot Wheels Convention, #787 (1998) 25 - 30
af. black; yellow chassis, clear windshield, black int.; multicolored tampo w/"22," "Caterpillar," logo & race decals; rrch; Thailand. #1 in NASCAR Twin Mill series (2001) 5 - 7

TwinMill-ag

ag. white; dark blue chassis; blue-tinted windshield; white int.; multicolored tampo w/"10," "Valvoline," logo & race decals; rrch; Thailand. #2 in NASCAR Twin Mill Series (2001) 5 - 7
ah. dark blue w/white chassis; clear windshield; white int.; multicolored tampo w/"99," "Supergard," Citgo logo & race decals; rrch; Thailand. #3 in NASCAR Twin Mill series (2001) 5 - 7
ai. orange; unpainted chassis; blue-tinted windshield; white int.; multicolored tampo with "32," "Tide," logo & race decals & rrch; Thailand. #4 in NASCAR Twin Mill series (2001) 5 - 7

5266-a

TwinMill II 5266 - 73mm - 1993
This new design of the 1969 TwinMill has two chrome plastic engines with side pipes, black-tinted windows and uh; Malaysia.

a. Day-Glow yellow, #211 $12 - 15
a2. as a, gray plastic base, #211 6 - 8
a3. as a, black plastic base, #211 40 - 45
b. 13285, mtlfk black, red Hot Wheels logo in back, chrome black engines, mtlfk black windows, iwb. #2 Dark Rider series, #298 (1995) 10 - 12
b2. as b, black sp7, #298 (1995) 4 - 6
c. 12353; navy blue; red & white stripe on top; red-tinted windows; chrome engine & pipes; uh; #260 (1995) 3 - 5
c2. as c, bw, Canada only (1996) 3 - 5
c3. as c, ho5, #260 (1996) 2 - 4
c4. as c, ho5w, #260 (1997) 8 - 10
c5. as c, sp5, #260 (1997) 2 - 4
c6. as c, chrome base, ho5, #260 (1997) 2 - 4
d. green, gold-plated engines, green-tinted windows, dw3gd. Designer Collection 8-pack, Target Stores only (1996) 5 - NA

TwinMill II-e

e. 16937, white, red-tinted windows, red chrome engine & pipes, sp5. #4 in White Ice series, #564 (1997) 2 - 4

TwinMill II-f

f. mtlfk gold, black plastic base & windows, magenta & black tampo on sides, lwch, #861 (1998) 2 - 3
g. gray, same as f, #783 (1998) 2 - 3
h. red; blacked-out windows; black, yellow, white & blue tampo w/"Final Flight IV" & "Flight 2 DA Finish" on sides, boxer on roof, "FF IV" on nose; lwch. #4 in Game Over series, #960 (1999) 2 - 3

TwinMill II-i

i. orange, gray base, gold & white flame tampo w/face on sides, ho5gd. #4 in Mad Maniax series, #020 (2000) 2 - 3

TwinMill II-j

j. mtlfk dark red; black chassis & windows; gold chrome engine; gold, black & white tampo design on sides & top with "Drag'n" on top; lwgd. #3 in Extreme Sports series, #083 (2001) 2 - 3

Vector "Avtech" WX-3 3050 - 1993
Based on the full-size Vector, this model has a black plastic base, black-tinted windows, tan interior and uh; Malaysia.

3050-a

a. gray, small "v" on both sides of rear bumper, black stripe on doors. Vector exclusive, 500 only in this color, not in blisterpack $120 - NA
b. grayish purple, same as a, #207 (1994) 4 - 6
b2. same as b, sp5, #207 (1994) 3 - 5

Vector "Avtech" WX-3-c

c. mtlfk black, same as a, red tampo, red Hot Wheels logo on spoiler, clear windows, red int., sp5. Super Show Cars 5-pack only (1995) 2 - NA
c2. same as c, mtlc magenta replaces red in tampo. Super Show Cars 5-pack only (1997) 2 - NA

1994

Mattel introduced only one new series: the Vintage Collection. This was actually a continuation of the 1993 25th Anniversary collector's series with the same packaging, buttons, etc. Eight new vehicles were included. Each model, including 1993's 25th Anniversary cars, had the Hot Wheels logo and "Vintage" embossed on the base. Also introduced was a new Top Fuel dragster and some redesigns of earlier vehicles.

10494-g

'32 Ford Vicky 10494 - 62mm - 1994
This customized 1932 Ford Victoria is a remake of the 1969 model. It has a metal chassis, white plastic interior, exposed metal engine, clear plastic windows, smooth black roof, and nrl. Made in China, it also has the Hot Wheels logo and "Vintage" embossed on the base. Each comes with a plastic button. Similar casting: 6250 Classic '32 Ford Vicky (1969)

a. metalflake orange $3 - 5
b. metalflake light green 3 - 5
c. metallic olive 3 - 5
d. metalflake dark red 3 - 5
e. metalflake brown 3 - 5
f. metalflake gold 3 - 5
g. metalflake pink 3 - 5
h. metalflake lime 3 - 5
i. metalflake purple 3 - 5
j. mtlc magenta, Vintage series 8-pack only 2 - NA
k. yellow, same as a, black Hot Wheels logo in back, FAO Schwarz History of Hot Wheels 8-pack, ltd to 7000 (1995) 4 - NA
l. gold-plated, chrome engine, white int., red Hot Wheels logo in back, rsw, gold hubs. 1 of 16 in FAO Schwarz Gold Series Collection II, limited to 4000 (1995) 8 - NA
m. turquoise, white top, clear windows, white int., iw. 100th Anniv. of Auto gift pack (1996) 12 - NA
n. no #, mtlc purple, orange flames, green outline on sides & roof, clear windows, lt. purple int., sp5. Real Rods ltd ed set only, K•B excl. (1996) 12 - NA

Values are shown in U.S. dollars, first price is for mint, second is for mint packaged vehicles only. See pages 15-16 for grading guide to determine value for cars in lesser conditions.

10494-o

o. no #; black; red, yellow & white flame tampo w/"The Inside Track" & Hot Wheels logo on sides. Hot Wheels Inside Track Newsletter mail-in, baggie only (1997) 25 - NA

'32 Ford Vicky-p

p. 17262; pearl white; yellow to orange flames on front & sides; yellow, orange & black tampo on roof w/"Early Times '97 Mid Winter Rod Run"; clear windows; white int.; iw. Ltd ed of 10,000 (1997) 25 - 30
q. mtlc red, gold Hot Wheels 30th Anniv. logo on back. Ltd ed for 30th Anniv. w/blistercard & metal button in window box (1998) 5 - 7

'32 Ford Vicky-r

r. white; black roof & int.; blue-tinted windows; dk. blue, yellow & white tampo w/"Syracuse Police" on sides, "513" & Syracuse, NY Police logo on roof; rrch w/white stripe. Limited to 25,000 in Cop Rods series for K•B Toys (1999) 5 - 7

'32 Ford Vicky-s

s. yellow, blue int., clear windows, sp5, Pop n' Play set (1999) 5 - NA

'32 Ford Vicky-s2

s2. same as s, white int, black roof; nrsw (1999) 5 - NA

'32 Ford Vicky-t

t. mtlfk red, white int., clear windows, gold & white tampo design w/"Ford Vicky" on sides, lwgd. Vintage Hot Rods 3-pack from Avon (2000) 6 - NA
u. flat black, red int., clear windows, orange to yellow flame tampo on sides & roof, pr5s, Malaysia, #125 (2001) 2 - 3
u2. same as u, sp5, Malaysia, #125 (2001) 4 - 8

'32 Ford Vicky-v

v. black; clear windows; white int, orange spray mask in front & on sides; blue, white, red, orange & yellow 15th Annual Collector's Convention logo on roof; rrch w/red stripe. Limited to 4000, for 15th Annual Collector's Convention in Irvine, CA. (2001) 18 - 25

12341-a

Blimp 12341 - 80mm - 1994
This model has a metal gondola with gray fuselage and was made in Malaysia. A message can be seen by rotating the tail. Similar casting: 1384 Goodyear Blimp (1992)
a. white, thick green stripe in middle, "Fuji Film" outlined in black on stripe, red Fuji logo on one side of gondola, Hot Wheels logo on turning side, #249 $4 - 6

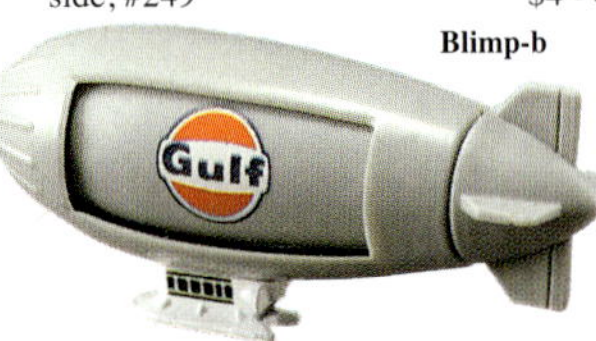
Blimp-b

b. white; red & yellow Hot Wheels logo on one side; orange, white & dk. blue Gulf logo on other; from Gulf stations in baggie only (1994) 4 - NA

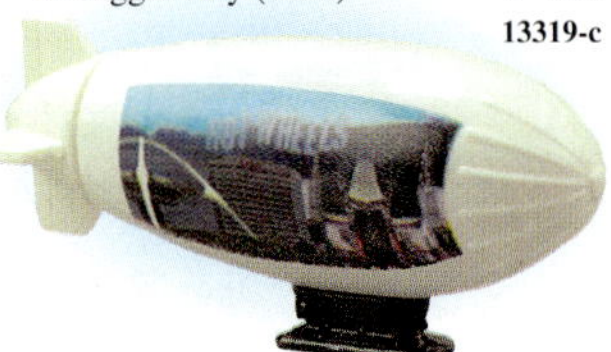
13319-c

c. 13319, mtlfk black base, white fuselage, photo of LA Airport & "Hot Wheels" on sides, Flyin' Aces Blimp. #2 in Photo Finish Series, #332 (1995) 3 - 6

Blimp-d

d. black fuselage w/large Hot Wheels logo, red base & tail, #1074 (1999) 2 - 3

10496-d

Custom Mustang 10496 - 71mm - 1994
This 1967 Ford Mustang Fastback is a remake of the original 1968 model. It has a metal chassis, gray plastic interior, opening hood, white Hot Wheels logo on the trunk, nrl, and was made in China. The Hot Wheels logo and "Vintage" are embossed on the base. Each comes with a plastic button. Similar casting: 6206 Custom Mustang (1968)
a. metalflake light blue $3 - 5
b. metallic magenta 3 - 5
c. metalflake orange 3 - 5
d. metalflake light green 3 - 5
e. metallic olive 3 - 5
f. metalflake dark red 3 - 5
g. metalflake brown 3 - 5
h. metalflake gold 3 - 5
i. metalflake pink 5 - 7
j. metallic aqua, Vintage series 8-pack only 3 - NA
k. gold-plated, black int., red Hot Wheels logo in back, rsw w/gold hubs in back. 1 of 16 in FAO Schwarz Gold Series Collection II, ltd to 4000 (1995) 6 - NA

10496-l

l. black; clear windows; black int.; red stripe; yellow outline w/"GT" on sides, "Greater Seattle Toy Show 1994" on roof; rsw. Limited to 10,000 (1994) 15 - 20

10496-m

m. mtlfk gray, 2 black stripes on top, clear windows, gray int., bw. Mattel bonus car mail-in only, in baggie (1996) 12 - NA

10496-n

n. mtlc blue; white int.; blue-tinted windows; black stripe; white design; yellow outline w/"GT" on sides, "Greater Seattle Toy Show 1996" on roof; bw w/white stripe. Limited to 10,000 (1996) 15 - 20

10496-o

o. white; two blue stripes on hood, roof & trunk; clear windows; blue int.; black grill & engine; rsw. '60s Muscle Cars 4-pack only (1996) 12 - NA

Custom Mustang-p

p. blue; white, red & yellow tampo w/"1" in white circle, Hot Wheels logo & racing decals on sides, "1" in white circle on roof, logo on trunk; black grill; clear windows; white int.; rsw. Vintage series 4-pack (1996) 12 - NA

10496-q

q. red; two gold stripes on hood, roof & trunk; black grill; clear windows; cream int.; iwch. 100th Anniv. of Auto gift pack (1996) 10 - NA

16899-r

r. 16899; white; blue tampo w/"1" in circle, "Van de Kamp's" on sides, "Van de Kamp's" on blue stripe twice on hood; orange, yellow & black fish sticker on roof; '67 Mustang.Van de Kamp's offer on fish sticks pkg only (1997) 6 - 8
s. no #, dk. green, clear windows, black & white int., black & white license plate

Custom Mustang-s

w/"1965" on front & back, gych. Four Decades of Pony Power 3-car gift set only (1997) 12 - NA

Custom Mustang-t

t. lt. yellow, clear windows, black int., black stripes w/"GT" on sides, black vents & side scoops, silver door handles, gych. 30th Anniv. of '67 Muscle Cars 3-pack only (1997) 12 - NA
u. no #, blue, clear windows, gray int., white stripe w/"67" & "GT 500" on sides, two stripes w/"428 cu. in." on hood, bw. FAO Schwarz 8-pack only (1997) 8 - NA

12354-a

Cybercruiser® 12354 - 73mm - 1994
This concept race car has a metal chassis, purple chrome driver, interior and rear engine, uh, and was made in Malaysia. Similar casting: 3036 Pipe Jammer (1993)
a. 12354, mtlfk purple, metal base, white Hot Wheels logo in back, pinkish chrome driver & engine, uh, #261 (1995) $3 - 5
a2. 12354, same as a, black metal base, #261 (1995) 30 - 35
b. 13294; black; orange metalflakes; rose chrome int., engine & metal base; blue hhb; orange tires. #1 Hot Hubs series, #307 (1995) 6 - 10

10495-e

Deora 10495 - 70mm - 1994
A remake of the 1968 model based on the custom surfing truck designed by Harry Bradley for Dodge and built by the Alexander Brothers. It has a metal chassis, black plastic interior, and flat bed with two removable surfboards (one yellow, one orange). It also has a white Hot Wheels logo on the side behind the rear wheels, nrl and was made in China. The Hot Wheels logo and "Vintage" are embossed on the back. Each comes with a plastic button. Similar casting: 6210 Deora (1968)
a. metallic magenta $3 - 5
b. metalflake orange 3 - 5
c. metalflake light green 3 - 5
d. metallic olive 3 - 5
e. metalflake dark red 3 - 5
f. metalflake brown 3 - 5
g. metalflake gold 3 - 5
h. metalflake pink 3 - 5
i. metalflake lime 3 - 5
j. mtlfk lt. blue, Vintage series 8-pack only 2 - NA
k. mtlc aqua, same a; white Hot Wheels logo on side. FAO Schwarz History of Hot Wheels 8-pack, ltd to 7000 (1995) 4 - NA

Deora-l

l. gold-plated, black int., red Hot Wheels logo on side, rsw, gold hubs. 1 of 16 in

FAO Schwarz Gold Series Collection II, limited to 4000 (1995) 8 - NA

10495-m

m. gold-plated, clear windows, black int., plastic surfboards, rsw. Mattel employees only, ltd ed of 1500, gold box (1995) 150 - 175

Deora-n

n. mtlfk blue; white, red & yellow race team tampo w/"1," Hot Wheels logo & race decals on sides, "1" on roof, logo on bed; "Hot Wheels" on windshield; clear windows; white int.; 2 orange surfboards; bw. Mattel bonus car, mail-in only, in baggie (1996) 10 - NA

n2. same as m, rsw, Vintage series 4-pack (1996) 8 - NA

Deora-o

o. no #; blue; red, yellow, white & orange tampo w/flames, "New York Toy Fair 1997," "Pro Racing" & Hot Wheels logo on black shiny bed; "44," "Kyle's Favorite Hot Wheels," logo & racing decals on sides; Kyle Petty's signature on roof; clear windows; black int.; bw; "Goodyear" & unreadable white type on tires. Park 'n Plates box give-away at 1997 Toy Fair only (1997) 125 - 150

Deora-p

p. 18584, pink, clear windows, white int., blue & white Van De Kamp's tampo on sides, lime green surfboards, bw. Ltd ed of 50,000, Van de Kamp's Fish Sticks mail-in (1998) 8 - NA

q. metallic green, gold Hot Wheels 30th Anniv. logo on sides. Ltd ed for 30th Anniv., w/button & blistercard in window box (1998) 5 - 7

Deora-r

r. white; blue on top; white int.; clear windows; multicolored tampo w/"99," "Supergard" & race decals on sides; blue surfboards; Citgo logo on roof; bw, Thailand. #1 in NASCAR Deora Series (2001) 7 - 9

s. yellow; black roof & truck bed cover; white int.; clear windows; black, red & white tampo w/"17," "Dewalt" & race decals on sides & roof; "Guaranteed Tough" on yellow surfboards; bw; Thailand. #2 in NASCAR Deora series (2001) 7 - 9

Deora-t

t. dark blue; white nose & int.; blue-tinted windows; red, white & blue tampo w/"12," pegasus & race decals on sides, "Mobil 1" on roof, "Speedpass" on red surfboards; bw; Thailand. #3 in NASCAR Deora series (2001) 7 - 9

u. lt. blue; dk. blue in back; white int.; clear windows; multicolored tampo w/"43," "Cheerios," STP logo & race decals on sides; "Betty Crocker" & STP logo on blue surfboards; STP logo on roof; Thailand. #4 in NASCAR Deora series (2001) 7 - 9

Deora-v

v. mtlfk blue, lt. blue int., blue-tinted windows, black & white tampo w/"Deora 1" & Treasure Hunt logo on sides, rsw, Thailand. #11 in 2001 Treasure Hunt series, #011 (2001) 20 - 25

w. dark red; white int. & surf boards; clear windows; yellow, black, orange & white tampo w/"Cowabunga" on sides; dw3; #122 (2002) 2 - 3

11847-a

Driven To The Max 11847 - 84mm - 1994

This Malaysia-made Top Fuel dragster has a metal base, metal engine in back of the cockpit, gray plastic spoiler and driver, bw in back & small dragster wheels in front. Similar castings: 13265 Dragster (1995), 14973 Mongoose Dragster (1996), 14972 Snake Dragster (1996)

a. orange; red & blue "Driven To The Max" & red Hot Wheels logo on sides; #245 $10 - 12

b. lime green; yellow plastic spoiler; purple, black & blue tampo w/"Hot Set-Up" & racing decals on sides & nose; sp5; #245 (1997) 4 - 6

b2. same as b, Thailand, Racing World 5-pack only (1998) 2 - NA

c. white, same as b, red plastic int. & spoiler, sp5, #808 (1998) 4 - 6

d. unpainted, red int. & spoiler, sp5, 1998 Hot Wheels Convention, #808 (1998) 60 - 70

Flyin' Aces Blimp - See Blimp

Fuji Blimp - See Blimp

10783-a

Mongoose 10783 - 76mm - 1994

This remake of a 1970 model is based on Tom (The Mongoose) McEwen's Plymouth Duster funny car. It has a metal chassis, lift-up body, black plastic interior, clear windows, nrl, and was made in China. The Hot Wheels logo and "Vintage" are embossed on the base. Each comes with a plastic button. Similar castings: 6410 Mongoose (1970), 5954 Mongoose 2 (1971)

a. mtlc red; white rectangle w/"Tom McEwen," "The Mongoose," blue & yellow mongoose & red Hot Wheels logo on sides; blue stripe & 2 white stripes on each side; yellow stars on top $3 - 5

b. dark metallic red, same as a 3 - 5

c. metalflake pink, same as a 8 - 10

d. metalflake light blue, same as a 3 - 5

e. metallic aqua, same as a 3 - 5

f. metalflake orange, same as a, Vintage series 8-pack only 4 - NA

g. dk. blue; white tampo w/red Hot Wheels logo, "Tom McEwen," "The Mongoose," & yellow & blue mongoose on sides; red & white stripe & yellow stars on top; clear windows; black int.; rsw. Target Snake & Mongoose race set 25 - NA

h. dk. blue; white tampo w/red Hot Wheels logo, "Tom McEwen," "The Mongoose," red & lt. blue mongoose on sides; red & dk. blue stripe & red stars on top; clear windows; black int.; rsw. Target Snake & Mongoose race set only 25 - NA

i. dk. mtlc red; yellow, black, brown & white tampo w/"Tom Mongoose McEwen," Carefree Gum logo, Hot Wheels logo, Coca-Cola logo & Pennzoil logo on sides; "Coca-Cola" & mongoose on hood; clear windows; black int.; rsw. Limited to 10,000 15 - 18

j. gold-plated, black int., red Hot Wheels logo in back, rsw w/gold hubs. 1 of 16 in FAO Schwarz Gold Series Collection II, limited to 4000 (1995) 8 - NA

10786-k

k. dk. mtlc blue; white tampo w/red Hot Wheels logo, "Tom McEwen," "the Mongoose II," black & brown mongoose on sides; red flames & white outline on hood, roof & trunk; clear windows; black int.; nrsw. Limited to 10,000 (1996) 15 - 18

11524-a

Mutt Mobile 11524 - 72mm - 1994

This concept car is a remake of a 1971 model and was issued as part of the Vintage Collection. Designed by Larry Wood, it has a metal chassis, exposed metal engine, white plastic top with "Mutt Mobile" in black embossed on the sides, two white plastic dogs in a black plastic cage, black plastic interior, rsw, and was made in China. Similar casting: 6185 Mutt Mobile (1971)

a. metallic light blue $3 - 5

b. metallic magenta 3 - 5

c. metallic orange 3 - 5

d. metallic dark red, Vintage series 8-pack only 4 - NA

e. gold-plated; white int., dogs & gate; black roof; gold "Mutt Mobile" on sides; Hot Wheels logo on top; chrome engine & pipes; rsw w/gold hubs in back. 1 of 16 in FAO Schwarz Gold Series Collection II, limited to 4000 (1995) 8 - NA

f. mtlc dk. magenta, gold "Mutt Mobile" on white plastic top, black int., rsw. Target Stores excl. 4-pack only (1996) 6 - NA

g. mtlc blue, gold Hot Wheels 30th Anniv. logo on roof. Ltd ed for 30th Anniv, w/ blistercard & metal collectors button in window box (1998) 5 - 7

11846-a

No Fear Race Car 11846 - 80mm - 1994

This Malaysia-made Indy-type racer has a black metal chassis and interior, and bw.

a. black; red & white tampo w/"No Fear" on sides & spoiler; "No Fear," "1" & "Racer" on sides; "1," Hot Wheels logo & "Goodyear" on front; #244 4 - 6

a2. same as a, sp7, #244 (1997) 2 - 4

a3. same as a, sp5, #244 (1997) 2 - 4

a4. same as a, sp5, "No Fear" missing 2 - 4

a5. same as a, sp5, "No Fear" & "Racer" missing 2 - 4

a6. same as a, ho5, #244 (1998) 2 - 3

11849-a

Rigor Motor 11849 - 78mm - 1994

This concept race car features a metal base with metal engine and tail pipes, white front grill with two skulls, metal interior, clear canopy, bw, and was made in Malaysia.

a. mtlfk ruby red, white Hot Wheels logo in back, #247 $2 - 6

a2. same as a, gold Hot Wheels 30th Anniv. logo under canopy. Ltd ed for 30th Anniv., w/blistercard in window box (1998) 5 - 7

b. 13287, mtlfk black, red Hot Wheels logo in back, chrome black engine, iwb. #4 in Dark Rider series, #300 (1995) 6 - 15

b2. same as b, black-tinted canopy, sp7, #300 3 - 10

b3. same as b, sp5, #300 (1996) 2 - 8

c. 15452, mtlfk purple, same as a, green chrome engine & int., sp5. Computer Cars series, computer chip in blisterpack (1996) 3 - 5

d. mtlfk gold, white skulls, gold int., black-tinted canopy, black pipes, sp5. Designer Collection 8-pack sold by Target Stores only (1996) 4 - NA

Rigor Motor-e

e. no number; black; red base & exhaust; gold engine; white skeleton hands on sides; sp5. Crazy Classics 5-pack only (1997) 2 - NA

Rigor Motor-f

f. black, red chrome engine, tinted canopy, white skulls, lwch, China, #300 (1997) 2 - 6

Rigor Motor-g

g. purple, gold-plated engine & int., yellow-tinted canopy, gold "Rigor Motors Racing" on sides, sp5gd, China, #852 (1998) 2 - 3

g2. same as g, sp5gd, Thailand, #852 (1998) 2 - 3

Rigor Motor-g3

g3. same as g, sp3gd, Malaysia, #852 (1999) 2 - 3

Values are shown in U.S. dollars, first price is for mint, second is for mint packaged vehicles only. See pages 15-16 for grading guide to determine value for cars in lesser conditions.

Rigor Motor-h

h. red; chrome engine & int.; tinted canopy; white, yellow & black tampo w/"Thorny Graves" on sides & top; sp5; China; #1052 (1999) 2 - 3
h2. same as h, Malaysia, 10-pack (1999) 2 - NA

Rigor Motor-i

i. lime green, chrome int. & engine, black pipes, yellow-tinted canopy, sp5gd. #4 in 1999 Treasure Hunt series, #932 (1999) 15 - 20
j. mtlfk blue, mtlfk gray chassis & side pipes, blue chrome engine & int., blue-tinted canopy, sp5, Malaysia. #1 in Tony Hawk Skate series, #041 (2000) 2 - 3
j2. same as j, unpainted chassis, #1 in Tony Hawk Skate series, #041 (2000) 2 - 3

Rigor-Motor-k

k. orange; black chassis & side pipes; gold chrome engine & int.; red canopy; gray, black & gold tampo design on sides & top; sp5gd. #1 in Skull & Crossbones series, #069 (2001) 2 - 3

11522-a

S'Cool Bus 11522 - 77mm - 1994
This Tom Daniel design of a funny-car dragster based on a school bus is a remake of the 1971 model. Issued as part of the Vintage Collection, it has a metal chassis, lift-up body to reveal a metal engine with an orange plastic air scoop, black plastic interior, black struts to support the body, sun roof, rsw, and was made in China.
Similar casting: 6468 S'Cool Bus (1971)
a. yellow; black & white tampo w/"S'Cool Bus" & black stripe on sides, "S'Cool Bus" & "854 C.I." twice on hood $25 - 30
a2. yellow, same as a, Target Stores excl. 4-pack only (1996) 12 - NA
b. metalflake yellow, same as a 15 - 20

11522-c

c. mtlfk gold, same as a, Vintage series 8-pack only 10 - NA
d. gold-plated, white int., red Hot Wheels logo in back, rsw w/gold hubs. 1 of 16 in FAO Schwarz Gold Series Collection II, limited to 4000 (1995) 10 - NA

13849-e

e. 13849, white, pink "Redline Spring Break" & green stripe on sides, no windows, turquoise int., rsw. Ltd to 10,000, on turquoise blistercard (1995) 18 - 20
f. blue; white roof; black int.; red, white, black & silver tampo w/flames & "2nd Nationals" sides, 2nd Annual Nationals logo on hood; rrch w/red stripe. Ltd ed of 4000, sold at 2nd Annual Nationals (2002) 20 - 25

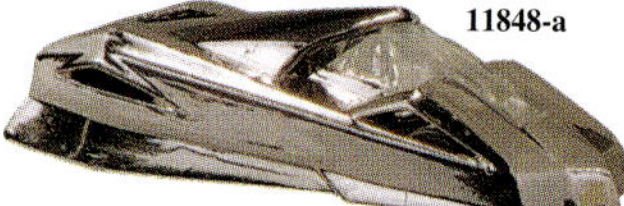
11848-a

Shadow Jet II 11848 - 76mm - 1994
This concept car was originally called Stealth. It has a metalflake black metal chassis, chrome interior and uh; Malaysia.
Similar casting: 16926, Stealth (1997)
a. chrome black; white Hot Wheels logo in back; #246 $2 - 4
a2. as a, red-on-white Hot Wheels logo 2 - 4
a3. as a, sp7, #246 2 - 4
a4. as a, sp5, #246 2 - 4
a5. as a, sp3, #246 2 - 4
a6. as a, ho5, #246 2 - 4

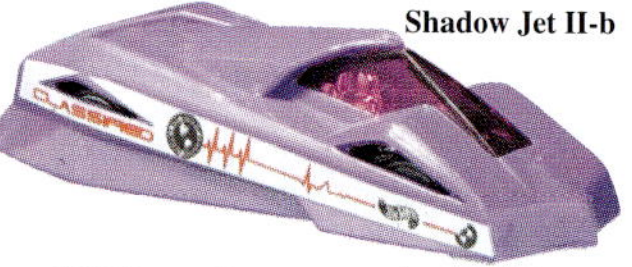
Shadow Jet II-b

b. 16926, purple, magenta-tinted windshield, chrome int., red & black tampo w/"Classified" on white stripe, sp3. #1 Spy Print series, #553 (1997) 2 - 4
b2. same as b, dw3, #553 (1997) 2 - 4
b3. same as b, silver base, #1 in Spy Print series, #553 (1997) 2 - 4
c. black; red, white & lt. green tampo w/"Cyber," "Accelerator" & "11848" on sides; sp5bk. #1 in Techno Bits series, #689 (1998) 2 - 4

Shadow Jet II-d

d. gray; metal chassis; white int.; green-tinted windshield; yellow, lt. green & black tampo on sides & top; "Stinger" on sides; sp5. #2 in Buggin' Out series, #942 (1999) 2 - 3
d2. same as d, sp5bk, #942 (1999) 2 - 3
e. purple plastic, clear windshield, chrome int. & figure, lwch. Towing Action Pack only (1999) 5 - NA
f. blue; silver base; red-tinted windshield; yellow, black & brown tampo design on sides & top; Malaysia. #3 in Kung Fu series, #35 (2000) 2 - 3
f2. same as f, unpainted chassis, Malaysia, #3 in Kung Fu series, #35 (2000) 2 - 3
g. red; tinted windshield; chrome int.; silver, black, white & pink tampo w/"Techno" on sides; Malaysia. Virtual Collection, #153 (2000) 2 - 3
g2. same as g, painted chassis 2 - 3

10497-b

Snake 10497 - 75mm - 1994
This remake of a 1970 model is based on Don (The Snake) Prudhomme's Plymouth Barracuda funny car. It has a metal chassis, lift-up body, black plastic interior, clear windows, nrl, and was made in China. The Hot Wheels logo and "Vintage" are embossed on the base. Each comes with a plastic button.
Similar castings: 6409 Snake (1970), 5953 Snake 2 (1971), 6969 Snake (1973), 6970 Mongoose (1973), 7630 Top Eliminator (1974), no # '70 Plymouth Barracuda Funny Car (1997)
a. mtlfk gold; white rectangle, snake, blue "Don Prudhomme," yellow "The Snake" & red Hot Wheels logo on sides; blue stripe & 2 white stripes on each side; gold stars showing thru on top $3 - 5
a2. same as a, Vintage series 8-pack only 4 - NA
b. yellow, same as a 6 - 8
b2. same as b (yellow little darker than b) 5 - 7
c. metalflake yellow, same as a 3 - 5
d. metalflake light green, same as a 3 - 5
e. white; dk. blue tampo w/red Hot Wheels logo, "Don Prudhomme," "The Snake" & yellow & white cobra on sides; red & yellow stripe, white stars on top; clear windows; black int.; rsw. Target Snake & Mongoose race set only 25 - NA
f. white; yellow tampo w/red Hot Wheels logo, "Don Prudhomme," "The Snake" & green & lt. green cobra on sides; green & yellow stripe, white stars on top; clear windows; black int.; rsw. Target Snake & Mongoose race set only 25 - NA

14071-g

g. yellow; red, black & white tampo w/"Don 'Snake' Prudhomme," Carefree Gum logo, Hot Wheels logo, Coca-Cola logo & Pennzoil logo on sides; "Coca-Cola" & snake on hood; clear windows; black int.; rsw. Limited to 10,000 (1995) 15 - 18
h. gold-plated, black int., red Hot Wheels logo in back, rsw w/gold hubs. 1 of 16 in FAO Schwarz Gold Series Collection II, limited to 4000 (1995) 8 - NA

10497-i

i . white; dk. blue tampo w/red Hot Wheels logo, "Don Prudhomme," "the Snake II" & yellow, red & white cobra on sides; red flames on hood, roof & trunk; clear windows; black int.; nrsw. Ltd ed of 10,000 (1996) 15 - 18

11850-a3

Splittin' Image II 11850 - 74mm - 1994
A remake of the original Hot Wheels concept car, this Malaysia-made model has a dark blue plastic base, chrome canopies & engine, and uhp.
a. dk. mtlfk purple, white Hot Wheels logo on front bumper, #248 10 - 12
a2. same as a, uh, #248 15 - 18
a3. same as a2; red-tinted canopies, engine & headlights; white Hot Wheels logo on front bumper; red uh; #248 (1995) 6 - 8
a4. same as a3, sp7o, #248 (1997) 4 - 6
a5. same as a3, sp7, #248 (1997) 4 - 6
a6. same as a, sp7, #248 (1997) 4 - 6
b. 13284, mtlfk black, black plastic base, red Hot Wheels logo on front fender, chrome black engine & canopies, iwb. #1 in Dark Rider series, #297 (1995) 8 - 10
b2. 13284, same as b, black-tinted canopies, sp7, #297 (1995) 2 - 4
c. yellow; plastic magenta-tinted canopies, engine & headlights. Designer Collection 8-pack, Target Stores only (1996) 4 - NA
d. 16936; white; chrome canopies, engine, etc.; sp3. #3 in White Ice series, #563 (1997) 2 - 4

11850-e

e. mtlc aqua; black plastic base; chrome canopies & engine; black pipes; black, white & red tampo w/"40 Valve" on sides; sp3. X-treme Machines 5-pack only (1998) 2 - NA
e2. same as e, dw3 (1998) 2 - NA

Splittin' Image II-f

f. metalflake blue; chrome engine & canopies; red, white & yellow tampo w/Hot Wheels logo, "Chip" & race decals on sides; sp5; Malaysia. Race Team III 5-pack (1999) 2 - 3
f2. same as f, Thailand (1999) 2 - 3

Splittin' Image II-g

g. mtlfk gold; black base; pink chrome engine & canopies; red, black & lt. green tampo w/"Attack of the Killer Flies" on sides; sp3; Malaysia. #4 in Terrorific series, #980 (1999) 2 - 3
h. gray; black chassis, canopies & engine; sp3gd; Virtual Collection; #155 (2000) 6 - 10

Splittin' Image II-i

i. mtlfk magenta; black chassis; beige canopies & engine; orange, black & blue tampo on sides & top; ho5; Malaysia; Fireball 5-pack (2001) 2 - NA

Splittin'Image II-j

j. blue, gray chassis, chrome engine & canopies, dark blue & black tampo w/"Vortex" on sides, sp3, Thailand, Super Launcher 5-pack (2001) 2 - NA

11523-a

Whip Creamer 11523 - 79mm - 1994
This concept car is a remake of a 1970 model and was issued as part of the Vintage Collection. Designed by Paul Tam, it has a metal chassis, sliding plastic canopy, orange plastic turbine, white plastic interior, and rsw. It was made in China.
Similar casting: 6457 Whip Creamer (1970)
a. metalflake aqua $3 - 5
a2. same as a, Target Stores excl. 4-pack only (1996) 4 - NA
b. metalflake dark red 3 - 5
c. metalflake light blue 3 - 5

Values are shown in U.S. dollars, first price is for mint, second is for mint packaged vehicles only. See pages 15-16 for grading guide to determine value for cars in lesser conditions.

d. mtlfk lt. green, Vintage series 8-pack only 4 - NA
e. gold-plated, white int., red Hot Wheels logo on side; rsw, gold hubs. 1 of 16 in FAO Schwarz Gold Series Collection II, limited to 4000 (1995) 8 - NA

1995

Mattel introduced the Treasure Hunt Cars and the 1995 Model Series. Twelve Treasure Hunt Cars were issued monthly and were limited to 10,000 each. They caused quite a commotion, with speculators buying all they could find and reselling them for $25 to $100 each. The 1995 Model Series consisted of 12 new castings and was also issued monthly. The Segment Series were also introduced: 12 different series of four cars each in the same theme. Three different series were scheduled every three months for a total of 48 cars. In 1995, six new wheels were introduced: three-spoke (sp3), five-spoke (sp5), six-spoke (sp6), seven-spoke (sp7), hot hubs (hh), and the progressive oval wheels (pow). The six-spoke and progressive ovals were only used for one vehicle each.

2015-a

'58 Corvette Coupe 2015 - 70mm - 1995
This Corvette convertible has a pink plastic base, chrome interior, large exposed chrome engine, clear windshield, and bw.

a. pinkish red, #3 in 1995 Model series, #341 $6 - 9
a2. as a, sp5, #341 7 - 10
a3. as a, sp7, #341 10 - 12
b. mtlfk purple, same as a2, #3 in 1995 Model series, #341 (1996) 4 - 6
b2. as b, sp7, #341 (1996) 10 - 12
b3. as b, ho5, #341 (1997) 6 - 8

14974-c

c. 14974, red, red chassis & hood (no plastic engine), white on sides, white int., clear windshield, pc. Ltd ed of 7000, #14 (1996) 40 - 45
d. mtlfk blue, same as a2, blue-tinted windshield, chrome int., sp5. Corvette 5-pack only (1996) 3 - NA
d2. as d, sp3 (1996) 3 - NA
e. pearl white, same as f, white chassis, red on sides, red int., clear windshield, rrgd w/red stripe. FAO Schwarz History of Hot Wheels II 8-pack (1996) 8 - NA

15082-f

f. 15082, mtlfk silver, gray plastic base, red tampo on sides, red int., clear windshield, rrch w/white stripe. #9 in Treasure Hunt series, #436 (1996) 60 - 65
g. no #, gold-plated, clear windshield, black int., gygd. FAO Schwarz Olympic 3-pack only (1996) 50 - NA
h. no #, mtlfk dk. blue, chrome int., blue-tinted windshield, opening hood, gray sides, sp5. Cruisin' America 6-pack (1997) 5 - NA
i. no #, white, gold int., blue-tinted windshield, opening hood, red & dk. blue stars & stripes, pcgd. American Spirit 4-pack gift set only (1997) 12 - NA
j. mtlfk dk. red, chrome int., clear windshield, sp7 w/red stripe. General Mills

'58 Corvette Coupe-j

Designer Collection 5-pack mail-in (1997) 5 - NA
k. turquoise, chrome int., tinted windshield, ho5, #780 (1997) 2 - 3
k2. as k, closed hood 2 - 4
l. gray; blue int.; tinted windshield; blue, red & white tampo w/"1" & Cubs logo on sides, "1" & "Chicago" on hood, "1," & different Cubs logo on trunk; sp5. June 1998 Chicago Cubs baseball game 2-pack give-away only (1998) 18 - NA
m. black, red int., clear windshield lined in gray, gray tampo, sp7 w/white sidewall tires. China. Cruisin' the '50s 8-pack from FAO Schwarz only (1998) 6 - NA

'58 Corvette Coupe-n

n. lt. blue, lt. blue metal base & int., clear windshield, gray on sides, blue tampo w/Corvette Central logo on trunk. Ltd ed of 10,000 for Corvette Central (1998) 12 - 15

'58 Corvette Coupe-o

o. black, chrome int., tinted windshield, lwch, #1092 (1999) 2 - 3

'58 Corvette Coupe-p

p. white, clear windshield, mtlfk blue int. & stripe over top, gray on sides, "58" on sides & hood, sp5. Ames Stores exclusive 4-pack only (1999) 4 - NA

'58 Corvette Coupe-q

q. black; white on sides, hood & trunk; white int.; blue-tinted windshield; white, gold & black tampo w/Las Vegas police badge & "Police" on sides & hood; "22," "Las Vegas Police" & "To Protect and Serve" on trunk; rrch. Limited to 25,000 in Cop Rods series for K•B Toys (1999) 5 - 7

'58 Corvette Coupe-r

r. yellow, yellow chassis, chrome int., blue-tinted windshield; sp3. Target excl. w/Arco Hauler, China 5 - NA

'58 Corvette-s

s. purple, black chassis, chrome int., sp3, K Mart Long Haulers 2-pack only (2000) 3 - NA

'58 Corvette-t

t. chrome; black int.; clear windshield; red, yellow & white tampo w/"Wild Weekend of" & Hot Wheels logo on sides; pr5s. Wild Weekend of Hot Wheels (2001) 20 - 25
u. black, black chassis, chrome exposed engine & int., blue-tinted windshield, tampo on sides & trunk w/"Heavy Metal" on sides, dw3, Thailand. Motorin' Music 5-pack (2001) 3 - NA
v. black, black chassis, chrome int., tinted windshield, white & red tampo w/"TH" on sides, sp3. Pavement Pounder pack (2001) 20 - NA
w. gray, gray chassis, chrome int., blue-tinted windshield, purple & black tampo on sides, sp3. China. Pavement Pounder pack (2001) 5 - NA

2015-x

x. white, chrome chassis, purple chrome int. & bumpers, clear windshield, purple & gold tampo w/"TH" on sides, sp3, China, Treasure Hunt, Pavement Pounder pack (2001) 20 - NA

'58 Corvette-y

y. yellow, black chassis, chrome int., clear windshield, white on sides, black stripes over top, sp3. China. #3 in Corvette series, #069 (2002) 2 - 3

13347-a

Big Chill® 13347 - 80mm - 1995
This snowmobile has a metalflake black plastic chassis; chrome interior, driver & windshield; engine in back and pink skis in front.

a. white, #12 in 1995 Model series, #352 $6 - 8
a2. as a, orange skis, #352 10 - 15

13347-a3

a3. as a2, blue design, orange "Shredder" on sides, #352 8 - 10
a4. as a2, black design on sides. #12 in 1995 Model series, #352 (1996) 4 - 6
b. 15243, black, black blades, chrome engine & int. #3 in Dark Rider Series II, #400 (1996) 2 - 4

Big Chill-c

c. mtlfk silver, red blades. China. #1 in Dark Rider II series, #400 (1997) 3 - 6
d. blue, white blades, chrome int. & engine, white tampo on sides, Malaysia, #779 (1999) 2 - 3
d2. as d, Thailand (1999) 2 - 3
d3. as d, China, in 10-pack (1999) 2 - 3

Big Chill-e

e. blue; black blades; gray tracks; orange, yellow, red & white tampo w/"Big Chill" on sides. Snow Plowers Action Pack (1999) 5 - NA

Big Chill-f

f. mtlfk gray; blue blades & track; chrome int. & engine; black, white, blue & red tampo w/"Search & Rescue" & "Avalanche Resort" on sides; Thailand. Snow Patrol 5-pack (2000) 2 - NA

Big Chill-g

g. gray; gray blades; chrome int. & engine; purple, white & lt. blue tampo w/"2000" on top; Thailand. Forces of Nature 5-pack (2001) 2 - NA
h. yellow; black chassis, blades & track; multicolored tampo w/"36," "M&M's" & race decals on sides & top; Thailand. #1 in NASCAR Snowmobile series (2001) 5 - 7
i. red; black chassis, blades & track; multicolored tampo w/"45," "Sprint" & race decals on sides & top; Thailand. #2 in NASCAR Snowmobile series (2001) 5 - 7
j. orange; black chassis, blades & track; multicolored tampo w/"5," "Kellogg's," Tony the Tiger & race decals on sides & top; Thailand. #3 in NASCAR Snowmobile series (2001) 5 - 7

Big Chill-k

k. yellow; black top, chassis, blades & track; red, white, black & blue tampo w/"22," "Caterpillar," "CAT" & race decals on sides & top; Thailand. #4 in NASCAR Snowmobile series (2001) 5 - 7
l. white; white chassis, blades & track; multicolored tampo w/"10," "Valvoline," Valvoline V & race decals on the sides & top; Thailand. #5 in NASCAR Snowmobile series (2001) 5 - 7

13340-a

('95) Camaro Convertible 13340 - 80mm - 1995
This 1995 Camaro convertible has a black plastic base, clear windshield, gray interior, uh, and "Camaro" engraved in back.

a. mtlc aqua, red Hot Wheels logo on windshield, #8 in 1995 Model series, #344 $8 - 10
a2. as a, sp5, #344 4 - 6
a3. as a, sp3, #344 4 - 7
a4. as a, sp7gd. Canada & Europe only (1996) 2 - 4

Camaro Convertible-b

b. black, gold Hot Wheels logo on black-tinted windshield, black plastic base & int., sp5. Black Convertible Collection, Target Stores only 4 - NA
c. mtlc red, gold "Season's Greetings" on sides, green sparkle wreath, gold "'95" on hood, clear windshield, white int.

Values are shown in U.S. dollars, first price is for mint, second is for mint packaged vehicles only. See pages 15-16 for grading guide to determine value for cars in lesser conditions.

Camaro Convertible-c

w/presents, Christmas tree on seats, pc w/green hubs. Red display box w/ornament & plastic top for 1995 Christmas 15 - 20

Camaro Convertible-d

d. chrome, same as c, green "Season's Greetings" on sides, red "'95" on hood, red int., pc w/red hubs. Red display box w/ornament & plastic top for 1995 Christmas 15 - 20
e. red, black int., clear windshield, yellow Hot Wheels logo on side, sp5. #8 of 1995 Model series, #344 4 - 6
e2. as e, sp3, #344 (1996) 4 - 6
e3. as e, dw3, #344 (1996) 2 - 4
e4. as e, no "Camaro" engraved in back, sp5, China, #344 (1997) 2 - 4
e5. as e4, not in Model series, India, #344 (1997) 2 - 4
e6. as e, ho5, Malaysia, #344 (1998) 2 - 4
e7. as e, sp5, India (1999) 2 - 3

13340-f

f. white; red, green, yellow, black & blue "USA," five Olympic circles on sides; black int.; clear windshield; pcgd. American Victory Olympic 3-pack only (1996) 5 - NA
g. no #, purple, clear windshield, black trim, gray int.; tw. 30th Anniv. of Camaro Collectible line gift pack only (1997) 10 - NA

Camaro Convertible-h

h. black; tinted windshield; red int.; red, yellow & white tampo w/"360," "Buckle Up Hold On" on sides; sp3; India; as '95 Camaro; #881 (1998) 2 - 3
h2. as h, sp5 (1999) 2 - 3
h3. as h, sp3, Malaysia (1999) 2 - 3

Camaro Convertible-i

i. mtlfk dk. blue; black int.; clear windshield; red & white tampo w/"Nestle Crunch" on sides & hood, "Milk Chocolate with Crisped Rice" on sides, "Nestle" & "Milk Chocolate with Crisped Rice" on trunk; sp5; Malaysia. #3 in Sugar Rush series, as '95 Camaro, #743 (1998) 2 - 3
i2. as i, India 2 - 3

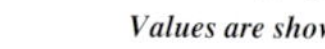
Camaro Convertible-j

j. white, gray plastic chassis, red int., tinted windshield, red striping tampo on sides & top, sp5w, India, #796 (1999) 2 - 3

Camaro Convertible-k

k. green, clear windshield, black int., sp5. Parking Garage playset (1999) 5 - NA

Camaro Convertible-l

l. orange, same as k; sp5. in playset (1999) 5 - NA

Camaro Convertible-m

m. red, same as l, gray int., sp5 (1999) 5 - NA

Camaro Convertible-n

n. white; black chassis & int.; tinted windshield; black, magenta, silver & brown tampo w/basketball, "27," "Gilstein University" & "Lords" on sides; dw3; India. Issued as '95 Camaro Convertible, #179 (2000) 2 - 3
n2. as n, Thailand, Sports Stars 5-pack (2001) 2 - NA
o. yellow; black chassis & int.; clear windshield; black, dark brown & brown tampo w/"Pace Car" on sides; sp3gd; Malaysia; #141 (2001) 2 - 3
p. red, black chassis & int., clear windshield, black & yellow tampo w/"SS" on sides, sp5, China, Kool Toyz Power Launcher pack (2001) 3 - NA
q. dk. blue, black int., clear windshield, silver & red tampo w/"SS" on sides, sp5, China, Power Launcher pack (2001) 3 - NA

13325-a

Camaro Racer 13325 - 75mm - 1995

This Malaysia-made Camaro has a metal base, clear windows, white interior, and sp5.

a. chrome blue; white int.; clear windows; white, red & yellow tampo w/"1," Hot Wheels logo & white border on sides; Hot Wheels logo on hood; Chevy logo on roof; "Hot Wheels" & 2 Hot Wheels logos on rear spoiler; "Jack Baldwin" on roof. #3 in Racing Metals series, #338 $15 - 20
a2. as a, no "Jack Baldwin" on roof 8 - 10

Camaro Racer-b

b. white; black int.; clear windows; black & orange tampo w/"4" & "Bousquette Racing" on sides, black stripe w/"Bousquette Racing" on hood, "4" on roof; sp5, Camaro Race Car; #792 (1998) 2 - 3
c. unpainted, black int., clear windows, ho5. Issued as Camaro Race Car, 1998 Hot Wheels Convention, #792 (1998) 65 - 75

Dodge Ram 1500 13344 - 80mm - 1995

This Dodge truck features a gray plastic base with chrome strip separating it from the body, gray-tinted windows, chrome interior, and sp5.

13344-a

a. mtlfk aqua, plastic camper shell, #7 of 1995 Model series, #348 $4 - 6
a2. as a, ho5, #348 (1996) 4 - 6
a3. as a, ho5w, #348 (1997) 10 - 12
a4. as a3, dark gray base, #348 (1997) 2 - 4

15219-b

b. 15218; red; yellow, gray & black tampo w/Hot Wheels logo, "4," "Dodge" & racing decals on sides; clear windows; red int.; sp7bk w/yellow "Goodyear #1" & "Eagle" on tires. #1 in Race Truck series, #380 (1996) 20 - 25

15219-b2

b2. as b, yellow & black shield w/ram head & "Goodyear" twice on hood, #380 6 - 8
b3. as b, no tampo on wheels, #1 in Race Truck series, #380 (1996) 12 - 15

15084-c

c. 15084, mtlfk dk. red, plastic camper shell, gray plastic base & int., clear windows, rrch. #11 in 1996 Treasure Hunt series, #438 (1996) 45 - 50

13344-d

d. black; red & yellow tampo w/flames, ram & winner's flag on sides, "Big Daddy" in back, white "Dodge" on rear window, white "Don Garlits" on windshield, Swamp Rat logo behind rear wheels; chrome int. & truck bed; clear windshield; tw. Limited to 10,000 (1996) 20 - 25

13344-e

e. mtlfk gray; gray chassis; "4," "Dodge" & racing decals on sides; "4" on roof; Dodge Ram shield & "Goodyear" on hood; red truck bed & int.; black-tinted windows; yellow "Goodyear" & "Eagle" on sides; sp7bk. Kmart excl. Thunder Trucks 4-pack (1996) 12 - NA
e2. as e, no tampo on roof or tailgate, front grille is different, sp5. #1 in Race Truck series, China, #380 (1998) 8 - 10

13348-f

f. white; red chassis; "01," Kmart logo, Hot Wheels logo & racing decals on sides; "01" on roof; Kmart logo on hood; chrome truck bed & int.; black-tinted windows; sp7bk w/yellow "Goodyear" & "Eagle" on sides; in K mart excl. Thunder Trucks 4-pack (1996) 12 - NA

Dodge Ram 1500-g

g. mtlfk dk. blue; white & red tampo w/"2," "Dodge" & racing decals on sides; Dodge Ram logo on hood; "2" on roof; "Dodge," "2" & Hot Wheels logo on back; red int. & truck bed; clear windows; black & red grill; gych. Dodge 3-pack only (1996) 15 - NA

Dodge Ram 1500-h

h. orange; gray chassis; clear windows; black int.; black, white & yellow tampo on sides; sp5. Road Repair 5-pack (1998) 2 - NA

Dodge Ram 1500-i

i. red, red camper shell, white chassis, yellow int. & grill, tinted windows, white tampo w/"Dodge Ram X-tra" on sides, sp5, #797 (1998) 2 - 3
i2. as i, ho5, China, #797 (1998) 2 - 3
i3. as i, sp5, China, #797 (1998) 2 - 3
i4. as i, no camper shell, China, 10-pack (1999) 2 - NA

Dodge Ram 1500-j

j. black; lt. brown chassis; chrome int. & truck bed; tinted windows; gold, white & red tampo w/"Hi Bank Racing," "Pit crew," "Auto Parts" & "Radio" on sides; sp3; Thailand. Race Team Crew 5-pack only (1999) 2 - NA

Dodge Ram 1500-k

k. black; lt. gray chassis, int. & truck bed; clear windows; gray & red tampo with "Federal Drug Enforcement," "1037" & "Drug Sniffing K9" on sides; logo on sides and hood; sp5; China; #1045 (1999) 2 - 3
k2. as k, Thailand, City Police 5-pack (1999) 2 - 3

Dodge Ram 1500-l

l. white; blue chassis & int.; white camper shell; clear windows; blue, red & yellow flame tampo on sides & hood; rrch. Ltd ed of 15,000, #1059 (1999) 6 -10

Values are shown in U.S. dollars, first price is for mint, second is for mint packaged vehicles only. See pages 15-16 for grading guide to determine value for cars in lesser conditions.

m. green; gray chassis; chrome int. & truck bed; clear windows; lt. green, black & white tampo; ho5; China #1059 (2000) 2 - 3
n. red, blue chassis, white int. & truck bed, clear windows, blue & white tampo w/"Dodge Different" & Dodge Ram logo on sides, Texas Rangers logo on hood, "Texas Rangers" & Dodge Ram logo on roof, pc. Texas Rangers baseball team promo (2000) 6 - 8

Dodge Ram 1500-o

o. blue; white chassis & int.; blue-tinted windows; white, black & red tampo w/baseball & "Dodgers 2000" on sides; "LA" on hood; rrw. Los Angeles baseball team promo (2000) 6 - 8

Dodge Ram 1500-p

p. mtlfk dk. red, clear windows, black bed & int., yellow & black tampo w/black scorpion & "Scorpion" on sides, sp5. China. #4 in Attack Pack series, #024 (2000) 2 - 3

Dodge Ram 1500-q

q. orange; black int.; clear windows; white, purple & black tampo on sides, Editor's Choice logo on hood; pc; Thailand. Target Exclusive Editor's Choice series (2000) 6 - 8

Dodge Ram 1500-r

r. dk. blue; dk. blue chassis; gray int.; clear windows; red, yellow & white tampo w/large Hot Wheels logo on sides, hood, truck bed & in back; "43" on sides & roof; sp5rd. In NASCAR pack (2001) 8 - 10
s. dk. blue; dk. blue chassis; gray int.; clear windows; multicolored tampo w/"12" & race decals on sides & roof; large Hot Wheels logo on sides, hood & truck bed cover; gyrd; Thailand. In NASCAR line as Mexican Special Edition (2002) 8 - 10

Dodge Ram 1500-t

t. dk. blue; dk. blue chassis; gray int.; clear windows; red, white & yellow tampo w/"43" on sides & roof; large Hot Wheels logo on sides, hood & truck bed cover; sp5rd; Thailand. In NASCAR line as Sticker Carlos Contreras (2002) 8 - 10
u. yellow; black chassis; chrome int. & truck bed; blue-tinted windows; black, red & white tampo w/"Radio Dispatched 24 Hrs.," "Hot Wheels Trans," "7" & "Maintenance Service" on sides; sp3; Thailand. Asphalt Assault 5-pack (2002) 2 - NA
v. yellow; black chassis; chrome int. & truck bed; blue-tinted windows; red, black, gold & white tampo w/"7," "HW Trans" & "Maintenance Service" on sides; sp3; China; #219 (2002) 2 - 3

13265-a3

Dragster 13265 - 84mm - 1995
This Top Fuel dragster has a metal base and engine in back of the cockpit, white plastic spoiler and driver, bw in back, small dragster wheels in front. Malaysia.
Similar castings: 11847 Driven To The Max (1994), 14973 Mongoose Dragster (1996), 14972 Snake Dragster (1996)

a. white, blue sides, red Hot Wheels logo & white "1 t/f" on sides, red stripes & Hot Wheels logo on top. #4 in Race Team series, #278 (1995) $5 - 7
a2. as a, dark blue sides, #278 3 - 5
a3. as a2, sp5 in back, #278 3 - 5
a4. as a3, extra-large sp5 in back, Thailand. Race Team Haulers 3-pack only (1998) 2 - NA
b. 13326; blue chrome; same as c; red stripes & Hot Wheels logo on white on top; red, white & yellow Hot Wheels logo & "1 t/f" on sides. #4 in Racing Metals series, #340 (1995) 8 - 10

Dragster-c

c. red; white front; yellow, black & white tampo w/"Interstate Batteries," "McDonald's" & McDonald's arch on sides, black spoiler; sp5 in back, dragster wheels in front. Kellogg's Raisin Bran mail-in offer only (1996) 6 - 8

Dragster-d

d. blue; blue spoiler; white, red & black tampo on sides & top w/"Warrior" & "Bousquette" on sides; China. Action Pack w/pink plastic parachute attached to rear (1999) 5 - NA

Dragster-e

e. lt. green; lt. green spoiler; red, black & white tampo w/"Graveyard" on sides & hood, "Handy" on top; orange plastic parachute attached to rear; China (1999) 4 - NA

Dragster-f

f. white; red spoiler & int.; red & black tampo w/"Jordan Drag Racing," "10" & race decals on sides; "WRF," "10" & race decals on top; sp5. World Racers 5-pack (1999) 2 - NA
g. black; green int. & spoiler; green, lt. blue, gray & white tampo w/"MX Drag" on sides; mw in front, sp5 in back; Malaysia. Max Steel 5 pack 2 - NA
h. purple, white int. & spoiler, white & orange tampo w/"Bratden Racing" & "Carris Weise" on sides, mw in front, sp5 in back, #164 (2001) 2 - 3
h2. purple, same as h, small sp5 in front, #164 (2001) 2 - 3

Dragster-i

i. red, white int. & spoiler, black & white tampo w/"1" & "Enjoy Coca Cola" on sides, Coke emblem & "1" on top, iw in front, sp5 in back, Malaysia. Coca Cola Race Team 4-pack (2001) 4 - NA

1338-a

Ferrari 355 13338 - 65mm - 1995
This Ferrari features a metal base, clear windows, black interior, and sp7.

a. yellow, red Hot Wheels logo on back license plate. #10 in 1995 Model series, #350 $8 - 10
a2. as a, sp5, #350 4 - 6
a3. as a, sp3, #350 4 - 6
a4. as a2, silver base, #350 (1996) 4 - 6
a5. as a, sp7gd, Canada & Europe only (1996) 2 - 4
a6. as a, dw3 (1996) 2 - 4
a7. as a, ho5w (1996) 10 - 12
a8. as a, ho5 (1996) 2 - 4

Ferrari 355-a9

a9. as a, black stripe, "Ferrari" & logo on sides, sp5, #350 (1997) 2 - 4
a10. as a9, sp7gd, Europe only (1997) 5 - 7

15081-b

b. 15081, white, clear windows, tan int., red tail lights, pcgd. #8 in 1996 Treasure Hunt series, #435 (1996) 40 - 45
c. 16943, black; purple int., clear windows; dk. red, green & white tampo: "Metal" on sides & roof, guitar, "Pedal," "Metal" on hood; sp5. #2 in Rockin' Rods series, #570 (1997) 2 - 4
d. blue-green; black int.; tinted windows; red, black & white stripe tampo with "3," "Straight Line Racing" on sides; lwch. Figure 8 Racers 5-pack only (1998) 2 - NA

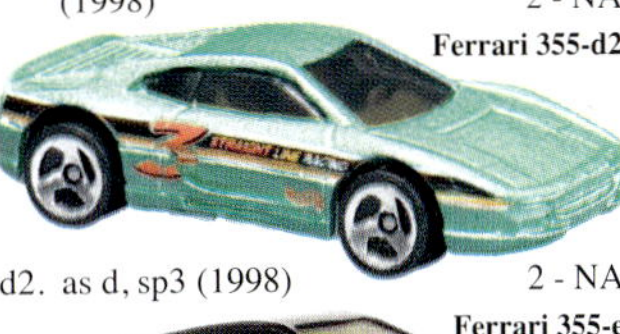
Ferrari 355-d2

d2. as d, sp3 (1998) 2 - NA

Ferrari 355-e

e. black, yellow-tinted windows, white int., yellow Ferrari logo on sides & hood, sp5, #813 (1998) 2 - 4

Ferrari 355-f

f. red, same as e, clear windows, #1094 (1999) 2 - 3

12803-a4

Hot Wheels 500 12803 - 75mm - 1995
This Indy-type racer has a metal chassis and interior, rear wing, and bw.
Similar casting: 11846 No Fear Race Car (1994)

a. blue; red, yellow & white tampo w/"Hot Wheels" on sides; Hot Wheels logo on sides, front & rear wing; "Goodyear" on front spoiler; "1" on front. #2 in Race Team series, #276 (1995) $12 - 15
a2. as a, sp7, #276 45 - 65
a3. dk. mtlfk blue, same as a, #276 10 - 12
a4. as a2, uh, #276 35 - 40
a5. as a2, bw, #276 10 - 12
b. unpainted; black chassis, int. & spoiler; ho5; 1998 Hot Wheels Convention; #244 (1998) 75 - 80

Hot Wheels 500-c

c. lt. green; metal chassis; black int.; black, white & orange race tampo w/"Handy" & race decals on sides, "8" & race decals on top; sp7bk w/yellow "Goodyear" on tires #773 (1999) 5 - 7

Hot Wheels 500-d

d. black; black int.; orange & white tampo w/"1" & "Heralda" on sides, "1" on nose & "Treasure Hunt Ninety-Nine" on front wing; sp7 w/"Treasure Hunt Ninety-Nine." #11 in 1999 Treasure Hunt series, #935 (1999) 12 - 15

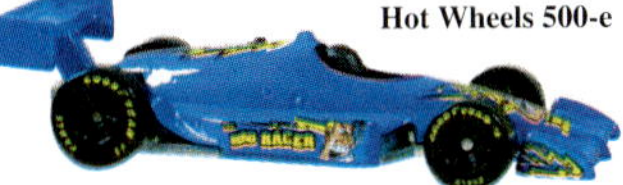
Hot Wheels 500-e

e. blue; black int.; yellow, brown, white & black tampo w/face & "The Mad Racer" on sides & top. #1 in Mad Maniax series, #017 (2000) 2 - 3

Hot Wheels 500-f

f. red, black chassis, blue int., blue & white logo w/"Target" on sides & wing, Colorado Rockies logo on sides. Issued in baggie for Target stores (2001) 10 - 12

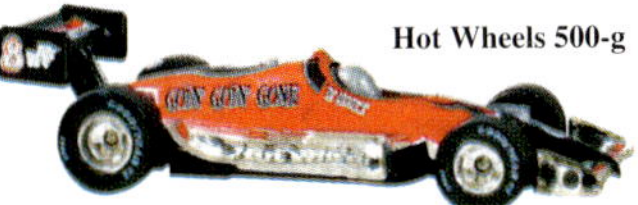
Hot Wheels 500-g

g. mtlc. red; chrome sides; gray int.; black spoiler; black & white tampo w/Hot Wheels logo on sides, "Goin' Goin' Gone" & "W. Scott" on body, "8" & "Final Run" on wing; gych. #7 in 2001 Final Run (2001) 7 - 9

13342-a

Hydroplane 13342 - 85mm - 1995
This model has a white plastic chassis, chrome plastic engine and interior, clear windshield, and small black wheels.
Similar casting: Hydroplane (2000)

a. blue; red, white & yellow Hot Wheels logo, "Team" & "Racing" on each side of top, Hot Wheels logo on wing. #6 of 1995 Model series, #346 $3 - 5
a2. as a, gold Hot Wheels 30th Anniv. logo on front. Ltd ed for 30th Anniv., w/blistercard in window box (1998) 5 - 7

Values are shown in U.S. dollars, first price is for mint, second is for mint packaged vehicles only. See pages 15-16 for grading guide to determine value for cars in lesser conditions.

b. 15456, red, same as a, orange & black tampo on top. Computer Cars series w/computer chip in blister (1996) 3 - 5

c. yellow; blue, orange & yellow flames on top; black metal chassis. #2 in Flamethrower series, #385 (1996) 4 - 6

c2. as c, flames on rear wing are backwards, #385 (1996) 20 - 25

c3. as c, China, #385 (1997) 2 - 4

d. no #; gray; black chassis; purple, red & orange tampo on top. Racing World 5-pack only (1996) 2 - NA

d2. no #, same as d, Thailand (1996) 2 - NA

e. 16922; white; blue base; chrome engine & int.; clear windshield; blue, yellow & black tampo w/waves & "Wet & Wild" on top. #1 in Speed Spray series, #549 (1997) 2 - 4

f. lt. green; brown, black & yellow tampo w/"Biohazard Removal," "Unit 4" & logo on top; Malaysia. #1 in Biohazard series, #717 (1998) 2 - 4

f2. as f, different shade, Thailand, #717 (1998) 2 - 4

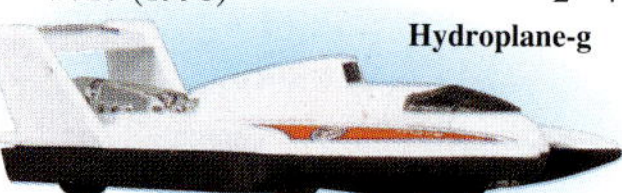

g. white, black chassis, tinted windshield, red & black tampo w/"Harbor Patrol" twice on top, large blue Hot Wheels logo on wing, Malaysia, #873 (1999) 2 - 3

g2. as g, Thailand, Police Squad 5-pack (1999) 2 - NA

h. gray; black bottom; orange-tinted windshield; chrome engine; black, white & orange tampo w/"Seahorse" & "Triton S Racing" on top; Thailand. Ocean Blasters 5-pack (1999) 2 - NA

i. black; yellow-tinted windshield; chrome int.; white, gold, red & yellow tampo w/"7" on front, large Hot Wheels logo on wing; China; #1053 (1999) 2 - 3

j. white; orange chassis; chrome int.; orange-tinted windshield; orange, red & blue tampo w/"Oceanics Research Vehicle One" on one side, "Preserving Nature is Our Business" on other, "Oceanics One" on rear fin; China; #202 (2000) 2 - 3

j2. as j, Thailand, issued in Forces of Nature pack (2001) 2 - NA

k. yellow; chrome engine & int.; clear windshield; multicolored tampo w/"4" & race decals on sides, "Kodak Max Film" on top, "Kodak" on wing; Thailand. #1 in NASCAR Hydroplane series (2000) 5 - 7

l. blue; same as k; lt. blue upper body; multicolored tampo w/"44" & race decals on sides; "44," Hot Wheels logo & race decals on top; Hot Wheels logo on wing; Thailand. #2 in NASCAR Hydroplane series (2000) 5 - 7

m. black; same as k; yellow on top; yellow, white & red tampo w/"Nations Rent" on sides, top & wing; "Nations Rent" & race decals on top; Thailand. #3 in NASCAR Hydroplane series (2000) 5 - 7

n. white; same as k; dk. blue chassis; dk. blue & red tampo w/"12" & race decals on sides; "12," pegasus & "Mobil 1" on top; "Mobil 1" on wing; Thailand. #4 in NASCAR Hydroplane series (2000) 5 - 7

Lumina Minivan 12352 - 75mm - 1995
This Chevy Lumina has a yellow plastic chassis, clear windows with black plastic frames, black interior, and bw.
Similar casting: 5675 Chevy Lumina (1992)

a. yellow, black "Taxi" & checkerboard design on sides & hood, red Hot Wheels logo on hood, #259 $4 - 6

a2. as a, sp5, #259 3 - 5

b. aqua, black plastic base, tan int., tinted windows, silver stripes w/"Lumina" on sides, sp5, Lumina Van, China, #702 (1998) 8 - 10

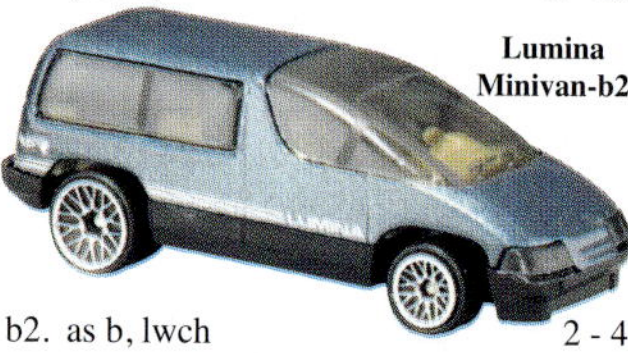

b2. as b, lwch 2 - 4

Lumina Stocker 12794 - 75mm - 1995
This Chevy Lumina has a metal base, clear windows, white interior, and uh. Malaysia.

a. blue; white, red & yellow tampo w/"1," Hot Wheels logo, racing decals & white border on sides; "1," "Goodyear," Hot Wheels logo & Chevy logo on hood; "1" on roof; logo on trunk. #1 in Race Team series, #275 (1995) 4 - 6

a2. as a, red int., Race Team series 2-pack (1995) 175 - 200

a3. as a, Pontiac Grand Prix, #1 of Race Team series, #275 (1995) 150 - 200

a4. dk. blue, same as a, #275 (1995) 6 - 8

a5. as a4, sp7, #275 6 - 8

b. white; red & black tampo w/"4," "Lane Automotive" & racing decals on sides; "Lane Automotive" & racing decals on hood; "4" on roof. Lane Automotive, in box, limited to 7000 15 - 20

c. black, white int., clear windows, white "76" on sides & roof, sp7. Unocal station only, baggie only (1994) 6 - NA

d. black, white "76" on sides & roof, clear windows, white int., sp7. Unocal 76 premium, baggie only (1995) 4 - NA

Pontiac Stocker 12873 - 75mm - 1995
This Malaysia-made stock car has a metal chassis, red plastic interior, clear windows and pcr.
Similar castings: 2628 #42 Mellow Yellow (1992), 2623 #42 STP (1992), 2630 #2 Pontiac Excitement (1993), 10159 Auto Palace/AC Delco (1993)

a. white; red, black & pink tampo w/"1," "Mattel," "Racing into the Future," "Barbie," Hot Wheels logo & racing decals on sides; Mattel Circle & "Goodyear" on hood; "1" & "Hank V" on roof; "The Toy Club" on trunk; "Racing into the Future" on rear bumper. Mattel Toy Club only, in box 35 - 40

Power Pipes® 13346 - 72mm - 1995
This concept car has silver metal base, two chrome wings, clear magenta dome, and sp5.
Similar casting: 15264 Pasta Pipes (1996)

a. dk. mtlfk blue, red Hot Wheels logo in white rectangle in back. #9 in 1995 Model series, #349 (1995) $4 - 6

a2. as a, sp7, #349 (1996) 4 - 8

a3. as a, sp3, #349 (1996) 2 - 4

a4. as a, sp7gd, Canada only (1996) 2 - 4

a5. as a, ho5, #349 (1998) 2 - 3

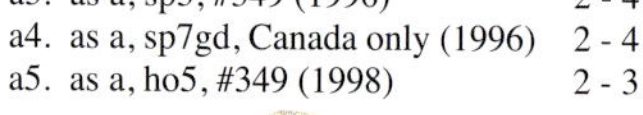

b. yellow, same as a, chrome int., transparent magenta dome, sp7, set only (1996) 7 - NA

c. gray, chrome int., yellow-tinted dome, lwgd. Designer Collection 8-pack, Target excl. (1996) 5 - NA

d. 16904, blue-tinted plastic, magenta-tinted dome, chrome int. & pipes, sp3. #3 in Phantom Racer series, #531 (1997) 2 - 4

e. no #, orange, mtlfk silver base, tinted dome, chrome int., sp5. Spin-Out Set & Dash 'n Crash set only (1997) 7 - NA

f. lt. green; dk.-tinted dome; black, red, white & yellow tampo w/"8" & "Starter Set" on sides, "8" on top; lwgd. Starter Set only (1997) 7 - NA

g. black, orange metal base, chrome int., orange-tinted dome, orange & yellow tampo on sides, dw3o, Thailand, #869 (1998) 2 - 3

h. black, chrome int., clear dome, gold & white tampo on sides & top w/"Mystery Car" & "Q4" on hood, sp3. In baggie as 4th quarter Mystery Car (1999) 6 - NA

i. white, same as g, red metal base, red-tinted dome, ho5, #1100 (2000) 2 - 3

j. chrome; black chassis, fins & dome; blue & black tampo w/"Power Pipes" on sides; sp3; #106 (2001) 2 - 3

k. lime green, chrome int., orange-tinted dome, black tampo design on sides, sp3, Malaysia. Motorized Wildcat Super Starter Set (2001) 10 - NA

Power Pistons® 13343 - 77mm - 1995
This concept car has a metal base, blue-tinted canopies, metal interior & headlights, and sp5.

a. bronze, silver Hot Wheels logo on sides, #5 in 1995 Model series, #347 (1995) $4 - 6

a2. as a, uh, #347 15 - 25

a3. as a, sp7, #347 (1996) 10 - 20

a4. as a, sp3, #347 (1996) 4 - 8

a5. as a, mtlfk silver base, #347 (1996) 2 - 6

a6. as a, sp7gd, Canada only (1996) 2 - 4

a7. as a, dw3, #347 (1997) 2 - 4

b. 15246, black chrome, clear canopies, black int., black base, sp7. #4 in Dark Rider Series II, #403 (1996) 2 - 6

c. no #, chrome blue, white sides, red & yellow "Toy Fair '96" & blue "New York" on sides, Hot Wheels logo on each rear fender, red plastic canopies, 1996 Toy Fair car, Park 'n Plates box only (1996) 150 - NA

d. 15454, yellow plastic, metal int., blue-tinted canopies, Computer Car, iw (1996) 3 - 5

Values are shown in U.S. dollars, first price is for mint, second is for mint packaged vehicles only. *See pages 15-16 for grading guide to determine value for cars in lesser conditions.*

e. 6903, dk. red-tinted plastic, chrome int., clear canopies, sp3. #2 in Phantom Racer series, #530 (1997) 2 - 4
e2. as e, sp5, #530 (1997) 2 - 4
e3. as e, silver base, #530 (1997) 2 - 4

Power Pistons-f

f. no #, dk. chrome, red Hot Wheels flame logo on sides, black int., sp7. Figure 8 Starter Set only (1997) 7 - NA
f2. as f, gray int. (1997) 7 - NA

Power Pistons-g

g. mtlfk purple; yellow & white tampo w/"Net" & "www.hotwheels.com" on sides; yellow-tinted canopies; sp3. #2 in Techno Bits series, #690 (1998) 2 - 3
g2. as g, lwch, #690 (1998) 2 - 3

Power Pistons-h

h. gray; lt. green int.; green-tinted canopies; lt. green, black, white & red tampo w/"3" & "Nuclear" on sides; sp5; Thailand. Alien Attack 5-pack (1999) 2 - NA
i. white; gray int.; blue-tinted canopies; black, orange & gray tampo on sides; sp3; Thailand. Tornado Twister 5-pack (1999) 3 - NA
j. gray; white int.; green-tinted canopies; red, black & white tampo on sides & top w/"3" & "77890" on sides; sp3; Thailand; Super Launcher pack (2000) 3 - NA
k. orange-tinted plastic body; clear canopies; gray int.; black, white & gold tampo w/"Power Flyz" on sides; sp3; Thailand; #154 (2001) 2 - 3
l. gray; red int.; red-tinted canopies; yellow, black & red tampo on sides & top w/"Viper Strike" on sides; sp5; Thailand. Motorized Viper Strike Starter set (2001) 10 - NA
m. white glow in dark plastic; black chassis; chrome int.; purple-tinted canopies; orange, black & yellow tampo on sides & rear fenders; dw3; Thailand. Fireball playset (2001) 10 - NA

Power Pistons-n

n. black; white int.; red-tinted canopies; red, gold, white & gray tampo w/"Yu-Gi-Ho" on sides; sp5rd; Thailand. #1 in Yu-Gi-Ho series. #083 (2002) 2 - 3

13348-a2

Power Rocket® 13348 - 84mm - 1995
This concept car features a metal chassis; chrome engine, pipes and interior; and sp5.
Similar casting: 24105 X-Ploder (1999)
a. purple; orange Hot Wheels logo, stripe, "EXP 3510," "Danger" & white "Watch for Flames" & "Experimental" on sides; sp5. #11 of 1995 Model Car series, #351 $4 - 6
a2. as a; "Experimental," "Watch for Flame" & logo in silver; #351 2 - 6
a3. as a, mtlfk silver base, #351 4 - 10
a4. as a3, sp3, #351 (1996) 2 - 4
a5. as a3, sp7gd (1996) 2 - 4
a6. as a3, dw3, Canada only (1996) 2 - 4
a7. as a3, ho5, #351 (1997) 2 - 4
a8. as a3, ho5w, #351 (1997) 8 - 12
b. orange-tinted plastic, chrome int., hw5. Designer Collection 8-pack only, Target Stores (1996) 3 - NA
c. 16902, green-tinted plastic, orange-tinted canopy, chrome engine & int., metal base, sp3. #1 in Phantom Racer series, #529 (1997) 2 - 4
c2. as c, silver base, #529 (1997) 2 - 4

Power Rocket-d

d. white; red canopy; pink chrome engine & int.; red, dk. blue & black tampo w/"Stunt Flyer" on sides; sp3. G-Force Stunt Riders 5-pack only (1998) 2 - NA
d2. as d, dw3 (1998) 2 - NA

Power Rocket-e

e. dk. red, chrome engine & int., orange-tinted canopy, yellow & orange flames on sides, sp3gd, Thailand. Volcano Blowout 5-pack only (1999) 2 - NA
f. clear blue plastic body; clear canopy; chrome int.; black, yellow & red tampo w/"Lotrap LSI ES" on sides; sp3; Malaysia. Max Steel 5-pack 3 - NA
g. dark red; chrome engine & int.; tinted canopy; white, red & black tampo with "3" & "Hot Wheels" on sides; ho5; Thailand; #207 (2001) 2 - 3

12795-a2

Side-Splitter 12795 - 79mm - 1995
This Funny Car concept model has a metal chassis and interior, lift-up body to show a metal engine, engine top sticking through the hood and windshield, clear windows and bw.
Similar casting: 3250 Firebird Funny Car (1982)
a. blue; red, white & yellow tampo w/Hot Wheels logo, "1 f/c" & racing decals on sides, Hot Wheels logo & Chevy logo on hood. #3 of Race Team series, #277 (1995) $8 - 10
a2. dk. blue, same as a, #277 8 - 10
a3. as a2, sp5 in front & sp5-large in back, #277 4 - 6

15254-b

b. 15254, white, same as a, red & yellow paint splattered all over, sp5. #2 in Splatter Paint series, #409 (1996) 2 - 4

Side-Splitter-c

c. white; blue-tinted windows; black, blue, lt. green & red tampo w/"Toys R Us" & race decals on sides & hood; sp5. Toys "R" Us 10-pack only (1999) 10 - NA

11390-a

Spawn Mobile 11390 - 79mm - 1995
A remake of the Firebird Funny Car, this model has a metal chassis & interior, lift-up body showing a metal engine, engine top sticking thru the hood & windshield, clear windows, and bw.
Similar casting: Firebird Funny Car (1982)
a. white; red, yellow, green & black tampo of red flames w/"Spawn" in blue & black on one side; yellow & black design w/"Spawn" in green, yellow & black on other side; chains, red flames & black on top; limited to 5000, card reads "Todd McFarlane's Spawn From Image Comics" & "America's Number 1 Comic Book!" (1994) $35 - 40
b. as a, black bats added to hood, headlights in front, sold w/Spawn comic book, about 95,000 made (1994) 20 - 25

13609-a2

Speed Blaster® 13609 -
72mm or 70mm - 1995
This concept model has a pinkish chrome plastic chassis, rear engine and windows, uh.
Similar casting: 3438 Dragon Wagon (1993)
a. metalflake blue, 1995 Model series, #343 $6 - 8
a2. as a, sp5, #343 6 - 8
a3. as a, chrome plastic chassis, #343 6 - 8
a4. as a, black plastic chassis, #343 85 - 90
a5. as a, chrome chassis, sp5, #343 (1996) 4 - 6
b. green, same as a, sp5, #343 3 - 5
b2. as b, sp7, #343 30 - 35
b3. as b, sp3, #343 2 - 4
b4. as b, sp7gd, Canada only (1996) 2 - 4
b5. as b, ho5, #343 4 - 6
b6. as b, dw3, #343 (1997) 2 - 4
b7. same as b, gray plastic base & engine, ho5 2 - 4
c. 16949, blue, black plastic base, chrome windows & engine, silver Hot Wheels logo on hood, sp3. #4 in Blue Streak series, #576 (1997) 2 - 4
c2. as c, chrome base, #576 (1997) 18 - 20

Speed Blaster-d

d. mtlfk purple; chrome base & windows; yellow, orange & white tampo w/"Extreme Entry Ceramic Shielding" on sides; sp3. X-Treme Machine 5-pack only (1998) 2 - NA
d2. as d, dw3, #778 (1998) 2 - 3

Speed Blaster-e

e. mtlfk purple, black plastic chassis, chrome windows, red & white tampo w/"C778" on sides, sp3, #778 (1998) 2 - 3

Speed Blaster-f

f. green; lt. yellow & green chassis; chrome windows & engine; yellow, black & lt. green tampo on sides & roof w/"Dinohunt" on sides; sp3. #3 in Game Over series #959 (1999) 2 - 3
g. mtlfk black, black chassis & windows, chrome engine, gold & white tampo w/"Q3" on sides & nose, "Mystery Car" behind engine, sp3. In a baggie as a Mystery Car (1999) 6 - NA
h. orange; black chassis; black windows; black, white & gold tampo on sides & hood w/"Birdhouse" on hood; sp3. #3 in Tony Hawk Skate series, #43 (2000) 2 - 3
i. pink; chrome chassis, windows & engine; yellow Hot Wheels logo in front; sp3; Malaysia. Alien Attack playset (2001) 6 - 8
j. mtlfk blue; chrome chassis & windows; red, white & black tampo w/Hot Wheels logo, "6" & race decals on sides; sp3; Malaysia; #168 (2002) 2 - 3

13341-a

Speed-A-Saurus® 13341 - 70mm - 1995
This model looks like a stegosaurus on wheels. It features a metal engine and tail pipes, and bw.
a. green, #4 of 1995 Model series, #345 (1995) $4 - 6
a2. as a, sp5, #345 2 - 4
b. 13341, purple, same as a, sp5. #4 of 1995 Model series, #345 (1997) 2 - 4
c. no #; lt. gray; red & yellow tampo w/red heart, arrowhead & "M" on body; sp5. Crazy Classics 5-pack only (1997) 2 - NA
d. dk. turquoise, orange base, sp5, #814 (1998) 2 - 4
e. bright green, yellow chassis, gold chrome engine & pipes, black & white tampo w/arrow & heart on sides, sp5gd. Virtual Collection #104 (2000) 2 - 3

T-Bird Stocker-a2

T-Bird Stocker - no number - 78mm - 1995
This newer version of a Ford stock car has a metal chassis, gray interior, clear windows, and uh.
Similar casting: 15265 Sweet Stocker (1996)
a. no #, mtlc dk. red; white, blue & red tampo w/"11," "Ford Thunderbird," racing decals & Hot Wheels logo on sides, Ford logo & "Goodyear" on hood, "11" & "Luis M." on roof, logo on trunk; clear windows; gray int. & roll cage; uh. Ford 5-pack only (1995) $3 - NA
a2. as a, sp5 (1995) 3 - NA
a3. as a, sp7 (1995) 8 - 10
b. gray, tinted windows, white int., red Hot Wheels logo in white rectangle, sp5. Then & Now 8-pack (1995) 3 - NA
b2. as b, gray int. (1995) 5 - NA

15026-c

c. 15026; black; red, yellow, blue, white, orange & green tampo w/"McDonald's," "94," Coca-Cola logo, Batman outline & racing decals on sides; McDonald's M logo on hood; "94" & "Bill Elliott" on roof; Reese's candy bar on trunk; clear win-

Values are shown in U.S. dollars, first price is for mint, second is for mint packaged vehicles only. See pages 15-16 for grading guide to determine value for cars in lesser conditions.

dows; red int. & roll cage; sp7bk w/yellow "Goodyear" & "Eagle" on sides. Thunderbat, box only, limited to 15,000 (1996) 15 - 20

d. no #; fluorescent lime; red, orange & magenta tampo design w/"Track System" on sides; uhgd. Track System 5-pack only (1995) 2 -NA

16203-e

e. 16203; red; white front; yellow, black, & white tampo w/"94," "McDonald's" & racing decals on sides, McDonald's M logo on hood, "94" & "Bill Elliott" on roof; clear windows; red int. & roll cage; sp7bk w/yellow "Goodyear" & "Eagle" on sides. Kellogg's Raisin Bran mail-in only (1996) 5 - 7

T-Bird Stocker-f

f. blue; gray chassis; red int.; clear windows; black, white, red & yellow tampo w/Hot Wheels logo, ".com" & "Connected" on sides; sp3; China; .com 5-pack (1999) 2 - NA

T-Bird Stocker-g

g. white; black chassis & int.; blue-tinted windows; dark blue, gray & black tampo on sides & roof; "Carris" on sides; ho5; Thailand. Shark Park 5-pack (2001) 2 - NA

T-Bird Stocker-h

h. red, metal chassis, chrome windows, black & white tampo w/"Photography" & "Artie Boott" on sides, ho5, Malaysia, #239 (2001) 2 - 3

i. mtlfk blue; black chassis; gray int.; clear windows; black hood; red, white & silver tampo w/"4," "Hot Wheels" & race decals on sides & hood; sp5; China; #155 (2002) 2 - 3

1996

Mattel began re-issuing basic cars from China. Most were from the late 1980s and early 1990s with new colors and tampos. Vehicles made from old Corgi tools also appeared. Other introductions were the VW bus, 1970 Dodge Daytona Charger, and Radio Flyer Wagon, all favorites among collectors. More new wheels appeared, including the lace wheel (lw), directional wheel (dw), and five-hole wheel (ho5). Many cars got all three plus a few from prior years.

149-a

1970 Dodge Charger Daytona 14908 - 82mm - 1996

This Daytona racer was issued with a chrome plastic base, clear windows, tan interior, lwgd. Malaysia.

a. red, "Daytona" on rear fenders, gold Hot Wheels logo on side. #3 in 1996 First Editions, #382 $3 - 5

a2. as a, sp7gd, #382 (1997) 6 - 10

a3. as a, dw3, #382 (1997) 4 - 6

a4. as a, sp7bk (2000) 4 - 6

b. red, yellow rear spoiler, red "Daytona" on rear bumper, clear windows, black int., gych. Dodge 3-pack only 12 - NA

c. lime green, black spoiler w/lime green "Daytona" on sides, clear windows, black int.; gych. '60s Muscle Cars 4-pack only (1996) 12 - NA

d. orange, tinted windows, black int., sp7. General Mills Designer Collection 5-pack mail-in (1997) 5 - NA

1970 Dodge Charger-e

e. mtlfk dk. green; tan chassis; black int.; clear windows; white, black, gold & red tampo on sides w/two white stripes on hood, brown on nose & top of wing; sp5. #1 in Flyin' Aces Series #737 (1998) 2 - 3

e2. as e, ho5, #737 (1999) 3 - 5

f. unpainted, blue int., tinted windows, ho5. #1 in Flyin' Aces series, 1998 Hot Wheels Convention, #737 (1998) 100 - 125

1970 Dodge Charger-g

g. blue; clear windows; orange int.; orange, black & white tampo on sides & hood w/"22" on sides; sp5; Malaysia. #2 in Seein' 3-D series, #010 (2000) 2 - 3

g2. as g, dw3, #010 (2000) 2 - 3

1970 Dodge Charger-h

h. gray; red int.; clear windows; "15," Michael Kollins dinner logo & race decals on sides; 14th Annual Hot Wheels Convention logo & "426 C.I." on hood; dinner logo on roof; "Michael Kollins" on wing; collectible wheels. Limited to 2000 for Michael Kollins Dinner (2000) 35 - 45

1970 Dodge Charger-i

i. mtlfk gray; clear windows; black int.; black, yellow, red & white tampo w/"P," "01," "823609," "Night Prowler" & black cat on 8 ball on sides; black hood; lwch; Malaysia. #1 in Rod Squadron series, #065 (2001) 2 - 3

14841-a

1996 Mustang GT ('96 Mustang) 14841 - 67mm - 1996

This convertible has a metal chassis, clear windshield, tan interior, and sp5. Malaysia.

a. dk. mtlfk red; silver headlights, black "Mustang GT" on rear bumper. #1 in 1996 First Editions series, #378 $4 - 10

a2. as a, sp3, #378 4 - 8

a3. as a, sp7gd, only in Canada 4 - 15

a4. as a, dw3, #378 2 - 5

a5. as a, sp7, #378 2 - 4

a6. as a, ho5, #378 2 - 6

b. fluor. orange, black chassis & int., clear windshield, sp5. Computer Cars series, w/disc (1996) 3 - 5

c. mtlfk orange, tan int., clear windshield, sp5. China. Father & Son Collector 2-pack by Avon or Ford Dealership playset only (1997) 7 - NA

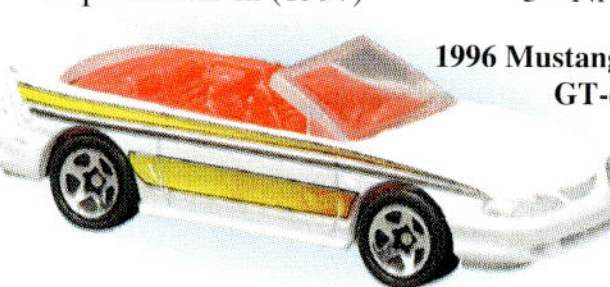
14841-d

d. purple, turquoise int., tinted windshield, sp5. General Mills Designer Collection, 5-pack mail-in (1997) 5 - NA

1996 Mustang GT-e

e. white; red int.; yellow, black & red stripes on sides; sp5; China; #821 (1997) 3 - 6

1996 Mustang GT-f

f. white, pink int., clear windshield, pink & lt. purple tampo w/stripes & "Barbie" on sides & hood, sp5. Hot Wheels Cars-Timeless Toys 4-pack (1998) 6 - NA

1996 Mustang GT-g

g. yellow; black int.; clear windshield; dk. blue & white tampo w/"Nestle's Butterfinger" on sides & stripes on top; sp5; China. #4 in Sugar Rush series, #744 (1999) 3 - 5

1996 Mustang GT-h

h. mtlfk dk. red; black int.; tinted windshield; gold, black & white flame tampo w/"Mustang 96" & mustang on sides & hood; lwgd; China; #1058 (1999) 2 - 3

i. white; tinted windshield; black int.; black, gold & gray flame tampo on sides & hood; pr5s; Malaysia; #114 (2001) 2 - 3

i2. as i, sp3, #114 (2001) 2 - 3

1996 Mustang GT-j

j. mtlfk black; black int.; tinted windshield; yellow, orange, black, gray & white tampo w/"Dragons Football" on sides; lwgd; Thailand; Sports Stars 5-pack (2001) 2 - NA

k. orange, white int., clear windshield, black & lt. orange tampo on sides, lwch, China, Pavement Pounder pack (2001) 3 - 5

1996 Mustang GT Coupe-a

1996 Mustang GT Coupe - no # - 67mm - 1996

This coupe has a metal chassis, clear windows, white interior, gray headlights, pcgd. Malaysia.

a. dk. mtlfk blue, FAO Schwarz History of Hot Wheels II 8-pack $10 - NA

1996 Mustang GT Coupe-b

b. purple, clear windows, white int., iw. Four Decades of Pony Power 3 car gift set only (1997) 12 - NA

'80s Camaro-a

'80s Camaro - no # - 75mm - 1996

This race car is the same casting as the Blown Camaro, but without the engine. It has a plastic body, metal base, blue-tinted windows, and sp3gd.

Similar castings: 2115 #25 Hot Wheels (1992), 2738 #33 Duracell (1992)

a. white; black, yellow, orange & red checkered flag & flame tampo on sides & hood. Track Systems Gift Pack only $4 - NA

a2. as a, sp7gd 4 - NA

a3. as a, sp5 2 - NA

b. white; blue int. & windows; orange, yellow & red flames & "Hot Wheels" on sides, hood & roof; uho. Only issued in a set 8 - NA

b2. as b, sp7o (1997) 2 - 4

b3. as b, black windows, sp7. Camaro 5-pack only (1997) 2 - NA

b4. white, metal body, clear windows, gray int., yellow & red flame tampo, sp3. Camaro 5-pack only (1997) 2 - NA

'80s Camaro-c

c. white, metal body, black & blue paint splattered on car. #4 in Splatter Paint series, #411 4 - 6

d. white; plastic body; blue, purple & orange stripes on sides; uho. Starter Set only (1996) 7 - NA

e. 16932; lime green; metal body; black int.; tinted windows; black & green design on sides & hood; black, green & red dragon on hood; dw3br. #3 in Street Beast series, #559 (1997) 2 - 4

'80s Camaro-f

f. lt. yellow, clear windows, black int., silver "IROC-Z" on sides, silver & black design on hood, iw. 30th Anniv. of Camaro Collectible gift pack only (1997) 10 - NA

g. mtlc aqua, gray int., clear windows, sp5. Camaro 5-pack only (1997) 2 - NA

'80s Camaro-g2

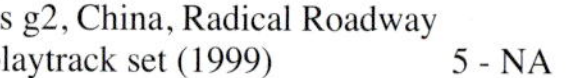

g2. as g, sp3, as Camaro Z28, #822 (1997) 2 - NA

g3. as g2, China, Radical Roadway playtrack set (1999) 5 - NA

Values are shown in U.S. dollars, first price is for mint, second is for mint packaged vehicles only. See pages 15-16 for grading guide to determine value for cars in lesser conditions.

h. yellow; tinted windows; blue int.; red, blue & lt. green tampo w/"Toys "R" Us" on sides. Toys "R" Us-excl. 10-pack only (1998) 2 - NA

i. white, same as h, black int., tampo colors reversed, Toys "R" Us-excl. 10-pack only (1998) 2 - NA

'80s Camaro-j

j. green, same as i, Toys "R" Us-excl. 10-pack only (1998) 3 - NA

'80s Camaro-k

k. dk. blue; tinted windows; black int.; orange, white & gray tampo w/"Q2" & "Bonus Car '98" on sides, design on hood & roof. 2nd Bonus car for 1998 (1998) 5 - NA

l. black; tan int.; tinted windows; white roof w/"02" & "Highway Patrol" in gold & black; white doors w/"Highway Patrol" & star in yellow, blue & red; "To Protect and Serve" in white on sides; sp5; Thailand. Police Squad 5-pack only (1999) 2 - NA

'80s Camaro-l2

l2. as k, ho5, 10-car gift pack (1999) 2 - NA

m. aqua; tinted windows; black int.; black, gray & gold tampo w/"Blown Camaro" & "650" on sides & hood; lwch. Issued as Blown Camaro, #1083 (2000) 2 - 3

n. red, same as m, lwch, Malaysia. Issued as Blown Camaro, #229 (2000) 2 - 3

o. yellow, clear windows, gray int., yellow & black flames on hood & roof, sp3. China. Power Launcher pack (2001) 3 - NA

'82 Corvette Stingray-a

'82 Corvette Stingray - no # - 80mm -1996

This model of the Corvette Stingray has a plastic body, a metal chassis, chrome interior, orange-tinted windows, and sp3gd.

Similar casting: #15263 Pizza Vette (1996)

a. green, black tire marks all over, Track Systems 5-pack only $4 - NA

a2. as a, sp7gd, Track Systems 5-pack only 4 - NA

16305-a

BMW 850i 16305 - 75mm - 1996

Made from a Corgi casting, this model has a black plastic base, clear windows, red interior and sp5. China. Similar to the 1991 850i, the main differences are this model is slightly larger than the 1991 version, does not have side mirrors or a sun roof, and has opening doors and separation between the front and back side windows.

Similar casting: 5667 BMW 850i (1991)

a. metalflake silver, #498 $2 - 4

a2. as a, lwch, #498 (1997) 2 - 4

b. no #, black, gray plastic base, tan int., sp5gd. FAO Schwarz Gold Collection III only 8 - NA

c. white; blue-tinted windows; red int.; black, red & yellow tampo w/black "850i" on front fenders; lwch; Europe. #1 in Street Racers series (1997) 2 - 4

BMW 850i-d

d. red, gray base, clear windows, tan int., sp5. Back Pak 5-pack only (1997) 2 - NA

14907-a

Chevy 1500 (Chevy Pick-Up) 14907 - 72mm - 1996

This Chevy pickup has a metal chassis, tinted windows, gray interior & truck-bed cover, sp7b with "Goodyear #1" & "Eagle" in yellow on the sides. Malaysia.

a. gray; red, black, blue & yellow tampo w/"Roadster Wheels," "10" & racing decals on sides; Hot Wheels logo on hood & bed cover; "10" on roof. #2 in 1996 First Editions series, #367 $12 - 15

a2. as a, smaller wheels, #367 6 - 8

a3. as a2, no logo on bed cover, sp5, China, #367 (1998) 5 - 7

14907-b

b. blue; white truck cover; red, white & yellow tampo w/"1," "Hot Wheels" & racing decals on sides, Hot Wheels logo on hood, "1" on roof; clear windows w/yellow "Hot Wheels"; white int.; sp7bk w/yellow "Goodyear" & "Eagle" on sides. K mart excl. Thunder Trucks 4-pack (1996) 12 - NA

14907-c

c. black; red truck cover; gray, red & white tampo w/"1," "Chevrolet" & racing decals on sides, "Chevrolet" on hood, "1" on roof; clear windows; red int.; sp7bk w/yellow "Goodyear" & "Eagle" on sides. K mart excl. Thunder Trucks 4-pack (1996) 12 - NA

d. 16907; blue; white, red & yellow racing tampo w/"1" on sides, Hot Wheels logo on hood, "1" on roof; white int.; bed cover; tinted windows; sp5. #2 in Race Team Series III, #534 (1997) 4 - 6

d2. as d, sp7, #534 (1997) 2 - 4

d3. as d, sp3, #534 (1997) 2 - 4

d4. as d, ho5, #534 (1997) 2 - 4

d5. as d, mtlfk silver base, sp5, #534 (1997) 2 - 4

Chevy 1500-e

e. gray; black metal base & int.; clear windows; red, black, yellow & white tampo w/"8" & "Power Charger Racing" on sides; dw3; #877 (1998) 2 - 3

e2. as e, India, #877 (1999) 2 - 3

f. orange, black int. & truck bed, clear windows, black & white tampo w/"Z" on sides, #1121 (1999) 2 - NA

Chevy 1500-f

Chevy 1500-g

g. yellow, clear windows, black int. & truck bed, black & silver tampo design on sides & hood w/"Barb'd & Wired" on sides, pr5s, Malaysia, #101 (2001) 2 - 3

g2. as g, sp3, #101 (2001) 2 - 3

h. dk. blue; black int.; tinted windows; white, red, yellow & black tampo w/"12," Hot Wheels logo & race decals on sides, Hot Wheels logo on hood, "12" on roof; sp5rd. Carlos Contreras Pickup challenge set (2001) 10 - NA

16048-a

Computer Warrior™ 16048 - 74mm - 1996

This re-issue of the Phantomachine is a concept car that looks like a reclining robot. It has an orange metal base, chrome engine in the stomach, sp5. China.

Similar casting: 3851 Phantomachine (1987)

a. dark grayish blue $2 - 4

16306-a

Corvette Coupe 16306 - 68mm - 1996

Made from a Corgi casting, this model has a black plastic base, clear windows, red interior, and sp5. Similar to the '80s Corvette, the main differences are this model is slightly smaller, has side mirrors and plastic windows on the sides with a slightly different shape between the front and back windows. China.

Similar casting: 3928 '80s Corvette (1983)

a. mtlfk dk. grayish green, #499 $2 - 4

a2. as a, lwch, #499 (1997) 2 - 4

b. mtlc green, black int. & Corgi wheels, issued in playset 6 - NA

c. white, black chassis & trim, red int., clear windows, iww. 100th Anniv. of Auto gift pack only 12 - NA

d. no #, black, tan int., sp5gd. FAO Schwarz Gold Collection III only 8 - NA

e. 16980; red; white int.; stripe on sides; orange, yellow & black "Chuck E Cheese's" & gray, yellow, blue & pink Chuck E Cheese mouse on hood. Chuck E Cheese Pizza only (1997) 6 - 8

f. 95522, white, clear windows, dk. blue int., orange & blue tampo /"Corvette" on sides, sp5, European blistercard only (1997) 5 - 7

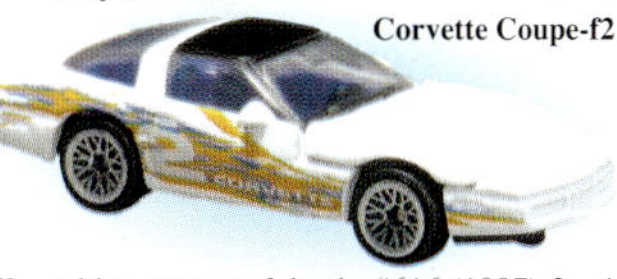
Corvette Coupe-f2

f2. white, same as f, lwch, #616 (1997) 2 - 4

g. mtlfk gold, black roof & int., lwch, 1980 Corvette on blistercard, #1103 (2000) 2 - 3

15266-a

Crunch Chief 15266 - 76mm - 1996

This Chevrolet Stocker has a black metal chassis, yellow-tinted windows, black interior, and sp3.

Similar casting: 1791 Chevy Stocker (1996)

a. white; red, green, yellow, purple & orange candy tampo all over. #4 in Fast Food series, #419 $4 - 6

a2. as a, sp7, #419 3 - 5

14914-a

Dogfighter® 14914 - 75mm - 1996

This model looks like an open-cockpit World War I airplane without the wings. It has a black plastic base, chrome interior, tan plastic propeller in front, and dw3.

a. dk. mtlfk red; "K-9" & Hot Wheels logo on tail; red star & red, white & yellow design on sides. #10 in 1996 First Editions, #375 $2 - 4

a2. as a, sp5, #375 4 - 6

a3. as a2, chrome is gray plastic, sp5, #375 (1997) 8 - 10

a4. as a, ho5, #375 (1998) 2 - 4

Dogfighter-b

b. 16682, mtlfk dk. green, same as a, yellow base, red plastic propeller w/"32" & logo in gold, black on sides, sp5. #8 in 1997 Treasure Hunt series, #585 (1997) 18 - 22

Dogfighter-c

c. black; yellow plastic base & propeller; white, red, gold & yellow tampo w/"Dog-Fighter" on sides; sp5. #2 in Flyin' Aces series, #738 (1998) 2 - 3

c2. as c, sp3, #738 (1999) 2 - 3

c3. as c, ho5, #738 (1999) 6 - 8

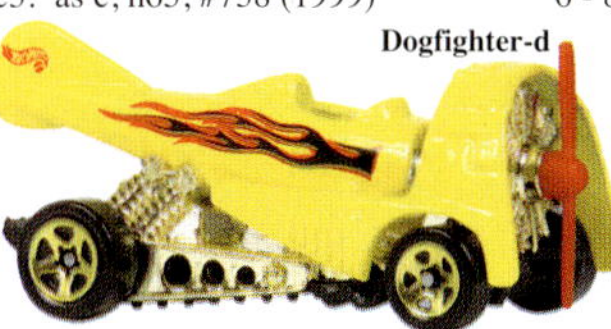
Dogfighter-d

d. yellow, black base, gold chrome engine, red propeller, red & black flame tampo on sides, sp5gd, Malaysia. Crazy Classics III 5-pack (1999) 2 - NA

d2. as d, China, Virtual Collection series, #137 (2000) 2 - 3

e. mtlfk gray, orange propeller, black & orange flame tampo on sides, lwch, China, #222 (2000) 2 - 3

f. flat black; black chassis; chrome int.; red propeller; yellow, red & white flame tampo on sides; sp3gd; China; #146 (2002) 2 - 3

Dragon Wagon 16047 - 80mm - 1996

Based on a lizard, this concept car has a green metal chassis, exposed engines, plastic body, and sp5. China.

Similar casting: #2059 Fangster (1986)

Values are shown in U.S. dollars, first price is for mint, second is for mint packaged vehicles only. See pages 15-16 for grading guide to determine value for cars in lesser conditions.

16047-a

a. lt. green; orange eyes; #478 $2 - 4

15968-a

Enforcer 15968 - 73mm - 1996
Based on a military sprint buggy, this concept model has a metal base, silver windows, gray plastic guns and movable plastic rockets on the sides, a movable plastic machine gun in back, and sp5. China.
Similar castings: 5268 Megadestroyer 1 (1982), 5269 Megadestroyer 2 (1982), 9373 Super Cannon (1985)
a. dk. metallic magenta $2 - 4

Enforcer-b

b. mtlfk green; black chassis, guns & windows; black, white & gold tampo with "Police," "Enforcer," "Riot Control" & emblems on sides; sp5; #150 (2001) 2 - 3

17962-a

Ferrari 308 GTB 17962 - 74mm - 1997
This hardtop has a black metal base, red interior, tinted windows, and sp5. Malaysia.
Similar castings: 2021 Race Bait 308 (1978), 7295 Quik Trik (1984), 9538 Street Beast (1985), 3494 Hot Wheels (1993 Tattoo Machines)
a. black, yellow Ferrari logo on hood, "Ferrari" on trunk. Small European blistercard only, #2 in Ferrari series (1997) $5 - 7

Ferrari 308 GTB-b

b. no #, fluor. yellow, clear windows, black int., yellow & black Ferrari logo on hood, sp5. Ferrari 5-pack only (1997) 2 - NA
b2. as b, ho5 2 - NA
b3. as b, ho5w 2 - NA
b4. as b, dw3 2 - NA

Ferrari 308 GTB-c

c. mtlfk brown, tinted windows, tan int., yellow & black Ferrari logo on hood, ho5, #816 (1998) 4 - 6
c2. as c, sp5, #816 (1999) 2 - 3
c3. as c2, black int., #816 (1999) 20 - 25

Ferrari 308 GTB-d

d. red, red metal base, tinted windows, black int., sp5, #816 (1999) 2 - 3
d2. as d, tan int., #816 (1999) 2 - 3
e. yellow; yellow chassis; black int.; clear windows; gray, orange & black

Ferrari 308 GTB-e

tampo w/"Twister" on sides; sp5; Thailand. Tornado Twister 5-pack (1999) 2 - NA
f. gray, black chassis, black int., tinted windows, yellow & black Ferrari logo on hood, sp5, Malaysia, #190 (2001) 2 - 3
g. black, black int., clear windows, red & yellow tampo w/"308 Turbo" on sides, Ferrari logo on hood, lwch, Malaysia, #166 (2002) 2 - 3

Ferrari 308 GTS-b

Ferrari 308 GTS - no # - 74mm - 1996
This convertible, an old Corgi casting, was made in China and has a black plastic base, black interior, clear windshield, and sp5.
a. no #, black, tan int., sp5gd. FAO Schwarz Gold Collection III only $8 - NA
b. red, same as a, #496 2 - 4

Ferrari 308 GTS-c

c. yellow, same as a, black lower half of body, Ferrari logo on hood, sp5, #604 (1998) 3 - 6
c2. as c, lwch, #604 (1998) 2 - 3

95519-a

Ferrari 328 GTB - 95519 - 72mm - 1996
This remake of the old Street Beast casting has a plastic body, gold chrome windows and sp3gd. Malaysia.
a. dark red, Track System 5-pack only $2 - NA
a2. as a, sp7gd 2 - NA
a3. as a, lwgd 2 - NA
b. orange, blue windows, black tire-tracks tampo, sw. G-Force set only (1996) 6 - NA

95519-c

c. white; black metal base; blacked-out windows; pink, black & lt. blue tornado design w/"Tornado" on sides & hood; ho5. Ferrari 308 GTB, #3 in Quicksilver series, #547 (1997) 2 - 4

95546-b

Ferrari 348 TB - 95546 - #80mm - 1996
This model, an old Corgi casting, has a gray plastic base, tan interior, clear windows and sp5gd. China.
a. black, FAO Schwarz Gold Collection III only $8 - NA
b. red; black plastic base & int.; tinted windows; yellow, silver & black stripe tampo on hood & roof; "348" on hood; sp5. #1 in Racing Series, Europe only (1997) 5 - 7

b2. as b, tan int., no tampo, Corgi Wheels, playset only (1997) 6 - NA
c. red, tan int., clear windows, yellow & black Ferrari tampo on hood, ho5. China. Sto 'n Go Ferrari Dealership set (2001) 2 - NA

14917-a

Ferrari F50 (convertible) 14917 - 64mm - 1996
This model of the Italian convertible has a gray plastic base, clear windshield, black plastic interior, and lwch. Malaysia.
Similar casting: #23932 Ferrari F50 (hardtop) (1999)
a. red, #12 in 1996 First Editions, #377 $2 - 4
a2. as a, China, #377 (1997) 2 - 4
a3. 17064, same as a, Ferrari logo in yellow & black on hood, "Ferrari" in yellow on spoiler, lwch. #4 in Ferrari series, Europe only (1997) 5 - 7
a4. as a, India, #377 (1999) 2 - 3

Ferrari F50-b

b. no #, yellow, clear windshield, black int., Ferrari logo on nose, "Ferrari" on spoiler, sp5. Toys "R" Us 10-car set (1997) 5 - NA

Ferrari F50-c

c. mtlc purple; black int.; tinted windshield; silver, black & red tampo with "Stunt Machines" & "Team Leader" on sides; dw3; #855 (1998) 2 - 3
c2. as c, India (1999) 2 - 3

16304-a

Ferrari Testarossa 16304 - 77mm - 1996
This model, an old Corgi casting, has a black plastic base, black interior, clear windows and sp5. China.
a. white, #497 $2 - 4
a2. as a, lwch, #497(1997) 2 - 4
a3. as a, yellow & black Ferrari logo on hood, #136 (2000) 2 - 3
b. no #, black, tan int., sp5gd, FAO Schwarz Gold Collection III only 8 - NA

Ferrari Testarossa-c

c. yellow, same as a, sp5, Super Highway playset, in backpack only (1997) 8 - NA

Ford LTL - See Kenworth T 600

95585-b

Ford Sierra 23 Ghia XR4ti - 95585 - 77mm - 1996
This Ford 4-door sedan, an old Corgi casting, was made in China and has a black plastic chassis with a trailer hitch, tan interior, clear windows, and sp5gd.
a. black, FAO Schwarz Gold Collection III only 8 - NA
b. 95518; mtlfk gray; clear windows; red int.; dk. blue & gold tampo w/"XR4Ti," "Sierra" & "4" on sides; "4" on hood; sp5. Ford XR4Ti only, #615 (1997) 4 - 6

95585-c

c. dark metallic blue, same as b, blue plastic base, sp5, Backpack 5-pack only (1997) 6 - NA

95538-a

Ford Thunderbird Convertible - 95538 - 66mm - 1996
This model was originally from the Corgi line. It has a metal base, black interior, clear windshield, and iwch. China.
a. pink, 100th Anniv. of the Automobile gift set only $10 - NA
b. black, tan int., bwgd, FAO Schwarz Gold Collection III only 10 - NA
c. red, black int., clear windshield, Corgi wheels, playset only 5 - NA
d. mtlc blue, same as c, Corgi wheels, playset only 5 - NA
e. black, same as c, Corgi wheels, playset only 5 - NA

95538-f

f. aqua, white int., clear windshield, rrch w/white stripe, opening hood w/engine displayed. 40th Anniv. of 2-Seat Thunderbird 2-car gift set only (1997) 12 - NA
g. yellow, clear windshield, white int., ww, open engine. Motorin' Music 4-pack from Target only (1997) 25 - NA

95538-h

h. 95538, dk. turquoise, white int., clear windshield, opening hood, no tampo, bw, #612 (1997) 12 - 15

16055-a

Grizzlor® 16055 - 68mm - 1996
Shaped like a gargoyle, this concept car has a plastic body, metal chassis, orange interior, sp5. China.
Similar casting: 2058 Cargoyle (1986)
a. white, red Hot Wheels logo in back, #484 $4 - 6

16055-a2

a2. as a, big black spots on body, orange collar, chrome int., #484 2 - 4

Values are shown in U.S. dollars, first price is for mint, second is for mint packaged vehicles only. See pages 15-16 for grading guide to determine value for cars in lesser conditions.

15219-a

Kenworth T 600A 15219 - 81mm - 1996
This model of the T 600A tractor rig with sleeper cab has a red chassis, blue plastic windows, and black sp7 with "Goodyear #1" & "Eagle" in yellow on the sides.
Similar castings: 1790 Big Rig (1989), 15219 Kenworth T600 (1996)
a. mtlfk silver; red, white & blue tampo w/Hot Wheels logo, "11," "Kenworth" & race decals on sides; Kenworth logo on hood; "Kenworth" on roof. #2 in Race Truck series, #381 $12 - 15

Kenworth T 600-b

b. metallic purple, chrome plastic chassis, black windows, silver and orange tampo with "Treasure Hunt '98" on sides, sp3. #3 in Treasure Hunt series, #751 (1998) 20 - 30

Kenworth T 600-c

c. mtlfk gold & black; gray, gold, black & white tampo w/Final Run logo on sides, roof & back of cab; "Longhaul" on sides; "FR" & "9921341" on sides of doors; sp7; "Final Run" in gold on tires. #3 in 1999 Final Run series, (1999) 5 - 7

95512-b

London Bus - 95512 - 75mm - 1996
This model of the Daimler Fleetline double deck bus, an old Corgi casting, was made in China and has a black plastic base, chrome windows, and sp5gd.
a. black, FAO Schwarz Gold Collection III only $8 - NA
b. 95512; red; black-tinted windows; black "The London Standard," "A Great Newspaper" & "For A Great City" in red rectangles on white stripe on sides; sp5; #613 (1997) 10 - 12

95510-b

London Taxi - 95510 - 72mm - 1996
This model, an old Corgi casting, was made in China and has a metal base, tan interior, clear windows, opening doors, and sp5gd.
a. black, "FAO Schwarz" and logo on sides. FAO Schwarz Gold Collection III only $8 - NA
b. 95510; yellow; black int.; red, black & white tampo w/"London Cab Co.," "See City of Hot Wheels" on sides; #619 (1997) 8 - 10

16301-a

Mercedes 500SL 16301 - 77mm - 1996
Originally a Corgi casting, this model has a clear windshield with a black frame, red interior, and sp5. China.
a. metalflake gray, #494 (1996) $3 - 5
b. no #, black, tan int., sp5gd. FAO Schwarz Gold Collection III only (1997) 7 - NA
c. mtlc gray, metal base, purple int., tinted windshield, orange & purple pinstripes, sp5. #3 in Cabriolet series, Europe (1997) 5 - 7
d. metallic blue, black base, clear windshield, gray interior, Corgi wheels, playset only 7 - NA
e. mtlfk dk. green; black chassis; tan int.; tinted windshield; red, black & gold tampo on sides & hood; sp3; #815 (1998) 2 - 3
f. unpainted, black base, tan int., clear windshield, sp3. 1998 Hot Wheels Convention, #815 (1998) 60 - 70

Mercedes 500SL-g

g. mtlfk gray, black chassis & int., tinted windshield, lwch, Malaysia #1013 (1999) 2 - 3

14973-a

Mongoose Dragster 14973 - 84mm - 1996
This Malaysia-made Top Fuel dragster has a metal base, metal engine in back of the cockpit, white plastic spoiler and driver, sp5 in back and small dragster wheels in front.
Similar castings: 11847 Driven To The Max (1994), 13265 Dragster (1995), 14972 Snake Dragster (1996)
a. blue, "Tom McEwen The Mongoose" in white on sides, white design w/red stars on nose, limited to 8000, #90 $20 - 25

14860-a3

Monte Carlo Stocker 14860 - 75mm - 1996
This Chevy stock car has a gray plastic base, clear windows, white interior & roll cage, and sp7b. Malaysia.
a. blue; Race Team colors in white, yellow & red; yellow "Goodyear" & "Eagle" on tires; 1996 Model Series, #440 $8 - 10
a2. as a, sp7gd, Canada only 3 - 5
a3. as a, sp7b w/out tire tampo 6 - 8

14860-b

b. black; "1," "Chevrolet" & racing decals on sides; "Chevrolet" & Chevy logo on hood; "1" on roof; Chevy logo on trunk; clear windows; red int.; iw; China. 100th Anniv. of Auto gift pack (1996) 10 - NA
c. black; yellow on bottom of car; clear windows; red int. & roll cage; red, yellow, white, blue & black tampo w/"Caterpillar," "95" & racing decals on sides, "Cat" on hood, "95" on roof; sp5y w/"Goodyear" & "Eagle" in yellow; China. FAO Schwarz History of Hot Wheels III only (1997) 8 - NA
d. yellow; brown plastic chassis & int.; clear windows; brown stripe around bottom of car; brown, lt. green, red & white tampo w/"1" & "Snyder's Of Hanover Sourdough" on sides; "Snyder's Of Hanover Sourdough Hard Pretzels Fat Free" on hood; 1 on roof; "1" & "Snyder's Of Hanover" in back; Goodyear racing tires. Snyder's of Hanover mail-in (1999) 6 - 8

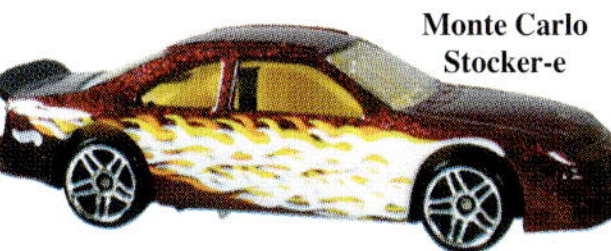
Monte Carlo Stocker-e

e. mtlfk brown; yellow int.; clear windows; white, yellow & orange flame tampo; pr5s; Thailand. Forces of Nature 5-pack (2001) 2 - NA

95540-b

(Ford) Mustang Cobra
95540 - 73mm - 1996
This model, an old Corgi casting, has a black plastic base, tan interior, clear windows, and sp5gd. China.
a. black, FAO Schwarz Gold Collection III only $10 - NA
b. 95540, mtlc magenta, clear windows, black int., orange stripe with black "Mustang R.D." on sides, black stripe with "5.0 Mustang" on hood, lwch, #623 (1997) 2 - 4
b2. as b, sp5, #623 (1997) 10 - 12
c. silver, no tampos, Backpack 5-pack only (1997) 2 - NA

15264-a

Pasta Pipes® 15264 - 72mm - 1996
This concept car has a black metal base, two chrome wings, clear blue plastic bubble top, and sp3.
Similar casting: 13346 Power Pipes (1995)
a. white; orange and yellow spaghetti tampo all over; #2 in Fast Food series, #417 $6 - 10

15263-a

Pizza Vette 15263 - 76mm - 1996
This Corvette Stingray has a black metal base, blacked-out windows, and sp3.
Similar casting: '82 Corvette Stingray (1996)
a. white; brown, orange & dk. red pepperoni pizza tampo all over. #2 in Fast Food series, #416 $8 - 15
a2. as a, sp7, #416 (1997) 3 - 5
a3. as a, sp5, #416 (1997) 3 - 5

15785-a

Police Cruiser (Car) 15785 - 73mm - 1996
This model was based on the Holden Commodore and uses the old casting. It has clear windows, tan interior, blue plastic light on top, and sp7bk.
Similar casting: 9713 Holden Commodore (1991)
a. black; white doors w/Hot Wheels logo; red & gold "Auto City Police" on doors; gold "Emergency" on rear fender; white & gold "96," Hot Wheels logo & white, red & gold "Police" on trunk; #577 $2 - 6
b. 16016; same as a; white doors & roof; black int.; "96" on roof; white sticker, "To Protect & To Serve," "Police," black, yellow, red & green shield; sp7bk. Ltd ed of 10,000 for Los Angeles Police Department (1996) 35 - 40
c. 16910; green; purple plastic chassis & int.; light on top; clear windows; orange flames w/purple outline on sides & hood; sp5. #1 in Heat Fleet series, #537 (1997) 4 - 6
c2. as c, sp7, #537 (1997) 4 - 6
c3. as c, ho5, #537 (1997) 2 - 4
c4. as c, sp3, #537 (1997) 2 - 4

Police Cruiser-d

d. white; black int.; blue-tinted windows & lights; red, gold & black tampo w/"Fire Dept. Chief," "01" & logo on sides, "01" on roof, "Fire Dept." on trunk; sp5; #577 (1998) 2 - 6
d2. as d, sp3, #577 (1998) 2 - 4
e. black; dk. blue chassis; lt. gray int.; tinted windows; red plastic light on top; white roof w/"01" in black; white & red tampo w/"State Police" & logo on sides; sp5; Malaysia; #875 (1999) 2 - 3
f. white; black chassis & int.; blue-tinted windows & lights; red & dk. blue stars & stripes tampo w/"Police," "02" & "Hot Wheels Police Force" on sides; sp3; Thailand; #1046 (1999) 2 - 3

Police Cruiser-f2

f2. as f, ho5 (1999) 2 - NA

Police Cruiser-g

g. blue-gray, black chassis, gray int., tinted windows, red lights on top, gray & black tampo w/"Police" & "K9 Unit" on sides, dw3, #207 (2000) 2 - 3
h. white, black chassis & int., clear windows, clear red lights on top, gold & black tampo w/"Hot Wheels County Sheriff" on sides & roof, "Emergency Response Vehicle" on sides, "240" on roof, sp5, Thailand, #149 (2001) 2 - 3

Police Cruiser-i

i. black; dark blue chassis; gray int.; tinted windows; white roof w/red lights; white, gold & red tampo w/"State Police" & shield on sides; sp5; Thailand; #875 (2001) 2 - 3
j. blue; gray chassis & int.; clear windows; orange-tinted lights; orange, lt. orange & white tampo w/Hot Wheels logo, "No. 6" & "Fire Chief" on sides; sp3; Thailand. Heat Fleet 5-pack (2002) 3 - NA

Values are shown in U.S. dollars, first price is for mint, second is for mint packaged vehicles only. See pages 15-16 for grading guide to determine value for cars in lesser conditions.

95532-b

Porsche 935 - 95532 - 78mm - 1996
This model, an old Corgi casting, has a black plastic base, tan interior, clear windows, and sp5gd. China.

a. black, FAO Schwarz Gold Collection III only $8 - NA
b. mtlfk silver; blue-tinted windows; white int.; black "935" on white rectangle on hood & sides; red & blue stripes on sides, hood, roof & trunk w/racing decals; lwgd. FAO Schwarz History of Hot Wheels III only (1997) 6 - NA

95532-c

c. mtlc black; clear windows; purple int.; green, silver & purple tampo w/"4" on sides & hood; "Kollins Kompressor Werke Competition Induction Systems"; lwch. #4 in Racing series, Europe only (1997) 5 - 7

95520-c

Porsche (911) Carrera - 95520 - 72mm - 1996
This model, an old Corgi casting, has a black metal base, tan interior, clear windows, and sp5gd. China.

a. black, FAO Schwarz Gold Collection III only $8 - NA
b. mtlfk silver, red int., clear windows, sp5, Malaysia. Porsche 5-pack only (1997) 2 - NA
b2. as b, dw3, #829 (1997) 2 - 3
c. 95520; black; same as b; orange & flame tampo w/"3" & "Dynamic Racing" in white on sides & hood; sp5. Small European card only (1997) 5 - 7
c2. as c, dw3, Europe only (1997) 5 - 7
d. unpainted, black int., tinted windows, dw3, 1998 Hot Wheels Convention, #829 (1998) 60 - 75
e. dk. mtlfk red, tan int., tinted windows, sp5gd, #818 (1999) 4 - 8

95520-f

f. dk. mtlfk red; same as e; black, orange & yellow tampo; sp5gd; #818 (1999) 20 - 35

95520-g

g. gray; tan int.; tinted windows; red, white & black tampo on sides & hood, "Dirtbike Team" on hood; sp5gd. #3 in X-Treme Speed series, #967 (1999) 2 - 3
h. mtlfk blue, white int., clear windows, sp3, #146 (2000) 2 - 3
i. mtlfk blue, mtlfk gray chassis, white int., clear windows, red & silver flame tampo on sides, sp3, China, #130 (2002) 2 - 3

95537-a

Porsche Targa - 95537 - 72mm - 1996
This convertible has clear windows, green interior with Santa in the driver's seat, presents on the trunk, and sp5 with green hubs. Issued with an ornament in a red display box for Christmas, 1996. China.

a. mtlc red; gold "Happy Holidays" on sides; green & gold tampo w/"96" inside wreath on hood $15 - 20

95537-b

b. mtlc green; same as a; gold & red hood tampo; red int.; sp5 w/red hubs 15 - 20

16300-c

c. 16300, lime yellow, black plastic base, clear windows, black int., sp5, China, #493 (1997) 2 - 4
d. no number, black, tan int., sp5gd. FAO Schwarz Gold Collection III 7 - NA
e. red, black int., clear windows, Corgi wheels, playset only 7 - NA
f. mtlc gray, same as e, playset only 7 - NA

Porsche Targa-g

g. no #, red, same as a, black base & window frame, lwgd. Cruisin' America 6-pack only (1997) 10 - NA

Porsche Targa-h

h. 95537, mtlfk silver, same as c, sp5, #608 (1997) 2 - 4

Porsche Targa-i

i. mtlc green, black int., clear windows, sp5, 5-car backpack only (1997)6 - NA

14914-a

Radio Flyer Wagon 14914 - 55mm - 1996
This model has a metal base & pipes, chrome plastic engine & wing, black interior and sp5. Similar castings: 1668 Hot Rod Wagon (1997), Draggin' Wagon (2000)

a. red, "Radio Flyer" in white on sides, #9 in 1996 First Editions, #374 $2 - 6
a2. as a, bw, China (1997) 4 - 8
a3. as a2, sp5 in front, bw in back, China (1997) 2 - 4
a4. as a, silver base (1997) 2 - 4
a5. as a, Thailand, Crazy Classics II 5-pack (1999) 2 - NA

Radio Flyer Wagon-b

b. mtlfk blue, white int., Radio Flyer logo in white on sides, sp5, China, #837 (1999) 2 - 4

Radio Flyer Wagon-c

c. lt. blue; chrome engine; gray seat & handle; white, yellow & black tampo w/"43" & race decals on sides, front & back; sp5bl; Thailand. #1 in NASCAR Draggin' Wagon series (2000) 7 - 9
d. black; same as c; white, yellow, blue & red tampo w/"75," "Cartoon Network" & race decals on sides, front & back; sp5; Thailand. #2 in NASCAR Draggin' Wagon series (2000) 7 - 9
e. lt. & dk. blue; same as c; white & red tampo w/"33" & race decals on sides, front & back; sp5; Thailand. #3 in NASCAR Draggin' Wagon series (2000) 7 - 9
f. red; same as c; multicolored tampo w/"5" & race decals on sides, front & back; sp5; Thailand. #4 in NASCAR Draggin' Wagon series (2000) 7 - 9
g. purple, same as a, Malaysia, #172 (2001) 2 - 3

14910-a

Rail Rodder® 14910 - 73mm - 1996
This train engine has a metal base, black plastic body, chrome engine, molded and dragster wheels. Malaysia.

a. black; red, yellow & orange tampo w/Hot Wheels logo & "Rail Rodder" on sides; #370 $2 - 8
a2. as a, chrome is gray plastic, #370 (1997) 8 - 10
a3. as a, China, #370 (1997) 2 - 4
a4. as a2, gray plastic, chrome plastic wheels, #370 (1997) 2 - 4

16676-b

b. 16676, white, same as a, pink chrome engine & smokestack, red flame outline on sides, mw. #12 in Treasure Hunt series, #589 (1997) 20 - 25

14910-c

c. gray; green, black & yellow tampo w/"Rail Rodder," "Engine" & railroad decals on sides; #850 (1998) 2 - 3
c2. as c; made in China #850 (1999) 2 - 3

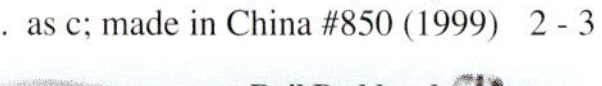

Rail Rodder-d

d. white; gray & blue tampo w/"Ice Breaker" & "Engine 32 Below" on sides; Malaysia; #1043 (1999) 2 - 3
e. black, same as c, tampo colors are red, lime & white, #1062 (2000) 2 - 3

Rail Rodder-f

f. black; mtlfk gray base; gold chrome wheels, engine & smokestack; red, yellow & white flame tampo w/"Rail Rodder" & "12EX" on sides; China; #221 (2001) 2 - 3

14911-a

Road Rocket® 14911 - 75mm - 1996
This concept model has a metal chassis and front & rear bumpers, plastic body and engine, blue-tinted top, and lwgd.

a. light green, #7 in 1996 First Editions, #371 $4 - 6
a2. as a, sp7gd (1997) 4 - 12

Road Rocket-b

b. 16905, orange-tinted plastic, yellow plastic top, chrome engine, orange int., sp3. #4 in Phantom Racer series, #532 (1997) 2 - 4
b2. as b, dw3 (1997) 2 - 4

Road Rocket-c

c. white plastic, dk. blue top, white int., lt. green & silver tampo w/"Intercooled Turbo" on sides, sp3. X-Treme Machines 5-pack only (1998) 2 - NA
c2. as c, dw3 (1998) 2 - NA
c3. as c, sp3, Thailand, #860 (1999) 2 - 3

Road Rocket-d

Values are shown in U.S. dollars, first price is for mint, second is for mint packaged vehicles only. See pages 15-16 for grading guide to determine value for cars in lesser conditions.

d. chrome, chrome int., clear top, black & red Hot Wheels logo in back, "TH 98" on sides, sp3. #8 in 1998 Treasure Hunt series, #756 (1998) 15 - 20

Road Rocket-e

e. orange, orange int., tinted top, black tampo on sides, sp3gd, Malaysia. Volcano Blowout 5-pack only (1999) 2 - NA

Road Rocket-f

f. red, black on top, red int., black tampo, lwch, Malaysia, #1099 (1999) 2 - 3

g. gold chrome; gray int.; clear top; black, yellow & orange flame tampo on top; pr5s; Malaysia; #102 (2001) 2 - 3

g2. as g, ho5, Malaysia, #102 (2001) 6 - 8

Road Rocket-h

h. white glow in dark plastic, black chassis, white int., yellow-tinted top, orange & white flame tampo on fenders, sp3, Thailand, Fireball playset (2001) 10 - NA

i. white; white int.; tinted top; yellow, orange & blue flame tampo on sides & dome; lwch; Malaysia; Fireball 5-pack (2001) 10 - NA

16298-a

Rocket Shot™ 16298 - 64mm - 1996
A re-issue of the Rocketank, this army rocket-launching tank has a gray metal base, gray rocket, small wheelsChina.
Similar casting: 9380 Rocketank (1988)

a. dk. mtlfk gray, red top, gray rocket $4 - 6

16298-b

b. black, maroon camouflage, Hot Wheels logo & "Night Force" in front, purple rocket, #491 2 - 6

Sizzler - See Turbo Flame

14972-a

Snake Dragster 14972 - 84mm - 1996
This Malaysia-made Top Fuel dragster has a metal base, metal engine in back of the cockpit, blue plastic spoiler and driver, sp5 in back and small dragster wheels in front.
Similar castings: 11847 Driven To The Max (1994), 13265 Dragster (1995), 14973 Mongoose Dragster (1996)

a. yellow, "Don Prudhomme The Snake" in blue on sides, blue design w/red stars on nose, limited to 8000, #91 $20 - 25

15258-a

Speed Machine® 15258 - 75mm - 1996
This Malaysia-made concept car has a metal chassis, two red-tinted movable canopies, and sp7.
Similar castings: 6423 Mantis (1970), 6975 Double Vision (1973), 7299 Speed Seeker (1984)

a. 15258; mtlfk aqua; red, yellow & black tampo w/teeth along sides & eyes, nostrils & teeth in front. #1 in Street Eater series, #412 $4 - 6

a2. as a, sp5, #412 2 - 4

b. 16934, white, sp3. #1 in White Ice series, #561 (1997) 2 - 4

Speed Machine-c

c. purple, white int., tinted canopies, orange & white tampo w/"Q4" on nose, "'98 Bonus Car" on sides, sp3. In baggie as 1998 Bonus Car (1998) 6 - NA

Speed Machine-d

d. black, lt. brown int., clear canopies, mtlfk brown spots on car, dw3, Malaysia. #3 in Tech Tones series, #747 (1999) 2 - 3

Speed Machine-e

e. black & white; yellow-tinted canopies; yellow, red, orange & white flame tampo on sides & hood w/"Speed Seeker" on sides; ho5gd; #1088 (1999) 2 - 3

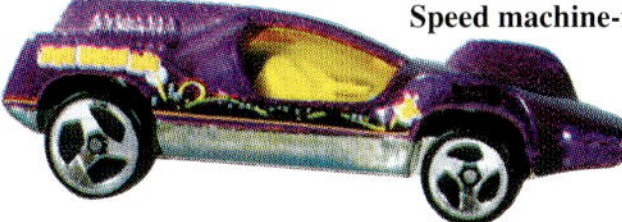
Speed machine-f

f. mtlfk purple; white int.; yellow-tinted canopies; black, white & orange tampo w/"Space Invasion 2000" on sides; sp3; Thailand. Star Explorers 5-pack (1999) 2 - NA

Speed machine-g

g. green; blue-tinted canopies; white int; yellow, black & dark blue tampo with "Hammerhead" on sides; hammerhead shark on nose; sp5; Thailand; Shark Park 5-pack (2001) 2 - NA

Speed machine-h

h. flat black; orange chassis & int.; red-tinted canopies; white, gray & red-brown tampo w/"Insectiride Beetle" on top; ho5; Thailand; Insectiride 5-pack (2002) 2 - NA

Street Cleaver® 14913 - 85mm - 1996
This model has a plastic body & wing, metal base, chrome plastic engine, yellow interior, and sp5.

a. yellow; orange & blue flames; #4 in 1996 First Editions; #373 $10 - 12

14913-a

a2. as a, sp3, #373 8 - 10

a3. as a, no tampo, #373 6 - 8

a4. as a3, dw3, #373 6 - 8

a5. as a3, ho5, #373 3 - 5

a6. as a3, ho5w, #373 (1997) 12 - 15

a7. as a3, gray plastic engine, ho5, #373 (1997) 8 - 10

Street Cleaver-b

b. 16678; black; mtlfk gold base, interior & blade; red & gold tampo on sides; sp5. #4 in Treasure Hunt series, #581 (1997) 15 - 20

Street Cleaver-c

c. yellow; metal base; black, white & red tampo w/"CAT" on engine cover, "Caterpillar" on sides; sp7y. Caterpillar charity donation, baggie only (1998) 3 - NA

15265-a

Sweet Stocker® 15265 - 78mm - 1996
This T-Bird Stocker has a black metal base, yellow-tinted windows, white interior and sp3.
Similar casting: T-Bird Stocker (1995)

a. white; red, yellow, brown, green & orange candies. #3 in Fast Food series, #418 $50 - 55

14916-a

Swingfire 16299 - 78mm - 1996
This army half-track vehicle has a gray plastic chassis and interior, sp5 in front and small plastic wheels under the tread in back. China.
Similar casting: 9374 Tank Gunner (1985)

a. red-orange $3 - 5

16299-b

b. white, lt. blue int. & windshield, "Snow Patrol" & lt. blue design on sides, sp5 in front, #492 2 - 4

Swingfire-c

c. lt. blue; orange int. & windshield; white, black, yellow & red tampo w/"Snowplow" & "Road Maintenance" on sides; gray tracks in back, sp5 in front. Snow Plowers Action Pack only (1999) 5 - NA

14909-a

Turbo Flame® (Sizzler) 14909 - 76mm - 1996
This concept model has a metal chassis and side pipes, plastic body, chrome plastic engine, orange-tinted windshield & interior, and sp5. Originally issued as Turbo Flame, the name was changed to Sizzler soon after.

a. pearl white, large red & yellow Hot Wheels logo on sides. #8 in 1996 First Editions, #369 $4 - 6

a2. as a, ho5, #369 2 - 4

a3. as a, gray plastic intake & exhaust, sp5, #369 (1997) 2 - 4

a4. as a, silver base, #373 (1997) 2 - 4

Turbo Flame-b

b. 16944; purple; black metal base; yellow-tinted windshield & tail; chrome engine; yellow, black, red & white guitar on sides; sp5. #3 in Rockin' Rods series, #571 (1997) 2 - 4

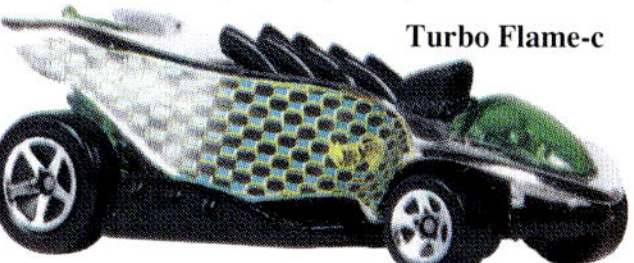
Turbo Flame-c

c. chrome; black metal base & engine; green-tinted windshield & tail; black, green & yellow tampo on sides; sp5. #5 in Treasure Hunt series, #753 (1998) 15 - 20

Turbo Flame-d

d. black; yellow-tinted windshield; yellow, black & red tampo w/"12" & "Team Swisher" on sides; sp5gd. #3 in Mega Graphics series, #975 (1999) 2 - 3

e. clear red plastic with orange windshield & tail, yellow & rose flame tampo with "Turbo Flame" on sides, sp5gd, Malaysia, Virtual Collection, #112 (2000) 2 - 3

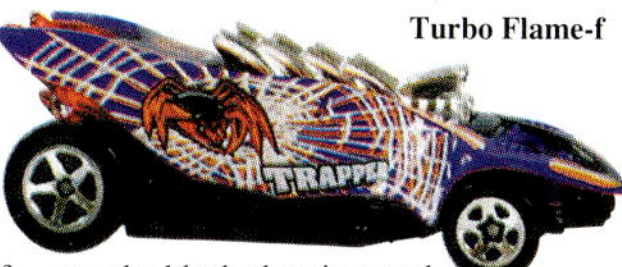
Turbo Flame-f

f. purple; black chassis; purple int.; no windshield; clear red tail; white, orange & black tampo w/"Trapper" on sides & top; sp5; Thailand; Spider Slam 5-pack (2001) 2 - NA

Turbo Flame-g

g. black, metal chassis, black int., orange-tinted windshield & tail, purple sides w/black & lt. green spider, sp5, Thailand, Spider Slam playset (2001) 6 - NA

Values are shown in U.S. dollars, first price is for mint, second is for mint packaged vehicles only. See pages 15-16 for grading guide to determine value for cars in lesser conditions.

h. purple, purple int., orange windshield & tail, red & yellow Hot Wheels logo on sides, sp5, China, Kool Toyz Racing pack (2001) 5 - 7
i. lime green, chrome int., black windshield & tail, black tampo design on sides, sp5, Malaysia, Motorized Wildcat Super Starter set (2001) 8 - NA

Turbo Flame-j

j. chrome; green chassis; green-tinted tail; yellow-tinted windshield; yellow, orange & black tampo w/"Insectiride" on sides; sp5; Thailand; Insectiride 5-pack (2002) 2 - NA

14916-a

Twang Thang® 14916 - 76mm - 1996
This concept car has an exposed chrome engine and side pipes, guitars on the sides, clear windshield, chrome interior, gray plastic base, and sp5.
a. mtlc silver, dk. red guitar w/silver strings on sides. #11 in 1996 First Editions, #376 $2 - 4
b. 16942, mtlfk red, black base & guitar, skull on front, sp5. #1 in Rockin' Rods series, #569 (1997) 2 - 4

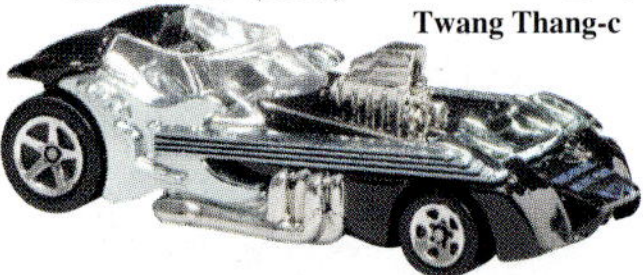
Twang Thang-c

c. black; chrome guitar, int. & trim; clear windshield; sp5. #1 in Treasure Hunt series (1998) 15 - 20

Twang Thang-d

d. orange, purple chassis, tinted windshield, gold chrome engine & int., purple guitars, sp5gd, #1104 (1999) 2 - 3

Twang Thang-e

e. mtlfk green, black chassis, chrome engine & int., green-tinted windshield, gold chrome guitars, gold & white flame tampo on top, sp5, Malaysia, Crazy Classics III 5-pack (1999) 2 - NA
f. mtlfk green; black base; green-tinted windshield; chrome int., engine & pipes; gold chrome guitars; gold & white tampo; sp5; China; #1042 (2000) 2 - 3
g. mtlfk blue, blue chassis, chrome int., tinted windshield, white guitars w/silver strings on sides, sp5, China, #223 (2001) 2 - 3
g2. as g, gold chrome strings, China, #223 (2001) 2 - 3

16039-a

Velocitor® 16039 - 78mm - 1996
This Chinese-made Thunderbird Stocker has a white metal chassis, clear windows, orange interior, sp5 & "Thunderburner" on the bottom.
Similar castings: 5900 Thunderbird Stocker (1984), 1456 Thunderburner (1987), 2565 #6 Valvoline (1992), 2568 #21 Citgo
a. mtlfk blue; red, yellow & white Hot Wheels logo on hood; #471 $2 - 4

16039-b

b. black, same as a, "Mattel" in red on sides, red & yellow Hot Wheels logo on roof & hood, #471 (1997) 35 - 40
b2. as b, lwch, #471 (1997) 2 - 4

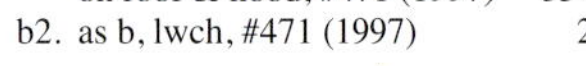

Velocitor-c

c. no number, mtlfk blue, same tampo & color as b, sp5, Action Pack racing set (1997) 5 - NA

Velocitor-d

d. no #; black; clear windows; gray int.; white doors & roof; blue, yellow & white star & "Police" on doors; sp5. Target stores' Police Station set or Police Chase set only (1997) 4 - NA

14912-a

VW Bus 14912 - 85mm - 1996
This model Volkswagen Bus Funny Car has a large rear spoiler, metal base, tinted windows, orange interior, sp5 in front and large new wheels in back. It is the heaviest Hot Wheels vehicle made to date.
a. mtlc blue; "Phil's VW Performance Parts," "Fahrvergnugen," & large Hot Wheels logo in red, white & yellow on sides. #6 in 1996 Model Series, #372 $55 - 65
a2. as a, ltd ed for 30th Anniv., w/blistercard in window box (1998) 10 - 15

VW Bus-b

b. 16724; mtlfk bronze; metal spoiler; "http://www.hotwheels.com" on sides in gold on black stripe & orange underneath; black, gold & orange tampo on sides; orange dots in black on top; clear windows; wheels & int. same as a. Mattel Web page exclusive 150 - NA
c. 16956, white, black in front fading to white, red stripe around top, "JC Whitney Warshawsky Established 1915" in red & blue on sides, clear windows, sp5 in front, large new wheels in back. Ltd ed of 10,000 for J.C. Whitney 120 - 135

VW Bus-c

d. pearl white, red int., Custom Car Design CD-Rom (1997) 15 - NA

VW Bus-e

e. black; red-tinted windows; yellow int.; red, orange & yellow flames on sides; sp5gd. Ltd ed 50,000 for All Tune & Lube (1997) 20 - 25

VW Bus-f

f. 18585; lt. green; clear windows; red int.; blue & white Van de Kamp's logo on sides & roof; blue, yellow & orange "Fish-O-Saurs" on sides; pink & white design on roof. Limited edition of 50,000, Van de Kamp's Fish Sticks mail-in (1998) 20 - 25

VW Bus-g

g. lt. blue; yellow int.; tinted windows; yellow, dk. blue & white tampo w/3 planes & Blue Angels crest on sides, "Blue Angels" & 4 planes on roof. Ltd ed of 20,000 for Blue Angels, M & D Toys & Collectibles (1998) 40 - 60

VW bus-h

h. yellow; red-tinted windows; black, red & white int.; "13" & race decals on sides; sp5. Ltd ed of 50,000 for Jiffy Lube (1998) 20 - 25

VW bus-i

i. dk. blue; red int.; clear windows; red & white tampo w/four planes & Thunderbirds logo on sides, four planes & "Thunderbirds" on top; sp5. Ltd ed of 30,000 for M & D Toys for USAF Thunderbirds (1998) 20 - 25

VW Bus-j

j. mtlfk dk. red; tinted-windows; gold spoiler; white, gold & blue tampo with crane & "High Rise Express" on sides, "Malleco Tower Cranes the Name in Tower Cranes" on both sides of roof; sp5gd. Ltd ed as High Rise Express for Malleco Cranes (1999) 25 - 30

VW Bus-k

k. blue, same as b, black & white tampo. Mattel web page exclusive, baggie only (1999) 100 - NA

VW Bus-l

l. black; orange stripe around top; yellow, orange & red tampo w/Golden Knights logo & "United States Army Parachute team" on sides, "Golden Knights" & parachutes on top; sp5. Limited to 30,000 (1999) 20 - 25

14912-m

m. aqua, multicolored underwater scene, Navy SEALs on sides, Navy SEALs in raft & parachuting into water on roof. M & D ltd ed of 30,000 (1999) 20 - 25

VW Bus-n

n. mtlc magenta; black roof; gold, black & white tampo w/Hot Wheels 30th Anniv. logo & "Interactive" on sides; red stripe around tires; w/Official Collector's Guide CD-ROM (1999) 20 - 25

VW Bus-o

o. black; white roof; orange spoiler; orange, black, gray & white tampo w/"COM," "Hot Wheels," "It's on the Web" & Web address on sides & roof; VW logo in front; China. Mattel Web page excl., baggie only (1999) 90 - NA
p. black, red int., clear windows, gray spoiler, gray spray mask, gray & red tampo w/"Penske Auto Center" on sides, Penske Auto Center stores (2001) 15 - 20

Values are shown in U.S. dollars, first price is for mint, second is for mint packaged vehicles only. See pages 15-16 for grading guide to determine value for cars in lesser conditions.

VW Bus-p

VW Bus-q

q. mtlfk blue; white roof; gray spoiler; red int.; tinted windows; black, gray, red, orange, yellow & white tampo w/large Hot Wheels logo & "15th Annual Collector's Convention" on sides, Convention logo on roof; rrch w/red stripe in front. About 2000 made for 15th Annual Collector's Convention (2001) 125 - 175

VW Bus-q2

q2. as q, Hot Wheels logo larger & more yellow. About 4000 made for 15th Annual Collector's Convention (2001) 75 - 100

r. gray, white int., clear windows, black spoiler & spray mask, white & black tampo w/"Penske Auto Center" on sides, Penske Auto Centers (2001) 15 - 20

s. dk. red, white int., clear windows, gray spoiler, black spray mask, yellow & white tampo w/"Penske Auto Center" on sides, Penske Auto Centers (2001) 30 - 35

VW Bus-t

t. white & yellow, black roof, white int., tinted windows, lt. blue & black tampo w/"M.A.C.E." & "Midwest Air-Cooled Enthusiasts" on sides. Ltd ed sold by Midwest Air-Cooled Enthusiasts 15 - 20

u. mtlc gold; black roof; orange int.; yellow-tinted windows; black, white, yellow, red, silver & orange tampo w/large Hot Wheels logo & "Philip Riehlman" on sides; Hot Wheels logo, "collectors.com," flames, "Philip Riehlman 10th Anniversary" & 2nd Annual Nationals logo on roof; rrch w/red stripe. Limited to 2000, for Phil Riehlman dinner at 2nd Annual Nationals (2002) 100 - 150

u2. as u, no Nationals logo on roof. Sold by hotwheelscollectors.com at 2nd Annual Nationals (2002) 100 - 150

v. chrome; red-tinted windows; black roof; red, white & black tampo w/checkerboards, pinstripes & Hot Wheels logo; "collectors.com" on sides; pinstripes & 2nd Annual Nationals logo on roof; rrch w/red stripe. Sold by hotwheelscollectors.com at 2nd Annual Nationals & online (2002) 50 - 70

w. mtlc blue, same as u2. Ltd ed sold by hotwheelscollectors.com (2002) 50 - 70

x. chrome; red-tinted windows; red, yellow, dk. red, black & white tampo w/flames & "Hot Wheels Flying Colors" on sides; rrchrl. Ltd ed of 10,000 by Hot Wheels Collectors.com (2002) 65 - 70

1997

Kyle Petty and PE[2] signed licensing agreements with Mattel. As a result, Hot Wheels returned to the racing scene with the introduction of the Pro Racing series (separate section), featuring cars from the NASCAR circuit. The line was divided into two segments: basic cars for kids, and more elaborate models targeted at collectors. The basic cars had plastic bases and wheels, came packaged on a card shaped like the number "1," and sold for about $1.99. The collector's line was more detailed, with metal bases and synthetic rubber wheels. Each included a collector's card and retailed for approximately $2.99. Apart from the Treasure Hunt cars, the hot releases this year were the Scorchin' Scooter, 1970 Plymouth Barracuda, Excavator, and the '59 Chevy Impala.

19640-a

20th Anniv. Race Car 19640 - 75mm - 1997

This Pontiac Grand Prix stock car has a gray plastic base, interior & roll cage, clear windows, gytbk. China.

a. red; yellow, blue, black & white tampo w/"Chuck E Cheese's" & mouse on sides, mouse's head on hood, "Chuck E Cheese" twice & "20" on roof. Chuck E Cheese's Pizza only $5 - 7

16663-b

25th Anniversary Lamborghini Countach 16663 - 68mm - 1997

This new China casting of the latest Lamborghini Countach (no wing) has clear windows, a black interior, and ho5.

a. yellow, #12 in 1997 First Editions, #510 $2 - 4

a2. as a, red int., China, w/Power Launcher only (1999) 3 - NA

b. black; red int., clear windows, ho5, #768 (1998) 2 - 4

b2. as b, China, Target excl. Long Hauler (1999) 5 - NA

16663-c

c. red; clear windows; tan int.; lt. green, white & silver tampo w/"Lamborghini" & "World Racers 12" on sides & hood, race decals on car; lwch; Thailand. Flag Flyers 5-pack only (1998) 2 - NA

d. mtlc dk. blue, red int., China, Target excl. Long Hauler (1999) 5 - NA

e. gray, black base & int., ho5, 25th Anniv. Countach, #1089 (1999) 2 - 3

f. white; black chassis & int.; orange-tinted windows; orange, black & red tampo w/"07," "Lamborghini" & race decals on sides, ho5; Thailand. World Racers 2 5-pack (1999) 2 - NA

g. dk. blue, black chassis, white int., clear windows, silver & black tampo w/1" & "Lamborghini" on sides & hood, pr5s, Malaysia, #130 (2001) 2 - 3

g2. as g, ho5, Malaysia, #130 (2001) 3 - 8

h. yellow, black plastic base, gray windows, red & black tampo on sides, ho5. China. Kool Toyz Super Race Rigs pack (2001) 3 - 5

i. orange, black chassis, clear windows, gray int., black tampo on sides, ho5. China. Kool Toyz Power Launcher pack (2001) 3 - 5

j. blue, black chassis, clear windows, red int., two gray stripes over top, ho5. China. Power Launcher pack (2001) 3 - 5

k. mtlfk dk. blue; black windows; white, gray & orange tampo w/"Hyper" on sides; ho5; China. Power Launcher pack (2001) 3 - 5

l. red, tan int., tinted windows, black & gray flame tampo w/"Shogun" on sides, ho5. China. Pavement Pounder pack (2001) 3 - 5

m. mtlfk gray, black chassis & int., orange-tinted windows, orange and black tampo w/"Lamborghini," "07" & race decals on sides, sp5, Malaysia. Pavement Pounder pack (2001) 3 - 5

n. yellow, black chassis, black int., tinted windows, silver & black tampo w/"Automobile Milestones 2002" on roof, iw, Thailand. Auto Milestones series (2002) 7 - 9

'33 Ford Convertible-a

'33 Ford Convertible (Roadster) - no # - 67mm - 1997

This convertible has a metal base, blue plastic fenders, black interior, a clear windshield, a metal dash, steering wheel and engine, and sp5. China.

a. mtlfk blue; Home Improvement Action Pack only $10 - NA

'33 Ford Convertible-b

b. mtlc purple; red grille & int.; gold-plated engine; blue-tinted windshield; gold & red tampo on sides; red-on-black "'97" and gold & red wreath on trunk; red iw; Santa w/presents in front seat. Holiday Hot Wheels gift pack only (1997) 20 - 25

'33 Ford Convertible-c

c. mtlc green; gold grille; red engine; blue-tinted windshield; tan int.; red & gold tampo on sides; red-on-green "'97" and gold & red wreath on trunk; gold iw; Santa w/presents in front seat. Holiday Hot Wheels gift pack only (1997) 20 - 25

'33 Ford Convertible-d

d. black; red int.; clear windshield; yellow, orange & blue flames on hood & sides; white Boise Roadster Show logo on trunk; iw. Midnight Cruzer for Boise Roadster Show & M & D Toys, limited to 12,000 (1999) 15 - 20

e. ruby red; black int.; clear windshield; gold engine; gold & black tampo with flames on sides, Grand National Roadster Show 50th Anniv. logo on trunk. For Grand National Roadster show & M & D Toys, limited to 15,000 (1999) 15 - 20

'33 Ford Convertible-e

'33 Ford Convertible-f

f. pearl green; black int.; clear windshield; gold chrome engine & steering wheel; black, yellow & red flame tampo w/"Lucky Flame" on sides; dw3. #4 in Hot Rod series, #008 (2000) 2 - 3

f2. as f, sp5, #008 (2000) 3 - 5

'33 Ford Convertible-g

g. white; black on top; clear windshield; black int.; blue, red & white tampo w/"Emergency Trenton Police" on sides, "Trenton Emergency" on hood, "Trenton Police" & "58" on trunk; rrch. Cop Rods Series 2 only (2000) 7 - 9

h. black, tinted windshield, black int., orange & yellow tampo design on sides & hood, pr5s, #234 (2000) 2 - 3

'33 Ford Convertible-i

i. yellow; gray fenders; black int. & trunk; clear windshield; black, gray & orange flame tampo on sides & hood; sp5; KayBee 2-pack (2001) 9 - NA

j. unpainted, black fenders & int., clear windshield, sp5, KayBee 2-pack (2001) 9 - NA

'33 Ford Convertible-k

k. flat black, brown chassis, red int. & floor board, clear windshield, "Lil Black & Red" in gray on sides, ww, Malaysia. #2 in Rat Rods series, #058 (2001) 2 - 3

'33 Ford Convertible-l

l. white, dk. red fenders, black int. & running boards, tinted windshield, red & black playing card tampo on sides & hood, sp5, Malaysia. #4 in Trump Card series, #074 (2002) 2 - 3

'33 Ford Convertible-m

m. yellow, black int., clear windshield, black & red tampo on sides, red & white Motor City Classics logo on trunk, rrgych. Wal-Mart excl. Motor City Classics series (2002) 6 - 8

Values are shown in U.S. dollars, first price is for mint, second is for mint packaged vehicles only. See pages 15-16 for grading guide to determine value for cars in lesser conditions.

16670-a

'59 Chevy Impala 16670 - 76mm - 1997
This model has a plastic base, white interior, clear windows and lwgd. Malaysia.

a. plum; gray & black stripe, orange design on sides. #5 in 1997 First Editions, #517 $3 - 6
a2. as a, sp7gd, #517 3 - 6

16670-b

b. turquoise, tinted windows, white int., violet & black tampo on sides, lwgd. #2 in Low 'n Cool Series, #698 (1998) 2 - 3
b2. as b, China, train set (1999) 5 - NA

16670-c

c. chrome, tinted windows, tan int., black striping tampo on sides & top, lwgd. K•B excl. 2-pack only 8 - NA

16670-d

d. white, gold chrome chassis, tinted windows, black int., red & gold tampo w/"'59 Impala" on sides, lwgd, #1000 (1999) 3 - 7

16670-e

e. mtlfk purple; gold chrome chassis; white int.; tinted windows; gold, black, lt. purple & orange tampo on sides & hood, "99 Treasure Hunt" on sides; lwgd. #6 in 1999 Treasure Hunt series, #934 (1999) 20 - 25

16670-f

f. white; gold & blue tampo w/police shield from Birmingham, AL Police Dept. & "Birmingham Police" on sides, "22" on roof, striping tampo on hood & trunk; rrgd. Limited to 25,000 in Cop Rods series for K•B Toys (1999) 5 - 7
g. mtlfk gray; black-tinted windows; black int.; yellow, gold & red tampo design on sides & hood; dw3; Malaysia; #116 (2000) 2 - 3
h. black, gold chassis, tinted windows, red int., orange & gold tampo design on sides & hood, lwgd, Malaysia, #249 (2000) 2 - 3

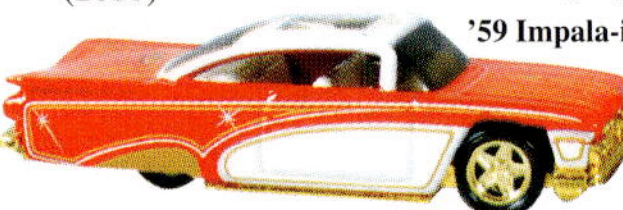
'59 Impala-i

i. red; white int.; tinted windows; white roof; white, black & gold tampo on sides & top w/"MEA's Hollywood Premiere Dinner Dance 2000 December 16th" & logo on roof; pcgd. In clear plastic box, limited to about 1000 (2000) 200 - NA

'59 Impala-j

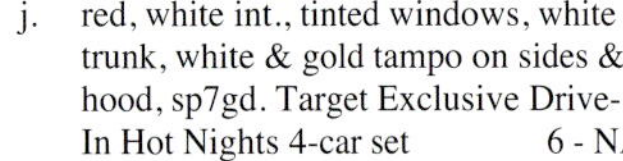

j. red, white int., tinted windows, white trunk, white & gold tampo on sides & hood, sp7gd. Target Exclusive Drive-In Hot Nights 4-car set 6 - NA

'59 Impala-k

k. black; white int.; green-tinted windows; gray, yellow & orange tampo with mummy's hand on side & hood, flames on roof. #1 in Monsters series, #077 (2001) 2 - 3
l. black, clear windows, chrome int., orange & silver tampo w/"Super Enforcement" on sides, lwch. China. Kool Toyz Super Race Rigs pack (2001) 6 - NA
m. yellow, tinted windows, white int., maroon & black tampo on sides, lwch, China, Pavement Pounder pack (2001) 3 - NA
n. lt. green, white int., tinted windows, white & gold tampo on hood & roof, lwgd, China, Power Launcher pack (2001) 3 - NA
o. black, black int., clear windows, yellow tampo on sides & hood, lwgd, China, Power Launcher pack (2001) 3 - NA

'59 Impala-p

p. mtlfk brown; gold chassis; white int.; tinted windows; red, white & black tampo on sides & roof, "Posse" on sides; sp5gd; Malaysia. #1 in Frontier series, #055 (2002) 2 - 3

'67 GTO-a

'67 (Pontiac) GTO - no # - 84mm - 1997
This Pontiac was one of the top muscle cars of the '60s. It has a metal chassis, clear windows, black interior and roof, an air scoop on the hood, and rrch. China.

a. red, red stripe around tire, 30th Anniv. of '67 Muscle Cars 3-pack only $15 - NA

'67 GTO-b

b. blue, black roof, sp5 w/red sidewalls. Motorin' Music 4-pack from Target stores only (1997) 25 - NA

'67 GTO-c

c. mtlc dk. green, gray int., clear windows, gold stripe on sides, rrch w/red stripe. Ltd ed in box by Hill's Department Stores (1997) 25 - 30
d. unpainted, white int., clear windows, sp5. 1998 Hot Wheels Convention 4-pack (1998) 15 - NA

'67 GTO-e

e. black, red int., clear windows, rrch. China. Limited to 25,000, Jiffy Lube (1999) 15 - 18
f. mtlfk blue, white int., clear windows, white tampo w/"8" & "Van de Kamp's" on sides, two stripes over top, rrch w/red stripe, China, Van de Kamp's premium (2000) 15 - 18

'67 GTO-f

'67 GTO-g

g. white; black roof; clear windows; black int.; red, gold & dk. blue tampo w/"Atlanta Police" & star on sides, roof & trunk; rrgd w/red stripe; Cop Rods Series 2 only (2000) 7 - 9

'67 GTO-h

h. mtlfk blue, black roof & int., clear windows, red & white Editor's Choice logo on rear window, rrch w/red stripes, Thailand. Target Exclusive Editor's Choice series (2000) 7 - 9

'67 GTO-i

i. gray, black roof, red int., clear windows, red stripe on sides, "Lexmark" in white on windshield, gych. In box for Lexmark (2001) 15 - 20
j. white, black roof, red int., clear windows, red stripe on sides, "Lexmark" in white on windshield, gych. Ltd ed for Lexmark Printers (2000) 15 - 20

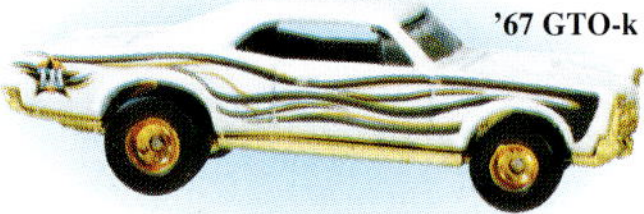
'67 GTO-k

k. white, gold chassis, black int., tinted windows, gold & black tampo w/2000 Treasure Hunt logo on sides, "GTO" in white on windshield, rrgd. #10 in 2000 Treasure Hunt series, #058 (2000) 25 - 30

'67 GTO-l

l. mtlfk gold; black chassis, roof & int.; tinted windows; red, black & white tampo w/"Hot Rod Magazine Test Car" on sides, "Winner" on trunk; sp5 w/red stripe. 2000 given away by Hot Rod Magazine, baggie only (2000) 15 - NA
m. orange, clear windows, black int., black & white tampo w/"Tiger Racing" & race decals on sides, sp5, Thailand, #226 (2001) 2 - 3
m2. as m, Malaysia, #226 (2001) 2 - 3

'67 GTO-n

n. yellow; tinted windows; black int.; white, orange & black tampo w/flowers, a face & "GTO" on sides, "Flower Power" on hood; sp5; Malaysia. #4 in Hippie Mobiles series, #092 (2001) 2 - 3

'67 GTO-o

o. mtlfk green; white spray mask & roof; white int.; clear windows; "2001 Official Convention Car" on sides; 15th Annual Convention logo in red, black & green on roof. Limited to 2000, in baggie for 15th Annual Hot Wheels Convention (2001) 175 - NA

'67 GTO-p

p. green, black int. & roof, tinted windows, "GTO" in white on rear fender, red & white Motor City Classics logo on rear window, rrchrl. Wal-Mart excl. Motor City Classics series (2002) 7 - 9

17273-a

'70 Plymouth Barracuda 17273 - 82mm - 1997
This 1970 Hemi Cuda hardtop has a metal base, black interior, clear windows, a black plastic roof and engine, and gych. China.

a. yellow, black stripe on sides. Ltd ed of 10,000 by Hill's Dept. stores $25 - 30

17273-b

b. purple; clear windows; black int. & roof; white tampo w/"Toy Cars and Vehicles" on sides & trunk; rrch. In box, limited to 10,000 for Toy Cars & Vehicles magazine (1999) 15 - 18

17273-c

c. black; black chassis & int.; clear windows; white, red, lt. blue & yellow tampo w/"48," "Plymouth" & race decals on sides; "48" on hood & trunk; sp7w w/"Goodyear Eagle"; China. Ltd ed for Sports Car Club of America (2000) 15 - 18

17273-d

d. white; black chassis; red top; red plastic roof; yellow, black & white tampo w/"70 Hemi Cuda" on hood; Editor's Choice logo on trunk; rrch; Thailand. Target Exclusive Editor's Choice series (2000) 7 - 9

16322-b2

'70 Plymouth Barracuda Convertible 16322 - 82mm - 1997
This 1970 Hemi Cuda convertible model has a metal base, black interior, clear windshield and engine, gychChina.

a. lt. green, black stripe & "426" on sides, sp5, #523 $3 - 9
b. black; orange int.; tinted windshield; white, orange & blue tampo on sides, hood & trunk; sp3; Malaysia. #4 in Artistic License series, #732 (1998) 2 - 3
b2. as b, orange & blue tampo on right side is reversed, #732 (1998) 2 - 3

16322-b3

b3. as b, sp5, #732 (1999) 2 - 3
b4. as b, sp5, China, #732 (1998) 2 - 3

16322-c

c. green, plastic base, white int., clear windshield, black plastic hood scoop,

Values are shown in U.S. dollars, first price is for mint, second is for mint packaged vehicles only. See pages 15-16 for grading guide to determine value for cars in lesser conditions.

stripe on rear fenders, sp5 w/white "Goodyear" on sides. Avon Park 'n Plates box only (1998) 6 - 8

d. purple; black chassis; white int.; red, yellow & white Hot Wheels logo on sides; "Winner" in white on trunk. Limited to 2000, Hot Rod Magazine give-away, baggie only (1999) 175 - NA

16322-e

e. purple, black int., tinted windshield, gray & white tampo w/"Purple Octopus Beach Rentals" on sides, sp3, Thailand. Ocean Blasters 5-pack (1999) 2 - NA

e2. as e, China 2 - NA

16322-f

f. orange, tinted windshield, black int., white stripe w/"426" on sides, sp3, China, #1063 (2000) 2 - 3

16322-g

g. as f, yellow, sp5 2 - 3

'70 Plymouth Funny-a

'70 Plymouth Barracuda Funny - no # - 75mm - 1997

This Funny Car has a metal chassis, lift - up body, gold plastic interior, blue-tinted windows, and pcgd. China.

Similar castings: 6409 Snake (1970), 5953 Snake 2 (1971), 6969 Snake (1973), 6970 Mongoose (1973), 7630 Top Eliminator (1974), 10497 Snake (1994)

a. white; red & dk. blue stars & stripes; American Spirit 4-pack only $15 - NA

'70 Plymouth Funny-b

b. orange; black hood; black, blue & yellow tampo w/small lines & "Hemi 'Cuda" on sides. FAO Schwarz History of Hot Wheels III only (1997) 10 - NA

16668-a

'97 Corvette 16668 - 77mm - 1997

This Corvette has a black plastic base, tinted windows, tan interior & lwch. Malaysia.

a. mtlfk aqua, #11 in 1997 First Editions, #515 $6 - 8

b. white, blue-tinted windows, black int., blue pinstripes, red & blue tampo w/Chicago Cubs logo on sides & hood, "2" on roof, small different Cubs logo on trunk, sp5. Chicago Cubs baseball game 2-pack give-away in June, 1998 only (1998) 12 - NA

16668-c

c. mtlfk blue; red plastic base; white int.; tinted windows; white, gray, black & red tampo w/"World Racers 1," "Corvette" & race decals on sides & hood; "USA 1" & Chevy logo on hood; sp5; Thailand; #867 (1998) 2 - 3

d. unpainted, red interior, clear windows, sp5. 1998 Hot Wheels Convention, #867 (1998) 60 - 75

16668-e

e. lt. purple; tinted windows; tan int.; gold, white, orange & black tampo on sides & hood; shield & "Nineteen 99" on sides; ho5; Thailand. #3 in 1999 Treasure Hunt series, #931 (1999) 18 - 20

16668-f

f. black; white int.; blue-tinted windows; silver, orange & white tampo w/"1" & race decals on sides; "USA 1," "Corvette," Chevy logo & race decals on hood; sp3; #1090 (1999) 2 - 3

16668-g

g. yellow, white int., clear windows, sp3, Deluxe Downtown set (1999) 5 - NA

16668-h

h. black, same as g, tan int., sp3, Sto 'n Go set only (1999) 5 - NA

16668-i

i. blue, same as g, sp3, Sto 'n Go set only (1999) 5 - NA

16668-j

j. aqua, same as g, sp3, Sto 'n Go set only (1999) 5 - NA

16668-k

k. pink, white int., clear windows, white tampo w/"Barbie" on sides & hood, lwch. Toys "R" Us 4-pack (1999) 5 - NA

l. red, black int. & base, clear windows, lwgd, #188 (2000) 2 - 3

l2. as l, sp3, China, Detail Center Sto 'n Go set (2001) 4 - NA

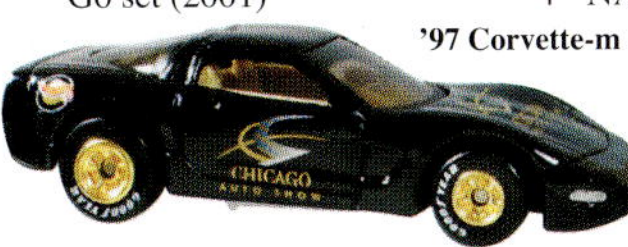
'97 Corvette-m

m. black; tan int.; tinted windows; silver, gold & red tampo w/"Chicago Auto Show" & logo on sides & hood; "Millennium" on trunk; gygd. Chicago Auto Show, in box (2000) 12 - 15

n. blue; black chassis; white int.; clear windows; yellow, white & magenta tampo w/"Chicago Auto Show" & logo on sides & hood, "Millennium" on trunk; gych; Chicago Auto Show (2000) 12 - 15

o. mtlfk red; red chassis; white int.; clear windows; yellow, white & magenta tampo w/"Chicago Auto Show" & logo on sides & hood; "Year 2000" on trunk; sp5 w/"Goodyear"; Chicago Auto Show (2000) 12 - 15

p. mtlfk gray; black chassis; white int.; tinted windows; red, blue, black & white ribbon tampo w/"97" on sides; lwch; #133 (2001) 2 - 3

'97 Corvette-q

q. blue; gray chassis; white int.; clear windows; orange, black & white tampo w/"41" on sides, Mets logo on sides & hood, Corvette logo on sides & roof; sp5. New York Mets baseball premium (2001) 10 - 15

r. dark mustard; clear windows; beige int.; dark red & gray tampo on hood, roof & trunk; ap3; China; Power Launcher pack (2001) 4 - NA

s. black, white int., clear windows, gray & yellow tampo on hood & roof, sp3, China, Sto 'n Go Auto Dealership set (2001) 4 - NA

'97 Corvette-t

t. mtlfk purple, black chassis, gray int., clear windows, black & gray tampo on sides & roof, "Corvette" on trunk, sp3. #2 in Corvette series, #068 (2002) 2 - 3

t2. as t, sp5. #2 in Corvette series, #068 (2002) 2 - 4

Armored Truck-a

Armored Truck (Car) - no # - 67mm - 1997

This truck has a metal chassis, black interior, slightly tinted windows, and sp5. China.

a. gray; red & white Hot Wheels logo; white "Don't Get Held Up!"on sides. Action Pack Police Force set only $6 - NA

Armored Truck-b

b. gray; lt. blue, black, green, red, yellow & purple tampo w/earth, "Global IT Information Security" & "Lexmark" on sides; design on hood; rrgy. Ltd ed for Lexmark, in box (2000) 15 - 20

Armored Truck-c

c. black; yellow-tinted windows; white & gold tampo w/"Always Safe," "Armored Transport," "Driver Only Carries Hot Wheels Cars" & numbers on sides; "Always Safe" & numbers on hood; large sp5; #185 (2001) 2 - 4

c2. as c, smaller sp5 in front, #185 (2001) 2 - 3

16811-a

Beach Blaster 16811 - 73mm - 1997

This India-made van has a gray plastic chassis, clear windows, red plastic interior, a vent on top, and bw.

Similar casting: #2510 Inside Story (1979)

a. white; red & magenta tampo on sides; #528 $2 - 4

16671-a

BMW M(Z3) Roadster 16671 - 66mm - 1997

This Malaysia-made convertible has a metal base, red interior, clear windshield, and sp5.

a. mtlfk silver; red, blue & dk. blue vertical slanted stripes. #6 in 1997 First Editions, #518 $2 - 6

a2. as a, black base, #518 2 - 15

a3. as a, sp3, #518 2 - 4

a4. as a, ho5 2 - 4

16671-b

b. white; red int.; tinted windshield; black & red tampo w/stripes on sides, hood & trunk; "Nicholas Leasing" & "Roadster" on sides; sp3; #890 (1998) 2 - 3

b2. as b, Thailand, #890 (1999) 2 - 3

c. red, black metal base, black int., clear windshield, sp5, #100 (2000) 2 - 3

d. aqua, black int., tinted windshield, pr5s, Malaysia, #113 (2001) 2 - 3

d2. as c, sp3, #113 (2001) 2 - 3

e. mtlfk gold, black chassis & int., tinted windshield, ho5, Malaysia, #161 (2002) 2 - 3

95517-b

BMW M3 - 95517 - 77mm - 1997

This model, an old Corgi casting, was made in China and has a black plastic base, tan interior, clear windows, and sp5gd.

a. black; FAO Schwarz Gold Collection III only $8 - NA

b. white; blue windows; lt. blue, dk. blue & red tampo w/"3" on hood; lwch. #2 in Racing series, Europe only (1997) 5 - 7

18551-a

Camaro Wind 18551 - 75mm - 1997

This Trans Am series style racer has a metal chassis, rose chrome windows and pipes, and lwch. China.

Similar casting: #2104 Firebird (1990)

a. white; yellow & orange flames on sides & hood; #599 $6 - 8

95647-a

Cement Mixer - 95647 - 70mm - (1997)

This Chinese-made Corgi casting has clear windows, black interior, a gray drum, & sp5.

a. yellow, black tampo on sides & front. Action Pack Construction set only (1997) $6 - NA

Values are shown in U.S. dollars, first price is for mint, second is for mint packaged vehicles only. See pages 15-16 for grading guide to determine value for cars in lesser conditions.

City Police 95530 - 74mm - 1997
This is a Corgi casting of a '70s Buick Police car. It has a black plastic base, clear windows, a gray interior, a blue light bar on top, sp5bk. China.

a. black; white roof; white, yellow & red stripe tampo w/"Police," "Interceptor 27" & logo on sides; "Interceptor 27" on roof; "Police" on trunk; #622 $6 - 8

Commando 18553 - 70mm - 1997
This casting of a generic pickup truck has a metal chassis, clear windows, black interior, and cts. China.
Similar casting: #4059 Tail Gunner 5T (1987)

a. dk. magenta; gold & black tampo on sides; #601 $3 - 5

b. orange; black windows & truck bed; black, blue, orange & white tampo w/"3" & race decals on sides, "3" on hood, Unocal 76 logo & "Racing" on truck bed; cts. Off-Road Racing 4-pack (1998) 4 - NA

c. yellow; black chassis; black, gray & orange tampo w/"12," "Off Track Racing Commando," "Heralda" & "Lil Noah" on sides & top; cts. Issued with Micro Racers CD-ROM (2001) 15 - 18

Dirt Rover 95544 - 45mm - 1997
This model has a yellow base, gray plastic boom and shovel, blacked-out windows, and sp5. China.

a. yellow, red "4" on side, Action Pack Construction set only (1997) $6 - NA

b. yellow, lt. gray shovel & boom, black "E32" & City of Hot Wheels, sp5, China, #643 (1998) 2 - 4

Dixie Chopper - no # - 65mm - 1997
This riding lawn mower has a metal chassis, black front seat, dark gray engine, sp5 in front and cts in back. China.

a. gray, red "Dixie Chopper" & "Sta - Bil" in front, red & blue design on engine $8 - NA

Excavator 16665 - 45mm - 1997
This Malaysia-made model has a black plastic base and tracks, gray plastic boom and shovel, and small hidden wheels.

a. white, blue stripe w/"BX - 1" on sides, #3 in 1997 First Editions, #512 $20 - 30

b. yellow; yellow shovel & boom; red, black & white stripe tampo w/CAT logo on sides. Caterpillar Action Machines series only, w/vial of dirt (1998) 4 - 6

Fire-Eater II 95505 - 75mm - 1997
This Chinese-made Corgi ladder fire truck casting has a gray plastic base, interior, boom & bucket; slightly tinted windows; and sp5.

a. red, gray fire truck tampo, #611 $2 - 4

Firebird Funny Car 16662 - 83mm - 1997
This model has a metal chassis with a lift-up body showing a metal engine and interior, clear windows, no rear window, sp5. Malaysia.

a. blue; red, white & yellow tampo with Hot Wheels logo on sides & hood, racing decals on sides. #1 in 1997 First Editions, #509 $4 - 6

b. mtlfk silver; tinted windows; red & black tampo w/"Bad Bird" & racing decals on sides, "Pontiac" & Firebird logo on hood; sp5. Exclusive Funny Car Race Team 4-pack 6 - NA

c. red; white, gray & black tampo w/winner's flag, Hurst logo & racing decals on sides, Hurst logo & "Pontiac" on hood; sp5. Exclusive Funny Car Race Team 4-pack 6 - NA

d. purple; tinted windows; orange & white tampo on hood & sides w/"Bonus Car '98" & "Q1" on sides; sp5. 1st quarter Mystery Car, baggie only (1998) 6 - NA

e. dk. mtlfk red; tinted windows; white, black, gray & yellow tampo w/"Martin Racing" & race decals on sides & hood; sp5gd; #998 (1999) 2 - 3

f. black; tinted windows; white, brown & orange tampo w/large Hot Wheels logo on sides, "1 F/C Team Handy" on sides & hood; sp5bk; Malaysia. #4 in Mega Graphics series, #976 (1999) 2 - 3

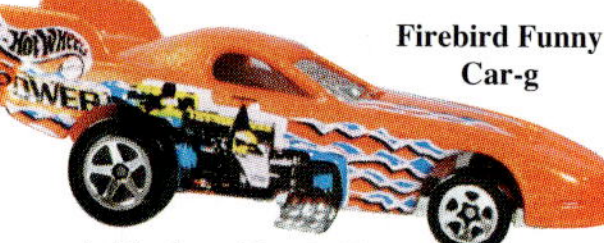

g. red; black, white & blue tampo on sides & hood, "Power" on sides; sp5; Malaysia. #1 in Speed Blaster series, #037 (2000) 2 - 3

h. yellow; clear windows; dk. red, black & white tampo w/face & teeth and "Chuy Drag Team" on sides & hood; sp5 (2001) 2 - 3

i. orange; metal int.; yellow-tinted windows; red, black & gray tampo with "Rock Em Sock Em Robots" on sides & hood; sp5. Toys "R" Us Timeless Toys Series III 4-pack (2001) 3 - NA

j. black; metal int.; red-tinted windows; red, white & brown tampo on sides & hood w/"Hot Wheels Racing" on sides; sp5rd; Malaysia. #1 in Cold Blooded series, #075 (2002) 2 - 3

Flame Stopper II 95506 - 73mm - 1997
This Corgi bucket fire truck casting has a gray plastic base, interior and ladder, blue-tinted windows, blue lights on top, sp5. China.

a. red; black & white fire truck tampo; #617 $2 - 4

Ford F-150 16666 - 77mm - 1997
This Malaysia-made Ford truck model has a gray plastic base, chrome plastic interior and truck bed, tinted windows, and sp5.

a. red, #2 in 1997 First Editions, #513 $2 - 4

b. black; clear windows; yellow int.; yellow, red, white & blue tampo w/"28," "Team Hot Wheels" & racing decals on sides; "28" on roof; "Team" & Hot Wheels logo on hood & bed; sp7bk w/yellow "Goodyear" & "Eagle" on tires. Ltd ed of 5000 for Ernie Irvan (1997) 15 - 20

c. white, black plastic base, tinted windows, chrome int. & bed, orange & black tampo w/"M" & "Marcus Construction" on sides, sp3. #865 (1998) 2 - 3

c2. white, same as c, sp5. Rad Trucks 5-pack only (1998) 2 - NA

d. green; white, blue & red striping tampo w/"JC Whitney" on sides; rrch. Ltd ed of 10,000 by JC Whitney (1998) 15 - 20

e. mtlfk gold, chrome int. & truck bed, tinted windows, black & red tampo w/"Masters of the Universe" on sides & hood, sp5. Hot Wheels Cars-Timeless Toys 4-pack (1998) 4 - NA

f. mtlfk purple; black plastic base; black chrome int. & truck bed; tinted windows; yellow, orange & lt. green tampo w/"E" on sides & roof; sp5; #908 (1999) 2 - 3

f2. as f, sp3, #908 (1999) 10 - 12

Values are shown in U.S. dollars, first price is for mint, second is for mint packaged vehicles only. See pages 15-16 for grading guide to determine value for cars in lesser conditions.

g. black; black chassis; chrome truck bed & int.; tinted windows; yellow, lt. green & gray tampo w/"Rusty's Pipes Plumbing" on sides; sp5; Malaysia. House Calls 5-pack only (1999) 2 - NA
g2. as g, Thailand (1999) 2 - NA

Ford F-150-h

h. black; black chassis; chrome int. & truck bed; tinted windows; yellow, gray & lt. green tampo w/"Rusty Pipes Plumbing" on sides; sp5; 5-pack (1999) 2 - NA

Ford F-150-i

i. red; black chassis; chrome bed & int.; blue-tinted windows; black, white & lt. blue tampo w/"Avalanche Resort" & "Ski Patrol" on sides & hood; dw3; Thailand. Snow Patrol 5-pack (2000) 2 - NA
j. black, black chassis, chrome bed & int., yellow-tinted windows, sp3, Thailand, #247 (2001) 2 - 3
k. white; black chassis & int.; clear windows; blue, red & black tampo on sides, hood & bed; "Editor's Choice" on hood; pc; Thailand. Target Exclusive Editor's Choice series (2001) 7 - 9

Ford F-150-l

l. white; black chassis; chrome int. & truck bed; tinted windows; gold, dk. blue, orange, yellow & blue tampo on sides, hood & roof; "U.S. Customs" & logo on sides; "U.S. Customs" on hood; different symbols on roof; sp5. U.S. Customs Service only (2001) 20 - 25

Ford F-150-m

m. orange; black chassis; chrome int. & bed; black, silver & white flame tampo w/"Motor Accessories" on sides, Harley-Davidson logo on sides & hood; sp3; Thailand. Harley-Davidson 5-pack (2001) 2 - NA
n. orange, black chassis, chrome int. & bed; black & yellow flame tampo on sides, sp5, Thailand. Wreck 'n Roll track set only (2001) 5 - NA
o. purple; black chassis; chrome int. & truck bed; orange-tinted windows; black, orange & white tampo w/"Radio Dispatched 24 Hrs.," "HW Trans," "9" & "Maintenance Service" on sides, "HW Trans" on hood; sp3; Thailand. Asphalt Assault 5-pack (2002) 2 - NA

95514-a

Ford Transit Wrecker 95514 - 80mm - 1997
This Corgi casting of a tow truck with a white plastic chassis and boom, blacked-out windows, black hook, sp5. China.
a. lt. blue; white & red tow truck tampo w/"Kevin's 24hr Towing" & "Deluxe Towing" on sides 4 - 6

95541-a

Highway Builder 95541 - 75mm - 1997
This Corgi wheel loader has a gray plastic base, interior and scoop and large Corgi wheels. China.
a. yellow; black, red & white logo w/"Road Repair" & "E44" on top, small European card only 5 - 7

16680-a

Hot Rod Wagon 16680 - 55mm - 1997
This model of the Radio Flyer Wagon has a metal base and pipes, gold chrome engine and wing, black interior, and sp5y. Malaysia. Similar casting: 14914 Radio Flyer Wagon (1996)
a. yellow, #6 in Treasure Hunt series, #583 (1997) 30 - 35

Jaguar XJ40 95534 - 78mm - 1997
This former Corgi casting has a black plastic chassis, blue-tinted windows, white interior, and sp5. China.
a. black, small European blistercard $5 - 7
a2. as a, lwch, #609 2 - 4

95548-a

Jaguar XJR9 or Jaguar XJR12 95548 - 78mm - 1997
This Corgi casting of the Jaguar endurance race car has a black plastic base, a silver plastic rear wing, clear windows, black interior, and lwch. China.
a. purple; white, lt. blue & silver tampo w/"9," "Smokin' Ghost Racing" & race decals on sides. #3 in Racing series, Europe only $5 - 7

95528-a2

Land Rover Mark II 95528 - 75mm - 1997
This former Corgi utility truck casting has a black plastic chassis, tinted windshield, black interior, sp5. China.
a. orange; white & dk. blue tampo w/"Smith Electric for your lighting needs," "Service Dept.," "23" & light bulb on sides; large sp5; #616 $2 - 4
a2. as a, small sp5, #616 2 - 4

95533-b

Mercedes 2.6 190E 95533 - 76mm - 1997
This model, an old Corgi casting, has a black plastic base, tan interior, clear windows, and sp5gd. China.
a. black, FAO Schwarz Gold Collection III only $8 - NA
b. mtlfk gold, tan int., sp5, small European card 5 - 7
b2. as b, black int., lwch, #605 2 - 4

95535-a2

Mercedes 300TD 95535 - 77mm - 1997
This Corgi casting of a Mercedes station wagon has a gray plastic chassis & interior, clear windows, sp5. China.
a. dk. green, all small sp5 $2 - 4
a2. as a, all large sp5 2 - 4

16669-a

Mercedes C - Class 16669 - 70mm - 1997
This Mercedes model has a gray plastic chassis, clear windows, gray interior, and lwgd. Malaysia.
a. black, silver tampo w/"3" on sides & roof, "Mercedes Benz" & logo on sides. #10 in 1997 First Editions, #516 $2 - 4

16669-b

b. mtlfk blue; black chassis; white int.; tinted windows; white, red & yellow tampo w/Hot Wheels logo on sides & hood; "1" on sides; sp5. #2 in Race Team IV series, #726 (1998) 2 - 4
b2. as b, Thailand, #726 (1999) 2 - 4

16669-c

c. purple; clear windows; yellow int.; black & white tampo on sides, roof & hood; lwgd; Malaysia. #1 in X-Ray Cruiser series, #945 (1999) 3 - 10

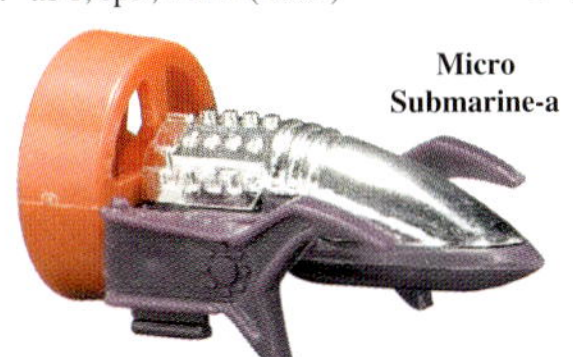
16669-d

d. yellow, black chassis, clear windows, red int., lwch, #1015 (1999) 2 - 3
e. red, black plastic chassis, black int., clear windows, ho5, Malaysia, #131 (2000) 2 - 3
f. lt. blue, black chassis & int., tinted windows, gold & orange tampo w/Hot Wheels logo on sides & hood, lwch, #171 (2001) 2 - 3
f2. as f, sp5, #171 (2001) 2 - 3

Micro Submarine-a

Micro Submarine - no # - 50mm - 1997
This futuristic mini-submarine has a dark purple chassis and sides, and a red propeller in back. China.
a. chrome, Undersea Adventure Action Pack only $4 - NA

Off Road Racer-a

Off Road Racer - no # - 68mm - 1997
This Corgi model has a black plastic chassis, red interior, a black cage, ctsChina.
a. white, red "Lifeguard" on sides & hood. Action Pack Surf Patrol only (1997) $5 - NA

Off Road Racer-b

b. white; same as a; yellow int.; red, blue, yellow & pink Sunbelt Snacks & Cereal logo on sides; cts. Little Debbie Bakery Series II 3-pack only (1997) 5 - NA

Off Road Racer-c

c. white; black int.; gray plastic roll cage; orange plastic flag & tampo in back; orange, lt. orange, yellow & black tampo w/"5" & racing decals on sides; stripes, "5" & "Goodyear" on hood. FAO Schwarz History of Hot Wheels III only (1997) 6 - NA

16913-a

Ramblin' Wrecker 16913 - 72mm - 1997
This wrecker was used for semi tractors has a chrome plastic chassis and interior, clear windows, a red plastic boom and lights on top and sp7. Malaysia. Similar casting: #3916 Rig Wrecker (1983)
a. black; yellow & orange flames w/blue outline; Heat Fleet series; #540 $2 - 8

95550-a

Road Roller 95550 - 75mm - 1997
This Corgi model has a gray plastic seat, engine and roller and large Corgi wheels in back. China.
a. yellow; black, red & white logo with "Road Repair" on sides; black "E34" on top; small European blistercard $5 - 7

Values are shown in U.S. dollars, first price is for mint, second is for mint packaged vehicles only. See pages 15-16 for grading guide to determine value for cars in lesser conditions.

16673-a

Saltflat Racer 16673 - 77mm - 1997
This convertible concept race car has a metalflake silver metal chassis; plastic body; chrome engine, pipes and interior; clear windshield; sp5. Malaysia.

a. red, racing decals on sides. #4 in 1997 First Editions, #520 $2 - 4
a2. as a, Thailand 2 - 4

16673-b

b. black, mtlfk gold chassis, red-tinted windshield, gold-plated engine & pipes, red & black design on sides, sp5, Thailand. #6 in Treasure Hunt series, #754 (1998) 15 - 20

16673-c

c. purple; mtlfk silver chassis; chrome engine, pipes & int.; clear windshield; black, white & orange tampo w/Natasha on sides & top, "Natasha Fatale" on top; sp5. #1 in Car-Toon Friends series, #985 (1999) 2 - 3
d. black; mtlfk gray chassis; chrome int.; orange-tinted windshield; mtlfk silver, orange & yellow tampo on sides & top; sp5gd; India; #148 (2001) 3 - 5
d2. as d, Thailand, Super Launcher 5-pack (2001) 3 - NA

Saltflat Racer-e

e. black; black chassis; gold chrome engine & pipes; orange-tinted windshield; gold, yellow & gray tampo w/"Sting" on sides & top; sp5; Thailand. Spider Slam 5-pack (2001) 3 - NA
f. black; mtlfk gray chassis; chrome int., engine & pipes; silver, orange & yellow tampo on sides & top w/"Max Velocity" on top; sp5gd; #204 (2001) 2 - 3

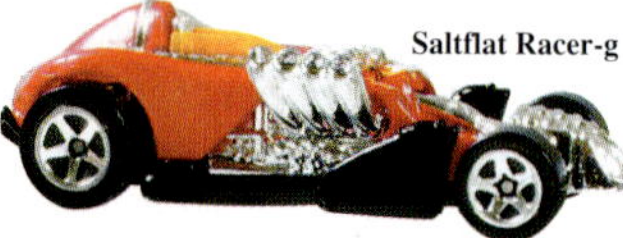
Saltflat Racer-g

g. maroon; black chassis; chrome int., engine & pipes; orange-tinted windshield; black, white & orange tampo w/"Fire Ants" on top; sp5; Thailand; #238 (2002) 2 - 3

95549-a

Sandstinger 95549 - 60mm - 1997
This Corgi dump truck has a metal chassis, red seat and steering wheel, gray dump, and large Corgi wheels. China.

a. yellow; black, red & white logo w/"Road Repair" in front; yellow "E27" on dump; small European blistercard only $5 - 7

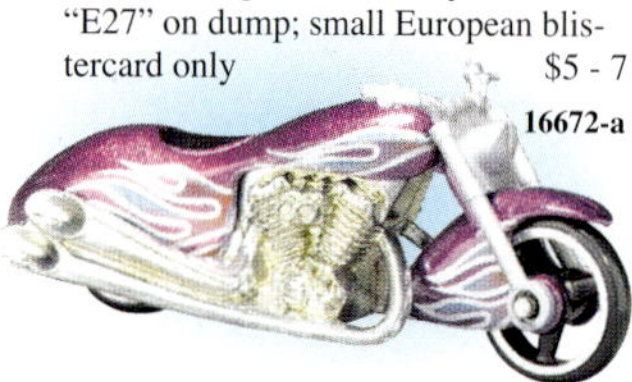
16672-a

Scorchin' Scooter® 16672 - 70mm - 1997
This motorcycle has a metal base, chrome engine and pipes, black seat, gray plastic handlebars, black interior. China.

a. purple; lt. blue & silver design on sides. #9 in 1997 First Editions, #519 $10 - 12
a2. as a, gold Hot Wheels 30th Anniv. logo on gas tank. Ltd ed for 30th Anniv., with blistercard in window box (1998) 5 - 7
a3. as a, China, w/Long Hauler only (1999) 5 - NA

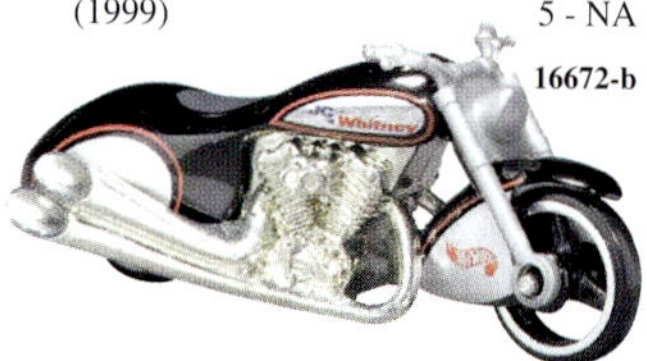
16672-b

b. black, gray sides w/red outline, "JC Whitney" on sides. Ltd ed of 10,000 by JC Whitney, in box 15 - 20

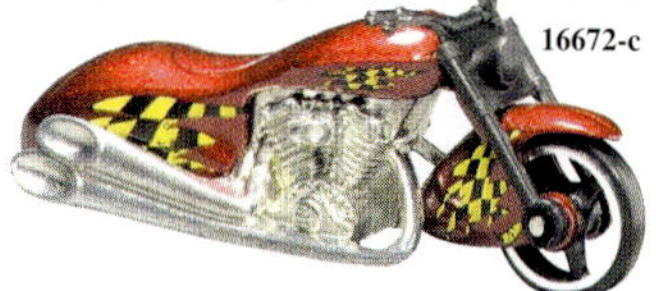
16672-c

c. mtlfk red; black & yellow squares on sides; black handlebars. #2 in 1998 Treasure Hunt series, #750 35 - 40
d. black; metal engine & pipes; chrome plastic handlebars & fork; yellow, orange, blue, black & white flame tampo w/"The Official Collectors Club" on seat. Mattel's Inside Track newsletter, on white card, give-away only (1998) 20 - 25
e. black; gold handlebars; yellow, orange & blue flames; red seat. Limited to 25,000, issued by Jiffy Lube (1998) 15 - 20
f. unpainted, 1998 Hot Wheels Convention, 4-pack (1998) 15 - NA

16672-g

g. black; white, yellow, orange & red tampo w/"Toys for Tots" on front fender, "1998 Chicagoland Motorcycle Parade" on rear side fender, POW*MIA logo on gas tank, Marine Corps logo in back. Ltd ed in box for Toys For Tots (1998) 15 - 20

16672-h

h. yellow, black seat, black & gray flame tampo. '50s Cruisers 5-pack only (1999) 2 - NA
h2. as h, Thailand (1999) 2 - NA
i. white; black sides, handle bars & seat; turquoise & gold tampo on sides; gold rims around wheels. Mervyn's 50th Anniv., in box (1999) 15 - 20

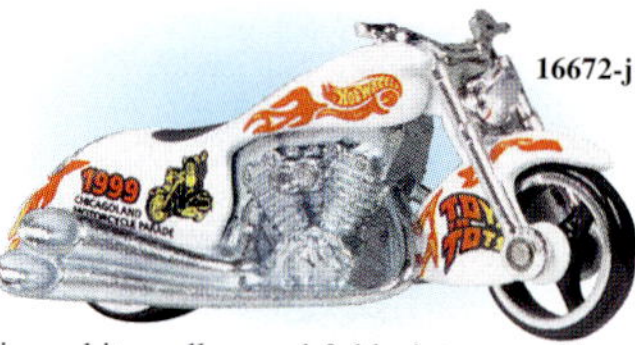
16672-j

j. white; yellow, red & black tampo with "Toys For Tots" on front fender, "1999 Chicagoland Motorcycle Parade" on rear fender, logos on seat & in back. Toys For Tots, ltd ed, in box (1999) 15 - 20

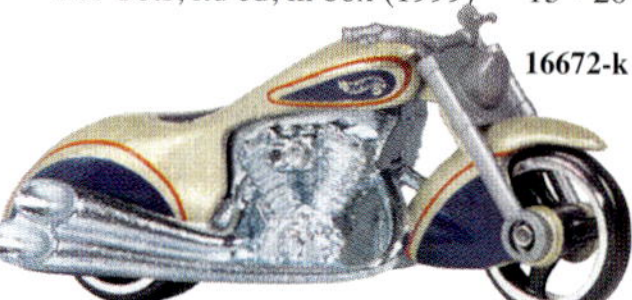
16672-k

k. mtlfk gold, red pinstripes, dk. blue tampo. Ltd ed for White's Guide (1999) 15 - 20
l. black, same as k, gold tampo. Ltd ed for White's Guide (1999) 15 - 20

detail-m

m. chrome green; red sides; gold engine & pipes; white & gold tampo w/"Season's Greetings" on sides, wreath w/"99" on gas tank, red stripe around tires; Santa on scooter. Christmas present in 1999 Holiday Assortment (1999) 15 - 20

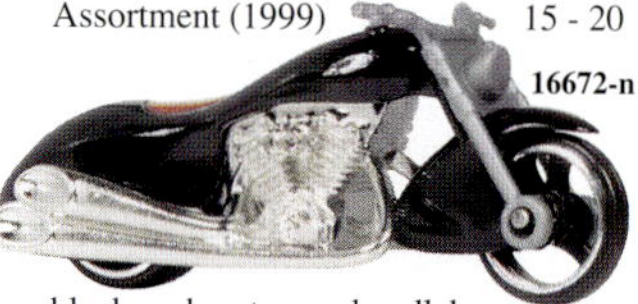
16672-n

n. black, red seat, gray handlebars, China, w/Long Hauler (1999) 5 - NA

16672-o

o. blue, white seat, red & white stripe tampo, JC Whitney logo in white, Thailand. Ltd ed for JC Whitney 15 - 20
o2. red, same as o, colors reversed, tampo same, Thailand. Ltd ed for JC Whitney 15 - 20

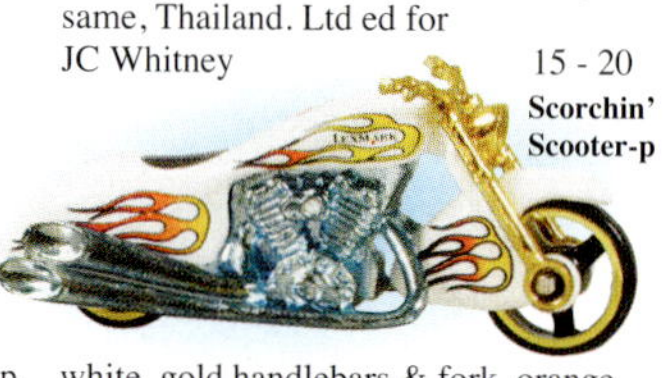
Scorchin' Scooter-p

p. white, gold handlebars & fork, orange & yellow flames outlined in black, "Lexmark" on sides. Ltd ed by Lexmark Printers (2000) 15 - 20
q. black, orange & yellow flames outlined in black, "Lexmark" on sides. Ltd ed by Lexmark Printers (2000) 15 - 20

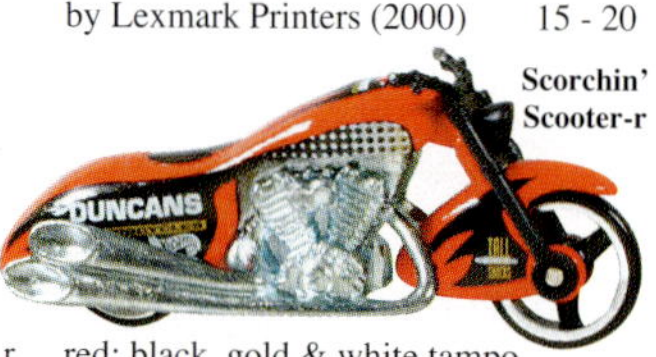
Scorchin' Scooter-r

r. red; black, gold & white tampo w/"Duncan's Motorcycles" on sides & gas tank; #1075 (2000) 2 - 8

Scorchin' Scooter-s

s. black; white seat; white & blue tampo w/shield, "South Carolina Police," "Team A," "Charleston S.C." & "Charles Towne" on sides; "356 Police" on top; "Team A" in back. Cop Rods Series 2 only (2000) 7 - 9
t. mtlfk orange; black seat; black, white & gold tampo w/"Duncans Motorcycles" on sides & top, "Tall Shocks" on front fender; Malaysia; #240 (2000) 3 - 5

Scorchin' Scooter-u

u. mtlfk dk. red; black seat; yellow, white & red tampo w/"Toys For Tots" & "Chicagoland 2000 Motorcycle Parade" on sides; decals on top. Ltd ed for Toys for Tots, in box (2000) 15 - 20

Scorchin' Scooter-v

v. yellow; black seat; multicolored tampo w/"4," "Kodak Film" & race decals on sides, "4" & "Kodak Max Film" on top; gold rims; Thailand. NASCAR Scorchin' Scooter series (2001) 9 - 12
w. red; yellow front; black seat; yellow, lt. green, black & white tampo w/"5," "Kellogg's" & race decals on sides, "5" & "Advance Auto Parts" on top; yellow rims; Thailand. NASCAR Scorchin' Scooter series (2001) 9 - 12
x. white; dk. blue rear; red seat; multicolored tampo w/"6," "Valvoline" & race decals on sides, "6" & "Cummins" on top; metal rims; Thailand. NASCAR Scorchin' Scooter series (2001) 9 - 12
y. dark blue; same as u; white front; multicolored tampo w/"12," pegasus & race decals on sides, "12" & "Mobil 1" on top; metal rims; Thailand. NASCAR Scorchin' Scooter series (2001) 9 - 12
z. lt. red; black seat; white, black, blue & red tampo w/"21," "Citgo" & race decals on sides & top; gold rims; Thailand. NASCAR Scorchin' Scooter series 9 - 12
aa. yellow; black top; yellow seat; multicolored tampo w/"22," "Caterpillar" & race decals on sides, "CAT" & "CAT Financial" on top; gold rims; Thailand. NASCAR Scorchin' Scooter series (2001) 9 - 12
ab. lt. blue; black seat; multicolored tampo w/"43," STP logo & race decals on sides & top; blue rims; Thailand. NASCAR Scorchin' Scooter series (2001) 10 - 15
ac. dk. blue; black seat; multicolored tampo w/"44," Hot Wheels logo & race decals on sides & top; metal rims; Thailand. NASCAR Scorchin' Scooter series (2001) 10 - 15
ad. green; black seat; multicolored tampo w/"45," "Sprint" & race decals on sides & top; "No Fear" on top; gold rims; Thailand. NASCAR Scorchin' Scooter series (2001) 10 - 15
ae. blue; red seat; yellow, red & white tampo w/"55," "Square D" & race decals on sides & top; gold rims;

Values are shown in U.S. dollars, first price is for mint, second is for mint packaged vehicles only. See pages 15-16 for grading guide to determine value for cars in lesser conditions.

Thailand. NASCAR Scorchin' Scooter series (2001) 9 - 12

af. black; black seat; red, yellow & white tampo w/"60," "Power Team" & race decals on sides; "Exelon" & emblem on top; metal rims; Thailand. NASCAR Scorchin' Scooter series (2001) 9 - 12

ag. lt. blue & red; black seat; multicolored tampo w/"66," "Big K" & race decals on sides, "66" & Highway 66 emblem on top; metal rims; Thailand. NASCAR Scorchin' Scooter series (2001) 9 - 12

ah. red & black; red seat; multicolored tampo w/"94," "Drive Thru," McDonald's M & race decals on sides; "94" & Reese's Peanut Butter bar on top & gold rims; Thailand. NASCAR Scorchin' Scooter series (2001) 9 - 12

ai. lt. green; yellow front end; black seat; multicolored tampo w/"97," "John Deere" & race decals on sides; "97" & John Deere logo on top; gold rims; Thailand. NASCAR Scorchin' Scooter series (2001) 9 - 12

aj. yellow; green on top; blue back; black seat; multicolored tampo w/"98," "Universal" & race decals on sides, "98" & "Woody" on top; metal rims; Thailand. NASCAR Scorchin' Scooter series (2001) 10 - 15

ak. black; pink front end; gray seat; multi-colored tampo w/"99," "Exide" & race decals on sides & top; metal rims; Thailand. NASCAR Scorchin' Scooter (2001) 9 - 12

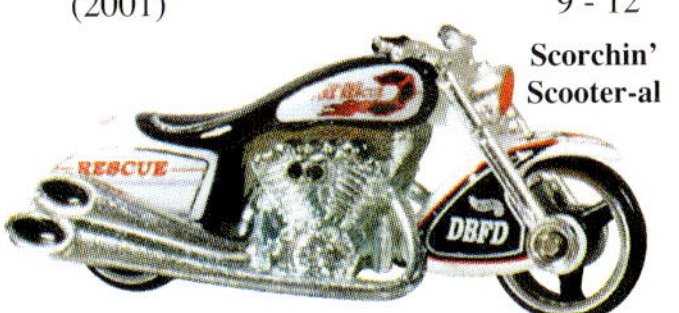
Scorchin' Scooter-al

al. white; black seat & top; red, white & gray tampo w/"Rescue" & "DBFD" on sides; "Rosie" on gas tank; "Daytona Beach" in back; Fire Rods series (2001) 9 - 12

am. black, gray seat, gold & white tampo w/"State Police 01" & "CA" on sides, Thailand, Police Cruisers 5-pack (2001) 3 - NA

an. lt. blue, black & white flame tampo on sides. China. Treasure Hunt car, with Pavement Pounder pack only (2001) 22 - NA

18362-a

Skullrider 18362 - 72mm - 1997
This Malaysia-made concept race car has a metal base, black interior & engine, and sp5.

a. chrome pink, #593 $4 - 6

18362-b

b. red, chrome int., black & white tampo w/"8" on sides & front, sp5, Malaysia. Crazy Classics III 5-pack (1999) 2 - NA

c. red plastic, gray chassis, chrome int., black & white tampo w/"8" on sides & hood, sp5. China. Virtual Collection, #138 (2000) 2 - 3

d. black w/chrome int., dk. red & silver tampo on sides, sp5, China, #227 (2000) 2 - 3

e. purple; purple chassis; gray pipes; gold int.; yellow, red & black flame tampo w/"Skull Rider" on sides, "FR" on

Skullrider-e

hood, "Gots to Go" on top; pr5s; Thailand. #12 in 2001 Final Run series (2001) 5 - 7

16926-a

Stealth 16926 - 76mm - 1997
This concept car has a metal chassis, chrome interior, magenta tinted windows, and sp3. Malaysia.
Similar casting: #11848 Shadow Jet II (1994)

a. purple; orange & black spy tampo w/"Classified" on white sides. #1 in Techno Bits series, #553 $2 - 4

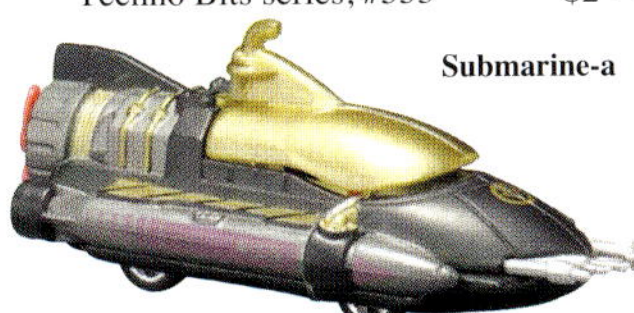
Submarine-a

Submarine - no # - 86mm - 1997
This futuristic submarine on wheels has a gray interior and gold-speckled canopy, red plastic propeller and steering wheel, and bw. China.

a. black; gold & magenta tampo; Action Pack Undersea Adventure set (1997) $5 - NA

16808-a

Trailbuster 16808 - 78mm - 1997
This pickup truck has a metal chassis, red plastic interior and truck bed, clear windows, and bw. India.
Similar casting: #4370 Jeep Scrambler (1983)

a. black, orange tampo on sides, #525 $2 - 4

95551-a

Trailer with Dinghy - 95551 - 56mm - 1997
This Corgi casting is a trailer that hooks on some Corgi cast cars. It has two sp5. On the trailer is a red and white dinghy. China.

a. black; Action Pack Surf Patrol set (1997) $5 - NA

16667-a

Way 2 Fast® 16667 - 80mm - 1997
This model has a metal base, chrome interior, two chrome engines and pipes in front, and sp5. Malaysia.

a. orange; black & white checkerboard tampo on roof. #7 in 1997 First Editions, #514 $4 - 6

a2. as a, Thailand, #514 4 - 6

a3. as a, silver base, #514 (1997) 4 - 6

16667-b

b. purple; yellow, orange & lt. green flames on sides; black, orange & yellow tampo w/"Early Times '98 Mid - Winter Rod Run" on roof; sp5. Ltd ed of 10,000, Early Times 29th Annual Mid-Winter Rod Run (1998) 20 - 25

16667-c

c. mtlfk gold; orange & white tampo w/"1" on sides & roof; sp5. #12 in 1997 Treasure Hunt series, #760 (1997) 20 - 25

d. unpainted; black metal chassis, engine & int.; black, orange & white tampo on sides, roof & back; "Dream Halloween 1998" on roof & back; sp5. Dream Halloween give-away only (Mattel charity), collectible plastic box only 175 - 200

16667-e

e. mtlfk dk. blue; chrome int.; yellow, red & white tampo w/flames on sides, two Hot Wheels logos on roof; sp5. Hot Wheels Cars-Timeless Toys 4-pack (1998) 8 - NA

16667-f

f. mtlfk aqua, chrome int., white side pipes, yellow & red flame tampo on sides & roof, sp5. Target exclusive Street Rods set only (1999) 6 - NA

16667-g

g. red; black top & pipes; chrome engine; black roof; yellow, lt. blue & white flame tampo on sides & roof; rrgd. Ltd ed of 15,000, #994 (1999) 10 - 12

16667-h

h. black & white; white pipes; chrome engine; gold, black & white tampo w/police shield from Indianapolis, PA Police Dept. & "Indianapolis Police" on sides, "7" & "Indianapolis Police" on roof; sp5. Limited to 25,000 in Cop Rods series for K•B Toys (1999) 5 - 7

16667-i

i. black; gold chassis & pipes; orange, white & gold tampo on sides & top; sp5gd; #994 (1999) 2 - 3

j. white; chrome int.; purple, red, blue & black tampo w/"Championship Auto Shows" on roof; sp5. Ltd ed for Championship Auto Show (2000) 15 - 18

Way 2 Fast-j

k. mtlfk dk. red, same as i, sp5, Malaysia. Virtual Collection. #115 (2000)

k2. as k, Thailand, Virtual Collection, #115 (2000) 2 - 3

Way 2 Fast-l

l. red; chrome int. & engine; black pipes; white, black & dk. blue tampo w/"Brach's" on roof; sp5; Brach's premium (2000) 6 - 10

Way 2 Fast-m

m. mtlfk dk. red, gold chassis & pipes, black int., clear windows, gold & white tampo w/"MC" & "Mystery Car 2000" on roof, sp5. 2000 Mystery Car, in baggie (2000) 6 - NA

n. dk. blue; black int.; multicolored tampo w/"12," pegasus & race decals on sides, "12" & "Mobil 1" on roof; sp5; Thailand. #1 in NASCAR Way 2 Fast series (2001) 5 - 7

o. white; chrome int.; red, blue, orange & black tampo w/"01" & Hot Wheels logo on sides & roof; sp5; Thailand. #2 in NASCAR Way 2 Fast series (2001) 5 - 7

Way 2 Fast-p

p. yellow; black int.; multicolored tampo with "36," "M&M's" & race decals on sides & roof; sp5; Thailand. #3 in NASCAR Way 2 Fast series (2001) 5 - 7

Way 2 Fast-q

q. black; black chassis & int.; multicolored tampo w/"96," "Drive Thru" & race decals on sides, "96" & McDonald's M on roof; sp5; Thailand. #4 in NASCAR Way 2 Fast series (2001) 5 - 7

Way 2 Fast-r

r. gray, black chassis & pipes, chrome engine & int., black & blue tampo w/"Heralda Way 2 Fast Racing" on sides, "Heralda Racing" on roof, sp5, Malaysia, #248 (2001) 2 - 3

Way 2 Fast-s

s. white; black chassis & pipes; gold chrome int. & engine; gold, black & orange tampo w/"Celebration Special" on sides and top, "Edition Series" on sides; pr5s. Thailand. Kmart excl. 10-pack (2001) 8 - NA

Values are shown in U.S. dollars, first price is for mint, second is for mint packaged vehicles only. See pages 15-16 for grading guide to determine value for cars in lesser conditions.

1998

For the 30th Anniversary of Hot Wheels cars, Mattel issued 40 new castings instead of the usual 12. Many of these models had variations, including color, wheels, and country of origin. The smallest Hot Wheels model, Go Kart, and one of the strangest models, Hot Seat, a toilet on wheels, came out early in the year. Other popular models included the '32 Ford, '40 Ford, '63 T-Bird, '65 Impala Lowrider, '68 Mustang, '70 Roadrunner, Dairy Delivery, Slideout and Tail Dragger. All of these models were produced as premiums later in the year or early 1999, which means they were very popular with the older collectors. This was also the first year the convention cars were produced by Mattel. The Hot Wheels Pro Racing and Hot Wheels Collectibles® lines were both continued (see separate section).

18587-a

'32 Ford 18587 - 59mm - 1998
This Malaysia-made 1932 Ford has a black plastic chassis, an exposed plastic chrome engine, clear windows, red interior, and sp5.

- a. black; yellow, orange and blue flames on sides. #7 in 1998 First Editions, #636 — $4 - 8
- a2. as a, dw3 — 4 - 8
- a3. as a2, China, #636 (1999) — 2 - 3
- a4. as a, Thailand, #636 (1999) — 2 - 3
- a5. as a2, Thailand, #636 (1999) — 2 - 3
- b. unpainted, black int., clear windows, sp5. 1998 Hot Wheels Convention in 4-pack (1998) — 12 - NA

18587-c

- c. pearl white; clear windows; brown int.; red, lt. blue & blue flame tampo on sides & roof; sp5; Thailand. '50s Cruisers 5-pack only (1999) — 2 - NA
- c2. as c, Malaysia (1999) — 2 - NA

18587-d

- d. mtlfk ruby red; black int.; clear windows; blue, orange, yellow & white tampo w/flames on sides; Firebird Raceway logo, Hot Wheels logo & "Hot Rod Coupe" on trunk; rrch. Hot Rod Coupe for Firebird Raceway & M & D toys, limited to 12,000 (1999) — 15 - 20

18587-e

- e. gray, black int., clear windows, blue & purple flame tampo on sides & hood, sp5. Target excl. Street Rods set only (1999) — 4 - NA

18587-f

- f. red; dk. red, white & black tampo w/"Toy Shop" on sides & roof; rrch. Boxe ltd ed for *Toy Shop*, (1999) — 15 - 18

18587-g

- g. mtlfk dk. red, gray chassis, clear windows, black int., gray & black tampo w/"Frankie's Garage" on sides, ho5, China, #1070 (1999) — 2 - 3

18587-h

- h. white; black pipes; blue & gold tampo w/Milwaukee Police logo & "191" on sides, "191" on roof, "Police" on trunk; rrch. Limited to 25,000 in Cop Rods series for K•B Toys (1999) — 5 - 7
- i. white; purple, light blue and black flame tampo on sides and roof; #1018 (1999) — 2 - 3
- j. mtlfk lime; gold & black pipes; black, white & orange tampo w/pumpkin, spider webs & "Dream Halloween" on sides, "Benefiting the Children," Aids Foundation & logo on trunk; rrch w/red stripe. Limited to 2000, in acrylic display case, Children Affected by Aids Foundation, 1999 Dream Halloween give-away (1999) — 175 - NA

18587-k

- k. blue; blue base; white int.; blue-tinted windows; white, red & yellow tampo w/large Hot Wheels logo on sides; dw3. Timeless Toys II 4-pack, sold by Toys "R" Us through web site (1999) — 5 - NA

18587-l

- l. black; red int.; clear windows; red, orange & white tampo w/"Chuck E Cheese" on sides; red & white sticker, Chuck E Cheese on roof; sp5. Chuck E Cheese Pizza only (1999) — 7 - 10

'32 Ford-m

- m. mtlfk red; white chassis & roof; black int.; clear windows; silver & white tampo on sides; red, white & black Editor's Choice logo on trunk; rrch; Thailand. Target excl. Editor's Choice (2000) — 7 - 9
- n. green; purple roof; black int.; tinted windows; gray, red & gold tampo on sides, roof & trunk; sp3. Ames Stores excl. Cruise Night 4-pack (2000) — 4 - NA
- o. purple; clear windshield; black int.; black, red & yellow tampo w/Hot Wheels logo, ".Com" & "Surf the Net" on sides; lwch; China; #195 (2001) — 2 - 3

'32 Ford-p

- p. yellow; black plastic chassis & int.; clear windows; black top; red, black & white tampo w/"Wild Weekend of" & Hot Wheels logo on sides; rrch w/red stripe. (2001) — 20 - 25
- q. black, white roof & int., green-tinted windows, white & green tampo on sides, sp5. Target excl. Elvis Drive-In 4 pack (2001) — 6 - NA

'32 Ford-r

- r. black; black chassis; orange int.; clear windows; white, orange & silver tampo w/pinstripes, "51," white doors w/"State Troopers Talluville, CA" & flying wheel on sides; sp5; #216 (2001) — 2 - 3
- s. black; white roof; red int.; clear windows; white, gold & black tampo w/"V8" & wings on sides & trunk, "Automobile Milestones 2002" on roof; rrch w/red stripe. Auto Milestones series (2002) — 6 - 8

56567-t

- t. yellow; tan int.; tinted windows; white, black & red tampo w/"5" & checker squares on sides; rrgych. Rod & Custom series from Preferred Line (2002) — 6 - 8

18674-a2

'40 Ford (Truck) 18674 - 74mm - 1998
This Malaysia-made 1940 Ford truck has a plastic base, gray plastic interior and truck bed, blue-tinted windows, and sp5.

- a. metalflake blue; yellow & orange design on sides. #20 in 1998 First Editions, #654 — $2 - 4
- a2. silver blue, same as a — 18 - 20
- a3. as a, Thailand, #654 (1999) — 2 - 3
- a4. as a, China, #654 (1999) — 16 - 20

18674-b

- b. red; chrome base; white truck bed & int.; yellow-tinted windows; yellow, black & white tampo w/"Pizza on Wheels" & "Fast Delivery" on sides; sp5. House Calls 5-pack only (1999) — 2 - NA
- b2. as b, China, #1029 (2000) — 2 - 3

18674-c

- c. black; gold truck bed, int. & hood scoop; gold tampo w/"JC Whitney" on sides & roof; iwgd. Limited to 10,000 for JC Whitney, in box (1999) — 15 - 18

18674-d

18674-e

- d. brown, same as c (1999) — 15 - 18
- e. yellow; black plastic base & int.; black, red & gold design on sides, "Haulin' 40" on roof; ho5; China; #1069 (1999) — 3 - 5

18674-f

- f. white; chrome chassis & spoiler; Ford logo in blue on spoiler; orange hood, roof & truck bed; purple stripe; orange & black tampo w/"SCTA" on door; gych. Ltd ed of 15,000 for Full Grid, China, #1004 (1999) — 10 - 12

18674-g

- g. red; black fender; chrome base; clear windows; black, white & silver tampo w/"1" & Cherry Coke tampo; ho5; Thailand. Coca Cola 4-pack (1999) — 4 - NA
- h. gray; black chassis; blue int. & truck bed; black, blue & white tampo on sides & roof; "Triston Auto" on roof; dw3; China; #192 (2000) — 2 - 3
- i. white; black chassis; blue int. & truck bed; blue-tinted windows; blue & gray tampo w/Cheyenne Police Department emblem on sides, "Cheyenne Police" on roof; rrch. Cop Rods 2 (2000) — 6 - 8

18674-j

- j. yellow & black; red int.; tinted windows; red, black, white & yellow tampo w/"Unit 08," "Official Unit Fire Dept." & San Ramon Fire Dept. emblem on sides, flames on hood & sides, San Ramon Fire Dept. emblem on truck bed; iwgd; Fire Rods series (2001) — 6 - 8
- k. white & black, black chassis, clear windows, orange int. & truck bed, orange & white Harley-Davidson logo on doors, sp5, China, #156 (2001) — 2 - 3
- k2. as k, Thailand, Harley-Davidson 5-pack (2001) — 2 - NA
- l. mtlfk red; chrome chassis; clear windows; black int., fenders & running board; black & white tampo w/"1," Cherry Coke & coke decals on sides, "!" & "Coca Cola" on roof; ho5; Malaysia. Coca Cola Race Team 4-pack (2001) — 4 - NA
- m. blue; red chassis; black int. & truck bed; tinted windows; red, black & white tampo on sides, "Haulin' 40" on roof; sp5; Thailand. Pavement Pounder pack (2001) — 3 - NA

18674-n

- n. turquoise; black chassis; white top; black int.; clear windows; black & silver flames on fenders; black, lt. blue & gray Treasure Hunt logo on roof. #9 in 2002 Treasure Hunt Series, #009 (2002) — 20 - 25

Values are shown in U.S. dollars, first price is for mint, second is for mint packaged vehicles only. See pages 15-16 for grading guide to determine value for cars in lesser conditions.

18543-a

'63 T-Bird 18543 - 80mm - 1998
This Malaysia-made 1963 Ford Thunderbird convertible has a metal base, white interior, clear windshield, and ho5.

a. mtlfk aqua, gray design on doors, "Thunderbird" behind rear wheels. #9 in 1998 First Editions, #644 $2 - 4

18543-b

b. chrome, tinted windshield, tan int., black striping tampo on sides & top, lwgd. K•B excl. 2-pack only 5 - NA

c. mtlfk gold, white int., tinted windshield, black & white tampo on sides & hood, "Hot Wheels Reels" on sides, lwch, Thailand, #1022 (1999) 2 - 5

18543-c2

c2. as c, lwgd, Malaysia (1999) 2 - NA

18543-d

d. red, black int., tinted windshield, gray tampo; lwch. Ames Stores excl. 4-pack only (1999) 4 - NA

18543-e

e. black, clear windshield, white int., white Toy Shop logo on sides, gych. Ltd ed for *Toy Shop* magazine, in box (1999) 15 - 18

f. mtlfk black, white int., clear windshield, white tampo design on sides & top, lwch, Thailand, #130 (2000) 2 - 3

g. mtlfk dark red; white int.; clear windshield; white, orange & silver tampo on sides & top; lwch; #142 (2001) 2 - 3

g2. as g, sp3, #142 (2001) 3 - 5

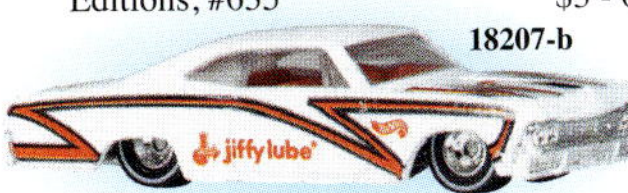
18207-a

'65 Impala Lowrider 18207 - 80mm - 1998
This model has a chrome plastic base, tan interior, clear windows, lwgd. Malaysia.

a. mtlfk purple; yellow & orange striping on sides; yellow, orange & black design on hood. #8 in 1998 First Editions, #635 $3 - 6

18207-b

b. pearl white; red int.; clear windows; red & black tampo on sides & hood w/"Jiffy Lube" & Jiffy lube logo on sides, "Signature service" on trunk; rrch w/white stripe around tires. Ltd ed of 25,000 cars for Jiffy Lube (1999) 15 - 18

18207-c

c. mtlfk green, gold chrome base, tan int., tinted windows, gold & white tampo on sides & hood, lwgd. #3 in Pinstripe Power series, #955 (1999) 3 - 4

d. white; black roof; clear windows; black int.; black, blue, white, yellow & gray tampo w/flames on sides, roof & hood; shield & "Denver Police" on

'65 Impala-d

sides & trunk; rrch w/white walls. Cop Rods Series 2 only (2000) 6 - 8

e. mtlfk green w/gold chassis; yellow int.; yellow-tinted windows; white, black, red & yellow tampo on sides & hood w/Hot Wheels logo & ".COM" on sides; sp3; #197 (2000) 2 - 3

f. mtlfk purple; white int.; tinted windows; gray & white tampo on sides, hood & trunk; lwch. Ames Stores excl. Cruise Night 4-pack (2000) 8 - NA

'65 Impala-g

g. white w/red in back; tinted windows; white int.; black, gold & red tampo w/"Los Angeles County Fire Dept.," "Official Fire Safety Advisor" & Los Angeles Fire Department emblem on sides, "Official Fire Safety Advisor" & "042" on hood, "042" & "Los Angeles County Fire Dept." on roof & trunk; rrch w/white stripe; Fire Rods (2001) 9 - 12

h. white, gray int., red-tinted windows, black & gold tampo on sides, lwgd. China, #226 (2001) 2 - 4

'68 Mustang-a

'68 Mustang - no # - 73mm - 1998
This new casting of a 1968 Mustang has a metal base, black interior, clear windows, an opening hood with a white engine, and sp5. China.

a. white; dk. blue stripes: "GT" on sides, 2 dk. blue stripes on top. Park 'n Plates box by Avon only (1998) $6 - 8

b. unpainted, 1998 Hot Wheels Convention, 4-pack (1998) 15 - NA

'68 Mustang-c

c. white; purple, orange & yellow stripes w/"Lexmark" in black on sides & white on rear window; gych. In box, limited to 10,000 for Lexmark (1999) 15 - 20

'68 Mustang-d

d. blue; gray int.; black & white tampo w/"67" & stripes on sides, two stripes over top; bw (1999) 2 - 3

'68 Mustang-e

e. yellow; black int.; white, black & red tampo w/"67" & race decals on sides, two stripes over top; sp5. Target V8 3-pack (1999) 5 - NA

'68 Mustang-f

f. mtlfk green; black int.; black, gold & white Editor's Choice logo on trunk; pc; Thailand. Target Exclusive Editor's Choice series (2000) 7 - 9

g. red, black int., gray & black tampo design on sides, sp5, Thailand, #126 (2001) 2 - 3

'68 Mustang-h

h. gray; black int.; blue-tinted windows; blue, red & white tampo w/"United Groove" on sides & hood, sp5, Malaysia. #1 in Hippie Mobiles series, #089 (2001) 2 - 3

18535-a

'70 Roadrunner 18535 - 77mm - 1998
This model of a 1970 Plymouth Roadrunner has a plastic base, black interior, clear windows, and sp5. Malaysia.

a. orange, wide black stripe on hood & trunk, gray "426 Hemi" twice on hood. #17 in 1998 First Editions, #661 $2 - 4

a2. as a, ho5 (1998) 10 - 15

18535-b

b. red, black int., clear windows, JC Whitney logo in black on sides, black stripes over trunk, pcgy 15 - 18

c. purple, same as a, white int., white tampo, JC Whitney logo on sides. JC Whitney ltd ed, in box (1999) 15 - 18

'70 Roadrunner-d

d. green, same as a, no "426 Hemi" on hood, Ames Stores ltd ed, in black box (1999) 12 - 18

e. yellow, clear windows, black int., purple & red tampo w/"Nestle's Oh Henry" on sides & trunk, ho5. #1 in Sugar Rush Series II, #969 (2000) 2 - 3

f. black & white, black int., blue-tinted windows, gold & black shield on sides & trunk, "Jackson Police" on hood, iw. Cop Rods Series 2 only (2000) 9 - 12

g. purple; black roof & int.; clear windows; gray, red & black tampo w/Editor's Choice logo on trunk; rrch; Thailand; Target excl. Editor's Choice (2000) 7 - 9

'70 Roadrunner-h

h. red w/black int., tinted windows, black tampo w/"440" & "Roadrunner" on sides, "Plymouth 440" on hood, sp5, Malaysia, #100 (2001) 2 - 3

'70 Roadrunner-i

i. white; clear windows; black int.; black & red tampo w/stripes & Little Debbie Snacks logo on sides, stripes & "420 C.I." on hood, Little Debbie Snacks logo on roof; pr5s. Series III Little Debbie 3-pack (2001) 4 - NA

j. mtlfk gray, black roof & int., clear windows, "Plymouth" in black on rear fender, red & white Motor City Classics logo on rear window, rrch. Wal-Mart excl. Motor City Classics series (2002) 7 - 9

18843-a

At-A-Tude 18843 - 80mm - 1998
This customized vehicle has a black plastic base, metal spoiler, chrome interior, orange-tinted windows, lwch. Malaysia.

a. mtlfk blue; yellow, black & white tampo w/"5" & race decals on sides. #34 in 1998 First Editions, #667 2 - 3

18843-b

b. green; black spoiler; green-tinted windows; white, lt. green, black & orange tampo w/"Freaks of Horror on sides & hood; sp5bk. #1 in Terrorific series, #977 (1999) 2 - 3

At-A-Tude-c

c. gray; chrome int.; orange-tinted windows; orange wing; yellow, black & blue tampo w/"Performance" on sides; sp5; Malaysia. #2 in Speed Blaster series, #038 (2000) 2 - 3

d. white; chrome int.; clear windows; red, orange & black tampo w/"Target Drive into the Millennium" on sides, flames on hood, Hot Wheels logo & "Mattel Wheels" on trunk; gych. Target stores giveaway, in baggie (2000) 75 - NA

e. white, black plastic chassis & spoiler, chrome int., yellow-tinted windows, black hood & roof, yellow & red flame tampo on sides & hood, white square on roof, Editor's Choice logo on trunk, rrch, Thailand. Target excl. Editor's Choice series (2001) 7 - 9

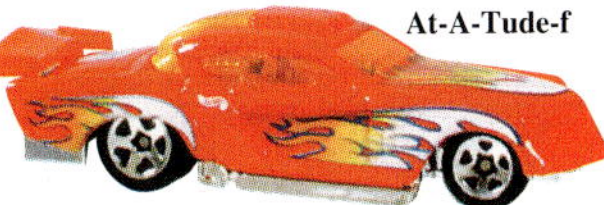
At-A-Tude-f

f. red; chrome int.; orange-tinted windows; white, orange & blue flame tampo on sides & hood; "Power Wheels" in black & white on trunk; sp5. Toys "R" Us Timeless Toys Series III 4-pack (2001) 4 - NA

g. dark yellow; black chassis & int.; blue-tinted windows; brown, black, white, gray & red tampo w/"Parking Patrol" & Planet Hot Wheels logo on sides; sp5; Thailand. City Service 5-pack (2001) 2 - NA

At-A-Tude-h

h. turquoise, black chassis & int., tinted windows, black & white tampo w/"Mosquito" & race decals w/designers' names on sides, sp5, Thailand, #237 (2002) 2 - 3

18847-a

Bad Mudder® 18847 - 76mm - 1998
This Ford off-road pickup truck has a black plastic chassis, interior, roll cage and engine in back; clear windshield, and dw3ct. Malaysia.

a. white; red, dk. blue & black tampo w/"8," Ford logo & race decals on sides; "8," "Bousquette" & "Handy

Cams" on roof. #33 in 1998 First Editions, #662 2 - 3
a2. as a, China, #662 2 - 3

18847-a3

a3. as a; red, dk. blue & mtlc blue tampo colors, no roof tampo; #662 (1999) 20 - 35

95509-a

BMW 325i 95509 - 73mm - 1998
This Corgi casting of a BMW sedan has a gray metal base, clear windows, black interior and lwch. China.
a. yellow; red & black tampo on sides & hood; #603 $3 - 5

18536-a

Callaway C-7 18536 - 73mm - 1998
This modified race car is based on a Corvette and has a black plastic base, wing & interior with black headlights as part of interior, clear windows, and sp5. Malaysia.
a. gray; black & orange tampo w/"C7R" & "Callaway" on sides & "OSD Fast Racing" on hood. #31 in 1998 First Editions, #677 2 - 3
a2. as a, painted headlights (1999) 2 - 3

18536-b

b. green; yellow, black & white tampo w/"ZRO" on sides; sp5. #2 in X-Treme Speed series, #966 (1999) 2 - 3
b2. as b, dw3, #966 (1999) 2 - 3

18536-c

c. white; same as c; red, black & gray tampo w/"1" & Diet Coke tampos; sp5. Coca Cola 4-pack (1999) 2 - NA

Callaway C-7-d

d. mtlfk green; orange int. & wing; yellow, orange & black tampo w/"Chowtime Pretzels" on sides & hood; sp5. #1 in Snack Time series, #013 (2000) 2 - 3
d2. as d, ho5, #013 (2000) 2 - 3
e. mtlfk green; black chassis & int.; clear windows; black, white & gold tampo w/"C" & "Team Corrosive" on sides & top; pr5s; China. Cyborg City 5-pack (2001) 3 - NA
f. black, red spoiler & int., tinted windows, gray & orange tampo w/"1" & race decals on sides, "1" on hood, pr5s, Malaysia. Victory Lane 5-pack (2001) 3 - NA

g. blue; black chassis; orange int. & spoiler; orange-tinted windows; black, white & orange tampo w/baseball player, "Home Run" & logo on sides; sp3; Thailand. Sports 5-pack (2002) 2 - NA

18222-a

Cat-A-Pult 18222 - 60mm - 1998
This convertible race car has a metal base, black interior, orange-tinted windows and sp5. Malaysia.
a. red; white stripe w/black "64" on hood. #38 in 1998 First Editions, #681 2 - 3
a2. as a, sp3, #681 (1999) 2 - 3

18222-b

b. orange; black & lt. green tampo with "Hunchback" on sides & hood; sp5. #2 in Terrorific series, #978 (1999) 2 - 3
c. green; black int.; yellow-tinted windows & int.; black, gray & yellow tampo w/"Strike Decoy" on sides, "Cat-A-Pult" on hood; Thailand. Super Launcher 5-pack (2001) 2 - NA

18531-a

Chaparral 2 18531 - 65mm - 1998
This mid-sixties race car has a black metal chassis, black interior, clear windshield, and lwch. Malaysia.
a. white, black circle w/"6" on hood, #28 in 1998 First Editions, #669 2 - 3

18531-b

b. red, white metal chassis, two white stripes on top, #1008 (1999) 2 - 3

Chaparral 2-c

c. mtlfk blue; white chassis; gray int.; blue-tinted windshield; black, white & orange tampo w/"Chaparral 2" on sides & trunk; 2000 Treasure Hunt logo on nose; rrch. #7 in 2000 Treasure Hunt series, #055 (2000) 12 - 15
d. mtlfk green; black chassis & interior; clear windshield; black, white & gold tampo design w/"C" & "Team Corrosine" on sides & top; pr5s; China; #178 (2001) 2 - 3

Chaparral 2-e

e. yellow; black chassis & int.; clear windshield; black, orange & white tampo w/"Wasp" on sides & trunk; sp5; Thailand. Insectiride 5-pack (2002) 2 - NA

18844-a

Chrysler Thunderbolt 18844 - 73mm - 1998
This Chrysler show car has a black plastic base, purple-tinted windows, ho5. Malaysia.
a. gray, #32 in 1998 First Editions, #671 2 - 3
b. blue, black chassis, white int., tinted windows, white tampo w/"Lucero" on sides, sp3, Malaysia, #1107 (1999) 2 - 3

Chrysler Thunderbolt-c

c. black w/gray chassis, white int., yellow-tinted windows, purple & silver design w/"Future Fleet 2000" on sides, sp3. #4 in Future Fleet 2000 series, #004 (2000) 2 - 3
d. red; clear windows; black int.; black & gray tampo w/"Thunderstreak," "Lucero" & "36" on sides; sp5; Thailand; #225 (2001) 2 - 3
d2. as d, Malaysia, #225 (2001) 2 - 3
e. black, white int., blue-tinted windows, blue & white tampo w/shark on sides & hood, sp3, Thailand, Shark Park 5-pack (2001) 2 - NA
f. mtlfk dark red; black chassis & int.; yellow-tinted windows; yellow, orange, black & white tampo with "18," "Hot Wheels" & race decals on sides & hood; hotgd; #136 (2002) 2 - 3

16979-a

Custom Van 16979 - 70mm - 1998
This Corgi casting of a van has a chrome plastic base with "Hot Rod Custom Van" embossed on the bottom, blacked-out windows, sp5. China.
a. purple; yellow, orange & red flame tampo w/"Chuck E. Cheese's" logo on sides. Chuck E. Cheese excl $5 - 7

16979-b

b. mtlc aqua; gold plastic base, pipes & tinted windows; black int.; blue, white & gray window tampo on sides; gold striping; red & black "JC Whitney" on sides; bumper sticker tampo w/"I" heart "Love JC Whitney" in back. Ltd ed of 10,000, JC Whitney only 12 - 15

18848-a

Customized C3500 18848 - 79mm - 1998
This Malaysia-made truck has a gray plastic base and interior, tinted windows, and ho5.
a. mtlfk aqua; red, blue and gray striping on sides. #26 in 1998 First Editions, #663 $20 - 25

18848-a2

a2. as a, stripe is thicker. #26 in 1998 First Editions, #663 2 - 4
b. plum; black plastic chassis & int.; blue -tinted windows; yellow tampo on hood & roof; yellow, black & white tampo w/"Jerry's Electric 24 Hr

18848-b

Service Since 1998" & "How Am I Driving?" on sides; sp5; #1027 (1999) 3 - 5
c. white w/red & black sides, black chassis & int., clear windows, gray & red Editor's Choice logo on back cover, pc. China. Target excl. Editor's Choice series (2000) 5 - 7

Customized C3500-d

d. white; black tonneau cover; white int.; tinted windows; red, blue & white tampo w/"JC Whitney www.jcwhitney.com" on sides & cover; gych. Ltd ed for JC Whitney, in box (2000) 12 - 15
e. blue, blue tonneau cover, white int., tinted windows, red & gray tampo with "JC Whitney www.jcwhitney.com" on sides & cover, gych. Ltd ed for JC Whitney, in box (2000) 12 - 15
f. yellow; clear windows; black int.; orange, dark red, white & black tampo design w/"Thorn Bros. Industrial Maintenance" on sides & hood; dw3; China; #209 (2001) 2 - 3
g. blue; black chassis & int.; yellow-tinted windows; black, gold, pink & white tampo w/"Radio Dispatched 24 Hrs.," "HW Trans," "9" & "Maintenance Service" on sides; sp5. Thailand. Asphalt Assault 5-pack (2002) 2 - NA

18675-a

Dairy Delivery™ 18675 - 75mm - 1998
This '40s milk truck has a gray plastic base, clear windows, light blue interior and sp5. Malaysia.
a. white; lt. blue, dk. blue & pink tampo w/"Got Milk?" on sides. #10 in 1998 First Editions, #645 $4 - 6
a2. as a, China 4 - 6

18675-b

b. red; yellow int.; clear windows; yellow, white & dk. blue tampo w/"Ronald McDonald House Charities" & House on sides & roof; "12th Annual Collector's Convention Oct. 16-18, 1998" on roof; sp5; 1998 Hot Wheels Convention 25 - 30

18675-c

c. red; white int.; clear windows; black, white & gold tampo w/"Jiffy Lube" & "Fleet Service" on sides; rrch w/white walls. Edition of 25,000 for Jiffy Lube (1999) 15 - 18
d. white; top half & roof blue; red, white & yellow tampo w/"1999 National Balloon Rally Statesville, NC" on sides; rrch. M & D ltd ed of 15,000 for 1999 Balloon Rally (1999) 15 - 18

Values are shown in U.S. dollars, first price is for mint, second is for mint packaged vehicles only. See pages 15-16 for grading guide to determine value for cars in lesser conditions.

18675-d

18675-e

e. white, clear windows, black int., large black spots, "Got Milk?" in red on sides, sp5, China, #1004 (1999) 3 - 6
e2. as e, Malaysia, #1004 (1999) 4 - 6

18675-f

f. mtlfk gray; gray plastic chassis; black int.; tinted windows; orange, yellow, white, red & black flame tampo w/Hot Wheels logo & "Delivery Since 1968" on sides; rrch; Malaysia. Ltd ed of 15,000 for Full Grid, #1004 (1999) 15 - 18

18675-g

g. white, red on sides & hood, red & blue tampo w/JC Whitney logo on sides. Ltd ed for JC Whitney, in box (1999) 15 - 18

18675-h

h. pearl white; black int., roof & rear doors; clear windows; gold, black & blue tampo w/"Town of Madison" on sides, "Town of Madison Police" & logo on sides & roof, "Town of Madison Police in back. Ltd ed of 25,000, Cop Rods series for K•B Toys (1999) 5 - 7
i. lt. green; black base; clear windows; red int.; white, gray, black, plum & lt. blue tampo w/"World of Wheels" on sides, "Championship Auto Shows Inc." on roof, gych. Ltd ed for World of Wheels (2000) 12 - 15

Dairy Delivery-j

j. orange, same as i, limited edition for World of Wheels (2000) 12 - 15

Dairy Delivery-k

k. blue; chrome chassis; tinted windows; white int.; red, lt. blue, lt. green, white & black tampo w/"Otter Pops" on sides & roof, 3 Pops figures on sides; sp5. Otter Pops premium (2000) 4 - 6

Dairy Delivery-l

l. purple; clear windshield; tan int.; red, lt. green, black & white tampo w/"World's Smallest Clowns" & "Circus on Wheels" on sides; sp5gd; China. #4 in Circus on Wheels series, #28 (2000) 2 - 3

Dairy Delivery-m

m. white, clear windows, black int., red & dark blue star tampo w/Puerto Rico" on roof, sp5. Excl. to Puerto Rico, in box (2000) 20 - 25

Dairy Delivery-n

n. red; white roof; black int.; tinted windows; orange, black, white & gold tampo w/"Unit 76," "www.houseon-fire.com" & Houston Fire Department emblem on sides; "Unit 76," flames & Houston Fire Department emblem on roof; iw. Fire Rods series (2001) 5 - 7

Dairy Delivery-o

o. yellow; tinted windows; red int.; red, black, gray & white tampo on sides & hood w/"Big Lou's Speedy Delivery," "Mr. Big" & decals on sides; pr5s; China; #199 (2001) 2 - 3
o2. as o, Malaysia, Truck Stoppers 5-pack; #199 (2001) 2 - 3

18173-a

Dodge Caravan 18173 - 72mm - 1998
This Dodge van has a gray plastic base, white interior, tinted windows and sunroof, and dw3. Malaysia.
a. mtlfk brown; yellow & black tampo w/"Dodge" & "Caravan" on sides. #4 in 1998 First Editions, #633 $2 - 4
a2. as a, sp5, #633 2 - 4

18173-b

b. gray; lt. blue, yellow, black & red tampo w/"8," "Cal State L.A." & "Solar Eagle III" on sides; sp5gd. Solar Racing Action Pack 5 - NA
c. mtlfk red; tinted windows; white int.; silver, black, yellow & white tampo w/"Metro Hotel Shuttle" on sides; sp5; #1026 (1999) 7 - 10

18173-c

d. red; gray chassis; white int.; blue-tinted windows; white, blue & black tampo w/"Mobile TV Unit Channel 7" on sides; sp5; China. Kool Toyz Racing pack (2001) 4 - 6
e. yellow; black chassis & int.; clear windows; red & black tampo w/"Ambulance," "Rescue" & "Unit 9" on sides; sp5; China. Sto 'n Go Rescue Center set (2001) 4 - 6
f. mtlfk white; white int.; blue-tinted windows; pink & blue tampo with "Barbie" on sides & front, "Dodge Caravan" on sides; sp5. Toys "R" Us Timeless Toys Series III 4-pack (2001) 6 - NA
g. mtlfk blue; tan int.;, clear windows; gray, lt. green & white tampo w/"Yosemite" on sides; sp3; Thailand. World Tour 5-pack (2001) 2 - NA
h. black, gray chassis & int., tinted windows, white & gold tampo w/"Police" & City of Hot Wheels logo on sides & hood, sp5. China. Super Police Headquarters set (2001) 4 - NA
i. mtlfk orange; gray chassis; tan int.; clear windows; black, white & lt. green tampo w/"Goaaal!!!!!", soccer ball, "Dodge" & logo on sides; sp5; Thailand. Sports 5-pack (2002) 2 - NA

18845-a

Dodge Concept Car (Copperhead) 18845 - 77mm - 1998
This model, based on a Dodge show car, has a metal base, black interior, tinted windshield, and sp5. Malaysia.
a. mtlfk red-orange, gray headlights, #35 in 1998 First Editions, #672 2 - 3
a2. as a, China, #672 2 - 3
b. black, brown int., tinted windshield, sp5. Ames Stores excl. 4-pack only (1999) 8 - NA

18845-c

c. white, blue int., clear windshield, blue & red tampo w/stripes & "Baby Ruth" on sides & hood, stripes on trunk. #4 in Sugar Rush series, #972 (1999) 2 - 3

18845-d

d. mtlfk gray; black & gold tampo design on sides, hood & trunk, "Dodge" on sides & hood, lwgd, #1068 (2000) 2 - 3
d2. same as d 2 - 3
e. white; tan int.; clear windshield, black & gold tampo design on sides, hood & trunk; "Dodge" on sides & hood; sp3gd; #167 (2000) 2 - 3
f. mtlfk lt. green, black int., tinted windshield, silver & black flame tampo on sides & trunk, "R/T" on sides, sp3, China, #120 (2002) 2 - 3

18174-a

Dodge Sidewinder 18174 - 68mm - 1998
This Dodge minitruck has a gray plastic base, black plastic interior and truck bed cover, tinted windshield, and sp5. Malaysia.
a. candy red; #3 in 1998 First Editions #634 $2 - 4

18174-b

b. white; black plastic base; purple int. & truck bed cover; lt. green, magenta & black tampo w/"Snowboarding Team" on sides, "Benboards" on hood. #1 in X-Treme Speeds series, #965 (1999) 2 - 3

Dodge Sidewinder-c

c. mustard; gray base; red int.; clear windshield; black, red & white tampo w/popcorn & "Popcorn" on sides & hood; dw3. #4 in Snack Time series, #016 (2000) 2 - 3
d. yellow, same as c, #4 in Snack Time series, #016 (2000) 2 - 3

Dodge Sidewinder-e

e. dark maroon; black chassis, int. & cover; tinted windshield; orange, black & white tampo w/"Dodge" & Dodge logo on sides & "Dodge Sidewinder" on hood; pr5s. #4 in Company Cars series, #088 (2001) 2 - 3
e2. as e, sp3, #4 in Company Cars series, #088 (2001) 2 - 3

19643-a

Double Vision 19643 - 77mm - 1998
This concept car has two bodies: one with two chrome engines, the other with a clear dome. It also has a gray plastic base and lwgd. Malaysia.
a. mtlfk dk. red; white & black tampo with "20/20" & race decals on side & one body. #40 in 1998 First Editions, #684 2 - 3

19643-b

b. black; brown, white, red & tan tampo w/Bullwinkle on sides, "Bullwinkle" on top; lwgd. #3 in Car-Toon Friends series, #987 (1999) 2 - 3

Double Vision-c

c. purple; silver & black tampo w/star & "TH 2000" on sides. #1 in 2000 Treasure Hunt series, #049 (2000) 15 - 18
d. mtlfk green; gray chassis; white, black & orange tampo w/"20/20" & race decals on sides & top; sp3; Malaysia; #212 (2000) 2 - 3

Double Vision-e

Values are shown in U.S. dollars, first price is for mint, second is for mint packaged vehicles only. See pages 15-16 for grading guide to determine value for cars in lesser conditions.

e. mtlfk green; black chassis; yellow-tinted dome; black, gold & white flame tampo on sides & top w/"Lucky Laprechoun" on top; lwgd. #2 in Extreme Sports series, #082 (2001) 2 - 3
e2. as e, ho5gd (2001) 2 - 3

18143-a

(Ford) Escort Rally 18143 - 70mm - 1998
This rally car has a gray plastic base, red interior, tinted windows and rear spoiler, and lwch. Malaysia.
a. white; blue front; black, blue, red & yellow tampo w/"8," "Swisher Motors" & race decals on sides & front. #1 in 1998 First Editions, #637 $4 - 8

18143-b

b. red; gray plastic chassis; black int.; clear windows & rear spoiler; yellow, black, white & lt. green tampo w/"The Original Uno" on sides; lwch; Malaysia. #4 in Classic Games series, #984 (1999) 8 - 12

18143-c

c. black; blue-tinted windows; gray int.; red, white & gold tampo w/"Police," "To Protect and Serve," "Unit 9" & City of Hot Wheels logo on sides; "02" on roof; lwch. Police Squad 5-pack (1999) 5 - NA

Escort Rally-d

d. black; clear wing & windows; white int. & doors; red, white & black tampo w/"1 Uno/Ze Policia," "Al N Al Rescate" & "Emergencia" on sides & lwch; Thailand. World Racers 2 5-pack (1999) 2 - NA
e. gray; tinted windows; black int.; orange, black, white & red tampo w/"VRally" & "1" on sides & roof; ho5; Malaysia; #192 (2001) 2 - 3

18537-a

Express Lane® 18537 - 45mm - 1998
This shopping cart with an engine has a metal chassis, handles and engine, black interior and steering wheel, and sp5. Malaysia.
a. red, "Express Lane" on white on sides, #37 in 1998 First Editions, #678 2 - 3
a2. as a, China 2 - 3
b. orange; red int.; yellow, black & red tampo w/"Floyd's Market" on sides; China; #1067 (1999) 2 - 3

18537-b

Express Lane-c

c. purple, black int., red & yellow tampo w/"Treasure Hunt" on sides, sp5gd. #11 in 1999 Treasure Hunt series, #940 (1999) 20 - 25
d. red, black int., white tampo w/"Cub Foods" on sides, sp5. In Cubs Foods 2-pack w/basic line car (2001) 3 - 5
e. orange; tan steering wheel; green, white & black tampo w/"Gator Bait Market" on sides; sp5; China; #111 (2001) 2 - 3

18849-a

Fathom This® 18849 - 76mm - 1998
This Malaysia-made concept submarine is all plastic with two sets of black blades, two sets of white blades, and orange windows.
a. white, "experimental" in red on both sides of stand, #682 2 - 3

18849-b

b. yellow; black & yellow blades, black stand with "Rescue Unit" in silver; Thailand. Ocean Blasters 5-pack (1999) 2 - NA
c. white, orange & white blades, orange windows, Virtual Collection, Malaysia, #152 (2001) 2 - 3
d. orange, gray & orange blades, black windows, Malaysia, pkg reads "Submarine," #236 (2001) 2 - 3

19953-c

Ferrari F512M 19953 - 72mm - 1998
This Ferrari has a black metal base, black interior, clear windows, and ho5. Malaysia.
a. mtlfk silver; yellow & black Ferrari logo on hood; #784 2 - 3
a2. as a, sp5, #784 3 - 6
b. red, tan int., tinted windows, sp5, #992 (1999) 2 - 3
c. yellow, as a, pc, #5 in 1999 Treasure Hunt series, #933 (1999) 18 - 20
c2. as c, unpainted metal base (1999) 18 - 20
d. bluish gray, black chassis & int., clear windows, yellow & black Ferrari logo on hood, sp5, Malaysia, #162 (2002) 2 - 3

18850-a

Ford GT-90 18850 - 66mm - 1998
This Ford show car has a metal base, black dome, and sp3. Malaysia.
a. white, #14 in 1998 First Editions, #668 2 - 3
a2. as a, China, #668 2 - 3

18850-b

b. mtlc blue; gray int.; clear dome; chrome hood; white, black & orange tampo w/"New York Toy Fair 1999" on hood; sp3. 1999 Toy Fair give-away, in plastic box (1999) 120 - NA

18850-c

c. red; black interior; tinted dome; white, gold & black tampo all over car, "Ford GT-90" on sides; dw3; China; #1073 (1999) 2 - 3

18850-d

d. yellow; black int.; clear dome; black, white & red tampo w/"15" & "Collision Patrol" on sides, "15" on hood; sp3; China; #1032 (1999) 2 - 3
e. red, clear dome, black int., White's Guide logo in white on rear of dome, gray-to-black stripe on sides, sp3, Malaysia. Ltd ed of 12,500 for White's Guide (1999) 15 - 18
f. black, same as e, ltd ed of 12,500 for White's Guide, Malaysia (1999) 15 - 18

Ford GT-90-g

g. black; green-tinted dome; gray, red & black tampo w/"Future Fleet 2000" on sides & rear of dome; numbers on sides; sp3; China. #1 in Future Fleet 2000 series, #001 (2000) 2 - 3
g2. as g, lwch, #1 in Future Fleet 2000 series, #001 (2000) 2 - 3
g3. as g2, lwch, Malaysia, #1 in Future Fleet 2000 series, #001 (2000) 2 - 3
g4. as g, Malaysia, #1 in Future Fleet 2000 series, #001 (2000) 2 - 3
h. green, same as c, white int., ho5., China, #224 (2000) 2 - 3

Ford GT-90-i

i. white; gray int.; blue-tinted dome; gold, black & blue design on sides & hood; pr5s; China. #2 in Anime series, #062 (2001) 2 - 3
j. blue; mtlfk gray chassis; gray int.; clear dome; black, red, white & gray tampo w/"EFX Recovery Team" on sides & hood; "1" & "GT90" on sides; sp3; China; Cyborg City 5-pack. (2001) 2 - NA

Ford GT-90-k

k. black; clear dome; red int.; yellow, white & red tampo w/"Power Department" & Planet Hot Wheels logo on sides; hood design; sp3; Thailand. City Service 5-pack (2001) 2 - NA
l. yellow; black int.; clear dome; black, orange & white tampo w/"Demolition Derby" on sides; lwch; Thailand. Demolition Derby playset (2001) 6 - NA

18679-a

Go Kart 18679 - 43mm - 1998
The smallest and lightest Hot Wheels model produced to date. It has a green painted metal base, black seat, metal engine, sp5 in back and mw in front. Malaysia.
Similar casting: Go Kart (2000) (Racing Series)
a. green; black, orange & white tampo w/"123 Racing" & "M Engineering." #21 in 1998 First Editions, #651 $8 - 10
a2. as a, sp3 2 - 3

18679-b

b. orange, orange chassis, metal int., black seat & sides, orange & white race decals, ho5 #1106 (1999) 6 - 8

18679-c

c. blue; blue chassis; chrome int.; black seat; white, red & yellow tampo w/race decals on sides, "5" in front; pc with "Goodyear" in white on sides. Ltd ed of 12,500 for Yamahauler (1999) 15 - 18
c2. as c; gold plated int.; pcgd 15 - 18

Go Cart-d

d. white; black seat; gold-plated engine & steering wheel; orange, gold & black tampo w/"TH" on sides & "Go Cart" on top; rrgd. #6 in 2000 Treasure Hunt series, #054 (2000) 25 - 30
e. purple, gray seat, lt. blue metal engine, gray tampo, ho5. Virtual Collection, #151 (2000) 3 - 5
f. white; blue sides; black seat; multicolored tampo w/"6" & race decals on sides, "Valvoline" on nose; sp5; Thailand. #1 in NASCAR Go Cart series (2000) 5 - 7

Go Cart-g

g. yellow; black seat; red, yellow & white tampo w/"4" & race decals on sides, "Kodak" on nose; sp5; Thailand. #2 in NASCAR Go Cart series (2000) 5 - 7
h. green, yellow nose, black seat, multi-colored tampo w/"98" & race decals on sides & "Woody" on nose, sp5, Thailand. #3 in NASCAR Go Cart series (2000) 5 - 7
i. black; white nose; black seat; dark blue, red & white tampo w/"99" & race decals on sides, "Exide" on nose; sp5; Thailand. #4 in NASCAR Go Cart series (2000) 5 - 7

Values are shown in U.S. dollars, first price is for mint, second is for mint packaged vehicles only. See pages 15-16 for grading guide to determine value for cars in lesser conditions.

j. red, red chassis, black seat, chrome engine, Hot Wheels logo in black on sides, sp5 in back, mw in front, Malaysia. Go Cart Test Track playset & Kmart City Service 6-car set (2001) 8 - NA
k. orange, black seat, metal engine, black & gray tampo on sides & top w/"Kieran Racing" in front, mw in front and sp5 in back, #141 (2001) 3 - 5
k2. as k, small sp5 in front & sp5 in back, #141 (2001) 3 - 5

18678-a

Hot Seat® 18678 - 70mm - 1998
This toilet-on-wheels has a metal base, plastic toilet with a metal engine in back, black plunger for a steering wheel, black toilet seat, and sp5. Malaysia.
a. white, #13 in 1998 First Editions, #648 $2 - 4
a2. as a, Thailand, #648 2 - 3
a3. as a, China, Scum Chums Action Pack (1999) 7 - NA

18678-b

b. chrome, red seat & plunger, sp5, #999 (1999) 2 - 3

18678-c

c. clear plastic, black seat & plunger, sp5. #10 in 1999 Treasure Hunt series, #938 (1999) 15 - 20
d. blue, white seat & plunger, bluish metal engine, sp5, Malaysia. Virtual Collection, #101 (2001) 2 - 3
e. orange, purple seat & plunger, sp5, #140 (2001) 2 - 3

18544-a

(IROC) Firebird 18544 - 78mm - 1998
This model has a gray plastic base, slightly tinted windows, gray interior, and sp5b with "Goodyear" & "Eagle" in yellow on the tires. The IROC designation was only used on the original version. China.
a. gold; black & white tampo w/"True Value," "Firebird" & "1" on sides; "True Value" on hood; "1" & "Goodyear" on roof. #16 in 1998 First Editions, #653 $2 - 4

18544-b

b. white; tinted windows; black int.; gray, red, dk. blue & black tampo w/"Huffman Racing," "1" & race decals on sides & hood; sp5bk w/"Goodyear" & "Eagle" in yellow on tires; Firebird; China; #1065 (1999) 2 - 3

Firebird-c

c. orange; black plastic base; white int.; clear windows; yellow, black, red & white tampo w/"Yip's BBQ Cheesy Potato Chips" on sides & hood; sp5. #2 in Snack Time series, #014 (2000) 2 - 3

Firebird-d

d. mtlfk gray; black chassis & int.; lightly tinted windows; red, black & white tampo w/"Handy" & race decals on sides & hood, "1" on hood; pr5bk w/"Goodyear Eagle" on tires; China; #121 (2001) 2 - 3
d2. as d, Malaysia (2001) 2 - 3
e. white; black chassis, int. & windows; gray, black & red tampo w/"1," "Behrendt Racing" & race decals on sides; sp5bk; Malaysia. Crash Test set (2001) 4 - NA

Firebird-f

f. red; black chassis; white int.; clear windows; black & white tampo w/"03," "Pep Boys" & race decals on sides; "Pep Boys" & picture on hood; "03" on roof; sp5bk w/"Goodyear" in white. Pep Boys 2-pack (2001) 3 - NA

18144-a

Jaguar D-Type 18144 - 65mm - 1998
This Malaysia-made model of the Jaguar race car has a blue metal base, clear windshield & headlights, gray plastic interior, and sp5.
a. blue; black "4" on solid white circle in front & back; #6 in 1998 First Editions; #638 $6 - 8
a2. as a, dw3 2 - 3
a3. as a, lwch 2 - 3
a4. as a, sp5, China, #638 2 - 3

18144-b

b. red; red chassis; gray int.; yellow, black & white tampo w/"Jaguar D-Type," "27" & race decals on sides, "27" on hood; lwch; China; #997 (1999) 2 - 3
b2. as b, Malaysia (1999) 2 - 3

18144-c

c. mtlfk black; gold int.; clear windshield; red, gold & white striping tampo w/stripes & logo, "TH" on sides & hood; sp5; Malaysia. #8 in 1999 Treasure Hunt series, #936 (1999) 15 - 20
d. mtlfk dark red; black chassis; gray int.; tinted windshield; yellow, white & black tampo w/"Huffman Racing" on top; lwch; China; #180 (2000) 2 - 3
d2. as d, Thailand, Sports Stars 5-pack (2001) 2 - NA

e. mtlfk gray; clear windshield; black int.; red, black & white tampo w/"6" behind drivers seat; stripes & "6" on top; sp5; China; #184 (2001) 2 - 3

18221-a

Jaguar XK8 18221 - 74mm - 1998
This Jaguar convertible has a gray plastic base, black interior, clear windshield, lwch. Malaysia.
a. blue-green; black & white tampo w/"Jaguar XK-8" on sides. #5 in 1998 First Editions, #639 $3 - 6
a2. as a, white int. 75 - 90

Jaguar XK8-b

b. red; black plastic base; tan int.; tinted windshield; white, yellow & black tampo w/"Nestle's 1000 Grand" on sides & hood; lwgd. #2 in Sugar Rush Series II, #970 (2000) 2 - 3
c. gray, tinted windshield, blue int., black & blue stripe w/"XK8" on sides & top, ho5, Malaysia, #165 (2000) 2 - 3

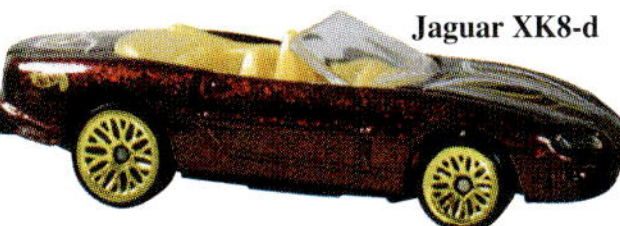
Jaguar XK8-d

d. dk. mtlfk red, black chassis, tan int., clear windshield, gold & gray pinstripes on hood & trunk, "MC 2000" on the trunk. 2000 Mystery Car, in baggie (2000) 6 - NA
e. dk. mtlfk red, black chassis, beige int., clear windshield, dk. blue stripe w/"XK8" in white on sides & top, pr5s, China, #161 (2001) 2 - 3

18540-a

Lakester® 18540 - 78mm - 1998
This 1960s-style race car, used to set speed records, has a red metal base, six metal pipes on each side, clear windshield, chrome interior, and large sp5. Malaysia.
a. red; yellow, white, orange & black tampo w/"'61 Spirit of Eagle Rock, XXA/GL" & race decals on top & sides. #12 in 1998 First Editions, #647 $2 - 3
a2. as a, China 2 - 3

18540-b

b. mtlfk silver; mtlfk silver chassis; blue-tinted windshield; chrome int.; black, blue, white & green tampo w/"Alien Xplorer" & "93005" on sides; sp5; China; #1064 (1999) 2 - 3

18540-c

c. white; black center; black chassis; chrome int.; red-tinted windshield; orange, white & black tampo w/"The Bomb" & bomb on sides, Boris & "Boris" on top. #4 in Car-Toon Friends series, #988 (1999) 2 - 3

Lakester-d

d. mtlfk aqua; black chassis; gold chrome int. & pipes; yellow-tinted windshield; white, orange & black tampo w/2000 Treasure Hunt logo on top; sp5gd. #5 in 2000 Treasure Hunt series, #053 (2000) 12 - 14
e. black; gold chrome int. & side pipes; yellow-tinted windshield; black, gold & white tampo w/"Skunk" on top; sp5; Malaysia. Virtual Collection, #168 (2001) 2 - 3

Lakester-f

f. olive & brown camouflage, gray chassis, clear windshield, chrome int., black & white tampo w/eagle & "Golden Eagle" on sides, sp5, Malaysia. #2 in Rod Squadron series, #066 (2001) 2 - 3
f2. as f, China, #2 in Rod Squadron series, #066 (2001) 2 - 3
g. gray, chrome int., red-tinted windshield, red & yellow flames on top, sp5, Thailand. Hot Rods 5-pack 2 - NA

18530-a

Mercedes SLK 18530 - 68mm - 1998
This Malaysia-made model has a metal chassis, tan interior, tinted windows, black plastic headlights, black door handles, and ho5.
a. mtlc yellow, Hot Wheels logo tampo, #11 in 1998 First Editions, #646 $2 - 4
a2. as a, sp5, #646 2 - 4
a3. yellow, same as a, black int., gray side tampo, #646 12 - 15
a4. as a, black int., #646 2 - 4
a5. as a, India, #646 2 - 4

18530-b

b. mtlfk dk. blue, white int., tinted windows; dw3, Malaysia, #1025 (1999) 2 - 3
b2. as b, India, #1025 (1999) 2 - 3
b3. as b2, silver base, #1025 (1999) 2 - 3
c. gray, black base, tinted windows, dw3, #1095 (2000) 2 - 3
d. aqua, same as c, India, #120 (2000) 2 - 3
e. mtlfk gray, metal chassis, black int., aqua-tinted windows, black & yellow tampo design on hood & roof, ho5, #225 (2001) 2 - 3

18542-a

Mustang Cobra 18542 - 72mm - 1998
This Trans-Am racing Mustang has a gray plastic base and interior, clear windows and lwgd. Malaysia.
a. black; lt. green, orange, yellow & white tampo w/"OSO Fast Racing Mustang," "11" & race decals on sides, "Mustang Team OSO" & race decals on hood, Ford logo & "Team OSO" on trunk. #18 in 1998 First Editions, #665 2 - 3

Values are shown in U.S. dollars, first price is for mint, second is for mint packaged vehicles only. See pages 15-16 for grading guide to determine value for cars in lesser conditions.

a2. as a, Thailand (1999) 2 - 3
a3. as a, India (1999) 2 - 3

18542-b

b. white; black chassis & int.; black & orange tampo w/"Team Wagner" on sides & hood; dw3. #2 in Mega Graphics series, #974 (1999) 2 - 3
b2. as b, India, #974 (1999) 2 - 3
b3. as b, dw3, #974 (2000) 2 - 3

18542-c

c. mtlc gold, black plastic base & int., black tampo w/"Mustang" on sides, sp5, India, #1066 (1999) 2 -3
d. gold, black int., black tampo with "Mustang" on sides, sp5, India, #1066 (2000) 2 - 3
e. mtlfk blue; clear windows; gray int.; yellow, black & orange tampo w/"30" & "Attitude" on sides; sp5; Malaysia. #3 in Speed Blaster series, #039 (2000) 2 - 3
e2. as e, India (2000) 2 - 3
f. dk. mtlfk red, dark red chassis, white int., tinted windows, black tampo w/"Mustang" on sides, dw3, India, #121 (2000) 2 - 3
g. mtlfk purple; black chassis; gray int.; red-tinted windows; gray, red & black tampo w/"Happy Birthday" & "1" thru "12" on sides; lwch; China; #217 (2002) 2 - 3

18539-a2

(1970) Mustang Mach I 18539 - 70mm - 1998

This 1970 Ford Mustang has a black chassis, interior, rear window and spoiler; blue-tinted windows; and sp5. Malaysia.

a. yellow, black tampo w/stripes & "428" on hood. #29 in 1998 First Editions, #670 2 - 3
a2. as a, ho5, #670 35 - 40
b. red-orange, same as a, #29 in 1998 First Editions, #670 35 - 40

18539-c

c. dk. ruby red, same as a, "Mustang" in white on sides, black stripe on hood, gych. Ltd ed for Hills Department Stores (1999) 25 - 30

18539-d

d. red; clear windows; yellow, black & white tampo w/stripe on bottom of sides, "Penske Auto Center" on sides, stripe on hood. Ltd ed for Penske Auto Centers (1999) 15 - 18

18539-e

e. mtlfk aqua, clear windows, black int., silver & black tampo w/"T H Mustang" on sides, sp5. #11 in 1999 Treasure Hunt series, #939 (1999) 20 - 25

18539-f

f. mtlfk blue; clear windows; black int.; silver, orange & black tampo w/"Mustang" on sides; lwch; #1105 (1999) 3 - 5

18539-g

g. mtlfk blue; white, orange & yellow tampo w/large Hot Wheels logo & race decals on sides, stripes on hood & roof; rrch. Ltd ed in box for 1999 Power Tour. Some boxes have Tour Ed car on front of box (1999) 15 - 18

18539-h

h. gray; blue int.; blue-tinted windows; blue & red tampo w/"4" & Cubs logo on sides, "4," Cubs logo & "Chicago" on hood, "4" on roof; sp5. Ltd ed 2-pack, Chicago Cubs baseball give-away (1999) 10 - NA
i. black; orange & white flame tampo on sides & roof; White's Guide logo on roof; gych; Malaysia. Ltd ed of 12,500 for Whites Guide (1999) 12 - 15
j. white, same as i, black tampo w/White's Guide logo & "Mustang" on sides, stripes & "428" on hood, Malaysia. Ltd ed of 12,500 for Whites Guide (1999) 12 - 15

Mustang Mach 1-k

k. red; black hood; white roof; clear windows; black int.; black, white, yellow & blue tampo w/"15" on sides & hood, race decals on sides. Parnelli Jones Mustang, limited to 15,000, #1 in Full Grid Racing series (2000) 10 - 12

Mustang Mach 1-l

l. mtlfk dark red; black chassis & int.; clear windows; white, gold & black pinstripe tampo on sides & top, "MC" & "Mystery Car 2000" on roof; sp5gd. 2000 Mystery Car, in baggie (2000) 5 - 7
m. mtlfk gray; black chassis; clear windows; black int.; orange, black & white tampo on sides & hood; pr5s; Malaysia; #112 (2001) 2 - 3
m2. as m, sp5, Malaysia, #112 (2001) 4 - 6

Mustang Mach 1-n

n. black; clear windows; black int.; orange & white pinstripe on sides; two wide white stripes on hood & roof; red & gold Editor's Choice logo on trunk; rrch; Thailand. Target excl. Editor's Choice series (2001) 7 - 9
o. red, black base & int., tinted windows, black & white stripe tampo on sides & top w/"Little Debbie" on sides, pr5s. Series III Little Debbie 3-pack (2001) 5 - NA

Mustang Mach 1-o

p. mtlfk gold, black chassis & int., clear windows, turquoise & black tampo on sides & hood, lwch, Malaysia, Gas Station set (2001) 4 - NA

95553-a

Oil Refinery Truck - 95553 - 1998

This Corgi casting has a black plastic base, black interior, clear windows, and sp5. China.

a. white; gray plastic tank; yellow on bottom of cab; red, yellow & white striping on bottom of tank. Oil Refinery playset only $5 - NA

18545-a

Panoz GTR-1 18545 - 75mm - 1998

This race car has a black plastic chassis, clear windows, blue interior, a spoiler in back, and lwch. China.

a. white; lt. blue, red, silver & black tampo w/"66" & race decals on sides; stripes on hood & trunk; "66" on hood. #19 in 1998 First Editions, #657 $2 - 3
a2. as a, black int., Malaysia, #657 2 - 3
a3. as a, black int., #657 (1999) 2 - 3

18545-b

b. mtlfk green; black chassis, int. & spoiler; clear windows; red, white & black tampo w/"17" & race decals on sides & hood, "WRF" on rear fenders; sp3; China; #1040 (1999) 2 - 3
b2. as b, Malaysia, World Racers 5-pack 2 - 3
c. black, red wing & int., clear windows, gray & red tampo on sides & top w/"Samurai Racing" on top, sp3, Thailand. World Racers 2 5-pack (1999) 3 - NA
d. black, red int. & spoiler, silver & red tampo w/"2" & race decals on sides & hood, sp3, China, #1071 (2000) 2 - 3

Panoz GTR-1-e

e. yellow; clear windows; black int.; red wing; white, black, red & gray tampo w/"SEK Polizei" on sides & hood; sp3; China; #187 (2000) 2 - 3
f. mtlfk blue, clear windows, white int., dark red & silver tampo w/"2" on sides & hood, sp3, China, #169 (2000) 2 - 3
g. red, black chassis, clear windows, blue int. & spoiler, gray & blue tampo w/"1" on sides & hood, pr5s, China, #206 (2001) 2 - 3

18532-a

Pikes Peak Celica 18532 - 75mm - 1998

This race car has a black plastic base, red interior and spoiler, tinted windows, and lwgd. Malaysia.

a. yellow; purple, red, black & white tampo w/"#1," "Pennzoil" & race decals on sides; "Pennzoil" & "Celica" on hood; "1," "Toyota," "BF Goodrich" & "Express Lube" on roof. #15 in 1998 First Editions, #652 2 - 3
a2. as a, magenta not purple in tampo, #15 in 1998 First Editions, #652 3 - 6

18532-b

b. white; clear windows; black int.; lt. blue & red tampo w/"Sweet Tarts" on sides & hood; lwch; Malaysia. #3 in Sugar Rush series, #971 (1999) 2 - 3

18532-c

c. mtlc gold; white int. & wing; black, red & white tampo w/"1" & caffeine-free Coca Coca decals; Malaysia. Coca Cola Race Team 4-pack (1999) 5 - NA
d. white; black chassis, wing & int.; clear windows; blue, black & red tampo w/"8," "Dynodon Tuned" & race decals on sides, "Toyota" on hood & roof, "8" on roof; sp3; Malaysia; #166 (2000) 2 - 3

Pikes Peak Celica-e

e. mtlfk blue; black int.; clear windows; white, black & orange tampo w/"7" & 2000 Treasure Hunt logo on sides & hood; rrgd. #9 in 2000 Treasure Hunt series, #057 (2000) 16 - 20
f. white; clear windows; blue int. & spoiler; yellow, black & brown tampo w/"Slingshot Racing" & "Jinn Shocks" on sides; lwch; Thailand; #205 (2001) 2 - 3

Pikes Peak Celica-g

g. purple; black chassis & int.; tinted windows; gold & white tampo w/"Dynodon Tuned," "8" & race decals on sides, hood & roof; sp3; Thailand. Nitro Hill Race Track set (2001) 6 - NA
h. mtlfk blue; black chassis; gray wing & int.; clear windows; red, white & black tampo w/Hot Wheels logo, "5" & race decals on sides; "5," "Hot Wheels" & race decals on black roof; lwch; Thailand; #160 (2002) 2 - 3

Side Kick-c

Side Kick - 80mm - 1998

This customized Larry Wood concept car, a remake of the 1972 model, has a metal chassis and interior, blue-tinted windows, and nrsw. China.

Similar casting: #6022 Side Kick (1972)

a. metallic magenta, ltd ed for 30th Anniv., w/blistercard in window box 5 - 7

Values are shown in U.S. dollars, first price is for mint, second is for mint packaged vehicles only. See pages 15-16 for grading guide to determine value for cars in lesser conditions.

b. mtlfk gold, metal chassis & int., red-tinted windows, black & red tampo w/"Side Kick" on hood, sp5, Malaysia, #219 (2000) 3 - 4
b2. as b, black plastic chassis (2001) 2 - 3
c. mtlfk gray; black chassis; metal int.; red-tinted windows; red, yellow, black & white tampo w/"Postal Express" on sides, eagle & "Hot Wheels Postal Express" on hood, Planet Hot Wheels logo on top; Thailand; #198 (2001) 2 - 3

18293-a

Slideout® 18293 - 60mm - 1998
This sprint car has a gray plastic base; orange plastic spoiler, wing and engine; and sp5. Malaysia.
a. mtlfk magenta; "6" & race decals on sides & wing. #2 in 1998 First Editions, #640 $2 - 4

18293-b

b. mtlfk blue; white plastic base; yellow plastic spoiler, wing & engine; black, yellow & white tampo w/"27" & logo on sides, "27" & "RMAN Racing" on sides of spoiler; sp5 #1001 (1999) 2 - 3

18293-c

c. black; chrome wing; gray engine; red, white & black tampo w/"6th" on sides, "Trophy City 6th" & "Ray Williams Properties" on wing; gych. Ltd ed for Make-a-Wish Trophy Cup (1999) 15 - 20
c2. as c, gyrd. Ltd ed for Make-a-Wish Trophy Cup (1999) 15 - 20

Slideout-d

d. black; red plastic base; white plastic spoiler; gray plastic engine; red, yellow & white flame tampo on sides, monster spouting flames on side of wing. #3 in Mad Maniax series, #019 (2000) 2 - 3

e. lt. green; blue chassis; black spoiler; green, yellow & white tampo w/"6," "Austin Curtis" & Hot Wheels logo on sides & top; sp3; Malaysia; #129 (2001) 2 - 3

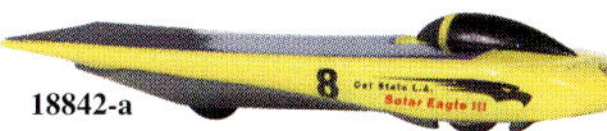
18842-a

Solar Eagle III 18842 - 83mm - 1998
This solar-powered car has a metalflake black plastic base and dome, metallic blue panels on top, small black wheels. Malaysia.
a. dk. yellow; black & red tampo w/"8 Cal State L.A. Solar Eagle III" & eagle head on sides & front, logo on front. #23 in 1998 First Editions, #650 $2 - 4
a2. as a, gray base, China, Solar Racing Action Pack (1999) 5 - NA

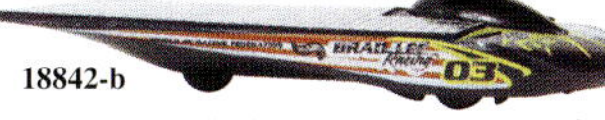
18842-b

b. dk. gray; black base; chrome top; red, white, black, yellow & lt. green tampo w/"World of Racing Federation," "Brad Lee Racing" & "03" on sides; "Brad Lee Racing," "WRF" & "03" on nose; Malaysia. World Racers 5-pack 2 - NA
c. red; black chassis & dome; gold, black & white tampo w/"Cal State L.A." & "Solar Eagle" on sides, "Solar Eagle" in front; #176 (2000) 2 - 3
d. orange; black, gray & white tampo with "Cal State L.A." on sides, "Solar Eagle" on hood; Malaysia; #170 (2001) 2 - 3

18840-a

Super Comp Dragster 18840 - 81mm - 1998
This Malaysia-made hot rod-style dragster has a chrome plastic chassis and side pipes, gray plastic interior and roll cage, and sp5.
a. black; 5 red, black & white race decals on sides. #22 in 1998 First Editions, #655 $3 - 5
a2. as a, 3 race decals on sides 12 - 15

18840-b

b. mtlfk gray; black int.; red, black & white tampo w/"24" & race decals on sides, "24" & Power Speed Attitude" on top; sp5; #1041 (1999) 2 - 3

Super Comp Dragster-c

c. white; blue int. & cage; black fenders; red, dk. blue, black & gray tampo w/"Bismarck Police" & emblem on sides, "Bismarck Police" & "12" on top; sp5. Cop Rods Series 2 (2000) 6 - 8
d. yellow, black int. & fenders, black & red flame tampo w/race decals on sides & "5" on top, sp5, Malaysia, #214 (2001) 2 - 3

Super Comp Dragster-e

e. mtlfk gold; black int. & fenders; black, white & red flame tampo on sides & top w/"Hot Wheels" on hood, 2 skulls behind seat, sp5. #1 in Skin Deep series, #093 (2001) 2 - 3

18541-a

Super Modified 18541 - 74mm - 1998
This race car has a metal base, metal wing and pipes, two red front spoilers, red interior, and lwch. Malaysia.
a. black; yellow, white & purple tampo w/race decals on top. #27 in 1998 First Editions, #664 2 - 3

18541-b

b. yellow; black spoiler & int.; red, white & black race decals on sides & top, "Stunt Driver" on top, gold Hot Wheels logo on wing; lwgd. Stunt Driver CD-ROM (1998) 10 - NA

18541-c

c. lt. blue; black spoiler & int.; red, orange, white & lt. green tampo w/"Kerplunk" on sides & nose. #1 in Classic Games series, #981 (1999) 2 - 3
d. red; white spoiler, roll cage & int.; lwgd; Malaysia. Virtual Collection, #158 (2000) 2 - 3

Super Modified-e

e. dark mtlfk red; black chassis & int.; gold pinstripes on body; white & black tampo on wing w/"MC" & "Mystery Car 2000" on roof; sp5gd. 2000 Mystery Car, in baggie (2000) 6 - NA
f. orange; black spoiler, roll cage & int.; lwgd; Malaysia; #183 (2001) 2 - 3

19641-a

Sweet 16 II 19641 - 78mm - 1998
This Malaysia-made concept car has a metalflake purple base, eight chrome pipes on each side, purple-tinted windshield, and sp5.
a. mtlfk purple, #30 in 1998 First Editions, #674 $2 - 4

19641-b

b. black, metal chassis, gold chrome pipes, yellow-tinted windshield, gray int., white & red tampo w/"Dr Vamp" on sides & hood, sp5, Malaysia. #3 in Terrorific series, #979 (1999) 2 - 3

19641-c

c. mtlfk purple; mtlfk purple base; tinted windshield; black int.; yellow, orange & red flame tampo on sides & top, "Toys R Us" on sides. Toys "R" Us excl., baggie only, w/purchase of Play Station game only 5 - NA

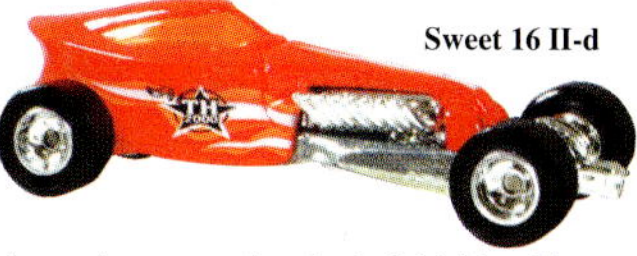
Sweet 16 II-d

d. red; orange-tinted windshield; white, orange & black tampo w/"TH 2000" on sides; rrch. #4 in 2000 Treasure Hunt series, #052 (2000) 18 - 20

Sweet 16 II-e

e. yellow; green-tinted windshield; orange, green & red tampo w/flames on sides & top, "Chuck E Cheese's" on sides, "CEC" on top, sp5. Chuck E Cheese's Pizza (2000) 4 - 6
f. gray; chrome engine & int.; orange-tinted windshield; black, green & orange tampo on sides; sp5; Malaysia. Max Steel 5-pack 2 - NA

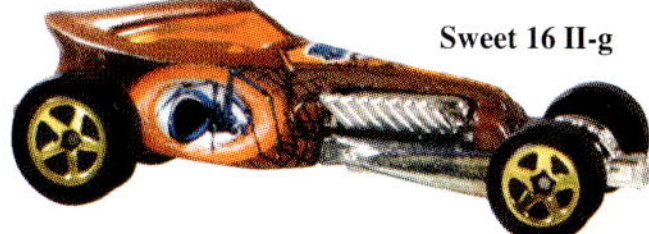
Sweet 16 II-g

g. mtlfk brown; orange-tinted windshield; orange, black, blue & white tampo w/spider on sides, "Black Widow" on top, sp5gd, Thailand, Spider Slam 5-pack (2001) 2 - NA

Sweet 16 II-h

h. mtlfk purple; green-tinted windshield; black, white & lt. green tampo w/"AK" & race decals on sides, "16" & "MechaniX" on top; sp5 w/red stripe. MechaniX CD-ROM only (2001) 10 - NA

18846-a

Tail Dragger® 18846 - 70mm - 1998
This Malaysia-made model has a metal base, white interior, clear windows, and lwch.
a. purple; orange & lt. blue pinstripes on sides & hood. #24 in 1998 First Editions, #659 $3 - 6
b. red & yellow-green, black int., tinted windows, "12th Annual October 16-18, 1998" & "12th" in red on back, "30 Years of Cool" in red on sides, "Anaheim, California" in yellow over front fenders, 1998 Convention logo on hood, lwch. 1998 Hot Wheels Convention give-away only (1998) 100 - NA

18846-c

c. black; lt. brown roof; tan int.; tinted windows; yellow, orange, white, black & red tampo w/flames on sides, hood & trunk; "12th Annual" on trunk; 1998 convention logo & Hot Wheels Newsletter logo on roof; rrww. 1998 Hot Wheels Convention (1998) 30 - 35
d. red; yellow front end; white int.; clear windows; white, black & yellow tampo w/Early Times Car Club logo on roof, "Mid-Winter Rod run" on

18846-d

trunk; rrch. Limited to 10,000 for Early Times Car Club (1999) 18 - 20

18846-e

e. black; gold & lt. purple tampo design on hood, front & rear fenders; lwch. #2 in Pinstripe Power series, #954 (1999) 3 - 5

18846-f

f. black; clear windows; white int.; yellow, red & purple tampo w/"Lexmark" on sides & hood; gyw. Limited to 10,000 for Lexmark printers, in box (1999) 20 - 25

18846-g

g. white, clear windows, red int., red flame spray mask, rrch w/white walls. Limited run of 25,000 for Jiffy Lube (1999) 15 - 18

18846-h

h. black & white; gold, black, blue & white tampo w/police shield from Bakersfield, CA Police Dept., "Bakersfield Police," "To Serve and Protect" & "For Emergency" on sides; "27" on roof; pinstripes on hood; rrch. Limited run of 25,000 in Cop Rods series for K•B Toys (1999) 5 - 7

i. mtlfk blue, white int., clear windows, yellow spray mask in front, "Whites Guide" outlined in black on sides, rrch, Malaysia. Ltd ed of 12,500 for Whites Guide (1999) 15 - 18

j. white, clear windows, black int., magenta spray mask, blue & magenta tampo, rrch, Malaysia. Ltd ed of 12,500 for Whites Guide (1999) 15 - 18

18846-k

k. chrome red; green int.; tinted windows; white, gold, green, lt. green & red tampo w/"Season's Greetings" on sides, "99" & wreath on hood, Santa & skis on car; green ww. Christmas Past in 1999 Holiday Assortment (1999) 15 - 20

l. mtlfk dk. red; white int.; blue-tinted windows; white roof; yellow flame spray mask in front; blue, orange, yellow & white tampo w/"Flame Dragger" on sides, Firebird Raceway logo on trunk; rrch w/white walls. Ltd ed of 15,000 for Firebird Raceway (1999) 15 - 20

Tail Dragger-m

m. white, black int., yellow-tinted windows, black & orange flame tampo on top, lwgd. #3 in Hot Rod series, #007 (2000) 2 - 3

Tail Dragger-n

n. white, clear windows, white int., red & dk. blue flame tampo on sides & top, "Puerto Rico" on sides, lwgd. Puerto Rico excl., in box (2000) 20 - 25

o. mtlfk orange; white int.; tinted windows; green, lt. green & purple tampo on sides, hood & roof; lwgd. Ames Stores excl. Cruise Night 4-pack (2000) 10 - NA

Tail Dragger-q

p. mtlfk blue; gray int.; blue-tinted windows; gray & lt. blue tampo on sides & hood; sp3; Thailand; #239 (2001) 2 - 3

p2. as p, Malaysia, #239 (2001) 2 - 3

q. blue; blue, lt. blue & white top; white int.; blue-tinted windows; multicolored tampo w/"44," Hot Wheels logo & race decals on sides, Hot Wheels logo on hood; lwch; Thailand. #1 in NASCAR Tail Dragger series (2001) 10 - 15

r. yellow; black upper body, hood & trunk; white int.; tinted windows; multicolored tampo w/"22," "Caterpillar" & race decals on sides, "Cat" on hood & trunk, "22" on roof; lwch; Thailand. #2 in NASCAR Tail Dragger series (2001) 8 - 12

s. blue; black int.; tinted windows; multicolored tampo w/"55," "Cooper Lighting" & race decals on sides, "D" on hood, "55" on roof, "Square D" on trunk; Thailand. #3 in NASCAR Tail Dragger series (2001) 8 - 12

t. yellow; red roof, rear & hood; white int.; tinted windows; multicolored tampo w/"5," "Kellogg's" & race decals on sides, "Kellogg's" on hood, "5" on roof, "Advance Auto Parts" on trunk; Thailand. #4 in NASCAR Tail Dragger series (2001) 8 - 12

u. dk. blue; white front end; red int.; tinted windows; multicolored tampo w/"12," pegasus & race decals on sides, "Mobil 1" on hood, "12" on roof, "Mobil Speedpass" on trunk; Thailand. #5 in NASCAR Tail Dragger series (2001) 8 - 12

v. lt. blue; dk. blue rear & hood; white int.; tinted windows; multicolored tampo w/"43," STP logo, "Cheerios" & race decals on sides, STP logo on hood, "43" on roof, Betty Crocker logo on trunk; Thailand. #6 in NASCAR Tail Dragger series (2001) 10 - 15

w. red; black hood, trunk & on sides; white int.; tinted windows; gray, black, white & blue tampo w/"45," "Sprint" & race decals on sides; "Sprint" on hood; "45" on roof; "Sprint" & "SprintPCS" on trunk; Thailand. #7 in NASCAR Tail Dragger series (2001) 10 - 15

x. white; dk. blue on sides; white int.; tinted windows; multicolored tampo w/"6," "Valvoline" & race decals on sides, "Valvoline" & V on hood, "6" on roof, "Cummins" & "Eagle 1" on trunk; Thailand. #8 in NASCAR Tail Dragger series (2001) 8 - 12

y. black; white hood & front fenders; white int.; tinted windows; multicolored tampo w/"99," "Exide" & race decals on sides, "Exide SKF" on hood, "99" on roof, "CR" & "SKF" on trunk; Thailand. #9 in NASCAR Tail Dragger series (2001) 8 - 12

z. dk. blue; white int.; tinted windows; multicolored tampo w/"33," "Oakwood Homes" & race decals on sides, "Oakwood Homes" on hood, "33" on roof, "Schult" on trunk; Thailand. #10 in NASCAR Tail Dragger series (2001) 8 - 12

aa. black; white int.; tinted windows; multicolored tampo w/"7" & race decals on sides, "Nations Rent" on hood, "7" on roof, "Phillips Halogen" on trunk; Thailand. #11 in NASCAR Tail Dragger series (2001) 10 - 15

ab. yellow; black hood & roof; white int.; tinted windows; black, white & red tampo w/"17," "Dewalt" & race decals on sides, "Dewalt" on hood, "17" on roof, "Guaranteed Tough" on trunk; Thailand. #12 in NASCAR Tail Dragger series (2001) 8 - 12

Tail Dragger-ac

ac. pearl blue; red-tinted windows; yellow, dk. red, black & gray tampo design on sides & roof, "Zombie Attack" on roof; lwch. #2 in Monster series, #078 (2001) 2 - 3

Tail Dragger-ad

ad. white; black chassis & int.; tinted windows; silver & black flame tampo on sides, hood & roof; lwch. Fred Meyer stores only (2001) 4 - 6

Tail Dragger-ae

ae. mtlfk red; white fenders; black int.; clear windows; black, yellow, white & lt. blue tampo w/"Firehouse 23," "NOFD" & emblem on sides, emblem on hood, stripes on top, rrgd w/white stripe. Fire Rods series (2001) 7 - 9

95650-a

Tipper 95650 - 74mm - 1998
This dump truck, formerly a Corgi casting, has "Tipping Lorry" embossed on a black plastic base, a white dump, blacked-out windows, and sp5. China.

a. blue; black, blue & yellow tampo with "BD Construction" on sides of dump; #712 $2 - 3

18841-a

Tow Jam™ 18841 - 75mm - 1998
This hot rod tow truck has a chrome plastic base, tow bar and bumpers; black windows; and six sp3. Malaysia.

18841-a 18841-a2

a. red, #25 in 1998 First Editions, #658 $2 - 4

a2. as a, larger Hot Wheels logo on roof 28 - 35

18841-b

b. lt. brown, same as a, lwch. Towing Action Pack only (1999) 5 - NA

18841-c

c. mtlc dk. green; black windows; lt. green, yellow & black flame tampo on hood & sides; sp3; #1007 (1999) 2 - 3

18841-d

d. black; black int. & windows; gray hood; lt. blue, blue, red & white tampo w/Hot Wheels logo & "Interactive" on sides & roof, race decals on hood; sp3 in mtlc blue. Crash CD-ROM (1999) 12 - NA

e. mtlfk blue, same as c, sp5, Malaysia, #211 (2000) 2 - 3

Tow Jam-f

f. yellow, black boom, black & orange tampo on hood, 2000 Treasure Hunt logo on roof, rrch. #2 in 2000 Treasure Hunt series, #050 (2000) 20 - 22

g. yellow, black windows, red & black flame tampo on sides & hood, sp3, Malaysia. Tow & Tune set (2001) 6 - NA

Tow Jam-h

h. flat black; gray windows; white, orange & gray tampo w/"Speed Tow Service" on sides, "Speed Tow Handy" on hood, Hot Wheels logo on roof; sp3; Malaysia; #128 (2002) 2 - 3

18856-a

Whatta Drag® 18856 - 73mm - 1998
This concept vehicle, based on a BMW Isetta, has a metal base, small body in front, a large chrome engine, and a spoiler in back. It has two sp3 in front and one VW Bus wheel in back. Malaysia.

a. mtlfk dk. red, red-tinted windows, yellow & lt. green tampo on roof. #36 in 1998 First Editions, #673 2 - 3

18856-b

b. black; red-tinted windows; gold chrome engine & spoiler; white, black & red tampo w/"6" on front & on roof; race decals on front; sp5 in front; Malaysia. Crazy Classics III 5-pack (1999) 2 - NA

b2. as b; ho5 (1999), #1044 2 - 3

Values are shown in U.S. dollars, first price is for mint, second is for mint packaged vehicles only. See pages 15-16 for grading guide to determine value for cars in lesser conditions.

c. orange, chrome int., tinted windows, black & white tampo w/"6" on top & in front, sp5, Malaysia, #213 (2000) 2 - 3
d. dark yellow; clear windows; chrome int.; black, gray & red tampo w/"12" & race decals in front, Hot Wheels logo on roof; sp5; Malaysia; #145 (2002) 2 - 3
d2. as d, sp5, #145 (2002) 2 - 3

1999

In 1999, Mattel added 26 new models as well as several new casting that were not a part of the 1999 First Editions. Mattel continued with the Treasure Hunt series as well as the four-car segments, five-packs and Action Packs. Also, Hot Wheels vehicles were added to the ARCO products (Long Haulers), Power Launchers and sets. Most of these models were different from the regular-line vehicles. This was the year of the Premiums/Limited editions, with more than sixty different models produced.

19642-a

1936 Cord 19642 - 80mm - 1999
This Malaysia-made vintage car has a plastic chassis, black interior, clear windows, & lwch.

a. mtlfk dk. red, #1 in 1999 First Editions, #649 2 - 3
b. gray, rrchww, FAO Schwarz Classic Collection 8 - NA

19642-c

c. black, tan int., rrchww. Ltd ed for Auburn Cord Duesenberg Museum 10 - 12

19642-d

d. mtlfk gray; orange-tinted windows; orange, black & white tampo w/star & "TH 2000" on sides; flames on hood; rrch. #3 in 2000 Treasure Hunt series, #051 (2000) 18 - 24
d2. as d, rrchww. #3 in 2000 Treasure Hunt series, #051 (2000) 28 - 30
e. green, white int., bw, China, Virtual Collection, #097 (2000) 2 - 3
f. black, red int., clear windows, lwch, China, #234 (2001) 2 - 3
g. mtlfk dark red, black-tinted windows, silver & black tampo w/"Automobile Milestones 2002" on roof, rrch w/white stripe, Thailand. Was 1937 810 Cord in Auto Milestones series (2002) 6 - 10

21062-a

1970 ('70) Chevelle SS 21062 - 77mm - 1999
This replica of the real car has a metal chassis, white interior, blue-tinted windows, and sp5. Malaysia.

a. dk. blue, white stripes, pinstripes on hood & trunk. #4 in 1999 First Editions, #915 2 - 3
a2. as a, no pinstripes on hood, #915 4 - 8
b. mtlfk gold, same as a, black stripes, #4 in 1999 First Editions, #915 2 - 3
c. red; white, dk. blue, yellow & red tampo w/yellow stripes on top & sides; "Ronald McDonald House Charities," logo, McDonald's "M" & 13th Annual Hot Wheels Convention logo on sides; "Ronald McDonald House Charities" & McDonald's "M" on hood; Ronald McDonald House logo on roof; "Ronald McDonald House Charities" & "13th Annual Collectors Convention Oct. 14-16 1999" on trunk (1999) 20 - 25

21062-b
21062-c

21062-d

d. black w/white front; black, white, yellow, orange & red striping tampo w/"Lexmark" on sides & trunk; gych. Ltd ed for Lexmark, in box 20 - 25

21062-e

e. red; black int.; clear windows; gray, black & white tampo w/"Logan Motorsports" & race decals on sides, stripes over top, "454 C.I." on hood; sp7 w/"Goodyear" & "Eagle" on tires. Racing American Style 4-pack from Toys "R" Us website 5 - NA
f. mtlfk gold, same as a, tampo is black, sp5, China, #107 (2000) 2 - 3
f2. as f, greenish tint, #107 (2000) 2 - 3

1970 Chevelle-g

g. white; black roof; blue-tinted windows; white int.; blue, gray & black tampo w/"183," "New Orleans Police" & "to Protect and to Serve" on sides, "Police" on hood & trunk, "183" on roof; rrch. Cop Rods Series 2 only (2000) 9 - 12
h. yellow, black roof & int., clear windows, black stripes on top, red & white Editor's Choice logo on back window, rrch, Thailand. Target excl. Editor's Choice series (2000) 9 - 12

1970 Chevelle-i

i. white; blue-tinted windows; blue int.; blue, red & black tampo w/stripes & Cubs logo on sides, "5" on hood, Cubs logo on roof, emblem on trunk. Chicago Cubs baseball promo, in 2-pack (2000) 6 - NA

1970 Chevelle-j

j. black, white int., tinted windows, orange tampo on sides & hood, 2000 Treasure Hunt logo on roof, rrch. #12 in 2000 Treasure Hunt series, #060 (2000) 20 - 25

1970 Chevelle-k

k. mtlfk blue; white int.; blue-tinted windows; black, white & gold tampo w/"Chinatown Blue Taxi" on sides & hood; sp5; China. #4 in Turbo Taxi series, #056 (2001) 2 - 3

1970 Chevelle-l

l. yellow; clear windows, red int.; black, red & white tampo w/stripes on sides, hood & trunk; Little Debbie Snacks logo on sides & trunk; pr5s. Series III Little Debbie 3 pack (2001) 4 - NA

1979 Ford Truck-a

1979 Ford Truck - 98mm - 1999
This truck was issued with a chrome plastic chassis, clear windows, red and white interior, red truck bed, white box behind rear window, gray kennel with dog in back, and gych. Malaysia.

a. red, white sides, black stripe, Wal-Mart excl., in box 5 - 8

1979 Ford Truck-b

b. black, black plastic canopy over bed, clear windows, black int., yellow & turquoise tampo w/"Mantis" & praying mantis on sides, sp5, Malaysia. #3 in Attack Pack series, #023 (2000) 2 - 3

1979 Ford Truck-c

c. black, black chassis, white int., orange plastic shell, orange flames on sides, white & orange Harley-Davidson logo on roof, sp5, Thailand. Harley-Davidson 5-pack (2001) 3 - NA

23902-a

360 Modena 23902 - 70mm - 1999
This Malaysia-made model has a black plastic base and interior, clear windows, and sp5.

a. red, yellow logo on hood, #21 in 1999 First Editions, #1113 (1999) 2 - 3
b. gray; metal chassis; white int.; clear windows; black, white & orange tampo w/"48" & "360 Modena" on sides; ho5; Thailand. World Racers 2 5-pack 3 - NA
c. black, black metal chassis, tan int., clear windows, yellow & red Ferrari logo on hood, sp5, Malaysia, #204 2 - 3
c2. as c, pr5s 2 - 3

360 Modena-d

d. red; black chassis; white int.; clear windows; yellow, black & white tampo w/Ferrari logo on hood, Auto Milestones logo on roof; pr5s; Thailand. Auto Milestones series (2002) 7 - 9

18534-a

'38 Phantom Corsair 18534 - 80mm - 1999
This vintage car has a metal chassis, gray interior, clear windows, and black chrome sp5 with a white stripe around the tire. Malaysia.

a. black, #3 in 1999 First Editions, #656 2 - 3
a2. as a, no white stripe around tire, #656 2 - 3

18534-b

b. purple, black int., rrch. FAO Schwarz Classic Collection (1999) 8 - NA
c. blue, #3 in 1999 First Editions, #656 10 - 12
d. mtlfk dk. red, white int., clear windows, lwch, China, #099 (2000) 2 - 3
d2. as d, Malaysia, #099 (2000) 2 - 3
e. mtlfk brown; clear windows; black int.; gray, black & gold tampo on sides & hood; sp5 w/white walls; China; #205 (2001) 2 - 3

21074-a

'56 Ford Truck 21074 - 70mm - 1999
This Malaysia-made 1956 truck has a gray plastic chassis, chrome interior, blue-tinted windows, an opening hood with an exposed engine sticking through the hood, and sp5.

a. lt. blue; purple, blue & white tampo w/Ford Auto Parts logo. #22 in 1999 First Editions, #927 3 - 5
b. white; black roof; gold chrome int. & engine; clear windows; lt. blue, yellow & black tampo w/"529" & "Key West Police" on sides & roof; rrch. Cop Rods Series 2 only (2000) 8 - 10

'56 Ford Truck-c

c. red; gold-plated int. & engine; tinted windows; yellow & black tampo w/"Andretti Racing," "40 Years of Winning" & "Sprint Cars, Indy Cars, Formula 1" on sides; gych. Ltd ed of 15,000 (2000) 10 - 12
d. black; clear windows; red int.; red, yellow, black & blue tampo w/flames & "Jiffy Lube" on sides; gych. Jiffy Lube promo (2000) 15 - 18

'56 Ford Truck-e

e. white; tan int.; tinted windows; red, black & yellow tampo w/"Jiffy Lube Signature Service" & Pennzoil decal on sides; gych. Jiffy Lube promo (2000) 15 - 18
f. red, same as e, chrome int., white replaces red in tampo. Jiffy Lube promo (2000) 15 - 18
g. purple; clear windows; chrome int.; yellow, red & white tampo w/flames & "Autorama" in yellow & black on

'56 Ford Truck-g

sides, "Championship Auto Shows Inc." on roof; gych. Championship Auto Shows Inc. promo (2000) 15 - 18

h. white, same as g, "Autorama" in red & black. Championship Auto Shows Inc. promo (2000) 15 - 18

i. white, dark yellow chassis, gold chrome engine & int., yellow-tinted windows, dk. red & gold tampo on sides, sp5gd, China, #171 (2001) 2 - 3

j. gray, black chassis & int., clear windows, orange & black tampo w/Harley-Davidson logo on sides, sp5, China, #155 (2001) 3 - 5

j2. as j, Thailand, Harley-Davidson 5-pack (2001) 3 - NA

'56 Ford Truck-k

k. blue; black chassis & int.; blue-tinted windows; black top; white, red, lt. blue & black tampo w/stripes on sides, Editor's Choice logo on roof; rrch; Thailand. Target Exclusive Editor's Choice series (2001) 7 - 9

l. red; white roof, rear doors & rear fenders; black int.; clear windows; gold & black tampo w/"Albuquerque N.M. Fire Dept.," "No.6" & emblem on sides, hood & roof; rrch. Fire Rods series (2001) 7 - 9

m. red, white chassis, chrome int., clear windows, white & yellow tampo w/flames & "Walgreens" on sides, sp5, Thailand. Walgreen's Drug Stores 2-pack only 3 - NA

'56 Ford Truck-n

n. mtlfk dk. red; mtlfk white camper shell; cold chrome int. & engine; clear windows; black & gold tampo w/"Duckwall Alco Stores Inc.," "Serving Small Town America with Down Home Savings" on sides; 100 Years Anniversary logo & "Serving Small Town America with Down Home Savings" on roof; rrgd. Duckwall Stores only, on large blistercard (2001) 3 - 5

21056-a

'99 Mustang (GT) #21056 - 70mm - 1999
This Malaysia-made model has a black plastic base, tan interior, clear windows, and sp5.

a. purple, gold logo on sides, "Mustang" in white on rear bumper. #2 in 1999 First Editions, #909 3 - 5

a2. as a, red interior, #909 25 - 40

a3. as a, sp3, #909 2 - 3

21056-b

b. blue, same as a, #2 in 1999 First Editions, #909 20 - 30

b2. as b, "1" on roof, "Mattel Toys" on hood 12 - 15

21056-c

c. mtlfk blue; black windows; red, yellow & white tampo w/large Hot Wheels logo on sides & hood, "1" & "12" on roof; Malaysia; sold in Mexico 10 - 12

c2. as c, "1" on roof, "Mattel Toys" on hood 10 - 12

21056-d

d. yellow; gray int.; clear windows; gray, black & red tampo w/"88" & race decals on sides, design on hood, "88" on roof. Racing American Style 4-pack from Toys "R" Us Web site 5 - NA

e. mtlfk dk. red; clear windows; black int.; orange, black, yellow & gray tampo w/"Lesser 420" & "PSSC" on sides; sp5; China; #098 (2000) 2 - 3

e2. as e, sp3, #098 (2000) 2 - 3

'99 Mustang-f

f. white; green roof; gray int.; clear windows; "Herdez," "Avis," "36" & race decals on sides; "Herdez" & "Avis" on hood; "36" on roof; "Herdez" in back; sp3; Thailand; on racing blistercard; Mexico only (2001) 8 - 10

g. green; black roof & rear; gray int.; clear windows; "Q," "70," "Quaker State" & race decals on sides; "Q" & "Quaker State" on hood; "Q" on roof; sp3; Thailand; on racing blistercard; Mexico only (2001) 8 - 10

h. white; red roof; gray int.; clear windows; "Motocraft," "9" & race decals on sides, hood & in back; "9" on roof; sp3; Thailand; on racing blistercard; Mexico only (2001) 8 - 10

i. red; clear windows; black int.; yellow, black & orange tampo design on sides & hood; sp3; Thailand. #1 in Kung Fu series, #034 (2001) 2 - 3

i2. as i, dw3, Thailand, #034, #1 in Kung Fu series (2001) 2 - 3

j. gray; white int.; tinted windows; purple rear; black, lt. green & white tampo on sides & roof; Editors Choice logo on roof; gyg; Thailand. Target excl. Editor's Choice series (2001) 6 - 8

'99 Mustang-k

k. white; tan int.; lightly tinted windows; red, black & blue tampo on sides & hood w/"Mustang GT" on sides; sp3; China. #2 in the Company Cars series, #086 (2001) 2 - 3

Al's Custom Cruiser-a

Al's Custom Cruiser - 78mm - 1999
This model has a chrome chassis, white interior, clear windows, and sp7 with white wall tires. China.

a. white, turquoise sides & roof, Toy Story 2 Action Pack (1999) 10 - NA

a2. as a, no whitewall tires, Toy Story 2 Action Pack 10 - NA

Attack Beast-a

Attack Beast - 86mm - 1999
This concept military truck has a metal chassis, tinted windshield, black interior, gray and red saw-blade weapon on the roof, and dw3ct. China.

a. black; red, gray & white logo on doors; yellow, blue & black logo on hood. Team Knight Rider Action Pack 5 - NA

18853-a

Baby Boomer™ - 18853 - 73mm - 1999
This baby carriage on wheels has a metal chassis; chrome spoiler, engine and front end; gray plastic headers; blue interior; and sp5. Malaysia.

a. mtlfk blue; orange, yellow & white flame tampo. #24 in 1999 First Editions, #680 2 - 3

b. red, gold chrome engine, gray plastic headers, white & black tampo w/"Bad Bad Boy" on sides, sp5. China. Virtual Collection, #173 (2000) 2 - 3

Baby Boomer-c

c. blue; blue int.; white, gray, red & black tampo w/letters on sides; sp5; Malaysia. #2 in Secret Code series, #046 (2000) 2 - 3

c2. as c, China 2 - 3

d. turquoise; mtlfk gray chassis; gray engine; red, white & blue tampo with "Happy Birthday" on sides; sp5; China. Birthday Cake 5-pack (2001) 2 - 3

d2. as d, #218 (2002) 2 - 3

21075-a

Chrysler Pronto 21075 - 67mm - 1999
This Chrysler show car has a black chassis and roof, blacked-out windows, and sp5. Malaysia.

a. yellow; #23 in 1999 First Editions, #928 2 - 3

Chrysler Pronto-b

b. white, red int., clear windows, black roof, wide red stripe on hood, red & blue tampo w/JC Whitney logo on sides & trunk, JC Whitney phone number & e-mail address on sides, pc. Ltd ed for JC Whitney, in box 15 - 18

c. black; clear windows; white int.; silver tampo on sides, hood & trunk w/JC Whitney logo on sides. Ltd ed for JC Whitney, in box 15 - 18

21075-d

d. gray; clear windows; red int.; black roof; white, blue, red & black tampo w/"Chrysler" & logo on sides, "Phillies 2000" on hood; sp3. Philadelphia Phillies baseball promo, in 2-pack (2000) 3 - 5

e. dk. purple, gray int., clear windows, sp3, China, #150 2 - 3

21075-f

f. mtlfk green, black chassis & int., clear windows, black & white tampo w/large Hot Wheels logo on sides & hood, sp3, Malaysia. #1 in CD Customs series, #029 (2000) 2 - 3

f2. as f, no country on base. #1 in CD Customs series, #029 (2000) 2 - 3

21075-g

g. mtlfk ruby red; black chassis; gray int.; clear windows; red, white & blue flag tampo on sides & hood; lwch; China. #1 in Star Spangled series, #079 (2002) 2 - 3

Dante-a

Dante - 80mm - 1999
This concept truck has a gray chassis, clear windows, black interior and truck bed, and large sp5. China.

a. gray; blue, lt. green & black logo on sides; yellow, blue & black logo on hood; two different pieces for truck bed. Team Knight Rider Action Pack 5 - NA

23930-a

Ferrari 456M 23930 - 75mm - 1999
This Ferrari sports car has a metal chassis, clear windows, tan interior, sp5. Malaysia.

a. red; black & yellow Ferrari logo on hood; #1118 2 - 3

b. pearl blue, mtlfk gray chassis, tan int., clear windows, yellow & black Ferrari logo on hood, pr5s, #186 (2001) 2 - 3

24108-a

Ferrari F355 Berlinetta 24108 - 75mm - 1999
This Ferrari sports car has a metal chassis, clear windows, black interior, sp5. Malaysia.

a. red; black & yellow Ferrari logo on sides & hood; #1094 2 - 3

b. mtlfk gray; black int.; clear wind; yellow, green, red & black Ferrari logo on hood; sp5; Malaysia; #172 (2002) 2 - 3

Values are shown in U.S. dollars, first price is for mint, second is for mint packaged vehicles only. See pages 15-16 for grading guide to determine value for cars in lesser conditions.

Ferrari F355 Challange-a

Ferrari F355 Challenge 1115 - 68mm - 1999

This Malaysia-made Ferrari has a metal chassis, tinted windshield, black interior, and sp5.

a. gray; red, green, white & yellow tampo w/"7" & race decals on sides, "7" on hood, stripes on hood & roof 2 - 3
b. yellow; gray int.; tinted windows; white, black, red & green tampo w/"7" & race decals on sides, "7" & stripes over top; #162 (2000) 2 - 3
c. yellow; white int.; tinted windows; lt. green, red, white & black tampo on hood & roof w/"1," "Racing" & logo on hood; "Goodyear" on roof; pr5s; Malaysia; #191 (2001) 2 - 3
c2. as c, sp5, #191 (2001) 2 - 3
c3. as c, Thailand, #191 (2001) 2 - 3

23931-a

Ferrari F355 Spider 23931 - 75mm - 1999

This Ferrari convertible has a metal chassis, clear windshield, tan interior, sp5. Malaysia.

a. red; black & yellow Ferrari logo on sides & hood; #1119 2 - 3
b. gray, black interior, tinted windshield, sp5, #230 (2000) 2 - 3
c. mtlfk dark blue, black chassis & int., tinted windshield, yellow & black hood tampo, red & white Hot Wheels logo on trunk, sp5, China, #164 (2002) 2 - 3

Ferrari F50-a

Ferrari F50 - 75mm - 1999

This Ferrari sports car has a black metal chassis, clear windows, black interior, and sp5. Malaysia.

Similar casting: #14917 Ferrari F50 (convertible) (1996)

a. red; black & yellow Ferrari logo on sides & hood; #1120 2 - 3
b. yellow, same as a, #161 (2000) 2 - 3
c. mtlfk purple; clear windows, black int.; red, yellow & black Ferrari logo on hood; sp5; Malaysia; #238 (2001) 2 - 3

21066-a

Fiat 500C 21066 - 67mm - 1999

This model has a metal chassis, a large gray plastic wing in back, clear windshield, metal interior, chrome engine & pipes, and sp5. Malaysia.

a. purple, gold pinstripe on sides. #11 in 1999 First Editions, #919 2 - 3

Fiat 500C-b

b. yellow, no wing, metal int., blue-tinted windshield, black & white tampo w/"Mooneyes Santa Fe Springs, CA" & emblem on sides, gych. Ltd ed of 15,000 for Full Grid (2000) 10 - 15
c. red, metal int., black wing, clear windshield, black & white tampo on sides, sp5, Malaysia, #045 (2000) 2 - 3

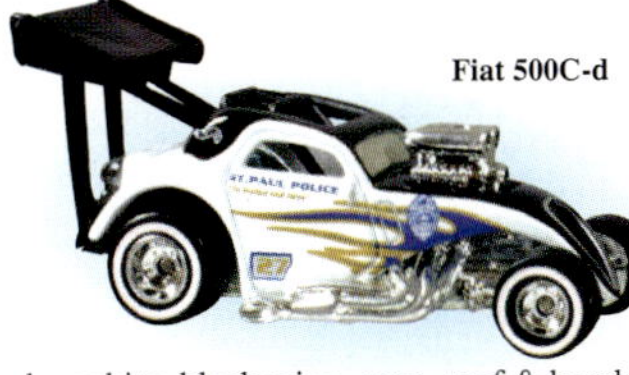
Fiat 500C-d

d. white; black wing, cage, roof & hood; metal int.; dk. blue & gold tampo w/"27," "St. Paul Police" & emblem on sides; rrch w/white stripe. Cop Rods Series 2 (2000) 9 - 12

Fiat 500C-e

e. mtlfk blue; gray int.; chrome windshield; white wing; yellow, orange & white flame tampo w/"Hot Wheels" on sides & hood; sp5. Toys "R" Us Timeless Toys Series III 4-pack (2001) 5 - NA
f. red, gold chassis & engine, red wing & cage, metal int., clear windshield, white top, gold & black tampo w/"Chicago Fire Dept." on sides & hood, "03" on sides, rrch. Fire Rods series (2001) 9 - 12
g. red; chrome int. & engine; purple roll cage & wing; yellow, purple & gray tampo on sides; sp5; Thailand. Hot Rods 5-pack 3 - NA

21068-a

Ford GT-40 21068 - 72mm - 1999

This model has a gray plastic chassis and interior, blue-tinted windows, sp5. Malaysia.

a. mtlfk blue; black & white tampo: stripes & "59" on sides & top, "Ford" on sides. #16 in 1999 First Editions, #921 2 - 3

Ford GT-40-b

b. mtlfk gold, black chassis & int., clear windows, black tampo on top, 2000 Treasure Hunt logo on hood, rrch. #11 in 2000 Treasure Hunt series, #059 (2000) 10 - 18
c. red; black base & int.; clear windows; white, blue & black tampo w/stripes & "78" on sides & hood, stripes on roof & trunk; sp5; #139 (2000) 2 - 3
c2. red, same as c, lwch, China, #139 (2000) 2 - 3
d. orange; gray chassis & int.; clear windows; black, yellow & gray tampo on sides & hood w/"Twister" on sides; sp5; Thailand. Motorized Tornado Twister set (2001) 10 - NA
e. purple; black base; white int.; clear windows; white, blue & black tampo w/stripes & "78" on sides & hood, stripes on roof & trunk; sp5; China #139 (2001) 2 - 3
f. red; black chassis; white int.; clear windows; black, white & gray tampo w/"Qracing" & "3" on sides; lwch; Thailand. Powershift Garage 5-pack (2001) 3 - NA
f2. as f, sp5, Thailand. Powershift Garage 5-pack (2001) 3 - NA
g. black; white int.; blue-tinted windows; gray, white & orange tampo w/"7" on sides, hood & trunk; stripes on top; Auto Milestones logo on roof; rrch;

Ford GT-40-g

Thailand. Auto Milestones series (2002) 9 - 12

21069-a

Jeepster 21069 - 60mm - 1999

This Malaysia-made convertible has a metal chassis, black interior, tinted windows and sp5.

a. red, lower part black, gray border around window. #17 in 1999 First Editions, #922 2 - 3

Jeepster-b

b. as a; white, blue & black tampo w/Chrysler logo & "P" on sides, "Phillies 2000" on hood; sp5. Philadelphia Phillies baseball promo, in 2-pack (2000) 15 - 20

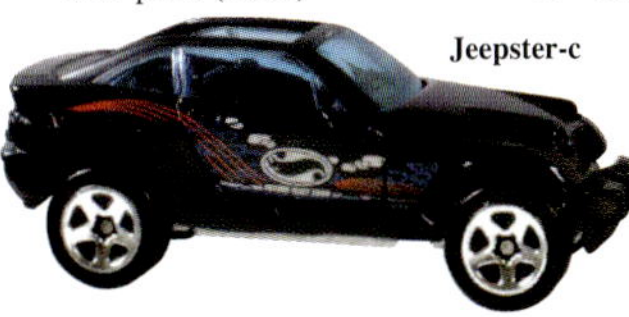
Jeepster-c

c. black; black int.; blue-tinted windows; silver, red & blue tampo w/"Future Fleet 2000" on sides; sp5. #3 in Future Fleet 2000 series, #003 (2000) 2 - 3
d. green; mtlfk gray chassis; black int.; tinted windows; black, gray & white tampo on sides & hood, "Jeepster" on sides; ho5; China; #140 (2001) 2 - 3

Jeepster-e

e. white; black chassis & int.; clear windows w/"Jeepster" in white on windshield; orange, black & gray tampo w/"4x4 Jeepster" on sides, "Editor's Choice" on hood; gych; Thailand. Target excl. Editor's Choice series (2001) 10 - 15

Jeepster-f

f. white, blue fenders & int., blue-tinted windows, gold & black tampo w/"HWPD Special Police Force" & "Unit 6" on sides & hood, "Radio Dispatched" on sides, "Hot Wheels Police Dept." on hood, sp5, Thailand. Police Cruisers 5-pack (2001) 2 - NA

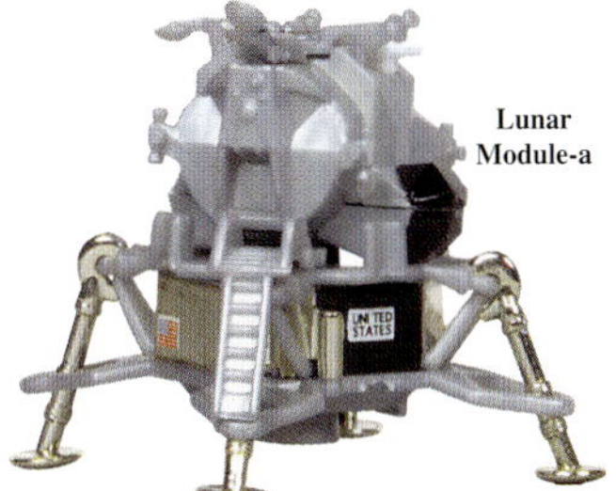
Lunar Module-a

g. yellow; gray plastic trim & int.; tinted windows; black, white, red & gray tampo w/"Jeepster 02" & Hot Wheels logo on sides, "Team Hot Wheels 02" on hood & trunk; sp5; #144 (2002) 2 - 3

Lunar Module - 45mm - 1999

a. gray plastic, gold-plated legs, U.S. flag on sides. Apollo Mission Action Pack 5 - NA

Lunar Roving Vehicle-a

Lunar Roving Vehicle - 65mm - 1999

a. flat metal base; white interior, gray plastic satellite dish, brass fenders, clear plastic wheels. Apollo Mission Action Pack 5 - NA

21073-a

Mercedes CLK-LM 21073 - 75mm - 1999

This Mercedes has a black plastic base, black spoiler & interior; clear windows, and lwgd. Malaysia.

a. gray 2 - 3
b. red, same as a, lwch, China, #163 (2000) 2 - 3
c. mtlfk dark red; black chassis, spoiler & int.; tinted windows; lwch; China; #118 (2002) 2 - 3

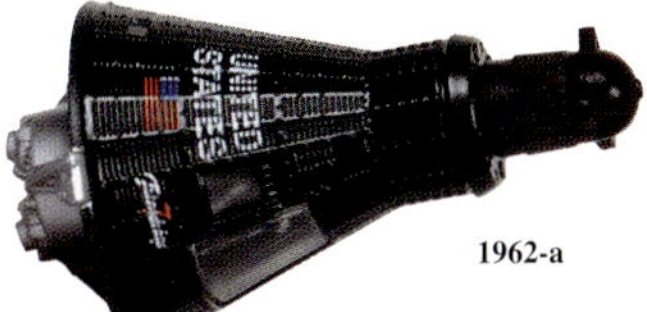
1962-a

Mercury Friendship 7 1962 - 66mm - 1999

a. black; clear windows; gray astronaut; silver, red & blue space shuttle tampo. John Glenn Action Pack only 5 - NA

21057-a

Monte Carlo Concept Car 21057 - 73mm - 1999

This model has a mtlfk gray metal chassis, gray interior, tinted windows, and sp5. Malaysia.

a. red, #6 in 1999 First Editions, #910 2 - 3

21057-b

b. mtlfk dk. red, same as a, tan int. #6 in 1999 First Editions, #910 2 - 5

21057-c

c. blue; yellow chassis; clear windows; gray int.; yellow, white, black & red tampo w/"27," "Manacop" & race decals on sides, "Manacop" & Chevy logo on hood, "27" on roof, "Goodyear" on trunk; sp7 w/"Goodyear" & "Eagle" on tires. Racing American Style 4-pack from Toys "R" Us Web site 5 - NA

Values are shown in U.S. dollars, first price is for mint, second is for mint packaged vehicles only. See pages 15-16 for grading guide to determine value for cars in lesser conditions.

Monte Carlo Concept Car-d

d. mtlfk blue; red chassis; white int.; clear windows; lt. brown, red, white & black tampo w/"Alan's Favorite Deluxe Cookies" & cookies on sides; lwch. #3 in Snack Time series, #015 (2000) 2 - 3

Monte Carlo Concept Car-e

e. gray; blue metal chassis; white int.; blue-tinted windows; black, blue, red & white tampo w/"6" & Cubs logo on sides, "Chicago" & Cubs logo on hood, "6" on roof, Hot Wheels logo & ".Com" on trunk; dw3. Chicago Cubs baseball promo, in 2-pack (2000) 10 - 15

f. red, gray metal chassis, black int., clear windows, black and gold tampo on sides, dw3. China. Virtual Collection, #109 (2000) 2 - 5

f2. as f, orange not gold in tampo. Virtual Collection, #109 (2000) 2 - 3

Monte Carlo Concept Car-g

g. yellow, black metal chassis, black int., tinted windows, red & black tampo w/"Monte Carlo" on sides & hood, Chevy logo on hood, sp5. #3 in Company Cars series, #087 (2001) 2 - 3

g2. as g, orange not red in tampo. #3 in Company Cars series, #087 (2001) 2 - 3

21058-a

Olds Aurora GTS-1 21058 - 76mm - 1999

This Malaysia-made model of the Jack Baldwin race car has a black plastic base, interior & roll cage; black wing; clear windows; and lwgd.

a. white & blue; red, yellow, black & blue tampo w/Hot Wheels logo, "11" & race decals on sides & hood. #5 in 1999 First Editions, #911 2 - 3

21058-b

b. mtlfk silver, same as a. #5 in 1999 First Editions, #911 2 - 5

21058-c

c. red; blue, black & white tampo w/large Hot Wheels design on sides. #5 in 1999 First Editions, #911 2 - 3

21058-d

d. black; orange chassis; white spoiler & int.; clear windows; gray & orange tampo w/"24," "Aurora" & race decals on sides, design on hood, "24" on roof; lwch. Racing American Style 4-pack from Toys "R" Us Web site 5 - NA

e. yellow, same as c, red added to tampo, dw3, China, GTS-1 not on package, #108 (2000) 2 - 3

f. orange; black chassis, spoiler & int.; clear windows; black, blue & white tampo w/large Hot Wheels logo on sides & hood, "1" on roof; lwch; China; #175 (2001) 2 - 3

Olds Aurora GTS-1-g

g. lt. blue-gray, black chassis & int., clear windows, black & red tampo design on sides & hood, "Unit 1" on sides, pr5s. China. #4 in Anime series, #064 (2001) 2 - 3

h. mtlfk green; black chassis, spoiler & interior; clear windows; gold, white, red & black tampo w/"Olds GTS 1" & "17" on sides; sp3; Thailand. Powershift Garage 5-pack, (2001) 3 - NA

21063-a

Phaeton 21063 - 65mm - 1999

This convertible has a removable tan plastic roof, tan interior, clear windshield, and sp5. Malaysia.

a. mtlfk turquoise 2 - 3

a2. as a, "1-877-Powers31" in silver on sides. Given at 2000 SEMA Show, in baggie (2000) 150 - NA

Phaeton-b

b. dk. mtlfk red, gray int., lwgd, Malaysia. #1 in Hot Rod Magazine series, #005 (2000) 2 - 3

b2. as b. China. #1 in Hot Rod Magazine series, #005 (2001) 2 - 3

Phaeton-c

EARLY TIMES 2000 MID-WINTER ROD RUN

c. mtlfk purple; black int.; clear windshield; tan roof; red, yellow & black tampo w/"Early Times 2000 Mid-Winter Rod Run" on roof; rrch. Ltd ed of 15,000 for Early Times Car Club (2000) 15 - 20

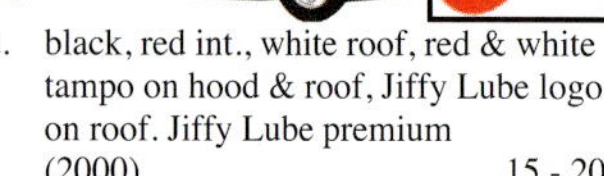

Phaeton-d

jiffy lube

d. black, red int., white roof, red & white tampo on hood & roof, Jiffy Lube logo on roof. Jiffy Lube premium (2000) 15 - 20

e. black, mtlfk gray chassis, black plastic roof, clear windshield, purple int., gray & purple tampo design on sides & hood, sp5. China. Virtual Collection, #164 (2000) 2 - 3

f. white, black roof & int., tinted windshield, blue & silver tampo w/"Police," "Wichita" & emblem on sides, rrch w/white stripe. Cop Rods Series 2 (2000) 7 - 9

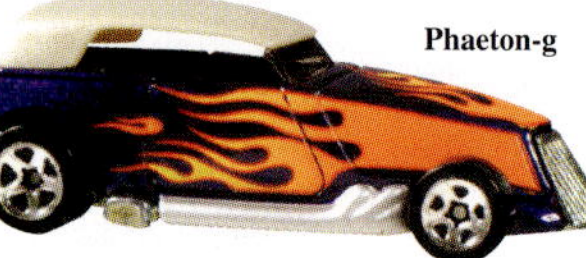

Phaeton-g

g. mtlfk purple, tan roof, black int., clear windshield, orange & red flames on sides & hood, sp5. K•B Toys excl. 2-pack (2001) 9 - NA

h. unpainted, black roof, white int., clear windshield, sp5. K•B Toys excl. 2-pack (2001) 9 - NA

i. flat burgundy; black chassis; clear windshield; black int., grille & roof; red flames w/black outline on sides; ww; China. #3 in Rat Rods series, #059 (2001) 2 - 3

Phaeton-j

j. mtlc red, tan roof & int., clear windshield, white & orange tampo w/"Coca Cola" on sides, Houston Astros logo

detail-j

on hood, Thailand. Houston Astros baseball premium (2001) 15 - 20

Phaeton-k

k. mtlc red, white int., clear windshield, black roof, white tampo on sides & hood w/"Walgreen's" on sides, ww. Walgreen's 2-pack only (2001) 5 - NA

l. blue; tan int.; clear windshield; multicolored tampo w/"99," "Supergard" & race decals on sides, "SKF" & Citgo logo on hood & back, "99" on roof, "Citgo" on back; dw3; Thailand. #1 in NASCAR Phaeton series (2001) 7 - 9

Phaeton-m

m. gray; white int.; clear windshield; multicolored tampo w/"6," "Pfizer" & race decals on sides, "Pfizer" on hood & back, "6" on roof; dw3; Thailand. #2 in NASCAR Phaeton series (2001) 7 - 9

n. red & black; tan int.; clear windshield; multicolored tampo w/"45," "Sprint PCS" & race decals on sides, "Sprint" on hood & back, "45" & "Sprint" on roof; dw3; Thailand. #3 in NASCAR Phaeton series (2001) 7 - 9

o. yellow & lt. blue; tan int.; clear windshield; multicolored tampo w/"43" & race decals on sides, "Cheerios" & Betty Crocker spoon on hood, "43" & "Chex" on roof, "Cheerios" on back; dw3; Thailand. #4 in NASCAR Phaeton series (2001) 7 - 9

p. black; white front; tan int.; clear windshield; multicolored tampo w/"02," "Alltel" & race decals on sides, "Alltel" & "Mobil 1" on hood, "02" & "Chex" on roof, "www.alltel.com" on back; dw3; Thailand. #5 in NASCAR Phaeton series (2001) 7 - 9

q. yellow; tan int.; clear windows; multicolored tampo w/"36," "M&M's" & race decals on sides, "M&M's" on hood, "36" & "M&M's" on roof & in back; dw3; Thailand. #6 in NASCAR Phaeton series (2001) 7 - 9

r. orange; blue roof; tan int.; clear windows; multicolored tampo w/"5" & race decals on sides, Tony the Tiger on hood, "5" on roof, "Kellogg's" in back; dw3; Thailand. #7 in NASCAR Phaeton series (2001) 7 - 9

Phaeton-s

s. yellow; tan int.; clear windshield; multicolored tampo w/"10," "Nesquik" & race decals on sides; "Nesquik" on hood & back; "10," "Nesquik" & race decals on roof; dw3; Thailand. #8 in NASCAR Phaeton series (2001) 7 - 9

t. gray; tan int.; clear windshield; multicolored tampo w/"40" & race decals on sides, "Sterling Marlin" on hood & back, "40" on roof; dw3; Thailand. #9 in NASCAR Phaeton series (2001) 7 - 9

u. black & red; tan int.; clear windshield; multicolored tampo w/"25," "UAW-Delphi" & race decals on sides; "UAW-Delphi" on hood & back; "25," "UAW-Delphi" & race decals on roof; dw3; Thailand. #10 in NASCAR Phaeton series (2001) 7 - 9

Phaeton-v

v. mtlfk aqua; mtlfk gray chassis; black roof & int.; red-tinted windshield; yellow, red & black tampo w/cobra on sides; dw3gd; China. #4 in Cold Blooded series, #078 (2002) 2 - 3

Phaeton-w

w. white, black roof & int., clear windshield, green & black tampo on sides & hood; rrchww; Thailand. #7 in 2002 Treasure Hunt series, #007 (2002) 20 - 25

21071-a

Pikes Peak Tacoma 21071 - 80mm - 1999

This racing truck has a black interior; clear windshield; black plastic interior, truck bed cover & rear window; rear spoiler; and lwgd. Malaysia.

a. yellow; white roof & hood; black, white, yellow & red tampo with "Pennzoil" & "1" on sides; race decals on sides & hood. #19 in 1999 First Editions, #924 (1999) 2 - 3

b. red; gray plastic chassis; clear windows; yellow int. & truck bed; red in insert; yellow, orange, black & white tampo on hood & sides; "64 Tacoma" on sides; sp3; Malaysia; #148 (2000) 2 - 3

b2. as b, silver in insert, #148 (2000) 2 - 6

Pikes Peak Tacoma-c

c. black; black chassis; red int.; clear windows; orange & white tampo w/"Crash CD ROM" & "2" on sides, "2" & "CD ROM" on hood; ho5gd; Malaysia. #2 in CD Customs series, #030 (2000) 2 - 4

c2. as c, lwgd, Malaysia. #2 in CD Customs Series 2 - 4

d. black; gray chassis; red int. & truck bed; clear windows; yellow, orange &

Values are shown in U.S. dollars, first price is for mint, second is for mint packaged vehicles only. See pages 15-16 for grading guide to determine value for cars in lesser conditions.

white tampo on sides & hood; "64" & "Toyota" on sides; ho5; Malaysia; #223 (2001) 2 - 3
d2. as d, China, #223 (2001) 2 - 3

19580-a2

Pit Crew Truck 19580 - 70mm - 1999
Based on a generic stepside delivery van, this Thailand-made model has a red plastic base, red plastic opening doors in back, blue-tinted windshield, red interior, and ho5. Similar castings: 9643 Letter Getter (1977), 2854 S.W.A.T. Van (1979), 2850 The Incredible Hulk (1979), 3303 Racing Team (1981), 9643 Delivery Van (1984), 2519 Combat Medic (1986), 2808 Delivery Truck (1989), 9114 The Simpson's Homer's Nuclear Waste Van (1990)
a. gray; blue, red & white tampo w/"Hi Bank Racing," "Tool Supply" & "Pit Crew" on sides; #874 2 - 3
a2. as a, dw3, #874 2 - 3

Plymouth Duster-a

Plymouth Duster - 76mm - 1999
This Funny Car has a metal chassis, lift-up body, orange interior, clear windows and sp5
a. purple; orange, white, red, green & black tampo w/"Duster" & race decals on sides. Target V-8 3-pack 5 - NA

18851-a

Pontiac Rageous 18851 - 72mm - 1999
This Malaysia-made model has a black plastic chassis & rear spoiler, gray interior, tinted dome, and sp3.
a. dk. mtlfk red, white "Rageous" on sides. #7 in 1999 First Editions, #675 2 - 3
a2. as a, black dome, #675 2 - 3

Pontiac Rageous-b

b. black; gray chassis; red-tinted dome; blue, gold & gray tampo w/"Future Fleet 2000" on sides; sp3; Malaysia. #2 in Future Fleet 2000 series, #002 (2000) 2 - 3
b2. as b. China. #2 in Future Fleet 2000 series, #002 (2000) 2 - 3
c. mtlfk blue, white int., black base, tinted black dome, black & silver tampo w/"Rageous" on sides, sp3, #119 (2000) 2 - 3
c2. as c, solid black dome 2 - 3

Pontiac Rageous-d

d. mtlfk brown; gray plastic chassis; black-tinted dome; silver, black & orange tampo design on sides & hood; rrch. #10 in 2001 Treasure Hunt series, #010 (2001) 10 - 15
e. white; black chassis; white int.; tinted dome; gold, black & blue tampo w/"Unit 6," "Special Service Police" & logo on sides; sp3; Malaysia. Metro City Police Force set (2001) 6 - NA

f. yellow; black chassis; gray int.; clear dome; black, red, green & gray tampo on sides & dome; sp5; Malaysia. Motorized Tornado Twister set (2001) 6 - NA
g. mtlfk gray, black chassis, gray int., tinted dome, red & black flame tampo on sides, lwch, Malaysia, #119 (2002) 2 - 3

21060-a

Popcycle™ 21060 - 65mm - 1999
This concept model has a metal base, interior, and engine; an orange plastic dome over the driver's seat; a metal motorcycle; and sp3. Malaysia.
a. mtlfk purple, orange stripe. #13 in 1999 First Editions, #913 2 - 3
b. mtlfk burgundy, same as a. #13 in 1999 First Editions, #913 6 - 12
c. mtlfk green, gold chrome engine & pipes, yellow-tinted dome, sp3gd, Malaysia, #157 (2000) 2 - 3
c2. as c, China, #157 (2000) 2 - 3
d. purple, chrome engine & int., purple-tinted dome, white tampo on top, ho5, China, #215 (2001) 2 - 3
d2. as d, name on base changed to Motor Psycho, #215 (2002) 2 - 3

18852-a

Porsche 911 GT1-98 18852 - 75mm - 1999
This model has a black plastic chassis and spoiler, clear windows, black interior, and lwch. Malaysia.
a. white; magenta, orange, black & gray tampo with "2" & race decals on sides & front. #25 in 1999 First Editions, #676 2 - 3
b. mtlfk blue; black wing; white int.; yellow-tinted windows; white, black, gray & red tampo w/"27," "24 Heures Du Mans" & race decals on top; lwch. World Racers 2 5-pack (1999) 2 - NA
c. purple; tan int.; tinted windows; white, black & red tampo w/"27" & race decals on top; pr5s; Malaysia; #172 (2000) 4 - 10
c2. as c, lwch, #172 (2000) 2 - 3
c3. as c, dw3, #172 (2000) 3 - 6

Porsche 911 GT1-98-d

d. white; white spoiler; dk. blue, lt. green, red, yellow & black tampo w/U.S. flag & race decals on sides, "Porsche" & "Champion" on nose, "Champion Parts" on spoiler; lwch; China; #250 (2001) 2 - 3
d2. as d, Malaysia, #250 (2001) 2 - 3
e. mtlfk orange; gray spoiler & int.; clear windows; yellow, black & white tampo w/"5" on sides; lwch; Malaysia; #135 (2002) 2 - 3

21059-a

Porsche 911 GT3 Cup 21059 - 70mm - 1999
This European sports car has a black plastic chassis, red interior, clear windows, yellow spoiler, and lwch. Malaysia.
a. gray; lt. green, yellow & red tampo w/"8 Cup" on sides. #10 in 1999 First Editions, #912 2 - 3

21059-a2

a2. as a, black spoiler, #912 3 - 10

21059-b

b. mtlfk purple, same as a, #10 in 1999 First Editions, #912 (1999) 2 - 3
c. white, same as a, clear windows, red interior & spoiler, sp3, India, #128 (2000) 2 - 3
d. mtlfk orange, black windows & spoiler, white & dk. blue tampo w/"1" & "Hot Wheels" on sides, pr5s, Malaysia, #214 (2001) 2 - 3
d2. as d, sp3, #214 (2001) 2 - 3
e. mtlfk gray; black chassis, spoiler & int.; clear windows; black, white & orange tampo w/"GT3," "Porsche" & "27" on sides; ho5; Thailand. Powershift Garage 5-pack (2001) 2 - NA

Reptar Wagon-a

Reptar Wagon - 65mm - 1999
a. lt. green, purple int., white teeth, orange eyes, lt. blue hands & fins, baby in seat, dw3. Rugrats Movie Action Pack 5 - NA

21065-a

Screamin' Hauler™ 21065 - 80mm - 1999
This concept race car/pickup truck has metal chassis and interior, blue-tinted windshield, chrome engines on both sides, and sp5. Malaysia.
a. mtlfk purple; mtlfk purple truck bed, #918 2 - 3
b. mtlfk dark red, mtlfk gray chassis & int., tinted windshield, sp5. China. Virtual Collection, #156 (2000) 2 - 3

Screamin' Hauler-c

c. yellow; mtlfk gray chassis & int.; black, gold, orange & white tampo w/"57334111 104 1110111" & "3" on sides; sp5; China. #4 in Secret Code series, #48 (2000) 2 - 3
c2. as c, Malaysia (2001) 2 - 3

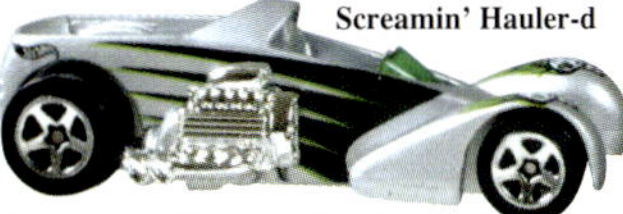
Screamin' Hauler-d

d. gray, mtlfk gray chassis & int., clear green windshield, black & lt. green tampo design on sides & front fenders, sp5. China. #4 in Skull & Crossbones series, #072 (2001) 2 - 3

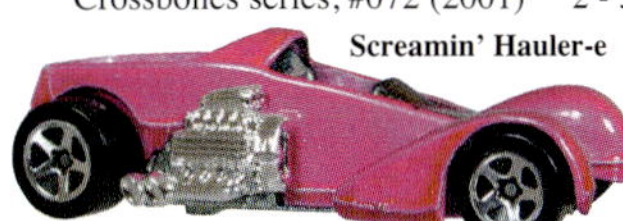
Screamin' Hauler-e

e. mtlc magenta, metal int., gray & black tampo on nose, sp5, Malaysia, #090 (2002) 2 - 3

21061-a2

Semi-Fast™ 21061 - 78mm - 1999
This concept race truck cab has a metal chassis, tinted windows, black interior, gray plastic engine behind the cab, and sp5.
a. red; yellow & silver upper grill; black & white tampo w/"17" in circle on sides. #8 in 1999 First Editions, #914 2 - 3
a2. as a, red upper grill, #914 8 - 10

21061-b

b. black, same as a, red cab. #8 in 1999 First Editions, #914 2 - 3
c. blue; mtlfk silver base; white cab; clear windows; gray int.; yellow, black & white tampo w/"17" on sides; China. Virtual Collection, #118 (2000) 2 - 3
c2. as c, Malaysia, #118 (2000) 2 - 3
d. aqua; mtlfk gray chassis; white cab; lt. green, yellow & black tampo w/"KH" & "Kieran Hauling" on sides; sp5; China; #189 (2001) 2 - 3
e. orange; white cab; gray int.; blue-tinted windows; dark blue, white & orange tampo with "12" & race decals on sides; sp5; Malaysia. Victory Lane 5-pack (2001) 2 - NA
f. clear dk. red, mtlfk gray chassis, black cab, gray int., yellow-tinted windows, black tampo on sides, sp5, #235 (2001) 2 - 3
g. blue; black cab; gold chassis & int.; gold-tinted windows; gold, white & blue tampo on cab w/"Volley" & logo on sides; sp5gd; Thailand. Sports 5-pack (2002) 3 - NA

21072-a

Shadow Mk IIa 21072 - 75mm - 1999
This race car has a gray plastic chassis and interior, a mtlfk silver wing in back, and sp5. Malaysia.
a. black; white & red tampo: "101" & race decals on sides, "Shadow" on spoiler. #20 in 1999 First Editions, #925 2 - 3

Shadow Mk IIa-b

b. white; black chassis; gray int.; red wing; black, orange, gray & white tampo w/"Stunt Track Driver CD ROM" & "17" on sides & wing; sp5; Malaysia. #3 in CD Customs series, #31 (2000) 2 - 3
c. red, gray chassis & int., black spoiler, blue & yellow tampo design on sides & top, sp5gd, Malaysia, #149 (2000) 2 - 3
d. black, black chassis, red spoiler, gray int., red & white tampo on top, pr5s, #224 (2001) 2 - 3
e. orange; gray chassis & int.; blue wing; yellow, blue, black & white tampo w/Hot Wheels logo on sides; "Happy Birthday" on top; pr5; China. Birthday Cake 5-pack (2001) 3 - NA

Values are shown in U.S. dollars, first price is for mint, second is for mint packaged vehicles only. See pages 15-16 for grading guide to determine value for cars in lesser conditions.

Space Shuttle Discovery 1998-a

Space Shuttle Discovery 1998 - 78mm - 1999

a. white; black, silver red & blue space shuttle tampo. John Glenn Action Pack only 5 - NA

Sudzster-a

Sudzster™ 80mm - 1999

This Chinese-made bathtub has a metal chassis & rear engine, four green alligator feet, & sp5.

a. white, w/Alligator in tub. Scum Chums Action Pack (1999) 15 - NA

18854-a

Tee'd Off™ 18854 - 55mm - 1999

This golf cart has a metal chassis, chrome engine in back, white roof, gray interior, and sp5. Malaysia.

Similar casting: Fore Wheeler (2000)

a. pearl white; lt. green, purple & yellow tampo w/"Miller CC" & "Country Club" on roof. #9 in 1999 First Editions, #683 8 - 15

18854-a2

a2. as a, burgundy int., #683 2 - 6

18854-b

b. blue, same as a, white int., #9 in 1999 First Editions, #683 2 - 3

c. red; purple int.; white roof; gray, orange & black design on roof & in front; sp5; China. Virtual Collection, #117 (2000) 2 - 3

d. dk. blue; chrome engine; gray int.; multicolored tampo w/"44," Hot Wheels logo & race decals on sides, Hot Wheels logo in front, "44" on roof; sp5; Thailand. #1 in NASCAR Pit Cruisers series (2000) 10 - 15

Tee'd Off-e

e. lt. blue; same as c; multicolored tampo w/"43," STP logo & race decals on sides, STP logo in front, "43" on roof; sp5; Thailand. #2 in NASCAR Pit Cruisers series (2000) 10 - 15

f. orange; same as c; multicolored tampo w/"10," "Tide" & race decals on sides, "Tide" in front, "10" on roof; sp5; Thailand. #3 in NASCAR Pit Cruisers series (2000) 8 - 12

g. dk. blue; same as a; white front end; multicolored tampo w/"6," "Valvoline" & race decals on sides, "Valvoline" & "V" in front, "6" on roof; sp5; Thailand. #4 in NASCAR Pit Cruisers series (2000) 8 - 12

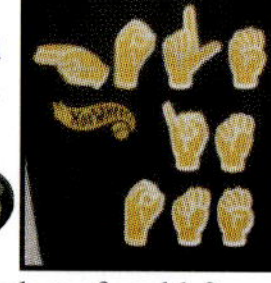
Tee'd Off-h

h. black, white int., black roof, gold & orange tampo w/hand signals on roof, sp5. #3 in Hand Signals series, Malaysia, #47 (2001) 2 - 3

h2. black, same as h, hand signals are gold and white, China, #47 (2001) 2 - 3

21064-a

Track T™ 21064 - 57mm - 1999

This Malaysia-made roadster has a metal chassis, engine & seat; tan plastic steering wheel & cover over the passenger seat; sp5.

a. black; yellow, red & blue flames over hood. #12 in 1999 First Editions, #917 (1999) 2 - 3

Tract T-b

b. yellow, white int., lt. green & black tampo w/flames on sides, "Wayne's Body Shop" on trunk, dw3. #2 in Hot Rod Magazine series, #006 (2000) 2 - 3

b2. as b. China. #2 in Hot Rod Magazine series, #006 (2001) 2 - 3

c. white; metal int.; black top; red, yellow, black & silver tampo on sides & top, "07" on roof; dw3. Virtual Collection, #127 (2000) 2 - 3

d. white; metal int.; black cover; blue & gray tampo w/"414" & emblem on sides, "Vigilans" on hood, "Tucson Police" on trunk; rrch. Cop Rods 2 series (2000) 7 - 9

e. black, metal int., dk. red & white tampo, ww, Malaysia. #1 in Rat Rods series, #057 (2001) 2 - 3

e2. as e, red not dk. red in tampo. #1 in Rat Rods series, #057 (2001) 2 - 3

f. yellow, metal int., black tampo, sp5, Malaysia. Speed Shift Duel track set (2001) 6 - NA

21070-a

Turbolence™ 21070 - 80mm - 1999

This concept racer has a metal chassis, chrome interior, windshield and engine and ho5gd. Malaysia.

a. black, gold tampo w/"1" & "Dayla Special" on top. #18 in 1999 First Editions, #923 (1999) 2 - 3

b. gray; chrome int. & engine; red, white, black & turquoise tampo on sides & hood; ho5; Malaysia. Virtual Collection, #129 (2000) 2 - 3

b2. as b, gray engine & int., Malaysia. Virtual Collection, #129 (2000) 2 - 3

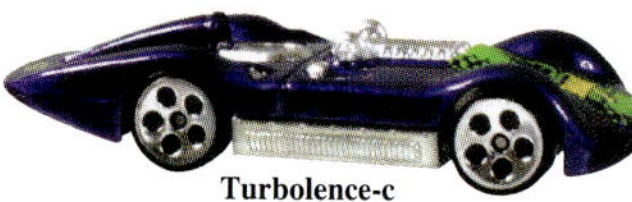
Turbolence-c

c. mtlfk purple; chrome int. & engine; green, black, white & red tampo w/"Max" in front; ho5; Malaysia. Max Steel 5-pack 2 - NA

Turbolence-d

d. black, chrome int. & engine, white & gold tampo w/Hot Wheels logo on sides & top, ho5. #3 in Loco-Motive series, #075 (2001) 2 - 3

d2. as d, gold interior and engine, ho5. #3 in Loco-Motive series, #075 (2001) 3 - 7

e. dk. blue; chrome int. & engine; yellow, orange & lt. green flame tampo on sides & hood; Malaysia, Fireball 5-pack (2001) 2 - NA

24105-a

X-Ploder™ 24105 - 84mm - 1999

This Malaysia-made concept car features a metal chassis; chrome engine, pipes & interior; red-tinted dome; and dw3. It also has "Power Rocket" embossed on the base. Similar casting: 13348 Power Rocket™ (1995)

a. black; orange & yellow flames on sides; #1091 2 - 3

2000

Not counting variations, close to 500 different basic cars were issued in 2000. There were 36 2000 First Editions, 12 Treasure Hunt cars, and 12 sets of four-segment cars included in the 250 number packs for this year. In addition, there were 5-packs and Convention cars, plus a large number of limited editions. Target introduced an Editor's Choice series, and 15 baseball teams had Hot Wheels promotions.

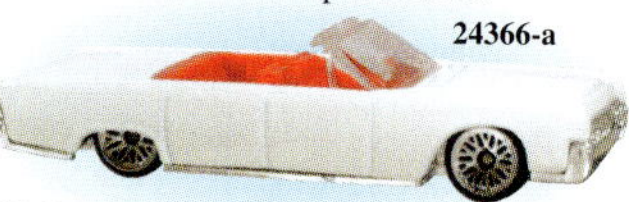
24366-a

1964 ('64) Lincoln Continental 24366 - 82mm - 2000

This Malaysia-made convertible has a plastic chassis, red interior, clear windshield and lwch.

a. white, #3 in 2000 First Editions, #063 2 - 3

b. black, ho5, #237 2 - 3

c. blue; blue-tinted windshield; white int.; black & gray tampo on sides, hood & trunk w/"Right On" on trunk; China; #091 (2001) 2 - 3

Isuzu VehiCROSS 24392 - 68mm - 2000

This Malaysia-made Japanese sport utility vehicle has a metal chassis, black plastic

24392-a

around the sides, black interior, tinted windows, and pr5s.

a. mtlfk gray, #16 in 2000 First Editions, #076 2 - 3

b. yellow, same as a, #144 (2001) 2 - 3

24383-a

'41 Willys 24383 - 80mm - 2000

This Malaysia-made 1941 coupe dragster has a gray plastic base, chrome engine sticking through the hood, black windows, and sp5.

a. mtlfk orange; yellow, magenta, blue & black tampo w/"Wild Willy" & race decals on sides. #14 in 2000 First Editions, #074 2 - 3

b. black; red-tinted windows; yellow, white, dk. red & black tampo w/"Wild Willy" & race decals on sides; sp5; Malaysia; #110 (2001) 2 - 3

24383-c

c. mtlfk dark red; black plastic base; clear windows; black int.; lt. blue, yellow, red & black design on sides & trunk; Editor's Choice logo behind rear window; sp5. Target excl. Editor's Choice series (2001) 5 - 7

d. mtlfk gray; red-tinted windows; dk. red, gray & black tampo; sp5. #2 in Skin Deep series, #094 (2001) 2 - 3

e. gray, gray chassis, chrome engine & int., red-tinted windows, yellow & brown tampo w/"Wild Willy Racing" & race decals on sides, sp5, Malaysia. Pavement Pounder pack (2001) 5 - NA

24372-a

'65 'Vette ('65 Corvette) 24372 - 68mm - 2000

This 1965 Corvette convertible has a gray plastic chassis, red interior, clear windshield, and sp5. Malaysia.

a. mtlfk black, #19 in 2000 First Editions, #079 2 - 3

24372-b

b. red, gray chassis, white int., gray pinstripe design on sides & hood, rrch, Malaysia. #1 in 2001 Treasure Hunt series, #001 (2001) 20 - 25

c. white; black int.; black, yellow & orange flame tampo on sides, hood & trunk; sp5; Malaysia; #109 (2001) 2 - 3

24372-d

d. white; red int.; dk. blue, gold & red tampo w/"Bloomington Gold Corvettes USA 2001" on sides & hood; rrch

Values are shown in U.S. dollars, first price is for mint, second is for mint packaged vehicles only. See pages 15-16 for grading guide to determine value for cars in lesser conditions.

w/white stripe; Malaysia. Ltd ed for Bloomington's (2001) 15 - 20

e. mtlfk silver, same as d. Ltd ed for Bloomington's (2001) 15 - 20

f. red; black chassis & int.; black, yellow & orange flame tampo on sides & top; sp5. McDonald's set (2001) 5 - NA

g. mtlfk blue, gray chassis, black int., clear windshield, gray & gold flame tampo on sides & top, sp5, Malaysia. #2 in Corvette series, #067 (2002) 2 - 3

('67) Dodge Charger 24381 - 80mm - 2000
This 1967 muscle car has a chrome plastic chassis, clear windows, red interior, and pr5s. Malaysia.

a. lt. gray, "Dodge" in red on sides. #28 in 2000 First Editions, #088 2 - 3

b. yellow; black int.; red, black & white tampo w/"Dodge" & "7" in circle; race decals on sides; "7" in circle on hood; rrch. #8 in 2001 Treasure Hunt series, #008 (2001) 15 - 20

c. red; white roof; white int.; yellow, white & dark blue tampo w/McDonald's "M" on sides & hood; Ronald McDonald House logo & "Ronald McDonald House Charities" on sides & roof; 15th Annual Hot Wheels Convention logo on trunk; rrch w/red stripe. Ltd to 5000, Hot Wheels Convention, in baggie (2001) 25 - 30

d. yellow, black int., tinted windows, dk. red & black tampo on sides & roof, sp3, Malaysia, #117 (2001) 2 - 3

d2. as d, Thailand, #117 (2001) 2 - 3

'68 El Camino 24371 - 77mm - 2000
This 1968 El Camino truck has a metal chassis, gray interior and rear wing, blue-tinted windows, chrome metal engine in back, and sp5. Malaysia.

a. pearl white, #8 in 2000 First Editions, #068 2 - 3

b. mtlfk orange, black stripe on bottom, same as a, China, #268 (2001) 2 - 3

c. mtlfk blue; gray int.; clear windows; yellow, black & orange tampo on sides & hood. Hot Haulers 4-pack (2001) 7 - NA

d. red; yellow int. & wing; orange-tinted windows; gray, gold & black tampo w/"E90" & "Torrance Fire Dept." on sides & hood; "1" on sides; rrch. Fire Rods series (2001) 7 - 9

e. orange, clear windows, yellow int. & wing, purple & yellow flame tampo on sides & hood, "Xtreme Xpress" on sides, pr5s, China, #200 (2001) 2 - 3

e2. as e, tinted windows, Thailand, #200 (2001) 2 - 3

e3. as e, tinted windows, Malaysia. Truck Stoppers 5-pack (2001) 3 - NA

f. white, red int. & spoiler, clear windows, chrome engine, blue & red stars, flames tampo, sp5, China, #082 (2002) 2 - 3

Anglia Panel Truck 24397 - 66mm - 2000
This English truck has a gray chassis, orange-tinted windows, chrome interior, and sp5. Malaysia.

a. purple; orange, white & black tampo w/"Jonathan's Express Delivery Toys & Collectibles" on sides. #17 in 2000 First Editions, #077 2 - 3

b. red, gray chassis, white int., clear windows, white & blue tampo on sides & hood, Intl. Show Car Association logo on sides. Ltd ed for ISCA (2000) 10 - 15

c. turquoise, same as b, tampo colors are black, red, white & dk. blue. Ltd ed for ISCA (2000) 10 - 15

d. mtlc purple; white int.; clear windows; white, red, lt. green & yellow tampo design on sides, hood, roof & in back; "2000" on sides; "Dream Halloween" on roof; gych. Ltd to 2000 for Dream Halloween, in plastic box (2000) 200 - 250

e. yellow, chrome int., blue-tinted windows, dark green & black tampo w/"Express" & "Jonathan's Toys & Collectibles" on sides, sp5, China, #097 (2001) 2 - 3

f. red, black & white; chrome int.; clear windows; black, red, white & gold tampo w/"No. 4," "Pittsfield, MA Fire Chief" & "Official Business" on sides; "Fire Chief Pittsfield, Mass" on hood; Pittsfield emblem, "Fire Chief" & "No. 4" on roof & back; rrch. Fire Rods series (2001) 9 - 12

g. black & white; black chassis & fenders; clear windows; chrome int.; purple, red & gray tampo w/Anglia Rods" on sides; "Editor's Choice" in back; rrch; Thailand. Target excl. Editor's Choice series (2001) 9 - 12

h. yellow; gray int.; blue-tinted windows; multicolored tampo w/"36," "M&M's" & race decals on sides & top; sp5gd. Thailand. #2 in NASCAR Anglia Panel Truck series (2001) 9 - 12

i. mtlfk dk. blue; black chassis & int.; clear windows; black roof; red, black & white tampo w/"2," Hot Wheels logo & "Racing" on sides & roof; sp5; China; #143 (2002) 2 - 3

i2. mtlfk blue, same as i, #143 (2002) 2 - 3

Arachnorod 24398 - 85mm - 2000
This Malaysia-made concept race car has a gray plastic chassis, tinted dome, tan plastic interior, black tailpipes, chrome decoration that looks like a spider over the top, and pr5s.

a. dk. mtlfk red; black, yellow & white tampo w/"4" on rear fenders. #34 in 2000 First Editions, #094 2 - 3

b. black; orange-tinted dome, int. & tail pipes; purple, silver & red spider web tampo on top; sp5; #137 (2001) 2 - 3

c. flat black, purple top, orange-tinted dome, chrome deco, purple & orange tampo on sides & top, pr5s w/gray background. Target excl. Originals series (2001) 5 - 7

Austin Healey 24391 - 74mm - 2000
This convertible British sports car has a metal base, chrome engine sticking through the hood, red interior, tinted windshield, and sp5. Malaysia.

a. black, gray sides, #32 in 2000 First Editions, #092 2 - 3

b. red with white sides, black int., clear windshield, lwch, #167 (2001) 2 - 3

c. blue; red int.; clear windshield; orange, yellow, black & gray tampo w/flames, "Office of the Mayor" & Planet Hot Wheels logo on sides; sp5; Thailand; #197 (2001) 2 - 3

Blast Lane 27497 - 68mm - 2000
This Malaysia-made motorcycle has a metal chassis, engine & fork; orange seat, gas tank & rear fenders; and gray plastic handlebars.

a. orange; black & white tampo w/"Hot Wheels" on seat. #36 in 2000 First Editions, #096 2 - 4

b. gold; black seat; black, red, white & gold tampo; Malaysia. #5 in 2001 Treasure Hunt series, #005 (2001) 20 - 35

c. yellow, dk. blue stars & red Jiffy Lube logo on gas tank. Jiffy Lube premium (2001) 15 - 20

d. white, same as c, Jiffy Lube premium (2001) 15 - 20

e. black; silver & magenta skull-&-crossbones tampo; chrome magenta rims. #2 in Skull and Crossbones series, #070 (2001) 2 - 6

f. dk. blue; red & white flame tampo on gas tank & seats; Hot Wheels logo on seat, #169 (2001) 2 - 5

Cabbin' Fever 24370 - 78mm - 2000
This Malaysia-made concept model of a ramp truck has a gray plastic chassis & ramp, chrome windows & truck bed, and pr5s.

a. black; orange, yellow & white tampo w/"Motor'ed Transport" on sides. #22 in 2000 First Editions, #082 2 - 3

b. mtlfk green; orange, yellow & white tampo w/"Motor'ed Transport" on sides; #159 (2001) 2 - 3

c. white; black top; gold chrome chassis, int. & ramp; aqua, black, gold & white tampo w/Treasure Hunt logo on sides, "Cabbin' Fever" on roof; pr5s. #12 in 2001 Treasure Hunt series, #012 (2001) 20 - 25

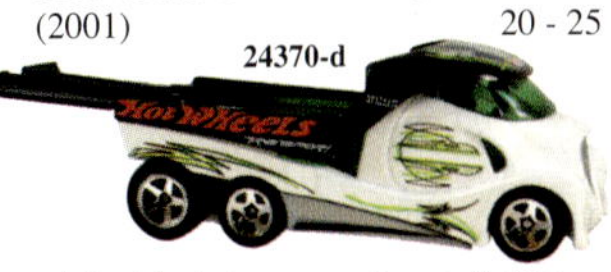

d. white; black top; gray chassis & int.; black ramp; green-tinted windows; lt. green, red, black & white tampo on sides & top w/"Hot Wheels Transport" & "Cellular Dispatch" on sides; sp5; Malaysia. Costco 20-pack, in bp (2001) 10 - 15

e. dark red; white chassis & cab; dk.red windows; blue ramp; black, blue, orange & green tampo "Daytona 500" & "Daytona" on sides & top; pr5s; Thailand. #1 in 2002 NASCAR Treasure Hunt series (2002) 12 - 18

f. red; black chassis; royal blue ramp; yellow top & windows; red, blue, white & yellow tampo w/"Darlington a NASCAR Tradition" & "a NASCAR Tradition" on sides & top; pr5s; Thailand. #2 in 2002 NASCAR Treasure Hunt series (2002) 12 - 18

g. mtlfk dk. red; gray chassis; black ramp; chrome windows; black, white & red tampo w/"Talladega Superspeedway" & "Superspeedway" on sides & top; pr5s; Thailand. #3 in 2002 NASCAR Treasure Hunt series (2002) 12 - 18

h. yellow, black chassis, dark red ramp, black windows, multicolored tampo w/"Daytona at Speed of Light" on sides" & top, pr5s, Thailand. #4 in 2002 NASCAR Treasure Hunt series (2002) 12 - 18

Values are shown in U.S. dollars, first price is for mint, second is for mint packaged vehicles only. See pages 15-16 for grading guide to determine value for cars in lesser conditions.

i. white; gray chassis; red ramp & windows; black, white & red tampo w/"Watkins Glen New York's Thunder Road" & "New York's Thunder Road" on sides & top; pr5s; Thailand. #5 in 2002 NASCAR Treasure Hunt series (2002) 12 - 18

j. black; gray chassis; white cab; black ramp & windows; blue top; black, orange & lt. blue tampo w/"Phoenix International Raceway" on sides & top; pr5s; Thailand. #6 in 2002 NASCAR Treasure Hunt series (2002) 12 - 18

k. yellow, gray chassis & ramp, chrome windows, black top, black & blue tampo w/"Kansas Speedway" on sides & top, pr5s. Thailand. #7 in 2002 NASCAR Treasure Hunt series (2002) 12 - 18

l. blue; white chassis; black cab; dark red ramp & top; chrome windows; dark red, black & white tampo w/"Talladega Speedway" on sides & top; pr5s; Thailand. #8 in 2002 NASCAR Treasure Hunt series (2002) 12 - 18

m. dk. red; gray chassis; chrome windows; black ramp; black, white & red tampo w/"California Speedway" on sides & top; pr5s; Thailand. #9 in 2002 NASCAR Treasure Hunt series (2002) 12 - 18

n. purple, gray chassis, turquoise windows, black ramp, turquoise & white tampo w/"Homestead Miami Speedway" on sides & top, pr5s, Thailand. #10 in 2002 NASCAR Treasure Hunt series (2002) 12 - 18

24370-a

Chevy Pro Stock Truck 24370 - 84mm - 2000

This Malaysia-made racing truck has a plastic chassis, gray interior, black-tinted windshield, large sp5 in back and smaller sp5 in front.

a. fluor. orange; dk. red, red & white tampo on sides & hood w/"Pro Stock" & race decals on sides. #7 in 2000 First Editions, #067 2 - 3

b. purple, clear windows, orange int., red & white tampo on sides & hood w/Pro Truck" & Race decals on sides, sp5, China, #244 (2001) 2 - 3

24370-c

c. yellow; black int.; tinted windows; red, blue, gray & white tampo on sides & top w/"PR Truck" on sides; sp5. Puerto Rico only, in box (2000) 20 - 25

d. white; black int. & truck bed; clear windows; green & red tampo on sides, hood & roof w/"Karma" on sides & roof; sp5. Hot Haulers 4 pack (2001) 5 - NA

e. lime yellow, gray & black tampo on sides & back cover, picture of big cat's head on back cover, pr5s. China. #3 in Skin Deep series, #095 (2001) 2 - 3

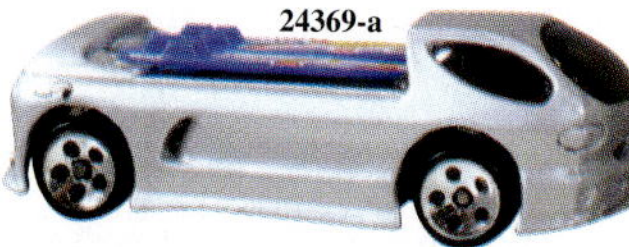
24369-a

Deora II 24369 - 70mm - 2000

The Malaysia-made 1/64th scale version of this concept model has a black plastic chassis, clear windows, black interior, and two removable surfboards on the back tonneau cover.

a. gray, two blue surfboards w/two different multicolored designs. #5 in the 2000 First Editions, #065 2 - 3

24369-b

b. burgundy; clear windows; gold int.; black, purple, white, yellow & orange tampo w/"Hot Wheels 2000 New York Toy Fair" on sides; two gold surfboards on bed w/"Hot Wheels" on each; gold pc. 2000 New York Toy Fair, in plastic box 100 - 150

24369-c

c. red; black chassis, bed & int.; clear windows; gray surfboards; red, white & yellow tampo on sides, roof & surfboards w/"Puerto Rico Isla del Encanto" on sides; sp5. Puerto Rico only, in box (2000) 20 - 25

d. mtlfk blue; clear windows; chrome int.; two orange surfboards w/white, red & yellow design; pr5s; China; #243 (2001) 2 - 3

e. red with black windows and truck bed, a yellow and black tampo on the sides, gray surfboards with red and yellow flames and sp5. Hot Haulers 4-pack (2001) 6 - NA

f. dk. mtlfk red; clear windows; chrome int. & surfboards; black, white & gold tampo w/Hot Wheels logo on sides; "H 33 W" on roof; sp5; China; #152 (2001) 2 - 3

f2. as f, no surfboards, sp5, Thailand. Skateboarders 5-pack (2001) 3 - NA

24369-g

g. mtlfk black; chrome int.; blue-tinted windows; black surfboards; gray, yellow, orange, lt. blue & white flame tampo on sides; "Hot Wheels" on one surfboard; lwch; Thailand. Sam's Club 20-pack only, in blister (2001) 10 - 15

24369-h

h. gray, chrome chassis & int., clear windows, red & blue surfboard, red & blue flag tampo on sides & roof, ho5. China. #3 in Star Spangled series, #081 (2002) 2 - 3

i. mtlfk gold; black surfboards & windows; red, purple, black, yellow & white tampo with "Geo" & "Thermal" on surfboards; CD-ROM logo on roof; ho5; Thailand; with CD-ROM disc. #4 in CD-ROM series (2002) 7 - 9

24389-a

Deuce Roadster 24389 - 58mm - 2000

This 2-seat roadster convertible has a metal chassis, black interior, clear windshield, and sp5. Malaysia.

a. unpainted, #6 in 2000 First Editions, #066 2 - 3

b. mtlfk gold; black int.; red-tinted windshield; red, black & white tampo w/devil's head & flames on sides, flames on hood; sp5gd; Malaysia; #238 (2000) 2 - 3

c. yellow; black int.; tinted windshield; black, orange & red tampo w/flames on sides, Editor's Choice logo on hood; rrch; Thailand. Target excl. Editor's Choice series (2000) 7 - 9

d. purple, red seat, clear windshield, white & red tampo on sides & hood w/skull on sides; sp5; Thailand. #3 in Skull and Crossbones series, #071 (2001) 2 - 3

24389-e

e. white; black int.; clear windshield; red, yellow, black & dk. red tampo w/50th Detroit Autorama emblem on sides; red flame tampo on hood; rrch. Ltd ed for Championship Auto Show (2001) 10 - 15

f. red; white int.; clear windshield; white, yellow, black & dk. red tampo w/50th Detroit Autorama emblem on sides; yellow flame tampo on hood; rrch. Ltd ed for Championship Auto Show (2001) 10 - 15

g. dk. purple; white int.; tinted windshield; red & white flames on sides & hood; sp5; Thailand; #195 (2001) 2 - 3

24389-h

h. mtlc green; red chassis & engine; black int.; clear windshield; yellow & red flame tampo on sides; sp5; Santa sitting in seat pulling toy bag. 2001 Holiday Hot Wheels line (2001) 10 - 15

24389-i

i. lt. blue, clear windshield, orange int., orange & yellow flames on sides & hood, spt. Target exclusive Pop's Garage 4-car set (2002) 6 - NA

24377-T/a

Dodge Charger R/T 24377 - 72mm - 2000

This modern muscle car has a gray plastic chassis and interior, tinted windows, and sp5. Malaysia.

a. dark mtlfk red, #12 in 2000 First Editions, #072 2 - 3

a2. as a, pr5s, #12 in 2000 First Editions, #072 10 - 20

b. dk. yellow; black chassis & int.; green-tinted windows; red, green, black & white tampo w/man & sword on sides & hood, "Unit Two" on side; sp3; Malaysia. #3 in Anime series, #063 (2001) 2 - 3

c. mtlfk purple, black chassis, white int., clear windows, pr5s, Malaysia, #108 (2001) 2 - 3

c2. as c, sp5, #108 (2001) 6 - 12

24377-T/d

d. black; gray chassis & int.; red-tinted windows; red, white & gray tampo on sides & hood; ho5; China. #1 in Trump Card series, #071 (2002) 2 - 3

24393-a

Dodge Power Wagon 24393 - 80mm - 2000

This 1940s style Dodge truck has a gray plastic chassis, black windows & tonneau cover, and dw3ct. Malaysia.

a. mtlfk gray, "Power Wagon" in black on sides. #25 in 2000 First Editions, #085 2 - 3

b. mtlfk black, "Power Wagon" in orange on sides, dw3ct, China, #189 (2001) 2 - 3

24393-c

c. black; black plastic chassis; red-tinted windows; white, gold & blue tampo w/"D.C. Police" on sides & hood, "Group 7" & "Tactical Response" on sides; dw3ct; Thailand. Police Cruisers 5-pack (2001) 2 - NA

24374-a

Ferrari 333 SP 24374 - 72mm - 2000

This convertible race car has a black plastic chassis, spoiler & interior; and lwch. Malaysia.

a. red; yellow, aqua & white tampo w/"17" & race decals on sides & hood. #11 in 2000 First Editions, #071 2 - 3

b. black; yellow int. & spoiler; yellow, orange & white tampo w/flames, "17" & race decals on sides & hood; pr5s; #157 (2001) 2 - 3

23928-a

Ferrari 365 GTB/4 23928 - 73mm - 2000

This Malaysia-made sports car has a metal chassis, clear windows, tan interior, and sp5.

a. red; yellow & black Ferrari logo & Italian flag on hood. #1 in 2000 First Editions, #061 2 - 3

a2. as a, Italian flag is missing. #1 in 2000 First Editions, #061 2 - 3

b. yellow; black int.; black, lt. green & red Ferrari logo on hood; sp5; Malaysia; #236 (2001) 2 - 3

23929-a

Ferrari 550 Maranello 23929 - 70mm - 2000

This Malaysia-made sports car has a metal chassis, clear windows, tan interior, and sp5.

a. red; yellow & black Ferrari logo & Italian flag on hood. #2 in 2000 First Editions, #062 2 - 3

a2. as a, Italian flag is missing, #1 in 2000 First Editions, #062 2 - 3

b. gray, clear windows, red int., sp5, Malaysia, #235 2 - 3

Greased Lightnin' 24399 - 85mm - 2000

This concept model has a metal chassis,

Values are shown in U.S. dollars, first price is for mint, second is for mint packaged vehicles only. See pages 15-16 for grading guide to determine value for cars in lesser conditions.

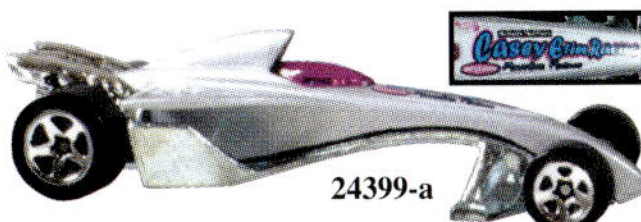
24399-a

chrome tail pipes & interior, clear magenta dome, and pr5s. Malaysia.

a. gray; blue, black & magenta tampo on top. #35 in 2000 First Editions, #095 2 - 3
a2. as a, sp5, #35 in 2000 First Editions, #095 2 - 3
b. black; yellow chassis; yellow-tinted dome; black int.; red, white & black bee on sides; "Buzzbomb" on top; pr5s; Malaysia. #3 in the Rod Squadron series, #067 (2001) 2 - 3
b2. as b, sp5, Malaysia. #3 in Rod Squadron series, #067 (2001) 3 - 5
c. mtlfk orange; tinted dome; blue, black & pink tampo w/"Casey Racing" on front; pr5s; #131 (2001) 2 - 3
c2. as c, sp5, #131 (2001) 5 - 10

24394-a

Hammered Coupe 24394 - 87mm - 2000
This Malaysia-made concept model has a metal chassis; clear windows; black interior, engine and side pipes sticking out the sides; and sp5.

a. mtlfk purple, #33 in 2000 First Editions, #093 2 - 3
b. mtlfk blue, pr5s, #120 (2001) 2 - 3
b2. as b, sp5, #120 (2001) 4 - 10

24394-c

c. gray, black fenders, orange-tinted windows, black & white tampo w/2001 Treasure Hunt logo in back, pr5s, Malaysia. #6 in 2001 Treasure Hunt series, #006 (2001) 10 - 20
d. mtlfk orange; black chassis & int.; tinted windows; green, black, white & red tampo with "Casey Racing" on nose; sp5; #131 (2001) 2 - 3

24394-e

e. mtlfk dark red; black chassis; gold pipes & int.; clear windows; black, orange, yellow & white playing-card tampo on top; "Joker" on trunk; sp5gd; Malaysia. #2 in Trump Cards series, #072 (2002) 2 - 3

24376-a

(Holden) SS Commodore (VT) 24376 - 75mm - 2000
This Australian high-performance sedan has a black plastic chassis, tan interior, black-tinted windows, red rear spoiler, and sp5. Malaysia.

a. gray; orange, red & dark blue tampo w/"12" & race decals on sides. #21 in 2000 First Editions, #081 2 - 3
b. yellow; blue spoiler & int.; blue-tinted windows; orange, black & white tampo w/"12," "Oz Some" & race decals on sides; pr5s; China; #143 (2001) 2 - 3
c. white; blue spoiler; black int.; blue-tinted windows; black, dk. blue & red tampo w/"5," "BRG" & race decals on sides; lwch; Malaysia. Victory Lane 5-pack (2001) 2 - NA

24376-d

d. mtlfk blue; black windows; yellow, orange, black, gray & white flame tampo w/"Hot Wheels" on sides, wing & windshield; "Racing" & Hot Wheels logo on hood; logo on roof; sp5; Australia; in box (2001) 10 - 15

24376-e

e. yellow; black windows; blue, orange, black, gray & white tampo w/"Hot Wheels" on sides, wing & windshield; "100%" & Hot Wheels logo on hood; logo on roof; pr5; Australia; in box (2001) 10 - 15
f. green; black chassis & int.; clear windows; black & white tampo w/"Hockey" on sides, goalie's mask on hood; lwch; Thailand. Sports 5-pack (2002) 2 - NA

27110-a

Ice Cream Truck 27110 - 68mm - 2000
This Malaysia-made truck has a black plastic chassis, clear windows, red interior with plastic figure in window, and ho5.
Similar casting: #5904 Good Humor Truck (1984)

a. tan; red, white & dk. blue tampo w/clown & "I Scream" on sides; Malaysia. Virtual Collection, #144 2 - 3
a2. as a, sp3, Virtual Collection, #144 2 - 3
b. white, red int., red & black tampo w/clown & "I Scream" on sides, Malaysia. Virtual Collection, #144 2 - 3
d. white; black plastic chassis; clear windows; black int.; red & black tampo w/clown, ice cream cone & stars on sides; stars & Hot Wheels logo in back; #136 (2001) 2 - 3
e. orange; black chassis; white int.; tinted windows; black, yellow & white tampo w/"Come'n Git It," "Rollin' Round-Up Rodeo Grill" & "Dave "Saucy" Sanders on Board" on sides; sp5gd; Malaysia; #57 (2001) 2 - 3

24388-a

Lotus Elise 340R 24388 - 64mm - 2000
This English sports utility convertible has a metal chassis, clear windshield, gray interior, black seats & spoiler, and pr5s. Malaysia.

a. mtlfk gray, green & white hood tampo. #15 in 2000 First Editions, #075 2 - 3
a2. as a, mtlfk gray chassis, #15 in 2000 First Editions, #075 20 - 30
b. red; tinted windshield; black spoiler, sides & seats; gray int.; pr5s; #128 (2001) 2 - 3
b2. as b, mtlfk gray chassis, China, #128 (2001) 2 - 3

24384-a

Metrorail 24384 - 78mm - 2000
This Nash Metropolitan dragster has a chrome plastic chassis, interior, side pipes and engine sticking through the hood; tinted windows; and sp5. Malaysia.

a. turquoise, white on bottom, "Metrorail" in dk. red on sides. #23 in 2000 First Editions, #083 2 - 3
a2. as a, large front wheels, #23 in 2000 First Editions, #083 2 - 3
b. white, orange-tinted windows, orange and black flame tampo w/large Hot Wheels logos on sides & hood, sp5. #4 in Loco Motive series, #076 (2001) 2 - 3
c. red, white on bottom of sides, magenta-tinted windows, "Metrorail" in black on sides, sp5, #160 (2001) 2 - 3

24386-a

Mini Cooper 24386 - 56mm - 2000
This Malaysia-made English two-door sedan has a metal base, blue-tinted windows, blue interior, gray and blue hood scoop, and lwch.

a. yellow; black & white checkerboard tampo on roof. #30 in 2000 First Editions, #090 2 - 3
b. mtlfk dk. blue, black int., orange-tinted windows, black & white checkerboard tampo on roof, lwch, #158 (2001) 2 - 3
b2. as b, ho5, #158 (2001) 3 - 8
c. orange, gray int., tinted windows, black and white checkerboard tampo on roof, lwch. Power Launcher pack (2001) 5 - NA

24386-d

d. black; orange int.; clear windows, white, orange & gray tampo with Hot Wheels logo, Treasure Hunt logo & flames on sides; "20" & flames on roof; rrch with red stripe; Malaysia. #11 in 2002 Treasure Hunt series, #011 (2002) 20 - 30

24390-a

Muscle Tone 24390 - 70mm - 2000
This concept model has a gray plastic base, blue interior, tinted windows, and sp5. Malaysia.

a. mtlfk orange, black stripe on sides & over hood. #24 in 2000 First Editions #084 2 - 3
a2. as a, pr5s, #24 in 2000 First Editions, #084 2 - 3
a3. as a, black int., #24 in 2000 First Editions, #084 3 - 6

24390-b

b. chrome; black int.; tinted windows; white, black, blue & lt. green tampo w/"TF1" & "Toy Fair MM 1" on sides & hood, "Toy Fair MM 1" on windshield, "TF1" on trunk; pr5. 2001 Toy Fair (2001) 100 - 150
c. black, red int., clear windows, red stripe on sides & hood, pr5s, Malaysia, #118 (2001) 2 - 3
c2. as c, sp5, Malaysia, #118 (2001) 3 - 5
d. mtlfk green; white int.; yellow-tinted windows; black, gray & brown tampo w/"E Unit Four" on sides & hood; dw3; Malaysia. #1 in Anime series, #061 (2001) 2 - 3
e. mtlfk black, gray chassis & int., tinted windows, yellow stripe on sides & hood, pr5s, Malaysia. Power Launcher pack (2001) 3 - NA

24390-f

f. red; white int.; orange-tinted windows; black, white & gray tampo w/"3," "Street" & race decals on sides & hood; dw3. Avon excl. Super Tuners 3-pack (2001) 6 - NA

24390-g

g. spectraflame gold; white int.; tinted windows; "Muscle Tone" in white on windshield; green, black & white Spectraflame II emblem on trunk; pr5gd. #4 in Spectraflame II series, #088 (2002) 2 - 3

24375-a

MX48 Turbo 24375 - 70mm - 2000
This convertible sports car has a metal metalflake gray chassis, gray interior, blue-tinted windshield, and pr5s wheels.

a. blue; mtlfk gray chassis; gray int.; green-tinted windshield; green, black & brown hood tampo. #20 in 2000 First Editions, #080 2 - 3
a2. as a, sp5, #20 in 2000 First Editions, #080 5 - 10
b. mtlfk purple w/red tint, same as a, #20 in 2000 First Editions, #080 20 - 40
c. mtlfk gray, black chassis, tinted windshield, black int., black & lt. green logo on hood, sp3, #132 (2001) 2 - 3

24375-d

d. dk. yellow, red chassis, black int., green-tinted windshield, black & orange tampo w/"Chuck E. Cheese's" on sides, Chuck E. Cheese sticker on hood, pr5s (2001) 10 - 15
e. mtlfk gray; black int.; yellow-tinted windshield; black, red, orange & white tampo on sides & hood, "Hipno Ride" on hood; sp3. #1 in Extreme Sports series, #081 (2001) 2 - 3

24375-f

f. yellow; black chassis & int.; clear windshield; white, red & magenta tampo w/"Happy Birthday" on sides; dw; China. Birthday Cake 5-pack (2001) 3 - NA
g. white; mtlfk blue chassis; black int.; blue-tinted windshield; black, blue & lt. green tampo w/"Blueye Racing" on sides & hood, "6" on hood; sp3. Avon excl. Super Tuners 3-pack (2001) 6 - NA

Values are shown in U.S. dollars, first price is for mint, second is for mint packaged vehicles only. See pages 15-16 for grading guide to determine value for cars in lesser conditions.

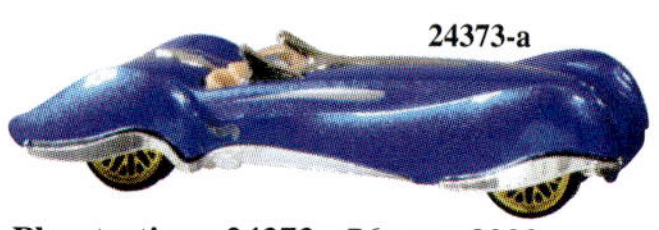
24373-a

Phantastique 24373 - 76mm - 2000
This futuristic concept car has a plastic chassis, tan interior, clear windshield with chrome on the sides of the windows, and lwgd. Malaysia.

a. mtlfk blue, gray tampo on sides, #9 in 2000 First Editions #069 2 - 3
b. mtlfk dk. red, same as a, China, #245 (2001) 2 - 3
c. red, tinted windshield, black int., black & white Hot Wheels logo on sides & hood, lwch. #1 in Loco-Motive series, #073 (2001) 2 - 3

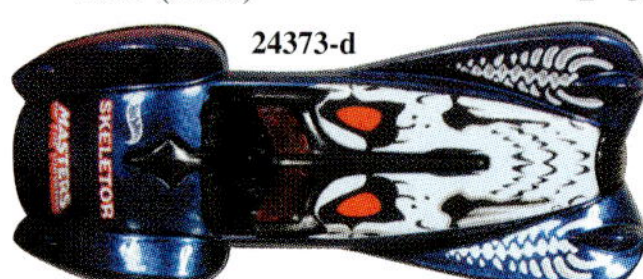
24373-d

d. mtlfk dark blue, black chassis & int., red-tinted windshield, white & red tampo on hood & trunk w/"Skeletor" & "Masters of the Universe" on trunk, dw3. China. #4 in He-Man series, #094 (2002) 2 - 3

24368-a

Pro Stock Firebird 24368 - 86mm - 2000
This drag racer has a metal base, white interior, tinted windows, an orange snorkel on the hood, and sp5. Malaysia.

a. yellow; white, magenta, red & black tampo w/"Kaboom" & race decals on sides & hood. #4 in 2000 First Editions, #064 2 - 3
b. black, same as a, #4 in 2000 First Editions, #064 2 - 3
c. white, mtlfk gray chassis, clear windows, black int., red spoiler, red & black tampo w/"Proch Racing" & race decals on sides, design on hood, pr5s, China, #099 (2001) 2 - 3
d. black, mtlfk gray chassis, tinted windows, white int., gray scoop, pink & silver tampo design on sides & hood, pr5s. China. #4 in Skin Deep series, #096 (2001) 2 - 3

24387-a

Roll Cage 24387 - 80mm - 2000
This Malaysia-made off-road vehicle has a metal chassis, black interior, chrome rear engine, wheel on top of the trunk, and dw3ct.

a. yellow, #31 in 2000 First Editions, #091 2 - 3
b. red, same as a, #127 (2001) 2 - 3

24387-c

c. orange; white chassis; gold chrome engine; black & gold chrome int.; red, black & white Treasure Hunt logo on sides & hood; rrctch. #2 in 2001 Treasure Hunt series, #002 (2001) 16 - 20
d. red, mtlfk gray chassis, black int., yellow & red tampo w/Hot Wheels logo on sides, dw3ct. Crash Canyon track set only 6 - NA
e. blue; mtlfk gray chassis; red int.; red, white & black tampo w/"1" & "Team Interactive" on sides; blue dwct. Stunt Track Driver CD-ROM only (2001) 15 - NA

24396-a

Sho-Stopper (Seared Tuner) 24396 - 70mm - 2000
This concept car has a gray plastic base, rear spoiler, blacked-out windows, and sp3. Malaysia.

a. dk. yellow; red, black & white tampo on sides & hood. #27 in 2000 First Editions, #087 2 - 3
a2. as a, pr5s, #27 in 2000 First Editions, #087 2 - 3

24396-b

b. mtlfk gold; chrome base; black int.; clear windows; red, yellow & lt. blue flame tampo on sides; large Hot Wheels logo on hood. Ltd ed for Washington Auto Show, (2001) 10 - 15
c. black, same as b. Ltd ed for Washington Auto Show (2001) 10 - 15
d. red, clear windows, black int., black stripe on sides, yellow stripe on right side of front fender, black & white diamond design on hood, pr5s, China, #119 (2001) 2 - 3
d2. as d, Malaysia, #119 (2001) 2 - 3
d3. as d, front fender stripe is gray. Power Launcher pack (2001) 3 - NA

24396-e

e. white; red int.; red-tinted windows; red, black, yellow & gray tampo w/"Chuck E. Cheese's" on sides, Chuck E. Cheese's face on hood; Malaysia. Chuck E. Cheese's premium only (2001) 10 - 15
f. pearl gray, black windows, red & black tampo on sides, sp3. Spinnin' Rim Track Set (2001) 6 - NA
g. red; black chassis & int.; clear windows; yellow, gray & black tampo w/"Message Madness" & Planet Hot Wheels logo on sides; sp3; Thailand. City Service 5-pack (2001) 2 - NA

24396-h

h. black; black int.; clear windows; gold & white tampo w/"5" & race decals on sides, "5" on hood; sp3. Avon excl. Super Tuners 3-pack (2001) 6 - NA

24396-i

i. red; black chassis & int.; yellow-tinted windows; yellow, black & blue tampo w/"Time Wizard" on sides; ho5gd; Malaysia. #2 in Yu-Gi-Ho series, #084 (2002) 2 - 3

24395-a

Shoe Box 24395 - 80mm - 2000
This Malaysia-made '49 Ford has a black plastic chassis, chrome interior & engine sticking thru the hood, magenta windows, and lwch.

a. yellow; red & magenta flame tampo. #26 in 2000 First Editions, #086 3 - 6
a2. as a, pr5s, #26 in 2000 First Editions, #086 2 - 3
b. white; black int.; tinted windows; orange & black flame tampo on sides, roof & hood; sp5. Target excl. Drive-In Jailhouse Rock or Blue Hawaii 4-car set 6 - NA
c. lt. purple; chrome int.; blue-tinted windows; black, red & white tampo w/pinstripes, pair of dice & "Lucky Nines" on sides; ww. #4 in Rat Rods series, #60 (2001) 2 - 3

24395-d

d. red, clear windows, white int., white front & roof, white & silver flame logo on sides, gold & red flame logo on hood & roof, Editor's Choice logo on trunk, rrch w/ww, Thailand. Target excl. Editor's Choice series (2001) 9 - 12
e. pearl white, black chassis, tinted windows, chrome int., red & purple flame tampo on sides, pr5s, Malaysia, #117 (2001) 2 - 3
e2. as e, sp5, Malaysia, #117 (2001) 8 - 12

24395-f

f. yellow; white roof; clear windows; chrome int.; gold, black & white tampo w/"Times Square Taxi" & "No. 6" on sides & roof, "First Mile Free" on roof; rrch w/white stripe; Malaysia. Toys "R" Us grand opening in New York's Times Square only (2001) 10 - 15
g. blue, same as e. Toys "R" Us grand opening in New York's Times Square only (2001) 10 - 15

24395-h

h. blue, black int., clear windows, yellow & red flame spray mask in front, JC Whitney logo in white on sides, gych. Ltd ed for JC Whitney, in box (2001) 10 - 15

24395-i

i. red, same as h. Ltd ed for JC Whitney, in box (2001) 10 - 15
j. dk. yellow, black chassis, chrome int., tinted windows, red & black flame tampo on sides, pr5s, Malaysia. Power Launcher pack (2001) 3 - NA
k. orange, same as h, green added to flame tampo, pr5s. Detail Center set (2001) 4 - NA
l. mtlfk purple; black chassis; chrome int.; clear windows; yellow, orange & lt. blue flame tampo on sides, hood & roof; lwch; Malaysia. Sam's Club 20-pack only, in blister (2001) 10 - 15

24395-l

m. red, tan int., clear windows, purple & silver tampo on top, sp3, in set (2001) 6 - NA
n. flat black; black chassis; chrome int.; clear windows; yellow, lt. green & gray tampo w/flames & spider webs on sides; spider web & "Ghost Rider" on hood; sp5; Malaysia; #180 (2002) 2 - 3

24395-l

o. pastel green, white int., clear windows, white tampo on sides, rrch. Rod & Custom series from the Preferred Line (2002) 7 - 9

24400-a

So Fine 24400 - 87mm - 2000
This '51 Buick has a plastic chassis, clear windows, red interior, and lwch. Malaysia.

a. black, silver stripe on sides. #18 in 2000 First Editions, #078 2 - 3

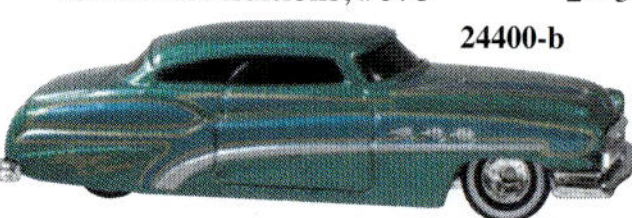
24400-b

b. mtlfk green, black-tinted windows, tan int., white & gold striping tampo on sides & hood w/"Lil Green Dream" on sides, 2001 Treasure Hunt logo on trunk, rrch w/ww, Malaysia. #3 in 2001 Treasure Hunt series, #003 (2001) 20 - 30

24400-c

c. mtlfk blue; white roof & int.; clear windows; silver tampo on sides, hood & trunk; Nationals logo in red, black & gray on roof; rrch w/ww. Ltd to 4000 for First Annual Nationals (2001) 30 - 40
d. mtlfk green, clear windows, white int., gray stripe on sides, lwch, #168 (2001) 2 - 3
d2. as d, sp5, #168 (2001) 3 - 5
e. pearl blue; white roof & int.; clear windows; white & gray tampo on sides, hood & trunk; lwch. Target excl. Elvis Drive-In 4-pack (2001) 6 - NA

24400-f

f. turquoise, clear windows, white int., black & white tampo on sides & hood w/"Three Lane King" on sides, sp5. #2 in Spares 'n Strikes series, #060 (2002) 2 - 3

27246-a

Suburban 27246 - 84mm - 2000
This model has a chrome plastic chassis, tan interior, tinted windows, and rrch. China.

a. red; black & white tampo w/"Walker Racing" & "#5" on sides & hood. Ltd ed of 15,000 10 - 15
b. blue; white int.; clear windows; multicolored tampo w/"55," "Oakwood Homes," "Cooper Lighting" & race

decals on sides, "D" in square on hood, "55" & "Square D" on roof & in back; sp5; Thailand. #1 in NASCAR Suburban series (2000) 7 - 9

27246-c

c. red; same as b; tinted windows; multi-colored tampo w/"5," "Kellogg's," Tony the Tiger & race decals on sides, "Kellogg's" on hood, "5" & "Advance Auto Parts" on roof, "Kellogg's" in back; sp5; Thailand. #2 in NASCAR Suburban series (2000) 7 - 9

d. black; same as b; yellow, gray & red tampo w/"40," "Marlin" & race decals on sides, "Sterling Marlin" on hood, "40" & "Sabco" on roof, "Marlin" & "40" in back; sp5; Thailand. #3 in NASCAR Suburban series (2000) 7 - 9

e. black; same as b; white, red & yellow tampo w/"60," "Power Team" & race decals on sides, "Power Team" & "Peco Energy" on hood, "Exelon" on roof, "Peco Energy no Doubt about it" in back; sp5; Thailand. #4 in NASCAR Suburban series (2000) 7 - 9

24378-a

Surf Crate 24378 - 76mm - 2000

This concept race car looks like a flattened woody and has a metal chassis, exposed engine & pipes, metal interior, removable surfboard sticking out the back, and sp5. It was first seen as a one-of-a-kind 1/18th scale model auctioned for charity at the 1998 convention. Malaysia.

a. purple, lt. brown & red-brown sides, red surfboard in back. #13 in 2000 First Editions, #073 2 - 3

a2. as a, dark purple, #13 in 2000 First Editions, #073 3 - 6

a3. as a, no surfboard, Pep Boys 2-pack (2000) 3 - NA

24378-b

b. brown, black roof, red surfboard, red & white tampo w/Jiffy Lube logo & "Does your car get it" on roof, sp5. Jiffy Lube giveaway 10 - 15

c. mtlfk gold, tan & red-brown sides, orange surfboard in back, sp5, no country on base, #107 2 - 3

d. black; black int.; orange surfboard; yellow, orange & lt. green flame tampo on sides & roof; sp5. Hot Haulers 4 pack, (2001) 6 - NA

24378-e

e. mtlfk dr. red; black int.; no surfboard; black, gold & white tampo on roof; sp5. In 2-pk. by K•B stores (2001) 9 - NA

f. unpainted, same as e, no tampo. In 2-pk. by K•B stores (2001) 9 - NA

g. mtlfk gray; black int.; black, orange & white tampo on sides & roof; sp5; Thailand; #151 (2001) 2 - 3

24378-h

h. mtlc red, chrome engine, white int., clear windows, gold surfboard, white & lt. blue tampo on sides & roof, sp5. Surf in the 2001 Holiday Hot Wheels line, plastic display box (2001) 15 - NA

24378-i

i. red; gold chassis; gold chrome engine & pipes; black int.; white surfboard; yellow, white & black tampo w/"Curly" on sides, a face & flames on roof; sp5gd; #126 (2002) 2 - 3

j. chrome; chrome engine & pipes; black int.; chrome surfboard; black, white & red tampo design on sides & roof; rrch w/red stripe. Ltd ed for hotwheels.com (2002) 25 - 35

24367-a

Thomassima III - 24367 - 76mm - 2000

This concept sports car has a chrome chassis, black & chrome interior, clear windows, sp5. Malaysia.

a. dark mtlfk red, #10 in 2000 First Editions, #070 2 - 3

a2. as a, lwch, #070, #10 in 2000 First Editions, #070 2 - 3

a3. as a, pr5s, #070, #10 in 2000 First Editions, #070 3 - 10

b. mtlfk blue, clear windows, black int., "Thomassima" in white on sides, pr5s, China, #098 (2001) 2 - 3

c. aqua, black int., clear windows, "Thomassima 3" in gray on sides, pr5s, China, #159 (2002) 2 - 3

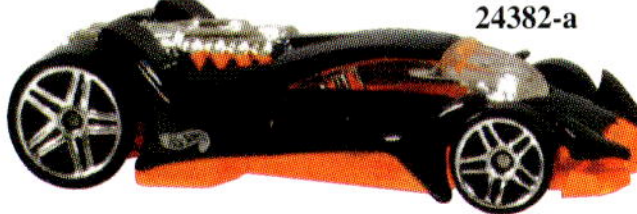
24382-a

Vulture 24382 - 67mm - 2000

This concept car has an orange-tinted chassis, chrome interior & rear engine, clear windows, pr5s. Malaysia

a. black, "Vulture" in orange on windows. #29 in 2000 First Editions, #089 2 - 3

a2. as a, sp5, #29 in 2000 First Editions, #089 2 - 3

24382-b

b. white; red-tinted windows; black & red tampo w/"Vulture" on sides & top, "Treasure Hunt 2001" on hood; pr5s. #7 in 2001 Treasure Hunt series, #007 (2001) 10 - 15

c. mtlfk blue, clear green chassis & dome, chrome int., sp5, China, #138 (2001) 2 - 3

24382-d

d. mtlfk blue; same as c; gray & black tampo w/"Vulture" on dome, "THQ" on top; sp5; Malaysia; w/CD-ROM (2001) 7 - 9

24382-e

e. gray, yellow-tinted plastic chassis & int., clear windows, yellow & black tampo on sides & top w/"Vulture" on roof, pr5s. Costco 20-pack, in bp (2001) 10 - 15

f. mtlfk gray, orange-tinted chassis & windows, chrome int., pr5s, Malaysia, Fireball 5-pack (2001) 3 - NA

h. mtlfk orange; black chassis; chrome int.; purple windows; purple, black, orange & white tampo w/"Particle" on sides & windshield; CD-ROM logo on front; pr5s; Thailand; with CD-ROM disc. #4 in CD-ROM series (2002) 7 - 9

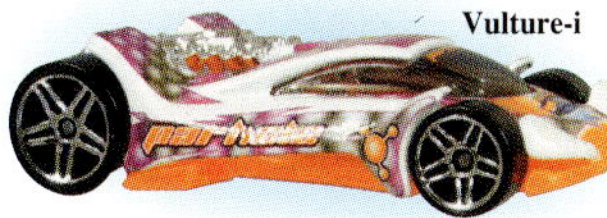
Vulture-i

i. white; clear orange chassis; chrome int.; tinted windshield; purple, orange & black w/"Particle" on sides & windshield; CD-ROM logo on front; pr5s; Thailand. With pencil box & CD-ROM disc in CD-ROM series (2002) 7 - 9

2001

Just over 450 new basic cars were issued (not counting variations). Included were 40 2001 First Editions, 12 Treasure Hunt cars, and 12 sets of four-segment cars as part of the 240 number packs for this year. Five-packs and set cars were continued as well as limited editions, although not as many limiteds as in recent years. K•B, Wal-Mart, Target and Kmart all had their exclusive series and cars.

28768-a

'57 Roadster 28768 - 80mm - 2001

This 1957-style roadster has a metal chassis, chrome plastic engine sticking through the hood, tan interior, tinted windshield, sp5 in back, mw in front. Malaysia

a. red, gray tampo on sides, #32 in 2001 First Editions, #052 2 - 3

a2. as a, small sp5 in front, #32 in 2001 First Editions, #052 2 - 3

28751-a

('71) 1971 Plymouth GTX 28751 - 82mm - 2001

This model has a chrome plastic chassis, black interior, blue-tinted windows, and sp5. Malaysia.

a. green, black hood scoop, #14 in 2001 First Editions, #026 2 - 3

28751-b

b. mtlfk blue; black roof & int.; clear windows; white, orange & black tampo w/"GTX" & "440" on sides, "440" on hood, Treasure Hunt logo on trunk; rrch. #2 in 2002 Treasure Hunt series, #002 (2002) 20 - 25

c. yellow, black int., tinted windows, black tampo on roof, sp5, China, #116 (2002) 2 - 3

28751-d

d. red, black roof & int., tinted windows, black hood scoop w/"440" in white, rrch. Target exclusive Pop's Garage 4-car set (2002) 6 - NA

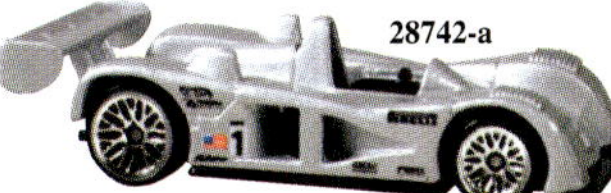
28742-a

Cadillac LMP 28742 - 70mm - 2001

This Malaysia-made race car has a black plastic chassis, wing in back, black interior, and lwch.

a. gray; red, black & blue race decals on sides, "Cadillac Toshiba" & logo on front. #1 in 2001 First Editions, #013 2 - 3

b. black, lt. brown chassis & int., mtlfk gold wing, gold flame tampo, lwgd, #208 2 - 3

28746-a

Cunningham CAR 28746 - 67mm - 2001

This 1950s English sports car has a black plastic chassis & interior, clear windshield, and sp5. Malaysia.

a. white, two blue stripes over top, #31 in 2001 First Editions, #051 2 - 3

b. mtlfk blue, same as a, two white stripes over top, sp5, #156 (2002) 2 - 3

28743-a

Dodge Viper GTS-R 28743 - 70mm - 2001

This model has a black plastic chassis & interior, rear spoiler, clear windows, and sp5. Malaysia.

a. red; gray & black tampo on hood & roof. #11 in 2001 First Editions, #023 2 - 3

28747-a

Evil Twin 28747 - 82mm - 2001

This luxury car has a black plastic chassis with chrome pipes, clear windows, tan interior, two chrome engines sticking through the hood, lwch. Malaysia.

a. mtlfk purple, #16 in 2001 First Editions, #028 2 - 3

b. mtlfk gold, black chassis, white int., tinted windows, lwgd, #123 (2002) 2 - 3

c. yellow, same as b, #123 (2002) 6 - 12

d. mtlfk lt. green; black top & int.; tinted windows; black, lt. green & gold flame tampo on sides & roof; rrchrl. Limited to 10,000, HotWheelsCollectors.com (2002) 20 - 35

Evil Twin-e

e. pearl white; red int.; clear windows; yellow, red & blue tampo on sides; pc. Target excl. Originals (2001) 9 - 12

28756-a

Fandango 28756 - 68mm - 2001

This concept panel truck has a gray plastic chassis, black interior, orange-tinted windows, and pr5s. Malaysia.

a. orange; lt. green, black & white tampo w/"Fandango" on sides. #36 in 2001 First Editions, #048 2 - 3

28756-b

b. black; black chassis; orange int.; clear windows; gray, orange & red tampo

Values are shown in U.S. dollars, first price is for mint, second is for mint packaged vehicles only. See pages 15-16 for grading guide to determine value for cars in lesser conditions.

w/"Auto Zone" on sides; pr5s. Auto Zone Stores only, 2-pack (2001) 3 - NA

c. red; black chassis; gray int.; clear windows; black, white, gray & orange tampo w/Hot Wheels logo on sides; pr5s. On blistercard in 3-pack w/2002 Hot Wheels blue book (2002) 3 - NA

d. yellow; black chassis & int.; black tinted windows; black, orange & silver tampo on sides; pr5gd; Malaysia; #158 (2002) 2 - 3

28756-e

e. blue; black int.; green-tinted windows; gold, white, orange & black tampo with "Yu-Gi-Oh!" on sides; sp5mg; Malaysia. #3 in Yu-Gi-Oh! series, #085 (2002) 2 - 3

28762-a

Ferrari 156 28762 - 62mm - 2001
This old Ferrari Indy-style race car has a metal chassis, tail pipes & interior; clear windshield; gray plastic roll bar; and lwch.

a. red, "2" in white on sides, #30 in 2001 First Editions, #050 2 - 3

b. red; same as a; white, yellow & black tampo w/"36" on sides & nose; Ferrari logo on nose; lwch; #141 (2002) 2 - 3

28770-a

Ford Focus 28770 - 78mm - 2001
This Malaysia-made Ford drag car has a black plastic chassis, large black rear wing, clear windows, black interior, and ho5.

a. black; yellow, red & blue tampo w/"Meguiar's" on sides, hood & roof; race decals on sides & hood; ho5. #25 in 2001 First Editions, #037 2 - 3

28770-b

b. white, red rear wing & int., clear windows, red & black tampo w/"Yokohama Elbach Springs" & race decals on sides & hood, lwch. Malaysia. #1 in Tuners series, #063 (2002) 2 - 3

28769-a

Ford Thunderbolt 28769 - 75mm - 2001
This Malaysia-made model has a chrome plastic chassis, red interior, tinted windows, and sp5.

a. black; red & white tampo w/"Thunderbird," "Robert Ford" & other names on sides. #34 in 2001 First Editions, #046 2 - 3

b. mtlfk dk. red; white int.; tinted windows; white tampo w/"Thunderbolt," "Robert Ford" & other names on sides; sp3; Malaysia; #142 (2002) 2 - 3

b2. as b, sp5, Malaysia, #142 (2002) 2 - 3

c. mtlfk silver; black hood; white int.; blue-tinted windows; black, white & lt. blue tampo w/"Heralda Racing" on

28769-c

sides, Hot Wheels logo & Treasure Hunt logo on trunk; rrch; Malaysia. #5 in 2002 Treasure Hunt series, #005 (2002) 18 - 25

28767-a

Fright Bike 28767 - 80mm - 2001
This motorcycle has a metal chassis and engine, black cowling, comes on a gray plastic stand. Malaysia

a. clear purple, #21 in 2001 First Editions, #033 2 - 3

b. clear red, same as a, #133 (2002) 2 - 3

28758-a

Honda Civic Si 28758 - 78mm - 2001
This model has a black plastic chassis, rear spoiler, white interior, tinted windows, and pr5s. Malaysia.

a. red; black & white tampo w/"Hot Wheels" & "Honda" on sides, "Hot Wheels" on hood. #15 in 2001 First Editions, #027 2 - 3

a2. as a, lwch, #15 in 2001 First Editions, #027 2 - 8

28758-b

b. mtlfk gray; clear windows; white int.; blue, red & white tampo w/Blue Jays' logo on sides, 25th Season logo on hood. Toronto Blue Jays baseball team for 25th Season, (2001) 15 - 20

28758-c

c. mtlfk blue, black chassis & int., clear windows, yellow tampo w/race decals on sides & hood, sp3. #2 in Tunerz series, #064 (2002) 2 - 3

d. black, black chassis, white int., green-tinted windows, yellow & green tampo w/"Hot Wheels" on sides & hood, ho5, #115 (2002) 2 - 3

28758-e

e. white; chrome chassis; blue int.; clear windows; dk. blue & red tampo w/"Fantastic Sams" on sides, "Gotta Be The Hair!" on hood; sp3. Sold at Fantastic Sams salons (2002) 15 - 20

28758-f

f. purple; black hood & int.; tinted windows; yellow & dk. red tampo w/race decals on sides, "H" on hood, "Team Speed" on windshield, "Wings West" on wing; pr5s. Target exclusive Pop's Garage 4-car set (2002) 6 - NA

28740-a

Hooligan 28740 - 60mm - 2001
This roadster truck has a metal base, black fenders, red interior & grill, no windows, red and chrome exposed engine under the hood, and sp5. Malaysia.

a. black; dark red & gold flame tampo on sides. #6 in 2001 First Editions, #018 2 - 3

a2. as a, red engine w/chrome intake. #6 in 2001 First Editions, #018 12 - 25

b. dark mtlfk purple, mtlfk gray chassis, red int., red & gold flames on sides, sp5, China, #203 (2001) 2 - 3

28740-c

c. brown; black int., fenders & running board; black, white, red & gold tampo w/rat, Hot Wheels logo & "Lucky Rat" on sides; rrchww. Target exclusive Pop's Garage 4-car set (2002) 6 - NA

28757-a

Hyper Mite 28757 - 40mm - 2001
This Malaysia-made concept vehicle is tall and short with a black plastic chassis, metal engine in back with two exhaust pipes on top, magenta dome, mw in front and sp5 in back.

a. lt. green; white, red & magenta tampo w/"2" on sides. #17 in 2001 First Editions, #029 2 - 4

a2. as a, blue replaces magenta in tampo. #17 in 2001 First Editions, #029 2 - 3

b. mtlfk purple, black chassis, gold chrome engine, red-tinted dome, dk. red & orange tampo w/"2" on sides, sp5gd, #125 (2002) 2 - 3

b2. as b, Thailand, #125 (2002) 2 - 3

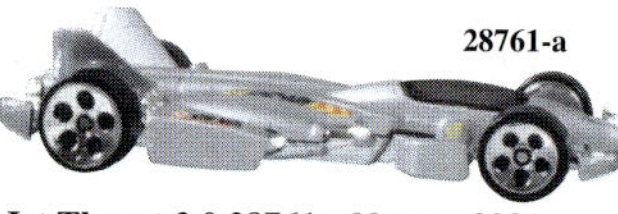
28761-a

Jet Threat 3.0 28761 - 80mm - 2001
This concept race car has a gray plastic chassis, chrome interior, tinted dome, and ho5. Malaysia.

a. gray; black, white, yellow & red tampo w/"Step Back" & "OC-121" on top. #22 in 2001 First Editions, #034 2 - 3

a2. as a, mtlfk gray chassis, #22 in 2001 First Editions, #034 3 - 6

28761-b

b. black; yellow chassis; chrome int.; yellow-tinted dome; yellow, red & white tampo on sides & top w/"Jetz," "Hydraulic Fin Engine" & "Caution" on top; lwch. Jetz CD-ROM pack only (2001) 15 - NA

c. lt. blue, gray body & chassis, chrome int., tinted dome, orange & black tampo on top, ho5, Thailand, #149 (2002) 2 - 3

28761-d

d. mtlc lt. blue, metal int., yellow-tinted dome, gray & black tampo w/"Spectraflame II" on top, lwch, Malaysia. #3 in Spectraflame II series, #089 (2002) 2 - 3

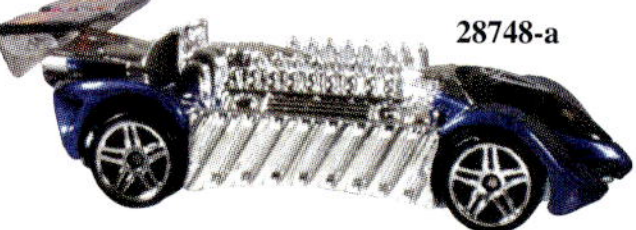
28748-a

Krazy 8s 28748 - 85mm - 2001
This race car-style model has a metal engine with eight carburetors on each side; metal chassis, spoiler and interior; tinted dome; and pr5s. Malaysia.

a. dk. blue; gray design on dome; "Krazy 8s" in yellow, black & orange on spoiler. #7 in 2001 First Editions, #019 2 - 3

b. lt. yellow-green, clear green dome & spoiler; red and black tampo on all 4 fenders and pr5s, #179 2 - 3

b2. as b, no dome, Fireball 5-pack 3 - NA

c. black; black metal chassis; gold chrome engine, pipes & int.; yellow-tinted dome & spoiler; pr5gd; China; #211 (2001) 2 - 3

d. orange; chrome int.; tinted wing & dome; yellow, orange & black honeycomb tampo on dome & wing; pr5s. Hot Wheels Starter Set, in baggie 9 - NA

28741-a

La Troca ('50 Chevy Pickup) 28741 - 84mm - 2001
This Malaysia-made truck has a gold chrome plastic chassis & grill, black windows, and lwgd.

a. mtlfk dk. red, gold tampo on overhang. #3 in 2001 First Editions, #015 2 - 3

a2. as a, Hot Wheels logo embossed in back. #3 in 2001 First Editions, #015 2 - 3

b. green; chrome chassis; white spray mask w/white, gold & black flames on sides & hood; Editor's Choice logo on roof; rrch; Thailand. Target excl. Editor's Choice series (2001) 10 - 12

c. lilac primer, chrome chassis, black windows, lwch, China, #202 2 - 3

28741-d

d. yellow; gold chassis; black windows; white, black & gold tampo on sides, hood & roof w/Treasure Hunt logo on sides, "La Troca" on roof; rrch; Malaysia. #1 in 2002 Treasure Hunt series, #001 (2002) 15 - 25

28753-a

Lotus (Project) M250 28753 - 70mm - 2001
This model has a black plastic chassis, red interior, black-tinted windows, and sp5. Malaysia.

Values are shown in U.S. dollars, first price is for mint, second is for mint packaged vehicles only. See pages 15-16 for grading guide to determine value for cars in lesser conditions.

a. gray; green & white hood tampo; #13 in 2001 First Editions #025 3 - 6

b. yellow, gray int., tinted windows, pr5s, China, #231 2 - 3

b2. as b, "Lotus" in back highlighted in gray, China, #231 2 - 3

c. mtlfk dk. red; black chassis; gray int.; black-tinted windows; gold, black & white Treasure Hunt tampo on roof; rrch w/red stripe. #4 in 2002 Treasure Hunt series, #004 (2002) 15 - 20

Maelstrom 28754 - 72mm - 2001

This Malaysia-made model has a chrome plastic chassis, twin tailpipes & two exposed engines, black-tinted windows, and sp3.

a. blue; red & gray tampo on sides; #12 in 2001 First Editions; #024 2 - 3

b. fluor. lime yellow, black chassis & windows, chrome engine & pipes, orange & black flame tampo on sides, ho5, #233 2 - 3

c. red, chrome chassis & int., tinted windows, black & silver tampo on sides & roof, sp3. Metro City Police Force set 5 - NA

d. black, same as c, silver & red tampo colors, sp3. Pavement Pounders set 4 - NA

e. red, white & blue; chrome int.; blue-tinted windows; white & gray tampo w/"Toyfair 2000" on sides; "Toyfair" in red, white & blue on windshield; pr5s, 2002 Toy Fair, in plastic box (2001) 75 - 100

f. white, chrome int., blue-tinted windows, red & silver tampo on sides & front, sp3. Crash Curve playset (2001) 5 - NA

Mega-Duty 52715 - 66mm - 2001

This heavy-duty pickup truck has a metal chassis, black plastic trim all around the bottom of the body, black truck bed & interior, orange-tinted windows & headlights, and large pr5s. Malaysia.

a. gray; black & orange tampo on hood. #26 in 2001 First Editions, #038 2 - 3

b. orange; black fenders, truck bed & int.; black windows; black & white tampo on hood; pr5s; Malaysia; #150 (2002) 2 - 3

Mo' Scoot 28766 - 66mm - 2001

This Malaysia-made scooter has a metal base, shaft & handlebars; gray plastic motor & pipes; and special lime-tinted wheels.

a. orange-tinted plastic, #33 in 2001 First Editions, #045 2 - 3

b. clear blue plastic; white, gray & black tampo w/Hot Wheels logo on top;

orange wheels; Malaysia; #157 (2002) 2 - 3

28764-a

Monoposto 28764 - 66mm - 2001

This concept race car has the driver's seat on the left side, a black plastic chassis, chrome driver and interior, green-tinted windshield, and pr5s. Malaysia.

a. mtlfk orange; black, white, lt. green & blue tampo w/"Hot Wheels" on top next to driver. #19 in 2001 First Editions, #031 2 - 3

a2. as a, lwch, #19 in 2001 First Editions, #031 3 - 6

b. yellow, black chassis, chrome int., orange-tinted windshield, pr5. Power Launcher pack (2001) 2 - 3

c. red; black chassis; white int.; blue-tinted windshield; gold, blue & white tampo w/"Hot Wheels" on top; sp3; #124 (2002) 2 - 3

c2. as c, pr5s, Thailand, #124 (2002) 2 - 3

c3. as c2, sp3, Thailand, #124 (2002) 2 - 3

d. black; black chassis; yellow-tinted windshield; gold chrome int. & driver; red, orange, yellow & white tampo with "Electrical" on sides, CD-ROM logo on hood; pr5gd; Thailand; with CD-ROM disc; Thailand. #1 in CD-ROM series (2002) 7 - 9

e. lt.green; black chassis; chrome int.; magenta-tinted windows; red, gray, black & white tampo w/Hot Wheels logo & "Spectre Flame II" on sides; pr5s. #1 in Spectraflame II series, Malaysia, #087 (2002) 2 - 3

f. red; gold int.; red-tinted windows; black, white, orange & gray tampo w/"02 bday" on top; pr5s. Kmart excl. 10-Car Party Pack (2002) 3 - NA

g. red; chrome int.; red-tinted windows; silver & black stripes on sides; red, black & white tampo on top; iw. Target excl. Originals series (2001) 5 - 7

Montezooma 28760 - 77mm - 2001

This concept Monte Carlo convertible lowrider has a chrome plastic chassis, light brown interior, tinted windshield without a frame, and lwch. Malaysia.

a. mtlfk dark yellow; gold & orange tampo on sides. #23 in 2001 First Editions, #035 2 - 3

b. mtlfk gold; black chassis & int.; red-tinted windshield; white, yellow, black & red playing-cards tampo on sides &

hood; ho5; Malaysia. #3 in Trump Cards series, #073 (2002) 2 - 3

Morris Wagon 28759 - 65mm - 2001

This model has a metal chassis, chrome large exposed engine and interior, yellow-tinted windshield, plastic wood-like back half and sp5. Malaysia.

a. black, tan back half, black roof, #35 in 2001 First Editions, #047 2 - 3

MS-T Suzuka 28745 - 75mm - 2001

This model has a black plastic chassis and interior, rear spoiler, clear windows, and pr5s. Malaysia.

a. lt. green; black & yellow tampo w/race decals on sides & hood, "2" on hood. #8 in 2001 First Editions, #020 2 - 3

b. red; red spoiler; yellow, black & gray tampo w/race decals on sides & hood, "2" on hood; #213 2 - 3

c. mtlc red; chrome chassis; gray spoiler & int.; orange-tinted windows; silver, orange, black & white tampo with "Protonic Energy" on sides, "New York Toy Fair 2000" on hood, Planet Hot Wheels logo on roof; pc. Ltd ed of 800 for 2002 Toy Fair, in plastic box (2002) 100 - 175

d. yellow; black chassis & int.; tinted windows; black & gray tampo w/"Hot Wheels," "Eibach Springs" & race decals on sides & hood; sp3. #3 in Tunerz series, #065 (2002) 2 - 3

e. dark red-brown; white int.; orange-tinted windows; black, yellow, red, blue & white tampo w/"Protonic Energy" on sides, CD-ROM logo on roof; pr5s; Thailand; with CD-ROM disc. #3 in CD-ROM series (2002) 5 - 7

Old #3 28750 - 60mm - 2001

This early 1900s race car has a black metal chassis, black interior, gray steering wheel, long metal tail pipe running from the front to the back, and sp5. Malaysia.

a. red, "3" in white on sides, #29 in 2001 First Editions 2 - 3

b. orange, mtlfk gray chassis, metal int., black steering wheel & pipes, "3" in black on sides, large sp5, China, #134 (2002) 2 - 3

Outsider 28739 - 68mm - 2001

This Malaysia-made futuristic concept motorcycle and sidecar has a metal chassis & interior, gray driver & rider, and three wheels.

a. mtfk orange; black, white, lt. green & orange tampo w/"Roberts," "Jones," "Saffer" & "Heralda" (designers) on top. #18 in 2001 First Editions, #030 2 - 3

a2. as a, "VJ" added to top, #18 in 2001 First Editions, #030 2 - 3

b. fluor. lt. green; green figures; metal int.; black, white & orange tampo w/"1" on top; lwch; #222 2 - 3

Panoz LMP-1 Roadster S 28744 - 78mm - 2001

This race car has a black chassis, wing and interior; and lwch. Malaysia.

a. red; white & black tampo w/"11" & "Panoz Racing Schools" on sides; "11," "Hella," U.S. flag & emblem on hood. #9 in 2001 First Editions, #021 2 - 3

b. green; black chassis, wing & int.; red, white & black tampo w/"11" & "Panoz Racing Schools" on sides, "11" & race decals on top; ho5; #232 (2001) 2 - 3

Riley & Scott Mk III 28765 - 78mm - 2001

This race car, driven by Jack Baldwin, has a black plastic chassis, white interior, roll bar, white plastic wing in back, lwch. Malaysia

a. mtlfk blue; red, white & black tampo w/race decals & Hot Wheels logo on top, Hot Wheels logo on spoiler. #27 in 2001 First Editions, #039 2 - 3

a2. as a, larger lwch in front. #27 in 2001 First Editions, #039 2 - 3

b. red; black chassis, blue wing & int.; dk. blue, white & black tampo w/14" & race decals on sides, "74 Ranch Resort" & "Gar" on top; lwch; #221 2 - 3

Shredster 28749 - 80mm - 2001

This Malaysia-made concept car has a gray plastic chassis, black interior, tinted windows, fenders separated from the body, and pr5s.

a. red, black sides, dark yellow fenders, "Shredster" in gray on sides. #10 in 2001 First Editions, #022 3 - 6

a2. as a, sp5, #10 in 2001 First Editions, #022 2 - 3

b. fluor. lime yellow, purple fenders, chrome chassis, black int. & sides, clear windows, "Shredster" in gray on sides, pr5s, China, #212 2 - 3

Sooo Fast 28737 - 64mm - 2001

This dry-lakes race car has a metalflake red chassis, chrome interior, clear windows, and sp5. Malaysia.

a. pearl white; blue & gold tampo design on hood. #4 in 2001 First Editions, #016 2 - 3

28737-b

b. white, metal chassis, clear windows, red & chrome int., red spray mask w/gold & black tampo w/"Early Times 2001 So. Calif." on sides, rrch. Ltd ed of 2,000 for Early Times Car Club 15 - 20
c. black, tinted windows, black int., red & white tampo design on hood, sp5, #182 2 - 3
d. red; tinted windows; black int.; black & white tampo on sides & hood, "Street Strike" on sides; sp5. #4 in Spares 'n Strikes series, #062 (2002) 2 - 3

28737-e

e. red; clear windows; yellow & orange tampo on sides & hood, Hallmark logo on sides, "2001" on hood; sp5. Hallmark stores in baggie only (2002) 10 - NA

28738-a

Super Tuned 28738 - 75mm - 2001
This truck has a gray plastic chassis; red interior, truck bed & spoiler; tinted windows; and pr5s. Malaysia.
a. mtlfk blue; closed spoiler; white, red & black tampo w/"TAU14" & race decals on sides, "PHA" on hood. #5 in 2001 First Editions, #017 2 - 3
a2. as a, open spoiler, #5 in 2001 First Editions #017 15 - 20
b. yellow, gray chassis, tinted windows, red int. & truck bed, same tampo as a, pr5s, #201 2 - 3

28738-c

c. green; gray chassis; black int.; yellow-tinted windows; black, blue, white & gold tampo of pterodactyl & "Yu Gi Oh!" on sides; sp5bl; China. #4 in Yu Gi Oh series, #086 (2002) 2 - 3

28736-a

Surfin' School Bus 28736 - 85mm - 2001
This Malaysia-made bus has a gray plastic chassis, black fenders, gray & chrome engine, pipes behind the rear wheels & in back, two black surfboards sticking through the rear window, magenta-tinted windows, and sp5.
a. yellow, #2 in 2001 First Editions, #014 2 - 3
b. mtlfk dk. blue; gray chassis & fenders; orange-tinted windows, lights & surfboards; brown & lt. brown wood-like side tampo; pr5s; #181 2 - 3

28736-c

c. white; chrome chassis; black surfboards; black windows; orange & black tampo on sides, roof, front & back w/Hot Wheels Nationals logo on roof. Ltd to 2000, First Annual Nationals, Oak Brook, IL, in baggie 100 - 150

28736-d

d. black; black windows; white fenders, red, white & yellow tampo w/"Wild Weekend of" & Hot Wheels logo on sides, flames & "Toys For Tots" on roof; rrch w/red stripe. Wild Weekend of Hot Wheels, in baggie (2001) 50 - 75

28736-e

e. mtlfk gray; gold chassis & engine; black int.; yellow-tinted windows; orange, yellow & black tampo on sides & roof w/"Nathan's Smokin' Bowl-A-Rama," "Burnin' up the Lanes of the World," "Nathan's Crew" & designers' names: Wilmot, Heralda, Carris, McClone, Thienprasiddhi, Sanders; sp5gd. #1 in Spares 'n Strikes series, #059 (2002) 2 - 3

28755-a

Toyota Celica 28755 - 72mm - 2001
This Japanese car has a black plastic chassis, white interior, yellow-tinted windows, yellow plastic spoiler in back, and pr5s. Malaysia.
a. yellow; black & gray tampo w/"RHL Man Turbo" & race decals on sides. #24 in 2001 First Editions, #036 2 - 3

28755-b

b. red; black chassis & int.; white spoiler; tinted windows; blue, white & black tampo w/"Modern" & race decals on sides & hood; lwch. #4 in Tuners series, #066 (2002 2 - 3
c. purple, gray chassis, white int., yellow-tinted windows, yellow tampo w/"RHLmam Turbo" on sides, lwch, Malaysia, #151 (2002) 2 - 3

28752-a

Vulture Roadster 28752 - 70mm - 2001
This Malaysia-made concept model has an orange-tinted chassis, front bumper, windshield & interior; semi-exposed chrome engine with an overhead exhaust; and sp5.
a. purple; white & orange tampo on sides & top w/"Roadster VR1" on sides. #20 in 2001 First Editions, #032 2 - 3

28752-b

b. blue; red & chrome int.; red-tinted windshield; red, black & white tampo with "Vulture" on sides; sp5; #132 (2002) 2 - 3

28767-a

XS-IVE 28767 - 76mm - 2001
This Malaysia-made futuristic fire-fighting forest truck has a pivoting chassis, exposed chrome engine, black dome & roll bars, and four large dwct with two smaller dwct in the center.
a. red; yellow, black & green tampo with "Rescue Field & Forest," "28768" & Hot Wheels Rescue emblem on sides. #28 in 2001 First Editions, #040 2 - 3
b. beige; gold engine; yellow-tinted dome; black roll bars; white, black & red tampo w/"WSMR," "Missile Range ATEC" & "LC33" on sides, "WSMR" & "LC33" on nose; dw3gdct; #140 (2002) 2 - 3
b2. as d, dw3ct, #140 (2002) 2 - 3
b3. as b, ort5gd, #140 (2002) 2 - 3

2002

Mattel continued the same selection as in 2001 with 12 Treasure Hunt cars, 48 series cars and 42 First Editions. Limited Editions were plentiful with hotwheelscollectors.com introducing the Red Line club and more than 15 different limited editions. Limiteds were also made for the Japanese market, and Baseball team promotions continued. Power Launchers, Pavement Pounders, track sets and Sto 'n Go sets all came with their own exclusive cars. All together, there were at least 500 different models for 2002 (including variations).

52921-a

2001 Mini Cooper 52921 - 60mm - 2002
This Malaysia-made model has a metal chassis, black interior, clear windows, and pr5s.
a. dk. yellow, white roof, black posts & fenders. #28 in 2002 First Editions, #040 8 - 10
a2. as a, sp5, #28 in 2002 First Editions, #040 2 - 3

52919-a

'40 Ford Coupe 52919 - 75mm - 2002
This Malaysia-made model has a chrome plastic chassis, white interior, tinted windows, and sp5.
a. red; yellow, black & orange flames on sides. #12 in 2002 First Editions, #024 2 - 3

52919-b

b. blue, white int., tinted windows, yellow-to-orange spray mask, red & white tampo w/"Tomart's Price Guide To" & Hot Wheels logo on roof, gych, Malaysia. Limited to 6000, sold only w/Tomart's price guide (2002) 15 - 18
c. white, same as b, roof tampo is red & black. Limited to 6000, sold only w/Tomart's price guide (2002) 15 - 18

52919-c

52922-a

'57 Cadillac Eldorado Brougham 52922 - 86mm - 2002
This luxury car has a chrome chassis, gray roof, white interior, clear windows, and lwch. Malaysia.
a. black, gray Hot Wheels logo on trunk, #23 in 2002 First Editions, #035 2 - 3

52914-a

'64 Riviera 52914 - 80mm -2002
This Buick has a chrome chassis, white interior, magenta-tinted windows, and pr5s. Malaysia.
a. mtlfk orange; gold tampo on hood, roof & trunk. #30 in 2002 First Editions, #042 2 - 3
a2. as a, sp5, #30 in 2002 First Editions, #042 2 - 3

52935-a

'68 Cougar 52935 - 73mm - 2001
This Mercury has a black roof, chrome plastic chassis, black plastic interior, tinted windows, and sp5. Malaysia.
a. lt. green, #17 in 2002 First Editions, #029 2 - 3
a2. as a, flat black roof, #17 in 2002 First Editions, #029 2 - 3

52639-a3

a3. as a; red, white & black tampo w/Hot Wheels logo, "collectors.com" on sides, sp5 w/red stripe. Hot Wheels Collectors.com via mail only (2001) 30 - 50

52906-a

Altered State 52906 - 56mm - 2002
This '60s nostalgia-style dragster with a blown engine has a metal chassis, black interior & roll bar, no windshield, huge engine in front, and sp5. Malaysia.
a. purple; orange & white tampo w/"Altered State" on sides. #6 in 2002 First Editions, #018 2 - 3

52909-a

Backdraft 52909 - 70mm - 2002
This Malaysia-made concept sports car has a metal chassis, chrome interior with surfboard in back, tinted windshield, and pr5s.
a. mtlfk lt. blue, white tampo on sides of hood, blue surfboard. #15 in 2002 First Editions, #027 2 - 3
a2. as a, sp3, Malaysia. #15 in 2002 First Editions, #027 2 - 3

Values are shown in U.S. dollars, first price is for mint, second is for mint packaged vehicles only. See pages 15-16 for grading guide to determine value for cars in lesser conditions.

52939-a

Ballistik #52939 - 74mm - 2002
This concept car has a black plastic chassis, chrome engine & interior, blue-tinted dome, and y5s. Malaysia.
a. mtlfk dark green, #41 in 2002 First Editions, #053 2 - 3

52942-a

Corvette SR-2 52942 - 70mm - 2002
This race car has a chrome chassis, gray interior, clear windshield, and sp5. Malaysia.
a. red, gray on sides, white & black tampo w/"2" on hood. #9 in 2002 First Editions, #021 2 - 3

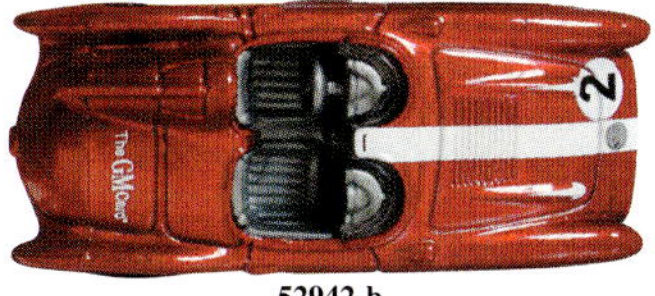
52942-b

b. dark red, same as a, "The GM Card" in gray on trunk. GM MasterCard premium 15 - 20

Corvette SR-2-c

c. black; gray int.; clear windshield; gray, white & gold tampo with "www.bloomingtongold.com" on rear fenders; "2002"; Bloomington Gold logo on trunk; rrgych. Bloomington Gold premium 10 - 15

Corvette SR-2-d

d. blue, same as d, Bloomington Gold premium 10 - 15

52907-a

Custom '59 Cadillac 52907 - 88mm - 2002
This Malaysia-made modified 1959 Cadillac Series 62 Deville has a chrome plastic chassis, white interior, clear windows, and lwgd.
a. violet, #20 in 2002 First Editions, #032 (2002) 2 - 3

52916-a

Custom '69 Chevy 52916 - 75mm - 2002
This Malaysia-made truck has a black plastic chassis, gray interior, tinted windows and pr5s.
a. red, #19 in 2002 First Editions, #031 2 - 3

52927-a

Custom Cougar 52927 - 75mm - 2002
This tuner version of a Mercury Cougar has a black chassis, magenta wing in back, chrome interior, orange-tinted windows, pr5mg. Malaysia
a. black; orange & yellow tampo on sides. #16 in 2002 First Editions 2 - 3

52915-a

Ferrari P4 52915 - 70mm - 2002
This race car has a black plastic chassis, black interior, clear windows, and sp5gd. Malaysia.
a. red; black & white tampo w/"24" on sides, hood & back; race decals on sides. #13 in 2002 First Editions, #025 2 - 3

Fore Wheeler 55012 - 55mm - 2002
Formerly Tee'd Off, this Chinese-made golf cart has a metal chassis, chrome engine in back, green roof, white interior, and sp5gd.
Similar casting: Tee'd Off (1999)
a. mtlfk gold; white & orange tampo w/"La Paz Resort" in front, flames & "Caliente" on roof; #127 (2002) 2 - 3

52905-a

Honda Spocket 52905 - 65mm - 2002
This small Malaysia-made show car (truck) has a black plastic chassis, metalflake silver sides & bed, plastic top, light gray interior, black-tinted wraparound windshield, and pr5s.
a. red, #8 in 2002 First Editions, #020 2 - 3

52923-a

HW Prototype 12 52923 - 70mm - 2002
This concept car has a metal chassis, black plastic on sides, gray spoiler in back, chrome interior, purple-tinted windows, and pr5s. Malaysia.
a. mtlfk orange, #24 in 2002 First Editions, #036 2 - 3
a2. as a, sp5. #24 in the 2002 First Editions. #036 2 - 3

52902-a

Hyperliner 52902 - 75mm - 2002
This Malaysia-made concept minivan-Formula 1 (the ultimate "mom" car) has a wing on the roof, black plastic chassis, black & red plastic interior, dark-tinted windows, and sp5bk with "Goodyear" in yellow on the sides.
a. yellow; red & black tampo w/"1" & "Hyperliner" on roof. #2 in 2002 First Editions, #014 2 - 3

52912-a

Hyundai Spyder Concept 52912 - 65mm - 2002
This concept convertible has a black chassis & interior, tinted windshield, and pr5s. Malaysia.
a. dark gold, #37 in 2002 First Editions, #049 2 - 3

52911-a

I Candy 52933 - 71mm - 2002
This concept hot-rod model has a metal chassis, exposed metal engine, purple interior & fenders, orange-tinted windows, and sp5. Malaysia.
a. anodized lime green, black & orange flames & Hot Wheels logo on front. #35 in 2002 First Editions, #047 2 - 3

52911-a

Jaded 52911 - 70mm - 2002
This Malaysia-made customized 1953 Henry J has a gray plastic chassis, chrome wing & interior, magenta-tinted windows, and sp5.
a. purple; red & black tampo w/"Jaded" on sides. #22 in 2002 First Editions, #034 2 - 3

52918-a

Jester 52918 - 65mm - 2002
This concept pickup truck has a black plastic chassis, metal truck bed, green-tinted windows, pr5s. Malaysia
a. clear purple, gray roof, white & lt. green tampo on sides. #5 in 2002 First Editions, #017 2 - 3

52938-a

Lancia Stratos 52938 - 62mm - 2002
This Italian rally car has a black plastic chassis, black interior, clear windows, and sp5. Malaysia.
a. red, gray dot on hood, gray Hot Wheels logo on trunk. #25 in 2002 First Editions, #037 (2002) 6 - 10
a2. as a, pr5gd, #25 in 2002 First Editions, #037 (2002) 2 - 3
a3. as a, pr5s. #25 in 2002 First Editions, #037 (2002) 2 - 4
a4. as a2, white, aqua & gray tampo on top. #25 in 2002 First Editions, #037 (2002) 2 - 3

52917-a

Lotus Esprit 52917 - 75mm - 2002
This Lotus has a black plastic chassis and spoiler, clear windows, tan interior, and sp5. Malaysia.
a. black, #32 in 2002 First Editions, #044 2 - 3

52901-a

Midnight Otto 52901 - 60mm - 2002
This Malaysia-made customized '32 Ford sedan has a metal chassis, black windows, and pr5s.
a. white with a orange and black tampo on the sides and roof. #1 in 2002 First Editions, #013 2 - 3
a2. as a, sp5. #1 in 2002 First Editions, #013 2 - 3

52901-b

b. blue; green top & hood; black windows; yellow to orange flames on sides; gold & black tampo w/"Early Times Mid-Winter Rod Run" on roof, "2002" in back; rrch. Ltd ed for Early Times Club (2002) 10 - 15

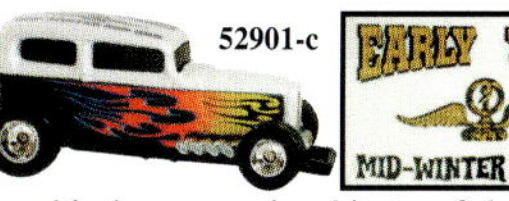

52901-c

c. black, same as b, white top & hood. Ltd ed for Early Times Club (2002) 10 - 15

52920-a

Nissan Skyline 52920 - 70mm - 2002
This Malaysia-made Nissan has a black plastic base, spoiler & interior; clear windows; and pr5s.
a. mtlfk dark blue, "APT" & race decals on sides & hood, "2" on hood, pr5s. #7 in 2002 First Editions, #019 5 - 10
a2. as a, sp5 2 - 3

52931-a

Nissan Z 52931 - 70mm - 2002
This Malaysia-made Japanese car has a black plastic chassis, interior & windows; and pr5s.
a. mtlfk silver, #26 in 2002 First Editions 2 - 3

52903-a

Nomadder What 52903 - 74mm - 2002
This Malaysia-made concept model of a souped-up Chevy Nomad has an orange-tinted chassis, black interior, clear windows and pr5s.
a. mtlfk orange; black & white stripe tampo. #10 in 2002 First Editions, #022 2 - 3
a2. as a, sp5. #10 in 2002 First Editions, #022 2 - 3
b. mtlfk purple; yellow-tinted chassis & windows; black, orange, yellow & white tampo with "Chemical" on sides; CD-ROM logo on roof; pr5s; Thailand; with CD-ROM disc. #2 in CD-ROM series (2002) 7 - 9

52908-a

Open Road-Ster 52908 - 72mm - 2002
This convertible concept car has a metal chassis, chrome engine, chrome and yellow interior, green-tinted wraparound windshield, and pr5s. Malaysia.
a. dk. yellow; black, green & gray tampo in front. #21 in 2002 First Editions, #033 2 - 3
a2. as a, sp5. #21 in 2002 First Editions, #033 2 - 3

Values are shown in U.S. dollars, first price is for mint, second is for mint packaged vehicles only. See pages 15-16 for grading guide to determine value for cars in lesser conditions.

52910-a

Overbored 454 52910 - 70mm - 2002
This modern muscle car with a blown engine has a black plastic chassis, chrome exposed engine & interior, blue-tinted windows, and pr5s. Malaysia.

a. mtlfk blue, two wide white stripes over roof & trunk, white & gray Hot Wheels logo on trunk. #4 in 2002 First Editions, #016 — 2 - 3

52910-b

b. red, chrome int., black windows, "Sears Portrait Studio" in white on sides, 2 white stripes over top, pr5s. Sears Portrait Studio give-away (2002) — 10 - 15

52926-a

Pony-Up 52926 - 72mm - 2002
This Malaysia-made impression of a contemporary pony car has a metal chassis, tan interior, black-tinted windows, and pr5.

a. mtlfk dk. orange, blue stripe on top. #34 in 2002 First Editions, #046 (2002) — 2 - 3

52934-a

Rocket Oil Special 52934 - 68mm - 2002
This race car has a metal chassis & sides, chrome engine & interior, tinted windshield, and sp5. Malaysia.

a. purple; red & white tampo w/"Rocket Oil" on sides. #36 in 2002 First Editions, #048 — 2 - 3

52929-a

Saleen S7 52929 - 75mm - 2002
This model has a black plastic chassis, black windows, and pr5s. Malaysia.

a. gray, #14 in 2002 First Editions, #026 — 2 - 3

52929-a

Side Draft 52940 - 76mm - 2002
This concept race car has an opening hatch, black plastic chassis & interior, tinted dome, and pr5s. Malaysia.

a. red-orange; black & gray tampo; pr5s. #40 in 2002 First Editions, #052 — 2 - 3

52928-a

Super Smooth 52928 - 75mm - 2002
This '30s-style hot rod truck has a black chassis & interior, clear windows, and pr5s. Malaysia.

a. blue; white & black design on truck bed. #11 in 2002 First Editions, #023 — 2 - 3

a2. as a, black stripe along roof, sp5. #14 in 2002 First Editions, #026 — 2 - 3

b. mtlfk gray; black chassis & int.; green-tinted windows; turquoise, black, white & red tampo with "Cyber" on hood; CD-ROM logo on truck bed; sp3; Thailand; with CD-ROM disc. #6 in CD-ROM series (2002) — 7 - 9

52925-a

Super Tsunami 52925 - 78mm - 2002
This import tuner concept car has a black chassis, gray wing & interior, blue-tinted windows, and pr5s. Malaysia.

a. dark gold; blue, gray & white tampo with "HW Tsunami" & race decals on sides; "Super Tsunami" & "www.hotwheels.com" on windshield; hotwheels.com logo on rear window. #29 in 2002 First Editions, #041 — 2 - 3

52904-a

Tantrum 52904 - 60mm - 2002
This Malaysia-made tuner roadster has a black plastic chassis, black & chrome interior, aqua-tinted windshield, and pr5s.

a. fluor. lime; silver & black tampo with "Hot Wheels" & race decals on sides. #3 in 2002 First Editions, #015 — 2 - 3

a2. as a, sp3. #3 in 2002 First Editions, #015 — 2 - 6

52913-a

Torpedo Jones 52913 - 77mm - 2002
This Malaysia-made 1912 30-liter race car has a red chassis, chrome exposed engine & interior, beige figure in the driver's seat and lwch.

a. red; gold & black pin striping on hood. #18 in 2002 First Editions, #030 — 2 - 3

52930-a

Toyota RSC 52930 - 68mm - 2002
This Malaysia-made Japanese show car has a black chassis, interior & windows; and ort5.

a. gray; black & orange design on rear fenders. #27 in 2002 First Editions, #039 — 2 - 3

52937-a

Volkswagen New Beetle Cup 52937 - 68mm - 2002
This 2002 VW has a rear spoiler, yellow roll cage, gray chassis & interior, blue-tinted windows, and pr5s. Malaysia.

a. yellow; red, black & white tampo with stripes, "1" & race decals on sides, "1" on hood. #33 in 2002 First Editions, #045 — 2 - 3

Additional New Models for 2002

Cold Blooded™ Series

Vulture

Spares 'N Strikes™ Series

Rodger Dodger

Sooo Fast

Star-Spangled™ Series

3-Window '34

Fed Fleet™ Series

Armored Truck

Dodge Power Wagon

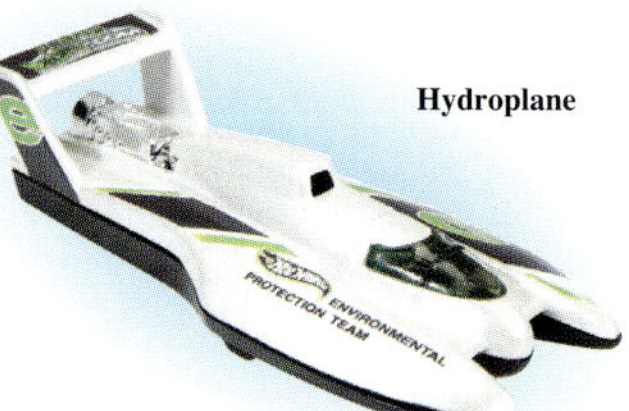
Hydroplane

Propper Chopper

Grave Rave™ Series

Evil Twin

Krazy 8s

Rigor Motor

Wagon

Values are shown in U.S. dollars, first price is for mint, second is for mint packaged vehicles only. See pages 15-16 for grading guide to determine value for cars in lesser conditions.

2002

Masters of the Universe™ Series

'41 Willys Coupe

Double Vision

Phantastique

Twin Mill II

Hot Rod Magazine™ Series

'70 Plymouth Road Runner

Deuce Roadster

Hooligan

Purple Passion

Red Lines™ Series

'32 Ford Vicky

Classic Nomad

Side Kick

The Demon

Sweet Rides™ Series

'70 Chevelle SS

Chevy Pro Stock Truck

Mustang Cobra

Pro Stock Firebird

Treasure Hunt Series

'57 Roadster

Panoz LMP-1 Roadster S

Phaeton

Tail Dragger

Wild Frontier™ Series

'32 Ford Delivery

'59 Chevy Impala

Ice Cream Truck

Power Plower

Other 2002 Releases

'40 Somethin'™

Moto-Crossed™

Slingshot

Syd Mead Sentinel 400 Limo

HOT WHEELS COLLECTIBLES®

All of these models were made with higher detail, including painted lights, door handles, and detailed chassis. Most had synthetic rubber tires with their own detailed hubs and many have opening hoods with accurate engines. There were more parts to these models than the regular line and fewer were produced. Each model has its own wheel type. Unless noted, all were issued either in a collectible set with two, three or four cars per set, or singly in a plastic box inside a collectible box as part of the Hot Wheels Collectibles line.

1996

1949 Mercury-a

1949 Mercury - 80mm - 1996 (Legends)
This chopped 1949 Mercury has a black chassis, clear windows, black & white interior, and chrome hubs.

a. purple; yellow, orange, red & blue flame tampo; black & yellow license plate w/"To Cool." Legends series, with 1/24th-scale version of same model 55 - NA

1949 Mercury-b

b. candy red, red & white int., chrome wheels w/rubber whitewall tires. Barris Customs Legends set 15 - NA

1949 Mercury-c

c. black, clear windows, tan int., plum & white flame spray mask in front, whitewall tires. Gone in 60 Seconds 4-car set (2000) 15 - NA

1949 Mercury-d

d. mtlfk green, white int., clear windows, white & purple spray mask tampo & whitewall tires. Drive In 3-car set (2000) 12 - NA

e. black primer; dark red int.; yellow, orange & red spray mask; red wheels w/whitewall tires. Lead Sledz 2-car set (2001) 30 - NA

CadZZilla-a

CadZZilla© - 85mm - 1996 (Legends)
This 1948 Cadillac has a black chassis with gray pipes, detailed side mirrors, white interior, clear windows, and chrome wheels with rubber tires.

a. dark purple, chrome trim, Boyd Coddington Custom Rods set 35 - NA

a2. as a, Legends series, with 1/24th-scale version of same model 15 - NA

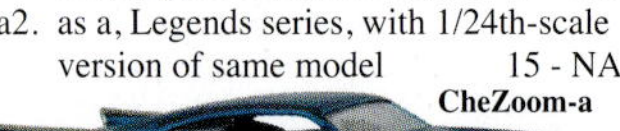

CheZoom-a

CheZoom - 80mm - 1996 (Legends)
This 1957 Chevy has a black chassis with gray pipes, clear windows, gray & green interior, and chrome wheels with rubber tires.

a. metallic aqua, chrome trim, Boyd Coddington Custom Rods set 35 - NA

CheZoom-b

b. yellow chrome; white, gray, black & orange tampo with "East Coast Convention" on sides, flames on hood & trunk, Wild Weekend logo on roof; 3-spoke collectible wheels w/redlines. Ltd ed for Wild Weekend (2002) 25 - 30

Smoothster-a

Smoothster (Customized 1937 Ford) - 65mm - 1996 (Legends)
This 1937 Ford Roadster has a yellow chassis with gray pipes, light brown plastic roof, black & tan interior, clear windows, headlight rings, hand-wiped grille with black paint between grille bars, and rubber tires with chrome six-spoke wheels.

a. yellow, chrome trim, Boyd Coddington Custom Rods Set 35 - NA

b. mtlc red, tan int. & roof, chrome front end. Cool Collectibles box (2001) 8 - 12

Vern Luce Coupe-a

Vern Luce Coupe ('33 Ford Hi-Boy Coupe) 60mm - 1996 (Legends)
This '33 Ford 3-window has a red chassis with gray pipes, highly detailed suspension with real springs, quick-change rear end, clear windows, tan interior, and chrome wheels with rubber tires.

a. red, Boyd Coddington Custom Rods set 35 - NA

b. purple, clear windows, black int., yellow to red spray mask, Cool Collectibles box (2001) 8 - 12

c. black, clear windows, black int., yellow spray mask, red flames & "MACD Racing" on trunk. Designer Dreamz II 4-car set (1997) 8 - NA

1997

'38 Ford Cabover-a

'38 Ford Cabover - 55mm - 1997
This Ford truck has a sleeper cab, tilt flat bed, metal base, tan interior & bed, and blue-tinted windows.

a. dk. aqua; turquoise, red, yellow & black tampo w/"Elwood's Garage" & address on sides. Elwoody Custom Cars 2-pack (1997) 20 - NA

'38 Ford Cabover-b

b. green; clear windows; tan int.; wood-color truck bed; yellow, black & white tampo w/"Hallwell's Garage Restoration and Repair" on sides, green-hubbed wheels. Gone in 60 Seconds 4-car set (2000) 10 - NA

c. yellow; yellow box; gray, red & black trim on cab; chrome siding on box; red, black & white tampo w/"Mooneyes," logo & address on sides. Mooneyes 2-car set (2001) 10 - NA

d. white, clear windows, chrome int., white bed, light blue & purple tampo, Designer Dreamz II 4-car set 10 - NA

e. red, car trailer, chrome & black bed, "Richard's Hot Rod" in black & yellow on side of cab. Lost Treasures 2-car set 10 - NA

f. orange & black, box added to truck, tan int., clear windows, black & chrome box with white & orange Harley-Davidson logo on sides. Hotwheels.com only, in white box. #1 in Harley-Davidson 4-car series (2001) 60 - NA

g. red; red & white box w/chrome strip on side; black int.; clear windows; black, red & white tampo w/"So-Cal Speed Shop" on sides of cab & trailer. So-Cal Speed Shop set (2002) 10 - NA

'50s Buick Woody-a

'50s Buick Woody - 80mm - 1997
This customized 1950 station wagon has a tan interior, clear windows, decorated white surfboard sticking out of the rear window, and chrome "wire" wheels.

a. turquoise; silver & aqua tampo on sides, tan trim. Elwoody Custom Cars™ 2-pack only (1997) 20 - NA

b. dk. red & tan; lt. brown int., clear windows, lt. brown surfboard. In plastic box inside collectible box, Hot Wheels Collectibles (1998) 10 - 12

c. magenta, same as b, tan int., surfboard is dk. red (1998) 10 - 12

'50s Buick Woody-c2

c2. as c, white interior (1998) 10 - 12

'50s Buick Woody-d

d. dk. blue; yellow, red & lt. blue flames w/"Firewood" in red on sides. In plastic box inside collectible box, Hot Wheels Collectibles (1998) 8 - 10

'50s Buick Woody-e

e. chrome, tinted windows, black int., red & black tampo w/"Larry Wood 30 Years of (Hot Wheels logo) Design" on roof. Ltd to 2000, 13th Annual Hot Wheels Collectors Convention, 400 given w/special stickers at Larry Wood dinner (1999) 75 - 85

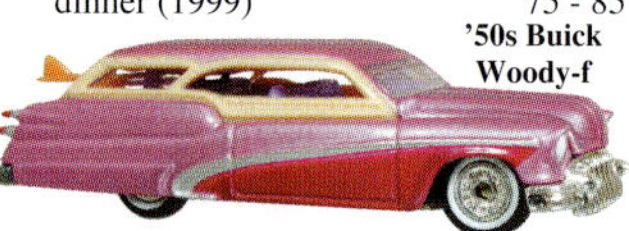

'50s Buick Woody-f

f. mtlfk light purple, purple int., clear windows, light brown surfboard, whitewall tires, Drive In 3-car set (2000) 10 - NA

g. orange, white roof & tampo on sides, dark red molding around windows, dark red surfboard, white interior, clear windows, ww tires, in Cool Collectibles box, #03 (2002) 8 - 10

'57 Cadillac Eldorado-a

'57 Cadillac Eldorado - 87mm - 1997 (Legends)
This model has a chrome chassis, white interior, clear windows, chrome wheels with whitewall rubber tires.

a. mtlfk red, chrome trim, 40th Anniv. of Signature '57s Legends set 10 - NA

'57 Cadillac Eldorado-b

b. black, lt. green flames w/purple ends all over, Rock 'n Road 4-car set 10 - NA

c. mtlfk green, white int., clear windows, John D'Agostino Kustoms set 10 - NA

d. mtlc aqua, white int., clear windows, white tampo design all over, white walls, Troy Lee set (2002) 10 - NA

'57 Chevy Funny Car-a

'57 Chevy Funny Car - 86mm - 1997 (Legends)
This model has a black & chrome chassis, chrome engine & interior, clear windows, black rear window & spoiler, large wheels with chrome hubs, and rubber tires with "Goodyear Eagle" in yellow on the sides & small wheels in front.

a. red; black, white, red, blue, gray & yellow tampo w/"Tom Mongoose McEwen" & race decals on sides; mongoose & "Mongoose" on hood; "The Heartbeat of America '57 Chevrolet" & Chevy logo on spoiler. 40th Anniv. of Signature '57s Legends set 15 - NA

b. mtlfk blue; clear windows; gray int.; red, yellow, white & black tampo w/large Hot Wheels logo & race decals on sides; Hot Wheels logo & "Design Center" on black rear. In Cool Collectibles box (2001) 15 - 20

'57 Ford Fairlane-a

'57 Ford Fairlane - 87 mm - 1997 (Legends)
This convertible has a black chassis, clear windshield, red & white interior, and chrome wheels with rubber whitewall tires.

a. white; red & chrome trim; 40th Anniv. of Signature '57s Legends set 10 - NA

'57 Ford Fairlane-b

b. red, clear windshield, white & red int., chrome trim. In Cool Collectibles box (2001) 8 - 12

c. black, clear windshield, white & black int., chrome trim. In Cool Collectibles box (2001) 8 - 12

16742-a

1965 Shelby Cobra Daytona 16742 - 71mm - 1997
This 1965 hardtop has a black metal base, clear windows, black interior, opening hood with a gray engine, extra wheel in the trunk (smaller than those on the car), and iw.

a. blue, 2 white stripes over top. 35th Anniv. of Shelby Cobra 2-pack only $20 - NA

Values are shown in U.S. dollars, first price is for mint, second is for mint packaged vehicles only. See pages 15-16 for grading guide to determine value for cars in lesser conditions.

16742-b

b. red, same as a, one white stripe over top, iww (1999) 6 - 8

16742-c

c. dk. green, same as a, yellow stripes, iwy (1999) 6 - 8
d. blue, same as a, black & white tampo w/"15" on sides & hood, two stripes over top, rubber tires. In Cool Collectibles box, #04 (2002) 8 - 12

Ala Kart-a

Ala Kart - 62mm - 1997 (Legends)
This custom 1929 Ford Roadster Pickup has a pearl white chassis, clear windows, black & white interior, and chrome wheels with rubber whitewall tires.
a. pearl white, gold & purple tampo on hood & fenders, Barris Customs Legends set 15 - NA

Dodge Viper GTS-a

Dodge Viper GTS - no # - 75mm - 1997
This 1996 hardtop has a black metal base, clear windows, gray & black interior, opening hood with a black & red engine, extra wheel in the trunk (smaller than those on the car), and iw.
a. blue, 2 white stripes over top. 35th Anniv. of Shelby Cobra 2-pack only $20 - NA
b. 19785, black, same as a, black int. & back wheel, white "Viper" & red Viper Club logo on sides, gygd. Ltd ed of 10,000 for Viper Club of America 20 - 25

Dodge Viper GTS-c

c. red; gray & black int.; clear windows; iw (1998) 8 - 10

Dodge Viper GTS-d

d. green, same as c, two black stripes on top, iw (1998) 8 - 10
d2. as d, pc 8 - 10

Dodge Viper GTS-e

e. black, same as c, two white stripes on top, iw (1998) 8 - 10
f. gray, same as c, two blue stripes on top, iw (1999) 6 - 8
g. red, white & blue; black interior; iw (1999) 6 - 8

Dodge Viper GTS-f

Dodge Viper GTS-h

h. blue, black int., clear windows, white stripes over top, 6-spoke collectibles-line wheels, Gone in 60 Seconds 4-car set (2000) 12 - NA

Elvis Dream Cadillac-a

Elvis Dream Cadillac - 88mm - 1997 (Legends)
This 1965 Eldorado convertible has a black chassis, clear windshield, gold & white interior, two gold guitars over the windshield, a gold statue between the rear seats, and chrome wheels with rubber whitewall tires.
a. pearl gold, red & white tampo w/"Elvis Dream Cadillac," George Barris signature & "E.P. Cosmetics" on sides, emblem on hood. Barris Customs Legends set 10 - NA

Hirohata Merc-a

Hirohata ('51) Merc - 85mm - 1997 (Legends)
This chopped Mercury Club Coupe has a black chassis, clear windows, white & dark green interior, and chrome wheels with rubber whitewall tires.
a. seafoam green, dk. green side panels, chrome trim. Barris Customs Legends set 15 - NA
b. black primer, white int., yellow & green flame tampo, whitewall tires. Lead Sledz 2-car set (2001) 30 - NA
c. gray primer, clear windows, black int., white & maroon spray mask, in Cool Collectibles box (2001) 25 - 30
d. magenta primer, black int., clear windows, chrome molding, lighter purple on sides, red & white tampo hood ornament, whitewalls. Rod & Custom set (2002) 15 - NA

Plymouth Fury-a

(1957) Plymouth Fury - 82mm - 1997 (Legends)
This custom '57 Fury with classic fins has a black chassis, clear windows, light brown & beige interior, opening hood with a red engine, and chrome wheels with rubber tires.
a. brown, light brown trim, 40th Anniv. of Signature '57s Legends set 10 - NA
b. red; white roof; white int.; clear windows; chrome engine & blower sticking thru opening hood; chrome trim. In Cool Collectibles box (2001) 8 - 10

Snake-a

Snake - 74mm - 1997 (Legends)
This Plymouth Barracuda Funny Car has a metal chassis, gray frame, lift-up body, clear windows, black interior, and chrome wheels with synthetic rubber tires.
a. yellow; multicolored tampo w/"Don Prudhomme the Snake"; snake & race decals on sides; blue, red & white stripe with stars over top. Issued with 1/24th-scale version of same model in Legends series 15 - NA
b. white; black & gray int.; clear windows; dk. blue, red & black tampo with Hot Wheels logo, "Don Prudhomme Snake II" & race decals on sides; flames on hood, roof & trunk. In Cool Collectibles box, #16 (2001) 10 - 15

1998

'32 Ford Coupe-a

'32 Ford Coupe
This car has a black metal chassis, chrome plastic engine, black interior & clear windows.
a. yellow, American Graffiti 2-pack 20 - NA

'32 Ford Coupe-b

b. magenta; tan int. & roof; clear windows; black, white & red tampo w/"PP" on sides 8 - 10

'32 Ford Coupe-c

c. turquoise, same as b, white roof, two moon eyes & logo on sides 8 - 10

'32 Ford Coupe-d

d. black, white int., white roof, red & yellow flame tampo on sides, red hubs & white-stripe tires. In bp as ltd ed for Hot Rod magazine (2000) 10 - 15

'32 Ford Coupe-e

e. red; white roof & int.; clear windows; white, yellow & black tampo w/logo & "Hot Rod" on license plate; red hubs with whitewall tires. Drive In 3-car set (2000) 10 - NA
f. flat black; black int.; clear windows; red, white & yellow tampo w/"Deuces Wild" & "2 A/G" on sides; checkerboard roof; white on trunk. In Cool Collectibles box, #02 (2002) 10 - 15

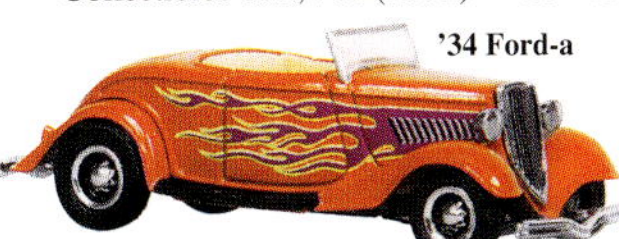
'34 Ford-a

'34 Ford Convertible - 71mm - 1998
This convertible has a metal chassis, tan interior, clear windshield with a metal rim, and black running boards.
a. orange; yellow & purple flames. Street Rodder 2-pack 10 - NA
b. red, plum fenders, tan int. In Cool Collectibles box (2000) 10 - 12
c. black, yellow on top, yellow int., clear windshield, rubber tires. In Cool Collectibles box (2000) 10 - 12

'47 Ford Convertible-a

'47 Ford Convertible - 76mm - 1998
This car has a purple metal chassis, purple & gray interior, clear windshield, and an opening hood with a chrome engine.
a. purple; gray, blue & orange tampo on hood. Street Rodder 2-pack 15 - NA

'47 Ford Convertible-b

b. purple; purple int.; white spray mask; lt. green & white tampo w/flames, dice & "Lucky '46" on sides; dice & "Lucky '46" on hood; 13th Annual Hot Wheels Collectors Convention logo on trunk. '46 Ford Convertible, ltd ed of 5000 for 13th Hot Wheels Collectors Convention (1999) 20 - 25
c. red, same as a, red & tan int., silver & orange side stripe. In plastic box inside collectible box, Hot Wheels Collectibles (1998) 6 - 8

'47 Ford Convertible-d

d. black; clear windshield, red int.; red, white & yellow tampo w/"Tomart's Price Guide" & Hot Wheels logo on trunk; wire mag wheels. Mail-in, ltd ed of 20,000 for Tomart Publications (1999) 15 - 18
e. lime green, same as c, in Cool Collectibles box (2000) 8 - 10

'47 Ford Convertible-f

f. white; red int.; clear windshield; tan plastic removable roof; yellow, orange & lt. blue spray mask tampo. In bp as ltd ed for *Hot Rod* magazine (2000) 10 - 15

'53 Corvette-a

'53 Corvette - 68mm - 1998
This convertible has a black metal base, red interior, clear windshield with chrome trim, and an opening hood with a chrome engine.
a. white, silver trim, red & black Corvette logo on hood, black license plate with "1953" on trunk. Corvette Showcase #1 2-pack $12 - NA

'53 Corvette-b

b. lt. yellow, black interior (1999) 8 - 10

'53 Corvette-c

c. red, black int., white & yellow tampo w/"Tomart's Price Guide" & Hot

Values are shown in U.S. dollars, first price is for mint, second is for mint packaged vehicles only. See pages 15-16 for grading guide to determine value for cars in lesser conditions.

Wheels logo on trunk, wire mag wheels. Mail-in, ltd ed of 25,000 for Tomart Publications (1999) 15 - 18

d. mtlfk blue gray; gray-blue interior (1999) 6 - 8

e. black; black int.; white, yellow & orange spray mask. Haulin Heat 4-car set 10 - NA

'57 Oldsmobile-a

'57 Oldsmobile - 78mm - 1998

This stock car, driven by Lee Petty, has a black base with gray pipes, clear windows, and black interior.

a. white; black & red tampo w/"42," "Petty Engineering" & Air Lift decal on sides, "277 H.P." twice on hood, "42" on roof. Petty Generation 3-pack only $8 - NA

'57 Oldsmobile-b

b. lt. blue; red, black & white tampo w/"43" & race decals on sides, "277 H.P." on hood, "43" & Richard Petty's signature on roof 6 - 8

'57 Oldsmobile-c

c. lt. blue (darker shade), same as b, white wheels 6 - 8

d. black, yellow roof & rear, opening hood, clear windows, black int., gray trim, in Cool Collectibles box (2001) 8 - 10

'67 Corvette Stingray-b

'67 Corvette Stingray - 69mm - 1998

This car has a black metal base; red interior; clear windows; opening hood with black, red & gray engine; and new mag-style wheels.

a. blue, wide white stripe w/"427" in silver on both sides of stripe, "Corvette" in silver on trunk, silver license plate w/"1967" in black. Corvette Showcase #2 2-pack only $10 - NA

b. black; gray & red engine; "Corvette" & special wheels in white in back 8 - 10

'67 Corvette Stingray-c

c. white, same as b, white & black int., "Corvette" is black (1998) 8 - 10

'67 Corvette Stingray-d

d. lt. yellow; black int.; black, red, blue & silver tampo w/large stripe & logo on hood; "Corvette" in back. Popular Hot Rodding Magazine 4-pack only 6 - NA

e. dk. lime yellow, black hood, clear windows, black int., "427" in red on hood. Cool 'n' Custom III set (2002) 10 - NA

'70 Plymouth Superbird-a

'70 Plymouth Superbird - 85mm - 1998

This stock car, driven by Richard Petty, has a blue base with gray pipes, clear windows, black & blue interior, gray roll cage, and rrch.

a. lt. blue; white & black tampo w/"43," "Plymouth" & race decals on sides; "426 C.L." twice on hood; "43" on headlights, roof & trunk. Petty Generation 3-pack only $8 - NA

'70 Plymouth Superbird-b

b. green, black int., "Plymouth" in black on rear fender, black & red logo on side of spoiler (1998) 6 - 8

'70 Plymouth Superbird-c

c. red, same as b (1998) 6 - 8

'98 Corvette Convertible-b

'98 Corvette Convertible - 71mm - 1998

This 1998 Corvette convertible model has a black metal base, red interior, clear windshield with black outline, opening hood with a black engine and pc.

a. gray; red & black Corvette logo on hood & trunk; black license plate w/"1998" in white. Corvette Showcase #2 2-pack #2 only $10 - NA

b. gray, same as a, tan int., smaller rear wheels, no logo on hood. In plastic box inside collectible box as single 8 - 10

c. mtlfk black, same as b, red interior (1999) 8 - 10

1955 Chevy Bel Air-a

1955 Chevy Bel Air - 78mm - 1998

This replica has a black metal chassis, open hood with a chrome engine, clear windows, and black interior.

a. black, American Graffiti 2-pack 20 - NA

1955 Chevy Bel Air-b

b. purple; white int.; orange, yellow & white flames on sides & hood (1999) 10 - 12

1955 Chevy Bel Air-c

c. white, lt. green int., yellow to lt. green tampo on sides & hood (1999) 10 - 12

1955 Chevy Bel Air-d

d. turquoise, white roof & rear, white int., gray trim. Tri Chevy 3-car set 10 - NA

1955 Chevy Bel Air-e

e. dk. red, gray int., orange flames, ltd ed in bp by Adkins Collectibles (2000) 10 - 15

1957 Chevy 150-a

1957 Chevy 150 (Sedan) - 80mm - 1998 (Legends)

This Chevy 150 Black Widow was driven by Buck Baker in 1957, when he set the record for the most wins in a season with 17 wins on the NASCAR circuit. It has a red chassis, opening hood with a black, gray & red engine, lightly tinted windows, black & white interior, and special racing wheels with white hubs.

a. black; white rear; white, silver & black tampo w/"87," "Buck Baker," "Fuel Injection" & race decals on sides; "220 H.P." twice on hood; "87' on roof & trunk. Vintage Record Holders Legends set 10 - NA

b. white, turquoise roof & rear, opening hood, clear windows, turquoise & white int., in Cool Collectibles box (2001) 8 - 10

c. lt. yellow, black roof & rear, yellow & black int., clear windows. In Cool Collectibles box (2002) 8 - 10

1982 Corvette Stingray-a

1982 Corvette Stingray - 75mm - 1998

This Stingray has a black metal base, black interior, clear windows, and an opening hood with a black, red and gray engine.

a. red; white & black Corvette logo on hood; silver "Corvette," black license plate w/"1982" on trunk. Corvette Showcase #1 2-pack $10 - NA

1982 Corvette Stingray-b

b. black; same as a; white int.; chrome, red & gray engine; "Corvette" in white in back; "Cross Fire Injection" in white on sides 6 - 8

c. yellow, black interior (1999) 6 - 8

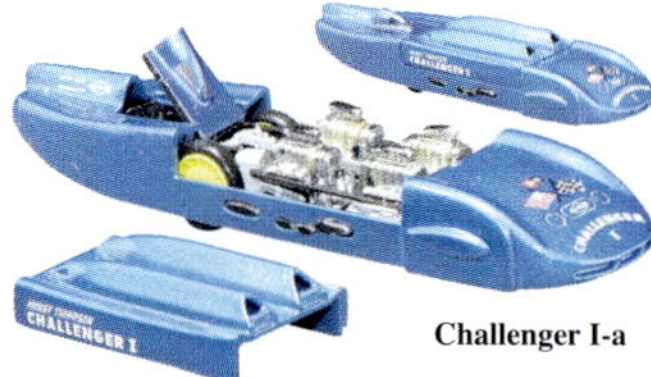

Challenger I-a

Challenger 1 - 100mm - 1998 (Legends)

This race car was driven by Mickey Thompson in 1960 to set a land speed record of 401 mph. It has a blue chassis, opening canopy, black interior, tinted windows, lift-up hood, four engines in the middle, and special racing wheels with yellow hubs.

a. blue; white & black tampo w/"Mickey Thompson Challenger 1" on sides; "Challenger 1," two flags & race decals on top. Vintage Record Holders Legends set 15 - NA

Heavy Chevy-a

Heavy Chevy - 72mm - 1998

This customized Chevrolet Camaro, a remake of the 1970 model, has a metal chassis, cream interior, clear windows, exposed chrome engine, and nrsw.

Similar casting: '68 Camaro (w/hood), (1999)

a. gold, 30th Anniv. of Hot Wheels 4-pack 10 - NA

King Kuda-a

King Kuda - 74mm - 1998

This customized Plymouth Barracuda, a remake of the 1970 model, has a metal chassis, cream interior, clear windows, exposed chrome engine, and nrsw.

Similar casting: King Kuda (w/hood), (1999)

a. blue; 30th Anniv. of Hot Wheels 4-pack 10 - NA

Light My Firebird-a

Light My Firebird - 75mm - 1998

This customized Pontiac Firebird convertible, a remake of the 1970 model, has a metal chassis, cream interior, clear windshield, exposed chrome engine, and nrsw.

Similar casting: '68 Custom Firebird Convertible (w/hood), (1999)

a. green; 30th Anniv. of Hot Wheels 4-pack 10 - NA

Mongoose-a

Mongoose - 78mm - 1998 (Legends)

This Plymouth Duster Funny Car has a metal chassis, blue frame, lift-up body, clear windows, black interior, and chrome wheels with rubber tires.

a. red; multicolored tampo w/"Tom McEwen the Mongoose," mongoose & race decals on sides; blue & white stripe w/stars over top. With 1/24th-scale version of same model in Legends series 15 - NA

Nitty Gritty Kitty-a

Nitty Gritty Kitty - 75mm - 1998

This customized Mercury Cougar, a remake of the 1970 model, has a metal chassis, cream interior, clear windows, exposed chrome engine, and nrsw.

a. red; 30th Anniv. of Hot Wheels 4-pack 10 - NA

Twin Mill-a

Twin Mill - 80mm - 1998 (Legends)

The Legends version has a metalflake lime metal chassis with chrome engine and pipes, clear windows, black interior, and chrome wheels with rubber tires with a red stripe.

a. mtlc lime, two red Hot Wheels logos as hood ornaments. With 1/24th- scale version of same model in Legends series 15 - NA

Values are shown in U.S. dollars, first price is for mint, second is for mint packaged vehicles only. See pages 15-16 for grading guide to determine value for cars in lesser conditions.

Watson Roadster-a

Watson Roadster - 70mm - 1998 (Legends)
This Indy race car has a white chassis, clear windshield, black interior, an opening hood with a chrome engine and special racing wheels with chrome hubs.
a. white; blue nose; gold, red & blue tampo with "98" on nose & rear, "Agajanian's Willard Battery Special" on hood, race decal on sides. Vintage Record Holders Legends set 15 - NA

Willys Gasser-a

Willys Gasser ('41 Willys) - 68mm - 1998 (Legends)
This Stone, Woods and Cook Willys Gasser has a black & red chassis, clear windows, black interior, opening hood with a chrome & black engine, and special racing wheels with chrome hubs.
a. grayish blue; black tampo w/"Swindler II" on rear fenders; "Owners Fred Stone, Leonard Woods & Doug Cook" on sides. Vintage Record Holders Legends set 15 - NA

Willys Gasser-b

b. dk. mtlfk red, white tampo w/"Big John Mazmanian," "36" & race decals on sides. Willys Gassers 2-car set (2000) 15 - NA
c. black; clear windows; black int.; white, yellow, orange & blue spray mask. In Cool Collectibles box (2001) 10 - 12
d. mtlfk white, black int., clear windows, red & blue tampo w/flames & "American Racing" on sides, stars on hood. American Racing Equipped 2-car set (2002) 10 - NA

1999

'32 Ford Hi-Boy Roadster-a

'32 Ford Hi-Boy Roadster - 53mm - 1999
This Chinese-made convertible hot rod has an exposed metal engine, black interior, clear windshield, and Cool Collectibles wheels.
a. mtlfk dk. red; gold & orange stripe on sides. Reggie's Cars 4-pack 8 - NA

'32 Ford Hi-Boy Roadster-b

b. mtlfk olive; black int.; red, yellow & black Clay Smith Cams logo & "Clay Smith Cams" on sides; flames on trunk. Clay Smith Cams 2-car set 10 - NA

'32 Ford Hi-Boy Roadster-c

c. beige, red tampo in front, black & white checkerboard design behind engine. Rockin' Road 4-car set 10 - NA
d. black; red & white int.; clear windshield; yellow, red & blue flame tampo with skull on sides. In Cool Collectibles box (2001) 10 - 12
e. gray primer, multicolored int., clear windshield, red tampo on sides, black & white checkerboard tampo behind engine, whitewalls w/red hubs. Rod & Custom set (2002) 10 - NA

'40s Ford Convertible-a

'40s Ford Convertible - 75mm - 1999
This model has a black and gray chassis, opening hood with a chrome engine, white plastic removable top, clear windshield, light brown interior, and a new wheel style with synthetic rubber tires.
a. black; Reggie's Cars 4-pack 8 - NA
b. orange; magenta & pink tampo on sides. Issued as 1940 Ford Convertible in Cool Collectibles box (2000) 8 - 10
c. blue with a white roof and interior, clear windshield and gray trim. Issued in a Cool Collectibles box (2000) 8 - 10
d. black with black interior, clear windows and yellow spray mask with red tips. Rock'n Road 4-car set (2001) 15 - NA

'40s Ford Convertible-d2

d2. as a, white spray mask, Rockin' Road 4-car set (2001) 10 - NA
e. gray primer, red & white int., clear windshield, red spray mask, ww tires. Issued in a Cool Collectibles box, #12 (2002) 10 - 12

'53 Bel Air-a

'53 Bel Air ('53 Chevy Lowrider) - 80mm - 1999
This replica of a lowrider has a black metal chassis, clear windows, white interior, and a new wheel style with gray hubs & a white stripe around the tires.
a. dk. mtlfk red, gray roof, gray striping tampo on sides. Lowrider Magazine 3-pack 8 - NA
b. lt. mtlc brown, darker roof, reddish brown & white int., clear windows, white tampo on sides & roof. Issued as '53 Chevy Lowrider in Cool Collectibles box (2000) 15 - 18

'53 Bel Air-c

c. lt. blue, white interior, clear windows, gray tampo on sides. Issued as '53 Chevy Lowrider in Cool Collectibles box (2000) 10 - 12

'53 Bel Air-d

d. black, red int., clear windows, white & red stripes all over. Issued in Rockin' Road 4-car set (2001) 10 - NA

'56 Chevy 210 2-Door Sedan-a

'56 Chevy 210 2-Door Sedan - 75mm - 1999
This model has a black & gray chassis, opening hood with an engine hole, chrome engine, clear windows, and purple & white interior.
a. purple, Reggie's Cars 4-pack 12 - NA
a2. as a, no front bumper 8 - NA
b. turquoise, white roof & rear, white & black int., in Collectible box (2001) 10 - 12
c. orange; white roof & rear; white int.; clear windows; gray trim; in Collectible box (2001) 10 - 12

'56 Chevy 210 2-Door Sedan-d

d. black; red int.; white, yellow, orange & blue spray mask; Tri Chevy 3-car set 10 - NA

'57 Eldorado-a

'57 Eldorado
This replica of a Cadillac Eldorado Biarritz convertible with a closed white roof has a black metal chassis, clear windows, red & white interior, and a new wheel style with chrome hubs & white sidewalls.
a. pink, Hard Rock Cafe 3-pack 10 - NA
b. mtlfk black, white roof, dk. red int., clear windows, whitewall tires. In Cool Collectibles box (2000) 10 - 12
c. silver, black roof, white & blue int., clear windows. In Cool Collectibles box (2000) 10 - 12
d. tan roof, red int., clear windows, gray trim. In Cool Collectibles box, #08 (2002) 10 - 12

'59 Chevrolet El Camino-a

'59 (1959) Chevrolet El Camino - 82mm - 1999
This replica of a Chevrolet El Camino pickup truck has a black & gray metal chassis; opening hood with a black, red & gray engine; clear windows; red interior; and a new wheel style with synthetic rubber tires.
a. white, black roof & truck bed, black stripe w/"El Camino" in silver on sides. Cool Classics El Camino 40th Anniversary 2-pack Series 1 12 - NA

'59 Chevrolet El Camino-b

b. black, same as a, yellow & red flame tampo on sides & hood. Cool Classics Series 1 Fireworkz 2-pack only 15 - NA

'59 Chevrolet El Camino-e

c. black, white roof & truck bed, red int., clear windows, gray stripe, "El Camino" on sides. In Cool Collectibles box (2000) 10 - 12
d. red, black roof & truck bed, red int., clear windows, black & gray stripe w/"El Camino" on sides. In Cool Collectibles box (2000) 10 - 12
e. mtlfk olive; black int.; red, yellow & black Woody Woodpecker head & "Clay Smith Cams" on sides; flames on hood. Clay Smith Cams 2-car set 12 - NA
f. red; black int., truck bed & roof; clear windows; yellow sides; black & white tampo w/Mooneyes logo & "Mooneyes Racing Team" on sides. Custom Classic Trucks 2-car set (2002) 12 - NA

'59 Chevy Apache Fleetside-a

'59 Chevy Apache Fleetside Pickup - 75mm - 1999
This replica has a black & gray metal chassis, opening hood with a red & gray engine, clear windows, and a black & white interior and truck bed.
a. red, Chevy logo in front, white "Chevrolet" in back, black & white tonneau cover in back. Smoke 'n Water 2-pack only 10 - NA
b. yellow, clear windows, white & black int. and tonneau cover. In Cool Collectibles box (2000) 10 - 12
c. lt. blue, dk. blue int. & truck bed, clear windows. In Cool Collectibles box (2000) 10 - 12
d. mtlfk olive, black int., clear windows, red flame spray mask on sides, red & yellow tampo w/Clay Smith Cams logo & "Clay Smith Cams" on sides. Custom Classic Trucks 2-car set (2002) 10 - NA

'68 Custom Firebird Convertible-a

'68 Custom Firebird Convertible - 75mm - 1998
This customized Pontiac Firebird convertible, a remake of the 1970 model, has a metal chassis, cream interior, clear windshield, exposed chrome engine and nrsw. Similar casting: Light My Firebird (exposed engine), (1999)
a. mtlc lt. green, brown int., opening hood (1999) 8 - 10
b. unpainted, same as a, red int. (1999) 8 - 10

'70 Monte Carlo-a

'70 Monte Carlo - 83mm - 1999
This replica of a Chevrolet lowrider has a black metal chassis, clear windows, black & white interior, and a new wheel style with gold hubs & a white stripe around the tires.
a. mtlfk orange; dk. green tampo on sides; green & lt. green tampo on hood, roof & trunk. Lowrider Magazine 3-pack 10 - NA
b. red; bright yellow int.; yellow, gold & orange tampo on sides; chrome hubs

Values are shown in U.S. dollars, first price is for mint, second is for mint packaged vehicles only. *See pages 15-16 for grading guide to determine value for cars in lesser conditions.*

'70 Monte Carlo-b

w/white stripe around tires. Voodoo Highway 3-car set 8 - NA

c. mtlfk yellow, green int., clear windows, orange & yellow tampo on top. In Cool Collectibles box (2000) 10 - 12

d. purple, tan int., clear windows, green & red flame tampo on sides & top, white stripe around tires. In Cool Collectibles box (2000) 12 - 15

1959 Cadillac Eldorado Woody-a

1959 Cadillac Eldorado Woody - 98mm - 1999

This replica has a black metal chassis, clear windows, light green & white interior, and a new wheel style with chrome hubs & white side walls. It also has one red and one blue surfboard sticking out the rear windows. It is one of the longest 1/64th scale vehicles Mattel has produced.

a. lt. green; dk & lt. brown side panels. Hard Rock Cafe 3-pack 10 - NA

1959 Cadillac Eldorado Woodie-b

b. orange, beige int., brown & tan wood sides, orange fades to white in middle of roof, ww 10 - 12

c. yellow, black & white interior and surfboards, clear windows, tan & brown sides, whitewall tires. In Collectible box (2001) 10 - 12

d. blue, white & black int., tan & brown sides. Airstream Dream 2-car set 15 - NA

1963 Cadillac Fleetwood-a

1963 Cadillac Fleetwood (Hearse)

This replica of a 1957 Cadillac Fleetwood has a black metal chassis, clear windows, tan interior, black roof, and a new wheel style with chrome hubs and white side walls.

a. mtlfk black; yellow, red & blue flames on sides & roof. Hard Rock Cafe 3-pack 10 - NA

1963 Cadillac Fleetwood-b

b. black; red int.; gold, yellow & gold flame tampo w/"Voodoo Hearzz" on sides. Voodoo Highway™ 3-car set 10 - NA

1963 Cadillac Fleetwood-c

c. black, white interior, green-tinted windows w/"Phantom Coaches" in white on side window, gray trim. In Cool Collectibles box (2001) 10 - 12

d. white, white int., tinted windows w/"Phantom Coaches" in white on side window, gray trim. In Cool Collectibles box (2001) 10 - 12

e. orange chrome; clear windows; black interior & roof; lt. green flames on sides, hood & top; white & orange tampo w/"Dream Halloween" on roof; 5-spoke wheels. Issued for 2001 Dream Halloween (2001) 200 - 250

1963 Plymouth 426 Max Wedge-a

1963 Plymouth 426 Max Wedge - 82mm - 1999

This model has a black & gray chassis, opening hood with a red & gray engine, clear windows, and black interior.

a. white, Reggie's Cars 4-pack 8 - NA

b. orange, tan int., purple spray mask & flames on sides. Car Craft magazine 2-car set (2001) 10 - NA

c. white; red engine; black, red & yellow tampo w/"Melrose Missile 1963 International Champ," "SS 611" & flames on sides. In Cool Collectibles box (2000) 8 - 12

1963 Plymouth 426 Max Wedge-d

d. mtlfk gray, black int., clear windows, red & black race decals on sides. In Cool Collectibles box (2000) 8 - 12

1965 Shelby GT-350-a

1965 Shelby GT-350 - 74mm - 1999 (Legends)

This model has a black chassis with gray details, an opening hood with a black and chrome engine, black interior with a wheel inside back window, clear windows and chrome wheels with rubber tires.

a. white, 2 blue stripes over top, Jay Leno set 15 - NA

b. blue, opening hood, clear windows, black int., white flame spray mask w/yellow tips. Mustang Monthly 2-car set (2001) 10 - NA

c. black, opening hood, clear windows, black int., 2 gold stripes over top. In Cool Collectibles box (2001) 8 - 10

1968 Camaro-a

1968 Camaro - 70mm - 1999

This replica of a 1968 Chevrolet has a metal chassis, clear windows, black interior, opening hood with a gray & red engine, and new mag wheels with synthetic rubber tires. Similar casting: Heavy Chevy (exposed engine), (1998)

a. white; yellow, red & lt. blue flame tampo on sides & hood. Popular Hot Rodding Magazine 4-pack only 15 - NA

b. unpainted, same as a, red int., no tampo, Collectible singles (1999) 10 - 12

1968 Camaro-c

c. black; yellow & green flame tampo on sides. Limited ed. in bp by Adkins Collectibles 10 - 15

1969 Buick Riviera Lowrider-a

1969 Buick Riviera Lowrider - 85mm - 1999

This replica of a Buick Riviera lowrider has a black metal chassis, clear windows, black & white interior, and a new wheel style with gold hubs & a white stripe around the tires.

a. black; red to pink to white to green tampo on car. Lowrider Magazine 3-pack 8 - NA

1969 Buick Riviera Lowrider-b

b. lt. brown, beige int., orange pinstripe on sides & top, chrome hubs w/white stripe around tires 10 - 12

c. white, purple int., clear windows, gold & gray tampo on sides & top, white stripe around tires. In Cool Collectibles box (2000) 10 - 12

1969 Oldsmobile 442-a

1969 Oldsmobile 442 - 80mm - 1999

This replica of the 1969 Hearst version of the Oldsmobile 442 has a black metal chassis; opening hood with a black, red & chrome engine; clear windows; black interior; and a rally-style wheel with rubber tires.

a. white; gold & black striping on sides & top; "H/O 455" on both sides of hood. 30th Anniv. of '69 Muscle Car 2-pack, Series 1, set 1 only 10 - NA

1969 Oldsmobile 442-b

b. mtlfk gray, same as a, red int., in plastic box inside collectible box, Hot Wheels Collectibles (1998) 8 - 10

1969 Oldsmobile 442-c

c. red, white int., gold & black pinstripe on sides, large stripe on roof & trunk, "H/O 456" on hood. Ltd ed in bp by Adkins Collectibles (2000) 10 - 15

d. black, black interior, clear windows, red & white tampo on sides & top, "H/O 455" on hood. In Cool Collectibles box (2000) 8 - 10

e. green, black int., gray trim, gold & black tampo w/"H/O 455" on hood, stripe on roof & trunk. *Car Craft* magazine 2-car set (2001) 10 - NA

1970 Chevrolet El Camino-a

1970 Chevrolet El Camino - 78mm - 1999

This pickup truck has a black & red metal chassis, opening hood with a red & gray engine, clear windows, black & white interior, and five-spoke mag wheels with synthetic rubber tires.

a. black, white stripes on hood, "El Camino SS 454" in silver on sides. Cool Classics El Camino 40th Anniv. 2-pack Series 1 only 12 - NA

1970 Chevrolet El Camino-b

b. red, same as a; black int & white stripes on hood. Popular Hot Rodding Magazine 4-pack only 8 - NA

1970 Chevrolet El Camino-c

c. blue, same as b, two white stripes on hood 8 - 10

d. dk. gold, black int., clear windows, black stripes on hood, rubber tires. In Cool Collectibles box (2000) 10 - 12

e. mtlfk white; clear windows; black int.; yellow, orange & red spray mask. In Cool Collectibles box (2001) 8 - 10

AMX-a

(1969) AMX - 77mm - 1999

This replica has a black, gray & red metal chassis; opening hood with a black, red & chrome engine; black interior; and clear windows.

a. pea green; black stripes over top. 30th Anniv. of Muscle Car 2-pack Series 1 set 2 only 12 - NA

AMX-b

b. red, white & blue; "Lexmark" on sides & trunk. Ltd ed in box for Lexmark 20 - 25

c. blue, black stripes over top. Issued as 1969 AMX in Cool Collectibles box (2000) 10 - 12

d. dull blue, same as c. Issued as 1969 AMX in Cool Collectibles box (2000) 20 - 25

e. orange, black int., clear windows, black striping tampo over top. Issued in Cool Collectibles box (2000) 8 - 10

Chevrolet Chevelle-a

(1969) Chevrolet Chevelle - 77mm - 1999

This replica has a black metal chassis; opening hood with a black, red, gray & chrome engine; black interior; and clear windows.

a. gold, black stripe on sides, black vents, "Chevelle" in black & white on hood & trunk. 30th Anniv. of '69 Muscle Car 2-pack, Series 1, set 1 only 12 - NA

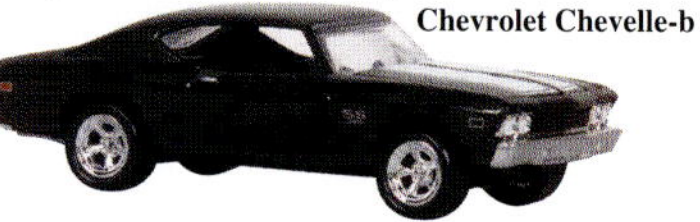
Chevrolet Chevelle-b

b. mtlfk dk. green, same as a, white stripes on hood & trunk. Popular Hot Rodding Magazine 4-pack only 10 - NA

Chevrolet Chevelle-c

c. blue; white roof; black hood & trunk; white, orange & black tampo w/"396," "Street Pro Racing" & race decals on sides, "Air" & stars on hood, stripes on roof, 13th Annual Hot Wheels Collectors Convention logo on trunk; 5-spoke mag hubs. Ltd ed of 5000 for 13th Annual Hot Wheels Collectors Convention (1999) 20 - 25

Chevrolet Chevelle-d

d. white, black int. & roof, "SS 427" in

Values are shown in U.S. dollars, first price is for mint, second is for mint packaged vehicles only. See pages 15-16 for grading guide to determine value for cars in lesser conditions.

silver on sides. Ltd ed in bp by Adkins Collectibles (2000) 10 - 15
e. dk. blue, black int., clear windows, "SS 396" in silver on sides, white stripes on hood & trunk. In Cool Collectibles box (2000) 25 - 30
f. red, black int., clear windows, "SS 396" in silver on sides, black stripes on hood & trunk. In Cool Collectibles box (2000) 10 - 12
g. yellow; black int.; clear windows; black & silver striping tampo on sides, hood & trunk; "SS" on sides. In Cool Collectibles box (2000) 10 - 12

Crackerbox Race Boat-a

Crackerbox Race Boat - 76mm - 1999
This is the first boat in the collectible line. It has a reddish brown bottom, exposed engine in the middle, and a black-&-beige interior.
a. lt. brown, brown stripes, yellow pinstripes on top, black pinstripes on sides. Smoke 'n' Water™ 2-pack only 8 - NA

Crackerbox Race Boat-b

b. black, same as a, red interior, yellow & red flame tampo. Fireworkz 2-pack only 8 - NA

Go Mad-a

Go-Mad™ - 88mm - 1999
This customized Chevy Nomad has a chopped top, altered wheelbase, four exposed Hemi engines, red-tinted windows, and five-spoke slot mag wheels. Made in China, it was issued in the Baur's Beasts™ 2-pack.
a. yellow, "Go Mad" in red & black on rear bumper 10 - NA
b. turquoise, white roof & int., white tampo on sides, rubber tires. In Collectibles box, #01 (2002) 8 - 10

Jaguar XJ-13-a

Jaguar XJ-13 - 68mm - 1999
This convertible has a dark green chassis, black interior, clear windows with a rear engine behind driver's seat, and a new style of mag wheels.
a. dk. green, Jaguar 4-car set 8 - NA
b. metal, clear windshield, red int. In Collectibles Box (2000) 8 - 10

Jaguar XKE-a

Jaguar XKE - 68mm - 1999
A Jaguar with light yellow chassis, red-brown interionr, clear windows, opening hood, gray engine, and new mag wheels.
a. lt yellow; Jaguar 4-car set 8 - NA

Jaguar XKE Convertible-a

Jaguar XKE Convertible - 70mm - 1999 (Legends)
This customized convertible has a black chassis, opening hood, black interior, clear windshield, and chrome wheels with rubber tires.
a. red, gray trim, Jay Leno set 15 - NA

Jaguar XKR-a

Jaguar XKR - 76mm - 1999
This Jaguar has a black chassis, light brown interior, clear windows, an opening hood with a chrome & black engine, and a new style of mag wheels.
a. mtlfk dk. blue, Jaguar 4-car set 8 - NA

Jaguar XKR-b

b. red, brown int., clear windows, black trim. In Motor Trend series from Preferred Line (2002) 5 - 7

Jaguar XKSS-a

Jaguar XKSS - 76mm - 1999
This convertible has a black plastic roof cover, red chassis, black interior, clear windows, an opening hood with a gray & red engine, and a new style of mag wheels.
a. red, Jaguar 4-car set 8 - NA

King Kuda-a

King Kuda - 74mm - 1999
This customized Plymouth Barracuda, a remake of the 1970 model, has a metal chassis, cream interior, clear windows, an opening hood & chrome engine, and nrsw. Similar casting: King Kuda (exposed engine) (1998)
a. mtlfk gold, black interior (1998) 10 - 12

King Kuda-b

b. unpainted, same as a, red interior 10 - 12

Lamborghini Miura-a

Lamborghini Miura - 70mm - 1999 (Legends)
This model has a black chassis, opening rear engine compartment, black interior, clear windows, and chrome wheels with rubber tires.
a. yellow, Jay Leno set 15 - NA

Mercohaulic-a

Mercohaulic - 70mm - 1999
This Ed Newton-customized 1938 or 1939 Mercury has black interior, clear windows, an opening hood with a chrome and red engine and wire style wheels in front and five-spoke wheels in back.
a. mtlfk dk. blue, silver headlights, grille tampo. Ed Newton's Lowboyz™ 3-car set only 10 - NA
b. white; red-tinted windows; orange & chrome engine; yellow, orange & blue flame tampo on sides & roof. In Cool Collectibles box (2000) 15 - 25
c. black; black int.; clear windows; white, yellow, orange & blue flame spray mask. In Cool Collectibles box (2000) 15 - 20

Plymouth Hemi GTX-a

(1969) Plymouth Hemi GTX - 82mm - 1999
This model has a black & gray metal chassis, opening hood with a black & chrome engine, clear windows, and a black interior.
a. blue; silver & red stripe on sides; 30th Anniv. of '69 Muscle Car 2-pack, Series 1, set 1 only 10 - NA

Plymouth Hemi GTX-b

b. white; black roof; orange, black & gold tampo w/"426," "Hemi Bros" & race decals on sides, "Dearborn Street Runner" on hood, 13th Annual Hot Wheels Collectors Convention logo on trunk; mag-style hubs. Ltd ed of 5000 for 13th Hot Wheels Collectors Convention (1999) 20 - 25
c. dk. green, black int., clear windows, red & silver tampo w/"GTX" on sides. In Cool Collectibles box (2000) 8 - 10
d. orange, black rectangle on hood, "Hemi" in black on sides. Issued as 1969 Plymouth Hemi GTX in Cool Collectibles box (2000) 10 - 12
e. black, red int., clear windows, red & gray stripe and "GTX" on sides. In Cool Collectibles box (2000) 15 - 18

Plymouth Hemi GTX-f

f. purple, black int., silver stripe w/"Hemi" & "GTX" on sides. Ltd ed issued in bp by Adkins Collectibles (2000) 10 - 15

Porsche 550 Spyder-a

Porsche 550 Spyder - 58mm - 1999
This sports-car replica has a black & gray metal chassis, opening rear hood with a black & gray engine, clear windshield, and black & gray interior with a red steering wheel.
a. gray, Porsche 50th Anniversary 4-pack only 10 - NA

Porsche 550 Spyder-b

b. lt. blue, same as a, white stripes, black "2" in white circle on sides & top 10 - 15
c. red, same as b 10 - 15

Porsche 917-a

Porsche 917 - 67mm - 1999
This replica of the original race car has a blue & black metal chassis with white pipes, an opening rear hood with a black & gray engine, clear windows, black interior, and rubber tires with a new style black hub.
a. lt. blue; red & black stripes over top; "2" in black in white circle on sides, front & back; race decals. Porsche 50th Anniv. 4-pack only 10 - NA
b. red, clear windows, black int., white & black tampo w/"23" & race decals on sides & top, "Porsche" on sides. In a Cool Collectibles box (2001) 10 - 12

Porsche 930 Turbo-a

Porsche 930 Turbo - 67mm - 1999
This model has a black & gray metal chassis, opening rear hood with a black & gray engine, black interior, and clear windows.
a. red, black stripe around car, black & red spoiler. Porsche 50th Anniv. 4-pack only 8 - NA

Porsche 930 Turbo-b

b. white, same as a, collectible singles, Porsche 911 Turbo 6 - 8

Porsche 930 Turbo-c

c. gray, black int, clear windows, black trim. In Motor Trend series from Preferred Line (2002) 5 - 7

Porsche Boxster-a

Porsche Boxster - 67mm - 1999
This model has a black & gray metal chassis, clear windshield, and tan interior.
a. yellow, "Boxster" in black on trunk. Porsche 50th Anniv. 4-pack only 8 - NA
b. silver, as a, collectible singles 6 - 8

Rareflow-a

Rareflow - 70mm - 1999
This Ed Newton-customized car has a red interior, clear windows, opening front end with a chrome engine, and five-spoke wheels.
a. mtlfk olive, silver headlights, grille tampo. Ed Newton's Lowboyz 3-car set only 8 - NA

Rareflow-b

b. mtlc red, clear windows, white int., in Collectible box (2000) 7 - 9

Rareflow-c

c. orange; black int.; clear windows, white front; purple, black & gray tampo. In Collectible box (2001) 7 - 9
d. gray, dark gray in back, clear windows, black int., magenta & blue tampo. In Collectible box (2001) 7 - 9

Shelby Cobra Replica-a

Shelby Cobra Replica (427 S/C) - 63mm - 1999 (Legends)
This model has a black chassis with gray details, white pipes, opening hood, gray interior, clear windshield, and rubber tires with chrome mags.
a. blue, white stripes over top, Jay Leno set 15 - NA

Values are shown in U.S. dollars, first price is for mint, second is for mint packaged vehicles only. See pages 15-16 for grading guide to determine value for cars in lesser conditions.

b. mtlfk silver, clear windshield, black int., opening hood w/chrome engine, 2 blue stripes over top. In Cool Collectibles box (2001) 10 - 15

Torqued Off-a

Torqued Off™ - 95mm - 1999
This customized semi-truck has two Allison aircraft engines behind the cab, sides scoop, a rear spoiler, clear windows, chrome interior, and special beige wheels with synthetic rubber tires. Made in China, it was issued in the Baur's Beasts 2-pack.

a. blue, "Torq'd Off" in black & white on sides 10 - NA

Triclopz-a

Triclopz™ - 75mm - 1999
This Ed Newton-customized 1948 Tucker has a tan interior, clear windows, rear hood with a chrome engine, and three-spoke wheels.

a. mtlfk red-brown; Ed Newton's Lowboyz 3-car set only 8 - NA

Triclopz-b

b. mtlfk blue; white int.; red, yellow & white flame tampo on sides. Voodoo Highway 3-car set only 8 - NA

Triclopz-c

c. purple; clear windows; lt. purple int.; white, yellow, red & lt. blue spray mask. In Collectible box (2001) 8 - 10

2000

'34 Ford Hot Rod Coupe-a

'34 Ford Hot Rod Coupe (Blown '34 Ford) - 65mm - 2000 (Legends)

This customized five-window coupe has a yellow chassis, chrome & red engine, clear windows, black interior, and chrome wheels with rubber tires.

a. yellow. Issued with 1/24th-scale version of same model in Legends series 30 - NA
b. white, red front, black int., clear windows, red tampo w/"So-Cal Speed Shop" on sides. So-Cal Speed Shop set (2002) 10 - NA
c. black, black int., clear windows, red sides with yellow flames & light stripe on sides. In Cool Collectibles box, #05 (2002) 10 - NA

'48 Ford Woodie-b

'48 Ford Woody (Merc Woody) - 75mm - 2000
This 1949 Ford Woody has clear windows, a brown interior, opening hood with a chrome engine, dark & light brown wood-like sides, black roof, and Cool Collectibles five-spoke wheels.

a. yellow, pulling a trailer, Night at the Races 2-pack 10 - NA
b. turquoise, same as a, black roof. Issued in Collectible box, wrongly named Merc Woodie (2001) 10 - 12
c. red, same as b. Issued in a Collectible box, wrongly named Merc Woodie (2001) 10 - 12

'67 Mustang GT500-a

'67 Mustang GT500 - 70mm - 2000 (Legends)
This Mustang has an opening hood with a black engine, clear windows, black interior, and Cool Collectibles wheels with rubber tires.

a. white, 2 blue stripes over top. with a 1/24th scale version of the same model in blue in the Legends series 30 - NA

'67 Mustang GT500-b

b. gray, black int., clear windows, 2 black stripes over top. Gone in 60 Seconds 4-car set (2000) 15 - NA
c. red, white stripe w/"GT 500" on sides, 2 white stripes on top. Mustang Monthly 2-car set (2001) 10 - NA

'67 Mustang GT500-d

d. black; black int.; clear windows; "eBay" in red, purple, yellow & green & white stripe w/"G.T. 500" on sides; 2 white stripes over top. eBay only (2001) 30 - 35

'70 Dodge Challenger R.T-a

'70 Dodge Challenger R/T - 78mm - 2000
This muscle car has an opening hood with a hole for the engine, black interior, clear windows, and five-spoke collectible wheels.

a. yellow, black stripe & "Challenger R/T" in gray on sides. 30th Anniv. of '70 Muscle Cars 4-car set (2000) 10 - NA

1933 Willys Coupe-a

1933 Willys Coupe - 72mm - 2000
This coupe comes with an opening hood, chrome engine with a black snorkel sticking through the hood, wheelie bar in back, clear windows, black interior, and Cool Collectibles wheels.

a. mtlfk gray-blue, black & white tampo w/"Malco" & race decals on sides, "Dayco" on hood. Hot Rod magazine 4-car set 10 - NA

1933 Willys Coupe-b

b. orange; clear windows; black int. & roof; yellow, black & blue tampo with "K.S. Pittman" & race decals on sides. In Collectible box (2001) 10 - 12

1933 Willys Coupe-c

c. yellow, white roof, gold & black tampo w/"John Coonrod" & race decals on sides. Willys Gassers 2-car set (2001) 15 - NA
d. yellow; black hood, roof & trunk; white int.; clear windows; red & black tampo w/"Killer Bee," a bee & "201 BG/S" on sides; small wheels in front & large wheels in back. In Cool Collectibles box, #15 (2002) 10 - 12

1956 Ford Pickup-c

1956 Ford Pickup
This model has a black chassis, clear windows, purple interior & tonneau cover, opening hood with a chrome engine, and Cool Collectibles wheels.

a. purple; yellow, orange & lt. blue spray mask. In Cool Collectibles box (2000) 15 - 20
b. aqua with light brown truck bed, gray interior, a white spray mask with yellow flames. Issued in a Cool Collectibles box (2000) 15 - 20
c. beige, red spray mask, black outlines in front, black int. & truck bed, clear windows. With trailer, Photo Finish (Main Event) 2-car set 12 - NA
d. yellow; black hood, roof & truck bed cover; red striping; black & white Mooneyes logo on sides. Mooneyes 2-car set (2001) 12 - NA

1956 Ford Pickup-e

e. mtlfk gray; red flames on sides, hood & roof; "Pinstriping by Roth Lu 15381" in black on sides; "Ed "Big Daddy" Roth in black & lt. green on truck bed. Ed Roth 4-car set 15 - NA
f. black; orange & white spray mask; clear windows; tan int.; Harley-Davidson logo on truck bed; rubber tires. Hotwheels.com only, in white box. #2 in Harley-Davidson 4-car series (2001) 75 - NA

1957 Chevy Nomad (custom)-a

1957 Chevy Nomad (Custom) - 78mm - 2000
The rear body lifts up on this customized Nomad. It has clear windows, a black interior, engine inside in back, air vent on roof, and Cool Collectibles five-spoke wheels.

a. mtlfk dark red, chrome trim, "Hot Wheels" in white & chrome on sides. Cool 'n' Custom 2-car set 12 - NA
b. black; yellow, orange & blue flame spray mask in front; gray Hot Wheels logo in back. In Collectibles box (2001) 15 - 20
c. spectraflame aqua, clear windows, white int., gray trim w/"Hot Wheels" on sides. In Collectible box (2001) 15 - 20
d. black; yellow int.; clear windows; yellow, orange & lt. green flame tampo all over, Troy Lee set (2002) 10 - NA

1957 Chevy Nomad (Custom)-e

e. chrome gold; white roof; white, gray, black & orange tampo w/Hot Wheels logo & "East Coast Convention" on sides, flames on hood, flames & Wild Weekend logo on roof; 5-spoke collectible wheels w/redlines. Ltd ed for Wild Weekend (2002) 30 - 35

1957 Chevy Nomad-b

1957 Chevy Nomad (Stock) - 75mm - 2000
This Nomad has an opening hood with a chrome engine, white roof, turquoise interior, clear windows, and Cool Collectibles wheels.

a. turquoise, chrome trim, Cool 'n' Custom 2-car set 10 - NA
b. red, white roof, white int., gray trim, Tri Chevy 3-car set 10 - NA
c. yellow, clear windows, white int., gray trim. In Cool Collectibles box (2001) 10 - 12

1970 Firebird T/A-a

1970 Firebird T/A - 78mm - 2000
This model has clear windows, a white interior & headers, an opening hood with a black engine, and Cool Collectibles five-spoke wheels.

a. white, clear windows, blue int., blue stripe over top, 5-spoke tires. 30th Anniv. of '70 Muscle Cars 4-car set (2000) 10 - NA

1970 Firebird T/A-b

b. blue, thick white stripe over top. In Cool Collectibles box (2001) 10 - 12
c. black, clear windows, black int., gold stripes over top. In Cool Collectibles box (2001) 10 - 12

1970 Ford Mustang-a

1970 Ford Mustang ('70 Mustang Boss 429) - 78mm - 2000
This model has clear windows, a white interior, opening hood with a chrome & black engine, black spoiler & hood scoop, and Cool Collectibles five-spoke wheels.

a. blue, white & black int., clear windows & "Boss 429" in white on sides. 30th Anniv. of '70 Muscle Car 4-car set 10 - NA
b. turquoise w/"Boss 429" in white on sides. In Cool Collectibles box 8 - 10

1970 Ford Mustang-c

c. yellow; black hood, spoiler & int.; clear windows; black stripe on sides. In Cool Collectibles box (2001) 8 - 10

Values are shown in U.S. dollars, first price is for mint, second is for mint packaged vehicles only. See pages 15-16 for grading guide to determine value for cars in lesser conditions.

1970 Ford Mustang-d

d. orange, same as a, black int. & tampo. #4 in *Hot Rod* magazine Limited Edition series, in bp 10 - 15
e. red, black int., clear windows, white tampo w/flames on sides & hood, "American Racing" on sides. "'65 Mustang" in American Racing Equipped 2-car set (2002) 10 - NA
f. dark yellow; black & white tampo with "15" & black stripe on sides & hood; racing decals on sides. Vintage Pony Wars II 2-car set 10 - NA

1970 Plymouth Super Bee-a

1970 Plymouth Super Bee - 80mm - 2000
This model has an opening hood with a chrome engine, white interior, clear windows, and Cool Collectibles five-spoke wheels.
a. purple, "Hemi" in white on hood. 30th Anniv. of '70 Muscle Cars 4-car set (2000) 10 - NA

Bizarro-a

Bizarro - 80mm - 2000
This convertible has chrome halfway up the sides, an opening hood with a chrome engine, clear windshield, white interior, and Cool Collectibles rrww.
a. red, Designer Dreamz 2-car set 12 - NA
b. turquoise, tan dirty int., black (dirt) all over. Lost Treasures 2-car set 12 - NA
b2. as b, less black (dirt) over car. Lost Treasures 2-car set 10 - NA

Harley-Davidson 1920 Racer - 70mm - 2000
a. olive, brown seat & brown wheels. Harley-Davidson 4-car set 10 - NA
b. gray, brown seat, "Harley-Davidson" in brown on gas tank, chrome spokes & white tires. In Cool Collectibles box (2001) 10 - 12

Harley-Davidson Buell - 60mm - 2000
a. yellow, black seat, chrome spokes & blue stripes on tires. Harley-Davidson 4-car set 10 - NA

Harley Davidson Fatboy-b

Harley-Davidson Fatboy
a. gray, black seat, chrome wheels. Harley-Davidson 4-car set 10 - NA
b. red, black seat, gray tampo, gray wheels & ww tires. In Cool Collectibles box (2001) 10 - 12
c. purple, brown seat, gray tampo, gray wheels & ww tires. In Cool Collectibles box (2001) 10 - 12

Harley-Davidson Panhead - 70mm - 2000
a. blue, black seat, white trim, silver & red tampo on gas tank, silver spokes. Harley-Davidson 4-car set 10 - NA
b. black; orange & gray trim; tan seat & int.; gray handlebars & gas tank. Hotwheels.com only, in white box. #4 in Harley-Davidson 4-car series (2001) 75 - NA

Hummer-a

Hummer - 78mm - 2000
This model has an opening hood with a black engine, clear windows, tan interior, and dark red Cool Collectibles wheels with rubber tires.
a. mtlfk dk. red, white tampo w/"Hummer" on sides. Extreme Trucks 2-pack 10 - NA
b. yellow, clear windows, tan int., black tampo w/"Hummer" on sides, yellow hubs. In Cool Collectibles box (2000) 8 - 10
c. black; red int.; clear windows; white, yellow, orange, red & light blue flame tampo on hood & roof. In Cool Collectibles box (2000) 8 - 10

Invader-a

Invader - 72mm - 2000
This model has a clear wrap-around windshield, white interior, chrome twin engines & pipes, and Cool Collectibles wheels.
a. red, white stripes, red int., clear windshield. *Hot Rod* magazine 4-car set 10 - NA
b. purple; white, red & yellow flame spray mask & flames on sides. Cool Collectibles box (2001) 8 - 10

Invader-c

c. mtlfk gold, clear windshield, white int., white & red flame spray mask and flame tampo on sides. In Cool Collectibles box (2001) 8 - 10

Pontiac Funny Car-a

Pontiac Funny Car - 2000
This funny car has clear windows, a black interior, and Cool Collectibles wheels with rubber tires.
a. black; red, yellow, white, orange & blue tampo w/large Hot Wheels logo & race decals on sides; "E" & "e.moola.com" on hood; "Pontiac" on roof. In Cool Collectibles box (2001) 8 - 10

Pro Street Camaro-a

Pro Street Camaro - 72mm - 2000
This Camaro has a chrome engine and blower sticking through an opening hood, black interior, clear windows, wheelie bars in back, and Cool Collectibles wheels.
a. yellow, black stripes over top, black int., clear windows. *Hot Rod* magazine 4-car set 10 - NA

Pro Street Camaro-b

b. orange-brown; white, yellow, orange & red spray mask & "Aaron Automotive" & race decals on sides, "Driver: Parakeet" on roof. In Cool Collectibles box (2001) 15 - 18

c. green, same as b, in Cool Collectibles box (2001) 12 - 15

Rocket Oil-a

Rocket Oil - 112mm - 2000
This futuristic tanker has yellow-tinted windows, chrome interior, and Cool Collectibles wheels with chrome hubs. In 2000, it was issued in the Designer Dreamz two-car set.
a. black and white 12 - NA
b. pearl white & purple, black int., clear windshield, orange & white tampo w/"Racing Fuel" Harley-Davidson logo on sides. Hotwheels.com only, in white box. #3 in Harley-Davidson 4-car series (2001) 75 - NA

Sprint Car-b

Sprint Car & Trailer - 60mm - 2000
This sprint race car has a clear windshield, red interior, chrome roll bar & steering wheel, and chrome hubs with rubber tires.
a. black & white, red tampo w/"27" on sides. Night at the Races 2-car set 10 - NA
b. beige, black int., clear windshield, red & black w/"13" on back sides. Photo Finish (Main Event) 2-car set 10 - NA
c. white, white trailer, black int., clear windshield, red & black winner's flag tampo & "32" on sides. In Cool Collectibles box (2001) 12 - 15
d. black; no trailer; dark beige int.; yellow, orange & red spray mask and 2 white circles w/"3" in back. Haulin' Heat 4-car set 10 - NA

Toyota Baja Truck-a

Toyota Baja Truck - 75mm - 2000
This Japanese model has a red chassis, no windows, black interior, gray roll cage, gray engine in back, and Cool Collectibles wheels with rubber construction tires and an extra wheel on the truck bed.
a. black; light gray, gray, red & blue tampo w/"Toyota," "MCI Worldcom" & race decals on sides, hood & roof; "11" on sides & roof. Xtreme Trucks 2-car set 10 - NA

Toyota Baja Truck-b

b. red; white, black, mustard & blue tampo w/"Tundra Racing," "13" & race decals on sides; "Tundra Racing" & race decals on hood; "13" & driver's name on roof. Cool Collectibles box (2001) 8 - 10
c. white; gray int. & engine in truck bed; clear windshield; yellow, orange, red & black tampo w/"Toyota" on sides, roof & fenders; "MCI" on hood; "1" on roof; race decals all over. In Cool Collectibles box (2001) 10 - 12

2001

'37 Chevy-a

'37 Chevy - 60mm - 2001
This five-window coupe has an opening hood, clear windows, black interior, and Cool Collectibles five-spoke wheels.
a. yellow, Cool 'n' Custom set 10 - NA

'37 Chevy (Customized)-a

'37 Chevy (Customized) - 72mm - 2001
This five-window funny car has a blower sticking through an opening hood, rear wing, clear windows, red interior, & Cool Collectibles wheels.
a. red; white top; white, black, blue & yellow tampo w/"BDS Blower Drive Service" & decal on sides. Cool 'n' Custom set 10 - NA
b. yellow; gray, red, orange & black tampo w/"Jeg's" & race decals on sides; "Jeg's" on black background on wing. *Hot Rod* Magazine Pro Mods set 10 - NA

'52 Agajanian Special-a

'52 Agajanian Special - 64mm - 2001
This 1952 Indianapolis 500 race car has a red interior, black steering wheel, chrome pipes, and Cool Collectibles wheels with gray hubs and rubber tires.
a. white, red spray mask, red & black flame tampo with "98" on sides & nose. Bruce Meyer 4-car set 10 - NA

'56 Ford Cabover - 2001
This cab has clear windows, yellow interior, a two-piece auto hauler, and large Cool Collectibles wheels with rubber tires.
a. yellow; magenta stripe on cab & trailers; "Classic Auto Transport" in red, black & gray on both pieces of trailer. Haulin' Heat 4-car set 15 - NA

'59 Cadillac Convertible-a

'59 Cadillac Convertible - 85mm - 2001
This model has a clear windshield, black & white interior, and Collectible wheels.
a. purple; gray trim; yellow, orange, red & blue flames on sides & hood; magenta, yellow & white tampo with "Hard Rock Cafe Singapore" on trunk. Hard Rock Cafe II 3-car set 10 - NA

'60s-Style Dragster-a

'60s-Style Full Body Dragster - 68mm - 2001
This Greer/Black/Prudhomme dragster has a clear windshield, black interior, exposed

'56 Ford Cabover-a

Values are shown in U.S. dollars, first price is for mint, second is for mint packaged vehicles only. See pages 15-16 for grading guide to determine value for cars in lesser conditions.

chrome engine in the middle, Cool Collectibles wire wheels in front, and five-spoke wheels with large rubber tires in back.
a. yellow; silver & black tampo w/"33" & race decals. Bruce Meyer 4-car set 10 - NA

'71 Buick GSX-a

'71 Buick GSX - 74mm - 2001
This model has an opening hood with a black and gold engine, clear windows, black interior, and Cool Collectibles five-spoke wheels.
a. yellow; red & black tampo w/stripe & "GSX" on sides; 2 thick black stripes on hood. '71 Muscle Cars 4-car set 10 - NA

'71 Chevelle-a

'71 Chevelle - 72mm - 2001
This model of a 1971 Chevrolet has an opening hood with a blue & chrome engine, clear windows, white interior, and Cool Collectibles five-spoke wheels.
a. mtlfk blue, gray trim, "SS 494" on sides, 2 white stripes on hood & trunk. '71 Muscle Cars 4-car set 10 - NA

'71 Dodge Charger R/T-a

'71 Dodge Charger R/T - 76mm - 2001
This Dodge has an opening hood with an orange & chrome engine, clear windows, black interior, and Cool Collectibles five-spoke wheels.
a. lt. green, black & red tampo w/"Charger" & stripes on sides, black stripe & "R/T" on hood. '71 Muscle Cars 4-car set 10 - NA

'71 Ford Torino-a

'71 Ford Torino - 76mm - 2001
This Torino has a black & blue engine sticking through an opening hood, clear windows, black interior, and Cool Collectibles five-spoke wheels.
a. red, black hood w/"Ford" in gray. '71 Muscle Cars 4-car set 10 - NA
b. yellow, black int., clear windows, black hood, black & orange stripe on sides. In Cool Collectibles box, #07 (2002) 10 - 12

1959 Cadillac-a

1959 Cadillac - 90mm - 2001
This Eldorado hardtop has clear windows, a red interior, opening hood with a chrome engine, and whitewall tires.
a. black; red int.; gray trim; magenta, yellow & white "Hard Rock Cafe Paris" on trunk. Hard Rock Cafe II 3-car set 10 - NA
b. black; white, yellow, orange, red & blue flame spray mask in front. In Cool Collectibles box 10 - 12
c. mtlfk lt. purple, clear windows, white int., in Cool Collectibles box (2001) 8 - 10

1963 Coupe De Ville-a

1963 Cadillac Coupe De Ville - 85mm - 2001
This hardtop has an opening hood with a chrome engine, clear windows, blue interior, and Cool Collectibles spoke wheels.
a. pink; gray trim; magenta, yellow & white tampo w/"Hard Rock Cafe La Jolla" on trunk. Hard Rock Cafe II 3-car set 10 - NA
b. black; opening hood; clear windows; white int.; white & blue flame tampo on sides. In Cool Collectibles box (2001) 10 - 12

1972 Dodge Funny Car-a

1972 Dodge Funny Car - 75mm - 2001
This Dodge has clear windows, a black interior, and Cool Collectibles wheels with chrome hubs & rubber tires.
a. dk. blue; red, white & lt. blue tampo w/"Hawaiian" & race decals on sides; red tampo on hood; black int.; clear windows. *Hot Rod* magazine 4-car set 10 - NA
b. gray; magenta, black, yellow, blue, white & red tampo w/"Chi-Town Hustler" & race decals on sides; flames & "Dodge" on hood; blue stripes on roof; "Rislone" on rear window. In Cool Collectibles box 8 - 10

Airstream Trailer-a

Airstream Trailer - 94mm - 2001
This model has a trailer hitch, clear windows with light orange-brown shades, and two Cool Collectibles wheels.
a. chrome, Airstream Dream 2-car set 12 - NA

Big Mutha-a

Big Mutha - 95mm - 2001
This late 1940s car has an opening hood, clear windows, black interior, and Cool Collectibles wheels with whitewall tires.
a. black; red & lt. blue tampo design on sides. Designer Dreamz II 4-car set 10 - NA
b. pearl white, yellow & red flame spray mask, no whitewall tires. In Cool Collectibles box (2002) 15 - 18

Manta Ray-a

Manta Ray - 65mm - 2001
This 1964 Oakland Roadster Show winner has an exposed engine, clear dome, black interior, two small Cool Collectibles wheels in front, and large wheels with rubber tires in back.
a. pearl white, Rod & Custom 2-car set 10 - NA

Mysterion-a

Mysterion - 50mm - 2001
This model has a blue-tinted lift-up dome, gray interior, two exposed chrome engines, one raised headlight, & Cool Collectibles wheels.
a. yellow, Ed Roth 4-car set 10 - NA

Orange Crate-a

Orange Crate ('32 Ford) - 55mm - 2001
This model has clear windows, a black interior, two small Cool Collectibles wheels in front, and large wheels with rubber tires in back.
a. orange, black roof, Rod & Custom 2-car set 10 - NA
b. white, chrome int., clear windows, black roof, red & black tampo with "So-Cal Speed Shop Team" & "32 AG/S" on sides. In Cool Collectibles box, #13 (2002) 12 - 15

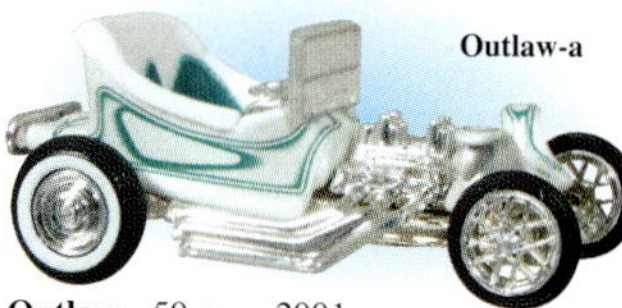
Outlaw-a

Outlaw - 50mm - 2001
This dune buggy has a clear windshield, white & turquoise interior, chrome engine with six side pipes, and Cool Collectibles wheels.
a. mtlfk white , turquoise pinstriping, Ed Roth 4-car set 10 - NA

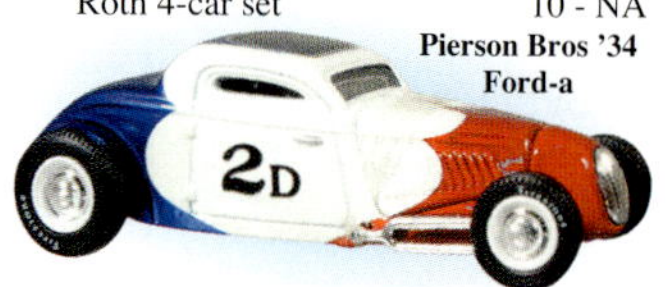

Pierson Bros '34 Ford-a

Pierson Brothers '34 Ford 3-Window Coupe - 63mm - 2001
This race car has a black interior, clear windows, and Cool Collectibles white wheels with rubber tires.
a. dk. red, white & blue w/"2D" in black on sides. Bruce Meyer 4-car set 10 - NA

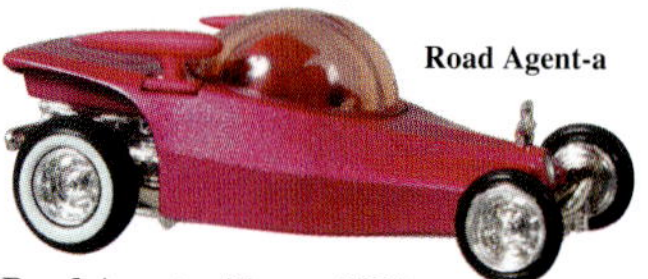
Road Agent-a

Road Agent - 47mm - 2001
This model has a red-tinted dome, magenta interior, and Cool Collectibles wheels.
a. mtlfk magenta, Ed Roth 4-car set 10 - NA

So-Cal Belly Tank-a

So-Cal Belly Tank (Lakester) - 60mm - 2001
This dry-lake racer features a clear windshield, black interior, and Cool Collectibles chrome hubs with rubber tires.
a. white, red rear, black & red tampo w/"28" & "So-Cal" on sides. Bruce Meyer 4 car set 10 - NA
b. black; clear windshield; black int.; red, yellow & light blue spray mask and "200" in white on sides. In Cool Collectibles box, #10 (2002) 10 - 12

Streetliner-a

Streetliner - 98mm - 2001
This strange three-wheeled concept race car has two chrome engines with pipes in back, a long front suspension, purple windshield & interior, two thin Cool Collectibles five-spoke wheels in front, and one thick Cool Collectibles five-spoke wheel in back.
a. white; blue & purple spray mask. Designer Dreamz II set 15 - NA

Volkswagen Microbus-a

Volkswagen Microbus - 65mm - 2001
This German van has clear windows, a white interior, and Cool Collectibles wheels.
a. blue, top half white, Bugs and Buses 4-car set 10 - NA
b. dark red; white top; clear windows; black int.; yellow, orange & gold flame tampo on sides & roof; "2001 MEA Dinner Dance December 8, 2001" on roof; spoke wheels. 2001 Mattel Dinner Dance, in plastic box (2001) 125 - 175

Volkswagen Microbus-c

c. blue; white top; clear windows; chrome int.; yellow, red & white tampo with flames & "Davids-Wheels.com" on sides & front; flames on roof. Website only (2002) 25 - 30

Volkswagen Bug-b

Volkswagen Bug - 60mm - 2001
This classic German car has an opening trunk with an exposed engine, clear windows, black interior, and Cool Collectibles wheels.
a. red, Bugs and Buses 4-car set 10 - NA
b. mtlfk gray; red int.; orange & yellow flames on sides, hood & roof. Bugs and Buses 4-car set 10 - NA
c. mtlfk blue; red int.; clear windows; yellow-to-red spray mask tampo & flames on sides, hood & trunk; black & white checkerboard tampo on sides & hood; "Hot" on trunk. In Cool Collectibles box, #14 (2002) 15 - 18

Volkswagen Microbus - 65mm - 2001
This German van has clear windows, a black interior and Cool Collectibles wheels.
a. lt. green, dk. green flames on sides & roof. Bugs and Buses 4-car set 10 - NA
b. white, pink front, black int., clear windows, pink & orange design, 5-spoke Cool Collectible wheels. In Cool Collectibles box, #06 (2002) 18 - 20

2002

'69 Camaro - 70mm - 2002
This Chevrolet has clear windows, a black interior & roof, opening hood, and eight-spoke yellow Cool Collectible wheels. This Trans Am version of the Hot Wheels Pro Street Camaro from 2000 has a new chassis, grille, wheelie bars, rear bumper, hood, and engine.

Values are shown in U.S. dollars, first price is for mint, second is for mint packaged vehicles only. See pages 15-16 for grading guide to determine value for cars in lesser conditions.

a. blue; white & yellow tampo w/"6," "Sunoco Camaro" & race decals on sides. Vintage Pony Wars II 2-car set 10 - NA

'70 Dodge Charger - 70mm - 2002
This model has an opening power hood, black interior, clear windows, and eight-spoke Cool Collectible wheels.
a. lt. green; black, red & white tampo with stripe, "77," "Dodge" & race decals on sides; "77" on hood & trunk; "Dodge" in front. Vintage Pony Wars 2-car set 10 - NA

'70 Pontiac Firebird - 72mm - 2002
This model has an opening power hood with a hole, black interior, clear windows, and eight-spoke collectible wheels.
a. white; lt. blue, yellow, black & red tampo with "8" & race decals on sides; "8" on hood & trunk. Vintage Pony Wars 2-car set 10 - NA

1953 Biarritz-a

1953 Biarritz - 80mm - 2002
This 1953 Cadillac convertible has an opening hood with a chrome engine, tan interior, clear windshield, and chrome wheels with white wall rubber tires.
a. yellow, John D'Agostino Kustoms set 10 - NA

1967 Pro Street Corvette-a

1967 Pro Street Corvette - 80mm - 2002
This customized Corvette Stingray has an opening hood with engine sticking through, black interior, blue-tinted windows, and five-spoke chrome wheels with rubber tires.
a. mtlc blue; yellow, orange & white flame spray mask tampo with "Hard Knocks" & race decals on sides. Cool & Custom III set 10 - NA
a2. as a, white in front on spray mask. Cool & Custom III set 12 - NA
b. black; yellow, red & white tampo with "Eagle One" & race decals on sides; "Eagle One" on hood. *Hot Rod* Magazine Pro Mods set (2002) 10 - NA

Ford Focus-a

Ford Focus - 62mm - 2002
This tuner model has an opening hood with a chrome engine, black interior, tinted windows, black rear wing, and five-spoke chrome wheels with rubber tires.
a. yellow; black, red & white tampo with "Hot Wheels" & race decals on sides & hood; "Wings West" on windshield; "hotwheels.com" on wing. *Super Street* Magazine set 10 - NA

HemisFear - 70mm - 2002
This concept car has a beige interior, clear windows, chrome engine inside the rear window, and five-spoke collectible wheels.
a. mtlfk orange, "Hemisfear" in black on sides. Foose Design 2-car set 10 - NA

Honda Civic Si - 68mm - 2002
This tuner model has an opening hood with a chrome engine, black interior, tinted windows, black rear wing, and five-spoke chrome wheels with rubber tires.

Honda Civic SI-a

a. green; black hood; black, gray & white tampo w/"Hot Wheels" & race decals on sides & hood; "Super Street" on windshield & wing. *Super Street* Magazine set 10 - NA

Manhattan - 85mm - 2002
This concept car has an opening hood with a light blue, black & chrome engine; white interior; clear windows; and collectible wheels.
a. dark blue, chrome trim, Foose Design 2-car set 10 - NA

Pure Hell-a

Pure Hell - 53mm - 2002
This '50s-style drag racer has a black interior & roll cage, clear windshield, large exposed engine in front, large rrch in back & small bicycle-style wheels in front.
a. dark red; white, red & yellow tampo with flames & "Pure Hell" on sides; Dale Emory's signature on top. Fuel Altereds collectible set, 2002 10 - NA

Winged Express-a

Winged Express - 64mm - 2002
This '50s-style drag racer has a black interior & roll cage, chrome roof, large exposed engine in front, large rrgd in back & thin gold wheels in front.
a. red; white & black tampo with "Marcellus & Bosch Winged Express" on sides; "Marcellus & Bosch" on top; "Howards Cams" on roof. Fuel Altereds collectible set, 2002 10 - NA

PRO CIRCUIT

1992

2565-a

#6 Valvoline 2565 - 78mm - 1992
This Ford Thunderbird stock car has a black plastic chassis, clear windows, gray plastic interior, and pcg. China.
Similar castings: 5900 Thunderbird Stocker (1984), 1456 Thunderburner (1987), 2568 #21 Citgo (1992 Pro Circuit), 16039 Velocitor (1996)
a. white; dk. blue in back; red, lt. blue & dk. blue tampo w/"6," "Valvoline" on sides; "Valvoline," racing decals on hood & trunk; "6," "Mark Martin" twice on roof; racing sponsors' sticker on sides $6 - 8
a2. as a, no sticker on sides 6 - 8

2568-a

#21 Citgo 2568 - 78mm - 1992
This Ford Thunderbird stock car has a black plastic chassis, clear windows, orange plastic interior, racing sponsors' sticker on sides, and pcg. China.
Similar castings: 5900 Thunderbird Stocker (1984), 1456 Thunderburner (1987), 2565 #6 Valvoline (1992 Pro Circuit), 16039 Velocitor (1996)
a. white; red, orange & dk. blue tampo w/"21," "Citgo" & race decals on sides; "Citgo" & race decals on hood; "21" & "Morgan Shephard" twice on roof $6 - 8
a2. as a, "Shepherd" spelled correctly on roof 6 - 8

2568-a3

a3. as a2, GE logo on trunk lid 6 - 8
a4. as a2, large Ford logo on hood 6 - 8

2115-a

#25 Hot Wheels 2115 - 75mm - 1992
This Camaro has a white metal chassis, clear windows, white interior, pcr in front, pcw in back. China.
Similar castings: 5182 Blown Camaro Z-28 (1984), #33 Duracell (1992 Pro Circuit)
a. blue; white in back; red, yellow & white tampo w/Hot Wheels logo, "25," "Duracell" on sides; logo on hood; "Camaro" on windshield; Chevy logo, "Jack Baldwin" twice on roof; "Hot Wheels" & Hot Wheels logo twice on trunk $10 - 12
a2. as a, pcr, Pro Circuit Speedway set 15 - NA

2698-a

#26 Quaker State Indy Car 2698 - 75mm - 1992
This racer has a metal chassis, front & rear spoilers, white plastic sides, white driver with a green helmet, exposed metal engine, iwc. China.
Similar castings: 3915 Formula Fever (1983), 9545 Thunderstreak (1985)
a. green; white tampo w/"Quaker State" & race decals; spoilers $8 - 10

2567-a

#26 Quaker State Stock Car 2567 - 78mm - 1992
This Ford Thunderbird has a black metal chassis, clear windows, gray plastic interior, and pcg. China.
Similar castings: 5900 Thunderbird Stocker (1984), 1456 Thunderburner (1987), 2565 #6 Valvoline (1992 Pro Circuit), 2568 #21 Citgo (1992 Pro Circuit)
a. green; white & black tampo w/"Quaker State," "26" & race decals $8 - 10

2738-a

#33 Duracell 2738 - 75mm - 1992
This Camaro stock car has a white metal base, white plastic interior, clear windows, pc. China.
Similar castings: 5182 Blown Camaro Z-28 (1984), 2115 #25 Hot Wheels (1992 Pro Circuit)
a. orange; black border around bottom; red, white & black tampo w/"33," "Duracell," "Goodyear," Hot Wheels logo on sides; Chevy logo twice; "Duracell" twice; battery on top; "Camaro" on windshield $6 - 8

2628-a

#42 Mello Yello 2628 - 76mm - 1992
This Pontiac stock car has a black plastic chassis, clear windows, gray plastic interior, pcg. China.
Similar castings: 2623 #43 STP (1992), 2630 #2 Pontiac Excitement (1993), 10159 Auto Palace/AC Delco (1993), 12873 Pontiac Stocker (1995)
a. black; lt. green border around bottom; "42," "Mello Yello," "UNIDEN" & race decals on sides; "Enjoy Mello Yello" on hood; "42" & "Kyle" on roof; sponsors' sticker on sides $6 - 8
a2. as a; no "UNIDEN" on sides 6 - 8

2623-a

#43 STP 2623 - 76mm - 1992
This Pontiac stock car has a black plastic chassis, clear windows, gray plastic interior, iwg. China.
Similar castings: 2628 #42 Mello Yello (1992), 2630 #2 Pontiac Excitement (1993), 10159 Auto Palace/AC Delco (1993), 12873 Pontiac Stocker (1995)
a. blue; red stripe around bottom & over top; white, red & dk. blue tampo w/"43" & racing decals on sides, "STP" on hood, "43" on roof; sponsors' stickers on sides. "Oil Treatment" has dk blue border $35 - 40
a2. as a, lt. blue int. 7 - 9
a3. as a2, no border around "Oil Treatment" 7 - 9
a4. lt. blue, same as a3 6 - 8

2743-a

Castrol GTX Funny Car 2743 - 80mm - 1992
This funny car has a metal chassis & engine, gray plastic interior, clear windows, pc. China.
Similar castings: 7608 Probe Funny Car (1990), King Kenny Funny Car (1992 Pro Circuit)
a. white; "Castrol GTX" & race decals on sides & hood; "Oldsmobile," Castrol GTX bottle & "John Force" on roof; "Castrol GTX" in back; 4 headlights $15 - 18
a2. as a, 2 headlights 15 - 18

Values are shown in U.S. dollars, first price is for mint, second is for mint packaged vehicles only. *See pages 15-16 for grading guide to determine value for cars in lesser conditions.*

2841-a

King Kenny Funny Car 2841 - 80mm - 1992
This funny car has a metal chassis & engine, gray plastic interior, clear windows, pc. China.
Similar castings: 7608 Probe Funny Car (1990), 2743 Castrol GTX Funny Car (1992 Pro Circuit)
a. red; white, green & black tampo w/"King Kenny," "Kenny Bernstein" & race stickers on sides & top; 4 headlights $15 - 18
a2. as a, 2 headlights 15 - 18

1993

2638-a

#1 Texaco 2638 - 75mm - 1993
This Indy-style racer has a metal chassis, front & rear spoiler, black plastic sides, black driver with a white helmet, exposed black metal engine, and iwb. China.
Similar castings: 3915 Formula Fever (1983), 9545 Thunderstreak (1985), 2698 #26 Quaker State Indy Car (1992 Pro Circuit), 2690 #3 Valvoline (1993), 2692 #4 Penske (1993), 2694 #5 Penske (1993), 2677 #2 Texaco (1993)
a. white; red, white & black tampo w/"Texaco," "1," "Kmart," race decals; white roll bar $10 - 12

2630-a

#2 Pontiac Excitement 2630 - 75mm - 1993
This Pontiac stock car has a black metal chassis, clear windows, black plastic interior, pcg. China.
Similar castings: 2623 #43 STP (1992), 2628 #42 Mello Yello (1992), 10159 Auto Palace/AC Delco (1993), 12873 Pontiac Stocker (1995)
a. black; yellow, red & white tampo: "Pontiac," "2," "Pontiac Excitement," "Rusty Wallace" & race decals all over $8 - 10

2677-a

#2 Texaco 2677 - 75mm - 1993
This Indy-style racer has a metal chassis, front & rear spoiler, black plastic sides, black driver with a white helmet, exposed black metal engine, and iwb. China.
Similar castings: 3915 Formula Fever (1983), 9545 Thunderstreak (1985), 2698 #26 Quaker State Indy Car (1992 Pro Circuit), 2690 #3 Valvoline (1993), 2692 #4 Penske (1993), 2694 #5 Penske (1993), 2638 #1 Texaco (1993)
a. white; red, white & black tampo with "Texaco," "2," "K mart," race decals; red roll bar $10 - 12

2739-a

#3 Cytomax 2739 - 75mm - 1993
This Chinese-made Camaro race car has a blue metal chassis, clear windows, gray interior, and pc.
Similar castings: 5182 Blown Camaro Z-28 (1984), 2115 #25 Hot Wheels (1992 Pro Circuit), 2738 #33 Duracell (1992 Pro Circuit)
a. white; lt. green, black & pink tampo w/"Cytomax" & "3" on hood & sides; "Greg Pickett" twice on roof; "Champion Nutrition" on trunk; yellow "Pickett Racing" on windshield $10 - 12

2690-a

#3 Valvoline 2690 - 75mm - 1993
This Indy-style racer has a metal chassis, front & rear spoilers, white plastic sides, black driver with a white helmet, exposed metal engine, iwc. China.
Similar castings: 3915 Formula Fever (1983), 9545 Thunderstreak (1985), 2698 #26 Quaker State Indy Car (1992 Pro Circuit), 2692 #4 Penske (1993), 2694 #5 Penske (1993), 2677 #2 Texaco (1993), 2638 #1 Texaco (1993)
a. white w/black sides; red, black & blue tampo w/"Valvoline," "3" & decals on sides $10 - 12

2692-a

#4 Penske 2692 - 75mm - 1993
This Indy-style racer has a metal chassis, front & rear spoiler, white plastic sides, orange driver with a white helmet, exposed metal engine, and iwc. China.
Similar castings: 3915 Formula Fever (1983), 9545 Thunderstreak (1985), 2698 #26 Quaker State Indy Car (1992 Pro Circuit), 2690 #3 Valvoline (1993), 2694 #5 Penske (1993), 2677 #2 Texaco (1993), 2638 #1 Texaco (1993)
a. white & orange w/"Penske," "4" & race decals $10 - 12

2694-a

#5 Penske 2694 - 75mm - 1993
This Indy-style racer has a metal chassis, front & rear spoiler, white plastic sides, orange driver with a blue helmet, exposed metal engine, iwc. China.
Similar castings: 3915 Formula Fever (1983), 9545 Thunderstreak (1985), 2698 #26 Quaker State Indy Car (1992 Pro Circuit), 2690 #3 Valvoline (1993), 2692 #4 Penske (1993), 2677 #2 Texaco (1993), 2638 #1 Texaco (1993)
a. orange & white; "Penske," "5" & race decals on sides $10 - 12

HOT WHEELS RACING

In 1997, Mattel decided to enter NASCAR and sponsored Kyle Petty's Pontiac. Even though the Pro Circuit line from 1992 wasn't a big hit, Mattel went ahead in a big way, issuing both a kid's line and a deluxe line. The kid's line had plastic bases, plastic wheels, were issued on blistercards that looked like a 1, and retailed for around $1.99 each. The deluxe line was a more detailed version with metal bases and synthetic rubber tires. They also came with a collector's card, featuring the driver and his car on the front, with a short story about the driver and statistics on the back. These models sold for approximately $2.99 each.

Mattel issued at least three different versions each year of most of these models, with some of the sponsors changing drivers. Most of the cars had very slight differences like tinted or clear windows, different front ends, etc. Some of the drivers drove special cars for one race; a few were featured by Mattel.

1997 Pro Racing Collector line

#04 Kodak-a4

#4 Kodak 17408 - Sterling Marlin - 78mm - 1997
This Chevrolet Monte Carlo has a black metal base, black plastic interior & roll cage, clear windows with black outline, black stripes, gybk, and a collector's card.
a. dk. yellow; black spoiler; red, black, gold, blue, orange & white tampo w/"4," "Kodak Gold Film" & racing decals on sides, "4" on roof, "Kodak Film" & Chevy logo on hood, "Monte Carlo" in front. Sterling Marlin's signature on both sides of roof. Car faces wrong direction in blistercard. Collector's 1st Ed. card $40 - 50
a2. as a; brighter paint & tampo: "Kodak Film," "4" in back; car is facing right direction on blistercard. Collector's 1st Ed. card 3 - 5
a3. as a2, tinted windows, Superspeedway card 3 - 5
a4. as a, black Short Track front end, line under "$" on door is wavy instead of straight. Superspeedway; Short Track card 3 - 5

#04 Kodak-b

b. gray, same as a; red & black tampo w/"4" on sides; red, black & gold tampo w/"Kodak" & "Gold Film" on hood. Test Track 1998 card (1998) 5 - 7
c. dk. yellow, same as a4, different race decals. Bobby Hamilton's signature on both sides of roof. Trackside box (1998) 2 - 10
c2. as c, gray base, 1st Ed 1998 card, w/card (1998) 3 - 5
d. as c, gray roll cage & int., smaller "4" on sides, "Kodak Max" not "Kodak Gold" on sides & hood, different race decals. Trackside box or Daytona 99 Edition blistercard (1999) 3 - 5
d2. as d, Thailand (1999) 3 - 5

#04 Kodak-e

e. black; yellow, blue, red, green, magenta & white tampo w/"4," "Kodak Advantix" & race decals on sides; "Kodak Advantix System" on hood; "4" & Bobby Hamilton's signature on roof; "Advanced" in yellow on trunk; "Kodak Advantix" & "4" in back; gyrd. Trackside box (1999) 8 - 10
e2. black, same as e, lighter yellow & red in tampo, "Kodak" on hood, signature on roof & "Advanced" on trunk are gray not yellow, Thailand. Daytona 99 Edition blistercard (1999) 4 - 6

#05 Kellogg's-a2

#5 Kellogg's 17407 - Terry Labonte - 78mm - 1997
This Chevrolet Monte Carlo has a gray metal base, white interior & roll cage, clear windows with black outlines, black stripes, and gybk. Each car is on a Collector's 1997 1st Ed. blistercard; with collector's card.
a. yellow w/red back half; yellow, black, white, red & green tampo w/"5," "Kellogg's" & racing decals on sides; "5" on roof; "Kellogg's" in back; sun & tiger on trunk; Corn Flakes logo on hood. Terry Labonte's sig. on both sides of roof. Car faces wrong direction in blistercard. Collector's 1st Ed card $60 - 75
a2. as a, lt. green in tampo, "Starburst" on trunk, two black stripes in front are missing. Collector's card is different, car is facing right direction on blistercard. Collector's 1st Ed card 3 - 5
a3. as a2, tinted windows, Superspeedway card 3 - 5
a4. as a2, black Short Track front end & card 3 - 5

#05 Kellogg's-b

b. blue; same as a2; large orange stripe on bottom; red, yellow, white, lt. blue, green & black tampo w/"5," "Kellogg's," race decals on sides; "5" on roof; "Starburst" on yellow block on trunk; Tony the Tiger on hood. Short Track card 10 - 12
c. yellow, same as a2, spoiler is black, hood tampo is different. Terry Labonte's signature on both sides of roof. Trackside Box (1998) 2 - 10
c2. as c, Preview Ed 1998 card, w/card (1998) 3 - 5
d. white; green top; green, yellow, red & black tampo w/"5," Kellogg's rooster & race decals on sides; Kellogg's rooster & "Corny" on hood; "5" & Terry Labonte's signature on roof; starburst logo on trunk; "Kellogg's," rooster & "Corny" in back 5 - 7

#05 Kellogg's-e

e. gold, same as a2, race decals different, "Starburst" on trunk. Pit Crew Collector Ed (1999) 8 - 10

#05 Kellogg's-e2

e2. as a2, darker red tampo, larger "5" on sides, no "Starburst" on trunk, different race decals. Trackside box or Daytona 99 Ed blistercard (1999) 3 - 5
e3. as e, Thailand (1999) 3 - 5
f. yellow, same as c, green stripe is darker, "Advanced Auto Parts" on trunk. Pit Crew 1999 Collector Ed (1999) 3 - 5
f2. as f, Thailand (1999) 3 - 5
f3. as f, black & gray scratches tampoed on sides & hood, Thailand. Trading Paint blistercard, #3 in Trading Paint series, limited to 15,000 (1999) 12 - 18

Values are shown in U.S. dollars, first price is for mint, second is for mint packaged vehicles only. See pages 15-16 for grading guide to determine value for cars in lesser conditions.

#06 Valvoline-a2

#6 Valvoline 17411 - Mark Martin - 80mm - 1997

This Ford Thunderbird has a gray metal base, light gray plastic interior & roll cage, clear windows with black outlines, black stripes, and gybk; with collector's card.

a. white; back half blue; black, white, red, dk. blue & lt. blue tampo w/"6," "Valvoline" broken up by rear wheel well; racing decals on sides; "6" on roof; "Valvoline" in back; "Cummins" on trunk; "Valvoline," "Cummins" & Valvoline logo on hood; Mark Martin's signature on both sides of roof. Car faces wrong direction in blistercard. Collector's 1st Ed blistercard $60 - 75

a2. as a, lighter blue in tampo w/"6" on sides, roof is larger & slants more, "Valvoline" above wheel well & black design in front is smaller. Car is facing right direction on blistercard. Collector's 1st Ed card 3 - 5

a3. as a2, tinted windows, Superspeedway card 3 - 5

a4. as a, black Short Track front end, Short Track card 3 - 5

#06 Valvoline-b

b. gray; same as a; red, black & white tampo w/"6" on sides; lt. blue, dk. blue & red tampo w/"V" & "Valvoline" on hood. Test Track 1998 card (1998) 5 - 7

#06 Valvoline-c

c. white Ford Taurus; same as a2; different "6," "Valvoline's "V" & race decals; "Eagle One," "V," "6" in back. Trackside Box only (1998) 3 - 10

c2. as c, Preview Ed 1998 Collector's card (1998) 3 - 5

c3. as c, red hubs, 1st Edition card (1998) 4 - 6

d. gray; red, dk. blue, lt. blue & white tampo w/"6," "Synpower" & race decals on sides; "Valvoline," "V" & "Cummins" on hood; "6" on roof; "Cummins" on trunk; "Eagle 1" in back; red hubs 10 - 12

e. black; yellow, red, orange & blue tampo w/"6," "Eagle 1" & race decals on sides; Eagle 1 logo & "Cummins" on hood; "6" & Mark Martin's signature on roof; "Cummins" on trunk; "Valvoline" & race decals in back; red hubs. 1st Ed card, Trackside Box 3 - 5

#06 Valvoline-e2

e2. gold, same as c, race decals different. Collector Edition 1999 Pit Crew card (1999) 7 - 9

f. white, same as c, larger "6" on sides & roof, race decals different, gyrd. Collector Ed 1999 Pro Racing card, Trackside box, w/transporter or Collector Ed 1999 Pit Crew card (1999) 3 - 5

f2. as f, Thailand (1999) 3 - 5

g. as f, lighter color, race decals different, Bugles logo smaller, red hubs. Daytona 500 1999 Edition blistercard; Trackside box or 2-pack with 1/24th scale model (1999) 3 - 5

g2. as g, Thailand (1999) 3 - 5

g3. as g, black & gray scratches tampoed on sides & hood, Thailand. #2 in Trading Paint series, limited to 15,000 (1999) 12 - 15

h. as g, black replaces dk. blue (1999) 3 - 5

#07 QVC-a

#7 QVC 17410 - Geoff Bodine - 80mm - 1997

This Ford Thunderbird has a gray metal base, gray interior & roll cage, clear windows with black outlines & stripes, and gybk with black hubs and "Goodyear" & "Eagle" in yellow; with collector's card.

a. black; lt. red, white & blue tampo w/red border on bottom; "7" & "QVC" race decals on sides; "QVC" on hood & in back; "7" & Geoff Bodine's signature on roof; "WWW.QVC.COM" on trunk; "QVC" & "7" in back 3 - 5

#08 Circuit City-a

#8 Circuit City 18087 - Hut Stricklin - 80mm - 1997

This Ford Thunderbird has a gray metal base, gray interior & roll cage, clear windows with black outline & stripes, and gybk with black hubs and "Goodyear" & "Eagle" in yellow; with collector's card.

a. red; black in back; white, black, blue & red tampo w/"8," "Circuit City," race decals on sides; "Circuit City" on hood, trunk & back; "8" on roof. Hut Stricklin's signature on both sides of roof. Collector's 1st Ed card $3 - 5

a2. as a, tinted windows, Superspeedway card 3 - 5

a3. as a, black Short Track front end, Short Track card 3 - 5

b. red Chevrolet Monte Carlo, same as a, "Monte Carlo" in front, Trackside Box, Hut Stricklin's last name spelled Strickland (1998) 3 - 10

b2. as b, Preview Ed 1998 card, collector's card (1998) 3 - 5

#10 Tide-a4

#10 Tide 17816 - Ricky Rudd - 80mm - 1997

This Ford Thunderbird has a gray metal base, light gray plastic interior & roll cage, clear windows with black outlines & three stripes, and gybk; with collector's card.

a. orange; white back; black, white, dk. blue & yellow tampo w/"10," "Tide" & racing decals on sides; "10" on roof; "Whirlpool" on trunk; "Tide" & "10" in back; "Tide America's Favorite" & Ford logo on hood. Ricky Rudd's signature on both sides of roof. Collector's 1st Ed blistercard $3 - 5

a2. as a, tinted windows, Superspeedway card 3 - 5

a3. as a2, black Short Track front end, Short Track card 3 - 5

a4. as a, "Mountain Spring" under "Tide" in tampo, Short Track card 6 - 8

a5. as a, 6 black vertical stripes in front. Season Summary 1997 card (1998) 3 - 5

#10 Tide-b

b. gray Ford Taurus; same as a5; black & white tampo w/"10" on sides; yellow, lt. blue, dk. blue, orange & white tampo w/Tide logo on hood. Test Track 1998 blistercard (1998) 5 - 7

c. orange, same as a2, clear windows, "Taurus" in front, "10" is smaller, race decals are different. Trackside Box only (1998) 3 - 10

c2. as c, Preview Ed 1998 card or 1st Edition, w/card (1998) 3 - 5

#10 Tide-d

d. mtlfk gold, same as c, decals slightly different. Pit Crew Blistercard (1999) 7 - 9

e. orange; same as c; larger 10 on sides & roof; smaller, thicker "Tide" on hood; different race decals; Thailand. Hot Wheels Racing 1999 blistercard, Trackside box w/transporter or a Pit Crew blistercard (1999) 3 - 5

#10 Tide-e2

e2. as e, hood tampo larger, numbers smaller. Daytona 500 blistercard, Trackside box & 2-pack, 1/24 model (1999) 3 - 5

#10 Tide-f

f. off-white; black & white "10" on sides; "Tide America's Favorite" in dk. blue, lt. blue & white. Test Track 1999 blistercard. #1 in 99 Test Track series, limited to 15,000 (1999) 12 - 15

#16 Primestar-a2

#16 Primestar 17413 - Ted Musgrave - 80mm - 1997

This Ford Thunderbird has a gray metal base, black interior & roll cage, clear windows with black outlines & stripes, and gybk; with collector's card.

a. dk. blue w/red back; yellow, white, blue, black & red tampo w/"16," "Primestar," Family Channel logo & racing decals on sides; "16" on roof; "Primestar" & Family Channel logo on trunk, in back & on hood; "16" in back; Ford logo on hood. No sig. on roof. Car faces wrong direction in blistercard. Collector's 1st Ed card $60 - 75

a2. as a, darker red in back, larger "16" on sides, red lines not black inside "Primestar" on sides, smaller black tampo in front. Ted Musgrave's signature on both sides of roof. Car is facing right direction on blistercard. Collector's 1st Ed card 3 - 5

a3. as a2, tinted windows, Superspeedway card 3 - 5

a4. as a2, black Short Track front end, Short Track card 3 - 8

a5. as a2, more black tampo in front, black headlights, Season Summary 1997 card (1998) 3 - 5

b. blue Ford Taurus; same as a2; yellow nose, roof & sides; "Primestar" on trunk, back & hood; Trackside box only (1998) 8 - 10

b2. dk. blue, same as c, Preview Ed 1998 card, w/card (1998) 3 - 5

c. orange; yellow, white, black & blue tampo w/"16," "Primestar" & race decals on sides; "16" & "Primestar" on hood; "16" & driver's signature on roof; "Primestar" on trunk; "1 800 Primestar" in back; Thailand. 1999 Hot Wheels Racing blistercard or on Trackside box (1999) 3 - 5

c2. as c, China (1999) 3 - 5

#21 Citgo-b

#21 Citgo 18088 - Michael Waltrip - 80mm - 1997

This Ford Thunderbird has a gray metal base, red interior & roll cage, clear windows with black outlines & stripes, and gybk; with collector's card.

a. red-orange; black, white, dk. red & dk. blue tampo w/"21," "Citgo," Citgo logo & racing decals on sides; "21" on roof; "Citgo," "21" & logo in back; logo on trunk; Citgo & Ford logos on hood. Michael Waltrip's sig. on both sides of roof. Collector's 1st Ed card $3 - 5

a2. as a, tinted windows, Superspeedway card 3 - 5

a3. as a, black Short Track front end, Short Track card 3 - 5

b. white; red top; clear windows; red int.; black, dk. red, dk. blue, gold & orange tampo w/"21" on top; "Citgo," logo & racing decals on sides; '21," "Citgo," logo & "Saysgo" in back; "Citgo" & logo on trunk; Citgo & Ford logos on hood. Short Track front end, Short Track card 4 - 6

#21 Citgo-c

c. gray; same as a; black & white "21" on sides; blue, red, orange & white Citgo logo on hood. Test Track 1998 card (1998) 5 - 7

#21 Citgo-d

d. red-orange Ford Taurus, same as a, different race decals, smaller logo on hood, "Taurus" in front. Michael Waltrip's signature on both sides of roof. Trackside Box only (1998) 8 - 10

d2. as d, red int., Preview Ed 1998 card, w/Collector's card (1998) 3 - 5

d3. as d, gray int., 1st Ed card 3 - 5

e. red; pink, white, black, dk. blue & yellow tampo w/"Citgo," "21" & race decals on sides; Citgo logo on hood; "21" & "Elliott Sadler" on roof; "WWW.CITGO.COM" on trunk; "Citgo" & "21" in back. Collector Ed. Blistercard & Trackside box (1999) 3 - 5

Values are shown in U.S. dollars, first price is for mint, second is for mint packaged vehicles only. See pages 15-16 for grading guide to determine value for cars in lesser conditions.

#28 Havoline-a2

#28 Havoline 17581 - Ernie Irvan - 80mm - 1997

This Ford Thunderbird has a red metal base, red plastic interior & roll cage, clear windows with black outlines & stripes, and gybk; with collector's card.

a. black; red, white, yellow & blue tampo w/"28," "Havoline" broken up by rear wheel well; racing decals on sides; "28" on roof; "Clean System 3" & Havoline logo on trunk; "Havoline," logo & Raybestos logo in back; "Havoline," logo & Ford logo on hood. Ernie Irvan's sig. on both sides of roof. Car faces wrong direction in blistercard. Collector's 1st Ed card $40 - 50

a2. black, same as a, brighter red & yellow in tampo w/"28" not as slanted on sides, Havoline is above wheel well, signatures on roof are yellow. Car facing right direction on blistercard. Collector's 1st Ed. card 3 - 5

a3. as a2, tinted windows, Superspeedway card 3 - 5

a4. as a2, Short Track front end, Short Track card 3 - 5

#28 Havoline-b

b. gray; same as a; red, black & white tampo w/"Havoline" & Texaco star on hood, red "28" on sides. Test Track (1998) 5 - 7

#30 Pennzoil-b

#30 Pennzoil 17817 - Johnny Benson - 80mm - 1997

This Pontiac Grand Prix has a yellow metal base, yellow plastic interior & roll cage, clear windows with black outlines & stripes, and gybk; with Collector's 1st Ed blistercard.

a. yellow; black halfway up sides; red, black & white tampo w/"30," "Pennzoil," decals on sides; "Pennzoil" on hood & in back; "36" on roof & in back $3 - 5

b. as a, tinted windows, Superspeedway card 3 - 5

c. as a, black Short Track front end, Short Track card 3 - 5

#37 Kmart-c

#37 Kmart 17412 - Jeremy Mayfield - 80mm - 1997

This Ford Thunderbird has a red metal base, red interior & roll cage, tinted windows with black outlines & stripes, and gybk; with collector's card.

a. white; thin red stripe around bottom of car; red, dk. blue, lt. blue & black tampo w/"37," "Kmart" & "RC Cola" on sides; "Kmart" & Ford logo on hood; "Energizer" & "Long Life Alkaline Batteries" on trunk; "Kmart," "RC Cola" & "#37" in back. Collector's 1st Ed card $3 - 5

a2. as a, tinted windows, Superspeedway card 3 - 5

a3. as a, black Short Track front end, clear windows, Short Track card 3 - 5

#43 STP-b

#43 STP 17409 - Bobby Hamilton - 80mm - 1997

This Pontiac Grand Prix has a gray metal base, gray plastic interior & roll cage, clear windows with black outlines & stripes, and gybk; with collector's card.

a. lt. blue & bright red; red, dk. blue, black & white tampo w/"43," STP logo & decals on sides; "43" on roof; blue "Hughes Network Systems" on trunk; "Kohler from Fergussen" in back; yellow stripe in front; STP logo on hood. Bobby Hamilton's sig. in front on both sides of roof. Car facing wrong direction on blistercard. Collector's 1st Ed card $75 - 85

a2. as a, gybu, no yellow stripe in front, dk. blue not blue on trunk. Bobby Hamilton's signature more toward back of roof. Car facing wrong direction on blistercard 3 - 6

a3. as a2, collector's card is different, car facing right direction on blistercard. Collector's 1st Ed card 3 - 5

a4. as a2, tinted windows, Superspeedway card 3 - 5

a5. as a2, black Short Track front end. Short Track card 3 - 5

b. gray; same as a2; black & white tampo w/"43" on sides; red, black & white tampo w/STP logo on hood; blue hubs. Test Track 1998 blistercard (1998) 5 - 7

#43 STP-c

c. lt. blue; orange front & trunk; John Andretti is driver; red, white, black & orange tampo w/"43," "STP" & decals on sides, "www.stp.com" on hood, "43" & "John Andretti" on roof, "WWW.PETTYRACING.COM" on trunk; "Kohler" & decals in back. Preview Ed (1998) 3 - 5

c2. as c, more decals on sides. 1st Ed Card (1998) 2 - 4

c3. dk. blue & red, same as a2, John Andretti is driver, STP logo & "WWW.STP.COM" on hood, "WWW.PETTYRACING.COM" on trunk, "Kohler," STP logo in back. John Andretti's signature on both sides of roof. Trackside Box only (1999) 8 - 10

c4. lt. blue, same as c, bright orange stripes. Preview Edition 1998 card w/Collector's card (1999) 3 - 5

c5. as c, orange trunk & nose, orange & white lines on sides, "Grand Prix" on nose, larger STP logo on hood, smaller "43" on sides, Petty Generations logo on trunk, "John Andretti" printed on both sides of roof. Petty Generations 3-pack. Target Stores only (1999) 8 - NA

c6. as c2, "Red Lobster" on trunk, Trackside box (1999) 3 - 5

c7. as c4, more & different decals, "Goodyear" in yellow over front wheels, Thailand, 2-pack with 1/24 model, Daytona 500 blistercard or Trackside box (1999) 3 - 5

c6. as c5, brown front (1999) 4 - 6

c8. as c5, no orange nose, gold ribbon trim around car, gold hubs not blue hubs. Wal-Mart excl. Petty Racing 50th Anniv. 4-pack (1999) 8 - NA

d. lt. blue; red, black, yellow, blue & white tampo w/football player, "43," STP logo & decals on sides; Player's logo & STP logo on hood; "43" & "John Andretti" on roof; Red Lobster logo on trunk; "Kohler," Player's logo & STP in back 4 - 6

#43 STP-e

e. gold; orange nose & spoiler; "43," stripes, STP logo & decals on sides; STP logo & "WWW.STP.COM" on hood; "43" & "John Andretti" on roof; Petty logo, web address & "Kohler" in back. Collector Ed Pit Crew blistercard (1999) 5 - 7

#44 Hot Wheels-a

#44 Hot Wheels 17580 - Kyle Petty - 80mm - 1997

This Pontiac Grand Prix has a gray metal base, gray plastic interior & roll cage, clear windows with black outline & stripes, and gybk. It came boxed.

a. lt. blue; white stripe around bottom; orange, black, white, red & yellow tampo w/"44," Hot Wheels logo, Hot Wheels track & decals on sides; "44" on roof; "Hot Wheels" in back; logo on hood. Kyle Petty's sig. on both sides of roof $225 - 250

a2. blue, same as a, "44" on sides slanted forward, "Hot Wheels" in back smaller; gyr 2 - 10

a3. as a2, collector's card on blistercard, car facing right direction on card. Collector's 1st Ed. card 3 - 5

a4. as a2, tinted windows, "Spree" on lower rear fender, Superspeedway card 3 - 5

a5. as a2, black Short Track front end, clear windows, Short Track card 3 - 5

a6. as a4, clear windows, "STP" on trunk, Short Track card 3 - 5

#44 Hot Wheels-a7

a7. as a5, white "Showtime" on red rectangle on trunk. Ltd ed on Collector's 1st Ed card, "Showtime" on card 25 - 30

a8. as a5; white "Carborundum Abrasives" red logo on trunk. Ltd ed on Collector's 1st Ed card, "Showtime" on card 25 - 30

b. gray; same as a; red, black & white tampo w/"10" on sides; red, yellow & white tampo; Hot Wheels logo on hood. Test Track 1998 card (1998) 8 - 10

#44 Hot Wheels-c

c. dk. blue, same as a in 1997; "44" larger, slanted more; Hot Wheels logo, "30 Years of Cool!" on hood, blue rear bumper. Kyle Petty's signature on both sides of roof. "Hot Wheels" in back. Trackside Box (1998) 3 - 10

c2. as c, Preview Ed 1998 card w/Collector's card (1998) 3 - 5

c3. as c, red hubs. 1st Ed card, Trackside box (1998) 3 - 5

c4. as c; "44," Hot Wheels logo, Goal Posts & decals on sides; black hood; lines logo on hood; "Players Inc" & football helmet on trunk. Trackside Box or 1st Ed card (1998) 4 - 6

c5. as c, Petty Generations logo on trunk. Petty Generations 3-pack & Target Stores only (1998) 8 - NA

c6. blue; same as c; "Kyle Petty 500 Starts," "79," "97" & smaller Hot Wheels logo on hood; "Spree Prepaid Foncard" on trunk. Petty Racing Family 3-pack only (1998) 8 - NA

d. white; black, orange, yellow, red & blue tampo w/"44," Hot Wheels logo, track & racing decals on sides; "Blues Brothers 2000" & logo on hood; "44" on roof; "Hot Wheels" & logo in back; black hubs. Kyle Petty's sig. on both sides of roof. Trackside box (1998) 4 - 10

d2. as d, Preview Ed or 1st Ed 1998 card w/Collector's card (1998) 4 - 6

#44 Hot Wheels-e

e. gold; orange, white, red, yellow & black tampo w/track, "44," Hot Wheels logo & race decals on sides; Hot Wheels logo & "30 years of Cool!" on hood; "44" & Kyle Petty's signature on roof; "Hot Wheels" & "44" in back. Collector's Edition Pit Crew card (1999) 6 - 8

f. as a; darker blue; smaller "44," Hot Wheels logo & track on sides; smaller Hot Wheels logo on hood; smaller "44" on roof; "World's Coolest Car Co." not "30 Years of Cool" on hood; Red Lobster logo on trunk; different decals. 1999 Pro Racing card w/transporter or Trackside box (1999) 3 - 5

f2. as f, Thailand (1999) 3 - 5

f3. as f, decals different, lighter orange & darker red in tampo, Thailand (1999) 3 - 5

f4. as f; decals different, w/tiny STP logo next to Hot Wheels logo; Thailand. Daytona 500 card or Trackside box (1999) 3 - 5

f5. lt. blue, same as f, orange track color changed to gold, gold hubs not blue hubs. Wal-Mart excl. Petty Racing 50th Anniversary 4-pack (1999) 8 - NA

f6. as f, track is shape of helmet on sides, Player's logo & Hot Wheels logo on hood, China (1999) 3 - 5

f7. as f4, black & gray scratches tampoed on sides & hood, Thailand. Trading Paint card, #1 in Trading Paint series, limited to 15,000 (1999) 12 - 15

g. white; yellow, red, blue & black tampo w/"44" & "Daytona 500" on sides; Hot Wheels logo & "Daytona 500" on hood; "44" on roof, "Celebrating 41 years of racing February 14, 1999" on trunk; "Hot Wheels" in back; rrrd, Thailand (1999) 4 - 6

#44 Hot Wheels-h

h. gray; "44" in red, black & white; yellow & orange Hot Wheels logo on hood. Test Track card, #3 in 99 Test Track series, limited to 15,000 (1999) 12 - 15

Values are shown in U.S. dollars, first price is for mint, second is for mint packaged vehicles only. See pages 15-16 for grading guide to determine value for cars in lesser conditions.

#91 Spam-a

#91 Spam 18089 - Mike Wallace - 78mm - 1997

This Chevrolet Monte Carlo has a gray metal base, white interior & roll cage, tinted windows with black outlines & stripes, and gybk; with collector's card.

a. blue; thick pinkish red stripes on sides & trunk; pinkish red, yellow, gray & black tampo w/"91," "Spam," "Kid's Kitchen" & decals on sides; "Spam" & Chevy logo on hood; "91" on roof; "Kid's Kitchen" on trunk; "Spam" in back. Superspeedway card $3 - 5

a2. as a, tinted windows, black Short Track front end, Short Track card 3 - 5

#94 McDonald's-a

#94 McDonald's 17583 - Bill Elliott - 80mm - 1997

This Ford Thunderbird has a gray metal base, red interior & roll cage, clear windows with black outlines, black stripes, and gybk; with collector's card.

a. red; yellow, black, white, orange & blue tampo w/"94," "McDonald's" & decals on sides; "94" on roof; Reese's Peanut Butter bar on trunk; "Super 8 Motels," McDonald's "M" & "94" in back; McDonald's "M," Coca Cola logo & Ford logo on hood. Bill Elliott's signature twice on roof. Collector's 1st Ed card $3 - 5

a2. as a, tinted windows, Superspeedway card 3 - 5

a3. as a, black Short Track front end, clear windows, Short Track card 3 - 5

#94 McDonald's-b

b. dk. blue; same as a; red base; yellow, white, red, lt. blue, orange & black tampo w/"94," "Mac Tonight" & decals on sides; McDonald's "M," "Mac Tonight," "Coca Cola" & figure on hood; "94" & Bill Elliott's sig. twice on roof; Reese's Peanut Butter bar on trunk; "Super 8 Motels," "94" & McDonald's "M" in back 10 - 12

#94 McDonald's-c

c. red Ford Taurus, same as a, bigger "94" on sides & roof, different race decals, smaller "M" on hood, bigger Coca Cola logo on hood, different Reese's Peanut Butter bar & "Service Merchandise" in back. Trackside box or Preview Ed box (1998) 3 - 5

c2. as c; yellow stripe on sides; "94" in black, "Drive Thru," McDonald's "M" & different decals on sides; "94" on top of square on black roof; larger "M" on hood. 1999 Hot Wheels Racing card, 2-pack with 1/24 model or Trackside box (1999) 3 - 5

c3. as c, Thailand (1999) 3 - 5

c4. as c, different decals, orange in stripe on sides, "94" & Super 8 Motel decal larger on sides, Coca-Cola decal under smaller "M" on hood, Thailand. Daytona 500 card or Trackside box (1999) 3 - 5

#94 McDonald's-d

d. gold; yellow, blue, white, orange & red tampo w/"94," "McDonald's" & race decals on sides; large "M" & Coca-Cola logo on hood; "94" & Bill Elliott's sig. on roof; Reese's Peanut Butter Bar on trunk; "Service Merchandise" &"94" in back. Collector Ed card (1999) 5 - 7

#96 Caterpillar-a

#96 Caterpillar 17582 - David Green - 78mm - 1997

This Chevrolet Monte Carlo has a black metal base, white interior & roll cage, tinted windows with black outlines & stripes, and gybk with black hubs and "Goodyear" & "Eagle" in yellow; with collector's card.

a. black; large yellow stripe around bottom; red, white, yellow & blue tampo w/"96," "Caterpillar" & decals on sides; Cat logo & Chevy logo on hood; "96" on roof. Superspeedway card $3 - 5

a2. as a, black Short Track front end, clear windows. Short Track card 3 - 5

a3. black, same as a, clear windows, smaller "96" on sides, different turquoise & decals in tampo. David Green's sig. on both sides of roof. Trackside box (1998) 2 - 10

a4. as a, Preview Ed 1998 card w/Collector's card (1998) 3 - 5

#98 RCA 17814 - John Andretti - 80mm - 1997

This Ford Thunderbird has a gray metal base, gray plastic interior & roll cage, clear windows with black outlines & stripes, and gybk; with collector's card.

a. red; white back & hood; black, white, blue & red tampo w/"98," "RCA" & decals on sides; "98" on roof; "RCA" on hood & in back; John Andretti's sig. on both sides of roof. Collector's 1st Ed card $3 - 5

a2. as a, tinted windows, Superspeedway card 3 - 5

a3. as a, black Short Track front end, Short Track card 3 - 5

#99 Exide-a

#99 Exide 17414 - Jeff Burton - 80mm - 1997

This Ford Thunderbird has a gray metal base, black plastic interior & roll cage, clear windows with black outlines & stripes, and gybk; with collector's card.

a. black; magenta hood & sides; white, lt. blue, yellow & black tampo w/"99," "Exide" & decals on sides; "99" on roof; "Exide" on trunk & in back; "Exide Batteries" & Ford logo on hood; Jeff Burton's sig. twice on roof. Collector's 1st Ed card $3 - 5

a2. as a, lighter magenta in tampo, not as long on sides. Collector's 1st Ed card 3 - 5

a3. as a, tinted windows, Superspeedway card 3 - 5

a4. as b, black Short Track front end & card 3 - 5

#99 Exide-b

b. gray; same as a; black & white tampo w/"99" on sides, "Exide Batteries" on hood. Test Track 1998 card (1998) 6 - 8

c. black Ford Taurus; same as a; pink fenders; "99," "Exide" & different decals on sides, hood, roof & trunk; back tampos different sizes than 1997 model; hood & trunk tampo includes "SKF" Trackside Box (1998) 3 - 10

c2. as c, Preview Ed or 1st Ed 1998 card w/Collector's card (1998) 3 - 5

#99 Exide-d

d. gold; pink front end; white, yellow, red, blue, pink & black tampo w/"99," "Exide" & race decals on sides; "Exide Batteries" & "SKF" on hood; "99" & Jeff Burton's sig. on roof; "SKF Bearings" on trunk; "Exide" & "94" in back. Collector's Ed Pit Crew card (1999) 4 - 6

e. black; lt. plum front end; white, yellow, red, blue & black tampo: "99," "Exide" & race decals on sides; "Exide Batteries" & "SKF" on hood; "99" & Jeff Burton's sig. on roof; "CR" & "SKF" on trunk; "Exide" & "94" in back; Thailand. Trackside box (1999) 3 - 5

e2. as e, different race logos on sides, Thailand (1999) 3 - 5

e3. as b2, brighter pink on hood, China 3 - 5

#99 Exide-f

f. beige; white & brown "99" on sides; "Exide Batteries" in black & white on hood, Thailand. 1999 Test Track card. #2 in 1999 Test Track series, limited to 15,000 (1999) 12 - 15

1997 Pro Racing basic line on #1 cards

04 Kodak-a

#4 Kodak 17417 - 76mm - 1997

This Chevrolet Monte Carlo has a black plastic base, interior & roll cage; clear windows; and plastic gytbk.

a. dk. yellow; red, black & white tampo: "4," Kodak Gold Film," racing decals on sides; "4" on roof; "Kodak Film" in back & on hood. Sterling Marlin's sig. on both sides of roof $2 - 4

b. as a, lt. gray base, painted headlights, black spoiler, smaller "4" on sides, race decals & "Kodak Max Film" on sides & hood (not "Kodak Gold Film"); no black in front of windshield; no tampo in back (1998) 2 - 4

#5 Kellogg's-a

#5 Kellogg's 17416 - 76mm - 1997

This Chevrolet Monte Carlo has a light gray plastic base, interior & roll cage; clear windows; and plastic gytbk.

a. yellow; back half red; yellow, black, white, red, & lt. green tampo w/"5," "Kellogg's" & decals on sides; "5" on roof; "Kellogg's" in back; Corn Flakes logo on hood. Terry Labonte's sig. on both sides of roof $2 - 4

#5 Kellogg's-b

b. purple; green spoiler; black, white, yellow, lt. green & orange tampo w/"5," "Spooky Froot Loops" & race decals on sides & hood; Frankenstein monster on hood; "5" & Terry Labonte on both sides of roof; "Starburst" on trunk; monster & toucan on back 10 - 12

c. as a, painted headlights, black stripe on lower sides, smaller "5" on sides, hood tampo different, race decals, no black in front of windshield, no tampo in back (1998) 2 - 4

d. as b; "5" & lt. green stripe larger, lt. green stripe in front, different decals, "Kellogg's" in back (1999) 10 - 12

#6 Valvoline-a

#6 Valvoline 17420 - 76mm - 1997

This Ford Thunderbird has a light gray plastic base, interior & roll cage; clear windows; and plastic gytb.

a. white; back half blue; black, white, red, dk. blue, & lt. blue tampo w/"6," "Valvoline" & decals on sides; "6" on roof; "Valvoline" in back; "Valvoline" & logo on hood; Mark Martin's sig. on both sides of roof $2 - 4

b. blue Ford Taurus, same as a, white front, "6" on sides, different roof, red splatters in back of front wheel to roof, no tampo on trunk or in back, decals different (1998) 2 - 4

c. dk. blue, same as b, "6" on sides larger, race decals different, "Cummins" on trunk; "Eagle 1" & race decals in back (1999) 10 - 12

#7 QVC-a

#7 QVC 17419 - 76mm - 1997

This Ford Thunderbird has a light gray plastic base, interior & roll cage, clear windows and plastic gytbk.

a. black; lt. red, white & blue tampo w/red border on bottom; "7," "QVC" & decals on sides, hood & back; "7" on roof; "WWW.QVC.COM" on trunk $2 - 4

#8 Circuit City 18084 - 76mm - 1997

This Ford Thunderbird has a light gray plastic base, interior & roll cage; clear windows; and plastic gytbk.

a. red; black in back; white, black, blue & red tampo w/"8," "Circuit City" &

Values are shown in U.S. dollars, first price is for mint, second is for mint packaged vehicles only. See pages 15-16 for grading guide to determine value for cars in lesser conditions.

#8 Circuit City-a

decals on sides; "Circuit City" on hood, trunk & back; "Hut Stricklin" & "8" on roof $2 - 4

#10 Tide-a

#10 Tide 17812 - 76mm - 1997
This Ford Thunderbird has a light gray plastic base, interior & roll cage; clear windows; and plastic gytbk.

a. orange; white back; black, white, dk. blue & yellow tampo w/"10," "Tide" & racing decals on sides; "10" on roof; "Whirlpool" on trunk; "Tide America's Favorite" on hood. Ricky Rudd's sig. on both sides of roof $2 - 4
b. orange Ford Taurus; lt. gray plastic base; black spoiler; painted headlights; white back; dk. blue, pink, yellow & black tampo w/"Tide," "10" & race decals on sides; "Tide America's Favorite" on hood; "10" & Ricky Rudd's sig. on roof (1998) 2 - 4
c. as b, "10" & "Tide" on sides larger, race decals different, "Whirlpool" on trunk, "Tide" in back (1999) 10 - 12

#16 Primestar-a

#16 Primestar 17422 - 76mm - 1997
This Ford Thunderbird has a light gray plastic base, black interior & roll cage; clear windows; and plastic gytbk.

a. dk. blue; red back; yellow, white, blue, black & red tampo w/"16," "Primestar," Family Channel & racing decals on sides & hood; "16" on roof; Ted Musgrave's sig. on sides of roof $2 - 4
b. yellow & blue; gray plastic int. & roll cage; white, yellow, blue, black, red & lt. green tampo w/"16," "Primestar" & race decals on sides; "Primestar" on hood; "16" & Ted Musgrave's sig. on roof (1998) 2 - 4

#21 Citgo-a

#21 Citgo 18085 - 76mm - 1997
This Ford Thunderbird has a light gray plastic base, red interior & roll cage, clear windows, and plastic gytbk.

a. red; black, white, dk. red & blue tampo w/"21," "Citgo," Citgo logo & racing decals on sides; "21" on roof; Citgo logo & Ford logo on hood; Michael Waltrip's sig. on sides of roof $2 - 4

#28 Havoline-a

#28 Havoline 17585 - 76mm - 1997
This Ford Thunderbird has a red plastic base, interior & roll cage; clear windows; and plastic gytbk.

a. black; red, white & yellow tampo w/"28," "Havoline" & racing decals on sides & hood; "28" on roof; "Clean System 3" & logo on trunk. Ernie Irvan's sig. on sides of roof $2 - 4

#30 Pennzoil-a

#30 Pennzoil 17813 - 75mm - 1997
This Pontiac Grand Prix has a yellow plastic base, interior & roll cage; clear windows; and plastic gytbk.

a. yellow; black stripe around bottom; red, black & white tampo w/"30," "Pennzoil" & decals on sides; "30" on roof & back; logo on hood; Johnny Benson's sig. on sides of roof $2 - 4

#37 Kmart-a

#37 Kmart 17421 - 76mm - 1997
This Ford Thunderbird has a red plastic base, interior & roll cage; clear windows; and plastic gytbk.

a. white; lt. blue, dk. blue, red & black tampo w/"37," "Kmart" & "RC Cola" on sides; "Kmart," "RC Cola" & Ford logo on hood; "37" on roof; Jeremy Mayfield's sig. on sides of roof $3 - 5

#43 STP-a

#43 STP 17418 - 75mm - 1997
This Pontiac Grand Prix has a light gray plastic base, interior & roll cage; clear windows; and plastic gytbk.

a. lt. blue & bright red; red, dk. blue, black & white tampo w/"43," STP logo & decals on sides & hood; "43" on roof; Bobby Hamilton's sig. on sides of roof $2 - 4
b. lt. blue, same as a, smaller "43" and red & white straight lines on sides, race decals & red tampo different, "www.stp.com" on hood (1998) 2 - 4

#44 Hot Wheels-a

#44 Hot Wheels 17584 - 75mm - 1997
This Pontiac Grand Prix has a light gray plastic base, interior & roll cage; clear windows; and plastic gytbk.

a. blue; white stripe around bottom; orange, black, white, red & yellow tampo w/"44," Hot Wheels logo, Hot Wheels track & decals on sides; "44" on roof; logo on hood; Kyle Petty's sig. on roof $2 - 4
a2. as a, Spree race decal on side of rear bumper 2 - 4
b. blue, same as a, much darker blue, lighter tampo colors, "Spree" on side of rear fenders, decals different, "30 Years of Cool" on hood (1998) 2 - 4
c. dk. blue, same as a, darker tampo colors, no white on bottom, race decals different, "World's Coolest Car Co." on hood, Red Lobster logo on trunk, "Hot Wheels" in back (1999) 10 - 12
d. dk. blue, same as b, Barbie tampo on trunk. NASCAR Barbie purchase giveaway by K•B Stores (1999) 12 - 15
e. black; white nose; red spoiler; red, white, blue & black tampo w/"44" & "Pepsi" on sides; "Pepsi 400 at Daytona" on hood; "44" on roof; Daytona logo on trunk; "Hot Wheels" in back. Pepsi 400 in Daytona giveaway w/program (1999) 10 - 12

#91 Spam-a

#91 Spam 18086 - 76mm - 1997
This Chevrolet Monte Carlo has a light gray plastic base, interior & roll cage; clear windows; and plastic gytbk.

a. blue; thick pinkish red stripes on sides & trunk; pinkish red, yellow, gray & black tampo w/"91," "Spam," "Kid's Kitchen" & decals on sides; "Spam" & Chevy logo on hood; "91" on roof $2 - 4

#94 McDonald's-a

#94 McDonald's 17587 - 76mm - 1997
This Ford Thunderbird has a red plastic base, interior & roll cage; clear windows; and plastic gytbk.

a. red; yellow, black, white & blue tampo w/"94," "McDonald's" & race decals on sides; McDonald's "M" on hood; "94" in back (1999) $2 - 4
b. red Ford Taurus, same as a, darker red, larger "94" & "McDonald's" on sides, smaller "M" on hood, larger "94" on roof, black spoiler in back, different race decals (1998) 2 - 4

#96 Caterpillar-a

#96 Caterpillar 17586 - 76mm - 1997
This Chevrolet Monte Carlo has a black plastic base, gray interior & roll cage; clear windows; and plastic gytbk.

a. black; large yellow stripe around bottom; red, white, yellow & blue tampo w/"96," "Caterpillar" & decals on sides; Cat logo & Chevy logo on hood; "96" & David Green's name on both sides of roof $2 - 4
b. black; same as a; "96" smaller on sides, larger on roof; no "Cat" in back; Deluxe Paints decal on rear fender; turquoise Siemans decal on sides; different race decals (1998) 2 - 4

#98 RCA-a

#98 RCA 17818 - 76mm - 1997
This Ford Thunderbird has a light gray plastic base, interior & roll cage; clear windows; and plastic gytbk.

a. red; white back & hood; black, white & red tampo w/"98," "RCA" & decals on sides; "98" on roof; "RCA" on hood. John Andretti's sig. on sides of roof $2 - 4

#99 Exide-a

#99 Exide 17423 - 76mm - 1997
This Ford Thunderbird has a gray base, black interior & roll cage; clear windows; and plastic gytbk.

a. black; magenta hood & sides; white, lt. blue, yellow & black tampo w/"99," "Exide" & decals on sides; "Exide Batteries" on hood; "99" on roof; Jeff Burton's sig. twice on roof $2 - 4
b. black; multicolored tampo w/"99," "Exide" & decals on sides; "NASCAR Rocks America," "True Value" & "SKF" on hood; "99" & sig. on roof; "CR" & "SKF" on trunk; "Exide," "True Value" & decals in back. Mailed in kit for purchase of certain amounts from True Value Stores 10 - 12

#4 Kodak-a #6 Valvoline-a
#10 Tide-a #94 McDonald's-a

Pit Crew® Tool Boxes (1997–99)

In late 1997 Mattel issued a two pack with a deluxe Hot Wheels Racing car and a tool box on wheels. All tool boxes were made in China and have a metal base, gray metal top, black plastic handle, and small black wheels. Each was issued only with its counterpart NASCAR vehicle. They are valued at $6-8 each (the blisterpack value is for the two-pack).

1998 Pro Racing Collector line

#11 Paychex-b

#11 Paychex - Brett Bodine - 80mm - 1999
This Ford Taurus has a light gray metal base, light gray plastic interior/roll cage, clear windows with black outlines, stripes, and gybk.

a. white; gold back; blue, white, red & black tampo w/"11," "Paychex" & race decals on sides, "Paychex" on hood; "11" & driver's sig on roof, 50th Anniv. NASCAR logo on trunk; "Paychex" & "11" in back. Thailand $4 - 6
b. white; blue, gray, red & black tampo w/"11," "Paychex" & race decals on sides; "Paychex Payroll" & "401 (k)" on hood; "11" & driver's sig. on roof; "Paychex" & "11" in back; Thailand. Daytona 500 card, Trackside box 3 - 5
b2. white, same as a, darker blue tampo, "11" on sides smaller, different decals. Hot Wheels Racing 1999 card 2 - 4

#12 Mobil 1-a

#12 Mobil 1 20054 - Jeremy Mayfield - 80mm - 1998
This Ford Taurus has a gray metal base, light gray plastic interior/roll cage, clear windows w/black outlines & 3 black stripes, and gybk.

a. blue; white nose; red, white, black & blue tampo w/"12," Mobil flying horse logo & race decals on sides; "Mobil 1" on nose & back; "12" on roof; "Mobil Speedpass" on trunk. Jerry Mayfield's sig. on both sides of roof. Trackside Box or 1st Ed Card $4 - 6

Values are shown in U.S. dollars, first price is for mint, second is for mint packaged vehicles only. See pages 15-16 for grading guide to determine value for cars in lesser conditions.

#12 Mobil 1-b

b. gold, same as b, red in tampo darker. Pit Crew 1999 card (1999) 8 - 10
c. blue, same as a, red roll cage, brighter red tampo, larger "12" & winged horse on sides, different Ford logo & race decals. Daytona 500 card, Trackside box & Pit Crew 1999 card (1999) 2 - 4
c2. as c, Thailand (1999) 2 - 4
c3. as c, darker blue, name on roof larger & in red & white, Thailand. Trackside box, Hot Wheels Racing 1999 card or 2-pack, 1/24 model (1999) 2 - 4

#12 Mobil 1-d

d. black; "12" in red & white on sides, gray "Mobil 1" on hood, Thailand (1999). Test Track card. #4 in 99 Test Track series, limited to 15,000 (1999) 12 - 15

#13 FirstPlus 20060 - Jerry Nadeau - 80mm - 1998
This Ford Taurus has a red metal base, red plastic interior & roll cage, clear windows with black outlines & three stripes, and gybk.
a. dk. green; white & orange tampo in middle; white, black, dk. green, orange & red tampo w/"13," "First Plus" & race decals on sides; "First Plus Loans" on hood; "13" on roof; "Vanstar" on trunk; "First Plus" & "13" back. Jerry Nadeau's signature on both sides of roof. Trackside Box only $2 - 10
a2. as a, Preview Ed w/1998 Collector's card 3 - 5

#26 Cheerios-a3

#26 Cheerios 20064 - Johnny Benson - 80mm - 1998
This Ford Taurus has a gray metal base, gray interior & roll cage, clear windows with black outlines & stripes, and gybk.
a. yellow; black, blue, red, white & green tampo w/"26," "Pop Secret," "Hamburger Helper" & race decals on sides; "Cheerios" on hood & back; spoon w/"Betty Crocker" on trunk; Johnny Benson's signature twice on roof. Trackside box only $2 - 10
a2. same as a, Preview Ed 1998 card w/Collector's card 3 - 5
a3. as a, spoon w/"Betty Crocker" on sides, "Hamburger Helper" on trunk, other product names repositioned & race decals different, 2-pack with 1/24 model. 1999 Hot Wheels Racing card or in Trackside box (1999) 2 - 4
a4. as a3, Thailand (1999) 2 - 4
a5. as a3, "26" & decals different, red heart outline on hood. Daytona 500 card or in Trackside box (1999) 2 - 4

#30 Gumout-a3

#30 Gumout 20070 - Derrike Cope - 80mm - 1998
A Pontiac Grand Prix with gray metal base, gray plastic interior/roll cage, clear windows with black outlines & stripes, and gybk.
a. black; silver, white, yellow & red tampo w/"30," "Gumout" & decals on sides; logo & "Long Life Formula" on hood; "30" on roof; "Bryan" on trunk; "Pennzoil" in back. Derrike Cope's sig. twice on roof. Trackside box only $3 - 10
a2. as a, Preview Ed or 1st Ed Card 1998 card w/Collector's card 3 - 5

#35 Tabasco-b

#35 Tabasco 20062 - Todd Bodine - 80mm - 1998
This Pontiac Grand Prix has a light gray metal chassis, orange interior & roll cage, clear windows with black outline & stripes, and gybk with black hubs and "Goodyear" & "Eagle" in yellow.
a. orange; white back; lt. green, white, black & yellow tampo w/"35," "Tabasco" & decals on sides; "Tabasco" & label on hood; "35" on roof; "Tabasco" on trunk & back. Todd Bodine's sig. on both sides of roof. Trackside box only $8 - 10
a2. as a, black & gray scratches tampoed on sides & hood. China. Trading Paint card (1998) 5 - 7
b. red; same as a; red int.; black in back; lt. green, black, white & yellow tampo w/"35," "Tabasco," tube of sauce, flames & decals on sides; "Tabasco" & label on hood; "35" on roof; 'Tabasco" on trunk & back. Todd Bodine's sig. on both sides of roof. Trackside box 8 - 10
b2. as b, gray int., Preview Ed 1998 card 1st Ed card 2 - 4
c. black; red int.; lt. green splashes on sides; white, green, yellow & red tampo w/"35," "Tabasco" & decals on sides; "Tabasco" & label on hood; "35" on roof; "Tabasco" on trunk & back. Todd Bodine's sig. on both sides of roof. 98 1st Ed card & Trackside box only 8 - 10

#36 Skittles-a

#36 Skittles 20061 - Ernie Irvan - 80mm - 1998
This Pontiac Grand Prix has a light gray metal chassis, light gray plastic interior & roll cage, clear windows with black outlines & stripes, and gybk with Goodyear & Eagle in yellow w/black hubs.
a. red; orange, green, blue, white, black & yellow rainbow tampo w/"36," "Skittles" & decals on sides; "Skittles "Taste the Rainbow" on hood; "36" on roof; "Starburst" on trunk; "Skittles" in back. Ernie Irvan's sig. on both sides of roof. Trackside Box only $4 - 10
a2. as a, Preview Ed or 1st Ed card 1998 card 3 - 5
a3. as a2, Monte Carlo, Preview Ed 1998 card 3 - 5

#40 SABCO Racing 20063 - Sterling Marlin - 78mm - 1998
This Chevrolet Monte Carlo has a gray metal chassis, light gray plastic interior & roll cage, clear windows with black outlines & stripes, and gybk with black hubs and "Goodyear" & "Eagle" in yellow.

#40 SABCO Racing-a

a. blue; lt. yellow rear; white, black, yellow, gray, red & blue tampo w/"40," "Marlin" & decals on sides; "Team Sabco" on hood & trunk; "Monte Carlo" in front; "40" on roof; "Marlin" in back. Sterling Marlin's sig. on both sides of roof. Trackside box $3 - 10
a2. as a, Preview Ed 1998 card w/Collector's card 3 - 5
a3. as a, "Sabco" on trunk missing, "Marlin" is black w/red outline (not yellow w/black outline). 1st Ed Card (1998) 3 - 5

#40 SABCO Racing-b

b. black; same as a; lt. yellow in back; red, white, yellow, gray & blue tampo w/"40," "Marlin" & decals on sides; "Sterling Marlin" & Chevy logo on hood; "40" & "Sterling Marlin" on roof; logo on trunk. 1999 Hot Wheels Racing card or Trackside box (1999) 2 - 4
b2. as b, Thailand (1999) 2 - 4
c. black, same as b, wider gray stripe, different decals. Daytona 500 card (1999) 2 - 4

#42 BellSouth-a

#42 BellSouth 20066 - Joe Nemechek - 78mm - 1998
This Chevrolet Monte Carlo has a gray metal base, gray interior & roll cage, clear windows with black outlines & stripes, and gybk with black hubs & "Goodyear" & "Eagle" in yellow.
a. black; white, turquoise, lt. blue, white & yellow tampo w/"42," "BellSouth" & decals on sides; "1-800-Bellsouth" on hood; "42" on roof; "1-800-Bell-South" in back. Joe Nemechek's sig. on both sides of roof. Trackside box $3 - 10
a2. as a, Preview Ed 1998 Collector's card 3 - 5

#42 BellSouth-b

b. blue; gray roll cage & int.; yellow, orange, red, white & blue tampo w/"42," "Bell South" & decals on sides; "Bell South" on hood; "42" & driver's sig. on roof; "42" & "Bell South" in back; Thailand. 2-pack w/1/24 model, 1999 Hot Wheels Racing card or Trackside box (1999) 2 - 4
d. blue, same as c; race decals different, "Bell South on trunk. Thailand. Daytona 500 card (1999) 2 - 4

#43 Petty Racing - 74mm - 1998
This Dodge racing truck has a gray metal chassis, gray interior, clear windows, silver & black painted grill, and Pro Racing wheels with blue hubs.
a. red; white, blue & black tampo w/"Cummins," "43" & decals on sides; Cummins "C" on hood; "43" & "Jimmy Hensley" on roof; Petty Racing logo & "1-800 Be-Petty" on truck bed; decals in back $5 - 7
b. red; black hood; black, green, yellow, blue & dk. blue tampo w/"43," "Players," "C" & race decals on sides; theatrical masks on hood; "43" & "Jimmy Hensley" on roof; green football field w/helmet & race decals on back. Player's 3-pack only 5 - NA
c. lt. blue; white, dk. blue, red, gold & black tampo w/"43," "Dodge" & race decals on sides; "Dodge" & Dodge logo on hood; "43" & "Jimmy Hensley" on roof; "Dodge," Dodge logo, Petty Racing logo & "1-800 Be-Petty" on truck bed; race decals in back; gold hubs not blue hubs. Wal-Mart excl. Petty Racing 50th Anniv. 4 pack (1999) 4 - NA

#45 Spree no # - Adam Petty - 80mm - 1998
This Pontiac Grand Prix has a gray metal base, gray plastic interior & roll cage, clear windows with black outlines & stripes, and gyrd.
a. lt. green w/red nose & purple rear; black, red, purple, yellow, pink & white tampo w/"45," "Spree" & decals on sides; "Happy Father's Day From Spree," "Prepaid Foncard" & "Sprint" on trunk; "AC Delco" on top of windshield; "45" on roof; Petty Generations logo on trunk. Adam Petty's name printed on both sides of roof. Petty Generations 3-pack & Target Stores only (1998) $8 - NA
b. lt. green Chevrolet Monte Carlo; red front; yellow, purple, red, blue, pink & white tampo w/"Spree," "45" & race decals on sides; "Spree Prepaid Foncard" & "Sprint" on hood & back; "45" "WWW.ADAMPETTY.COM" on roof & trunk; "45," in back; Thailand. 2-pack with 1/24 model (1999) 6 - NA
c. lt. blue, same as a, gold ribbon trim around car, gold hubs replace blue hubs. Wal-Mart excl. Petty Racing 50th Anniversary 4-pack (1999) 4 - NA

#46 First Union 20069 - Wally Dallenbach - 78mm - 1998
This Chevrolet Monte Carlo has a gray metal chassis, gray plastic interior/roll cage, clear windows with black outlines & stripes, gybk.
a. black & green; white, black, silver, red & yellow tampo w/"46," "First Union" & race decals on sides; "First Union" on green hood & back; "46" on roof; "Color Works" on trunk. Wally Dallenbach's name printed on both sides of roof. 1st Ed card (1998) $3 - 5
a2. as a, blue hood, Trackside box 8 - 10
b. black; purple front; green, white, black, orange & yellow tampo w/"46," "First Union" & decals on sides; "First Union" & Devil Rays logo on hood & back; "46" on roof; "Devil Rays" on trunk 3 - 5

#50 Boy Scouts-b

#50 Boy Scouts 20067 - 80mm - 1998
This Ford Taurus has a light gray metal base, light gray plastic interior/roll cage, clear windows with black outlines & stripes, gybk.
a. yellow; blue, red & white tampo: "50" on sides & roof, "Character Counts" & Boy Scouts logo on sides & hood; "Be

Values are shown in U.S. dollars, first price is for mint, second is for mint packaged vehicles only. See pages 15-16 for grading guide to determine value for cars in lesser conditions.

Prepared for the 21st Century" & "Character Counts" on hood; "Boy Scouts of America" in back. Trackside box or 1st Ed card (1998) 6 - 8
b. white; lt. blue sides; yellow, black, red, lt. blue & orange tampo: "50," "Strong Values-Strong Leaders" & logos on sides; logo & "Character Counts" on hood; "50" on roof; 2 logos & "Working Together" on trunk (1999) 5 - 7
c. as b, larger logos on sides, more red in hood logo (1999) 7 - NA

#50 Hendrick Motorsports-a

#50 Hendrick Motorsports 20059 - Ricky Craven - 78mm - 1998
This Chevrolet Monte Carlo has a black metal chassis, light gray plastic interior & roll cage, clear windows with black outlines & stripes, and gybk with black hubs and "Goodyear" & "Eagle" in yellow.
a. red; white, black, yellow & blue tampo: "50," Craven" & decals on sides; "Hendrick Motorsports" on hood & back; "Monte Carlo" in front; "50" on roof; Pedigree logo on trunk. "Ricky Craven" on sides of roof. Trackside box $3 - 10
a2. as a, Preview Ed 1998 card w/Collector's card 3 - 5

#89 McRib! 20148 - Bill Elliott - 78mm - 1998
This Ford Taurus has a red metal chassis, red plastic interior & roll cage, clear windows with black outlines & stripes, and gybk with black hubs & "Goodyear" & "Eagle" in yellow.
a. dk. green; yellow, red & white tampo w/"89," "Get Wild at," McDonald "M" & race decals on sides; "Get McRib" Sandwich," McDonald "M," "89" & driver's sig. on roof; "Get Wild" & "Get Wild at McDonald's," McDonald's "M" on hood. 1st Edition card (1998) 4 - 6

#90 Heilig-Meyers-a

#90 Heilig-Meyers 20071 - Dick Trickle - 78mm - 1998
This Ford Taurus has a black metal chassis, light gray plastic interior & roll cage, clear windows with black outlines & stripes, and gybk with black hubs and "Goodyear" & "Eagle" in yellow.
a. black; wide red stripe over thin turquoise stripe at bottom; white, red, turquoise & yellow tampo w/"90," "Heilig-Meyers," race decals & "Love This Store" on hood; "90" on roof; "Beautyrest" on trunk & back. Dick Trickle's sig. on sides of roof. Trackside box $3 - 10
a2. as a, Preview Ed 1998 card w/Collector's card 3 - 5

#97 John Deere-a

#97 John Deere 20065 - Chad Little - 80mm - 1998
This Ford Taurus has a gray metal base, black plastic interior & roll cage, clear windows with black outlines & stripes, and gybk.
a. lt. green; yellow front; green rear; yellow, black, white, red & green tampo w/"97," "John Deere" & decals on sides; John Deere logo on hood; "97" on roof; John Deere logo on trunk; "John Deere" & "Nothing Runs Like a Deere" in back. Trackside box $3 - 10
a2. as a, Preview Ed or 1st Ed Card 1998 card w/Collector's card 3 - 5
a3. as a; brighter yellow, larger "97" on sides, different race decals. 1999 Hot Wheels Racing card or Trackside box (1999) 2 - 4
a4. as a3, Thailand (1999) 2 - 4
a5. as a3, different decals: new Hardee's logo in red, lighter hood tampo, Thailand. 2-pack with 1/24 model or Trackside box (1999) 2 - 4
a6. as a3, black & gray scratches tampoed on sides & hood, Thailand. Trading Paint card, #4 in Trading Paint series, limited to 15,000 (1999) 12 - 15

#97 John Deere-c

c. gold; lt. green rear & roof; yellow, red, black, lt. green & white tampo w/"97," logo & decals on sides & hood; "97" & driver's sig. on roof; "John Deere" & logo on trunk; "John Deere" & "97" in back. Collector's Ed card (1999) 6 - 8

1998 Pro Racing basic line

#12 Mobil 1 17421 - 76mm - 1998
This Ford Taurus has a light gray plastic base, black interior & roll cage; clear windows; and plastic gytbk.
a. blue; white nose; red, white, black & blue tampo w/"12," Mobil flying horse logo & race decals on sides; "Mobil 1" on hood; "12" & Jerry Mayfield's sig. on roof (1998) $2 - 4
b. as a, red int., orange-red replaces red in tampo, race decals different, "Mobil Speedpass" on trunk, "Mobil 1" on back (1999) 10 - 12

#26 Cheerios 20080 - 1998
This Ford Taurus has a light gray plastic base, interior & roll cage; clear windows; and plastic gytbk.
a. yellow; dk. blue, black, red & lt. green tampo w/"26," "Pop Secret" & race decals on sides, "Cheerios" on hood; painted headlights; "26" & Johnny Benson's sig. on roof $2 - 4

#35 Tabasco 20078 - 75mm - 1998
This Pontiac Grand Prix has a light gray plastic base, red interior & roll cage, clear windows, and plastic gytbk.
a. orange; white back; lt. green, white, black, yellow tampo w/"35," "Tabasco" & race decals on sides; "Tabasco" & label on hood; "35" & Todd Bodine's sig. on roof $2 - 4

#36 Skittles 20077 - 75mm - 1998
This Pontiac Grand Prix has a light gray plastic base, interior & roll cage; clear windows; and plastic gytbk.
a. red; orange, green, blue, white, black & yellow rainbow-style tampo w/"36," "Skittles" & race decals on sides; "Skittles Taste the Rainbow" on hood; "36" & Ernie Irvan's sig. on roof $2 - 4

#50 Boy Scouts 20083 - 76mm - 1998
This Ford Taurus has a light gray plastic base, black interior & roll cage, clear windows, and plastic gytbk.
a. yellow; blue, red & white tampo w/"50" on sides & roof; "Character Counts" & Boy Scouts' logo on sides & hood; "Be Prepared for the 21st Century" on hood $2 - 4

1999 Pro Racing Collector line

#4 Chevrolet Monte Carlo
a. yellow; black spoiler; gray chassis & int.; clear windows; red, black, white, green & purple tampo with "4," "Kodak Max Film" & race decals on sides; "Kodak Max Film" on hood; "4" on roof; "Kodak" in back; red hubs; Thailand; Deluxe series (2000) 2 - 4

#5 Chevrolet Monte Carlo
a. red; yellow front; gray chassis & int.; clear windows; white, yellow, black & lt. green tampo w/"5," "Kellogg's" & race decals on sides; "Kellogg's" on hood & in back; "5" on roof; "Advance Auto Parts" in back; black hubs; Thailand; Deluxe series (2000) 3 - 5

#6 Ford Taurus
a. dk. blue; white hood, roof & rear; gray chassis & int.; clear windows; dk. blue, red, lt. blue & black tampo with "6," "Valvoline" & race decals on sides; "Valvoline Cummins" & Valvoline V on hood; "6" on roof; "Cummins" on trunk; "Eagle One" in back; black hubs; Thailand; Deluxe series (2000) 3 - 5

#7 Chevrolet Monte Carlo
a. black; gray chassis & int.; clear windows; yellow roof; yellow, white & red tampo w/"7," "Philips Light Bulbs" & race decals on sides; "Nations Rent" on hood; "7" on roof; "Philips Halogena Light Bulbs" on trunk; race decals in back; black hubs; Thailand; Deluxe series (2000) 2 - 4

#7 Philips-a

#7 Philips 25261 - 78mm - 1999
This Chevrolet Monte Carlo has a light gray metal chassis, interior & roll cage; clear windows with black outlines; and gyrd.
a. blue; white sides & back; red, white, black, blue & yellow tampo w/"7," "Klaussner" & race decals on sides; "Philips" & Chevy Logo on hood; "7" & "Michael Waltrip" on roof; "Philips Halogena Light Bulbs" on trunk; Thailand. Daytona 500 1999 Edition card w/Geoff Bodine collector card or Trackside box 3 - 5
a2. blue, same as a, red int. & roll cage, "Philips" & "Klaussner" on sides, no tampo on trunk, different decals, Thailand. Collector Ed 1999 Pro Racing card w/Geoff Bodine collector card 2 - 4
a3. blue, same as a, red int. & roll cage 3 - 5

#9 Cartoon Network - 82mm - 1999
This Ford Taurus has a light gray metal base, light gray plastic interior/roll cage, clear windows with black outlines & stripes, and gybk.
a. blue; multicolored tampo: "9," cartoons & race decals on sides (each side different); "Cartoon Network" & cartoons on hood; "9" & driver's sig. on roof; "Cartoon Network.COM" on trunk; cartoons & race decals in back 2 - 4

#9 Track Gear - 82mm - 1999
This Ford Taurus has a light gray metal base, light gray plastic interior & roll cage, clear windows with black outlines & stripes, black spoiler, and gybk.
a. yellow; multicolored tampo w/"9," "Track Gear" & race decals on sides; "Track Gear Racing Apparel" on hood; "9" & signature on roof; "Tutlex" on trunk; "www.trackgear.com" in back. #4 in Grand National series, limited to 15,000 2 - 4

#12 Ford Taurus
a. dk. blue; white front; red chassis & int.; clear windows; white, red & black tampo with "12," pegasus & race decals on sides; "Mobil 1" on hood & in back; "12" on roof; "Mobil Speedpass" on trunk; black hubs; Thailand; Deluxe series (2000) 2 - 4

#14 Pontiac Grand Prix
a. dk. green; lt. green spoiler; gray chassis & int.; clear windows; white, red, lt. green & black tampo w/"14," "Conseco" & race decals on sides; "Conseco" on hood & in back; "14" on roof; "Conseco.step.up" on trunk; black hubs; Thailand; Deluxe series (2000) 2 - 4

#14 Tennessee Volunteers - Sterling Marlin - 78mm - 1999
This Chevrolet Monte Carlo has a light gray metal chassis, interior & roll cage; clear windows with black outlines; and gybk.
a. orange; white, black, yellow & red tampo w/"Vols," "14," "Tennessee Volunteers" & race decals on sides; white hood; large "T" & "National Champions" on hood; "14" & "Sterling Marlin" on roof; "Vols" & "Tennessee Volunteers" on white trunk; "Tennessee" & "1998 National Champions" in back (1999) 6 - 8

#17 Dewalt - 78mm - 1999
This Chevrolet Monte Carlo has a light gray metal chassis, interior & roll cage; clear windows with black outlines; and gybk.
a. yellow; black hood, roof & trunk; black, red, white & dk. blue tampo w/"DeWalt," "17" & race decals on sides; "DeWalt" & Chevy logo on hood; "17" & Matt Kenseth's sig. on roof, "Guaranteed Tough" on trunk; "DeWalt," "17" & Chevy logo in back. Pit Crew pack. #2 in Grand National series, limited to 15,000 4 - 6

#17 Ford Taurus
a. yellow; black hood, roof & trunk; gray chassis & int.; clear windows; black, red & white tampo with "17," "Dewalt" & race decals on sides; "Dewalt" on hood & in back; "17" on roof; "Guaranteed Tough" on trunk; yellow hubs; Thailand; Deluxe series (2000) 2 - 4

#21 Ford Taurus
a. orange; black roof & spoiler; gray chassis & int.; clear windows; black, white, yellow, red & dark red tampo w/"21," "Supergard" & race decals on sides; Citgo logo on hood; "21" on roof; "Citgo" in back; black hubs; Thailand; Deluxe series (2000) 2 - 4

#22 Caterpillar 22518 - Ward Burton - 80mm - 1999
This Pontiac Grand Prix has a light gray metal chassis, light gray plastic interior &

Values are shown in U.S. dollars, first price is for mint, second is for mint packaged vehicles only. See pages 15-16 for grading guide to determine value for cars in lesser conditions.

#22 Caterpillar-a

roll cage, clear windows with black outlines & stripes, and gybk with black hubs and "Goodyear" & "Eagle" in yellow.

a. black; large yellow stripe around bottom; yellow roof; red, white & yellow tampo w/"22," "Caterpillar" & decals on sides; "CAT" on hood & trunk; "22" & Ward Burton's sig. on roof; Thailand. Trackside box, w/1/24th scale car & on Daytona 500 1999 Ed card 3 - NA
b. black, same as a, race decals different, no decals in front of back wheel, Thailand. Trackside box 3 - 5

#22 Pontiac Grand Prix

a. yellow; black hood & trunk; gray chassis & int.; clear windows; white, red, blue & black tampo with "22," "Caterpillar" & race decals on sides; "CAT" on hood & in back; "22" on roof; "CAT Financial" on trunk; black hubs; Thailand; Deluxe series (2000) 2 - 4

#25 Chevrolet Monte Carlo

a. dk. blue; white front; black trunk & spoiler; gray chassis & int.; clear windows; white, red, yellow & black tampo w/"25," "Michael Holigan" & race decals on sides; "Michael Holigan Nobody Knows Homes Like Holigan" on hood; "25" on roof; "Michael Holigan's Your New House" on trunk; "Michael Holigan.com" in back; black hubs; Thailand; Deluxe series (2000) 2 - 4

#25 Hendrick Motorsports-a

#25 Hendrick Motorsports 22528 - Wally Dallenbach - 78mm - 1999.
This Chevrolet Monte Carlo has a light gray metal chassis, interior & roll cage; clear windows with black outlines; and gybk.

a. red; white, black, yellow & lt. green tampo w/"25," "Dallenbach" & race decals on sides; "Hendrick Motorsports" on hood; "25" & Wally Dallenbach's sig. on roof. Trackside box or on 1999 Pro Racing card 2 - 4

#26 Ford Taurus

a. dk. blue; red border on bottom; white hood; gray chassis & int.; clear windows; red, white, dk. blue & yellow tampo w/"26," "Big KMart" & race decals on sides; "Big KMart" on hood, trunk & in back; "26" on roof; black hubs; Thailand; Deluxe series (2000) 2 - 4

#28 Havoline - 25696 - Davey Allison - 80mm 1999
This Ford Thunderbird has a gray metal base, white plastic interior & roll cage, clear windows with black outlines & stripes, and gybk; with collector's card.

a. white; black rear; gold stripe; gold, red, white, yellow, black & blue tampo w/"28," "Havoline" & race decals on sides; "Havoline Motor Oil" & Texaco Star on hood & back; "28" & Davey Allison's sig. on roof; Thailand. #4 in Hall of Fame series 5 - 7

#30 Bahari Racing - 80mm - 1999
This Pontiac Grand Prix has a light gray metal chassis, light gray plastic interior & roll cage, clear windows with black outlines & stripes, and gybk with black hubs and "Goodyear" & "Eagle" in yellow.

a. red; black back & sides; black, yellow, white & red tampo w/"Bryan," "30" & race decals on sides; Bryan logo on hood; "30" & driver's sig. on roof; race decals in back; Thailand 3 - 5
b. yellow; lt. blue in back; red, lt. blue, black & white tampo w/"30," "State Fair" & race decals on sides; "State Fair Corn Dogs" on hood; "30" & driver's sig. on roof; race decals in back; Thailand 3 - 5
c. yellow; black back; red, black & white tampo w/"30," "Jimmy Dean" & race decals on sides; "Jimmy Dean" & two cowboy boots on hood; "30" & driver's sig. on roof; "Jimmy Dean" & race decals in back 3 - 5

#32 Ford Taurus

a. orange; white rear; black spoiler; gray chassis & int.; clear windows; dk. blue, yellow & white tampo w/"32," "Tide" & race decals on sides; "Tide" on hood & in back, "32" on roof; black hubs; Thailand; Deluxe series (2000) 4 - 6

#33 Chevrolet Monte Carlo

a. black; white hood & trunk; gray chassis & int.; clear windows; white, lt. blue & red tampo w/"33," "Oakwood Homes" & race decals on sides; "Oakwood Homes" on hood & trunk; "33" on roof; "www.oakwoodhomes.com" in back; black hubs; Thailand; Deluxe series (2000) 2 - 4

#34 Goulds Pumps - 78mm - 1999
This Chevrolet Monte Carlo has a light gray metal chassis, interior & roll cage; clear windows with black outlines; and gybk.

a. white; blue, red, black, green, orange & yellow tampo w/"Goulds Pumps," "34" & race decals on sides; "Goulds Pumps" & two race decals on hood; "34" & driver's sig. on roof; "Little Trees" on trunk; "Goulds Pumps" & trees in back (1999) 2 - 4

#36 M&M's-a

#36 M&M's - Ernie Irvan - 80mm - 1999
This Pontiac Grand Prix has a light gray metal chassis, light gray plastic interior & roll cage, clear windows with black outlines & stripes, and gybk with black hubs and "Goodyear" & "Eagle" in yellow.

a. yellow; blue, red, lt. green, dk. red, white, brown & black tampo w/"M&M's" & candies on sides & hood; purple M&M on right side; "36" on sides & roof; "Pedigree" on trunk. 1999 Pro Racing card, Trackside box (1999) 3 - 5
a2. as a, blue M&M on right side, Thailand 2 - 4
b. as a, "36" on roof, "Pedigree" on trunk larger, "Call Carry" behind rear tires (1999) 2 - 4
b2. as b, Thailand 2 - 4

#36 Stanley Racing - 80mm - 1997
This Pontiac Grand Prix has a gray metal base, gray plastic interior & roll cage, clear windows with black outlines & stripes, and gybk.

a. yellow; black, red, blue & white tampo: "Stanley," "36" & race decals on sides; "Stanley" on hood, "36" & driver's sig on hood; "Stanley" & "36" in back (1999) 2 - 4

#40 Chevrolet Monte Carlo

a. black; yellow rear; gray chassis & int.; clear windows; yellow, red, gray & white tampo w/"40," "Marlin" & race decals on sides; "Sterling Marlin" on hood; "40" on roof; "Sabco" on trunk; "Marlin" in back; black hubs; Thailand; Deluxe series (2000) 2 - 4

#42 Chevrolet Monte Carlo

a. lt. green; opening hood; dk. blue front; gray chassis & int.; clear windows; white, orange, red, yellow & black tampo w/"42," "Bell South" & race decals on sides; "Bell South" on hood, trunk & in back; "42" on roof; black hubs; Thailand; Deluxe series (2000) 2 - 4

#43 Pontiac Grand Prix

a lt. blue; dk. blue rear; gray chassis & int.; clear windows; white, red, orange, yellow & black tampo w/"43," "Cheerios," "STP" & race decals on sides; "STP" on hood; "43" on roof; Betty Crocker spoon on trunk; race decals in back; lt. blue hubs; Thailand; Deluxe series (2000) 2 - 4
b. lt. blue; orange hood; gray chassis & int.; clear windows; orange, white, black, red & yellow tampo w/"43," "Wheaties" & race decals on sides; "Wheaties" on hood; "43" on roof; "Wheaties Legends of Racing" on trunk; race decals in back; dk. blue hubs; Thailand; Deluxe series (2000) 2 - 4
c. lt. blue; yellow hood; gray chassis & int.; clear windows; yellow, white, red & black tampo w/"43," "Pop Secret" & race decals on sides; "Cheerios" on hood; "43" on roof; "Hamburger Helper" on trunk; race decals in back; dark blue hubs; Thailand; Deluxe series (2000) 2 - 4

#44 Pontiac Grand Prix

a. multicolored; dk. blue hood & spoiler; gray chassis & int.; clear windows; lt. blue, orange, white, red, dk. blue & black tampo w/"44," Hot Wheels logo & race decals on sides; Hot Wheels logo on hood; "44" on roof; Hot Wheels logo & ".com" in back; gray hubs; Thailand; Deluxe series (2000) 2 - 4
b. unpainted; gray chassis & int.; clear windows; yellow, red, white & black tampo with "44," Hot Wheels logo & race decals on sides; Hot Wheels logo on hood; "44" on roof; Red Lobster logo on trunk; "Hot Wheels" in back; red hubs; Pit Crew series (2000) 5 - 7
c. chrome; black chassis; gray int.; engraved "44," Hot Wheels logo & race decals on sides; Hot Wheels logo on hood; "44" on roof; black hubs; Thailand; Deluxe series (2000) 2 - 4

#45 Chevrolet Monte Carlo

a. red & black; gray chassis & int.; clear windows; white, black, red & gray tampo w/"45," "Sprint PCS" & race decals on sides; "Sprint" on hood, trunk & in back; "45" on roof; black hubs; Thailand; Deluxe series (2000) 12 - 15

#55 Chevrolet Monte Carlo

a. dark blue; gray chassis & int.; clear windows; yellow, red, white & black tampo with "55," "Cooper Lighting" & race decals on sides; Square D logo on hood; "55" on roof; "Square D" on trunk & in back; black hubs; Thailand; Deluxe series (2000) 2 - 4
b. black; silver roof & rear; gray chassis & int.; clear windows; red, white & silver tampo w/"55," "Square D" & race decals on sides; "Aerosmith" on hood; "55" on roof; "America's Greatest Rock Band" on trunk; "Square D" in back; black hubs; Thailand; Deluxe series (2000) 6 - 8

#58 Turbine Solutions - 82mm - 1999
This Ford Taurus has a light gray metal base, light gray plastic interior & roll cage, clear windows with black outlines & stripes, gybk.

a. black; yellow roof; yellow, white & red tampo w/"Turbine Solutions, "58" & race decals on sides & back; "Turbine Solutions Racing to New Solutions" on hood; "58" & sig. on roof; "Mirsa Chem" on trunk. Pit Crew pack 4 - 6

#60 Chevrolet Monte Carlo

a. black; gray chassis & int.; clear windows; red, white & yellow tampo w/"60," "Power Team" & race decals on sides; "Power Team" & "Peco Energy on hood; "60" on roof; "Exelon" on trunk; "Peco Energy No Doubt About It" in back; gray hubs; Thailand; Deluxe series (2000) 2 - 4

#60 Winn Dixie - 82mm - 1999
This Ford Taurus has a light gray metal base, light gray plastic interior & roll cage, clear windows with black outlines & stripes, gybk.

a. black; yellow, white, red & dk. blue tampo w/"60," "Winn Dixie," logo & race decals on sides; "Winn Dixie," logo & "The Beef People" on hood; "60" & sig. on yellow roof; "Chek Drinks" on trunk; "Winn Dixie," logo, "60" & "The Beef People" in back. 2-pack with 1/24 model, Pit Crew pack. #2 in Grand National series, limited to 15,000 (1999) 4 - 6

#66 Ford Taurus

a. red, orange & lt. blue; white hood; gray chassis & int.; clear windows; multicolored tampo w/"66," "Big KMart" & race decals on sides; "Darrell Waltrip Victory Tour 2000" & Route 66 road sign on hood; "66" on roof; Route 66 road sign on trunk; "Big KMart" in back; black hubs; Thailand; Deluxe series (2000) 2 - 4

#66 Kmart-a

#66 Kmart - 82mm - 1999
This Ford Taurus has a light gray metal base, light gray plastic interior & roll cage, clear windows with black outlines & stripes, gybk.

a. red, orange & blue; white hood; white, red, orange, black & dk. blue tampo w/"66," "Big Kmart" & decals on sides; "Big" & Kmart logo on hood; "66" & driver's name on roof; highway sign: "South 66" on trunk; Thailand. 1999 Pro Racing card or Trackside box 2 - 4
a2. as a; race decals different, "Big" on hood is lt. blue not dk. blue. Daytona 500 card or 2-pack with 1/24th scale car (1999) 2 - 4
b3. as b, lighter orange tampo, China (1999) 2 - 4

Values are shown in U.S. dollars, first price is for mint, second is for mint packaged vehicles only. See pages 15-16 for grading guide to determine value for cars in lesser conditions.

#66 Phillips 66 - 78mm - 1999
This Chevrolet Monte Carlo has a light gray metal chassis, interior & roll cage; clear windows with black outlines; and gybk.
a. white; red roof; red, white, black, yellow & blue tampo w/"66," "Tropartic," Phillips 66 logo & race decals on sides; Phillips 66 logo on hood; "66" on roof; "1-800-Do-Apply" & "66" in back (1999) 2 - 4

#75 Ford Taurus
a. black; gray chassis & int.; clear windows; multicolored tampo w/"75," cartoon figures & race decals on sides; Cartoons & "Cartoon Network" on hood; "75" on roof; cartoon on trunk; "Powerpuff Girls" in back; black hubs; Thailand; Deluxe series (2000) 2 - 4

#77 Ford Taurus
a. blue; black spoiler; gray chassis & int.; clear windows; red, white, gray & black tampo w/"77," "Jasper" & race decals on sides; "Jasper Engines Transmissions Sealed Power" on hood, "77" on roof; race decals on trunk; "Jasper" in back; black hubs; Thailand; Deluxe series (2000) 2 - 4

#94 Ford Taurus
a. red; black roof & trunk; gray chassis & int.; clear windows; black, white, yellow & orange tampo w/"94," "Drive-Thru" & race decals on sides; McDonald's M on hood; "94" on roof; "Reese's" on trunk; black hubs; Thailand; Deluxe series (2000) 2 - 4

#97 Ford Taurus
a. red; black roof & trunk; gray chassis & int.; clear windows; black, white & yellow tampo w/"97," "Drive-Thru" & race decals on sides; McDonald's M on hood; "97" on roof; "mciworld-com" in back; black hubs; Thailand; Deluxe series (2000) 3 - 5
b. lt. green; yellow front; gray chassis & int.; clear windows; yellow, black, red, white & dk. green tampo w/"97," "John Deere" & race decals on sides; John Deere logo on hood; "97" on roof, "John Deere" & logo on trunk; "John Deere" in back; black hubs; Thailand; Deluxe series (2000) 2 - 4

#99 Ford Taurus
a. white, black & blue; gray chassis & int.; clear windows; white, black, lt. blue, purple & red tampo w/"99," "Exide" & race decals on sides; "Exide SKF" on hood; "99" on roof; "CR Chicago Rawhide" & "SKF" on trunk; "Exide" in back; black hubs; Thailand; Deluxe series (2000) 3 - 5

1999 Pro Racing basic line

#11 Paychex 23332 - 76mm - 1999
This Ford Taurus has a light gray plastic base, black interior & roll cage, clear windows, and plastic gytbk.
a. white; dk. blue, silver, red & yellow tampo w/"11," "Paychex" & race decals on sides; "Paychex" on hood; "11" & driver's sig. on roof; blue rear spoiler; "Paychex" in back $10 - 12

#36 M&M's 22511 - 75mm - 1999
This Pontiac Grand Prix has a light gray plastic base, interior & roll cage; clear windows; and plastic gytbk.
a. yellow; blue, red, lt. green, dk. red, white, brown & black tampo: "M&M's" & M&M's on sides & hood; "36" on sides & roof; "Pedigree" on trunk; "M&M's" & "54" in back $10 - 12

#97 John Deere 22514 - 76mm - 1999
This Ford Taurus has a light gray plastic base, interior & roll cage; clear windows; and plastic gytbk.
a. lt. green; yellow front & fenders; green rear; yellow, black, white, red & green tampo w/"97," "John Deere" & decals on sides; logo on hood & trunk; "97" on roof; "John Deere" in back $10 - 12

1999 Formula 1 Racing (Basic)

All these cars were issued on a #1 card, were made in Thailand, and use the same casting.

22794-a

Ferrari 22794 - 78mm - 1999
Red plastic chassis, black interior, front & rear spoilers, no windshield, and lwch.
a. red; yellow, white, black & lt. blue tampo w/race decals all over. On #1 card 3 - 5
a2. as a, white stripe on top, w/driver (2001) 3 - 5
a3. as a2, U.S. flag on sides, no driver, in plastic box, October Toy Fair give-away (2001) 75 - 100

Jaguar 50179 - 78mm - 2001
This Formula 1 race car has a green plastic chassis, black interior, and lwgd.
a. green; white, black & red tampo w/"HSBC" & "Best's" on sides, race decals on top 3 - 5

22798-a

Jordan 22798 - 78mm - 1999
Black plastic chassis, black interior, front & rear spoilers, no windshield, and lwch.
a. yellow; black & white tampo w/"Buzzin Hornets" on sides; "Buzzin" on nose; race decals; on #1 card 3 - 5
a2. as a, red & orange added to tampo, "Bitten Heroes" replaces "Buzzin Hornets" on sides, "Bitten" replaces "Buzzin" on nose, "Honda" on top, w/driver (2001) 3 - 5

22795-a

McLaren 22795 - 78mm - 1999
a. Black plastic chassis, black interior, front & rear spoilers, no windshield, and lwch. 3 - 5

McLaren - 73mm - 1999
Black metal chassis, black plastic interior, front & rear spoilers, no windshield, lw. China.
a. mtlfk black; gray on top; white, gray & red tampo w/"7," "Mobil 1" & race decals on sides & hood. In acrylic 2-pack, on #1 card $3 - 5
a2. as a, "8" not "7" in tampo 3 - 5
a3. as a, "Mika" on sides & wing, "3" replaces "7" in tampo, more race decals, w/driver (2001) 3 - 5

22797-a

Stewart 22797 - 78mm - 1999
White plastic chassis, black interior, front & rear spoilers, no windshield, and lwch.
a. white; red, blue & black tampo w/"SBC" & "16" on sides, on #1 card 3 - 4

22793-a

Williams 22793 - 78mm - 1999
Dark red plastic chassis, black interior, front & rear spoilers, no windshield, and lwch.
a. red; white, yellow, blue & black tampo w/"Williams F1" on sides; race decals; on #1 card 3 - 5
b. blue & white; red, white & black tampo w/"Compaq" on sides & spoiler, "5" on sides & nose, race decals 3 - 5
b2. as b, white int. & driver 3 - 5

Toys "R" Us Special 29018 - 78mm - 2001
This Formula 1 race car has a blue plastic chassis, black interior, and lwch.
a. blue; yellow, blue, orange & red tampo w/flame logo on sides; "Toys "R" Us" on top & behind driver 5 - 7

1999 Pit Crew Collection

#4 Chevrolet Monte Carlo
a. black; gray chassis & int.; clear windows; multicolored tampo w/"4," "Advantix" & race decals on sides; "Kodak Advantix" on hood & in back; "4" on roof; "Advanced" on trunk; red hubs; Thailand; Pit Crew series (1999) 2 - 4

#5 Chevrolet Monte Carlo
a. red; yellow front; gray chassis & int.; clear windows; white, yellow, black & lt. green tampo w/"5," "Kellogg's" & race decals on sides; "Kellogg's Corn Flakes" on hood; "5" on roof; "Kellogg's" in back; black hubs; Thailand; Pit Crew series (1999) 2 - 4

#6 Ford Taurus
a. dk. blue; white front; gray chassis & int.; clear windows; white, red, lt. blue & black tampo w/"6," "Valvoline" & race decals on sides; "Valvoline Cummins" & Valvoline V on hood; "6" on roof; "Cummins" on trunk; "Eagle One" in back; red hubs; Thailand; Pit Crew series (1999) 2 - 4

#07 Chevrolet Monte Carlo-a

#7 Chevrolet Monte Carlo
a. white; dk. blue hood & roof; gray chassis & int.; clear windows; red, black, yellow & lt. blue tampo with "7," "Klaussner" & race decals on sides; "Philips" on hood; "7" on roof; "Philips Halogena Light Bulbs" on trunk; "Philips Lighting in back; red hubs; Thailand; Pit Crew series (1999) 2 - 4

#9 Ford Taurus
a. blue; gray chassis & int.; clear windows; multicolored tampo w/"9," cartoon figures & race decals on sides, cartoons & "Cartoon Network" on hood & in back; "9" on roof; cartoon & "Cartoon Network.com" on trunk; black hubs; Thailand; Pit Crew series (1999) 8 - 10

#10 Ford Taurus
a. orange; white rear; black spoiler; gray chassis & int.; clear windows; dark blue, yellow & white tampo w/"10," "Tide" & race decals on sides; "Tide" on hood & in back; "10" on roof; "Whirlpool" on trunk; black hubs; Thailand; Pit Crew series (1999) 2 - 4

#11 Ford Taurus
a. white; dk. blue spoiler; gray chassis & int.; clear windows; dk. blue, black, red & gray tampo w/"11," "Paychex" & race decals on sides; "Paychex" on hood & in back; "11" on roof; black hubs; Thailand; Pit Crew series (1999) 2 - 4

#12 Ford Taurus
a. dk. blue; white front; red chassis & int.; clear windows; white, red & black tampo w/"12," pegasus & race decals on sides; "Mobil 1" on hood & in back; "12" on roof; "Mobil Speedpass" on trunk; black hubs; Thailand; Pit Crew series (1999) 2 - 4

#17 Ford Taurus
a. yellow; black hood, roof & trunk; gray chassis & int.; clear windows; black, red & white tampo w/"17," "DeWALT" & race decals on sides; "DeWALT" on hood & in back; "17" on roof; "Guaranteed Tough" on trunk; yellow hubs; Thailand; Pit Crew series (1999) 5 - 7

#21 Ford Taurus
a. red; gray chassis & int.; clear windows; white, black & dk. red tampo w/"21," "Citgo" & race decals on sides; "Citgo" on hood & in back; "21" on roof; "www.citgo.com" on trunk; black hubs; Thailand; Pit Crew series (1999) 2 - 4

#22 Pontiac Grand Prix
a. black; yellow stripe around car; gray chassis & int.; clear windows; yellow, red & white tampo w/"22," "Caterpillar" & race decals on sides; "CAT" on hood, trunk & in back; "22" on roof; black hubs; Thailand; Pit Crew series (1999) 2 - 4

#25 Chevrolet Monte Carlo
a. red; gray chassis & int.; clear windows; white, blue & black tampo with "25," "Dallenbach" & race decals on sides; "Hendrick Motorsports" on hood & in back; "25" on roof; "Advance Auto Parts" on trunk; black hubs; Thailand; Pit Crew series (1999) 2 - 4

#30 Pontiac Grand Prix
a. black; yellow front & roof; gray chassis & int.; clear windows; yellow, red, white & black tampo w/"30," "Jimmy Dean" & race decals on sides; "Jimmy Dean" & emblem on hood & in back; "30" on roof; black hubs; Thailand; Pit Crew series (1999) 2 - 4

#34 Chevrolet Monte Carlo
a. white; gray chassis & int.; clear windows; lt. blue, red & black tampo w/"34," "Goulds Pumps" & race decals on sides; "Goulds Pumps" on hood & in back; "34" on roof; "Little Trees" on trunk; black hubs; Thailand; Pit Crew series (1999) 2 - 4

Values are shown in U.S. dollars, first price is for mint, second is for mint packaged vehicles only. See pages 15-16 for grading guide to determine value for cars in lesser conditions.

#36 Pontiac Grand Prix

a. yellow; gray chassis & int.; clear windows; multicolored tampo with "36," "M&M's" & race decals on sides; "M&M's" on hood & in back; "36" on roof; "Pedigree" on trunk; black hubs; Thailand; Pit Crew series (1999) 2 - 4

#42 Chevrolet Monte Carlo

a. lt. blue; gray chassis & int.; clear windows; yellow, orange, red, white & black tampo w/"42," "Bell South" & race decals on sides; "Bell South" on hood, trunk & in back; "42" on roof; black hubs; Thailand; Pit Crew series (1999) 2 - 4

#43 Pontiac Grand Prix

a. lt. blue; red front; gray chassis & int.; clear windows; red, white & black tampo w/"43," "STP" & race decals on sides; "STP" on hood; "43" on roof; "Red Lobster" on trunk; "Kohler" in back; dk. blue hubs; Thailand; Pit Crew series (1999) 2 - 4

#44 Pontiac Grand Prix

a. dk. blue; gray chassis & int.; clear windows; multicolored tampo with "44," Hot Wheels logo & race decals on sides; Hot Wheels logo on hood; "44" on roof; "Red Lobster" on trunk; "wwwhotwheels.com" in back; red hubs; Thailand; Pit Crew series (1999) 2 - 4

#58 Ford Taurus

a. black; yellow roof; gray chassis & int.; clear windows; yellow, white & red tampo w/"58," "Turbine Solutions" & race decals on sides; "Turbine Solutions Racing to New Altitudes" on hood, "58" on roof; "MiraChem on trunk; "Turbine Solutions" in back; black hubs; Thailand; Pit Crew series (1999) 2 - 4

#60 Chevrolet Monte Carlo

a. black; gray chassis & int.; clear windows; red, white & yellow tampo with "60," "Winn Dixie" & race decals on sides; "Winn Dixie" & "The Beef People" on hood; "60" on roof; "Chek Drinks" on trunk; "Winn Dixie" in back; black hubs; Thailand; Pit Crew series (1999) 2 - 4

#66 Ford Taurus

a. red, orange & lt. blue; white hood; gray chassis & int.; clear windows; multicolored tampo with "66," "Big Kmart" & race decals on sides; "Big Kmart" on hood & in back; "66" on roof; Route 66 road sign on trunk; black hubs; Thailand; Pit Crew series (1999) 2 - 4

#94 Ford Taurus

a. red; black roof & trunk; red chassis & int.; clear windows; black, white, yellow & orange tampo with "94," "Drive-Thru" & race decals on sides; McDonald's M on hood; "94" on roof; "Reese's" on trunk; "Service Merchandise" in back; black hubs; Thailand; Pit Crew series (1999) 2 - 4

#97 Ford Taurus

a. lt. green; yellow front; gray chassis & int.; silver stripe in front; clear windows; yellow, black, red, white & dk. green tampo w/"97," "John Deere" & race decals on sides; John Deere logo on hood; "97" on roof; "John Deere" & logo on trunk, "John Deere Nothing Runs Like a Deere" in back; black hubs; Thailand; Pit Crew series (1999) 2 - 4

1999 Team Transporters

All have die-cast sleeper cabs with black plastic chassis, clear windows and black interiors. Each has chrome wheels and synthetic rubber tires (front wheels are different).

#5 Kellogg's Kenworth 12000 $15 - 18
#6 Valvoline Kenworth 12000 $15 - 18
#7 Philips International Eagle $15 - 18
#10 Tide Kenworth 12000 $15 - 18
#12 Mobil 1 Kenworth 12000 $15 - 18
#22 Caterpillar Kenworth 12000 $15 - 18
#26 Cheerios International Eagle $15 - 18
#43 50th Anniversary of Petty Racing International Eagle $15 - 18
#44 Hot Wheels International Eagle $15 - 18
#94 McDonald's Kenworth 12000 $15 - 18
#97 John Deere Kenworth 12000 $15 - 18
#99 Exide Kenworth 12000 $15 - 18

2000 Pit Crew Collection

#4 Chevrolet Monte Carlo

a. unpainted; gray chassis & int.; clear windows; red, black, white, blue & purple tampo with "4," "Kodak Max Film" & race decals on sides; "Kodak Max Film" on hood; "4" on roof; "Kodak" in back; red hubs; Thailand; Pit Crew series (2000) 3 - 5

b. yellow; gray chassis & int.; clear windows; black spoiler; red, black, white, blue & purple tampo with "4," "Kodak Max Film" & race decals on sides; "Kodak Max Film" on hood; "4" on roof; "Kodak" in back; red hubs; Thailand; Pit Crew series (2000) 3 - 5

#5 Chevrolet Monte Carlo

a. unpainted; white front end; gray chassis & int.; clear windows; red, black, white & blue tampo with "12," pegasus & race decals on sides; "Mobil 1" on hood & in back; "12" on roof; "Mobil Speed Pass" on trunk in back; black hubs; Thailand; Pit Crew series (2000) 3 - 5

#12 Ford Taurus

a. unpainted; yellow front; white hood; gray chassis & int.; clear windows; red, yellow, black, white & green tampo with "5," "Kellogg's" & race decals on sides; "Kellogg's Corn Flakes" on hood; "5" on roof; "Advance Auto Parts" on trunk; "Kellogg's" in back; black hubs; Thailand; Pit Crew series (2000) 3 - 5

#17 Ford Taurus

a. yellow; black hood, roof & trunk; gray chassis & int.; clear windows; black, red & white tampo w/"17," "DeWALT" & race decals on sides; "DeWALT" on hood & in back; "17" on roof; "Guaranteed Tough" on trunk; yellow hubs; Thailand; Pit Crew series (2000) 3 - 5

#22 Pontiac Grand Prix

a. unpainted; yellow front & hood; gray chassis & int.; clear windows; yellow, red, black & white tampo with "22," "Caterpillar" & race decals on sides; "CAT" on hood, trunk & in back; "22" on roof; black hubs; Thailand; Pit Crew series (2000) 3 - 5

#43 Pontiac Grand Prix

a. unpainted; red front; gray chassis & int.; clear windows; red, white, yellow & black tampo with "43," "STP" & race decals on sides; "STP" on hood; "43" on roof; Petty logo on trunk; "Kohler" in back; black hubs; Thailand; Pit Crew series (2000) 3 - 5

#06 Valvoline-a
#43 STP-a
#44 Hot Wheels-a
#94 McDonald's-a
#97 John Deere-a

#44 Pontiac Grand Prix

a. unpainted; gray chassis & int.; clear windows; yellow, orange, white, black & blue tampo with "44," Hot Wheels logo & race decals on sides; Hot Wheels logo on hood; "44" on roof; Red Lobster logo on hood; "Hot Wheels" in back; red hubs; Thailand; Pit Crew series (2000) 3 - 5

#55 Chevrolet Monte Carlo

a. unpainted; gray chassis & int.; clear windows; yellow, red, white & black tampo with "55," "Cooper Lighting" & race decals on sides; Square D logo on hood; "55" on roof; "Square D" on trunk & in back; black hubs; Thailand; Pit Crew series (2000) 3 - 5

a2. blue, same as a, Thailand, Pit Crew series (2000) 3 - 5

#60 Chevrolet Monte Carlo

a. unpainted; gray chassis & int.; clear windows; red, white, black & yellow tampo with "60," "Power Team" & race decals on sides; "Peco Energy Power Team" on hood; "60" on roof; "Exelon" on trunk; "Peco Energy no doubt about it" in back; gray hubs; Thailand; Pit Crew series (2000) 3 - 5

#66 Ford Taurus

a. red, orange & lt. blue; white hood; gray chassis & int.; clear windows; multicolored tampo with "66," "Big Kmart" & race decals on sides; "Darrell Waltrip" & Route 66 road sign on hood; "66" on roof; Route 66 road sign on trunk; "Big K" in back; black hubs; Thailand; Pit Crew series (2000) 3 - 5

#97 Ford Taurus

a. lt. green; yellow front; gray chassis & int.; black stripe in front; clear windows; yellow, black, red, white & dk. green tampo with "97," "John Deere" & race decals on sides; John Deere logo on hood; "97" on roof; "John Deere" & logo on trunk, "John Deere Nothing Runs Like a Deere" in back; black hubs; Thailand; Pit Crew series (2000) 3 - 5

#98 Ford Taurus

a. unpainted; gray chassis & int.; clear windows; red, white, yellow, black & blue tampo with "98," Woody Woodpecker & race decals on sides; Woody Woodpecker & "Woody" on hood; "98" on roof; "Woody" in back; black hubs; Thailand; Pit Crew series (2000) 3 - 5

2000 Select Series

#4 Chevrolet Monte Carlo

a. yellow; opening hood; black spoiler; gray chassis & int.; clear windows; red, black, white, green & purple tampo w/"4," "Kodak Max Film" & race decals on sides; "Kodak Max Film" on hood; "4" on roof; "Kodak" in back; yellow hubs; Thailand; Select 2000 series (2000) 3 - 5

#6 Ford Taurus-a

#6 Ford Taurus

a. white; white opening hood & rear; gray chassis & int.; clear windows; dk. blue, red, lt. blue & black tampo w/"6," "Valvoline" & race decals on sides; "Valvoline Cummins" & Valvoline V on hood; "6" on roof

Values are shown in U.S. dollars, first price is for mint, second is for mint packaged vehicles only. See pages 15-16 for grading guide to determine value for cars in lesser conditions.

"Cummins" on trunk; "Eagle 1" in back; black hubs; Thailand; Select 2000 series (2000) 7 - 9

#12 Ford Taurus-a

#12 Ford Taurus

a. dk. blue; white front; red chassis & int.; clear windows; white, red & black tampo w/"12," pegasus & race decals on sides; "Mobil 1" on hood & in back; "12" on roof; "Mobil Speedpass" on trunk; black hubs; Thailand; Select 2000 series (2000) 7 - 9

#14 Pontiac Grand Prix

a. dk. green; opening hood; lt. green spoiler; gray chassis & int.; clear windows; white, red, lt. green & black tampo with "14," "Conseco" & race decals on sides; "Conseco" on hood & in back; "14" on roof; "Conseco.step.up" on trunk; black hubs; Thailand; Select 2000 series (2000) 3 - 5

#17 Ford Taurus

a yellow; black opening hood, roof & trunk; gray chassis & int.; clear windows; black, red & white tampo with "17," "DeWALT" & race decals on sides; "DeWALT" on hood & in back; "17" on roof; "Guaranteed Tough" on trunk; yellow hubs; Thailand; Select 2000 series (2000) 7 - 9

#22 Pontiac Grand Prix-a

#22 Pontiac Grand Prix

a. yellow; black opening hood & trunk; gray chassis & int.; clear windows; white, red, lt. blue & black tampo with "22," "Caterpillar" & race decals on sides; "CAT" on hood, trunk & in back; "22" on roof; black hubs; Thailand; Select 2000 series (2000) 3 - 5

#32 Ford Taurus

a. orange; opening hood; white rear; black spoiler; gray chassis & int.; clear windows; dk. blue, yellow & white tampo with "32," "Tide" & race decals on sides, "Tide" on hood & in back, "32" on roof; black hubs; Thailand; Select 2000 series (2000) 3 - 5

#33 Chevrolet Monte Carlo

a. dk. aqua; white opening hood & trunk; gray chassis & int.; clear windows; white, lt. blue & red tampo with "33," "Oakwood Homes" & race decals on sides; "Oakwood Homes" on hood & trunk; "33" on roof; "www.oakwood-homes.com" in back; black hubs; Thailand; Select 2000 series (2000) 3 - 5

#40 Chevrolet Monte Carlo-a

#40 Chevrolet Monte Carlo

a. black; opening hood; yellow rear; gray chassis & int.; clear windows; yellow, gray, red & white tampo w/"40," "Marlin" & race decals on sides; "Sterling Marlin" on hood; "40" on roof; "Sabco" on trunk; "Marlin" in back; black hubs; Thailand; Select 2000 series (2000) 3 - 5

#42 Chevrolet Monte Carlo

a. lt. green; opening hood; dk. blue front end; gray chassis & int.; clear windows, white, black, red & yellow tampo w/"42," "Bell South" & race decals on sides; "Bell South" on hood, trunk & in back; "42" on roof; black hubs; Thailand; Select 2000 series (2000) 10 - 12

#43 Pontiac Grand Prix

a. lt. blue; opening hood; yellow front; gray chassis & int.; clear windows; yellow, white, red & black tampo w/"43," "Pop Secret" & race decals on sides; "Cheerios" on hood; "43" on roof; "Hamburger Helper" on trunk; Betty Crocker spoon in back; dk. blue hubs; Thailand; Select 2000 series (2000) 8 - 10

b. lt. blue; opening hood; dk. blue rear; gray chassis & int.; clear windows; yellow, white, red & black tampo with "43," "STP," "Cheerios" & race decals on sides; "STP" on hood; "43" on roof; Betty Crocker spoon on trunk; lt. blue hubs; Thailand; Select 2000 series (2000) 8 - 10

#44 Pontiac Grand Prix

a. multicolored; dark blue opening hood; gray chassis & int.; clear windows; lt. blue, orange, white, red, dk. blue & black tampo w/"44," Hot Wheels logo & race decals on sides; Hot Wheels logo on hood; "44" on roof; Hot Wheels logo & ".com" on back trunk; chrome hubs; Thailand; Select 2000 series (2000) 8 - 10

#45 Chevrolet Monte Carlo

a. red & black; opening hood; gray chassis & int.; clear windows; white, black, red & gray tampo with "45," "Sprint PCS" & race decals on sides; "Sprint" on hood, trunk & in back; "45" on roof; black hubs; Thailand; Select 2000 series (2000) 18 - 20

#55 Chevrolet Monte Carlo-a

#55 Chevrolet Monte Carlo

a. dk. blue; opening hood; gray chassis & int.; clear windows; yellow, red, white & black tampo w/"55," "Cooper Lighting" & race decals on sides; Square D logo on hood; "55" on roof; "Square D" on trunk & in back; black hubs; Thailand; Select 2000 series (2000) 2 - 4

#60 Chevrolet Monte Carlo-a

#60 Chevrolet Monte Carlo

a. black; opening hood; gray chassis & int.; clear windows; red, white & yellow tampo with "60," "Power Team" & race decals on sides; "Peco Energy Power Team" on hood; "60" on roof; "Exelon" on trunk; "Peco Energy no doubt about it" in back; gray hubs; Thailand; Select 2000 series (2000) 2 - 4

#66 Ford Taurus

a. red, orange & lt. blue; white hood; gray chassis & int.; clear windows; multicolored tampo with "66," "Big Kmart" & race decals on sides; "Darrell Waltrip" & Route 66 road sign on hood; "66" on roof; Route 66 road sign on trunk; "Big K" in back; black hubs; Thailand; Select 2000 series (2000) 2 - 4

#77 Ford Taurus

a. blue; opening hood; black spoiler; gray chassis & int.; clear windows; red, white, gray & black tampo with "77," "Jasper" & race decals on sides; "Jasper Engines Transmissions Sealed Power" on hood; "77" on roof; race decals on trunk; "Jasper" in back; black hubs; Thailand; Select 2000 series (2000) 2 - 4

#94 Ford Taurus

a. red; opening hood; black roof & trunk; gray chassis & int.; clear windows; black, white, yellow & orange tampo w/"94," "Drive-Thru" & race decals on sides; McDonald's M on hood; "94" on roof; "Reese's" on trunk; black hubs; Thailand; Select 2000 series (2000) 2 - 4

#97 Ford Taurus-a

#97 Ford Taurus

a. red; black roof & trunk; gray chassis & int.; clear windows; yellow, black & white tampo with "97," "Drive-Thru" & race decals on sides; McDonald's M on hood; "97" on roof; "mciworld-com" in back; black hubs; Thailand; Select 2000 series (2000) 2 - 4

b. green; dk. green rear; yellow front; gray chassis & int.; clear windows; yellow, black, olive, white & red tampo with "97," "John Deere" & race decals on sides; John Deere logo on hood; "97" on roof; "John Deere" on trunk & in back; dk. olive hubs; Thailand; Select 2000 series (2000) 2 - 4

#99 Ford Taurus

a. black; opening hood; white front; gray chassis & int.; clear windows; white, black, lt. blue, purple & red tampo w/"99," "Exide" & race decals on sides; "Exide SKF" on hood; "99" on roof; "SKF" on trunk; "Exide" in back; black hubs; Thailand; Select 2000 series (2000) 2 - 4

2000 Small Cards

#4 Chevrolet Monte Carlo

a. yellow; black spoiler; gray chassis & int.; clear windows; red, black, white, green & purple tampo w/"4," "Kodak Max Film" & race decals on sides, "Kodak Max Film" on hood, "4" on roof, "Kodak" in back; black hubs; Thailand; Racing series (2000) 6 - 8

#5 Chevrolet Monte Carlo

a. red; white hood; gray chassis & int.; clear windows; lt. green, yellow, black & white tampo w/"5," "Kellogg's" & race decals on sides, "Kellogg's" on hood & in back, "5" on roof, "Advance Auto Parts" on trunk; black hubs; Thailand; Racing series (2000) 6 - 8

#6 Ford Taurus

a. dark blue; white hood, roof & trunk; gray chassis & int.; clear windows; red, white, yellow, black & blue tampo with "6," "Valvoline" & race decals on sides, Valvoline V & "Valvoline" on hood, "6" on roof, "Cummins" on trunk, "Eagle One" in back; black hubs; Thailand; Racing series (2000) 6 - 8

#22 Pontiac Grand Prix

a. yellow; black hood & trunk; gray chassis & int.; clear windows; white, red, blue & black tampo with "22," "Caterpillar" & race decals on sides, "CAT" on hood & in back, "22" on roof, "CAT Financial" on trunk; black hubs; Thailand; Racing series (2000) 6 - 8

#32 Ford Taurus

a. orange; white rear; black spoiler; gray chassis & int.; clear windows; dark blue, white, yellow & black tampo with "32," "Tide" & race decals on sides, "Tide" on hood & in back, "32" on roof; black hubs; Thailand; Racing series (2000) 6 - 8

#33 Chevrolet Monte Carlo

a. black; white hood & trunk; gray chassis & int.; clear windows; white, lt. blue, red & yellow tampo w/"33," "Oakwood Homes" & race decals on sides, "Oakwood Homes" on hood & trunk, "33" on roof, "www.oakwood-homes.com" in back; black hubs; Thailand; Racing series (2000) 6 - 8

#42 Chevrolet Monte Carlo

a. lt. green; dark blue front; gray chassis & int.; clear windows; yellow, orange, red & white tampo with "42," "Bell South" & race decals on sides; "Bell South" on hood, trunk & in back; "42" on roof; black hubs; Thailand; Racing series (2000) 6 - 8

#43 Pontiac Grand Prix

a. lt. blue; dk. blue rear; gray chassis & int.; clear windows; yellow, white, red & black tampo w/"43," "Cheerios" & race decals on sides, "STP" on hood, "43" on roof, Betty Crocker spoon on trunk, race decals in back; black hubs; Thailand; Racing series (2000) 6 - 8

b. lt. blue; yellow hood; gray chassis & int.; clear windows; yellow, white, red & black tampo w/"43," "Pop Secret" & race decals on sides, "Cheerios" on hood, "43" on roof, "Hamburger Helper" on trunk, race decals in back; black hubs; Thailand; Racing series (2000) 6 - 8

#44 Pontiac Grand Prix

a. multicolored; dk. blue hood; gray chassis & int.; clear windows; lt. blue, orange, white, red, dk. blue & black tampo w/"44," Hot Wheels logo & race decals on sides, Hot Wheels logo on hood, "44" on roof, Hot Wheels logo & ".com" in back; black hubs; Thailand; Racing series (2000) 6 - 8

#45 Chevrolet Monte Carlo

a. red & black; gray chassis & int.; clear windows; white, black, red & gray tampo with "45," "Sprint PCS" & race decals on sides; "Sprint" on hood, trunk & in back; "45" on roof; black hubs; Thailand; Racing series (2000) 6 - 8

#94 Ford Taurus

a. red; black roof, trunk & spoiler; gray chassis & int.; clear windows; yellow, white & black tampo w/"94," "Drive-Thru" & race decals on sides, McDonald's M on hood, "94" on roof, "Reese's" on trunk; black hubs; Thailand; Racing series (2000) 6 - 8

#97 Ford Taurus

a. red; black roof, trunk & spoiler; gray chassis & int.; clear windows; yellow, white & black tampo with "97," "Drive-Thru" & race decals on sides, McDonald's M on hood, "97" on roof, "mci.worldcom" in back; black hubs; Thailand; Racing series (2000) 6 - 8

Values are shown in U.S. dollars, first price is for mint, second is for mint packaged vehicles only. See pages 15-16 for grading guide to determine value for cars in lesser conditions.

#97 Ford Taurus
a. lt. green; dk. green rear; gray chassis & int.; clear windows; yellow, white, red & black tampo with "97," "John Deere" & race decals on sides; "John Deere" & logo on hood & trunk; "97" on roof; "John Deere Nothing Runs Like a Deere" in back; black hubs; Thailand; Racing series (2000) 6 - 8

#98 Ford Taurus
a. red; yellow hood; lt. green roof; lt. blue rear; gray chassis & int.; clear windows; red, white, yellow, black & blue tampo with "98," Woody Woodpecker & race decals on sides; Woody Woodpecker & "Woody" on hood; "98" on roof; about 20 Ha Ha's on trunk; "Woody" in back; black hubs; Thailand; Racing series (2000) 6 - 8

#99 Ford Taurus
a. white, blue & black; gray chassis & int.; clear windows; red, white, yellow, black & blue tampo w/"99," "Exide" & race decals on sides; "Exide SKF" on hood & in back; "99" on roof; "CR Chicago Rawhide SKF" on trunk; black hubs; Thailand; Racing series (2000) 6 - 8

2000 Racing Treasure Hunt Series

These Pontiac Grand Prixs have light gray chassis & interiors, "44" on the sides & roofs, a decal on the trunks, and gych.

a. lt. blue; red, white, yellow & black tampo w/"Daytona 500" on sides & hood 18 - 20
b. yellow; red, white & black tampo with flames, "Darlington a NASCAR Tradition" on hood & sides 18 - 20
c. black; red, white, yellow & blue tampo w/"Talladega Super Speedway" on hood 18 - 20
d. red, white, blue & black w/"Talladega" on sides; "Talladega Super Speedway" on hood 18 - 20
e. dk. blue; lt. blue, red, black & white tampo w/"California Speedway" on hood & sides 18 - 20
f. gray & white; red & black tampo with "Michigan Speedway" on hood 18 - 20
g. white; black & red tampo w/"Watkins Glen" on sides; "Watkins Glen New York Thunder Road" on hood 18 - 20
h. black & white; red, yellow & black tampo w/"Phoenix International Raceway" on hood 18 - 20
i. purple; white, lt. blue & red tampo with "Homestead Miami Speedway" on hood 18 - 20
j. white; black, yellow, gray, red & green tampo w/checkerboard & "Daytona" on sides; "Daytona Light" on hood 18 - 20

2000 Team Transporters

#43 Cheerios International Eagle	15-18
#44 Kyle Petty International Eagle	15-18
#45 Sprint PCS International Eagle	18-25
#94 McDonald's Kenworth 12000	15-18
Little Debbie International Eagle, Mail-in	18-25

2001 Pit Board Series

#02 Ford Taurus
a. black; gray chassis & int.; clear windows; white hood; white, red & blue tampo w/"02," "Alltel" & race decals on sides; "Alltel Mobil 1" on hood; "02" on roof; "www.alltel.com" in back; Thailand; Pit Board series (2001) 3 - 5

#5 Chevrolet Monte Carlo-a

#5 Chevrolet Monte Carlo
a. orange & dk. blue; gray chassis & int.; clear windows; multicolored tampo w/"5," "Kellogg's" & race decals on sides; Tony the Tiger on hood; "5" on roof; "Kellogg's" in back; Thailand; Pit Board series (2001) 4 - 6

#6 Ford Taurus-a

#6 Ford Taurus
a. gray & blue; gray chassis & int.; clear windows; multicolored tampo w/"6," "Pfizer" & race decals on sides; "Pfizer" on hood, trunk & in back; "6" on roof; Thailand; Pit Board series (2001) 3 - 5
b. dk. blue; gray chassis; clear windows; gray int.; red, yellow, black & white tampo w/"6," "Tombstone" & race decals on sides; "Kraft" on hood; "6" on roof; "Kraft Singles" on trunk; "Maxwell House" in back; Team Kraft Racing premium; Thailand; Pit Board series (2001) 3 - 5

#10 Ford Taurus-a

#10 Ford Taurus
a. white; gray chassis; dk. blue back; clear windows; gray int.; multicolored tampo w/"10," "Valvoline" & race decals on sides; "Valvoline" & Valvoline "V" on hood; "10" on roof; "Eagle One" on trunk & in back; Thailand; Pit Board series (2001) 3 - 5
b. yellow; gray chassis & int.; clear windows; white, dk. blue, brown, white & black tampo w/"10," "Nestle Nesquik" & race decals on sides; "Nestle Nesquik" & rabbit on hood & in back; "10" on roof; "Nestea" & race decals on trunk; Thailand; Pit Board series (2001) 3 - 5

#11 Ford Taurus
a. white; gray chassis; clear windows; white int.; red & black tampo w/"11," "Red Cell Batteries" & race decals on sides; "Ralphs" on hood & trunk; "11" on roof; "red Cell" in back; Thailand. In Bonus pack w/8 Red Cell AA batteries, Pit Board series (2001) 3 - 5

#12 Ford Taurus-a

#12 Ford Taurus
a. dk. blue; red chassis; clear windows; gray int.; white hood; multicolored tampo w/"12," pegasus & race decals on sides; "Mobil 1" on hood & in back; "12" on roof; "Speedpass" on trunk; Thailand; Pit Board series (2001) 3 - 5

#17 Ford Taurus-a

#17 Ford Taurus
a. yellow; gray chassis & int.; clear windows; black roof & trunk; black, white & red tampo w/"17," "DeWALT" & race decals on sides; "DeWALT" on hood & in back; "17" on roof; "Guaranteed Tough" on trunk; Thailand; Pit Board series (2001) 3 - 5

#21 Ford Taurus
a. red; black chassis; clear windows; gray int.; white, red, black & yellow tampo w/"21," "Motorcraft" & race decals on sides; "Motorcraft Quality Parts" & emblem on hood; "21" on roof; "Motorcraft" in back; Thailand; Pit Board series (2001) 3 - 5

#22 Dodge Intrepid-a

#22 Dodge Intrepid
a. yellow; black hood & trunk; gray chassis & int.; clear windows; red, white, black & blue tampo w/"22," "Caterpillar" & race decals on sides; "CAT" on hood & in back; "40" on roof; "CAT Financial on trunk; Thailand; Pit Board series (2001) 3 - 5

#25 Chevrolet Monte Carlo-a

#25 Chevrolet Monte Carlo
a. black & red; gray chassis & int.; clear windows; red, yellow, black & white tampo w/"25," "UAW-Delphi" & race decals on sides; "UAW-Delphi" on hood, trunk & in back; "25" on roof; Thailand; Pit Board series (2001) 3 - 5

#26 Ford Taurus
a. blue; gray chassis & int.; clear windows; white hood; dk. blue rear; white, dk. blue, red, black & yellow tampo with "26," Kmart logo & race decals on sides; Kmart logo on hood & trunk; "26" on roof; "Kmart" in back; Thailand; Pit Board series (2001) 3 - 5

#32 Ford Taurus
a. orange; white rear; gray chassis & int.; clear windows; white, dk. blue, red, black & yellow tampo w/"32," "Tide" & race decals on sides; "Tide" on hood & in back; "32" on roof; "Kenmore" on trunk; Thailand; Pit Board series (2001) 3 - 5

#33 Chevrolet Monte Carlo-a

#33 Chevrolet Monte Carlo
a. white; gray chassis & int.; clear windows; blue roof & rear; blue, red & yellow tampo w/"33," "Oakwood Homes" & race decals on sides; "Oakwood Homes" on hood & in back; "33" on roof; "Schult Homes"; Thailand; Pit Board series (2001) 3 - 5

#36 Pontiac Grand Prix-a

#36 Pontiac Grand Prix
a. yellow; gray chassis; clear windows; gray int.; turquoise on one side, pink on other; multicolored tampo with "36," "M&M's" & race decals on sides; "M&M's" & M&M's on hood; "36" on roof; "Snickers" on trunk; "M&M's" in back; Thailand; Pit Board series (2001) 3 - 8
b. blue; gray chassis & int.; clear windows; red & white stripes on one side, blue on other; red, white & yellow tampo w/"36," "M&M's" & race decals on sides; M&M's on hood; "36" on roof; "M&M's" & M&M's on trunk & in back; Thailand; Pit Board series; (2001) 3 - 5

#40 Dodge Intrepid-a

#40 Dodge Intrepid
a. gray; black chassis; clear windows; gray int.; red, white, black & yellow tampo w/"40," "Marlin" & race decals on sides; "Sterling Marlin" on hood & in back; "40" on roof; Thailand; Pit Board series (2001) 3 - 5

#43 Dodge Intrepid-a

#43 Dodge Intrepid
a. lt. blue; gray chassis; clear windows; gray int.; yellow hood & trunk; multicolored tampo w/"43" & race decals on sides; "Cheerios" & Betty Crocker spoon on hood; "43" on roof; "Chex" on trunk; "Cheerios" in back; Thailand; Pit Board series (2001) 3 - 5

#44 Dodge Intrepid-a

#44 Dodge Intrepid
a. blue; gray chassis; clear windows; gray int.; white, red, black & yellow tampo w/"44," "Sparkle" & race decals on sides; "GP" & "Georgia Pacific Building Products" on hood; "44" on roof; Hot Wheels logo on trunk; "Georgia Pacific" in back; Thailand; Pit Board series (2001) 3 - 5

#44 Dodge Intrepid-b

b. blue; black chassis; clear windows; red int.; white, red, black & yellow tampo with "44," Hot Wheels logo & race decals on sides; "GP" & "Four Generations Petty 42 43 44 45" on hood; "44" on roof; "GP Georgia Pacific" in back; Thailand; Pit Board series (2001) 3 - 5

#45 Dodge Intrepid
a. black; red chassis; clear windows; gray int.; red roof; black, white & yellow tampo w/"45," "Sprint PCS" & race decals on sides; "Sprint" on hood, trunk & in back; "45" on roof; Thailand; Pit Board series (2001) 3 - 5
b. black; black chassis; clear windows; red int.; red, gray & white tampo w/"45," "Sprint," stars & race decals on sides; "2001 Kyle Petty" & "Charity Ride Across America" on hood; "45" on roof; "Sprint" on trunk & in back; Thailand; Pit Board series (2001) 3 - 5

#60 Ford Taurus
a. gray; gray chassis & int.; clear windows; red roof; black rear; white, red, black & yellow tampo w/"60," "Grainger.com" & race decals on sides; "Granger Industrial Supply" & emblem on hood; "60" on roof; "Grainger.com" & "More Stuff Faster" on trunk; "Grainger" in back; Thailand; Pit Board series (2001) 3 - 5

Values are shown in U.S. dollars, first price is for mint, second is for mint packaged vehicles only. See pages 15-16 for grading guide to determine value for cars in lesser conditions.

#96 Ford Taurus

a. red; red chassis; clear windows; red int.; black roof; yellow, black & white tampo w/"96," "Drive-Thru" & race decals on sides; McDonald's M on hood; "96" on roof; "www.ppl.racing.com" in back; Thailand; Pit Board series (2001) 3 - 5

#99 Ford Taurus-a

#99 Ford Taurus

a. blue; red chassis; clear windows; gray int.; white, red, black, gray & yellow tampo w/"99," "Supergard" & race decals on sides; "Citgo SKF" on hood; "99" on roof; "CR Chicago Rawhide" & "vsm.skf.com" on trunk; "Citgo" in back; Thailand; Pit Board series (2001) 3 - 5

2001 Team Transporters

#5 Kellogg's Kenworth 12000	15-18
#6 Pfizer Kenworth 12000	15-18
#10 Nesquick Kenworth 12000	15-18
#10 Valvoline Kenworth 12000	15-18
#11 Darrel Waltrip International Eagle	15-18
#12 Mobil 1 Kenworth 12000	15-18
#17 DeWALT Kenworth 12000	15-18
#22 CAT Kenworth 12000	15-18
#28 Davey Allison International Eagle	15-18
#32 Tide Kenworth 12000	15-18
#36 M&M's Kenworth 12000	15-18
#43 Richard Petty International Eagle	15-18
#44 Georgia-Pacific International Eagle	15-18
#44 Kyle Petty International Eagle	15-18
#45 Sprint PCS International Eagle	18-25
#55 Square D International Eagle	15-18
#96 McDonald's Kenworth 12000	15-18
#99 Citgo Kenworth 12000	15-18

2002 Sticker Series

#5 Chevrolet Monte Carlo

a. white; clear windows; gray int.; lt. green roof; mtlfk blue sides; multicolored tampo w/"5," "Monsters, Inc" & race decals on sides; "Monsters, Inc." & "Kellogg's" on hood & in back; "5" on roof; Thailand; Sticker series (2002) 2 - 4

b. orange & dk. blue; clear windows; gray int.; multicolored tampo w/"5," "Kellogg's" & race decals on sides; Tony the Tiger on hood; "5" on roof; "Kellogg's" in back; Pit Board series; Thailand; Sticker series (2002) 2 - 4

#6 Ford Taurus-a

#6 Ford Taurus

a. black; clear windows; gray int.; multicolored tampo with "6," "Pfizer" & race decals on sides; "Pfizer" on hood, trunk & in back; "6" on roof; Thailand; Sticker series (2002) 2 - 4

#12 Ford Taurus-a

#10 Ford Taurus

a. yellow; gray chassis & int.; clear windows; dk. blue, brown, white & red tampo w/"10," "Nesquik" & race decals on sides; "Nesquik" on hood & in back; "10" on roof; "Nestea," "Coffee Mate" & "Juicy Juice" on trunk; Thailand; Sticker series (2002) 2 - 4

#12 Ford Taurus

a. black; gray chassis & int.; clear windows; white hood; white, blue & red tampo w/"12," "Alltel" & race decals on sides; "Alltel" & "Mobil II" on hood & in back; "12" on roof; "Print by Sony" on trunk; Thailand; Sticker series (2002) 2 - 4

#14 Chevrolet Monte Carlo

a. violet; gray chassis & int.; clear windows; red, white & black tampo w/"14," "Harrahs.Com" & race decals on sides; "Harrahs Oh Yeah!" on hood; "14" on roof; "Harrahs.com" on trunk & in back; Thailand; Sticker series (2002) 2 - 4

#17 Ford Taurus-a

#17 Ford Taurus

a. black; gray chassis & int.; clear windows; yellow roof; yellow, red & white tampo w/"17," "DeWALT" & race decals on sides; "DeWALT" on hood & in back; "17" on roof; "Guaranteed Tough" on trunk; Thailand; Sticker series (2002) 2 - 4

#21 Ford Taurus--a

#21 Ford Taurus

a. red; clear windows; gray int.; black, white & blue tampo w/"21," "Motorcraft" & race decals on sides; "Motorcraft Quality Parts" on hood; "21" on roof; "Quality Care" on trunk; "Motorcraft" in back; Thailand; Sticker series (2002) 2 - 4

#22 Dodge Intrepid-a

#22 Dodge Intrepid

a. yellow & black; clear windows; gray int.; multicolored tampo w/"22," "Caterpillar" & race decals on sides; "CAT" on hood & trunk; "22" on roof; Polaris ATVs in back; Thailand; Sticker series (2002) 2 - 4

#99 Citgo-a

#5 Kellogg's-a

#25 Chevrolet Monte Carlo-b

#25 Chevrolet Monte Carlo

a. black; clear windows; gray int.; multicolored tampo with "25," "UAW-Delphi" & race decals on sides, hood, trunk & in back; "25" on roof; Thailand; Sticker series (2002) 2 - 4

b. red, white & blue; gray chassis & int.; clear windows; multicolored tampo w/"25," "Marines.com" & race decals on sides; "Marines" & emblem on hood; "25" on roof; "Team Remsi" on trunk; "1-800-marines" in back; Thailand; Sticker series (2002) 2 - 4

#32 Ford Taurus-a

#32 Ford Taurus

a. orange; gray chassis & int.; clear windows; white rear with black spoiler; white, dark blue, red & yellow tampo with "32," "Tide" & race decals on sides; "Tide" on hood & in back; "32" on roof; "Kenmore" on trunk; Thailand; Sticker series (2002) 2 - 4

#36 Pontiac Grand Prix-a

#36 Pontiac Grand Prix

a. yellow; gray chassis & int.; clear windows; multicolored tampo with "36," "M&M's" & race decals on sides; "Pfizer" on hood, trunk & in back; "36" on roof; "Snickers" on trunk; Thailand; Sticker series (2002) 2 - 4

#40 Dodge Intrepid

a. gray; clear windows; gray int.; multicolored tampo w/"40" & race decals on sides; "Sterling Marlin" on hood, trunk & in back; "40" on roof; Thailand; Sticker series (2002) 2 - 4

#43 Dodge Intrepid

a. dk. blue; gray chassis & int.; clear windows; multicolored tampo w/"43," "Pop Secret" & race decals on sides; "Pop Secret" on hood, trunk & in back; "43" on roof; popcorn all over; Thailand; Sticker series (2002) 2 - 4

b. lt. blue; gray chassis & int.; clear windows; yellow, red, black & white tampo w/"43," "Pop Secret" & race decals on sides; "Cheerios" & Betty Crocker spoon on hood; "43" on roof; "Chex" on trunk; "Cheerios" in back; Thailand; Sticker series (2002) 2 - 4

c. orange; gray chassis & int.; clear windows; yellow & black striped rear; multicolored tampo with "43," "Honey Nut Cheerios" & race decals on sides; "Honey Nut Cheerios" on hood, trunk and in back; "43" on roof; Thailand; Sticker series (2002) 2 - 4

#44 Dodge Intrepid

a. blue; gray chassis & int.; clear windows; black, red & white tampo w/"44," "Brawny" & race decals on sides; "GP Georgia-Pacific" on hood; "44" on roof; Hot Wheels logo on trunk; "GP gp.com in back; Thailand; Sticker series (2002) 2 - 4

#45 Dodge Intrepid

a. red; red chassis; gray int.; clear windows; black hood & trunk; white, gray,

#45 Dodge Intrepid-a

black & blue tampo w/45," "Sprint PCS" & race decals on sides; "Sprint" on hood, trunk & in back; "45" on roof; Thailand; Sticker series (2002) 2 - 4

#55 Chevrolet Monte Carlo

a. yellow; clear windows; gray int.; multicolored tampo w/"55," "Square D" & race decals on sides; Square & "D" on hood; "55" on roof; "Square D" on trunk & in back; Thailand; Sticker series (2002) 2 - 4

#60 Ford Taurus

a. red; gray chassis & int.; clear windows; black hood & trunk; white, gray, black, yellow & blue tampo w/"60," "Grainger" & race decals on sides; "Grainger Industrial Supply" on hood; "60" on roof; "Grainger" on trunk; "www.grainger.com" in back; Thailand; Sticker series (2002) 2 - 4

#97 Ford Taurus

a. black; gray chassis & int.; clear windows; white, blue & red tampo with "97," "Sharpie" & race decals on sides; "Rubbermade" on hood & in back; "97" on roof; "Graco" on trunk; Thailand; Sticker series (2002) 2 - 4

#99 Ford Taurus-a

#99 Ford Taurus

a. blue; red chassis; white roof & int.; multicolored tampo w/"99," "Citgo" & race decals on sides; Citgo logo on hood; "99" on roof; "Supergard Racing" on trunk; "www.citgo.com" in back; Thailand; Sticker series (2002) 2 - 4

2002 Team Transporters

#5 Kellogg's Kenworth 12000	15-18
#14 Harrah's Kenworth 12000	15-18
#22 CAT Kenworth 12000	15-18
#25 Marines Kenworth 12000	15-18
#25 UAW-Delphi Kenworth 12000	15-18
#32 Tide Kenworth 12000	15-18
#36 M&M's Kenworth 12000	15-18
#60 Grainger Kenworth 12000	15-18
Buddy Baker International Eagle	15-18
Cale Yarborough Int. Eagle	15-18
Disneyland Resort Int. Eagle	15-18
Four Generations of Petty Racing International Eagle	15-18
Hendrick Motorsports Int. Eagle	15-18

Promotional Cars & Limited Editions

#00 Chevrolet Monte Carlo - Milwaukee Brewers

a. black; gold hood & trunk; clear windows; white int.; white, lt. blue, red & dk. red tampo w/"00" & Milwaukee Brewers logo on sides; "American Family Insurance Auto Home Business Health Life" on hood; "00" & "Brewers" on roof; Hot Wheels logo on trunk; gytbk. Milwaukee Brewers give-away, in box 5 - 7

#00 Pontiac Grand Prix - Daytona

a. dk. blue; gray chassis & int.; clear windows; red rear; red, yellow, white, lt. blue & black tampo w/"00" & Hot Wheels logo on sides; "Daytona 500"

Values are shown in U.S. dollars, first price is for mint, second is for mint packaged vehicles only. *See pages 15-16 for grading guide to determine value for cars in lesser conditions.*

on hood; "'00" on roof; "February 20, 2000" on trunk; Hot Wheels logo & ".com" in back; gytbk. On #1 card for Daytona 500 (2000) 8 - 10

#00 Pontiac Grand Prix - Talladega

a. black; yellow spoiler; clear windows; gray int.; red, yellow, white & gray tampo w/"'00" & "Talladega" on sides; "Talladega Superspeedway" on hood; "'00" on roof, "www.iscmotor-sports.com" on trunk; red back w/race decals; gytbk. On #1 card for Talladega Superspeedway 8 - 10

b. blue; white roof; beige int.; clear windows; red, white & black tampo w/"'00," Talladega" & race decals on sides; "Talladega White Knuckle Weekend" on hood, "'00" on roof; "www.ISC.motorsports.com" on trunk. On #1 card for Talladega Superspeedway (2000) 8 - 10

c. white; black chassis & int.; clear windows; blue, red & black tampo w/"'01," "Talladega" & race decals on sides; "Track Attack Weekend" & "April 22, 2001" on hood; "'01" on roof; racing wheels; Thailand. Talladega Speedway, on basic card (2001) 8 - 10

d. black; black chassis; clear windows; black int.; blue, red & white tampo with "'01," "Talladega" & race decals on sides; "Talladega" & "October 21, 2001" on hood; "'01" on roof; racing wheels; Thailand. Talladega Speedway, on basic card (2001) 8 - 10

e. blue; gray chassis & int.; black stripe on bottom; white, black, dk. blue & red tampo w/"00," "Pepsi" & race decals on sides; "Pepsi 400 at Michigan" on hood; "00" on roof; "Michigan Speedway" on trunk; Hot Wheels logo & ".com" in back; racing wheels. On #1 card for Michigan Speedway (2000) 8 - 10

f. white, gray chassis & int., black & red tampo w/"00" & "Michigan Speedway" on sides, "Michigan Speedway" on hood, "00" on roof, "www.iscmotorsports.com" on trunk, Hot Wheels logo & ".com" in back, racing wheels. On #1 card for Michigan Speedway (2000) 8 - 10

#01 Pontiac Grand Prix - California Speedway

a. white; black chassis & int.; clear windows; red, gray & black tampo w/"'01," "California Speedway" & race decals on sides; "California Speedway" & "April 29, 2001" on hood, "'01" on roof; racing wheels; Thailand. On basic card for California Speedway (2001) 8 - 10

#01 Pontiac Grand Prix - Michigan International Speedway

a. white; black chassis & int.; clear windows; red & dk. blue tampo with "'01," "Michigan International Speedway" & race decals on sides; "Michigan International Speedway" & "June 10, 2001" on hood; "'01" on roof; racing wheels; Thailand. On basic card for Michigan International Speedway (2001) 8 - 10

#01 Pontiac Grand Prix - Daytona Speedway

a. black; black chassis & int.; clear windows; red, yellow, blue & white tampo w/"'01," "Light" & race decals on sides; "Daytona at the speed of Light" & "July 7th, 2001" on hood; "'01" on roof; racing wheels; Thailand. On basic card for Daytona Speedway (2001) 8 - 10

#01 Ford Taurus - That's Racin'

a. white; black chassis & int.; clear windows; red, yellow & black tampo with "'01," "That's Racin'" & race decals on sides; "That's Racin'" & "www.thatsracin.com" on hood; "'01" on roof; racing wheels; Thailand. On basic card for www.thatsracin.com (2001) 8 - 10

#01 Dodge Intrepid - Los Angeles Dodgers

a. white; blue front & trunk; clear windows; white int.; red, white & blue tampo w/"01," "LA" & race decals on sides; "Dodgers" on hood; "01" on roof; "Los Angeles" on trunk; racing wheels; Thailand. On basic card for Los Angeles Dodgers & Dodge (2001) 7 - 9

#1 Hot Wheels

a. dk. blue; white front; dk. blue hood; orange, red, white, black & yellow tampo w/"#1," Hot Wheels track, logo, small race decals & Hot Wheels product lines on sides; Hot Wheels logo on hood; "#1" on roof; "Call:1-877-Power31" on trunk; "Hot Wheels" in back. Mattel sales-force give-aways, baggie only, Thailand (1999) $35 - 40

#02 Pontiac Grand Prix - Chef Boyardee

a. black; red hood & spoiler; black chassis; white int.; red, white & green tampo w/Chef Boyardee logo on sides, hood & trunk; race decals in back. Chef Boyardee, at NASCAR events (2002) 10 - 12

#6 '93 T-Bird Stocker - Valvoline

a. white; lt. gray plastic chassis, dk. blue rear end, white int., clear windows; lt. blue, dk. blue & red tampo: "6," "Valvoline" & race decals on sides; "Valvoline Cummins" & Valvoline "V" on hood; "6" & Mark Martin's sig on roof; "Valvoline" in back; Pro racing wheels. Thailand, w/Valvoline Oil on horizontal card (1999) $10 - 12

#6 '97 T-Bird Stocker - Valvoline

a. white; lt. gray plastic chassis; dk. blue rear; white int.; clear windows; lt. blue, dk. blue & red tampo: "6," "Valvoline" & decals on sides; "Valvoline Cummins" & Valvoline "V" on hood; "6" & Mark Martin's sig. on roof; "Cummins" on trunk; "Valvoline" on back; Pro racing wheels; Thailand. Valvoline Oil on horizontal card (1999) $10 - 12

c. gray; same as a; clear windows; red, white, lt. blue & dk. blue tampo w/"6," "Synpower" & decals on sides; "Valvoline," "Cummins," Ford & Valvoline logos on hood; "Taurus" on front; "6" on roof; "Cummins" on trunk; "Eagle One" & decals on back. Valvoline Synpower on horizontal card w/form for chance to win Valvoline Synpower Mark Martin race car (1998) 8 - 10

d. white; lt. gray plastic chassis; dk. blue rear; white int.; clear windows; lt. blue, dk. blue, orange, brown & red tampo w/"6," "Valvoline" & race decals on sides; "Valvoline Cummins" & Valvoline "V" on hood; "6" & Mark Martin's sig. on roof; "Cummins" on trunk; "Eagle One" on back; Pro Racing wheels; Thailand. Valvoline Oil on horizontal card (1999) 8 - 10

#6 Ford Taurus

a. gray; lt. gray plastic chassis; white int.; clear windows; lt. blue, dk. blue, orange & red tampo w/"6," "Synpower" & race decals on sides; "Valvoline Cummins" & Valvoline "V" on hood; "6" & Mark Martin's sig. on roof; "Cummins" on trunk; "Eagle One" on back; Pro Racing wheels; Thailand. Valvoline Oil on horizontal card (1998) $8 - 10

b. black; same as a; yellow, orange, lt. orange, red & white tampo w/"6," "Eagle 1" & race decals on sides; "Eagle 1" & logo on hood; "6" & Mark Martin's sig. on roof; "Cummins" on trunk; "Eagle One" in back; Thailand. Eagle 1 Polish & Wax, horizontal card (1998) 8 - 10

#10 Chevrolet Monte Carlo - Nesquik

a. yellow; clear windows; gray int.; blue, white, yellow, red & black tampo w/"10," "Nestle's Nesquick" & race decals on sides; "Nestle's Nesquick" & rabbit on hood & in back; "10" on roof; race decals on trunk; gytbk. Mail-in with Proof of Purchase only, 8500 in bp, Thailand 10 - 12

#10 Chevrolet Monte Carlo - Nestea

a. lt. blue; clear windows; gray int.; dk. blue, yellow & white tampo w/"10" & "Nestea" on sides; "Nestea" on hood, trunk & in back; "10" on roof; gytbk. Mail-in w/Proof of Purchase only, 4500 bp & 5000 loose, Thailand 10 - 12

#11 Ford Taurus - Red Cell Batteries - 2001

a. white; black chassis; white int.; clear windows; red & black tampo w/"11," "Red Cell Batteries" & race decals on sides; "Ralphs" on hood & trunk; "11" on roof; "Red Cell Batteries" in back. On card w/8 Red Cell batteries, Ralphs Grocery Stores only (2001) 10 - 12

#17 Chevrolet Monte Carlo - Matt Kenseth - Kraft Racing

a. blue; dk. blue rear; clear windows; white int.; multicolored tampo w/"17," "Visine" & race decals on sides; "Visine gets the red out" on hood; "17" on roof; "Visine" on trunk; "Kraft" in back; Thailand (2001) 8 - 10

#22 Chevrolet Monte Carlo-a

#22 Chevrolet Monte Carlo - 2002

a. orange; white, blue & black with "22," Chevy logo & New York skyline on sides; "Mets" & "Team Monte Carlo" on hood; Mets logo on roof; "Chevrolet" Chevy logo on trunk; "Team Monte Carlo" in back. New York Mets baseball team giveaway 7 - 9

#26 Cheerios

a. yellow; multicolored tampo w/"26," "Cheerios," *Toy Story 2* characters & race decals on sides; "Woody," toy story characters & logo on hood; "26" & sig. on roof; "Cheerios" on trunk; race decals in back. General Mills mail-in from Lucky Charms cereal box, 2-pack (1999) $4 - 12

#32 Ford Taurus - Tide - 2000

a. orange; white back w/black spoiler; dk. blue, yellow & white tampo w/"32," "Tide" & race decals on sides; "Tide" on hood & in back; "32" on roof. 2000 Tide Collectors Edition, on special card (2000) 8 - 10

b. dk. blue; silver spoiler; white, orange, yellow, lt. blue & green tampo w/"32," "Tide," stars & decals on sides; "Tide" on hood; "32" on roof; "Kenmore" on trunk; "Kids Village" & "1-800 995-Kids" in back. Tide & Give Kids the World charity, on special card (2000) 10 - 12

c. dk. orange, same as a, slightly different design, "Kenmore" on trunk. 2001 Tide Collectors Edition, on special card (2001) 10 - 12

d. orange; white back w/black spoiler; clear windows, white int.; dk. blue, yellow & white tampo w/"32," "Tide" & race decals on sides; "Tide" on hood & in back; "32" on roof; "Kenmore" on trunk. 2001 Tide Collectors Edition, on special card (2001) 8 - 10

e. white; white int.; clear windows; multicolored tampo w/32," "Tide" & race decals on sides; "Tide" & "Give Kids the World" on hood; "32" on roof; "Kenmore" on trunk; "Give Kids the World" in back. Ltd ed for Give Kids the World Charity (2001) 8 - 10

#36 Pontiac Grand Prix

a. multicolored, turquoise M&M's on sides, clear windows, white int., multicolored tampo w/M&M's all over, "36" & "M&M's" on sides, "M&M's" on hood & in back, "36" on roof, Snickers candy bar on trunk, #1 in M&M's Color Vote series (2002) 12 - 15

b. multicolored, same as a, pink M&M's, #2 in M&M's Color Vote series (2002) 12 - 15

c. multicolored, same as a, purple M&M's. #3 in M&M's Color Vote series (2002) 12 - 15

d. yellow, turquoise on sides, clear windows, white int., multicolored tampo with M&M's all over, "36" & "M&M's" on sides, "M&M's" on hood & in back, "36" on roof, Snickers candy bar on trunk. #4 in M&M's Color Vote series (2002) 12 - 15

#43 1964 Belvedere - 80mm - 1999

This 1964 Plymouth has a metal chassis, clear windows, white interior, and racing wheels with "Goodyear" & "Eagle" in white on the sides. Thailand.

a. lt. blue; "Plymouth," "43" & race decals on sides; "400 H.P." on hood; "43" on roof. Trackside box $6 - 8

#43 1967 Plymouth - 78mm -1999

This model has a metal chassis, clear windows, white interior, and racing wheels with "Goodyear" & "Eagle" in white on the sides. Thailand.

a. lt. blue; "Plymouth," "43" & race decals on sides; "426 C.I." on hood; "43" on roof & trunk. Trackside box $6 - 8

#43 1972 Dodge Charger - 80mm - 1999

This model has a metal chassis, clear windows, white interior, and racing wheels with "Goodyear" & "Eagle" in white on the sides. Thailand.

a. red; thick lt. blue stripe over top; white, red & dk. blue tampo: "43," "Oil Filters Oil Treatment" & race decals on sides; "426 C.I." & STP logo on hood; "43" on roof & trunk. Trackside box $6 - 8

#44 Dodge Intrepid - 2002

a. blue; gray chassis & int.; clear windows; white front; red, white & black tampo with "44," "Sparkle" & race decals on sides; "GP Georgia-Pacific" on hood & in back; "44" on roof; Hot Wheels logo on trunk; Thailand. Mail-in premium for Sparkle paper towels, in baggie (2001) 4 - 6

#44 Hot Wheels
a. dk. blue; multicolored tampo w/"44," Hot Wheels logo, *Toy Story 2* characters & race decals on sides; "Buzz Lightyear," logo & characters on hood; "44" & Kyle Petty's sig. on roof; Red Lobster logo on trunk; race decals on back. General Mills mail-in from Lucky Charms cereal box, 2-pack (1999) $15 - 18

#64 Pontiac Grand Prix - 2000
a. lt. green; yellow, red, blue, black & white tampo with "64" on sides & roof; VISA card & "Use the card. Drive the Sport." on sides, hood, trunk & in back. VISA premium 12 - 15

#92 Chevrolet Monte Carlo-a

#92 Chevrolet Monte Carlo - 2002
a. red; white, black, yellow & green tampo with "92," "Excedrin" & race decals on sides; "Excedrin" on hood, trunk & in back; "92" on roof. Excedrin premium, in window box 10 - 12

#99 Ford Taurus-a

#99 Ford Taurus
a. yellow; dk. green, white, gray & brown tampo w/Oakland A's emblem & elephant baseball player on sides; "Generation 99 A's" on hood; "Athletics 99" on roof; "A's 4 times World Series Champions" on trunk; black hubs. Oakland A's Baseball Team premium, in box (1999) 7 - 9

#99 Ford Taurus-b

b. blue & white; black spoiler; red, white, gray, black & yellow tampo with "99," "Supergard" & race decals on sides; Citgo logo on hood; "99" on roof; "United We Stand" on trunk; "Citgo" in back; black hubs. October Toy Fair give-away, in plastic box (2001) 75 - 100

#99 Speedway Editions - 80mm - 1999
These models were sold in a four-car boxed set, and were all the same car: a Pontiac Grand Prix with gray metal base, gray plastic interior & roll cage, clear windows with black outlines & stripes, and gybk.
Set with collector's card $25

#99 California Speedway - 1999
a. yellow; white, red & black tampo: "99" & "California Speedway" on sides; "California Speedway" on hood & trunk; "99" on roof; Penske Motorsports on back 5 - NA

#99 Michigan Speedway - 1999
a. white; red & black tampo w/"Michigan Speedway" & "99" on sides & roof; "Michigan Speedway" on hood & trunk; Penske Motorsports in back $5 - NA

#99 Nazareth Speedway - 1999
a. red; yellow, black & white tampo with "Nazareth Speedway" & "99" on sides; "Nazareth Speedway" on hood & trunk; "99" on roof; Penske Motorsports in back $5 - NA

#99 North Carolina Speedway - 1999
a. black; red & white tampo w/"99" & "North Carolina Speedway" on sides; North Carolina Speedway" on hood & trunk; "99" on roof; Penske Motorsports in back $5 - NA

Chevrolet Monte Carlo - Detroit Tigers
a. dk. blue; clear windows; white int.; orange, white, lt. blue & red tampo w/"D," Pepsi logo & "Detroit" on sides; "Comerica Park" & tiger's head on hood; "D" on roof; "Detroit Tigers" on trunk; Thailand. Detroit Tigers Baseball Team premium (2001) 5 - 7

Daytona 500
This Pontiac Grand Prix has a light gray base, interior & roll cage; clear windows; gytbk.
a. dk. blue; white front end, multicolored tampo w/"44," Hot Wheels logo & race decals on sides; "Daytona 500" & "February 14th" on hood; "44" on roof; Hot Wheels logo on trunk; "Hot Wheels" in back; baggie. 1999 Daytona 500 give-away w/program $8 - 10
b. black; same as a; white front; "41" not "44"; no logo on trunk; baggie, mail-in in back of Pro Racing cards only 8 - 10

Pace Car
This Pontiac Grand Prix has a light gray plastic base, interior & roll cage; clear windows with plastic gytbk.
a. black; yellow spray mask in front; yellow, red, green & black tampo w/Pace logo race decals on front & roof; "Daytona 500" on hood; Thailand. Large card, give-away w/Pace Picante Sauce $6 - 8

Pepsi 400
This Monte Carlo has a light gray base, interior & roll cage; clear windows; and gytbk.
a. blue; multicolored tampo w/"98," "Pepsi" & race decals on sides; "Pepsi 400 at Daytona" on hood; "98" on roof; Daytona logo on trunk; "Pepsi 400" in back $8 - 10

MULTIPACKS

Multipacks were first introduced in 1970 and have been issued yearly since 1975. Assortments are normally pictured on package backs. Mattel has taken the liberty of substituting different cars at times. The prices are for packs with the listed cars in their basic colors. Prices vary if the pack contains more valuable cars (for example, the green Vega Bomb in place of the orange one).

1970

Indy Team Gift Pack: four Indy cars fastened by rubber bands in a window box and mounted on an angled picture of a track. Matching buttons were fastened above each car. Mattel also issued the Sizzlin' Six Set which was basically a way to get rid of excess stock.

Indy Team Gift Set 6447 Brabham Repco F1, Indy Eagle, Lotus Turbine, Shelby Turbine $1200

Sizzlin' Six Set 6431 6-pack picturing '31 Ford Woody, Custom Cougar, Beatnik Bandit, Splittin' Image, Turbofire & McLaren M6A. Pictured models are not necessarily the ones in the box. 1200

6447

2-Pack 7611 Horizontal blue header card w/2 '69 or '70 cars, in baggie. 75+POC

1971

Four 4-packs were issued with slightly smaller window boxes. They were also fastened at an angle with matching buttons above each car.

6428

Go Team 6428 Custom Corvette, Beatnik Bandit, Hot Heap, Python $2000

5935

Mongoose & Snake Dragster Pak 5935 1800

6429

Ontario Team 6429 McLaren M6A, Lola GT70, Ford Mk IV, Chapparal 2G 2000

6427

Show Team 6427 Silhouette, Torero, Turbofire, Splittin' Image 2000

1973

2-Pack 7609 Vertical blue header card with two '73 cars, in baggie. $75+POC

1975

Mattel issued four different 6-packs, the first multipacks since 1971. The boxes are white with cellophane windows in front, and the cars are arranged horizontally.

2-Pack 7609 w/2 '74 or '75 cars, in baggie $75+POC

Fun Machines 9033 Dune Daddy, Super Van (purple), Ranger Rig, Baja Bruiser, Band Drifter, Backwoods Bomb 900

H.E.L.P. Machines 9031 Ramblin' Wrecker, Chief's Special, Mustang Stocker, Emergency Squad, Police Cruiser, Paramedic (white) 900

Streak Machines 9034 Vega Bomb, El Rey Special, American Victory, Monte Carlo Stocker, Torino Stocker, P-917 900

Street Machines 9032 Mercedes C-111, Rodger Dodger, Super Van (black), Gremlin Grinder, Mighty Maverick, P-911 900

1976

Mattel issued five different 6-packs. The boxes are light blue with cellophane windows, and the cars are arranged horizontally. Three had been issued in 1975; this reissue was in new packs, and some cars were changed. All cars have rsw, although Staff Car has also been found with bw.

H.E.L.P. Machines 9031 Ramblin' Wrecker, Chief's Special, Ranger Rig, Fire-Eater, Police Cruiser (red light), Paramedic (white) $350

9504

Military Machines 9504 Gun Slinger, Gun Bucket, Khaki Cooler, Aw Shoot, Tough Customer, Staff Car 1200

Streak Machines 9034 Vega Bomb, Formula P.A.C.K., American Victory, Monte Carlo Stocker, Torino Stocker, P-911 450

Street Machines 9032 Mercedes C111, Rodger Dodger, Super Van (black), Grass Hopper, Maxi Taxi, Lowdown 350

9505

Super Chromes Machines 9505 Corvette Stingray, Rock Buster, Neet Streeter, Formula 5000, Twin Mill II, Poison Pinto 400

1977

This year's boxes are light blue with cellophane windows in front, and the cars are arranged horizontally. Two had been issued in 1976, although some cars were different. Truckin' Machines contain two of the more valuable vehicles: GMC Motor Home and Letter Getter, both with rsw.

Classic Machines 9855 '31 Doozie, '57 Chevy, '56 Hi-Tail Hauler, Street Rodder, T-Totaller (brown, bw only), Neet Streeter, w/rsw $300
w/bw 125

H.E.L.P. Machines 9031 Ramblin' Wrecker, Chief's Special, Emergency Squad, Fire-Eater, Police Cruiser (blue light), Paramedic (yellow), w/rsw 250
w/bw 125

Super Chromes Machines 9505 Corvette Stingray, Rock Buster, Neet Streeter, Formula 5000, Twin Mill II, Poison Pinto, w/rsw 400
w/bw 300

Truckin' Machines 9856 American Hauler, American Tipper, GMC Motor Home, Funny Money (gray), Letter Getter, Backwoods Bomb (green), w/rsw 1200
w/bw 175

1978

Mattel issued four 6-packs and a 10th Anniversary 3-pack. The boxes are light blue with cellophane windows in front, and the cars are arranged horizontally. Three had been issued in 1977; cars in these packs remained the same. The 3-pack is vertical with the cars and a belt buckle inside a blister. All cars had bw only.

Belt Buckle 2385 Jaguar XJS, '57 T-Bird (white), Hot Bird, metal belt buckle $120

Classic Machines 9855 same as 1977 120

H.E.L.P. Machines 9031 same as '77 120

Sprint Machines 2360 Lickety Six, Jaguar XJS, Mercedes C-111, Race Bait 308, Hot Bird, Porsche 917 120

Super Chromes Machines 9505 same as 1977 300

1979

Mattel issued four 6-packs, a 4-pack, and three 2-packs. Two of the 6-packs are the same as 1978, and one, Golden Machines, includes cars never issued on blistercards. The 4-pack includes a Scene Machine and three regular line cars. The 2-packs have two Marvel Comics Heroes cars of 1979 facing each other on a special blistercard that's twice as wide as the regular card and pictures all the Heroes. All packs have the same number and were sold only at Kmart.

Class of '79 Machines 2860 Royal Flash, Greased Gremlin, Spacer Racer, Auburn 852, Flat Out 442, Dumpin' A $100

Classic Machines 9855 same as 1977 110

2861

Golden Machines 2861 Jaguar XJS, Corvette Stingray, Hot Bird, Spoiler Sport, Z Whiz, Race Bait 308 225

H.E.L.P. Machines 9031 same as 1977 140

Heroes 1397 The Incredible Hulk & Spider-Man 140

Heroes 1397 The Thing & Thor 140

Heroes 1397 The Thing & Incredible Hulk 140

Scene Machines Pack 2858 The Incredible Hulk (Scene Machine), Greased Gremlin, Royal Flash, Upfront 924 150

1980

Mattel issued four horizontal and one vertical 6-pack, a 3-pack, and five new 2-packs. The Heroes 2-pack remained in the line. Three of the 6-packs are the same as 1979. The vertical 6-pack includes all six Marvel Comics Hero vehicles and has a plastic insert holding the cars. The 3-pack includes a Hi-Raker and two standard cars on plastic inserts. New 2-packs were all regular-line cars and are on one small card with two blisters.

2-Pak 1878 '57 T-Bird & Stutz Blackhawk $15

2-Pak 1890 Spoiler Sport & Inside Story 15

2-Pak 1891 Formula 5000/Street Rodder 20

2-Pak 1893 Neet Streeter (blue or magenta) & 3-Window '34 35

Class Of '80 Machines 1501 P-911 Turbo, Super Scraper, Tricar X8, Turbo Mustang, Stutz Blackhawk, Greyhound MC-8 75

Classic Machines 9855 same as 1979 120

Golden Machines 2861 same as 1979 120

H.E.L.P. Machines 9031 same as 1979 140

Heroes 6-Pack 1493 The Thing, Thor, The Incredible Hulk, Captain America, Spider-Man, The Human Torch 120

Hi-Rakers 3-Pack 1349 40's Woodie, Turbo Mustang, Stutz Blackhawk, Canada 120

1493 1634

1981

Mattel issued four horizontal 6-packs, two of which were completely new. Two were the same as 1980 except the boxes were now half as tall as in previous years. The 1981 boxes pictured three of the assortments on the box back; the assortment in the box was not pictured. A special three-pack contained the first Hot Wheels collectors' book.

4 Cars for the Price of 3 pack yellow card $35+POC

6-Pak 1262 Vertical window box w/assorted cars 10+POC

12-Car Carrying Case - no #, magenta 12-car case w/window showing 6 cars, Canada only 40+POC

Classic Machines 9885 '31 Doozie, '57 Chevy, '56 Hi-Tail Hauler, Street Rodder, T-Totaller (brown, bw only), Neet Streeter 75

Collector's Book 1495 Chevy Citation, Turbo Mustang, Airport Rescue 70

Collector's Book 1495 Bronco 4-Wheeler, Cannonade, Airport Rescue; Canada only 85

H.E.L.P. Machines 9031 Ramblin' Wrecker, Fire Chaser, Emergency Squad, Fire-Eater, Airport Rescue, Highway Patrol 60

U.S.A. Machines 1990 Hot Bird, Mirada Stocker, Corvette Stingray, Chevy Citation, Turbo Mustang, Omni 024 60

Weekend Machines 2860 Bronco 4-Wheeler, Minitrek, Baja Breaker, Bywayman, Dodge D-50, '56 Hi-Tail Hauler 60

1982

Mattel again issued four horizontal 6-packs; two were from the previous year (although some of the cars were different) and two were completely new. Different sets were pictured instead of six packs.

City Machines 3757 Super Scraper, Hiway Hauler, Fire-Eater, Ramblin' Wrecker, Letter Getter, Sheriff Patrol $40

Classic Machines 9885 '31 Doozie, Auburn 852, '35 Classic Caddy, Street Rodder, Old Number 5, '37 Bugatti 40

Hot Ones Patch pack 5086 Front Runnin' Fairmont, Datsun 200SX, Corvette Stingray 35

Hot Ones Machines 3756 Corvette Stingray, P-911, Flat Out 442, Mirada Stocker, Turbo Mustang, Hot Bird 40

Weekend Machines 1989 Bronco 4-Wheeler, Dixie Challenger, Jeep CJ7, Bywayman, '56 Hi-Tail Hauler 40

1983

There were six different 6-packs in this year's line. The name "Gift Packs" replaced "Machines." The Hot Ones gift pack was discontinued and five new assortments were issued. Again, different sets were on the box back. Three Play Settings were issued for 1983 only, consisting of three cars, a full-color backdrop, assorted plastic figures and scenery.

'60's Teen Gift Pack 5760 3-Window '34, '57 T-Bird, '40s Woodie, '55 Chevy, Split Window '63, '57 Chevy $50

Belt Buckle 5709 '67 Camaro, P-928, Long Shot 55

Bonus Offer 3-Pack 0771 3 cars & key chain, Zellers stores, Canada 50+POC

Bonus Offer 3-Pack 0772 3 cars & cloth patch, Zellers stores, Canada 50+POC

Bonus Offer 3-Pack 0773 3 cars & button, Zellers stores, Canada 50+POC

City Gift Pack 3757 Hiway Hauler, Fire-Eater, Peterbilt Tank Truck, Ramblin' Wrecker, Letter Getter, Sheriff Patrol 35

Classic Gift Pack 9855 '37 Bugatti, Classic Caddy, '40's Ford 2 Door, Auburn 852, Mercedes 540K, '31 Doozie 35

Competition Gift Pack 5849 P-911 Turbo, Frontrunnin' Fairmont, Flat Out 442, Camaro Z-28, Mirada Stocker, NASCAR Stocker 35

Play Settings Camping Set 4224 Bronco 4-Wheeler, Jeep CJ-7, Sunagon 45

Play Settings City Set 4223 Taxi, Rapid Transit, Trash Truck 45

Play Settings Firefighters Set 4225 Fire-Eater, Emergency Squad, Fire Chief Car 45

Racer Gift Pack 5759 Malibu Grand Prix, Vetty Funny (gray), Turbo Streak, Land Lord, Pepsi Challenger, Firebird Funny Car (magenta) 40

Special 15th Birthday Offer 5709 '67 Camaro, P-928, and Long Shot 50

Weekend Gift Pack 1989 Jeep CJ-7, Bronco 4-Wheeler, Bywayman, Minitrek, Beach Patrol, Baja Breaker 35

1984

Mattel reissued all 6-packs from 1983 with some color changes. Six 4-packs were also issued.

'60s Teen Gift Pack 5760 same as 1983 $35

City Gift Pack 3757 same as 1983 35

City Service 4 Car Gift Pack 7125 CAT Dump Truck, Fire-Eater, Ramblin' Wrecker, Construction Crane 30

Classic Gift Pack 9855 same as 1983 35

Collector Series 4 Car Gift Pack 7122 Auburn 852, '37 Bugatti, Mercedes 540K, '35 Classic Caddy 30

Competition Gift Pack 5849 same as 1983 30

Construction 4 Car Gift Pack 7120 Construction Crane, CAT Wheel Loader, CAT Dump Truck, Peterbilt Tank Truck 30

Military 4 Car Gift Pack 7121 Big Bertha, Tank Gunner, Roll Patrol Jeep CJ, Shell Shocker 30

Off Road 4x4 4 Car Gift Pack 7123 Jeep CJ-7, Baja Bug, Bronco 4-Wheeler, Bywayman 25

Racer Gift Pack 5759 same as 1983 40

7124

Racing Series 4-Car Gift Pack 7124 Firebird Funny Car, Blown Camaro, Tricar X8, Turbo Streak 25

Scratch and Win 8002 3 cars and chance to win, Zellers stores, Canada 65+POC

Weekend Gift Pack 1989 same as 1983 30

1985

Mattel reissued all the 6-packs, though many vehicles were changed or had new colors/tampos. There were six 4-packs issued: two reissues and four new. The Stamper 3-packs consisted of a rubber stamp (picturing a car) and three cars that had never been issued in a single blisterpack before were introduced on one large card.

'60s Teen Gift Pack 5760 3-Window '34 (black), '57 T-Bird (red), '40s Woodie (metallic blue), '55 Chevy (red), Split Window '63 (black), '57 Chevy (yellow) $55

Action Command Battleground Gift Pack 9412 Big Bertha, TankGunner, Super Cannon (black), Command Tank (black) 85

City Gift Pack 3757 Hiway Hauler (Racing Team), Peterbilt Tank Truck, Fire-Eater, Ramblin' Wrecker (yellow), Delivery Van (Frito Lay), Sheriff Patrol 140

Classic Gift Pack 9855 '37 Bugatti (black), Classic Caddy (maroon), Rolls-Royce Phantom II, Auburn 852 (white), Mercedes 540K (red), '31 Doozie (red) 40

Competition Gift Pack 5849 P-911 Turbo (black), Frontrunnin' Fairmont (red), Flat Out 442 (green), Camaro Z-28 (red), Mirada Stocker (metalflake gold), NASCAR Stocker 80

Construction 4 Car Gift Pack 7120 same as 1984 25

Estuche De Regalo 4-Pack 8100 Odd Rod, Lickety Six, Fat Fendered '40, Sunagon 150

Hot Ones Stamper 3-Pack 9326 Camaro Z-28, P-911, '80's Firebird 35

Off Road 4x4 4 Car Gift Pack 7123 same as 1984 25

Racer Gift Pack 5759 Lightning Gold, Vetty Funny (white), Turbo Streak (black), Screamin' (red), Landlord, Firebird Funny Car (magenta) 35

Real Riders Stamper 3-Pack 9328 Baja Bug, Bywayman, Dream Van XGW 100

Speed Busters 4 Car Gift Pack 9417 Tricar X8, Corvette Stingray, Firebird Funny Car, Turbo Heater 25

Ultra Hots 9416 - 4 Car Gift Pack Wind Splitter, Speed Seeker, Flame Runner, Nightstreaker 25

Ultra Hots Stamper 3-Pack 9327 Sol-Aire CX4, Speed Seeker, Flame Runner 40

Weekend Gift Pack 1989 Minitrek (white), Bronco 4-Wheeler (red), Jeep CJ-7 (yellow), Bywayman (mtlfk blue), Beach Patrol, Baja Breaker (black) 30

1986

Mattel replaced the vertical 6-packs and 4-packs with four 5-packs. Also, two special 4-packs ("Buy 3 Get One Free") were issued on a blistercard. Another 4-pack had a Hot Wheels wrecker and three Crack-Ups.

Classic 5 Car Gift Pack 1156 '37 Bugatti, Auburn 852, Classic Caddy, '31 Doozie, Mercedes 540K $5+POC

Off Road 4x4 2848 Pavement Pounder, Jeep Scrambler, Baja Breaker, Baja Bug (all w/Real Rider tires) 85

Racers 2849 P-911, T-Bird Stocker, Firebird Funny Car, Thunderstreak 30

Racers 5 Car Gift Pack 1159 Firebird Funny Car, Corvette Stingray, XT-3, Stock Rocket, Black Lightning 5+POC

Smash & Tow Gift Pack 2817 Ramblin' Wrecker and 3 Crack-Ups 20

Super Sportscar 5 Car Gift Pack 1161 Turbo Heater, '80s Corvette, '80s Firebird, Fiero 2M4, Nissan 300ZX 5+POC

Ultra Hots 5 Car Gift Pack 1158 Back Burner, Sol-Aire CX4, Speed Seeker, Jet Sweep X5, Quik Trik 5+POC

1987

Multipacks were the same as in 1986. All cars were the same, although there may be color/tampo variations.

1988

Six 3-Car packs were issued in chrome or gold chrome models with "20th Anniversary" and the Hot Wheels logo on top. Two different cars were in each pack and there was a different stock number for each assortment. Mattel reissued three 5-packs from 1987 and introduced three new ones.

20th Anniversary 3-pack 4590 Firebird Funny Car (chrome or gold chrome), Bywayman, Peterbilt Dump Truck $25

20th Anniversary 3-pack 4591 Firebird Funny Car (chrome or gold chrome), Rescue Ranger, Vampyra 25

20th Anniversary 3-pack 4592 Ferrari Testarossa (chrome), Sharkruiser, Jeep CJ7 25

20th Anniversary 3-pack 4594 Ferrari Testarossa (chrome), Thunderburner, Blazer 4x4 25

20th Anniversary 3-pack 4600 Tall Ryder (chrome), '31 Doozie, Hot Bird 25

20th Anniversary 3-pack 4601 Tall Ryder (chrome), Classic Cobra, Megadestroyer 25

20th Anniversary 3-pack 4602 Mercedes 540K (chrome), Gulch Stepper, '80s Corvette 25

20th Anniversary 3-pack 4603 Mercedes 540K (chrome), Baja Bug, Thunderstreak 25

20th Anniversary 3-pack 4604 Monster 'Vette (chrome or gold chrome), XT-3, Nightstreaker 25

20th Anniversary 3-pack 4604 Monster 'Vette (chrome or gold chrome, XT-3, Thunderstreak (white "25th Anniv.") 45

20th Anniversary 3-pack 4605 Monster 'Vette (chrome or gold chrome), Nissan 300ZX, Tank Gunner 25

20th Anniversary 3-pack 4606 Combat Medic (gold chrome, vertical lines), Sol-Aire CX4, Camaro Z-28 25

20th Anniversary 3-pack 4607 Combat Medic (gold chrome, smooth sides), Blown Camaro Z-28, Turboa 60

20th Anniversary 3-pack 7796 Monster 'Vette (chrome), XT-3, Nightstreaker (Canada) 25

20th Anniversary 3-pack 7798 Mercedes 540K (gold chrome), Gulch Stepper, '80s Corvette (Canada) 25

Action Command Gift Pack 3870 Big Bertha, Command Tank, Roll Patrol Jeep CJ, Tail Gunner, Combat Medic 5+POC

Classics 5 Car Gift Pack 1629 '37 Bugatti, Mercedes 540K, Classic Caddy, '31 Doozie, Auburn 852 5+POC

Racers 5 Car Gift Pack 1631 Firebird Funny Car, Corvette Stingray, XT-3, Sol-Aire CX4, Turbo Streak 5+POC

Super Sportscar 5 Car Gift Pack 1634 Ferrari Testarossa, '80's Corvette, '80s Firebird, Fiero 2M4, Nissan 300ZX 5+POC

Trailbusters Gift Pack 3872 Jeep CJ-7, Baja Bug, Blazer 4x4, Monster 'Vette, Bywayman 5+POC

Workhorses Gift Pack 3871 Team Bus, Earthmover, Sheriff Patrol, Fire-Eater, Good Humor Truck 5+POC

1989

Mattel issued six 5-packs. Five were the same, but car assortments were different.

Classics 5-Car Gift Pack 1629 Split Window '63, '57 T-Bird, '65 Mustang Convertible, Talbot Lago, Rolls-Royce Phantom II $5+POC

Emergency Vehicles 5-Car Gift Pack 3268 Flame Stopper, Rescue Ranger, Fire-Eater, Ambulance, Fire Chaser (black int.) 15

Emergency Vehicles 5-Car Gift Pack 3268 Flame Stopper, Rescue Ranger, Fire-Eater, Ambulance, Fire Chaser (tan int.) 40

Racers 5-Car Gift Pack 1631 Firebird Funny Car, Shadow Jet, Ferrari F40, Sol-Aire CX4, Thunderburner 5+POC

Super Sportscar 5-Car Gift Pack 1634 Ferrari Testarossa, Classic Cobra, Corvette Convertible, Porsche 959, Lamborghini Countach 5+POC

Trailbusters 5-Car Gift Pack 3872 Nissan Hardbody, Baja Bug, Suzuki QuadRacer, Bronco 4-Wheeler, Blazer 4x4 5+POC

Workhorses 5-Car Gift Pack 3871 CAT Dump Truck, CAT Wheel Loader, Peterbilt Tank Truck, CAT Road Roller, Cement Truck 5+POC

Showcase Carry Case (blue) 3464 20

1990

Two of 1989's 5-packs were discontinued and two new packs were added. Car-assortment packs stayed basically the same, although there were a few color changes.

Classics 5-Car Gift Pack 1629 '57 T-Bird, Split Window '63 (white w/flames), '65 Mustang Convertible, Talbot Lago, Rolls-Royce Phantom II $5+POC

Construction Crew 5-Car Gift Pack 3871 CAT Dump Truck, CAT Road Roller, CAT Wheeler, CAT Forklift (yellow or green), Peterbilt Cement Mixer 5+POC

Emergency Team 5-Car Gift Pack 3870 Ambulance, Rescue Ranger, Fire-Eater, Flame Stopper, Fire Chief Car 5+POC

Racers 5-Car Gift Pack 1631 Firebird Funny Car, Shadow Jet, Ferrari F40, Sol-Aire CX4, Thunderburner 5+POC

Super Sportscar 5-Car Gift Pack 1634 Ferrari Testarossa, Classic Cobra, Corvette Convertible, Porsche 959, Lamborghini Countach 5+POC

Trailbusters 5-Car Gift Pack 3872 Nissan Hardbody, Baja Bug, Blazer 4x4, Bronco 4-Wheeler, Suzuki QuadRacer 5+POC

1991

Mattel reissued five of the six 5-packs from 1990. The pack name "Trailbusters" was changed to "Off Road" although the stock number remained the same. Most of the vehicles in the assortments were changed. Mattel also issued a 3-pack with three different funny cars.

Classics 5-Car Gift Pack 1629 '32 Ford Delivery, Auburn 852, '37 Bugatti, Mercedes 540K, '65 Mustang Convertible $5+POC

Dragsters Gift Pack 7449 5+POC

Emergency Team 5-Car Gift Pack 3870 Ambulance, Rescue Ranger, Fire-Eater, Ramp Truck, Sheriff Patrol 5+POC

Funny Car Gift Pack 7456 5+POC

Off Road 5-Car Gift Pack 3872 Range Rover, Trailbuster, Power Plower, Surf Patrol, Suzuki QuadRacer 5+POC

Racers 5-Car Gift Pack 1631 Pontiac Banshee, Shadow Jet, Lamborghini Countach, Sol-Aire CX4, XT-3 5+POC

Super Sportscar 5-Car Gift Pack 1634 Ferrari 348, Lamborghini Diablo, Nissan Custom Z, Toyota MR2 Rally, Mazda MX-5 Miata 5+POC

1992

Mattel reissued five 5-packs from 1991 and one from 1990. Most of these had new names and many of the cars were different.

Classic Collection 5-Car Gift Pack 1629 '59 Caddy, Classic Cobra, '57 Chevy, Mercedes 540K, '65 Mustang Convertible $5+POC

Construction Crew 5-Car Gift Pack 3871 Dump Truck, Road Roller, Wheel Loader, Bulldozer, Oshkosh Cement Truck 5+POC

Emergency Squad 5-Car Gift Pack 3870 Ambulance, Rescue Ranger, Fire-Eater, Ramp Truck, Sheriff Patrol 5+POC

Off Road Explorers 5-Car Gift Pack 3872 Trailbuster, Power Plower, Range Rover, Gulch Stepper, Suzuki QuadRacer 5+POC

Racing Team 5-Car Gift Pack 1631 Ferrari F40, Shadow Jet, Turbo Streak, Chevy Stocker, Zender Fact 4 5+POC

Super Sportscars 5-Car Gift Pack 1634 Ferrari Testarossa, '80s Firebird, Porsche 959, Mazda MX-5 Miata, Lamborghini Countach 5+POC

Wacky Warehouse Limited Edition 2-pack Suzuki QuadRacer, Trailbuster, Kool-Aid 15

1993

25th Anniversary Dream Car 5-pack 10784 Alien, Speed Shark, Sol-Aire CX4, Flashfire, Zender Fact 4 $25

25th Anniversary Chevy 5-pack 10787 '93 Camaro, Custom Corvette, '57 Chevy, Blazer 4x4, Corvette Split Window 35

25th Anniversary Exotic 5-pack 10788 '93 Camaro, Lamborghini Countach, Lamborghini Diablo, Ferrari F40, Ferrari Testarossa 40

10960

25th Anniversary Collector's Edition 8-pack 10960 Paddy Wagon, Red Baron, Twin Mill, Beatnik Bandit, Splittin' Image, The Demon, Classic Nomad, Silhouette 15

25th Anniversary Ford 5-pack 12404 Fat Fendered '40, Classic Cobra, '65 Mustang Convertible, '32 Ford Delivery, 3-Window '34 50

1994

Racing Team 5-pack 1631 Shadow Jet, Turbo Streak, Chevy Stocker, Sol-Aire CX4, Ferrari F40 or Firebird $3+POC

Off Road Explorers 5-pack 3872 Trailbuster, Power Plower, Gulch Stepper, Suzuki QuadRacer, Nissan Hardbody 3+POC

Service Merchandise 25th Anniversary All American Showcase Collection 10996 '57 T-Bird, Classic Cobra, '65 Mustang Convertible, Auburn 852, '80s Firebird, Corvette Split Window, 3-Window '34, Custom Corvette, Thunderburner, '59 Caddy, Hot Bird, '32 Ford Vicky, Camaro Z-28, '93 Camaro, Chevy Stocker, Blazer 4x4 85

Speed Demons® 5-pack 11363 Rodzilla, Vampyra, Evil Weevil, Double Demon, Cargoyle 3+POC

Blimp and Support Team 5-pack 11364 Blimp, Rig Wrecker, Tank Truck, Emergency Squad, Flame Stopper 3+POC

Action Command® 5-pack 11365 Tail Gunner, Tank Gunner, Troop Convoy, Super Cannon, Command Tank 3+POC

FAO Schwarz Gold Series I Collection 12293 Red Baron, Classic Cobra, Passion, Beatnik Bandit, TwinMill, '57 T-Bird, '37 Bugatti, Silhouette, Deora, Swingfire, Mercedes 540K, Paddy Wagon, Talbot Lago, Chevy Nomad, '55 Chevy, Splittin' Image 170

Chevrolet 5-pack 12403 Corvette Stingray, '57 Chevy, Corvette Convertible, Camaro Z-28, Chevy Stocker 3+POC

Ford 5-pack 12404 '32 Ford Delivery, 3-Window '34, '57 T-Bird, Bronco 4-Wheeler, T-Bird Stocker 3+POC

Ferrari 5-pack 12405 Ferrari Testarossa, Ferrari F40, Ferrari 250, Ferrari 348, Street Beast 3+POC

12496

Hot Wheels Vintage Collection 12496 Mutt Mobile, '32 Ford Vicky, Deora, Mongoose, Whip Creamer, Snake, S'Cool Bus, Custom Mustang 25

Track System Gift Pack 13366 Aeroflash, Sting Ray 'Vette, T-Bird Stocker,

12404 11363 12405 13366

Values are shown in U.S. dollars, first price is for mint, second is for mint packaged vehicles only. See pages 15-16 for grading guide to determine value for cars in lesser conditions.

13821

13505 15066 15069 15070 17458 17490

Thunderbird Stocker, Baja Bug, Porsche 959, Flashfire 3+POC

World Cup 5-pack 12498 '93 Camaro, Corvette Convertible, '63 Split Window, Blazer 4x4, '57 Chevy $15

1995

FAO Schwarz History of Hot Wheels 13821 Deora, Neet Streeter, '93 Camaro, Stutz Blackhawk, '32 Vicky, Second Wind, Vetty Funny, Shadow Jet II $70

FAO Schwarz Gold Series Collection II 13828 '67 Camaro, Splittin' Image, TwinMill, S'Cool Bus, Silhouette, The Demon, Classic Nomad, Red Baron, Paddy Wagon, '32 Ford Vicky, Snake, Mongoose, Deora, Mutt Mobile, Custom Mustang, Whip Creamer 165

Service Merchandise Classic American Cars 14021 Old Number 5, '31 Doozie, '32 Ford Delivery, Auburn 852, 3-Window '34, Classic Caddy, Fat Fendered '40, Passion, '56 Flashsider, '57 T-Bird, '57 Chevy, '59 Caddy, '63 Split Window, '65 Mustang Convertible, '67 Camaro, Olds 442 100

Hill's Year in Review 14065 the twelve 1995 Model Series cars 35

JC Penney's Trea$ure Hunt Series 14066-0980 the twelve 1995 Treasure Hunt series cars, w/certificate 900

JC Penney's Performance Collection 15930 Classic Cobra & Olds 442 gold-plated 140

FAO Schwarz 24K Gold Classics 19063 Talbot Lago, Mercedes 540K & Rolls Royce Phantom 150

1996

Super Show Cars 5-pack 13502 Zender Fact 4, Mercedes SL, Audi Avus Quattro, Jaguar XJ220, Dodge Viper 3+POC

Muscle Cars 5-pack 13503 '65 Mustang Convertible, '67 Camaro, Olds 442, Corvette Split Window, Classic Cobra 3+POC

Baywatch 5-pack 13505 Helicopter, Suzuki Quadracer, Trailbuster, Surf Patrol, Rescue Ranger 3+POC

Hot Wheels Race Team 5-pack 13506 Firebird Funny Car, Sol-Aire CX4, Dragster, Hot Wheels 500, Lumina Stocker or '57 Chevy 3+POC

Porsche 5-pack 15066 Porsche 911, Porsche 959, Porsche 928, Porsche Carrera, Porsche 930 3+POC

'50s Favorites 5-pack 15068 Swingfire, '57 T-Bird, Chevy Nomad, '57 Chevy, '56 Flashsider 3+POC

Auto-City 5-pack 15069 Peterbilt Dump Truck, Fire-Eater, Rig Wrecker, Mazda MX-5 Miata, Sheriff Patrol 3+POC

Corvette 5-pack 15070 Corvette Split Window, '80s Corvette, '58 Corvette Convertible, Corvette Stingray, Custom Corvette 3+POC

Camaro 5-pack 15071 '93 Camaro, '67 Camaro, Camaro Z-28, '80s Camaro, Camaro Convertible 3+POC

Target Then & Now Collection 15162 '67 Camaro, Ferrari 250, '57 T-Bird, Old Number 5, '93 Camaro, Ferrari Testarossa, T-Bird Stocker, Fire-Eater 25

Black Convertible Collection 15171 Mercedes SL, '65 Mustang Convertible, '95 Camaro Convertible, Mazda MX-5 Miata, Dodge Viper RT/10, Shelby Cobra, Roll Patrol, Custom Corvette 25

FAO Schwarz Hot Wheels Olympic Medals 3-pack 15723 '58 Corvette Convertible, Corvette Split Window, Corvette Stingray 165

15732

FAO Schwarz History of Hot Wheels II 15732 '58 Corvette, Classic Cobra, '63 Split Window, Dodge Viper RT/10, Corvette Stingray, Ferrari Testarossa, '96 Mustang Convertible, Ferrari 250 70

Target Retro Wheels 15741 Mutt Mobile, S'Cool Bus, Red Baron, Whip Creamer 20

American Victory 3-pack 15746 Camaro Convertible, '67 Camaro, '93 Camaro 45

Kmart 70th Anniversary of the Pontiac 3-pack 15746 Hot Bird, Pontiac Banshee, Fiero 2M4 45

JC Penney's Treasure Hunt Series 15911 12 1996 Treasure Hunt Series cars 400

JC Penney's Gold 2-pack 15930 Snake & Mongoose gold-plated 120

Target Designer Collection 15942 Street Beast, Power Rocket, Power Pipes, XT-3, Splittin' Image II, Twin Mill II, Silhouette II, Rigor-Motor 30

FAO Gold Series III 16020 London Taxi, Ford Sierra, Ferrari Testarossa, Porsche Carrera, '57 T-Bird Convertible, Mercedes 500SL, Ferrari 348, '80s Corvette, Ford Mustang Cobra, BMW 850i, Mercedes-Benz 190E, Ferrari 308, Double Decker Bus, Porsche 911 Targa, BMW M3, Porsche 935 120

Vintage Race Team 4-pack 16139 Twin Mill, Deora, Classic Nomad, '67 Mustang 50

K•B Real Rods Demon 16186 Chevy Nomad, '32 Ford Vicky, Demon 12

Dodge Showroom 3-pack 16251 Dodge Charger Daytona, Dodge Ram 1500, Dodge Viper RT/10 40

'60s Muscle Cars 4-pack 16255 '67 Camaro, Custom Mustang, Olds 442, Dodge Charger Daytona 50

American Classics 3-pack 16262 Classic Caddy, Auburn 852, '31 Doozie 35

100th Anniversary of the Automobile 16266 '32 Ford Vicky, T-Bucket, Old Number 5, Custom Mustang, Ford Thunderbird Convertible, Fat Fendered '40, '80s Corvette, Monte Carlo Stocker, Hot Bird 135

Kmart Thunder Trucks™ 4-pack 16323 two Chevy 1500s, two Dodge Ram 1500s 30

Hill's Year in Review II 46108 twelve 1996 Model Series cars 20

Bloomingdale's Fabulous '57 Collection - no # '57 Chevy, '57 Thunderbird. Ltd ed of 5000, initial distribution limited 200

Little Debbie's 3-pack - no # Delivery Truck, Hiway Hauler, '32 Delivery 10

20th Anniversary 20-car gift set 5+POC

1997

Action Pack JPL Sojourner Mars Rover 16145 Mars Rover, Mars Pathfinder, Lander $2+POC

Action Pack Home Improvement 16146 '33 Ford Convertible, Dixie Chopper 5+POC

Action Pack Undersea Adventure 16154 Micro Submarine, Submarine 2+POC

Action Pack Surf Patrol 16156 Off-Road Racer, Trailer w/Dinghy 2+POC

Action Pack Construction 16153 Dirt Rover, Cement Mixer 2+POC

Action Pack Firefighting 16148 Fire-Eater 2, Flame Stopper 2 2+POC

Action Pack Racing 16155 Buick Stocker, Velocitor 2+POC

Action Pack Police Force 16149 Armored Truck, Sheriff Patrol 2+POC

Avon 2-pack 15344 '63 Corvette, Custom Corvette 8

Avon 2-pack 15341 Mercedes SL, Mercedes 540K 8

Avon 2-pack 15338 '65 Mustang Convertible, '96 Mustang 10

Action News Team 5-pack 17456 Olds Aurora, Delivery Van, Big Rig, Propper Chopper, Trailbuster 2+POC

California Dreamin' 5-pack 17492 Mazda MX-5 Miata, Mercedes 500SL, Dodge Viper, BMW 850, '59 Caddy 2+POC

City Action 5-pack 17458 Rescue Ranger, Blimp, Rig Wrecker, '32 Ford Delivery, Recycling Truck 2+POC

Firefighting 5-pack 17459 Ambulance, Fire-Eater, Emergency Squad, Holden Commodore (Police Cruiser), Flame Stopper 2+POC

Farm Country 5-pack 17455 Ford Stake Bed Truck, Bronco 4x4, Tractor, Oshkosh Snow Plow, Ford F-150 2+POC

14066-0980

15911

17216

Values are shown in U.S. dollars, first price is for mint, second is for mint packaged vehicles only. See pages 15-16 for grading guide to determine value for cars in lesser conditions.

Crazy Classics 5-pack 17490 Speed-a-Saurus, Rigor Motor, Treadator, Radio Flyer Wagon, Big Chill 2+POC

Just Trucks 5-pack 16287 Ford LTL, Dodge Ram 1500, '56 Flashsider, Minitruck, Bronco 4-Wheeler 2+POC

Police Force 5-pack 17461 Hummer, School Bus, Propper Chopper, Delivery Van, Aurora police car 2+POC

Race Team II 5-pack 17491 Rig Wrecker, Camaro, Firebird Funny Car, Chevy 1500, Ramp Truck 2+POC

Racing World 5-pack 17457 Driven To The Max, Hydroplane, Nissan Hardbody, Thunderstreak, Toyota MR-2 2+POC

Rescue Squad 5-pack 17489 Propper Chopper, Roll Patrol, Emergency Squad, Surf Patrol, Ambulance 2+POC

General Mills 5-pack 17940 Daytona Charger, '96 Mustang, Stutz Blackhawk, '58 Corvette, '60s Camaro 15

JC Penney 24K Performance Collection '63 Corvette, Custom Corvette 60

Service Merchandise Spirit of America 4-car set 17158 Bywayman, T-Bucket, Snake Funny Car, '58 Corvette 70

Target Motorin' Music 4-car set 17279 '57 Thunderbird Convertible, Classic Cobra, GTO, '40s Woodie 60

Target Cruisin America 6 car set 17263 Mercedes 540K, Passion, Olds 442, '57 Chevy, '58 Corvette, Porsche Targa 35

Little Debbie 3-pack 16189 Fork Lift, Thunder Roller, Off-Road Racer 10

40th Anniversary of the '57 Chevy Set 4-pack 17401 4 different '57 Chevys 50

30th Anniversary of the '67 Muscle Car Set 3-pack 16730 '67 GTO, '67 Camaro, '67 Mustang 45

40th Anniversary of the Thunderbird Set 2-pack 16989 '57 T-Bird, '57 T-Bird Convertible 25

30th Anniversary of the Camaro Set 4-pack 16737 '67 Camaro, '97 Camaro, Camaro Convertible, & '80s Camaro 50

'37 European Classics 2-pack 16992 Talbot Lago, '37 Bugatti 25

Four Decades of Pony Power 3-pack 16986 '65 Mustang Convertible, '67 Mustang, '96 Mustang 40

Elwoody Custom Cars 2-pack 18076 1950 2-door Buick station wagon, Ford cab-over tow truck 35

JC Penney's 1997 Treasure Hunt series 17216 12 1997 Treasure Hunt cars 400

Kmart Funny Cars 4-pack 17274 Funny Car, Side-Splitter, two 1997 Firebird Funny Cars 30

Toys "R" Us 10 pack 18317 '32 Delivery, Tractor, Mazda MX-5 Miata, Avus Quattro, Radar Ranger, Oshkosh Cement Mixer, Ferrari F50, Baja Bug, Mini Truck, Shadow Jet II 15

Toys "R" Us 10 pack 18476 '32 Delivery, Tractor, Ramp Truck, Speed Blaster, School Bus, '80s Corvette, Lexus SC400, Lamborghini Diablo, Ferrari 250, P-911 15

JC Penney's Watch and Car Set - no # Classic Nomad and watch 30

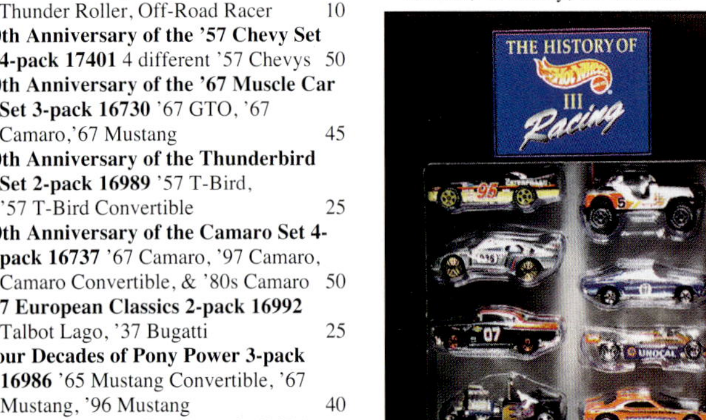

18317

1998

1998 Convention Zamak 4-car set Scorchin' Scooter, '67 GTO, '32 Ford, '67 Mustang $60 - 75

Chicago Cubs 2-pack 20001 '58 Corvette, '97 Corvette 60

Crazy Classics II 5-pack 18827 Radio Flyer Wagon, Wienermobile, Treadator, Rigor-Motor, Rail Rodder 2+POC

FAO Schwarz Cruisin' the 50s 8-pack 19758 Street Beast, '57 Chevy, Classic Nomad, '56 Flashsider, '57 T-Bird, Passion, '59 Caddy, '58 Corvette 75

The History of Hot Wheels III

FAO Schwarz History of Hot Wheels III Racing 8-pack '96 Monte Carlo Stocker, '67 Mustang, Turbo Streak, T-Bucket, '57 Chevy, '70 Barracuda, Off Road Racer, Porsche 935 80

FAO Schwarz Radical Rides 6-pack 18956 Dairy Delivery, Sweet 16 II, Tow Jam, Solar Eagle III, Go-Kart, Hot Seat 20

Figure 8 Racers 5-pack 18828 Ferrari 355, Chevy 1500, Camaro Z-28, Porsche 959, Chevy Stocker 2+POC

Flag Flyers 5-pack 18834 Porsche 928, Range Rover, '97 Corvette, Lamborghini Countach, Toyota MR2 Rally 2+POC

G-Force Stunt Riders 5-pack 18829 Power Rocket, Ferrari F50, Porsche 930, Camaro Convertible, T-Bird Stocker 2+POC

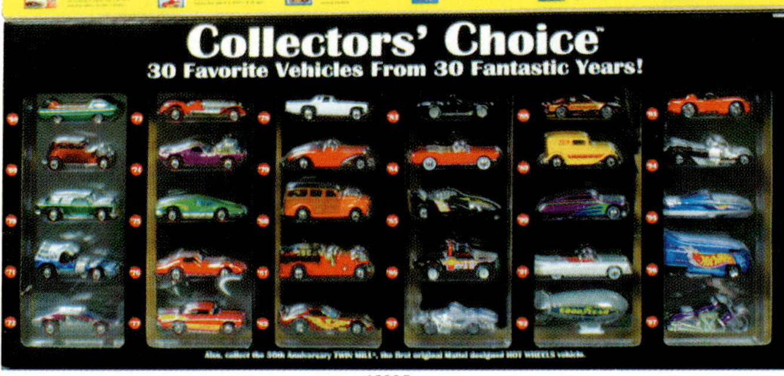

18995

Hills Cool 'n' Custom Set 19328 '65 Impala, Custom C3500, Tail Dragger, '40s Ford Pickup, '63 T-Bird, Dodge Caravan, '32 Ford, Dodge Sidewinder 25

19328

JC Penney's Watch and Car Set 20652 Splittin' Image and watch 30

Kmart Off-Road Racing 4-pack Shock Factor, Roll Patrol, Commando, Suzuki QuadRacer 40

Off-Road 4x4s 5-pack 18830 Hummer, Gulch Stepper, Bronco 4-Wheeler, Path Beater, Roll Patrol Jeep 2+POC

Racing Series 1 8-pack 20425 Slideout, '70 Roadrunner, Escort Rally, Firebird, Jaquar XK8, Lakester, Panoz GTR-1, Super Comp Dragster 8

Rad Rigs 5-pack 18832 Ford F-150, Tank Truck, Oshkosh Cement Mixer, Ford Stake Bed Truck, Peterbilt Dump Truck 2+POC

Road Repair 5-pack 17460 Tank Truck, Oshkosh Cement Mixer, Oshkosh Snow Plow, Peterbilt Dump Truck, Dodge Ram 1500 2+POC

Showroom Specials 5-pack 18833 Ramp Truck, 380 SEL, BMW M Roadster, Ferrari 250, Lexus SC400 2+POC

Target Fathers Day 3-car set Monte Carlo Stocker, two Pontiac Grand Prix 30

Target V-8 4-pack Classic Nomad, Plymouth Duster, '67 Mustang 30

18355

Values are shown in U.S. dollars, first price is for mint, second is for mint packaged vehicles only. See pages 15-16 for grading guide to determine value for cars in lesser conditions.

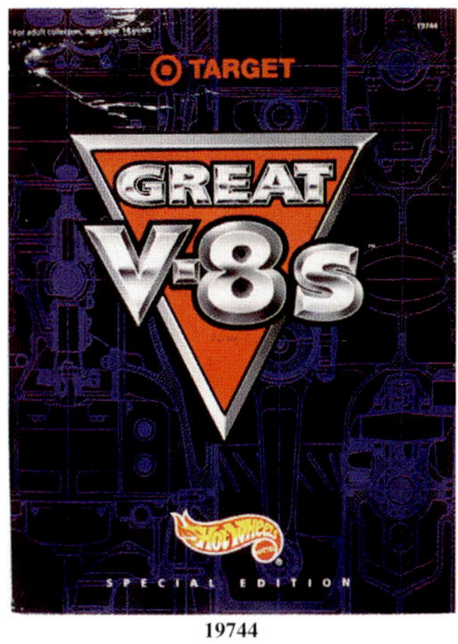

19744

21068 21080

21081 21083

Target's Petty Generations 3-pack Richard, Kyle & Adam Petty's Pontiac Grand Prix 25
The Petty Racing Family 3-pack 19021 '57 Oldsmobile, '70 Plymouth Superbird, '97 Pontiac Grand Prix 35
Toys "R" Us 10 Car Gift Set 18730 Street Rodder, '97 Corvette, Porsche 959, Ferrari Testarossa, Chevy 1500, Baja Bug, Sol-Aire CX4, BMW M Roadster, Aeroflash, '80s Camaro 15
Toys "R" Us 10 Car Gift Set 18731 Propper Chopper, Lamborghini Countach, Fire-Eater, Mercedes 380 SEL, Dodge Ram 1500, Mercedes-Benz Unimog, Lexus SC400, Range Rover, Ferrari Testarossa, '80s Camaro 15
Toys R Us Racing Series 1 8-pack all regular-line cars 2+POC
Toys R Us Racing Series 2 8-pack all regular-line cars 2+POC
Toys R Us Timeless Toys 4-pack Way 2 Fast, Ford F-150, '96 Mustang Convertible, Baja Bug 35
X-Treme Machines 5-pack 18831 Road Rocket, Twin Mill II, Speed Blaster, Splittin' Image II, Pontiac Salsa 2+POC

Collectible Sets

35th Anniversary of the Shelby Cobra 2-pack 16742 Dodge Viper GTS, 1965 Cobra Daytona 40
American Graffiti 2-pack '32 Ford Coupe, 1955 Chevy Bel Air 45
Collectors' Choice set 18995 '32 Ford Delivery Truck, '40s Woodie, '57 Chevy, '57 T-Bird, '59 Caddy, '65 Mustang, Auburn 852, Corvette Sting Ray, Deora, Dodge Viper RT/10, Firebird Funny Car, Ford Vicky, Goodyear Blimp, Hydroplane, Large Charge, Mutt Mobile, Nomad, Old Number 5, Path Beater, Porsche 959, Purple Passion, Rigor Motor, Rodger Dodger, Scorchin' Scooter, Sharkruiser, Shelby Cobra, Side Kick, Sweet 16, VW Bus, XT-3 170
Corvette Showcase 2-pack set 1 of 2 '53 Corvette, '82 Corvette Stingray 30
Corvette Showcase 2 pack set 2 of 2 '67 Corvette Stingray, '98 Corvette Convertible 30
JC Penney's 1998 Treasure Hunt Series 21136 12, 1998 Treasure Hunt Cars 400
Street Rodder 2-pack '34 Ford Convertible,'47 Ford Convertible 35

1999

Ames Department Stores 4-pack '63 Thunderbird, Dodge Viper RT/10, '58 Corvette, Dodge Concept Car 35
Chicago Cubs 2-pack '67 Camaro, 1970 Mustang Mach I 50
K•B Toys 2-pack '63 T-Bird, '59 Impala 10
Players Inc. Special Edition 3-pack Dodge Ram 1500, two Grand Prix 25
Target Fathers Day 3-car set Monte Carlo Stocker, two Pontiac Grand Prix 25
Target Street Rods 4-pack Way 2 Fast, '32 Ford, '32 Ford Delivery, 3-Window '34 25
Target Great V8s 3-pack 19744 '68 Mustang, Classic Nomad, Plymouth Duster 20
Toys "R" Us 10-car pack '80s Camaro plus 9 regular-line cars 3+POC
Toys "R" Us 10-car pack Side Splitter plus 10 regular-line cars 6+POC
Toys "R" Us Coca Cola Race Team 4-car Set '40s Ford, Driven To The Max, Olds Aurora GTS1, Mercedes CLK-LM 25
Toys "R" Us Racing American Style 4-pack '70 Chevelle, '99 Mustang, Monte Carlo Concept Car, Olds Aurora GTS-1 25
Toys "R" Us Timeless Toys II 4-pack '97 Corvette, '32 Ford, School Bus, Shock Factor 25
Wal-Mart 50th Anniversary of Petty Racing 4-pack Monte Carlo Stocker, Dodge Ram 1500, two Pontiac Grand Prix 25

5-Packs

'50s Cruiser '59 Caddy, '57 T-Bird, '57 Chevy, '32 Ford Coupe, Scorchin' Scooter 2+POC
Alien Attack Porsche 930, Lexus SC400, Camaro Z-28, Power Pistons, Flashfire 2+POC
Baja Blazers 21083 Bywayman, Roll Patrol, Nissan Hardbody, Gulch Stepper, Bronco 4-Wheeler 2+POC
City Center Good Humor Truck, Fire-Eater, Mercedes SLK, Dodge Caravan, Recycling Truck 2+POC
City Police 21068 Dodge Ram 1500, Holden Police Car, Surf Patrol, Olds Aurora, Rescue Ranger 2+POC
Crazy Classics III Twang Thang, Rail Rodder, Whatta Drag, Skull Rider, Dogfighter 2+POC
Criss Cross Crash 21081 Porsche 959, Aeroflash, Ford GT90, Chevy Stocker, Chevy 1500 2+POC
FAO Schwarz Classic Collection Auburn 852, Classic Caddy, '31 Doozie, Talbot Lago, Phaetom 50
House Calls 21080 Dodge Ram 1500, Chevy 1500, '56 Flashsider, Delivery Van, '40s Ford truck 2+POC
Ocean Blasters Fathom This, Corvette Sting Ray III, Hydroplane, Corvette Stingray, '70 Cuda Convertible 2+POC
Police Squad Hydroplane, Olds Aurora, '80s Camaro, Police Cruiser, Alien, or GM Ultralite 2+POC
Race Team 3 Olds 442, Porsche 930, '56 Flashsider, Silhouette II, Splittin' Image II 2+POC
Race Team Crew Kenworth T600A, Bywayman, Dodge Ram 1500, Rig Wrecker, Delivery Truck 2+POC
Show Biz 21078 Classic Caddy, Limozeen, '63 T-Bird, Ferrari 250, Classic Cobra 2+POC
Showroom Specials Ramp Truck, Mercedes 380SL, Lexus SC400, Ferrari 250, BMW M Roadster 2+POC
Snow Patrol Big Chill, Roll Patrol, Oshkosh Snow Plow, Treadator, Ford F-150 2+POC
Sports Stars Stingray III, Jaguar D-Type, 1996 Mustang GT, Camaro Convertible, Dodge Viper RT/10 2+POC
Volcano Blowout Chevy Stocker, T-Bird Stocker, Road Rocket, Power Rocket, Power Pipes 2+POC
World Racers 21084 Dodge Viper, Solar Eagle III, Panoz GTR-1, Super Comp Racer, Rail Dragster 2+POC

Action Packs

Drag Racing 18736 2 Dragsters 8
Fire 'n Rescue 21532 Ambulance, Fire-Eater 6
Galileo Mission 21252 no cars 6
Team Knight Rider Attack Beast 19398 Attack Beast 10
Team Knight Rider Dante 19396 Dante 10
The Rugrats Movie 18742 Reptar Wagon 6
Scum Chums™ Hot Seat, Bathtub Wagon 8
Sky Search 18735 Propper Chopper, Blimp 6
Snow Plowers 18737 Big Chill, Power Plower 6
Surf's Up Classic Nomad, '40s Woodie 18
Towing 21262 Shadow Jet 2, Tow Jam 15
Toy Story Shock Factor 10
Toy Story 2 Al's Custom Cruiser 10

Collectible Sets

30th Anniversary of '69 Muscle Car 2-pack Series 1, set 1 1969 Oldsmobile 442, Chevrolet Chevelle 25
30th Anniversary of '69 Muscle Car 2-pack Series 1, set 2 AMX, Plymouth Hemi GTX 25
30th Anniversary of Hot Wheels 4-pack Heavy Chevy, King Kuda, Light My Firebird, Nitty Gritty Kitty 35
Baur's Beasts 2-pack Go-Mad, Torqued Off 20
Ed Newton's Lowboyz™ 3 car set Mercoholic, Rareflow, Triclopz 25
El Camino 40th Anniversary 2-pack 1959 El Camino, 1970 El Camino 25
Fireworkz 1959 El Camino, Crackerbox Race Boat 2-pack 25
Hard Rock Cafe 3-pack 1959 Cadillac Eldorado Woodie, '57 Eldorado, '63 Fleetwood 25
Jaguar 4-car set Jaguar XJ-13, Jaguar XKE, Jaguar XKR, Jaguar XKSS 35
Lowrider Magazine 3-pack 1969 Buick Riviera Lowrider, '53 Bel Air, '70 Monte Carlo 30
Popular Hot Rodding Magazine 4-pack '67 Corvette Stingray, 1970 El Camino, 1968 Camaro, Chevrolet Chevelle 45
Porsche 50th Anniversary 4-pack Porsche 917, Porsche 930 Turbo, Porsche 550 Spyder Porsche Boxster 35
Reggie's Cars 4-pack 1932 Ford Hi-Boy Roadster, 1963 Plymouth 426 Max Wedge '40s Ford Deluxe Convertible, '56 Chevy 210 2-Door Sedan 40
Smoke 'n Water 2-pack '59 Chevy Apache Fleetside Pickup & Crackerbox Race Boat 20

Multi Packs

JC Penney's 1999 Treasure Hunt Series 23297 12, 1999 Treasure Hunt Cars 300
Penske Motor sports 23416 four different Pontiac Grand Prix 20
Target Drive-In 26622 '57 Chevy, Purple Passion, '59 Cadillac, '59 Impala 20
Cub Foods 2 pack 26638 Express Lane & various asst. cars 5
K•B 2 pack 27005 Two Pheatons 12
Toys "R" Us Hot Haulers 27663 Chevy Pro Stock Truck, Deora II, '68 El Camino, Surf Crate 20

2000

5-Packs

Star Explorers 25363 Shadow Jet, Radar Ranger, Solar Eagle III, Speed Seaker, Flashfire 2 + POC
Max Steel 25366 Turbolence, Dragster, Power Rocket, Sweet 16 II, GT Racer 2 + POC
Tornado Twister 25367 Power Pistons, Aeroflash, Buick Wildcat, Zender Fact 4 2 + POC
Powershift Garage 25368 Olds Aurora GT3, Rig Wrecker, Police Car, Porsche 911 GT3, Ford GT-40 2 + POC
World Tour 25369 Bronco 4-Wheeler, Roll Patrol, Dodge Caravan, Oldsmobile Aurora, '80s Corvette 2 + POC
Hotwheels.com 25371 '40s Woodie, '65 Impala, T-Bird Stocker, Chevy Nomad, '32 Ford 2 + POC
World Racers 2 25370 Escort Rally, Porsche 911 GT1-98, Ferrari 360 Modena, Panoz GTR-1, 25th Anniversary Lamborghini Countach 2 + POC
Motorin' Music 25372 '67 Camaro, '65 Mustang, Purple Passion, '58 Corvette, '59 Cadillac 2 + POC
Forces of Nature 25373 Hydroplane, Funny Car, T-Bird Stocker, Big Chill, Path Beater 2 + POC
Super Launcher 25374 Saltflat Racer, Pikes Peak Celica, Cat-A-Pult, Silhouette II, Splittin' Image II 2 + POC

Multi Packs

JC Penney's 2000 Treasure Hunt Series 27629 12, 2000 Treasure Hunt Cars 300
Ames Cruise Night 27795 '65 Impala, Tail Dragger, '32 Ford, Chevy Nomad 20
Avon Vintage Hot Rods 27797 '32 Ford Vicky, Purple Passion, Sweet 16 15
Toys "R" Us Timeless Toys III 27798 Dodge Caravan, Fiat 500, At-A-Tude, Funny Car 20
K•B 2 pack 27805 Two '33 Ford Roadster's 12
Target Toy Story 2 27958 Pontiac Grand Prix, Ford Taurus, and Ford Taurus 18
Chicago Cubs 2 pack 28363 Monte Carlo Concept Car & '70 Chevelle SS 15
Phillies 2 pack 28790 Jeepster & Chrysler Pronto 12
Avon Super Tuners 29871 Sho-Stopper, MX48 Turbo, Muscle Tone 15
Walgreens 2 pack 29872 '56 Ford Panel & various asst. cars 7
Pep Boys 2 pack 29883 Firebird & various asst. cars 5
K•B 2 pack 29894 Two Surf Crates 12
Cub Foods 2 pack 29948 Hiway Hauler & various asst. cars 5

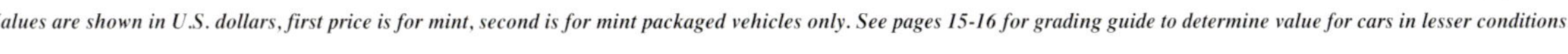
Values are shown in U.S. dollars, first price is for mint, second is for mint packaged vehicles only. See pages 15-16 for grading guide to determine value for cars in lesser conditions.

50060 50072 54417 56140 50078 54399 54429 54459

2001

5-Packs

Shark Park 50012 T-Bird Stocker, Sharkruiser, Speed Seeker, Chrysler Thunderbolt, Speed Shark 2 + POC

Police Cruisers 50024 Dodge Power Wagon, Scorchin' Scooter, Police Car, Enforcer, Jeepster 2 + POC

Spider Slam 50018 Chevy Stocker, Turbo Flame, Power Pistons, Sweet 16 II, Saltflat Racer 2 + POC

Harley-Davidson 50030 Bronco 4-Wheeler, '79 Ford F-150, '56 Ford, Ford F-150, '40 Ford 2 + POC

Skateboarders 50036 '40s Woodie, '32 Ford Delivery, Deora II, Surf Crate, Chevy Nomad 2 + POC

Cyborg City 50042 Porsche 930, Ford GT-90, Dodge Viper RT/10, Zender Fact 4, Chaparral 2 2 + POC

Fireball 50048 Krazy 8s, Splittin' Image II, Turbolence, Road Rocket, Corvette Stingray III 3 + POC

Fireball 50048 Krazy 8s, Splittin' Image II, Turbolence, Road Rocket, Vulture 2 + POC

Victory Lane 50054 Holden, Callaway C-7, Ferrari F355 Challenge, Escort Rally, Semi-Fast 2 + POC

Rescue Rods 50060 Rig Wrecker, Ambulance, Roll Patrol, Rescue Ranger, Path Beater 2 + POC

Truck Stoppers 50066 '56 Flashsider, '68 El Camino, Fat Fendered '40, Delivery Van, Dairy Delivery 2 + POC

Hot Rods 50072 Lakester, Fat Fendered '40, Deuce Roadster, 3-Window '34, Fiat 500 2 + POC

Multi Packs

Target Blue Hawaii 29895 Fat Fendered '40, So Fine, Shoe Box, '32 Ford 20

Target Jailhouse Rock 29895 Fat Fendered '40, So Fine, Shoe Box, '32 Ford 20

Costco 20 pack 29896 Cabbin' Fever & 19 asst. Blister packs 18

Costco 20 pack 29896 Vulture & 19 asst. Blister packs 18

Sam's Club 20 pack 29896 Deora II & 19 asst. Blister packs 18

Sam's Club 20 pack 29896 Shoe Box & 19 asst. Blister packs 18

Kmart 10 pack 52579 Way 2 Fast & 9 asst. singles 12

Walgreens 2 pack 54958 Pheaton & various asst. cars 6

Auto Zone 2 pack 55699 Fandango & various asst. cars 6

Pep Boys 2 pack 55700 '63 Corvette & various asst. cars 6

2002

5-Packs

City Service 50078 At-A-Tude, Ford GT-90, Sho-Stopper, Austin Healy, Side-Kick 2 + POC

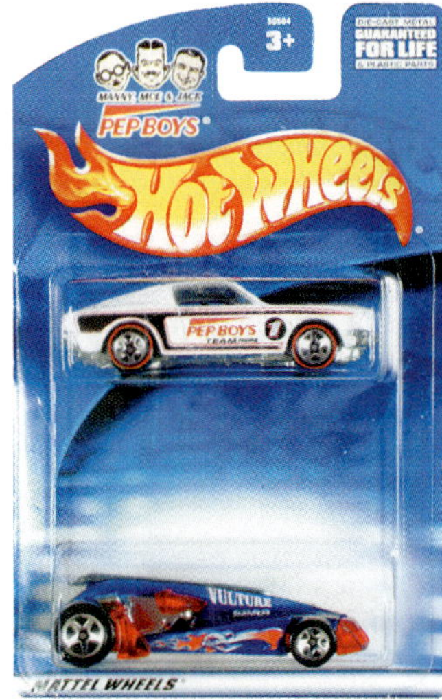

56504

Birthday 54393 Pack Shadow Mk IIa, Baby Boomer, MX48 Turbo, Mustang Cobra 2 + POC

Insectiride 54399 Speed Seaker, At-A-Tude, Saltflat Racer, Chaparral 2, Turbo Flame 2 + POC

Sports Gift Pack 54417 Blimp, Holden, Callaway C-7, Dodge Caravan, Semi-Fast 2 + POC

56003

Heat Fleet 54429 Olds Aurora, Police Car, Rescue Range, Fire Eater, Flame Stopper 2 + POC

Asphalt Assault 54459 Toyota MR2 Rally, Customized C3500, Dodge Ram 1500, Ford F-150, Peterbilt Dump Truck 2 + POC

Multi Packs

Blue Book 56003 3 pack Fandango & 2 asst. blister packs 10

Pop's Garage 56149 4 pack Civic, Hooligan, Deuce Roadster, '71 Plymouth GTX 20

Kmart 56268 10 pack Monoposto & 9 asst singles 12

SETS AND CASES

1968

5013 **Service Station** fold down $60

5014 **Construction Company** fold down 60

5134 **Pop-Up Service Station** 1 car 75+POC

5135 **Pop-Up Speed Shop** 1 car 60+POC

5136 **Pop-Up House & Car Port** 1 car 60+POC

5137 **12 Car Rally Case** wheel case w/red line, inset sticker of mag wheel 10

5138 **24 Car Case** vinyl, orange & brown, shows white & purple car crossing finish line 50

5139 **Pop-Up 12 Car Collector's Case** shows yellow & blue car on race-track, pop-up grandstand when opened 60

5141 **Pop-Up Speedway Action Set** 2 cars 50+POC

6200 **Strip Action Set** 1 car 50+POC

6201 **Stunt Action Set** 1 car 50+POC

6202 **Drag Race Action Set** 2 cars 45+POC

6223 **Hot Curves Race Action Set** 2 cars 45+POC

6224 **Hot Strip Track Pak** 15

6225 **Full Curve Pak** 12

6226 **Daredevil Loop Pak** 15

6227 **Half Curve Pak** 12

6475 **Hot Strip Super Pak** 15

1969

5142 **24 Car Super Rally Case** same as 5137 but larger $5

5143 **12 Car Adjustable Case** yellow, shows red car 30

5144 **24 Car Adjustable Case** yellow, shows blue & white car 35

5145 **48 Car Adjustable Case** yellow; shows yellow, purple & white car 45

5146 **Custom Shop Showcase Plaque** 50

5147 **Car Carrier Showcase Plaque** 50

5158 **Action City** 65

5159 **Talking Service Center** 85

5439 **Hot Wheels Wipe-Out Race Game** 50

56268

54886

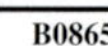

B0865

Values are shown in U.S. dollars, first price is for mint, second is for mint packaged vehicles only. See pages 15-16 for grading guide to determine value for cars in lesser conditions.

6226

6438

6279 **Stunt Action Set** 1 car 50+POC
6280 **Double-Dare Race Set** 2 cars 50+POC
6281 **Hot Curves Race Action Set** 2 cars 45+POC
6283 **Jump Ramp Pak** 12
6284 **Trestle Pak** 12
6285 **Competition Pak** 12
6290 **Super-Charger Sprint Set** 1 car 50+POC
6291 **Super-Charger Speedway-Freeway Set** 2 cars 45+POC
6292 **Super-Charger Grand Prix Race Set** 4 cars 45+POC

1970

4355 **Hot Wheels Factory** w/Plastix™ & wheels to make ten Hot Wheels cars $150
4952 **Action Set Gear Box** no vehicles 80
4975 **12-Car Collector's Race Case** black w/trays, shows Mantis & Swingin' Wing on race track 30
4976 **24-Car Collector's Race Case** black w/trays, shows Custom Mustang & Custom Camaro on race track 30
4977 **48-Car Collector's Race Case** black w/trays, shows Porsche 917 & Ferrari 312P on race track 35
4978 **72-Car Collector's Race Case** black w/trays, shows Snake & Mongoose funny cars on track 35
4979 **Speed Shop** no cars 90
6248 **Hazard Hill** 2 cars 60+POC
6270 **Lap Counter** 15
6278 **Strip Action Set** 1 car 55+POC
6284 **Trestle 5-Pak** 15
6294 **Super-Charger** 40
6295 **2-Way Super-Charger** 50
6297 **Racing Sticker Pak** 5
6429 **Super Charger Race Set** 2 cars 50+POC
6430 **Super Charger Rally 'n Freeway** 2 cars 50+POC
6436 **Sky Show Set Sky Show Fleetside** with 6 planes 800
6437 **Drag 'Chute Stunt Set** 1 car 55+POC
6438 **Mongoose vs Snake Drag Race Set** Snake & Mongoose 600
6439 **Rod Runner Speedway Set** 1 car 50+POC
6440 **Dual-Lane Rod Runner Race Set** 2 cars 50+POC
6441 **Super Charger Speed Test Set** one car 60+POC
6442 **Road Trials Set** Tune-Up Tower & car 85+POC
6443 **Hi-Performance Set** Tune-Up Tower, 2-way Super-Charger, 4 cars 85+POC
6446 **Dual-Lane Rod Runner Drag Set** 2 cars 50+POC

6473 **Decal Pak** Stick-Arounds 5
6475 **Hot Strip Track Super Pak** 25
6476 **Dual-Lane Lap Counter** 20
6477 **Dual-Lane Curve Pak** 20
6479 **Rod Runner** 20
6480 **Dual-Lane Rod Runner** 30
6481 **Tune-Up Tower** 80
6482 **Bridge Pak** 15
6483 **Speedometer** 20
6484 **Dual-Lane Speedometer** 30
6492 **Joiner Pak** 20
6599 **Club Kit** 1 car: Chrome Boss Hoss, Heavy Chevy, or King Kuda 175

1971

6013 **Victory Pak** $25
6015 **Danger-Changer 2-Pak** 25
6034 **Big Belter & Matchmaker** 30
6037 **Mongoose & Snake Wild Wheelie Set** Snake & Mongoose rail dragsters 600
6159 **Crossover Pak** 25
6107 **Ontario Trio** 2 cars 50+POC
6490 **Great Getaway Set** The Demon & Paddy Wagon w/special top (exclusive to set) 650
6493 **Flyin' Circus Set** Sky Show Fleetside, 3 planes, 2 Zopters 1000
6494 **Racing Posters** Snake & Mongoose 125
6494 **Racing Posters** all others 35

1972

5645 **Bug Bite Set** 1 car $50+POC
5824 **Zappit Pak** 1 car 15+POC
5870 **Drivin' Gear** 50
6692 **Snake Bite Set** 2 cars 50+POC

1973

8227 **24-Car Collector's Case** red, same as 4976 on blue background $25
8232 **Campground Set** 120
8247 **24-Car Display** 275

1974

4975 **12-Car Collectors Case** same as 4976 but red $30
7615 **Mountain Mining Set** Road King Truck 750
7623 **City Police Set** 2 cars 150+POC
7624 **Road King Highway Drive-ins Set** 1 car 150+POC
7631 **Speed Stunter Set** 1 car 100+POC
7632 **Double Dare Set** 2 cars 90+POC

1975

7672 **Cutoff Canyon** 2 cars $100+POC
7673 **Thundershift 500** 2 cars 60+POC
8227 **Collector's Race Case** blue w/P-917, Heavy Chevy & Baja Bruiser on white background 50
9084 **Country Life** no vehicles 100

1976

4975 **12-Car Collector's Case** shows P-917, Emergency Squad & black Super Van in color on blue vinyl case $15
8227 **24-Car Collector's Case** shows P-917, Emergency Squad & black Super Van in color on blue vinyl case 15
8227 **24-Car Collector's Case** same scene as 4976, blue or gray vinyl w/picture in red; red or yellow vinyl w/picture in blue 25
9245 **Super Chrome Stunt Set** chrome Rock Buster 80
9274 **Double Duel Speedway** 2 cars 70+POC
9275 **Loco-Motion** 1 car 60+POC
9530 **Super Rally Case** silver line around tire, mag wheel insert 10

1977

9676 **Double Scare Speedway** 2 chrome cars $80+POC
9793 **Thrill Drivers Corkscrew Race Set** 2 red & white Thrill Driver Torinos 250
9876 **Turbo Blast 600 Race Set** black P-911+another car 400+2nd car price

1978

2011 **Stingray Stunt** red Corvette Stingray $60
2363 **Thundershift Roarin' Raceway** 2 cars 40+POC
2386 **T-Bird Tossup** '57 T-Bird 50

1979

1082 **Captain America Stunt Set** Captain America car $50
2886 **Spider-Man's Web of Terror Set** Spider-Man car 50
2945 **Criss-Cross Crash Set** 2 cars 40+POC
4445 **Getaway 12-Car Case** black, clear plastic front, 12 vehicles
w/vehicles 30
w/o vehicles 10

1980

1437 **The Great American Truck Race** Hammer Down & Movin' On $385
1503 **Service Center** Hot Bird 35
1547 **Wipeout Side by Side Raceway** 2 cars 35+POC

1981

3324 **City Sto & Go Set** no vehicles $15
3342 **Flyin' Bronco Set** black Bronco 4-wheeler 20
3370 **Dixie Challenger Thrill** Dixie Challenger 25
3854 **Dixie Challenger Getaway Spinout** Dixie Challenger, Highway Patrol 35
4975 **12-Car Collector's Case** blue vinyl w/Wheel Loader, Dump Truck, Mirada Stocker, '31 Doozie 7
8227 **24-Car Collector's Case** blue vinyl, same picture as 4975 7

1982

1503 **Service Center Sto & Go** no vehicles $15
1898 **Photo Finish Race Set** 2 cars 20+POC
3464 **Showcase Carry Case** (black) 10
3534 **Hot Ones Drag Race Set** 2 cars 20+POC
3741 **Hot Wheels U.S.A. Deluxe Set** no vehicles 15
3808 **Inside Track Sto & Go** 2 cars 20+POC
3896 **Loop & Chute Stunt Set** 1 car 20+POC
5051 **Radio Control Hauler** 15
5054 **Hot Wheels U.S.A. Starter Set** 2 no vehicles 15
5055 **Hot Wheels U.S.A. Builder Set** no vehicles 15
5306 **Megaforce Vertibird** no vehicles 35
5324 **Megaforce Desert Strike** Megadestroyer 35
5360 **Hot Wheels U.S.A. Starter Set 1** no vehicles 15

1983

2275 **Hot Wheels U.S.A. Starter Set 2** no vehicles $15
4001 **Construction Site Sto & Go** no vehicles 15
4061 **Spiral Speedway** 2 cars 35+POC
4062 **Jumpmasters** 1 car 20+POC
4490 **Flying Firebird Variable Jump** black '80s Firebird 40
5323 **Cargo Plane** no vehicles 50
5563 **Dash & Crash Speedway** 2 cars 20+POC

1984

3464 **Showcase Carry Case** (brown) $10
4445 **Getaway 12-Car Case** red, clear plastic front & 8 vehicles,
w/vehicles 30
w/o vehicles 10
7001 **Racer's Engine Case** 25
7003 **Thrill Driver's Corkscrew** 2 Turbo Mustangs 30
7101 **Speed Shifter 500** 2 cars 25+POC
7226 **Cobra Stunt Set** red Turbo Mustang, tampo colors reversed from blisterpack model 40
7282 **24-Car Collector's Case** yellow w/'37 Bugatti, Sol-Aire CX4, Tricar X8, Turbo Streak 10
9793 **Tirabuzon Thrill Drivers** 2 Mexican cars, Mexico only 40+POC

1985

9176 **Dynamite Crossing** black Super Van w/orange stripe $25
9250 **Action Command Sto & Go** no vehicles 20
9511 **Snake Mountain Challenge** Snake Busters car 20

1986

1264 **Turbotrax Mach 1** white Fiero 2M4 $25
2137 **Super Turbotrax 3000** Wind Splitter, Sol-Aire CX4 30
2148 **Turbotrax** '80s Corvette, Nissan 300ZX 30
2159 **Turbotrax Straight Trax** accessory pack 5
2160 **Turbotrax Curved Trax** accessory pack 5
2161 **Turbotrax Crossroads Trax** accessory pack 5
2162 **Turbotrax Columns** accessory pack 5

1987

1142 **Fix & Fill Center Sto & Go** no vehicles $15
1673 **CarGo Carrier** 15
2063 **Leapin' Demons Chase Set** lt. green Double Demon, yellow Cargoyle 45
3051 **Speed Trigger** launcher w/blue Nissan 300ZX 15
3243 **Turbotrax Turboglo Jump Set** Ferrari Testarossa & Blown Camaro, w/glow-in-dark tampos 50
3342 **Car Wash & Service Station Sto & Go** no cars 15
9980 **Turbotrax Turbo Drive Power Booster** 10

6436

Values are shown in U.S. dollars, first price is for mint, second is for mint packaged vehicles only. See pages 15-16 for grading guide to determine value for cars in lesser conditions.

4513

1988

4451 **Alpine Mountain Adventure Sto & Go** no vehicles $15
4513 **Dinosaur Mud Pit Set** olive Blazer 4x4 25
5190 **Sight & Smash Booster Set** 1 car 5+POC
5463 **Building Site Sto & Go** no vehicles 10
5464 **Mini-Market Sto & Go** no vehicles 10
5465 **Drive & Eat Sto & Go** no vehicles 10

1989

1684 **G-Force Stunt Set** mtlc red Blown Camaro $10
1903 **Emergency Station Sto & Go** no vehicles 10
2642 **Sprint & Spin Speed Trigger** no vehicles 8
2683 **Fire Fighter Sto & Go** no vehicles 15
2756 **Pop 'n Play School House** Team Bus 6
2757 **Pop 'n Play Construction Co. Peterbilt** Cement Mixer 6
2759 **Pop 'n Play Police Station** Sheriff Patrol 6
3254 **Double Barrel Stunt Set** 20
3254 **Gravity Blaster** Hot Bird, Camaro Z-28 25
3495 **Track** pack 5
3496 **Loop** pack 5
3497 **Launch** pak 5
3498 **Curve** pack 5

1990

2758 **Pop 'n Play Drive-In-Bank** Custom Corvette $6
4980 **California Custom Freeway** 9
5469 **Mini Market Sto & Go** w/Getty Labels 10
7554 **Custom Car Center** no vehicles 10
9093 **Wildwave Stunt** '40s Woodie 5+POC
9938 **Round-Up Ranch Sto & Go** no vehicles 10

1991

2680 **Dash 'N Crash** GT Racer $15
2756 **Starter City School** School Bus 8
2758 **Starter City Police Station** Sheriff Patrol 8
3285 **Wal-Mart Playset** "Wal-Mart" Hiway Hauler 15
7456 **Funny Car Gift Pack** Motorcraft, Castrol GTX, and Pennzoil funny cars 5+POC
7493 **Jumpbuster Stunt** yellow Ferrari Testarossa 15
7552 **Starter City Bank** Mercedes 380SEL 8
9511 **Starter City Hospital** Ambulance 5+POC
9512 **Starter City Burger Stand** Minitruck 5+POC
9515 **Starter City Mini Market** Passion 5+POC
9568 **City® Wash 'n Wax** no vehicles 10
9576 **City Highway Builder** no vehicles 10
9577 **City Airport** no vehicles 8
9578 **City Race Center** no vehicles 8
9579 **City Construction Co.** no vehicles 8
9650 **Turbo Tube Raceway** P-911 15

1992

2114 **Pro Circuit Speedway Set** #25 Hot Wheels, #33 Duracell $25
5736 **Quick-Fire Crash Curve** Fiero 2M4, Camaro 20

1993

2585 **Engine Car Case** $10
10996 **Service Merchandise All-American Car Showcase Collection** 65

1994

3254 **Double Barrel® Stunt Set** purple '65 Mustang Convertible, mtlfk green Porsche 930 $5+POC
65603 **Sto & Go Parking & Service Garage** 5
65606 **Sto & Go Drag Race Case & Playset** 5
11644 **Target Snake & Mongoose Drag Race Set** Snake & Mongoose 25+POC

1995

13040 **Track System Jump Pack** $3
13087 **Track System Track Pack** 3
13088 **Track System Starter** white '80s Camaro 3+POC
13091 **Track System Loop Pack** 3
13092 **Track System Launcher Pack** 3
13093 **Track System Curve Pack** 3
13094 **Track System C-Clamp & Track Pack** 3
15741 **Track System Track Pack** 3
65605 **Gas Station Sto & Go** blue Frontrunnin' Fairmont 3+POC
65613 **McDonald's Sto & Go** red '65 Mustang Convertible 3+POC

1996

08707 **Hot Wheels Drag Race Set** red Porsche Targa, black Custom Hot Rod Van (both Corgi) $5+POC
08707 **Hot Wheels Goodyear Playset** dark red '82 Supra & dark blue '57 T-Bird (Corgi) 5+POC
08707 **Hot Wheels Truck Stop** red Ferrari (Corgi) & red Peterbilt Dump Truck 5+POC
14181 **Track System Speedometer** pack 4
15089 **Dino-Soar Jump® Set** green Speed-A-Saurus 3+POC
15112 **Mega Rig™ Construction Set** 6
15468 **Super Electronic Garage** 1 car 2+POC
15472 **Spin-Out Set** yellow Power Pipes 5+POC
16539 **Toy Story Super Stunt Set** Red Baron 5+POC
16741 **Service Center** Camaro Convertible 2+POC
65603 **Sto & Go Parking Garage** red '57 T-Bird (Corgi) or orange '80s Firebird 5+POC
65603 **Sto 'n Go Parking & Service Garage** w/BMW 850 2+POC
65610 **Car Wash** light mtlfk green Fiero 2M4 5+POC
65610 **Car Wash** Pontiac Fiero 2+POC
65616 **Chevrolet Dealership** black '57 Chevy 5+POC
65620 **Street Traxx Super Highway Playset** red Ferrari 348 4+POC
65623 **Street Traxx™ City Streets** dk. red '82 Supra 4+POC
65624 **Sto 'n Go Super City Playset** '80s Firebird 2+POC
65625 **Baywatch Lifeguard Rescue Station** 4+POC
65693 **Blimp Port** Blimp 2+POC
65694 **Gas Station** '57 T-Bird Convertible 2+POC
65701 **Baywatch Set** 5+POC
65709 **Heliport** white Propper Chopper 3+POC
65710 **Shark's Lair** gray Sharkruiser 5+POC
65711 **Snake Pit** yellow Turboa 5+POC
65727 **Cargo Chopper** 5
65730 **Goodyear Service Set** dk. red '82 Supra 4+POC
65738 **Road Construction Playtrack** Peterbilt Dump Truck 2+POC
65740 **Super Highway Playtrack** Porsche 2+POC
65875 **Police Chase Playtrack** Police Car 2+POC
65876 **Sto 'n Go Race Case** 5
93170 **Auto City™ Garage** red P-911 or Mercedes Fire Chief (Corgi) & red Helicopter (Corgi) 5

1997

1673-97 **Cargo Carrier** red or black $10
1684 **G-Force®** orange Mazda MX-5 Miata 20
14181 **Track Systems Speedometer Pack** 3
14478 **Track Systems Turbo Curve Pack** 3
17113 **Volcano Blowout Set** Aeroflash & Road Rocket 2+POC
17325 **Figure 8 Starter Set** Power Pipes 5+POC
18090 **Super Starter Set** Ferrari 355 & Turboflame 5+POC
20020 **48 Car Carry Case** 6
20375 **100 Car Carry Case** 10
65601 **Emergency Hospital Sto 'n Go** white Ambulance 3+POC
65602 **Sto 'n Go City Playset** blue Corvette Split Window or dk. red '82 Supra 3+POC
65603 **Parking & Service Garage** with '57 T-Bird Convertible 5+POC
65604 **Cargo Plane** 25
65605 **Gas Station Sto & Go – Race** 3+POC
65617 **Car Wash** Mercedes 500 2+POC
65710 **Shark's Lair** Sharkruiser 2+POC
65711 **Snake Pit Set** Turboa 2+POC
65823 **Super City Playset** Camaro Convertible 3+POC
65868 **Power Launcher** Camaro Convertible 2+POC
65875 **Construction Site** Peterbilt Dump Truck 3+POC
65884 **Super Construction Site** Dodge Ram, Peterbilt Dump Truck & Ford Stake Bed Truck 3+POC
67345 **Motorized Starter Set** Power Pistons 3+POC
7996 **Criss Cross Crash® set** pink Toyota MR2, mtlfk silver Zender Fact 4, lime yellow Ferrari Testarossa 5+POC

1998

1684 **Anniversary Edition G-Force Stunt Set** Prowler 15
16539 **Toy Story Super Stunt Set** Red Baron 14
16871 **Construction Playset** Peterbilt Dump Truck 2+POC
17325 **Starter Set** Power Pipes 18
17429 **Kyle Petty Speedway Set** Pontiac Stocker 5+POC
18329 **Dash 'n Crash Set** Lexus SC400 2+POC
19309 **Fire Station** Fire-Eater 2+POC
24235 **Criss Cross Crash Set** 50
24851 **G-Force Burnout** Porsche 930 15
65696 **Police Station** Oldsmobile Aurora 10
65784 **Car Wash** different cars 2+POC
65790 **McDonald's Drive-In** different cars 2+POC
65790 **Super Highway Set** different cars 2+POC
65867 **Long Hauler** with either
a. Rig Wrecker 4
b. Ambulance 4
c. '57 Chevy 4
d. Dragster 4

65870 **Cement Loading Dock** Ford Stake Bed Truck 2+POC
65874 **Car Crusher Set** VW Bug 2+POC
65885 **Deluxe Auto Service Center** Peterbilt Dump Truck, Zender Fact 4 2+POC
65898 **30th Anniv. Cargo Carrier** 10
65742 **Race & Play Case** 4

1999

1684 **G-Force Nite Glow Set** Mercedes SLK 15
22082 **Alien Attack Track Set** Speed Machine 15
23580 **Toy Story 2 Super Stunt Set** Classic Nomad 15
25497 **Viper Strike Starter Set** 2+POC
25770 **Big Air Stunt Ramp** 15
65659 **Deluxe World Train Set** Train + '97 Corvette, Classic Cobra, 25th Anniv. Countach, Toyota MR2, '57 T-Bird 55
65660 **America's Highway Set** Oldsmobile Aurora, Ambulance 18
65698 **Road Race Play Track** Toyota MR2 10
65768 **Super Police Set** Ambulance, Oldsmobile Aurora 20
65786 **Fed Ex World Service Center** Ambulance 10
65789 **Shell Gas Station** different cars 2+POC
65820 **Super Track Set** '58 Corvette plus 2 other cars 18
68992 **Deluxe World Downtown Playset** Ambulance, Toyota MR2, '97 Corvette 20
69553 **Ferrari Dealership** Ferrari 348 6
69555 **Radical Roadway** '80s Camaro 10
68689 **Metro Bus Station** '96 Mustang Convertible 18
'99 Power Express Train Set '59 Impala 50

2000

25771 **Motorized Tornado Twister** Pontiac Rageous, Ford GT-40 15
28603 **Cosmic Blast Set** Speed Shark 9
28774 **Spider Slam Set** Twang Thang 9
28775 **Wrech 'n' Roll Set** Ford F-150 9
29010 **Pick-up Truck Challenge** Chevy 1500 15
29422 **Fireball Set** Road Rocket, Power Pistion 20
52575 **Motorized Starter Set** Krazy 8s 9
52580 **Spinnin' Rim** Seared Tuner 9
52581 **Crash Canyon** Roll Cage 9

2001

88217 **Rescue Center** Ford Aerostar 7
88459 **Gas Station** Dodge Viper RT/10 7
88460 **Auto Dealership** '97 Corvette 7
88461 **McDonald's** '57 Chevy 7
88462 **Go Kart Test Track** Go Kart 12
88463 **Rock 'n' Roll Cafe** '57 T-Bird 12
88464 **Metro Tech Police Force** Aurora Police Car 7

2002

88465 **Hot Rod Boulevard** 9
89706 **Detail Center** 7
65740 **Super Highway** '59 Caddy 9
89075 **Detail Center** Shoebox 7
89076 **McDonald's** '65 Corvette 7
89077 **Gas Station** Mustang Mach 1 7
89078 **Crash Test Track** Firebird 7
89087 **Speed Shift Duel** Track T 12
89088 **Tow & Tune** Tow Jam 12
89089 **Nitro Hill Race** Pikes Peak Celica 12
89090 **Metro City Police Force** Malestrom, Pontiac Rageous 15
Soakin' Speedway Set Silhouette II, Flashfire 15
Ultimate Police Chase Set '97 Corvette 12

Values are shown in U.S. dollars, first price is for mint, second is for mint packaged vehicles only. See pages 15-16 for grading guide to determine value for cars in lesser conditions.

Number Packs

This list consists of all Collector Number packs from 1989 through 2002. Unlike Collector Number packs issued prior to 1989, these new packs command a premium, and are thus listed here with value estimates. Collector packs for earlier series (1976-79, 1987-88, and 1988 experimental packs), currently sell for the same price as identical packs without numbers. Values for these are listed in the color section.

1 Old Number 5, red; bw 175
2 Sol-Aire CX4, black; uh, dk. blue in tampo 22
2 Sol-Aire CX4, black; uhg 185
2 Sol-Aire CX4, black; hoc 45
3 Wheel Loader, yellow; ct 15
4 XT-3, purple; bw, lighter purple 20
5 Good Humor Truck, white; bw, large rear window 18
5 Good Humor Truck, white; bw, small rear window 12
5 Good Humor Truck, white; sp5 6
5 Good Humor Truck, white; sp7 16
5 Good Humor Truck, white; dw3 5
6 Blazer 4x4, black; ct 85
6 Blazer 4x4, black; cts 110
6 Blazer 4x4, blue; ct 30
6 Blazer 4x4, blue; cts 40
7 Troop Convoy, olive 235
8 Vampyra, purple; uh, lighter color 15
8 Vampyra, purple; bw 15
9 Hiway Hauler, red; gyg 35
10 Baja Breaker, white; ct 100
11 '31 Doozie, maroon; ww 50
12 Roll Patrol, olive; ctb 375
13 Delivery Van, red; gych 25
14 '58 Corvette Coupe, red; rrch 45
15 Peterbilt Tank Truck, yellow; bw 50
16 (CAT) Earth Mover, yellow; cty 40
17 Suzuki QuadRacer, yellow; cty 32
18 Mercedes 540K, black; bw 25
19 Shadow Jet, yellow; bw, blue in tampo 30
19 Shadow Jet, yellow; bw, maroon in tampo 100
20 Rocketank, olive 25
21 Nissan Hardbody, white; ct 45
21 Nissan Hardbody, white; cts 65
22 Talbot Lago, white; ww 28
23 '80s Firebird, black; bw 20
23 '80s Firebird, yellow; bw 18
23 '80s Firebird, yellow; bw, w/black tail lights 35
24 Highway Hauler, red; bw, long Pepsi logo 30
24 Highway Hauler, turquoise; bw, OP lt. red in tampo 20
26 '65 Mustang Conv., lt.blue; ww 32
26 '65 Mustang Conv., metf.blue; ww 30
26 '65 Mustang Conv., white; ww 235
27 Command Tank, olive 40
28 '37 Bugatti, blue; ww, blue fenders 22
28 '37 Bugatti, blue; sp7, blue fenders 12
28 '37 Bugatti, blue; ww, yellow fenders 25
28 '37 Bugatti, blue; bw 50
28 '37 Bugatti, yellow; ww 40
28 '37 Bugatti, yellow; bw 110
29 Tail Gunner, olive; ctsb 145
29 Tail Gunner, olive; ctb 100
30 '80s Corvette, blue; gw, tan bag in back 300
31 Classic Cobra, red; bw, no #427 on hood 10
31 Classic Cobra, red; sp7, black plastic base 10
31 Classic Cobra, red; sp7, metal base 25
31 Classic Cobra, red; sp7, black metal base 6
32 Sharkruiser, grey; uh 10
32 Sharkruiser, grey; hoc 20
33 Camaro Z-28, red; gw 40
33 Camaro Z-28, red; gw, metal base 30
33 Camaro Z-28, red; bw, plastic base 12
33 Camaro Z-28, red; uh, plastic base 8
33 Camaro Z-28, red; uh, black metal base 18
33 Camaro Z-28, orange; uh 135
33 Camaro Z-28, orange; bw 12
33 Camaro Z-28, purple; bw 12
34 Bulldozer, yellow 50
35 Ferrari Testarossa, red; uh, tan interior 15
35 Ferrari Testarossa, red; uh, black interior 10
35 Ferrari Testarossa, black; uhg 6
35 Ferrari Testarossa, black; sp3g 8
35 Ferrari Testarossa, black; lwgd 4
36 Baja Bug, white; bw 50
37 Hot Bird, black; gw, red interior 30
37 Hot Bird, black; gw, tan interior 125
37 Hot Bird, blue; gw, tan interior 30
37 Hot Bird, blue; uh, tan interior 22
37 Hot Bird, white; gw 18
37 Hot Bird, white; hoc 25
37 Hot Bird, white; uh 12
37 Hot Bird, white; uh, tan interior 60
37 Hot Bird, white; uhg 250
38 (CAT) Dump Truck, yellow; cty, metal dump 20
38 (CAT) Dump Truck, yellow; cty, plastic dump 10
39 Monster 'Vette, purple; ct 45
39 Monster 'Vette, purple; cts 60
39 Monster 'Vette, yellow; cts 185
39 Monster 'Vette, yellow; ct 165
40 Power Plower, black; ct 20
42 Oshkosh Snow Plow, orange; cto, all metal 35
42 Oshkosh Snow Plow, orange; cto, plastic top 18
42 Oshkosh Snow Plow, green; ct, green top & bottom 25
42 Oshkosh Snow Plow, green; ct, plastic top & green bottom 15
42 Oshkosh Snow Plow, green; cts, green top & bottom 25
42 Oshkosh Snow Plow, green; cts, plastic top & green bottom 15
43 Tall Ryder, silver; ct 50
43 Tall Ryder, silver; cts 60
44 Classic Caddy, blue; ww 18
44 Classic Caddy, blue; sp5 12
44 Classic Caddy, blue; dw3 6
45 Rescue Ranger, red; bw 22
46 Rig Wrecker, white; bw 95
47 '57 Chevy, turquoise; uh 200
47 '57 Chevy, turquoise; gw 250
48 Passion, white; sp5, white stripe around tire 40
49 Gulch Stepper, red; ct 18
49 Gulch Stepper, red; cts 22
49 Gulch Stepper, red; ct, no Penzoil tampo 22
50 Rolls Royce Phaetom II, met. blue; ww 500
51 '40s Woodie, yellow; bw 1300
52 Delivery Truck, white; bw 45
53 Zombot, gold; uh 10
53 Zombot, gold; hoc 18
54 Nissan 300ZX, met. red; uh 18
54 Nissan 300ZX, white; gw 200
54 Nissan 300ZX, white; uh 28
55 Road Roller, yellow 12
56 Bronco 4-Wheeler, turquoise; ct 40
56 Bronco 4-Wheeler, white; ct 110
57 3-Window '34, purple; bw 40
58 Blown Camaro Z-28, turquoise; gw 110
58 Blown Camaro Z-28, turquoise; uh 55
58 Blown Camaro Z-28, turquoise; bw 90
59 Sheriff Patrol, blue; bw 45
59 Sheriff Patrol, black; bw 12
59 Sheriff Patrol, black; sp7 15
60 Lamborghini Countach, white; uh 18
62 Alien, red; uh 10
62 Alien, red; sp5 5
62 Alien, red; ho5 5
63 Radar Ranger, silver; dw3ct 8
63 Radar Ranger, silver; ct 12
63 Radar Ranger, silver; cts 40
63 Radar Ranger, silver; ctb 40
65 VW Bug, turquoise; bw 50
65 VW Bug, red; bw, dk. blue in tampo 20
65 VW Bug, red; bw, turquoise in tampo 40
66 Custom Corvette, red; uh 55
67 '32 Ford Delivery, yellow; bw 35
68 T-Bucket, yellow; bw 12
68 T-Bucket, yellow; sp5 10
69 Ferrari F40, red; uh 8
69 Ferrari F40, red; uhg 10
69 Ferrari F40, red; sp5g 5
69 Ferrari F40, red; sp3g 5
70 Chevy Stocker, black; bw, with Union or Valvoline tampo 35
70 Chevy Stocker, black; bw, no Union or Valvoline tampo 20
71 Ambulance, white; bw 10
71 Ambulance, white; sp7 22
71 Ambulance, white; dw3 6
71 Ambulance, yellow; sp5 8
72 School Bus, yellow; bw 6
72 School Bus, black; ho5 8
73 Street Roader, white; ct 12
73 Street Roader, white; cts 65
74 GT Racer, purple; uh, with V in tampo 18
74 GT Racer, purple; uh, no V in tampo 12
74 GT Racer, purple; bw, no V in tampo 15
75 Pontiac Banshee, red; uh 10
75 Pontiac Banshee, red; uhg 225
75 Pontiac Banshee, red; sp5 6
75 Pontiac Banshee, red; sp7 6
76 (Kenworth) Big Rig, black; bw 7
76 (Kenworth) Big Rig, black; sp7 6
77 Bywayman, maroon; ct 45
77 Bywayman, maroon; ctw 175
77 Bywayman, black; ct, lg. headlights & grill bars 18
77 Bywayman, metf.blue; ct 20
77 Bywayman, metf.blue; ct, red interior 125
78 Peterbilt Cement Truck, red; bw 55
79 Big Bertha, olive 25
80 Porsche 959, metf.red; uh 22
80 Porsche 959, red; uh, #7 tampo 18
80 Porsche 959, red; uh, #59 in tampo 18
80 Porsche 959, red; hoc, #59 in tampo 30
81 Ratmobile, white; uh 4
81 Ratmobile, white; hoc 12
82 Fire Eater, red; bw 8
83 Tank Gunner, olive; bw 75
84 Funny Car, red; bw 55
86 Propper Chopper, white with yellow triangle 40
86 Propper Chopper, white no yellow triangle 15
87 Purple Passion, purple; ww, lines 20
87 Purple Passion, purple; ww, flames 15
88 T-Bird Stocker, red; bw, Motorcraft 40
88 T-Bird Stocker, red; bw, Motorcraft/all small wheels 50
88 T-Bird Stocker, white; uh, Havoline tampo 22
88 T-Bird Stocker, white; bw 300
89 Mini Truck, turquoise; uh 10
89 Mini Truck, turquoise; hoc 300
90 Mongoose Dragster, blue; sp5 25
91 Snake Dragster, yellow; sp5 25
92 Mercedes 380SEL, black; gw 45
92 Mercedes 380SEL, black; uh 18
92 Mercedes 380SEL, black; hoc 20
94 Auburn 852, red; ww 15
94 Auburn 852, red; bw 175
95 '55 Chevy, yellow; bw 20
95 '55 Chevy, white; bw 30
98 Nissan Custom Z, met. red; uh 15
98 Nissan Custom Z, met. red; hoc 25
98 Nissan Custom Z, met. red; uhg 260
99 Ford Stake Bed Truck, metf. blue; bw 12
100 Peterbilt Dump Truck, red; bw 7
100 Peterbilt Dump Truck, red; bww 100
100 Peterbilt Dump Truck, red; sp7 6
100 Peterbilt Dump Truck, red; dw3 4
100 Peterbilt Dump Truck, red; sp3 4
102 Surf Patrol, yellow; ct 8
103 Range Rover, white; ct 6
104 Turbostreak, fl.red; bw, painted rear wing 110
104 Turbostreak, fl.red; bw, unpainted rear wing-wt.decal 20
105 Peugeot 205, white; bw 100
106 VW Golf, red; bw 15
106 VW Golf, white; bw 65
108 Ramp Truck, white; bw, dark windows 18
108 Ramp Truck, white; bw, clear windows 25
110 Trailbuster, turquoise; ct, blue tampo 15
110 Trailbuster, turquoise; ct, black tampo 35
111 Street Beast, white; ww 8
112 Limozeen, white; ww 12
113 Speed Shark, maroon; bw 65
113 Speed Shark, purple; bw 8
113 Speed Shark, black; bw 5
113 Speed Shark, black; sp5 4
114 Pontiac Fiero 2M4, red; uh 12
114 Pontiac Fiero 2M4, red; bw 150
114 Pontiac Fiero 2M4, black; bw, black base 12
114 Pontiac Fiero 2M4, black; bw, metal base 25
114 Pontiac Fiero 2M4, black; uh 15
114 Pontiac Fiero 2M4, black; hoc 22
115 Roll Patrol, olive; ctb 25
116 Mazda MX-5 Miata, red; bw, tampo on left side 10
116 Mazda MX-5 Miata, red; bw, tampo hood only 15
117 Classic Ferrari, yellow; bw, chrome base 20
117 Classic Ferrari, yellow; bw, yellow plastic base 12
117 Classic Ferrari, yellow; bw, black pipes 8
117 Classic Ferrari, yellow; sp7 6
118 Ferrari 348, yellow; uh 10
118 Ferrari 348, yellow; hoc 20
122 Toyota MR2 Rally, white; uh, black plastic light bar 40
122 Toyota MR2 Rally, white; uh, chrome light bar 12
122 Toyota MR2 Rally, white; hoc, chrome light bar 20
123 Lamborghini Diablo, red; uh 12
125 Zender Fact 4, metf.grey; uh, Zender in yellow on side 12
125 Zender Fact 4, metf.grey; uh, no tampo 8
125 Zender Fact 4, metf.grey; hoc, no tampo 18
125 Zender Fact 4, metf.grey; uhg, no tampo 200
126 Chevy Lumina, red; bw, small wheels 8
126 Chevy Lumina, red; bw, large wheels-narrow seat guard 30
127 Power Plower, metf.purple; ct 25
127 Power Plower, dk. purple; ct 15
127 Power Plower, lt.purple; ct 12
128 Baja Breaker, purple; bw 10
129 Suzuki QuadRacer, white; cty 15
129 Suzuki QuadRacer, white; ct 10
131 Nissan Hardbody, black; ct, plastic base-pale lt.pink tampo 15
131 Nissan Hardbody, black; ct, metal base 30
131 Nissan Hardbody, white; ct, plastic base 60
131 Nissan Hardbody, black; ct, yellow interior 12
131 Nissan Hardbody, black; cts 15
131 Nissan Hardbody, black; dw3ct 10
131 Nissan Hardbody, red; dw3ct 6
133 Shadow Jet, met. purple; bw, green "Inter" 8
133 Shadow Jet, met. purple; bw, yellow "Inter" 30
133 Shadow Jet, met. purple; bw, green "Inter", small front wheels 25
134 Mercedes 540K, white; bw 20
135 '32 Ford Delivery, turquoise; bw 15
135 '32 Ford Delivery, turquoise; sp7 10
135 '32 Ford Delivery, purple; rrgy 50
135 '32 Ford Delivery, purple; rrgy, Temecula on roof 200
136 '56 Flashsider, turquoise; uh 10
136 '56 Flashsider, turquoise; hoc 30
136 '56 Flashsider, turquoise; ho5 8
136 '56 Flashsider, turquoise; ho5w 6
136 '56 Flashsider, turquoise; sp5 6
136 '56 Flashsider, turquoise; sp5, chrome windows 20
137 Goodyear Blimp, white; Rev it up/Hot Wheels on the inside 6
137 Goodyear Blimp, white; #1 in tires/Hot Wheels on the inside 6
140 Flashfire, black; uh 8
140 Flashfire, black; hoc 20
140 Flashfire, black; dw3 4
140 Flashfire, black; sp3 20
140 Flashfire, black; ho5 12
140 Flashfire, black; ho5w 8
141 Shock Factor, black; ct, pink tampo 12
141 Shock Factor, black; ct, red tampo 60
142 Hiway Hauler, red; bw 15
143 Recycling Truck, orange; bw 8
143 Recycling Truck, lt. green; sp7 6
144 Oshkosh Cement Truck, white; bw, dk. red barrel 8
145 Tractor, yellow; ct 15
145 Tractor, red; ct 6
145 Tractor, red; dw3 4
145 Tractor, green; dw3yct, yellow cage 6
145 Tractor, unpainted 85
146 Bulldozer, yellow 5
147 Tank Truck, red; bw, Unocal 12
147 Tank Truck, red; sp7 8
147 Tank Truck, orange; sp7 5
147 Tank Truck, orange; dw3 5
148 Porsche 930, purple; bw 90
148 Porsche 930, red; bw 12
148 Porsche 930, red; sp5 6
148 Porsche 930, fluorescent green; bw 110
149 BMW 850i, blue; uh 8
149 BMW 850i, blue; hoc 15
149 BMW 850i, blue; pow 10
150 BMW 323, black; uh, BMW on rear 15
150 BMW 323, black; bw, BMW on rear 12
150 BMW 323, black; uh, no BMW on rear 12
150 BMW 323, black; hoc, no BMW on rear 22
151 Ford Aerostar, met. purple; bw 10
153 Thunderstreak, yellow; bw 12
153 Thunderstreak, blue; bw, no 1 in front 10
153 Thunderstreak, blue; bw, 1 in front 10
154 '59 Caddy, pearl white; ww 8
155 Turboa, yellow; uh 8
155 Turboa, yellow; hoc 15
156 Rodzilla, purple; uh, purple base 6
156 Rodzilla, purple; uh, reddish purple base 15
156 Rodzilla, purple; hoc 20
157 '57 Chevy, yellow; uh 20
157 '57 Chevy, yellow; hoc 30
158 Mercedes Unimog, white; ct 8
159 Big Bertha, olive 8
160 Command Tank, white cam.; dk. grey tampo 8
161 Roll Patrol, tan; ct 18
161 Roll Patrol, tan; ctb 12
161 Roll Patrol, tan; bwb 10
161 Roll Patrol, tan; ctb, star tampo on hood 18
162 '65 Mustang Convertible, red; ww 15
162 '65 Mustang Convertible, dark red; ww 10
162 '65 Mustang Convertible, red; sp7 8
162 '65 Mustang Convertible, red; sp5 6
163 Talbot Lago, metf.red; ww 20
164 Mercedes 540K, metf.blue; bw 6
164 Mercedes 540K, metf.blue; sp5 6
164 Mercedes 540K, metf.blue; sp7 8
164 Mercedes 540K, metf.blue; sp3 5
164 Mercedes 540K, metf.blue; dw3 5
164 Mercedes 540K, metf.blue; ho5 5
165 Suzuki QuadRacer, dk. pink; ct 12
166 Vampyra, black; bw, purple, green and yellow tampo 5
166 Vampyra, black; uh 6
166 Vampyra, black; hoc, yellow, green and purple tampo 30
166 Vampyra, black; uh, no tampo on wings 12
167 '80s Firebird, orange; bw, with extra lightning bolt 35
167 '80s Firebird, orange; bw, without extra lightning bolt 25
168 GT Racer, black; bw, green, yellow and pink tampo 10
169 Sol-Aire CX4, blue; uh, metal base 25
169 Sol-Aire CX4, blue; uh, plastic base 12
169 Sol-Aire CX4, blue; hoc, plastic base 20
170 Chevy Stocker, metf.orange; bw 15

Collector Number Packs

171 VW Bug, purple; bw 18
171 VW Bug, purple; sp3 6
172 Mazda MX-5 Miata, yellow; bw 8
172 Mazda MX-5 Miata, yellow; liw 18
172 Mazda MX-5 Miata, yellow; sp7 60
172 Mazda MX-5 Miata, dk. mf.red; sp7 5
172 Mazda MX-5 Miata, dk. mf.red; sp5 5
172 Mazda MX-5 Miata, dk. mf.red; sp3 4
174 Limozeen, metf.blue; ww 18
175 Ferrari 348, white; hoc 18
175 Ferrari 348, white; uh 6
176 Lamborghini Diablo, blue; uh, lt.blue rear fin 8
176 Lamborghini Diablo, blue; uh, dk. blue rear fin 15
177 Zender Fact 4, magenta; hoc 18
177 Zender Fact 4, magenta; uh 6
178 Hot Bird, black; uh 12
179 Porsche 959, purple; hoc 20
179 Porsche 959, purple; uh 8
181 Fiero 2M4, metf.green; uh 8
181 Fiero 2M4, metf.green; hoc 20
182 Shadow Jet, green; bw, yellow in tampo 6
182 Shadow Jet, green; bw, blue in tampo 6
182 Shadow Jet, green; sp5 6
183 VW Golf, metf.dk. green; bw 35
183 VW Golf, metf.pink; bw, chrome plastic base 20
183 VW Golf, metf.pink; bw, black plastic basr 10
184 380 SEL, metf.blue; hoc 20
184 380 SEL, metf.blue; uh 8
185 Propper Chopper, white; police tampo 8
185 Propper Chopper, yellow; black blades, red base 12
185 Propper Chopper, yellow; black blades, black base 8
186 Ford Aerostar, white; bw, Phone # 15
186 Ford Aerostar, white; bw, no Phone # 10
187 Ramp Truck, yellow; bw 12
187 Ramp Truck, yellow; sp7 6
188 Hummer, lt.tan; ct 10
188 Hummer, lt.brown; ct 8
188 Hummer, lt.brown; ct, no hood tampo-plastic body-black metal base 6
188 Hummer, lt.brown; dw3 5
188 Hummer, white; dw3ct 5
189 Gleamer Patrol, silver; bw, tan interior 18
189 Gleamer Patrol, silver; bw, black interior 10
189 Gleamer Patrol, dark silver; bw, black interior 8
190 '57 T-Bird, gl.gold; bw 10
191 Aeroflash, gl.rose; uh 12
191 Aeroflash, gl.rose; uhg, metallic silver base 20
191 Aeroflash, gl.rose; uhg, metal base 10
192 Corvette Stingray, gl.dk. green; bw 22
192 Corvette Stingray, gl.silver; bw 12
192 Corvette Stingray, gl.silver; uh 10
193 Porsche 959, gl.dk. pink; uh 10
193 Porsche 959, gl.silver; uh 16
194 Goodyear Blimp, white; #1 in tires 5
194 Goodyear Blimp, white; Rev it up! 5
195 Troop Convoy, lt.brown; bwb 8
196 3-Window '34, white; bw, purple fenders-thick lines 18
196 3-Window '34, white; bw, pink fenders 80
196 3-Window '34, yellow-green; bw 225
197 Split Window '63, blue; bw 22
197 Split Window '63, blue; ww 10
197 Split Window '63, blue; ww, grey plastic base 10
197 Split Window '63, blue; sp5, grey plastic base 6
198 Path Beater, fl.lime; ct 10
198 Path Beater, fl.lime; ctb 18
198 Path Beater, fl.lime; dw3ct 10
199 Double Demon, fl.yellow; uh, chrome interior 6
199 Double Demon, fl.yellow; uh, black interior 6
199 Double Demon, yellow; uh, black interior 6
200 Custom Corvette, white; uh 8
200 Custom Corvette, metf.dk. purple; uh 8
200 Custom Corvette, metf.dk. purple; sp5 8
200 Custom Corvette, metf.dk. purple; sp7 12
200 Custom Corvette, metf.dk. purple; lwch 6
201 Oshkosh Snow Plow, orange; cto 8
201 Oshkosh Snow Plow, orange; ctb 15
201 Oshkosh Snow Plow, orange; dw3ct 6
202 1993 Camaro, purple; uh, white interior-dark windows 8
202 1993 Camaro, purple; uh, white interior-clear windows 12
203 Jaguar XJ220, silver; uh, open spoiler 10
203 Jaguar XJ220, silver; uh, closed spoiler 8
203 Jaguar XJ220, silver; uhg 35
203 Jaguar XJ220, dk. blue; uhg 20
203 Jaguar XJ220, dk. blue; uh 8
203 Jaguar XJ220, dk. blue; lwgd 10
204 Oscar Mayer Wienermobile, red; bwb 6
204 Oscar Mayer Wienermobile, red; bw 6
204 Oscar Mayer Wienermobile, red; sp7 6
204 Oscar Mayer Wienermobile, red; ho5 6
205 Treadator, red 6
205 Treadator, fl.lt.green 6
205 Treadator, green 4
206 Pipe Jammer, yellow; uh 10
207 Vector (Avtech), met. purple; uh 6
207 Vector (Avtech), met. purple; sp5 5
208 Avus Quattro, grey; uh 6
208 Avus Quattro, grey; sp5 4
209 Lexus SC400, black; uh 6
210 Viper RT/10, red; uh 8
210 Viper RT/10, red; uhg 20
210 Viper RT/10, red; sp5 100
210 Viper RT/10, red; lwch 6
210 Viper RT/10, yellow; uhg 15
210 Viper RT/10, met. green; uhg 8
210 Viper RT/10, met. green; sp5g 10
210 Viper RT/10, met. green; sp3g 6
210 Viper RT/10, met. green; lwgd 5
211 Twin Mill II, fl.lime; uh, chrome base 15
211 Twin Mill II, fl.lime; uh, grey base 8
211 Twin Mill II, fl.lime; uh, black base 45
212 Silhouette II, purple; uh, chrome plastic base 8
212 Silhouette II, purple; uh, grey plastic base 6
212 Silhouette II, purple; ho5, grey plastic base 6
213 '57 Chevy, aqua; uh, with tampo on door 18
213 '57 Chevy, aqua; uh, w/o tampo on door 20
213 '57 Chevy, aqua; uhg, w/o tampo on door 18
213 '57 Chevy, aqua; sp5, w/o tampo on door 8
214 Swingfire, blue; ww 8
214 Swingfire, blue; sp7 6
214 Swingfire, blue; dw3 4
214 Street Beast, unpainted; dw3 95
215 Auburn 852, unpainted 95
215 Auburn 852, red; ww 15
215 Auburn 852, red; sp5 8
216 Fat Fendered '40, purple; bw 25
217 '40s Woodie, aqua; bw 8
217 '40s Woodie, aqua; sp7 8
217 '40s Woodie, aqua; sp5 6
217 '40s Woodie, aqua; ho5 4
217 '40s Woodie, candy red; bw, Hemet Run 35
218 Street Roader, metf.green; ct 10
219 Gulch Stepper, fl.lime; ct 10
220 Bywayman, white; ct, blue interior 6
220 Bywayman, white; dw3ct 6
220 Bywayman, white; ct, black interior 8
221 Range Rover, black; ct 6
221 Range Rover, black; dw3ct 5
222 Blazer 4X4, met. blue; ct 8
222 Blazer 4X4, met. blue; btb 15
223 Baja Bug, metf.red; bw 35
224 Zombot, chrome blue; uh 14
224 Zombot, black chrome; uh, pink gun 10
224 Zombot, black chrome; uh, orange gun 5
224 Zombot, black chrome; sp7, orange gun 5
225 Limozeen, metf.black; ww 8
226 Ferrari 348, metf.pink; uh 8
226 Ferrari 348, metf.pink; sp5 6
226 Ferrari 348, black; sp5 6
226 Ferrari 348, black; sp7 10
227 Lamborghini Diablo, yellow; uh 6
227 Lamborghini Diablo, yellow; sp5 8
227 Lamborghini Diablo, purple; sp5 6
227 Lamborghini Diablo, purple; dw3 4
227 Lamborghini Diablo, purple; ho5 4
228 Zender Fact 4, dk. blue; uh, tinted windows 10
228 Zender Fact 4, dk. blue; uh, clear windows 35
228 Zender Fact 4, fl.green; uh, dark windows-orange in tampo 12
228 Zender Fact 4, fl.green; uh, clear windows-orange in tampo 30
228 Zender Fact 4, fl.green; uh, clear windows-yellow in tampo 10
228 Zender Fact 4, dk. red; sp5 6
229 Mercedes 380 SEL, metf.pink; uh 8
230 XT-3, white; bw, red dome 8
230 XT-3, white; bw, blue dome 55
230 XT-3, metf.blue; bw 6
230 XT-3, metf.blue; sp5 6
231 Mini Truck, orange; uh 8
231 Mini Truck, orange; dw3 4
231 Mini Truck, orange; ho5 6
231 Mini Truck, orange; ho5w 18
231 Mini Truck, orange; sp5 6
232 Lamborghini Countach, red; uh 8
232 Lamborghini Countach, red; uhg 10
232 Lamborghini Countach, white; ho5 6
233 Toyota MR2 Rally, white; uh 8
233 Toyota MR2 Rally, white; sp3 8
233 Toyota MR2 Rally, white; dw3 4
233 Toyota MR2 Rally, white; ho5 4
233 Toyota MR2 Rally, white; lwch, purple, green and blue tampo 4
233 Toyota MR2 Rally, white; lwch, met. blue in tampo 4
233 Toyota MR2 Rally, black; sp5 130
233 Toyota MR2 Rally, black; sp3 75
233 Toyota MR2 Rally, black; uh 85
234 Nissan Custom Z, purple; uh 8
234 Nissan Custom Z, purple; uhg 8
234 Nissan Custom Z, purple; sp5g 4
234 Nissan Custom Z, purple; lwgd 4
234 Nissan Custom Z, purple; sp3gd 4
235 Turbo Streak, fl.lime; bw 6
236 Ford Aerostar, black; bw 12
237 Ford Stake Bed Truck, red; bw 8
237 Ford Stake Bed Truck, red; sp7 6
237 Ford Stake Bed Truck, red; sp3 8
237 Ford Stake Bed Truck, red; sp5 6
238 Hiway Hauler, purple; bw 12
239 Mercedes-Benz Unimog, ct 12
239 Mercedes-Benz Unimog, ctb 10
239 Mercedes-Benz Unimog, ctw 8
239 Mercedes-Benz Unimog, dw3ctw 6
242 1993 Camaro, met. blue; bw 8
242 1993 Camaro, met. blue; uh 175
242 1993 Camaro, blue; bw 35
242 1993 Camaro, blue; uh 150
244 No Fear Race Car, black; bw 8
244 No Fear Race Car, black; sp7 5
244 Hot Wheels 500, unpainted; ho5 80
245 Driven To The Max, orange; bw 12
245 Driven To The Max, lime; sp5 6
246 Shadow Jet II, chrome black; uh 4
246 Shadow Jet II, chrome black; sp7 4
246 Shadow Jet II, chrome black; sp5 4
246 Shadow Jet II, chrome black; sp3 3
246 Shadow Jet II, chrome black; ho5 3
247 Rigor Motor, dk. red; bw 6
248 Splittin' Image II, black; uhpk 12
248 Splittin' Image II, black; uhpk, red windows 8
248 Splittin' Image II, black; uh 18
248 Splittin' Image II, black; sp7o 6
248 Splittin' Image II, black; sp7 6
249 Fuji Blimp, white 6
250 Talbot Lago, metf.black; ww 8
250 Talbot Lago, metf.black; sp7 5
251 Gulch Stepper, red; ct 6
251 Gulch Stepper, black; ct, roof tampo yellow in red 12
251 Gulch Stepper, black; ct, roof tampo reversed 50
251 Gulch Stepper, black; dw3ct 6
252 Street Roader, white; ct 4
252 Street Roader, white; dw3 4
253 Mercedes 380SEL, metf.dk. red; uh 6
253 Mercedes 380SEL, metf.dk. red; sp5 6
253 Mercedes 380SEL, metf.dk. red; dw3 4
253 Mercedes 380SEL, metf.dk. red; sp7 4
254 Sol-Aire CX4, metf.blue; uhg 6
254 Sol-Aire CX4, metf.blue; sp7 6
254 Sol-Aire CX4, metf.blue; lwgd 4
255 BMW 850i, dk. metf.blue; uh 4
255 BMW 850i, dk. metf.blue; uhg 6
255 BMW 850i, dk. metf.blue; sp3g 6
255 BMW 850i, dk. metf.blue; lwgd 6
256 80s Firebird, orange-rose; bw 20
257 3-Window '34, metf.grey; bw 15
257 3-Window '34, metf.grey; sp7 10
257 3-Window '34, unpainted 190
258 Blazer 4X4, grey-blue; ct 6
258 Blazer 4X4, grey-blue; ctb 20
259 Lumina Minivan, yellow; bw 6
259 Lumina Minivan, yellow; sp5 5
260 Twin Mill II, black; uh 5
260 Twin Mill II, black; ho5 4
260 Twin Mill II, black; ho5w 10
261 Cyber Cruiser, metf.purple; uh 5
261 Cyber Cruiser, metf.purple; uh, black base 35
262 1993 Camaro, red; uh, tan interior 12
262 1993 Camaro, red; uh, white interior 10
262 1993 Camaro, red; uh, grey base-tan interior 30
262 1993 Camaro, red; sp5, tan interior 6
262 1993 Camaro, red; sp7 55
262 1993 Camaro, metf.blue; uhg 6
262 1993 Camaro, dk. metf.blue; uhg 10
263 Mean Green Passion, green; ww 30
264 Lexus SC400, dk. metf.red; uh 6
264 Lexus SC400, dk. metf.red; sp5 6
264 Lexus SC400, dk. metf.red; sp3 6
264 Lexus SC400, dk. metf.red; bw 4
264 Lexus SC400, dk. metf.red; dw3 4
264 Lexus SC400, dk. metf.red; ho5 5
264 Lexus SC400, dk. metf.red; ho5w 15
265 Olds Aurora, teal green; bw, clear windows 18
265 Olds Aurora, teal green; bw, tinted windows 28
265 Olds Aurora, black; sp7b 6
266 '59 Cadillac, lt.purple; ww 10
266 '59 Cadillac, lt.purple; sp7 8
266 '59 Cadillac, blue; lwgd 8
267 Olds 442 W-30, yellow; bw 8
267 Olds 442 W-30, yellow; sp7 6
268 GM Lean Machine, lime; uh 6
268 GM Lean Machine, lime; sp7 5
268 GM Lean Machine, lime; sp5 5
268 GM Lean Machine, lime; dw3 4
269 Oshkosh Cement Mixer, yellow; bw 8
269 Oshkosh Cement Mixer, yellow; sp5 6
269 Oshkosh Cement Mixer, yellow; sp7 8
269 Oshkosh Cement Mixer, yellow; dw3 4
269 Oshkosh Cement Mixer, yellow; sp3 4
270 Chevy Stocker, metf.orange; uhg 12
270 Chevy Stocker, metf.orange; uhg, red interior 65
270 Chevy Stocker, metf.gold; uhg 50
271 Dragster, mf blue; bw 1200
273 Tail Gunner, white; ctw 10
274 Super Cannon, olive; bww 6
274 Super Cannon, olive; sp5w 6
275 Lumina Stocker, dark blue; sp7 8
275 Lumina Stocker, dark blue; uh 8
275 Lumina Stocker, blue; uh 6
275 Lumina Stocker, blue; uh, Pontiac front 200
276 Hot Wheels 500, dark blue; bw 12
276 Hot Wheels 500, dark blue; sp7 8
276 Hot Wheels 500, dark blue; uh 40
276 Hot Wheels 500, blue; bw 15
276 Hot Wheels 500, blue; sp7 65
277 Side-Splitter, dark blue; bw 10
277 Side-Splitter, blue; bw 10
277 Side-Splitter, dark blue; sp5 6
278 Dragster, dark blue; bw 5
278 Dragster, dark blue; sp5 5
278 Dragster, blue; bw 7
280 Sharkruiser, turquoise; uh, painted base 4
280 Sharkruiser, turquoise; uh 4
280 Sharkruiser, turquoise; sp7 8
281 Turboa, purple; uh 6
281 Turboa, purple; sp7 8
282 '63 Split Window, aqua; bw 6
282 '63 Split Window, aqua; sp5 6
282 '63 Split Window, aqua; sp7 15
284 Flashfire, purple; uh 6
284 Flashfire, purple; sp5, yellow dome 4
284 Flashfire, purple; sp5, orange dome 25
285 Steel Passion, metf.black; ww 12
285 Steel Passion, metf.black; sp7 10
287 Zender Fact 4, metf.black; uh 8
287 Zender Fact 4, metf.black; sp5, clear windows 20
287 Zender Fact 4, metf.black; sp5, tinted windows 6
287 Zender Fact 4, metf.black; sp3 4
289 '56 Flashsider, met. bronze; uh 10
289 '56 Flashsider, met. bronze; sp5 8
289 '56 Flashsider, met. bronze; sp7 10
290 '57 Chevy, metf.black; uh 12
290 '57 Chevy, metf.black; sp5 10
290 '57 Chevy, metf.black; sp7 22
290 '57 Chevy, metf.black; sp5, black interior and windows 50
292 Pearl Passion, pearl purple; ww 8
292 Pearl Passion, pearl purple; sp7 10
293 VW Bug, pearl rose; bw 10
293 VW Bug, pearl rose; sp7 10
293 VW Bug, pearl rose; sp5 25
295 Talbot Lago, pearl blue; ww 6
295 Talbot Lago, pearl blue; sp7 8
296 Jaguar XJ220, pearl white; uh 8
296 Jaguar XJ220, pearl white; sp5 7
296 Jaguar XJ220, pearl white; sp7 12
296 Jaguar XJ220, pearl white; sp3 6
297 Splittin' Image II, metf.black; iwb 12
297 Splittin' Image II, metf.black; sp7 6
298 Twin Mill II, metf.black; iwb 12
298 Twin Mill II, metf.black; sp7 6
299 Silhouette II, metf.black; iwb 15
299 Silhouette II, metf.black; sp7 10
299 Silhouette II, metf.black; iwb, chrome plastic base 20
300 Rigor Motor, metf.black; iwb, black base 15
300 Rigor Motor, metf.black; sp7, black tinted base 10
300 Rigor Motor, metf.black; sp5 8
300 Rigor Motor, metf.black; lwch, red engine 6
302 Mini Truck, lt.brown; uh 8
302 Mini Truck, lt.brown; sp5 6
302 Mini Truck, lt.brown; sp5, orange chassis 60
302 Mini Truck, lt.brown; sp7 8
303 Street Roader, orange; cto 8
303 Street Roader, orange; ct 50
304 Roll Patrol, white; cty 8
304 Roll Patrol, white; ct 35
305 Classic Cobra, fl.lime; sp7, black tinted metal base 15
305 Classic Cobra, fl.lime; sp7, metal base 10
305 Classic Cobra, fl.lime; sp7, plastic base 10
305 Classic Cobra, fl.lime; sp5 65
307 Cyber Cruiser, maroon; hhb 10
308 Vampyra, purple; hhsg 10
308 Vampyra, purple; sp6g 15
308 Vampyra, purple; sp6g, painted base 12
308 Vampyra, purple; lwch 4
310 Shadow Jet, lt.green; hhy 6
310 Shadow Jet, lt.green; hhy, blue chrome engine 75
311 Suzuki QuadRacer, yellow; hhy 10
311 Suzuki QuadRacer, yellow; cts 6
311 Suzuki QuadRacer, yellow; hhy,

blue seat 60
311 Suzuki QuadRacer, lime green; hhy 40
311 Suzuki QuadRacer, lime green; pie 75
312 3-Window '34, turquoise chrome; sp7 12
313 T-Bucket, met. purple; sp5 6
313 T-Bucket, met. purple; sp5, blue engine 12
313 T-Bucket, met. purple; sp5, clear windshield 45
313 T-Bucket, met. purple; sp7 15
315 Ratmobile, black; sp7 6
315 Ratmobile, black; uh 5
316 Limozeen, metf.gold; ww 15
316 Limozeen, metf.gold; sp7 15
317 (Peterbilt) Dump Truck, lime; rtl 25
318 Mercedes Unimog, grey; rto 25
320 '59 Caddy, pearl pink; nrr 35
321 Corvette Stingray, mf aqua; gyg 75
322 Fire Eater, chrome; bw 6
322 Fire Eater, chrome; sp7 10
323 Rodzilla, chrome; uh 5
323 Rodzilla, chrome; sp7 8
323 Rodzilla, chrome; sp7, painted base 12
323 Rodzilla, chrome; uh, painted base 8
325 Propper Chopper, chrome 8
328 School Bus, chrome; bw, tinted windows 35
328 School Bus, chrome; bw, clear windows 18
328 School Bus, chrome; sp7 8
328 School Bus, chrome; sp5 8
326 School Bus, chrome; sp3 15
331 Ford Aerostar, white; sp7 12
332 Blimp, black 6
333 Tank Truck, light blue; sp7 6
335 Hiway Hauler, green; sp7 10
336 Race Truck (Bywayman), grey chrome; ct 10
337 Ramp Truck, purple chrome; sp7 10
337 Ramp Truck, pink chrome; sp7 15
338 Camaro Racer, blue chrome; sp5, name on roof 20
338 Camaro Racer, blue chrome; sp5, no name on roof 10
340 Dragster, blue chrome 10
341 '58 Corvette, fl.pink; sp5 10
341 '58 Corvette, fl.pink; sp7 12
341 '58 Corvette, fl.pink; bw 9
341 '58 Corvette, metf. purple; sp7 12
341 '58 Corvette, metf. purple; sp5 6
341 '58 Corvette, metf. purple; ho5 8
342 Mercedes SL, red; uh 8
342 Mercedes SL, red; sp5 8
342 Mercedes SL, red; sp3 6
342 Mercedes SL, mf black; sp5, red interior 7
342 Mercedes SL, mf black; sp5, tan interior 50
342 Mercedes SL, mf black; sp7 8
342 Mercedes SL, mf black; lwch 4
343 Speed Blaster, metf.blue; uh, pink chrome base 8
343 Speed Blaster, metf.blue; sp5, pink chrome base 8
343 Speed Blaster, metf.blue; uh, chrome base 8
343 Speed Blaster, metf.blue; uh, black base 90
343 Speed Blaster, metf.blue; sp5 6
343 Speed Blaster, green; sp5 5
343 Speed Blaster, green; sp7 35
343 Speed Blaster, green; sp3 4
343 Speed Blaster, green; ho5 6
343 Speed Blaster, green; dw3 4
344 Camaro Convertible, metf.aqua; sp5 6
344 Camaro Convertible, metf.aqua; uh 10
344 Camaro Convertible, metf.aqua; sp3 7
344 Camaro Convertible, red; sp3 6
344 Camaro Convertible, red; sp5 6
344 Camaro Convertible, red; dw3 4
345 Speed-A-Saurus, olive; bw 6
345 Speed-A-Saurus, olive; sp5 4
345 Speed-A-Saurus, purple; sp5 4
346 Hydroplane, dk. blue 5
347 Power Pistons, bronze; sp5 6
347 Power Pistons, bronze; sp7 20
347 Power Pistons, bronze; uh 25
347 Power Pistons, bronze; sp3 8
347 Power Pistons, bronze; sp3, painted base 6
347 Power Pistons, bronze; dw3 4
348 Dodge Ram 1500, met. aqua; sp5 6
348 Dodge Ram 1500, met. aqua; ho5 6
348 Dodge Ram 1500, met. aqua; ho5w 12
349 Power Pipes, dk. purple; sp5 6
349 Power Pipes, dk. purple; sp7 8
349 Power Pipes, dk. purple; sp3 4
349 Power Pipes, dk. purple; ho5 3
350 Ferrari 355, yellow; sp7 10
350 Ferrari 355, yellow; sp5 6
350 Ferrari 355, yellow; sp3 6
350 Ferrari 355, yellow; sp5, painted base 6
350 Ferrari 355, yellow; dw3 4
350 Ferrari 355, yellow; ho5w 12
350 Ferrari 355, yellow; ho5 4
351 Power Rocket, purple; sp5 6
351 Power Rocket, purple; sp5, painted base 10
351 Power Rocket, purple; sp3 4
351 Power Rocket, purple; dw3 4
351 Power Rocket, purple; ho5 4
351 Power Rocket, purple; ho5w 12
351 Power Rocket, purple; sp7gd 5
352 Big Chill, white 8
352 Big Chill, white; orange skis 15
352 Big Chill, white; w/shredder tampo 10
352 Big Chill, white; black tampo 6
353 Olds 442, metf.blue; rtgy 130
354 Gold Passion, gold/black; rtgd 135
355 '67 Camaro, pearl white; rtgy 350
356 '57 T-Bird, metf.black; rtgy 75
357 VW Bug, lt.green; twp 160
358 Split Window '63, dk. met. blue; rtgy 95
359 Stutz Blackhawk, metf.black; rtc 70
360 Rolls Royce, metf.dk. red; iwr 75
361 Classic Caddy, metf.lt.green; iwgd 60
362 Nomad, met. aqua; twc 105
363 Classic Cobra, metf.green; iwgd 125
364 '31 Doozie, yellow; iwy 65
367 Chevy 1500, grey; sp7b, large wheels 15
367 Chevy 1500, grey; sp7b, small wheels 8
367 Chevy 1500, grey; sp5 7
368 Dodge Charger Daytona, red; dw3 6
369 Turbo Flame, white; sp5 6
369 Sizzler, white; ho5 18
369 Road Rocket, green; lwgd 6
369 Road Rocket, green; sp7gd 12
370 Rail Rodder, black; dw, gray replaces chrome 10
370 Rail Rodder, black; dw 8
372 VW Bus, blue; sp5 65
373 Street Cleaver, yellow; sp5, no tampo 8
373 Street Cleaver, yellow; sp5 12
373 Street Cleaver, yellow; sp3 10
373 Street Cleaver, yellow; dw3 8
373 Street Cleaver, yellow; ho5 5
373 Street Cleaver, yellow; ho5w 15
374 Radio Flyer Wagon, red; sp5 6
374 Radio Flyer Wagon, red; bw 8
375 Dogfighter, dk. red; dw3 4
375 Dogfighter, dk. red; sp5 6
375 Dogfighter, dk. red; sp5, gray replaces chrome 10
375 Dogfighter, dk. red; ho5 4
376 Twang Thang, mf silver; sp5 4
377 Ferrari F50, red; lwch 4
378 1996 Mustang GT, metf. red; sp5 10
378 1996 Mustang GT, metf. red; sp3 8
378 1996 Mustang GT, metf. red; sp7 15
378 1996 Mustang GT, metf. red; dw3 5
378 1996 Mustang GT, metf. red; ho5 6
380 Dodge Ram 1500, red; sp7b, no hood tampo 25
380 Dodge Ram 1500, red; sp7b, w/hood tampo 8
380 Dodge Ram 1500, red; sp7bk, no tampo on wheels 15
380 Dodge Ram 1500, grey; sp5 10
381 Ford LTL, grey; sp7b 35
381 Kenworth T600, grey; sp7b 15
382 '56 Flashsider, black; sp7b 10
382 '56 Flashsider, black; sp7b, no tampo on wheels 15
382 Dodge Charger Daytona, red; lwgd 5
382 Dodge Charger Daytona, red; sp7gd 10
382 Dodge Charger Daytona, red; sp7bk 6
383 Nissan Truck, black; ct 7
383 Nissan Truck, black; ct, yellow interior 135
383 Nissan Truck, black; ctb 20
384 '57 T-Bird, white; sp7, orange & green flames 8
384 '57 T-Bird, white; sp7, pink and green flames 8
384 '57 T-Bird, white; sp7, Hot Wheels logo on sides 10
385 Hydroplane, yellow 6
385 Hydroplane, yellow; flames on spoiler are on backwards 25
386 Range Rover, red; ct, part of flames missing 8
386 Range Rover, red; ct 6
387 Oshkosh Snowplow, black; ct 6
387 Oshkosh Snowplow, black; ctb 12
388 Radar Ranger, white; ct 6
389 GM Lean Machine, white; sp5 6
390 Alien, white; sp5 4
391 Treadator, blue chrome 6
391 Treadator, white 45
392 Ramp Truck, metf. blue; sp5 8
392 Ramp Truck, metf. blue; sp7 25
393 Baja Bug, metf. blue; sp5 8
394 '57 Chevy, metf. blue; sp5 10
395 Bywayman, metf. blue; ct 8
395 Bywayman, metf. blue; dw3 12
396 Hummer, pink; ct 8
396 Hummer, pink; dw3 25
397 School Bus, mf purple; sp7 6
398 VW Bug, metf.blue; sp7 10
399 '67 Camaro, green; sp5 10
399 '67 Camaro, green; sp5, tinted windows 30
399 '67 Camaro, green; sp7 75
400 Big Chill, black 4
400 Big Chill, silver 6
401 Street Beast, black; sp7 6
402 Thunderstreak, black; sp7 6
403 Power Pistons, black chrome; sp7 6
404 Porsche 930, mf silver; sp7 8
405 Custom Corvette, purple; sp7 8
405 Custom Corvette, purple; sp7, red interior 60
406 Classic Cobra, white; sp7 10
406 Classic Cobra, white; sp5 90
407 '59 Caddy, black; sp7 8
407 '59 Caddy, black; sp7, white stripe around tire 55
408 Rescue Ranger, orange; sp5 7
408 Rescue Ranger, orange; dw3 4
409 Side-Splitter, white; sp5 4
410 '55 Chevy, orange; sp5 6
410 '55 Chevy, orange; dw3 6
411 '80s Camaro Z-28, white; sp5 6
412 Speed Machine, green; sp7 6
412 Speed Machine, green; sp5 4
413 Silhouette II, purple; sp5 4
414 Propper Chopper, blue 6
415 Roll Patrol, lt.brown; dw3y 6
415 Roll Patrol, lt.brown; cty 10
416 Pizza Vette, lt.brown; sp3 15
417 Pasta Pipes, white; sp3 10
418 Sweet Stocker, white; sp3 55
419 Crunch Chief, white; sp3 6
419 Crunch Chief, white; sp7 5
420 (CAT) Dump Truck, chrome; dw3 30
420 (CAT) Dump Truck, chrome; dw3, black dumper 8
421 '40s Woodie, chrome; sp5 10
421 '40s Woodie, chrome; sp7 20
422 '57 Chevy, chrome; sp5 10
423 Wienermobil, chrome; sp5b 8
424 Ambulance, green; sp5 10
424 Ambulance, green; sp7 4
424 Ambulance, red; sp7 6
425 Rescue Ranger, yellow; sp5 4
426 Flame Stopper, yellow; dw3cty 6
426 Flame Stopper, yellow; cts 15
427 Fire Eater, red; sp5 4
427 Fire Eater, red; sp7 6
428 '40s Woodie, lime yellow; rry, yellow rims 50
428 '40s Woodie, lime yellow; rry, silver rims 75
428 '40s Woodie, lime yellow; rry, gold rims 100
429 Lamborghini Countach, red; iw 35
430 Ferrari 250, grey; rrch 45
431 Jaguar XJ220, green; iwgd 40
432 '59 Caddy, red; rrch 60
433 Dodge Viper, white; iww 75
434 '57 Chevy, mf purple; gych 65
435 Ferrari 355, white; pcgd 45
436 '58 Corvette Coupe, silver; rrch 65
437 Auburn 852, mf gold; gygd 45
438 Dodge Ram 1500, mf red; rrch 50
439 '37 Bugatti, blue; iw 40
440 Monte Carlo Stocker, blue; sp7b 10
440 Monte Carlo Stocker, blue; sp7bgy, no tampo on tires 8
441 Chevy Stocker, black; sp7 8
442 Ferrari F40, white; sp7 6
442 Ferrari F40, white; sp5 4
442 Ferrari F40, white; ho5w 12
443 Ferrari 348, black; sp7 8
443 Ferrari 348, black; sp5 6
443 Ferrari 348, black; ho5 4
444 Aeroflash, white; sp7 7
444 Aeroflash, white; sp7gd 5
445 Jaguar XJ220, green; sp5 8
445 Jaguar XJ220, green; sp7 15
445 Jaguar XJ220, green; dw3 10
446 '32 Ford Delivery, black; sp7 15
447 '63 Split Window, green; sp7 8
447 '63 Split Window, green; sp5 4
447 '63 Split Window, green; sp3 5
448 '67 Camaro, yellow; sp5 8
448 '67 Camaro, yellow; ho5 8
449 Camaro Z-28, orange; sp5 10
449 Camaro Z-28, orange; sp3 6
450 Corvette Stingray, white; sp3 4
450 Corvette Stingray, white; sp5 6
450 Corvette Stingray, white; sp7 15
451 3-Window '34, pink; sp3 12
451 3-Window '34, pink; sp7 10
452 Ferrari 250, mf aqua; sp7 6
452 Ferrari 250, mf aqua; sp5 6
452 Ferrari 250, mf aqua; ho5 4
452 Ferrari 250, mf aqua; ho5w 4
453 Avus Quattro, red; sp5 4
453 Avus Quattro, red; sp7 4
453 Avus Quattro, red; dw3 4
454 Zender Fact 4, white; sp5 4
454 Zender Fact 4, white; sp7 4
455 '65 Mustang Convertible, mf gold; sp7 15
455 '65 Mustang Convertible, mf gold; sp3 10
455 '65 Mustang Convertible, mf gold; sp5 12
455 '65 Mustang Convertible, met. dk. blue; sp5 4
457 Pontiac Banshee, black; sp5 6
457 Pontiac Banshee, purple; sp5 4
458 Speed Shark, purple; sp5 4
460 Zombot, dark grey; sp5 4
461 Enforcer, met. purple; sp5 4
462 '80s Firebird, blue; sp5 8
463 Pontiac Fiero 2M4, lime yellow; sp5 6
463 Pontiac Fiero 2M4, lime yellow; sp5, tampo on sides 6
463 Pontiac Fiero 2M4, lime yellow; lwch 3
464 Blazer 4 x 4, blue; ct 6
464 Blazer 4 x 4, blue; cts 6
467 Peugeot 405, mf dk green; sp5 6
467 Peugeot 405, grey; sp5 6
467 Peugeot 405, grey; lwch 6
468 GT Racer, red; sp5 4
468 GT Racer, red; sp5, tampo on sides 4
468 GT Racer, red; lwch, tampo on sides 4
468 GT Racer, gold; sp5 4
469 Hot Bird, mf gold; sp5, tampo on sides 4
469 Hot Bird, mf gold; sp5 6
469 Hot Bird, mf gold; lwch 4
470 Turbo Streak, white & blue; sp5 4
470 Turbo Streak, white & blue; sp5, tampo on sides 4
471 Velocitor, mf dk blue; sp5 4
471 Velocitor, black; sp5, tampo on sides 40
471 Velocitor, black; lwch 4
472 Buick Stocker, yellow; sp5 4
472 Buick Stocker, yellow; sp5, tampo on sides 4
472 Buick Stocker, yellow; lwch 3
473 Street Beast, green; sp5 4
473 Street Beast, mf silver; sp5 4
474 VW Golf, black; sp5 8
474 VW Golf, black; sp5, tampo on sides 4
474 VW Golf, black; lwch 4
475 Fork Lift, yellow; sp5 4
477 Double Demon, light green; sp5 4
478 Dragon Wagon, lt. green; sp5 4
479 Computer Warrior, grey blue; sp5 4
481 Tall Ryder, green; cts 6
481 Tall Ryder, dark yellow; cts 6
482 (CAT) Earth Mover, yellow; cts 4
483 Thunder Roller, mf dk. red; bw&sp5 8
484 Grizzlor, white; sp5 6
484 Grizzlor, white; sp5, black spots 4
485 Eevil Weevil, orange; sp5 4
486 Command Tank, bk & magenta 4
487 Troop Convoy, mf grey; sp5 6
487 Troop Convoy, mf aqua; sp5 4
488 Sting Rod, mf grey; cts 4
489 Big Bertha, bk & magenta 4
491 Rocket Shot, mf dk. grey 6
491 Rocket Shot, black 4
492 Swingfire, red-orange; sp5 5
492 Swingfire, white; sp5 4
493 Porsche 911 Taarga, lime; sp5 4
494 Mercedes 500SL, mf grey; sp5 5
496 Ferrari 308 GTS, red; sp5 4
497 Ferrari Testarossa, white; sp5 4
497 Ferrari Testarossa, white; lwch 25
498 BMW 850i, mf silver; sp5 4
499 Corvette Coupe, mf aqua; sp5 4
499 Corvette Coupe, mf aqua; lwch 4
502 Chevy Nomad, dk. red; sp7gd 8
503 '80s Corvette, red; sp3 4
503 '80s Corvette, red; lwch 4
503 '80s Corvette, red; dw3 4
504 Camaro Z-28, white; sp5 6
504 Camaro Z-28, white; sp3 4
504 Camaro Z-28, white; sp7 4
505 '93 Camaro, black; sp5 8
505 '93 Camaro, black; dw3 6
505 '93 Camaro, black; lwch 4
506 Nissan 300ZX, purple; sp5 6
507 Peugeot 205 Rally, bk,blue and mag; sp5, painted base 18
507 Peugeot 205 Rally, bk,blue and mag; sp5, unpainted base 18
509 Firebird Funny Car, blue; sp5 6
510 Lamborghini Countach, yellow; ho5 4
512 Excavator, white 30
513 Ford F-150, red; sp5 4
514 Way 2 Fast, orange; sp5 6
515 '97 Corvette, aqua; lwch 8
516 Mercedes C-Class, black; lwgd 4
517 '59 Impala, plum; lwgd 6
518 BMW M Roadster, silver; sp3 4
518 BMW M Roadster, silver; sp5 6
518 BMW M Roadster, silver; sp5, black base 15
519 Scorchin' Scooter, purple 12
520 Saltflat Racer, red; sp5 4
523 1970 Plymouth Barracuda, lime green; sp5 9
524 GMC Motor Home, blue; bw 30
525 Trailbuster, black; bw 4
526 Neet Streeter, yellow; bw 4
527 Second Wind, white; bw 4
528 Beach Blaster, white; bw 4
529 Power Rocket, green; sp3 4
530 Power Pistons, red; sp3 4
531 Power Pipes, blue; sp3 4
532 Road Rocket, orange; sp3 4
532 Road Rocket, orange; dw3 4
533 Hummer, blue; dw3 6
534 Chevy 1500, blue; sp5 6
534 Chevy 1500, blue; sp7 4
534 Chevy 1500, blue; sp3 4
534 Chevy 1500, blue; ho5 4
534 Chevy 1500, blue; sp5, mf silver base 4
535 3-Window '34, blue; sp5 8
536 '80s Corvette, blue; sp5 6
536 '80s Corvette, blue; ho5 4
537 Police Cruiser, green; sp5 6
538 School Bus, aqua; sp5 5
538 School Bus, aqua; sp3 5
538 School Bus, aqua; sp7 25
538 School Bus, aqua; ho5 4
539 Peterbilt Tank Truck, dk. red; sp7 8
540 Ramblin' Wrecker, black; sp7 8
541 Mini Truck, red; sp3 5
542 Limozeen, blue; sp5 4
543 VW Bug, green; sp5 8
544 Range Rover, magenta; dw3ct 4
545 Chevy Stocker, red; sp3 4
546 Aeroflash, purple; sp3 4

COLLECTOR NUMBER PACKS

547 Ferrari 308 GTB, white; ho5 4
548 T-Bird Stocker, blue; sp5 4
549 Hydroplane, white 4
550 Street Roader, white; dw3ct 4
551 XT-3, blue; sp5 4
552 (Probe) Funny Car, magenta; sp5 6
553 Stealth, purple; sp3 4
554 Alien, blue & white; sp3 4
554 Alien, blue & white; dw3 4
555 Sol-Aire CX4, dk. magenta; sp3 4
556 Custom Corvette, black; sp3 4
557 Mercedes-Benz Unimog, black; dw3ct 6
558 Jaguar XJ220, orange; dw3y 4
559 '80s Camaro, yellow; dw3bn 4
560 Corvette Stingray, white; dw3y 4
561 Speed Machine, white; sp3 4
562 Shadow Jet, white; sp5 4
563 Splittin' Image II, white; sp3 4
564 Twin Mill II, white; sp5 4
565 Silhouette II, blue; ho5 4
566 Street Beast, gold & white; ho5 4
567 Baja Bug, red; sp5 8
568 '63 Corvette, black; ho5 4
569 Twang Thang, dk. red; sp5 4
570 Ferrari 355, black; sp5 4
571 Turbo Flame, purple; sp5 4
572 Porsche 930, aqua; sp5 4
572 Porsche 930, aqua; ho5 4
573 Olds 442, blue; sp3 6
574 Nissan Truck, blue; dw3ct 35
575 '55 Chevy, blue; sp3 6
576 Speed Blaster, blue; sp3, chrome base 20
576 Speed Blaster, blue; sp3, black base 4
577 Police Cruiser, black; sp7b 6
578 '56 Flashsider, dk. green; sp5 35
579 Silhouette II, white; sp3w 25
580 Mercedes 500 SL, black; sp5 25
581 Street Cleaver, black; sp5 20
582 GM Lean Machine, dk. red 25
583 Hot Rod Wagon, yellow; sp5y 35
584 Olds Aurora, black; sp5 28
585 Dogfighter, green; sp5 22
586 Buick Wildcat, silver; sp3 22
587 Blimp, blue 25
588 Avus Quattro, gold; dw3 20
589 Rail Rodder, white 25
590 Porsche 911, red; dw3 4
590 Porsche 911, red; sp5 4
590 Porsche 911, red; ho5 4
591 Porsche 959, blue-grey; sp5 4
591 Porsche 959, blue-grey; dw3 4
592 Porsche 930, blue; sp5 4
593 Skullrider, ch pink; sp5 6
594 GM Ultralite, black & white; sp7 8
594 GM Ultralite, black & white; sp3 6
594 GM Ultralite, black & white; ho5 4
595 Corvette Stingray III, blue; sp3 4
595 Corvette Stingray III, purple; sp5 4
596 Pontiac Salsa, orange; sp7 4
596 Pontiac Salsa, orange; sp3, metal base 4
596 Pontiac Salsa, orange; sp3, chrome base 18
597 Buick Wildcat, red; sp7 6
597 Buick Wildcat, dk. green; sp3 4
598 Turboa, mustard; sp5 4
599 Camaro Wind, white; lwch 8
600 Nissan Custom Z, blue; lwch 6
600 Nissan Custom Z, lt.blue; lwch 4
600 Nissan Custom Z, lt.blue; sp5 30
601 Commando, dk. red; cts 5
602 Sharkruiser, black; lwch 4
603 BMW 325i, yellow; lwch 5
604 Ferrari 308 GTS, red; sp5 6
604 Ferrari 308 GTS, red; lwch 6
605 Mercedes 2.6, gold; lwch 4
606 Mercedes 300TD, dk. green; sp5 4
607 Fat Fendered '40, turquoise; sp5 12
608 Porsche 911 Targa, silver; sp5 4
609 Jaguar XJ40, black; lwch 4
610 Land Rover MKII, orange; sp5 4
611 Fire-Eater II, red; sp5 4
612 '57 T-Bird, turquoise; bw 20
613 London Bus, red; sp5 12
615 Ford XR4Ti, silver; sp5 6
616 Corvette Coupe, white; lwch 4
617 Flame Stopper, red; sp5 4
618 Chevy Stocker, white; sp5 22
619 London Taxi, yellow; sp5 10
620 Ford Transit Wrecker, lt.blue; sp5 6
622 City Police, black; sp5bk 8
623 Mustang Cobra, dk. pink; lwch 4
623 Mustang Cobra, dk. pink; sp5 12
624 Assault Crawler, olive 4
625 Classic Packard, black; sp5 10
633 Dodge Caravan, red-brown; dw3 4
633 Dodge Caravan, red-brown; sp5 4
634 Dodge Sidewinder, red; sp5 4
635 '65 Impala Lowrider, purple; lwgd 6
636 '32 Ford, black; sp5 8
636 '32 Ford, black; dw3 8
637 Escort Rally, white; lwch, Escort Rally on base 8
637 Escort Rally, white; lwch, Ford Rally on base 10
638 Jaguar D-Type, blue; sp5 8
638 Jaguar D-Type, blue; dw3 3
638 Jaguar D-Type, blue; lwch 3
639 Jaguar XK8, blue-green; lwch 6
639 Jaguar XK8, blue-green; lwch, white interior 90
640 Slideout, purple; sp5 4
641 Wheel Loader, orange; cts 4
642 Forklift, white; bw & sp5 4
643 Digger (Dirt Rover), yellow; sp5 4
644 '63 T-Bird, aqua; ho5 4
645 Dairy Delivery, white; sp5 6
646 Mercedes SLK, met. yellow; ho5 4
646 Mercedes SLK, met. yellow; sp5, tan interior 4
646 Mercedes SLK, yellow; sp5, tan interior 25
646 Mercedes SLK, yellow; sp5, black interior 20
647 Lakester, red; sp5 3
648 Hot Seat, white; sp5 3
649 1936 Cord, dk. red; lwch 3
650 Solar Eagle III, yellow 3
651 Go Kart, green; sp5 10
652 Pikes Peak Celica, yellow; lwgd, magenta in tampo 6
652 Pikes Peak Celica, yellow; lwgd, lt.purple in tampo 6
653 IROC Firebird, gold; sp5bk 4
654 '40 Ford, blue; sp5 4
654 '40 Ford, silver blue; sp5 20
654 '40 Ford, dk. blue; sp5 20
655 Super Comp Dragster, black; sp5, 3 sponsor decals 15
655 Super Comp Dragster, black; sp5, 5 sponsor decals 5
656 '38 Phantom Corsair, black; ho5w 3
656 '38 Phantom Corsair, blue; ho5w 12
657 Panoz GTR-1, white; lwch 3
658 Tow Jam, red; sp3, chrome base 4
658 Tow Jam, red; sp3, chrome base, lg. Hot Wheels logo 35
659 Tail Dragger, purple; lwch 6
661 '70 Roadrunner, orange; sp5 4
661 '70 Roadrunner, orange; ho5 15
662 Bad Mudder, white; dw3ct, no roof tampo 35
662 Bad Mudder, white; dw3ct 3
663 Customized C3500, aqua; ho5, thin stripe 25
663 Customized C3500, aqua; ho5, thick stripe 4
664 Super Modified, black ; lwch 3
665 Mustang Cobra, black; lwgd 3
667 At-A-Tude, blue; lwch 3
668 Ford GT-90, white; sp3 3
669 Chaparral 2, white; lwch 3
670 Mustang Mach I, orange; sp5 40
670 Mustang Mach I, yellow; sp5 3
670 Mustang Mach I, yellow; ho5 40
671 Chrysler Thunderbolt, grey; ho5 3
671 Chrysler Thunderbolt, grey; sp5 50
672 Dodge Concept Car, orange; sp5, black interior 3
672 Dodge Concept Car, orange; sp5, purple interior 350
673 Whatta Drag, dark red; sp3 3
674 Sweet 16 II, purple; sp5 4
675 Pontiac Rageous, dk. mf red; sp3 3
675 Pontiac Rageous, dk. mf red; sp3, black roof 3
676 Porsche 911 GT1-98, white; lwch 3
677 Callaway C-7, gray; sp5 3
678 Express Lane, red; sp5 3
681 Cat-A-Pult, red; sp5 3
681 Cat-A-Pult, red; sp5, red logo on hood 25
681 Cat-A-Pult, red; sp3 4
682 Fathom This, white 3
683 Tee'd Off, white; sp5, magenta interior 6
683 Tee'd Off, white; sp5, gray interior 15
683 Tee'd Off, blue; sp5 6
684 Double Vision, dk. red; lwgd 3
685 '57 T-Bird, blue; sp3 3
686 '93 Camaro, lt. green; sp3 5
687 Stutz Blackhawk, dk. red; sp3 4
688 Corvette Stingray, orange; sp3 5
689 Shadow Jet II, black; sp5 3
690 Power Pistons, purple; sp3 3
690 Power Pistons, purple; lwch 3
691 Shadow Jet, purple; sp5 4
692 Radar Ranger, light green; dw3ct 3
693 Ice Cream Truck, white; sp5 5
694 Baja Bug, white; sp5 4
695 Classic Caddy, red; lwch 4
695 Classic Caddy, red; sp3 3
696 Custom Corvette Convertible, green; sp3 4
696 Custom Corvette Convertible, green; lwch 3
697 Mini Truck, yellow; sp3 3
697 Mini Truck, yellow; sp3gd 6
698 '59 Impala, aqua; lwgd 3
699 '59 Caddy, red; lwgd 4
699 '59 Caddy, unpainted; lwgd 85
700 Shock Factor, yellow; bw 4
702 Lumina Minivan, aqua; sp5 10
712 Tipper, blue; sp5 3
714 Talbot Lago, blue; lwch 375
716 Limozeen, black; lwgd 4
716 Limozeen, unpainted; lwgd 70
717 Hydroplane, green 4
718 Flame Stopper, red; dw3cty 3
719 Recycling Truck, lime green; dw3 3
720 Rescue Ranger, black; sp5 3
720 Rescue Ranger, black; ho5 3
721 Jaguar XJ220, gray; sp3 3
721 Jaguar XJ220, gray; lwch 3
721 Jaguar XJ220, gray; dw3 3
721 Jaguar XJ220, unpainted; lwch 75
722 Ferrari F40, unpainted; lwgd 85
722 Ferrari F40, gold; lwgd 3
723 Avus Quattro, black; lwgd 3
723 Avus Quattro, unpainted; lwgd 70
724 Dodge Viper RT/10, unpainted; dw3 200
724 Dodge Viper RT/10, white; dw3, Thailand 3
724 Dodge Viper RT/10, white; dw3, Malaysia 3
725 '67 Camaro, blue; sp5 6
725 '67 Camaro, unpainted; sp5 300
726 Mercedes C-Class, blue; sp5 4
727 Shelby Cobra 427, blue; sp5 4
727 Shelby Cobra 427, unpainted; sp5 150
728 '63 Corvette, blue; sp5 3
729 Alien, white; sp3 3
730 '57 Chevy, gray; dw3 4
731 VW Bug, white; ho5 6
731 VW Bug, unpainted; ho5 300
732 1970 Plymouth Barracuda, black; sp3 3
732 1970 Plymouth Barracuda, black; sp3, tampo colors reversed 3
732 1970 Plymouth Barracuda, black; sp5 3
732 1970 Plymouth Barracuda, black; sp5, tampo colors reversed 3
733 Street Roader, white; dw3ct 3
734 '80s Corvette, green; lwch 3
735 Nissan Truck, red; dw3ct 3
736 School Bus, yellow; ho5 3
737 Dodge Charger Daytona, green; sp5 3
737 Dodge Charger Daytona, green; ho5 5
737 Dodge Charger Daytona, unpainted; sp5 125
738 Dogfighter, black; sp5 3
738 Dogfighter, black; sp3 3
738 Dogfighter, black; ho5 8
739 Sol-Aire CX4, yellow; sp5 3
739 Sol-Aire CX4, yellow; sp3 3
739 Sol-Aire CX4, yellow; ho5 8
740 XT-3, grey; sp5 3
741 Mazda MX-5 Miata, orange; sp5 3
741 Mazda MX-5 Miata, unpainted; sp5 75
742 (Probe) Funny Car, white; sp5 5
743 '95 Camaro, dk. blue; sp5 3
744 '96 Mustang, yellow; sp5 5
745 Buick Wildcat, black; sp3 3
746 Silhouette II, black; ho5 3
747 Speed Machine, black; dw3 3
748 Avus Quattro, black; lwgd 3
749 Twang Thang, black; sp5 20
750 Scorchin' Scooter, red 40
751 Kenworth T600A, purple; sp3 30
752 3-Window '34, orange; ho5 35
753 Turbo Flame, chrome; sp5 20
754 Saltflat Racer, black; sp5 20
755 Street Beast, red and white; lwgd 25
756 Road Rocket, chrome; sp3 20
757 Sol-Aire CX4, white; lwch 25
758 '57 Chevy, green; sp3 35
759 Corvette Stingray III, grey; sp3 25
760 Way 2 Fast, gold; sp5 25
760 Way 2 Fast, gold; sp5, black speckles in paint 25
761 Flame Stopper, red; dw3cty 5
765 Oshkosh P-Series (Snow Plow), blue; dw3ct 3
767 Mercedes 380 SEL, white; dw3 4
768 Lamborghini Countach, black; ho5 3
770 Lexus SC400, purple; lwch, clear window 30
770 Lexus SC400, purple; lwch, tinted window 4
771 '56 Flashsider, yellow; ho5 3
773 Hot Wheels 500, light green; sp7bk 7
774 Ramp Truck, dark green; sp5 3
778 Speed Blaster, purple; sp3 3
779 Big Chill, white 3
780 '58 Corvette Coupe, turquoise; ho5 3
781 Lamborghini Diablo, red; sp5 4
781 Lamborghini Diablo, red; ho5 4
782 Radar Ranger, gold; dw3ct 3
783 Twin Mill II, grey; lwch 3
784 Ferrari Testarossa, silver; ho5 4
784 Ferrari 512M, silver; ho5 3
784 Ferrari 512M, silver; sp5 6
787 '57 Chevy, purple; dw3 8
787 '57 Chevy, unpainted; dw3 150
788 Mercedes 540K, purple; lwch 3
788 Mercedes 540K, purple; sp3 3
791 Treadator, blue 3
792 Camaro Race Car, white; sp5 3
792 Camaro Race Car, unpainted; sp5 75
793 Auburn 852, black; lwgd 4
795 Tractor, grey; dw3ct 3
796 '95 Camaro Convertible, white; sp5w 3
797 Dodge Ram, red; ho5 3
797 Dodge Ram, red; sp5 3
798 Propper Chopper, blue 3
802 Flashfire, gold; ho5 4
803 '40s Woodie, white; sp5 6
806 Ferrari 308, brown; ho5 6
808 Driven To The Max, white; sp5 6
808 Driven To The Max, unpainted; sp5 75
812 GM Lean Machine, turq. & gold; dw3 3
813 Ferrari 355, black; sp5 4
814 Speed-A-Saurus, dk. turquoise; sp5 4
815 Mercedes 500SL, green; sp3 3
815 Mercedes 500SL, unpainted; sp3 70
816 Ferrari 308, brown; ho5 3
816 Ferrari 308, brown; sp5 3
816 Ferrari 308, brown; sp5, black interior 25
816 Ferrari 308, red; sp5 3
817 Porsche 928, white; lwch 3
818 Porsche Carrera, dk. mf red; sp5gd 8
818 Porsche Carrera, dk. mf red; sp5gd, Flames 35
820 Zender Fact 4, dk. green; lwch 3
821 '96 Mustang, white; sp5 6
822 Camaro Z28, dk. turquoise; sp3 6
823 Sol-Aire CX4, blue; lwgd 3
829 Porsche Carrera, silver; dw3 3
829 Porsche Carrera, unpainted; dw3 75
834 Ferrari Testarossa, black; bw 5
835 Baja Bug, blue; bw 6
835 Baja Bug, red; bw 10
837 Radio Flyer Wagon, blue; sp5 4
850 Rail Rodder, grey 3
851 Treadator, purple 3
852 Rigor Motor, purple; sp5gd 3
853 Camaro Z28, lt.green; ho5 5
854 Porsche 959, white; sp3 3
854 Porsche 959, white; dw3 3
854 Porsche 959, white; lwch 3
855 Ferrari F50, purple; dw3 3
856 Porsche 930, dk. red; sp3 3
857 T-Bird Stocker, orange; ho5 3
858 Hummer, white; dw3cy 3
859 Bronco 4-Wheeler, red; dw3ct 3
860 Road Rocket, white; sp3 3
861 Twin Mill II, gold; lwch 3
862 Pontiac Salsa, dark red; ho5 3
863 Oshkosh Cement Mixer, lime; sp3 3
864 Tank Truck, mf dk. red; ho5 3
865 Ford F-150, white; sp3 3
866 Ferrari 250, gold; lwch 3
867 '97 Corvette, dk blue; sp5 3
867 '97 Corvette, unpainted; sp5 75
868 Range Rover, dk. green; dw3ct 3
868 Range Rover, unpainted; dw3ct 80
869 Power Pipes, black; dw3o 3
870 Chevy Stocker, purple; dw3gd 3
871 Olds 442, blue; sp5 10
872 Rig Wrecker, white; dw3 3
872 Rig Wrecker, white; ho5 3
873 Hydroplane, white 4
874 Pit Crew Truck, grey; ho5 3
874 Pit Crew Truck, grey; dw3 3
875 Police Car, white; sp5 3
876 Bywayman, red; dw3 3
877 Chevy 1500, grey; dw3 3
881 '95 Camaro Convertible, black; sp3 3
884 Gulch Stepper, yellow; dwct 3
889 Mercedes 380 SEL, black; lwgd 4
890 BMW M Roadster, white; sp3 3
894 Toyota MR2, white; lwch 3
899 '56 Flashsider, gray; sp5 5
899 '56 Flashsider, unpainted; sp5 170
908 Ford F-150, purple; sp5 3
908 Ford F-150, purple; sp3 12
909 '99 Mustang, purple; sp5, red interior 40
909 '99 Mustang, purple; sp5, tan interior 5
909 '99 Mustang, purple; sp3 3
909 '99 Mustang, blue; sp5, tan interior 30
910 Monte Carlo Concept Car, red; sp5 3
910 Monte Carlo Concept Car, met. red; sp5 5
911 Olds Aurora GT3, blue & white; lwgd 3
911 Olds Aurora GT3, blue & white; lwgd, pkg. readsGTS-3 8
911 Olds Aurora GT3, mf grey; lwgd 5
911 Olds Aurora GT3, red; lwgd 3
912 Porsche 911 GT3, gray; lwch, yellow spoiler 3
912 Porsche 911 GT3, gray; lwch, black spoiler 10
912 Porsche 911 GT3, purple; lwch 3
913 Popcycle, magenta; lwch 12
913 Popcycle, purple; sp3 4
914 Semi-Fast, red; sp5 3
914 Semi-Fast, black; sp5 3
915 1970 Chevelle SS, dk. blue; sp5 3
915 1970 Chevelle SS, dk. blue; sp5, no pinstripes 8
915 1970 Chevelle SS, gold; sp5 3
916 Phaeton, turquoise; sp5 3
917 Track T, black; sp5 3
918 Screamin' Hauler, purple; sp5 3
919 Flat 500C, purple; sp5 3
921 Ford GT-40, blue; sp5 3
921 Ford GT-40, dk. red; sp3 3
922 Jeepster, red; sp5 3
923 Turbolence, black; ho5gd, silver engine 15
923 Turbolence, black; ho5gd, gold engine 3
924 Pikes Peak Tacoma, yellow; lwgd 3
925 Shadow Mk IIA, black; sp5 3
926 Mercedes CLK-LM, mf gray; lwgd 3
927 '56 Ford Truck, lt. blue; sp5 5
928 Chrysler Pronto, yellow; sp5 3
929 Mercedes 540K, red; sp5 20
930 T-Bird Stocker, blue; sp5 15
931 '97 Corvette, lt.purple; ho5 20
932 Rigor Motor, lime; sp5gd 20
933 Ferrari 512M, yellow; pc 20
934 '59 Impala, Lt.purple; lwgd 25
935 Hot Wheels 500, black; sp7bk 15
936 Jaguar D-Type, black; sp5 20
937 '32 Delivery, blue; sp5gd 30
938 Hot Seat, clear; sp5 20
939 Mustang Mach I, black; sp5 25
940 Express Lane, purple; sp5gd 25
941 Treadator, red 3
942 Shadow Jet II, gray; sp5 3
943 Radar Ranger, purple; dw3ct 3
944 Baja Bug, blue; sp5 6
945 Mercedes C-Class, black; lwgd 10

946 Lamborghini Diablo, aqua; sp5 3
947 '67 Camaro, blue; sp5 6
947 '67 Camaro, blue; sp3 4
948 Jaguar XJ220, yellow; sp3 3
949 Mini Truck, black; dw3 3
950 Propper Chopper, green 3
951 Ambulance, purple; sp5 3
951 Ambulance, purple; sp3 3
952 School Bus, yellow; ho5 3
952 School Bus, yellow; ho5, rear door outline 3
952 School Bus, grey; ho5 3
952 School Bus, grey; ho5, rear door outline 3
953 3-Window '34, purple; sp5 5
954 Tail Dragger, black; lwch 5
955 '65 Impala, green; lwgd 4
956 Auburn 852, black; lwch 3
957 Lean Machine, purple 3
958 Shadow Jet, yellow; sp5 3
959 Speed Blaster, green; dw3gd 3
960 Twin Mill II, red; lwch 3
961 '40s Woodie, purple; sp5 6
962 VW Bug, blue; sp5 6
963 '55 Chevy, mf red; sp3 6
964 Chevy Nomad, white; sp5gd 6
965 Dodge Sidewinder, white; sp5 3
966 Callaway C7, green; dw3 3
967 Porsche Carrera, grey; sp5gd 3
968 Mazda MX-5 Miata, blue; lwch 3
969 '70 Roadrunner, yellow; ho5 3
970 Jaguar XK8, red; lwgd 3
971 Pikes Peak Celica, white; lwch 3
972 Dodge Concept Car, white; ho5 3
973 (Probe) Funny Car, lime; sp5 3
974 Mustang Cobra, white; dw3 3
975 Turbo Flame, black; sp5gd 3
976 Firebird Funny Car, black; sp5bk 3
977 At-A-Tude, green; sp5b 3
978 Cat-A-Pult, orange; sp5 3
979 Sweet 16 II, black; sp5 3
980 Splittin' Image II, mf gold; sp3 3
981 Super Modified, lt. blue; lwgd 3
982 Silhouette II, lt.blue-gray; ho5 3
983 Sol-Aire CX4, white; sp3 3
984 Escort Rally, red; lwch 12
991 Rodzilla, chrome; lwgd 3
992 Ferrari F512M, red; sp5 3
993 Ferrari 348, yellow; sp5 3
993 Way 2 Fast, red; rrgd 12
994 Way 2 Fast, black; sp5gd 3
995 Porsche 911, yellow; sp5 3
996 '32 Ford Delivery, blue; lwch 6
997 Jaguar D-Type, red; lwch 3
998 Firebird Funny Car, dk. mf red; sp5gd 3
999 Hot Seat, chrome; sp5 3
1000 '59 Impala, white; lwgd 7
1001 Slideout, mf blue; sp5 3
1003 Ferrari F40, black; sp5 3
1004 Dairy Delivery, white; sp5 6
1005 Mercedes-Benz Unimog, red; dw3ct 3
1006 Dodge Viper, blue; sp5 3
1007 Tow Jam, dk. green; sp3 3
1008 Chaparral 2, red; lwch 3
1009 Peterbilt Dump Truck, blue; sp5 3
1010 Ford Stake Bed Truck, aqua; ho5 3
1011 Oshkosh Cement Truck, black; dw3 3
1012 Flame Stopper, white; dw3ct 3
1013 Mercedes 500 SL, grey; lwch 3
1014 '67 Camaro, gray; sp5 3
1015 Mercedes C-Class, yellow; lwch 3
1018 '32 Ford Coupe, white; sp5 3
1022 '63 T-Bird, gold; lwch 5
1024 Shelby Cobra, white; sp5 7
1025 Mercedes SLK, dk. blue; dw3 3
1026 Dodge Caravan, red; sp5 10
1027 Customized C-3500, plum; sp5 5
1028 '56 Flashsider, yellow; sp3 5
1029 '40s Ford, red; sp5 3
1030 Porsch 959, gray; ho5 3
1031 Aeroflash, green; sp3 3
1032 Ford GT-90, yellow; sp3 3
1035 '70 Plymouth Barracuda, black; sp3 3
1037 Roll Patrol, yellow; dw3ct 12
1038 Dodge Viper RT/10, gray; sp3 3
1040 Panoz GTR-1, green; sp3 3
1041 Super Comp Dragster, gray; sp5 3
1042 Twang Thang, green; sp5 4
1043 Rail Rodder, white 3
1044 Whatta Drag, black; ho5 3
1045 Dodge Ram 1500, black; sp5 3
1046 Police Cruiser, white; sp3 3
1047 Olds Aurora, black; ho5 3
1048 Rescue Ranger, white; sp5 3
1048 Rescue Ranger, white; ho5 3
1049 Treadator, black 3
1051 '65 Mustang, black; sp5g 3
1052 Rigor Motor, red; sp5 3
1053 Hydroplane, black 3
1054 Porsche 959, black; lwch 3
1055 School Bus, black; ho5 3
1056 Corvette Stingray, yellow; lwgd 3
1057 Thunderstreak, dk. red; sp5bk 3
1058 '96 Mustang, dk. red; lwgd 3
1059 Dodge Ram 1500, green; ho5 3
1059 Dodge Ram 1500, white; rrch 10
1060 Ramp Truck, black; ho5 3
1061 Rescue Ranger, white; ho5 3
1062 Rail Rodder, black 3
1063 1970 Plymouth Barracuda, orange; sp5 3
1064 Lakester, mf silver; sp5 3
1065 Firebird, white; sp5bk 3
1066 Mustang Cobra, gold; sp5 3
1067 Express Lane, orange; sp5 3
1068 Dodge Concept Car, mf gray; lwgd 3
1069 '40 Ford, yellow; ho5 5
1069 '40 Ford, white & orange; rrch 12
1070 '32 Ford, dk. red; ho5 3
1071 Panoz GTR-1, black; sp3 3
1073 Ford GT-90, red; dw3 3
1074 Blimp, red 3
1075 Scorchin' Scooter, red 8
1076 '59 Eldorado, blue; lwch 3
1077 '57 Chevy, red; lwgd 3
1078 Camaro Z28, blue; sp3 3
1079 '63 Corvette, gray; ho5 3
1080 Humvee, aqua; dw3ct 3
1081 Power Plower, green; dw3ct 3
1082 Jaguar XJ220, mf gold; sp3gd 3
1083 '80s Camaro, aqua; lwch 3
1084 Mazda MX-5 Miata, white; sp3 3
1085 Porsche 928, gold; ho5 3
1086 Toyota MR2, purple; sp3 3
1087 Rig Wrecker, yellow; ho5 3
1088 Speed Machine, black; ho5gd 3
1089 25th Ann. Countach, gray; ho5 3
1090 '97 Corvette, black; sp3 3
1091 X-Ploder, black; dw3 3
1092 '58 Corvette Coupe, black; lwch 3
1093 BMW 850i, gold; lwch 3
1094 Ferrari F355 Berlinetta, red; sp5 3
1095 Mercedes SLK, gray; dw3 3
1096 Avus Quattro, chrome; sp5 3
1097 '31 Doozie, mf red; lwch 3
1098 '37 Bugatti, black; lwch 3
1099 Road Rocket, red; lwch 3
1100 Power Pipes, white; ho5 3
1101 Radar Ranger, aqua; dw3ct 3
1102 Mini Truck, black; lwgd 3
1103 1980 Corvette Coupe, gold; lwch 3
1104 Twang Thang, orange; sp5g 3
1105 Mustang Mach I, blue; lwch 5
1106 Go Kart, orange; ho5 8
1107 Chrysler Thunderbolt, blue; sp3 3
1113 360 Modena, red; sp5 3
1114 '63 Corvette, black; sp5g 3
1115 Ferrari 355 Challenge, gray; sp5 3
1116 Ferrari 456M, red; sp5 3
1117 Ferrari F355 Spider, red; sp5 3
1118 Ferrari F50, red; sp5 3
1121 Ferrari F355 Spider, red; sp5 3
1120 Ferrari F50, red; sp5 3
1121 Chevy 1500, orange; ho5 3

2000

Starting in 2000, the code numbers used on collector packs were reset each year.

1 Ford GT-90, black; sp3 3
1 Ford GT-90, black; lwch, China 3
1 Ford GT-90, black; lwch, Malaysia 3
1 Ford GT-90, black; sp3 3
2 Pontiac Rageous, black; sp3, Malaysia 3
2 Pontiac Rageous, black; sp3, China 3
3 Jeepster, black; sp5 3
3 Jeepster, black; sp5, painted base 3
4 Chrysler Thunderbolt, purple; sp3 3
5 Phaeton, dk. red; lwgd, Malaysia 3
5 Phaeton, dk. red; lwgd, Thailand 3
6 Track T, yellow; dw3, Malaysia 3
6 Track T, yellow; dw3, Thailand 3
7 Tail Dragger, white; lwgd, painted base 3
8 '33 Ford Roadster, green; dw3 3
8 '33 Ford Roadster, green; sp5 5
9 Propper Chopper, red 3
10 1970 Charger Daytona, blue; sp5 3
10 1970 Charger Daytona, blue; dw3 3
10 1970 Charger Daytona, blue; lwch 40
11 Lexus SC400, yellow; sp3 3
12 Olds 442, green; sp3 3
13 Callaway C-7, mf green; sp5 3
13 Callaway C-7, mf green; ho5 3
14 Firebird, orange; sp5 3
15 Monte Carlo Concept Car, blue; lwch 3
16 Dodge Sidewinder, tan; dw3 3
16 Dodge Sidewinder, yellow; dw3 3
17 Hot Wheels 500, blue; sp7bk 3
18 Camaro Z-28, gray; lwch, black base 3
18 Camaro Z-28, gray; dw3 30
19 Slideout, black; sp5, red base 3
20 Twin Mill II, orange; ho5gd 3
21 Nissan Truck, brown; dw3ct 3
22 Power Plower, purple; dw3ct, painted chassis 3
22 Power Plower, purple; dw3ct, unpainted chassis 3
23 '79 Ford F-150, dark blue; sp5 3
24 Dodge Ram 1500, dk. red; sp5 3
25 '56 Flashsider, mf red; ho5gd 3
26 '32 Ford Delivery, black; lwch, painted chassis 3
26 '32 Ford Delivery, black; lwch, unpainted chassis 3
27 Fat Fendered '40, blue; lwch 3
27 Fat Fendered '40, blue; dw3 5
28 Dairy Delivery, purple; sp5gd 3
29 Chrysler Pronto, mf aqua; sp3 3
29 Chrysler Pronto, mf aqua; sp3, no country on base 3
30 Pikes Peak Tacoma, black; ho5gd 4
30 Pikes Peak Tacoma, black; lwgd, w/paint on door insert 5
30 Pikes Peak Tacoma, black; lwgd, wo/paint on door insert 4
31 Shadow Mk IIa, white; sp5, black base 3
31 Shadow Mk IIa, white; sp5, gray base 3
32 Pontiac Banshee, orange; ho5 3
33 Toyota MR2, black; sp3 3
34 '99 Mustang, red; sp3 3
35 Shadow Jet II, blue; sp3, painted base 3
35 Shadow Jet II, blue; sp3, unpainted base 3
36 Mini Truck, green; dw3 3
37 Firebird Funny Car, mf orange; sp5, unpainted base 3
38 At-A-Tude, gray; sp5 3
39 Mustang Cobra, blue; sp5, India 3
39 Mustang Cobra, blue; sp5, Malaysia 3
40 Shelby Cobra 427 S/C, white; sp5 3
41 Rigor Motor, blue; sp5, painted base 3
41 Rigor Motor, blue; sp5, unpainted base 3
42 Sol-Aire CX4, white; sp3 3
43 Speed Blaster, orange; sp3 3
44 Combat Medic, gray; sp5 3
45 Fiat 500C, red; sp5 3
46 Baby Boomer, blue; sp5, China 3
46 Baby Boomer, blue; sp5, Malaysia 3
47 Tee'd Off, black; sp5 3
47 Tee'd Off, black; sp5 3
48 Screamin' Hauler, yellow; sp5, painted base 3
48 Screamin' Hauler, yellow; sp5, unpainted base 3
49 Double Vision, purple; rrch 18
50 Tow Jam, yellow; rrch 22
51 1936 Cord, grey; rrch 24
51 1936 Cord, grey; rrchww 40
52 Sweet 16 II, red; rrch 20
53 Lakester, mf aqua; sp5gd 14
54 Go Kart, white; rrgd 30
55 Chaparral 2, mf blue; rrch 15
56 '57 T-Bird, mf green; rrch 20
57 Pikes Peak Celica, mf blue; rrgd 20
58 '67 Pontiac GTO, white; rrgd 30
59 Ford GT-40, mf gold; rrch 18
60 '70 Chevelle, black; rrch 25
61 Ferrari 365 GTB/4, red; sp5, w/flag on hood 3
61 Ferrari 365 GTB/4, red; sp5, w/o flag on hood 3
62 Ferrari 550 Maranello, red; sp5, w/flag on hood 3
62 Ferrari 550 Maranello, red; sp5, w/o flag on hood 3
63 1964 Lincoln Continental, white; lwch 3
64 Pro Stock Firebird, yellow; sp5, w/ or w/o ww 3
64 Pro Stock Firebird, black; sp5 3
65 Deora II, gray; ho5, Malaysia on driver's side 3
65 Deora II, gray; ho5, Malaysia on passenger side 3
66 Deuce Roadster, unpainted; sp5 3
67 Chevy Pro Stock Truck, orange; sp5 3
68 '68 El Camino, pearl white; sp5 3
69 Phantastique, blue; lwgd 3
70 Thomassima III, mf dk. red; sp5 3
70 Thomassima III, mf dk. red; lwch 3
70 Thomassima III, mf dk. red; lwch, Thomassima VI on door 3
70 Thomassima III, mf dk. red; pr5s 10
71 Ferrari 333 SP, red; lwch 3
72 Dodge Charger R/T, dk. red; sp5 3
72 Dodge Charger R/T, dk. red; pr5s 20
73 Surf Crate, purple; sp5 3
73 Surf Crate, dark purple; sp5 6
74 '41 Willys, mf orange; sp5 3
75 Lotus Elise, gray; pr5s, unpainted base 3
painted base 30
75 Lotus Elise, gray; sp5 30
76 1999 Isuzu VehiCROSS, mf gray; pr5s 3
77 Anglia Panel Truck, purple; sp5 3
78 So Fine, black; lwch 3
79 '65 Corvette, black; sp5 3
80 MX48 Turbo, blue; pr5s 3
80 MX48 Turbo, blue; sp5 10
80 MX48 Turbo, purple; sp5 40
81 Holden, gray; sp5, solid red spoiler 3
81 Holden, gray; sp5, clear red spoiler 75
82 Cabbin' Fever, black; pr5s, large not for hire 3
83 Metrorail, turquoise; sp5, small front wheels 3
83 Metrorail, turquoise; sp5, large front wheels 3
84 Muscle Tone, mf orange; sp5, blue interior 3
84 Muscle Tone, mf orange; sp5, black interior 6
84 Muscle Tone, mf orange; pr5s, black interior 3
84 Muscle Tone, mf orange; pr5s, blue interior 3
85 Dodge Power Wagon, mf gray; dw3ct, big squares in grill 3
85 Dodge Power Wagon, mf gray; dw3ct, little squares in grill 3
86 Shoe Box, yellow; lwch 6
86 Shoe Box, yellow; pr5s 3
87 Sho-Stopper, dk. yellow; sp3 3
88 Sho-Stopper, dk. yellow; pr5s 3
88 '67 Dodge Charger, grey; pr5s 3
89 Vulture, black; pr5s 3
89 Vulture, black; sp5 3
90 Mini Cooper, yellow; lwch 3
91 Roll Cage, yellow; dw3ct 3
92 Austin Healey, black; sp5 3
93 Hammered Coupe, mf purple; sp5 3
94 Arachnorod, dk. red; pr5s 3
95 Greased Lightnin', gray; pr5s 3
95 Greased Lightnin', gray; sp5 3
96 Blast Lane, orange 4
97 1936 Cord, green; bw 3
98 '99 Mustang, dk. red; sp5 3
98 '99 Mustang, dk. red; sp3 3
99 '38 Phantom Corsair, mf dk. red; lwch 3
99 '38 Phantom Corsair, mf dk. red; lwch, Malaysia 3
100 BMW M Roadster, red; sp5 3
101 Hot Seat, blue; sp5 3
102 '90 T-Bird, chrome; lwgd 3
103 Tractor, lime; dw3ct 3
104 Speed-A-Saurus, green; sp5gd 3
105 '57 Chevy, turquoise; ho5, flames painted or unpaited chassis 3
105 '57 Chevy, turquoise; ho5, painted chassis 3
105 '57 Chevy, turquoise; ho5, with face 8
106 Ferrari 348, black; sp3, different logo & flag 3
107 '70 Chevelle, gold; sp5, greenish gold 3
107 '70 Chevelle, gold; sp5, gold 3
108 Olds Aurora, yellow; dw3 3
109 Monte Carlo Concept Car, red; dw3, gold in tampo-painted base 5
109 Monte Carlo Concept Car, red; dw3, yellow in tampo-painted base 3
110 Fork Lift, orange; sp5 3
111 Wheel Loader, red; dw3ct 3
112 Turbo Flame, clear red; sp5gd 3
113 Flame Stopper, orange; dw3ct 3
114 Lamborghini Diablo, blue; ho5 3
115 Way 2 Fast, dk. red; sp5 3
116 '59 Impala, gray; dw3 3
117 Tee'd Off, red; sp5 3
118 Semi-Fast, dk. blue; sp5, painted base 3
118 Semi-Fast, dk. blue; sp5, unpainted base 3
119 Pontiac Rageous, blue; sp3, black roof 3
119 Pontiac Rageous, blue; sp3, clear roof 3
120 Mercedes SLK, mf aqua; sp3 3
121 Mustang Cobra, dk. mf red; dw3 3
122 Ferrari F40, yellow; sp5 3
123 Oshkosh Cement truck, black; ho5 3
124 Camaro Z28, black; lwgd 3
125 Porsche 930, white; sp3 3
126 Rodzilla, green; sp3gd, dark gold engine 3
126 Rodzilla, green; sp3gd, light gold engine 3
127 Track T, white; dw3 3
128 Porsche 911 GT3, white; sp3 3
129 Turbolence, gray; ho5, chrome engine 3
129 Turbolence, gray; ho5, gray engine 12
130 '63 T-Bird, black; lwch 3
131 Mercedes C-Class, red; ho5 3
132 3-Window '34, green; sp3 3
132 MX48 Turbo, gray; sp3 3
133 Mercedes-Benz Unimog, dk. mf.red; dw3ct 3
134 Mercedes 500SL, blue; ho5, blue base 3
134 Mercedes 500SL, blue; ho5, gray base 3
135 Thunderstreak, plum; lwch 3
136 Ferrari Testarossa, white; sp5 3
137 Dogfighter, yellow; sp5gd 3
138 Skullrider, red; sp5 3
139 Ford GT-40, red; sp5 3
139 Ford GT-40, red; lwch 3
140 Jeepster, green; ho5 3
141 '95 Camaro Convertible, yellow; sp3gd 3
142 Blimp, red 3
143 Recycling Truck, black; dw3 3
144 Ice Cream Truck, tan; ho5 3
144 Ice Cream Truck, tan; sp3 3
144 Ice Cream Truck, white; sp3 3
145 Fire-Eater, white; sp3 3
146 Porsche Carrera, blue; sp3 3
148 Pikes Peak Tacoma, red; sp3, silver insert 6
148 Pikes Peak Tacoma, red; sp3, red insert 3
148 Saltflat Racer, black; sp5gd 5
149 Shadow Mk IIa, red; sp5gd 3
150 Chrysler Pronto, purple; sp3 3
151 Go Kart, purple; ho5 5
152 Fathom This, white 3
153 Shadow Jet II, red; ho5, unpainted chassis 3
153 Shadow Jet II, red; ho5, painted chassis 3
154 Corvette Stingray, blue; ho5 3
154 Corvette Stingray, blue; sp3 3
155 Splittin' Image II, gray; sp3gd 10
156 Screamin' Hauler, mf dk. red; sp5 3
157 Popcycle, mf green; sp3gd, dark gold 3
157 Popcycle, mf green; sp3gd, light gold 3
158 Super Modified, red; lwgd 3
159 BMW 850i, lt.blue; sp3 3

160 Jaguar XJ220, red; lwgd 3
161 Ferrari F50, yellow; sp5 3
162 Ferrari 355 Challenge, yellow; sp5 3
163 Mercedes CLK-LM, red; lwch 3
164 Phaeton, black; sp5 3
165 Jaguar XK8, gray; ho5 3
166 Pikes Peak Celica, white; sp3 3
167 Dodge Concept Car, white; sp3gd 3
167 Dodge Concept Car, white; sp3gd 3
168 Lakester, black; sp5 3
169 Panoz GTR-1, blue; sp3 3
171 '56 Ford Truck, white; sp5gd 3
172 Porsche 911 GT1-98, purple; pr5s 10
172 Porsche 911 GT1-98, purple; dw3 6
172 Porsche 911 GT1-98, purple; lwch 3
173 Baby Boomer, red; sp5 3
174 '63 'Vette, black; dw3 3
174 '63 'Vette, black; lwch 3
175 Olds Aurora, mf orange; lwch 3
176 Solar Eagle III, red 3
177 Flashfire, white; sp5 3
177 Flashfire, white; sp3 3
178 Dodge Viper, gray; sp3 3
179 '95 Camaro Convertible, white; dw3 3
180 Jaguar D-Type, dk. mf brown; lwch 3
183 Buick Wildcat, green; sp3 3
187 Panoz GTR-1, yellow; sp3 3
188 '97 Corvette, red; lwgd 3
189 Semi Fast, aqua; sp5 3
190 Peterbilt Dump Truck, aqua; sp3 3
191 Ford Stake Bed Truck, mf dk. red; sp3 3
192 '40 Ford, gray; dw3 3
193 '40s Woodie, mf.or.brown; lwch 3
194 T-Bird Stocker, blue; sp3 3
195 '32 Ford Coupe, purple; lwch 3
196 Chevy Nomad, orange; sp3gd 3
197 '65 Impala, mf green; sp3 3
198 Ford Bronco 4-Wheeler, white; dw3ct 3
199 Roll Patrol, red; dw3ct 3
200 Purple Passion, white; lwgd 5
201 '65 Mustang, green; dw3 3
202 Hydroplane, white 3
203 Surf Patrol, gray; dw3ct 3
204 Saltflat Racer, black; sp5gd 3
205 Pikes Peak Celica, white; lwch 3
206 Rig Wrecker, black; sp3gd 3
207 Police Car, gray; dw3 3
208 Zender Fact 4, red; dw3 3
209 Customized C3500, yellow; dw3 3
210 Lexus SC400, blue; dw3 5
210 Lexus SC400, blue; lwch 3
211 Tow Jam, blue; sp5 3
212 Double Vision, green; sp3 3
213 Whatta Drag, orange; sp5 3
214 Super Comp Dragster, yellow; sp5 3
215 XT-3, mf dk. red; sp5 3
216 School Bus, red; ho5 3
217 '57 T-Bird, purple; lwch 3
218 Rescue Ranger, mf gray; sp3 3
219 Side Kick, mf gold; sp5, metal chassis 4
219 Side Kick, mf gold; sp5, black plastic chassis 3
220 Sweet 16, black; lwch 3
221 Rail Rodder, black 3
222 Dogfighter, mf gray; lwch 3
223 Twang Thang, mf blue; sp5, silver strings 3
223 Twang Thang, mf blue; sp5, gold strings 3
224 Ford GT-90, green; ho5 3
225 Chrysler Thunderbolt, red; sp5, Malaysia 3
225 Chrysler Thunderbolt, red; sp5, Thailand 3
226 '67 Pontiac GTO, orange; sp5, Malaysia 3
226 '67 Pontiac GTO, orange; sp5, Thailand 3
227 Skullrider, black; sp5 3
228 '57 Chevy, mf orange; sp5 3
229 '80s Camaro, red; dw3 3
230 Ferrari F355 Spider, gray; sp5 3
231 Treadator, gold 3
231 Treadator, gold 3
232 Porsche 959, black; ho5 3
233 Oshkosh Snow Plow, yellow; dw3ct 3
233 Oshkosh Snow Plow, yellow; dw3ct, black plastic base 3
234 '33 Ford Roadster, black; pr5s 3
235 Ferrari 550 Maranello, gray; sp5 3
236 Ferrari 365 GTB/4, yellow; sp5 3
237 1964 Lincoln Continental, black; ho5 3
237 1964 Lincoln Continental, black; ho5, Hot Wheels logo on licence plate 35
238 Deuce Roadster, gold; sp5gd 3
239 Tail Dragger, blue; sp3, Malaysia 3
239 Tail Dragger, blue; sp3, Thailand 3
240 Scorchin' Scooter, orange 5
241 Propper Chopper, black 3
242 Olds 442, white; pr5s 3
242 Olds 442, white; sp5 3
243 Deora II, blue; pr5s 3
244 Chevy Pro Stock Truck, purple; sp5 3
245 Phantastique, mf red; lwch 3
246 '68 El Camino, orange; sp5 3
247 Ford F-150, black; sp3 3
248 Way 2 Fast, gray; sp5, Thailand 3
248 Way 2 Fast, gray; pr5s 22
248 Way 2 Fast, gray; sp5, Malaysia 3
249 '59 Impala, black; lwgd 3
250 Porsche 911 GT1-98, white; lwch, light green or olive green in tampo 3
250 Porsche 911 GT1-98, white; lwch 3

2001

1 '65 Corvette, red; rrch 25
2 Roll Cage, orange; rrch 20
3 So Fine, green; rrchww 30
4 Rodger Dodger, black; rrch 25
5 Blast Lane, gold 35
6 Hammered Coupe, gray; pr5s 20
7 Vulture, white; pr5s 15
8 Dodge Charger, yellow; rrch 20
9 Olds 442, blue; rrch 20
10 Pontiac Rageous, mf brown; rrch 15
11 Deora, blue; rsw 25
12 Cabbin' Fever, white; pr5s, light or dark gold 25
13 Cadillac LMP, gray; lwch 3
14 Surfin' School Bus, yellow; sp5 3
15 La Troca, mf.dk. red; lwgd 3
15 La Troca, mf.dk. red; lwgd, HW logo in back 3
16 Sooo Fast, white; sp5 3
17 Super Tuned, mf blue; pr5s, open spoiler 20
17 Super Tuned, mf blue; pr5s, closed spoiler 3
18 Hooligan, black; sp5, chrome on engine 3
18 Hooligan, black; sp5, no chrome on engine 25
19 Krazy 8s, dk. blue; pr5s 3
20 MS-T Suzuka, lt.green; pr5s 3
21 Panoz LMP-1 Roadster S, red; lwch 3
22 Shredster, yellow; pr5s 6
22 Shredster, yellow; sp5 3
23 Dodge Viper GTS-R, red; sp5 3
24 Maelstrom, blue; sp3 3
25 Lotus M250, gray; sp5, raised Lotus 25
25 Lotus Project M250, gray; sp5, lutus with o stamped over 5
25 Lotus Project M250, gray; sp5, writing not highlighted in gray 6
26 1971 Plymouth GTX, green; sp5, w/door lock 3
26 1971 Plymouth GTX, green; sp5, no door lock 25
27 Honda Civic Si, red; pr5s, Hot Wheels in red 3
27 Honda Civic Si, red; pr5s, Hot Wheels in orange 3
27 Honda Civic Si, red; lwch 8
28 Evil Twin, purple; lwch 3
29 Hyper Mite, green; sp5, magenta in tampo 4
29 Hyper Mite, green; sp5, blue in tampo 3
30 Outsider, orange; lwch 3
30 Outsider, orange; lwch, with VJ 3
31 Monoposto, mf orange; pr5s 3
31 Monoposto, mf orange; lwch 6
32 Vulture Roadster, purple; sp5 3
33 Fright Bike, purple; 1 on base 3
33 Fright Bike, deep purple; 2 on base 3
34 Jet Threat 3.0, gray; ho5, painted chassis 6
34 Jet Threat 3.0, gray; ho5, unpainted chassis 3
35 Montezooma, yellow; lwch 3
36 Toyota Celica, yellow; pr5s, yellow or black (Canada) grill 3
37 Ford Focus, black; ho5 3
38 Mega-Duty, gray; pr5s 3
39 Riley & Scott Mk III, blue; lwch, small wheels 3
39 Riley & Scott Mk III, blue; lwch, large wheels 3
40 XS-IVE, red; dw3ct 3
41 School Bus, green; ho5 3
42 Ambulance, purple; dw3 3
43 Funny Car, mf gray; sp5 3
44 Camaro Z-28, red; sp3, pink or white in tampo 3
45 Mo' Scoot, cl. orange; raised Hot Wheels logo 35
45 Mo' Scoot, cl. orange 3
46 Ford Thunderbolt, black; sp5 3
47 Morris Wagon, black; sp5 3
48 Fandango, orange; pr5s 3
49 Old #3, red; sp5 3
50 Ferrari 156, red; lwch 3
51 Cunningham C4R, white; sp5, blue and met blue 3
52 '57 Roadster, red; sp5, mw in front 3
52 '57 Roadster, red; sp5, sp5 in front 3
53 '57 Chevy, black; sp3, light or dark brown oval 3
54 Limozeen, mf green; dw3gd 3
54 Limozeen, mf green; sp5gd 3
55 '57 T-Bird, yellow; sp3, w/porthole 3
55 '57 T-Bird, yellow; sp3, no porthole 30
56 '70 Chevelle SS, blue; sp5 3
57 Track T, black; ww, red tampo 3
57 Track T, black; ww, dark red tampo 3
58 '33 Roadster, black; ww 3
59 Phaeton, dk. red; ww 3
60 Shoe Box, lt.purple; ww 3
61 Muscle Tone, green; dw3 3
62 Ford GT-90, white; pr5s 3
63 Dodge Charger r/t, yellow; sp3 3
64 Olds Aurora GTS-1, blue-gray; pr5s 3
65 Dodge Charger Daytona, gray; lwch 3
66 Lakester, gray; sp5 3
66 Lakester, gray; sp5 3
67 Greased Lightnin', black; pr5s 3
67 Greased Lightnin', black; sp5 5
68 Propper Chopper, blue 3
69 Rigor Motor, orange; sp5gd 3
70 Blast Lane, black 6
71 Deuce Roadster, purple; sp5 3
72 Screamin' Hauler, gray; sp5, painted base 3
72 Screamin' Hauler, gray; sp5 3
73 Phantastique, red; lwch 3
74 Pontiac Banshee, blue; sp5 3
75 Turbolence, black; ho5, chrome motor-int. 3
75 Turbolence, black; ho5, gold chrome motor-int. 7
76 Metrorail, white; sp5 3
77 '59 Impala, black; lwch 3
78 Tail Dragger, blue; lwch 3
79 '59 Caddy, green; sp5gd, Malaysia 3
79 '59 Caddy, green; sp5gd, Thailand 3
80 Purple Passion, red; sp5gd, Malaysia 4
80 Purple Passion, red; sp5gd, Thailand 4
81 MX48 Turbo, gray; sp3 3
82 Double Vision, green; lwgd 3
82 Double Vision, green; ho5gd 3
83 Twin Mill II, dk. red; lwgd1 3
84 Funny Car, yellow; sp5 3
85 Jaguar XJ220, black; sp3g 3
86 '99 Mustang, white; sp3 3
87 Monte Carlo Concept Car, yellow; sp5, orange tampo 3
87 Monte Carlo Concept Car, yellow; sp5, red tampo 3
88 Dodge Sidewinder, mf dk. red; pr5s 3
88 Dodge Sidewinder, mf dk. red; sp3 3
89 '68 Mustang, gray; sp5, hood tampo-peace sign 3
90 '63 Corvette, green; sp5 3
91 '64 Lincoln Continrntal, blue; lwch 3
92 '67 Pontiac GTO, yellow; sp5 3
93 Super Comp Dragster, mf gold; sp5 3
94 Willys Coupe, mf gray; sp5 3
95 Chevy Pro Stock Truck, lt.green; pr5s 3
96 Pro Stock Firebird, black; pr5s, painted chassis 3
97 Anglia Panel, yellow; sp5 3
98 Thomassima III, blue; pr5s 3
98 Thomassima III, blue; lwch 4
99 Pro Stock Firebird, white; pr5s, painted base 3
100 '70 Roadrunner, red; sp5 3
101 Chevy(1500) Pick-Up, yellow; pr5s 3
101 Chevy(1500) Pick-Up, yellow; sp3 3
102 Road Rocket, ch.gold; pr5s 3
102 Road Rocket, ch.gold; ho5 8
103 Porsche 928, green; ho5, painted chassis 3
104 Avus Quattro, dk. purple; pr5s 3
105 Demon, black; sp3, red or dark red tampo 3
105 Demon, black; sp3 3
106 Power Pipes, chrome; sp3 3
107 Surf Crate, tan; sp5 3
108 Dodge Charger R/T, purple; pr5s, white interior 3
108 Dodge Charger R/T, purple; sp5 12
108 Dodge Charger R/T, purple; pr5s, black interior 30
108 Dodge Charger R/T, purple; sp3 20
109 '65 Corvette, white; sp5 3
110 '41 Willys, black; sp5 3
111 Express Lane, orange; sp5 3
112 Mustang Mach I, mf gray; pr5s 3
112 Mustang Mach I, mf gray; sp5 6
113 BMW Z3 Roadster, aqua; pr5s 3
113 BMW Z3 Roadster, aqua; sp3 3
114 '96 Mustang, white; pr5s 3
114 '96 Mustang, white; sp3 3
115 1935 Cadillac, mf gold; lwch 3
116 Auburn 852, white; lwch 3
117 Shoe Box, white; pr5s 3
117 Shoe Box, white; sp5 12
118 Muscle Tone, black; pr5s 3
118 Muscle Tone, black; sp5 5
119 Sho-Stopper, red; pr5s 3
119 Sho-Stopper, red; pr5s 3
120 Hammered Coupe, blue; pr5s 3
120 Hammered Coupe, blue; sp5 10
121 Firebird, gray; sb5bk 3
121 Firebird, gray; sb5bk 3
122 Fork Lift, red; sp5 3
123 Wheel Loader, gray; dw3ct 3
124 Lamborghini Diablo, purple; sp3, painted chassis 3
124 Lamborghini Diablo, purple; sp3 3
124 Lamborghini Diablo, purple; pr5s 12
125 '32 Ford Vicky, black; pr5s 3
125 '32 Ford Vicky, black; sp5 8
126 '68 Mustang, red; sp5 3
127 Roll Cage, red; dw3ct 3
128 Lotus Elise 340R, red; pr5s 3
129 Slide Out, lt.green; sp3 3
129 Slide Out, lt.green; pr5s 18
130 25th Ann. Lamborghini Countach, blue; pr5s 3
130 25th Ann. Lamborghini Countach, blue; ho5 8
131 Greased Lightnin', orange; pr5s 3
131 Greased Lightnin', orange; sp5 10
132 MX48 Turbo, mf gray; sp3, black base 3
133 '97 Corvette, gray; lwch 3
134 Oshkosh Cement Truck, yellow; sp3 3
135 Corvette Stingray, black; sp5 3
136 Ice Cream Truck, white; sp3 3
137 Arachnorod, black; sp5 3
138 Vulture, blue; sp5 3
139 Ford GT-40, purple; lwch 3
140 Hot Seat, orange; sp5 3
141 Go Kart, orange; sp5, mw in front 5
141 Go Kart, orange; sp5, sp5 in front 5
142 '63 T-Bird, dk. red; lwch 3
142 '63 T-Bird, dk. red; sp3, rear trunk white to silver 5
143 SS Commodore (VT), yellow; pr5s 3
144 Isuzu VehiCROSS, yellow; pr5s 3
145 Toyota MR2, red; sp3 3
146 Camaro Z28, purple; sp5, painted chassis 3
146 Camaro Z28, purple; sp5, unpainted chassis 3
147 Sharkruiser, orange; dw3gd 3
148 Speed Shark, red; sp3 3
148 Speed Shark, red; dw3gd 3
149 Police Car, white; sp5 3
150 Enforcer, green; sp5 3
151 Surf Crate, mf gray; sp5 3
152 Deora II, dk mf red; sp5 3
153 Chevy Stocker, white; dw3gd 3
154 Power Pistons, cl.orange; sp3 3
155 '56 Ford Truck, gray; sp5 5
156 '40s Ford, white; sp5 3
157 Ferrari 333 SP, black; pr5s 3
158 Mini Cooper, blue; lwch 3
158 Mini Cooper, blue; ho5 8
159 Cabbin' Fever, green; pr5s 3
160 Metrorail, red; sp5 3
161 Jaguar XK8, dk. mf red; pr5s 3
162 Hummer, yellow; dw3ct 3
163 '37 Bugatti, white; ho5 3
164 Dragster, purple; sp5, mw in front 3
164 Dragster, purple; sp5, sp5 in front 3
165 Flashfire, black; lwch 3
165 Flashfire, black; ho5 4
166 Ferrari 456-m, blue; pr5s, painted base 3
167 Austin Healy, red; lwch 3
168 So Fine, green; lwch 3
168 So Fine, green; sp5 5
169 Blast Lane, dk. blue 5
170 Solar Eagle III, orange 3
171 Mercedes C-Class, lt.blue; lwch 3
171 Mercedes C-Class, lt.blue; sp5 3
172 Radio Flyer Wagon, purple; sp5 3
173 Talbot Lago, red; lwch 3
174 Baja Bug, mf gray; dw3ct, painted chassis 5
174 Baja Bug, mf gray; dw3ct, unpainted chassis 3
175 VW Bug, flat dk. red; ho5 5
176 1931 Duesenberg Model 1, mf dk red; sp5 3
177 Dodge Viper RT/10, lime; pr5s 3
178 Chaparral 2, green; pr5s 3
179 Krazy 8s, yellow green; pr5s 3
180 Corvette Stingray III, mf gray; lwch 3
181 Surfin' School Bus, mf blue; pr5s 3
182 Sooo Fast, black; sp5 3
183 Super Modified, orange; lwch 3
184 Jaguar D-Type, mf gray; sp5 3
185 Armored Car, black; sp5, small wheels in front 3
185 Armored Car, black; sp5, large wheels in front 4
186 Rodger Dodger, yellow; sp5 3
187 Bywayman, black; dw3ct 3
188 Flame Stopper, brown; dw3cty 3
188 Flame Stopper, brown; dw3ct 3
198 Dodge Power Wagon, mf black; dw3ct 3
190 Ferrari 308, gray; sp5 3
191 Ferrari F355, yellow; pr5s 3
191 Ferrari F355, yellow; pr5s 3
191 Ferrari F355, yellow; sp5 3
192 Escort Rally, gray; ho5 3
193 Rescue Ranger, red; ho5 3
194 Roll Patrol, blue; dw3ct 3
195 Deuce Roadster, dk. purple; sp5 3
196 3-Window '34, green; sp5 3
197 Austin Healey, light blue; sp5 3
198 Side Kick, blue-gray; ho5 3
199 Dairy Delivery, yellow; pr5s 3
199 Dairy Delivery, yellow; pr5s 3
200 '68 El Camino, orange; pr5s, China 3
200 '68 El Camino, orange; pr5s, Thailand 3
201 Super Tuned, yellow; pr5s 3
202 La Troca, purple; lwch 3
203 Hooligan, mf dk. red; sp5, painted chassis 3
204 Ferrari 360 Modena, black; pr5s 3
204 Ferrari 360 Modena, black; sp5 3
205 '38 Phantom Corsair, mf dk red 3
206 Panoz GTR-1, red; pr5s 3
207 Power Rocket, clear red; ho5 3
208 Cadillac LMP, flat black; lwgd 3
209 Ferrari F40, blue; pr5s 3
210 Blimp, orange 3
211 Krazy 8s, black; pr5gd 3
212 Shredster, purple; pr5s 3
213 MS-T Suzuka, red; pr5s 3
214 Porsche 911 GT3, orange; pr5s 3
214 Porsche 911 GT3, orange; sp3 3

215 Popcycle, purple; ho5, Popcycle on base 3
215 Popcycle, purple; ho5, Motor Psycho on base 3
216 '32 Ford, black; sp5 3
217 Shadow Jet, gray; sp5 3
218 Ferrari 250, gray; lwch 3
219 Corvette, mf orange; pr5s 5
219 Corvette, mf orange; sp3 4
220 GT Racer, blue; ho5 3
221 Riley & Scott Mk III, red; lwch 3
222 Outsider, fl.lt.green; lwch 3
223 Pikes Peak Tacoma, black; ho5, Malaysia 3
223 Pikes Peak Tacoma, black; ho5, China 3
224 Shadow Mk IIa, black; pr5s 3
225 Mercedes SLK, mf gray; ho5 3
226 '65 Impala, white; lwgd 4
227 Mini Truck, mf orange; sp5 3
228 Ford Stake Truck, blue; ho5 3
229 Silver Bullet, black; dw3 3
230 Olds Aurora, yellow; lwch, Malaysia 3
230 Olds Aurora, yellow; lwch, Thailand 3
231 Lotus Project M250, yellow; pr5s 3
232 Panoz LMP-1 Roadster S, green; ho5 3
233 Maelstom, fl.lime; ho5 3
234 1936 Cord, black; lwch 3
235 Semi-Fast, cl.red; sp5 3
236 Submarine, orange 3
237 Fire-Eater, fl.lime; ho5 3
237 Fire-Eater, fl.lime; sp5 3
238 Ferrari F50, purple; ho5 3
239 T-Bird Stocker, red; ho5 3
240 Shelby Cobra 427 S/C, mf dk. red; lwch 3

2002

1 La Troca, yellow; rrch 25
2 '71 Plymouth GTX, blue; rrch 25
3 '57 Roadster, lt. green; rrch 25
4 Lotus Project M250, dk. red; rrch 20
5 Ford Thunderbolt, mf gray; rrch 25
6 Panoz LMP Roadster S, white; rrch 20
7 Phaeton, white; rrchww 25
8 Fat Fendered '40, flat black; rrch 25
9 '40s Ford, turquoise; rrch 25
10 Tail Dragger, purple; rrch 20
11 Mini Cooper, black; rrch 30
12 Anglia Panel, dk. red; rrch 25
13 Midnight Otto, white; pr5s 3
13 Midnight Otto, white; sp5 4
14 Hyperliner, yellow; sp5bk 3
15 Tantrum, fl.lt.green; pr5s 3
15 Tantrum, fl.lt.green; sp3 5
16 Overbored 454, blue; pr5s 3
17 Jester, purple; pr5s 3
18 Altered State, purple; sp5 3
19 Nissan Skyline, dk. blue; pr5s 10
19 Nissan Skyline, dk. blue; sp5 3
20 Honda Spocket, red; pr5s 3
21 Corvette SR-2, red; sp5 3
22 Nomadder What, orange; pr5s 3
22 Nomadder What, orange; sp5 3
23 Super Smooth, blue; pr5s 3
23 Super Smooth, blue; sp5 3
24 '40 Ford Coupe, red; sp5 3
25 Ferrari P4, red; sp5gd 3
26 Saleen S7, gray; pr5s 3
26 Saleen S7, gray; sp5 3
27 Backdraft, blue-gray; pr5s 3
27 Backdraft, blue-gray; sp3 3
28 Custom Cougar, black; pr5mg 3
29 '68 Cougar, green; sp5, black roof 3
29 '68 Cougar, green; sp5, flat black roof 3
29 '68 Cougar, green; sp5, Collector's.com 50
30 Torpedo Jones, red; lwch 3
31 Custom '69 Chevy, red; pr5s 3
32 Custom '59 Cadillac, violet; lwgd 3
33 Open Roadster, yellow; pr5s 3
33 Open Roadster, yellow; sp5 3
34 Jaded, purple; sp5 3
35 '57 Eldorado Brougham, black; lwch 3
36 HW Prototype 12, mf orange; pr5s 3
36 HW Prototype 12, mf orange; sp5 3
37 Lancia Stratos, red; sp5 10
37 Lancia Stratos, red; pr5gd 3
37 Lancia Stratos, red; pr5s 4
37 Lancia Stratos, red; pr5gd, w/tampo 3
38 Nizzan Z, mf gray; pr5s 3
39 Toyota RSC, gray; orts 3
40 2001 Mini Cooper, yellow; pr5s 10
40 2001 Mini Cooper, yellow; sp5 3
41 Super Tsunami, gold; pr5 3
42 '64 Riviera, mf orange; pr5s 3
42 '64 Riviera, mf orange; sp5 3
43 Moto-Crossed 3
44 Lotus Esprit, black; sp5 3
45 Volkswagen New Beetle Cup 3
46 Pony-Up, orange; pr5s 3
47 I Candy 3
48 Rocket Oil Special, purple; sp5 3
49 Hyundai Spyder Concept 3
50 Sling Shot 3
51 '40 Somethin', yellow; pr5 3
52 Side Draft 3
53 Ballistik 3
54 Syd Mead's Sentinel 400 Limo 3
55 '59 Impala, mf brown; sp5gd 3
56 '32 Delivery, black; sp3 3
57 Ice Cream Truck, orange; sp5gd 3
58 Power Plower, dark red; dw3ctgd 3
58 Power Plower, dark red; or5gd 3
59 Surfin' School Bus, mf gray; sp5gd 3
60 So Fine, turquoise; sp5 3
61 Rodger Dodger, green; sp5 3
62 Sooo Fast, red; sp5 3
63 Ford Focus, white; lwch 3
64 Honda Civic, blue; sp3 3
65 MS-T Suzuka, yellow; sp3 3
66 Toyota Celica, red; lwch 3
67 '65 Corvette, mf blue; sp5 3
68 '97 Corvette, mf purple; sp3 3
68 '97 Corvette, mf purple; sp5 4
69 '58 Corvette Coupe, yellow; sp3 3
70 '63 Corvette, red; sp3 3
71 Dodge Charger R/T, black; ho5 3
72 Hammered Coupe, dk. red; sp5gd 3
73 Montezooma, gold; ho5 3
73 '33 Ford Roadster, white; sp5 3
75 Firebird Funny Car, black; sp5rd 3
76 Speed Shark, mf orange; sp5 3
77 Vulture, yellow; sp5 3
78 Phaeton, mf aqua; dw3gd 3
79 Chrysler Pronto, mf red; lwch 3
80 3-Window '34, blue; dw3 3
81 Deora II, gray; ho5 3
82 '68 El Camino, white; sp5 3
83 Power Pistons, black; sp5rd 3
84 Seared Tuner, red; ho5gd 3
85 Fandango, blue; sp5mg 3
86 Super Tuned, green; sp5bl 3
87 Monoposto, green; pr5 3
89 Jet Threat 3.0, blue; lwch 3
90 Hammered Coupe, magenta; sp5 3
94 Phantastique, blue; dw3 3
115 Honda Civic, black; ho5 3
116 '71 Plymouth GTX, yellow; sp5 3
116 '71 Plymouth GTX, yellow; sp3 3
117 '67 Dodge Charger, yellow; sp3 3
118 Mercedes CLK-LM, mf dark red; lwch 3
119 Pontiac Rageous, mf gray; lwch 3
120 Dodge Concept Car, lt. olive green; sp3 3
121 Shock Factor, fl green; dw3ct 3
122 Deora, dk. red; dw3 3
123 Evil Twin, gold; lwgd 3
123 Evil Twin, yellow; lwgd 12
124 Monoposto, red; sp3, Malaysia 3
124 Monoposto, red; pr5s 3
124 Monoposto, red; sp3, Thailand 3
125 Hyper Mite, purple; sp5gd, Malaysia 3
125 Hyper Mite, purple; sp5gd, Thailand 3
126 Surf Crate, red; sp5gd 3
127 Fore Wheeler, mf gold; sp5gd 3
128 Tow Jam, black; sp3 3
129 Sweet 16, white; lwch 3
130 Porsche 911 Carrera, blue; sp3 3
131 Thunderstreak, dk. blue; lwch 3
131 Thunderstreak, mf blue; lwch 3
132 Vulture Roadster, blue; sp5 3
133 Fright Bike, clear red 3
134 Old #3, orange; sp5, painted chassis 3
135 Porsche 911 GT1-98, mf orange; lwch 3
136 Chrysler Thunderbolt, mf dark red; ho5gd 3
137 Ferrari 348, yellow; sp3 3
138 Buick Wildcat, mf purple; sp3, black Chassis 3
139 '67 Camaro, dk. mf blue; sp3 3
140 XS-IVE, beige; dw3gdct 3
140 XS-IVE, beige; dw3ct 3
140 XS-IVE, beige; ortsgd 3
141 Ferrari 156, red; lwch 3
142 Ford Thunderbolt, mf dark red; sp3 3
142 Ford Thunderbolt, mf dark red; sp5 3
143 Anglia Panel, dk. blue; sp5 3
143 Anglia Panel, mf blue; sp5 3
144 Jeepster, yellow; sp5 3
145 Whatta Drag, yellow; sp5 3
145 Whatta Drag, yellow; sp3 3
146 Dogfighter, black; sp3gd 3
147 '65 Mustang Cnv., mf gray; sp5 3
148 Porsche 959, red; sp5 3
149 Jet Threat 3.0, blue-gray; ho5 3
150 Mega Duty, orange; pr5s 3
151 Toyota Celica, purple; lwch 3
152 Silhouette II, lime; sp3 3
153 Sol-Aire CX4, blue; sp3 3
154 Olds 442, dark red; sp3 3
155 T-Bird Stocker, blue; sp5 3
156 Cunningham Car, dk. blue; sp5 3
157 Mo' Scoot, cl.blue 3
158 Fandango, yellow; pr5gd 3
159 Thomassima III, aqua; pr5s 3
160 Pikes Peak Celica, dk. blue; lwch 3
161 (BMW) M Roadster, mf gold; ho5 3
162 Ferrari F512M, gray; sp5 3
163 Lexus SC400, gold; lwgd 3
164 Ferrari F355 Spider, blue; sp5 3
165 '57 T-Bird, mf blue; sp5 3
166 Ferrari 308, black; lwch 3
168 Speed Blaster, blue; sp3 3
170 Splittin' Image, lime green; sp5 3
172 Ferrari F355 Berlinetta, mf gray; sp5 3
180 Shoe Box, black; sp5 3
217 Mustang Cobra, mf purple; lwch 3
218 Baby Boomer, turquoise; sp5 3
219 Dodge Ram 1500, yellow; sp3 3
237 At-A-Tude, lt.blue; sp5 3
238 Saltflat Racer, dk. red; sp5 3

Promotional Series

Very early in their history, groups of vehicles were marketed under a series name. The following are standard-line Hot Wheels vehicles, listed under the series name and year they were sold.

Grand Prix Series 1969

Colors are assorted and not listed here. See regular section for colors and other variations.

Brabham-Repco F1
Chapparal 2G
Ford Mark IV
Indy Eagle
Lola GT70
Lotus Turbine
McLaren M6A
Porsche 917
Shelby Turbine

Spoilers 1970

Colors are assorted and not listed here. See regular section for colors and other variations.

Boss Hoss
Evil Weevil
Heavy Chevy
King Kuda
Light-My-Firebird
Nitty Gritty Kitty
Sugar Caddy
TNT Bird

Heavyweights 1970

Colors are assorted and not listed here. See regular section for colors and other variations.

Ambulance
Cement Mixer
Dump Truck
Fire Engine
Fuel Tanker
Moving Van
Racer Rig
S'Cool Bus
Scooper
Snorkel
Team Trailer
Tow Truck
Waste Wagon

Super Chromes 1976

These models come with either rsw, bw or both.

Alive '55
Chevy Monza 2+2
Corvette Stingray (6-pack only)
Formula 5000 (6-pack only)
Gremlin Grinder
Heavy Chevy (green)
Heavy Chevy (red)
Large Charge
Mighty Maverick
Mustang Stocker (450 HP)
Mustang Stocker (stars & stripes)
Neet Streeter (6-pack only)
P-911 (stripes)
P-911 (swirls)
P-917
Poison Pinto (6-pack only)
Prowler (burglar)
Prowler (flames)
Rock Buster (6-pack or set only)
Steam Roller
Super Van (California Cruisin')
Super Van (flames)
Twin Mill (6-pack only)

Rescue Team 1978

Only color variations are listed here. Wheel, tampo or other variations are in the regular listing.

Chief's Special - red
Emergency Squad - red
Fire Chaser - red
Fire Eater - red
Highway Patrol - white
Paramedic - yellow

Speedway Specials 1978

American Victory - magenta
Baja Breaker - gray
Bywayman - light blue
Flat Out 442 - orange
Formula 5000 - white
Formula P.A.C.K. - black (8)
Greased Gremlin - red
Lickety Six - dk blue
Mercedes C111 - red
Monte Carlo Stocker - dk blue
Monte Carlo Stocker - yellow
P-917 - orange
Race Bait 308 - red
Rock Buster - yellow
Steam Roller - yellow
Torino Stocker - black
Torino Stocker - red

Super Streeters 1978

Corvette Stingray - gray
Corvette Stingray - red
Corvette Stingray - yellow
Hare Splitter - white
Hot Bird - black
Jaguar XJS - gray
Mustang Stocker - chrome
P-911 - chrome
Royal Flash - white
Super Van - black
Super Van - chrome (California Cruisin')
Upfront 924 - yellow
Z Whiz - gray

Oldies But Goodies 1978

'31 Doozie - green
'31 Doozie - orange
'57 Chevy - red
'57 T-Bird - yellow
A-OK - light green
Alive '55 - chrome
Auburn 852 - red
Dumpin' A - yellow
T-Totaller - black
T-Totaller - brown

The Heavies 1978

'56 Hi-Tail Hauler
'56 Hi-Tail Hauler - orange
Funny Money - gray
GMC Motor Home - orange
Letter Getter - white
Maxi Taxi
Ramblin' Wrecker - white

Drag Strippers 1978

Army Funny Car - white
Cool One - green
Cool One - purple
Inferno - yellow
Jet Threat II - blue
Neet Streeter - light blue
Odd Rod
Packin' Pacer - yellow
Poison Pinto - light green
Prowler - chrome (burglar)
Rodger Dodger - gold-plated
Show Hoss II - light green
Street Rodder - black
Top Eliminator - gold chrome
Twin Mill - orange
Vetty Funny - gray

Classy Customs 1978

Bubble Gunner - purple
Buzz Off - gold plated
Ice "T" - light green
Inside Story - gray
Large Charge - orange
Paddy Wagon - dk blue
Red Baron - red
Science Friction - white
Second Wind - white
Spacer Racer - metallic red
Spoiler Sport - light green
Stagefright - brown

Heroes 1979
Captain America - white
Human Torch - black
Incredible Hulk, The - yellow
Iron Man - white
Silver Surfer - chrome
Spiderman - black
Thing, The - blue
Thor - yellow
Scene Machines 1979
Captain America - white
Circus Cats - white
Hot Wheels Race Team - yellow
Incredible Hulk, The - white
Motocross - red
Rescue Squad - red
Space Vehicle - gray
Spiderman - white
S.W.A.T. - blue
Hi-Rakers 1980
3-Window '34 - red
3-Window '34 - mf red
'40s Woodie - orange
'40s Woodie - blue
'40s Woodie - yellow
Dodge D-50 - red
Dodge D-50 - mf blue
Split Window '63 - gray
Split Window '63 - yellow
Split Window '63 - mf gold
Turbo Wedge - green
Turbo Wedge - orange
'Vette Van - black
'Vette Van - red
Workhorses 1980
Airport Rescue - yellow
Ambulance - white
Big Rig - black
CAT Bulldozer - yellow
CAT Dump Truck - yellow
CAT Earth Mover - yellow
CAT Fork Lift - yellow
CAT Road Roller - yellow
CAT Wheel Loader - yellow
Construction Crane - yellow
Delivery Truck - white (Wonder Bread)
Flame Stopper - red
Ford Dump Truck - green
Ford Stake Bed Truck - metallic red
Highway Hauler - blue (Goodyear)
Highway Hauler - green (Mountain Dew)
Highway Hauler - (Pepsi)
Highway Hauler - yellow (Mayflower)
Highway Hauler - yellow (Pennzoil)
Highway Hauler - white
(Hot Wheels Racing Team)
Highway Hauler - white
(Masters of the Universe)
Highway Hauler - white (NASA)
Highway Hauler - white (North American)
Oshkosh Snow Plow - orange
Peterbilt Cement Truck - red
Peterbilt Dump Truck - metallic blue
Peterbilt Dump Truck - red
Peterbilt Tank Truck - orange
(construction)
Peterbilt Tank Truck - orange (Shell)
Peterbilt Tank Truck - red (railroad)
Peterbilt Tank Truck - yellow (Shell)
Peterbilt Tank Truck - yellow (railroad)
Phone Truck - white
Rescue Ranger - green
Rescue Ranger - red
Rig Wrecker - white
School Bus - yellow
Trash Truck - orange
Hot Ones 1980
380 SEL - gray
380 SEL - mf silver
'57 Chevy - mf red
'55 Chevy - red
'55 Chevy - red & white
'57 Chevy - yellow
'80s Corvette - gray
'80s Corvette - mf silver
'80s Corvette - red
'80s Firebird - black
'80s Firebird - red
'82 Supra - black
'82 Supra - red
Blown Camaro Z-28 - black
Camaro Z-28 - mf silver
Camaro Z-28 - metallic dk red
Camaro Z-28 - red
Camaro Z-28 - white
Cannonade - red
Cannonade - yellow
Chevy Citation - mf brown
Chevy Citation - white
Chevy Citation - yellow
Corvette Stingray - orange
Corvette Stingray - red
Datsun 200SX - mf gold
Datsun 200SX - white
Dodge Mirada - red
Fiero 2M4 - white
Flat Out 442 - light green
Flat Out 442 - mf gold
Flat Out 442 - yellow
Frontrunnin' Fairmont - red
Highway Heat - orange
Mirada Stocker - mf gold
Mirada Stocker - yellow
Mountain Dew Stocker - white
Mustang S.V.O. - black
NASCAR Stocker - white
Nissan 300ZX - red
P-911 Turbo - black
P-911 Turbo - white
P-928 - red
Packin' Pacer - orange
Packin' Pacer - white
Race Ace - white
Race Bait 308 - gray
Racing Stocker - white
Science Friction - maroon
Science Friction - metallic maroon
Stock Rocket - red
Taxi - yellow
Thunderbird Stocker - white
Torino Tornado - yellow
Turbo Mustang - red
Turbo Mustang - yellow
Turbo Mustang - mf blue
Turbo Mustang - mf red
Turbo Mustang - white
Real Riders 1982
3-Window '34 (gyg) - mf red
3-Window '34 (gyw) - mf red
3-Window '34 (gyg) - black
3-Window '34 (gyw) - black
380 SEL (Mercedes) (gyg) - black (France)
380 SEL (Mercedes) (gyg) - mf silver
'40s Ford 2-Door (gyg) - black
'40s Ford 2-Door (gyw) - black
'40s Woodie (gyg) - mf blue
'40s Woodie (gyw) - mf blue
'57 T-Bird (gyg) - metallic red
'57 T-Bird (gyw) - metallic red
'57 T-Bird (gyg) - black
'57 T-Bird (gyw) - black
A-OK (gyg) - metallic red
Baja Breaker (gyg) - black
Baja Breaker (gyg) - mf orange
Baja Breaker (gyw) - black
Baja Bug (gyg) - yellow
Baja Bug (gyw) - yellow
Baja Bug (gyw) - black (3-pack)
Baja Bug (gyw) - red (Baja)
Baja Bug (gyw) - red (Blazin')
Baja Bug (gyw) - white
Beach Patrol (gyg) - white
Beach Patrol (gyw) - white
Black Lightning (gyg) - black
Black Lightning (gyg) - yellow (Kellogg's Promo)
BMW M1 (gyg) - red
Bronco 4-Wheeler (gyg) - red
Bronco 4-Wheeler (gyw) - red
Bywayman (gyg) - mf blue
Bywayman (gyw) - mf blue
Bywayman (gyw) - yellow (3-pack)
Cadillac Seville (gyg) - gray (France)
Cadillac Seville (gyg) - mf gold
(Mexico)
Classic Cobra (gyg) - blue
Classic Cobra (gyw) - blue
Classic Cobra (gyg) - blue
(Mexico, smaller wheels)
Classic Cobra (gyg) - blue
(Mexico, yellow stripes)
Classic Cobra (gyw) - red
Dodge D-50 (gyg) - mf blue
Dodge D-50 (gyw) - mf blue
Dodge D-50 (gyw) - white
Dodge Rampage (gyg) - red
Dodge Rampage (gyw) - red
Dodge Rampage (gyw) - red (Mexico)
Dream Van XGW (gyg) - mf blue
Dream Van XGW (gyw) - mf blue
Dream Van XGW (gyg) - light green
Dream Van XGW (gyg) - light green
(Mexico)
Dream Van XGW (gyw) - burgundy
(3-pack)
Formula Fever (gyg) - yellow
Formula Fever (gyw) - yellow
Good Ol' Pick-Um-Up (gyw) - maroon
Greased Gremlin (gyg) - red (Mexico)
Jeep CJ-7 (gyg) - mf brown
Jeep CJ-7 (gyw) - mf brown
Jeep CJ-7 (gyw) - white
Jeep CJ-7 (gyw) - yellow
Jeep Scrambler (gyg) - gray
Jeep Scrambler (gyg) - mf silver
Jeep Scrambler (gyw) - mf silver
Jeep Scrambler (gyw) - black
Jeep Scrambler (gyw) - metallic blue
Jeep Scrambler (gyw) - plum
Lightning Gold (gyg) - yellow
Lightning Gold (gyw) - yellow
Malibu Grand Prix (gyg) - black
P-928 (gyg) - red
Path Beater (gyw) - black
Pavement Pounder (gyw) - light green
Power Plower (gyw) - red
Race Bait 308 (gyg) - mf silver
Rescue Ranger (gyw) - green
Split Window '63 (gyg) - black
Split Window '63 (gyw) - black
Split Window '63 (gyg) - mf gold
Split Window '63 (gyw) - mf gold
Street Rodder (gyg) - white
Super Scraper (gyg) - black
Super Scraper (gyw) - black
Thunderstreak (gyg) - maroon
Thunderstreak (gyg) - white
Turbo Streak (gyg) - yellow
Turbo Streak (gyw) - yellow
Megaforce Series 1982
Battle Tank - olive
Megadestroyer 1 - black
Megadestroyer 1 - tan
Megafighter - tan
Personal Carrier - white
Extras 1983
'31 Doozie - red
'56 Hi-Tail Hauler - mf blue
Ford Stake Bed Truck - blue
Oshkosh Snow Plow - orange
Peterbilt Dump Truck - yellow
Sunagon - mf blue
Upfront 924 - mf gold
Trailbusters 1984
Baja Breaker - black
Baja Breaker - white
Baja Bug - white
Blazer 4x4 - black
Bronco 4-Wheeler - white
Bywayman - maroon
Bywayman - mf blue
Good Humor Truck - white
Gulch Stepper - red
Jeep CJ-7 - white
Jeep Scrambler - metallic blue
Jeep Scrambler metallic dk red
Monster 'Vette - yellow
Nissan Hardbody - red & white
Nissan Hardbody - white
Path Beater - black
Power Plower - black
Street Roader - white
Suzuki ATV (Quad Racer) - yellow
Tall Ryder - mf silver
Thunderbird Stocker - red
Ultra Hots 1984
Back Burner - metallic dk red
Flame Runner - metallic gold
Jet Sweep X5 - metallic yellow
Predator metallic green
Quik Trik - metallic magenta
Redliner - metallic gold
Silver Bullet - unpainted metal
Sol-Aire CX4 - mf silver
Sol-Aire CX4 - unpainted metal
Speed Seeker - metallic red
Street Beast - metallic blue
Street Scorcher - metallic dk red
Wind Splitter - metallic blue
Wind Splitter - metallic green
Action Command 1985
Assault Crawler - olive
Assault Crawler - tan
Big Bertha - olive
Big Bertha - tan
Combat Medic - olive
Combat Medic - tan
Command Tank - olive
Radar Ranger - mf silver
Rocketank - olive
Rocketank - tan
Roll Patrol Jeep CJ - olive
Roll Patrol Jeep CJ - tan
Shell Shocker - olive
Sting Rod - olive
Sting Rod - tan
Super Cannon - olive
Tail Gunner - olive
Tail Gunner - tan
Tank Gunner - olive
Troop Convoy - olive
Troop Convoy - tan
Speed Demons 1986
Cargoyle - orange
Double Demon - red
Evil Weevil - blue
Evil Weevil - yellow
Fangster - green
Phantomachine - chrome
Ratmobile - white
Rodzilla - magenta
Sharkruiser - gray
Turboa - yellow
Vampyra - purple
Zombot - gold chrome
Classics 1987
3-Window '34 - purple
3-Window '34 - red
'32 Ford Delivery - yellow
'37 Bugatti - yellow
'57 Chevy - mf blue
'57 Chevy - turquoise
'65 Mustang Convertible - turquoise
Classic Caddy - mf silver
Classic Cobra - red
Mercedes 540K - black
Talbot Lago - maroon
Talbot Lago - white
T-Bucket - orange
T-Bucket - yellow
Speed Fleet 1987
3-Window '34 - red
'80s Corvette - black
'80s Corvette - blue
'80s Firebird - black
Alien - blue
Alien - red
Blown Camaro Z-28 - turquoise
Chevy Stocker - black
Custom Corvette - metallic dk red
Ferrari Testarossa - red
Fiero 2M4 - red
Firebird Funny Car - mf blue
Firebird Funny Car - yellow
GT Racer - mf blue
GT Racer - purple
Hot Bird - mf blue
Lamborghini Countach - white
Mercedes 380 SEL - white

Nissan 300ZX - white
Peugeot 205 Rallye - white
Pontiac Banshee - red
Porsche 959 - metallic dk red
Power Plower - red
Shadow Jet - yellow
Silver Bullet - mf silver
Sol-Aire CX4 - black
Sol-Aire CX4 - red
Thunderburner - black
Thunderburner - white
Tricar X8 - yellow
XT-3 - black
XT-3 - purple

Speed Machines

Only major variations are listed.
American Victory - dk green
Bubble Gunner - yellow (black base)
Bubble Gunner - yellow (maroon base)
Dumpin 'A' - gray (chrome engine)
Dumpin 'A' - gray (gray engine)
Hare Splitter - light blue
Inside Story - red (chrome interior, blue-tinted windows)
Inside Story - red (chrome interior, yellow-tinted windows)
Inside Story - red (white interior, yellow-tinted windows)
Lowdown - red
Mustang Stocker - black
Packin' Pacer - light blue
Poison Pinto - red
Rock Buster - white (black interior)
Rock Buster - white (red interior)
Second Wind - orange
Show Hoss II - light blue
Spacer Racer - yellow
Spoiler Sport - light blue
Super Van - red
T-Totaller - magenta
Top Eliminator - plum
Turbo Wedge - yellow
Vega Bomb - dk green
'Vette Van - plum
Z Whiz - light green

French Hot Wheels

Listed are the models and colors. For tampo, wheel or other variations see the main section.
380 SEL - black
380 SEL - mf silver
'80s Firebird - red
Airport Food Service - blue
Airport Rescue - red
Airport Security - blue
Airport Transport - white
Alive '55 - green
American Victory - burgundy
American Victory - light blue
Beach Patrol - white
BMW M1 - red
Cadillac Seville - gray
Cargo Lift - yellow
Chevy Citation - white
Chevy Monza 2+2 - orange
Double Decker Bus - white
Double Vision - blue
Double Vision - dk blue
Dune Daddy - blue
Dune Daddy - light green
Fiat Ritmo - gray
Fire Eater - red
Fireball Torino - white
Ford Escort - black
Formula 5000 - white
Ice 'T' - blue
Ice 'T' - tan
Ice 'T' - yellow
Jaguar XJS - gray
Lickety Six - blue
Lowdown - blue
Lowdown - white
Mercedes 540K - red
Minitrek - gray
Mirada Stocker - red
Mustang Stocker - white
Mustang Stocker - yellow
Odd Rod - yellow
Old Number 5 - red
P-911 - black
Paddy Wagon - blue
Paddy Wagon - brown
Paddy Wagon - tan
Peugeot 505 - reddish brown
Poison Pinto - dk green
Poison Pinto - light green
Prowler - orange
Prowler - white
Renault LeCar - black
Renault LeCar - light blue
Renault LeCar - light olive green
Renault LeCar - red
Rolls-Royce Phaeton - gray
Rolls-Royce Phaeton - mf silver
Royal Flash - white
Sand Drifter - orange
Sand Drifter - yellow
Sand Witch - burgundy
Second Wind - white
Show Hoss II - yellow
Sir Rodney Roadster - metal
Spoiler Sport - green
Stutz Blackhawk - gray
Taxi - yellow
Top Eliminator - red
Turismo - plum
Upfront 924 - orange
Upfront 924 - white
Vega Bomb - maroon
Vega Bomb - red
Vega Bomb - tan
Warpath - blue
Warpath - light blue
Z Whiz - black

Mexican Hot Wheels

Listed are the models and colors. For tampo, wheel or other variations see the main section.
Airport Rescue - yellow
American Victory - dk blue
Aries Wagon - yellow
Autobus - red
Cadillac Seville - mf gold
Cannonade - maroon
Cannonade - yellow
CAT Fork Lift - yellow
Celica Supra - black
Chevy Citation - mf brown
Chevy Monza 2+2 - beige
Chevy Monza 2+2 - orange
Classic Cobra - blue
Classic Packard - black
Datsun 200SX - red-brown
Dixie Challenger - orange
Dodge D-50 - white
Dodge Rampage - red
Dream Van XGW - light green
Dumpin' 'A' - orange
Dune Daddy - light green
Fat Fendered '40 - metallic plum
Fiat Ritmo - mf gray
Fireball Torino - white
Ford Escort - red
Ford Escort - white
Ford Escort - yellow
Formula 5000 - white
GMC Motor Home - dk green
Good Ol' Pick-Um-Up - metallic plum
Greased Gremlin - red
Greyhound MC-8 - Chrome & white
Hare Splitter - white
Ice 'T' - dk green
Inside Story - black
Inside Story - gray-tan
Jaguar XJS - mf brown
Jaguar XJS - white
Large Charge - orange
Lickety Six - gray-blue
Lickety Six - white
Long Shot - white
Mercedes 380 SEL - gray
Minitrek - black
Mirada Stocker - red
Monte Carlo Stocker - dk blue
Mustang Stocker - white
Neet Streeter - blue
Neet Streeter - mf magenta
Odd Rod - yellow
Omni 024 - mf gold
Packin' Pacer - yellow
Paddy Wagon - blue
Peugeot 505 - black
Peugeot 505 - blue
Pontiac J-2000 - green
Pontiac J-2000 - red
Pontiac J-2000 - white
Pontiac J-2000 - yellow
Prowler - chrome
Renault LeCar - red
Rock Buster - yellow
Royal Flash - orange
Sand Witch - red
Second Wind - white
Show Hoss II - dk blue
Sir Rodney Roadster - yellow
Space Van - gray
Spacer Racer - red
Spiderman - black
Spoiler Sport - pink
Stagefright - dk brown
Street Rodder - white
Street Scorcher - brown
Stutz Open - mf brown
Sunagon - dk blue
Sunagon - mf blue
T-Totaller - dk brown
Telephone Truck - white
Thrill Driver Torino - red
Thrill Driver Torino - white
Torino Stocker - black
Torino Tornado - yellow
Trash Truck - orange
Turbo Mustang - red
Turismo - yellow
Upfront 924 - mf gold
Warpath - white
Z Whiz - green

Pro Circuit

Only color variations are listed.
#1 Texaco (Michael Andretti) - white
#2 Pontiac Excitement (Rusty Wallace) - black
#2 Texaco (Mario Andretti) - white
#3 Cytomax (Greg Pickett) - white
#3 Valvoline (Al Unser Jr.) - white
#4 Penske (Rick Mears) - white
#5 Penske (Emerson Fittipaldi) - orange
#6 Valvoline (Mark Martin
#21 Citgo (Morgan Shepherd) - white
#25 Hot Wheels (Jack Baldwin) - blue
#26 Quaker State (Brett Bodine) - green
#26 Quaker State (Roberto Guerrero) - green
#33 Duracell (Scott Sharp) orange
#42 Mello Yello (Kyle Petty) - black
#43 STP (Richard Petty) - blue
#43 STP (Richard Petty) - light blue
Castrol GTX Funny Car (John Force) - white
King Kenny Funny Car (Kenny Bernstein) - red

California Custom

Only color variations are listed.
3-Window '34 - fluorescent lime
3-Window '34 - metallic blue
'35 Classic Caddy - gold-plated
'40s Woodie - bright red
'40s Woodie - bright yellow green (set only)
'40s Woodie - turquoise
'55 Nomad - rose red
'57 Chevy - bright orange
'59 Caddy - pink
'65 Mustang Convertible - green
'65 Mustang Convertible - orange (set only)
'67 Camaro - mf blue
Baja Bug - fluorescent pink
Beach Patrol - fluorescent green
Blown Camaro Z-28 - dk red
Blown Camaro Z-28 - white
BMW 323 - white
Classic Cobra - lime yellow
Classic Cobra - white
Corvette Convertible - chrome blue
Corvette Convertible - orange
Corvette Funny Car - white
Ferrari Testarossa - chrome magenta
Ferrari Testarossa - neon red
Firebird - fluorescent lime
Mercedes 380 SEL - chrome
P-911 Turbo - bright red
P-911 Turbo - chrome magenta
Pontiac Banshee - gold chrome
Sol-Aire CX4 - bright pink
Split Window '63 - chrome rose
Split Window '63 - hot pink (set only)
Street Roader - orange
Street Roader - white
Stutz Blackhawk - neon red

Park 'n Plates

Only color variations are listed.
3-Window '34 - metallic blue
'40s Woodie - ruby red
'57 Chevy - metallic dk red
'57 T-Bird - turquoise
'65 Mustang Convertible - white
'80s Corvette - red
'80s Firebird - mf dk red
Blazer 4X4 - light green
Bywayman - white
Camaro Z-28 - orange
Classic Cobra - black
Ferrari Testarossa - mf silver
Ferrari Testarossa - red
GT Racer - red
Lamborghini Countach - red
Mercedes 380 SEL - black
Nissan 300 ZX - white
Porsche 959 - white
Sheriff Patrol - black
Sol-Aire CX4 - yellow
T-Bucket - purple
Thunderstreak - blue & yellow
VW Bug - yellow

25th Anniversary Series

Beatnik Bandit
Classic Nomad
Demon, The
Paddy Wagon
Red Baron
Silhouette
Splittin' Image
Twin Mill
Vintage Series A
Beatnik Bandit
Classic Nomad
Demon, The
Paddy Wagon
Red Baron
Silhouette
Splittin' Image
Twin Mill
Vintage Series B
'32 Ford Vicky
Custom Mustang
Deora
Mongoose
Mutt Mobile
S'Cool Bus
Snake
Whip Creamer

Race Team Series®

#1 Lumina Stocker
#2 Hot Wheels 500
#3 Side-Splitter
#4 Dragster

Steel Stamp Series®

#1 Steel Passion
#2 Zender Fact 4
#3 '56 Flashsider
#4 '57 Chevy

Krackle Car Series

#1 Sharkruiser
#2 Turboa
#3 '63 Split Window
#4 Flashfire

Pearl Driver Series®

#1 Talbot Lago
#2 Pearl Passion
#3 VW Bug
#4 Jaguar XJ220

Promotional Series

Dark Rider Series®
#1 Splittin' Image
#2 Twin Mill II
#3 Silhouette II
#4 Rigor Motor
Roarin' Rods Series™
#1 Street Roader
#2 Roll Patrol
#3 Cobra
#4 Mini Truck
Hot Hubs Series®
#1 Cybercruiser
#2 Vampyra
#3 Shadow Jet
#4 Suzuki Quad Racer
Speed Gleamer Series®
#1 3-Window '34
#2 T-Bucket
#3 Ratmobile
#4 Limozeen
Silver Series
#1 Fire Eater
#2 Rodzilla
#3 Propper Chopper
#4 School Bus
Photo Finish Series®
#1 Aerostar
#2 Flyin' Aces Blimp
#3 Tank Truck
#4 Hiway Hauler
Racing Metals Series®
#1 Race Truck
#2 Ramp Truck
#3 Camaro Racer
#4 Dragster
"Real Riders" Series
#1 Dump Truck
#2 Mercedes-Benz Unimog
#3 '59 Caddy
#4 Corvette Stingray
Treasure Hunt Series (1995)
#1 Olds 442
#2 Gold Passion
#3 '67 Camaro
#4 '57 T-Bird
#5 VW Bug
#6 '63 Split Window
#7 Stutz Blackhawk
#8 Rolls-Royce
#9 Classic Caddy
#10 Nomad
#11 Cobra
#12 '31 Doozie
1995 First Editions
#1 Speed Blaster
#2 Mercedes SL
#3 '58 Corvette Coupe
#4 Speed-A-Saurus
#5 Power Rocker
#6 Hydroplane
#7 Dodge Ram Truck
#8 Camaro Convertible
#9 Power Pipes
#10 Ferrari 355
#11 Power Pistons
#12 Snowmobile
1996 Race Truck Series®
#1 Dodge Ram 1500
#2 Kenworth T 600A
#3 '56 Flashsider
#4 Nissan Truck
Flame Thrower Series
#1 '57 T-Bird
#2 Hydroplane
#3 Range Rover
#4 Oshkosh Snow Plow
Space Series®
#1 Radar Ranger
#2 GM Lean Machine
#3 Alien
#4 Treadator
Race Team Series® II
#1 Ramp Truck
#2 Baja Bug
#3 '57 Chevy
#4 Bywayman

Mod Bod Series™
#1 Hummer
#2 School Bus
#3 VW Bug
#4 '67 Camaro
Dark Rider Series® II
#1 Big Chill
#2 Street Beast
#3 Thunderstreak
#4 Power Pistons
Sports Car Series
#1 Porsche 930
#2 Custom Corvette
#3 Shelby Cobra 427 S/C
#4 '59 Caddy
Splatter Paint Series™
#1 Rescue Ranger
#2 Side-Splitter
#3 '55 Chevy
#4 '80s Camaro
Street Eaters® Series
#1 Speed Machine
#2 Silhouette II
#3 Propper Chopper
#4 Roll Patrol
Fast Food Series
#1 Pizza Vette
#2 Pasta Pipes
#3 Sweet Stocker
#4 Crunch Chief
Silver Series II
#1 Dump Truck
#2 '40s Woodie
#3 '57 Chevy
#4 Oscar Mayer Wienermobile
Fire Squad Series
#1 Ambulance
#2 Rescue Ranger
#3 Flame Stopper
#4 Fire Eater
1996 Treasure Hunt Series
#1 '40s Woodie
#2 Auburn 852
#3 Ferrari 250
#4 Jaguar XJ220
#5 '59 Caddy
#6 Dodge Viper RT/10
#7 '57 Chevy
#8 Ferrari 355
#9 '58 Corvette
#10 Speed Fleet
#11 Dodge Ram 1500
#12 '37 Bugatti
1996 First Editions
#1 1996 Mustang GT
#2 Chevy 1500
#3 1970 Dodge Charger Daytona
#4 Street Cleaver
#5 Rail Rodder
#6 VW Bus
#7 Road Rocket
#8 Turbo Flame
#9 Radio Flyer Wagon
#10 Dogfighter
#11 Twang Thang
#12 Ferrari F50
1997 Speed Spray Series
Hydroplane
Street Roader
XT-3
Funny Car
Heat Fleet Series™
Police Cruiser
School Bus
Peterbilt Tank Truck
Ramblin' Wrecker
Quicksilver Series
Ferrari 308
T-Bird Stocker
Aeroflash
Chevy Stocker
Blue Streak Series
Nissan Truck
'55 Chevy
Olds 442
Speed Blaster
Race Team III Series
Hummer

Chevy 1500
'80s Corvette
3-Window '34
White Ice Series™
Splittin' Image II
Twin Mill II
Speed Machine
Shadow Jet
Phantom Racer Series™
Power Rocket
Power Pipes
Power Pistons
Road Rocket
Dealer's Choice Series™
'63 Corvette
Street Beast
Baja Bug
Silhouette II
Rockin' Rods Series™
Turbo Flame
Twang Thang
Ferrari 355
Porsche 930
Street Beast™ Series
Jaguar XJ220
Blown Camaro
Corvette Stingray
Mercedes-Benz Unimog
Biff! Bam! Boom! Series™
Range Rover
Mini Truck
VW Bug
Limozeen
Spy Print Series
Custom Corvette
Sol-Aire CX4
Stealth
Alien
1997 Treasure Hunt Series
'56 Flashsider
Silhouette II
Mercedes 500SL
Street Cleaver
GM Lean Machine
Hot Rod Wagon
Olds Aurora
Dogfighter
Buick Wildcat
Blimp
Avus Quattro
Rail Rodder
1997 First Editions
Excavator
Ford F-150
Way 2 Fast
'97 Corvette
Mercedes C-Class
'59 Chevy Impala
BMW M Roadster
Scorchin' Scooter
Saltflat Racer
1970 Plymouth Barracuda
25th Anniversary Lamborghini Countach
Firebird Funny Car
1998 Tattoo Machines® Series
'57 T-Bird
'93 Camaro
Stutz Blackhawk
Corvette Stingray
Techno Bits™ Series
Shadow Jet II
Power Pistons
Shadow Jet
Radar Ranger
Tropicool™ Series
Ice Cream Truck
Baja Bug
Classic Caddy
Corvette Convertible
Low 'n Cool Series
Mini Truck
'59 Impala
'59 Caddy
Limozeen
Biohazard™ Series
Hydroplane
Flame Stopper
Recycling Truck

Rescue Ranger
Dash 4 Cash™ Series
Jaguar XJ220
Ferrari F40
Audi Avus
Dodge Viper RT/10
Race Team IV Series
Shelby Cobra 427
'63 Corvette
Mercedes C-Class
'67 Camaro
Artistic License™ Series
'57 Chevy
Alien
VW Bug
1970 Plymouth Barracuda
Mixed Signals
Street Roader
School Bus
Ambulance
'80s Corvette
Flyin' Aces™ Series
1979 Dodge Charger Daytona
Dogfighter
Sol-Aire CX4
XT-3
Sugar Rush™ Series
Mazda MX-5 Miata
Funny Car
'95 Camaro
'96 Mustang Convertible
Tech Tones™ Series
Buick Wildcat
Silhouette II
Speed Machine
Avus Quattro
1997 Mystery Cars
Speed Machine
Firebird Funny
Custom Corvette
Blown Camaro
1998 First Editions
#1 Escort Rally
#2 Slideout
#3 Dodge Sidewinder
#4 Dodge Caravan
#5 Jaguar XK8
#6 Jaguar D-Type
#7 '32 Ford
#8 '65 Impala Lowrider
#9 '63 T-Bird
#10 Dairy Delivery™
#11 Mercedes SLK
#12 Lakester™
#13 Hot Seat™
#14 Ford GT-90
#15 Pikes Peak Celica
#16 IROC Firebird
#17 '70 Roadrunner
#18 Mustang Cobra
#19 Panoz GTR-1
#20 '40 Ford
#21 Go Kart
#22 Super Comp Dragster
#23 Solar Eagle III
#24 Tail Dragger™
#25 Tow Jam™
#26 Customized C3500
#27 Super Modified
#28 Chaparral 2
#29 Mustang Mach I
#30 Sweet 16 II
#31 Callaway C-7
#32 Chrysler Thunderbolt
#33 Bad Mudder™
#34 At-A-Tude
#35 Dodge Concept Car
#36 Whatta Drag™
#37 Express Lane™
#38 Cat-A-Pult
#39 Fathom This™
#40 Double Vision™
1998 Treasure Hunt Series
Twang Thang
Scorchin' Scooter
Kenworth T600A
3-Window '34
Turbo Flame

Saltflat Racer
Street Beast
Road Rocket
Sol-Aire CX4
'57 Chevy
Stingray III
Way 2 Fast
1998 Mystery Car
Speed Machine
Firebird Funny
Custom Corvette
Blown Camaro
30th Anniversary Cars
1968 Deora
1969 '32 Vicky
1970 Classic Nomad
1971 Mutt Mobile
1972 Side Kick
1973 Sweet 16
1974 Rodger Dodger
1975 Large Charge
1976 Corvette Stingray
1977 '57 Chevy
1978 '57 T-Bird
1979 Auburn 852
1980 '40s Woodie
1981 Old Number 5
1982 Firebird Funny Car
1983 Shelby Cobra 427 S/C
1984 '65 Mustang Convertible
1985 XT-3
1986 Path Beater
1987 Sharkruiser
1988 Porsche 959
1989 '32 Ford Delivery
1990 Purple Passion
1991 '59 Caddy
1992 Goodyear Blimp
1993 Dodge Viper RT/10
1994 Rigor Motor
1995 Hydroplane
1996 VW Bus
1997 Scorchin' Scooter
1998 Zamak Cars
3-Window '34
'40s Woodie
'56 Flashsider
'57 Chevy
'59 Caddy
'67 Camaro
'70 Dodge Daytona
'97 Corvette
Auburn 852
Audi Avus
Camaro Race Car
Classic Cobra
Dodge Viper RT/10
Driven To The Max
Ferrari F40
Hot Wheels 500
Jaguar XJ220
Limozeen
Mazda MX-5 Miata
Mercedes 500SL
Porsche Carrera
Range Rover
Street Beast
Tractor
VW Bug
Silhouette II (Baggie only)
4-pack see multipacks
1999 First Editions
#1 1936 Cord
#2 '99 Mustang
#3 '38 Phantom Corsair
#4 1970 Chevelle SS
#5 Olds Aurora GTS-1
#6 Monte Carlo Concept Car
#7 Pontiac Rageous
#8 Semi-Fast
#9 Tee'd Off
#10 Porsche 911 GT3 Cup
#11 Fiat 500C
#12 Track T
#13 Popcycle
#14 Phaeton
#15 Screamin' Hauler
#16 Ford GT40
#17 Jeepster
#18 Turbolence
#19 Pikes Peak Tacoma
#20 Shadow Mk IIa
#21 Ferrari 350 Modena
#22 '56 Ford Truck
#23 Chrysler Pronto
#24 Baby Boomer
#25 Porsche 911 GT1-98
#26 Mercedes CLK-LM
Treasure Hunt Series
Mercedes 540K
T-Bird Stocker
'97 Corvette
Rigor Motor
Ferrari Testarossa
'59 Impala
Hot Wheels 500
Jaguar D Type
'32 Ford Delivery
Hot Seat
Mustang Mach I
Express Lane
4 Car segments
Buggin' Out Series
Treadator
Shadow Jet II
Radar Ranger
Baja Bug
X-Ray Cruisers Series
'63 Corvette
Lamborghini Diablo
'67 Camaro
Jaguar XJ220
Street Art Series
Mini Truck
Propper Chopper
Ambulance
School Bus
Game Over Series
Lean Machine
Shadow Jet
Speed Blaster
Twin Mill II
Pin Stripe Power
3-Window '34
Tail Dragger
'65 Impala
Auburn 852
Surf 'n Fun
'40s Woodie
VW Bug
'55 Chevy
Chevy Nomad
X-Treme Speed
Dodge Sidewinder
Callaway C7
Porsche Carrera
Mazda MX-5 Miata
Mega Graphics
Probe Funny Car
Classic Cobra
Turbo Flame
Firebird Funny Car
Terrorific
At-A-Tude
Cat-A-Pult
Sweet 16 II
Splittin' Image II
Classic Games Series
Super Modified
Silhouette II
Sol-Aire CX4
Escort Rally
Sugar Rush Series 2
'70 Roadrunner
Jaguar XK8
Pikes Peak Celica
Dodge Concept Car
Car-toon Friends Series
Saltflat Racer
XT-3
Double Vision
Lakester
Bonus Cars
'56 Flashsider
Shock Factor
Buick Wildcat
Power Pipes
Future Fleet Series
Ford GT-90
Pontiac Rageous
Jeepster
Chrysler Thunderbolt
Hot Rod Magazine Series
Phaeton
Track T
Tail Dragger
33 Ford Roadster
Seein' 3-D Series
Propper Chopper
1970 Charger Daytona
Lexus SC400
Olds 442
Snack Time Series
Callaway C-7
Firebird
Monte Carlo Concept Car
Dodge Sidewinder
Mad Maniax Series
Hot Wheels 500
Camaro Z-28
Slideout
Twin Mill II
Attack Pack Series
Nissan Truck
Power Plower
'79 Ford F-150
Dodge Ram 1500
Circus on Wheels
'56 Flashsider
'32 Ford Delivery
Fat Fendered '40
Dairy Delivery
CD Customs Series
Chrysler Pronto
Pikes Peak Tacoma
Shadow Mk IIa
Pontiac Banshee
Kung Fu Force Series
Toyota MR2
'99 Mustang
Shadow Jet II
Mini Truck
Speed Blaster series
Firebird Funny Car
At-A-Tude
Mustang Cobra
Shelby Cobra 427 S/C
Tony Hawk Skate Series
Rigor Motor
Sol-Aire CX4
Speed Blaster
Combat Medic
Secret Code Series
Fiat 500C
Baby Boomer
Tee'd Off
Screamin' Hauler
2000 Treasure Hunt Series
Double Vision
Tow Jam
1936 Cord
Sweet 16 II
Lakester
Go Kart
Chaparral 2
'57 T-Bird
Pikes Peak Celica
'67 Pontiac GTO
Ford GT-40
'70 Chevelle
2000 First Editions
Ferrari 365 GTB/4
Ferrari 550 Maranello
1964 Lincoln Continental
Pro Stock Firebird
Deora II
Deuce Roadster
Chevy Pro Stock Truck
'68 El Camino
Phantastique
Thomassima III
Ferrari 333 SP
Dodge Charger R/T
Surf Crate
'41 Willys
Lotus Elise
1999 Isuzu VehiCROSS
Anglia Panel Truck
So Fine
'65 'Vette
MX48 Turbo
SS Commodore (VT)
Cabbin' Fever
Metrorail
Muscle Tone
Dodge Power Wagon
Shoe Box
Sho-Stopper
'67 Dodge Charger
Vulture
Mini Cooper
Roll Cage
Austin Healey
Hammered Coupe
Arachnorod
Greased Lightnin'
Blast Lane
2001 Treasure Hunt Series
'65 Corvette
Roll Cage
So Fine
Rodger Dodger
Blast Lane
Hammered Coupe
Vulture
Dodge Charger
Olds 442
Pontiac Rageous
Deora
Cabbin' Fever
2001 First Editions
Cadillac LMP
Surfin' School Bus
La Troca
Sooo Fast
Super Tuned
Hooligan
Krazy 8s
MS-T Suzuka
Panoz LMP-1 Roadster S
Shredster
Dodge Viper GST-R
Maelstrom
Lotus M250
1971 Plymouth GTX
Honda Civic Si
Evil Twin
Hyper Mite
Outsider
Monoposto
Vulture Roadster
Fright Bike
Jet Threat 3.0
Montezooma
Toyota Celica
Ford Focus
Mega Duty
Riley & Scott Mk III
XS-IVE
School Bus
Ambulance
Funny Car
Camaro Z-28
Mo' Scoot
Ford Thunderbolt
Morris Wagon
Fandango
Old #3
Ferrari 156
Cunningham C4R
'57 Roadster
Turbo Taxi Series
'57 Chevy
Limozeen
'57 T-Bird
'70 Chevelle SS
Rat Rods Series
Track T
'33 Roadster
Phaeton
Shoe Box

Promotional Series

Anime Series
Muscle Tone
Ford GT-90
Dodge Charger R/T
Olds Aurora GTS-1
Rod Squadron Series
Dodge Daytona Charger
Lakester
Greased Lightnin'
Propper Chopper
Skull and Crossbones Series
Rigor Motor
Blast Lane
Deuce Roadster
Screamin' Hauler
Loco-Motive Series
Phantastique
Pontiac Banshee
Turbolence
Metrorail
Monsters Series
'59 Impala
Tail Dragger
Cadillac 1959
Purple Passion
Extreme Sports Series
MX48 Turbo
Double Vision
Twin Mill II
Funny Car
Company Cars series
Jaguar XJ 220
'98 Mustang
Monte Carlo Concept Car
Dodge Sidewinder
Hippie Mobiles series
'68 Mustang
'63 Corvette
'64 Lincoln Continrntal
'67 Pontiac GTO
Skin Deep Series
Super Comp Dragster
Willys Coupe
Chevy Pro Stock Truck
Pro Stock Firebird
2002 Treasure Hunt Series
La Troca
'71 Plymouth GTX
'57 Roadster
Lotus Project M250
Ford Thunderbolt
Panoz LMP-1 Roadster S
Phaeton
Fat Fendered '40
'40 Ford
Tail Dragger
Mini Cooper
Anglia Panel
2002 First Editions
Midnight Otto
Hyperliner
Tantrum
Overbored 454
Jester
Altered State
Nissan Skyline
Honda Spocket
Corvette SR-2
Nomadder What
Super Smooth
'40 Ford Coupe
Ferrari P4
Saleen S7
Backdraft
Custom Cougar
'68 Cougar
Torpedo Jones
Custom '69 Chevy
Custom '59 Cadillac
Open Roadster
Jaded
'57 Eldorado Brougham
HW Prototype 12
Lancia Stratos
Nizzan Z
Toyota RSC
2001 Mini Cooper
Super Tsunami
'64 Riviera
Moto-Crossed
Lotus Esprit
Volkswagen New Beetle Cup
Pony-Up
I Candy
Rocket Oil Special
Hyundai Spyder Concept
Sling Shot
'40 Somethin'
Side Draft
Ballistik
Syd Mead's Sentinel 400 Limo
Wild Frontier Series
'59 Chevy Impala
'32 Delivery
Ice Cream Truck
Power Plower
Spares 'n Strikes Series
Surfin' School Bus
So Fine
Rodger Dodger
Sooo Fast
Tuners Series
Ford Focus
Honda Civic
MS-T Suzuka
Toyota Celica
Corvette Series
'65 Corvette
'97 Corvette
'58 Corvette
'63 Corvette
Trump Cards Series
Dodge Charger R/T
Hammered Coupe
Montezooma
'33 Ford
Cold Blooded Series
Firebird Funny Car
Speed Shark
Vulture
Phaeton
Star-Spangled Series
Chrysler Pronto
3-Window '34
Deora II
'68 El Camino
Yu-Gi-Oh Series
Power Pistons
Seared Tuner
Fandango
Super Tuned
Spectraflame II Series
Monoposto
Muscle Tone
Jet Threat 3.0
Hammered Coupe
He-Man Series
'41 Willys Coupe
Twin Mill II
Double Vision
Phantastique
Sweet Rides Series
Chevy Pro Stock Truck
Pro Stock Firebird
Mustang Cobra
'70 Chevelle SS
Grave Rave Series
Evil Twin
Krazy 8s
Rigor Motor
Delivery Van
Red Line Series
The Demon
'32 Ford Vicky
Side Kick
Chevy Nomad
Hot Rod Magazine Series
Passion
Hooligan
Deuce Roadster
'70 Plymouth Roadrunner
Fed Fleet Series
Propper Chopper
Armored Truck
Hydroplane
Dodge Power Wagon

Hot Wheels

ABOUT THE AUTHOR

Mike Strauss has always been a strong family man...and collector. Over the years he has collected non-sports cards, coins, stamps, Classic Comics and cartoon glasses.

He was born in Berlin, Germany during World War II. His family moved to the U.S.A. when he was six. He sells gourmet foods full-time and spends many hours on the highway where his natural interest in cars and other vehicles developed.

Mike began collecting Hot Wheels cars when they were given away by Shell stations in the early '70s. Several years later, he saw the same cars commanding impressive prices at a toy show. This got him hooked on Hot Wheels collecting and he worked in earnest to expand his own collection which is now one of the largest in the world.

In 1985, he and Russ Looker started the Hot Wheels Newsletter because there was no reliable source of information on this growing collectible field. It has been a major force in bringing Hot Wheels collectors together.

Many articles about Hot Wheels and Mike have appeared in various automobile and toy related magazines. There have also been definitive exhibits of his extensive collection at the Museum of American Heritage in Palo Alto, CA and at the 1993 Toy Fair in New York which celebrated the 25th anniversary of Hot Wheels production.